THE COMPLETE WORKS OF OSCAR WILDE

THE COMPLETE WORKS OF
Oscar Wilde

Introduced by Merlin Holland

Collins

HarperCollins Publishers
77–85 Fulham Palace Road, London w6 8jb

First Collected Edition 1948
Second Edition 1966
Third Edition 1994
Centenary Edition (Fourth Edition) published 1999
Fifth Edition (with corrections) 2003

The full text of *De Profundis* © Estate of Oscar Wilde 1962 and the four-act version of *The Importance of being Earnest* © Estate of Oscar Wilde 1957, are both reproduced by permission of Merlin Holland. The chronological order of Wilde's poems was established by Prof. Bobby Fong of Hope College, Michigan and is here reproduced with grateful acknowledgement to him. The texts of Wilde's two American lectures 'The Decorative Arts' and 'The House Beautiful' were established from manuscript sources and contemporary accounts by Prof. Kevin O'Brien of St Francis Xavier University, Nova Scotia, who has kindly allowed their reproduction. The cover photography is reproduced by permission of William Andrews Clark Memorial Library, Los Angeles, as are picture numbers 5, 9, 10 and 16. All other photographs are from the Collection Merlin Holland and are reproduced by permission of Merlin Holland.

11 10 09 08 07
10 9 8 7 6

© HarperCollins Publishers 2003

Hardback Edition: isbn–13: 978-0-00-714435-8
Hardback Edition: isbn–10: 0-00-714435-0
Paperback Edition: isbn–13: 978-0-00-714436-5
Paperback Edition: isbn–10: 0-00-714436-9

A catalogue record for this book is available from the British Library.

Typeset in Erhardt by Tradespools Limited, Graphic House, Station Approach, Frome, Somerset BA11 1RE

Printed and bound in China by Imago

CONTENTS

THE CONTRIBUTORS

Owen Dudley Edwards, a Dubliner, was initially trained in historical research by Sir Rupert Hart-Davis, who was then editing *The Letters of Oscar Wilde* (1962). His own books include *The Fireworks of Oscar Wilde* (1989), and he has a biography of Oscar Wilde in preparation. He is now Reader in History at the University of Edinburgh, and is also a writer, broadcaster and theatre critic, whose first play will be staged at the Edinburgh Festival Fringe in 1994.

Terence Brown holds a personal chair in the School of English in Trinity College, Dublin. He is a Fellow of Trinity College and also a member of the Royal Irish Academy. He has written and edited many books. Among his publications are *Louis MacNeice: Sceptical Vision* (1975), *Northern Voices: Poets from Ulster* (1975), *Ireland: a Social and Cultural History* (1981, 2nd edition 1985), and *Ireland's Literature: Selected Essays* (1986). He has recently published an edition of James Joyce's *Dubliners* (1992), was a contributing editor of the *Field Day Anthology of Irish Writing* (1992), and is currently at work on a book on Yeats. He has lectured on Anglo-Irish Literature in many parts of the world.

Declan Kiberd lectures in Anglo-Irish Literature at University College, Dublin. He is author of *Synge and the Irish Language* (1979, second edition 1993) and *Men and Feminism in Modern Literature* (1985). He edited the section on Wilde in the *Field Day Anthology of Irish Writing* (1991) and has lectured on the author in more than fifteen countries. Among his other scholarly commentaries are *The Students' Annotated Ulysses* (Penguin 1992) and *Anglo-Irish Attitudes* (Derry, 1984).

Merlin Holland, son of Vyvyan Holland and grandson of Oscar Wilde, writes, lectures and broadcasts regularly on all aspects of Wilde's life and works. For twenty-five years he has been in the unique position, through having to administer the few remaining copyrights in Wilde's writings (mostly letters and unpublished fragmentary manuscripts), of being in close touch with the latest academic research while presenting his grandfather to a wider general audience. He is the wine-correspondent of *Country Life*.

After Wilde's conviction, his wife, Constance, and their sons were forced to change their name to Holland after being refused accommodation at a Swiss hotel. The family has never reverted to the name Wilde.

INTRODUCTION TO THE 1994 EDITION

by

MERLIN HOLLAND

At an international conference on Wilde in May 1993, a highly respected academic and specialist in Anglo-Irish literature put to his audience the question: 'Is Oscar Wilde really a great writer?' I suspect that his own mind had already been made up, for he added by way of a guideline, 'Why do so many of those who study his works end up by calling him "Oscar" in a rather over-familiar fashion?', as if an author worthy of serious study should make himself less accessible and behave with somewhat more decorum. It is a question which his critics have been asking repeatedly for a hundred years and for which there still seems to be no satisfactory answer.

Within days of his death the *Pall Mall Gazette* was saying 'Mr Wilde's gifts included supreme intellectual ability, but nothing he ever wrote had strength to endure.' In 1910 Edmund Gosse wrote to André Gide: 'Of course he was not a "great writer" . . . . his works, taken without his life, present to a sane criticism, a mediocre figure.' An *Evening Standard* article by Arnold Bennett in 1927 treats him as outmoded and his style as lacking in permanence but grudgingly concedes 'Wilde, even if he was not a first rate writer, had given keen pleasure to simpletons such as my younger self; and he was a first rate figure.' And as late as 1950, the *Times Literary Supplement* said rather condescendingly, 'Apart from one perfect play, one memorable poem and *De Profundis*, Wilde left little with which, as literature, posterity need seriously concern itself.'

Yet forty-four years on, Oscar Wilde's reputation stands higher than at any time since his theatrical triumphs of the 1890s. His works are never out of print and some of them have been rendered in to languages as diverse as Catalan and Arabic, Yiddish and Chinese. Scarcely a day passes when he is not quoted in the press or on the airwaves and the spring of 1993 saw the simultaneous West End revival of *An Ideal Husband* and *The Importance of Being Earnest*—the very same plays which were delighting packed houses on the eve of his arrest nearly a century before.

This popularity in defiance of the critics is his ultimate, unanswerable paradox, thrown down like a challenge from beyond the grave. His readers love him as much for his weakness and his fallibility as they do for his wit, his satire and his *fin de siècle* daring, and they remain endlessly fascinated by his outrageous behaviour. The same public which crucified him for his lack of conformity and respect for Victorian values in 1895, today holds him up as a martyr for individuality. 'I was a man.' he says in *De Profundis*, 'who stood in symbolic relations to the art and culture of my age. I treated Art as the supreme reality, and life as a mere mode of fiction: I awoke the imagination of my century so that it created myth and legend around me: I summed up all systems in a phrase, and all existence in an epigram.' The unabashed arrogance of that when it was published in 1905, a mere five years after his death, must have been difficult to swallow, but today we are forced to see the truth of it. Wilde's life and his work survive side by side, in a symbiotic relationship with each other, and despite all attempts by his critics to prise them apart and subject each to scrutiny, they remain more closely entwined than ever.

How could it be otherwise? The story of his life is, in a sense, the one great play he lived out and never wrote. It has all the elements of Greek theatre so familiar to him as a classical scholar: the hero apparently in control of his destiny; the hubris; the tragic flaw; and finally the nemesis. His end, though, was not a mercifully quick death but rather a Promethean torment. Five long years of suffering followed his downfall: prison, bankruptcy, disgrace and, the ultimate indignity for one of his generosity, poverty and having to borrow money from friends. Small wonder then that public opinion refuses to allow his life and his work to be separated. To some extent, however, it has created an imbalance which threatens to play into the hands of the critics. The great majority of books written about Wilde has concentrated on the man, and passed fleetingly over the works as being merely secondary expressions of his life as an art form, a problem for which he himself is partly to blame. He has left us with that enduring vision of Wilde as the supreme showman whom nobody, at his peril, should attempt to take seriously. 'Art,' as he said, 'is the only serious thing in the world. And the artist is the only person who is never serious.' Both were themes which dominated his life.

It is this apparent lack of seriousness on which the greater part of his popular reputation rests and anecdote has done little to change it. Two of the permanent hallmarks of Wildean humour, for example, were an affected indifference to hard work as well as the effortless ease of his own genius. Asked by the critic W. E. Henley how often he went into the office during his editorship of the *Woman's World*, Oscar replied, 'I used to go three times a week for an hour a day, but I have since struck off one of the days.' And when George Alexander asked him to cut the 'Gribsby' scene from *The Importance of Being Earnest* (restored in the present edition) Wilde could not resist remarking, 'Do you realise, Alec, this scene you feel is superfluous cost me terrible exhausting labour and heart-rending nerve-racking strain. I assure you on my honour that it must have taken fully five minutes to write.'

Even while he was still at Oxford, Wilde was at pains to cultivate this image of creative idleness. He would read the 19th century poets rather than studying the classical texts for his degree course, or at least that was the impression he liked to give. One of his contemporaries though, David Hunter-Blair, recalled many years later, 'Of course Wilde worked hard for the high academic honours which he achieved at Oxford. He liked to pose as a dilettante trifling with his books; but I knew of the hours of assiduous reading often into the early hours of the morning. He read surreptitiously in his small and stuffy bedroom. Books lay in apparently hopeless confusion though he knew where to lay his hands on each in every corner.'

This is the Wilde most of us are accustomed to see, the Wilde who admitted to André Gide 'J'ai mis tout mon génie dans ma vie, je n'ai mis que mon talent dans mes oeuvres.' He persuaded us of its authenticity a hundred years ago and it is still the form in which the public wishes to enjoy his company—witty, nonconformist and faintly perfumed with decadence. Understandably, they are not qualities which persuade those who inhabit the rarefied atmosphere of pure literary criticism to grant him first division status.

But in the last thirty years, parts of the academic world have started to reassess Oscar Wilde on their own terms, digging beneath the veneer of superficiality and revealing a very different character to the one we thought we knew. All the old magic remains but it is given an added dimension by seeing him occasionally without his mask. We begin to see that, far from lounging nonchalantly through life, very early on he showed a strong determination to succeed as a writer. Put him alongside any ambitious young journalist of the 1990s and compare their paths to success. A couple of youthful literary indiscretions, a period of probation as a critic and reviewer, the editorship of a national magazine and the *succès de scandale* of a first novel, and the whole liberally peppered with self-publicity—*plus ça change*. And if Wilde did not have the power of radio and television to rely on, at least he had the lecture hall and the theatre to reach his public direct.

From the moment he left Oxford he was hard at work promoting himself. He made it his business to be seen at any social gathering of importance and at first nights, and courted the friendship of actresses in the public eye – Ellen Terry, Lillie Langtry and Sarah Bernhardt. Then, with little more than a volume of self-published poems to his credit, he was offered a lecture tour in America by Richard D'Oyly Carte to coincide with his production of *Patience*. Naturally he seized the opportunity. But the programme, originally planned to last four months stretched to nearly a year and it was far from being just as a sedate lecture tour for the self-appointed 'Professor of Aesthetics', a young dandy in velvet knee-breeches, rising languidly at mid-day to parade himself across the country as a live 'aesthete' for the audiences of Gilbert and Sullivan's comic opera. In reality detailed research has shown that he faced a punishing schedule of 140 lectures in 260 days from the East to the West coast and up into Canada without the help of air travel and fast trains. He also made sure that he met Walt Whitman, Henry Longfellow and Oliver Wendell Holmes; he arranged for *Vera* to be staged in New York the following year; and was commissioned to write *The Duchess of Padua*. He had taken the calculated risk of ridicule and turned it entirely to his advantage both financially and in terms of his reputation.

On his return to England Wilde added his 'Personal Impressions of America' to his repertoire and continued lecturing as a source of income until 1888. Indeed, from 1883 until early in 1885 it was almost his only source of income. He was acutely aware of this and tried on several occasions to have himself made an inspector of schools, as Matthew Arnold had done before him, but without success. In 1885 he even writes to an unidentified correspondent: 'Believe me that it is impossible to live by literature. By journalism a man may make an income but rarely by pure literary work. I would strongly advise you to make some profession, such as that of a tutor, the basis and mainstay of your life, and to keep literature for your finest, rarest moments. Remember that London is full of young men working for literary success, and that you must carve your way to fame. Laurels don't come for the asking.' Shortly afterwards he took his own advice and his career in journalism lasted from 1885 until 1891. In addition to helping with the family finances it enabled him to publish most of the stories and essays contained in this volume and played a part in his literary development, the importance of which has been largely underestimated.

Other research is beginning to probe into the influence on his writing of Wilde's Irish background, and his reading of other authors which was prodigious (at the sheriff's sale of all his possessions after his arrest, nearly two thousand volumes were disposed of). The old arguments over whether his literary 'borrowings' are plagiarism or not, have been reopened and are being reassessed. Wilde as the lightweight author of society comedies, a few memorable poems and some fairy stories may eventually have to make extra room for Wilde as a hard-working professional writer, deeply interested by the issues of his day and carrying in his intellectual baggage something that we all too frequently overlook, a quite extraordinary classical and philosophical education. I realise that for most people the idea of Wilde as a scholar and thinker sits uncomfortably beside their view of him as wit and bon viveur, 'the spendthrift of my own genius' as he put it, but that is just another of the delicious paradoxes with which he has left us. His interest in social matters, in the power of the theatre to question and criticise as well as to entertain, his belief in the importance of women's role in society and his own fragile position within it as an outsider, are all coming to light.

For anyone concerned that all this may destroy the lightness of touch with which they have come to associate Oscar Wilde, an antidote is to hand in the form of his letters. Two collections have been published in 1962 and 1985, and if they have helped to validate the view of him as a more profound writer, they have also added immeasurably to our knowledge of him as a man. Wonderfully fluent in style, when read aloud they must be the nearest we shall ever come to hearing that legendary conversation. I should like to have included some of them here but for reasons of space this was not possible. One, however, the publisher has allowed me and I offer it to you as a little *bonnebouche* of what is to be found there. He wrote it to an old friend, Frances Forbes-Robertson, on her marriage in 1899, when he was living in Paris and at his poorest. It has humour, beauty and sadness.

My dear, sweet, beautiful Friend, Eric [her brother] has just sent me your charming letter and I am delighted to have a chance of sending you my congratulations on your marriage, and all the good wishes of one who has always loved and admired you. I met Eric quite by chance and he told me he had been over to the marriage. He was as picturesque and sweet as usual but more than usually vague. I was quite furious with him. He could not quite remember who it was you had married, or whether he was fair or dark, young or old, tall or small. He could not remember where you were married, or what you wore, or whether you looked more than usually beautiful. He said there were a great many people at the wedding but he could not remember their names. He remembered, however, Johnston [another brother] being present. He spoke of the whole thing as a sort of landscape in a morning mist. Your husband's name he could not for the moment recall: but he said he thought he had it written down at home. He went dreamily away down the Boulevard followed by violent reproaches from me, but they were no more to him than the sound of fluting: he wore the sweet smile of those who are always looking for the moon at mid-day.

So, dear Frankie, you are married, and your husband is a king of men. That is as it should be; those who wed the daughters of the gods are kings, or become so.

I have nothing to offer you but one of my books, that absurd comedy *The Importance of Being Earnest*, but I send it to you in the hopes that it may live on your bookshelves and be allowed to look at you from time to time. The dress is pretty, it wears Japanese vellum and belongs to a limited family of nine and is not on speaking terms with the popular edition: it refuses to recognise the poor relations whose value is only seven and sixpence. Such as the pride of birth. It is a lesson.

Ah! how delightful it would be to be with you and your husband in your own home! But my dear child how could I get to you? Miles of sea, miles of land, the purple of the mountains and the silver of the rivers divide us: you don't know how poor I am: I have no money at all: I live, or am supposed to live, on a few francs a day: a bare remnant saved from a shipwreck. Like St Francis of Assisi I am wedded to poverty: but in my case the marriage is not a success; I hate the bride that has been given to me. I see no beauty in her hunger and her rags: I have not the soul of St Francis: my thirst is for the beauty of life: my desire for the joy. But it was dear of you to ask me, and do tell the king of men how touched and grateful I am by the invitation you and he have sent me.

And, also sometimes, send me a line to tell me of the beauty you have found in life. I live now in echoes and have little music of my own. Your old friend

OSCAR

*   *   *

The Collins *Complete Works of Oscar Wilde* has remained unchanged since 1966 and as it has now been entirely reset, I felt it important to add what I believe to be the best of both his journalism and his lectures. They have hardly been seen at all since their appearance in the first collected works of 1908, brought out by Wilde's literary executor, Robert Ross, and quite apart from the important role which they played in Wilde's life, they contain some memorable passages which have been 'lost' for too long. Professor Kevin

O'Brien of St Francis Xavier University in Nova Scotia has very kindly allowed me to use the texts of 'The Decorative Arts' and 'The House Beautiful' which he reconstructed from existing manuscripts and contemporary newspaper reports.

The other change which I felt was timely was to put his poems into chronological order. When they were first published in 1881, Wilde grouped them thematically. This sequence was followed in the edition of 1882 which was the last the author oversaw. In the 1908 edition Ross included 24 previously unpublished pieces as well as 'Ravenna' 'The Sphinx' and 'The Ballad of Reading Gaol' all of which had been published as separate volumes. By the following year two more unpublished poems, 'Pan' and 'Désespoir' had surfaced and were included in editions from then on. All these additional poems were simply tacked on to the end of Wilde's original order. In the last Collins revision of 1966, for whatever reason, neither Wilde's nor Ross's order was respected, and since I have taken the liberty of including a number of poems discovered since then, it seemed sensible to present all the poetry in the order in which Wilde wrote it. For this, and for the new poems, I am indebted to Professor Bobby Fong of Hope College, Michigan, who most generously shared his research with me.

A final word needs to be said about the introduction which my father wrote in 1966. At the time it struck exactly the right note. It was a good balance between broad literary assessment and biography and if it skimmed over the reasons for Wilde's disgrace and imprisonment, it is understandable. Homosexuality in the United Kingdom was still a criminal offence (though legalised the following year) and, odd though it must sound today, it was an aspect of Oscar Wilde's private life which still made some of his readers distinctly uneasy. It is a sobering thought that the same prosecution could have been brought at the time my father was writing.

It appears, too, that my father made one or two slips of a historical nature in the family history and it would seem appropriate, in the light of later research, to correct them.

The idea that Wilde's family is descended from Colonel de Wilde is a pleasingly romantic one for which there is sadly no evidence. The furthest back that his paternal lineage can be traced is to a Dublin merchant, John Wilde, in the first half of the 18th century. The statement about King Oscar of Sweden is also incorrect. There is no record of Sir William operating on the King's cataract, nor was he the inventor of that operation. He was, however, decorated by the Swedish government in 1862 with the order of the Northern Star.

I hope that I show him no disrespect in pointing this out. If I do, let me offer him a suitable misquotation from our common ancestor: 'Parents begin by loving their children. After a time they are exasperated by them. It is rarely impossible to forgive them.'

INTRODUCTION TO THE 1966 EDITION

by

VYVYAN HOLLAND

Oscar Wilde's family is Dutch in origin. The first Wilde to settle in Ireland was a certain Colonel de Wilde, the son of an artist, examples of whose work hang in the Art Gallery at The Hague; he was a soldier of fortune who was granted lands in Connaught at the end of the seventeenth century for his services to King William III of England. He is said to have repented his adherence to the English king and to have become 'more Irish than the Irish'. From that time the family were land agents and doctors.

My father's parents were both distinguished in their own way. Sir William Wilde was the foremost eye and ear specialist of his time, and a physician of international repute. He invented the operation for cataract and performed it on King Oscar of Sweden, for which he received the Order of the Polar Star. His mother, Lady Wilde, born Jane Francesca Elgee, was a staunch Irish Nationalist, who wrote fierce poems and articles in the Irish Nationalist newspaper *The Nation*, under the name of 'Speranza', a name she had adopted from her motto 'Fidanza, Constanza, Speranza' – Faith, Constancy, Hope. Lady Wilde had three children, William, Oscar and Isola, who died when she was ten, to Oscar's lasting grief. Oscar Wilde was born on 16 October 1854, and was given the names Oscar Fingal O'Flahertie Wills Wilde.

His education began at Portora Royal School in Enniskillen, from which he obtained a scholarship to Trinity College, Dublin, where he won the Berkeley Gold Medal for Greek. From there he received a demyship to Magdalen College, Oxford. While at Oxford he came under the influence of John Ruskin and Walter Pater. Pater preached the love of Art for Art's sake, and Oscar Wilde, going one step further, set out to idolise beauty for beauty's sake and filled his rooms looking over the Cherwell with blue china and reproductions of paintings by Rossetti and Burne-Jones. Aestheticism was the key-note of his creed and he declared that beauty was the ideal after which everyone should strive.

My father's life at Oxford, one gathers from his letters, was a joyous one. He entered whole-heartedly into the undergraduate life of the University and distinguished himself by winning the Newdigate Prize for English verse and getting a double first in Classics. Upon this note he came to London in 1879 with the remains of a small patrimony and started to make his living by his pen. True to his doctrine of beauty he established himself as the 'Apostle of Aestheticism' and drew attention to himself by the eccentricity of his dress. It must be remembered that at this period the clothing of the British upper middle classes was rigidly conventional, and the sight of him in the evening in a velvet coat edged with braid, knee-breeches, black silk stockings, a soft loose shirt with a wide turn-down collar and a large flowing tie, was bound to arouse indignant curiosity.

At the same time he was writing poems, and in 1880 he also wrote *Vera*, a rather immature play, which ran for one week in New York in 1883 and never reached the boards in London. In 1881 his collected poems were published, and in 1882, being short of money, he was persuaded to go on a lecture tour to America. This proved to be a brilliant success and he returned to England in 1883, covered, if not with glory, at least with considerable notoriety.

On his return to Europe, he retired to Paris to finish another play, *The Duchess of Padua*, for the American actress Mary Anderson; but when she received the play, she turned it down flatly. This was really a disaster for Oscar Wilde, and he returned to England and went on a series of lecture tours in the provinces. However, this nomadic life soon palled and he returned to London where, in 1884, he married Constance Mary, daughter of a distinguished Irish barrister, Horace Lloyd, Q.C. Oscar was romantically in love with his beautiful young wife and for some years he was ideally happy. He had two sons by his wife – Cyril, born in 1885, and myself in 1886.

Oddly enough, although his literary activities had been almost entirely confined to writing poetry until his marriage, he now turned largely to prose and, with the exception of *The Sphinx*, the idea of which had occurred to him much earlier, he wrote few poems until after his imprisonment, when he wrote *The Ballad of Reading Gaol*. Boris Brasol, who wrote one of the only two carefully considered lives of my father, sums up his poetic period as follows:

'He began his literary career as a composer of sonorous and pleasing verses in which, however, as he himself admitted, 'there was more rhyme than reason'; yet as he grew older, he seemed to have lost all taste for poetry, and though there is nothing that would justify the contention that he ever regarded his early poems as callow productions, the fact remains that upon reaching maturity he took no further interest in that delightful occupation which Browning aptly called "the unlocking of hearts with sonnet keys".'

Upon what, then, does his reputation as an author rest? His early poems were mostly lyrical, and certain of them will undoubtedly pass the test of time. His true literary life was spread over seven years only, from 1888 until 1894. In 1887 he had become editor of *Woman's World* in which capacity he continued until 1889 when he resigned. He had gathered a reputation for eccentricity and, still more, as a conversationalist. There are few people alive now who remember his conversation, but when in 1954 a plaque was unveiled by Sir Compton Mackenzie on the house in Tite Street where my family lived for eleven years, he read the following message from Sir Max Beerbohm (the Incomparable Max!), who felt too frail to undertake the journey to London to be present:

'I have had the privilege of listening to many masters of table talk – Meredith and Swinburne, Edmund Gosse and Henry James, Augustine Birrell and Arthur Balfour, Gilbert Chesterton and Desmond MacCarthy and

Hilaire Belloc – all of them splendid in their own way. But Oscar was the greatest of them all – the most spontaneous and yet the most polished, the most soothing and yet the most surprising. . . . Nobody was willing to interrupt the music of so magnificent a virtuoso. To have heard him consoled me for not having heard Dr Johnson or Edmund Burke, Lord Brougham or Sidney Smith.'

Winston Churchill was once asked whom he would like to meet and talk with in after life, and he replied, without hesitation: 'Oscar Wilde.'

Wilde's first memorable work was *The Happy Prince*, which appeared in 1888. The stories in *The Happy Prince* are really poems in prose more than fairy tales for children; and yet the remarkable thing is that they appeal equally to children and adults.

In 1891 he produced a small volume of four stories which he had written some time previously. The book was called *Lord Arthur Savile's Crime and Other Stories*, the other three tales being 'The Canterville Ghost', 'The Sphinx without a Secret' and 'The Model Millionaire'. The first two of these stories have been dramatised and their substance has been copied on several occasions; they possess the light-hearted gaiety and insouciance that find their fullest expression in *The Importance of Being Earnest*, and show the buoyancy of my father's spirit at that time.

A House of Pomegranates, my father's other book of short stories – one can hardly call them fairy tales – appeared with illustrations by Charles Shannon, R.A. in the same year. This book completely puzzled the critics, who thought that the stories were meant for children and protested, quite rightly, that no child could understand them. This was followed by *The Sphinx*, which really dated from his Oxford days, and upon which he had worked at intervals ever since. The critics were again confused by the poem, which was really nothing more than an experiment with words. He revelled in finding rhymes for words such as hieroglyph and catafalque, which he rhymed with hippogriff and Amenalk.

In 1891, too, Oscar Wilde's only novel, *The Picture of Dorian Gray*, appeared in book form, enlarged from the original which had been already published in *Lippincott's Magazine*. The publication of this work was greeted with a storm of protest by the critics. The English Press was almost unanimous in its condemnation of the book. The idea of the book had first come to my father some years before. Hesketh Pearson tells the story of it in his *Life of Oscar Wilde*; 'In the year 1884 Wilde used to drop in at the studio of a painter, Basil Ward, one of whose sitters was a young man of exceptional beauty . . . When the portrait was done and the youth had gone, Wilde happened to say, "What a pity that such a glorious creature should ever grow old!" The artist agreed, adding, "How delightful it would be if he could remain exactly as he is, while the portrait aged and withered in his stead!" Wilde expressed his obligation by calling the painter in his story Basil Hallward.'

By far the most interesting and entertaining book of essays that Oscar Wilde wrote was *Intentions*, in which he really gave rein to his imagination.

In my own opinion, it is the most absorbing of all his works. *The Critic as Artist* occupies considerably more than half of it; its sub-title 'with some remarks upon the importance of doing nothing' shows the curious charm the word 'importance' had for him; it occurs in the titles of two of his plays, and is constantly cropping up in his essays. It is almost as though the word held a strange sonorousness for him and that he liked to roll it, if not round his tongue, then round his mind.

But the most interesting essay in the book is *The Decay of Lying*. The essay is in the form of a dialogue, the dominant theme being the vast superiority of Art over Nature, leading to the conclusion that Nature follows Art.

Oscar Wilde now entered into his final stage, the one for which he was destined, that of a dramatist. In 1891 he wrote *Lady Windermere's Fan*, which he described as 'one of those modern drawing-room plays with pink lampshades'. It was produced at the St James's Theatre in February, 1892 by George Alexander. There were loud cries of 'Author!' at the end of the play and Wilde came onto the stage with a cigarette in his gloved hand and said: 'Ladies and Gentlemen. I have enjoyed this evening immensely. The actors have given us a charming rendering of a delightful play, and your appreciation has been most intelligent. I congratulate you on the great success of your performance which persuades me that you think almost as highly of the play as I do.'

When Wilde had finished *Lady Windermere's Fan* he retired to Paris and wrote his Biblical play *Salomé* in French, dedicated to Pierre Louÿs who made certain corrections in the French, but did not otherwise interfere with it. Sarah Bernhardt was immensely attracted to this play, and she put it into rehearsal at the Palace Theatre in London, with herself in the title-role. However, the Lord Chamberlain refused to grant it a licence, on the ground that no play which contained Biblical characters was allowed to be performed on the English stage. This so annoyed Wilde that he announced his intentions of renouncing his British nationality and becoming a Frenchman, there being no such restrictions in France. As matters turned out, it is a pity that he did not carry out his threat.

In the summer of 1892 he wrote *A Woman of No Importance*, which was produced with immediate success by Herbert Beerbohm Tree at the Haymarket in 1893. Once again the audience rose to its feet and called for the author. This time remembering the bad impression he had made on the first night of *Lady Windermere's Fan*, he got up in the box in which he was sitting and announced: 'Ladies and Gentlemen, I regret to inform you that Mr Oscar Wilde is not in the house.'

On 3 January 1895, Oscar Wilde's third important play *An Ideal Husband* was produced by Lewis Waller. The Prince of Wales was present at the first night. It was almost unprecedented for Royalty to be present at a first night, and it seemed now that Wilde's future was assured. George Bernard Shaw's comment on the play is worth repeating: 'Mr Oscar Wilde's new play at the Haymarket is a dangerous subject, because he has the property of making his critics dull. . . . He plays with everything; with wit, with philosophy, with drama, with actors and audience, with the whole theatre.'

And so we come to Oscar Wilde's last, and his most brilliant play, *The Importance of Being Earnest*. Wilde originally wrote the play in four acts, as he had written his other three major plays. He submitted it in this form to George Alexander who, with the object of making room for a 'curtain raiser', as was usual in those days, asked Wilde to cut it to three acts. When, four years later, Leonard Smithers published the play in book form, it was this three-act version that he had printed, and each subsequent edition has followed this pattern. Why this has been so is not clear, but the play as written by Oscar Wilde, with two extra characters in it, is the play as given in this volume. As Mr Philip Drake, who is responsible for this edition of Wilde's works, remarked, it seems a pity that George Alexander should have a permanent influence on the play.

The Importance of Being Earnest was produced at the St James's Theatre on 14 February 1895. Wilde had now reached the pinnacle of his success. Two plays of his were drawing crowded audiences in the West End, and actor-managers were falling over one another to beg him to write for them. Then the Marquess of Queensberry, with the object of attacking his son, Lord Alfred Douglas, because of his friendship with Wilde, launched a campaign of ungovernable fury on Wilde. The story has been told often enough; Alfred Douglas, whose only object was to see his father in the dock, persuaded Oscar Wilde to bring a prosecution for criminal libel against him. Lord Queensberry was triumphantly acquitted and his place in the dock was taken by Oscar Wilde, who was sentenced to two years imprisonment.

While in prison, Wilde wrote the letter to Lord Alfred Douglas, part of which was published in 1905 by Robert Ross, under the title of *De Profundis*. In a letter to Robert Ross he wrote: 'This is indeed an Encyclical letter, and as the Bulls of the Holy Father are named from their opening words, it may be spoken of as *Epistola: in Carcere et Vinculis*.' The manuscript was not revised by Wilde, although he intended to do this, as is shown by the letter he wrote to Robert Ross: 'As soon as you have read it, I want you to have it copied for me. As regards the method of copying, I wish the copy to be done on good paper and a wide rubricated margin should be left for corrections.' A copy of *De Profundis* was made and sent to Alfred Douglas; but after reading the first few pages, he destroyed it, probably thinking, rather naïvely, that there was no other copy in existence. Douglas strenuously denied ever having received the letter, and he could not go back on this without contradicting himself.

After my father's death in 1900, Alfred Douglas tried to get hold of the manuscript, but Robert Ross settled the matter by sealing it up and presenting it to the British Museum, with the proviso that it should remain sealed for sixty years, that is to say until 1960, at the end of which time it might safely be presumed that everyone mentioned in it would be dead.

The copying was done hastily and without much care, because the version printed in 1949 varied in several particulars from the original manuscript, although, of course, the substance was the same. The version here printed has been carefully compared with the original and is exactly as Wilde wrote it.

The Portrait of Mr. W. H. was first published as an article of 12,000 words in *Blackwood's Magazine* for July, 1889. Oscar Wilde became more and more obsessed with the idea contained in the article and during the next four years he re-wrote the story and added to it, bringing the total up to 25,000 words. The manuscript disappeared at the time of the sale of my father's effects at Tite Street, together with others, and did not re-appear until the year 1920 in America, where it was published in a limited edition by Mitchell Kennerley. The expanded version is printed in this edition.

The only work that my father wrote after 1897 was the poem *The Ballad of Reading Gaol*, which he wrote at Berneval, so that Douglas's claim to have had a large share in writing it may be ignored, as he and Wilde did not meet again until later.

All his life, my father had an intense leaning towards religious mysticism and was strongly attracted to the Catholic Church, into which he was received on his death bed in 1900. His remains now lie in the French National Cemetery of Père Lachaise.

Vyvyan Holland

THE STORIES OF OSCAR WILDE

Introduction by

OWEN DUDLEY EDWARDS

THE Lake District of England may not suggest Oscar Wilde (although, with pleasing irony, his is the literary name most obviously prompted by Lake Windermere) but it doesn't really matter where I witnessed it. It could have been anywhere. The date was about 25 July 1993. The people were adults and children, mostly Roman Catholics, of the Dominican Peace Action Group. The weather was an incessant downpour. The speaker was Sue Dowell, an Anglican Rector's wife, talking about literary failure to think of children from the child's standpoint, and then, for an example of a story-teller who saw things from a child's interest (in all senses) rather than an adult's, she offered to read the little ones a story. The room was split with infant yells of 'The Selfish Giant'. She read it well, and her audience was the most silent and attentive it ever proved itself in the entire week. At the close there was one united sigh of rapture. It was perfect ecumenicism, transcending cultures, ethnicities, nationalities, religions, genders – and ages. To my generation and the next, Wilde is an old friend – but to those children, some half-a-century my junior, he was evidently a (fairly) old friend, less by his own name than as the man who wrote 'The Selfish Giant'. His sensational biography, dazzling theatre, *fin-de-siècle*, fireworks of epigram, were all irrelevant. His future in the next century is secure in the hands of these truest of all lovers of Art for Art's sake. It neatly disposes of the superstition that his literary survival is a spin-off of scandal.

'I'm glad they didn't ask for 'The Happy Prince',' said Ms Dowell afterwards. 'It always makes me cry.' It was 'The Selfish Giant' which made Wilde himself cry when he told it, recalled his son Vyvyan in *Son of Oscar Wilde* (1954). His recollection is most valuable. Wilde's success arose primarily from thinking of stories as things to tell.

It is hardly surprising. His mother was an Irish folklorist, his father was an Irish topographer. He himself graduated in classical scholarship whose earliest texts were the oral narratives of a probably illiterate Homer. It gave him a much more immediate sense of audience than most writers. This is not to say that the stories were first told to his two sons, though simple versions of them may have been: Cyril was almost three when the five stories in *The Happy Prince and Other Tales* were published in May 1888, Vyvyan one and a half. But they were written with the *intention* of telling them to his sons. They are stories from an unselfconscious father who knows how to move the storyteller in and out of the narrative with mild self-mockery, as opposed to some assertive male chauvinist brute thundering his own dignity and morality for the edification of his wretched offspring. Wilde is on the child's side:

but he knows the child will only be truly happy if it hates cruelty, treachery and poverty, if it loves loyalty, laughter – and love. These are stories by someone in love with love. As Tolstoy would say, it is where God is.

His sons were a projected audience for the stories, but not an imaginary one. He was already singing them to sleep with lullabies in the Irish language. We have therefore to think of Wilde's rebellion against Victorian materialism being partially grounded in the older cultures that materialism claimed to supersede. He could play games with the English language because he stood on its frontier; however limited his Irish he was profoundly aware of it. It is noteworthy that the two most successful adaptations of Wilde's work into another language are Patrick Pearse's into Irish: *Iosagán* and *Eoghainín na nÉan* from 'The Selfish Giant' and 'The Happy Prince'. Pearse was borrowing from a source Puritan Ireland forbad his acknowledging, but he was also taking the spirit of the stories back to the tongue whence it came.

Wilde in London society or in Paris Bohemia might seem far from Irish roots, but his impact was still that of the story-teller even when the story might be compressed into a sentence. And however clothed in raiment acceptable to fashionable London, the stories in almost all cases travel back to a Celtic folk-world dominated by ghosts and God: the Man Predestined to be a Murderer, the Murderer whose only Salvation can come from the Self-sacrifice of an Innocent, the Salvation of Body by Damnation of Soul – strange but undeniable descriptions of 'Lord Arthur Savile's Crime', of 'The Canterville Ghost', and of *The Picture of Dorian Gray*. They sparkle with comedy and epigrams; they toy with philosophy and lightly flick off profound social comment; they martial incidental figures with the precision of point visible in the pencils of his reluctant disciple Beardsley and his rebellious disciple Beerbohm. But go to the hearts of the stories and they play with ideas as old as time and as deep as hell, and yet may hope from time to time for heaven.

The true folk story rejects any genre division between comedy and tragedy just as the miracle play fell on its knees in slapstick and remained on them in worship. Wilde knew – and was ultimately to prove (as one may see from Toulouse-Lautrec's portrait) – that there is no tragedy greater than that of the weeping clown. Hamlet, Othello, Lear and Macbeth are either conscious or unconscious clowns at various times, and are set in deliberately comic contexts here and there. 'Lord Arthur Savile's Crime' speaks of how 'Our Guildensterns play Hamlet for us, and our Hamlets have to jest like Prince Hal. The world is a stage, but the play is badly cast.' But Wilde also acknowledged the philosopher in Falstaff and the buffoon in Hamlet. So his own Canterville Ghost might render his audience defenceless by paralysing it with farce, and then strike with pity; and his 'Lord Arthur Savile's Crime' promenades on the verge of horror before saving its reader in laughter; and Dorian Gray goes to his death as we are still smiling over grace-notes of satire such as 'young Lord Poole, Bournemouth's eldest son'.

The last line no doubt inspired Evelyn Waugh's Lord Tangent, son of

Lord Circumference, destined to die so comically, just as Wilde inaugurates
the wit of so many other comparable figures in our century from 'Saki' to Joe
Orton, but unlike most of them it is not a wit which takes any pleasure in suf-
fering and it holds out – far more than does the formally Roman Catholic
Waugh – continual if desperate hopes of salvation. In their different ways the
four stories of *A House of Pomegranates* turn on those hopes, even if the
young King can only find it by the recognition of suffering, and the Star-
Child by himself suffering enough to cut short his life, while the Dwarf and
the Fisherman can only be saved by death itself. The satire on predestination
in 'Lord Arthur Savile's Crime' is subsequently asserted in explicit language
in *The Picture of Dorian Gray*: Dorian Gray can save himself, enchantment
or no, but fails because he will not separate repentance from hypocrisy while
it is in his power to do so. Perhaps the most neglected biographical item in
Oscar Wilde's life is that he was the nephew of three clergymen.

The origin of the stories in the art of story-telling accounts for one of
their most startling dichotomies – dialogue and description. The exotic cata-
logues of *outré* phenomena might seem almost the antithesis of the rippling,
quicksilver dialogue: but we must remember the catalogues were conceived
of as spoken, as are those in Homer. Persons with access to a film of Micheál
Mac Liammóir's *The Importance of Being Oscar* can appreciate it from his
rolling French rendition of Herod's jewel speech in *Salome*. If a story's pace
seems to slow down in the reading of narrative, read it aloud. The dialogue of
the stories is story-teller craft in itself, by a story-teller with a great gift for
varying voices: in *Dorian Gray*, among other things, one can see the great
modern master of comedy bursting the constraints of prose in his anxiety to
realise himself fully in the theatre.

But the underlying question on how far the story *is* the narrator, and the
work of art its performer, reaches its most subtle expression in the enlarged
Portrait of Mr W. H. over which Wilde laboured for five years only to have its
full version vanish from sight at the time of his trial. Wilde has, idiotically,
been called a snob; but when it comes to snobbery, everyone – or almost
everyone – was out of step but our Oscar. Scholarship virtually united in
crediting Shakespeare with an Earl as the recipient of his sonnets: scholars
split one another's hairs as to which Earl, but agreed that it must be *some*
Earl. Wilde insisted that the obvious place to look was in the poet's own pro-
fession, and the obvious context the performance of his plays. Having found
the most likely solution he then charmingly played with the emotional pres-
sures of conviction in a scholarly thesis. Conversion brings loss of the con-
verter's faith, much as in the old folk stories the granting of a wish bankrupts
its recipient. And we are left asking whether Shakespeare must remain in
perpetual dependence on the Mr W. H. who interprets him just as Wilde can
only be kept alive by his readers. But Mr W. H. was a boy actor, and Wilde's
future is in no doubt when left in the hands of the children. The converse is
equally true: unless we be as little children we shall never fully enter the
kingdom of Oscar Wilde.

THE PICTURE OF DORIAN GRAY

The Preface

THE artist is the creator of beautiful things.

To reveal art and conceal the artist is art's aim.

The critic is he who can translate into another manner or a new material his impression of beautiful things.

The highest, as the lowest, form of criticism is a mode of autobiography.

Those who find ugly meanings in beautiful things are corrupt without being charming. This is a fault.

Those who find beautiful meanings in beautiful things are the cultivated. For these there is hope.

They are the elect to whom beautiful things mean only Beauty.

There is no such thing as a moral or an immoral book.

Books are well written, or badly written. That is all.

The nineteenth century dislike of Realism is the rage of Caliban seeing his own face in a glass.

The nineteenth century dislike of Romanticism is the rage of Caliban not seeing his own face in a glass.

The moral life of man forms part of the subject-matter of the artist, but the morality of art consists in the perfect use of an imperfect medium.

No artist desires to prove anything. Even things that are true can be proved.

No artist has ethical sympathies. An ethical sympathy in an artist is an unpardonable mannerism of style.

No artist is ever morbid. The artist can express everything.

Thought and language are to the artist instruments of an art.

Vice and virtue are to the artist materials for an art.

From the point of view of form, the type of all the arts is the art of the musician. From the point of view of feeling, the actor's craft is the type.

All art is at once surface and symbol.

Those who go beneath the surface do so at their peril.

Those who read the symbol do so at their peril.

It is the spectator, and not life, that art really mirrors.

Diversity of opinion about a work of art shows that the work is new, complex, and vital.

When critics disagree the artist is in accord with himself.

We can forgive a man for making a useful thing as long as he does not admire it. The only excuse for making a useless thing is that one admires it intensely.

All art is quite useless.

1

THE studio was filled with the rich odour of roses, and when the light summer wind stirred amidst the trees of the garden, there came through the open door the heavy scent of the lilac, or the more delicate perfume of the pink-flowering thorn.

From the corner of the divan of Persian saddle-bags on which he was lying, smoking, as was his custom, innumerable cigarettes, Lord Henry Wotton could just catch the gleam of the honey-sweet and honey-coloured blossoms of a laburnum, whose tremulous branches seemed hardly able to bear the burden of a beauty so flame-like as theirs; and now and then the fantastic shadows of birds in flight flitted across the long tussore-silk curtains that were stretched in front of the huge window, producing a kind of momentary Japanese effect, and making him think of those pallid jade-faced painters of Tokio who, through the medium of an art that is necessarily immobile, seek to convey the sense of swiftness and motion. The sullen murmur of the bees shouldering their way through the long unmown grass, or circling with monotonous insistence round the dusty gilt horns of the straggling woodbine, seemed to make the stillness more oppressive. The dim roar of London was like the bourdon note of a distant organ.

In the centre of the room, clamped to an upright easel, stood the full-length portrait of a young man of extraordinary personal beauty, and in front of it, some little distance away, was sitting the artist himself, Basil Hallward, whose sudden disappearance some years ago caused, at the time, such public excitement, and gave rise to so many strange conjectures.

As the painter looked at the gracious and comely form he had so skilfully mirrored in his art, a smile of pleasure passed across his face, and seemed about to linger there. But he suddenly started up, and, closing his eyes, placed his fingers upon the lids, as though he sought to imprison within his brain some curious dream from which he feared he might awake.

'It is your best work, Basil, the best thing you have ever done,' said Lord Henry, languidly. 'You must certainly send it next year to the Grosvenor. The Academy is too large and too vulgar. Whenever I have gone there, there have been either so many people that I have not been able to see the pictures, which was dreadful, or so many pictures that I have not been able to see the people, which was worse. The Grosvenor is really the only place.'

'I don't think I shall send it anywhere,' he answered, tossing his head back in that odd way that used to make his friends laugh at him at Oxford. 'No: I won't send it anywhere.'

Lord Henry elevated his eyebrows, and looked at him in amazement through the thin blue wreaths of smoke that curled up in such fanciful whirls from his heavy opium-tainted cigarette. 'Not send it anywhere? My dear fellow, why? Have you any reason? What odd chaps you painters are! You do anything in the world to gain a reputation. As soon as you have one, you seem to want to throw it away. It is silly of you, for there is only one thing in the world worse than being talked about, and that is not being talked about. A portrait like this would set you far above all the young men in England, and make the old men quite jealous, if old men are ever capable of any emotion.'

'I know you will laugh at me,' he replied, 'but I really can't exhibit it. I have put too much of myself into it.'

Lord Henry stretched himself out on the divan and laughed.

'Yes, I knew you would; but it is quite true, all the same.'

'Too much of yourself in it! Upon my word, Basil, I didn't know you were so vain; and I really can't see any resemblance between you, with your rugged strong face and your coal-black hair, and this young Adonis, who looks as if he was made out of ivory and rose-leaves. Why, my dear Basil, he is a Narcissus, and you – well, of course you have an intellectual expression, and all that. But beauty, real beauty, ends where an intellectual expression begins. Intellect is in itself a mode of exaggeration, and destroys the harmony of any face. The moment one sits down to think, one becomes all nose, or all forehead, or something horrid. Look at the successful men in any of the learned professions. How perfectly hideous they are! Except, of course, in the Church. But then in the Church they don't think. A bishop keeps on saying at the age of eighty what he was told to say when he was a boy of eighteen, and as a natural consequence he always looks absolutely delightful. Your mysterious young friend, whose name you have never told me, but whose picture really fascinates me, never thinks. I feel quite sure of that. He is some brainless, beautiful creature, who should be always here in winter when we have no flowers to look at, and always here in summer when we want something to chill our intelligence. Don't flatter yourself, Basil: you are not in the least like him.'

'You don't understand me, Harry,' answered the artist. 'Of course I am not like him. I know that perfectly well. Indeed, I should be sorry to look like him. You shrug your shoulders? I am telling you the truth. There is a fatality about all physical and intellectual distinction, the sort of fatality that seems to dog through history the faltering steps of kings. It is better not to be different from one's fellows. The ugly and the stupid have the best of it in this world. They can sit at their ease and gape at the play. If they know nothing of victory, they are at least spared the knowledge of defeat. They live as we all should live, undisturbed, indifferent, and without disquiet. They neither bring ruin upon others, nor ever receive it from alien hands. Your rank and wealth, Harry; my brains, such as they are – my art, whatever it may be worth; Dorian Gray's good looks – we shall all suffer for what the gods have given us, suffer terribly.'

'Dorian Gray? Is that his name?' asked Lord Henry, walking across the studio towards Basil Hallward.

'Yes, that is his name. I didn't intend to tell it to you.'

'But why not?'

'Oh, I can't explain. When I like people immensely I never tell their names to any one. It is like surrendering a part of them. I have grown to love secrecy. It seems to be the one thing that can make modern life mysterious or marvellous to us. The commonest thing is delightful if one only hides it. When I leave town now I never tell my people where I am going. If I did, I would lose all my pleasure. It is a silly habit, I dare say, but somehow it seems to bring a great deal of romance into one's life. I suppose you think me awfully foolish about it?'

'Not at all,' answered Lord Henry, 'not at all, my dear Basil. You seem to forget that I am married, and the one charm of marriage is that it makes a life of deception absolutely necessary for both parties. I never know where my wife is, and my wife never knows what I am doing. When we meet – we do meet occasionally, when we dine out together, or go down to the Duke's – we tell each other the most absurd stories with the most serious faces. My wife is very good at it – much better, in fact, than I am. She never gets confused over her dates, and I always do. But when she does find me out, she makes no row at all. I sometimes wish she would; but she merely laughs at me.'

'I hate the way you talk about your married life, Harry,' said Basil Hallward, strolling towards the door that led into the garden. 'I believe that you are really a very good husband, but that you are thoroughly ashamed of your own virtues. You are an extraordinary fellow. You never say a moral thing, and you never do a wrong thing. Your cynicism is simply a pose.'

'Being natural is simply a pose, and the most irritating pose I know,' cried Lord Henry, laughing; and the two young men went out into the garden together, and ensconced themselves on a long bamboo seat that stood in the shade of a tall laurel bush. The sunlight slipped over the polished leaves. In the grass white daisies were tremulous.

After a pause, Lord Henry pulled out his watch. 'I am afraid I must be going, Basil,' he murmured, 'and before I go, I insist on your answering a question I put to you some time ago.'

'What is that?' said the painter, keeping his eyes fixed on the ground.

'You know quite well.'

'I do not, Harry.'

'Well, I will tell you what it is. I want you to explain to me why you won't exhibit Dorian Gray's picture. I want the real reason.'

'I told you the real reason.'

'No, you did not. You said it was because there was too much of yourself in it. Now, that is childish.'

'Harry,' said Basil Hallward, looking him straight in the face, 'every portrait that is painted with feeling is a portrait of the artist, not of the sitter. The sitter is merely the accident, the occasion. It is not he who is revealed by the painter; it is rather the painter who, on the coloured canvas, reveals himself. The reason I will not exhibit this picture is that I am afraid that I have shown in it the secret of my own soul.'

Lord Henry laughed. 'And what is that?' he asked.

'I will tell you,' said Hallward; but an expression of perplexity came over his face.

'I am all expectation, Basil,' continued his companion, glancing at him.

'Oh, there is really very little to tell, Harry,' answered the painter; 'and I am afraid you will hardly understand it. Perhaps you will hardly believe it.'

Lord Henry smiled, and, leaning down, plucked a pink-petalled daisy from the grass, and examined it. 'I am quite sure I shall understand it,' he replied, gazing intently at the little golden white-feathered disk, 'and as for believing things, I can believe anything, provided that it is quite incredible.'

The wind shook some blossoms from the trees, and the heavy lilac-blooms, with their clustering stars, moved to and fro in the languid air. A grasshopper began to chirrup by the wall, and like a blue thread a long thin dragon-fly floated past on its brown gauze wings. Lord Henry felt as if he could hear Basil Hallward's heart beating, and wondered what was coming.

'The story is simply this,' said the painter after some time. 'Two months ago I went to a crush at Lady Brandon's. You know we poor artists have to show ourselves in society from time to time, just to remind the public that we are not savages. With an evening coat and a white tie, as you told me once, anybody, even a stockbroker, can gain a reputation for being civilised. Well, after I had been in the room about ten minutes, talking to huge overdressed dowagers and tedious Academicians, I suddenly became conscious that some one was looking at me. I turned half-way round, and saw Dorian Gray for the first time. When our eyes met, I felt that I was growing pale. A curious sensation of terror came over me. I knew that I had come face to face with some one whose mere personality was so fascinating that, if I allowed it to do so, it would absorb my whole nature, my whole soul, my very art itself. I did not want any external influence in my life. You know yourself, Harry, how independent I am by nature. I have always been my own master; had at least always been so, till I met Dorian Gray. Then – but I don't know how to explain it to you. Something seemed to tell me that I was on the verge of a terrible crisis in my life. I had a strange feeling that Fate had in store for me exquisite joys and exquisite sorrows. I grew afraid, and turned to quit the room. It was not conscience that made me do so; it was a sort of cowardice. I take no credit to myself for trying to escape.'

'Conscience and cowardice are really the same things, Basil. Conscience is the trade-name of the firm. That is all.'

'I don't believe that, Harry, and I don't believe you do either. However, whatever was my motive – and it may have been pride, for I used to be very proud – I certainly struggled to the door. There, of course, I stumbled against Lady Brandon. "You are not going to run away so soon, Mr. Hallward?" she screamed out. You know her curiously shrill voice?'

'Yes; she is a peacock in everything but beauty,' said Lord Henry, pulling the daisy to bits with his long, nervous fingers.

'I could not get rid of her. She brought me up to Royalties, and people with Stars and Garters, and elderly ladies with gigantic tiaras and parrot noses. She spoke of me as her dearest friend. I had only met her once before, but she took it into her head to lionise me. I believe some picture of mine had made a great success at the time, at least had been chattered about in the penny newspapers, which is the nineteenth-century standard of immortality. Suddenly I found myself face to face with the young man whose personality had so strangely stirred me. We were quite close, almost touching. Our eyes met again. It was reckless of me, but I asked Lady Brandon to introduce me to him. Perhaps it was not so reckless, after all. It was simply inevitable. We would have spoken to each other without any introduction. I am sure of that. Dorian told me so afterwards. He, too, felt that we were destined to know each other.'

'And how did Lady Brandon describe this wonderful young man?' asked his companion. 'I know she goes in for giving a rapid *précis* of all her guests. I remember her bringing me up to a truculent and red-faced old gentleman covered all over with orders and ribbons, and hissing into my ear, in a tragic whisper which must have been perfectly audible to everybody in the room, the most astounding details. I simply fled. I like to find out people for myself. But Lady Brandon treats her guests exactly as an auctioneer treats his goods. She either explains them entirely away, or tells one everything about them except what one wants to know.'

'Poor Lady Brandon! You are hard on her, Harry!' said Hallward, listlessly.

'My dear fellow, she tried to found a *salon*, and only succeeded in opening a restaurant. How could I admire her? But tell me, what did she say about Mr. Dorian Gray?'

'Oh, something like, "Charming boy – poor dear mother and I absolutely inseparable. Quite forget what he does – afraid he – doesn't do anything – oh, yes, plays the piano – or is it the violin, dear Mr. Gray?" Neither of us could help laughing, and we became friends at once.'

'Laughter is not at all a bad beginning for a friendship, and it is far the best ending for one,' said the young lord, plucking another daisy.

Hallward shook his head. 'You don't understand what friendship is, Harry,' he murmured – 'or what enmity is, for that matter. You like every one; that is to say, you are indifferent to every one.'

'How horribly unjust of you!' cried Lord Henry, tilting his hat back, and looking up at the little clouds that, like ravelled skeins of glossy white silk, were drifting across the hollowed turquoise of the summer sky. 'Yes; horribly unjust of you. I make a great difference between people. I choose my friends for their good looks, my acquaintances for their good characters, and my enemies for their good intellects. A man cannot be too careful in the choice of his enemies. I have not got one who is a fool. They are all men of some intellectual power, and consequently they all appreciate me. Is that very vain of me? I think it is rather vain.'

'I should think it was, Harry. But according to your category I must be merely an acquaintance.'

'My dear old Basil, you are much more than an acquaintance.'

'And much less than a friend. A sort of brother, I suppose?'

'Oh, brothers! I don't care for brothers. My elder brother won't die, and my younger brothers seem never to do anything else.'

'Harry!' exclaimed Hallward, frowning.

'My dear fellow, I am not quite serious. But I can't help detesting my relations. I suppose it comes from the fact that none of us can stand other people having the same faults as ourselves. I quite sympathise with the rage of the English democracy against what they call the vices of the upper orders. The masses feel that drunkenness, stupidity, and immorality should be their own special property, and that if any one of us makes an ass of himself he is poaching on their preserves. When poor Southwark got into the Divorce Court, their indignation was quite magnificent. And yet I don't suppose that ten per cent of the proletariat live correctly.'

'I don't agree with a single word that you have said, and, what is more, Harry, I feel sure you don't either.'

Lord Henry stroked his pointed brown beard, and tapped the toe of his patent-leather boot with a tasselled ebony cane. 'How English you are, Basil! That is the second time you have made that observation. If one puts forward an idea to a true Englishman – always a rash thing to do – he never dreams of considering whether the idea is right or wrong. The only thing he considers of any importance is whether one believes it oneself. Now, the value of an idea has nothing whatsoever to do with the sincerity of the man who expresses it. Indeed, the probabilities are that the more insincere the man is, the more purely intellectual will the idea be, as in that case it will not be coloured by either his wants, his desires, or his prejudices. However, I don't propose to discuss politics, sociology, or metaphysics with you. I like persons better than principles, and I like persons with no principles better than anything else in the world. Tell me more about Mr. Dorian Gray. How often do you see him?'

'Every day. I couldn't be happy if I didn't see him every day. He is absolutely necessary to me.'

'How extraordinary! I thought you would never care for anything but your art.'

'He is all my art to me now,' said the painter, gravely. 'I sometimes think, Harry, that there are only two eras of any importance in the world's history. The first is the appearance of a new medium for art, and the second is the appearance of a new personality for art also. What the invention of oil-painting was to the Venetians, the face of Antinoüs was to late Greek sculpture, and the face of Dorian Gray will some day be to me. It is not merely that I paint from him, draw from him, sketch from him. Of course I have done all that. But he is much more to me than a model or a sitter. I won't tell you that I am dissatisfied with what I have done of him, or that his beauty is such that Art cannot express it. There is nothing that Art cannot express, and I know that the work I have done, since I met Dorian Gray, is good work, is the best work of my life. But in some curious way – I wonder will you understand me? – his personality has suggested to me an entirely new manner in art, an entirely new mode of style. I see things differently, I think of them differently. I can now recreate life in a way that was hidden from me before. "A dream of form in days of thought:" – who is it who says that? I forget; but it is what Dorian Gray has been to me. The merely visible presence of this lad – for he seems to me little more than a lad, though he is really over twenty – his merely visible presence – ah! I wonder can you realise all that that means? Unconsciously he defines for me the lines of a fresh school, a school that is to have in it all the passion of the romantic spirit, all the perfection of the spirit that is Greek. The harmony of soul and body – how much that is! We in our madness have separated the two, and have invented a realism that is vulgar, an ideality that is void. Harry! if you only knew what Dorian Gray is to me! You remember that landscape of mine, for which Agnew offered me such a huge price, but which I would not part with? It is one of the best things I have ever done. And why is it so? Because, while I was painting it, Dorian Gray sat beside me. Some subtle influence passed from him to me, and for the first time in my life I saw in the plain woodland the wonder I had always looked for, and always missed.'

'Basil, this is extraordinary! I must see Dorian Gray.'

Hallward got up from the seat, and walked up and down the garden. After some time he came back. 'Harry,' he said, 'Dorian Gray is to me simply a motive in art. You might see nothing in him. I see everything in him. He is never more present in my work than when no image of him is there. He is a suggestion, as I have said, of a new manner. I find him in the curves of certain lines, in the loveliness and subtleties of certain colours. That is all.'

'Then why won't you exhibit his portrait?' asked Lord Henry.

'Because, without intending it, I have put into it some expression of all this curious artistic idolatry, of which, of course, I have never cared to speak to him. He knows nothing about it. He shall never know anything about it. But the world might guess it; and I will not bare my soul to their shallow prying eyes. My heart shall never be put under their microscope. There is too much of myself in the thing, Harry – too much of myself!'

'Poets are not so scrupulous as you are. They know how useful passion is for publication. Nowadays a broken heart will run to many editions.'

'I hate them for it,' cried Hallward. 'An artist should create beautiful things, but should put nothing of his own life into them. We live in an age when men treat art as if it were meant to be a form of autobiography. We have lost the abstract sense of beauty. Some day I will show the world what it is; and for that reason the world shall never see my portrait of Dorian Gray.'

'I think you are wrong, Basil, but I won't argue with you. It is only the intellectually lost who ever argue. Tell me, is Dorian Gray very fond of you?'

The painter considered for a few moments. 'He likes me,' he answered, after a pause; 'I know he likes me. Of course I flatter him dreadfully. I find a strange pleasure in saying things to him that I know I shall be sorry for having said. As a rule, he is charming to me, and we sit in the studio and talk of a thousand things. Now and then, however, he is horribly thoughtless, and seems to take a real delight in giving me pain. Then I feel, Harry, that I have given away my whole soul to some one who treats it as if it were a flower to put in his coat, a bit of decoration to charm his vanity, an ornament for a summer's day.'

'Days in summer, Basil, are apt to linger,' murmured Lord Henry. 'Perhaps you will tire sooner than he will. It is a sad thing to think of, but there is no doubt that Genius lasts longer than Beauty. That accounts for the fact that we all take such pains to over-educate ourselves. In the wild struggle for existence, we want to have something that endures, and so we fill our minds with rubbish and facts, in the silly hope of keeping our place. The thoroughly well-informed man – that is the modern ideal. And the mind of the thoroughly well-informed man is a dreadful thing. It is like a bric-à-brac shop, all monsters and dust, with everything priced above its proper value. I think you will tire first, all the same. Some day you will look at your friend, and he will seem to you to be a little out of drawing, or you won't like his tone of colour, or something. You will bitterly reproach him in your own heart, and seriously think that he has behaved very badly to you. The next time he calls, you will be perfectly cold and indifferent. It will be a great pity, for it will alter you. What you have told me is quite a romance, a romance of art one might call it, and the worst of having a romance of any kind is that it leaves one so unromantic.'

'Harry, don't talk like that. As long as I live, the personality of Dorian Gray will dominate me. You can't feel what I feel. You change too often.'

'Ah, my dear Basil, that is exactly why I can feel it. Those who are faithful know only the trivial side of love: it is the faithless who know love's tragedies.' And Lord Henry struck a light on a dainty silver case, and began to smoke a cigarette with a self-conscious and satisfied air, as if he had summed up the world in a phrase. There was a rustle of chirruping sparrows in the green lacquer leaves of the ivy, and the blue cloud-shadows chased themselves across the grass like swallows. How pleasant it was in the garden! And how delightful other people's emotions were! – much more delightful than their ideas, it seemed to him. One's own soul, and the passions of one's friends – those were the fascinating things in life. He pictured to himself with silent amusement the tedious luncheon that he had missed by staying so long with Basil Hallward. Had he gone to his aunt he would have been sure to have met Lord Goodbody there, and the whole conversation would have been about the feeding of the poor, and the necessity for model lodging-houses. Each class would have preached the importance of those virtues, for whose exercise there was no necessity in their own lives. The rich would have spoken on the value of thrift, and the idle grown eloquent over the dignity of labour. It was charming to have escaped all that! As he thought of his aunt, an idea seemed to strike him. He turned to Hallward, and said, 'My dear fellow, I have just remembered.'

'Remembered what, Harry?'

'Where I heard the name of Dorian Gray.'

'Where was it?' asked Hallward, with a slight frown.

'Don't look so angry, Basil. It was at my aunt, Lady Agatha's. She told me she had discovered a wonderful young man, who was going to help her in the East End, and that his name was Dorian Gray. I am bound to state that she never told me he was good looking. Women have no appreciation of good looks; at least, good women have not. She said that he was very earnest, and had a beautiful nature. I at once pictured to myself a creature with spectacles and lank hair, horribly freckled, and tramping about on huge feet. I wish I had known it was your friend.'

'I am very glad you didn't, Harry.'

'Why?'

'I don't want you to meet him.'

'You don't want me to meet him?'

'No.'

'Mr. Dorian Gray is in the studio, sir,' said the butler, coming into the garden.

'You must introduce me now,' cried Lord Henry, laughing.

The painter turned to his servant, who stood blinking in the sunlight. 'Ask Mr. Gray to wait, Parker: I shall be in in a few moments.' The man bowed, and went up the walk.

Then he looked at Lord Henry. 'Dorian Gray is my dearest friend,' he said. 'He has a simple and a beautiful nature. Your aunt was quite right in what she said of him. Don't spoil him. Don't try to influence him. Your influence would be bad. The world is wide, and has many marvellous people in it. Don't take away from me the one person who gives to my art whatever charm it possesses; my life as an artist depends on him. Mind, Harry, I trust you.' He spoke very slowly, and the words seemed wrung out of him almost against his will.

'What nonsense you talk!' said Lord Henry, smiling, and, taking Hallward by the arm, he almost led him into the house.

2

AS they entered they saw Dorian Gray. He was seated at the piano, with his back to them, turning over the pages of a volume of Schumann's 'Forest Scenes.' 'You must lend me these, Basil,' he cried. 'I want to learn them. They are perfectly charming.'

'That entirely depends on how you sit to-day, Dorian.'

'Oh, I am tired of sitting, and I don't want a life-sized portrait of myself,' answered the lad, swinging round on the music-stool, in a wilful, petulant manner. When he caught sight of Lord Henry, a faint blush coloured his cheeks for a moment, and he started up. 'I beg your pardon, Basil, but I didn't know you had any one with you.'

'This is Lord Henry Wotton, Dorian, an old Oxford friend of mine. I have just been telling him what a capital sitter you were, and now you have spoiled everything.'

'You have not spoiled my pleasure in meeting you, Mr. Gray,' said Lord Henry, stepping forward and extending his hand. 'My aunt has often spoken to me about you. You are one of her favourites, and, I am afraid, one of her victims also.'

'I am in Lady Agatha's black books at present,' answered Dorian, with a funny look of penitence. 'I promised to go to a club in Whitechapel with her last Tuesday, and I really forgot all about it. We were to have played a duet together – three duets, I believe. I don't know what she will say to me. I am far too frightened to call.'

'Oh, I will make your peace with my aunt. She is quite devoted to you. And I don't think it really matters about your not being there. The audience probably thought it was a duet. When Aunt Agatha sits down to the piano she makes quite enough noise for two people.'

'That is very horrid to her, and not very nice to me,' answered Dorian, laughing.

Lord Henry looked at him. Yes, he was certainly wonderfully handsome, with his finely-curved scarlet lips, his frank blue eyes, his crisp gold hair. There was something in his face that made one trust him at once. All the candour of youth was there, as well as all youth's passionate purity. One felt that he had kept himself unspotted from the world. No wonder Basil Hallward worshipped him.

'You are too charming to go in for philanthropy, Mr. Gray – far too charming.' And Lord Henry flung himself down on the divan and opened his cigarette-case.

The painter had been busy mixing his colours and getting his brushes ready. He was looking worried, and when he heard Lord Henry's last remark he glanced at him, hesitated for a moment, and then said, 'Harry, I want to finish this picture to-day. Would you think it awfully rude of me if I asked you to go away?'

Lord Henry smiled, and looked at Dorian Gray. 'Am I to go, Mr. Gray?' he asked.

'Oh, please don't, Lord Henry. I see that Basil is in one of his sulky moods; and I can't bear him when he sulks. Besides, I want you to tell me why I should not go in for philanthropy.'

'I don't know that I shall tell you that, Mr. Gray. It is so tedious a subject that one would have to talk seriously about it. But I certainly shall not run away, now that you have asked me to stop. You don't really mind, Basil, do you? You have often told me that you liked your sitters to have some one to chat to.'

Hallward bit his lip. 'If Dorian wishes it, of course you must stay. Dorian's whims are laws to everybody, except himself.'

Lord Henry took up his hat and gloves. 'You are very pressing, Basil, but I am afraid I must go. I have promised to meet a man at the Orleans. Good-bye, Mr. Gray. Come and see me some afternoon in Curzon Street. I am nearly always at home at five o'clock. Write to me when you are coming. I should be sorry to miss you.'

'Basil,' cried Dorian Gray, 'if Lord Henry Wotton goes I shall go too. You never open your lips while you are painting, and it is horribly dull standing on a platform and trying to look pleasant. Ask him to stay. I insist upon it.'

'Stay, Harry, to oblige Dorian, and to oblige me,' said Hallward, gazing intently at his picture. 'It is quite true, I never talk when I am working, and never listen either, and it must be dreadfully tedious for my unfortunate sitters. I beg you to stay.'

'But what about my man at the Orleans?'

The painter laughed. 'I don't think there will be any difficulty about that. Sit down again, Harry. And now, Dorian, get up on the platform, and don't move about too much, or pay any attention to what Lord Henry says. He has a very bad influence over all his friends, with the single exception of myself.'

Dorian Gray stepped up on the dais, with the air of a young Greek martyr, and made a little *moue* of discontent to Lord Henry, to whom he had rather taken a fancy. He was so unlike Basil. They made a delightful contrast. And he had such a beautiful voice. After a few moments he said to him, 'Have you really a very bad influence, Lord Henry? As bad as Basil says?'

'There is no such thing as a good influence, Mr. Gray. All influence is immoral – immoral from the scientific point of view.'

'Why?'

'Because to influence a person is to give him one's own soul. He does not think his natural thoughts or burn with his natural passions. His virtues are not real to him. His sins, if there are such things as sins, are borrowed. He becomes an echo of some one else's music, an actor of a part that has not been written for him. The aim of life is self-development. To realise one's nature perfectly – that is what each of us is here for. People are afraid of themselves, nowadays. They have forgotten the highest of all duties, the duty that one owes to one's self. Of course they are charitable. They feed the hungry, and clothe the beggar. But their own souls starve, and are naked. Courage has gone out of our race. Perhaps we never really had it. The terror of society, which is the basis of morals, the terror of God, which is the secret of religion – these are the two things that govern us. And yet –'

'Just turn your head a little more to the right, Dorian, like a good boy,' said the painter, deep in his work, and conscious only that a look had come into the lad's face that he had never seen there before.

'And yet,' continued Lord Henry, in his low, musical voice, and with that graceful wave of the hand that was always so characteristic of him, and that he had even in his Eton days, 'I believe that if one man were to live out his life fully and completely, were to give form to every feeling, expression to every thought, reality to every dream – I believe that the world would gain such a fresh impulse of joy that we would forget all the maladies of mediaevalism, and return to the Hellenic ideal – to something finer, richer, than the Hellenic ideal, it may be. But the bravest man amongst us is afraid of himself. The mutilation of the savage has its tragic survival in the self-denial that mars our lives. We are punished for our refusals. Every impulse that we strive to strangle broods in the mind, and poisons us. The body sins once, and has done with its sin, for action is a mode of purification. Nothing remains then but the recollection of a pleasure, or the luxury of a regret. The only way to get rid of a temptation is to yield to it. Resist it, and your soul grows sick with longing for the things it has forbidden to itself, with desire for what its monstrous laws have made monstrous and unlawful. It has been said that the great events of the world take place in the brain. It is in the brain, and the brain only, that the great sins of the world take place also. You, Mr. Gray, you yourself, with your rose-red youth and your rose-white boyhood, you have had passions that have made you afraid, thoughts that have filled you with terror, day-dreams and sleeping dreams whose mere memory might stain your cheek with shame –'

'Stop!' faltered Dorian Gray, 'stop! You bewilder me. I don't know what to say. There is some answer to you, but I cannot find it. Don't speak. Let me think. Or, rather, let me try not to think.'

For nearly ten minutes he stood there, motionless, with parted lips, and eyes strangely bright. He was dimly conscious that entirely fresh influences were at work within him. Yet they seemed to him to have come really from himself. The few words that Basil's friend had said to him – words spoken by chance, no doubt, and with wilful paradox in them – had touched some secret chord that had never been touched before, but that he felt was now vibrating and throbbing to curious pulses.

Music had stirred him like that. Music had troubled him many times. But music was not articulate. It was not a new world, but rather another chaos, that it created in us. Words! Mere words! How terrible they were! How clear, and vivid, and cruel! One could not escape from them. And yet what a subtle magic there was in them! They seemed to be able to give a plastic form to formless things, and to have a music of their own as sweet as that of viol or of lute. Mere words! Was there anything so real as words?

Yes; there had been things in his boyhood that he had not understood. He understood them now. Life suddenly became fiery-coloured to him. It seemed to him that he had been walking in fire. Why had he not known it?

With his subtle smile, Lord Henry watched him. He knew the precise psychological moment when to say nothing. He felt intensely interested. He was amazed at the sudden impression that his words had produced, and, remembering a book that he had read when he was sixteen, a book which had revealed to him much that he had not known before, he wondered whether Dorian Gray was passing through a similar experience. He had merely shot an arrow into the air. Had it hit the mark? How fascinating the lad was!

Hallward painted away with that marvellous bold touch of his, that had the true refinement and perfect delicacy that in art, at any rate, comes only from strength. He was unconscious of the silence.

'Basil, I am tired of standing,' cried Dorian Gray, suddenly. 'I must go out and sit in the garden. The air is stifling here.'

'My dear fellow, I am so sorry. When I am painting, I can't think of anything else. But you never sat better. You were perfectly still. And I have caught the effect I wanted – the half-parted lips, and the bright look in the eyes. I don't know what Harry has been saying to you, but he has certainly made you have the most wonderful expression. I suppose he has been paying you compliments. You mustn't believe a word that he says.'

'He has certainly not been paying me compliments. Perhaps that is the reason that I don't believe anything he has told me.'

'You know you believe it all,' said Lord Henry, looking at him with his dreamy, languorous eyes. 'I will go out to the garden with you. It is horribly hot in the studio. Basil, let us have something iced to drink, something with strawberries in it.'

'Certainly, Harry. Just touch the bell, and when Parker comes I will tell him what you want. I have got to work up this background, so I will join you later on. Don't keep Dorian too long. I have never been in better form for painting than I am to-day. This is going to be my masterpiece. It is my masterpiece as it stands.'

Lord Henry went out to the garden, and found Dorian Gray burying his face in the great cool lilac-blossoms, feverishly drinking in their perfume as if it had been wine. He came close to him, and put his hand upon his shoulder. 'You are quite right to do that,' he murmured. 'Nothing can cure the soul but the senses, just as nothing can cure the senses but the soul.'

The lad started and drew back. He was bare-headed, and the leaves had tossed his rebellious curls and tangled all their gilded threads. There was a look of fear in his eyes, such as people have when they are suddenly awakened. His finely-chiselled nostrils quivered, and some hidden nerve shook the scarlet of his lips and left them trembling.

'Yes,' continued Lord Henry, 'that is one of the great secrets of life – to cure the soul by means of the senses, and the senses by means of the soul. You are a wonderful creation. You know more than you think you know, just as you know less than you want to know.'

Dorian Gray frowned and turned his head away. He could not help liking the tall, graceful young man who was standing by him. His romantic olive-coloured face and worn expression interested him. There was something in his low, languid voice that was absolutely fascinating. His cool, white, flower-like hands, even, had a curious charm. They moved, as he spoke, like music, and seemed to have a language of their own. But he felt afraid of him, and ashamed of being afraid. Why had it been left for a stranger to reveal him to himself? He had known Basil Hallward for months, but the friendship between them had never altered him. Suddenly there had come some one across his life who seemed to have disclosed to him life's mystery. And, yet, what was there to be afraid of? He was not a schoolboy or a girl. It was absurd to be frightened.

'Let us go and sit in the shade,' said Lord Henry. 'Parker has brought out the drinks, and if you stay any longer in this glare you will be quite spoiled, and Basil will never paint you again. You really must not allow yourself to become sunburnt. It would be unbecoming.'

'What can it matter?' cried Dorian Gray, laughing, as he sat down on the seat at the end of the garden.

'It should matter everything to you, Mr. Gray.'

'Why?'

'Because you have the most marvellous youth, and youth is the one thing worth having.'

'I don't feel that, Lord Henry.'

'No, you don't feel it now. Some day, when you are old and wrinkled and ugly, when thought has seared your forehead with its lines, and passion branded your lips with its hideous fires, you will feel it, you will feel it terribly. Now, wherever you go, you charm the world. Will it always be so? . . . You have a wonderfully beautiful face, Mr. Gray. Don't frown. You have. And Beauty is a form of Genius – is higher, indeed, than Genius, as it needs no explanation. It is of the great facts of the world, like sunlight, or springtime, or the reflection in dark waters of that silver shell we call the moon. It cannot be questioned. It has its divine right of sovereignty. It makes princes of those who have it. You smile? Ah! when you have lost it you won't smile . . . People say sometimes that Beauty is only superficial. That may be so. But at least it is not so superficial as Thought is. To me Beauty is the wonder of wonders. It is only shallow people who do not judge by appearances. The true mystery of the world is the visible, not the invisible . . . Yes, Mr. Gray, the gods have been good to you. But what the gods give they quickly take away. You have only a few years in which to live really, perfectly, and fully. When your youth goes, your beauty will go with it, and then you will suddenly discover that there are no triumphs left for you, or have to content yourself with those mean triumphs that the memory of your past will make more bitter than defeats. Every month as it wanes brings you nearer to something dreadful. Time is jealous of you, and wars against your lilies and your roses. You will become sallow, and hollow-cheeked, and dull-eyed. You will suffer horribly. . . . Ah! realise your youth while you have it. Don't squander the gold of your days, listening to the tedious, trying to improve the hopeless failure, or giving away your life to the ignorant, the common, and the vulgar. These are the sickly aims, the false ideals, of our age. Live! Live the wonderful life that is in you! Let nothing be lost upon you. Be always searching for new sensations. Be afraid of nothing. . . . A new Hedonism – that is what our century wants. You might be its visible symbol. With your personality there is nothing you could not do. The world belongs to you for a season. . . . The moment I met you I saw that you were quite unconscious of what you really are, of what you really might be. There was so much in you that charmed me that I felt I must tell you something about yourself. I thought how tragic it would be if you were wasted. For there is such a little time that your youth will last – such a little time. The common hill-flowers wither, but they blossom again. The laburnum will be as yellow next June as it is now. In a month there will be purple stars on the clematis, and year after year the green night of its leaves will hold its purple stars. But we never get back our youth. The pulse of joy that beats in us at twenty, becomes sluggish. Our limbs fail, our senses rot. We degenerate into hideous puppets, haunted by the memory of the passions of which we were too much afraid, and the exquisite temptations that we had not the courage to yield to. Youth! Youth! There is absolutely nothing in the world but youth!'

Dorian Gray listened, open-eyed and wondering. The spray of lilac fell from his hand upon the gravel. A furry bee came and buzzed round it for a moment. Then it began to scramble all over the oval stellated globe of the tiny blossoms. He watched it with that strange interest in trivial things that we try to develop when things of high import make us afraid, or when we are stirred by some new emotion for which we cannot find expression, or when some thought that terrifies us lays sudden siege to the brain and calls on us to yield. After a time the bee flew away. He saw it creeping into the stained trumpet of a Tyrian convolvulus. The flower seemed to quiver, and then swayed gently to and fro.

Suddenly the painter appeared at the door of the studio, and made staccato signs for them to come in. They turned to each other, and smiled.

'I am waiting,' he cried. 'Do come in. The light is quite perfect, and you can bring your drinks.'

They rose up, and sauntered down the walk together. Two green and white butterflies fluttered past them, and in the pear-tree at the corner of the garden a thrush began to sing.

'You are glad to have met me, Mr. Gray,' said Lord Henry, looking at him.

'Yes, I am glad now. I wonder shall I always be glad?'

'Always! That is a dreadful word. It makes me shudder when I hear it. Women are so fond of using it. They spoil every romance by trying to make it last for ever. It is a meaningless word, too. The only difference between a caprice and a life-long passion is that the caprice lasts a little longer.'

As they entered the studio, Dorian Gray put his hand upon Lord Henry's arm. 'In that case, let our friendship be a caprice,' he murmured, flushing at his own boldness, then stepped up on the platform and resumed his pose.

Lord Henry flung himself into a large wicker armchair, and watched him. The sweep and dash of the brush on the canvas made the only sound that broke the stillness, except when, now and then, Hallward stepped back to look at his work from a distance. In the slanting beams that streamed through the open doorway the dust danced and was golden. The heavy scent of the roses seemed to brood over everything.

After about a quarter of an hour Hallward stopped painting, looked for a long time at Dorian Gray, and then for a long time at the picture, biting the end of one of his huge brushes, and frowning. 'It is quite finished,' he cried at last, and stooping down he wrote his name in long vermilion letters on the left-hand corner of the canvas.

Lord Henry came over and examined the picture. It was certainly a wonderful work of art, and a wonderful likeness as well.

'My dear fellow, I congratulate you most warmly,' he said. 'It is the finest portrait of modern times. Mr. Gray, come over and look at yourself.'

The lad started, as if awakened from some dream. 'Is it really finished?' he murmured, stepping down from the platform.

'Quite finished,' said the painter. 'And you have sat splendidly to-day. I am awfully obliged to you.'

'That is entirely due to me,' broke in Lord Henry. 'Isn't it, Mr. Gray?'

Dorian made no answer, but passed listlessly in front of his picture, and turned towards it. When he saw it he drew back, and his cheeks flushed for a moment with pleasure. A look of joy came into his eyes, as if he had recognised himself for the first time. He stood there motionless and in wonder, dimly conscious that Hallward was speaking to him, but not catching the meaning of his words. The sense of his own beauty came on him like a revelation. He had never felt it before. Basil Hallward's compliments had seemed to him to be merely the charming exaggerations of friendship. He had listened to them, laughed at them, forgotten them. They had not influenced his nature. Then had come Lord Henry Wotton with his strange panegyric on youth, his terrible warning of its brevity. That had stirred him at the time, and now, as he stood gazing at the shadow of his own loveliness, the full reality of the description flashed across him. Yes, there would be a day when his face would be wrinkled and wizen, his eyes dim and colourless, the grace of his figure broken and deformed. The scarlet would pass away from his lips, and the gold steal from his hair. The life that was to make his soul would mar his body. He would become dreadful, hideous, and uncouth.

As he thought of it, a sharp pang of pain struck through him like a knife, and made each delicate fibre of his nature quiver. His eyes deepened into amethyst, and across them came a mist of tears. He felt as if a hand of ice had been laid upon his heart.

'Don't you like it?' cried Hallward at last, stung a little by the lad's silence, not understanding what it meant.

'Of course he likes it,' said Lord Henry. 'Who wouldn't like it? It is one of the greatest things in modern art. I will give you anything you like to ask for it. I must have it.'

'It is not my property, Harry.'

'Whose property is it?'

'Dorian's, of course,' answered the painter.

'He is a very lucky fellow.'

'How sad it is!' murmured Dorian Gray, with his eyes still fixed upon his own portrait. 'How sad it is! I shall grow old, and horrible, and dreadful. But this picture will remain always young. It will never be older than this particular day of June. . . . If it were only the other way! If it were I who was to be always young, and the picture that was to grow old! For that – for that – I would give everything! Yes, there is nothing in the whole world I would not give! I would give my soul for that!'

'You would hardly care for such an arrangement, Basil,' cried Lord Henry, laughing. 'It would be rather hard lines on your work.'

'I should object very strongly, Harry,' said Hallward.

Dorian Gray turned and looked at him. 'I believe you would, Basil. You like your art better than your friends. I am no more to you than a green bronze figure. Hardly as much, I dare say.'

The painter stared in amazement. It was so unlike Dorian to speak like that. What had happened? He seemed quite angry. His face was flushed and his cheeks burning.

'Yes,' he continued, 'I am less to you than your ivory Hermes or your silver Faun. You will like them always. How long will you like me? Till I have my first wrinkle, I suppose. I know, now, that when one loses one's good looks, whatever they may be, one loses everything. Your picture has taught me that. Lord Henry Wotton is perfectly right. Youth is the only thing worth having. When I find that I am growing old, I shall kill myself.'

Hallward turned pale, and caught his hand. 'Dorian! Dorian!' he cried, 'don't talk like that. I have never had such a friend as you, and I shall never have such another. You are not jealous of material things, are you? – you who are finer than any of them!'

'I am jealous of everything whose beauty does not die. I am jealous of the portrait you have painted of me. Why should it keep what I must lose? Every moment that passes takes something from me, and gives something to it. Oh, if it were only the other way! If the picture could change, and I could be always what I am now! Why did you paint it? It will mock me some day – mock me horribly!' The hot tears welled into his eyes; he tore his hand away, and, flinging himself on the divan, he buried his face in the cushions, as though he was praying.

'This is your doing, Harry,' said the painter, bitterly.

Lord Henry shrugged his shoulders. 'It is the real Dorian Gray – that is all.'

'It is not.'

'If it is not, what have I to do with it?'

'You should have gone away when I asked you,' he muttered.

'I stayed when you asked me,' was Lord Henry's answer.

'Harry, I can't quarrel with my two best friends at once, but between you both you have made me hate the finest piece of work I have ever done, and I will destroy it. What is it but canvas and colour? I will not let it come across our three lives and mar them.'

Dorian Gray lifted his golden head from the pillow, and with pallid face and tear-stained eyes looked at him, as he walked over to the deal painting-table that was set beneath the high curtained window. What was he doing there? His fingers were straying about among the litter of tin tubes and dry brushes, seeking for something. Yes, it was for the long palette-knife, with its thin blade of lithe steel. He had found it at last. He was going to rip up the canvas.

With a stifled sob the lad leaped from the couch, and, rushing over to Hallward, tore the knife out of his hand, and flung it to the end of the studio. 'Don't, Basil, don't!' he cried. 'It would be murder!'

'I am glad you appreciate my work at last, Dorian,' said the painter, coldly, when he had recovered from his surprise. 'I never thought you would.'

'Appreciate it? I am in love with it, Basil. It is part of myself. I feel that.'

'Well, as soon as you are dry, you shall be varnished, and framed, and sent home. Then you can do what you like with yourself.' And he walked across the room and rang the bell for tea. 'You will have tea, of course, Dorian? And so will you, Harry? Or do you object to such simple pleasures?'

'I adore simple pleasures,' said Lord Henry. 'They are the last refuge of the complex. But I don't like scenes, except on the stage. What absurd fellows you are, both of you! I wonder who it was defined man as a rational animal. It was the most premature definition ever given. Man is many things, but he is not rational. I am glad he is not, after all: though I wish you chaps would not squabble over the picture. You had much better let me have it, Basil. This silly boy doesn't really want it, and I really do.'

'If you let any one have it but me, Basil, I shall never forgive you!' cried Dorian Gray; 'and I don't allow people to call me a silly boy.'

'You know the picture is yours, Dorian. I gave it to you before it existed.'

'And you know you have been a little silly, Mr. Gray, and that you don't really object to being reminded that you are extremely young.'

'I should have objected very strongly this morning, Lord Henry.'

'Ah! this morning! You have lived since then.'

There came a knock at the door, and the butler entered with a laden tea-tray and set it down upon a small Japanese table. There was a rattle of cups and saucers and the hissing of a fluted Georgian urn. Two globe-shaped china dishes were brought in by a page. Dorian Gray went over and poured out the tea. The two men sauntered languidly to the table, and examined what was under the covers.

'Let us go to the theatre to-night,' said Lord Henry. 'There is sure to be something on, somewhere. I have promised to dine at White's but it is only with an old friend, so I can send him a wire to say that I am ill, or that I am prevented from coming in consequence of a subsequent engagement. I think that would be a rather nice excuse: it would have all the surprise of candour.'

'It is such a bore putting on one's dress-clothes,' muttered Hallward. 'And, when one has them on, they are so horrid.'

'Yes,' answered Lord Henry, dreamily, 'the costume of the nineteenth century is detestable. It is so sombre, so depressing. Sin is the only real colour-element left in modern life.'

'You really must not say things like that before Dorian, Harry.'

'Before which Dorian? The one who is pouring out tea for us, or the one in the picture?'

'Before either.'

'I should like to come to the theatre with you, Lord Henry,' said the lad.

'Then you shall come; and you will come too, Basil, won't you?'

'I can't really. I would sooner not. I have a lot of work to do.'

'Well, then, you and I will go alone, Mr. Gray.'

'I should like that awfully.'

The painter bit his lip and walked over, cup in hand, to the picture. 'I shall stay with the real Dorian,' he said, sadly.

'Is it the real Dorian?' cried the original of the portrait, strolling across to him. 'Am I really like that?'

'Yes; you are just like that.'

'How wonderful, Basil!'

'At least you are like it in appearance. But it will never alter,' sighed Hallward. 'That is something.'

'What a fuss people make about fidelity!' exclaimed Lord Henry. 'Why, even in love it is purely a question for physiology. It has nothing to do with our own will. Young men want to be faithful, and are not: old men want to be faithless, and cannot: that is all one can say.'

'Don't go to the theatre to-night, Dorian,' said Hallward. 'Stop and dine with me.'

'I can't, Basil.'

'Why?'

'Because I have promised Lord Henry Wotton to go with him.'

'He won't like you the better for keeping your promises. He always breaks his own. I beg you not to go.'

Dorian Gray laughed and shook his head.

'I entreat you.'

The lad hesitated, and looked over at Lord Henry, who was watching them from the tea-table with an amused smile.

'I must go, Basil,' he answered.

'Very well,' said Hallward; and he went over and laid down his cup on the tray. 'It is rather late, and, as you have to dress, you had better lose no time. Good-bye, Harry. Good-bye, Dorian. Come and see me soon. Come to-morrow.'

'Certainly.'

'You won't forget?'

'No, of course not,' cried Dorian.

'And . . . Harry!'

'Yes, Basil?'

'Remember what I asked you, when we were in the garden this morning.'

'I have forgotten it.'

'I trust you.'

'I wish I could trust myself,' said Lord Henry, laughing. 'Come, Mr. Gray, my hansom is outside, and I can drop you at your own place. Good-bye, Basil. It has been a most interesting afternoon.'

As the door closed behind them, the painter flung himself down on a sofa, and a look of pain came into his face.

3

AT half-past twelve next day Lord Henry Wotton strolled from Curzon Street over to the Albany to call on his uncle, Lord Fermor, a genial if some-what rough-mannered old bachelor, whom the outside world called selfish, because it derived no particular benefit from him, but who was considered generous by Society as he fed the people who amused him. His father had been our ambassador at Madrid when Isabella was young, and Prim unthought of, but had retired from the Diplomatic Service in a capricious moment of annoyance at not being offered the Embassy at Paris, a post to which he considered that he was fully entitled by reason of his birth, his in-dolence, the good English of his despatches, and his inordinate passion for pleasure. The son, who had been his father's secretary, had resigned along with his chief, somewhat foolishly as was thought at the time, and on suc-ceeding some months later to the title, had set himself to the serious study of the great aristocratic art of doing absolutely nothing. He had two large town houses, but preferred to live in chambers, as it was less trouble, and took most of his meals at his club. He paid some attention to the management of his collieries in the Midland counties, excusing himself for this taint of in-dustry on the ground that the one advantage of having coal was that it en-abled a gentleman to afford the decency of burning wood on his own hearth. In politics he was a Tory, except when the Tories were in office, during which period he roundly abused them for being a pack of Radicals. He was a hero to his valet, who bullied him, and a terror to most of his relations, whom he bullied in turn. Only England could have produced him, and he always said that the country was going to the dogs. His principles were out of date, but there was a good deal to be said for his prejudices.

When Lord Henry entered the room, he found his uncle sitting in a rough shooting-coat, smoking a cheroot, and grumbling over *The Times*. 'Well, Harry,' said the old gentleman, 'what brings you out so early? I thought you dandies never got up till two, and were not visible till five.'

'Pure family affection, I assure you, Uncle George. I want to get some-thing out of you.'

'Money, I suppose,' said Lord Fermor, making a wry face. 'Well, sit down and tell me all about it. Young people, nowadays, imagine that money is everything.'

'Yes,' murmured Lord Henry, settling his buttonhole in his coat; 'and when they grow older they know it. But I don't want money. It is only people who pay their bills who want that, Uncle George, and I never pay mine. Cre-dit is the capital of a younger son, and one lives charmingly upon it. Besides, I always deal with Dartmoor's tradesmen, and consequently they never bother me. What I want is information; not useful information, of course; useless information.'

'Well, I can tell you anything that is in an English Blue-book, Harry, al-though those fellows nowadays write a lot of nonsense. When I was in the Diplomatic, things were much better. But I hear they let them in now by ex-amination. What can you expect? Examinations, sir, are pure humbug from beginning to end. If a man is a gentleman, he knows quite enough, and if he is not a gentleman, whatever he knows is bad for him.'

'Mr. Dorian Gray does not belong to Blue-books, Uncle George,' said Lord Henry, languidly.

'Mr. Dorian Gray? Who is he?' asked Lord Fermor, knitting his bushy white eyebrows.

'That is what I have come to learn, Uncle George. Or rather, I know who he is. He is the last Lord Kelso's grandson. His mother was a Devereux; Lady Margaret Devereux. I want you to tell me about his mother. What was she like? Whom did she marry? You have known nearly everybody in your time, so you might have known her. I am very much interested in Mr. Gray at present. I have only just met him.'

'Kelso's grandson!' echoed the old gentleman. – 'Kelso's grandson! . . . Of course. . . . I knew his mother intimately. I believe I was at her christening. She was an extraordinarily beautiful girl, Margaret Devereux; and made all the men frantic by running away with a penniless young fellow; a mere no-body, sir, a subaltern in a foot regiment, or something of that kind. Certainly. I remember the whole thing as if it happened yesterday. The poor chap was killed in a duel at Spa, a few months after the marriage. There was an ugly story about it. They said Kelso got some rascally adventurer, some Belgian brute, to insult his son-in-law in public; paid him, sir, to do it, paid him; and that the fellow spitted his man as if he had been a pigeon. The thing was hushed up, but, egad, Kelso ate his chop alone at the club for some time af-terwards. He brought his daughter back with him, I was told, and she never spoke to him again. Oh yes; it was a bad business. The girl died too; died within a year. So she left a son, did she? I had forgotten that. What sort of boy is he? If he is like his mother he must be a good-looking chap.'

'He is very good looking,' assented Lord Henry.

'I hope he will fall into proper hands,' continued the old man. 'He should have a pot of money waiting for him if Kelso did the right thing by him. His mother had money too. All the Selby property came to her, through her grandfather. Her grandfather hated Kelso, thought him a mean dog. He was, too. Came to Madrid once when I was there. Egad, I was ashamed of him. The Queen used to ask me about the English noble who was always quar-relling with the cabmen about their fares. They made quite a story of it. I didn't dare to show my face at Court for a month. I hope he treated his grandson better than he did the jarvies.'

'I don't know,' answered Lord Henry. 'I fancy that the boy will be well off. He is not of age yet. He has Selby, I know. He told me so. And . . . his mother was very beautiful?'

'Margaret Devereux was one of the loveliest creatures I ever saw, Harry. What on earth induced her to behave as she did, I never could understand. She could have married anybody she chose. Carlington was mad after her. She was romantic, though. All the women of that family were. The men were a poor lot, but, egad! the women were wonderful. Carlington went on his knees to her. Told me so himself. She laughed at him, and there wasn't a girl in London at the time who wasn't after him. And by the way, Harry, talking about silly marriages, what is this humbug your father tells me about Dart-moor wanting to marry an American? Ain't English girls good enough for him?'

'It is rather fashionable to marry Americans just now, Uncle George.'

'I'll back English women against the world, Harry,' said Lord Fermor, striking the table with his fist.

'The betting is on the Americans.'

'They don't last, I am told,' muttered his uncle.

'A long engagement exhausts them, but they are capital at a steeplechase. They take things flying. I don't think Dartmoor has a chance.'

'Who are her people?' grumbled the old gentleman. 'Has she got any?'

Lord Henry shook his head. 'American girls are as clever at concealing their parents as English women are at concealing their past,' he said, rising to go.

'They are pork-packers, I suppose?'

'I hope so, Uncle George, for Dartmoor's sake. I am told that pork-packing is the most lucrative profession in America, after politics.'

'Is she pretty?'

'She behaves as if she was beautiful. Most American women do. It is the secret of their charm.'

'Why can't these American women stay in their own country? They are always telling us that it is the Paradise for women.'

'It is. That is the reason why, like Eve, they are so excessively anxious to get out of it,' said Lord Henry. 'Good-bye, Uncle George. I shall be late for lunch if I stop any longer. Thanks for giving me the information I wanted. I always like to know everything about my new friends, and nothing about my old ones.'

'Where are you lunching, Harry?'

'At Aunt Agatha's. I have asked myself and Mr. Gray. He is her latest *protégé*.'

'Humph! tell your Aunt Agatha, Harry, not to bother me any more with her charity appeals. I am sick of them. Why, the good woman thinks that I have nothing to do but to write cheques for her silly fads.'

'All right, Uncle George, I'll tell her, but it won't have any effect. Philanthropic people lose all sense of humanity. It is their distinguishing characteristic.'

The old gentleman growled approvingly, and rang the bell for his servant. Lord Henry passed up the low arcade into Burlington Street, and turned his steps in the direction of Berkeley Square.

So that was the story of Dorian Gray's parentage. Crudely as it had been told to him, it had yet stirred him by its suggestion of a strange almost modern romance. A beautiful woman risking everything for a mad passion. A few wild weeks of happiness cut short by a hideous, treacherous crime. Months of voiceless agony, and then a child born in pain. The mother snatched away by death, the boy left to solitude and the tyranny of an old and loveless man. Yes; it was an interesting background. It posed the lad, made him more perfect as it were. Behind every exquisite thing that existed, there was something tragic. Worlds had to be in travail, that the meanest flower might blow. . . . And how charming he had been at dinner the night before, as, with startled eyes and lips parted in frightened pleasure, he had sat opposite to him at the club, the red candleshades staining to a richer rose the wakening wonder of his face. Talking to him was like playing upon an exquisite violin. He answered to every touch and thrill of the bow. . . . There was something terribly enthralling in the exercise of influence. No other activity was like it.

To project one's soul into some gracious form, and let it tarry there for a moment; to hear one's own intellectual views echoed back to one with all the added music of passion and youth; to convey one's temperament into another as though it were a subtle fluid or a strange perfume; there was a real joy in that – perhaps the most satisfying joy left to us in an age so limited and vulgar as our own, an age grossly carnal in its pleasures, and grossly common in its aims.... He was a marvellous type, too, this lad, whom by so curious a chance he had met in Basil's studio; or could be fashioned into a marvellous type, at any rate. Grace was his, and the white purity of boyhood, and beauty such as old Greek marbles kept for us. There was nothing that one could not do with him. He could be made a Titan or a toy. What a pity it was that such beauty was destined to fade!... And Basil? From a psychological point of view, how interesting he was! The new manner in art, the fresh mode of looking at life, suggested so strangely by the merely visible presence of one who was unconscious of it all; the silent spirit that dwelt in dim woodland, and walked unseen in open field, suddenly showing herself, Dryad-like and not afraid, because in his soul who sought for her there had been wakened that wonderful vision to which alone are wonderful things revealed; the mere shapes and patterns of things becoming, as it were, refined, and gaining a kind of symbolical value, as though they were themselves patterns of some other and more perfect form whose shadow they made real: how strange it all was! He remembered something like it in history. Was it not Plato, that artist in thought, who had first analysed it? Was it not Buonarotti who had carved it in the coloured marbles of a sonnet-sequence? But in our own century it was strange.... Yes; he would try to be to Dorian Gray what, without knowing it, the lad was to the painter who had fashioned the wonderful portrait. He would seek to dominate him – had already, indeed, half done so. He would make that wonderful spirit his own. There was something fascinating in this son of Love and Death.

Suddenly he stopped, and glanced up at the houses. He found that he had passed his aunt's some distance, and, smiling to himself, turned back. When he entered the somewhat sombre hall the butler told him that they had gone in to lunch. He gave one of the footmen his hat and stick, and passed into the dining-room.

'Late as usual, Harry,' cried his aunt, shaking her head at him.

He invented a facile excuse, and having taken the vacant seat next her, looked round to see who was there. Dorian bowed to him shyly from the end of the table, a flush of pleasure stealing into his cheek. Opposite was the Duchess of Harley – a lady of admirable good nature and good temper, much liked by every one who knew her, and of those ample architectural proportions that in women who are not Duchesses are described by contemporary historians as stoutness. Next to her sat, on her right, Sir Thomas Burdon, a Radical member of Parliament, who followed his leader in public life, and in private life followed the best cooks, dining with the Tories, and thinking with the Liberals, in accordance with a wise and well-known rule. The post on her left was occupied by Mr. Erskine of Treadley, an old gentleman of considerable charm and culture, who had fallen, however, into bad habits of silence, having, as he explained once to Lady Agatha, said everything that he had to say before he was thirty. His own neighbour was Mrs. Vandeleur, one of his aunt's oldest friends, a perfect saint amongst women, but so dreadfully dowdy that she reminded one of a badly bound hymn-book. Fortunately for him she had on the other side Lord Faudel, a most intelligent middle-aged mediocrity, as bald as a Ministerial statement in the House of Commons, with whom she was conversing in that intensely earnest manner which is the one unpardonable error, as he remarked once himself, that all really good people fall into, and from which none of them ever quite escape.

'We are talking about poor Dartmoor, Lord Henry,' cried the Duchess, nodding pleasantly to him across the table. 'Do you think he will really marry this fascinating young person?'

'I believe she has made up her mind to propose to him, Duchess.'

'How dreadful!' exclaimed Lady Agatha. 'Really, some one should interfere.'

'I am told, on excellent authority, that her father keeps an American dry-goods store,' said Sir Thomas Burdon, looking supercilious.

'My uncle has already suggested pork-packing, Sir Thomas.'

'Dry goods! What are American dry-goods?' asked the Duchess, raising her large hands in wonder, and accentuating the verb.

'American novels,' answered Lord Henry, helping himself to some quail.

The Duchess looked puzzled.

'Don't mind him, my dear,' whispered Lady Agatha. 'He never means anything that he says.'

'When America was discovered,' said the Radical member, and he began to give some wearisome facts. Like all people who try to exhaust a subject, he exhausted his listeners. The Duchess sighed, and exercised her privilege of interruption. 'I wish to goodness it never had been discovered at all!' she exclaimed. 'Really, our girls have no chance nowadays. It is most unfair.'

'Perhaps, after all, America never has been discovered,' said Mr. Erskine. 'I myself would say that it had merely been detected.'

'Oh! But I have seen specimens of the inhabitants,' answered the Duchess, vaguely. 'I must confess that most of them are extremely pretty. And they dress well, too. They get all their dresses in Paris. I wish I could afford to do the same.'

'They say that when good Americans die they go to Paris,' chuckled Sir Thomas, who had a large wardrobe of Humour's cast-off clothes.

'Really! And where do bad Americans go to when they die?' inquired the Duchess.

'They go to America,' murmured Lord Henry.

Sir Thomas frowned. 'I am afraid that your nephew is prejudiced against that great country,' he said to Lady Agatha. 'I have travelled all over it, in cars provided by the directors, who, in such matters, are extremely civil. I assure you that it is an education to visit it.'

'But must we really see Chicago in order to be educated?' asked Mr.

Erskine, plaintively. 'I don't feel up to the journey.'

Sir Thomas waved his hand. 'Mr. Erskine of Treadley has the world on his shelves. We practical men like to see things, not to read about them. The Americans are an extremely interesting people. They are absolutely reasonable. I think that is their distinguishing characteristic. Yes, Mr. Erskine, an absolutely reasonable people. I assure you there is no nonsense about the Americans.'

'How dreadful!' cried Lord Henry. 'I can stand brute force, but brute reason is quite unbearable. There is something unfair about its use. It is hitting below the intellect.'

'I do not understand you,' said Sir Thomas, growing rather red.

'I do, Lord Henry,' murmured Mr. Erskine, with a smile.

'Paradoxes are all very well in their way . . .' rejoined the Baronet.

'Was that a paradox?' asked Mr. Erskine. 'I did not think so. Perhaps it was. Well, the way of paradoxes is the way of truth. To test Reality we must see it on the tight-rope. When the Verities become acrobats we can judge them.'

'Dear me!' said Lady Agatha, 'how you men argue! I am sure I never can make out what you are talking about. Oh! Harry, I am quite vexed with you. Why do you try to persuade our nice Mr. Dorian Gray to give up the East End? I assure you he would be quite invaluable. They would love his playing.'

'I want him to play to me,' cried Lord Henry, smiling, and he looked down the table and caught a bright answering glance.

'But they are so unhappy in Whitechapel,' continued Lady Agatha.

'I can sympathise with everything, except suffering,' said Lord Henry, shrugging his shoulders. 'I cannot sympathise with that. It is too ugly, too horrible, too distressing. There is something terribly morbid in the modern sympathy with pain. One should sympathise with the colour, the beauty, the joy of life. The less said about life's sores the better.'

'Still, the East End is a very important problem,' remarked Sir Thomas, with a grave shake of the head.

'Quite so,' answered the young lord. 'It is the problem of slavery, and we try to solve it by amusing the slaves.'

The politician looked at him keenly. 'What change do you propose, then?' he asked.

Lord Henry laughed. 'I don't desire to change anything in England except the weather,' he answered. 'I am quite content with philosophic contemplation. But as the nineteenth century has gone bankrupt through an over-expenditure of sympathy, I would suggest that we should appeal to Science to put us straight. The advantage of the emotions is that they lead us astray, and the advantage of Science is that it is not emotional.'

'But we have such grave responsibilities,' ventured Mrs. Vandeleur, timidly.

'Terribly grave,' echoed Lady Agatha.

Lord Henry looked over at Mr. Erskine. 'Humanity takes itself too seriously. It is the world's original sin. If the caveman had known how to laugh, History would have been different.'

'You are really very comforting,' warbled the Duchess. 'I have always felt rather guilty when I came to see your dear aunt, for I take no interest at all in the East End. For the future I shall be able to look her in the face without a blush.'

'A blush is very becoming, Duchess,' remarked Lord Henry.

'Only when one is young,' she answered. 'When an old woman like myself blushes, it is a very bad sign. Ah! Lord Henry, I wish you would tell me how to become young again.'

He thought for a moment. 'Can you remember any great error that you committed in your early days, Duchess?' he asked, looking at her across the table.

'A great many, I fear,' she cried.

'Then commit them over again,' he said, gravely. 'To get back one's youth, one has merely to repeat one's follies.'

'A delightful theory!' she exclaimed. 'I must put it into practice.'

'A dangerous theory!' came from Sir Thomas's tight lips. Lady Agatha shook her head, but could not help being amused. Mr. Erskine listened.

'Yes,' he continued, 'that is one of the great secrets of life. Nowadays most people die of a sort of creeping common sense, and discover when it is too late that the only things one never regrets are one's mistakes.'

A laugh ran round the table.

He played with the idea, and grew wilful; tossed it into the air and transformed it; let it escape and recaptured it; made it iridescent with fancy, and winged it with paradox. The praise of folly, as he went on, soared into a philosophy, and Philosophy herself became young, and catching the mad music of Pleasure, wearing, one might fancy, her wine-stained robe and wreath of ivy, danced like a Bacchante over the hills of life, and mocked the slow Silenus for being sober. Facts fled before her like frightened forest things. Her white feet trod the huge press at which wise Omar sits, till the seething grape-juice rose round her bare limbs in waves of purple bubbles, or crawled in red foam over the vat's black, dripping, sloping sides. It was an extraordinary improvisation. He felt that the eyes of Dorian Gray were fixed on him, and the consciousness that amongst his audience there was one whose temperament he wished to fascinate, seemed to give his wit keenness, and to lend colour to his imagination. He was brilliant, fantastic, irresponsible. He charmed his listeners out of themselves, and they followed his pipe laughing. Dorian Gray never took his gaze off him, but sat like one under a spell, smiles chasing each other over his lips, and wonder growing grave in his darkening eyes.

At last, liveried in the costume of the age, Reality entered the room in the shape of a servant to tell the Duchess that her carriage was waiting. She wrung her hands in mock despair. 'How annoying!' she cried. 'I must go. I have to call for my husband at the club, to take him to some absurd meeting at Willis's Rooms, where he is going to be in the chair. If I am late, he is sure to be furious, and I couldn't have a scene in this bonnet. It is far too fragile. A harsh word would ruin it. No, I must go, dear Agatha. Good-bye, Lord Henry; you are quite delightful, and dreadfully demoralising. I am sure I don't know what to say about your views. You must come and dine with us some night. Tuesday? Are you disengaged Tuesday?'

'For you I would throw over anybody, Duchess,' said Lord Henry, with a bow.

'Ah! that is very nice, and very wrong of you,' she cried; 'so mind you come;' and she swept out of the room, followed by Lady Agatha and the other ladies.

When Lord Henry had sat down again, Mr. Erskine moved round, and taking a chair close to him, placed his hand upon his arm.

'You talk books away,' he said: 'why don't you write one?'

'I am too fond of reading books to care to write them, Mr. Erskine. I should like to write a novel certainly; a novel that would be as lovely as a Persian carpet, and as unreal. But there is no literary public in England for anything except newspapers, primers, and encyclopædias. Of all people in the world the English have the least sense of the beauty of literature.'

'I fear you are right,' answered Mr. Erskine. 'I myself used to have literary ambitions, but I gave them up long ago. And now, my dear young friend, if you will allow me to call you so, may I ask if you really meant all that you said to us at lunch?'

'I quite forget what I said,' smiled Lord Henry. 'Was it all very bad?'

'Very bad, indeed. In fact, I consider you extremely dangerous, and if anything happens to our good Duchess we shall all look on you as being primarily responsible. But I should like to talk to you about life. The generation into which I was born was tedious. Some day, when you are tired of London, come down to Treadley, and expound to me your philosophy of pleasure over some admirable Burgundy I am fortunate enough to possess.'

'I shall be charmed. A visit to Treadley would be a great privilege. It has a perfect host and a perfect library.'

'You will complete it,' answered the old gentleman, with a courteous bow. 'And now I must bid good-bye to your excellent aunt. I am due at the Athenaeum. It is the hour when we sleep there.'

'All of you, Mr. Erskine?'

'Forty of us, in forty arm-chairs. We are practising for an English Academy of Letters.'

Lord Henry laughed, and rose. 'I am going to the Park,' he cried.

As he was passing out of the door Dorian Gray touched him on the arm. 'Let me come with you,' he murmured.

'But I thought you had promised Basil Hallward to go and see him,' answered Lord Henry.

'I would sooner come with you; yes, I feel I must come with you. Do let me. And you will promise to talk to me all the time? No one talks so wonderfully as you do.'

'Ah! I have talked quite enough for to-day,' said Lord Henry, smiling. 'All

I want now is to look at life. You may come and look at it with me, if you care to.'

4

ONE afternoon, a month later, Dorian Gray was reclining in a luxurious arm-chair, in the little library of Lord Henry's house in Mayfair. It was, in its way, a very charming room, with its high-panelled wainscoting of olive-stained oak, its cream-coloured frieze and ceiling of raised plaster-work, and its brick-dust felt carpet strewn with silk long-fringed Persian rugs. On a tiny satinwood table stood a statuette by Clodion, and beside it lay a copy of *Les Cent Nouvelles*, bound for Margaret of Valois by Clovis Eve, and powdered with the gilt daisies that Queen had selected for her device. Some large blue china jars and parrot-tulips were arranged on the mantelshelf, and through the small leaded panels of the window streamed the apricot-coloured light of a summer day in London.

Lord Henry had not yet come in. He was always late on principle, his principle being that punctuality is the thief of time. So the lad was looking rather sulky, as with listless fingers he turned over the pages of an elaborately-illustrated edition of *Manon Lescaut* that he had found in one of the bookcases. The formal monotonous ticking of the Louis Quartorze clock annoyed him. Once or twice he thought of going away.

At last he heard a step outside, and the door opened. 'How late you are, Harry!' he murmured.

'I am afraid it is not Harry, Mr. Gray,' answered a shrill voice.

He glanced quickly round, and rose to his feet. 'I beg your pardon. I thought –'

'You thought it was my husband. It is only his wife. You must let me introduce myself. I know you quite well by your photographs. I think my husband has got seventeen of them.'

'Not seventeen, Lady Henry?'

'Well, eighteen, then. And I saw you with him the other night at the Opera.' She laughed nervously as she spoke, and watched him with her vague forget-me-not eyes. She was a curious woman, whose dresses always looked as if they had been designed in a rage and put on in a tempest. She was usually in love with somebody, and, as her passion was never returned, she had kept all her illusions. She tried to look picturesque, but only succeeded in being untidy. Her name was Victoria, and she had a perfect mania for going to church.

'That was at *Lohengrin*, Lady Henry, I think?'

'Yes; it was at dear *Lohengrin*. I like Wagner's music better than anybody's. It is so loud that one can talk the whole time without other people hearing what one says. That is a great advantage; don't you think so, Mr. Gray?'

The same nervous staccato laugh broke from her thin lips, and her fingers began to play with a long tortoise-shell paper-knife.

Dorian smiled, and shook his head. 'I am afraid I don't think so, Lady Henry. I never talk during music, at least during good music. If one hears bad music, it is one's duty to drown it in conversation.'

'Ah! that is one of Harry's views, isn't it, Mr. Gray? I always hear Harry's views from his friends. It is the only way I get to know of them. But you must not think I don't like good music. I adore it, but I am afraid of it. It makes me too romantic. I have simply worshipped pianists – two at a time, sometimes, Harry tells me. I don't know what it is about them. Perhaps it is that they are foreigners. They all are, ain't they? Even those that are born in England become foreigners after a time, don't they? It is so clever of them, and such a compliment to art. Makes it quite cosmopolitan, doesn't it? You have never been to any of my parties, have you, Mr. Gray? You must come. I can't afford orchids, but I spare no expense in foreigners. They make one's rooms look so picturesque. But here is Harry! – Harry, I came into look for you, to ask you something – I forget what it was – and I found Mr. Gray here. We have had such a pleasant chat about music. We have quite the same ideas. No; I think our ideas are quite different. But he has been most pleasant. I am so glad I've seen him.'

'I am charmed, my love, quite charmed,' said Lord Henry, elevating his dark crescent-shaped eyebrows and looking at them both with an amused smile. 'So sorry I am late, Dorian. I went to look after a piece of old brocade in Wardour Street, and had to bargain for hours for it. Nowadays people know the price of everything, and the value of nothing.'

'I am afraid I must be going,' exclaimed Lady Henry, breaking an awkward silence with her silly sudden laugh. 'I have promised to drive with the Duchess. Good-bye, Mr. Gray. Good-bye, Harry. You are dining out, I suppose? So am I. Perhaps I shall see you at Lady Thornbury's.'

'I dare say, my dear,' said Lord Henry, shutting the door behind her, as, looking like a bird of paradise that had been out all night in the rain, she flitted out of the room, leaving a faint odour of frangipani. Then he lit a cigarette, and flung himself down on the sofa.

'Never marry a woman with straw-coloured hair, Dorian,' he said, after a few puffs.

'Why, Harry?'

'Because they are so sentimental.'

'But I like sentimental people.'

'Never marry at all, Dorian. Men marry because they are tired; women, because they are curious; both are disappointed.'

'I don't think I am likely to marry, Henry. I am too much in love. That is one of your aphorisms. I am putting it into practice, as I do everything that you say.'

'Who are you in love with?' asked Lord Henry, after a pause.

'With an actress,' said Dorian Gray, blushing.

Lord Henry shrugged his shoulders. 'That is a rather common-place *début*.'

'You would not say so if you saw her, Harry.'

'Who is she?'

'Her name is Sibyl Vane.'

'Never heard of her.'

'No one has. People will some day, however. She is a genius.'

'My dear boy, no woman is a genius. Women are a decorative sex. They never have anything to say, but they say it charmingly. Women represent the triumph of matter over mind, just as men represent the triumph of mind over morals.'

'Harry, how can you?'

'My dear Dorian, it is quite true. I am analysing women at the present, so I ought to know. The subject is not so abstruse as I thought it was. I find that, ultimately, there are only two kinds of women, the plain and the coloured. The plain women are very useful. If you want to gain a reputation for respectability, you have merely to take them down to supper. The other women are very charming. They commit one mistake, however. They paint in order to try and look young. Our grandmothers painted in order to try and talk brilliantly. *Rouge* and *esprit* used to go together. That is all over now. As long as a woman can look ten years younger than her own daughter, she is perfectly satisfied. As for conversation, there are only five women in London worth talking to, and two of these can't be admitted into decent society. However, tell me about your genius. How long have you known her?'

'Ah! Harry, your views terrify me.'

'Never mind that. How long have you known her?'

'About three weeks.'

'And where did you come across her?'

'I will tell you, Harry; but you mustn't be unsympathetic about it. After all, it never would have happened if I had not met you. You filled me with a wild desire to know everything about life. For days after I met you something seemed to throb in my veins. As I lounged in the Park, or strolled down Piccadilly, I used to look at every one who passed me, and wonder, with a mad curiosity, what sort of lives they led. Some of them fascinated me. Others filled me with terror. There was an exquisite poison in the air. I had a passion for sensations. . . . Well, one evening about seven o'clock I determined to go out in search of some adventure. I felt that this grey, monstrous London of ours, with its myriads of people, its sordid sinners, and its splendid sins, as you once phrased it, must have something in store for me. I fancied a thousand things. The mere danger gave me a sense of delight. I remembered what you had said to me on that wonderful evening when we first dined together, about the search for beauty being the real secret of life. I don't know what I expected, but I went out and wandered eastward, soon losing my way in a labyrinth of grimy streets and black, grassless squares. About half-past eight I passed by an absurd little theatre, with great flaring gas-jets and gaudy play-bills. A hideous Jew, in the most amazing waistcoat I ever beheld in my life, was standing at the entrance, smoking a vile cigar. He had greasy ringlets, and an enormous diamond blazed in the centre of a soiled shirt. "Have a box, my Lord?" he said, when he saw me, and he took off his hat with an air of gorgeous servility. There was something about him, Harry, that amused me. He was such a monster. You will laugh at me, I know, but I really went in and paid a whole guinea for the stage-box. To the present day I can't make out why I did so; and yet if I hadn't – my dear Harry, if I hadn't, I should have missed the greatest romance of my life. I see you are laughing. It is horrid of you!'

'I am not laughing, Dorian; at least I am not laughing at you. But you should not say the greatest romance of your life. You should say the first romance of your life. You will always be loved, and you will always be in love with love. A *grande passion* is the privilege of people who have nothing to do. That is the one use of the idle classes of a country. Don't be afraid. There are exquisite things in store for you. This is merely the beginning.'

'Do you think my nature so shallow?' cried Dorian Gray, angrily.

'No; I think your nature so deep.'

'How do you mean?'

'My dear boy, the people who love only once in their lives are really the shallow people. What they call their loyalty, and their fidelity, I call either the lethargy of custom or their lack of imagination. Faithfulness is to the emotional life what consistency is to the life of the intellect – simply a confession of failures. Faithfulness! I must analyse it some day. The passion for property is in it. There are many things that we would throw away if we were not afraid that others might pick them up. But I don't want to interrupt you. Go on with your story.'

'Well, I found myself seated in a horrid little private box, with a vulgar drop-scene staring me in the face. I looked out from behind the curtain and surveyed the house. It was a tawdry affair, all Cupids and cornucopias, like a third-rate wedding cake. The gallery and pit were fairly full, but the two rows of dingy stalls were quite empty, and there was hardly a person in what I suppose they called the dress-circle. Women went about with oranges and ginger-beer, and there was a terrible consumption of nuts going on.'

'It must have been just like the palmy days of the British Drama.'

'Just like, I should fancy, and very depressing. I began to wonder what on earth I should do, when I caught sight of the play-bill. What do you think the play was, Harry?'

'I should think *The Idiot Boy or Dumb but Innocent*. Our fathers used to like that sort of piece, I believe. The longer I live, Dorian, the more keenly I feel that whatever was good enough for our fathers is not good enough for us. In art, as in politics, *les grandpères ont toujours tort*.'

'This play was good enough for us, Harry. It was *Romeo and Juliet*. I must admit that I was rather annoyed at the idea of seeing Shakespeare done in such a wretched hole of a place. Still, I felt interested, in a sort of way. At any rate, I determined to wait for the first act. There was a dreadful orchestra, presided over by a young Hebrew who sat at a cracked piano, that nearly drove me away, but at last the drop-scene was drawn up, and the play began. Romeo was a stout elderly gentleman, with corked eyebrows, a husky tragedy voice, and a figure like a beer-barrel. Mercutio was almost as bad. He was played by the low-comedian, who had introduced gags of his own and was on most friendly terms with the pit. They were both as grotesque as the scenery, and that looked as if it had come out of a country booth. But Juliet! Harry, imagine a girl, hardly seventeen years of age, with a little flower-like face, a small Greek head with plaited coils of dark-brown hair, eyes that were violet wells of passion, lips that were like the petals of a rose. She was the loveliest thing I had ever seen in my life. You said to me once that pathos left you unmoved, but that beauty, mere beauty, could fill your eyes with tears. I tell you, Harry, I could hardly see this girl for the mist of tears that came across me. And her voice – I never heard such a voice. It was very low at first, with deep, mellow notes, that seemed to fall singly upon one's ear. Then it became a little louder, and sounded like a flute or a distant hautbois. In the garden scene it had all the tremulous ecstasy that one hears just before dawn when nightingales are singing. There were moments, later on, when it had the wild passion of violets. You know how a voice can stir one. Your voice and the voice of Sibyl Vane are two things that I shall never forget. When I close my eyes, I hear them, and each of them says something different. I don't know which to follow. Why should I not love her? Harry, I do love her. She is everything to me in life. Night after night I go to see her play. One evening she is Rosalind, and the next evening she is Imogen. I have seen her die in the gloom of an Italian tomb, sucking the poison from her lover's lips. I have watched her wandering through the forest of Arden, disguised as a pretty boy in hose and doublet and dainty cap. She has been mad, and has come into the presence of a guilty king, and given him rue to wear, and bitter herbs to taste of. She has been innocent, and the black hands of jealousy have crushed her reed-like throat. I have seen her in every age and in every costume. Ordinary women never appeal to one's imagination. They are limited to their century. No glamour ever transfigures them. One knows their minds as easily as one knows their bonnets. One can always find them. There is no mystery in any of them. They ride in the Park in the morning, and chatter at tea-parties in the afternoon. They have their stereotyped smile, and their fashionable manner. They are quite obvious. But an actress! How different an actress is! Harry! why didn't you tell me that the only thing worth loving is an actress?'

'Because I have loved so many of them, Dorian.'

'Oh, yes, horrid people with dyed hair and painted faces.'

'Don't run down dyed hair and painted faces. There is an extraordinary charm in them, sometimes,' said Lord Henry.

'I wish now I had not told you about Sibyl Vane.'

'You could not have helped telling me, Dorian. All through your life you will tell me everything you do.'

'Yes, Harry, I believe that is true. I cannot help telling you things. You have a curious influence over me. If I ever did a crime, I would come and confess it to you. You would understand me.'

'People like you – the wilful sunbeams of life – don't commit crimes, Dorian. But I am much obliged for the compliment, all the same. And now tell me – reach me the matches, like a good boy: thanks – what are your actual relations with Sibyl Vane?'

Dorian Gray leaped to his feet, with flushed cheeks and burning eyes. 'Harry! Sibyl Vane is sacred!'

'It is only the sacred things that are worth touching, Dorian,' said Lord Henry, with a strange touch of pathos in his voice. 'But why should you be annoyed? I suppose she will belong to you some day. When one is in love, one always begins by deceiving one's self, and one always ends by deceiving others. That is what the world calls a romance. You know her, at any rate, I suppose?'

'Of course I know her. On the first night I was at the theatre, the horrid old Jew came round to the box after the performance was over, and offered to take me behind the scenes and introduce me to her. I was furious with him, and told him that Juliet had been dead for hundreds of years, and that her body was lying in a marble tomb in Verona. I think, from his blank look of amazement, that he was under the impression that I had taken too much champagne, or something.'

'I am not surprised.'

'Then he asked me if I wrote for any of the newspapers. I told him I never even read them. He seemed terribly disappointed at that, and confided to me that all the dramatic critics were in a conspiracy against him, and that they were every one of them to be bought.'

'I should not wonder if he was quite right there. But, on the other hand, judging from their appearance, most of them cannot be at all expensive.'

'Well, he seemed to think they were beyond his means,' laughed Dorian. 'By this time, however, the lights were being put out in the theatre, and I had to go. He wanted me to try some cigars that he strongly recommended. I declined. The next night, of course, I arrived at the place again. When he saw me he made me a low bow, and assured me that I was a munificent patron of art. He was a most offensive brute, though he had an extraordinary passion for Shakespeare. He told me once, with an air of pride, that his five bankruptcies were entirely due to "The Bard," as he insisted on calling him. He seemed to think it a distinction.'

'It was a distinction, my dear Dorian – a great distinction. Most people become bankrupt through having invested too heavily in the prose of life. To have ruined one's self over poetry is an honour. But when did you first speak to Miss Sibyl Vane?'

'The third night. She had been playing Rosalind. I could not help going round. I had thrown her some flowers, and she had looked at me; at least I fancied that she had. The old Jew was persistent. He seemed determined to take me behind, so I consented. It was curious my not wanting to know her, wasn't it?'

'No; I don't think so.'

'My dear Harry, why?'

'I will tell you some other time. Now I want to know about the girl.'

'Sibyl? Oh, she was so shy, and so gentle. There is something of a child about her. Her eyes opened wide in exquisite wonder when I told her what I thought of her performance, and she seemed quite unconscious of her power. I think we were both rather nervous. The old Jew stood grinning at the doorway of the dusty green-room, making elaborate speeches about us both, while we stood looking at each other like children. He would insist on calling me "My Lord," so I had to assure Sibyl that I was not anything of the kind. She said quite simply to me, "You look more like a prince. I must call you Prince Charming."'

'Upon my word, Dorian, Miss Sibyl knows how to pay compliments.'

'You don't understand her, Harry. She regarded me merely as a person in a play. She knows nothing of life. She lives with her mother, a faded tired woman who played Lady Capulet in a sort of magenta dressing-wrapper on the first night, and looks as if she had seen better days.'

'I know that look. It depresses me,' murmured Lord Henry, examining his rings.

'The Jew wanted to tell me her history, but I said it did not interest me.'

'You were quite right. There is always something infinitely mean about other people's tragedies.'

'Sibyl is the only thing I care about. What is it to me where she came from? From her little head to her little feet, she is absolutely and entirely divine. Every night of my life I go to see her act, and every night she is more marvellous.'

'That is the reason, I suppose, that you never dine with me now. I thought you must have some curious romance on hand. You have; but it is not quite what I expected.'

'My dear Harry, we either lunch or sup together every day, and I have been to the Opera with you several times,' said Dorian, opening his blue eyes in wonder.

'You always come dreadfully late.'

'Well, I can't help going to see Sibyl play,' he cried, 'even if it is only for a single act. I get hungry for her presence; and when I think of the wonderful soul that is hidden away in that little ivory body, I am filled with awe.'

'You can dine with me to-night, Dorian, can't you?'

He shook his head. 'To-night she is Imogen,' he answered, 'and to-morrow night she will be Juliet.'

'When is she Sibyl Vane?'

'Never.'

'I congratulate you.'

'How horrid you are! She is all the great heroines of the world in one. She is more than an individual. You laugh, but I tell you she has genius. I love her, and I must make her love me. You, who know all the secrets of life, tell me how to charm Sibyl Vane to love me! I want to make Romeo jealous. I want the dead lovers of the world to hear our laughter, and grow sad. I want a breath of our passion to stir their dust into consciousness, to wake their ashes into pain. My God, Harry, how I worship her!' He was walking up and down the room as he spoke. Hectic spots of red burned in his cheeks. He was terribly excited.

Lord Henry watched him with a subtle sense of pleasure. How different he was now from the shy, frightened boy he had met in Basil Hallward's studio. His nature had developed like a flower, had borne blossoms of scarlet flame. Out of its secret hiding-place had crept his Soul, and Desire had come to meet it on the way.

'And what do you propose to do?' said Lord Henry at last.

'I want you and Basil to come with me some night and see her act. I have not the slightest fear of the result. You are certain to acknowledge her genius. Then we must get her out of the Jew's hands. She is bound to him for three years – at least for two years and eight months – from the present time. I shall have to pay him something, of course. When all that is settled, I shall take a West End theatre and bring her out properly. She will make the world as mad as she has made me.'

'That would be impossible, my dear boy!'

'Yes, she will. She has not merely art, consummate art-instinct, in her, but she has personality also; and you have often told me that it is personalities, not principles, that move the age.'

'Well, what night shall we go?'

'Let me see. To-day is Tuesday. Let us fix to-morrow. She plays Juliet to-morrow.'

'All right. The Bristol at eight o'clock; and I will get Basil.'

'Not eight, Harry, please. Half-past six. We must be there before the curtain rises. You must see her in the first act, where she meets Romeo.'

'Half-past six! What an hour! It will be like having a meat-tea, or reading an English novel. It must be seven. No gentleman dines before seven. Shall you see Basil between this and then? Or shall I write to him?'

'Dear Basil! I have not laid eyes on him for a week. It is rather horrid of me, as he has sent me my portrait in the most wonderful frame, specially designed by himself, and, though I am a little jealous of the picture for being a whole month younger than I am, I must admit that I delight in it. Perhaps you had better write to him. I don't want to see him alone. He says things that annoy me. He gives me good advice.'

Lord Henry smiled. 'People are very fond of giving away what they need most themselves. It is what I call the depth of generosity.'

'Oh, Basil is the best of fellows, but he seems to me to be just a bit of a Philistine. Since I have known you, Harry, I have discovered that.'

'Basil, my dear boy, puts everything that is charming in him into his work. The consequence is that he had nothing left for life but his prejudices, his principles, and his common sense. The only artists I have ever known, who are personally delightful, are bad artists. Good artists exist simply in what they make, and consequently are perfectly uninteresting in what they are. A great poet, a really great poet, is the most unpoetical of all creatures. But inferior poets are absolutely fascinating. The worse their rhymes are, the more picturesque they look. The mere fact of having published a book of second-rate sonnets makes a man quite irresistible. He lives the poetry that he cannot write. The others write the poetry that they dare not realise.'

'I wonder is that really so, Harry?' said Dorian Gray, putting some perfume on his handkerchief out of a large gold-topped bottle that stood on the table. 'It must be, if you say it. And now I am off. Imogen is waiting for me. Don't forget about to-morrow. Good-bye.'

As he left the room, Lord Henry's heavy eyelids drooped, and he began to think. Certainly few people had ever interested him so much as Dorian Gray, and yet the lad's mad adoration of some one else caused him not the slightest pang of annoyance or jealousy. He was pleased by it. It made him a more interesting study. He had been always enthralled by the methods of natural science, but the ordinary subject-matter of that science had seemed to him trivial and of no import. And so he had begun by vivisecting himself, as he had ended by vivisecting others. Human life – that appeared to him the one thing worth investigating. Compared to it there was nothing else of any value. It was true that as one watched life in its curious crucible of pain and pleasure, one could not wear over one's face a mask of glass, nor keep the sulphurous fumes from troubling the brain, and making the imagination turbid with monstrous fancies and misshapen dreams. There were poisons so subtle that to know their properties one had to sicken of them. There were maladies so strange that one had to pass through them if one sought to understand their nature. And, yet, what a great reward one received! How wonderful the whole world became to one! To note the curious hard logic of passion, and the emotional coloured life of the intellect – to observe where they met, and where they separated, at what point they were in unison, and at what point they were at discord – there was a delight in that! What matter what the cost was? One could never pay too high a price for any sensation.

He was conscious – and the thought brought a gleam of pleasure into his brown agate eyes – that it was through certain words of his, musical words said with musical utterance, that Dorian Gray's soul had turned to this white girl and bowed in worship before her. To a large extent the lad was his own creation. He had made him premature. That was something. Ordinary people waited till life disclosed to them its secrets, but to the few, to the elect, the mysteries of life were revealed before the veil was drawn away. Sometimes this was the effect of art, and chiefly of the art of literature, which dealt immediately with the passions and the intellect. But now and then a complex personality took the place and assumed the office of art; was indeed, in its way, a real work of art, Life having its elaborate masterpieces, just as poetry has, or sculpture, or painting.

Yes, the lad was premature. He was gathering his harvest while it was yet spring. The pulse and passion of youth were in him, but he was becoming self-conscious. It was delightful to watch him. With his beautiful face, and his beautiful soul, he was a thing to wonder at. It was no matter how it all ended, or was destined to end. He was like one of those gracious figures in a pageant or a play, whose joys seem to be remote from one, but whose sorrows stir one's sense of beauty and whose wounds are like red roses.

Soul and body, body and soul – how mysterious they were! There was animalism in the soul, and the body had its moments of spirituality. The senses could refine, and the intellect could degrade. Who could say where the fleshly impulse ceased, or the physical impulse began? How shallow were the arbitrary definitions of ordinary psychologists! And yet how difficult to decide between the claims of the various schools! Was the soul a shadow seated in the house of sin? Or was the body really in the soul, as Giordano Bruno thought? The separation of spirit from matter was a mystery, and the union of spirit with matter was a mystery also.

He began to wonder whether we could ever make psychology so absolute a science that each little spring of life would be revealed to us. As it was, we always misunderstood ourselves, and rarely understood others. Experience was of no ethical value. It was merely the name men gave to their mistakes. Moralists had, as a rule, regarded it as a mode of warning, had claimed for it a certain ethical efficacy in the formation of character, had praised it as something that taught us what to follow and showed us what to avoid. But there was no motive power in experience. It was as little of an active cause as conscience itself. All that it really demonstrated was that our future would be the same as our past, and that the sin we had done once, and with loathing, we would do many times, and with joy.

It was clear to him that the experimental method was the only method by which one could arrive at any scientific analysis of the passions; and certainly Dorian Gray was a subject made to his hand and seemed to promise rich and fruitful results. His sudden mad love for Sibyl Vane was a psychological phenomenon of no small interest. There was no doubt that curiosity had much to do with it, curiosity and the desire for new experiences; yet it was not a simple but rather a very complex passion. What there was in it of the purely sensuous instinct of boyhood had been transformed by the workings of the imagination, changed into something that seemed to the lad himself to be remote from sense, and was for that very reason all the more dangerous. It was the passions about whose origin we deceived ourselves that tyrannised most strongly over us. Our weakest motives were those of whose nature we were conscious. It often happened that when we thought we were experimenting on others we were really experimenting on ourselves.

While Lord Henry sat dreaming on these things, a knock came to the door, and his valet entered, and reminded him it was time to dress for dinner. He got up and looked out into the street. The sunset had smitten into scarlet gold the upper windows of the houses opposite. The panes glowed like plates of heated metal. The sky above was like a faded rose. He thought of his friend's young fiery-coloured life, and wondered how it was all going to end.

When he arrived home, about half-past twelve o'clock, he saw a telegram lying on the hall table. He opened it, and found it was from Dorian Gray. It was to tell him that he was engaged to be married to Sybil Vane.

5

'MOTHER, mother, I am so happy!' whispered the girl, burying her face in the lap of the faded, tired-looking woman who, with back turned to the shrill intrusive light, was sitting in the one arm-chair that their dingy sitting-room contained. 'I am so happy!' she repeated, 'and you must be happy too!'

Mrs. Vane winced, and put her thin bismuth-whitened hands on her daughter's head. 'Happy!' she echoed, 'I am only happy, Sibyl, when I see you act. You must not think of anything but your acting. Mr. Isaacs has been very good to us, and we owe him money.'

The girl looked up and pouted. 'Money, mother?' she cried, 'what does money matter? Love is more than money.'

'Mr. Isaacs has advanced us fifty pounds to pay off our debts, and to get a proper outfit for James. You must not forget that, Sibyl. Fifty pounds is a very large sum. Mr. Isaacs has been most considerate.'

'He is not a gentleman, mother, and I hate the way he talks to me,' said the girl, rising to her feet, and going over to the window.

'I don't know how we could manage without him,' answered the elder woman, querulously.

Sibyl Vane tossed her head and laughed. 'We don't want him any more, mother. Prince Charming rules life for us now.' Then she paused. A rose shook in her blood, and shadowed her cheeks. Quick breath parted the petals of her lips. They trembled. Some southern wind of passion swept over her, and stirred the dainty folds of her dress. 'I love him,' she said, simply.

'Foolish child! foolish child!' was the parrot-phrase flung in answer. The waving of crooked, false-jewelled fingers gave grotesqueness to the words.

The girl laughed again. The joy of a caged bird was in her voice. Her eyes caught the melody, and echoed it in radiance; then closed for a moment, as though to hide their secret. When they opened the mist of a dream had passed across them.

Thin-lipped wisdom spoke at her from the worn chair, hinted at prudence, quoted from that book of cowardice whose author apes the name of common sense. She did not listen. She was free in her prison of passion. Her prince, Prince Charming, was with her. She had called on Memory to remake him. She had sent her soul to search for him, and it had brought him back. His kiss burned again upon her mouth. Her eyelids were warm with his breath.

Then Wisdom altered its method and spoke of espial and discovery. This young man might be rich. If so, marriage should be thought of. Against the shell of her ear broke the waves of worldly cunning. The arrows of craft shot by her. She saw the thin lips moving, and smiled.

Suddenly she felt the need to speak. The wordy silence troubled her. 'Mother, mother,' she cried, 'why does he love me so much? I know why I love him. I love him because he is like what Love himself should be. But what does he see in me? I am not worthy of him. And yet – why, I cannot tell – though I feel so much beneath him, I don't feel humble. I feel proud, terribly proud. Mother, did you love my father as I love Prince Charming?'

The elder woman grew pale beneath the coarse powder that daubed her cheeks, and her dry lips twitched with a spasm of pain. Sibyl rushed to her, flung her arms round her neck, and kissed her. 'Forgive me, mother, I know it pains you to talk about our father. But it only pains you because you loved him so much. Don't look so sad. I am as happy to-day as you were twenty years ago. Ah! let me be happy for ever!'

'My child, you are far too young to think of falling in love. Besides, what do you know of this young man? You don't even know his name. The whole thing is most inconvenient, and really, when James is going away to Australia, and I have so much to think of, I must say that you should have shown more consideration. However, as I said before, if he is rich . . .'

'Ah! Mother, mother, let me be happy!'

Mrs. Vane glanced at her, and, with one of those false theatrical gestures that so often become a mode of second nature to a stage-player, clasped her in her arms. At this moment the door opened, and a young lad with rough brown hair came into the room. He was thick-set of figure, and his hands and feet were large, and somewhat clumsy in movement. He was not so finely bred as his sister. One would hardly have guessed the close relationship that existed between them. Mrs. Vane fixed her eyes on him, and intensified the smile. She mentally elevated her son to the dignity of an audience. She felt sure that the *tableau* was interesting.

'You might keep some of your kisses for me, Sibyl, I think,' said the lad, with a good-natured grumble.

'Ah! but you don't like being kissed, Jim,' she cried. 'You are a dreadful old bear.' And she ran across the room and hugged him.

James Vane looked into his sister's face with tenderness. 'I want you to come out with me for a walk, Sibyl. I don't suppose I shall ever see this horrid London again. I am sure I don't want to.'

'My son, don't say such dreadful things,' murmured Mrs. Vane, taking up a tawdry theatrical dress, with a sigh, and beginning to patch it. She felt a little disappointed that he had not joined the group. It would have increased the theatrical picturesqueness of the situation.

'Why not, mother? I mean it.'

'You pain me, my son. I trust you will return from Australia in a position of affluence. I believe there is no society of any kind in the Colonies, nothing that I would call society; so when you have made your fortune you must come back and assert yourself in London.'

'Society!' muttered the lad. 'I don't want to know anything about that. I should like to make some money to take you and Sibyl off the stage. I hate it!'

'Oh, Jim!' said Sibyl, laughing, 'how unkind of you! But are you really going for a walk with me? That will be nice! I was afraid you were going to say good-bye to some of your friends – to Tom Hardy, who gave you that hideous pipe, or Ned Langton, who makes fun of you for smoking it. It is very sweet of you to let me have your last afternoon. Where shall we go? Let us go to the Park.'

'I am too shabby,' he answered, frowning. 'Only swell people go to the Park.'

'Nonsense, Jim,' she whispered, stroking the sleeve of his coat.

He hesitated for a moment. 'Very well,' he said at last, 'but don't be too long dressing.' She danced out of the door. One could hear her singing as she ran upstairs. Her little feet pattered overhead.

He walked up and down the room two or three times. Then he turned to the still figure in the chair. 'Mother, are my things ready?' he asked.

'Quite ready, James,' she answered, keeping her eyes on her work. For some months past she had felt ill at ease when she was alone with this rough, stern son of hers. Her shallow secret nature was troubled when their eyes met. She used to wonder if he suspected anything. The silence, for he made no other observation, became intolerable to her. She began to complain. Women defend themselves by attacking, just as they attack by sudden and strange surrenders. 'I hope you will be contented, James, with your sea-faring life,' she said. 'You must remember that it is your own choice. You might have entered a solicitor's office. Solicitors are a very respectable class, and in the country often dine with the best families.'

'I hate offices, and I hate clerks,' he replied. 'But you are quite right. I have chosen my own life. All I say is, watch over Sibyl. Don't let her come to any harm. Mother, you must watch over her.'

'James, you really talk very strangely. Of course I watch over Sibyl.'

'I hear a gentleman comes every night to the theatre, and goes behind to talk to her. Is that right? What about that?'

'You are speaking about things you don't understand, James. In the profession we are accustomed to receive a great deal of most gratifying attention. I myself used to receive many bouquets at one time. That was when acting was really understood. As for Sibyl, I do not know at present whether her attachment is serious or not. But there is no doubt that the young man in question is a perfect gentleman. He is always most polite to me. Besides, he has the appearance of being rich, and the flowers he sends are lovely.'

'You don't know his name, though,' said the lad, harshly.

'No,' answered his mother, with a placid expression in her face. 'He has not yet revealed his real name. I think it is quite romantic of him. He is probably a member of the aristocracy.'

James Vane bit his lip. 'Watch over Sibyl, mother,' he cried, 'watch over her.'

'My son, you distress me very much. Sibyl is always under my special care. Of course, if this gentleman is wealthy, there is no reason why she should not contract an alliance with him. I trust he is one of the aristocracy. He has all the appearance of it, I must say. It might be a most brilliant marriage for Sibyl. They would make a charming couple. His good looks are really quite remarkable; everybody notices them.'

The lad muttered something to himself, and drummed on the window-pane with his coarse fingers. He had just turned round to say something, when the door opened, and Sibyl ran in.

'How serious you both are!' she cried. 'What is the matter?'

'Nothing,' he answered. 'I suppose one must be serious sometimes. Good-bye, mother; I will have my dinner at five o'clock. Everything is packed, except my shirts, so you need not trouble.'

'Good-bye, my son,' she answered, with a bow of strained stateliness.

She was extremely annoyed at the tone he had adopted with her, and there was something in his look that had made her feel afraid.

'Kiss me, mother,' said the girl. Her flower-like lips touched the withered cheek and warmed its frost.

'My child! my child!' cried Mrs. Vane, looking up to the ceiling in search of an imaginary gallery.

'Come, Sibyl,' said her brother, impatiently. He hated his mother's affectations.

They went out into the flickering wind-blown sunlight, and strolled down the dreary Euston Road. The passers-by glanced in wonder at the sullen, heavy youth, who, in coarse, ill-fitting clothes, was in the company of such a graceful, refined-looking girl. He was like a common gardener walking with a rose.

Jim frowned from time to time when he caught the inquisitive glance of some stranger. He had that dislike of being stared at which comes on geniuses late in life, and never leaves the commonplace. Sibyl, however, was quite unconscious of the effect she was producing. Her love was trembling in laughter on her lips. She was thinking of Prince Charming, and, that she might think of him all the more, she did not talk of him, but prattled on about the ship in which Jim was going to sail, about the gold he was certain to find, about the wonderful heiress whose life he was to save from the wicked, red-shirted bush-rangers. For he was not to remain a sailor, or a super-cargo, or whatever he was going to be. Oh, no! A sailor's existence was dreadful. Fancy being cooped up in a horrid ship, with the hoarse, hump-backed waves trying to get in, and a black wind blowing the masts down, and tearing the sails into long screaming ribands! He was to leave the vessel at Melbourne, bid a polite good-bye to the captain, and go off at once to the gold-fields. Before a week was over he was to come across a large nugget of pure gold, the largest nugget that had ever been discovered, and bring it down to the coast in a wagon guarded by six mounted policemen. The bushrangers were to attack them three times, and be defeated with immense slaughter. Or, no. He was not to go to the gold-fields at all. They were horrid places, where men got intoxicated, and shot each other in bar-rooms, and used bad language. He was to be a nice sheep-farmer, and one evening, as he was riding home, he was to see the beautiful heiress being carried off by a robber on a black horse, and give chase, and rescue her. Of course she would fall in love with him, and he with her, and they would get married, and come home, and live in an immense house in London. Yes, there were delightful things in store for him. But he must be very good, and not lose his temper, or spend his money foolishly. She was only a year older than he was, but she knew so much more of life. He must be sure, also, to write to her by every mail, and to say his prayers each night before he went to sleep. God was very good, and would watch over him. She would pray for him, too, and in a few years he would come back quite rich and happy.

The lad listened sulkily to her, and made no answer. He was heart-sick at leaving home.

Yet, it was not this alone that made him gloomy and morose. Inexperienced though he was, he had still a strong sense of the danger of Sibyl's position. This young dandy who was making love to her could mean her no good. He was a gentleman, and he hated him for that, hated him through some curious race-instinct for which he could not account, and which for that reason was all the more dominant within him. He was conscious also of the shallowness and vanity of his mother's nature, and in that saw infinite peril for Sibyl and Sibyl's happiness. Children begin by loving their parents; as they grow older they judge them; sometimes they forgive them.

His mother! He had something on his mind to ask of her, something that he had brooded on for many months of silence. A chance phrase that he had heard at the theatre, a whispered sneer that had reached his ears one night as he waited at the stage-door, had set loose a train of horrible thoughts. He remembered it as if it had been the lash of a hunting-crop across his face. His brows knit together into a wedge-like furrow, and with a twitch of pain he bit his underlip.

'You are not listening to a word I am saying, Jim,' cried Sibyl, 'and I am making the most delightful plans for your future. Do say something.'

'What do you want me to say?'

'Oh! That you will be a good boy, and not forget us,' she answered, smiling at him.

He shrugged his shoulders. 'You are more likely to forget me, than I am to forget you, Sibyl.'

She flushed. 'What do you mean, Jim?' she asked.

'You have a new friend, I hear. Who is he? Why have you not told me about him? He means you no good.'

'Stop, Jim!' she exclaimed. 'You must not say anything against him. I love him.'

'Why, you don't even know his name,' answered the lad. 'Who is he? I have a right to know.'

'He is called Prince Charming. Don't you like the name? Oh! you silly boy! you should never forget it. If you only saw him, you would think him the most wonderful person in the world. Some day you will meet him: when you come back from Australia. You will like him so much. Everybody likes him, and I . . . love him. I wish you could come to the theatre to-night. He is going to be there, and I am to play Juliet. Oh! how I shall play it! Fancy, Jim, to be in love and play Juliet! To have him sitting there! To play for his delight! I am afraid I may frighten the company, frighten or enthrall them. To be in love is to surpass one's self. Poor dreadful Mr. Isaacs will be shouting "genius" to his loafers at the bar. He has preached me as a dogma; to-night he will announce me as a revelation. I feel it. And it is all his, his only, Prince Charming, my wonderful lover, my god of graces. But I am poor beside him. Poor? What does that matter? When poverty creeps in at the door, love flies in through the window. Our proverbs want re-writing. They were made in winter, and it is summer now; springtime for me, I think, a very dance of blossoms in blue skies.'

'He is a gentleman,' said the lad, sullenly.

'A prince!' she cried, musically. 'What more do you want?'

'He wants to enslave you.'

'I shudder at the thought of being free.'

'I want you to beware of him.'

'To see him is to worship him, to know him is to trust him.'

'Sibyl, you are mad about him.'

She laughed, and took his arm. 'You dear old Jim, you talk as if you were a hundred. Some day you will be in love yourself. Then you will know what it is. Don't look so sulky. Surely you should be glad to think that, though you are going away, you leave me happier than I have ever been before. Life has been hard for us both, terribly hard and difficult. But it will be different now. You are going to a new world, and I have found one. Here are two chairs; let us sit down and see the smart people go by.'

They took their seats amidst a crowd of watchers. The tulip-beds across the road flamed like throbbing rings of fire. A white dust, tremulous cloud of orrisroot it seemed, hung in the panting air. The brightly coloured parasols danced and dipped like monstrous butterflies.

She made her brother talk of himself, his hopes, his prospects. He spoke slowly and with effort. They passed words to each other as players at a game pass counters. Sibyl felt oppressed. She could not communicate her joy. A faint smile curving that sullen mouth was all the echo she could win. After some time she became silent. Suddenly she caught a glimpse of golden hair and laughing lips, and in an open carriage with two ladies Dorian Gray drove past.

She started to her feet. 'There he is!' she cried.

'Who?' said Jim Vane.

'Prince Charming,' she answered, looking after the victoria.

He jumped up, and seized her roughly by the arm. 'Show him to me. Which is he? Point him out. I must see him!' he exclaimed; but at that moment the Duke of Berwick's four-in-hand came between, and when it had left the space clear, the carriage had swept out of the Park.

'He is gone,' murmured Sibyl sadly. 'I wish you had seen him.'

'I wish I had, for as sure as there is a God in heaven, if he ever does you any wrong I shall kill him.'

She looked at him in horror. He repeated his words. They cut the air like a dagger. The people round began to gape. A lady standing close to her tittered.

'Come away, Jim; come away,' she whispered. He followed her doggedly, as she passed through the crowd. He felt glad at what he had said.

When they reached the Achilles Statue she turned round. There was pity in her eyes that became laughter on her lips. She shook her head at him. 'You are foolish, Jim, utterly foolish; a bad-tempered boy, that is all. How can you say such horrible things? You don't know what you are talking about. You are simply jealous and unkind. Ah! I wish you would fall in love. Love makes people good, and what you said was wicked!'

'I am sixteen,' he answered, 'and I know what I am about. Mother is no help to you. She doesn't understand how to look after you. I wish now that I was not going to Australia at all. I have a great mind to chuck the whole thing up. I would, if my articles hadn't been signed.'

'Oh, don't be so serious, Jim. You are like one of the heroes of those silly melodramas mother used to be so fond of acting in. I am not going to quarrel with you. I have seen him, and oh! to see him is perfect happiness. We won't quarrel. I know you would never harm any one I love, would you?'

'Not as long as you love him, I suppose,' was the sullen answer.

'I shall love him for ever!' she cried.

'And he?'

'For ever, too!'

'He had better.'

She shrank from him. Then she laughed and put her hand on his arm. He was merely a boy.

At the Marble Arch they hailed an omnibus, which left them close to their shabby home in the Euston Road. It was after five o'clock, and Sibyl had to lie down for a couple of hours before acting. Jim insisted that she should do so. He said that he would sooner part with her when their mother was not present. She would be sure to make a scene, and he detested scenes of every kind.

In Sibyl's own room they parted. There was jealousy in the lad's heart, and a fierce, murderous hatred of the stranger who, as it seemed to him, had come between them. Yet, when her arms were flung round his neck, and her fingers strayed through his hair, he softened, and kissed her with real affection. There were tears in his eyes as he went downstairs.

His mother was waiting for him below. She grumbled at his unpunctuality, as he entered. He made no answer, but sat down to his meagre meal. The flies buzzed round the table, and crawled over the stained cloth. Through the rumble of omnibuses, and the clatter of street-cabs, he could hear the droning voice devouring each minute that was left to him.

After some time, he thrust away his plate, and put his head in his hands. He felt that he had a right to know. It should have been told to him before, if it was as he suspected. Leaden with fear, his mother watched him. Words dropped mechanically from her lips. A tattered lace handkerchief twitched in her fingers. When the clock struck six, he got up, and went to the door. Then he turned back, and looked at her. Their eyes met. In hers he saw a wild appeal for mercy. It enraged him.

'Mother, I have something to ask you,' he said. Her eyes wandered vaguely about the room. She made no answer. 'Tell me the truth. I have a right to know. Were you married to my father?'

She heaved a deep sigh. It was a sigh of relief. The terrible moment, the moment that night and day, for weeks and months, she had dreaded, had come at last, and yet she felt no terror. Indeed in some measure it was a disappointment to her. The vulgar directness of the question called for a direct answer. The situation had not been gradually led up to. It was crude. It reminded her of a bad rehearsal.

'No,' she answered, wondering at the harsh simplicity of life.

'My father was a scoundrel then?' cried the lad, clenching his fists.

She shook her head. 'I knew he was not free. We loved each other very much. If he had lived, he would have made provision for us. Don't speak against him, my son. He was your father, and a gentleman. Indeed he was highly connected.'

An oath broke from his lips. 'I don't care for myself,' he exclaimed, 'but don't let Sibyl . . . It is a gentleman, isn't it, who is in love with her, or says he is? Highly connected, too, I suppose.'

For a moment a hideous sense of humiliation came over the woman. Her head drooped. She wiped her eyes with shaking hands. 'Sibyl has a mother,' she murmured; 'I had none.'

The lad was touched. He went towards her, and stooping down he kissed her. 'I am sorry if I have pained you by asking about my father,' he said, 'but I could not help it. I must go now. Good-bye. Don't forget that you will only have one child now to look after, and believe me that if this man wrongs my sister, I will find out who he is, track him down, and kill him like a dog. I swear it.'

The exaggerated folly of the threat, the passionate gesture that accompanied it, the mad melodramatic words, made life seem more vivid to her. She was familiar with the atmosphere. She breathed more freely, and for the first time for many months she really admired her son. She would have liked to have continued the scene on the same emotional scale, but he cut her short. Trunks had to be carried down, and mufflers looked for. The lodging-house drudge bustled in and out. There was the bargaining with the cabman. The moment was lost in vulgar details. It was with a renewed feeling of disappointment that she waved the tattered lace handkerchief from the window, as her son drove away. She was conscious that a great opportunity had been wasted. She consoled herself by telling Sibyl how desolate she felt her life would be, now that she had only one child to look after. She remembered the phrase. It had pleased her. Of the threat she said nothing. It was vividly and dramatically expressed. She felt that they would all laugh at it some day.

6

'I SUPPOSE you have heard the news, Basil?' said Lord Henry, that evening, as Hallward was shown into a little private room at the Bristol, where dinner had been laid for three.

'No, Harry,' answered the artist, giving his hat and coat to the bowing waiter. 'What is it? Nothing about politics, I hope? They don't interest me. There is hardly a single person in the House of Commons worth painting; though many of them would be the better for a little white-washing.'

'Dorian Gray is engaged to be married,' said Lord Henry, watching him as he spoke.

Hallward started, and then frowned. 'Dorian engaged to be married!' he cried. 'Impossible!'

'It is perfectly true.'

'To whom?'

'To some little actress or other.'

'I can't believe it. Dorian is far too sensible.'

'Dorian is far too wise not to do foolish things now and then, my dear Basil.'

'Marriage is hardly a thing that one can do now and then, Harry.'

'Except in America,' rejoined Lord Henry, languidly. 'But I didn't say he was married. I said he was engaged to be married. There is a great difference. I have a distinct remembrance of being married, but I have no recollection at all of being engaged. I am inclined to think that I never was engaged.'

'But think of Dorian's birth, and position, and wealth. It would be absurd for him to marry so much beneath him.'

'If you want to make him marry this girl tell him that, Basil. He is sure to do it, then. Whenever a man does a thoroughly stupid thing, it is always from the noblest motives.'

'I hope the girl is good, Harry. I don't want to see Dorian tied to some vile creature, who might degrade his nature and ruin his intellect.'

'Oh, she is better than good – she is beautiful,' murmured Lord Henry, sipping a glass of vermouth and orange bitters. 'Dorian says she is beautiful; and he is not often wrong about things of that kind. Your portrait of him has quickened his appreciation of the personal appearance of other people. It has had that excellent effect, amongst others. We are to see her to-night, if that boy doesn't forget his appointment.'

'Are you serious?'

'Quite serious, Basil. I should be miserable if I thought I should ever be more serious than I am at the present moment.'

'But do you approve of it, Harry?' asked the painter, walking up and down the room, and biting his lip. 'You can't approve of it, possibly. It is some silly infatuation.'

'I never approve, or disapprove, of anything now. It is an absurd attitude to take towards life. We are not sent into the world to air our moral preju-

dices. I never take any notice of what common people say, and I never inter-
fere with what charming people do. If a personality fascinates me, whatever
mode of expression that personality selects is absolutely delightful to me.
Dorian Gray falls in love with a beautiful girl who acts Juliet, and proposes to
marry her. Why not? If he wedded Messalina he would be none the less in-
teresting. You know I am not a champion of marriage. The real drawback to
marriage is that it makes one unselfish. And unselfish people are colourless.
They lack individuality. Still, there are certain temperaments that marriage
makes more complex. They retain their egotism, and add to it many other
egos. They are forced to have more than one life. They become more highly
organised, and to be highly organised is, I should fancy, the object of man's
existence. Besides, every experience is of value, and, whatever one may say
against marriage, it is certainly an experience. I hope that Dorian Gray will
make this girl his wife, passionately adore her for six months, and then sud-
denly become fascinated by some one else. He would be a wonderful study.'

'You don't mean a single word of all that, Harry; you know you don't. If
Dorian Gray's life were spoiled, no one would be sorrier than yourself. You
are much better than you pretend to be.'

Lord Henry laughed. 'The reason we all like to think so well of others is
that we are all afraid for ourselves. The basis of optimism is sheer terror. We
think that we are generous because we credit our neighbour with the posses-
sion of those virtues that are likely to be a benefit to us. We praise the banker
that we may overdraw our account, and find good qualities in the high-
wayman in the hope that he may spare our pockets. I mean everything that I
have said. I have the greatest contempt for optimism. As for a spoiled life, no
life is spoiled but one whose growth is arrested. If you want to mar a nature,
you have merely to reform it. As for marriage, of course that would be silly,
but there are other and more interesting bonds between men and women. I
will certainly encourage them. They have the charm of being fashionable.
But here is Dorian himself. He will tell you more than I can.'

'My dear Harry, my dear Basil, you must both congratulate me!' said the
lad, throwing off his evening cape with its satin-lined wings and shaking
each of his friends by the hand in turn. 'I have never been so happy. Of
course it is sudden; all really delightful things are. And yet it seems to me to
be the one thing I have been looking for all my life.' He was flushed with ex-
citement and pleasure, and looked extraordinarily handsome.

'I hope you will always be very happy, Dorian,' said Hallward, 'but I don't
quite forgive you for not having let me know of your engagement. You let
Harry know.'

'And I don't forgive you for being late for dinner,' broke in Lord Henry,
putting his hand on the lad's shoulder, and smiling as he spoke. 'Come, let us
sit down and try what the new *chef* here is like, and then you will tell us how
it all came about.'

'There is really not much to tell,' cried Dorian, as they took their seats at
the small round table. 'What happened was simply this. After I left you yes-
terday evening, Harry, I dressed, had some dinner at that little Italian res-

taurant in Rupert Street you introduced me to, and went down at eight o'clock to the theatre. Sibyl was playing Rosalind. Of course the scenery was dreadful, and the Orlando absurd. But Sibyl! You should have seen her! When she came on in her boy's clothes she was perfectly wonderful. She wore a moss-coloured velvet jerkin with cinnamon sleeves, slim brown cross-gartered hose, a dainty little green cap with a hawk's feather caught in a jewel, and a hooded cloak lined with dull red. She had never seemed to me more exquisite. She had all the delicate grace of that Tanagra figurine that you have in your studio, Basil. Her hair clustered round her face like dark leaves round a pale rose. As for her acting – well, you shall see her to-night. She is simply a born artist. I sat in the dingy box absolutely enthralled. I forgot that I was in London, and in the nineteenth century. I was away with my love in a forest that no man had ever seen. After the performance was over I went behind, and spoke to her. As we were sitting together, suddenly there came into her eyes a look that I had never seen there before. My lips moved towards hers. We kissed each other. I can't describe to you what I felt at that moment. It seemed to me that all my life had been narrowed to one perfect point of rose-coloured joy. She trembled all over, and shook like a white narcissus. Then she flung herself on her knees and kissed my hands. I feel that I should not tell you all this, but I can't help it. Of course our engagement is a dead secret. She has not even told her own mother. I don't know what my guardians will say. Lord Radley is sure to be furious. I don't care. I shall be of age in less than a year, and then I can do what I like. I have been right, Basil, haven't I, to take my love out of poetry, and to find my wife in Shakespeare's plays? Lips that Shakespeare taught to speak have whispered their secret in my ear. I have had the arms of Rosalind around me, and kissed Juliet on the mouth.'

'Yes, Dorian, I suppose you were right,' said Hallward, slowly.

'Have you seen her to-day?' asked Lord Henry.

Dorian Gray shook his head. 'I left her in the forest of Arden, I shall find her in an orchard in Verona.'

Lord Henry sipped his champagne in a meditative manner. 'At what particular point did you mention the word marriage, Dorian? And what did she say in answer? Perhaps you forgot all about it.'

'My dear Harry, I did not treat it as a business transaction, and I did not make any formal proposal. I told her that I loved her, and she said she was not worthy to be my wife. Not worthy! Why, the whole world is nothing to me compared with her.'

'Women are wonderfully practical,' murmured Lord Henry – 'much more practical than we are. In situations of that kind we often forget to say anything about marriage, and they always remind us.'

Hallward laid his hand upon his arm. 'Don't, Harry. You have annoyed Dorian. He is not like other men. He would never bring misery upon any one. His nature is too fine for that.'

Lord Henry looked across the table. 'Dorian is never annoyed with me,' he answered. 'I asked the question for the best reason possible, for the only reason, indeed, that excuses one for asking any question – simply curiosity. I have a theory that it is always the women who propose to us, and not we who propose to the women. Except, of course, in middle-class life. But then the middle classes are not modern.'

Dorian Gray laughed and tossed his head. 'You are quite incorrigible, Harry; but I don't mind. It is impossible to be angry with you. When you see Sibyl Vane you will feel that the man who could wrong her would be a beast, a beast without a heart. I cannot understand how any one can wish to shame the thing he loves. I love Sibyl Vane. I want to place her on a pedestal of gold, and to see the world worship the woman who is mine. What is marriage? An irrevocable vow. You mock at it for that. Ah! don't mock. It is an irrevocable vow that I want to take. Her trust makes me faithful, her belief makes me good. When I am with her, I regret all that you have taught me. I become different from what you have known me to be. I am changed, and the mere touch of Sibyl Vane's hand makes me forget you and all your wrong, fascinating, poisonous, delightful theories.'

'And those are . . . ?' asked Lord Henry, helping himself to some salad.

'Oh, your theories about life, your theories about love, your theories about pleasure. All your theories, in fact, Harry.'

'Pleasure is the only thing worth having a theory about,' he answered, in his slow, melodious voice. 'But I am afraid I cannot claim my theory as my own. It belongs to Nature, not to me. Pleasure is Nature's test, her sign of approval. When we are happy we are always good, but when we are good we are not always happy.'

'Ah! but what do you mean by good?' cried Basil Hallward.

'Yes,' echoed Dorian, leaning back in his chair, and looking at Lord Henry over the heavy clusters of purple-lipped irises that stood in the centre of the table, 'what do you mean by good, Harry?'

'To be good is to be in harmony with one's self,' he replied, touching the thin stem of his glass with his pale, fine-pointed fingers. 'Discord is to be forced to be in harmony with others. One's own life – that is the important thing. As for the lives of one's neighbours, if one wishes to be a prig or a Puritan, one can flaunt one's moral views about them, but they are not one's concern. Besides, Individualism has really the higher aim. Modern morality consists in accepting the standard of one's age. I consider that for any man of culture to accept the standard of his age is a form of the grossest immorality.'

'But, surely, if one lives merely for one's self, Harry, one pays a terrible price for doing so?' suggested the painter.

'Yes, we are overcharged for everything nowadays. I should fancy that the real tragedy of the poor is that they can afford nothing but self-denial. Beautiful sins, like beautiful things, are the privilege of the rich.'

'One has to pay in other ways but money.'

'What sort of ways, Basil?'

'Oh! I should fancy in remorse, in suffering, in . . . well, in the consciousness of degradation.'

Lord Henry shrugged his shoulders. 'My dear fellow, mediæval art is charming, but mediaeval emotions are out of date. One can use them in fiction, of course. But then the only things that one can use in fiction are the things that one has ceased to use in fact. Believe me, no civilised man ever regrets a pleasure, and no uncivilised man ever knows what a pleasure is.'

'I know what pleasure is,' cried Dorian Gray. 'It is to adore some one.'

'That is certainly better than being adored,' he answered, toying with some fruits. 'Being adored is a nuisance. Women treat us just as Humanity treats its gods. They worship us, and are always bothering us to do something for them.'

'I should have said that whatever they ask for they had first given to us,' murmured the lad, gravely. 'They create Love in our natures. They have a right to demand it back.'

'That is quite true, Dorian,' cried Hallward.

'Nothing is ever quite true,' said Lord Henry.

'This is,' interrupted Dorian. 'You must admit, Harry, that women give to men the very gold of their lives.'

'Possibly,' he sighed, 'but they invariably want it back in such very small change. That is the worry. Women, as some witty Frenchman once put it, inspire us with the desire to do masterpieces, and always prevent us from carrying them out.'

'Harry, you are dreadful! I don't know why I like you so much.'

'You will always like me, Dorian,' he replied. 'Will you have some coffee, you fellows? – Waiter, bring coffee, and *fine-champagne*, and some cigarettes. No: don't mind the cigarettes; I have some. Basil, I can't allow you to smoke cigars. You must have a cigarette. A cigarette is the perfect type of a perfect pleasure. It is exquisite, and it leaves one unsatisfied. What more can one want? Yes, Dorian, you will always be fond of me. I represent to you all the sins you have never had the courage to commit.'

'What nonsense you talk, Harry!' cried the lad, taking a light from a fire-breathing silver dragon that the waiter had placed on the table. 'Let us go down to the theatre. When Sibyl comes on the stage you will have a new ideal of life. She will represent something to you that you have never known.'

'I have known everything,' said Lord Henry, with a tired look in his eyes, 'but I am always ready for a new emotion. I am afraid, however, that, for me at any rate, there is no such thing. Still, your wonderful girl may thrill me. I love acting. It is so much more real than life. Let us go. Dorian, you will come with me. I am so sorry, Basil, but there is only room for two in the brougham. You must follow us in a hansom.'

They got up and put on their coats, sipping their coffee standing. The painter was silent and preoccupied. There was a gloom over him. He could not bear this marriage, and yet it seemed to him to be better than many other things that might have happened. After a few minutes they all passed downstairs. He drove off by himself, as had been arranged, and watched the flashing lights of the little brougham in front of him. A strange sense of loss came over him. He felt that Dorian Gray would never again be to him all that he had been in the past. Life had come between them. . . . His eyes darkened, and the crowded, flaring streets became blurred to his eyes. When the cab drew up at the theatre, it seemed to him that he had grown years older.

7

FOR some reason or other, the house was crowded that night, and the fat Jew manager who met them at the door was beaming from ear to ear with an oily, tremulous smile. He escorted them to their box with a sort of pompous humility, waving his fat jewelled hands, and talking at the top of his voice. Dorian Gray loathed him more than ever. He felt as if he had come to look for Miranda and had been met by Caliban. Lord Henry, upon the other hand, rather liked him. At least he declared he did, and insisted on shaking him by the hand, and assuring him that he was proud to meet a man who had discovered a real genius and gone bankrupt over a poet. Hallward amused himself with watching the faces in the pit. The heat was terribly oppressive, and the huge sunlight flamed like a monstrous dahlia with petals of yellow fire. The youths in the gallery had taken off their coats and waistcoats and hung them over the side. They talked to each other across the theatre, and shared their oranges with the tawdry girls who sat beside them. Some women were laughing in the pit. Their voices were horribly shrill and discordant. The sound of the popping of corks came from the bar.

'What a place to find one's divinity in!' said Lord Henry.

'Yes!' answered Dorian Gray. 'It was here I found her, and she is divine beyond all living things. When she acts you will forget everything. These common, rough people, with their coarse faces and brutal gestures, become quite different when she is on the stage. They sit silently and watch her. They weep and laugh as she wills them to do. She makes them as responsive as a violin. She spiritualises them, and one feels that they are of the same flesh and blood as one's self.'

'The same flesh and blood as one's self! Oh, I hope not!' exclaimed Lord Henry, who was scanning the occupants of the gallery through his opera-glass.

'Don't pay any attention to him, Dorian,' said the painter. 'I understand what you mean, and I believe in this girl. Any one you love must be marvellous, and any girl that has the effect you describe must be fine and noble. To spiritualise one's age – that is something worth doing. If this girl can give a soul to those who have lived without one, if she can create the sense of beauty in people whose lives have been sordid and ugly, if she can strip them of their selfishness and lend them tears for sorrows that are not their own, she is worthy of all your adoration, worthy of the adoration of the world. This marriage is quite right. I did not think so at first, but I admit it now. The gods made Sibyl Vane for you. Without her you would have been incomplete.'

'Thanks, Basil,' answered Dorian Gray, pressing his hand. 'I knew that you would understand me. Harry is so cynical, he terrifies me. But here is the orchestra. It is quite dreadful, but it only lasts for about five minutes. Then the curtain rises, and you will see the girl to whom I am going to give all my life, to whom I have given everything that is good in me.'

A quarter of an hour afterwards, amidst an extraordinary turmoil of applause, Sibyl Vane stepped on to the stage. Yes, she was certainly lovely to look at – one of the loveliest creatures, Lord Henry thought, that he had ever seen. There was something of the fawn in her shy grace and startled eyes. A faint blush, like the shadow of a rose in a mirror of silver, came to her cheeks as she glanced at the crowded, enthusiastic house. She stepped back a few paces, and her lips seemed to tremble. Basil Hallward leaped to his feet and began to applaud. Motionless, and as one in a dream, sat Dorian Gray, gazing at her. Lord Henry peered through his glasses, murmuring, 'Charming! Charming!'

The scene was the hall of Capulet's house, and Romeo in his pilgrim's dress had entered with Mercutio and his other friends. The band, such as it was, struck up a few bars of music, and the dance began.

Through the crowd of ungainly, shabbily dressed actors, Sibyl Vane moved like a creature from a finer world. Her body swayed, while she danced, as a plant sways in the water. The curves of her throat were the curves of a white lily. Her hands seemed to be made of cool ivory.

Yet she was curiously listless. She showed no sign of joy when her eyes rested on Romeo. The few words she had to speak –

> 'Good pilgrim, you do wrong your hand too much,
> Which mannerly devotion shows in this;
> For saints have hands that pilgrim's hands do touch,
> And palm to palm is holy palmers' kiss –'

with the brief dialogue that follows, were spoken in a thoroughly artificial manner. The voice was exquisite, but from the point of view of tone it was absolutely false. It was wrong in colour. It took away all the life from the verse. It made the passion unreal.

Dorian Gray grew pale as he watched her. He was puzzled and anxious. Neither of his friends dared to say anything to him. She seemed to them to be absolutely incompetent. They were horribly disappointed.

Yet they felt that the true test of any Juliet is the balcony scene of the second act. They waited for that. If she failed there, there was nothing in her.

She looked charming as she came out in the moonlight. That could not be denied. But the staginess of her acting was unbearable, and grew worse as she went on. Her gestures became absurdly artificial. She over-emphasised everything that she had to say. The beautiful passage –

> 'Thou knowest the mask of night is on my face,
> Else would a maiden blush bepaint my cheek
> For that which thou hast heard me speak to-night –'

was declaimed with the painful precision of a schoolgirl who has been taught to recite by some second-rate professor of elocution. When she leaned over the balcony and came to those wonderful lines –

> 'Although I joy in thee,
> I have no joy of this contract to-night:
> It is too rash, too unadvised, too sudden;
> Too like the lightning, which doth cease to be
> Ere one can say, "It lightens." Sweet, good-night!
> This bud of love by summer's ripening breath
> May prove a beauteous flower when next we meet –'

She spoke the words as though they conveyed no meaning to her. It was not nervousness. Indeed, so far from being nervous, she was absolutely self-contained. It was simply bad art. She was a complete failure.

Even the common, uneducated audience of the pit and gallery lost their interest in the play. They got restless, and began to talk loudly and to whistle. The Jew manager, who was standing at the back of the dress-circle, stamped and swore with rage. The only person unmoved was the girl herself.

When the second act was over there came a storm of hisses, and Lord Henry got up from his chair and put on his coat. 'She is quite beautiful, Dorian,' he said, 'but she can't act. Let us go.'

'I am going to see the play through,' answered the lad, in a hard, bitter voice. 'I am awfully sorry that I have made you waste an evening, Harry. I apologise to you both.'

'My dear Dorian, I should think Miss Vane was ill,' interrupted Hallward. 'We will come some other night.'

'I wish she were ill,' he rejoined. 'But she seems to me to be simply callous and cold. She has entirely altered. Last night she was a great artist. This evening she is merely a commonplace, mediocre actress.'

'Don't talk like that about any one you love, Dorian. Love is a more wonderful thing than Art.'

'They are both simply forms of imitation,' remarked Lord Henry. 'But do let us go. Dorian, you must not stay here any longer. It is not good for one's morals to see bad acting. Besides, I don't suppose you will want your wife to act. So what does it matter if she plays Juliet like a wooden doll? She is very lovely, and if she knows as little about life as she does about acting, she will be a delightful experience. There are only two kinds of people who are really fascinating – people who know absolutely everything, and people who know absolutely nothing. Good heavens, my dear boy, don't look so tragic! The secret of remaining young is never to have an emotion that is unbecoming. Come to the club with Basil and myself. We will smoke cigarettes and drink to the beauty of Sibyl Vane. She is beautiful. What more can you want?'

'Go away, Harry,' cried the lad. 'I want to be alone. Basil, you must go. Ah! Can't you see that my heart is breaking?' The hot tears came to his eyes. His lips trembled, and, rushing to the back of the box, he leaned up against the wall, hiding his face in his hands.

'Let us go, Basil,' said Lord Henry, with a strange tenderness in his voice;

and the two young men passed out together.

A few moments afterwards the footlights flared up, and the curtain rose on the third act. Dorian Gray went back to his seat. He looked pale, and proud, and indifferent. The play dragged on, and seemed interminable. Half of the audience went out, tramping in heavy boots, and laughing. The whole thing was a fiasco. The last act was played to almost empty benches. The curtain went down on a titter, and some groans.

As soon as it was over, Dorian Gray rushed behind the scenes into the green room. The girl was standing there alone, with a look of triumph on her face. Her eyes were lit with an exquisite fire. There was a radiance about her. Her parted lips were smiling over some secret of their own.

When he entered, she looked at him, and an expression of infinite joy came over her. 'How badly I acted to-night, Dorian!' she cried.

'Horribly!' he answered, gazing at her in amazement – 'horribly! It was dreadful. Are you ill? You have no idea what it was. You have no idea what I suffered.'

The girl smiled. 'Dorian,' she answered, lingering over his name with long-drawn music in her voice, as though it were sweeter than honey to the red petals of her mouth – 'Dorian, you should have understood. But you understand now, don't you?'

'Understand what?' he asked, angrily.

'Why I was so bad to-night. Why I shall always be bad. Why I shall never act well again.'

He shrugged his shoulders. 'You are ill, I suppose. When you are ill you shouldn't act. You make yourself ridiculous. My friends were bored. I was bored.'

She seemed not to listen to him. She was transfigured with joy. An ecstasy of happiness dominated her.

'Dorian, Dorian,' she cried, 'before I knew you, acting was the one reality of my life. It was only in the theatre that I lived. I thought that it was all true. I was Rosalind one night, and Portia the other. The joy of Beatrice was my joy, and the sorrows of Cordelia were mine also. I believed in everything. The common people who acted with me seemed to me to be godlike. The painted scenes were my world. I knew nothing but shadows, and I thought them real. You came – oh, my beautiful love! – and you freed my soul from prison. You taught me what reality really is. To-night, for the first time in my life, I saw through the hollowness, the sham, the silliness of the empty pageant in which I had always played. To-night, for the first time, I became conscious that the Romeo was hideous, and old, and painted, that the moonlight in the orchard was false, that the scenery was vulgar, and that the words I had to speak were unreal, were not my words, were not what I wanted to say. You had brought me something higher, something of which all art is but a reflection. You had made me understand what love really is. My love! my love! Prince Charming! Prince of life! I have grown sick of shadows. You are more to me than all art can ever be. What have I to do with the puppets of a play? When I came on to-night, I could not understand how it was that everything had gone from me. I thought that I was going to be wonderful. I found that I could do nothing. Suddenly it dawned on my soul what it all meant. The knowledge was exquisite to me. I heard them hissing, and I smiled. What could they know of love such as ours? Take me away, Dorian – take me away with you, where we can be quite alone. I hate the stage. I might mimic a passion that I do not feel, but I cannot mimic one that burns me like fire. Oh, Dorian, Dorian, you understand now what it signifies? Even if I could do it, it would be profanation for me to play at being in love. You have made me see that.'

He flung himself down on the sofa, and turned away his face. 'You have killed my love,' he muttered.

She looked at him in wonder, and laughed. He made no answer. She came across to him, and with her little fingers stroked his hair. She knelt down and pressed his hands to her lips. He drew them away, and a shudder ran through him.

Then he leaped up, and went to the door. 'Yes,' he cried, 'you have killed my love. You used to stir my imagination. Now you don't even stir my curiosity. You simply produce no effect. I loved you because you were marvellous, because you had genius and intellect, because you realised the dreams of great poets and gave shape and substance to the shadows of art. You have thrown it all away. You are shallow and stupid. My God! how mad I was to love you! What a fool I have been! You are nothing to me now. I will never see you again. I will never think of you. I will never mention your name. You don't know what you were to me, once. Why, once... Oh, I can't bear to think of it! I wish I had never laid eyes upon you! You have spoiled the romance of my life. How little you can know of love, if you say it mars your art! Without your art you are nothing. I would have made you famous, splendid, magnificent. The world would have worshipped you, and you would have borne my name. What are you now? A third-rate actress with a pretty face.'

The girl grew white, and trembled. She clenched her hands together, and her voice seemed to catch in her throat. 'You are not serious, Dorian?' she murmured. 'You are acting.'

'Acting! I leave that to you. You do it so well,' he answered bitterly.

She rose from her knees, and with a piteous expression of pain in her face, came across the room to him. She put her hand upon his arm, and looked into his eyes. He thrust her back. 'Don't touch me!' he cried.

A low moan broke from her, and she flung herself at his feet, and lay there like a trampled flower. 'Dorian, Dorian, don't leave me!' she whispered. 'I am so sorry I didn't act well. I was thinking of you all the time. But I will try – indeed, I will try. It came so suddenly across me, my love for you. I think I should never have known it if you had not kissed me – if we had not kissed each other. Kiss me again, my love. Don't go away from me. I couldn't bear it. Oh! don't go away from me. My brother.... No; never mind. He didn't mean it. He was in jest.... But you, oh! can't you forgive me for to-night? I will work so hard, and try to improve. Don't be cruel to me because I love you better than anything in the world. After all, it is only once that I have not pleased you. But you are quite right, Dorian. I should have shown myself more of an artist. It was foolish of me; and yet I couldn't help it. Oh, don't leave me, don't leave me.' A fit of passionate sobbing choked her. She crouched on the floor like a wounded thing, and Dorian Gray, with his beautiful eyes, looked down at her, and his chiselled lips curled in exquisite disdain. There is always something ridiculous about the emotions of people whom one has ceased to love. Sibyl Vane to him seemed to be absurdly melodramatic. Her tears and sobs annoyed him.

'I am going,' he said at last, in his calm, clear voice. 'I don't wish to be unkind, but I can't see you again. You have disappointed me.'

She wept silently, and made no answer, but crept nearer. Her little hands stretched blindly out, and appeared to be seeking for him. He turned on his heel, and left the room. In a few moments he was out of the theatre.

Where he went to he hardly knew. He remembered wandering through dimly-lit streets, past gaunt black-shadowed archways and evil-looking houses. Women with hoarse voices and harsh laughter had called after him. Drunkards had reeled by cursing, and chattering to themselves like monstrous apes. He had seen grotesque children huddled upon doorsteps, and heard shrieks and oaths from gloomy courts.

As the dawn was just breaking he found himself close to Covent Garden. The darkness lifted, and, flushed with faint fires, the sky hollowed itself into a perfect pearl. Huge carts filled with nodding lilies rumbled slowly down the polished empty street. The air was heavy with the perfume of the flowers, and their beauty seemed to bring him an anodyne for his pain. He followed into the market, and watched the men unloading their waggons. A white-smocked carter offered him some cherries. He thanked him, and wondered why he refused to accept any money for them, and began to eat them listlessly. They had been plucked at midnight, and the coldness of the moon had entered into them. A long line of boys carrying crates of striped tulips, and of yellow and red roses, defiled in front of him, threading their way through the huge jade-green piles of vegetables. Under the portico, with its grey sun-bleached pillars, loitered a troop of draggled bare-headed girls, waiting for the auction to be over. Others crowded round the swinging doors of the coffee-house in the Plazza. The heavy cart-horses slipped and stamped upon the rough stones, shaking their bells and trappings. Some of the drivers were lying asleep on a pile of sacks. Iris-necked, and pink-footed, the pigeons ran about picking up seeds.

After a little while, he hailed a hansom, and drove home. For a few moments he loitered upon the door-step, looking round at the silent Square with its blank, close-shuttered windows, and its staring blinds. The sky was pure opal now, and the roofs of the houses glistened like silver against it. From some chimney opposite a thin wreath of smoke was rising. It curled, a violet riband, through the nacre-coloured air.

In the huge gilt Venetian lantern, spoil of some Doge's barge, that hung from the ceiling of the great oak-panelled hall of entrance, lights were still burning from three flickering jets: thin blue petals of flame they seemed, rimmed with white fire. He turned them out, and, having thrown his hat and cape on the table, passed through the library towards the door of his bedroom, a large octagonal chamber on the ground floor that, in his new-born feeling for luxury, he had just had decorated for himself, and hung with some curious Renaissance tapestries that had been discovered stored in a disused attic at Selby Royal. As he was turning the handle of the door, his eye fell upon the portrait Basil Hallward had painted of him. He started back as if in surprise. Then he went on into his own room, looking somewhat puzzled. After he had taken the buttonhole out of his coat, he seemed to hesitate. Finally he came back, went over to the picture, and examined it. In the dim arrested light that struggled through the cream-coloured silk blinds, the face appeared to him to be a little changed. The expression looked different. One would have said that there was a touch of cruelty in the mouth. It was certainly strange.

He turned round, and, walking to the window, drew up the blind. The bright dawn flooded the room, and swept the fantastic shadows into dusky corners, where they lay shuddering. But the strange expression that he had noticed in the face of the portrait seemed to linger there, to be more intensified even. The quivering, ardent sunlight showed him the lines of cruelty round the mouth as clearly as if he had been looking into a mirror after he had done some dreadful thing.

He winced, and, taking up from the table an oval glass framed in ivory Cupids, one of Lord Henry's many presents to him, glanced hurriedly into its polished depths. No line like that warped his red lips. What did it mean?

He rubbed his eyes, and came close to the picture, and examined it again. There were no signs of any change when he looked into the actual painting, and yet there was no doubt, that the whole expression had altered. It was not a mere fancy of his own. The thing was horribly apparent.

He threw himself into a chair, and began to think. Suddenly there flashed across his mind what he had said in Basil Hallward's studio the day the picture had been finished. Yes, he remembered it perfectly. He had uttered a mad wish that he himself might remain young, and the portrait grow old; that his own beauty might be untarnished, and the face on the canvas bear the burden of his passions and his sins; that the painted image might be seared with the lines of suffering and thought, and that he might keep all the delicate bloom and loveliness of his then just conscious boyhood. Surely his wish had not been fulfilled? Such things were impossible. It seemed monstrous even to think of them. And, yet, there was the picture before him, with the touch of cruelty in the mouth.

Cruelty! Had he been cruel? It was the girl's fault, not his. He had dreamed of her as a great artist, had given his love to her because he had thought her great. Then she had disappointed him. She had been shallow and unworthy. And, yet, a feeling of infinite regret came over him, as he thought of her lying at his feet sobbing like a little child. He remembered with what callousness he had watched her. Why had he been made like that? Why had such a soul been given to him? But he had suffered also. During the three terrible hours that the play had lasted, he had lived centuries of pain, æon upon aeon of torture. His life was well worth hers. She had marred him for a moment, if he had wounded her for an age. Besides, women were better suited to bear sorrow than men. They lived on their emotions. They only thought of their emotions. When they took lovers, it was merely to have some one with whom they could have scenes. Lord Henry had told him that, and Lord Henry knew what women were. Why should he trouble about Sibyl Vane? She was nothing to him now.

But the picture? What was he to say of that? It held the secret of his life, and told his story. It had taught him to love his own beauty. Would it teach him to loathe his own soul? Would he ever look at it again?

No; it was merely an illusion wrought on the troubled senses. The horrible night that he had passed had left phantoms behind it. Suddenly there had fallen upon his brain that tiny scarlet speck that makes men mad. The picture had not changed. It was folly to think so.

Yet it was watching him, with its beautiful marred face and its cruel smile. Its bright hair gleamed in the early sunlight. Its blue eyes met his own. A sense of infinite pity, not for himself, but for the painted image of himself, came over him. It had altered already, and would alter more. Its gold would wither into grey. Its red and white roses would die. For every sin that he committed a stain would fleck and wreck its fairness. But he would not sin. The picture, changed or unchanged, would be to him the visible emblem of conscience. He would resist temptation. He would not see Lord Henry any more – would not, at any rate, listen to those subtle poisonous theories that in Basil Hallward's garden had first stirred within him the passion for impossible things. He would go back to Sibyl Vane, make her amends, marry her, try to love her again. Yes, it was his duty to do so. She must have suffered more than he had. Poor child! He had been selfish and cruel to her. The fascination that she had exercised over him would return. They would be happy together. His life with her would be beautiful and pure.

He got up from his chair, and drew a large screen right in front of the portrait, shuddering as he glanced at it. 'How horrible!' he murmured to himself, and he walked across to the window and opened it. When he stepped out on to the grass, he drew a deep breath. The fresh morning air seemed to drive away all his sombre passions. He thought only of Sibyl. A faint echo of his love came back to him. He repeated her name over and over again. The birds that were singing in the dew-drenched garden seemed to be telling the flowers about her.

8

IT was long past noon when he awoke. His valet had crept several times on tiptoe into the room to see if he was stirring, and had wondered what made his young master sleep so late. Finally his bell sounded, and Victor came softly in with a cup of tea, and a pile of letters, on a small tray of old Sèvres china, and drew back the olive-satin curtains, with their shimmering blue lining, that hung in front of the three tall windows.

'Monsieur has slept well this morning,' he said, smiling.

'What o'clock is it, Victor?' asked Dorian Gray, drowsily.

'One hour and a quarter, Monsieur.'

How late it was! He sat up, and, having sipped some tea, turned over his letters. One of them was from Lord Henry, and had been brought by hand that morning. He hesitated for a moment, and then put it aside. The others he opened listlessly. They contained the usual collection of cards, invitations to dinner, tickets for private views, programmes of charity concerts, and the like, that are showered on fashionable young men every morning during the season. There was a rather heavy bill, for a chased silver Louis-Quinze toilet-set, that he had not yet had the courage to send on to his guardians, who were extremely old-fashioned people and did not realise that we live in an age when unnecessary things are our only necessities; and there were several very courteously worded communications from Jermyn Street money-lenders offering to advance any sum of money at a moment's notice and at the most reasonable rates of interest.

After about ten minutes he got up, and, throwing on an elaborate dressing-gown of silk-embroidered cashmere wool, passed into the onyx-paved bathroom. The cool water refreshed him after his long sleep. He seemed to have forgotten all that he had gone through. A dim sense of having taken part in some strange tragedy came to him once or twice, but there was the unreality of a dream about it.

As soon as he was dressed, he went into the library and sat down to a light French breakfast, that had been laid out for him on a small round table close to the open window. It was an exquisite day. The warm air seemed laden with spices. A bee flew in, and buzzed round the blue-dragon bowl that, filled with sulphur-yellow roses, stood before him. He felt perfectly happy.

Suddenly his eye fell on the screen that he had placed in front of the portrait, and he started.

'Too cold for Monsieur?' asked his valet, putting an omelette on the table. 'I shut the window?'

Dorian shook his head. 'I am not cold,' he murmured.

Was it all true? Had the portrait really changed? Or had it been simply his own imagination that had made him see a look of evil where there had been a look of joy? Surely a painted canvas could not alter? The thing was absurd. It would serve as a tale to tell Basil some day. It would make him smile.

And, yet, how vivid was his recollection of the whole thing! First in the dim twilight, and then in the bright dawn, he had seen the touch of cruelty round the warped lips. He almost dreaded his valet leaving the room. He knew that when he was alone he would have to examine the portrait. He was afraid of certainty. When the coffee and cigarettes had been brought and the man turned to go, he felt a wild desire to tell him to remain. As the door was closing behind him he called him back. The man stood waiting for his orders. Dorian looked at him for a moment. 'I am not at home to any one, Victor,' he said, with a sigh. The man bowed and retired.

Then he rose from the table, lit a cigarette, and flung himself down on a luxuriously-cushioned couch that stood facing the screen. The screen was an old one, of gilt Spanish leather, stamped and wrought with a rather florid Louis-Quatorze pattern. He scanned it curiously, wondering if ever before it had concealed the secret of a man's life.

Should he move it aside, after all? Why not let it stay there? What was the use of knowing? If the thing was true, it was terrible. If it was not true, why trouble about it? But what if, by some fate or deadlier chance, eyes other than his spied behind, and saw the horrible change? What should he do if Basil Hallward came and asked to look at his own picture? Basil would be sure to do that. No; the thing had to be examined, and at once. Anything would be better than this dreadful state of doubt.

He got up, and locked both doors. At least he would be alone when he looked upon the mask of his shame. Then he drew the screen aside, and saw himself face to face. It was perfectly true. The portrait had altered.

As he often remembered afterwards, and always with no small wonder, he found himself at first gazing at the portrait with a feeling of almost scientific interest. That such a change should have taken place was incredible to him. And yet it was a fact. Was there some subtle affinity between the chemical atoms, that shaped themselves into form and colour on the canvas, and the soul that was within him? Could it be that what that soul thought, they realised? – that what it dreamed, they made true? Or was there some other, more terrible reason? He shuddered, and felt afraid, and, going back to the couch, lay there, gazing at the picture in sickened horror.

One thing, however, he felt that it had done for him. It had made him conscious how unjust, how cruel, he had been to Sibyl Vane. It was not too late to make reparation for that. She could still be his wife. His unreal and selfish love would yield to some higher influence, would be transformed into some nobler passion, and the portrait that Basil Hallward had painted of him would be a guide to him through life, would be to him what holiness is to some, and conscience to others, and the fear of God to us all. There were opiates for remorse, drugs that could lull the moral sense to sleep. But here was a visible symbol of the degradation of sin. Here was an ever-present sign of the ruin men brought upon their souls.

Three o'clock struck, and four, and the half-hour rang its double chime, but Dorian Gray did not stir. He was trying to gather up the scarlet threads of life, and to weave them into a pattern; to find his way through the sanguine labyrinth of passion through which he was wandering. He did not know what to do, or what to think. Finally, he went over to the table, and wrote a passionate letter to the girl he had loved, imploring her forgiveness, and accusing himself of madness. He covered page after page with wild words of sorrow, and wilder words of pain. There is a luxury in self-reproach. When we blame ourselves we feel that no one else has a right to blame us. It is the confession, not the priest, that gives us absolution. When Dorian had finished the letter, he felt that he had been forgiven.

Suddenly there came a knock to the door, and he heard Lord Henry's voice outside. 'My dear boy, I must see you. Let me in at once. I can't bear your shutting yourself up like this.'

He made no answer at first, but remained quite still. The knocking still continued, and grew louder. Yes, it was better to let Lord Henry in, and to explain to him the new life he was going to lead, to quarrel with him if it became necessary to quarrel, to part if parting was inevitable. He jumped up, drew the screen hastily across the picture, and unlocked the door.

'I am so sorry for it all, Dorian,' said Lord Henry, as he entered. 'But you must not think too much about it.'

'Do you mean about Sibyl Vane?' asked the lad.

'Yes, of course,' answered Lord Henry, sinking into a chair, and slowly pulling off his yellow gloves. 'It is dreadful, from one point of view, but it was not your fault. Tell me, did you go behind and see her, after the play was over?'

'Yes.'

'I felt sure you had. Did you make a scene with her?'

'I was brutal, Harry – perfectly brutal. But it is all right now. I am not sorry for anything that has happened. It has taught me to know myself better.'

'Ah, Dorian, I am so glad you take it in that way! I was afraid I would find you plunged in remorse, and tearing that nice curly hair of yours.'

'I have got through all that,' said Dorian, shaking his head, and smiling. 'I am perfectly happy now. I know what conscience is, to begin with. It is not what you told me it was. It is the divinest thing in us. Don't sneer at it, Harry, any more – at least not before me. I want to be good. I can't bear the idea of my soul being hideous.'

'A very charming artistic basis for ethics, Dorian! I congratulate you on it. But how are you going to begin?'

'By marrying Sibyl Vane.'

'Marrying Sibyl Vane!' cried Lord Henry, standing up, and looking at him in perplexed amazement. 'But, my dear Dorian –'

'Yes, Harry, I know what you are going to say. Something dreadful about marriage. Don't say it. Don't ever say things of that kind to me again. Two days ago I asked Sibyl to marry me. I am not going to break my word to her. She is to be my wife!'

'Your wife! Dorian! . . . Didn't you get my letter? I wrote to you this morning, and sent the note down, by my own man.'

'Your letter? Oh, yes, I remember. I have not read it yet, Harry. I was afraid there might be something in it that I wouldn't like. You cut life to pieces with your epigrams.'

'You know nothing then?'

'What do you mean?'

Lord Henry walked across the room, and, sitting down by Dorian Gray, took both his hands in his own, and held them tightly. 'Dorian,' he said, 'my letter – don't be frightened – was to tell you that Sibyl Vane is dead.'

A cry of pain broke from the lad's lips, and he leaped to his feet, tearing his hands away from Lord Henry's grasp. 'Dead! Sibyl dead! It is not true! It is a horrible lie! How dare you say it?'

'It is quite true, Dorian,' said Lord Henry, gravely. 'It is in all the morning papers. I wrote down to you to ask you not to see any one till I came. There will have to be an inquest, of course, and you must not be mixed up in it. Things like that make a man fashionable in Paris. But in London people are so prejudiced. Here, one should never make one's *début* with a scandal. One should reserve that to give an interest to one's old age. I suppose they don't know your name at the theatre? If they don't, it is all right. Did any one see you going round to her room? That is an important point.'

Dorian did not answer for a few moments. He was dazed with horror. Finally he stammered in a stifled voice, 'Harry, did you say an inquest? What did you mean by that? Did Sibyl – ? Oh, Harry, I can't bear it! But be quick. Tell me everything at once.'

'I have no doubt it was not an accident, Dorian, though it must be put in that way to the public. It seems that as she was leaving the theatre with her mother, about half-past twelve or so, she said she had forgotten something upstairs. They waited some time for her, but she did not come down again. They ultimately found her lying dead on the floor of her dressing-room. She had swallowed something by mistake, some dreadful thing they use at theatres. I don't know what it was, but it had either prussic acid or white lead in it. I should fancy it was prussic acid, as she seems to have died instantaneously.'

'Harry, Harry, it is terrible!' cried the lad.

'Yes; it is very tragic, of course, but you must not get yourself mixed up in it. I see by *The Standard* that she was seventeen. I should have thought she was almost younger than that. She looked such a child, and seemed to know so little about acting. Dorian, you mustn't let this thing get on your nerves. You must come and dine with me, and afterwards we will look in at the Opera. It is a Patti night, and everybody will be there. You can come to my sister's box. She has got some smart women with her.'

'So I have murdered Sibyl Vane,' said Dorian Gray, half to himself – 'murdered her as surely as if I had cut her little throat with a knife. Yet the roses are not less lovely for all that. The birds sing just as happily in my garden. And to-night I am to dine with you, and then go on to the Opera, and sup somewhere, I suppose, afterwards. How extraordinarily dramatic life is! If I had read all this in a book, Harry, I think I would have wept over it. Somehow, now that it has happened actually, and to me, it seems far too wonderful for tears. Here is the first passionate love-letter I have ever written in my life. Strange, that my first passionate love-letter should have been addressed to a dead girl. Can they feel, I wonder, those white silent people we call the dead? Sibyl! Can she feel, or know, or listen? Oh, Harry, how I loved her once! It seems years ago to me now. She was everything to me.

Then came that dreadful night – was it really only last night? – when she played so badly, and my heart almost broke. She explained it all to me. It was terribly pathetic. But I was not moved a bit. I thought her shallow. Suddenly something happened that made me afraid. I can't tell you what it was, but it was terrible. I said I would go back to her. I felt I had done wrong. And now she is dead. My God! My God! Harry, what shall I do? You don't know the danger I am in, and there is nothing to keep me straight. She would have done that for me. She had no right to kill herself. It was selfish of her.'

'My dear Dorian,' answered Lord Henry, taking a cigarette from his case, and producing a gold-latten match-box, 'the only way a woman can ever reform a man is by boring him so completely that he loses all possible interest in life. If you had married this girl you would have been wretched. Of course, you would have treated her kindly. One can always be kind to people about whom one cares nothing. But she would have soon found out that you were absolutely indifferent to her. And when a woman finds that out about her husband, she either becomes dreadfully dowdy, or wears very smart bonnets that some other woman's husband has to pay for. I say nothing about the social mistake, which would have been abject, which, of course, I would not have allowed, but I assure you that in any case the whole thing would have been an absolute failure.'

'I suppose it would,' muttered the lad, walking up and down the room, and looking horribly pale. 'But I thought it was my duty. It is not my fault that this terrible tragedy has prevented my doing what was right. I remember your saying once that there is a fatality about good resolutions – that they are always made too late. Mine certainly were.'

'Good resolutions are useless attempts to interfere with scientific laws. Their origin is pure vanity. Their result is absolutely *nil*. They give us, now and then, some of those luxurious sterile emotions that have a certain charm for the weak. That is all that can be said for them. They are simply cheques that men draw on a bank where they have no account.'

'Harry,' cried Dorian Gray, coming over and sitting down beside him, 'why is it that I cannot feel this tragedy as much as I want to? I don't think I am heartless. Do you?'

'You have done too many foolish things during the last fortnight to be entitled to give yourself that name, Dorian,' answered Lord Henry, with his sweet, melancholy smile.

The lad frowned. 'I don't like that explanation, Harry,' he rejoined, 'but I am glad you don't think I am heartless. I am nothing of the kind. I know I am not. And yet I must admit that this thing that has happened does not affect me as it should. It seems to me to be simply like a wonderful ending to a wonderful play. It has all the terrible beauty of a Greek tragedy, a tragedy in which I took a great part, but by which I have not been wounded.'

'It is an interesting question,' said Lord Henry, who found an exquisite pleasure in playing on the lad's unconscious egotism – 'an extremely interesting question. I fancy that the true explanation is this. It often happens that the real tragedies of life occur in such an inartistic manner that they hurt us by their crude violence, their absolute incoherence, their absurd want of meaning, their entire lack of style. They affect us just as vulgarity affects us. They give us an impression of sheer brute force, and we revolt against that. Sometimes, however, a tragedy that possesses artistic elements of beauty crosses our lives. If these elements of beauty are real, the whole thing simply appeals to our sense of dramatic effect. Suddenly we find that we are no longer the actors, but the spectators of the play. Or rather we are both. We watch ourselves, and the mere wonder of the spectacle enthralls us. In the present case, what is it that has really happened? Some one has killed herself for love of you. I wish that I had ever had such an experience. It would have made me in love with love for the rest of my life. The people who have adored me – there have not been very many, but there have been some – have always insisted on living on, long after I had ceased to care for them, or they to care for me. They have become stout and tedious, and when I meet them they go in at once for reminiscences. That awful memory of woman! What a fearful thing it is. And what an utter intellectual stagnation it reveals! One should absorb the colour of life, but one should never remember its details. Details are always vulgar.'

'I must sow poppies in my garden,' sighed Dorian.

'There is no necessity,' rejoined his companion. 'Life has always poppies in her hands. Of course, now and then things linger. I once wore nothing but violets all through one season, as a form of artistic mourning for a romance that would not die. Ultimately, however, it did die. I forget what killed it. I think it was her proposing to sacrifice the whole world for me. That is always a dreadful moment. It fills one with the terror of eternity. Well – would you believe it? – a week ago, at Lady Hampshire's, I found myself seated at dinner next the lady in question, and she insisted on going over the whole thing again, and digging up the past, and raking up the future. I had buried my romance in a bed of asphodel. She dragged it out again, and assured me that I had spoiled her life. I am bound to state that she ate an enormous dinner, so I did not feel any anxiety. But what a lack of taste she showed! The one charm of the past is that it is the past. But women never know when the curtain has fallen. They always want a sixth act, and as soon as the interest of the play is entirely over they propose to continue it. If they were allowed their own way, every comedy would have a tragic ending, and every tragedy would culminate in a farce. They are charmingly artificial, but they have no sense of art. You are more fortunate than I am. I assure you, Dorian, that not one of the women I have known would have done for me what Sibyl Vane did for you. Ordinary women always console themselves. Some of them do it by going in for sentimental colours. Never trust a woman who wears mauve, whatever her age may be, or a woman over thirty-five who is fond of pink ribbons. It always means that they have a history. Others find a great consolation in suddenly discovering the good qualities of their husbands. They flaunt their conjugal felicity in one's face, as if it were the most fascinating of sins. Religion consoles some. Its mysteries have all the charm of a flirtation, a woman once told me; and I can quite understand it. Besides, nothing makes one so vain as being told that one is a sinner. Conscience makes egotists of us all. Yes; there is really no end to the consolations that women find in modern life. Indeed, I have not mentioned the most important one.'

'What is that, Harry?' said the lad, listlessly.

'Oh, the obvious consolation. Taking some one else's admirer when one loses one's own. In good society that always whitewashes a woman. But really, Dorian, how different Sibyl Vane must have been from all the women one meets! There is something to me quite beautiful about her death. I am glad I am living in a century when such wonders happen. They make one believe in the reality of the things we all play with, such as romance, passion, and love.'

'I was terribly cruel to her. You forget that.'

'I am afraid that woman appreciate cruelty, downright cruelty, more than anything else. They have wonderfully primitive instincts. We have emancipated them, but they remain slaves looking for their masters, all the same. They love being dominated. I am sure you were splendid. I have never seen you really and absolutely angry, but I can fancy how delightful you looked. And, after all, you said something to me the day before yesterday that seemed to me at the time to be merely fanciful, but that I see now was absolutely true, and it holds the key to everything.'

'What was that, Harry?'

'You said to me that Sibyl Vane represented to you all the heroines of romance – that she was Desdemona one night, and Ophelia the other; that if she died as Juliet, she came to life as Imogen.'

'She will never come to life again now,' muttered the lad, burying his face in his hands.

'No, she will never come to life. She has played her last part. But you must think of that lonely death in the tawdry dressing-room simply as a strange lurid fragment from some Jacobean tragedy, as a wonderful scene from Webster, or Ford, or Cyril Tourneur. The girl never really lived, and so she has never really died. To you at least, she was always a dream, a phantom that flitted through Shakespeare's plays and left them lovelier for its presence, a reed through which Shakespeare's music sounded richer and more full of joy. The moment she touched actual life, she marred it, and it marred her, and so she passed away. Mourn for Ophelia, if you like. Put ashes on your head because Cordelia was strangled. Cry out against Heaven because the daughter of Brabantio died. But don't waste your tears over Sibyl Vane. She was less real than they are.'

There was a silence. The evening darkened in the room. Noiselessly, and with silver feet, the shadows crept in from the garden. The colours faded wearily out of things.

After some time Dorian Gray looked up. 'You have explained me to myself, Harry,' he murmured, with something of a sigh of relief. 'I felt all that you have said, but somehow I was afraid of it, and I could not express it to myself. How well you know me! But we will not talk again of what has happened. It has been a marvellous experience. That is all. I wonder if life has still in store for me anything as marvellous.'

'Life has everything in store for you, Dorian. There is nothing that you, with your extraordinary good looks, will not be able to do.'

'But suppose, Harry, I became haggard, and old, and wrinkled? What then?'

'Ah, then,' said Lord Henry, rising to go – 'then, my dear Dorian, you would have to fight for your victories. As it is, they are brought to you. No, you must keep your good looks. We live in an age that reads too much to be wise, and that thinks too much to be beautiful. We cannot spare you. And now you had better dress, and drive down to the club. We are rather late, as it is.'

'I think I shall join you at the Opera, Harry. I feel too tired to eat anything. What is the number of your sister's box?'

'Twenty-seven, I believe. It is on the grand tier. You will see her name on the door. But I am sorry you won't come and dine.'

'I don't feel up to it,' said Dorian, listlessly. 'But I am awfully obliged to you for all that you have said to me. You are certainly my best friend. No one has ever understood me as you have.'

'We are only at the beginning of our friendship, Dorian,' answered Lord Henry, shaking him by the hand. 'Good-bye. I shall see you before nine-thirty, I hope. Remember, Patti is singing.'

As he closed the door behind him, Dorian Gray touched the bell, and in a few minutes Victor appeared with the lamps and drew the blinds down.

He waited impatiently for him to go. The man seemed to take an interminable time over everything.

As soon as he had left, he rushed to the screen, and drew it back. No; there was no further change in the picture. It had received the news of Sibyl Vane's death before he had known of it himself. It was conscious of the events of life as they occurred. The vicious cruelty that marred the fine lines of the mouth had, no doubt, appeared at the very moment that the girl had drunk the poison, whatever it was. Or was it indifferent to results? Did it merely take cognizance of what passed within the soul? He wondered, and hoped that some day he would see the change taking place before his very eyes, shuddering as he hoped it.

Poor Sibyl! What a romance it had all been! She had often mimicked death on the stage. Then Death himself had touched her, and taken her with him. How had she played that dreadful last scene? Had she cursed him, as she died? No; she had died for love of him, and love would always be a sacrament to him now. She had atoned for everything, by the sacrifice she had made of her life. He would not think any more of what she had made him go through, on that horrible night at the theatre. When he thought of her, it would be as a wonderful tragic figure sent on to the world's stage to show the supreme reality of Love. A wonderful tragic figure? Tears came to his eyes as he remembered her child-like look, and winsome fanciful ways, and shy tremulous grace. He brushed them away hastily, and looked again at the picture.

He felt that the time had really come for making his choice. Or had his choice already been made? Yes, life had decided that for him – life, and his own infinite curiosity about life. Eternal youth, infinite passion, pleasures subtle and secret, wild joys and wilder sins – he was to have all these things. The portrait was to bear the burden of his shame: that was all.

A feeling of pain crept over him, as he thought of the desecration that was in store for the fair face on the canvas. Once, in boyish mockery of Narcissus, he had kissed, or feigned to kiss, those painted lips that now smiled so cruelly at him. Morning after morning he had sat before the portrait, wondering at its beauty, almost enamoured of it, as it seemed to him at times. Was it to alter now with every mood to which he yielded? Was it to become a monstrous and loathsome thing, to be hidden away in a locked room, to be shut out from the sunlight that had so often touched to brighter gold the waving wonder of its hair? The pity of it! The pity of it!

For a moment he thought of praying that the horrible sympathy that existed between him and the picture might cease. It had changed in answer to a prayer; perhaps in answer to a prayer it might remain unchanged. And, yet, who, that knew anything about Life, would surrender the chance of remaining always young, however fantastic that chance might be, or with what fateful consequences it might be fraught? Besides, was it really under his control? Had it indeed been prayer that had produced the substitution? Might there not be some curious scientific reason for it all? If thought could exercise its influence upon a living organism, might not thought exercise an influence upon dead and inorganic things? Nay, without thought or conscious desire, might not things external to ourselves vibrate in unison with our moods and passions, atom calling to atom in secret love of strange affinity? But the reason was of no importance. He would never again tempt by a prayer any terrible power. If the picture was to alter, it was to alter. That was all. Why inquire too closely into it?

For there would be a real pleasure in watching it. He would be able to follow his mind into its secret places. This portrait would be to him the most magical of mirrors. As it had revealed to him his own body, so it would reveal to him his own soul. And when winter came upon it, he would still be standing where spring trembles on the verge of summer. When the blood crept from its face, and left behind a pallid mask of chalk with leaden eyes, he would keep the glamour of boyhood. Not one blossom of his loveliness would ever fade. Not one pulse of his life would ever weaken. Like the gods of the Greeks, he would be strong, and fleet, and joyous. What did it matter what happened to the coloured image on the canvas? He would be safe. That was everything.

He drew the screen back into its former place in front of the picture, smiling as he did so, and passed into his bedroom, where his valet was already waiting for him. An hour later he was at the Opera, and Lord Henry was leaning over his chair.

9

AS he was sitting at breakfast next morning, Basil Hallward was shown into the room.

'I am so glad I have found you, Dorian,' he said, gravely. 'I called last night, and they told me you were at the Opera. Of course I knew that was impossible. But I wish you had left word where you had really gone to. I passed a dreadful evening, half afraid that one tragedy might be followed by another. I think you might have telegraphed for me when you heard of it first. I read of it quite by chance in a late edition of *The Globe* that I picked up at the club. I came here at once, and was miserable at not finding you. I can't tell you how heart-broken I am about the whole thing. I know what you must suffer. But where were you? Did you go down and see the girl's mother? For a moment I thought of following you there. They gave the address in the paper. Somewhere in the Euston Road, isn't it? But I was afraid of intruding upon a sorrow that I could not lighten. Poor woman! What a state she must be in! And her only child, too! What did she say about it all?'

'My dear Basil, how do I know?' murmured Dorian Gray, sipping some pale-yellow wine from a delicate gold-beaded bubble of Venetian glass, and looking dreadfully bored. 'I was at the Opera. You should have come on there. I met Lady Gwendolen, Harry's sister, for the first time. We were in her box. She is perfectly charming; and Patti sang divinely. Don't talk about horrid subjects. If one doesn't talk about a thing, it has never happened. It is simply expression, as Harry says, that gives reality to things. I may mention that she was not the woman's only child. There is a son, a charming fellow, I believe. But he is not on the stage. He is a sailor, or something. And now, tell me about yourself and what you are painting.'

'You went to the Opera?' said Hallward, speaking very slowly, and with a strained touch of pain in his voice. 'You went to the Opera while Sibyl Vane was lying dead in some sordid lodging? You can talk to me of other women being charming, and of Patti singing divinely, before the girl you loved has even the quiet of a grave to sleep in? Why, man, there are horrors in store for that little white body of hers!'

'Stop, Basil! I won't hear it!' cried Dorian, leaping to his feet. 'You must not tell me about things. What is done is done. What is past is past.'

'You call yesterday the past?'

'What has the actual lapse of time got to do with it? It is only shallow people who require years to get rid of an emotion. A man who is master of himself can end a sorrow as easily as he can invent a pleasure. I don't want to be at the mercy of my emotions. I want to use them, to enjoy them, and to dominate them.'

'Dorian, this is horrible! Something has changed you completely. You look exactly the same wonderful boy who, day after day, used to come down to my studio to sit for his picture. But you were simple, natural, and affectionate then. You were the most unspoiled creature in the whole world.

Now, I don't know what has come over you. You talk as if you had no heart, no pity in you. It is all Harry's influence. I see that.'

The lad flushed up, and, going to the window, looked out for a few moments on the green, flickering, sun-lashed garden. 'I owe a great deal to Harry, Basil,' he said, at last – 'more than I owe to you. You only taught me to be vain.'

'Well, I am punished for that, Dorian – or shall be some day.'

'I don't know what you mean, Basil,' he exclaimed, turning round. 'I don't know what you want. What do you want?'

'I want the Dorian Gray I used to paint,' said the artist, sadly.

'Basil,' said the lad, going over to him, and putting his hand on his shoulder, 'you have come too late. Yesterday when I heard that Sibyl Vane had killed herself –'

'Killed herself! Good heavens! Is there no doubt about that?' cried Hallward, looking up at him with an expression of horror.

'My dear Basil! Surely you don't think it was a vulgar accident? Of course she killed herself.'

The elder man buried his face in his hands. 'How fearful,' he muttered, and a shudder ran through him.

'No,' said Dorian Gray, 'there is nothing fearful about it. It is one of the great romantic tragedies of the age. As a rule, people who act lead the most commonplace lives. They are good husbands, or faithful wives, or something tedious. You know what I mean – middle-class virtue, and all that kind of thing. How different Sibyl was! She lived her finest tragedy. She was always a heroine. The last night she played – the night you saw her – she acted badly because she had known the reality of love. When she knew its unreality, she died, as Juliet might have died. She passed again into the sphere of art. There is something of the martyr about her. Her death has all the pathetic uselessness of martyrdom, all its wasted beauty. But, as I was saying, you must not think I have not suffered. If you had come in yesterday at a particular moment – about half-past five, perhaps, or a quarter to six – you would have found me in tears. Even Harry, who was here, who brought me the news, in fact, had no idea what I was going through. I suffered immensely. Then it passed away. I cannot repeat an emotion. No one can, except sentimentalists. And you are awfully unjust, Basil. You come down here to console me. That is charming of you. You find me consoled, and you are furious. How like a sympathetic person! You remind me of a story Harry told me about a certain philanthropist who spent twenty years of his life in trying to get some grievance redressed, or some unjust law altered – I forget exactly what it was. Finally he succeeded, and nothing could exceed his disappointment. He had absolutely nothing to do, almost died of *ennui*, and became a confirmed misanthrope. And besides, my dear old Basil, if you really want to console me, teach me rather to forget what has happened, or to see it from the proper artistic point of view. Was it not Gautier who used to write about *la consolation des arts*? I remember picking up a little vellum-covered book in your studio one day and chancing on that delightful phrase. Well, I am not like that young man you told me of when we were down at Marlow together, the young man who used to say that yellow satin could console one for all the miseries of life. I love beautiful things that one can touch and handle. Old brocades, green bronzes, lacquer-work, carved ivories, exquisite surroundings, luxury, pomp, there is much to be got from all these. But the artistic temperament that they create, or at any rate reveal, is still more to me. To become the spectator of one's own life, as Harry says, is to escape the suffering of life. I know you are surprised at my talking to you like this. You have not realised how I have developed. I was a schoolboy when you knew me. I am a man now. I have new passions, new thoughts, new ideas. I am different, but you must not like me less. I am changed, but you must always be my friend. Of course I am very fond of Harry. But I know that you are better than he is. You are not stronger – you are too much afraid of life – but you are better. And how happy we used to be together! Don't leave me, Basil, and don't quarrel with me. I am what I am. There is nothing more to be said.'

The painter felt strangely moved. The lad was infinitely dear to him, and his personality had been the great turning-point in his art. He could not bear the idea of reproaching him any more. After all, his indifference was probably merely a mood that would pass away. There was so much in him that was good, so much in him that was noble.

'Well, Dorian,' he said, at length, with a sad smile, 'I won't speak to you again about this horrible thing, after to-day. I only trust your name won't be mentioned in connection with it. The inquest is to take place this afternoon. Have they summoned you?'

Dorian shook his head and a look of annoyance passed over his face at the mention of the word 'inquest.' There was something so crude and vulgar about everything of the kind. 'They don't know my name,' he answered.

'But surely she did?'

'Only my Christian name, and that I am quite sure she never mentioned to any one. She told me once that they were all rather curious to learn who I was, and that she invariably told them my name was Prince Charming. It was pretty of her. You must do me a drawing of Sibyl, Basil. I should like to have something more of her than the memory of a few kisses and some broken pathetic words.'

'I will try and do something, Dorian, if it would please you. But you must come and sit to me yourself again. I can't get on without you.'

'I can never sit to you again, Basil. It is impossible!' he exclaimed, starting back.

The painter stared at him. 'My dear boy, what nonsense!' he cried. 'Do you mean to say you don't like what I did of you? Where is it? Why have you pulled the screen in front of it! Let me look at it. It is the best thing I have ever done. Do take the screen away, Dorian. It is simply disgraceful of your servant hiding my work like that. I felt the room looked different as I came in.'

'My servant has nothing to do with it, Basil. You don't imagine I let him arrange my room for me? He settles my flowers for me sometimes – that is all. No, I did it myself. The light was too strong on the portrait.'

'Too strong! Surely not, my dear fellow? It is an admirable place for it. Let me see it.' And Hallward walked towards the corner of the room.

A cry of terror broke from Dorian Gray's lips, and he rushed between the painter and the screen. 'Basil,' he said, looking very pale, 'you must not look at it. I don't wish you to.'

'Not look at my own work! You are not serious. Why shouldn't I look at it?' exclaimed Hallward, laughing.

'If you try to look at it, Basil, on my word of honour I will never speak to you again as long as I live. I am quite serious. I don't offer any explanation, and you are not to ask for any. But, remember, if you touch this screen, everything is over between us.'

Hallward was thunderstruck. He looked at Dorian Gray in absolute amazement. He had never seen him like this before. The lad was actually pallid with rage. His hands were clenched, and the pupils of his eyes were like disks of blue fire. He was trembling all over.

'Dorian!'

'Don't speak!'

'But what is the matter? Of course I won't look at it if you don't want me to,' he said, rather coldly, turning on his heel, and going over towards the window. 'But, really, it seems rather absurd that I shouldn't see my own work, especially as I am going to exhibit it in Paris in the autumn. I shall probably have to give it another coat of varnish before that, so I must see it some day, and why not to-day?'

'To exhibit it! You want to exhibit it?' exclaimed Dorian Gray, a strange sense of terror creeping over him. Was the world going to be shown his secret? Were people to gape at the mystery of his life? That was impossible. Something – he did not know what – had to be done at once.

'Yes; I don't suppose you will object to that. George Petit is going to collect all my best pictures for a special exhibition in the Rue de Sèze, which will open the first week in October. The portrait will only be away a month. I should think you could easily spare it for that time. In fact, you are sure to be out of town. And if you keep it always behind a screen, you can't care much about it.'

Dorian Gray passed his hand over his forehead. There were beads of perspiration there. He felt that he was on the brink of a horrible danger. 'You told me a month ago that you would never exhibit it,' he cried. 'Why have you changed your mind? You people who go in for being consistent have just as many moods as others have. The only difference is that your moods are rather meaningless. You can't have forgotten that you assured me most solemnly that nothing in the world would induce you to send it to any exhibition. You told Harry exactly the same thing.' He stopped suddenly, and a gleam of light came into his eyes. He remembered that Lord Henry had said to him once, half seriously and half in jest, 'If you want to have a strange quarter of an hour, get Basil to tell you why he won't exhibit your picture. He told me why he wouldn't, and it was a revelation to me.' Yes, perhaps, Basil, too, had his secret. He would ask him and try.

'Basil,' he said, coming over quite close, and looking him straight in the face, 'we have each of us a secret. Let me know yours and I shall tell you mine. What was your reason for refusing to exhibit my picture?'

The painter shuddered in spite of himself. 'Dorian, if I told you, you might like me less than you do, and you would certainly laugh at me. I could not bear you doing either of those two things. If you wish me never to look at your picture again, I am content. I have always you to look at. If you wish the best work I have ever done to be hidden from the world. I am satisfied. Your friendship is dearer to me than any frame or reputation.'

'No, Basil, you must tell me,' insisted Dorian Gray. 'I think I have a right to know.' His feeling of terror had passed away, and curiosity had taken its place. He was determined to find out Basil Hallward's mystery.

'Let us sit down, Dorian,' said the painter, looking troubled. 'Let us sit down. And just answer me one question. Have you noticed in the picture something curious? – something that probably at first did not strike you, but that revealed itself to you suddenly?'

'Basil!' cried the lad, clutching the arms of his chair with trembling hands, and gazing at him with wild, startled eyes.

'I see you did. Don't speak. Wait till you hear what I have to say. Dorian, from the moment I met you, your personality had the most extraordinary influence over me. I was dominated, soul, brain, and power by you. You became to me the visible incarnation of that unseen ideal whose memory haunts us artists like an exquisite dream. I worshipped you. I grew jealous of every one to whom you spoke. I wanted to have you all to myself. I was only happy when I was with you. When you were away from me you were still present in my art. . . . Of course I never let you know anything about this. It would have been impossible. You would not have understood it. I hardly understood it myself. I only knew that I had seen perfection face to face, and that the world had become wonderful to my eyes – too wonderful, perhaps, for in such mad worships there is peril, the peril of losing them, no less than the peril of keeping them. Weeks and weeks went on, and I grew more and more absorbed in you. Then came a new development. I had drawn you as Paris in dainty armour, and as Adonis with huntsman's cloak and polished boar-spear. Crowned with heavy lotus-blossoms you had sat on the prow of Adrian's barge, gazing across the green turbid Nile. You had leant over the still pool of some Greek woodland, and seen in the water's silent silver the marvel of your own face. And it had all been what art should be, unconscious, ideal, and remote. One day, a fatal day I sometimes think, I determined to paint a wonderful portrait of you as you actually are, not in the costume of dead ages, but in your own dress and in your own time. Whether it was the Realism of the method, or the mere wonder of your own personality, thus directly presented to me without mist or veil, I cannot tell. But I know that as I worked at it, every flake and film of colour seemed to me to reveal my secret. I grew afraid that others would know of my idolatry. I felt, Dorian, that I had told too much, that I had put too much of myself into it.

Then it was that I resolved never to allow the picture to be exhibited. You were a little annoyed; but then you did not realise all that it meant to me. Harry, to whom I talked about it, laughed at me. But I did not mind that. When the picture was finished, and I sat alone with it, I felt that I was right.... Well, after a few days the thing left my studio, and as soon as I had got rid of the intolerable fascination of its presence it seemed to me that I had been foolish in imagining that I had seen anything in it, more than that you were extremely good-looking, and that I could paint. Even now I cannot help feeling that it is a mistake to think that the passion one feels in creation is ever really shown in the work one creates. Art is always more abstract than we fancy. Form and colour tell us of form and colour – that is all. It often seems to me that art conceals the artist far more completely than it ever reveals him. And so when I got this offer from Paris I determined to make your portrait the principal thing in my exhibition. It never occurred to me that you would refuse. I see now that you were right. The picture cannot be shown. You must not be angry with me, Dorian, for what I have told you. As I said to Harry, once, you are made to be worshipped.'

Dorian Gray drew a long breath. The colour came back to his cheeks, and a smile played about his lips. The peril was over. He was safe for the time. Yet he could not help feeling infinite pity for the painter who had just made this strange confession to him, and wondered if he himself would ever be so dominated by the personality of a friend. Lord Henry had the charm of being very dangerous. But that was all. He was too clever and too cynical to be really fond of. Would there ever be some one who would fill him with a strange idolatry? Was that one of the things that life had in store?

'It is extraordinary to me, Dorian,' said Hallward, 'that you should have seen this in the portrait. Did you really see it?'

'I saw something in it,' he answered, 'something that seemed to me very curious.'

'Well, you don't mind my looking at the thing now?'

Dorian shook his head. 'You must not ask me that, Basil. I could not possibly let you stand in front of that picture.'

'You will some day, surely?'

'Never.'

'Well, perhaps you are right. And now good-bye, Dorian. You have been the one person in my life who has really influenced my art. Whatever I have done that is good, I owe to you. Ah! you don't know what it cost me to tell you all that I have told you.'

'My dear Basil,' said Dorian, 'what have you told me? Simply that you felt that you admired me too much. That is not even a compliment.'

'It was not intended as a compliment. It was a confession. Now that I have made it, something seems to have gone out of me. Perhaps one should never put one's worship into words.'

'It was a very disappointing confession.'

'Why, what did you expect, Dorian? You didn't see anything else in the picture, did you? There was nothing else to see?'

'No; there was nothing else to see. Why do you ask? But you mustn't talk about worship. It is foolish. You and I are friends, Basil, and we must always remain so.'

'You have got Harry,' said the painter, sadly.

'Oh, Harry!' cried the lad, with a ripple of laughter. 'Harry spends his days in saying what is incredible, and his evenings in doing what is improbable. Just the sort of life I would like to lead. But still I don't think I would go to Harry if I were in trouble. I would sooner go to you, Basil.'

'You will sit to me again?'

'Impossible!'

'You spoil my life as an artist by refusing, Dorian. No man came across two ideal things. Few come across one.'

'I can't explain it to you, Basil, but I must never sit to you again. There is something fatal about a portrait. It has a life of its own. I will come and have tea with you. That will be just as pleasant.'

'Pleasanter for you, I am afraid,' murmured Hallward, regretfully. 'And now good-bye. I am sorry you won't let me look at the picture once again. But that can't be helped. I quite understand what you feel about it.'

As he left the room, Dorian Gray smiled to himself. Poor Basil! How little he knew of the true reason! And how strange it was that, instead of having been forced to reveal his own secret, he had succeeded, almost by chance, in wresting a secret from his friend! How much that strange confession explained to him! The painter's absurd fits of jealousy, his wild devotion, his extravagant panegyrics, his curious reticences – he understood them all now, and he felt sorry. There seemed to him to be something tragic in a friendship so coloured by romance.

He sighed, and touched the bell. The portrait must be hidden away at all costs. He could not run such a risk of discovery again. It had been mad of him to have allowed the thing to remain, even for an hour, in a room to which any of his friends had access.

10

WHEN his servant entered, he looked at him steadfastly, and wondered if he had thought of peering behind the screen. The man was quite impassive, and waited for his orders. Dorian lit a cigarette, and walked over to the glass and glanced into it. He could see the reflection of Victor's face perfectly. It was like a placid mask of servility. There was nothing to be afraid of, there. Yet he thought it best to be on his guard.

Speaking very slowly, he told him to tell the housekeeper that he wanted to see her, and then to go to the frame-maker and ask him to send two of his men round at once. It seemed to him that as the man left the room his eyes wandered in the direction of the screen. Or was that merely his own fancy?

After a few moments, in her black silk dress, with old-fashioned thread mittens on her wrinkled hands, Mrs. Leaf bustled into the library. He asked her for the key of the schoolroom.

'The old schoolroom, Mr. Dorian?' she exclaimed. 'Why, it is full of dust. I must get it arranged, and put straight before you go into it. It is not fit for you to see, sir. It is not, indeed.'

'I don't want it put straight, Leaf. I only want the key.'

'Well, sir, you'll be covered with cobwebs if you go into it. Why, it hasn't been opened for nearly five years, not since his lordship died.'

He winced at the mention of his grandfather. He had hateful memories of him. 'That does not matter,' he answered. 'I simply want to see the place – that is all. Give me the key.'

'And here is the key, sir,' said the old lady, going over the contents of her bunch with tremulously uncertain hands. 'Here is the key. I'll have it off the bunch in a moment. But you don't think of living up there, sir, and you so comfortable here?'

'No, no,' he cried, petulantly. 'Thank you, Leaf. That will do.'

She lingered for a few moments, and was garrulous over some detail of the household. He sighed, and told her to manage things as she thought best. She left the room, wreathed in smiles.

As the door closed, Dorian put the key in his pocket, and looked round the room. His eye fell on a large purple satin coverlet heavily embroidered with gold, a splendid piece of late seventeenth-century Venetian work that his grandfather had found in a convent near Bologna. Yes, that would serve to wrap the dreadful thing in. It had perhaps served often as a pall for the dead. Now it was to hide something that had a corruption of its own, worse than the corruption of death itself – something that would breed horrors and yet would never die. What the worm was to the corpse, his sins would be to the painted image on the canvas. They would mar its beauty, and eat away its grace. They would defile it, and make it shameful. And yet the thing would still live on. It would be always alive.

He shuddered, and for a moment he regretted that he had not told Basil the true reason why he had wished to hide the picture away. Basil would have helped him to resist Lord Henry's influence, and the still more poisonous influences that came from his own temperament. The love that he bore him – for it was really love – had nothing in it that was not noble and intellectual. It was not that mere physical admiration of beauty that is born of the senses, and that dies when the senses tire. It was such love as Michael Angelo had known, and Montaigne, and Winckelmann, and Shakespeare himself. Yes, Basil could have saved him. But it was too late now. The past could always be annihilated. Regret, denial, or forgetfulness could do that. But the future was inevitable. There were passions in him that would find their terrible outlet, dreams that would make the shadow of their evil real.

He took up from the couch the great purple-and-gold texture that covered it, and, holding it in his hands, passed behind the screen. Was the face on the canvas viler than before? It seemed to him that it was unchanged; and yet his loathing of it was intensified. Gold hair, blue eyes, and rose-red lips – they all were there. It was simply the expression that had altered. That was horrible in its cruelty. Compared to what he saw in it of censure or rebuke, how shallow Basil's reproaches about Sibyl Vane had been! – how shallow, and of what little account! His own soul was looking out at him from the canvas and calling him to judgment. A look of pain came across him, and he flung the rich pall over the picture. As he did so, a knock came to the door. He passed out as his servant entered.

'The persons are here, Monsieur.'

He felt that the man must be got rid of at once. He must not be allowed to know where the picture was being taken to. There was something sly about him, and he had thoughtful, treacherous eyes. Sitting down at the writing-table he scribbled a note to Lord Henry, asking him to send him round something to read, and reminding him that they were to meet at eight-fifteen that evening.

'Wait for an answer,' he said, handing it to him, 'and show the men in here.'

In two or three minutes there was another knock, and Mr. Hubbard himself, the celebrated frame-maker of South Audley Street, came in with a somewhat rough-looking young assistant. Mr. Hubbard was a florid, red-whiskered little man, whose admiration for art was considerably tempered by the inveterate impecuniosity of most of the artists who dealt with him. As a rule, he never left his shop. He waited for people to come to him. But he always made an exception in favour of Dorian Gray. There was something about Dorian that charmed everybody. It was a pleasure even to see him.

'What can I do for you, Mr. Gray?' he said, rubbing his fat freckled hands. 'I thought I would do myself the honour of coming round in person. I have just got a beauty of a frame, sir. Picked it up at a sale. Old Florentine. Came from Fonthill, I believe. Admirably suited for a religious subject, Mr. Gray.'

'I am so sorry you have given yourself the trouble of coming round, Mr. Hubbard. I shall certainly drop in and look at the frame – though I don't go in much at present for religious art – but to-day I only want a picture carried to the top of the house for me. It is rather heavy, so I thought I would ask you to lend me a couple of your men.'

'No trouble at all, Mr. Gray. I am delighted to be of any service to you. Which is the work of art, sir?'

'This,' replied Dorian, moving the screen back. 'Can you move it, covering and all, just as it is? I don't want it to get scratched going upstairs.'

'There will be no difficulty, sir,' said the genial frame-maker, beginning, with the aid of his assistant, to unhook the picture from the long brass chains by which it was suspended. 'And, now, where shall we carry it to, Mr. Gray?'

'I will show you the way, Mr. Hubbard, if you will kindly follow me. Or perhaps you had better go in front. I am afraid it is right at the top of the house. We will go up by the front staircase, as it is wider.'

He held the door open for them, and they passed out into the hall and began the ascent. The elaborate character of the frame had made the picture extremely bulky, and now and then, in spite of the obsequious protests of Mr. Hubbard, who had the true tradesman's spirited dislike of seeing a gentleman doing anything useful, Dorian put his hand to it so to help them.

'Something of a load to carry, sir,' gasped the little man, when they reached the top landing. And he wiped his shiny forehead.

'I am afraid it is rather heavy,' murmured Dorian, as he unlocked the door that opened into the room that was to keep for him the curious secret of his life and hide his soul from the eyes of men.

He had not entered the place for more than four years – not, indeed, since he had used it first as a play-room when he was a child, and then as a study when he grew somewhat older. It was a large, well-proportioned room, which had been specially built by the last Lord Kelso, for the use of the little grandson whom, for his strange likeness to his mother, and also for other reasons, he had always hated and desired to keep at a distance. It appeared to Dorian to have but little changed. There was the huge Italian *cassone*, with its fantastically-painted panels and its tarnished gilt mouldings, in which he had so often hidden himself as a boy. There the satinwood bookcase filled with his dog-eared school-books. On the wall behind it was hanging the same ragged Flemish tapestry, where a faded king and queen were playing chess in a garden, while a company of hawkers rode by, carrying hooded birds on their gauntleted wrists. How well he remembered it all! Every moment of his lonely childhood came back to him as he looked round. He recalled the stainless purity of his boyish life, and it seemed horrible to him that it was here the fatal portrait was to be hidden away. How little he had thought, in those dead days, of all that was in store for him!

But there was no other place in the house so secure from prying eyes as this. He had the key, and no one else could enter it. Beneath its purple pall, the face painted on the canvas could grow bestial, sodden, and unclean. What did it matter? No one could see it. He himself would not see it. Why should he watch the hideous corruption of his soul? He kept his youth – that was enough. And, besides, might not his nature grow finer, after all? There was no reason that the future should be so full of shame. Some love might come across his life, and purify him, and shield him from those sins that seemed to be already stirring in spirit and in flesh – those curious unpictured sins whose very mystery lent them their subtlety and their charm. Perhaps, some day, the cruel look would have passed away from the scarlet sensitive mouth, and he might show to the world Basil Hallward's masterpiece.

No; that was impossible. Hour by hour, and week by week, the thing upon the canvas was growing old. It might escape the hideousness of sin, but the hideousness of age was in store for it. The cheeks would become hollow or flaccid. Yellow crow's-feet would creep round the fading eyes and make them horrible. The hair would lose its brightness, the mouth would gape or droop, would be foolish or gross, as the mouths of old men are. There would be the wrinkled throat, the cold, blue-veined hands, the twisted body, that he remembered in the grandfather who had been so stern to him in his boyhood. The picture had to be concealed. There was no help for it.

'Bring it in, Mr. Hubbard, please,' he said, wearily, turning round. 'I am sorry I kept you so long. I was thinking of something else.'

'Always glad to have a rest, Mr. Gray,' answered the framemaker, who was still gasping for breath. 'Where shall we put it, sir?'

'Oh, anywhere. Here: this will do. I don't want to have it hung up. Just lean it against the wall. Thanks.'

'Might one look at the work of art, sir?'

Dorian started. 'It would not interest you, Mr. Hubbard,' he said, keeping his eye on the man. He felt ready to leap upon him and fling him to the ground if he dared to lift the gorgeous hanging that concealed the secret of his life. 'I shan't trouble you any more now. I am much obliged for your kindness in coming round.'

'Not at all, not at all, Mr. Gray. Ever ready to do anything for you, sir.' And Mr. Hubbard tramped downstairs, followed by the assistant, who glanced back at Dorian with a look of shy wonder in his rough, uncomely face. He had never seen any one so marvellous.

When the sound of their footsteps had died away, Dorian locked the door, and put the key in his pocket. He felt safe now. No one would ever look upon the horrible thing. No eye but his would ever see his shame.

On reaching the library he found that it was just after five o'clock, and that the tea had been already brought up. On a little table of dark perfumed wood thickly encrusted with nacre, a present from Lady Radley, his guardian's wife, a pretty professional invalid, who had spent the preceding winter in Cairo, was lying a note from Lord Henry, and beside it was a book bound in yellow paper, the cover slightly torn and the edges soiled. A copy of the third edition of *The St. James's Gazette* had been placed on the tea-tray. It was evident that Victor had returned. He wondered, if he had met the men in the hall as they were leaving the house, and had wormed out of them what they had been doing. He would be sure to miss the picture – had no doubt missed it already, while he had been laying the tea things. The screen had not been set back, and a blank space was visible on the wall. Perhaps some night he might find him creeping upstairs and trying to force the door of the room. It was a horrible thing to have a spy in one's house. He had heard of rich men who had been blackmailed all their lives by some servant who had read a letter, or overheard a conversation, or picked up a card with an address, or found beneath a pillow a withered flower or a shred of crumpled lace.

He sighed, and, having poured himself out some tea, opened Lord Henry's note. It was simply to say that he sent him round the evening paper, and a book that might interest him, and that he would be at the club at eight-fifteen. He opened *The St. James's* languidly, and looked through it. A red pencil-mark on the fifth page caught his eye. It drew attention to the following paragraph: –

'INQUEST ON AN ACTRESS. – An inquest was held this morning at the Bell Tavern, Hoxton Road, by Mr. Danby, the District Coroner, on the body of Sibyl Vane, a young actress recently engaged at the Royal

Theatre, Holborn. A verdict of death by misadventure was returned. Considerable sympathy was expressed for the mother of the deceased, who was greatly affected during the giving of her own evidence, and that of Dr. Birrell, who had made the post-mortem examination of the deceased.'

He frowned, and, tearing the paper in two, went across the room and flung the pieces away. How ugly it all was! And how horribly real ugliness made things! He felt a little annoyed with Lord Henry for having sent him the report. And it was certainly stupid of him to have marked it with red pencil. Victor might have read it. The man knew more than enough English for that.

Perhaps he had read it, and had begun to suspect something. And, yet, what did it matter? What had Dorian Gray to do with Sibyl Vane's death? There was nothing to fear. Dorian Gray had not killed her.

His eye fell on the yellow book that Lord Henry had sent him. What was it, he wondered. He went towards the little pearl-coloured octagonal stand, that had always looked to him like the work of some strange Egyptian bees that wrought in silver, and taking up the volume, flung himself into an arm-chair, and began to turn over the leaves. After a few minutes he became absorbed. It was the strangest book that he had ever read. It seemed to him that in exquisite raiment, and to the delicate sound of flutes, the sins of the world were passing in dumb show before him. Things that he had dimly dreamed of were suddenly made real to him. Things of which he had never dreamed were gradually revealed.

It was a novel without a plot, and with only one character, being, indeed, simply a psychological study of a certain young Parisian, who spent his life trying to realise in the nineteenth century all the passions and modes of thought that belonged to every century except his own, and to sum up, as it were, in himself the various moods through which the world-spirit had ever passed, loving for their mere artificiality those renunciations that men have unwisely called virtue, as much as those natural rebellions that wise men still call sin. The style in which it was written was that curious jewelled style, vivid and obscure at once, full of argot and of archaisms, of technical expressions and of elaborate paraphrases, that characterises the work of some of the finest artists of the French school of *Symbolistes*. There were in it metaphors as monstrous as orchids, and as subtle in colour. The life of the senses was described in the terms of mystical philosophy. One hardly knew at times whether one was reading the spiritual ecstasies of some mediaeval saint or the morbid confessions of a modern sinner. It was a poisonous book. The heavy odour of incense seemed to cling about its pages and to trouble the brain. The mere cadence of the sentences, the subtle monotony of their music, so full as it was of complex refrains and movements elaborately repeated, produced in the mind of the lad, as he passed from chapter to chapter, a form of reverie, a malady of dreaming, that made him unconscious of the falling day and creeping shadows.

Cloudless, and pierced by one solitary star, a copper-green sky gleamed through the windows. He read on by its wan light till he could read no more. Then, after his valet had reminded him several times of the lateness of the hour, he got up, and, going into the next room, placed the book on the little Florentine table that always stood at his bedside, and began to dress for dinner.

It was almost nine o'clock before he reached the club, where he found Lord Henry sitting alone, in the morning-room, looking very much bored.

'I am so sorry, Harry,' he cried, 'but really it is entirely your fault. That book you sent me so fascinated me that I forgot how the time was going.'

'Yes: I thought you would like it,' replied his host, rising from his chair.

'I didn't say I liked it, Harry. I said it fascinated me. There is a great difference.'

'Ah, you have discovered that?' murmured Lord Henry. And they passed into the dining-room.

11

FOR years, Dorian Gray could not free himself from the influence of this book. Or perhaps it would be more accurate to say that he never sought to free himself from it. He procured from Paris no less than nine large paper copies of the first edition, and had them bound in different colours, so that they might suit his various moods and the changing fancies of a nature over which he seemed, at times, to have almost entirely lost control. The hero, the wonderful young Parisian, in whom the romantic and the scientific tempera-ments were so strangely blended, became to him a kind of pre-figuring type of himself. And, indeed, the whole book seemed to him to contain the story of his own life, written before he had lived it.

In one point he was more fortunate than the novel's fantastic hero. He never knew – never, indeed, had any cause to know – that somewhat grot-esque dread of mirrors, and polished metal surfaces, and still water, which came upon the young Parisian so early in his life, and was occasioned by the sudden decay of a beauty that had once, apparently, been so remarkable. It was with an almost cruel joy – and perhaps in nearly every joy, as certainly in every pleasure, cruelty has its place – that he used to read the latter part of the book, with its really tragic, if somewhat over-emphasised, account of the sorrow and despair of one who had himself lost what in others, and in the world, he had most dearly valued.

For the wonderful beauty that had so fascinated Basil Hallward, and many others besides him, seemed never to leave him. Even those who had heard the most evil things against him, and from time to time strange rumours about his mode of life crept through London and became the chatter of the clubs, could not believe anything to his dishonour when they saw him. He had always the look of one who had kept himself unspotted from the world.

Men who talked grossly became silent when Dorian Gray entered the room. There was something in the purity of his face that rebuked them. His mere presence seemed to recall to them the memory of the innocence that they had tarnished. They wondered how one so charming and graceful as he was could have escaped the stain of an age that was at once sordid and sensual.

Often, on returning home from one of those mysterious and prolonged absences that gave rise to such strange conjecture among those who were his friends, or thought that they were so, he himself would creep upstairs to the locked room, open the door with the key that never left him now, and stand, with a mirror, in front of the portrait that Basil Hallward had painted of him, looking now at the evil and ageing face on the canvas, and now at the fair young face that laughed back at him from the polished glass. The very sharpness of the contrast used to quicken his sense of pleasure. He grew more and more enamoured of his own beauty, more and more interested in the corruption of his own soul. He would examine with minute care, and sometimes with a monstrous and terrible delight, the hideous lines that seared the wrinkling forehead, or crawled around the heavy sensual mouth, wondering sometimes which were the more horrible, the signs of sin or the signs of age. He would place his white hands beside the coarse bloated hands of the picture, and smile. He mocked the misshapen body and the failing limbs.

There were moments, indeed, at night, when, lying sleepless in his own delicately-scented chamber, or in the sordid room of the little ill-famed tavern near the Docks, which, under an assumed name, and in disguise, it was his habit to frequent, he would think of the ruin he had brought upon his soul, with a pity that was all the more poignant because it was purely selfish. But moments such as these were rare. That curiosity about life which Lord Henry had first stirred in him, as they sat together in the garden of their friend, seemed to increase with gratification. The more he knew, the more he desired to know. He had mad hungers that grew more ravenous as he fed them.

Yet he was not really reckless, at any rate in his relations to society. Once or twice every month during the winter, and on each Wednesday evening while the season lasted, he would throw open to the world his beautiful house and have the most celebrated musicians of the day to charm his guests with the wonders of their art. His little dinners, in the settling of which Lord Henry always assisted him, were noted as much for the careful selection and placing of those invited, as for the exquisite taste shown in the decoration of the table, with its subtle symphonic arrangements of exotic flowers, and embroidered cloths, and antique plate of gold and silver. Indeed, there were many, especially among the very young men, who saw, or fancied that they saw, in Dorian Gray, the true realisation of a type of which they had often dreamed in Eton or Oxford days, a type that was to combine something of the real culture of the scholar with all the grace and distinction and perfect manner of a citizen of the world. To them he seemed to be of the company of those whom Dante describes as having sought to 'make themselves perfect by the worship of beauty.' Like Gautier, he was one for whom 'the visible world existed.'

And, certainly, to him Life itself was the first, the greatest, of the arts, and for it all the other arts seemed to be but a preparation. Fashion, by which what is really fantastic becomes for a moment universal, and Dandyism, which, in its own way, is an attempt to assert the absolute modernity of beauty, had, of course, their fascination for him. His mode of dressing, and the particular styles that from time to time he affected, had their marked influence on the young exquisites of the Mayfair balls and Pall Mall club windows, who copied him in everything that he did, and tried to reproduce the accidental charm of his graceful, though to him only half-serious, fopperies.

For, while he was but too ready to accept the position that was almost immediately offered to him on his coming of age, and found, indeed, a subtle pleasure in the thought that he might really become to the London of his own day what to imperial Neronian Rome the author of the *Satyricon* once had been, yet in his inmost heart he desired to be something more than a mere *arbiter elegantiarum*[1], to be consulted on the wearing of a jewel, or the knotting of a necktie, or the conduct of a cane. He sought to elaborate some new scheme of life that would have its reasoned philosophy and its ordered principles, and find in the spiritualising of the senses its highest realisation.

The worship of the senses has often, and with much justice, been decried, men feeling a natural instinct of terror about passions and sensations that seem stronger than themselves, and that they are conscious of sharing with the less highly organised forms of existence. But it appeared to Dorian Gray that the true nature of the senses had never been understood, and that they had remained savage and animal merely because the world had sought to starve them into submission or to kill them by pain, instead of aiming at making them elements of a new spirituality, of which a fine instinct for beauty was to be the dominant characteristic. As he looked back upon man moving through History, he was haunted by a feeling of loss. So much had been surrendered! And to such little purpose! There had been mad wilful rejections, monstrous forms of self-torture and self-denial, whose origin was fear, and whose result was a degradation infinitely more terrible than that fancied degradation from which, in their ignorance, they had sought to escape. Nature, in her wonderful irony, driving out the anchorite to feed with the wild animals of the desert and giving to the hermit the beasts of the field as his companions.

Yes: there was to be, as Lord Henry had prophesied, a new Hedonism that was to recreate life, and to save it from that harsh, uncomely puritanism that is having, in our own day, its curious revival. It was to have its service of the intellect, certainly; yet, it was never to accept any theory or system that would involve the sacrifice of any mode of passionate experience. Its aim, indeed, was to be experience itself, and not the fruits of experience, sweet or bitter as they might be. Of the asceticism that deadens the senses, as of the

---

[1] Leader of fashion.

vulgar profligacy that dulls them, it was to know nothing. But it was to teach man to concentrate himself upon the moments of a life that is itself but a moment.

There are few of us who have not sometimes wakened before dawn, either after one of those dreamless nights that make us almost enamoured of death, or one of those nights of horror and misshapen joy, when through the chambers of the brain sweep phantoms more terrible than reality itself, and instinct with that vivid life that lurks in all grotesques, and that lends to Gothic art its enduring vitality, this art being, one might fancy, especially the art of those whose minds have been troubled with the malady of reverie. Gradually white fingers creep through the curtains, and they appear to tremble. In black fantastic shapes, dumb shadows crawl into the corners of the room, and crouch there. Outside, there is the stirring of birds among the leaves, or the sound of men going forth to their work, or the sigh and sob of the wind coming down from the hills, and wandering round the silent house, as though it feared to wake the sleepers, and yet must needs call forth sleep from her purple cave. Veil after veil of thin dusky gauze is lifted, and by degrees the forms and colours of things are restored to them, and we watch the dawn remaking the world in its antique pattern. The wan mirrors get back their mimic life. The flameless tapers stand where we had left them, and beside them lies the half-cut book that we had been studying, or the wired flower that we had worn at the ball, or the letter that we had been afraid to read, or that we had read too often. Nothing seems to us changed. Out of the unreal shadows of the night comes back the real life that we had known. We have to resume it where we had left off, and there steals over us a terrible sense of the necessity for the continuance of energy in the same wearisome round of stereotyped habits, or a wild longing, it may be, that our eyelids might open some morning upon a world that had been refashioned anew in the darkness for our pleasure, a world in which things would have fresh shapes and colours, and be changed, or have other secrets, a world in which the past would have little or no place, or survive, at any rate, in no conscious form of obligation or regret, the remembrance even of joy having its bitterness, and the memories of pleasure their pain.

It was the creation of such worlds as these that seemed to Dorian Gray to be the true object, or amongst the true objects, of life; and in his search for sensations that would be at once new and delightful, and possess that element of strangeness that is so essential to romance, he would often adopt certain modes of thought that he knew to be really alien to his nature, abandon himself to their subtle influences, and then, having, as it were, caught their colour and satisfied his intellectual curiosity, leave them with that curious indifference that is not incompatible with a real ardour of temperament, and that indeed, according to certain modern psychologists, is often a condition of it.

It was rumoured of him once that he was about to join the Roman Catholic communion; and certainly the Roman ritual had always a great attraction for him. The daily sacrifice, more awful really than all the sacrifices of the an-

tique world, stirred him as much by its superb rejection of the evidence of
the senses as by the primitive simplicity of its elements and the eternal
pathos of the human tragedy that it sought to symbolise. He loved to kneel
down on the cold marble pavement, and watch the priest, in his stiff flowered
vestment, slowly and with white hands moving aside the veil of the taber-
nacle, or raising aloft the jewelled lantern-shaped monstrance with that pal-
lid wafer that at times, one would fain think, is indeed the '*panis cælestis*,' the
bread of angels, or, robed in the garments of the Passion of Christ, breaking
the Host into the chalice, and smiting his breast for his sins. The fuming cen-
sers, that the grave boys, in their lace, and scarlet, tossed into the air like
great gilt flowers, had their subtle fascination for him. As he passed out, he
used to look with wonder at the black confessionals, and long to sit in the dim
shadow of one of them and listen to men and women whispering through the
worn grating the true story of their lives.

But he never fell into the error of arresting his intellectual development by
any formal acceptance of creed or system, or of mistaking, for a house in
which to live, an inn that is but suitable for the sojourn of a night, or for a few
hours of a night in which there are no stars and the moon is in travail. Mysti-
cism, with its marvellous power of making common things strange to us, and
the subtle antinomianism that always seems to accompany it, moved him for
a season; and for a season he inclined to the materialistic doctrines of the
Darwinismus movement in Germany, and found a curious pleasure in tracing
the thoughts and passions of men to some pearly cell in the brain, or some
white nerve in the body, delighting in the conception of the absolute de-
pendence of the spirit on certain physical conditions, morbid or healthy,
normal or diseased. Yet, as has been said of him before, no theory of life
seemed to him to be of any importance compared with life itself. He felt
keenly conscious of how barren all intellectual speculation is when separated
from action and experiment. He knew that the senses, no less than the soul,
have their spiritual mysteries to reveal.

And so he would now study perfumes, and the secrets of their manufac-
ture, distilling heavily-scented oils, and burning odorous gums from the
East. He saw that there was no mood of the mind that had not its counterpart
in the sensuous life, and set himself to discover their true relation, won-
dering what there was in frankincense that made one mystical, and in amber-
gris that stirred one's passions, and in violets that woke the memory of dead
romances, and in musk that troubled the brain, and in champak that stained
the imagination; and seeking often to elaborate a real psychology of per-
fumes, and to estimate the several influences of sweet-smelling roots, and
scented pollen-laden flowers, or aromatic balms, and of dark and fragrant
woods, of spikenard that sickens, of hovenia that makes men mad, and of
aloes that are said to be able to expel melancholy from the soul.

At another time he devoted himself entirely to music, and in a long latticed
room, with a vermilion-and-gold ceiling and walls of olive-green lacquer, he
used to give curious concerts, in which mad gypsies tore wild music from
little zithers, or grave yellow-shawled Tunisians plucked at the strained

strings of monstrous lutes, while grinning negroes beat monotonously upon copper drums, and, crouching upon scarlet mats, slim turbaned Indians blew through long pipes of reed or brass, and charmed, or feigned to charm, great hooded snakes and horrible horned adders. The harsh intervals and shrill discords of barbaric music stirred him at times when Schubert's grace, and Chopin's beautiful sorrows, and the mighty harmonies of Beethoven himself, fell unheeded on his ear. He collected together from all parts of the world the strangest instruments that could be found, either in the tombs of dead nations or among the few savage tribes that have survived contact with Western civilisations, and loved to touch and try them. He had the mysterious *juruparis* of the Rio Negro Indians, that women are not allowed to look at, and that even youths may not see till they have been subjected to fasting and scourging, and the earthen jars of the Peruvians that have the shrill cries of birds, and flutes of human bones such as Alfonso de Ovalle heard in Chili, and the sonorous green jaspers that are found near Cuzco and give forth a note of singular sweetness. He had painted gourds filled with pebbles that rattled when they were shaken; the long *clarin* of the Mexicans, into which the performer does not blow, but through which he inhales the air; the harsh *turé* of the Amazon tribes, that is sounded by the sentinels who sit all day long in high trees, and can be heard, it is said, at a distance of three leagues; the *teponaztli*, that has two vibrating tongues of wood, and is beaten with sticks that are smeared with an elastic gum obtained from the milky juice of plants; the *yotl*-bells of the Aztecs, that are hung in clusters like grapes; and a huge cylindrical drum, covered with the skins of great serpents, like the one that Bernal Diaz saw when he went with Cortes into the Mexican temple, and of whose doleful sound he has left us so vivid a description. The fantastic character of these instruments fascinated him, and he felt a curious delight in the thought that Art, like Nature, has her monsters, things of bestial shape and with hideous voices. Yet, after some time, he wearied of them, and would sit in his box at the Opera, either alone or with Lord Henry, listening in rapt pleasure to *Tannhäuser*, and seeing in the prelude to that great work of art a presentation of the tragedy of his own soul.

On one occasion he took up the study of jewels, and appeared at a costume ball as Anne de Joyeuse, Admiral of France, in a dress covered with five hundred and sixty pearls. This taste enthralled him for years, and, indeed, may be said never to have left him. He would often spend a whole day settling and resettling in their cases the various stones that he had collected, such as the olive-green chrysoberyl that turns red by lamplight, the cymophane with its wire-like line of silver, the pistachio-coloured peridot, rose-pink and wine-yellow topazes, carbuncles of fiery scarlet with tremulous four-rayed stars, flame-red cinnamon-stones, orange and violet spinels, and amethysts with their alternate layers of ruby and sapphire. He loved the red gold of the sun-stone, and the moonstone's pearly whiteness, and the broken rainbow of the milky opal. He procured from Amsterdam three emeralds of extraordinary size and richness of colour, and had a turquoise *de la vieille roche* that was the envy of all the connoisseurs.

He discovered wonderful stories, also, about jewels. In Alphonso's *Clericalis Disciplina* a serpent was mentioned with eyes of real jacinth, and in the romantic history of Alexander, the Conqueror of Emathia, was said to have found in the vale of Jordan snakes 'with collars of real emeralds growing in their backs.' There was a gem in the brain of the dragon, Philostratus told us, and 'by the exhibition of golden letters and a scarlet robe' the monster could be thrown into a magical sleep, and slain. According to the great alchemist, Pierre de Boniface, the diamond rendered a man invisible, and the agate of India, made him eloquent. The cornelian appeased anger, and the hyacinth provoked sleep, and the amethyst drove away the fumes of wine. The garnet cast out demons, and the hydropicus deprived the moon of her colour. The selenite waxed and waned with the moon, and the meloceus, that discovers thieves, could be affected only by the blood of kids. Leonardus Camillus had seen a white stone taken from the brain of a newly-killed toad, that was a certain antidote against poison. The bezoar, that was found in the heart of the Arabian deer, was a charm that could cure the plague. In the nests of Arabian birds was the aspilates, that, according to Democritus, kept the wearer from any danger by fire.

The King of Ceilan rode through his city with a large ruby in his hand, at the ceremony of his coronation. The gates of the palace of John the Priest were 'made of sardius, with the horn of the horned snake inwrought, so that no man might bring poison within.' Over the gable were 'two golden apples, in which were two carbuncles,' so that the gold might shine by day, and the carbuncles by night. In Lodge's strange romance *A Margarite of America* it was stated that in the chamber of the queen one could behold 'all the chaste ladies of the world, inchased out of silver, looking through fair mirrors of chrysolites, carbuncles, sapphires, and greene emeraults.' Marco Polo had seen the inhabitants of Zipangu place rose-coloured pearls in the mouths of the dead. A sea-monster had been enamoured of the pearl that the diver brought to King Perozes, and had slain the thief, and mourned for seven moons over its loss. When the Huns lured the king into the great pit, he flung it away – Procopius tells the story – nor was it ever found again, though the Emperor Anastasius offered five hundred-weight of gold pieces for it. The King of Malabar had shown to a certain Venetian a rosary of three hundred and four pearls, one for every god that he worshipped.

When the Duke de Valentinois, son of Alexander VI., visited Louis XII. of France, his horse was loaded with gold leaves, according to Brantôme, and his cap had double rows of rubies that threw out a great light. Charles of England had ridden in stirrups hung with four hundred and twenty-one diamonds. Richard II. had a coat, valued at thirty thousand marks, which was covered with balas rubies. Hall described Henry VIII., on his way to the Tower previous to his coronation, as wearing 'a jacket of raised gold, the placard embroidered with diamonds and other rich stones, and a great bauderike about his neck of large balasses.' The favourites of James I. wore earrings of emeralds set in gold filigrane. Edward II. gave to Piers Gaveston a suit of red-gold armour studded with jacinths, a collar of gold roses set with turquoise-stones, and a skull-cap *parsemé* with pearls. Henry II. wore jew-elled gloves reaching to the elbow, and had a hawk-glove sewn with twelve rubies and fifty-two great orients. The ducal hat of Charles the Rash, the last Duke of Burgundy of his race, was hung with pear-shaped pearls, and stud-ded with sapphires.

How exquisite life had once been! How gorgeous in its pomp and decora-tion! Even to read of the luxury of the dead was wonderful.

Then he turned his attention to embroideries, and to the tapestries that performed the office of frescoes in the chill rooms of the Northern nations of Europe. As he investigated the subject – and he always had an extraordinary faculty of becoming absolutely absorbed for the moment in whatever he took up – he was almost saddened by the reflection of the ruin that Time brought on beautiful and wonderful things. He, at any rate, had escaped that. Sum-mer followed summer, and the yellow jonquils bloomed and died many times, and nights of horror repeated the story of their shame, but he was un-changed. No winter marred his face or stained his flower-like bloom. How different it was with material things! Where had they passed to? Where was the great crocus-coloured robe, on which the gods fought against the giants, that had been worked by brown girls for the pleasure of Athena? Where, the huge velarium that Nero had stretched across the Colosseum at Rome, that Titan sail of purple on which was represented the starry sky, and Apollo driving a chariot drawn by white gilt-reined steeds? He longed to see the curious table-napkins wrought for the Priest of the Sun, on which were dis-played all the dainties and viands that could be wanted for a feast; the mortu-ary cloth of King Chilperic, with its three hundred golden bees; the fantastic robes that excited the indignation of the Bishop of Pontus, and were figured with 'lions, panthers, bears, dogs, forests, rocks, hunters – all in fact, that a painter can copy from nature;' and the coat that Charles of Orleans once wore, on the sleeves of which were embroidered the verses of a song begin-ning '*Madame, je suis tout joyeux*,' the musical accompaniment of the words being wrought in gold thread, and each note, of square shape in those days, formed with four pearls. He read of the room that was prepared at the palace at Rheims for the use of Queen Joan of Burgundy, and was decorated with 'Thirteen hundred and twenty-one parrots, made in broidery, and blazoned with the king's arms, and five hundred and sixty-one butterflies, whose wings were similarly ornamented with the arms of the queen, the whole worked in gold.' Catherine de Médicis had a mourning-bed made for her of black velvet powdered with crescents and suns. Its curtains were of damask, with leafy wreaths and garlands, figured upon a gold and silver ground, and fringed along the edges with broideries of pearls, and it stood in a room hung with rows of the queen's devices in cut black velvet upon cloth of silver. Louis XIV. had gold embroidered caryatides fifteen feet high in his apart-ment. The state bed of Sobieski, King of Poland, was made of Smyrna gold brocade embroidered in turquoises with verses from the Koran. Its supports were of silver gilt, beautifully chased, and profusely set with enamelled and jewelled medallions. It had been taken from the Turkish camp before

Vienna, and the standard of Mohammed had stood beneath the tremulous gilt of its canopy.

And so, for a whole year, he sought to accumulate the most exquisite specimens that he could find of textile and embroidered work, getting the dainty Delhi muslins, finely wrought with gold-thread palmates, and stitched over with iridescent beetles' wings; the Dacca gauzes, that from their transparency are known in the East as 'woven air,' and 'running water,' and 'evening dew;' strange figured cloths from Java; elaborate yellow Chinese hangings; books bound in tawny satins or fair blue silks, and wrought with *fleurs de lys*, birds, and images; veils of *lacis* worked in Hungary point; Sicilian brocades, and stiff Spanish velvets; Georgian work with its gilt coins, and Japanese *Foukousas* with their green-toned golds and their marvellously-plumaged birds.

He had a special passion, also, for ecclesiastical vestments, as indeed he had for everything connected with the service of the Church. In the long cedar chests that lined the west gallery of his house he had stored away many rare and beautiful specimens of what is really the raiment of the Bride of Christ, who must wear purple and jewels and fine linen that she may hide the pallid macerated body that is worn by the suffering that she seeks for, and wounded by self-inflicted pain. He possessed a gorgeous cope of crimson silk and gold-thread damask, figured with a repeating pattern of golden pomegranates set in six-petalled formal blossoms, beyond which on either side was the pineapple device wrought in seed-pearls. The orphreys were divided into panels representing scenes from the life of the Virgin, and the coronation of the Virgin was figured in coloured silks upon the hood. This was Italian work of the fifteenth century. Another cope was of green velvet, embroidered with heart-shaped groups of acanthus-leaves, from which spread long-stemmed white blossoms, the details of which were picked out with silver thread and coloured crystals. The morse bore a seraph's head in gold-thread raised work. The orphreys were woven in a diaper of red and gold silk, and were starred with medallions of many saints and martyrs, among whom was St. Sebastian. He had chasubles, also, of amber-coloured silk, and blue silk and gold brocade, and yellow silk damask and cloth of gold, figured with representations of the Passion and Crucifixion of Christ, and embroidered with lions and peacocks and other emblems; dalmatics of white satin and pink silk damask, decorated with tulips and dolphins and *fleurs de lys*; altar frontals of crimson velvet and blue linen; and many corporals, chalice-veils, and sudaria. In the mystic offices to which such things were put, there was something that quickened his imagination.

For these treasures, and everything that he collected in his lovely house, were to be to him means of forgetfulness, modes by which he could escape, for a season, from the fear that seemed to him at times to be almost too great to be borne. Upon the walls of the lonely locked room where he had spent so much of his boyhood, he had hung with his own hands the terrible portrait whose changing features showed him the real degradation of his life, and in front of it had draped the purple-and-gold pall as a curtain. For weeks he would not go there, would forget the hideous painted thing, and get back his light heart, his wonderful joyousness, his passionate absorption in mere existence. Then, suddenly, some night he would creep out of the house, go down to dreadful places near Blue Gate Fields, and stay there, day after day, until he was driven away. On his return he would sit in front of the picture, sometimes loathing it and himself, but filled, at other times, with that pride of individualism that is half the fascination of sin, and smiling with secret pleasure, at the misshapen shadow that had to bear the burden that should have been his own.

After a few years he could not endure to be long out of England, and gave up the villa that he had shared at Trouville with Lord Henry, as well as the little white walled-in house at Algiers where they had more than once spent the winter. He hated to be separated from the picture that was such a part of his life, and was also afraid that during his absence some one might gain access to the room, in spite of the elaborate bars that he had caused to be placed upon the door.

He was quite conscious that this would tell them nothing. It was true that the portrait still preserved, under all the foulness and ugliness of the face, its marked likeness to himself; but what could they learn from that? He would laugh at any one who tried to taunt him. He had not painted it. What was it to him how vile and full of shame it looked? Even if he told them, would they believe it?

Yet he was afraid. Sometimes when he was down at his great house in Nottinghamshire, entertaining the fashionable young men of his own rank who were his chief companions, and astounding the county by the wanton luxury and gorgeous splendour of his mode of life, he would suddenly leave his guests and rush back to town to see that the door had not been tampered with, and that the picture was still there. What if it should be stolen? The mere thought made him cold with horror. Surely the world would know his secret then. Perhaps the world already suspected it.

For, while he fascinated many, there were not a few who distrusted him. He was very nearly blackballed at a West End club of which his birth and social position fully entitled him to become a member, and it was said that on one occasion when he was brought by a friend into the smoking-room of the Churchill, the Duke of Berwick and another gentleman got up in a marked manner and went out. Curious stories became current about him after he had passed his twenty-fifth year. It was rumoured that he had been seen brawling with foreign sailors in a low den in the distant parts of Whitechapel, and that he consorted with thieves and coiners and knew the mysteries of their trade. His extraordinary absences became notorious, and, when he used to reappear again in society, men would whisper to each other in corners, or pass him with a sneer, or look at him with cold searching eyes, as though they were determined to discover his secret.

Of such insolences and attempted slights he, of course, took no notice, and in the opinion of most people his frank debonair manner, his charming boyish smile, and the infinite grace of that wonderful youth that seemed never to leave him, were in themselves a sufficient answer to the calumnies, for so they termed them, that were circulated about him. It was remarked, however, that some of those who had been most intimate with him appeared, after a time, to shun him. Women who had wildly adored him, and for his sake had braved all social censure and set convention at defiance, were seen to grow pallid with shame or horror if Dorian Gray entered the room.

Yet these whispered scandals only increased, in the eyes of many, his strange and dangerous charm. His great wealth was a certain element of security. Society, civilised society at least, is never very ready to believe anything to the detriment of those who are both rich and fascinating. It feels instinctively that manners are of more importance than morals, and, in its opinion, the highest respectability is of much less value than the possession of a good *chef*. And, after all, it is a very poor consolation to be told that the man who has given one a bad dinner, or poor wine, is irreproachable in his private life. Even the cardinal virtues cannot atone for half-cold *entrées*, as Lord Henry remarked once, in a discussion on the subject; and there is possibly a good deal to be said for his view. For the canons of good society are, or should be, the same as the canons of art. Form is absolutely essential to it. It should have the dignity of a ceremony, as well as its unreality, and should combine the insincere character of a romantic play with the wit and beauty that make such plays delightful to us. Is insincerity such a terrible thing? I think not. It is merely a method by which we can multiply our personalities.

Such, at any rate, was Dorian Gray's opinion. He used to wonder at the shallow psychology of those who conceive the Ego in man as a thing simple, permanent, reliable, and of one essence. To him, man was a being with myriad lives and myriad sensations, a complex multiform creature that bore within itself strange legacies of thought and passion, and whose very flesh was tainted with the monstrous maladies of the dead. He loved to stroll through the gaunt cold picture-gallery of his country house and look at the various portraits of those whose blood flowed in his veins. Here was Philip Herbert, described by Francis Osborne, in his *Memoires on the Reigns of Queen Elizabeth and King James*, as one who was 'caressed by the Court for his handsome face, which kept him not long company.' Was it young Herbert's life that he sometimes led? Had some strange poisonous germ crept from body to body till it had reached his own? Was it some dim sense of that ruined grace that had made him so suddenly, and almost without cause, give utterance, in Basil Hallward's studio, to the mad prayer that had so changed his life? Here, in gold-embroidered red doublet, jewelled surcoat, and gilt-edged ruff and wrist-bands, stood Sir Anthony Sherard, with his silver-and-black armour piled at his feet. What had this man's legacy been? Had the lover of Giovanna of Naples bequeathed him some inheritance of sin and shame? Were his own actions merely the dreams that the dead man had not dared to realise? Here, from the fading canvas, smiled Lady Elizabeth Devereux, in her gauze hood, pearl stomacher, and pink slashed sleeves. A flower was in her right hand, and her left clasped an enamelled collar of white and damask roses. On a table by her side lay a mandolin and an apple. There were large green rosettes upon her little pointed shoes. He knew her life, and the strange stories that were told about her lovers. Had he something of her temperament in him? These oval heavy-lidded eyes seemed to look curiously at him. What of George Willoughby, with his powdered hair and fantastic patches? How evil he looked! The face was saturnine and swarthy, and the sensual lips seemed to be twisted with disdain. Delicate lace ruffles fell over the lean yellow hands that were so over-laden with rings. He had been a macaroni of the eighteenth century, and the friend, in his youth, of Lord Ferrars. What of the second Lord Beckenham, the companion of the Prince Regent in his wildest days, and one of the witnesses at the secret marriage with Mrs. Fitzherbert? How proud and handsome he was, with his chestnut curls and insolent pose! What passions had he bequeathed? The world had looked upon him as infamous. He had led the orgies at Carlton House. The star of the Garter glittered upon his breast. Beside him hung the portrait of his wife, a pallid, thin-lipped woman in black. Her blood, also, stirred within him. How curious it all seemed! And his mother with her Lady Hamilton face, and her moist wine-dashed lips – he knew what he had got from her. He had got from her his beauty, and his passion for the beauty of others. She laughed at him in her loose Bacchante dress. There were vine leaves in her hair. The purple spilled from the cup she was holding. The carnations of the painting had withered, but the eyes were still wonderful in their depth and brilliancy of colour. They seemed to follow him wherever he went.

Yet one had ancestors in literature, as well as in one's own race, nearer perhaps in type and temperament, many of them, and certainly with an influence of which one was more absolutely conscious. There were times when it appeared to Dorian Gray that the whole of history was merely the record of his own life, not as he had lived it in act and circumstance, but as his imagination had created it for him, as it had been in his brain and in his passions. He felt that he had known them all, those strange terrible figures that had passed across the stage of the world and made sin so marvellous, and evil so full of subtlety. It seemed to him that in some mysterious way their lives had been his own.

The hero of the wonderful novel that had so influenced his life had himself known this curious fancy. In the seventh chapter he tells how, crowned with laurel, lest lightning might strike him, he had sat, as Tiberius, in a garden at Capri, reading the shameful books of Elephantis, while dwarfs and peacocks strutted round him, and the flute-player mocked the swinger of the censer; and, as Caligula, had caroused with the green-shirted jockeys in their stables and supped in an ivory manger with a jewel-frontleted horse; and, as Domitian, had wandered through a corridor lined with marble mirrors, looking round with haggard eyes for the reflection of the dagger that was to end his days, and sick with that *ennui*, that terrible *tædium vitæ*, that comes on those to whom life denies nothing; and had peered through a clear emerald at the red shambles of the Circus, and then, in a litter of pearl and purple drawn by silver-shod mules, been carried through the Street of Pomegranates to a House of Gold, and heard men cry on Nero Cæsar as he passed by; and, as

Elagabalus, had painted his face with colours, and plied the distaff among the women, and brought the Moon from Carthage, and given her in mystic marriage to the Sun.

Over and over again Dorian used to read this fantastic chapter, and the two chapters immediately following, in which, as in some curious tapestries or cunningly-wrought enamels, were pictured the awful and beautiful forms of those whom Vice and Blood and Weariness had made monstrous or mad; Filippo, Duke of Milan, who slew his wife, and painted her lips with a scarlet poison that her lover might suck death from the dead thing he fondled; Pietro Barbi, the Venetian, known as Paul the Second, who sought in his vanity to assume the title of Formosus, and whose tiara, valued at two hundred thousand florins, was bought at the price of a terrible sin; Gian Maria Visconti, who used hounds to chase living men, and whose murdered body was covered with roses by a harlot who had loved him; the Borgia on his white horse, with Fratricide riding beside him, and his mantle stained with the blood of Perotto; Pietro Riario, the young Cardinal Archbishop of Florence, child and minion of Sixtus IV., whose beauty was equalled only by his debauchery, and who received Leonora of Aragon in a pavilion of white and crimson silk, filled with nymphs and centaurs, and gilded a boy that he might serve at the feast as Ganymede or Hylas; Ezzelin, whose melancholy could be cured only by the spectacle of death, and who had a passion for red blood, as other men have for red wine – the son of the Fiend, as was reported, and one who had cheated his father at dice when gambling with him for his own soul; Giambattista Cibo, who in mockery took the name of Innocent, and into whose torpid veins the blood of three lads was infused by a Jewish doctor; Sigismondo Malatesta, the lover of Isotta, and the lord of Rimini, whose effigy was burned at Rome as the enemy of God and man, who strangled Polyssena with a napkin, and gave poison to Ginevra d'Este in a cup of emerald, and in honour of a shameful passion built a pagan church for Christian worship; Charles VI., who had so wildly adored his brother's wife that a leper had warned him of the insanity that was coming on him, and who, when his brain had sickened and grown strange, could only be soothed by Saracen cards painted with the images of Love and Death and Madness; and, in his trimmed jerkin and jewelled cap and acanthus-like curls, Grifonetto Baglioni, who slew Astorre with his bride, and Simonetto with his page, and whose comeliness was such that, as he lay dying in the yellow piazza of Perugia, those who had hated him could not choose but weep, and Atlanta, who had cursed him, blessed him.

There was a horrible fascination in them all. He saw them at night, and they troubled his imagination in the day. The Renaissance knew of strange manners of poisoning – poisoning by a helmet and a lighted torch, by an embroidered glove and a jewelled fan, by a gilded pomander and by an amber chain. Dorian Gray had been poisoned by a book. There were moments when he looked on evil simply as a mode through which he could realise his conception of the beautiful.

12

IT was on the ninth of November, the eve of his own thirty-eighth birthday, as he often remembered afterwards.

He was walking home about eleven o'clock from Lord Henry's, where he had been dining, and was wrapped in heavy furs, as the night was cold and foggy. At the corner of Grosvenor Square and South Audley Street a man passed him in the mist, walking very fast, and with the collar of his grey ulster turned up. He had a bag in his hand. Dorian recognised him. It was Basil Hallward. A strange sense of fear, for which he could not account, came over him. He made no sign of recognition, and went on quickly in the direction of his own house.

But Hallward had seen him. Dorian heard him first stopping on the pavement, and then hurrying after him. In a few moments his hand was on his arm.

'Dorian! What an extraordinary piece of luck! I have been waiting for you in your library ever since nine o'clock. Finally I took pity on your tired servant, and told him to go to bed, as he let me out. I am off to Paris by the midnight train, and I particularly wanted to see you before I left. I thought it was you, or rather your fur coat, as you passed me. But I wasn't quite sure. Didn't you recognise me?'

'In this fog, my dear Basil? Why, I can't even recognise Grosvenor Square. I believe my house is somewhere about here, but I don't feel at all certain about it. I am sorry you are going away, as I have not seen you for ages. But I suppose you will be back soon?'

'No: I am going to be out of England for six months. I intend to take a studio in Paris, and shut myself up till I have finished a great picture I have in my head. However, it wasn't about myself I wanted to talk. Here we are at your door. Let me come in for a moment. I have something to say to you.'

'I shall be charmed. But won't you miss your train?' said Dorian Gray, languidly, as he passed up the steps and opened the door with his latchkey.

The lamp-light struggled out through the fog, and Hallward looked at his watch. 'I have heaps of time,' he answered. 'The train doesn't go till twelve-fifteen, and it is only just eleven. In fact, I was on my way to the club to look for you, when I met you. You see, I shan't have any delay about luggage, as I have sent on my heavy things. All I have with me is in this bag, and I can easily get to Victoria in twenty minutes.'

Dorian looked at him and smiled. 'What a way for a fashionable painter to travel! A Gladstone bag, and an ulster! Come in, or the fog will get into the house. And mind you don't talk about anything serious. Nothing is serious nowadays. At least nothing should be.'

Hallward shook his head as he entered, and followed Dorian into the library. There was a bright wood fire blazing in the large open hearth. The lamps were lit, and an open Dutch silver spirit-case stood, with some siphons of soda-water and large cut-glass tumblers, on a little marqueterie table.

'You see your servant made me quite at home, Dorian. He gave me everything I wanted, including your best gold-tipped cigarettes. He is a most hospitable creature. I like him much better than the Frenchman you used to have. What has become of the Frenchman, by the by?'

Dorian shrugged his shoulders. 'I believe he married Lady Radley's maid, and has established her in Paris as an English dressmaker. *Anglomanie* is very fashionable over there now, I hear. It seems silly of the French, doesn't it? But – do you know? – he was not at all a bad servant. I never liked him, but I had nothing to complain about. One often imagines things that are quite absurd. He was really very devoted to me, and seemed quite sorry when he went away. Have another brandy-and-soda? Or would you like hock-and-seltzer? I always take hock-and-seltzer myself. There is sure to be some in the next room.'

'Thanks, I won't have anything more,' said the painter, taking his cap and coat off, and throwing them on the bag that he had placed in the corner. 'And now, my dear fellow, I want to speak to you seriously. Don't frown like that. You make it so much more difficult for me.'

'What is it all about?' cried Dorian, in his petulant way, flinging himself down on the sofa. 'I hope it is not about myself. I am tired of myself to-night. I should like to be somebody else.'

'It is about yourself,' answered Hallward, in his grave, deep voice, 'and I must say it to you. I shall only keep you half an hour.'

Dorian sighed, and lit a cigarette. 'Half an hour!' he murmured.

'It is not much to ask of you, Dorian, and it is entirely for your own sake that I am speaking. I think it right that you should know that the most dreadful things are being said against you in London.'

'I don't wish to know anything about them. I love scandals about other people, but scandals about myself don't interest me. They have not got the charm of novelty.'

'They must interest you, Dorian. Every gentleman is interested in his good name. You don't want people to talk of you as something vile and degraded. Of course you have your position, and your wealth, and all that kind of thing. But position and wealth are not everything. Mind you, I don't believe these rumours at all. At least, I can't believe them when I see you. Sin is a thing that writes itself across a man's face. It cannot be concealed. People talk sometimes of secret vices. There are no such things. If a wretched man has a vice, it shows itself in the lines of his mouth, the droop of his eyelids, the moulding of his hands even. Somebody – I won't mention his name, but you know him – came to me last year to have his portrait done. I had never seen him before, and had never heard anything about him at the time, though I have heard a good deal since. He offered an extravagant price. I refused him. There was something in the shape of his fingers that I hated. I know now that I was quite right in what I fancied about him. His life is dreadful. But you, Dorian, with your pure, bright, innocent face, and your

marvellous untroubled youth – I can't believe anything against you. And yet
I see you very seldom, and you never come down to the studio now, and
when I am away from you, and I hear all these hideous things that people are
whispering about you, I don't know what to say. Why is it, Dorian, that a
man like the Duke of Berwick leaves the room of a club when you enter it?
Why is it that so many gentlemen in London will neither go to your house
nor invite you to theirs? You used to be a friend of Lord Staveley. I met him
at dinner last week. Your name happened to come up in conversation, in
connection with the miniatures you have lent to the exhibition at the
Dudley. Staveley curled his lip, and said that you might have the most art-
istic tastes, but that you were a man whom no pure-minded girl should be al-
lowed to know, and whom no chaste woman should sit in the same room
with. I reminded him that I was a friend of yours, and asked him what he
meant. He told me. He told me right out before everybody. It was horrible!
Why is your friendship so fatal to young men? There was that wretched boy
in the Guards who committed suicide. You were his great friend. There was
Sir Henry Ashton, who had to leave England, with a tarnished name. You
and he were inseparable. What about Adrian Singleton, and his dreadful
end? What about Lord Kent's only son, and his career? I met his father yes-
terday in St. James's Street. He seemed broken with shame and sorrow.
What about the young Duke of Perth? What sort of life has he got now? What
gentleman would associate with him?'

'Stop, Basil. You are talking about things of which you know nothing,'
said Dorian Gray, biting his lip, and with a note of infinite contempt in his
voice. 'You ask me why Berwick leaves a room when I enter it. It is because I
know everything about his life, not because he knows anything about mine.
With such blood as he has in his veins, how could his record be clean? You
ask me about Henry Ashton and young Perth. Did I teach the one his vices,
and the other his debauchery? If Kent's silly son takes his wife from the
streets what is that to me? If Adrian Singleton writes his friend's name across
a bill, am I his keeper? I know how people chatter in England. The middle
classes air their moral prejudices over their gross dinner-tables, and whisper
about what they call the profligacies of their betters in order to try and pre-
tend that they are in smart society, and on intimate terms with the people
they slander. In this country it is enough for a man to have distinction and
brains for every common tongue to wag against him. And what sort of lives
do these people, who pose as being moral, lead themselves? My dear fellow,
you forget that we are in the native land of the hypocrite.'

'Dorian,' cried Hallward, 'that is not the question. England is bad enough,
I know, and English society is all wrong. That is the reason why I want you to
be fine. You have not been fine. One had a right to judge of a man by the ef-
fect he has over his friends. Yours seem to lose all sense of honour, of good-
ness, of purity. You have filled them with a madness for pleasure. They have
gone down into the depths. You led them there. Yes: you led them there, and
yet you can smile, as you are smiling now. And there is worse behind. I know
you and Harry are inseparable. Surely for that reason, if for none other, you

should not have made his sister's name a by-word.'

'Take care, Basil. You go too far.'

'I must speak, and you must listen. You shall listen. When you met Lady Gwendolen, not a breath of scandal had ever touched her. Is there a single decent woman in London now who would drive with her in the Park? Why, even her children are not allowed to live with her. Then there are other stories – stories that you have been seen creeping at dawn out of dreadful houses and slinking in disguise into the foulest dens in London. Are they true? Can they be true? When I first heard them I laughed. I hear them now, and they make me shudder. What about your country house, and the life that is led there? Dorian, you don't know what is said about you. I won't tell you that I don't want to preach to you. I remember Harry saying once that every man who turned himself into an amateur curate for the moment always began by saying that, and then proceeded to break his word. I do want to preach to you. I want you to lead such a life as will make the world respect you. I want you to have a clean name and a fair record. I want you to get rid of the dreadful people you associate with. Don't shrug your shoulders like that. Don't be so indifferent. You have a wonderful influence. Let it be for good, not for evil. They say that you corrupt every one with whom you become intimate, and that it is quite sufficient for you to enter a house, for shame of some kind to follow after. I don't know whether it is so or not. How should I know? But it is said of you. I am told things that it seems impossible to doubt. Lord Gloucester was one of my greatest friends at Oxford. He showed me a letter that his wife had written to him when she was dying alone in her villa at Mentone. Your name was implicated in the most terrible confession I ever read. I told him that it was absurd – that I knew you thoroughly, and that you were incapable of anything of the kind. Know you? I wonder do I know you? Before I could answer that, I should have to see your soul.'

'To see my soul!' muttered Dorian Gray, starting up from the sofa and turning almost white from fear.

'Yes,' answered Hallward, gravely, and with deep-toned sorrow in his voice – 'to see your soul. But only God can do that.'

A bitter laugh of mockery broke from the lips of the younger man. 'You shall see it yourself, to-night!' he cried, seizing a lamp from the table. 'Come: it is your own handiwork. Why shouldn't you look at it? You can tell the world all about it afterwards, if you choose. Nobody would believe you. If they did believe you, they would like me all the better for it. I know the age better than you do, though you will prate about it so tediously. Come, I tell you. You have chattered enough about corruption. Now you shall look on it face to face.'

There was the madness of pride in every word he uttered. He stamped his foot upon the ground in his boyish insolent manner. He felt a terrible joy at the thought that someone else was to share his secret, and that the man who had painted the portrait that was the origin of all his shame was to be burdened for the rest of his life with the hideous memory of what he had done.

'Yes,' he continued, coming closer to him, and looking steadfastly into his stern eyes, 'I shall show you my soul. You shall see the thing that you fancy only God can see.'

Hallward started back. 'This is blasphemy, Dorian!' he cried. 'You must not say things like that. They are horrible, and they don't mean anything.'

'You think so?' He laughed again.

'I know so. As for what I said to you to-night, I said it for your good. You know I have been always a staunch friend to you.'

'Don't touch me. Finish what you have to say.'

A twisted flash of pain shot across the painter's face. He paused for a moment, and a wild feeling of pity came over him. After all, what right had he to pry into the life of Dorian Gray? If he had done a tithe of what was rumoured about him, how much he must have suffered! Then he straightened himself up, and walked over to the fireplace, and stood there, looking at the burning logs with their frost-like ashes and their throbbing cores of flame.

'I am waiting, Basil,' said the young man, in a hard, clear voice.

He turned round. 'What I have to say is this,' he cried. 'You must give me some answer to these horrible charges that are made against you. If you tell me that they are absolutely untrue from beginning to end, I shall believe you. Deny them, Dorian, deny them! Can't you see what I am going through? My God! Don't tell me that you are bad, and corrupt, and shameful.'

Dorian Gray smiled. There was a curl of contempt in his lips. 'Come upstairs, Basil,' he said, quietly. 'I keep a diary of my life from day to day, and it never leaves the room in which it is written. I shall show it to you if you come with me.'

'I shall come with you, Dorian, if you wish it. I see I have missed my train. That makes no matter. I can go to-morrow. But don't ask me to read anything to-night. All I want is a plain answer to my question.'

'That shall be given to you upstairs. I could not give it here. You will not have to read long.'

13

HE passed out of the room, and began the ascent, Basil Hallward following close behind. They walked softly, as men do instinctively at night. The lamp cast fantastic shadows on the wall and staircase. A rising wind made some of the windows rattle.

When they reached the top landing, Dorian set the lamp down on the floor, and taking out the key turned it in the lock. 'You insist on knowing, Basil?' he asked, in a low voice.

'Yes.'

'I am delighted,' he answered, smiling. Then he added, somewhat harshly, 'You are the one man in the world who is entitled to know everything about me. You have had more to do with my life than you think:' and, taking up the lamp, he opened the door and went in. A cold current of air passed them, and the light shot up for a moment in a flame of murky orange. He shuddered. 'Shut the door behind you,' he whispered, as he placed the lamp on the table.

Hallward glanced round him, with a puzzled expression. The room looked as if it had not been lived in for years. A faded Flemish tapestry, a curtained picture, an old Italian *cassone*, and an almost empty bookcase – that was all that it seemed to contain, besides a chair and a table. As Dorian Gray was lighting a half-burned candle that was standing on the mantelshelf, he saw that the whole place was covered with dust, and that the carpet was in holes. A mouse ran scuffling behind the wainscoting. There was a damp odour of mildew.

'So you think that it is only God who sees the soul, Basil? Draw that curtain back, and you will see mine.'

The voice that spoke was cold and cruel. 'You are mad, Dorian, or playing a part,' muttered Hallward, frowning.

'You won't? Then I must do it myself,' said the young man; and he tore the curtain from its rod and flung it on the ground.

An exclamation of horror broke from the painter's lips as he saw in the dim light the hideous face on the canvas grinning at him. There was something in its expression that filled him with disgust and loathing. Good heavens! It was Dorian Gray's own face that he was looking at! The horror, whatever it was, had not yet entirely spoiled that marvellous beauty. There was still some gold in the thinning hair and some scarlet on the sensual mouth. The sodden eyes had kept something of the loveliness of their blue, the noble curves had not yet completely passed away from chiselled nostrils and from plastic throat. Yes, it was Dorian himself. But who had done it? He seemed to re-cognise his own brushwork, and the frame was his own design. The idea was monstrous, yet he felt afraid. He seized the lighted candle, and held it to the picture. In the left-hand corner was his own name, traced in long letters of bright vermilion.

It was some foul parody, some infamous, ignoble satire. He had never done that. Still, it was his own picture! He knew it, and he felt as if his blood had changed in a moment from fire to sluggish ice. His own picture! What did it mean? Why had it altered? He turned, and looked at Dorian Gray, with the eyes of a sick man. His mouth twitched, and his parched tongue seemed unable to articulate. He passed his hand across his forehead. It was dank with clammy sweat.

The young man was leaning against the mantelshelf, watching him with that strange expression that one sees on the faces of those who are absorbed in a play when some great artist is acting. There was neither real sorrow in it nor real joy. There was simply the passion of the spectator, with perhaps a flicker of triumph in his eyes. He had taken the flower out of his coat, and was smelling it, or pretending to do so.

'What does this mean?' cried Hallward, at last. His own voice sounded shrill and curious in his ears.

'Years ago, when I was a boy,' said Dorian Gray, crushing the flower in his hand, 'you met me, flattered me, and taught me to be vain of my good looks.

One day you introduced me to a friend of yours, who explained to me the wonder of youth, and you finished the portrait of me that revealed to me the wonder of beauty. In a mad moment, that, even now, I don't know whether I regret or not, I made a wish, perhaps you would call it a prayer . . .'

'I remember it! Oh, how well I remember it! No, the thing is impossible! The room is damp. Mildew has got into the canvas. The paints I used had some wretched mineral poison in them. I tell you the thing is impossible.'

'Ah, what is impossible?' murmured the young man, going over to the window, and leaning his forehead against the cold, mist-stained glass.

'You told me you had destroyed it.'

'I was wrong. It has destroyed me.'

'I don't believe it is my picture.'

'Can't you see your ideal in it?' said Dorian, bitterly.

'My ideal, as you call it . . .'

'As you called it.'

'There was nothing evil in it, nothing shameful. You were to me such an ideal as I shall never meet again. This is the face of a satyr.'

'It is the face of my soul.'

'Christ! What a thing I must have worshipped! It has the eyes of a devil.'

'Each of us has Heaven and Hell in him, Basil,' cried Dorian, with a wild gesture of despair.

Hallward turned again to the portrait, and gazed at it. 'My God! If it is true,' he exclaimed, 'and this is what you have done with your life, why, you must be worse even than those who talk against you fancy you to be!' He held the light up again to the canvas, and examined it. The surface seemed to be quite undisturbed, and as he had left it. It was from within, apparently, that the foulness and horror had come. Through some strange quickening of inner life the leprosies of sin were slowly eating the thing away. The rotting of a corpse in a watery grave was not so fearful.

His hand shook, and the candle fell from its socket on the floor, and lay there sputtering. He placed his foot on it and put it out. Then he flung himself into the rickety chair that was standing by the table and buried his face in his hands.

'Good God, Dorian, what a lesson! What an awful lesson!' There was no answer, but he could hear the young man sobbing at the window. 'Pray, Dorian, pray,' he murmured. 'What is it that one was taught to say in one's boyhood? "Lead us not into temptation. Forgive us our sins. Wash away our iniquities." Let us say that together. The prayer of your pride has been answered. The prayer of your repentance will be answered also. I worshipped you too much. We are both punished.'

Dorian Gray turned slowly around, and looked at him with tear-dimmed eyes. 'It is too late, Basil,' he faltered.

'It is never too late, Dorian. Let us kneel down and try if we cannot remember a prayer. Isn't there a verse somewhere, "Though your sins be as scarlet, yet I will make them as white as snow?"'

'Those words mean nothing to me now.'

'Hush! Don't say that. You have done enough evil in your life. My God! Don't you see that accursed thing leering at us?'

Dorian Gray glanced at the picture, and suddenly an uncontrollable feeling of hatred for Basil Hallward came over him, as though it had been suggested to him by the image on the canvas, whispered into his ear by those grinning lips. The mad passions of a hunted animal stirred within him, and he loathed the man who was seated at the table, more than in his whole life he had ever loathed anything. He glanced wildly around. Something glimmered on the top of the painted chest that faced him. His eye fell on it. He knew what it was. It was a knife that he had brought up, some days before, to cut a piece of cord, and had forgotten to take away with him. He moved slowly towards it, passing Hallward as he did so. As soon as he got behind him, he seized it, and turned round. Hallward stirred in his chair as if he was going to rise. He rushed at him, and dug the knife into the great vein that is behind the ear, crushing the man's head down on the table, and stabbing again and again.

There was a stifled groan, and the horrible sound of someone choking with blood. Three times the outstretched arms shot up convulsively, waving grotesque stiff-fingered hands in the air. He stabbed him twice more, but the man did not move. Something began to trickle on the floor. He waited for a moment, still pressing the head down. Then he threw the knife on the table, and listened.

He could hear nothing but the drip, drip on the threadbare carpet. He opened the door and went out on the landing. The house was absolutely quiet. No one was about. For a few seconds he stood bending over the balustrade, and peering down into the black seething well of darkness. Then he took out the key and returned to the room, locking himself in as he did so.

The thing was still seated in the chair, straining over the table with bowed head, and humped back, and long fantastic arms. Had it not been for the red jagged tear in the neck, and the clotted black pool that was slowly widening on the table, one would have said that the man was simply asleep.

How quickly it had all been done! He felt strangely calm, and, walking over to the window, opened it, and stepped out on the balcony. The wind had blown the fog away, and the sky was like a monstrous peacock's tail, starred with myriads of golden eyes. He looked down, and saw the policeman going his rounds and flashing the long beam of his lantern on the doors of the silent houses. The crimson spot of a prowling hansom gleamed at the corner, and then vanished. A woman in a fluttering shawl was creeping slowly by the railings, staggering as she went. Now and then she stopped, and peered back. Once, she began to sing in a hoarse voice. The policeman strolled over and said something to her. She stumbled away, laughing. A bitter blast swept across the Square. The gas-lamps flickered, and became blue, and the leafless trees shook their black iron branches to and fro. He shivered, and went back, closing the window behind him.

Having reached the door, he turned the key, and opened it. He did not even glance at the murdered man. He felt that the secret of the whole thing was not to realise the situation. The friend who had painted the fatal portrait to which all his misery had been due had gone out of his life. That was enough.

Then he remembered the lamp. It was a rather curious one of Moorish workmanship, made of dull silver inlaid with arabesques of burnished steel, and studded with coarse turquoises. Perhaps it might be missed by his servant, and questions would be asked. He hesitated for a moment, then he turned back and took it from the table. He could not help seeing the dead thing. How still it was! How horribly white the long hands looked! It was like a dreadful wax image.

Having locked the door behind him, he crept quietly downstairs. The woodwork creaked, and seemed to cry out as if in pain. He stopped several times, and waited. No: everything was still. It was merely the sound of his own footsteps.

When he reached the library, he saw the bag and coat in the corner. They must be hidden away somewhere. He unlocked a secret press that was in the wainscoting, a press in which he kept his own curious disguises, and put them into it. He could easily burn them afterwards. Then he pulled out his watch. It was twenty minutes to two.

He sat down, and began to think. Every year – every month, almost – men were strangled in England for what he had done. There had been a madness of murder in the air. Some red star had come too close to the earth. . . . And yet what evidence was there against him? Basil Hallward had left the house at eleven. No one had seen him come in again. Most of the servants were at Selby Royal. His valet had gone to bed. . . . Paris! Yes. It was to Paris that Basil had gone, and by the midnight train, as he had intended. With his curious reserved habits, it would be months before any suspicions would be aroused. Months! Everything could be destroyed long before then.

A sudden thought struck him. He put on his fur coat and hat, and went out into the hall. There he paused, hearing the slow heavy tread of the policeman on the pavement outside, and seeing the flash of the bull's-eye reflected in the window. He waited, and held his breath.

After a few moments he drew back the latch, and slipped out, shutting the door very gently behind him. Then he began ringing the bell. In about five minutes his valet appeared half dressed, and looking very drowsy.

'I am sorry to have had to wake you up, Francis,' he said, stepping in; 'but I had forgotten my latchkey. What time is it?'

'Ten minutes past two, sir,' answered the man, looking at the clock and blinking.

'Ten minutes past two? How horribly late! You must wake me at nine to-morrow. I have some work to do.'

'All right, sir.'

'Did any one call this evening?'

'Mr. Hallward, sir. He stayed here till eleven, and then he went away to catch his train.'

'Oh! I am sorry I didn't see him. Did he leave any message?'

'No, sir, except that he would write to you from Paris, if he did not find you at the club.'

'That will do, Francis. Don't forget to call me at nine to-morrow.'

'No, sir.'

The man shambled down the passage in his slippers.

Dorian Gray threw his hat and coat upon the table, and passed into the library. For a quarter of an hour he walked up and down the room biting his lip, and thinking. Then he took down the Blue Book from one of the shelves, and began to turn over the leaves. 'Alan Campbell, 152, Hertford Street, Mayfair.' Yes: that was the man he wanted.

14

AT nine o'clock the next morning his servant came in with a cup of chocolate on a tray, and opened the shutters. Dorian was sleeping quite peacefully, lying on his right side, with one hand underneath his cheek. He looked like a boy who had been tired out with play, or study.

The man had to touch him twice on the shoulder before he awoke, and as he opened his eyes a faint smile passed across his lips, as though he had been lost in some delightful dream. Yet he had not dreamed at all. His night had been untroubled by any images of pleasure or of pain. But youth smiles without any reason. It is one of its chiefest charms.

He turned round, and, leaning upon his elbow, began to sip his chocolate. The mellow November sun came streaming into the room. The sky was bright, and there was a genial warmth in the air. It was almost like a morning in May.

Gradually the events of the preceding night crept with silent bloodstained feet into his brain, and reconstructed themselves there with terrible distinctness. He winced at the memory of all that he had suffered, and for a moment the same curious feeling of loathing for Basil Hallward that had made him kill him as he sat in the chair, came back to him, and he grew cold with passion. The dead man was still sitting there, too, and in the sunlight now. How horrible that was! Such hideous things were for the darkness, not for the day.

He felt that if he brooded on what he had gone through he would sicken or grow mad. There were sins whose fascination was more in the memory than in the doing of them; strange triumphs that gratified the pride more than the passions, and gave to the intellect a quickened sense of joy, greater than any joy they brought, or could ever bring, to the senses. But this was not one of them. It was a thing to be driven out of the mind, to be drugged with poppies, to be strangled lest it might strangle one itself.

When the half-hour struck, he passed his hand across his forehead, and then got up hastily, and dressed himself with even more than his usual care, giving a good deal of attention to the choice of his necktie and scarf-pin, and changing his rings more than once. He spent a long time also over breakfast, tasting the various dishes, talking to his valet about some new liveries that he was thinking of getting made for the servants at Selby, and going through his correspondence. At some of the letters he smiled. Three of them bored him. One he read several times over, and then tore up with a slight look of annoyance in his face. 'That awful thing, a woman's memory!' as Lord Henry had once said.

After he had drunk his cup of black coffee, he wiped his lips slowly with a napkin, motioned to his servant to wait, and going over to the table sat down and wrote two letters. One he put in his pocket, the other he handed to the valet.

'Take this round to 152, Hertford Street, Francis, and if Mr. Campbell is out of town, get his address.'

As soon as he was alone, he lit a cigarette, and began sketching upon a piece of paper, drawing first flowers, and bits of architecture, and then human faces. Suddenly he remarked that every face that he drew seemed to have a fantastic likeness to Basil Hallward. He frowned, and, getting up, went over to the bookcase and took out a volume at hazard. He was determined that he would not think about what had happened until it became absolutely necessary that he should do so.

When he had stretched himself on the sofa, he looked at the title-page of the book. It was Gautier's *Emaux et Camées*, Charpentier's Japanese-paper edition, with the Jacquemart etching. The binding was of citron-green leather, with a design of gilt trellis-work and dotted pomegranates. It had been given to him by Adrian Singleton. As he turned over the pages his eye fell on the poem about the hand of Lacenaire, the cold yellow hand *'du supplice encore mal lavée,'* with its downy red hairs and its *'doigts de faune.'* He glanced at his own white taper fingers, shuddering slightly in spite of himself, and passed on, till he came to those lovely stanzas upon Venice: –

> 'Sur une gamme chromatique,
>   Le sein de perles ruisselant,
> La Vénus de l'Adriatique
>   Sort de l'eau son corps rose et blanc.

> 'Les domes, sur l'azur des ondes
>   Suivant la phrase au pur contour,
> S'enflent comme des gorges rondes
>   Que soulève un soupir d'amour.

> 'L'esquif aborde et me dépose,
>   Jetant son amarre au pilier,
> Devant une façade rose,
>   Sur le marbre d'un escalier.'

How exquisite they were! As one read them, one seemed to be floating

down the green waterways of the pink and pearl city, seated in a black gon-
dola with silver prow and trailing curtains. The mere lines looked to him like
those straight lines of turquoise-blue that follow one as one pushes out to the
Lido. The sudden flashes of colour reminded him of the gleam of the opal-
and-iris-throated birds that flutter round the tall, honey-combed Campa-
nile, or stalk, with such stately grace, through the dim, dust-stained arcades.
Leaning back with half-closed eyes, he kept saying over and over to himself:

> 'Devant une façade rose,
> Sur le marbre d'un escalier.'

The whole of Venice was in those two lines. He remembered the autumn
that he had passed there, and a wonderful love that had stirred him to mad,
delightful follies. There was romance in every place. But Venice, like
Oxford, had kept the background for romance, and, to the true romantic,
background was everything, or almost everything. Basil had been with him
part of the time, and had gone wild over Tintoret. Poor Basil! what a horrible
way for a man to die!

He sighed, and took up the volume again, and tried to forget. He read of
the swallows that fly in and out of the little café at Smyrna where the Hadjis sit
counting their amber beads and the turbaned merchants smoke their long
tasselled pipes and talk gravely to each other; he read of the Obelisk in the
Place de la Concorde that weeps tears of granite in its lonely sunless exile,
and longs to be back by the hot lotus-covered Nile, where there are
Sphinxes, and rose-red ibises, and white vultures with gilded claws, and cro-
codiles, with small beryl eyes, that crawl over the green steaming mud; he
began to brood over those verses which, drawing music from kiss-stained
marble, tell of that curious statue that Gautier compares to a contralto voice,
the '*monstre charmant*' that couches in the porphyry-room of the Louvre. But
after a time the book fell from his hand. He grew nervous, and a horrible fit of
terror came over him. What if Alan Campbell should be out of England?
Days would elapse before he could come back. Perhaps he might refuse to
come. What could he do then? Every moment was of vital importance. They
had been great friends once, five years before – almost inseparable, indeed.
Then the intimacy had come suddenly to an end. When they met in society
now, it was only Dorian Gray who smiled; Alan Campbell never did.

He was an extremely clever young man, though he had no real appreci-
ation of the visible arts, and whatever little sense of the beauty of poetry he
possessed he had gained entirely from Dorian. His dominant intellectual
passion was for science. At Cambridge he had spent a great deal of his time
working in the Laboratory, and had taken a good class in the Natural Science
Tripos of his year. Indeed, he was still devoted to the study of chemistry, and
had a laboratory of his own, in which he used to shut himself up all day long,
greatly to the annoyance of his mother, who had set her heart on his standing
for Parliament, and had a vague idea that a chemist was a person who made
up prescriptions. He was an excellent musician, however, as well, and played
both the violin and the piano better than most amateurs. In fact, it was music

that had first brought him and Dorian Gray together – music and that inde-finable attraction that Dorian seemed to be able to exercise whenever he wished, and indeed exercised often without being conscious of it. They had met at Lady Berkshire's the night that Rubenstein played there, and after that used to be always seen together at the Opera, and wherever good music was going on. For eighteen months their intimacy lasted. Campbell was al-ways either at Selby Royal or in Grosvenor Square. To him, as to many others, Dorian Gray was the type of everything that is wonderful and fascin-ating in life. Whether or not a quarrel had taken place between them no one ever knew. But suddenly people remarked that they scarcely spoke when they met, and that Campbell seemed always to go away early from any party at which Dorian Gray was present. He had changed, too – was strangely mel-ancholy at times, appeared almost to dislike hearing music, and would never himself play, giving as his excuse, when he was called upon, that he was so absorbed in science that he had no time left in which to practise. And this was certainly true. Every day he seemed to become more interested in bio-logy, and his name appeared once or twice in some of the scientific reviews, in connection with certain curious experiments.

This was the man Dorian Gray was waiting for. Every second he kept glancing at the clock. As the minutes went by he became horribly agitated. At last he got up, and began to pace up and down the room, looking like a beautiful caged thing. He took long stealthy strides. His hands were curi-ously cold.

The suspense became unbearable. Time seemed to him to be crawling with feet of lead, while he by monstrous winds was being swept towards the jagged edge of some black cleft of precipice. He knew what was waiting for him there; saw it indeed, and, shuddering, crushed with dank hands his burning lids as though he would have robbed the very brain of sight, and dri-ven the eyeballs back into their cave. It was useless. The brain had its own food on which it battened, and the imagination, made grotesque by terror, twisted and distorted as a living thing by pain, danced like some foul puppet on a stand, and grinned through moving masks. Then, suddenly, Time stopped for him. Yes: that blind, slow-breathing thing crawled no more, and horrible thoughts, Time being dead, raced nimbly on in front, and dragged a hideous future from its grave, and showed it to him. He stared at it. Its very horror made him stone.

At last the door opened, and his servant entered. He turned glazed eyes upon him.

'Mr. Campbell, sir,' said the man.

A sigh of relief broke from his parched lips, and the colour came back to his cheeks.

'Ask him to come in at once, Francis.' He felt that he was himself again. His mood of cowardice had passed away.

The man bowed, and retired. In a few moments Alan Campbell walked in, looking very stern and rather pale, his pallor being intensified by his coal-black hair and dark eyebrows.

'Alan! this is kind of you. I thank you for coming.'

'I had intended never to enter your house again, Gray. But you said it was a matter of life and death.' His voice was hard and cold. He spoke with slow deliberation. There was a look of contempt in the steady searching gaze that he turned on Dorian. He kept his hands in the pockets of his Astrakhan coat, and seemed not to have noticed the gesture with which he had been greeted.

'Yes: it is a matter of life and death, Alan, and to more than one person. Sit down.'

Campbell took a chair by the table, and Dorian sat opposite to him. The two men's eyes met. In Dorian's there was infinite pity. He knew that what he was going to do was dreadful.

After a strained moment of silence, he leaned across and said, very quietly, but watching the effect of each word upon the face of him he had sent for, 'Alan, in a locked room at the top of this house, a room to which nobody but myself has access, a dead man is seated at a table. He has been dead ten hours now. Don't stir, and don't look at me like that. Who the man is, why he died, how he died, are matters that do not concern you. What you have to do is this –'

'Stop, Gray. I don't want to know anything further. Whether what you have told me is true or not true, doesn't concern me. I entirely decline to be mixed up in your life. Keep your horrible secrets to yourself. They don't interest me any more.'

'Alan, they will have to interest you. This one will have to interest you. I am awfully sorry for you, Alan. But I can't help myself. You are the one man who is able to save me. I am forced to bring you into the matter. I have no option. Alan, you are scientific. You know about chemistry, and things of that kind. You have made experiments. What you have got to do is to destroy the thing that is upstairs – to destroy it so that not a vestige of it will be left. Nobody saw this person come into the house. Indeed, at the present moment he is supposed to be in Paris. He will not be missed for months. When he is missed, there must be no trace of him found here. You, Alan, you must change him, and everything that belongs to him, into a handful of ashes that I may scatter in the air.'

'You are mad, Dorian.'

'Ah! I was waiting for you to call me Dorian.'

'You are mad, I tell you – mad to imagine that I would raise a finger to help you, mad to make this monstrous confession. I will have nothing to do with this matter, whatever it is. Do you think I am going to peril my reputation for you? What is it to me what devil's work you are up to?'

'It was suicide, Alan.'

'I am glad of that. But who drove him to it? You, I should fancy.'

'Do you still refuse to do this for me?'

'Of course I refuse. I will have absolutely nothing to do with it. I don't care what shame comes on you. You deserve it all. I should not be sorry to see you disgraced, publicly disgraced. How dare you ask me, of all men in the world, to mix myself up in this horror? I should have thought you knew more about people's characters. Your friend Lord Henry Wotton can't have taught you much about psychology, whatever else he has taught you. Nothing will induce me to stir a step to help you. You have come to the wrong man. Go to some of your friends. Don't come to me.'

'Alan, it was murder. I killed him. You don't know what he had made me suffer. Whatever my life is, he had more to do with the making or the marring of it than poor Harry has had. He may not have intended it, the result was the same.'

'Murder! Good God, Dorian, is that what you have come to? I shall not inform upon you. It is not my business. Besides, without my stirring in the matter, you are certain to be arrested. Nobody ever commits a crime without doing something stupid. But I will have nothing to do with it.'

'You must have something to do with it. Wait, wait a moment; listen to me. Only listen, Alan. All I ask of you is to perform a certain scientific experiment. You go to hospitals and dead-houses, and the horrors that you do there don't affect you. If in some hideous dissecting-room or fetid laboratory you found this man lying on a leaden table with red gutters scooped out in it for the blood to flow through, you would simply look upon him as an admirable subject. You would not turn a hair. You would not believe that you were doing anything wrong. On the contrary, you would probably feel that you were benefiting the human race, or increasing the sum of knowledge in the world, or gratifying intellectual curiosity, or something of that kind. What I want you to do is merely what you have often done before. Indeed, to destroy a body must be far less horrible than what you are accustomed to work at. And, remember, it is the only piece of evidence against me. If it is discovered, I am lost; and it is sure to be discovered unless you help me.'

'I have no desire to help you. You forget that. I am simply indifferent to the whole thing. It has nothing to do with me.'

'Alan, I entreat you. Think of the position I am in. Just before you came I almost fainted with terror. You may know terror yourself some day. No! don't think of that. Look at the matter purely from the scientific point of view. You don't inquire where the dead things on which you experiment come from. Don't inquire now. I have told you too much as it is. But I beg of you to do this. We were friends once, Alan.'

'Don't speak about those days, Dorian: they are dead.'

'The dead linger sometimes. The man upstairs will not go away. He is sitting at the table with bowed head and outstretched arms. Alan! Alan! if you don't come to my assistance I am ruined. Why, they will hang me, Alan! Don't you understand? They will hang me for what I have done.'

'There is no good in prolonging this scene. I absolutely refuse to do anything in the matter. It is insane of you to ask me.'

'You refuse?'

'Yes.'

'I entreat you, Alan.'

'It is useless.'

The same look of pity came into Dorian Gray's eyes. Then he stretched out his hand, took a piece of paper, and wrote something on it. He read it over twice, folded it carefully, and pushed it across the table. Having done this, he got up, and went over to the window.

Campbell looked at him in surprise, and then took up the paper, and opened it. As he read it, his face became ghastly pale, and he fell back in his chair. A horrible sense of sickness came over him. He felt as if his heart was beating itself to death in some empty hollow.

After two or three minutes of terrible silence, Dorian turned round, and came and stood behind him, putting his hand upon his shoulder.

'I am so sorry for you, Alan,' he murmured, 'but you leave me no alternative. I have a letter written already. Here it is. You see the address. If you don't help me, I must send it. If you don't help me, I will send it. You know what the result will be. But you are going to help me. It is impossible for you to refuse now. I tried to spare you. You will do me the justice to admit that. You were stern, harsh, offensive. You treated me as no man has ever dared to treat me – no living man, at any rate. I bore it all. Now it is for me to dictate terms.'

Campbell buried his face in his hands, and a shudder passed through him.

'Yes, it is my turn to dictate terms, Alan. You know what they are. The thing is quite simple. Come, don't work yourself into this fever. The thing has to be done. Face it, and do it.'

A groan broke from Campbell's lips, and he shivered all over. The ticking of the clock on the mantelpiece seemed to him to be dividing Time into separate atoms of agony, each of which was too terrible to be borne. He felt as if an iron ring was being slowly tightened round his forehead, as if the disgrace with which he was threatened had already come upon him. The hand upon his shoulder weighed like a hand of lead. It was intolerable. It seemed to crush him.

'Come, Alan, you must decide at once.'

'I cannot do it,' he said mechanically, as though words could alter things.

'You must. You have no choice. Don't delay.'

He hesitated a moment. 'Is there a fire in the room upstairs?'

'Yes, there is a gas-fire with asbestos.'

'I shall have to go home and get some things from the laboratory.'

'No, Alan, you must not leave the house. Write out on a sheet of notepaper what you want, and my servant will take a cab and bring the things back to you.'

Campbell scrawled a few lines, blotted them, and addressed an envelope to his assistant. Dorian took the note up and read it carefully. Then he rang the bell and gave it to his valet, with orders to return as soon as possible, and to bring the things with him.

As the hall door shut, Campbell started nervously, and, having got up from the chair, went over to the chimney-piece. He was shivering with a kind of ague. For nearly twenty minutes neither of the men spoke. A fly buzzed noisily about the room, and the ticking of the clock was like the beat of a hammer.

As the chime struck one, Campbell turned round, and, looking at Dorian Gray, saw that his eyes were filled with tears. There was something in the purity and refinement of that sad face that seemed to enrage him. 'You are infamous, absolutely infamous!' he muttered.

'Hush, Alan: you have saved my life,' said Dorian.

'Your life? Good heavens! What a life that is! You have gone from corruption to corruption, and now you have culminated in crime. In doing what I am going to do, what you force me to do, it is not of your life that I am thinking.'

'Ah, Alan,' murmured Dorian, with a sigh, 'I wish you had a thousandth part of the pity for me that I have for you.' He turned away as he spoke, and stood looking out at the garden. Campbell made no answer.

After about ten minutes a knock came to the door, and the servant entered, carrying a large mahogany chest of chemicals, with a long coil of steel and platinum wire and two rather curiously-shaped iron clamps.

'Shall I leave the things here, sir?' he asked Campbell.

'Yes,' said Dorian. 'And I am afraid, Francis, that I have another errand for you. What is the name of the man at Richmond who supplies Selby with orchids?'

'Harden, sir.'

'Yes – Harden. You must go down to Richmond at once, see Harden personally, and tell him to send twice as many orchids as I ordered, and to have as few white ones as possible. In fact, I don't want any white ones. It is a lovely day, Francis, and Richmond is a very pretty place, otherwise I wouldn't bother you about it.'

'No trouble, sir. At what time shall I be back?'

Dorian looked at Campbell. 'How long will your experiment take, Alan?' he said in a calm, indifferent voice. The presence of a third person in the room seemed to give him extraordinary courage.

Campbell frowned, and bit his lip. 'It will take about five hours,' he answered.

'It will be time enough, then, if you are back at half-past seven, Francis. Or stay: just leave my things out for dressing. You can have the evening to yourself. I am not dining at home, so I shall not want you.'

'Thank you, sir,' said the man, leaving the room.

'Now, Alan, there is not a moment to be lost. How heavy this chest is! I'll take it for you. You bring the other things.' He spoke rapidly, and in an authoritative manner. Campbell felt dominated by him. They left the room together.

When they reached the top landing, Dorian took out the key and turned it in the lock. Then he stopped, and a troubled look came into his eyes. He shuddered. 'I don't think I can go in, Alan,' he murmured.

'It is nothing to me. I don't require you,' said Campbell, coldly.

Dorian half opened the door. As he did so, he saw the face of his portrait leering in the sunlight. On the floor in front of it the torn curtain was lying. He remembered that the night before he had forgotten, for the first time in his life, to hide the fatal canvas, and was about to rush forward, when he drew back with a shudder.

What was that loathsome red dew that gleamed, wet and glistening, on one of the hands, as though the canvas had sweated blood? How horrible it was! – more horrible, it seemed to him for the moment, than the silent thing that he knew was stretched across the table, the thing whose grotesque misshapen shadow on the spotted carpet showed him that it had not stirred, but was still there, as he had left it.

He heaved a deep breath, opened the door a little wider, and with half-closed eyes and averted head walked quickly in, determined that he would not look even once upon the dead man. Then, stooping down, and taking up the gold and purple hanging, he flung it right over the picture.

There he stopped, feeling afraid to turn round, and his eyes fixed them-selves on the intricacies of the pattern before him. He heard Campbell bring-ing in the heavy chest, and the irons, and the other things that he had required for his dreadful work. He began to wonder if he and Basil Hallward had ever met, and, if so, what they had thought of each other.

'Leave me now,' said a stern voice behind him.

He turned and hurried out, just conscious that the dead man had been thrust back into the chair, and that Campbell was gazing into a glistening yellow face. As he was going downstairs he heard the key being turned in the lock.

It was long after seven when Campbell came back into the library. He was pale, but absolutely calm. 'I have done what you asked me to do,' he mut-tered. 'And now, good-bye. Let us never see each other again.'

'You have saved me from ruin, Alan. I cannot forget that,' said Dorian, simply.

As soon as Campbell had left, he went upstairs. There was a horrible smell of nitric acid in the room. But the thing that had been sitting at the table was gone.

15

THAT evening, at eight-thirty, exquisitely dressed and wearing a large but-ton-hole of Parma violets, Dorian Gray was ushered into Lady Narbo-rough's drawing-room by bowing servants. His forehead was throbbing with maddened nerves, and he felt wildly excited, but his manner as he bent over his hostess's hand was as easy and graceful as ever. Perhaps one never seems so much at one's ease as when one has to play a part. Certainly no one looking at Dorian Gray that night could have believed that he had passed through a tragedy as horrible as any tragedy of our age. Those finely-shaped fingers could never have clutched a knife for sin, nor those smiling lips have cried out on God and goodness. He himself could not help wondering at the calm of his demeanour, and for a moment felt keenly the terrible pleasure of a double life.

It was a small party, got up rather in a hurry by Lady Narborough, who was a very clever woman, with what Lord Henry used to describe as the remains of really remarkable ugliness. She had proved an excellent wife to one of our most tedious ambassadors, and having buried her husband properly in a marble mausoleum, which she had herself designed, and married off her daughters to some rich, rather elderly men, she devoted herself now to the pleasures of French fiction, French cookery, and French *esprit* when she could get it.

Dorian was one of her special favourites, and she always told him that she was extremely glad she had not met him in early life. 'I know, my dear, I should have fallen madly in love with you,' she used to say, 'and thrown my bonnet right over the mills for your sake. It is most fortunate that you were not thought of at the time. As it was, our bonnets were so unbecoming, and the mills were so occupied in trying to raise the wind, that I never had even a flirtation with anybody. However, that was all Narborough's fault. He was dreadfully short-sighted, and there is no pleasure in taking in a husband who never sees anything.'

Her guests this evening were rather tedious. The fact was, as she explained to Dorian, behind a very shabby fan, one of her married daughters had come up quite suddenly to stay with her, and, to make matters worse, had actually brought her husband with her. 'I think it is most unkind of her, my dear,' she whispered. 'Of course I go and stay with them every summer after I come from Homburg, but then an old woman like me must have fresh air sometimes, and besides, I really wake them up. You don't know what an existence they lead down there. It is pure unadulterated country life. They get up early, because they have so much to do, and go to bed early because they have so little to think about. There has not been a scandal in the neighbourhood since the time of Queen Elizabeth, and consequently they all fall asleep after dinner. You shan't sit next either of them. You shall sit by me, and amuse me.'

Dorian murmured a graceful compliment, and looked round the room. Yes; it was certainly a tedious party. Two of the people he had never seen before, and the others consisted of Ernest Harrowden, one of those middle-aged mediocrities so common in London clubs who have no enemies, but are thoroughly disliked by their friends; Lady Ruxton, an over-dressed woman of forty-seven, with a hooked nose, who was always trying to get herself compromised, but was so peculiarly plain that to her great disappointment no one would ever believe anything against her; Mrs. Erlynne, a pushing nobody, with a delightful lisp, and Venetian-red hair; Lady Alice Chapman, his hostess's daughter, a dowdy dull girl, with one of those characteristic British faces, that, once seen, are never remembered; and her husband, a red-cheeked, white-whiskered creature who, like so many of his class, was under the impression that inordinate joviality can atone for an entire lack of ideas.

He was rather sorry he had come, till Lady Narborough, looking at the great ormolu gilt clock that sprawled in gaudy curves on the mauve-draped mantelshelf, exclaimed: 'How horrid of Henry Wotton to be so late! I sent round to him this mo. ning on chance, and he promised faithfully not to disappoint me.'

It was some consolation that Harry was to be there, and when the door opened and he heard his slow musical voice lending charm to some insincere apology, he ceased to feel bored.

But at dinner he could not eat anything. Plate after plate went away untasted. Lady Narborough kept scolding him for what she called 'an insult to poor Adolphe, who invented the *menu* specially for you,' and now and then Lord Henry looked across at him, wondering at his silence and abstracted manner. From time to time the butler filled his glass with champagne. He drank eagerly, and his thirst seemed to increase.

'Dorian,' said Lord Henry at last, as the *chaudfroid* was being handed round, 'what is the matter with you to-night? You are quite out of sorts.'

'I believe he is in love,' cried Lady Narborough, 'and that he is afraid to tell me for fear I should be jealous. He is quite right. I certainly should.'

'Dear Lady Narborough,' murmured Dorian, smiling, 'I have not been in love for a whole week – not, in fact, since Madame de Ferrol left town.'

'How you men can fall in love with that woman!' exclaimed the old lady. 'I really cannot understand it.'

'It is simply because she remembers you when you were a little girl, Lady Narborough,' said Lord Henry. 'She is the one link between us and your short frocks.'

'She does not remember my short frocks at all, Lord Henry. But I remember her very well at Vienna thirty years ago, and how *décolletée* she was then.'

'She is still *décolletée*,' he answered, taking an olive in his long fingers; 'and when she is in a very smart gown she looks like an *édition de luxe* of a bad French novel. She is really wonderful, and full of surprises. Her capacity for family affection is extraordinary. When her third husband died, her hair turned quite gold from grief.'

'How can you, Harry!' cried Dorian.

'It is a most romantic explanation,' laughed the hostess. 'But her third husband, Lord Henry! You don't mean to say Ferrol is the fourth.'

'Certainly, Lady Narborough.'

'I don't believe a word of it.'

'Well, ask Mr. Gray. He is one of her most intimate friends.'

'Is it true, Mr. Gray?'

'She assures me so, Lady Narborough,' said Dorian. 'I asked her whether, like Marguerite de Navarre, she had their hearts embalmed and hung at her girdle. She told me she didn't, because none of them had any hearts at all.'

'Four husbands! Upon my word that is *trop de zèle*.'

'*Trop d'audace*, I tell her,' said Dorian.

'Oh! she is audacious enough for anything, my dear. And what is Ferrol like? I don't know him.'

'The husbands of very beautiful women belong to the criminal classes,' said Lord Henry, sipping his wine.

Lady Narborough hit him with her fan. 'Lord Henry, I am not at all surprised that the world says that you are extremely wicked.'

'But what world says that?' asked Lord Henry, elevating his eyebrows. 'It can only be the next world. This world and I are on excellent terms.'

'Everybody I know says you are very wicked,' cried the old lady, shaking her head.

Lord Henry looked serious for some moments. 'It is perfectly monstrous,' he said at last, 'the way people go about nowadays saying things against one behind one's back that are absolutely and entirely true.'

'Isn't he incorrigible?' cried Dorian, leaning forward in his chair.

'I hope so,' said his hostess, laughing. 'But really if you all worship Madame de Ferrol in this ridiculous way, I shall have to marry again so as to be in the fashion.'

'You will never marry again, Lady Narborough,' broke in Lord Henry. 'You were far too happy. When a woman marries again it is because she detested her first husband. When a man marries again, it is because he adored his first wife. Women try their luck; men risk theirs.'

'Narborough wasn't perfect,' cried the old lady.

'If he had been, you would not have loved him, my dear lady,' was the rejoinder. 'Women love us for our defects. If we have enough of them they will forgive us everything, even our intellects. You will never ask me to dinner again, after saying this, I am afraid, Lady Narborough; but it is quite true.'

'Of course it is true, Lord Henry. If we women did not love you for your defects, where would you all be? Not one of you would ever be married. You would be a set of unfortunate bachelors. Not, however, that that would alter you much. Nowadays all the married men live like bachelors, and all the bachelors like married men.'

'*Fin de siècle*,' murmured Lord Henry.

'*Fin du globe*,' answered his hostess.

'I wish it were *fin du globe*,' said Dorian with a sigh. 'Life is a great disappointment.'

'Ah, my dear,' cried Lady Narborough, putting on her gloves, 'don't tell me that you have exhausted Life. When a man says that one knows that life has exhausted him. Lord Henry is very wicked, and I sometimes wish that I had been; but you are made to be good – you look so good. I must find you a nice wife. Lord Henry, don't you think that Mr. Gray should get married?'

'I am always telling him so, Lady Narborough,' said Lord Henry, with a bow.

'Well, we must look out for a suitable match for him. I shall go through Debrett carefully to-night, and draw out a list of all the eligible young ladies.'

'With their ages, Lady Narborough?' asked Dorian.

'Of course, with their ages, slightly edited. But nothing must be done in a hurry. I want it to be what *The Morning Post* calls a suitable alliance, and I want you both to be happy.'

'What nonsense people talk about happy marriages!' exclaimed Lord Henry. 'A man can be happy with any woman, as long as he does not love her.'

'Ah! what a cynic you are!' cried the old lady, pushing back her chair, and nodding to Lady Ruxton. 'You must come and dine with me soon again. You are really an admirable tonic, much better than what Sir Andrew prescribes for me. You must tell me what people you would like to meet, though. I want it to be a delightful gathering.'

'I like men who have a future, and women who have a past,' he answered. 'Or do you think that would make it a petticoat party?'

'I fear so,' she said, laughing, as she stood up. 'A thousand pardons, my dear Lady Ruxton,' she added. 'I didn't see you hadn't finished your cigarette.'

'Never mind, Lady Narborough. I smoke a great deal too much. I am going to limit myself for the future.'

'Pray don't, Lady Ruxton,' said Lord Henry. 'Moderation is a fatal thing. Enough is as bad as a meal. More than enough is as good as a feast.'

Lady Ruxton glanced at him curiously. 'You must come and explain that to me some afternoon, Lord Henry. It sounds a fascinating theory,' she murmured, as she swept out of the room.

'Now, mind you don't stay too long over your politics and scandal,' cried Lady Narborough from the door. 'If you do, we are sure to squabble upstairs.'

The men laughed, and Mr. Chapman got up solemnly from the foot of the table and came up to the top. Dorian Gray changed his seat, and went and sat by Lord Henry. Mr. Chapman began to talk in a loud voice about the situation in the House of Commons. He guffawed at his adversaries. The word *doctrinaire* – word full of terror to the British mind – reappeared from time to time between his explosions. An alliterative prefix served as an ornament of oratory. He hoisted the Union Jack on the pinnacles of Thought. The inherited stupidity of the race – sound English common sense he jovially termed it – was shown to be the proper bulwark for Society.

A smile curved Lord Henry's lips, and he turned round and looked at Dorian.

'Are you better, my dear fellow?' he asked. 'You seemed rather out of sorts at dinner.'

'I am quite well, Harry. I am tired. That is all.'

'You were charming last night. The little Duchess is quite devoted to you. She tells me she is going down to Selby.'

'She has promised to come on the twentieth.'

'Is Monmouth to be there too?'

'Oh, yes, Harry.'

'He bores me dreadfully, almost as much as he bores her. She is very clever, too clever for a woman. She lacks the indefinable charm of weakness. It is the feet of clay that makes the gold of the image precious. Her feet are very pretty, but they are not feet of clay. White porcelain feet, if you like.

They have been through the fire. and what fire does not destroy, it hardens. She has had experiences.'

'How long has she been married?' asked Dorian.

'An eternity, she tells me. I believe, according to the peerage, it is ten years, but ten years with Monmouth must have been like eternity, with time thrown in. Who else is coming?'

'Oh, the Willoughbys, Lord Rugby and his wife, our hostess, Geoffrey Clouston, the usual set. I have asked Lord Grotrian.'

'I like him,' said Lord Henry. 'A great many people don't, but I find him charming. He atones for being occasionally somewhat over-dressed, by being always absolutely over-educated. He is a very modern type.'

'I don't know if he will be able to come, Harry. He may have to go to Monte Carlo with his father.'

'Ah! what a nuisance people's people are! Try and make him come. By the way, Dorian, you ran off very early last night. You left before eleven. What did you do afterwards? Did you go straight home?'

Dorian glanced at him hurriedly, and frowned. 'No, Harry,' he said at last. 'I did not get home till nearly three.'

'Did you go to the club?'

'Yes,' he answered. Then he bit his lip. 'No, I don't mean that. I didn't go to the club. I walked about. I forget what I did.... How inquisitive you are, Harry! You always want to know what one has been doing. I always want to forget what I have been doing. I came in at half-past two, if you wish to know the exact time. I had left my latch-key at home, and my servant had to let me in. If you want any corroborative evidence on the subject you can ask him.'

Lord Henry shrugged his shoulders. 'My dear fellow, as if I cared! Let us go up to the drawing-room. No sherry, thank you, Mr. Chapman. Something has happened to you, Dorian. Tell me what it is. You are not yourself to-night.'

'Don't mind me, Harry. I am irritable and out of temper. I shall come round and see you to-morrow or next day. Make my excuses to Lady Narborough. I shan't go upstairs. I shall go home. I must go home.'

'All right, Dorian. I daresay I shall see you to-morrow at tea-time. The Duchess is coming.'

'I will try to be there, Harry,' he said, leaving the room. As he drove back to his own house he was conscious that the sense of terror he thought he had strangled had come back to him. Lord Henry's casual questioning had made him lose his nerves for the moment, and he wanted his nerve still. Things that were dangerous had to be destroyed. He winced. He hated the idea of even touching them.

Yet it had to be done. He realised that, and when he had locked the door of his library, he opened the secret press into which he had thrust Basil Hallward's coat and bag. A huge fire was blazing. He piled another log on it. The smell of the singeing clothes and burning leather was horrible. It took him three-quarters of an hour to consume everything. At the end he felt faint and sick, and having lit some Algerian pastilles in a pierced copper brazier, he bathed his hands and forehead with a cool musk-scented vinegar.

Suddenly he started. His eyes grew strangely bright, and he gnawed nervously at his under-lip. Between two of the windows stood a large Florentine cabinet, made out of ebony, and inlaid with ivory and blue lapis. He watched it as though it were a thing that could fascinate and make afraid, as though it held something that he longed for and yet almost loathed. His breath quickened. A mad craving came over him. He lit a cigarette and then threw it away. His eyelids drooped till the long fringed lashes almost touched his cheek. But he still watched the cabinet. At last he got up from the sofa on which he had been lying, went over to it, and, having unlocked it, touched some hidden spring. A triangular drawer passed slowly out. His fingers moved instinctively towards it, dipped in, and closed on something. It was a small Chinese box of black and gold-dust lacquer, elaborately wrought, the sides patterned with curved waves, and the silken cords hung with round crystals and tasselled in plaited metal threads. He opened it. Inside was a green paste, waxy in lustre, the odour curiously heavy and persistent.

He hesitated for some moments, with a strangely immobile smile upon his face. Then shivering, though the atmosphere of the room was terribly hot, he drew himself up, and glanced at the clock. It was twenty minutes to twelve. He put the box back, shutting the cabinet doors as he did so, and went into his bedroom.

As midnight was striking bronze blows upon the dusky air, Dorian Gray dressed commonly, and with a muffler wrapped round his throat, crept quietly out of the house. In Bond Street he found a hansom with a good horse. He hailed it, and in a low voice gave the driver an address.

The man shook his head. 'It is too far for me,' he muttered.

'Here is a sovereign for you,' said Dorian. 'You shall have another if you drive fast.'

'All right, sir,' answered the man, 'you will be there in an hour,' and after his fare had got in he turned his horse round, and drove rapidly towards the river.

16

A COLD rain began to fall, and the blurred street-lamps looked ghastly in the dipping mist. The public-houses were just closing and dim men and women were clustering in broken groups round their doors. From some of the bars came the sound of horrible laughter. In others, drunkards brawled and screamed.

Lying back in the hansom, with his hat pulled over his forehead, Dorian Gray watched with listless eyes the sordid shame of the great city, and now and then he repeated to himself the words that Lord Henry had said to him on the first day they had met, 'To cure the soul by means of the senses, and the senses by means of the soul.' Yes, that was the secret. He had often tried it, and would try it again now. There were opium-dens, where one could buy oblivion, dens of horror where the memory of old sins could be destroyed by the madness of sins that were new.

The moon hung low in the sky like a yellow skull. From time to time a huge misshapen cloud stretched a long arm across and hid it. The gas-lamps grew fewer, and the streets more narrow and gloomy. Once the man lost his way, and had to drive back half a mile. A steam rose from the horse as it splashed up the puddles. The side-windows of the hansom were clogged with a grey-flannel mist.

'To cure the soul by means of the senses, and the senses by means of the soul!' How the words rang in his ears! His soul, certainly, was sick to death. Was it true that the senses could cure it? Innocent blood had been spilt. What could atone for that? Ah! for that there was no atonement; but though forgiveness was impossible, forgetfulness was possible still, and he was determined to forget, to stamp the thing out, to crush it as one would crush the adder that had stung one. Indeed, what right had Basil to have spoken to him as he had done? Who had made him a judge over others? He had said things that were dreadful, horrible, not to be endured.

On and on plodded the hansom, going slower, it seemed to him, at each step. He thrust up the trap, and called to the man to drive faster. The hideous hunger for opium began to gnaw at him. His throat burned, and his delicate hands twitched nervously together. He struck at the horse madly with his stick. The driver laughed, and whipped up. He laughed in answer, and the man was silent.

The way seemed interminable, and the streets like the black web of some sprawling spider. The monotony became unbearable, and, as the mist thickened, he felt afraid.

Then they passed by lonely brickfields. The fog was lighter here, and he could see the strange bottle shaped kilns with their orange fan-like tongues of fire. A dog barked as they went by, and far away in the darkness some wandering sea-gull screamed. The horse stumbled in a rut, then swerved aside, and broke into a gallop.

After some time they left the clay road, and rattled again over rough-paven streets. Most of the windows were dark, but now and then fantastic shadows were silhouetted against some lamp-lit blind. He watched them curiously. They moved like monstrous marionettes, and made gestures like live things. He hated them. A dull rage was in his heart. As they turned a corner a woman yelled something at them from an open door, and two men ran after the hansom for about a hundred yards. The driver beat at them with his whip.

It is said that passion makes one think in a circle. Certainly with hideous iteration the bitten lips of Dorian Gray shaped and reshaped those subtle words that dealt with soul and sense, till he had found in them the full expression, as it were, of his mood, and justified, by intellectual approval, passions that without such justification would still have dominated his temper. From cell to cell of his brain crept the one thought; and the wild desire to live, most terrible of all man's appetites, quickened into force each trembling nerve and fibre. Ugliness that had once been hateful to him because it made things real, became dear to him now for that very reason. Ugliness was the one reality. The coarse brawl, the loathsome den, the crude violence of disordered life, the very vileness of thief and outcast, were more vivid, in their intense actuality of impression, than all the gracious shapes of Art, the dreamy shadows of Song. They were what he needed for forgetfulness. In three days he would be free.

Suddenly the man drew up with a jerk at the top of a dark lane. Over the low roofs and jagged chimney stacks of the houses rose the black masts of ships. Wreaths of white mist clung like ghostly sails to the yards.

'Somewhere about here, sir, ain't it?' he asked huskily through the trap.

Dorian started, and peered round. 'This will do,' he answered, and, having got out hastily, and given the driver the extra fare he had promised him, he walked quickly in the direction of the quay. Here and there a lantern gleamed at the stern of some huge merchantman. The light shook and splintered in the puddles. A red glare came from an outward-bound steamer that was coaling. The slimy pavement looked like a wet mackintosh.

He hurried on towards the left, glancing back now and then to see if he was being followed. In about seven or eight minutes he reached a small shabby house, that was wedged in between two gaunt factories. In one of the top windows stood a lamp. He stopped, and gave a peculiar knock.

After a little time he heard steps in the passage, and the chain being unhooked. The door opened quietly, and he went in without saying a word to the squat misshapen figure that flattened itself into the shadow as he passed. At the end of the hall hung a tattered green curtain that swayed and shook in the gusty wind which had followed him in from the street. He dragged it aside, and entered a long, low room which looked as if it had once been a third-rate dancing-saloon. Shrill flaring gas jets, dulled and distorted in the fly-blown mirrors that faced them, were ranged round the walls. Greasy reflectors of ribbed tin backed them, making quivering discs of light. The floor was covered with ochre-coloured sawdust, trampled here and there into mud, and stained with dark rings of spilt liquor. Some Malays were crouching by a little charcoal stove playing with bone counters and showing their white teeth as they chattered. In one corner, with his head buried in his arms, a sailor sprawled over a table, and by the tawdrily-painted bar that ran across one complete side stood two haggard women mocking an old man who was brushing the sleeves of his coat with an expression of disgust. 'He thinks he's got red ants on him,' laughed one of them, as Dorian passed by. The man looked at her in terror and began to whimper.

At the end of the room there was a little staircase, leading to a darkened chamber. As Dorian hurried up its three rickety steps, the heavy odour of opium met him. He heaved a deep breath, and his nostrils quivered with pleasure. When he entered, a young man with smooth yellow hair, who was bending over a lamp, lighting a long thin pipe, looked up at him, and nodded in a hesitating manner.

'You here, Adrian?' muttered Dorian.

'Where else should I be?' he answered, listlessly. 'None of the chaps will speak to me now.'

'I thought you had left England.'

'Darlington is not going to do anything. My brother paid the bill at last. George doesn't speak to me either.... I don't care,' he added, with a sigh. 'As long as one has this stuff, one doesn't want friends. I think I have had too many friends.'

Dorian winced, and looked round at the grotesque things that lay in such fantastic postures on the ragged mattresses. The twisted limbs, the gaping mouths, the staring lustreless eyes, fascinated him. He knew in what strange heavens they were suffering, and what dull hells were teaching them the secret of some new joy. They were better off than he was. He was prisoned in thought. Memory, like a horrible malady, was eating his soul away. From time to time he seemed to see the eyes of Basil Hallward looking at him. Yet he felt he could not stay. The presence of Adrian Singleton troubled him. He wanted to be where no man would know who he was. He wanted to escape from himself.

'I am going on to the other place,' he said, after a pause.

'On the wharf?'

'Yes.'

'That mad-cat is sure to be there. They won't have her in this place now.'

Dorian shrugged his shoulders. 'I am sick of women who love one. Women who hate one are much more interesting. Besides, the stuff is better.'

'Much the same.'

'I like it better. Come and have something to drink. I must have something.'·

'I don't want anything,' murmured the young man.

'Never mind.'

Adrian Singleton rose up wearily, and followed Dorian to the bar. A half-caste, in a ragged turban and a shabby ulster, grinned a hideous greeting as he thrust a bottle of brandy and two tumblers in front of them. The women sidled up, and began to chatter. Dorian turned his back on them, and said something in a low voice to Adrian Singleton.

A crooked smile, like a Malay crease, writhed across the face of one of the women.

'We are very proud to-night,' she sneered.

'For God's sake don't talk to me,' cried Dorian, stamping his foot on the ground. 'What do you want? Money? Here it is. Don't ever talk to me again.'

Two red sparks flashed for a moment in the woman's sodden eyes, then flickered out, and left them dull and glazed. She tossed her head, and raked the coins off the counter with greedy fingers. Her companion watched her enviously.

'It's no use,' sighed Adrian Singleton. 'I don't care to go back. What does it matter? I am quite happy here.'

'You will write to me if you want anything, won't you?' said Dorian, after a pause.

'Perhaps.'

'Good-night, then.'

'Good-night,' answered the young man, passing up the steps, and wiping his parched mouth with a handkerchief.

Dorian walked to the door with a look of pain in his face. As he drew the curtain aside a hideous laugh broke from the painted lips of the woman who had taken his money. 'There goes the devil's bargain!' she hiccoughed, in a hoarse voice.

'Curse you!' he answered, 'don't call me that.'

She snapped her fingers. 'Prince Charming is what you like to be called, ain't it?' she yelled after him.

The drowsy sailor leapt to his feet as she spoke, and looked wildly round. The sound of the shutting of the hall door fell on his ear. He rushed out as if in pursuit.

Dorian Gray hurried along the quay through the drizzling rain. His meeting with Adrian Singleton had strangely moved him, and he wondered if the ruin of that young life was really to be laid at his door, as Basil Hallward had said to him with such infamy of insult. He bit his lip, and for a few seconds his eyes grew sad. Yet, after all, what did it matter to him? One's days were too brief to take the burden of another's errors on one's shoulders. Each man lived his own life, and paid his own price for living it. The only pity was one had to pay so often for a single fault. One had to pay over and over again, indeed. In her dealings with man Destiny never closed her accounts.

There are moments, psychologists tell us, when the passion for sin, or for what the world calls sin, so dominates a nature, that every fibre of the body, as every cell of the brain, seems to be instinct with fearful impulses. Men and women at such moments lose the freedom of their will. They move to their terrible end as automatons move. Choice is taken from them, and conscience is either killed, or, if it lives at all, lives but to give rebellion its fascination, and disobedience its charm. For all sins, as theologians weary not of reminding us, are sins of disobedience. When that high spirit, that morning-star of evil, fell from heaven, it was as a rebel that he fell.

Callous, concentrated on evil, with stained mien, and soul hungry for rebellion, Dorian Gray hastened on, quickening his step as he went, but as he darted aside into a dim archway, that had served him often as a short cut to the ill-famed place where he was going, he felt himself suddenly seized from behind, and before he had time to defend himself he was thrust back against the wall, with a brutal hand round his throat.

He struggled madly for life, and by a terrible effort wrenched the tightening fingers away. In a second he heard the click of a revolver, and saw the gleam of a polished barrel pointing straight at his head, and the dusky form of a short thick-set man facing him.

'What do you want?' he gasped.

'Keep quiet,' said the man. 'If you stir, I shoot you.'

'You are mad. What have I done to you?'

'You wrecked the life of Sibyl Vane,' was the answer, 'and Sibyl Vane was my sister. She killed herself. I know it. Her death is at your door. I swore I would kill you in return. For years I have sought you. I had no clue, no trace. The two people who could have described you were dead. I knew nothing of you but the pet name she used to call you. I heard it to-night by chance. Make your peace with God, for to-night you are going to die.'

Dorian Gray grew sick with fear. 'I never knew her,' he stammered. 'I never heard of her. You are mad.'

'You had better confess your sin, for as sure as I am James Vane, you are going to die.' There was a horrible moment. Dorian did not know what to say or do. 'Down on your knees!' growled the man. 'I give you one minute to make your peace – no more. I go on board to-night for India, and I must do my job first. One minute. That's all.'

Dorian's arms fell to his side. Paralysed with terror, he did not know what to do. Suddenly a wild hope flashed across his brain. 'Stop,' he cried. 'How long ago is it since your sister died? Quick, tell me!'

'Eighteen years,' said the man. 'Why do you ask me? What do years matter?'

'Eighteen years,' laughed Dorian Gray, with a touch of triumph in his voice. 'Eighteen years! Set me under the lamp and look at my face!'

James Vane hesitated for a moment, not understanding what was meant. Then he seized Dorian Gray and dragged him from the archway.

Dim and wavering as was the wind-blown light, yet it served to show him the hideous error, as it seemed, into which he had fallen, for the face of the man he had sought to kill had all the bloom of boyhood, all the unstained purity of youth. He seemed little older than a lad of twenty summers, hardly older, if older indeed at all, than his sister had been when they had parted so many years ago. It was obvious that this was not the man who had destroyed her life.

He loosened his hold and reeled back. 'My God! my God!' he cried, 'and I would have murdered you!'

Dorian Gray drew a long breath. 'You have been on the brink of committing a terrible crime, my man,' he said, looking at him sternly. 'Let this be a warning to you not to take vengeance into your own hands.'

'Forgive me, sir,' muttered James Vane. 'I was deceived. A chance word I heard in that damned den set me on the wrong track.'

'You had better go home, and put that pistol away, or you may get into trouble,' said Dorian, turning on his heel, and going slowly down the street.

James Vane stood on the pavement in horror. He was trembling from head to foot. After a little while a black shadow that had been creeping along the dripping wall moved out into the light and came close to him with stealthy footsteps. He felt a hand laid on his arm and looked round with a start. It was one of the women who had been drinking at the bar.

'Why didn't you kill him?' she hissed out, putting her haggard face quite close to his. 'I knew you were following him when you rushed out from Daly's. You fool! You should have killed him. He has lots of money, and he's as bad as bad.'

'He is not the man I am looking for,' he answered, 'and I want no man's money. I want a man's life. The man whose life I want must be nearly forty now. This one is little more than a boy. Thank God, I have not got his blood upon my hands.'

The woman gave a bitter laugh. 'Little more than a boy!' she sneered. 'Why, man, it's nigh on eighteen years since Prince Charming made me what I am.'

'You lie!' cried James Vane.

She raised her hand up to heaven. 'Before God I am telling the truth,' she cried.

'Before God?'

'Strike me dumb if it ain't so. He is the worst one that comes here. They say he has sold himself to the devil for a pretty face. It's nigh on eighteen years since I met him. He hasn't changed much since then. I have though,' she added, with a sickly leer.

'You swear this?'

'I swear it,' came in hoarse echo from her flat mouth. 'But don't give me away to him,' she whined; 'I am afraid of him. Let me have some money for my night's lodging.'

He broke from her with an oath, and rushed to the corner of the street, but Dorian Gray had disappeared. When he looked back, the woman had vanished also.

17

A WEEK later Dorian Gray was sitting in the conservatory at Selby Royal talking to the pretty Duchess of Monmouth, who with her husband, a jaded-looking man of sixty, was amongst his guests. It was tea-time, and the mellow light of the huge lace-covered lamp that stood on the table lit up the delicate china and hammered silver of the service at which the Duchess was presiding. Her white hands were moving daintily among the cups, and her full red lips were smiling at something that Dorian had whispered to her. Lord Henry was lying back in a silk-draped wicker chair looking at them. On a peach-coloured divan sat Lady Narborough pretending to listen to the Duke's description of the last Brazilian beetle that he had added to his collection. Three young men in elaborate smoking-suits were handing tea-cakes to some of the women. The house-party consisted of twelve people, and there were more expected to arrive on the next day.

'What are you two talking about?' said Lord Henry, strolling over to the table, and putting his cup down. 'I hope Dorian has told you about my plan for rechristening everything, Gladys. It is a delightful idea.'

'But I don't want to be rechristened, Harry,' rejoined the Duchess, looking up at him with her wonderful eyes. 'I am quite satisfied with my own name, and I am sure Mr. Gray should be satisfied with his.'

'My dear Gladys, I would not alter either name for the world. They are both perfect. I was thinking chiefly of flowers. Yesterday I cut an orchid, for my buttonhole. It was a marvellous spotted thing, as effective as the seven deadly sins. In a thoughtless moment I asked one of the gardeners what it was called. He told me it was a fine specimen of *Robinsoniana*, or something dreadful of that kind. It is a sad truth, but we have lost the faculty of giving lovely names to things. Names are everything. I never quarrel with actions. My one quarrel is with words. That is the reason I hate vulgar realism in literature. The man who could call a spade a spade should be compelled to use one. It is the only thing he is fit for.'

'Then what should we call you, Harry?' she asked.

'His name is Prince Paradox,' said Dorian.

'I recognise him in a flash,' exclaimed the Duchess.

'I won't hear of it,' laughed Lord Henry, sinking into a chair. 'From a label there is no escape! I refuse the title.'

'Royalties may not abdicate,' fell as a warning from pretty lips.

'You wish me to defend my throne, then?'

'Yes.'

'I give the truths of to-morrow.'

'I prefer the mistakes of to-day,' she answered.

'You disarm me, Gladys,' he cried, catching the wilfulness of her mood.

'Of your shield, Harry: not of your spear.'

'I never tilt against beauty,' he said, with a wave of his hand.

'That is your error, Harry, believe me. You value beauty far too much.'

'How can you say that? I admit that I think that it is better to be beautiful than to be good. But on the other hand no one is more ready than I am to acknowledge that it is better to be good than to be ugly.'

'Ugliness is one of the seven deadly sins, then?' cried the Duchess. 'What becomes of your simile about the orchid?'

'Ugliness is one of the seven deadly virtues, Gladys. You, as a good Tory, must not underrate them. Beer, the Bible, and the seven deadly virtues have made our England what she is.'

'You don't like your country, then?' she asked.

'I live in it.'

'That you may censure it the better.'

'Would you have me take the verdict of Europe on it?' he inquired.

'What do they say of us?'

'That Tartuffe has emigrated to England and opened a shop.'

'Is that yours, Harry?'

'I give it to you.'

'I could not use it. It is too true.'

'You need not be afraid. Our countrymen never recognise a description.'

'They are practical.'

'They are more cunning than practical. When they make up their ledger, they balance stupidity by wealth, and vice by hypocrisy.'

'Still, we have done great things.'

'Great things have been thrust on us, Gladys.'

'We have carried their burden.'

'Only as far as the Stock Exchange.'

She shook her head. 'I believe in the race,' she cried.

'It represents the survival of the pushing.'

'It has development.'

'Decay fascinates me more.'

'What of Art?' she asked.

'It is a malady.'

'Love?'

'An illusion.'

'Religion?'

'The fashionable substitute for Belief.'

'You are a sceptic.'

'Never! Scepticism is the beginning of Faith.'

'What are you?'

'To define is to limit.'

'Give me a clue.'

'Threads snap. You would lose your way in the labyrinth.'

'You bewilder me. Let us talk of some one else.'

'Our host is a delightful topic. Years ago he was christened Prince Charming.'

'Ah! don't remind me of that,' cried Dorian Gray.

'Our host is rather horrid this evening,' answered the Duchess, colouring. 'I believe he thinks that Monmouth married me on purely scientific principles as the best specimen he could find of a modern butterfly.'

'Well, I hope he won't stick pins into you, Duchess,' laughed Dorian.

'Oh, my maid does that already, Mr. Gray, when she is annoyed with me.'

'And what does she get annoyed with you about, Duchess?'

'For the most trivial things, Mr. Gray, I assure you. Usually because I come in at ten minutes to nine and tell her that I must be dressed by half-past eight.'

'How unreasonable of her! You should give her warning.'

'I daren't, Mr. Gray. Why, she invents hats for me. You remember the one I wore at Lady Hilstone's garden-party? You don't, but it is nice of you to pretend that you do. Well, she made it out of nothing. All good hats are made out of nothing.'

'Like all good reputations, Gladys,' interrupted Lord Henry. 'Every effect that one produces gives one an enemy. To be popular one must be a mediocrity.'

'Not with women,' said the Duchess, shaking her head; 'and women rule the world. I assure you we can't bear mediocrities. We women, as some one says, love with our ears, just as you men love with your eyes, if you ever love at all.'

'It seems to me that we never do anything else,' murmured Dorian.

'Ah! then, you never really love, Mr. Gray,' answered the Duchess, with mock sadness.

'My dear Gladys!' cried Lord Henry. 'How can you say that? Romance lives by repetition, and repetition converts an appetite into an art. Besides, each time that one loves is the only time one has ever loved. Difference of object does not alter singleness of passion. It merely intensifies it. We can have in life but one great experience at best, and the secret of life is to reproduce that experience as often as possible.'

'Even when one has been wounded by it, Harry?' asked the Duchess, after a pause.

'Especially when one has been wounded by it,' answered Lord Henry.

The Duchess turned and looked at Dorian Gray with a curious expression in her eyes. 'What do you say to that, Mr. Gray?' she inquired.

Dorian hesitated for a moment. Then he threw his head back and laughed. 'I always agree with Harry, Duchess.'

'Even when he is wrong?'

'Harry is never wrong, Duchess.'

'And does his philosophy make you happy?'

'I have never searched for happiness. Who wants happiness? I have searched for pleasure.'

'And found it, Mr. Gray?'

'Often. Too often.'

The Duchess sighed. 'I am searching for peace,' she said, 'and if I don't go and dress, I shall have none this evening.'

'Let me get you some orchids, Duchess,' cried Dorian, starting to his feet, and walking down the conservatory.

'You are flirting disgracefully with him,' said Lord Henry to his cousin. 'You had better take care. He is very fascinating.'

'If he were not, there would be no battle.'

'Greek meets Greek, then?'

'I am on the side of the Trojans. They fought for a woman.'

'They were defeated.'

'There are worse things than capture,' she answered.

'You gallop with a loose rein.'

'Pace gives life,' was the *riposte*.

'I shall write it in my diary to-night.'

'What?'

'That a burnt child loves the fire.'

'I am not even singed. My wings are untouched.'

'You can use them for everything except flight.'

'Courage has passed from men to women. It is a new experience for us.'

'You have a rival.'

'Who?'

He laughed. 'Lady Narborough,' he whispered. 'She perfectly adores him.'

'You fill me with apprehension. The appeal to Antiquity is fatal to us who are romanticists.'

'Romanticists! You have all the methods of science.'

'Men have educated us.'

'But not explained you.'

'Describe us as a sex,' was her challenge.

'Sphynxes without secrets.'

She looked at him, smiling. 'How long Mr. Gray is!' she said. 'Let us go and help him. I have not yet told him the colour of my frock.'

'Ah! you must suit your frock to his flowers, Gladys.'

'That would be a premature surrender.'

'Romantic Art begins with its climax.'

'I must keep an opportunity for retreat.'

'In the Parthian manner?'

'They found safety in the desert. I could not do that.'

'Women are not always allowed a choice,' he answered, but hardly had he finished the sentence before from the far end of the conservatory came a stifled groan, followed by the dull sound of a heavy fall. Everybody started up. The Duchess stood motionless in horror. And with fear in his eyes Lord Henry rushed through the flapping palms to find Dorian Gray lying face downwards on the tiled floor in a death-like swoon.

He was carried at once into the blue drawing-room, and laid upon one of the sofas. After a short time he came to himself, and looked round with a dazed expression.

'What has happened?' he asked. 'Oh! I remember. Am I safe here, Harry?' He began to tremble.

'My dear Dorian,' answered Lord Henry, 'you merely fainted. That was all. You must have overtired yourself. You had better not come down to dinner. I will take your place.'

'No, I will come down,' he said, struggling to his feet. 'I would rather come down. I must not be alone.'

He went to his room and dressed. There was a wild recklessness of gaiety in his manner as he sat at table, but now and then a thrill of terror ran through him when he remembered that, pressed against the window of the conservatory, like a white handkerchief, he had seen the face of James Vane watching him.

18

THE next day he did not leave the house, and indeed, spent most of the time in his own room, sick with a wild terror of dying, and yet indifferent to life itself. The consciousness of being hunted, snared, tracked down, had begun to dominate him. If the tapestry did but tremble in the wind, he shook. The dead leaves that were blown against the leaded panes seemed to him like his own wasted resolutions and wild regrets. When he closed his eyes, he saw again the sailor's face peering through the mist-stained glass, and horror seemed once more to lay its hand upon his heart.

But perhaps it had been only his fancy that had called vengeance out of the night, and set the hideous shapes of punishment before him. Actual life was chaos, but there was something terribly logical in the imagination. It was the imagination that set remorse to dog the feet of sin. It was the imagination that made each crime bear its misshapen brood. In the common world of fact the wicked were not punished, nor the good rewarded. Success was given to the strong, failure thrust upon the weak. That was all. Besides, had any stranger been prowling round the house he would have been seen by the servants or the keepers. Had any footmarks been found on the flower-beds, the gardeners would have reported it. Yes: it had been merely fancy. Sibyl Vane's brother had not come back to kill him. He had sailed away in his ship to founder in some winter sea. From him, at any rate, he was safe. Why, the man did not know who he was, could not know who he was. The mask of youth had saved him.

And yet if it had been merely an illusion, how terrible it was to think that conscience could raise such fearful phantoms, and give them visible form, and make them move before one! What sort of life would his be, if day and night, shadows of his crime were to peer at him from silent corners, to mock him from secret places, to whisper in his ear as he sat at the feast, to wake him with icy fingers as he lay asleep! As the thought crept through his brain, he grew pale with terror, and the air seemed to him to have become suddenly colder. Oh! in what a wild hour of madness he had killed his friend! How ghastly the mere memory of the scene! He saw it all again. Each hideous detail came back to him with added horror. Out of the black cave of Time, terrible and swathed in scarlet, rose the image of his sin. When Lord Henry came in at six o'clock, he found him crying as one whose heart will break.

It was not till the third day that he ventured to go out. There was something in the clear, pine-scented air of that winter morning that seemed to bring him back his joyousness and his ardour for life. But it was not merely the physical conditions of environment that had caused the change. His own nature had revolted against the excess of anguish that had sought to maim and mar the perfection of its calm. With subtle and finely-wrought temperaments it is always so. Their strong passions must either bruise or bend. They either slay the man, or themselves die. Shallow sorrows and shallow loves live on. The loves and sorrows that are great are destroyed by their own plenitude. Besides, he had convinced himself that he had been the victim of a terror-stricken imagination, and looked back now on his fears with something of pity and not a little of contempt.

After breakfast he walked with the Duchess for an hour in the garden, and then drove across the park to join the shooting-party. The crisp frost lay like salt upon the grass. The sky was an inverted cup of blue metal. A thin film of ice bordered the flat reed-grown lake.

At the corner of the pine-wood he caught sight of Sir Geoffrey Clouston, the Duchess's brother, jerking two spent cartridges out of his gun. He jumped from the cart, and having told the groom to take the mare home, made his way towards his guest through the withered bracken and rough undergrowth.

'Have you had good sport, Geoffrey?' he asked.

'Not very good, Dorian. I think most of the birds have gone to the open. I dare say it will be better after lunch, when we get to new ground.'

Dorian strolled along by his side. The keen aromatic air, the brown and red lights that glimmered in the wood, the hoarse cries of the beaters ringing out from time to time, and the sharp snaps of the guns that followed, fascinated him, and filled him with a sense of delightful freedom. He was dominated by the carelessness of happiness, by the high indifference of joy.

Suddenly from a lumpy tussock of old grass, some twenty yards in front of them, with black-tipped ears erect, and long hinder limbs throwing it forward, started a hare. It bolted for a thicket of alders. Sir Geoffrey put his gun to his shoulder, but there was something in the animal's grace of movement that strangely charmed Dorian Gray, and he cried out at once, 'Don't shoot it, Geoffrey. Let it live.'

'What nonsense, Dorian!' laughed his companion, and as the hare bounded into the thicket he fired. There were two cries heard, the cry of a hare in pain, which is dreadful, the cry of a man in agony, which is worse.

'Good heavens! I have hit a beater!' exclaimed Sir Geoffrey. 'What an ass the man was to get in front of the guns! Stop shooting there!' he called out at the top of his voice. 'A man is hurt.'

The head-keeper came running up with a stick in his hand.

'Where, sir? Where is he?' he shouted. At the same time the firing ceased along the line.

'Here,' answered Sir Geoffrey, angrily, hurrying towards the thicket. 'Why on earth don't you keep your men back? Spoiled my shooting for the day.'

Dorian watched them as they plunged into the alder-clump, brushing the lithe, swinging branches aside. In a few moments they emerged, dragging a body after them into the sunlight. He turned away in horror. It seemed to him that misfortune followed wherever he went. He heard Sir Geoffrey ask if the man was really dead, and the affirmative answer of the keeper. The wood seemed to him to have become suddenly alive with faces. There was the trampling of myriad feet, and the low buzz of voices. A great copper-breasted pheasant came beating through the boughs overhead.

After a few moments, that were to him, in his perturbed state, like endless hours of pain, he felt a hand laid on his shoulder. He started, and looked round.

'Dorian,' said Lord Henry. 'I had better tell them that the shooting is stopped for to-day. It would not look well to go on.'

'I wish it were stopped for ever, Harry,' he answered bitterly. 'The whole thing is hideous and cruel. Is the man. . . ?'

He could not finish the sentence.

'I am afraid so,' rejoined Lord Henry. 'He got the whole charge of shot in his chest. He must have died almost instantaneously. Come; let us go home.'

They walked side by side in the direction of the avenue for nearly fifty yards without speaking. Then Dorian looked at Lord Henry, and said, with a heavy sigh, 'It is a bad omen, Harry, a very bad omen.'

'What is?' asked Lord Henry. 'Oh, this accident, I suppose. My dear fellow, it can't be helped. It was the man's own fault. Why did he get in front of the guns? Besides, it's nothing to us. It is rather awkward for Geoffrey, of course. It does not do to pepper beaters. It makes people think that one is a wild shot. And Geoffrey is not; he shoots very straight. But there is no use talking about the matter.'

Dorian shook his head. 'It is a bad omen, Harry. I feel as if something horrible were going to happen to some of us. To myself, perhaps,' he added, passing his hand over his eyes, with a gesture of pain.

The elder man laughed. 'The only horrible thing in the world is *ennui*, Dorian. That is the one sin for which there is no forgiveness. But we are not likely to suffer from it, unless these fellows keep chattering about this thing at dinner. I must tell them that the subject is to be tabooed. As for omens, there is no such thing as an omen. Destiny does not send us heralds. She is too wise or too cruel for that. Besides, what on earth could happen to you, Dorian? You have everything in the world that a man can want. There is no one who would not be delighted to change places with you.'

'There is no one with whom I would not change places, Harry. Don't laugh like that. I am telling you the truth. The wretched peasant who has just died is better off than I am. I have no terror of Death. It is the coming of Death that terrifies me. Its monstrous wings seem to wheel in the leaden air around me. Good heavens! don't you see a man moving behind the trees there, watching me, waiting for me?'

Lord Henry looked in the direction in which the trembling gloved hand was pointing. 'Yes,' he said, smiling, 'I see the gardener waiting for you. I suppose he wants to ask you what flowers you wish to have on the table to-night. How absurdly nervous you are, my dear fellow! You must come and see my doctor, when we get back to town.'

Dorian heaved a sigh of relief as he saw the gardener approaching. The man touched his hat, glanced for a moment at Lord Henry in a hesitating manner, and then produced a letter, which he handed to his master. 'Her Grace told me to wait for an answer,' he murmured.

Dorian put the letter into his pocket. 'Tell her Grace that I am coming in,' he said, coldly. The man turned round, and went rapidly in the direction of the house.

'How fond women are of doing dangerous things!' laughed Lord Henry. 'It is one of the qualities in them that I admire most. A woman will flirt with anybody in the world as long as other people are looking on.'

'How fond you are of saying dangerous things, Harry! In the present instance you are quite astray. I like the Duchess very much, but I don't love her.'

'And the Duchess loves you very much, but she likes you less, so you are excellently matched.'

'You are talking scandal, Harry, and there is never any basis for scandal.'

'The basis for every scandal is an immoral certainty,' said Lord Henry, lighting a cigarette.

'You would sacrifice anybody, Harry, for the sake of an epigram.'

'The world goes to the altar of its own accord,' was the answer.

'I wish I could love,' cried Dorian Gray, with a deep note of pathos in his voice. 'But I seem to have lost the passion, and forgotten the desire. I am too much concentrated on myself. My own personality has become a burden to me. I want to escape, to go away, to forget. It was silly of me to come down here at all. I think I shall send a wire to Harvey to have the yacht got ready. On a yacht one is safe.'

'Safe from what, Dorian? You are in some trouble. Why not tell me what it is? You know I would help you.'

'I can't tell you, Harry,' he answered, sadly. 'And I dare say it is only a fancy of mine. This unfortunate accident has upset me. I have a horrible presentiment that something of the kind may happen to me.'

'What nonsense!'

'I hope it is, but I can't help feeling it. Ah! here is the Duchess, looking like Artemis in a tailor-made gown. You see we have come back, Duchess.'

'I have heard all about it, Mr. Gray,' she answered. 'Poor Geoffrey is terribly upset. And it seems that you asked him not to shoot the hare. How curious!'

'Yes, it was very curious. I don't know what made me say it. Some whim, I suppose. It looked the loveliest of little live things. But I am sorry they told you about the man. It is a hideous subject.'

'It is an annoying subject,' broke in Lord Henry. 'It has no psychological value at all. Now if Geoffrey had done the thing on purpose, how interesting he would be! I should like to know some one who had committed a real murder.'

'How horrid of you, Harry!' cried the Duchess. 'Isn't it, Mr. Gray? Harry, Mr. Gray is ill again. He is going to faint.'

Dorian drew himself up with an effort, and smiled. 'It is nothing, Duchess,' he murmured; 'my nerves are dreadfully out of order. That is all. I am afraid I walked too far this morning. I didn't hear what Harry said. Was it very bad? You must tell me some other time. I think I must go and lie down. You will excuse me, won't you?'

They had reached the great flight of steps that led from the conservatory on to the terrace. As the glass door closed behind Dorian, Lord Henry turned and looked at the Duchess with his slumberous eyes. 'Are you very much in love with him?' he asked.

She did not answer for some time, but stood gazing at the landscape. 'I wish I knew,' she said at last.

He shook his head. 'Knowledge would be fatal. It is the uncertainty that charms one. A mist makes things wonderful.'

'One may lose one's way.'

'All ways end at the same point, my dear Gladys.'

'What is that?'

'Disillusion.'

'It was my *début* in life,' she sighed.

'It came to you crowned.'

'I am tired of strawberry leaves.'

'They become you.'

'Only in public.'

'You would miss them,' said Lord Henry.

'I will not part with a petal.'

'Monmouth has ears.'

'Old age is dull of hearing.'

'Has he never been jealous?'

'I wish he had been.'

He glanced about as if in search of something. 'What are you looking for?' she inquired.

'The button from your foil,' he answered. 'You have dropped it.'

She laughed. 'I have still the mask.'

'It makes your eyes lovelier,' was the reply.

She laughed again. Her teeth showed like white seeds in a scarlet fruit.

Upstairs, in his own room, Dorian Gray was lying on a sofa, with terror in every tingling fibre of his body. Life had suddenly become too hideous a burden for him to bear. The dreadful death of the unlucky beater, shot in the thicket like a wild animal, had seemed to him to prefigure death for himself also. He had nearly swooned at what Lord Henry had said in a chance mood of cynical jesting.

At five o'clock he rang his bell for his servant and gave him orders to pack his things for the night-express to town, and to have the brougham at the door by eight-thirty. He was determined not to sleep another night at Selby Royal. It was an ill-omened place, Death walked there in the sunlight. The grass of the forest had been spotted with blood.

Then he wrote a note to Lord Henry, telling him that he was going up to town to consult his doctor, and asking him to entertain his guests in his absence. As he was putting it into the envelope, a knock came to the door, and his valet informed him that the headkeeper wished to see him. He frowned, and bit his lip. 'Send him in,' he muttered after some moments' hesitation.

As soon as the man entered Dorian pulled his cheque-book out of a drawer, and spread it out before him.

'I suppose you have come about the unfortunate accident of this morning, Thornton?' he said, taking up a pen.

'Yes, sir,' answered the gamekeeper.

'Was the poor fellow married? Had he any people dependent on him?' asked Dorian, looking bored. 'If so, I should not like them to be left in want, and will send them any sum of money you may think necessary.'

'We don't know who he is, sir. That is what I took the liberty of coming to you about.'

'Don't know who he is?' said Dorian, listlessly. 'What do you mean? Wasn't he one of your men?'

'No, sir. Never saw him before. Seems like a sailor, sir.'

The pen dropped from Dorian Gray's hand, and he felt as if his heart had suddenly stopped beating. 'A sailor?' he cried out. 'Did you say a sailor?'

'Yes, sir. He looks as if he had been a sort of sailor; tattooed on both arms, and that kind of thing.'

'Was there anything found on him?' said Dorian, leaning forward and looking at the man with startled eyes. 'Anything that would tell his name?'

'Some money, sir – not much, and a six-shooter. There was no name of any kind. A decent-looking man, sir, but rough-like. A sort of sailor, we think.'

Dorian started to his feet. A terrible hope fluttered past him. He clutched at it madly. 'Where is the body?' he exclaimed. 'Quick! I must see it at once.'

'It is in an empty stable in the Home Farm, sir. The folk don't like to have that sort of thing in their houses. They say a corpse brings bad luck.'

'The Home Farm! Go there at once and meet me. Tell one of the grooms to bring my horse round. No. Never mind. I'll go to the stables myself. It will save time.'

In less than a quarter of an hour Dorian Gray was galloping down the long avenue as hard as he could go. The trees seemed to sweep past him in spectral procession, and wild shadows to fling themselves across his path. Once the mare swerved at a white gate-post and nearly threw him. He lashed her across the neck with his crop. She cleft the dusky air like an arrow. The stones flew from her hoofs.

At last he reached the Home Farm. Two men were loitering in the yard. He leapt from the saddle and threw the reins to one of them. In the farthest stable a light was glimmering. Something seemed to tell him that the body was there, and he hurried to the door, and put his hand upon the latch.

There he paused for a moment, feeling that he was on the brink of a discovery that would either make or mar his life. Then he thrust the door open, and entered.

On a heap of sacking in the far corner was lying the dead body of a man dressed in a coarse shirt and a pair of blue trousers. A spotted handkerchief had been placed over the face. A coarse candle, stuck in a bottle, spluttered beside it.

Dorian Gray shuddered. He felt that his could not be the hand to take the handkerchief away, and called out to one of the farm-servants to come to him.

'Take that thing off the face. I wish to see it,' he said, clutching at the door-post for support.

When the farm-servant had done so, he stepped forward. A cry of joy broke from his lips. The man who had been shot in the thicket was James Vane.

He stood there for some minutes looking at the dead body. As he rode home, his eyes were full of tears, for he knew he was safe.

19

'THERE is no use your telling me that you are going to be good,' cried Lord Henry, dipping his white fingers into a red copper bowl filled with rose-water. 'You're quite perfect. Pray, don't change.'

Dorian Gray shook his head. 'No, Harry, I have done too many dreadful things in my life. I am not going to do any more. I began my good actions yesterday.'

'Where were you yesterday?'

'In the country, Harry. I was staying at a little inn by myself.'

'My dear boy,' said Lord Henry, smiling, 'anybody can be good in the country. There are no temptations there. That is the reason why people who live out of town are so absolutely uncivilised. Civilisation is not by any means an easy thing to attain to. There are only two ways by which man can reach it. One is by being cultured, the other by being corrupt. Country people have no opportunity of being either, so they stagnate.'

'Culture and corruption,' echoed Dorian. 'I have known something of both. It seems terrible to me now that they should ever be found together. For I have a new ideal, Harry. I am going to alter. I think I have altered.'

'You have not yet told me what your good action was. Or did you say you had done more than one?' asked his companion, as he spilt into his plate a little crimson pyramid of seeded strawberries, and through a perforated shell-shaped spoon snowed white sugar upon them.

'I can tell you, Harry. It is not a story I could tell to any one else. I spared somebody. It sounds vain, but you understand what I mean. She was quite beautiful, and wonderfully like Sibyl Vane. I think it was that which first at-tracted me to her. You remember Sibyl, don't you? How long ago that seems! Well, Hetty was not one of our own class, of course. She was simply a girl in a village. But I really loved her. I am quite sure that I loved her. All during this wonderful May that we have been having, I used to run down and see her two or three times a week. Yesterday she met me in a little orch-ard. The apple-blossoms kept tumbling down on her hair, and she was laughing. We were to have gone away together this morning at dawn. Suddenly I determined to leave her as flower-like as I had found her.'

'I should think the novelty of the emotion must have given you a thrill of real pleasure, Dorian,' interrupted Lord Henry. 'But I can finish your idyll for you. You gave her good advice, and broke her heart. That was the beginning of your reformation.'

'Harry, you are horrible! You mustn't say these dreadful things. Hetty's heart is not broken. Of course she cried, and all that. But there is no disgrace upon her. She can live, like Perdita, in her garden of mint and marigold.'

'And weep over a faithless Florizel,' said Lord Henry, laughing, as he leant back in his chair. 'My dear Dorian, you have the most curiously boyish moods. Do you think this girl will ever be really contented now with any one of her own rank? I suppose she will be married some day to a rough carter or a grinning ploughman. Well, the fact of having met you, and loved you, will teach her to despise her husband, and she will be wretched. From a moral point of view, I cannot say that I think much of your great renunciation. Even as a beginning, it is poor. Besides, how do you know that Hetty isn't floating at the present moment in some star-lit millpond, with lovely water-lilies round her, like Ophelia?'

'I can't bear this, Harry! You mock at everything, and then suggest the most serious tragedies. I am sorry I told you now. I don't care what you say to me. I know I was right in acting as I did. Poor Hetty! As I rode past the farm this morning, I saw her white face at the window, like a spray of jasmine. Don't let us talk about it any more, and don't try to persuade me that the first good action I have done for years, the first little bit of self-sacrifice I have ever known, is really a sort of sin. I want to be better. I am going to be better. Tell me something about yourself. What is going on in town? I have not been to the club for days.'

'The people are still discussing poor Basil's disappearance.'

'I should have thought they had got tired of that by this time,' said Dorian, pouring himself out some wine, and frowning slightly.

'My dear boy, they have only been talking about it for six weeks, and the British public are really not equal to the mental strain of having more than one topic every three months. They have been very fortunate lately, however. They have had my own divorce case, and Alan Campbell's suicide. Now they have got the mysterious disappearance of an artist. Scotland Yard still insists that the man in the grey ulster who left for Paris by the midnight train on the ninth of November was poor Basil, and the French police declare that Basil never arrived in Paris at all. I suppose in about a fortnight we shall be told that he has been seen in San Francisco. It is an odd thing, but every one who disappears is said to be seen in San Francisco. It must be a delightful city, and possess all the attractions of the next world.'

'What do you think has happened to Basil?' asked Dorian, holding up his Burgundy against the light, and wondering how it was that he could discuss the matter so calmly.

'I have not the slightest idea. If Basil chooses to hide himself, it is no business of mine. If he is dead, I don't want to think about him. Death is the only thing that ever terrifies me. I hate it.'

'Why?' said the younger man, wearily.

'Because,' said Lord Henry, passing beneath his nostrils the gilt trellis of an open vinaigrette box, 'one can survive everything nowadays except that. Death and vulgarity are the only two facts in the nineteenth century that one cannot explain away. Let us have our coffee in the music-room, Dorian. You must play Chopin to me. The man with whom my wife ran away played Chopin exquisitely. Poor Victoria! I was very fond of her. The house is rather lonely without her. Of course married life is merely a habit, a bad habit. But then one regrets the loss even of one's worst habits. Perhaps one regrets them the most. They are such an essential part of one's personality.'

Dorian said nothing, but rose from the table and, passing into the next room, sat down to the piano and let his fingers stray across the white and black ivory of the keys. After the coffee had been brought in, he stopped, and, looking over at Lord Henry, said, 'Harry, did it ever occur to you that Basil was murdered?'

Lord Henry yawned. 'Basil was very popular, and always wore a Waterbury watch. Why should he have been murdered? He was not clever enough to have enemies. Of course he had a wonderful genius for painting. But a man can paint like Velasquez and yet be as dull as possible. Basil was really rather dull. He only interested me once, and that was when he told me, years ago, that he had a wild adoration for you, and that you were the dominant motive of his art.'

'I was very fond of Basil,' said Dorian, with a note of sadness in his voice. 'But don't people say that he was murdered?'

'Oh, some of the papers do. It does not seem to me to be at all probable. I know there are dreadful places in Paris, but Basil was not the sort of man to have gone to them. He had no curiosity. It was his chief defect.'

'What would you say, Harry, if I told you that I had murdered Basil?' said the younger man. He watched him intently after he had spoken.

'I would say, my dear fellow, that you were posing for a character that doesn't suit you. All crime is vulgar, just as all vulgarity is crime. It is not in you, Dorian, to commit a murder. I am sorry if I hurt your vanity by saying so, but I assure you it is true. Crime belongs exclusively to the lower orders. I don't blame them in the smallest degree. I should fancy that crime was to them what art is to us, simply a method of procuring extraordinary sensations.'

'A method of procuring sensations? Do you think, then, that a man who has once committed a murder could possibly do the same crime again? Don't tell me that.'

'Oh! anything becomes a pleasure if one does it too often,' cried Lord Henry, laughing. 'That is one of the most important secrets of life. I should fancy, however, that murder is always a mistake. One should never do anything that one cannot talk about after dinner. But let us pass from poor Basil. I wish I could believe that he had come to such a really romantic end as you suggest; but I can't. I dare say he fell into the Seine off an omnibus, and that the conductor hushed up the scandal. Yes: I should fancy that was his end. I see him lying now on his back under those dull-green waters with the heavy barges floating over him, and long weeds catching in his hair. Do you know, I don't think he would have done much more good work. During the last ten years his painting had gone off very much.'

Dorian heaved a sigh, and Lord Henry strolled across the room and began to stroke the head of a curious Java parrot, a large grey-plumaged bird, with pink crest and tail, that was balancing itself upon a bamboo perch. As his pointed fingers touched it, it dropped the white scurf of crinkled lids over black glass-like eyes, and began to sway backwards and forwards.

'Yes,' he continued, turning round, and taking his handkerchief out of his pocket; 'his painting had quite gone off. It seemed to me to have lost something. It had lost an ideal. When you and he ceased to be great friends, he ceased to be a great artist. What was it that separated you? I suppose he bored you. If so, he never forgave you. It's a habit bores have. By the way, what has become of that wonderful portrait he did of you? I don't think I have ever seen it since he finished it. Oh! I remember your telling me years ago that you had sent it down to Selby, and that it had got mislaid or stolen on the way. You never got it back? What a pity! It was really a masterpiece. I remember I wanted to buy it. I wish I had now. It belonged to Basil's best period. Since then, his work was that curious mixture of bad painting and good intentions that always entitles a man to be called a representative British artist. Did you advertise for it? You should.'

'I forget,' said Dorian. 'I suppose I did. But I never really liked it. I am sorry I sat for it. The memory of the thing is hateful to me. Why do you talk of it? It used to remind me of those curious lines in some play – *Hamlet* I think – how do they run? –

> 'Like the painting of a sorrow,
> A face without a heart.'

Yes: that is what it was like.'

Lord Henry laughed. 'If a man treats life artistically, his brain is his heart,' he answered, sinking into an arm-chair.

Dorian Gray shook his head, and struck some soft chords on the piano. '"Like the painting of a sorrow,"' he repeated, '"a face without a heart."'

The elder man lay back and looked at him with half-closed eyes. 'By the way, Dorian,' he said, after a pause, '"what does it profit a man if he gain the whole world and lose" – how does the quotation run? – "his own soul"?'

The music jarred and Dorian Gray started, and stared at his friend. 'Why do you ask me that, Harry?'

'My dear fellow,' said Lord Henry, elevating his eyebrows in surprise, 'I asked you because I thought you might be able to give me an answer. That is all. I was going through the Park last Sunday, and close by the Marble Arch there stood a little crowd of shabby looking people listening to some vulgar street-preacher. As I passed by, I heard the man yelling out that question to his audience. It struck me as being rather dramatic. London is very rich in curious effects of that kind. A wet Sunday, an uncouth Christian in a mackintosh, a ring of sickly white faces under a broken roof of dripping umbrellas, and a wonderful phrase flung into the air by shrill, hysterical lips – it was really very good in its way, quite a suggestion. I thought of telling the prophet that Art had a soul, but that man had not. I am afraid, however, he would not have understood me.'

'Don't, Harry. The soul is a terrible reality. It can be bought, and sold, and bartered away. It can be poisoned, or made perfect. There is a soul in each one of us. I know it.'

'Do you feel quite sure of that, Dorian?'

'Quite sure.'

'Ah! Then it must be an illusion. The things one feels absolutely certain about are never true. That is the fatality of Faith, and the lesson of Romance. How grave you are! Don't be so serious. What have you or I to do with the superstitions of our age? No: we have given up our belief in the soul. Play me something. Play me a nocturne, Dorian, and, as you play, tell me, in a low voice, how you have kept your youth. You must have some secret. I am only ten years older than you are, and I am wrinkled, and worn, and yellow. You are really wonderful, Dorian. You have never looked more charming than you do to-night. You remind me of the day I saw you first. You were rather cheeky, very shy, and absolutely extraordinary. You have changed, of course, but not in appearance. I wish you would tell me your secret. To get back my youth I would do anything in the world, except take exercise, get up early, or be respectable. Youth! There is nothing like it. It's absurd to talk of the ignorance of youth. The only people to whose opinions I listen now with any respect are people much younger than myself. They seem in front of me. Life has revealed to them her latest wonder. As for the aged, I always contradict the aged. I do it on principle. If you ask them their opinion on something that happened yesterday, they solemnly give you the opinions current in 1820, when people wore high stocks, believed in everything, and knew absolutely nothing. How lovely that thing you are playing is! I wonder did Chopin write it at Majorca, with the sea weeping round the villa, and the salt spray dashing against the panes? It is marvellously romantic. What a blessing it is that there is one art left to us that is not imitative! Don't stop. I want music to-night. It seems to me that you are the young Apollo, and that I am Marsyas listening to you. I have sorrows, Dorian, of my own, that even you know nothing of. The tragedy of old age is not that one is old, but that one is young. I am amazed sometimes at my own sincerity. Ah, Dorian, how happy you are! What an exquisite life you have had! You have drunk deeply of everything. You have crushed the grapes against your palate. Nothing has been hidden from you. And it has all been to you no more than the sound of music. It has not marred you. You are still the same.'

'I am not the same, Harry.'

'Yes: you are the same. I wonder what the rest of your life will be. Don't spoil it by renunciations. At present you are a perfect type. Don't make yourself incomplete. You are quite flawless now. You need not shake your head: you know you are. Besides, Dorian, don't deceive yourself. Life is not governed by will or intention. Life is a question of nerves, and fibres, and slowly built-up cells in which thought hides itself and passion has its dreams. You may fancy yourself safe, and think yourself strong. But a chance tone of colour in a room or a morning sky, a particular perfume that you had once loved and that brings subtle memories with it, a line from a forgotten poem that you had come across again, a cadence from a piece of music that you had ceased to play – I tell you, Dorian, that it is on things like these that our lives depend. Browning writes about that somewhere; but our own senses will imagine them for us. There are moments when the odour of *lilas blanc* passes suddenly across me, and I have to live the strangest month of my life over again. I wish I could change places with you, Dorian. The world has cried out against us both, but it has always worshipped you. It always will worship you. You are the type of what the age is searching for, and what it is afraid it has found. I am so glad that you have never done anything, never carved a statue, or painted a picture, or produced anything outside of yourself! Life has been your art. You have set yourself to music. Your days are your sonnets.'

Dorian rose up from the piano, and passed his hand through his hair. 'Yes, life has been exquisite,' he murmured, 'but I am not going to have the same life, Harry. And you must not say these extravagant things to me. You don't know everything about me. I think that if you did, even you would turn from me. You laugh. Don't laugh.'

'Why have you stopped playing, Dorian? Go back and give me the nocturne over again. Look at that great honey-coloured moon that hangs in the dusky air. She is waiting for you to charm her, and if you play she will come closer to the earth. You won't? Let us go to the club, then. It has been a charming evening, and we must end it charmingly. There is some one at White's who wants immensely to know you – young Lord Poole, Bournemouth's eldest son. He has already copied your neckties, and has begged me to introduce him to you. He is quite delightful, and rather reminds me of you.'

'I hope not,' said Dorian, with a sad look in his eyes. 'But I am tired tonight, Harry. I shan't go to the club. It is nearly eleven, and I want to go to bed early.'

'Do stay. You have never played so well as to-night. There was something in your touch that was wonderful. It had more expression than I had ever heard from it before.'

'It is because I am going to be good,' he answered, smiling. 'I am a little changed already.'

'You cannot change to me, Dorian,' said Lord Henry. 'You and I will always be friends.'

'Yet you poisoned me with a book once. I should not forgive that. Harry, promise me that you will never lend that book to any one. It does harm.'

'My dear boy, you are really beginning to moralise. You will soon be going about like the converted, and the revivalist, warning people against all the sins of which you have grown tired. You are much too delightful to do that. Besides, it is no use. You and I are what we are, and will be what we will be. As for being poisoned by a book, there is no such thing as that. Art has no influence upon action. It annihilates the desire to act. It is superbly sterile. The books that the world calls immoral are books that show the world its own shame. That is all. But we won't discuss literature. Come round to-morrow. I am going to ride at eleven. We might go together, and I will take you to lunch afterwards with Lady Branksome. She is a charming woman, and wants to consult you about some tapestries she is thinking of buying. Mind you come. Or shall we lunch with our little Duchess? She says she never sees you now. Perhaps you are tired of Gladys? I thought you would be. Her clever tongue gets on one's nerves. Well, in any case, be here at eleven.'

'Must I really come, Harry?'

'Certainly. The Park is quite lovely now. I don't think there have been such lilacs since the year I met you.'

'Very well. I shall be here at eleven,' said Dorian. 'Good-night, Harry.' As he reached the door he hesitated for a moment, as if he had something more to say. Then he sighed and went out.

20

IT was a lovely night, so warm that he threw his coat over his arm, and did not even put his silk scarf round his throat. As he strolled home, smoking his cigarette, two young men in evening dress passed him. He heard one of them whisper to the other, 'That is Dorian Gray.' He remembered how pleased he used to be when he was pointed out, or stared at, or talked about. He was tired of hearing his own name now. Half the charm of the little village where he had been so often lately was that no one knew who he was. He had often told the girl whom he had lured to love him that he was poor, and she had believed him. He had told her once that he was wicked, and she had laughed at him, and answered that wicked people were always very old and very ugly. What a laugh she had! – just like a thrush singing. And how pretty she had been in her cotton dress and her large hats! She knew nothing, but she had everything that he had lost.

When he reached home, he found his servant waiting up for him. He sent him to bed, and threw himself down on the sofa in the library, and began to think over some of the things that Lord Henry had said to him.

Was it really true that one could never change? He felt a wild longing for the unstained purity of his boyhood – his rose-white boyhood, as Lord Henry had once called it. He knew that he had tarnished himself, filled his mind with corruption, and given horror to his fancy; that he had been an evil influence to others, and had experienced a terrible joy in being so; and that, of the lives that had crossed his own, it had been the fairest and the most full of promise that he had brought to shame. But was it all irretrievable? Was there no hope for him?

Ah! in what a monstrous moment of pride and passion he had prayed that the portrait should bear the burden of his days, and he keep the unsullied splendour of eternal youth! All his failure had been due to that. Better for him that each sin of his life had brought its sure, swift penalty along with it. There was purification in punishment. Not 'Forgive us our sins,' but 'Smite us for our iniquities,' should be the prayer of a man to a most just God.

The curiously carved mirror that Lord Henry had given to him, so many years ago now, was standing on the table, and the white-limbed Cupids laughed round it as of old. He took it up, as he had done on that night of horror, when he had first noted the change in the fatal picture, and with wild, tear-dimmed eyes looked into its polished shield. Once, some one who had terribly loved him had written to him a mad letter, ending with these idolatrous words: 'The world is changed because you are made of ivory and gold. The curves of your lips rewrite history.' The phrases came back to his memory, and he repeated them over and over to himself. Then he loathed his own beauty, and, flinging the mirror on the floor, crushed it into silver splinters beneath his heel. It was his beauty that had ruined him, his beauty and the youth that he had prayed for. But for those two things, his life might have been free from stain. His beauty had been to him but a mask, his youth but a mockery. What was youth at best? A green, an unripe time, a time of shallow moods and sickly thoughts. Why had he worn its livery? Youth had spoiled him.

It was better not to think of the past. Nothing could alter that. It was of himself, and of his own future, that he had to think. James Vane was hidden in a nameless grave in Selby Churchyard. Alan Campbell had shot himself one night in his laboratory, but had not revealed the secret that he had been forced to know. The excitement, such as it was, over Basil Hallward's disappearance would soon pass away. It was already waning. He was perfectly safe there. Nor, indeed, was it the death of Basil Hallward that weighed most upon his mind. It was the living death of his own soul that troubled him. Basil had painted the portrait that had marred his life. He could not forgive him that. It was the portrait that had done everything. Basil had said things to him that were unbearable, and that he had yet borne with patience. The murder had been simply the madness of a moment. As for Alan Campbell, his suicide had been his own act. He had chosen to do it. It was nothing to him.

A new life! That was what he wanted. That was what he was waiting for. Surely he had begun it already. He had spared one innocent thing, at any rate. He would never again tempt innocence. He would be good.

As he thought of Hetty Merton, he began to wonder if the portrait in the locked room had changed. Surely it was not still so horrible as it had been? Perhaps if his life became pure, he would be able to expel every sign of evil passion from the face. Perhaps the signs of evil had already gone away. He would go and look.

He took the lamp from the table and crept upstairs. As he unbarred the door a smile of joy flitted across his strangely young-looking face and lingered for a moment about his lips. Yes, he would be good, and the hideous thing that he had hidden away would no longer be a terror to him. He felt as if the load had been lifted from him already.

He went in quietly, locking the door behind him, as was his custom, and dragged the purple hanging from the portrait. A cry of pain and indignation broke from him. He could see no change save that in the eyes there was a look of cunning, and in the mouth the curved wrinkle of the hypocrite. The thing was still loathsome – more loathsome, if possible, than before – and the scarlet dew that spotted the hand seemed brighter, and more like blood newly spilt. Then he trembled. Had it been merely vanity that had made him do his one good deed? Or the desire for a new sensation, as Lord Henry had hinted, with his mocking laugh? Or that passion to act a part that sometimes makes us do things finer than we are ourselves? Or, perhaps, all these? And why was the red stain larger than it had been? It seemed to have crept like a horrible disease over the wrinkled fingers. There was blood on the painted feet, as though the thing had dripped – blood even on the hand that had not held the knife. Confess? Did it mean that he was to confess? To give himself up, and be put to death? He laughed. He felt that the idea was monstrous. Besides, even if he did confess, who would believe him? There was no trace of the murdered man anywhere. Everything belonging to him had been destroyed. He himself had burned what had been below-stairs. The world would simply say that he was mad. They would shut him up if he persisted in his story.... Yet it was his duty to confess, to suffer public shame, and to make public atonement. There was a God who called upon men to tell their sins to earth as well as to heaven. Nothing that he could do would cleanse him till he had told his own sin. His sin? He shrugged his shoulders. The death of Basil Hallward seemed very little to him. He was thinking of Hetty Merton. For it was an unjust mirror, this mirror of his soul that he was looking at. Vanity? Curiosity? Hypocrisy? Had there been nothing more in his renunciation than that? There had been something more. At least he thought so. But who could tell? ... No. There had been nothing more. Through vanity he had spared her. In hypocrisy he had worn the mask of goodness. For curiosity's sake he had tried the denial of self. He recognised that now.

But this murder – was it to dog him all his life? Was he always to be burdened by his past? Was he really to confess? Never. There was only one bit of evidence left against him. The picture itself – that was evidence. He would destroy it. Why had he kept it so long? Once it had given him pleasure to watch it changing and growing old. Of late he had felt no such pleasure. It had kept him awake at night. When he had been away, he had been filled with terror lest other eyes should look upon it. It had brought melancholy across his passions. Its mere memory had marred many moments of joy. It had been like conscience to him. Yes, it had been conscience. He would destroy it.

He looked round, and saw the knife that had stabbed Basil Hallward. He had cleaned it many times, till there was no stain left upon it. It was bright, and glistened. As it had killed the painter, so it would kill the painter's work, and all that that meant. It would kill the past and when that was dead he would be free. It would kill this monstrous soul-life, and, without its hideous warnings, he would be at peace. He seized the thing, and stabbed the picture with it.

There was a cry heard, and a crash. The cry was so horrible in its agony that the frightened servants woke, and crept out of their rooms. Two gentlemen, who were passing in the Square below, stopped, and looked up at the great house. They walked on till they met a policeman, and brought him back. The man rang the bell several times, but there was no answer. Except for a light in one of the top windows, the house was all dark. After a time, he went away and stood in an adjoining portico and watched.

'Whose house is that, constable?' asked the elder of the two gentlemen.

'Mr. Dorian Gray's, sir,' answered the policeman.

They looked at each other, as they walked away, and sneered. One of them was Sir Henry Ashton's uncle.

Inside, in the servants' part of the house, the half-clad domestics were talking in low whispers to each other. Old Mrs. Leaf was crying and wringing her hands. Francis was as pale as death.

After about quarter of an hour, he got the coachman and one of the footmen and crept upstairs. They knocked, but there was no reply. They called out. Everything was still. Finally, after vainly trying to force the door, they got on the roof, and dropped down on to the balcony. The windows yielded easily; their bolts were old.

When they entered they found, hanging upon the wall, a splendid portrait of their master as they had last seen him, in all the wonder of his exquisite youth and beauty. Lying on the floor was a dead man, in evening dress, with a knife in his heart. He was withered, wrinkled, and loathsome of visage. It was not till they had examined the rings that they recognised who it was.

LORD ARTHUR SAVILE'S CRIME

A Study of Duty

1

IT WAS Lady Windermere's last reception before Easter, and Bentinck House was even more crowded than usual. Six Cabinet Ministers had come on from the Speaker's Levée in their stars and ribands, all the pretty women wore their smartest dresses, and at the end of the picture-gallery stood the Princess Sophia of Carlsrühe, a heavy Tartar-looking lady, with tiny black eyes and wonderful emeralds, talking bad French at the top of her voice, and laughing immoderately at everything that was said to her. It was certainly a wonderful medley of people. Gorgeous peeresses chatted affably to violent Radicals, popular preachers brushed coat-tails with eminent sceptics, a perfect bevy of bishops kept following a stout prima-donna from room to room, on the staircase stood several Royal Academicians, disguised as artists, and it was said that at one time the supper-room was absolutely crammed with geniuses. In fact, it was one of Lady Windermere's best nights, and the Princess stayed till nearly half-past eleven.

As soon as she had gone, Lady Windermere returned to the picture-gallery, where a celebrated political economist was solemnly explaining the scientific theory of music to an indignant virtuoso from Hungary, and began to talk to the Duchess of Paisley. She looked wonderfully beautiful with her grand ivory throat, her large blue forget-me-not eyes, and her heavy coils of golden hair. *Or pur* they were – not that pale straw colour that nowadays usurps the gracious name of gold, but such gold as is woven into sunbeams or hidden in strange amber; and they gave to her face something of the frame of a saint, with not a little of the fascination of a sinner. She was a curious psychological study. Early in life she had discovered the important truth that nothing looks so like innocence as an indiscretion; and by a series of reckless escapades, half of them quite harmless, she had acquired all the privileges of a personality. She had more than once changed her husband; indeed, Debrett credits her with three marriages; but as she had never changed her lover, the world had long ago ceased to talk scandal about her. She was now forty years of age, childless, and with that inordinate passion for pleasure which is the secret of remaining young.

Suddenly she looked eagerly round the room, and said, in her clear contralto voice, 'Where is my chiromantist?'

'Your what, Gladys?' exclaimed the Duchess, giving an involuntary start.

'My chiromantist, Duchess; I can't live without him at present.'

'Dear Gladys! you are always so original,' murmured the Duchess, trying to remember what a chiromantist really was, and hoping it was not the same as a chiropodist.

'He comes to see my hand twice a week regularly,' continued Lady Windermere, 'and is most interesting about it.'

'Good heavens!' said the Duchess to herself, 'he is a sort of chiropodist after all. How very dreadful. I hope he is a foreigner at any rate. It wouldn't be quite so bad then.'

'I must certainly introduce him to you.'

'Introduce him!' cried the Duchess; 'you don't mean to say he is here?' and she began looking about for a small tortoise-shell fan and a very tattered lace shawl, so as to be ready to go at a moment's notice.

'Of course he is here; I would not dream of giving a party without him. He tells me I have a pure psychic hand, and that if my thumb had been the least little bit shorter, I should have been a confirmed pessimist, and gone into a convent.'

'Oh, I see!' said the Duchess, feeling very much relieved; 'he tells fortunes, I suppose?'

'And misfortunes, too,' answered Lady Windermere, 'any amount of them. Next year, for instance, I am in great danger, both by land and sea, so I am going to live in a balloon, and draw up my dinner in a basket every evening. It is all written down on my little finger, or on the palm of my hand, I forget which.'

'But surely that is tempting Providence, Gladys.'

'My dear Duchess, surely Providence can resist temptation by this time. I think every one should have their hands told once a month so as to know what not to do. Of course, one does it all the same, but it is so pleasant to be warned. Now if some one doesn't go and fetch Mr. Podgers at once, I shall have to go myself.'

'Let me go, Lady Windermere,' said a tall handsome young man, who was standing by, listening to the conversation with an amused smile.

'Thanks so much, Lord Arthur; but I am afraid you wouldn't recognise him.'

'If he is as wonderful as you say, Lady Windermere, I couldn't well miss him. Tell me what he is like, and I'll bring him to you at once.'

'Well, he is not a bit like a chiromantist. I mean he is not mysterious, or esoteric, or romantic-looking. He is a little, stout man, with a funny, bald head, and great gold-rimmed spectacles; something between a family doctor and a country attorney. I'm really very sorry, but it is not my fault. People are so annoying. All my pianists look exactly like poets; and all my poets look exactly like pianists; and I remember last season asking a most dreadful conspirator to dinner, a man who had blown up ever so many people, and always wore a coat of mail, and carried a dagger up his shirt-sleeve; and do you know that when he came he looked just like a nice old clergyman, and cracked jokes all the evening? Of course, he was very amusing, and all that, but I was awfully disappointed; and when I asked him about the coat of mail, he only laughed, and said it was far too cold to wear in England. Ah, here is Mr.

Podgers! Now, Mr. Podgers, I want you to tell the Duchess of Paisley's hand. Duchess, you must take your glove off. No, not the left hand, the other.'

'Dear Gladys, I really don't think it is quite right,' said the Duchess, feebly unbuttoning a rather soiled kid glove.

'Nothing interesting ever is,' said Lady Windermere: '*on a fait le monde ainsi*. But I must introduce you. Duchess, this is Mr. Podgers, my pet chiromantist. Mr. Podgers, this is the Duchess of Paisley, and if you say that she has a larger mountain of the moon than I have, I will never believe in you again.'

'I am sure, Gladys, there is nothing of the kind in my hand,' said the Duchess gravely.

'Your Grace is quite right,' said Mr. Podgers, glancing at the little fat hand with its short square fingers, 'the mountain of the moon is not developed. The line of life, however, is excellent. Kindly bend the wrist. Thank you. Three distinct lines on the *rascette*![1] You will live to a great age, Duchess, and be extremely happy. Ambition – very moderate, line of intellect not exaggerated, line of heart –'

'Now, do be indiscreet, Mr. Podgers,' cried Lady Windermere.

'Nothing would give me greater pleasure,' said Mr. Podgers, bowing, 'if the Duchess ever had been, but I am sorry to say that I see great permanence of affection, combined with a strong sense of duty.'

'Pray go on, Mr. Podgers,' said the Duchess, looking quite pleased.

'Economy is not the least of your Grace's virtues,' continued Mr. Podgers, and Lady Windermere went off into fits of laughter.

'Economy is a very good thing,' remarked the Duchess complacently; 'when I married Paisley he had eleven castles, and not a single house fit to live in.'

'And now he has twelve houses, and not a single castle,' cried Lady Windermere.

'Well, my dear,' said the Duchess, 'I like –'

'Comfort,' said Mr. Podgers, 'and modern improvements, and hot water laid on in every bedroom. Your Grace is quite right. Comfort is the only thing our civilisation can give us.'

'You have told the Duchess's character admirably, Mr. Podgers, and now you must tell Lady Flora's'; and in answer to a nod from the smiling hostess, a tall girl, with sandy Scotch hair, and high shoulder-blades, stepped awkwardly from behind the sofa, and held out a long, bony hand with spatulate fingers.

'Ah, a pianist! I see,' said Mr. Podgers, 'an excellent pianist, but perhaps hardly a musician. Very reserved, very honest, and with a great love of animals.'

'Quite true!' exclaimed the Duchess, turning to Lady Windermere, 'absolutely true! Flora keeps two dozen collie dogs at Macloskie, and would turn

---

1 (In palmistry) part of the hand with lines running crosswise.

our town house into a menagerie if her father would let her.'

'Well, that is just what I do with my house every Thursday evening,' cried Lady Windermere, laughing, 'only I like lions better than collie dogs.'

'Your one mistake, Lady Windermere,' said Mr. Podgers, with a pompous bow.

'If a woman can't make her mistakes charming, she is only a female,' was the answer. 'But you must read some more hands for us. Come, Sir Thomas, show Mr. Podgers yours;' and a genial-looking old gentleman, in a white waistcoat, came forward, and held out a thick rugged hand, with a very long third finger.

'An adventurous nature; four long voyages in the past, and one to come. Been shipwrecked three times. No, only twice, but in danger of a shipwreck your next journey. A strong Conservative, very punctual and with a passion for collecting curiosities. Had a severe illness between the ages of sixteen and eighteen. Was left a fortune when about thirty. Great aversion to cats and Radicals.'

'Extraordinary!' exclaimed Sir Thomas: 'you must really tell my wife's hand, too.'

'Your second wife's,' said Mr. Podgers quietly, still keeping Sir Thomas's hand in his. 'Your second wife's. I shall be charmed'; but Lady Marvel, a melancholy-looking woman, with brown hair and sentimental eyelashes, entirely declined to have her past or her future exposed; and nothing that Lady Windermere could do would induce Monsieur de Koloff, the Russian Ambassador, even to take his gloves off. In fact, many people seemed afraid to face the odd little man with his stereotyped smile, his gold spectacles, and his bright, beady eyes; and when he told poor Lady Fermor right out before every one, that she did not care a bit for music, but was extremely fond of musicians, it was generally felt that chiromancy was a most dangerous science, and one that ought not to be encouraged, except in a *tête-à-tête*.

Lord Arthur Savile, however, who did not know anything about Lady Fermor's unfortunate story, and who had been watching Mr. Podgers with a great deal of interest, was filled with an immense curiosity to have his own hand read, and feeling somewhat shy about putting himself forward, crossed over the room to where Lady Windermere was sitting, and, with a charming blush, asked her if she thought Mr. Podgers would mind.

'Of course he won't mind,' said Lady Windermere, 'that is what he is here for. All my lions, Lord Arthur, are performing lions, and jump through hoops whenever I ask them. But I must warn you beforehand that I shall tell Sybil everything. She is coming to lunch with me to-morrow, to talk about bonnets, and if Mr. Podgers finds out that you have a bad temper, or a tendency to gout, or a wife living in Bayswater, I shall certainly let her know all about it.'

Lord Arthur smiled, and shook his head. 'I am not afraid,' he answered. 'Sybil knows me as well as I know her.'

'Ah! I am a little sorry to hear you say that. The proper basis for marriage is a mutual misunderstanding. No, I am not at all cynical, I have merely got experience, which, however, is very much the same thing. Mr. Podgers, Lord Arthur Savile is dying to have his hand read. Don't tell him that he is engaged to one of the most beautiful girls in London, because that appeared in the *Morning Post* a month ago.'

'Dear Lady Windermere,' cried the Marchioness of Jedburgh, 'do let Mr. Podgers stay here a little longer. He has just told me I should go on the stage, and I am so interested.'

'If he has told you that, Lady Jedburgh, I shall certainly take him away. Come over at once, Mr. Podgers, and read Lord Arthur's hand.'

'Well,' said Lady Jedburgh, making a little *moue* as she rose from the sofa, 'if I am not to be allowed to go on the stage, I must be allowed to be part of the audience at any rate.'

'Of course; we are all going to be part of the audience,' said Lady Windermere; 'and now, Mr. Podgers, be sure and tell us something nice. Lord Arthur is one of my special favourites.'

But when Mr. Podgers saw Lord Arthur's hand he grew curiously pale, and said nothing. A shudder seemed to pass through him, and his great bushy eyebrows twitched convulsively, in an odd, irritating way they had when he was puzzled. Then some huge beads of perspiration broke out on his yellow forehead, like a poisonous dew, and his fat fingers grew cold and clammy.

Lord Arthur did not fail to notice these strange signs of agitation, and, for the first time in his life, he himself felt fear. His impulse was to rush from the room, but he restrained himself. It was better to know the worst, whatever it was, than to be left in this hideous uncertainty.

'I am waiting, Mr. Podgers,' he said.

'We are all waiting,' cried Lady Windermere, in her quick, impatient manner, but the chiromantist made no reply.

'I believe Arthur is going on the stage,' said Lady Jedburgh, 'and that, after your scolding, Mr. Podgers is afraid to tell him so.'

Suddenly Mr. Podgers dropped Lord Arthur's right hand, and seized hold of his left, bending down so low to examine it that the gold rims of his spectacles seemed almost to touch the palm. For a moment his face became a white mask of horror, but he soon recovered his *sang-froid*, and looking up at Lady Windermere, said with a forced smile, 'It is the hand of a charming young man.'

'Of course it is!' answered Lady Windermere, 'but will he be a charming husband? That is what I want to know.'

'All charming young men are,' said Mr. Podgers.

'I don't think a husband should be too fascinating,' murmured Lady Jedburgh pensively, 'it is so dangerous.'

'My dear child, they never are too fascinating,' cried Lady Windermere. 'But what I want are details. Details are the only things that interest. What is going to happen to Lord Arthur?'

'Well, within the next few months Lord Arthur will go on a voyage –'

'Oh yes, his honeymoon, of course!'

'And lose a relative.'

'Not his sister, I hope?' said Lady Jedburgh, in a piteous tone of voice.

'Certainly not his sister,' answered Mr. Podgers, with a deprecating wave of the hand, 'a distant relative merely.'

'Well, I am dreadfully disappointed,' said Lady Windermere. 'I have absolutely nothing to tell Sybil to-morrow. No one cares about distant relatives nowadays. They went out of fashion years ago. However, I suppose she had better have a black silk by her; it always does for church, you know. And now let us go to supper. They are sure to have eaten everything up, but we may find some hot soup. François used to make excellent soup once, but he is so agitated about politics at present, that I never feel quite certain about him. I do wish General Boulanger would keep quiet. Duchess, I am sure you are tired?'

'Not at all, dear Gladys,' answered the Duchess, waddling towards the door. 'I have enjoyed myself immensely, and the chiropodist, I mean the chiromantist, is most interesting. Flora, where can my tortoise-shell fan be? Oh, thank you, Sir Thomas, so much. And my lace shawl, Flora? Oh, thank you, Sir Thomas, very kind, I'm sure'; and the worthy creature finally managed to get downstairs without dropping her scent-bottle more than twice.

All this time Lord Arthur Savile had remained standing by the fireplace, with the same feeling of dread over him, the same sickening sense of coming evil. He smiled sadly at his sister, as she swept past him on Lord Plymdale's arm, looking lovely in her pink brocade and pearls, and he hardly heard Lady Windermere when she called to him to follow her. He thought of Sybil Merton, and the idea that anything could come between them made his eyes dim with tears.

Looking at him, one would have said that Nemesis had stolen the shield of Pallas, and shown him the Gorgon's head. He seemed turned to stone, and his face was like marble in its melancholy. He had lived the delicate and luxurious life of a young man of birth and fortune, a life exquisite in its freedom from sordid care, its beautiful boyish insouciance; and now for the first time he had become conscious of the terrible mystery of Destiny, of the awful meaning of Doom.

How mad and monstrous it all seemed! Could it be that written on his hand, in characters that he could not read himself, but that another could decipher, was some fearful secret of sin, some blood-red sign of crime? Was there no escape possible? Were we no better than chessmen, moved by an unseen power, vessels the potter fashions at his fancy, for honour or for shame? His reason revolted against it, and yet he felt that some tragedy was hanging over him, and that he had been suddenly called upon to bear an intolerable burden. Actors are so fortunate. They can choose whether they will appear in tragedy or in comedy, whether they will suffer or make merry, laugh or shed tears. But in real life it is different. Most men and women are forced to perform parts for which they have no qualifications. Our Guildensterns play Hamlet for us, and our Hamlets have to jest like Prince Hal. The world is a stage, but the play is badly cast.

Suddenly Mr. Podgers entered the room. When he saw Lord Arthur he started, and his coarse, fat face became a sort of greenish-yellow colour. The two men's eyes met, and for a moment there was silence.

'The Duchess has left one of her gloves here, Lord Arthur, and has asked me to bring it to her,' said Mr. Podgers finally. 'Ah, I see it on the sofa! Good evening.'

'Mr. Podgers, I must insist on your giving me a straightforward answer to a question I am going to put to you.'

'Another time, Lord Arthur, but the Duchess is anxious. I am afraid I must go.'

'You shall not go. The Duchess is in no hurry.'

'Ladies should not be kept waiting, Lord Arthur,' said Mr. Podgers, with his sickly smile. 'The fair sex is apt to be impatient.'

Lord Arthur's finely-chiselled lips curled in petulant disdain. The poor Duchess seemed to him of very little importance at that moment. He walked across the room to where Mr. Podgers was standing, and held his hand out.

'Tell me what you saw there,' he said. 'Tell me the truth. I must know it. I am not a child.'

Mr. Podger's eyes blinked behind his gold-rimmed spectacles, and he moved uneasily from one foot to the other, while his fingers played nervously with a flash watch-chain.

'What makes you think that I saw anything in your hand, Lord Arthur, more than I told you?'

'I know you did, and I insist on your telling me what it was. I will pay you. I will give you a cheque for a hundred pounds.'

The green eyes flashed for a moment, and then became dull again.

'Guineas?' said Mr. Podgers at last, in a low voice.

'Certainly. I will send you a cheque to-morrow. What is your club?'

'I have no club. That is to say, not just at present. My address is –, but allow me to give you my card'; and producing a bit of gilt-edge pasteboard from his waistcoat pocket, Mr. Podgers handed it, with a low bow, to Lord Arthur, who read on it, '*Mr. Septimus R. Podgers, Professional Chiromantist, 1030 West Moon Street.*'

'My hours are from ten to four,' murmured Mr. Podgers mechanically, 'and I make a reduction for families.'

'Be quick,' cried Lord Arthur, looking very pale, and holding his hand out.

Mr. Podgers glanced nervously round, and drew the heavy *portière* across the door.

'It will take a little time, Lord Arthur, you had better sit down.'

'Be quick, sir,' cried Lord Arthur again, stamping his foot angrily on the polished floor.

Mr. Podgers smiled, drew from his breast-pocket a small magnifying glass, and wiped it carefully with his handkerchief.

'I am quite ready,' he said.

2

TEN minutes later, with face blanched by terror, and eyes wild with grief, Lord Arthur Savile rushed from Bentinck House, crushing his way through the crowd of fur-coated footmen that stood round the large striped awning, and seeming not to see or hear anything. The night was bitter cold, and the gas-lamps round the square flared and flickered in the keen wind; but his hands were hot with fever, and his forehead burned like fire. On and on he went, almost with the gait of a drunken man. A policeman looked curiously at him as he passed, and a beggar, who slouched from an archway to ask for alms, grew frightened, seeing misery greater than his own. Once he stopped under a lamp, and looked at his hands. He thought he could detect the stain of blood already upon them, and a faint cry broke from his trembling lips.

Murder! that is what the chiromantist had seen there. Murder! The very night seemed to know it, and the desolate wind to howl it in his ear. The dark corners of the streets were full of it. It grinned at him from the roofs of the houses.

First he came to the Park, whose sombre woodland seemed to fascinate him. He leaned wearily up against the railings, cooling his brow against the wet metal, and listening to the tremulous silence of the trees. 'Murder! murder!' he kept repeating, as though iteration could dim the horror of the word. The sound of his own voice made him shudder, yet he almost hoped that Echo might hear him, and wake the slumbering city from its dreams. He felt a mad desire to stop the casual passer-by, and tell him everything.

Then he wandered across Oxford Street into narrow, shameful alleys. Two women with painted faces mocked at him as he went by. From a dark courtyard came a sound of oaths and blows, followed by shrill screams, and, huddled upon a damp door-step, he saw the crooked-back forms of poverty and eld. A strange pity came over him. Were these children of sin and misery predestined to their end, as he to his? Were they, like him, merely the puppets of a monstrous show?

And yet it was not the mystery, but the comedy of suffering that struck him; its absolute uselessness, its grotesque want of meaning. How incoherent everything seemed! How lacking in all harmony! He was amazed at the discord between the shallow optimism of the day, and the real facts of existence. He was still very young.

After a time he found himself in front of Marylebone Church. The silent roadway looked like a long riband of polished silver, flecked here and there by the dark arabesques of waving shadows. Far into the distance curved the line of flickering gas-lamps, and outside a little walled-in house stood a solitary hansom, the driver asleep inside. He walked hastily in the direction of Portland Place, now and then looking round, as though he feared that he was being followed. At the corner of Rich Street stood two men, reading a small bill upon a hoarding. An odd feeling of curiosity stirred him, and he crossed over. As he came near, the word "Murder," printed in black letters, met his eye. He started, and a deep flush came into his cheek. It was an advertisement offering a reward for any information leading to the arrest of a man of medium height, between thirty and forty years of age, wearing a billycock hat, a black coat, and check trousers, and with a scar upon his right cheek. He read it over and over again, and wondered if the wretched man would be caught, and how he had been scarred. Perhaps, some day, his own name might be placarded on the walls of London. Some day, perhaps, a price would be set on his head also.

The thought made him sick with horror. He turned on his heel, and hurried into the night.

Where he went he hardly knew. He had a dim memory of wandering through a labyrinth of sordid houses, and it was bright dawn when he found himself at last in Piccadilly Circus. As he strolled home towards Belgrave Square, he met the great waggons on their way to Covent Garden. The white-smocked carters, with their pleasant sunburnt faces and coarse curly hair, strode sturdily on, cracking their whips, and calling out now and then to each other; on the back of a huge grey horse, the leader of a jangling team, sat a chubby boy, with a bunch of primroses in his battered hat, keeping tight hold of the mane with his little hands, and laughing; and the great piles of vegetables looked like masses of jade against the morning sky, like masses of green jade against the pink petals of some marvellous rose. Lord Arthur felt curiously affected, he could not tell why. There was something in the dawn's delicate loveliness that seemed to him inexpressibly pathetic, and he thought of all the days that break in beauty, and that set in storm. These rustics, too, with their rough, good-humoured voices, and their nonchalant ways, what a strange London they saw! A London free from the sin of night and the smoke of day, a pallid, ghost-like city, a desolate town of tombs! He wondered what they thought of it, and whether they knew anything of its splendour and its shame, of its fierce, fiery-coloured joys, and its horrible hunger, of all it makes and mars from morn to eve. Probably it was to them merely a mart where they brought their fruit to sell, and where they tarried for a few hours at most, leaving the streets still silent, the houses still asleep. It gave him pleasure to watch them as they went by. Rude as they were, with their heavy, hob-nailed shoes, and their awkward gait, they brought a little of Arcady with them. He felt that they had lived with Nature, and that she had taught them peace. He envied them all that they did not know.

By the time he had reached Belgrave Square the sky was a faint blue, and the birds were beginning to twitter in the gardens.

3

WHEN Lord Arthur woke it was twelve o'clock, and the midday sun was streaming through the ivory-silk curtains of his room. He got up and looked out of the window. A dim haze of heat was hanging over the great city, and the roofs of the houses were like dull silver. In the flickering green of the square below some children were flitting about like white butterflies, and the pavement was crowded with people on their way to the Park. Never had life seemed lovelier to him, never had the things of evil seemed more remote.

Then his valet brought him a cup of chocolate on a tray. After he had drunk it, he drew aside a heavy *portière* of peach-coloured plush, and passed into the bathroom. The light stole softly from above, through thin slabs of transparent onyx, and the water in the marble tank glimmered like a moonstone. He plunged hastily in, till the cool ripples touched throat and hair, and then dipped his head right under, as though he would have wiped away the stain of some shameful memory. When he stepped out he felt almost at peace. The exquisite physical conditions of the moment had dominated him, as indeed often happens in the case of very finely-wrought natures, for the senses, like fire, can purify as well as destroy.

After breakfast, he flung himself down on a divan and lit a cigarette. On the mantel-shelf, framed in dainty old brocade, stood a large photograph of Sybil Merton, as he had seen her first at Lady Noel's ball. The small, exquisitely-shaped head drooped slightly to one side, as though the thin, reed-like throat could hardly bear the burden of so much beauty; the lips were slightly parted, and seemed made for sweet music; and all the tender purity of girlhood looked out in wonder from the dreaming eyes. With her soft, clinging dress of *crêpe de chine*, and her large leaf-shaped fan, she looked like one of those delicate little figures men find in the olive-woods near Tanagra; and there was a touch of Greek grace in her pose and attitude. Yet she was not *petite*. She was simply perfectly proportioned – a rare thing in an age when so many women are either over life-size or insignificant.

Now as Lord Arthur looked at her, he was filled with the terrible pity that is born of love. He felt that to marry her, with the doom of murder hanging over his head, would be a betrayal like that of Judas, a sin worse than any the Borgia had ever dreamed of. What happiness could there be for them, when at any moment he might be called upon to carry out the awful prophecy written in his hand? What manner of life would be theirs while Fate still held this fearful fortune in the scales? The marriage must be postponed, at all costs. Of this he was quite resolved. Ardently though he loved the girl, and the mere touch of her fingers, when they sat together, made each nerve of his body thrill with exquisite joy, he recognised none the less clearly where his duty lay, and was fully conscious of the fact that he had no right to marry until he had committed the murder. This done, he could stand before the altar with Sybil Merton, and give his life into her hands without terror of wrongdoing. This done, he could take her to his arms, knowing that she would never have to blush for him, never have to hang her head in shame. But done it must be first; and the sooner the better for both.

Many men in his position would have preferred the primrose path of dalliance to the steep heights of duty; but Lord Arthur was too conscientious to set pleasure above principle. There was more than mere passion in his love;

and Sybil was to him a symbol of all that is good and noble. For a moment he had a natural repugnance against what he was asked to do, but it soon passed away. His heart told him that it was not a sin, but a sacrifice; his reason reminded him that there was no other course open. He had to choose between living for himself and living for others, and terrible though the task laid upon him undoubtedly was, yet he knew that he must not suffer selfishness to triumph over love. Sooner or later we are all called upon to decide on the same issue – of us all the same question is asked. To Lord Arthur it came early in life – before his nature had been spoiled by the calculating cynicism of middle-age, or his heart corroded by the shallow, fashionable egotism of our day, and he felt no hesitation about doing his duty. Fortunately also, for him, he was no mere dreamer, or idle dilettante. Had he been so, he would have hesitated, like Hamlet, and let irresolution mar his purpose. But he was essentially practical. Life to him meant action, rather than thought. He had that rarest of all things, common sense.

The wild, turbid feelings of the previous night had by this time completely passed away, and it was almost with a sense of shame that he looked back upon his mad wanderings from street to street, his fierce emotional agony. The very sincerity of his sufferings made them seem unreal to him now. He wondered how he could have been so foolish as to rant and rave about the inevitable. The only question that seemed to trouble him was, whom to make away with; for he was not blind to the fact that murder, like the religions of the Pagan world, requires a victim as well as a priest. Not being a genius, he had no enemies, and indeed he felt that this was not the time for the gratification of any personal pique or dislike, the mission in which he was engaged being one of great and grave solemnity. He accordingly made out a list of his friends and relatives on a sheet of notepaper, and after careful consideration, decided in favour of Lady Clementina Beauchamp, a dear old lady who lived in Curzon Street, and was his own second cousin by his mother's side. He had always been very fond of Lady Clem, as every one called her, and as he was very wealthy himself, having come into all Lord Rugby's property when he came of age, there was no possibility of his deriving any vulgar monetary advantage by her death. In fact, the more he thought over the matter, the more she seemed to him to be just the right person, and, feeling that any delay would be unfair to Sybil, he determined to make his arrangements at once.

The first thing to be done was, of course, to settle with the chiromantist; so he sat down at a small Sheraton writing-table that stood near the window, drew a cheque for £105, payable to the order of Mr. Septimus Podgers, and, enclosing it in an envelope, told his valet to take it to West Moon Street. He then telephoned to the stables for his hansom, and dressed to go out. As he was leaving the room he looked back at Sybil Merton's photograph, and swore that, come what may, he would never let her know what he was doing for her sake, but would keep the secret of his self-sacrifice hidden always in his heart.

On his way to the Buckingham, he stopped at a florist's, and sent Sybil a beautiful basket of narcissi, with lovely white petals and staring pheasants' eyes, and on arriving at the club went straight to the library, rang the bell, and ordered the waiter to bring him a lemon-and-soda, and a book on Toxicology. He had fully decided that poison was the best means to adopt in this troublesome business. Anything like personal violence was extremely distasteful to him, and besides, he was very anxious not to murder Lady Clementina in any way that might attract public attention, as he hated the idea of being lionised at Lady Windermere's, or seeing his name figuring in the paragraphs of vulgar society-newspapers. He had also to think of Sybil's father and mother, who were rather old-fashioned people, and might possibly object to the marriage if there was anything like a scandal, though he felt certain that if he told them the whole facts of the case they would be the very first to appreciate the motives that had actuated him. He had every reason, then, to decide in favour of poison. It was safe, sure, and quiet, and did away with any necessity for painful scenes, to which, like most Englishmen, he had a rooted objection.

Of the science of poisons, however, he knew absolutely nothing, and as the waiter seemed quite unable to find anything in the library but *Ruff's Guide* and *Bailey's Magazine* he examined the book-shelves himself, and finally came across a handsomely-bound edition of the *Pharmacopœia*, and a copy of Erskine's *Toxicology*, edited by Sir Mathew Reid, the President of the Royal College of Physicians, and one of the oldest members of the Buckingham, having been elected in mistake for somebody else; a *contretemps* that so enraged the Committee, that when the real man came up they black-balled him unanimously. Lord Arthur was a good deal puzzled at the technical terms used in both books, and had begun to regret that he had not paid more attention to his classics at Oxford, when in the second volume of Erskine, he found a very interesting and complete account of the properties of aconitine, written in fairly clear English. It seemed to him to be exactly the poison he wanted. It was swift – indeed, almost immediate, in its effect – perfectly painless, and when taken in the form of a gelatine capsule, the mode recommended by Sir Mathew, not by any means unpalatable. He accordingly made a note, upon his shirt-cuff, of the amount necessary for a fatal dose, put the books back in their places, and strolled up St. James's Street, to Pestle and Humbey's, the great chemists. Mr. Pestle, who always attended personally on the aristocracy, was a good deal surprised at the order, and in a very deferential manner murmured something about a medical certificate being necessary. However, as soon as Lord Arthur explained to him that it was for a large Norwegian mastiff that he was obliged to get rid of, as it showed signs of incipient rabies, and had already bitten the coachman twice in the calf of the leg, he expressed himself as being perfectly satisfied, complimented Lord Arthur on his wonderful knowledge of Toxicology, and had the prescription made up immediately.

Lord Arthur put the capsule into a pretty little silver *bonbonnière* that he saw in a shop window in Bond Street, threw away Pestle and Humbey's ugly pill-box, and drove off at once to Lady Clementina's.

'Well, *monsieur le mauvais sujet*,' cried the old lady, as he entered the room, 'why haven't you been to see me all this time?'

'My dear Lady Clem, I never have a moment to myself,' said Lord Arthur, smiling.

'I suppose you mean that you go about all day long with Miss Sybil Merton, buying *chiffons* and talking nonsense? I cannot understand why people make such a fuss about being married. In my day we never dreamed of billing and cooing in public, or in private for that matter.'

'I assure you I have not seen Sybil for twenty-four hours, Lady Clem. As far as I can make out, she belongs entirely to her milliners.'

'Of course; that is the only reason you come to see an ugly old woman like myself. I wonder you men don't take warning. *On a fait des folies pour moi*, and here I am, a poor rheumatic creature, with a false front and a bad temper. Why, if it were not for dear Lady Jansen, who sends me all the worst French novels she can find, I don't think I could get through the day. Doctors are no use at all, except to get fees out of one. They can't even cure my heartburn.'

'I have brought you a cure for that, Lady Clem,' said Lord Arthur gravely. 'It is a wonderful thing, invented by an American.'

'I don't think I like American inventions, Arthur. I am quite sure I don't. I read some American novels lately, and they were quite nonsensical.'

'Oh, but there is no nonsense at all about this, Lady Clem! I assure you it is a perfect cure. You must promise to try it'; and Lord Arthur brought the little box out of his pocket, and handed it to her.

'Well, the box is charming, Arthur. Is it really a present? That is very sweet of you. And is this the wonderful medicine? It looks like a *bonbon*. I'll take it at once.'

'Good heavens! Lady Clem,' cried Lord Arthur, catching hold of her hand, 'you mustn't do anything of the kind. It is a homoeopathic medicine, and if you take it without having heartburn, it might do you no end of harm. Wait till you have an attack, and take it then. You will be astonished at the result.'

'I should like to take it now,' said Lady Clementina, holding up to the light the little transparent capsule, with its floating bubble of liquid aconitine. 'I am sure it is delicious. The fact is that, though I hate doctors, I love medicines. However, I'll keep it till my next attack.'

'And when will that be?' asked Lord Arthur eagerly. 'Will it be soon?'

'I hope not for a week. I had a very bad time yesterday morning with it. But one never knows.'

'You are sure to have one before the end of the month then, Lady Clem?'

'I am afraid so. But how sympathetic you are to-day, Arthur! Really, Sybil has done you a great deal of good. And now you must run away, for I am dining with some very dull people, who won't talk scandal, and I know that if I don't get my sleep now I shall never be able to keep awake during dinner. Good-bye, Arthur, give my love to Sybil, and thank you so much for the American medicine.'

'You won't forget to take it, Lady Clem, will you?' said Lord Arthur, rising from his seat.

'Of course I won't, you silly boy. I think it is most kind of you to think of me, and I shall write and tell you if I want any more.'

Lord Arthur left the house in high spirits, and with a feeling of immense relief.

That night he had an interview with Sybil Merton. He told her how he had been suddenly placed in a position of terrible difficulty, from which neither honour nor duty would allow him to recede. He told her that the marriage must be put off for the present, as until he had got rid of his fearful entanglements, he was not a free man. He implored her to trust him, and not to have any doubts about the future. Everything would come right, but patience was necessary.

The scene took place in the conservatory of Mr. Merton's house, in Park Lane, where Lord Arthur had dined as usual. Sybil had never seemed more happy, and for a moment Lord Arthur had been tempted to play the coward's part, to write to Lady Clementina for the pill, and to let the marriage go on as if there was no such person as Mr. Podgers in the world. His better nature, however, soon asserted itself, and even when Sybil flung herself weeping into his arms, he did not falter. The beauty that stirred his senses had touched his conscience also. He felt that to wreck so fair a life for the sake of a few months' pleasure would be a wrong thing to do.

He stayed with Sybil till nearly midnight, comforting her and being comforted in turn, and early the next morning he left for Venice, after writing a manly, firm letter to Mr. Merton about the necessary postponement of the marriage.

4

IN Venice he met his brother, Lord Surbiton, who happened to have come over from Corfu in his yacht. The two young men spent a delightful fortnight together. In the morning they rode on the Lido, or glided up and down the green canal in their long black gondola; in the afternoon they usually entertained visitors on the yacht; and in the evening they dined at Florian's, and smoked innumerable cigarettes on the Piazza. Yet somehow Lord Arthur was not happy. Every day he studied the obituary column in the *Times*, expecting to see a notice of Lady Clementina's death, but every day he was disappointed. He began to be afraid that some accident had happened to her, and often regretted that he had prevented her taking the aconitine when she had been so anxious to try its effect. Sybil's letters, too, though full of love, and trust, and tenderness, were often very sad in their tone, and sometimes he used to think that he was parted from her for ever.

After a fortnight Lord Surbiton got bored with Venice, and determined to run down the coast to Ravenna, as he heard that there was some capital cock-shooting in the Pinetum. Lord Arthur at first refused absolutely to come, but Surbiton, of whom he was extremely fond, finally persuaded him that if he stayed at Danielli's by himself he would be moped to death, and on the morning of the 15th they started, with a strong nor'east wind blowing, and a rather choppy sea. The sport was excellent, and the free, open-air life brought the colour back to Lord Arthur's cheek, but about the 22nd he became anxious about Lady Clementina, and, in spite of Surbiton's remonstrances, came back to Venice by train.

As he stepped out of his gondola on to the hotel steps, the proprietor came forward to meet him with a sheaf of telegrams. Lord Arthur snatched them out of his hand, and tore them open. Everything had been quite successful. Lady Clementina had died quite suddenly on the night of the 17th!

His first thought was for Sybil, and he sent her off a telegram announcing his immediate return to London. He then ordered his valet to pack his things for the night mail, sent his gondoliers about five times their proper fare, and ran up to his sitting-room with a light step and a buoyant heart. There he found three letters waiting for him. One was from Sybil herself, full of sympathy and condolence. The others were from his mother, and from Lady Clementina's solicitor. It seemed that the old lady had dined with the Duchess that very night, had delighted every one by her wit and *esprit*, but had gone home somewhat early, complaining of heartburn. In the morning she was found dead in her bed, having apparently suffered no pain. Sir Mathew Reid had been sent for at once, but, of course, there was nothing to be done, and she was to be buried on the 22nd at Beauchamp Chalcote. A few days before she died she had made her will, and left Lord Arthur her little house in Curzon Street, and all her furniture, personal effects, and pictures, with the exception of her collection of miniatures, which was to go to her sister, Lady Margaret Rufford, and her amethyst necklace, which Sybil Merton was to have. The property was not of much value; but Mr. Mansfield, the solicitor, was extremely anxious for Lord Arthur to return at once, if possible, as there were a great many bills to be paid, and Lady Clementina had never kept any regular accounts.

Lord Arthur was very much touched by Lady Clementina's kind remembrance of him, and felt that Mr. Podgers had a great deal to answer for. His love of Sybil, however, dominated every other emotion, and the consciousness that he had done his duty gave him peace and comfort. When he arrived at Charing Cross, he felt perfectly happy.

The Mertons received him very kindly. Sybil made him promise that he would never again allow anything to come between them, and the marriage was fixed for the 7th June. Life seemed to him once more bright and beautiful, and all his old gladness came back to him again.

One day, however, as he was going over the house in Curzon Street, in company with Lady Clementina's solicitor and Sybil herself, burning packages of faded letters and turning out drawers of odd rubbish, the young girl suddenly gave a cry of delight.

'What have you found, Sybil?' said Lord Arthur, looking up from his work, and smiling.

'This lovely little silver *bonbonnière*, Arthur. Isn't it quaint and Dutch? Do give it to me! I know amethysts won't become me till I am over eighty.'

It was the box that had held the aconitine.

Lord Arthur started, and a faint blush came into his cheek. He had almost entirely forgotten what he had done, and it seemed to him a curious coincidence that Sybil, for whose sake he had gone through all that terrible anxiety, should have been the first to remind him of it.

'Of course you can have it, Sybil. I gave it to poor Lady Clem myself.'

'Oh! thank you, Arthur; and may I have the *bonbon* too? I had no notion that Lady Clementina liked sweets. I thought she was far too intellectual.'

Lord Arthur grew deadly pale, and a horrible idea crossed his mind.

'*Bonbon*, Sybil? What do you mean?' he said in a slow, hoarse voice.

'There is one in it, that is all. It looks quite old and dusty, and I have not the slightest intention of eating it. What is the matter, Arthur? How white you look!'

Lord Arthur rushed across the room, and seized the box. Inside it was the amber-coloured capsule, with its poison-bubble. Lady Clementina had died a natural death after all!

The shock of the discovery was almost too much for him. He flung the capsule into the fire, and sank on the sofa with a cry of despair.

5

MR. MERTON was a good deal distressed at the second postponement of the marriage, and Lady Julia, who had already ordered her dress for the wedding, did all in her power to make Sybil break off the match. Dearly, however, as Sybil loved her mother, she had given her whole life into Lord Arthur's hands, and nothing that Lady Julia could say could make her waver in her faith. As for Lord Arthur himself, it took him days to get over his terrible disappointment, and for a time his nerves were completely unstrung. His excellent common sense, however, soon asserted itself, and his sound, practical mind did not leave him long in doubt about what to do. Poison having proved a complete failure, dynamite, or some other form of explosive, was obviously the proper thing to try.

He accordingly looked again over the list of his friends and relatives, and, after careful consideration, determined to blow up his uncle, the Dean of Chichester. The Dean, who was a man of great culture and learning, was extremely fond of clocks, and had a wonderful collection of timepieces, ranging from the fifteenth century to the present day, and it seemed to Lord Arthur that this hobby of the good Dean's offered him an excellent opportunity for carrying out his scheme. Where to procure an explosive machine was, of course, quite another matter. The London Directory gave him no information on the point, and he felt that there was very little use in going to Scotland Yard about it, as they never seemed to know anything about the movements of the dynamite faction till after an explosion had taken place, and not much even then.

Suddenly he thought of his friend Rouvaloff, a young Russian of very revolutionary tendencies, whom he had met at Lady Windermere's in the winter. Count Rouvaloff was supposed to be writing a life of Peter the Great, and to have come over to England for the purpose of studying the documents relating to that Tsar's residence in this country as a ship carpenter; but it was generally suspected that he was a Nihilist agent, and there was no doubt that the Russian Embassy did not look with any favour upon his presence in London. Lord Arthur felt that he was just the man for his purpose, and drove down one morning to his lodgings in Bloomsbury, to ask his advice and assistance.

'So you are taking up politics seriously?' said Count Rouvaloff, when Lord Arthur had told him the object of his mission; but Lord Arthur, who hated swagger of any kind, felt bound to admit to him that he had not the slightest interest in social questions, and simply wanted the explosive machine for a purely family matter, in which no one was concerned but himself.

Count Rouvaloff looked at him for some moments in amazement, and then seeing that he was quite serious, wrote an address on a piece of paper, initialled it, and handed it to him across the table.

'Scotland yard would give a good deal to know this address, my dear fellow.'

'They shan't have it,' cried Lord Arthur, laughing; and after shaking the young Russian warmly by the hand he ran downstairs, examined the paper, and told the coachman to drive to Soho Square.

There he dismissed him, and strolled down Greek Street, till he came to a place called Bayle's Court. He passed under the archway, and found himself in a curious *cul-de-sac*, that was apparently occupied by a French laundry, as a perfect network of clothes-lines was stretched across from house to house, and there was a flutter of white linen in the morning air. He walked to right to the end, and knocked at a little green house. After some delay, during which every window became a blurred mass of peering faces, the door was opened by a rather rough-looking foreigner, who asked him in very bad English what his business was. Lord Arthur handed him the paper Count Rouvaloff had given him. When the man saw it he bowed, and invited Lord Arthur into a very shabby front parlour on the ground floor, and in a few moments Herr Winckelkopf, as he was called in England, bustled into the room, with a very wine-stained napkin round his neck, and a fork in his left hand.

'Count Rouvaloff has given me an introduction to you,' said Lord Arthur, bowing, 'and I am anxious to have a short interview with you on a matter of business. My name is Smith, Mr. Robert Smith, and I want you to supply me with an explosive clock.'

'Charmed to meet you, Lord Arthur,' said the genial little German, laughing. 'Don't look so alarmed, it is my duty to know everybody, and I remember seeing you one evening at Lady Windermere's. I hope her ladyship is quite well. Do you mind sitting with me while I finish my breakfast? There is an excellent *paté*, and my friends are kind enough to say that my Rhine wine is better than any they get at the German Embassy,' and before Lord Arthur had got over his surprise at being recognised, he found himself seated in the back-room, sipping the most delicious Marcobrünner out of a pale yellow hock-glass marked with the Imperial monogram, and chatting in the friendliest manner possible to the famous conspirator.

'Explosive clocks,' said Herr Winckelkopf, 'are not very good things for foreign exportation, as, even if they succeed in passing the Custom House, the train service is so irregular, that they usually go off before they have reached their proper destination. If, however, you want one for home use, I can supply you with an excellent article, and guarantee that you will be satisfied with the result. May I ask for whom it is intended? If it is for the police, or for any one connected with Scotland Yard, I am afraid I cannot do anything for you. The English detectives are really our best friends, and I have always found that by relying on their stupidity, we can do exactly what we like. I could not spare one of them.'

'I assure you,' said Lord Arthur, 'that it has nothing to do with the police at all. In fact, the clock is intended for the Dean of Chichester.'

'Dear me! I had no idea that you felt so strongly about religion, Lord Arthur. Few young men do nowadays.'

'I am afraid you overrate me, Herr Winckelkopf,' said Lord Arthur, blushing. 'The fact is, I really know nothing about theology.'

'It is a purely private matter then?'

'Purely private.'

Herr Winckelkopf shrugged his shoulders, and left the room, returning in a few minutes with a round cake of dynamite about the size of a penny, and a pretty little French clock, surmounted by an ormolu figure of Liberty trampling on the hydra of Despotism.

Lord Arthur's face brightened up when he saw it. 'That is just what I want,' he cried, 'and now tell me how it goes off.'

'Ah! there is my secret,' answered Herr Winckelkopf, contemplating his invention with a justifiable look of pride; 'let me know when you wish it to explode, and I will set the machine to the moment.'

'Well, to-day is Tuesday, and if you could send it off at once –'

'That is impossible; I have a great deal of important work on hand for some friends of mine in Moscow. Still, I might send it off to-morrow.'

'Oh, it will be quite time enough!' said Lord Arthur politely, 'if it is delivered to-morrow night or Thursday morning. For the moment of the explosion, say Friday at noon exactly. The Dean is always at home at that hour.'

'Friday, at noon,' repeated Herr Winckelkopf, and he made a note to that effect in a large ledger that was lying on a bureau near the fireplace.

'And now,' said Lord Arthur, rising from his seat, 'pray let me know how much I am in your debt.'

'It is such a small matter, Lord Arthur, that I do not care to make any charge. The dynamite comes to seven and sixpence, the clock will be three pounds ten, and the carriage about five shillings. I am only too pleased to oblige any friend of Count Rouvaloff's.'

'But your trouble, Herr Winckelkopf?'

'Oh, that is nothing! It is a pleasure to me. I do not work for money; I live entirely for my art.'

Lord Arthur laid down £4.2s.6d on the table, thanked the little German for his kindness, and, having succeeded in declining an invitation to meet some Anarchists at a meat-tea on the following Saturday, left the house and went off to the Park.

For the next two days he was in a state of the greatest excitement, and on Friday at twelve o'clock he drove down to the Buckingham to wait for news. All the afternoon the stolid hall-porter kept posting up telegrams from various parts of the country giving the results of horse-races, the verdicts in divorce suits, the state of the weather, and the like, while the tape ticked out wearisome details about an all-night sitting in the House of Commons, and a small panic on the Stock Exchange. At four o'clock the evening papers came in, and Lord Arthur disappeared into the library with the *Pall Mall*, the *St. James's*, the *Globe*, and the *Echo*, to the immense indignation of Colonel Goodchild, who wanted to read the reports of a speech he had delivered that morning at the Mansion House, on the subject of South African Missions, and the advisability of having black Bishops in every province, and for some reason or other had a strong prejudice against the *Evening News*. None of the papers, however, contained even the slightest allusion to Chichester, and Lord Arthur felt that the attempt must have failed. It was a terrible blow to him, and for a time he was quite unnerved. Herr Winckelkopf, whom he went to see the next day, was full of elaborate apologies, and offered to supply him with another clock free of charge, or with a case of nitro-glycerine bombs at cost price. But he had lost all faith in explosives, and Herr Winckelkopf himself acknowledged that everything is so adulterated nowadays, that even dynamite can hardly be got in a pure condition. The little German, however, while admitting that something must have gone wrong with the machinery, was not without hope that the clock might still go off, and instanced the case of a barometer that he had once sent to the military Governor at Odessa, which, though timed to explode in ten days, had not done so for something like three months. It was quite true that when it did go off, it merely succeeded in blowing a housemaid to atoms, the Governor having gone out of town six weeks before, but at least it showed that dynamite, as a destructive force, was, when under the control of machinery, a powerful, though somewhat unpunctual agent. Lord Arthur was a little consoled by this reflection, but even here he was destined to disappointment, for two days afterwards, as he was going upstairs, the Duchess called him into her boudoir, and showed him a letter she had just received from the Deanery.

'Jane writes charming letters,' said the Duchess; 'you must really read her last. It is quite as good as the novels Mudie sends us.'

Lord Arthur seized the letter from her hand. It ran as follows: –

THE DEANERY, CHICHESTER,
27th May.

My dearest Aunt,

Thank you so much for the flannel for the Dorcas Society, and also for the gingham. I quite agree with you that it is nonsense their wanting to wear pretty things, but everybody is so Radical and irreligious nowadays, that it is difficult to make them see that they should not try and dress like the upper classes. I am sure I don't know what we are coming to. As papa has often said in his sermons, we live in an age of unbelief.

We have had great fun over a clock that an unknown admirer sent papa last Thursday. It arrived in a wooden box from London, carriage paid; and papa feels it must have been sent by some one who had read his remarkable sermon, 'Is Licence Liberty?' for on the top of the clock was a figure of a woman, with what papa said was the cap of Liberty on her head. I don't think it very becoming myself, but papa said it was historical, so I suppose it is all right. Parker unpacked it, and papa put it on the mantelpiece in the library, and we were all sitting there on Friday morning, when just as the clock struck twelve, we heard a whirring noise, a little puff of smoke came from the pedestal of the figure, and the goddess of Liberty fell off, and broke her nose on the fender! Maria was quite alarmed, but it looked so ridiculous, that James and I went off into fits of laughter, and even papa was amused. When we examined it, we found it was a sort of alarm clock, and that, if you set it to a particular hour, and put some gunpowder and a cap under a little hammer, it went off whenever you wanted. Papa said it must not remain in the library, as it made a noise, so Reggie carried it away to the schoolroom, and does nothing but have small explosions all day long. Do you think Arthur would like one for a wedding present? I suppose they are quite fashionable in London. Papa says they should do a great deal of good, as they show that Liberty can't last, but must fall down. Papa says Liberty was invented at the time of the French Revolution. How awful it seems!

I have now to go to the Dorcas, where I will read your most instructive letter. How true, dear aunt, your idea is, that in their rank of life they should wear what is unbecoming. I must say it is absurd, their anxiety about dress, when there are so many more important things in this world, and in the next. I am so glad your flowered poplin turned out so well, and that your lace was not torn. I am wearing my yellow satin, that you so kindly gave me, at the Bishop's on Wednesday, and think it will look all right. Would you have bows or not? Jennings says that every one wears bows now, and that the underskirt should be frilled. Reggie has just had another explosion, and papa has ordered the clock to be sent to the stables. I don't think papa likes it so much as he did at first, though he is very flattered at being sent such a pretty and ingenious toy. It shows that people read his sermons, and profit by them.

Papa sends his love, in which James, and Reggie, and Maria all unite, and, hoping that Uncle Cecil's gout is better, believe me, dear aunt, ever your affectionate niece,
Jane Percy.

PS. – Do tell me about the bows. Jennings insists they are the fashion.

Lord Arthur looked so serious and unhappy over the letter, that the Duchess went into fits of laughter.

'My dear Arthur,' she cried, 'I shall never show you a young lady's letter again! But what shall I say about the clock? I think it is a capital invention, and I should like to have one myself.'

'I don't think much of them,' said Lord Arthur, with a sad smile, and, after kissing his mother, he left the room.

When he got upstairs, he flung himself on a sofa, and his eyes filled with tears. He had done his best to commit this murder, but on both occasions he had failed, and through no fault of his own. He had tried to do his duty, but it seemed as if Destiny herself had turned traitor. He was oppressed with the sense of the barrenness of good intentions, of the futility of trying to be fine. Perhaps it would be better to break off the marriage altogether. Sybil would suffer, it is true, but suffering could not really mar a nature so noble as hers. As for himself, what did it matter? There is always some war in which a man can die, some cause to which a man can give his life, and as life had no pleasure for him, so death had no terror. Let Destiny work out his doom. He would not stir to help her.

At half-past seven he dressed, and went down to the club. Surbiton was there with a party of young men, and he was obliged to dine with them. Their trivial conversation and idle jests did not interest him, and as soon as coffee was brought he left them, inventing some engagement in order to get away. As he was going out of the club, the hall-porter handed him a letter. It was from Herr Winckelkopf, asking him to call down the next evening, and look at an explosive umbrella, that went off as soon as it was opened. It was the very latest invention, and had just arrived from Geneva. He tore the letter up into fragments. He had made up his mind not to try any more experiments. Then he wandered down to the Thames Embankment, and sat for hours by the river. The moon peered through a mane of tawny clouds, as if it were a lion's eye, and innumerable stars spangled the hollow vault, like gold dust powdered on a purple dome. Now and then a barge swung out into the turbid stream, and floated away with the tide, and the railway signals changed from green to scarlet as the trains ran shrieking across the bridge. After some time, twelve o'clock boomed from the tall tower at Westminster, and at each stroke of the sonorous bell the night seemed to tremble. Then the railway lights went out, one solitary lamp left gleaming like a large ruby on a giant mast, and the roar of the city became fainter.

At two o'clock he got up, and strolled towards Blackfriars. How unreal everything looked! How like a strange dream! The houses on the other side of the river seemed built out of darkness. One would have said that silver and shadow had fashioned the world anew. The huge dome of St. Paul's loomed like a bubble through the dusky air.

As he approached Cleopatra's Needle he saw a man leaning over the parapet, and as he came nearer the man looked up, the gas-light falling full upon his face.

It was Mr. Podgers, the chiromantist! No one could mistake the fat, flabby face, the gold-rimmed spectacles, the sickly feeble smile, the sensual mouth.

Lord Arthur stopped. A brilliant idea flashed across him, and he stole softly up behind. In a moment he had seized Mr. Podgers by the legs, and flung him into the Thames. There was a coarse oath, a heavy splash, and all was still. Lord Arthur looked anxiously over, but could see nothing of the chiromantist but a tall hat, pirouetting in an eddy of moonlit water. After a time it also sank, and no trace of Mr. Podgers was visible. Once he thought that he caught sight of the bulky misshapen figure striking out for the staircase by the bridge, and a horrible feeling of failure came over him but it turned out to be merely a reflection, and when the moon shone out from behind a cloud it passed away. At last he seemed to have realised the decree of Destiny. He heaved a deep sigh of relief, and Sybil's name came to his lips.

'Have you dropped anything, sir?' said a voice behind him suddenly.

He turned round, and saw a policeman with a bull's-eye lantern.

'Nothing of importance, sergeant,' he answered, smiling, and hailing a passing hansom, he jumped in, and told the man to drive to Belgrave Square.

For the next few days he alternated between hope and fear. There were moments when he almost expected Mr. Podgers to walk into the room, and yet at other times he felt that Fate could not be so unjust to him. Twice he went to the chiromantist's address in West Moon Street, but he could not bring himself to ring the bell. He longed for certainty, and was afraid of it.

Finally it came. He was sitting in the smoking-room of the club having tea, and listening rather wearily to Surbiton's account of the last comic song at the Gaiety, when the waiter came in with the evening papers. He took up the *St. James's*, and was listlessly turning over its pages, when this strange heading caught his eye:

'SUICIDE OF A CHIROMANTIST.'

He turned pale with excitement, and began to read. The paragraph ran as follows:

'Yesterday morning, at seven o'clock, the body of Mr. Septimus R. Podgers, the eminent chiromantist, was washed on shore at Greenwich, just in front of the Ship Hotel. The unfortunate gentleman had been missing for some days, and considerable anxiety for his safety had been felt in chiromantic circles. It is supposed that he committed suicide under the influence of a temporary mental derangement, caused by overwork, and a verdict to that effect was returned this afternoon by the coroner's jury. Mr. Podgers had just completed an elaborate treatise on the subject of the Human Hand, that will shortly be published, when it will no doubt attract much attention. The deceased was sixty-five years of age, and does not seem to have left any relations.'

Lord Arthur rushed out of the club with the paper still in his hand, to the immense amazement of the hall-porter, who tried in vain to stop him, and drove at once to Park Lane. Sybil saw him from the window, and something told her that he was the bearer of good news. She ran down to meet him, and, when she saw his face, she knew that all was well.

'My dear Sybil,' cried Lord Arthur, 'let us be married to-morrow!'

'You foolish boy! Why, the cake is not even ordered!' said Sybil, laughing through her tears.

6

WHEN the wedding took place, some three weeks later, St. Peter's was crowded with a perfect mob of smart people. The service was read in the most impressive manner by the Dean of Chichester, and everybody agreed that they had never seen a handsomer couple than the bride and bridegroom. They were more than handsome, however – they were happy. Never for a single moment did Lord Arthur regret all that he had suffered for Sybil's sake, while she, on her side, gave him the best things a woman can give to any man – worship, tenderness, and love. For them romance was not killed by reality. They always felt young.

Some years afterwards, when two beautiful children had been born to them, Lady Windermere came down on a visit to Alton Priory, a lovely old place, that had been the Duke's wedding present to his son; and one afternoon as she was sitting with Lady Arthur under a lime-tree in the garden, watching the little boy and girl as they played up and down the rose-walk, like fitful sunbeams, she suddenly took her hostess's hand in hers, and said, 'Are you happy, Sybil?'

'Dear Lady Windermere, of course I am happy. Aren't you?'

'I have no time to be happy, Sybil. I always like the last person who is introduced to me; but, as a rule, as soon as I know people I get tired of them.'

'Don't your lions satisfy you, Lady Windermere?'

'Oh dear, no! lions are only good for one season. As soon as their manes are cut, they are the dullest creatures going. Besides, they behave very badly, if you are really nice to them. Do you remember that horrid Mr. Podgers? He was a dreadful impostor. Of course, I didn't mind that at all, and even when he wanted to borrow money I forgave him, but I could not stand his making love to me. He has really made me hate chiromancy. I go in for telepathy now. It is much more amusing.'

'You mustn't say anything against chiromancy here, Lady Windermere; it is the only subject that Arthur does not like people to chaff about. I assure you he is quite serious over it.'

'You don't mean to say that he believes in it, Sybil?'

'Ask him, Lady Windermere, here he is'; and Lord Arthur came up the garden with a large bunch of yellow roses in his hand, and his two children dancing round him.

'Lord Arthur?'

'Yes, Lady Windermere.'

'You don't mean to say that you believe in chiromancy?'

'Of course I do,' said the young man, smiling.

'But why?'

'Because I owe to it all the happiness of my life,' he murmured, throwing himself into a wicker chair.

'My dear Lord Arthur, what do you owe to it?'

'Sybil,' he answered, handing his wife the roses, and looking into her violet eyes.

'What nonsense!' cried Lady Windermere. 'I never heard such nonsense in all my life.'

THE CANTERVILLE GHOST

A Hylo-Idealistic Romance

1

WHEN Mr. Hiram B. Otis, the American minister, bought Canterville
Chase, every one told him he was doing a very foolish thing, as there was no
doubt at all that the place was haunted. Indeed, Lord Canterville himself,
who was a man of the most punctilious honour, had felt it his duty to men-
tion the fact to Mr. Otis, when they came to discuss terms.

'We have not cared to live in the place ourselves,' said Lord Canterville,
'since my grand-aunt, the Dowager Duchess of Bolton, was frightened into a
fit, from which she never really recovered, by two skeleton hands being
placed on her shoulders as she was dressing for dinner, and I feel bound to
tell you, Mr. Otis, that the ghost has been seen by several living members of
my family, as well as by the rector of the parish, the Rev. Augustus Dampier,
who is a fellow of King's College, Cambridge. After the unfortunate accident
to the Duchess, none of our younger servants would stay with us, and Lady
Canterville often got very little sleep at night, in consequence of the myster-
ious noises that came from the corridor and the library.'

'My lord,' answered the Minister, 'I will take the furniture and the ghost
at a valuation. I come from a modern country, where we have everything that
money can buy; and with all our spry young fellows painting the Old World
red, and carrying off your best actresses and prima-donnas, I reckon that if
there were such a thing as a ghost in Europe, we'd have it at home in a very
short time in one of our public museums, or on the road as a show.'

'I fear that the ghost exists,' said Lord Canterville, smiling, 'though it may
have resisted the overtures of your enterprising impresarios. It has been well
known for three centuries, since 1584 in fact, and always makes its appear-
ance before the death of any member of our family.'

'Well, so does the family doctor for that matter, Lord Canterville. But
there is no such thing, sir, as a ghost, and I guess the laws of nature are not
going to be suspended for the British aristocracy.'

'You are certainly very natural in America,' answered Lord Canterville,
who did not quite understand Mr. Otis's last observation, 'and if you don't
mind a ghost in the house, it is all right. Only you must remember I warned
you.'

A few weeks after this, the purchase was completed, and at the close of the
season the Minister and his family went down to Canterville Chase. Mrs.
Otis, who, as Miss Lucretia R. Tappan, of West 53rd Street, had been a cel-
ebrated New York belle, was now a very handsome middle-aged woman,
with fine eyes, and a superb profile. Many American ladies on leaving their

native land adopt an appearance of chronic ill-health, under the impression that it is a form of European refinement, but Mrs. Otis had never fallen into this error. She had a magnificent constitution, and a really wonderful amount of animal spirits. Indeed, in many respects, she was quite English, and was an excellent example of the fact that we have really everything in common with America nowadays, except, of course, language. Her eldest son, christened Washington by his parents in a moment of patriotism, which he never ceased to regret, was a fair-haired, rather good-looking young man, who had qualified himself for American diplomacy by leading the German at the Newport Casino for three successive seasons, and even in London was well known as an excellent dancer. Gardenias and the peerage were his only weaknesses. Otherwise he was extremely sensible. Miss Virginia E. Otis was a little girl of fifteen, lithe and lovely as a fawn, and with a fine freedom in her large blue eyes. She was a wonderful amazon, and had once raced old Lord Bilton on her pony twice round the park, winning by a length and a half, just in front of the Achilles statue, to the huge delight of the young Duke of Cheshire, who proposed to her on the spot, and was sent back to Eton that very night by his guardians, in floods of tears. After Virginia came the twins, who were usually called 'The Stars and Stripes' as they were always getting swished. They were delightful boys, and with the exception of the worthy Minister the only true republicans of the family.

As Canterville Chase is seven miles from Ascot, the nearest railway station, Mr. Otis had telegraphed for a waggonette to meet them, and they started on their drive in high spirits. It was a lovely July evening, and the air was delicate with the scent of the pinewoods. Now and then they heard a wood pigeon brooding over its own sweet voice, or saw, deep in the rustling fern, the burnished breast of the pheasant. Little squirrels peered at them from the beech-trees as they went by, and the rabbits scudded away through the brushwood and over the mossy knolls, with their white tails in the air. As they entered the avenue of Canterville Chase, however, the sky became suddenly overcast with clouds, a curious stillness seemed to hold the atmosphere, a great flight of rooks passed silently over their heads, and, before they reached the house, some big drops of rain had fallen.

Standing on the steps to receive them was an old woman, neatly dressed in black silk, with a white cap and apron. This was Mrs. Umney, the housekeeper, whom Mrs. Otis, at Lady Canterville's earnest request, had consented to keep on in her former position. She made them each a low curtsey as they alighted, and said in a quaint, old-fashioned manner, 'I bid you welcome to Canterville Chase.' Following her, they passed through the fine Tudor hall into the library, a long, low-room, panelled in black oak, at the end of which was a large stained-glass window. Here they found tea laid out for them, and, after taking off their wraps, they sat down and began to look round, while Mrs. Umney waited on them.

Suddenly Mrs. Otis caught sight of a dull red stain on the floor just by the fireplace and, quite unconscious of what it really signified, said to Mrs. Umney, 'I am afraid something has been spilt there.'

'Yes, madam,' replied the old housekeeper in a low voice, 'blood has been spilt on that spot.'

'How horrid,' cried Mrs. Otis; 'I don't at all care for blood-stains in a sitting-room. It must be removed at once.'

The old woman smiled, and answered in the same low, mysterious voice, 'It is the blood of Lady Eleanore de Canterville, who was murdered on that very spot by her own husband, Sir Simon de Canterville, in 1575. Sir Simon survived her nine years, and disappeared suddenly under very mysterious circumstances. His body has never been discovered, but his guilty spirit still haunts the Chase. The blood-stain has been much admired by tourists and others, and cannot be removed.'

'That is all nonsense,' cried Washington Otis; 'Pinkerton's Champion Stain Remover and Paragon Detergent will clean it up in no time,' and before the terrified housekeeper could interfere he had fallen upon his knees, and was rapidly scouring the floor with a small stick of what looked like a black cosmetic. In a few moments no trace of the blood-stain could be seen.

'I knew Pinkerton would do it,' he exclaimed triumphantly, as he looked round at his admiring family; but no sooner had he said these words than a terrible flash of lightning lit up the sombre room, a fearful peal of thunder made them all start to their feet, and Mrs. Umney fainted.

'What a monstrous climate!' said the American Minister calmly, as he lit a long cheroot. 'I guess the old country is so overpopulated that they have not enough decent weather for everybody. I have always been of opinion that emigration is the only thing for England.'

'My dear Hiram,' cried Mrs. Otis, 'what can we do with a woman who faints?'

'Charge it to her like breakages,' answered the Minister; 'she won't faint after that'; and in a few moments Mrs. Umney certainly came to. There was no doubt, however, that she was extremely upset, and she sternly warned Mr. Otis to beware of some trouble coming to the house.

'I have seen things with my own eyes, sir,' she said, 'that would make any Christian's hair stand on end, and many and many a night I have not closed my eyes in sleep for the awful things that are done here.' Mr. Otis, however, and his wife warmly assured the honest soul that they were not afraid of ghosts, and, after invoking the blessings of Providence on her new master and mistress, and making arrangements for an increase of salary, the old housekeeper tottered off to her own room.

2

THE storm raged fiercely all that night, but nothing of particular note occurred. The next morning, however, when they came down to breakfast, they found the terrible stain of blood once again on the floor. 'I don't think it can be the fault of the Paragon Detergent,' said Washington, 'for I have tried it with everything. It must be the ghost.' He accordingly rubbed out the stain a second time, but the second morning it appeared again. The third morning also it was there, though the library had been locked up at night by Mr. Otis himself, and the key carried upstairs. The whole family were now quite interested; Mr. Otis began to suspect that he had been too dogmatic in his denial of the existence of ghosts, Mrs. Otis expressed her intention of joining the Psychical Society, and Washington prepared a long letter to Messrs. Myers and Podmore on the subject of the Permanence of Sanguineous Stains when connected with crime. That night all doubts about the objective existence of phantasmata were removed for ever.

The day had been warm and sunny; and, in the cool of the evening, the whole family went out for a drive. They did not return home till nine o'clock, when they had a light supper. The conversation in no way turned upon ghosts, so there were not even those primary conditions of receptive expectation which so often precede the presentation of psychical phenomena. The subjects discussed, as I have since learned from Mr. Otis, were merely such as form the ordinary conversation of cultured Americans of the better class, such as the immense superiority of Miss Fanny Davenport over Sarah Bernhardt as an actress; the difficulty of obtaining green corn, buckwheat cakes, and hominy, even in the best English houses; the importance of Boston in the development of the world-soul; the advantages of the baggage check system in railway travelling; and the sweetness of the New York accent as compared to the London drawl. No mention at all was made of the supernatural, nor was Sir Simon de Canterville alluded to in any way. At eleven o'clock the family retired and by half-past all the lights were out. Some time after, Mr. Otis was awakened by a curious noise in the corridor, outside his room. It sounded like the clank of metal, and seemed to be coming nearer every moment. He got up at once, struck a match, and looked at the time. It was exactly one o'clock. He was quite calm, and felt his pulse, which was not at all feverish. The strange noise still continued, and with it he heard distinctly the sound of footsteps. He put on his slippers, took a small oblong phial out of his dressing-case, and opened the door. Right in front of him he saw, in the wan moonlight, an old man of terrible aspect. His eyes were as red as burning coals; long grey hair fell over his shoulders in matted coils; his garments, which were of antique cut, were soiled and ragged, and from his wrists and ankles hung heavy manacles and rusty gyves.

'My dear sir,' said Mr. Otis, 'I really must insist on your oiling those chains, and have brought you for that purpose a small bottle of the Tammany Rising Sun Lubricator. It is said to be completely efficacious upon one application, and there are several testimonials to that effect on the wrapper from some of our most eminent native divines. I shall leave it here for you by the bedroom candles, and will be happy to supply you with more should you require it.' With these words the United States Minister laid the bottle down on a marble table, and, closing his door, retired to rest.

For a moment the Canterville ghost stood quite motionless in natural indignation; then, dashing the bottle violently upon the polished floor, he fled down the corridor, uttering hollow groans, and emitting a ghastly green light. Just, however, as he reached the top of the great oak staircase, a door was flung open, two little white-robed figures appeared, and a large pillow whizzed past his head! There was evidently no time to be lost, so, hastily adopting the Fourth Dimension of Space as a means of escape, he vanished through the wainscoting, and the house became quite quiet.

On reaching a small secret chamber in the left wing, he leaned up against a moonbeam to recover his breath, and began to try and realise his position. Never, in a brilliant and uninterrupted career of three hundred years, had he been so grossly insulted. He thought of the Dowager Duchess, whom he had frightened into a fit as she stood before the glass in her lace and diamonds; of the four housemaids, who had gone off into hysterics when he merely grinned at them through the curtains of one of the spare bedrooms; of the rector of the parish, whose candle he had blown out as he was coming late one night from the library, and who had been under the care of Sir William Gull ever since, a perfect martyr to nervous disorders; and of old Madame de Tremouillac, who, having wakened up one morning early and seen a skeleton seated in an arm-chair by the fire reading her diary had been confined to her bed for six weeks with an attack of brain fever, and, on her recovery, had become reconciled to the Church, and had broken off her connection with that notorious sceptic Monsieur de Voltaire. He remembered the terrible night when the wicked Lord Canterville was found choking in his dressing-room, with the knave of diamonds half-way down his throat, and confessed, just before he died, that he had cheated Charles James Fox out of £50,000 at Crockford's by means of that very card, and swore that the ghost had made him swallow it. All his great achievements came back to him again, from the butler who had shot himself in the pantry because he had seen a green hand tapping at the window pane, to the beautiful Lady Stutfield, who was always obliged to wear a black velvet band round her throat to hide the mark of five fingers burnt upon her white skin, and who drowned herself at last in the carp-pond at the end of the King's Walk. With the enthusiastic egotism of the true artist he went over his most celebrated performances, and smiled bitterly to himself as he recalled to mind his last appearance as 'Red Ruben, or the Strangled Babe,' his *début* as 'Gaunt Gibeon, the Blood-sucker of Bexley Moor,' and the *furore* he had excited one lonely June evening by merely playing ninepins with his own bones upon the lawn-tennis ground. And after all this, some wretched modern Americans were to come and offer him the Rising Sun Lubricator, and throw pillows at his head! It was quite unbearable. Besides, no ghosts in history had ever been treated in this manner. Accordingly, he determined to have vengeance, and remained till daylight in an attitude of deep thought.

3

THE next morning when the Otis family met at breakfast, they discussed the ghost at some length. The United States Minister was naturally a little annoyed to find that his present had not been accepted. 'I have no wish,' he said, 'to do the ghost any personal injury, and I must say that, considering the length of time he has been in the house, I don't think it is at all polite to throw pillows at him' – a very just remark, at which, I am sorry to say, the twins burst into shouts of laughter. 'Upon the other hand,' he continued, 'if he really declines to use the Rising Sun Lubricator, we shall have to take his chains from him. It would be quite impossible to sleep, with such a noise going on outside the bedrooms.'

For the rest of the week, however, they were undisturbed, the only thing that excited any attention being the continual renewal of the blood-stain on the library floor. This certainly was very strange, as the door was always locked at night by Mr. Otis, and the windows kept closely barred. The chameleon-like colour, also, of the stain excited a good deal of comment. Some mornings it was a dull (almost Indian) red, then it would be vermilion, then a rich purple, and once when they came down for family prayers, according to the simple rites of the Free American Reformed Episcopalian Church, they found it a bright emerald-green. These kaleidoscopic changes naturally amused the party very much, and bets on the subject were freely made every evening. The only person who did not enter into the joke was little Virginia, who, for some unexplained reason, was always a good deal distressed at the sight of the blood-stain, and very nearly cried the morning it was emerald-green.

The second appearance of the ghost was on Sunday night. Shortly after they had gone to bed they were suddenly alarmed by a fearful crash in the hall. Rushing downstairs, they found that a large suit of old armour had become detached from its stand, and had fallen on the stone floor, while, seated in a high-backed chair, was the Canterville ghost, rubbing his knees with an expression of acute agony on his face. The twins, having brought their peashooters with them, at once discharged two pellets on him, with that accuracy of aim which can only be attained by long and careful practice on a writing-master, while the United States Minister covered him with his revolver, and called upon him, in accordance with Californian etiquette, to hold up his hands! The ghost started up with a wild shriek of rage, and swept through them like a mist, extinguishing Washington Otis's candle as he passed, and so leaving them all in total darkness. On reaching the top of the staircase he recovered himself, and determined to give his celebrated peal of demoniac laughter. This he had on more than one occasion found extremely useful. It was said to have turned Lord Raker's wig grey in a single night, and had certainly made three of Lady Canterville's French governesses give warning before their month was up. He accordingly laughed his most horrible laugh, till the old vaulted roof rang and rang again, but hardly had the fearful echo died away when a door opened, and Mrs. Otis came out in a light blue dressing-gown. 'I am afraid you are far from well,' she said, 'and have brought you a bottle of Dr. Dobell's tincture. If it is indigestion, you will find it a most excellent remedy.' The ghost glared at her in fury, and began at once to make preparations for turning himself into a large black dog, an accomplishment for which he was justly renowned, and to which the family doctor always attributed the permanent idiocy of Lord Canterville's uncle, the Hon. Thomas Horton. The sound of approaching footsteps, however, made him hesitate in his fell purpose, so he contented himself with becoming faintly phosphorescent, and vanished with a deep church-yard groan, just as the twins had come up to him.

On reaching his room he entirely broke down, and became a prey to the most violent agitation. The vulgarity of the twins, and the gross materialism of Mrs. Otis, were naturally extremely annoying, but what really distressed him most was, that he had been unable to wear the suit of mail. He had hoped that even modern Americans would be thrilled by the sight of a Spectre In Armour, if for no more sensible reason, at least out of respect for their national poet Longfellow, over whose graceful and attractive poetry he himself had whiled away many a weary hour when the Cantervilles were up in town. Besides, it was his own suit. He had worn it with success at the Kenilworth tournament, and had been highly complimented on it by no less a person than the Virgin Queen herself. Yet when he had put it on, he had been completely overpowered by the weight of the huge breastplate and steel casque, and had fallen heavily on the stone pavement, barking both his knees severely, and bruising the knuckles of his right hand.

For some days after this he was extremely ill, and hardly stirred out of his room at all, except to keep the blood-stain in proper repair. However, by taking great care of himself, he recovered, and resolved to make a third attempt to frighten the United States Minister and his family. He selected Friday, the 17th of August, for his appearance, and spent most of that day in looking over his wardrobe, ultimately deciding in favour of a large slouched hat with a red feather, a winding-sheet frilled at the wrists and neck, and a rusty dagger. Towards evening a violent storm of rain came on, and the wind was so high that all the windows and doors in the old house shook and rattled. In fact, it was just such weather as he loved. His plan of action was this. He was to make his way quietly to Washington Otis's room, gibber at him from the foot of the bed, and stab himself three times in the throat to the sound of slow music. He bore Washington a special grudge, being quite aware that it was he who was in the habit of removing the famous Canterville blood-stain, by means of Pinkerton's Paragon Detergent. Having reduced the reckless and foolhardy youth to a condition of abject terror, he was then to proceed to the room occupied by the United States Minister and his wife, and there to place a clammy hand on Mrs. Otis's forehead, while he hissed into her trembling husband's ear the awful secrets of the charnel-house. With regard to little Virginia, he had not quite made up his mind. She had never insulted him in any way, and was pretty and gentle. A few hollow groans from the wardrobe, he thought, would be more than sufficient, or, if that failed to wake her, he might grabble at the counterpane with palsy-twitching fingers. As for the twins, he was quite determined to teach them a lesson. The first thing to be done was, of course, to sit upon their chests, so as to produce the stifling sensation of nightmare. Then, as their beds were quite close to each other, to stand between them in the form of a green, icy-cold corpse, till they became paralysed with fear, and finally, to throw off the winding-sheet, and crawl round the room, with white bleached bones and one rolling eyeball, in the character of 'Dumb Daniel, or the Suicide's Skeleton,' a *rôle* in which he had on more than one occasion produced a great effect, and which he considered quite equal to his famous part of 'Martin the Maniac, or the Masked Mystery.'

At half-past ten he heard the family going to bed. For some time he was disturbed by wild shrieks of laughter from the twins, who, with the light-hearted gaiety of schoolboys, were evidently amusing themselves before they retired to rest, but at a quarter-past eleven all was still, and, as midnight sounded, he sallied forth. The owl beat against the window panes, the raven croaked from the old yew-tree, and the wind wandered moaning round the house like a lost soul; but the Otis family slept unconscious of their doom, and high above the rain and storm he could hear the steady snoring of the Minister for the United States. He stepped stealthily out of the wainscoting, with an evil smile on his cruel, wrinkled mouth, and the moon hid her face in a cloud as he stole past the great oriel window, where his own arms and those of his murdered wife were blazoned in azure and gold. On and on he glided, like an evil shadow, the very darkness seeming to loathe him as he passed. Once he thought he heard something call, and stopped; but it was only the baying of a dog from the Red Farm, and he went on, muttering strange sixteenth-century curses, and ever and anon brandishing the rusty dagger in the midnight air. Finally he reached the corner of the passage that led to luckless Washington's room. For a moment he paused there, the wind blowing his long grey locks about his head, and twisting into grotesque and fantastic folds the nameless horror of the dead man's shroud. Then the clock struck the quarter, and he felt the time was come. He chuckled to himself, and turned the corner; but no sooner had he done so, than, with a piteous wail of terror, he fell back, and hid his blanched face in his long, bony hands. Right in front of him was standing a horrible spectre, motionless as a carven image, and monstrous as a madman's dream! Its head was bald and burnished; its face round, and fat, and white; and hideous laughter seemed to have writhed its features into an eternal grin. From the eyes streamed rays of scarlet light, the mouth was a wide well of fire, and a hideous garment, like to his own, swathed with its silent snows the Titan form. On its breast was a placard with strange writing in antique characters, some scroll of shame it seemed, some record of wild sins, some awful calendar of crime, and, with its right hand, it bore aloft a falchion of gleaming steel.

Never having seen a ghost before, he naturally was terribly frightened, and, after a second hasty glance at the awful phantom, he fled back to his room, tripping up in his long winding-sheet as he sped down the corridor, and finally dropping the rusty dagger into the Minister's jack-boots, where it was found in the morning by the butler. Once in the privacy of his own apartment, he flung himself down on a small pallet-bed and hid his face under the clothes. After a time, however, the brave old Canterville spirit asserted itself, and he determined to go and speak to the other ghost as soon as it was daylight. Accordingly, just as the dawn was touching the hills with silver, he returned towards the spot where he had first laid eyes on the grisly phantom, feeling that, after all, two ghosts were better than one, and that, by the aid of his new friend, he might safely grapple with the twins. On reaching the spot, however, a terrible sight met his gaze. Something had evidently happened to the spectre, for the light had entirely faded from its hollow eyes, the gleaming falchion had fallen from its hand, and it was leaning up against the wall in a strained and uncomfortable attitude. He rushed forward and seized it in his arms, when, to his horror, the head slipped off and rolled on the floor, the body assumed a recumbent posture, and he found himself clasping a white dimity bed-curtain, with a sweeping-brush, a kitchen cleaver, and a hollow turnip lying at his feet! Unable to understand this curious transformation, he clutched the placard with feverish haste, and there, in the grey morning light, he read these fearful words: –

> 𝔜𝔢 𝔒𝔗𝔍𝔖 𝔊𝔥𝔬𝔰𝔱𝔢,
> 𝔜𝔢 𝔒𝔫𝔩𝔦𝔢 𝔗𝔯𝔲𝔢 𝔞𝔫𝔡 𝔒𝔯𝔦𝔤𝔦𝔫𝔞𝔩𝔢 𝔖𝔭𝔬𝔬𝔨.
> 𝔅𝔢𝔴𝔞𝔯𝔢 𝔬𝔣 𝔜𝔢 𝔍𝔪𝔦𝔱𝔞𝔱𝔦𝔬𝔫𝔢𝔰.
> 𝔄𝔩𝔩 𝔬𝔱𝔥𝔢𝔯𝔰 𝔞𝔯𝔢 𝔠𝔬𝔲𝔫𝔱𝔢𝔯𝔣𝔢𝔦𝔱𝔢.

The whole thing flashed across him. He had been tricked, foiled, and outwitted! The old Canterville look came into his eyes; he ground his toothless gums together; and, raising his withered hands high above his head, swore, according to the picturesque phraseology of the antique school, that when Chanticleer had sounded twice his merry horn, deeds of blood would be wrought, and Murder walk abroad with silent feet.

Hardly had he finished this awful oath when, from the red-tiled roof of a distant homestead, a cock crew. He laughed a long, low, bitter laugh, and waited. Hour after hour he waited, but the cock, for some strange reason, did not crow again. Finally, at half-past seven, the arrival of the housemaids made him give up his fearful vigil, and he stalked back to his room, thinking of his vain hope and baffled purpose. There he consulted several books of ancient chivalry, of which he was exceedingly fond, and found that, on every occasion on which his oath had been used, Chanticleer had always crowed a second time. 'Perdition seize the naughty fowl,' he muttered, 'I have seen the day when, with my stout spear, I would have run him through the gorge, and made him crow for me an 'twere in death!' He then retired to a comfortable lead coffin, and stayed there till evening.

4

THE next day the ghost was very weak and tired. The terrible excitement of the last four weeks was beginning to have its effect. His nerves were completely shattered, and he started at the slightest noise. For five days he kept his room, and at last made up his mind to give up the point of the blood-stain on the library floor. If the Otis family did not want it, they clearly did not deserve it. They were evidently people on a low, material plane of existence, and quite incapable of appreciating the symbolic value of sensuous phenomena. The question of phantasmic apparitions, and the development of astral bodies, was of course quite a different matter, and really not under his control. It was his solemn duty to appear in the corridor once a week, and to gibber from the large oriel window on the first and third Wednesday in every month, and he did not see how he could honourably escape from his obligations. It is quite true that his life had been very evil, but, upon the other hand, he was most conscientious in all things connected with the supernatural. For the next three Saturdays, accordingly, he traversed the corridor as usual between midnight and three o'clock, taking every possible precaution against being either heard or seen. He removed his boots, trod as lightly as possible on the old worm-eaten boards, wore a large black velvet cloak, and was careful to use the Rising Sun Lubricator for oiling his chains. I am bound to acknowledge that it was with a good deal of difficulty that he brought himself to adopt this last mode of protection. However, one night, while the family were at dinner, he slipped into Mr. Otis's bedroom and carried off the bottle. He felt a little humiliated at first, but afterwards was sensible enough to see that there was a great deal to be said for the invention, and, to a certain degree, it served his purpose. Still, in spite of everything, he was not left unmolested. Strings were continually being stretched across the corridor, over which he tripped in the dark, and on one occasion, while dressed for the part of 'Black Isaac, or the Huntsman of Hogley Woods,' he met with a severe fall, through treading on a butter-slide, which the twins had constructed from the entrance of the Tapestry Chamber to the top of the oak staircase. This last insult so enraged him, that he resolved to make one final effort to assert his dignity and social position, and determined to visit the insolent young Etonians the next night in his celebrated character of 'Reckless Rupert, or the Headless Earl.'

He had not appeared in this disguise for more than seventy years; in fact, not since he had so frightened pretty Lady Barbara Modish by means of it, that she suddenly broke off her engagement with the present Lord Canterville's grandfather, and ran away to Gretna Green with handsome Jack Castleton, declaring that nothing in the world would induce her to marry into a family that allowed such a horrible phantom to walk up and down the terrace at twilight. Poor Jack was afterwards shot in a duel by Lord Canterville on Wandsworth Common, and Lady Barbara died of a broken heart at Tunbridge Wells before the year was out, so, in every way, it had been a great success. It was, however, an extremely difficult 'make-up,' if I may use such a theatrical expression in connection with one of the greatest mysteries of the supernatural, or, to employ a more scientific term, the higher-natural world, and it took him fully three hours to make his preparations. At last everything was ready, and he was very pleased with his appearance. The big leather riding-boots that went with the dress were just a little too large for him, and he could only find one of the two horse-pistols, but, on the whole, he was quite satisfied, and at a quarter-past one he glided out of the wainscoting and crept down the corridor. On reaching the room occupied by the twins, which I should mention was called the Blue Bed Chamber, on account of the colour of its hangings, he found the door just ajar. Wishing to make an effective entrance, he flung it wide open, when a heavy jug of water fell right down on him, wetting him to the skin, and just missing his left shoulder by a couple of inches. At the same moment he heard stifled shrieks of laughter proceeding from the four-post bed. The shock to his nervous system was so great that he fled back to his room as hard as he could go, and the next day he was laid up with a severe cold. The only thing that at all consoled him in the whole affair was the fact that he had not brought his head with him, for, had he done so, the consequences might have been very serious.

He now gave up all hope of ever frightening this rude American family, and contented himself, as a rule, with creeping about the passages in list slippers, with a thick red muffler round his throat for fear of draughts, and a small arquebuse, in case he should be attacked by the twins. The final blow he received occurred on the 19th of September. He had gone downstairs to the great entrance-hall, feeling sure that there, at any rate, he would be quite unmolested, and was amusing himself by making satirical remarks on the large Saroni photographs of the United States Minister and his wife, which had now taken the place of the Canterville family pictures. He was simply but neatly clad in a long shroud, spotted with churchyard mould, had tied up his jaw with a strip of yellow linen, and carried a small lantern and a sexton's spade. In fact, he was dressed for the character of 'Jonas the Graveless, or the Corpse-Snatcher of Chertsey Barn,' one of his most remarkable impersonations, and one which the Cantervilles had every reason to remember, as it was the real origin of their quarrel with their neighbour, Lord Rufford. It was about a quarter past two o'clock in the morning, and, as far as he could ascertain, no one was stirring. As he was strolling towards the library, however, to see if there were any traces left of the blood-stain, suddenly there leaped out on him from a dark corner two figures, who waved their arms wildly above their heads, and shrieked out 'BOO!' in his ear.

Seized with a panic, which, under the circumstances, was only natural, he rushed for the staircase, but found Washington Otis waiting for him there with the big garden-syringe; and being thus hemmed in by his enemies on every side, and driven almost to bay, he vanished into the great iron stove, which, fortunately for him, was not lit, and had to make his way home through the flues and chimneys, arriving at his own room in a terrible state of dirt, disorder, and despair.

After this he was not seen again on any nocturnal expedition. The twins lay in wait for him on several occasions, and strewed the passages with nut-shells every night to the great annoyance of their parents and the servants, but it was of no avail. It was quite evident that his feelings were so wounded that he would not appear. Mr. Otis consequently resumed his great work on the history of the Democratic Party, on which he had been engaged for some years; Mrs. Otis organised a wonderful clambake, which amazed the whole county; the boys took to lacrosse, euchre, poker, and other American national games; and Virginia rode about the lanes on her pony, accompanied by the young Duke of Cheshire, who had come to spend the last week of his holidays at Canterville Chase. It was generally assumed that the ghost had gone away, and, in fact, Mr. Otis wrote a letter to that effect to Lord Canterville, who, in reply, expressed his great pleasure at the news, and sent his best congratulations to the Minister's worthy wife.

The Otises, however, were deceived, for the ghost was still in the house, and though now almost an invalid, was by no means ready to let matters rest, particularly as he heard that among the guests was the young Duke of Cheshire, whose grand-uncle, Lord Francis Stilton, had once bet a hundred guineas with Colonel Carbury that he would play dice with the Canterville ghost, and was found the next morning lying on the floor of the card-room in such a helpless paralytic state, that though he lived on to a great age, he was never able to say anything again but 'Double Sixes.' The story was well known at the time, though, of course, out of respect to the feelings of the two noble families, every attempt was made to hush it up; and a full account of all the circumstances connected with it will be found in the third volume of Lord Tattle's *Recollections of the Prince Regent and his Friends*. The ghost, then, was naturally very anxious to show that he had not lost his influence over the Stiltons, with whom indeed, he was distantly connected, his own first cousin having been married *en secondes noces* to the Sieur de Bulkeley, from whom, as every one knows, the Dukes of Cheshire are lineally descended. Accordingly, he made arrangements for appearing to Virginia's little lover in his celebrated impersonation of 'The Vampire Monk, or, the Bloodless Benedictine,' a performance so horrible that when old Lady Startup saw it, which she did on one fatal New Year's Eve, in the year 1764, she went off into the most piercing shrieks, which culminated in violent apoplexy, and died in three days, after disinheriting the Cantervilles, who were her nearest relations, and leaving all her money to her London apothecary. At the last moment, however, his terror of the twins prevented his leaving his room, and the little Duke slept in peace under the great feathered canopy in the Royal Bedchamber, and dreamed of Virginia.

5

A FEW days after this, Virginia and her curly-haired cavalier went out riding on Brockley meadows, where she tore her habit so badly in getting through a hedge, that, on her return home, she made up her mind to go up by the back staircase so as not to be seen. As she was running past the Tapestry Chamber, the door of which happened to be opened, she fancied she saw some one inside, and thinking it was her mother's maid, who sometimes used to bring her work there, looked in to ask her to mend her habit. To her immense surprise, however, it was the Canterville Ghost himself! He was sitting by the window, watching the ruined gold of the yellow trees fly through the air, and the red leaves dancing madly down the long avenue. His head was leaning on his hand, and his whole attitude was one of extreme depression. Indeed, so forlorn, and so much out of repair did he look, that little Virginia, whose first idea had been to run away and lock herself in her room, was filled with pity, and determined to try and comfort him. So light was her footfall, and so deep his melancholy, that he was not aware of her presence till she spoke to him.

'I am so sorry for you,' she said, 'but my brothers are going back to Eton to-morrow, and then, if you behave yourself, no one will annoy you.'

'It is absurd asking me to behave myself,' he answered, looking round in astonishment at the pretty little girl who had ventured to address him, 'quite absurd. I must rattle my chains, and groan through keyholes, and walk about at night, if that is what you mean. It is my only reason for existing.'

'It is no reason at all for existing, and you know you have been very wicked. Mrs. Umney told us, the first day we arrived here, that you had killed your wife.'

'Well, I quite admit it,' said the Ghost petulantly, 'but it was a purely family matter, and concerned no one else.'

'It is very wrong to kill any one,' said Virginia, who at times had a sweet Puritan gravity, caught from some old New England ancestor.

'Oh, I hate the cheap severity of abstract ethics! My wife was very plain, never had my ruffs properly starched, and knew nothing about cookery. Why, there was a buck I had shot in Hogley Woods, a magnificent pricket, and do you know how she had it sent up to table? However, it is no matter now, for it is all over, and I don't think it was very nice of her brothers to starve me to death, though I did kill her.'

'Starve you to death? Oh, Mr. Ghost, I mean Sir Simon, are you hungry? I have a sandwich in my case. Would you like it?'

'No, thank you, I never eat anything now; but it is very kind of you, all the same, and you are much nicer than the rest of your horrid, rude, vulgar, dishonest family.'

'Stop!' cried Virginia, stamping her foot, 'it is you who are rude, and horrid, and vulgar; and as for dishonesty, you know you stole the paints out of my box to try and furbish up that ridiculous blood-stain in the library. First you took all my reds, including the vermilion, and I couldn't do any more sunsets, then you took the emerald-green and the chrome-yellow, and finally I had nothing left but indigo and Chinese white, and could only do moonlight scenes, which are always depressing to look at, and not at all easy to paint. I never told on you, though I was very much annoyed, and it was most ridiculous, the whole thing; for who ever heard of emerald-green blood?'

'Well, really,' said the Ghost, rather meekly, 'what was I to do? It is a very difficult thing to get real blood nowadays, and, as your brother began it all with his Paragon Detergent, I certainly saw no reason why I should not have your paints. As for colour, that is always a matter of taste: the Cantervilles have blue blood, for instance, the very bluest in England; but I know you Americans don't care for things of this kind.'

'You know nothing about it, and the best thing you can do is to emigrate and improve your mind. My father will be only too happy to give you a free passage, and though there is a heavy duty on spirits of every kind, there will be no difficulty about the Custom House, as the officers are all Democrats. Once in New York, you are sure to be a great success. I know lots of people there who would give a hundred thousand dollars to have a grandfather, and much more than that to have a family Ghost.'

'I don't think I should like America.'

'I suppose because we have no ruins and no curiosities,' said Virginia satirically.

'No ruins! No curiosities!' answered the Ghost; 'You have your navy and your manners.'

'Good evening; I will go and ask papa to get the twins an extra week's holiday.'

'Please don't go, Miss Virginia,' he cried; 'I am so lonely and so unhappy, and I really don't know what to do. I want to go to sleep and I cannot.'

'That's quite absurd! You have merely to go to bed and blow out the candle. It is very difficult sometimes to keep awake, especially at church, but there is no difficulty at all about sleeping. Why, even babies know how to do that, and they are not very clever.'

'I have not slept for three hundred years,' he said sadly, and Virginia's beautiful blue eyes opened in wonder; 'for three hundred years I have not slept, and I am so tired.'

Virginia grew quite grave, and her little lips trembled like rose-leaves. She came towards him, and kneeling down at his side, looked up into his old withered face.

'Poor, poor Ghost,' she murmured; 'have you no place where you can sleep?'

'Far away beyond the pine-woods,' he answered, in a low dreamy voice, 'there is a little garden. There the grass grows long and deep, there are the great white stars of the hemlock flower, there the nightingale sings all night long. All night long he sings, and the cold, crystal moon looks down, and the yew-tree spreads out its giant arms over the sleepers.'

Virginia's eyes grew dim with tears, and she hid her face in her hands.

'You mean the Garden of Death,' she whispered.

'Yes, Death. Death must be so beautiful. To lie in the soft brown earth, with the grasses waving above one's head, and listen to silence. To have no yesterday, and no to-morrow. To forget time, to forgive life, to be at peace. You can help me. You can open for me the portals of Death's house, for Love is always with you, and Love is stronger than Death is.'

Virginia trembled, a cold shudder ran through her, and for a few moments there was silence. She felt as if she was in a terrible dream.

Then the Ghost spoke again, and his voice sounded like the sighing of the wind.

'Have you ever read the old prophecy on the library window?'

'Oh, often,' cried the little girl, looking up; 'I know it quite well. It is painted in curious black letters, and it is difficult to read. There are only six lines:

> When a golden girl can win
> Prayer from out the lips of sin,
> When the barren almond bears,
> And a little child gives away its tears,
> Then shall all the house be still
> And peace come to Canterville.

But I don't know what they mean.'

'They mean,' he said sadly, 'that you must weep for me for my sins, because I have no tears, and pray for me for my soul, because I have no faith, and then, if you have always been sweet, and good, and gentle, the Angel of Death will have mercy on me. You will see fearful shapes in darkness, and wicked voices will whisper in your ear, but they will not harm you, for against the purity of a little child the powers of Hell cannot prevail.'

Virginia made no answer, and the Ghost wrung his hands in wild despair as he looked down at her bowed golden head. Suddenly she stood up, very pale, and with a strange light in her eyes. 'I am not afraid,' she said firmly, 'and I will ask the Angel to have mercy on you.'

He rose from his seat with a faint cry of joy, and taking her hand bent over it with old-fashioned grace and kissed it. His fingers were as cold as ice, and his lips burned like fire, but Virginia did not falter, as he led her across the dusky room. On the faded green tapestry were broidered little huntsmen. They blew their tasselled horns and with their tiny hands waved to her to go back. 'Go back! little Virginia,' they cried, 'go back!' but the Ghost clutched her hand more tightly, and she shut her eyes against them. Horrible animals with lizard tails, and goggle eyes, blinked at her from the carven chimney-piece, and murmured 'Beware! little Virginia, beware! we may never see you again,' but the Ghost glided on more swiftly, and Virginia did not listen. When they reached the end of the room he stopped, and muttered some words she could not understand. She opened her eyes, and saw the wall slowly fading away like a mist, and a great black cavern in front of her. A bitter cold wind swept round them, and she felt something pulling at her dress.

'Quick, quick,' cried the Ghost, 'or it will be too late,' and, in a moment, the wainscoting had closed behind them, and the Tapestry Chamber was empty.

6

ABOUT ten minutes later, the bell rang for tea, and, as Virginia did not come down, Mrs. Otis sent up one of the footmen to tell her. After a little time he returned and said that he could not find Miss Virginia anywhere. As she was in the habit of going out to the garden every evening to get flowers for the dinner-table, Mrs. Otis was not at all alarmed at first, but when six o'clock struck, and Virginia did not appear, she became really agitated, and sent the boys out to look for her, while she herself and Mr. Otis searched every room in the house. At half-past six the boys came back and said that they could find no trace of their sister anywhere. They were all now in the greatest state of excitement, and did not know what to do, when Mr. Otis suddenly remembered that, some few days before, he had given a band of gypsies permission to camp in the park. He accordingly at once set off for Blackfell Hollow, where he knew they were, accompanied by his eldest son and two of the farm-servants. The little Duke of Cheshire, who was perfectly frantic with anxiety, begged hard to be allowed to go too, but Mr. Otis would not allow him, as he was afraid there might be a scuffle. On arriving at the spot, however, he found that the gypsies had gone, and it was evident that their departure had been rather sudden, as the fire was still burning, and some plates were lying on the grass. Having sent off Washington and the two men to scour the district, he ran home, and despatched telegrams to all the police inspectors in the county, telling them to look out for a little girl who had been kidnapped by tramps or gypsies. He then ordered his horse to be brought round, and, after insisting on his wife and the three boys sitting down to dinner, rode off down the Ascot Road with a groom. He had hardly, however, gone a couple of miles when he heard somebody galloping after him, and, looking round, saw the little Duke coming up on his pony, with his face very flushed and no hat. 'I'm awfully sorry, Mr. Otis,' gasped out the boy, 'but I can't eat any dinner as long as Virginia is lost. Please, don't be angry with me; if you had let us be engaged last year, there would never have been all this trouble. You won't send me back, will you? I can't go! I won't go!'

The Minister could not help smiling at the handsome young scape-grace, and was a good deal touched at his devotion to Virginia, so leaning down from his horse, he patted him kindly on the shoulders, and said, 'Well, Cecil, if you won't go back I suppose you must come with me, but I must get you a hat at Ascot.'

'Oh, bother my hat! I want Virginia!' cried the little Duke, laughing, and they galloped on to the railway station. There Mr. Otis inquired of the station-master if any one answering the description of Virginia had been seen on the platform, but could get no news of her. The station-master, however, wired up and down the line, and assured him that a strict watch would be kept for her, and, after having bought a hat for the little Duke from a linen-draper, who was just putting up his shutters, Mr. Otis rode off to Bexley, a village about four miles away, which he was told was a well-known haunt of the gypsies, as there was a large common next to it. Here they roused up the rural policeman, but could get no information from him, and, after riding all over the common, they turned their horses' heads homewards, and reached the Chase about eleven o'clock, dead-tired and almost heartbroken. They found Washington and the twins waiting for them at the gate-house with lanterns, as the avenue was very dark. Not the slightest trace of Virginia had been discovered. The gypsies had been caught on Broxley meadows, but she was not with them, and they had explained their sudden departure by saying that they had mistaken the date of Chorton Fair, and had gone off in a hurry for fear they might be late. Indeed, they had been quite distressed at hearing of Virginia's disappearance, as they were very grateful to Mr. Otis for having allowed them to camp in his park, and four of their number had stayed be-hind to help in the search. The carp-pond had been dragged, and the whole Chase thoroughly gone over, but without any result. It was evident that, for that night at any rate, Virginia was lost to them; and it was in a state of the deepest depression that Mr. Otis and the boys walked up to the house, the groom following behind with the two horses and the pony. In the hall they found a group of frightened servants, and lying on a sofa in the library was poor Mrs. Otis, almost out of her mind with terror and anxiety, and having her forehead bathed with eau-de-Cologne by the old housekeeper. Mr. Otis at once insisted on her having something to eat, and ordered up supper for the whole party. It was a melancholy meal, as hardly any one spoke, and even the twins were awestruck and subdued, as they were very fond of their sister. When they had finished, Mr. Otis, in spite of the entreaties of the little Duke, ordered them all to bed, saying that nothing more could be done that night, and that he would telegraph in the morning to Scotland Yard for some detectives to be sent down immediately. Just as they were passing out of the dining-room, midnight began to boom from the clock tower, and when the last stroke sounded they heard a crash and a sudden shrill cry; a dreadful peal of thunder shook the house, a strain of unearthly music floated through the air, a panel at the top of the staircase flew back with a loud noise, and out on the landing, looking very pale and white, with a little casket in her hand, stepped Virginia. In a moment they had all rushed up to her. Mrs. Otis clasped her passionately in her arms, the Duke smothered her with violent kisses, and the twins executed a wild war-dance round the group.

'Good heavens! Child, where have you been?' said Mr. Otis, rather an-grily, thinking that she had been playing some foolish trick on them. 'Cecil and I have been riding all over the country looking for you, and your mother has been frightened to death. You must never play these practical jokes any more.'

'Except on the Ghost! Except on the Ghost!' shrieked the twins, as they capered about.

'My own darling, thank God you are found; you must never leave my side again,' murmured Mrs. Otis, as she kissed the trembling child, and smoothed the tangled gold of her hair.

'Papa,' said Virginia quietly, 'I have been with the Ghost. He is dead, and you must come and see him. He had been very wicked, but he was really sorry for all that he had done, and he gave me this box of beautiful jewels before he died.'

The whole family gazed at her in mute astonishment, but she was quite grave and serious; and, turning round, she led them through the opening in the wainscoting down a narrow secret corridor, Washington following with a lighted candle, which he had caught up from the table. Finally, they came to a great oak door, studded with rusty nails. When Virginia touched it, it swung back on its heavy hinges, and they found themselves in a little low room, with a vaulted ceiling, and one tiny grated window. Imbedded in the wall was a huge iron ring, and chained to it was a gaunt skeleton, that was stretched out at full length on the stone floor, and seemed to be trying to grasp with its long fleshless fingers an old-fashioned trencher and ewer, that were placed just out of its reach. The jug had evidently been once filled with water, as it was covered inside with green mould. There was nothing on the trencher but a pile of dust. Virginia knelt down beside the skeleton, and, folding her little hands together, began to pray silently, while the rest of the party looked on in wonder at the terrible tragedy whose secret was now disclosed to them.

'Hallo!' suddenly exclaimed one of the twins, who had been looking out of the window to try and discover in what wing of the house the room was situated. 'Hallo! the old withered almond-tree has blossomed. I can see the flowers quite plainly in the moonlight.'

'God has forgiven him,' said Virginia gravely, as she rose to her feet, and a beautiful light seemed to illumine her face.

'What an angel you are!' cried the young Duke, and he put his arm round her neck and kissed her.

7

FOUR days after these curious incidents a funeral started from Canterville Chase at about eleven o'clock at night. The hearse was drawn by eight black horses, each of which carried on its head a great tuft of nodding ostrich-plumes, and the leaden coffin was covered by a rich purple pall, on which was embroidered in gold the Canterville coat-of-arms. By the side of the hearse and the coaches walked the servants with lighted torches, and the whole procession was wonderfully impressive. Lord Canterville was the chief mourner, having come up specially from Wales to attend the funeral, and sat in the first carriage along with little Virginia. Then came the United States Minister and his wife, then Washington and the three boys, and in the last carriage was Mrs. Umney. It was generally felt that, as she had been frightened by the ghost for more than fifty years of her life, she had a right to see the last of him. A deep grave had been dug in the corner of the church-yard, just under the old yew-tree, and the service was read in the most impressive manner by the Rev. Augustus Dampier. When the ceremony was over the servants according to an old custom observed in the Canterville family, extinguished their torches, and, as the coffin was being lowered into the grave, Virginia stepped forward and laid on it a large cross made of white and pink almond-blossoms. As she did so, the moon came out from behind a cloud, and flooded with its silent silver the little churchyard, and from a distant copse a nightingale began to sing. She thought of the ghost's description of the Garden of Death, her eyes became dim with tears, and she hardly spoke a word during the drive home.

The next morning, before Lord Canterville went up to town, Mr. Otis had an interview with him on the subject of the jewels the ghost had given to Virginia. They were perfectly magnificent, especially a certain ruby necklace with old Venetian setting, which was really a superb specimen of sixteenth-century work, and their value was so great that Mr. Otis felt considerable scruples about allowing his daughter to accept them.

'My Lord,' he said, 'I know that in this country mortmain is held to apply to trinkets as well as to land, and it is quite clear to me that these jewels are, or should be, heirlooms in your family. I must beg you, accordingly, to take them to London with you, and to regard them simply as a portion of your property which has been restored to you under certain strange conditions. As for my daughter, she is merely a child, and has as yet, I am glad to say, but little interest in such appurtenances of idle luxury. I am also informed by Mrs. Otis, who, I may say, is no mean authority upon Art – having had the privilege of spending several winters in Boston when she was a girl – that these gems are of great monetary worth, and if offered for sale would fetch a tall price. Under these circumstances, Lord Canterville, I feel sure that you will recognise how impossible it would be for me to allow them to remain in the possession of any member of my family; and, indeed, all such vain gauds and toys, however suitable or necessary to the dignity of the British aristocracy, would be completely out of place among those who have been brought up on the severe, and I believe immortal, principles of republican simplicity. Perhaps I should mention that Virginia is very anxious that you should allow her to retain the box as a memento of your unfortunate but misguided ancestor. As it is extremely old, and consequently a good deal out of repair, you may perhaps think fit to comply with her request. For my own part, I confess I am a good deal surprised to find a child of mine expressing sympathy with mediævalism in any form, and can only account for it by the fact that Virginia was born in one of your London suburbs shortly after Mrs. Otis had returned from a trip to Athens.'

Lord Canterville listened very gravely to the worthy Minister's speech, pulling his grey moustache now and then to hide an involuntary smile, and when Mr. Otis had ended, he shook him cordially by the hand, and said, 'My dear sir, your charming little daughter rendered my unlucky ancestor, Sir Simon, a very important service, and I and my family are much indebted to her for her marvellous courage and pluck. The jewels are clearly hers, and, egad, I believe that if I were heartless enough to take them from her, the wicked old fellow would be out of his grave in a fortnight, leading me the devil of a life. As for their being heirlooms, nothing is an heirloom that is not so mentioned in a will or legal document, and the existence of these jewels has been quite unknown. I assure you I have no more claim on them than your butler, and when Miss Virginia grows up I daresay she will be pleased to have pretty things to wear. Besides, you forget, Mr. Otis, that you took the furniture and the ghost at a valuation, and anything that belonged to the ghost passed at once into your possession, as, whatever activity Sir Simon may have shown in the corridor at night, in point of law he was really dead, and you acquired his property by purchase.'

Mr. Otis was a good deal distressed at Lord Canterville's refusal, and begged him to reconsider his decision, but the good-natured peer was quite firm, and finally induced the Minister to allow his daughter to retain the present the ghost had given her, and when, in the spring of 1890, the young Duchess of Cheshire was presented at the Queen's first drawing-room on the occasion of her marriage, her jewels were the universal theme of admiration. For Virginia received the coronet, which is the reward of all good little American girls, and was married to her boy-lover as soon as he came of age. They were both so charming, and they loved each other so much, that every one was delighted at the match, except the old Marchioness of Dumbleton, who had tried to catch the Duke for one of her seven unmarried daughters, and had given no less than three expensive dinner-parties for that purpose, and, strange to say, Mr. Otis himself. Mr. Otis was extremely fond of the young Duke personally, but, theoretically, he objected to titles, and, to use his own words, 'was not without apprehension lest, amid the enervating influences of a pleasure-loving aristocracy, the true principles of republican simplicity should be forgotten.' His objections, however, were completely overruled, and I believe that when he walked up the aisle of St. George's, Hanover Square, with his daughter leaning on his arm, there was not a prouder man in the whole length and breadth of England.

The Duke and Duchess, after the honeymoon was over, went down to Canterville Chase, and on the day after their arrival they walked over in the afternoon to the lonely churchyard by the pine-woods. There had been a great deal of difficulty at first about the inscription on Sir Simon's tombstone, but finally it had been decided to engrave on it simply the initials of the old gentleman's name, and the verse from the library window. The Duchess had brought with her some lovely roses, which she strewed upon the grave, and after they had stood by it for some time they strolled into the ruined chancel of the old abbey. There the Duchess sat down on a fallen pillar, while her husband lay at her feet smoking a cigarette and looking up at her beautiful eyes. Suddenly he threw his cigarette away, took hold of her hand, and said to her, 'Virginia, a wife should have no secrets from her husband.'

'Dear Cecil! I have no secrets from you.'

'Yes, you have,' he answered, smiling, 'you have never told me what happened to you when you were locked up with the ghost.'

'I have never told any one, Cecil,' said Virginia gravely.

'I know that, but you might tell me.'

'Please don't ask me, Cecil, I cannot tell you. Poor Sir Simon! I owe him a great deal. Yes, don't laugh, Cecil, I really do. He made me see what Life is, and what Death signifies, and why Love is stronger than both.'

The Duke rose and kissed his wife lovingly.

'You can have your secret as long as I have your heart,' he murmured.

'You have always had that, Cecil.'

'And you will tell our children some day, won't you?'

Virginia blushed.

THE SPHINX WITHOUT A SECRET

An Etching

ONE afternoon I was sitting outside the Café de la Paix, watching the splendour and shabbiness of Parisian life, and wondering over my vermouth at the strange panorama of pride and poverty that was passing before me, when I heard some one call my name. I turned round and saw Lord Murchison. We had not met since we had been at college together, nearly ten years before, so I was delighted to come across him again, and we shook hands warmly. At Oxford we had been great friends. I had liked him immensely, he was so handsome, so high-spirited, and so honourable. We used to say of him that he would be the best of fellows, if he did not always speak the truth, but I think we really admired him all the more for his frankness. I found him a good deal changed. He looked anxious and puzzled, and seemed to be in doubt about something. I felt it could not be modern scepticism, for Murchison was the stoutest of Tories, and believed in the Pentateuch as firmly as he believed in the House of Peers; so I concluded that it was a woman, and asked him if he was married yet.

'I don't understand women well enough,' he answered.

'My dear Gerald,' I said, 'women are meant to be loved, not to be understood.'

'I cannot love where I cannot trust,' he replied.

'I believe you have a mystery in your life, Gerald,' I exclaimed; 'tell me about it.'

'Let us go for a drive,' he answered, 'it is too crowded here. No, not a yellow carriage, any other colour – there, that dark green one will do'; and in a few moments we were trotting down the boulevard in the direction of the Madeleine.

'Where shall we go to?' I said.

'Oh, anywhere you like!' he answered – 'to the restaurant in the Bois; we will dine there, and you shall tell me all about yourself.'

'I want to hear about you first,' I said. 'Tell me your mystery.'

He took from his pocket a little silver-clasped morocco case, and handed it to me. I opened it. Inside there was the photograph of a woman. She was tall and slight, and strangely picturesque with her large vague eyes and loosened hair. She looked like a *clairvoyante*, and was wrapped in rich furs.

'What do you think of that face?' he said; 'is it truthful?'

I examined it carefully. It seemed to me the face of some one who had a secret, but whether that secret was good or evil I could not say. Its beauty was a beauty moulded out of many mysteries – the beauty, in fact, which is psychological, not plastic – and the faint smile that just played across the lips was far too subtle to be really sweet.

'Well,' he cried impatiently, 'what do you say?'

'She is the Gioconda in sables,' I answered. 'Let me know all about her.'

'Not now,' he said, 'after dinner,' and began to talk of other things.

When the waiter brought us our coffee and cigarettes I reminded Gerald of his promise. He rose from his seat, walked two or three times up and down the room, and, sinking into an arm-chair, told me the following story:–

'One evening,' he said, 'I was walking down Bond Street about five o'clock. There was a terrific crush of carriages, and the traffic was almost stopped. Close to the pavement was standing a little yellow brougham, which, for some reason or other, attracted my attention. As I passed by there looked out from it the face I showed you this afternoon. It fascinated me immediately. All that night I kept thinking of it, and all the next day. I wandered up and down that wretched Row, peering into every carriage, and waiting for the yellow brougham; but I could not find *ma belle inconnue*, and at last I began to think she was merely a dream. About a week afterwards I was dining with Madame de Rastail. Dinner was for eight o'clock; but at half-past eight we were still waiting in the drawing-room. Finally the servant threw open the door, and announced Lady Alroy. It was the woman I had been looking for. She came in very slowly, looking like a moonbeam in grey lace, and, to my intense delight, I was asked to take her in to dinner. After we had sat down, I remarked quite innocently, "I think I caught sight of you in Bond Street some time ago, Lady Alroy." She grew very pale, and said to me in a low voice, "Pray do not talk so loud; you may be overheard." I felt miserable at having made such a bad beginning, and plunged recklessly into the subject of the French plays. She spoke very little, always in the same low musical voice, and seemed as if she was afraid of some one listening. I fell passionately, stupidly in love, and the indefinable atmosphere of mystery that surrounded her excited my most ardent curiosity. When she was going away, which she did very soon after dinner, I asked her if I might call and see her. She hesitated for a moment, glanced round to see if any one was near us, and then said, "Yes; to-morrow at a quarter to five." I begged Madame de Rastail to tell me about her; but all that I could learn was that she was a widow with a beautiful house in Park Lane, and as some scientific bore began a dissertation on widows, as exemplifying the survival of the matrimonially fittest, I left and went home.

'The next day I arrived at Park Lane punctual to the moment, but was told by the butler that Lady Alroy had just gone out. I went down to the club quite unhappy and very much puzzled, and after long consideration wrote her a letter, asking if I might be allowed to try my chance some other afternoon. I had no answer for several days, but at last I got a little note saying she would be at home on Sunday at four and with this extraordinary postscript: "Please do not write to me here again; I will explain when I see you." On Sunday she received me, and was perfectly charming; but when I was going away she begged of me, if I ever had occasion to write to her again, to address my letter to "Mrs. Knox, care of Whittaker's Library, Green Street." "There are reasons," she said, "why I cannot receive letters in my own house."

'All through the season I saw a great deal of her, and the atmosphere of mystery never left her. Sometimes I thought she was in the power of some man, but she looked so unapproachable that I could not believe it. It was really very difficult for me to come to any conclusion, for she was like one of those strange crystals that one sees in museums, which are at one moment clear, and at another clouded. At last I determined to ask her to be my wife: I was sick and tired of the incessant secrecy that she imposed on all my visits, and on the few letters I sent her. I wrote to her at the library to ask her if she could see me the following Monday at six. She answered yes, and I was in the seventh heaven of delight. I was infatuated with her: in spite of the mystery, I thought then – in consequence of it, I see now. No; it was the woman herself I loved. The mystery troubled me, maddened me. Why did chance put me in its track?'

'You discovered it, then?' I cried.

'I fear so,' he answered. 'You can judge for yourself.'

'When Monday came round I went to lunch with my uncle, and about four o'clock found myself in the Marylebone Road. My uncle, you know, lives in Regent's Park. I wanted to get to Piccadilly, and took a short cut through a lot of shabby little streets. Suddenly I saw in front of me Lady Alroy, deeply veiled and walking very fast. On coming to the last house in the street, she went up the steps, took out a latch-key, and let herself in. "Here is the mystery," I said to myself; and I hurried on and examined the house. It seemed a sort of place for letting lodgings. On the doorstep lay her handkerchief, which she had dropped. I picked it up and put it in my pocket. Then I began to consider what I should do. I came to the conclusion that I had no right to spy on her, and I drove down to the club. At six I called to see her. She was lying on a sofa, in a tea-gown of silver tissue looped up by some strange moonstones that she always wore. She was looking quite lovely. "I am so glad to see you," she said; "I have not been out all day." I stared at her in amazement, and pulling the handkerchief out of my pocket, handed it to her. "You dropped this in Cumnor Street this afternoon, Lady Alroy," I said very calmly. She looked at me in terror, but made no attempt to take the handkerchief. "What were you doing there?" I asked. "What right have you to question me?" she answered. "The right of a man who loves you," I replied; "I came here to ask you to be my wife." She hid her face in her hands, and burst into floods of tears. "You must tell me," I continued. She stood up, and, looking me straight in the face, said, "Lord Murchison, there is nothing to tell you." – "You went to meet some one," I cried; "this is your mystery." She grew dreadfully white, and said, "I went to meet no one." – "Can't you tell the truth?" I exclaimed. "I have told it," she replied. I was mad, frantic; I don't know what I said, but I said terrible things to her. Finally I rushed out of the house. She wrote me a letter the next day; I sent it back unopened, and started for Norway with Alan Colville. After a month I came back, and the first thing I saw in the *Morning Post* was the death of Lady Alroy. She had caught a chill at the Opera, and had died in five days of congestion of the lungs. I shut myself up and saw no one. I had loved her so much, I had loved her so madly. Good God! How I had loved that woman!'

'You went to the street, to the house in it?' I said.

'Yes,' he answered.

'One day I went to Cumnor Street. I could not help it; I was tortured with doubt. I knocked at the door, and a respectable-looking woman opened it to me. I asked her if she had any rooms to let. "Well, sir," she replied, "the drawing-rooms are supposed to be let; but I have not seen the lady for three months, and as rent is owing on them, you can have them." – "Is this the lady?" I said, showing the photograph. "That's her, sure enough," she exclaimed; "and when is she coming back, sir?" – "The lady is dead," I replied. "Oh, sir, I hope not!" said the woman; "she was my best lodger. She paid me three guineas a week merely to sit in my drawing-rooms now and then." – "She met some one here?" I said; but the woman assured me that it was not so, that she always came alone, and saw no one. "What on earth did she do here?" I cried. "She simply sat in the drawing-room, sir, reading books, and sometimes had tea," the woman answered. I did not know what to say, so I gave her a sovereign and went away. Now, what do you think it all meant? You don't believe the woman was telling the truth?'

'I do.'

'Then why did Lady Alroy go there?'

'My dear Gerald,' I answered, 'Lady Alroy was simply a woman with a mania for mystery. She took these rooms for the pleasure of going there with her veil down, and imagining she was a heroine. She had a passion for secrecy, but she herself was merely a Sphinx without a secret.'

'Do you really think so?'

'I am sure of it,' I replied.

He took out the morocco case, opened it, and looked at the photograph. 'I wonder?' he said at last.

THE MODEL MILLIONAIRE

A Note of Admiration

UNLESS one is wealthy there is no use in being a charming fellow. Romance is the privilege of the rich, not the profession of the unemployed. The poor should be practical and prosaic. It is better to have a permanent income than to be fascinating. These are the great truths of modern life which Hughie Erskine never realised. Poor Hughie! Intellectually, we must admit, he was not of much importance. He never said a brilliant or even an ill-natured thing in his life. But then he was wonderfully good-looking, with his crisp, brown hair, his clear-cut profile, and his grey eyes. He was as popular with men as he was with women, and he had every accomplishment except that of making money. His father had bequeathed him his cavalry sword and a *History of the Peninsular War* in fifteen volumes. Hughie hung the first over his looking-glass, put the second on a shelf between *Ruff's Guide* and *Bailey's Magazine*, and lived on two hundred a year that an old aunt allowed him. He had tried everything. He had gone on the Stock Exchange for six months; but what was a butterfly to do among bulls and bears? He had been a tea-merchant for a little longer, but had soon tired of pekoe and souchong. Then he had tried selling dry sherry. That did not answer; the sherry was a little too dry. Ultimately he became nothing, a delightful, ineffectual young man with a perfect profile and no profession.

To make matters worse, he was in love. The girl he loved was Laura Merton, the daughter of a retired Colonel who had lost his temper and his digestion in India, and had never found either of them again. Laura adored him, and he was ready to kiss her shoe-strings. They were the handsomest couple in London, and had not a penny-piece between them. The Colonel was very fond of Hughie, but would not hear of any engagement.

'Come to me, my boy, when you have got ten thousand pounds of your own, and we will see about it,' he used to say; and Hughie looked very glum in those days, and had to go to Laura for consolation.

One morning, as he was on his way to Holland Park, where the Mertons lived, he dropped in to see a great friend of his, Alan Trevor. Trevor was a painter. Indeed, few people escape that nowadays. But he was also an artist, and artists are rather rare. Personally he was a strange rough fellow, with a freckled face and a red, ragged beard. However, when he took up the brush he was a real master, and his pictures were eagerly sought after. He had been very much attracted by Hughie at first, it must be acknowledged, entirely on account of his personal charm. 'The only people a painter should know,' he used to say, 'are people who are *bête* and beautiful, people who are an artistic pleasure to look at and an intellectual repose to talk to. Men who are dandies and women who are darlings rule the world, at least they should do so.' However, after he got to know Hughie better, he liked him quite as much for his bright, buoyant spirits and his generous, reckless nature, and had given him the permanent *entrée* to his studio.

When Hughie came in he found Trevor putting the finishing touches to a wonderful life-size picture of a beggar-man. The beggar himself was standing on a raised platform in a corner of the studio. He was a wizened old man, with a face like wrinkled parchment, and a most piteous expression. Over his shoulder was flung a coarse brown cloak, all tears and tatters; his thick boots were patched and cobbled, and with one hand he leant on a rough stick, while with the other he held out his battered hat for alms.

'What an amazing model!' whispered Hughie, as he shook hands with his friend.

'An amazing model?' shouted Trevor at the top of his voice; 'I should think so! Such beggars as he are not to be met with every day. A *trouvaille, mon cher* a living Velasquez! My stars! what an etching Rembrandt would have made of him!'

'Poor old chap!' said Hughie, 'how miserable he looks! But I suppose, to you painters, his face is his fortune?'

'Certainly,' replied Trevor, 'you don't want a beggar to look happy, do you?'

'How much does a model get for sitting?' asked Hughie, as he found himself a comfortable seat on a divan.

'A shilling an hour.'

'And how much do you get for your picture, Alan?'

'Oh, for this I get two thousand!'

'Pounds?'

'Guineas. Painters, poets, and physicians always get guineas.'

'Well, I think the model should have a percentage,' cried Hughie, laughing; 'they work quite as hard as you do.'

'Nonsense, nonsense! Why, look at the trouble of laying on the paint alone, and standing all day long at one's easel! It's all very well, Hughie, for you to talk, but I assure you that there are moments when Art almost attains to the dignity of manual labour. But you mustn't chatter; I'm very busy. Smoke a cigarette, and keep quiet.'

After some time the servant came in, and told Trevor that the framemaker wanted to speak to him.

'Don't run away, Hughie,' he said, as he went out, 'I will be back in a moment.'

The old beggar man took advantage of Trevor's absence to rest for a moment on a wooden bench that was behind him. He looked so forlorn and wretched that Hughie could not help pitying him, and felt in his pockets to see what money he had. All he could find was a sovereign and some coppers. 'Poor old fellow,' he thought to himself, 'he wants it more than I do, but it means no hansoms for a fortnight'; and he walked across the studio and slipped the sovereign into the beggar's hand.

The old man started, and a faint smile flitted across his withered lips.

'Thank you, sir,' he said, 'thank you.'

Then Trevor arrived, and Hughie took his leave, blushing a little at what he had done. He spent the day with Laura, got a charming scolding for his extravagance, and had to walk home.

That night he strolled into the Palette Club about eleven o'clock, and found Trevor sitting by himself in the smoking-room drinking hock and seltzer.

'Well, Alan, did you get the picture finished all right?' he said, as he lit his cigarette.

'Finished and framed, my boy!' answered Trevor; 'and, by the bye, you have made a conquest. That old model you saw is quite devoted to you. I had to tell him all about you – who you are, where you live. What your income is, what prospects you have –'

'My dear Alan,' cried Hughie, 'I shall probably find him waiting for me when I go home. But, of course, you are only joking. Poor old wretch! I wish I could do something for him. I think it is dreadful that any one should be so miserable. I have got heaps of old clothes at home – do you think he would care for any of them? Why, his rags were falling to bits.'

'But he looks splendid in them,' said Trevor. 'I wouldn't paint him in a frock coat for anything. What you call rags I call romance. What seems poverty to you is picturesqueness to me. However, I'll tell him of your offer.'

'Alan,' said Hughie seriously, 'you painters are a heartless lot.'

'An artist's heart is his head,' replied Trevor; 'and besides, our business is to realise the world as we see it, not to reform it as we know it. *A chacun son métier.* And now tell me how Laura is. The old model was quite interested in her.'

'You don't mean to say you talked to him about her?' said Hughie.

'Certainly I did. He knows all about the relentless Colonel, the lovely Laura, and the £10,000.'

'You told that old beggar all my private affairs?' cried Hughie, looking very red and angry.

'My dear boy,' said Trevor, smiling, 'that old beggar, as you call him, is one of the richest men in Europe. He could buy all London to-morrow without overdrawing his account. He has a house in every capital, dines off gold plate, and can prevent Russia going to war when he chooses.'

'What on earth do you mean?' exclaimed Hughie.

'What I say,' said Trevor. 'The old man you saw to-day in the studio was Baron Hausberg. He is a great friend of mine, buys all my pictures and that sort of thing, and gave me a commission a month ago to paint him as a beggar. *Que voulez-vous? La fantaisie d'un millionnaire!* And I must say he made a magnificent figure in his rags, or perhaps I should say in my rags; they are an old suit I got in Spain.'

'Baron Hausberg!' cried Hughie. 'Good heavens! I gave him a sovereign!' and he sank into an arm-chair the picture of dismay.

'Gave him a sovereign!' shouted Trevor, and he burst into a roar of laughter. 'My dear boy, you'll never see it again. *Son affaire c'est l'argent des autres.*'

'I think you might have told me, Alan,' said Hughie sulkily, 'and not have let me make such a fool of myself.'

'Well, to begin with, Hughie,' said Trevor, 'it never entered my mind that you went about distributing alms in that reckless way. I can understand your kissing a pretty model, but your giving a sovereign to an ugly one – by Jove, no! Besides, the fact is that I really was not at home to-day to any one; and when you came in I didn't know whether Hausberg would like his name mentioned. You know he wasn't in full dress.'

'What a duffer he must think me!' said Hughie.

'Not at all. He was in the highest spirits after you left; kept chuckling to himself and rubbing his old wrinkled hands together. I couldn't make out why he was so interested to know all about you; but I see it all now. He'll invest your sovereign for you, Hughie, pay you the interest every six months, and have a capital story to tell after dinner.'

'I am an unlucky devil,' growled Hughie. 'The best thing I can do is to go to bed; and, my dear Alan, you mustn't tell any one. I shouldn't dare show my face in the Row.'

'Nonsense! It reflects the highest credit on your philanthropic spirit, Hughie. And don't run away. Have another cigarette, and you can talk about Laura as much as you like.'

However, Hughie wouldn't stop, but walked home, feeling very unhappy, and leaving Alan Trevor in fits of laughter.

The next morning, as he was at breakfast, the servant brought him up a card on which was written, 'Monsieur Gustave Naudin, *de la part de* M. le Baron Hausberg.' 'I suppose he has come for an apology,' said Hughie to himself; and he told the servant to show the visitor up.

An old gentleman with gold spectacles and grey hair came into the room, and said, in a slight French accent, 'Have I the honour of addressing Monsieur Erskine?'

Hughie bowed.

'I have come from Baron Hausberg,' he continued. 'The Baron –'

'I beg, sir, that you will offer him my sincerest apologies,' stammered Hughie.

'The Baron,' said the old gentleman with a smile, 'has commissioned me to bring you this letter'; and he extended a sealed envelope.

On the outside was written, 'A wedding present to Hugh Erskine and Laura Merton, from an old beggar,' and inside was a cheque for £10,000.

When they were married Alan Trevor was the best man, and the Baron made a speech at the wedding breakfast.

'Millionaire models,' remarked Alan, 'are rare enough; but, by Jove, model millionaires are rarer still!'

THE YOUNG KING

IT WAS the night before the day fixed for his coronation, and the young King was sitting alone in his beautiful chamber. His courtiers had all taken their leave of him, bowing their heads to the ground, according to the ceremonious usage of the day, and had retired to the Great Hall of the Palace, to receive a few last lessons from the Professor of Etiquette; there being some of them who had still quite natural manners, which in a courtier is, I need hardly say, a very grave offence.

The lad – for he was only a lad, being but sixteen years of age – was not sorry at their departure, and had flung himself back with a deep sigh of relief on the soft cushions of his embroidered couch, lying there, wild-eyed and open-mouthed, like a brown woodland Faun, or some young animal of the forest newly snared by the hunters.

And, indeed, it was the hunters who had found him, coming upon him almost by chance as, bare-limbed and pipe in hand, he was following the flock of the poor goatherd who had brought him up, and whose son he had always fancied himself to be. The child of the old King's only daughter by a secret marriage with one much beneath her in station – a stranger, some said, who, by the wonderful magic of his lute-playing, had made the young Princess love him; while others spoke of an artist from Rimini, to whom the Princess had shown much, perhaps too much honour, and who had suddenly disappeared from the city, leaving his work in the Cathedral unfinished – he had been, when but a week old, stolen away from his mother's side, as she slept, and given into the charge of a common peasant and his wife, who were without children of their own, and lived in a remote part of the forest, more than a day's ride from the town. Grief, or the plague, as the court physician stated, or, as some suggested, a swift Italian poison administered in a cup of spiced wine, slew, within an hour of her wakening, the white girl who had given him birth, and as the trusty messenger who bare the child across his saddle-bow stooped from his weary horse and knocked at the rude door of the goatherd's hut, the body of the Princess was being lowered into an open grave that had been dug in a deserted churchyard, beyond the city gates, a grave where it was said that another body was also lying, that of a young man of marvellous and foreign beauty, whose hands were tied behind him with a knotted cord, and whose breast was stabbed with many red wounds.

Such, at least, was the story that men whispered to each other. Certain it was that the old King, when on his death-bed, whether moved by remorse for his great sin, or merely desiring that the kingdom should not pass away from his line, had had the lad sent for, and, in the presence of the Council, had acknowledged him as his heir.

And it seems that from the very first moment of his recognition he had shown signs of that strange passion for beauty that was destined to have so great an influence over his life. Those who accompanied him to the suite of rooms set apart for his service, often spoke of the cry of pleasure that broke from his lips when he saw the delicate raiment and rich jewels that had been prepared for him, and of the almost fierce joy with which he flung aside his rough leathern tunic and coarse sheepskin cloak. He missed, indeed, at times the freedom of the forest life, and was always apt to chafe at the tedious Court ceremonies that occupied so much of each day, but the wonderful palace – *Joyeuse*, as they called it – of which he now found himself lord, seemed to him to be a new world fresh-fashioned for his delight; and as soon as he could escape from the council-board or audience-chamber, he would run down the great staircase, with its lions of gilt bronze and its steps of bright porphyry, and wander from room to room, and from corridor to corridor, like one who was seeking to find in beauty an anodyne from pain, a sort of restoration from sickness.

Upon these journeys of discovery, as he would call them – and, indeed, they were to him real voyages through a marvellous land, he would sometimes be accompanied by the slim, fair-haired Court pages, with their floating mantles, and gay fluttering ribands; but more often he would be alone, feeling through a certain quick instinct, which was almost a divination, that the secrets of art are best learned in secret, and that Beauty, like Wisdom, loves the lonely worshipper.

Many curious stories were related about him at this period. It was said that a stout Burgomaster, who had come to deliver a florid oratorical address on behalf of the citizens of the town, had caught sight of him kneeling in real adoration before a great picture that had just been brought from Venice, and that seemed to herald the worship of some new gods. On another occasion he had been missed for several hours, and after a lengthened search had been discovered in a little chamber in one of the northern turrets of the palace gazing, as one in a trance, at a Greek gem carved with the figure of Adonis. He had been seen, so the tale ran, pressing his warm lips to the marble brow of an antique statue that had been discovered in the bed of the river on the occasion of the building of the stone bridge, and was inscribed with the name of the Bithynian slave of Hadrian. He had passed a whole night in noting the effect of the moonlight on a silver image of Endymion.

All rare and costly materials had certainly a great fascination for him, and in his eagerness to procure them he had sent away many merchants, some to traffic for amber with the rough fisher-folk of the north seas, some to Egypt to look for that curious green turquoise which is found only in the tombs of kings, and is said to possess magical properties, some to Persia for silken carpets and painted pottery, and others to India to buy gauze and stained ivory moonstones and bracelets of jade, sandal-wood and blue enamel and shawls of fine wool.

But what had occupied him most was the robe he was to wear at his coronation, the robe of tissued gold, and the ruby-studded crown, and the sceptre with its rows and rings of pearls. Indeed, it was of this that he was thinking to-night, as he lay back on his luxurious couch, watching the great pinewood log that was burning itself out on the open hearth. The designs, which were from the hands of the most famous artists of the time, had been submitted to him many months before, and he had given orders that the artificers were to toil night and day to carry them out, and that the whole world was to be searched for jewels that would be worthy of their work. He saw himself in fancy standing at the high altar of the cathedral in the fair raiment of a King, and a smile played and lingered about his boyish lips, and lit up with a bright lustre his dark woodland eyes.

After some time he rose from his seat, and leaning against the carved penthouse of the chimney, looked round at the dimly-lit room. The walls were hung with rich tapestries representing the Triumph of Beauty. A large press, inlaid with agate and lapis lazuli, filled one corner, and facing the window stood a curiously wrought cabinet with lacquer panels of powdered and mosaiced gold, on which were placed some delicate goblets of Venetian glass, and a cup of dark-veined onyx. Pale poppies were broidered on the silk coverlet of the bed, as though they had fallen from the tired hands of sleep, and tall reeds of fluted ivory bare up the velvet canopy, from which great tufts of ostrich plumes sprang, like white foam, to the pallid silver of the fretted ceiling. A laughing Narcissus in green bronze held a polished mirror above its head. On the table stood a flat bowl of amethyst.

Outside he could see the huge dome of the cathedral, looming like a bubble over the shadowy houses, and the weary sentinels pacing up and down on the misty terrace by the river. Far away, in an orchard, a nightingale was singing. A faint perfume of jasmine came through the open window. He brushed his brown curls back from his forehead, and taking up a lute, let his fingers stray across the cords. His heavy eyelids drooped, and a strange languor came over him. Never before had he felt so keenly, or with such exquisite joy, the magic and mystery of beautiful things.

When midnight sounded from the clock-tower he touched a bell, and his pages entered and disrobed him with much ceremony, pouring rose-water over his hands, and strewing flowers on his pillow. A few moments after that they had left the room, he fell asleep.

And as he slept he dreamed a dream, and this was his dream.

He thought that he was standing in a long, low attic, amidst the whir and clatter of many looms. The meagre daylight peered in through the grated windows, and showed him the gaunt figures of the weavers bending over their cases. Pale, sickly-looking children were crouched on the huge crossbeams. As the shuttles dashed through the warp they lifted up the heavy battens, and when the shuttles stopped they let the battens fall and pressed the threads together. Their faces were pinched with famine, and their thin hands shook and trembled. Some haggard women were seated at a table sewing. A horrible odour filled the place. The air was foul and heavy, and the walls dripped and streamed with damp.

The young King went over to one of the weavers, and stood by him and watched him.

And the weaver looked at him angrily and said, 'Why art thou watching me? Art thou a spy set on us by our master?'

'Who is thy master?' asked the young King.

'Our master!' cried the weaver, bitterly. 'He is a man like myself. Indeed, there is but this difference between us – that he wears fine clothes while I go in rags, and that while I am weak from hunger he suffers not a little from overfeeding.'

'The land is free,' said the young King, 'and thou art no man's slave.'

'In war,' answered the weaver, 'the strong make slaves of the weak, and in peace the rich make slaves of the poor. We must work to live, and they give us such mean wages that we die. We toil for them all day long, and they heap up gold in their coffers, and our children fade away before their time, and the faces of those we love become hard and evil. We tread out the grapes, and another drinks the wine. We sow the corn, and our own board is empty. We have chains, though no eye beholds them; and we are slaves, though men call us free.'

'Is it so with all?' he asked.

'It is so with all,' answered the weaver, 'with the young as well as with the old, with the women as well as with the men, with the little children as well as with those who are stricken in years. The merchants grind us down, and we must needs do their bidding. The priest rides by and tells his beads, and no man has care of us. Through our sunless lanes creeps Poverty with her hungry eyes, and Sin with his sodden face follows close behind her. Misery wakes us in the morning, and Shame sits with us at night. But what are these things to thee? Thou art not one of us. Thy face is too happy.' And he turned away scowling, and threw the shuttle across the loom, and the young King saw that it was threaded with a thread of gold.

And a great terror seized upon him, and he said to the weaver, 'What robe is this that thou art weaving?'

'It is the robe for the coronation of the young King,' he answered; 'what is that to thee?'

And the young King gave a loud cry and woke, and lo! he was in his own chamber, and through the window he saw the great honey-coloured moon hanging in the dusky air.

And he fell asleep again and dreamed, and this was his dream.

He thought that he was lying on the deck of a huge galley that was being rowed by a hundred slaves. On a carpet by his side the master of the galley was seated. He was black as ebony, and his turban was of crimson silk. Great ear-rings of silver dragged down the thick lobes of his ears, and in his hands he had a pair of ivory scales.

The slaves were naked, but for a ragged loincloth, and each man was chained to his neighbour. The hot sun beat brightly upon them, and the negroes ran up and down the gangway and lashed them with whips of hide. They stretched out their lean arms and pulled the heavy oars through the water. The salt spray flew from the blades.

At last they reached a little bay, and began to take soundings. A light wind blew from the shore, and covered the deck and the great lateen sail with a fine red dust. Three Arabs mounted on wild asses rode out and threw spears at them. The master of the galley took a painted bow in his hand and shot one of them in the throat. He fell heavily into the surf, and his companions galloped away. A woman wrapped in a yellow veil followed slowly on a camel, looking back now and then at the dead body.

As soon as they had cast anchor and hauled down the sail, the negroes went into the hold and brought up a long rope-ladder, heavily weighted with lead. The master of the galley threw it over the side, making the ends fast to two iron stanchions. Then the negroes seized the youngest of the slaves and knocked his gyves off, and filled his nostrils and his ears with wax, and tied a big stone round his waist. He crept wearily down the ladder, and disappeared into the sea. A few bubbles rose where he sank. Some of the other slaves peered curiously over the side. At the prow of the galley sat a shark-charmer, beating monotonously upon a drum.

After some time the diver rose up out of the water, and clung panting to the ladder with a pearl in his right hand. The negroes seized it from him, and thrust him back. The slaves fell asleep over their oars.

Again and again he came up, and each time that he did so he brought with him a beautiful pearl. The master of the galley weighed them, and put them into a little bag of green leather.

The young King tried to speak, but his tongue seemed to cleave to the roof of his mouth, and his lips refused to move. The negroes chattered to each other, and began to quarrel over a string of bright beads. Two cranes flew round and round the vessel.

Then the diver came up for the last time, and the pearl that he brought with him was fairer than all the pearls of Ormuz, for it was shaped like the full moon, and whiter than the morning star. But his face was strangely pale, and as he fell upon the deck the blood gushed from his ears and nostrils. He quivered for a little, and then he was still. The negroes shrugged their shoulders, and threw the body overboard.

And the master of the galley laughed, and, reaching out, he took the pearl, and when he saw it he pressed it to his forehead and bowed. 'It shall be,' he said, 'for the sceptre of the young King,' and he made a sign to the negroes to draw up the anchor.

And when the young King heard this he gave a great cry and woke, and through the window he saw the long grey fingers of the dawn clutching at the fading stars.

And he fell asleep again, and dreamed, and this was his dream.

He thought that he was wandering through a dim wood, hung with strange fruits and with beautiful poisonous flowers. The adders hissed at him as he went by, and the bright parrots flew screaming from branch to branch. Huge tortoises lay asleep upon the hot mud. The trees were full of apes and peacocks.

On and on he went, till he reached the outskirts of the wood, and there he saw an immense multitude of men toiling in the bed of a dried-up river.

They swarmed up the crag like ants. They dug deep pits in the ground and
went down into them. Some of them cleft the rocks with great axes; others
grabbled in the sand. They tore up the cactus by its roots, and trampled on
the scarlet blossoms. They hurried about, calling to each other, and no man
was idle.

From the darkness of a cavern Death and Avarice watched them, and
Death said, 'I am weary; give me a third of them and let me go.'

But Avarice shook her head. 'They are my servants,' she answered.

And Death said to her, 'What hast thou in thy hand?'

'I have three grains of corn,' she answered; 'what is that to thee?'

'Give me one of them,' cried Death, 'to plant in my garden; only one of
them, and I will go away.'

'I will not give thee anything,' said Avarice, and she hid her hand in the
fold of her raiment.

And Death laughed, and took a cup, and dipped it into a pool of water, and
out of the cup rose Ague. She passed through the great multitude, and a
third of them lay dead. A cold mist followed her, and the water-snakes ran by
her side.

And when Avarice saw that a third of the multitude was dead she beat her
breast and wept. She beat her barren bosom, and cried aloud. 'Thou hast
slain a third of my servants,' she cried, 'get thee gone. There is war in the
mountains of Tartary, and the kings of each side are calling to thee. The Af-
ghans have slain the black ox, and are marching to battle. They have beaten
upon their shields with their spears, and have put on their helmets of iron.
What is my valley to thee, that thou shouldst tarry in it? Get thee gone, and
come here no more.'

'Nay,' answered Death, 'but till thou hast given me a grain of corn I will
not go.'

But Avarice shut her hand, and clenched her teeth. 'I will not give thee
anything,' she muttered.

And Death laughed, and took up a black stone, and threw it into the forest,
and out of a thicket of wild hemlock came Fever in a robe of flame. She
passed through the multitude, and touched them, and each man that she
touched died. The grass withered beneath her feet as she walked.

And Avarice shuddered, and put ashes on her head. 'Thou art cruel,' she
cried; 'thou art cruel. There is famine in the walled cities of India, and the
cisterns of Samarcand have run dry. There is famine in the walled cities of
Egypt, and the locusts have come up from the desert. The Nile has not over-
flowed its banks, and the priests have nursed Isis and Osiris. Get thee gone to
those who need thee, and leave me my servants.'

'Nay,' answered Death, 'but till thou hast given me a grain of corn I will
not go.'

'I will not give thee anything,' said Avarice.

And Death laughed again, and he whistled through his fingers, and a wo-
man came flying through the air. Plague was written upon her forehead, and
a crowd of lean vultures wheeled round her. She covered the valley with her

wings, and no man was left alive.

And Avarice fled shrieking through the forest, and Death leaped upon his red horse and galloped away, and his galloping was faster than the wind. And out of the slime at the bottom of the valley crept dragons and horrible things with scales, and the jackals came trotting along the sand, sniffing up the air with their nostrils.

And the young King wept, and said: 'Who were these men, and for what were they seeking?'

'For rubies for a king's crown,' answered one who stood behind him.

And the young King started, and, turning round, he saw a man habited as a pilgrim and holding in his hand a mirror of silver.

And he grew pale, and said: 'For what king?'

And the pilgrim answered: 'Look in this mirror, and thou shalt see him.'

And he looked in the mirror, and, seeing his own face, he gave a great cry and woke, and the bright sunlight was streaming into the room, and from the trees of the garden and pleasaunce the birds were singing.

And the Chamberlain and the high officers of State came in and made obeisance to him, and the pages brought him the robe of tissued gold, and set the crown and the sceptre before him.

And the young King looked at them, and they were beautiful. More beautiful were they than aught that he had ever seen. But he remembered his dreams, and he said to his lords: 'Take these things away, for I will not wear them.'

And the courtiers were amazed, and some of them laughed, for they thought that he was jesting.

But he spake sternly to them again, and said: 'Take these things away, and hide them from me. Though it be the day of my coronation, I will not wear them. For on the loom of sorrow, and by the white hands of Pain, has this my robe been woven. There is Blood in the heart of the ruby, and Death in the heart of the pearl.' And he told them his three dreams.

And when the courtiers heard them they looked at each other and whispered, saying: 'Surely he is mad; for what is a dream but a dream, and a vision but a vision? They are not real things that one should heed them. And what have we to do with the lives of those who toil for us? Shall a man not eat bread till he has seen the sower, nor drink wine till he has talked with the vinedresser?'

And the Chamberlain spake to the young King, and said, 'My lord, I pray thee set aside these black thoughts of thine, and put on this fair robe, and set this crown upon thy head. For how shall the people know that thou art a king, if thou hast not a king's raiment?'

And the young King looked at him. 'Is it so, indeed?' he questioned. 'Will they not know me for a king if I have not a king's raiment?'

'They will not know thee, my lord,' cried the Chamberlain.

'I had thought that there had been men who were kinglike,' he answered, 'but it may be as thou sayest. And yet I will not wear this robe, nor will I be crowned with this crown, but even as I came to the Palace so will I go forth from it.'

And he bade them all leave him, save one page whom he kept as his companion, a lad a year younger than himself. Him he kept for his service, and when he had bathed himself in clear water, he opened a great painted chest, and from it he took the leathern tunic and rough sheepskin coat that he had worn when he had watched on the hillside the shaggy goats of the goatherd. These he put on, and in his hand he took his rude shepherd's staff.

And the little page opened his big blue eyes in wonder, and said smiling to him, 'My lord, I see thy robe and thy sceptre, but where is thy crown?'

And the young King plucked a spray of wild briar that was climbing over the balcony, and bent it, and made a circlet of it, and set it on his own head.

'This shall be my crown,' he answered.

And thus attired he passed out of his chamber into the Great Hall, where the nobles were waiting for him.

And the nobles made merry, and some of them cried out to him, 'My lord, the people wait for their king, and thou showest them a beggar,' and others were wroth and said, 'He brings shame upon our state, and is unworthy to be our master.' But he answered them not a word, but passed on, and went down the bright porphyry staircase, and out through the gates of bronze, and mounted upon his horse, and rode towards the cathedral, the little page running beside him.

And the people laughed and said, 'It is the King's fool who is riding by,' and they mocked him.

And he drew rein and said, 'Nay, but I am the King.' And he told them his three dreams.

And a man came out of the crowd and spake bitterly to him, and said, 'Sir, knowest thou not that out of the luxury of the rich cometh the life of the poor? By your pomp we are nurtured, and your vices give us bread. To toil for a master is bitter, but to have no master to toil for is more bitter still. Thinkest thou that the ravens will feed us? And what cure hast thou for these things? Wilt thou say to the buyer, "Thou shalt buy for so much," and to the seller, "Thou shalt sell at this price?" I trow not. Therefore go back to thy Palace and put on thy purple and fine linen. What hast thou to do with us, and what we suffer?'

'Are not the rich and the poor brothers?' asked the young King.

'Ay,' answered the man, 'and the name of the rich brother is Cain.'

And the young King's eyes filled with tears, and he rode on through the murmurs of the people, and the little page grew afraid and left him.

And when he reached the great portal of the cathedral, the soldiers thrust their halberts out and said, 'What does thou seek here? None enters by this door but the King.'

And his face flushed with anger, and he said to them, 'I am the King,' and waved their halberts aside and passed in.

And when the old bishop saw him coming in his goatherd's dress, he rose up in wonder from his throne, and went to meet him, and said to him, 'My son, is this a king's apparel? And with what crown shall I crown thee, and what sceptre shall I place in thy hand? Surely this should be to thee a day of joy, and not a day of abasement.'

'Shall Joy wear what Grief has fashioned?' said the young King. And he told him his three dreams.

And when the Bishop had heard them he knit his brows, and said, 'My son, I am an old man, and in the winter of my days, and I know that many evil things are done in the wide world. The fierce robbers come down from the mountains, and carry off the little children, and sell them to the Moors. The lions lie in wait for the caravans, and leap upon the camels. The wild boar roots up the corn in the valley, and the foxes gnaw the vines upon the hill. The pirates lay waste the sea-coast and burn the ships of the fishermen, and take their nets from them. In the salt-marshes live the lepers; they have houses of wattled reeds, and none may come nigh them. The beggars wander through the cities, and eat their food with the dogs. Canst thou make these things not to be? Wilt thou take the leper for thy bedfellow, and set the beggar at thy board? Shall the lion do thy bidding, and the wild boar obey thee? Is not He who made misery wiser than thou art? Wherefore I praise thee not for this that thou hast done, but I bid thee ride back to the Palace and make thy face glad, and put on the raiment that beseemeth a king, and with the crown of gold I will crown thee, and the sceptre of pearl will I place in thy hand. And as for thy dreams, think no more of them. The burden of this world is too great for one man to bear, and the world's sorrow too heavy for one heart to suffer.'

'Sayest thou that in this house?' said the young King, and he strode past the Bishop, and climbed up the steps of the altar, and stood before the image of Christ.

He stood before the image of Christ, and on his right hand and on his left were the marvellous vessels of gold, the chalice with the yellow wine, and the vial with the holy oil. He knelt before the image of Christ, and the great candles burned brightly by the jewelled shrine, and the smoke of the incense curled in thin blue wreaths through the dome. He bowed his head in prayer, and the priests in their stiff copes crept away from the altar.

And suddenly a wild tumult came from the street outside, and in entered the nobles with drawn swords and nodding plumes, and shields of polished steel. 'Where is this dreamer of dreams?' they cried. 'Where is this King, who is apparelled like a beggar – this boy who brings shame upon our state? Surely we will slay him, for he is unworthy to rule over us.'

And the young King bowed his head again, and prayed, and when he had finished his prayer he rose up, and turning round he looked at them sadly.

And lo! through the painted windows came the sunlight streaming upon him, and the sunbeams wove round him a tissued robe that was fairer than the robe that had been fashioned for his pleasure. The dead staff blossomed, and bare lilies that were whiter than pearls. The dry thorn blossomed, and bare roses that were redder than rubies. Whiter than fine pearls were the lilies, and their stems were of bright silver, Redder than male rubies were the roses, and their leaves were of beaten gold.

He stood there in the raiment of a king, and the gates of the jewelled shrine flew open and from the crystal of the many-rayed monstrance shone a marvellous and mystical light. He stood there in a king's raiment, and the Glory of God filled the place, and the saints in their carven niches seemed to move. In the fair raiment of a king he stood before them, and the organ pealed out its music, and the trumpeters blew upon their trumpets, and the singing boys sang.

And the people fell upon their knees in awe, and the nobles sheathed their swords and did homage, and the Bishop's face grew pale, and his hands trembled. 'A greater than I hath crowned thee,' he cried, and he knelt before him.

And the young King came down from the high altar, and passed home through the midst of the people. But no man dared look upon his face, for it was like the face of an angel.

THE BIRTHDAY OF THE INFANTA

IT WAS the birthday of the Infanta. She was just twelve years of age, and the sun was shining brightly in the gardens of the palace.

Although she was a real Princess and the Infanta of Spain, she had only one birthday every year, just like the children of quite poor people, so it was naturally a matter of great importance to the whole country that she should have a really fine day for the occasion. And a really fine day it certainly was. The tall striped tulips stood straight up upon their stalks, like long rows of soldiers, and looked defiantly across the grass at the roses, and said: 'We are quite as splendid as you are now.' The purple butterflies fluttered about with gold dust on their wings, visiting each flower in turn; the little lizards crept out of the crevices of the wall, and lay basking in the white glare; and the pomegranates split and cracked with the heat, and showed their bleeding red hearts. Even the pale yellow lemons, that hung in such profusion from the mouldering trellis and along the dim arcades, seemed to have caught a richer colour from the wonderful sunlight, and the magnolia trees opened their great glove-like blossoms of folded ivory, and filled the air with a sweet heavy perfume.

The little Princess herself walked up and down the terrace with her companions, and played at hide and seek round the stone vases and the old moss-grown statues. On ordinary days she was only allowed to play with children of her own rank, so she had always to play alone, but her birthday was an exception, and the King had given orders that she was to invite any of her young friends whom she liked to come and amuse themselves with her. There was a stately grace about these slim Spanish children as they glided about, the boys with their large-plumed hats and short fluttering cloaks, the girls holding up the trains of their long brocade gowns, and shielding the sun from their eyes with huge fans of black and silver. But the Infanta was the most graceful of all, and the most tastefully attired, after the somewhat cumbrous fashion of the day. Her robe was of grey satin, the skirt and the wide puffed sleeves heavily embroidered with silver, and the stiff corset studded with rows of fine pearls. Two tiny slippers with big pink rosettes peeped out beneath her dress as she walked. Pink and pearl was her great gauze fan, and in her hair, which like an aureole of faded gold stood out stiffly round her pale little face, she had a beautiful white rose.

From a window in the palace the sad melancholy King watched them. Behind him stood his brother, Don Pedro of Aragon, whom he hated, and his confessor, the Grand Inquisitor of Granada, sat by his side. Sadder even than usual was the King, for as he looked at the Infanta bowing with childish gravity to the assembling courtiers, or laughing behind the fan at the grim Duchess of Albuquerque, who always accompanied her, he thought of the young Queen, her mother, who but a short time before – so it seemed to him – had come from the gay country of France, and had withered away in the sombre splendour of the Spanish court, dying just six months after the birth of her child, and before she had seen the almonds blossom twice in the orchard, or plucked the second year's fruit from the old gnarled fig-tree that stood in the centre of the now grass-grown courtyard. So great had been his love for her that he had not suffered even the grave to hide her from him. She had been embalmed by a Moorish physician, who in return for this service had been granted his life, which for heresy and suspicion of magical practices had been already forfeited, men said, to the Holy Office, and her body was still lying on its tapestried bier in the black marble chapel of the palace, just as the monks had borne her on that windy March day nearly twelve years before. Once every month the King, wrapped in a dark cloak and with a muffled lantern in his hand, went in and knelt by her side calling out, '*Mi reina! Mi reina!*' and sometimes breaking through the formal etiquette that in Spain governs every separate action of life, and sets limits even to the sorrow of a King, he would clutch at the pale jewelled hands in a wild agony of grief, and try to wake by his mad kisses the cold painted face.

To-day he seemed to see her again, as he had seen her first at the Castle of Fontainebleau, when he was but fifteen years of age, and she still younger. They had been formally betrothed on that occasion by the Papal Nuncio in the presence of the French King and all the Court, and he had returned to the Escurial bearing with him a little ringlet of yellow hair, and the memory of two childish lips bending down to kiss his hand as he stepped into his carriage. Later on had followed the marriage, hastily performed at Burgos, a small town on the frontier between the two countries, and the grand public entry into Madrid with the customary celebration of high mass at the Church of La Atocha, and a more than usually solemn *auto-da-fé*, in which nearly three hundred heretics, amongst whom were many Englishmen, had been delivered over to the secular arm to be burned.

Certainly he had loved her madly, and to the ruin, many thought, of his country, then at war with England for the possession of the empire of the New World. He had hardly ever permitted her to be out of his sight; for her, he had forgotten, or seemed to have forgotten, all grave affairs of State; and, with that terrible blindness that passion brings upon its servants, he had failed to notice that the elaborate ceremonies by which he sought to please her did but aggravate the strange malady from which she suffered. When she died he was, for a time, like one bereft of reason. Indeed, there is no doubt but that he would have formally abdicated and retired to the great Trappist monastery at Granada, of which he was already titular Prior, had he not been afraid to leave the little Infanta at the mercy of his brother, whose cruelty, even in Spain, was notorious, and who was suspected by many of having caused the Queen's death by means of a pair of poisoned gloves that he had presented to her on the occasion of her visiting his castle in Aragon. Even after the expiration of the three years of public mourning that he had ordained throughout his whole dominions by royal edict, he would never suffer his ministers to speak about any new alliance, and when the Emperor himself sent to him, and offered him the hand of the lovely Archduchess of Bohemia, his niece, in marriage, he bade the ambassadors tell their master that the King of Spain was already wedded to Sorrow, and that though she was but a barren bride he loved her better than Beauty; an answer that cost his crown the rich provinces of the Netherlands, which soon after, at the Emperor's instigation, revolted against him under the leadership of some fanatics of the Reformed Church.

His whole married life, with its fierce, fiery-coloured joys and the terrible agony of its sudden ending, seemed to come back to him to-day as he watched the Infanta playing on the terrace. She had all the Queen's pretty petulance of manner, the same wilful way of tossing her head, the same proud curved beautiful mouth, the same wonderful smile – *vrai sourire de France* indeed – as she glanced up now and then at the window, or stretched out her little hand for the stately Spanish gentlemen to kiss. But the shrill laughter of the children grated on his ears, and the bright pitiless sunlight mocked his sorrow, and a dull odour of strange spices such as embalmers use, seemed to taint – or was it fancy? – the clear morning air. He buried his face in his hands, and when the Infanta looked up again the curtains had been drawn, and the King had retired.

She made a little *moue* of disappointment, and shrugged her shoulders. Surely he might have stayed with her on her birthday. What did the stupid State-affairs matter? Or had he gone to that gloomy chapel, where the candles were always burning, and where she was never allowed to enter? How silly of him, when the sun was shining so brightly, and everybody was so happy! Besides, he would miss the sham bull-fight for which the trumpet was already sounding, to say nothing of the puppet-show and the other wonderful things. Her uncle and the Grand Inquisitor were much more sensible. They had come out on the terrace, and paid her nice compliments. So she tossed her pretty head, and taking Don Pedro by the hand, she walked slowly down the steps towards a long pavilion of purple silk that had been erected at the end of the garden, the other children following in strict order of precedence, those who had the longest names going first.

A procession of noble boys, fantastically dressed as *toreadors*, came out to meet her, and the young Count of Tierra-Nueva, a wonderfully handsome lad of about fourteen years of age, uncovering his head with all the grace of a born hidalgo and grandee of Spain, led her solemnly in to a little gilt and ivory chair that was placed on a raised dais above the arena. The children grouped themselves all round, fluttering their big fans and whispering to each other, and Don Pedro and the Grand Inquisitor stood laughing at the entrance. Even the Duchess – the Camerera-Mayor as she was called – a thin, hard-featured woman with a yellow ruff, did not look quite so bad-tempered as usual, and something like a chill smile flitted across her wrinkled face and twitched her thin bloodless lips.

It certainly was a marvellous bull-fight, and much nicer, the Infanta thought, than the real bull-fight that she had been brought to see at Seville, on the occasion of the visit of the Duke of Parma to her father. Some of the boys pranced about on richly-caparisoned hobby-horses brandishing long javelins with gay streamers of bright ribands attached to them; others went on foot waving their scarlet cloaks before the bull, and vaulting lightly over the barrier when he charged them; and as for the bull himself, he was just like a live bull, though he was only made of wickerwork and stretched hide, and sometimes insisted on running round the arena on his hind legs, which no live bull ever dreams of doing. He made a splendid fight of it too, and the children got so excited that they stood up upon the benches, and waved their lace handkerchiefs and cried out: *Bravo toro! Bravo toro!* just as sensibly as if they had been grown-up people. At last, however, after a prolonged combat, during which several of the hobby-horses were gored through and through, and their riders dismounted, the young Count of Tierra-Nueva brought the bull to his knees, and having obtained permission from the Infanta to give the *coup de grâce*, he plunged his wooden sword into the neck of the animal with such violence that the head came right off, and disclosed the laughing face of little Monsieur de Lorraine, the son of the French Ambassador at Madrid.

The arena was then cleared amidst much applause, and the dead hobby-horses dragged solemnly away by two Moorish pages in yellow and black liveries, and after a short interlude, during which a French posture-master performed upon the tight-rope, some Italian puppets appeared in the semi-classical tragedy of *Sophonisba* on the stage of a small theatre that had been built up for the purpose. They acted so well, and their gestures were so extremely natural, that at the close of the play the eyes of the Infanta were quite dim with tears. Indeed some of the children really cried, and had to be comforted with sweet-meats, and the Grand Inquisitor himself was so affected that he could not help saying to Don Pedro that it seemed to him intolerable that things made simply out of wood and coloured wax, and worked mechanically by wires, should be so unhappy and meet with such terrible misfortunes.

An African juggler followed, who brought in a large flat basket covered with a red cloth, and having placed it in the centre of the arena, he took from his turban a curious reed pipe, and blew through it. In a few moments the cloth began to move, and as the pipe grew shriller and shriller two green and gold snakes put out their strange wedge-shaped heads and rose slowly up, swaying to and fro with the music as a plant sways in the water. The children, however, were rather frightened at their spotted hoods and quick darting tongues, and were much more pleased when the juggler made a tiny orange-tree grow out of the sand and bear pretty white blossoms and clusters of real fruit; and when he took the fan of the little daughter of the Marquess de Las-Torres, and changed it into a blue bird that flew all round the pavilion and sang, their delight and amazement knew no bounds. The solemn minuet, too, performed by the dancing boys from the church of Nuestra Senora Del Pilar, was charming. The Infanta had never before seen this wonderful ceremony which takes place every year at Maytime in front of the high altar of the Virgin, and in her honour; and indeed none of the royal family of Spain had entered the great cathedral of Saragossa since a mad priest, supposed by many to have been in the pay of Elizabeth of England, had tried to administer a poisoned wafer to the Prince of the Asturias. So she had known only by hearsay of 'Our Lady's Dance,' as it was called, and it certainly was a beautiful sight. The boys wore old-fashioned court dresses of white velvet, and their curious three-cornered hats were fringed with silver and surmounted with huge plumes of ostrich feathers, the dazzling whiteness of their costumes, as they moved about in the sunlight, being still more accentuated by their swarthy faces and long black hair. Everybody was fascinated by the grave dignity with which they moved through the intricate figures of the dance, and by the elaborate grace of their slow gestures, and stately bows, and when they had finished their performance and doffed their great plumed hats to the Infanta, she acknowledged their reverence with much courtesy, and made a vow that she would send a large wax candle to the shrine of Our Lady of Pilar in return for the pleasure that she had given her.

A troop of handsome Egyptians – as the gipsies were termed in those days – then advanced into the arena, and sitting down cross-legs, in a circle, began to play softly upon their zithers, moving their bodies to the tune, and humming, almost below their breath, a low dreamy air. When they caught sight of Don Pedro they scowled at him, and some of them looked terrified, for only a few weeks before he had had two of their tribe hanged for sorcery in the market-place at Seville, but the pretty Infanta charmed them as she leaned back peeping over her fan with her great blue eyes, and they felt sure that one so lovely as she was could never be cruel to anybody. So they played on very gently and just touching the cords of the zithers with their long pointed nails, and their heads began to nod as though they were falling asleep. Suddenly, with a cry so shrill that all the children were startled, and Don Pedro's hand clutched at the agate pommel of his dagger, they leapt to their feet and whirled madly round the enclosure beating their tambourines, and chaunting some wild love-song in their strange guttural language. Then at another signal they all flung themselves again to the ground and lay there quite still, the dull strumming of the zithers being the only sound that broke the silence. After that they had done this several times, they disappeared for a moment and came back leading a brown shaggy bear by a chain, and carrying on their shoulders some little Barbary apes. The bear stood upon his head with the utmost gravity, and the wizened apes played all kinds of amusing tricks with two gipsy boys who seemed to be their masters, and fought with tiny swords, and fired off guns, and went through a regular soldier's drill just like the King's own bodyguard. In fact, the gipsies were a great success.

But the funniest part of the whole morning's entertainment, was undoubtedly the dancing of the little Dwarf. When he stumbled into the arena, waddling on his crooked legs and wagging his huge misshapen head from side to side, the children went off into a loud shout of delight, and the Infanta herself laughed so much that the Camerera was obliged to remind her that although there were many precedents in Spain for a King's daughter weeping before her equals, there were none for a Princess of the blood royal making so merry before those who were her inferiors in birth. The Dwarf, however, was really quite irresistible, and even at the Spanish Court, always noted for its cultivated passion for the horrible, so fantastic a little monster had never been seen. It was his first appearance, too. He had been discovered only the day before, running wild through the forest, by two of the nobles who happened to have been hunting in a remote part of the great cork-wood that surrounded the town, and had been carried off by them to the Palace as a surprise for the Infanta; his father, who was a poor charcoal-burner, being but too well pleased to get rid of so ugly and useless a child. Perhaps the most amusing thing about him was his complete unconsciousness of his own grotesque appearance. Indeed he seemed quite happy and full of the highest spirits. When the children laughed, he laughed as freely and as joyously as any of them, and at the close of each dance he made them each the funniest of bows, smiling and nodding at them just as if he was really one of themselves, and not a little misshapen thing that Nature, in some humorous mood, had fashioned for others to mock at. As for the Infanta, she absolutely fascinated him. He could not keep his eyes off her, and seemed to dance for her alone, and when at the close of the performance, remembering how she had seen the great ladies of the Court throw bouquets to Caffarelli, the famous Italian treble, whom the Pope had sent from his own chapel to Madrid that he might cure the King's melancholy by the sweetness of his voice, she took out of her hair the beautiful white rose, and partly for a jest and partly to tease the Camerera, threw it to him across the arena with her sweetest smile. He took the whole matter quite seriously, and pressing the flower to his rough coarse lips he put his hand upon his heart, and sank on one knee before her, grinning from ear to ear, and with his little bright eyes sparkling with pleasure.

This so upset the gravity of the Infanta that she kept on laughing long after the little Dwarf had run out of the arena, and expressed a desire to her uncle that the dance should be immediately repeated. The Camerera, however, on the plea that the sun was too hot, decided that it would be better that her Highness should return without delay to the Palace, where a wonderful feast had been already prepared for her, including a real birthday cake with her own initials worked all over it in painted sugar and a lovely silver flag waving from the top. The Infanta accordingly rose up with much dignity, and having given orders that the little dwarf was to dance again for her after the hour of siesta, and conveyed her thanks to the young Count of Tierra-Nueva for his charming reception, she went back to her apartments, the children following in the same order in which they had entered.

Now when the little Dwarf heard that he was to dance a second time before the Infanta, and by her own express command, he was so proud that he ran out into the garden, kissing the white rose in an absurd ecstasy of pleasure, and making the most uncouth and clumsy gestures of delight.

The Flowers were quite indignant at his daring to intrude into their beautiful home, and when they saw him capering up and down the walks, and waving his arms above his head in such a ridiculous manner, they could not restrain their feelings any longer.

'He is really far too ugly to be allowed to play in any place where we are,' cried the Tulips.

'He should drink poppy-juice, and go to sleep for a thousand years,' said the great scarlet Lilies, and they grew quite hot and angry.

'He is a perfect horror!' screamed the Cactus. 'Why, he is twisted and stumpy, and his head is completely out of proportion with his legs. Really he makes me feel prickly all over, and if he comes near me I will sting him with my thorns.'

'And he has actually got one of my best blooms,' exclaimed the White Rose-Tree. 'I gave it to the Infanta this morning myself, as a birthday present, and he has stolen it from her.' And she called out: 'Thief, thief, thief!' at the top of her voice.

Even the red Geraniums, who did not usually give themselves airs, and were known to have a great many poor relations themselves, curled up in disgust when they saw him, and when the Violets meekly remarked that though he was certainly extremely plain, still he could not help it, they retorted with a good deal of justice that that was his chief defect, and that there was no reason why one should admire a person because he was incurable; and, indeed, some of the Violets themselves felt that the ugliness of the little Dwarf was almost ostentatious, and that he would have shown much better taste if he had looked sad, or at least pensive, instead of jumping about merrily, and throwing himself into such grotesque and silly attitudes.

As for the old Sundial, who was an extremely remarkable individual, and had told the time of day to no less a person than the Emperor Charles V. himself, he was so taken aback by the little Dwarf's appearance, that he almost forgot to mark two whole minutes with his long shadowy finger, and could not help saying to the great milk-white Peacock, who was sunning herself on the balustrade, that every one knew that the children of Kings were Kings, and that the children of charcoal-burners were charcoal-burners, and that it was absurd to pretend that it wasn't so; a statement with which the Peacock entirely agreed, and indeed screamed out, 'Certainly, certainly,' in such a loud, harsh voice, that the gold-fish who lived in the basin of the cool splashing fountain put their heads out of the water, and asked the huge stone Tritons what on earth was the matter.

But somehow the Birds liked him. They had seen him often in the forest, dancing about like an elf after the eddying leaves, or crouched up in the hollow of some old oak-tree, sharing his nuts with the squirrels. They did not mind his being ugly a bit. Why, even the nightingale herself, who sang so sweetly in the orange groves at night that sometimes the Moon leaned down to listen, was not much to look at after all; and, besides, he had been kind to them, and during that terribly bitter winter, when there were no berries on the trees, and the ground was as hard as iron, and the wolves had come down to the very gates of the city to look for food, he had never once forgotten them, but had always given them crumbs out of his little hunch of black bread, and divided with them whatever poor breakfast he had.

So they flew round and round him, just touching his cheek with their wings as they passed, and chattered to each other, and the little Dwarf was so pleased that he could not help showing them the beautiful white rose, and telling them that the Infanta herself had given it to him because she loved him.

They did not understand a single word of what he was saying, but that made no matter, for they put their heads on one side, and looked wise, which is quite as good as understanding a thing, and very much easier.

The Lizards also took an immense fancy to him, and when he grew tired of running about and flung himself down on the grass to rest, they played and romped all over him, and tried to amuse him in the best way they could. 'Every one cannot be as beautiful as a lizard,' they cried; 'that would be too much to expect. And, though it sounds absurd to say so, he is really not so ugly after all, provided, of course, that one shuts one's eyes, and does not look at him.' The Lizards were extremely philosophical by nature, and often sat thinking for hours and hours together, when there was nothing else to do, or when the weather was too rainy for them to go out.

The Flowers, however, were excessively annoyed at their behaviour, and at the behaviour of the birds. 'It only shows,' they said, 'what a vulgarising effect this incessant rushing and flying about has. Well-bred people always stay exactly in the same place as we do. No one ever saw us hopping up and down the walks, or galloping madly through the grass after dragon-flies. When we do want change of air, we send for the gardener, and he carries us to another bed. This is dignified, and as it should be. But birds and lizards have no sense of repose, and indeed birds have not even a permanent address. They are mere vagrants like the gipsies, and should be treated in exactly the same manner.' So they put their noses in the air, and looked very haughty, and were quite delighted when after some time they saw the little Dwarf scramble up from the grass, and make his way across the terrace to the Palace.

'He should certainly be kept indoors for the rest of his natural life,' they said. 'Look at his hunched back, and his crooked legs,' and they began to titter.

But the little Dwarf knew nothing of all this. He liked the birds and the lizards immensely, and thought that the flowers were the most marvellous things in the whole world, except of course the Infanta, but then she had given him the beautiful white rose, and she loved him, and that made a great difference. How he wished that he had gone back with her! She would have put him on her right hand, and smiled at him, and he would have never left her side, but would have made her his playmate, and taught her all kinds of delightful tricks. For though he had never been in a palace before, he knew a great many wonderful things. He could make little cages out of rushes for the grasshoppers to sing in, and fashion the long-jointed bamboo into the pipe that Pan loves to hear. He knew the cry of every bird, and could call the starlings from the tree-top, or the heron from the mere. He knew the trail of every animal, and could track the hare by its delicate footprints, and the boar by the trampled leaves. All the wild-dances he knew, the mad dance in red raiment with the autumn, the light dance in blue sandals over the corn, the dance with white snow-wreaths in winter, and the blossom-dance, through the orchards in spring. He knew where the wood-pigeons built their nests, and once when a fowler had snared the parent birds, he had brought up the young ones himself, and had built a little dovecot for them in the cleft of a pollard elm. They were quite tame, and used to feed out of his hands every morning. She would like them, and the rabbits that scurried about in the long fern, and the jays with their steely feathers and black bills, and the hedgehogs that could curl themselves up into prickly balls, and the great wise tortoises that crawled slowly about, shaking their heads and nibbling at the young leaves. Yes, she must certainly come to the forest and play with him. He would give her his own little bed, and would watch outside the window till dawn, to see that the wild horned cattle did not harm her, nor the gaunt wolves creep too near the hut. And at dawn he would tap at the shutters and wake her, and they would go out and dance together all the day long. It was really not a bit lonely in the forest. Sometimes a Bishop rode through on his white mule, reading out of a painted book. Sometimes in their green velvet caps, and their jerkins of tanned deerskin, the falconers passed by, with hooded hawks on their wrists. At vintage-time came the grape-treaders, with purple hands and feet, wreathed with glossy ivy and carrying dripping skins of wine; and the charcoal burners sat round their huge braziers at night, watching the dry logs charring slowly in the fire, and roasting chestnuts in the ashes, and the robbers came out of their caves and made merry with them. Once, too, he had seen a beautiful procession winding up the long dusty road to Toledo. The monks went in front singing sweetly, and carrying bright banners and crosses of gold, and then, in silver armour, with matchlocks and pikes, came the soldiers, and in their midst walked three barefooted men, in strange yellow dresses painted all over with wonderful figures, and carrying lighted candles in their hands. Certainly there was a great deal to look at in the forest, and when she was tired he would find a soft bank of moss for her, or carry her in his arms, for he was very strong, though he knew that he was not tall. He would make her a necklace of red bryony berries, that would be quite as pretty as the white berries that she wore on her dress, and when she was tired of them, she could throw them away, and he would find her others. He would bring her acorn-cups and dew-drenched anemones, and tiny glow-worms to be stars in the pale gold of her hair.

But where was she? He asked the white rose, and it made him no answer. The whole palace seemed asleep, and even where the shutters had not been closed, heavy curtains had been drawn across the windows to keep out the glare. He wandered all round looking for some place through which he might gain an entrance, and at last he caught sight of a little private door that was lying open. He slipped through, and found himself in a splendid hall, far more splendid he feared, than the forest, for there was so much more gilding everywhere, and even the floor was made of great coloured stones, fitted together into a sort of geometrical pattern. But the little Infanta was not there, only some wonderful white statues that looked down on him from their jasper pedestals, with sad blank eyes and strangely smiling lips.

At the end of the hall hung a richly embroidered curtain of black velvet, powdered with suns and stars, the King's favourite devices, and broidered on the colour he loved best. Perhaps she was hiding behind that? He would try at any rate.

So he stole quietly across, and drew it aside. No; there was only another room, though a prettier room, he thought, than the one he had just left. The walls were hung with a many-figured green arras of needle-wrought tapestry representing a hunt, the work of some Flemish artists who had spent more than seven years in its composition. It had once been the chamber of *Jean le Fou*, as he was called, that mad King who was so enamoured of the chase, that he had often tried in his delirium to mount the huge rearing horses, and to drag down the stag on which the great hounds were leaping, sounding his hunting horn, and stabbing with his dagger at the pale flying deer. It was now used as the council-room, and on the centre table were lying the red portfolios of the ministers, stamped with the gold tulips of Spain, and with the arms and emblems of the house of Hapsburg.

The little Dwarf looked in wonder all round him, and was half-afraid to go on. The strange silent horsemen that galloped so swiftly through the long glades without making any noise, seemed to him like those terrible phantoms of whom he had heard the charcoal-burners speaking – the Comprachos, who hunt only at night, and if they meet a man, turn him into a hind, and chase him. But he thought of the pretty Infanta, and took courage. He wanted to find her alone, and to tell her that he too loved her. Perhaps she was in the room beyond.

He ran across the soft Moorish carpets, and opened the door. No! She was not here either. The room was quite empty.

It was a throne-room, used for the reception of foreign ambassadors, when the King, which of late had not been often, consented to give them a personal audience; the same room in which, many years before, envoys had appeared from England to make arrangements for the marriage of their Queen, then one of the Catholic sovereigns of Europe, with the Emperor's eldest son. The hangings were of gilt Cordovan leather, and a heavy gilt chandelier with branches for three hundred wax lights hung down from the black and white ceiling. Underneath a great canopy of gold cloth, on which the lions and towers of Castile were broidered in seed pearls, stood the throne itself, covered with a rich pall of black velvet studded with silver tulips and elaborately fringed with silver and pearls. On the second step of the throne was placed the kneeling-stool of the Infanta, with its cushion of cloth of silver tissue, and below that again, and beyond the limit of the canopy, stood the chair for the Papal Nuncio, who alone had the right to be seated in the King's presence on the occasion of any public ceremonial, and whose Cardinal's hat, with its tangled scarlet tassels, lay on a purple *tabouret* in front. On the wall, facing the throne, hung a life-sized portrait of Charles V. in hunting dress, with a great mastiff by his side, and a picture of Philip II. receiving the homage of the Netherlands, occupied the centre of the other wall. Between the windows stood a black ebony cabinet, inlaid with plates of ivory, on which the figures from Holbein's Dance of Death had been graved – by the hand, some said, of that famous master himself.

But the little Dwarf cared nothing for all this magnificence. He would not have given his rose for all the pearls on the canopy, nor one white pearl of his rose for the throne itself. What he wanted was to see the Infanta before she went down to the pavilion, and to ask her to come away with him when he had finished his dance. Here, in the Palace, the air was close and heavy, but in the forest the wind blew free, and the sunlight with wandering hands of gold moved the tremulous leaves aside. There were flowers, too, in the forest, not so splendid, perhaps, as the flowers in the garden, but more sweetly scented for all that; hyacinths in early spring that flooded with waving purple the cool glens, and grassy knolls; yellow primroses that nestled in little clumps round the gnarled roots of the oak-trees; bright celandine, and blue speedwell, and irises lilac and gold. There were grey catkins on the hazels, and the foxgloves drooped with the weight of their dappled bee-haunted cells. The chestnut had its spires of white stars, and the hawthorn its pallid moons of beauty. Yes; surely she would come if he could only find her! She would come with him to the fair forest, and all day long he would dance for her delight. A smile lit up his eyes at the thought, and he passed into the next room.

Of all the rooms this was the brightest and the most beautiful. The walls were covered with a pink-flowered Lucca damask, patterned with birds and dotted with dainty blossoms of silver; the furniture was of massive silver, festooned with florid wreaths, and swinging Cupids; in front of the two large fireplaces stood great screens broidered with parrots and peacocks, and the floor, which was of sea-green oynx, seemed to stretch far away into the distance. Nor was he alone. Standing under the shadow of the doorway, at the extreme end of the room, he saw a little figure watching him. His heart trembled, a cry of joy broke from his lips, and he moved out into the sunlight. As he did so, the figure moved out also, and he saw it plainly.

The Infanta! It was a monster, the most grotesque monster he had ever beheld. Not properly shaped as all other people were, but hunchbacked, and crooked-limbed, with huge lolling head and mane of black hair. The little Dwarf frowned, and the monster frowned also. He laughed, and it laughed with him, and held its hands to its sides, just as he himself was doing. He made it a mocking bow, and it returned him a low reverence. He went towards it, and it came to meet him, copying each step that he made, and stopping when he stopped himself. He shouted with amusement, and ran forward, and reached out his hand, and the hand of the monster touched his, and it was as cold as ice. He grew afraid, and moved his hand across, and the monster's hand followed it quickly. He tried to press on, but something smooth and hard stopped him. The face of the monster was now close to his own, and seemed full of terror. He brushed his hair off his eyes. It imitated him. He struck at it, and it returned blow for blow. He loathed it, and it made hideous faces at him. He drew back, and it retreated.

What is it? He thought for a moment, and looked round at the rest of the room. It was strange, but everything seemed to have its double in this invisible wall of clear water. Yes, picture for picture was repeated, and couch for couch. The sleeping Faun that lay in the alcove by the doorway had its twin brother that slumbered, and the silver Venus that stood in the sunlight held out her arms to a Venus as lovely as herself.

Was it Echo? He had called to her once in the valley, and she had answered him word for word. Could she mock the eye, as she mocked the voice? Could she make a mimic world just like the real world? Could the shadows of things have colour and life and movement? Could it be that – ?

He started, and taking from his breast the beautiful white rose, he turned round, and kissed it. The monster had a rose of its own, petal for petal the same! It kissed it with like kisses, and pressed it to its heart with horrible gestures.

When the truth dawned upon him, he gave a wild cry of despair, and fell sobbing to the ground. So it was he who was misshapen and hunchbacked, foul to look at and grotesque. He himself was the monster, and it was at him that all the children had been laughing, and the little Princess who he had thought loved him – she, too, had been merely mocking at his ugliness, and making merry over his twisted limbs. Why had they not left him in the forest, where there was no mirror to tell him how loathsome he was? Why had his father not killed him, rather than sell him to his shame? The hot tears poured down his cheeks, and he tore the white rose to pieces. The sprawling monster did the same, and scattered the faint petals in the air. It grovelled on the ground, and, when he looked at it, it watched him with a face drawn with pain. He crept away, lest he should see it, and covered his eyes with his hands. He crawled, like some wounded thing, into the shadow, and lay there moaning.

And at that moment the Infanta herself came in with her companions through the open window, and when they saw the ugly little Dwarf lying on the ground and beating the floor with his clenched hands, in the most fantastic and exaggerated manner, they went off into shouts of happy laughter, and stood all round him and watched him.

'His dancing was funny,' said the Infanta; 'but his acting is funnier still. Indeed, he is almost as good as the puppets, only, of course, not quite so natural.' And she fluttered her big fan and applauded.

But the little Dwarf never looked up, and his sobs grew fainter and fainter, and suddenly he gave a curious gasp, and clutched his side. And then he fell back again, and lay quite still.

'That is capital,' said the Infanta, after a pause; 'but now you must dance for me.'

'Yes,' cried all the children, 'you must get up and dance, for you are as clever as the Barbary apes, and much more ridiculous.'

But the little Dwarf made no answer.

And the Infanta stamped her foot, and called out to her uncle, who was walking on the terrace with the Chamberlain, reading some despatches that had just arrived from Mexico, where the Holy Office had recently been established. 'My funny little Dwarf is sulking,' she cried, 'you must wake him up, and tell him to dance for me.'

They smiled at each other, and sauntered in, and Don Pedro stooped down, and slapped the Dwarf on the cheek with his embroidered glove. 'You must dance,' he said, '*petit monstre*. You must dance. The Infanta of Spain and the Indies wishes to be amused.'

But the little Dwarf never moved.

'A whipping master should be sent for,' said Don Pedro wearily, and he went back to the terrace. But the Chamberlain looked grave, and he knelt beside the little Dwarf, and put his hand upon his heart. And after a few moments he shrugged his shoulders, and rose up, and having made a low bow to the Infanta, he said –

'*Mi bella Princesa*, your funny little Dwarf will never dance again. It is a pity, for he is so ugly that he might have made the King smile.'

'But why will he not dance again?' asked the Infanta, laughing.

'Because his heart is broken,' answered the Chamberlain.

And the Infanta frowned, and her dainty rose-leaf lips curled in pretty disdain. 'For the future let those who come to play with me have no hearts,' she cried, and she ran out into the garden.

THE FISHERMAN AND HIS SOUL

EVERY evening the young Fisherman went out upon the sea, and threw his nets into the water.

When the wind blew from the land he caught nothing, or but little at best, for it was a bitter and black-winged wind, and rough waves rose up to meet it. But when the wind blew to the shore, the fish came in from the deep, and swam into the meshes of his nets, and he took them to the market-place and sold them.

Every evening he went out upon the sea, and one evening the net was so heavy that hardly could he draw it into the boat. And he laughed, and said to himself, 'Surely I have caught all the fish that swim, or snared some dull monster that will be a marvel to men, or some thing of horror that the great Queen will desire,' and putting forth all his strength, he tugged at the coarse ropes till, like lines of blue enamel round a vase of bronze, the long veins rose up on his arms. He tugged at the thin ropes, and nearer and nearer came the circle of flat corks, and the net rose at last to the top of the water.

But no fish at all was in it, nor any monster or thing of horror, but only a little Mermaid lying fast asleep.

Her hair was as a wet fleece of gold, and each separate hair as a thread of fine gold in a cup of glass. Her body was as white ivory, and her tail was of silver and pearl. Silver and pearl was her tail, and the green weeds of the sea coiled round it; and like sea-shells were her ears, and her lips were like sea-coral. The cold waves dashed over her cold breasts, and the salt glistened upon her eyelids.

So beautiful was she that when the young Fisherman saw her he was filled with wonder, and he put out his hand and drew the net close to him, and leaning over the side he clasped her in his arms. And when he touched her, she gave a cry like a startled sea-gull, and woke, and looked at him in terror with her mauve-amethyst eyes, and struggled that she might escape. But he held her tightly to him, and would not suffer her to depart.

And when she saw that she could in no way escape from him, she began to weep, and said, 'I pray thee let me go, for I am the only daughter of a King, and my father is aged and alone.'

But the young Fisherman answered, 'I will not let thee go save thou makest me a promise that whenever I call thee, thou wilt come and sing to me, for the fish delight to listen to the song of the Sea-folk and so shall my nets be full.'

'Wilt thou in very truth let me go, if I promise thee this?' cried the Mermaid.

'In very truth I will let thee go,' said the young Fisherman.

So she made him the promise he desired, and sware it by the oath of the

Sea-folk. And he loosened his arms from about her, and she sank down into the water, trembling with a strange fear.

Every evening the young Fisherman went out upon the sea, and called to the Mermaid, and she rose out of the water and sang to him. Round and round her swam the dolphins, and the wild gulls wheeled above her head.

And she sang a marvellous song. For she sang of the Sea-folk who drive their flocks from cave to cave, and carry the little calves on their shoulders; of the Tritons who have long green beards, and hairy breasts, and blow through twisted conchs when the King passes by; of the palace of the King which is all of amber, with a roof of clear emerald, and a pavement of bright pearl; and of the gardens of the sea where the great filigrane fans of coral wave all day long, and the fish dart about like silver birds, and the anemones cling to the rocks, and the pinks bourgeon in the ribbed yellow sand. She sang of the big whales that come down from the north seas and have sharp icicles hanging to their fins; of the Sirens who tell of such wonderful things that the merchants have to stop their ears with wax lest they should hear them, and leap into the water and be drowned; of the sunken galleys with their tall masts, and the frozen sailors clinging to the rigging, and the mackerel swimming in and out of the open portholes; of the little barnacles who are great travellers, and cling to the keels of the ships and go round and round the world; and of the cuttlefish who live in the sides of the cliffs and stretch out their long black arms, and can make night come when they will it. She sang of the nautilus who has a boat of her own that is carved out of an opal and steered with a silken sail; of the happy Mermen who play upon harps and can charm the great Kraken to sleep; of the little children who catch hold of the slippery porpoises and ride laughing upon their backs; of the Mermaids who lie in the white foam and hold out their arms to the mariners; and of the sea-lions with their curved tusks, and the sea-horses with their floating manes.

And as she sang, all the tunny-fish came in from the deep to listen to her, and the young Fishermen threw his nets round them and caught them, and others he took with a spear. And when his boat was well-laden, the Mermaid would sink down into the sea, smiling at him.

Yet would she never come near him that he might touch her. Oftentimes he called to her and prayed of her, but she would not; and when he sought to seize her she dived into the water as a seal might dive, nor did he see her again that day. And each day the sound of her voice became sweeter to his ears. So sweet was her voice that he forgot his nets and his cunning, and had no care of his craft. Vermilion-finned and with eyes of bossy gold, the tunnies went by in shoals, but he heeded them not. His spear lay by his side unused, and his baskets of plaited osier were empty. With lips parted, and eyes dim with wonder, he sat idle in his boat and listened, listening till the sea-mists crept round him and the wandering moon stained his brown limbs with silver.

And one evening he called to her, and said: 'Little Mermaid, little Mermaid, I love thee. Take me for thy bridegroom for I love thee.'

But the Mermaid shook her head. 'Thou hast a human Soul,' she answered. 'If only thou wouldst send away thy Soul, then could I love thee.'

And the young Fisherman said to himself, 'Of what use is my soul to me? I cannot see it. I may not touch it. I do not know it. Surely I will send it away from me, and much gladness shall be mine.' And a cry of joy broke from his lips, and standing up in the painted boat, he held out his arms to the Mermaid. 'I will send my Soul away,' he cried, 'and you shall be my bride, and I will be thy bridegroom, and in the depth of the sea we will dwell together, and all that thou hast sung of thou shalt show me, and all that thou desirest I will do, nor shall our lives be divided.'

And the little Mermaid laughed for pleasure and hid her face in her hands.

'But how shall I send my Soul from me?' cried the young Fisherman. 'Tell me how I may do it, and lo! it shall be done.'

'Alas! I know not,' said the little Mermaid: 'the Sea-folk have no souls.' And she sank down into the deep, looking wistfully at him.

Now early on the next morning, before the sun was the span of a man's hand above the hill, the young Fisherman went to the house of the Priest and knocked three times at the door.

The novice looked out through the wicket, and when he saw who it was, he drew back the latch and said to him, 'Enter.'

And the young Fisherman passed in, and knelt down on the sweet-smelling rushes on the floor, and cried to the Priest who was reading out of the Holy Book and said to him, 'Father, I am in love with one of the Sea-folk, and my Soul hindereth me from having my desire. Tell me how I can send my Soul away from me, for in truth I have no need of it. Of what value is my soul to me? I cannot see it. I may not touch it. I do not know it.'

And the Priest beat his breast, and answered, 'Alack, alack, thou art mad, or hast eaten of some poisonous herb, for the Soul is the noblest part of man, and was given to us by God that we should nobly use it. There is no thing more precious than a human soul, nor any earthly thing that can be weighed with it. It is worth all the gold that is in the world, and is more precious than the rubies of the kings. Therefore, my son, think not any more of this matter, for it is a sin that may not be forgiven. And as for the Sea-folk, they are lost, and they who would traffic with them are lost also. They are the beasts of the field that know not good from evil, and for them the Lord has not died.'

The young Fisherman's eyes filled with tears when he heard the bitter words of the Priest, and he rose up from his knees and said to him, 'Father, the Fauns live in the forest and are glad, and on the rocks sit the Mermen with their harps of red gold. Let me be as they are, I beseech thee, for their days are as the days of flowers. And as for my Soul, what doth my Soul profit me, if it stand between me and the thing that I love?'

'The love of the body is vile,' cried the Priest, knitting his brows, 'and vile and evil are the pagan things God suffers to wander through His world. Accursed be the Fauns of the woodland, and accursed be the singers of the sea! I have heard them at night-time, and they have sought to lure me from my beads. They tap at the window and laugh. They whisper into my ears the tale of their perilous joys. They tempt me with temptations, and when I would pray they make mouths at me. They are lost, I tell thee, they are lost. For them there is no heaven nor hell, and in neither shall they praise God's name.'

'Father,' cried the young Fisherman, 'thou knowest not what thou sayest. Once in my net I snared the daughter of a King. She is fairer than the morning star, and whiter than the moon. For her body I would give my soul, and for her love I would surrender heaven. Tell me what I ask of thee, and let me go in peace.'

'Away! Away!' cried the Priest: 'thy leman is lost, and thou shalt be lost with her.' And he gave him no blessing, but drove him from his door.

And the young Fisherman went down into the market-place, and he walked slowly, and with bowed head, as one who is in sorrow.

And when the merchants saw him coming, they began to whisper to each other, and one of them came forth to meet him, and called him by name, and said to him, 'What hast thou to sell?'

'I will sell thee my Soul,' he answered: 'I pray thee buy it off me, for I am weary of it. Of what use is my Soul to me? I cannot see it. I may not touch it. I do not know it.'

But the merchants mocked at him, and said, 'Of what use is a man's soul to us? It is not worth a clipped piece of silver. Sell us thy body for a slave, and we will clothe thee in sea purple, and put a ring upon thy finger, and make thee the minion of the great Queen. But talk not of the Soul, for to us it is nought, nor has it any value for our service.'

And the young Fisherman said to himself: 'How strange a thing this is! The Priest telleth me that the Soul is worth all the gold in the world, and the merchants say that it is not worth a clipped piece of silver.' And he passed out of the market-place, and went down to the shore of the sea, and began to ponder on what he should do.

And at noon he remembered how one of his companions, who was a gatherer of samphire, had told him of a certain young Witch who dwelt in a cave at the head of the bay and was very cunning in her witcheries. And he set to and ran, so eager was he to get rid of his soul, and a cloud of dust followed him as he sped round the sand of the shore. By the itching of her palm the young Witch knew his coming, and she laughed and let down her red hair. With her red hair falling around her, she stood at the opening of the cave, and in her hand she had a spray of wild hemlock that was blossoming.

'What d'ye lack? What d'ye lack?' she cried, as he came panting up the steep, and bent down before her. 'Fish for thy net, when the wind is foul? I have a little reed-pipe, and when I blow on it the mullet come sailing into the bay. But it has a price, pretty boy, it has a price. What d'ye lack? What d'ye lack? A storm to wreck the ships, and wash the chests of rich treasure ashore? I have more storms than the wind has, for I serve one who is stronger than the wind, and with a sieve and a pail of water I can send the great galleys to the bottom of the sea. But I have a price, pretty boy, I have a price. What d'ye lack? What d'ye lack? I know a flower that grows in the valley, none knows it but I. It has purple leaves, and a star in its heart, and its juice is as white as milk. Shouldst thou touch with this flower the hard lips of the Queen, she would follow thee all over the world. Out of the bed of the King she would rise, and over the whole world she would follow thee. And it has a price, pretty boy, it has a price. What d'ye lack? What d'ye lack? I can pound a toad in a mortar, and make broth of it, and stir the broth with a dead man's hand. Sprinkle it on thine enemy while he sleeps, and he will turn into a black viper, and his own mother will slay him. With a wheel I can draw the Moon from heaven, and in a crystal I can show thee Death. What d'ye lack? What d'ye lack? Tell me thy desire, and I will give it thee, and thou shalt pay me a price, pretty boy, thou shalt pay me a price.'

'My desire is but for a little thing,' said the young Fisherman, 'yet hath the Priest been wroth with me, and driven me forth. It is but for a little thing, and the merchants have mocked at me, and denied me. Therefore am I come to thee, though men call thee evil, and whatever be thy price I shall pay it.'

'What wouldst thou?' asked the Witch, coming near to him.

'I would send my Soul away from me,' answered the young Fisherman.

The Witch grew pale, and shuddered, and hid her face in her blue mantle. 'Pretty boy, pretty boy,' she muttered, 'that is a terrible thing to do.'

He tossed his brown curls and laughed. 'My Soul is nought to me,' he answered. 'I cannot see it. I may not touch it. I do not know it.'

'What wilt thou give me if I tell thee?' asked the Witch, looking down at him with her beautiful eyes.

'Five pieces of gold,' he said, 'and my nets, and the wattled house where I live, and the painted boat in which I sail. Only tell me how to get rid of my Soul, and I will give thee all that I possess.'

She laughed mockingly at him, and struck him with the spray of hemlock. 'I can turn the autumn leaves into gold,' she answered, 'and I can weave the pale moonbeams into silver if I will it. He whom I serve is richer than all the kings of this world, and has their dominions.'

'What then shall I give thee,' he cried, 'if thy price be neither gold nor silver?'

The Witch stroked his hair with her thin white hand. 'Thou must dance with me, pretty boy,' she murmured, and she smiled at him as she spoke.

'Nought but that?' cried the young Fisherman in wonder, and he rose to his feet.

'Nought but that,' she answered, and she smiled at him again.

'Then at sunset in some secret place we shall dance together,' he said, 'and after that we have danced thou shalt tell me the thing which I desire to know.'

She shook her head. 'When the moon is full, when the moon is full,' she muttered. Then she peered all round, and listened. A blue bird rose screaming from its nest and circled over the dunes, and three spotted birds rustled through the coarse grey grass and whistled to each other. There was no other sound save the sound of a wave fretting the smooth pebbles below. So she reached out her hand, and drew him near to her and put her dry lips close to his ear.

'To-night thou must come to the top of the mountain,' she whispered. 'It is a Sabbath, and He will be there.'

The young Fisherman started and looked at her, and she showed her white teeth and laughed. 'Who is He of whom thou speakest?' he asked.

'It matters not,' she answered. 'Go thou to-night, and stand under the branches of the hornbeam, and wait for my coming. If a black dog run towards thee, strike it with a rod of willow, and it will go away. If an owl speak to thee, make it no answer. When the moon is full I shall be with thee, and we will dance together on the grass.'

'But wilt thou swear to me to tell me how I may send my Soul from me?' he made question.

She moved out into the sunlight, and through her red hair rippled the wind. 'By the hoofs of the goat I swear it,' she made answer.

'Thou art the best of the witches,' cried the young Fisherman, 'and I will surely dance with thee to-night on the top of the mountain. I would indeed that thou hadst asked of me either gold or silver. But such as thy price is thou shalt have it, for it is but a little thing.' And he doffed his cap to her, and bent his head low, and ran back to the town filled with a great joy.

And the Witch watched him as he went, and when he had passed from her sight she entered her cave, and having taken a mirror from a box of carved cedarwood, she set it up on a frame, and burned vervain on lighted charcoal before it, and peered through the coils of the smoke. And after a time she clenched her hands in anger. 'He should have been mine,' she muttered, 'I am as fair as she is.'

And that evening, when the moon had risen, the young Fisherman climbed up to the top of the mountain, and stood under the branches of the hornbeam. Like a targe of polished metal the round sea lay at his feet, and the shadows of the fishing-boats moved in the little bay. A great owl, with yellow sulphurous eyes, called to him by his name, but he made it no answer. A black dog ran towards him and snarled. He struck it with a rod of willow, and it went away whining.

At midnight the witches came flying through the air like bats. 'Phew!' they cried, as they lit upon the ground, 'there is some one here we know not!' and they sniffed about, and chattered to each other, and made signs. Last of all came the young Witch, with her red hair streaming in the wind. She wore a dress of gold tissue embroidered with peacocks' eyes, and a little cap of green velvet was on her head.

'Where is he, where is he?' shrieked the witches when they saw her, but she only laughed, and ran to the hornbeam, and taking the Fisherman by the hand she led him out into the moonlight and began to dance.

Round and round they whirled, and the young Witch jumped so high that he could see the scarlet heels of her shoes. Then right across the dancers came the sound of the galloping of a horse, but no horse was to be seen, and he felt afraid.

'Faster,' cried the Witch, and she threw her arms about his neck, and her breath was hot upon his face. 'Faster, faster!' she cried, and the earth seemed to spin beneath his feet, and his brain grew troubled, and a great terror fell on him, as of some evil thing that was watching him, and at last he became aware that under the shadow of a rock there was a figure that had not been there before.

It was a man dressed in a suit of black velvet, cut in the Spanish fashion. His face was strangely pale, but his lips were like a proud red flower. He seemed weary, and was leaning back toying in a listless manner with the pommel of his dagger. On the grass beside him lay a plumed hat, and a pair of riding-gloves gauntleted with gilt lace, and sewn with seed-pearls wrought into a curious device. A short cloak lined with sables hung from his shoulder, and his delicate white hands were gemmed with rings. Heavy eyelids drooped over his eyes.

The young Fisherman watched him, as one snared in a spell. At last their eyes met, and wherever he danced it seemed to him that the eyes of the man were upon him. He heard the Witch laugh, and caught her by the waist, and whirled her madly round and round.

Suddenly a dog bayed in the wood, and the dancers stopped, and going up two by two, knelt down, and kissed the man's hands. As they did so, a little smile touched his proud lips, as a bird's wing touches the water and makes it laugh. But there was disdain in it. He kept looking at the young Fisherman.

'Come! let us worship,' whispered the Witch, and she led him up, and a great desire to do as she besought him seized on him, and he followed her. But when he came close, and without knowing why he did it, he made on his breast the sign of the Cross, and called upon the holy name.

No sooner had he done so than the witches screamed like hawks and flew away, and the pallid face that had been watching him twitched with a spasm of pain. The man went over to a little wood, and whistled. A jennet with silver trappings came running to meet him. As he leapt upon the saddle he turned round, and looked at the young Fisherman sadly.

And the Witch with the red hair tried to fly away also, but the Fisherman caught her by her wrists, and held her fast.

'Loose me,' she cried, 'and let me go. For thou hast named what should not be named, and shown the sign that may not be looked at.'

'Nay,' he answered, 'but I will not let thee go till thou hast told me the secret.'

'What secret?' said the Witch, wrestling with him like a wild cat, and biting her foam-flecked lips.

'Thou knowest,' he made answer.

Her grass-green eyes grew dim with tears, and she said to the Fisherman, 'Ask me anything but that!'

He laughed, and held her all the more tightly.

And when she saw that she could not free herself, she whispered to him, 'Surely I am as fair as the daughter of the sea, and as comely as those that dwell in the blue waters,' and she fawned on him and put her face close to his.

But he thrust her back frowning, and said to her, 'If thou keepest not the promise that thou madest to me I will slay thee for a false witch.'

She grew grey as a blossom of the Judas tree, and shuddered. 'Be it so,' she muttered. 'It is thy Soul and not mine. Do with it as thou wilt.' And she took from her girdle a little knife that had a handle of green viper's skin, and gave it to him.

'What shall this serve me?' he asked of her, wondering.

She was silent for a few moments, and a look of terror came over her face. Then she brushed her hair back from her forehead, and smiling strangely she said to him, 'What men call the shadow of the body is not the shadow of the body, but is the body of the Soul. Stand on the sea-shore with thy back to the moon, and cut away from around thy feet thy shadow, which is thy Soul's body, and bid thy soul leave thee, and it will do so.'

The young Fisherman trembled. 'Is this true?' he murmured.

'It is true, and I would that I had not told thee of it,' she cried, and she clung to his knees weeping.

He put her from him and left her in the rank grass, and going to the edge of the mountain he placed the knife in his belt and began to climb down.

And his Soul that was within him called out to him and said, 'Lo! I have dwelt with thee for all these years, and have been thy servant. Send me not away from thee now, for what evil have I done thee?'

And the young Fisherman laughed. 'Thou hast done me no evil, but I have no need of thee,' he answered. 'The world is wide, and there is Heaven also, and Hell, and that dim twilight house that lies between. Go wherever thou wilt, but trouble me not, for my love is calling to me.'

And his Soul besought him piteously, but he heeded it not, but leapt from crag to crag, being surefooted as a wild goat, and at last he reached the level ground and the yellow shore of the sea.

Bronze-limbed and well-knit, like a statue wrought by a Grecian, he stood on the sand with his back to the moon, and out of the foam came white arms that beckoned to him, and out of the waves rose dim forms that did him homage. Before him lay his shadow, which was the body of his Soul, and behind him hung the moon in the honey-coloured air.

And his Soul said to him, 'If indeed thou must drive me from thee, send me not forth without a heart. The world is cruel, give me thy heart to take with me.'

He tossed his head and smiled. 'With what should I love my love if I gave thee my heart?' he cried.

'Nay, but be merciful,' said his Soul: 'give me thy heart, for the world is very cruel, and I am afraid.'

'My heart is my love's,' he answered, 'therefore tarry not, but get thee gone.'

'Should I not love also?' asked his Soul.

'Get thee gone, for I have no need of thee,' cried the young Fisherman, and he took the little knife with its handle of green viper's skin, and cut away his shadow from around his feet, and it rose up and stood before him, and looked at him, and it was even as himself.

He crept back, and thrust the knife into his belt, and a feeling of awe came over him. 'Get thee gone,' he murmured, 'and let me see thy face no more.'

'Nay, but we must meet again,' said the Soul. Its voice was low and flute-like, and its lips hardly moved while it spake.

'How shall we meet?' cried the young Fisherman. 'Thou wilt not follow me into the depths of the sea?'

'Once every year I will come to this place, and call to thee,' said the Soul. 'It may be that thou wilt have need of me.'

'What need should I have of thee?' cried the young Fisherman, 'but be it as thou wilt,' and he plunged into the water, and the Tritons blew their horns, and the little Mermaid rose up to meet him, and put her arms around his neck and kissed him on the mouth.

And the Soul stood on the lonely beach and watched them. And when they had sunk down into the sea, it went weeping away over the marshes.

And after a year was over the Soul came down to the shore of the sea and called to the young Fisherman, and he rose out of the deep, and said, 'Why dost thou call to me?'

And the Soul answered, 'Come nearer, that I may speak with thee, for I have seen marvellous things.'

So he came nearer, and couched in the shallow water, and leaned his head upon his hand and listened.

And the Soul said to him, 'When I left thee I turned my face to the East and journeyed. From the East cometh everything that is wise. Six days I journeyed, and on the morning of the seventh day I came to a hill that is in the country of the Tartars. I sat down under the shade of a tamarisk tree to shelter myself from the sun. The land was dry and burnt up with the heat. The people went to and fro over the plain like flies crawling upon a disk of polished copper.

'When it was noon a cloud of red dust rose up from the flat rim of the land. When the Tartars saw it, they strung their painted bows, and having leapt upon their little horses they galloped to meet it. The women fled screaming to the waggons, and hid themselves behind the felt curtains.

'At twilight the Tartars returned, but five of them were missing, and of those that came back not a few had been wounded. They harnessed their horses to the waggons and drove hastily away. Three jackals came out of a cave and peered after them. Then they sniffed up the air with their nostrils, and trotted off in the opposite direction.

'When the moon rose I saw a camp-fire burning on the plain, and went towards it. A company of merchants were seated round it on carpets. Their camels were picketed behind them, and the negroes who were their servants were pitching tents of tanned skin upon the sand, and making a high wall of the prickly pear.

'As I came near them, the chief of the merchants rose up and drew his sword and asked me my business.

'I answered that I was a Prince in my own land, and that I had escaped from the Tartars, who had sought to make me their slave. The chief smiled, and showed me five heads fixed upon long reeds of bamboo.

'Then he asked me who was the prophet of God, and I answered him Mohammed.

'When he heard the name of the false prophet, he bowed and took me by the hand, and placed me by his side. A negro brought me some mare's milk in a wooden dish, and a piece of lamb's flesh roasted.

'At daybreak we started on our journey. I rode on a red-haired camel by the side of the chief, and a runner ran before us carrying a spear. The men of war were on either hand, and the mules followed with the merchandise. There were forty camels in the caravan, and the mules were twice forty in number.

'We went from the country of the Tartars into the country of those who curse the Moon. We saw the Gryphons guarding their gold on the white rocks, and the scaled Dragons sleeping in their caves. As we passed over the mountains we held our breath lest the snows might fall on us, and each man tied a veil of gauze before his eyes. As we passed through the valleys the Pygmies shot arrows at us from the hollows of the trees, and at night-time we heard the wild men beating on their drums. When we came to the Tower of Apes we set fruits before them, and they did not harm us. When we came to the Tower of Serpents we gave them warm milk in bowls of brass, and they let us go by. Three times in our journey we came to the banks of the Oxus. We crossed it on rafts of wood with great bladders of blown hide. The river-horses raged against us and sought to slay us. When the camels saw them they trembled.

'The kings of each city levied tolls on us, but would not suffer us to enter their gates. They threw us bread over the walls, little maizecakes baked in honey and cakes of fine flour filled with dates. For every hundred baskets we gave them a bead of amber.

'When the dwellers in the villages saw us coming, they poisoned the wells and fled to the hill-summits. We fought with the Magadae who are born old, and grow younger and younger every year, and die when they are little children; and with the Laktroi who say that they are the sons of tigers, and paint themselves yellow and black; and with the Aurantes who bury their dead on the tops of trees, and themselves live in dark caverns lest the Sun, who is their god, should slay them; and with the Krimnians who worship a crocodile, and give it ear-rings of green grass, and feed it with butter and fresh fowls; and with the Agazonbae, who are dog-faced; and with the Sibans, who have horses' feet, and run more swiftly than horses. A third of our company died in battle, and a third died of want. The rest murmured against me, and said that I had brought them an evil fortune. I took a horned adder from beneath a stone and let it sting me. When they saw that I did not sicken they grew afraid.

'In the fourth month we reached the city of Illel. It was night-time when we came to the grove that is outside the walls, and the air was sultry, for the Moon was travelling in Scorpion. We took the ripe pomegranates from the trees, and brake them, and drank their sweet juices. Then we lay down on our carpets and waited for the dawn.

'And at dawn we rose and knocked at the gate of the city. It was wrought out of red bronze, and carved with sea-dragons and dragons that have wings. The guards looked down from the battlements and asked us our business. The interpreter of the caravan answered that we had come from the island of Syria with much merchandise. They took hostages, and told us that they would open the gate to us at noon, and bade us tarry till then.

'When it was noon they opened the gate, and as we entered in the people came crowding out of the houses to look at us, and a crier went round the city crying through a shell. We stood in the market-place, and the negroes uncorded the bales of figured cloths and opened the carved chests of syca-more. And when they had ended their task, the merchants set forth their strange wares, the waxed linen from Egypt, and the painted linen from the country of the Ethiops, the purple sponges from Tyre and the blue hangings from Sidon, the cups of cold amber and the fine vessels of glass and the curi-ous vessels of burnt clay. From the roof of a house a company of women watched us. One of them wore a mask of gilded leather.

'And on the first day the priests came and bartered with us, and on the se-cond day came the nobles, and on the third day came the craftsmen and the slaves. And this is their custom with all merchants as long as they tarry in the city.

'And we tarried for a moon, and when the moon was waning, I wearied and wandered away through the streets of the city and came to the garden of its god. The priests in their yellow robes moved silently through the green trees, and on a pavement of black marble stood the rose-red house in which the god had his dwelling. Its doors were of powdered lacquer, and bulls and peacocks were wrought on them in raised and polished gold. The tilted roof was of sea-green porcelain and the jutting eaves were festooned with little bells. When the white doves flew past, they struck the bells with their wings and made them tinkle.

'In front of the temple was a pool of clear water paved with veined onyx. I lay down beside it, and with my pale fingers I touched the broad leaves. One of the priests came towards me and stood behind me. He had sandals on his feet, one of soft serpent-skin and the other of birds' plumage. On his head was a mitre of black felt decorated with silver crescents. Seven yellows were woven into his robe, and his frizzed hair was stained with antimony.

'And after a little while he spake to me, and asked me my desire.

'I told him that my desire was to see the god.

'"The god is hunting," said the priest, looking strangely at me with his small slanting eyes.

'"Tell me in what forest, and I will ride with him," I answered.

'He combed out the soft fringes of his tunic with his long pointed nails. "The god is asleep," he murmured.

'"Tell me on what couch, and I will watch by him," I answered.

'"The god is at the feast," he cried.

'"If the wine be sweet, I will drink it with him, and if it be bitter I will drink it with him also," was my answer.

'He bowed his head in wonder, and, taking me by the hand, he raised me up, and led me into the temple.

'And in the first chamber I saw an idol seated on a throne of jasper bordered with great orient pearls. It was carved out of ebony, and in stature was of the stature of a man. On its forehead was a ruby, and thick oil dripped from its hair on to its thighs. Its feet were red with the blood of a newly-slain kid, and its loins girt with a copper belt that was studded with seven beryls.

'And I said to the priest, "Is this the god?" And he answered me, "This is the god."

'"Show me the god," I cried, "or I will surely slay thee." And I touched his hand, and it became withered.

'And the priest besought me, saying, "Let my lord heal his servant, and I will show him the god."

'So I breathed with my breath upon his hand, and it became whole again, and he trembled and led me into the second chamber, and I saw an idol standing on a lotus of jade hung with great emeralds. It was carved out of ivory, and in stature was twice the stature of a man. On its forehead was a chrysolite, and its breasts were smeared with myrrh and cinnamon. In one hand it held a crooked sceptre of jade, and in the other a round crystal. It wore buskins of brass, and its thick neck was circled with a circle of selenites.

'And I said to the priest, "Is this the god?" And he answered me, "This is the god."

'"Show me the god," I cried, "or I will surely slay thee." And I touched his eyes, and they became blind.

'And the priest besought me, saying, "Let my lord heal his servant, and I will show him the god."

'So I breathed with my breath upon his eyes, and the sight came back to them, and he trembled again, and led me into the third chamber, and lo! there was no idol in it, nor image of any kind, but only a mirror of round metal set on an altar of stone.

'And I said to the priest, "Where is the god?"

'And he answered me: "There is no god but this mirror that thou seest, for this is the Mirror of Wisdom. And it reflecteth all things that are in heaven and on earth, save only the face of him who looketh into it. This it reflecteth not, so that he who looketh into it may be wise. Many other mirrors are there, but they are mirrors of Opinion. This only is the Mirror of Wisdom. And they who possess this mirror know everything, nor is there anything hidden from them. And they who possess it not have not Wisdom. Therefore is it the god, and we worship it." And I looked into the mirror, and it was even as he had said to me.

'And I did a strange thing, but what I did matters not, for in a valley that is but a day's journey from this place have I hidden the Mirror of Wisdom. Do but suffer me to enter into thee again and be thy servant, and thou shalt be wiser than all the wise men, and Wisdom shall be thine. Suffer me to enter into thee, and none will be as wise as thou.'

But the young Fisherman laughed. 'Love is better than Wisdom,' he cried, 'and the little Mermaid loves me.'

'Nay, but there is nothing better than Wisdom,' said the Soul.

'Love is better,' answered the young Fisherman, and he plunged into the deep, and the Soul went weeping away over the marshes.

And after the second year was over, the Soul came down to the shore of the sea, and called to the young Fisherman and he rose out of the deep and said, 'Why dost thou call to me?'

And the Soul answered, 'Come nearer, that I may speak with thee, for I have seen marvellous things.'

So he came nearer, and couched in the shallow water, and leaned his head upon his hand and listened.

And the Soul said to him, 'When I left thee, I turned my face to the South and journeyed. From the South cometh everything that is precious. Six days I journeyed along the highways that lead to the city of Ashter, along the dusty red-dyed highways by which the pilgrims are wont to go did I journey, and on the morning of the seventh day I lifted up my eyes, and lo! the city lay at my feet, for it is in a valley.

'There are nine gates to this city, and in front of each gate stands a bronze horse that neighs when the Bedouins come down from the mountains. The walls are cased with copper, and the watch-towers on the wall are roofed with brass. In every tower stands an archer with a bow in his hand. At sunrise he strikes with an arrow on a gong, and at sunset he blows through a horn of horn.

'When I sought to enter, the guards stopped me and asked of me who I was. I made answer that I was a Dervish and on my way to the city of Mecca, where there was a green veil on which the Koran was embroidered in silver letters by the hands of the angels. They were filled with wonder, and entreated me to pass in.

'Inside it is even as a bazaar. Surely thou shouldst have been with me. Across the narrow streets the gay lanterns of paper flutter like large butterflies. When the wind blows over the roofs they rise and fall as painted bubbles do. In front of their booths sit the merchants on silken carpets. They have straight black beards, and their turbans are covered with golden sequins, and long strings of amber and carved peach-stones glide through their cool fingers. Some of them sell galbanum and nard, and curious perfumes from the islands of the Indian Sea, and the thick oil of red roses, and myrrh and little nail-shaped cloves. When one stops to speak to them, they throw pinches of frankincense upon a charcoal brazier and make the air sweet. I saw a Syrian who held in his hands a thin rod like a reed. Grey threads of smoke came from it, and its odour as it burned was as the odour of the pink almond in spring. Others sell silver bracelets embossed all over with creamy blue turquoise stones, and anklets of brass wire fringed with little pearls, and tigers' claws set in gold, and the claws of that gilt cat, the leopard, set in gold also, and ear-rings of pierced emerald, and finger-rings of hollowed jade. From the tea-houses comes the sound of the guitar, and the opium-smokers with their white smiling faces look out at the passers-by.

'Of a truth thou shouldst have been with me. The wine-sellers elbow their way through the crowd with great black skins on their shoulders. Most of them sell the wine of Schiraz, which is as sweet as honey. They serve it in little metal cups and strew rose leaves upon it. In the market-place stand the fruitsellers, who sell all kinds of fruit: ripe figs, with their bruised purple flesh, melons, smelling of musk and yellow as topazes, citrons and rose-apples and clusters of white grapes, round red-gold oranges, and oval lemons of green gold. Once I saw an elephant go by. Its trunk was painted with vermilion and turmeric, and over its ears it had a net of crimson silk cord. It stopped opposite one of the booths and began eating the oranges, and the man only laughed. Thou canst not think how strange a people they are. When they are glad they go to the bird-sellers and buy of them a caged bird, and set it free that their joy may be greater, and when they are sad they scourge themselves with thorns that their sorrow may not grow less.

'One evening I met some negroes carrying a heavy palanquin through the bazaar. It was made of gilded bamboo, and the poles were of vermilion lacquer studded with brass peacocks. Across the windows hung thin curtains of muslin embroidered with beetles' wings and with tiny seed-pearls, and as it passed by a pale-faced Circassian looked out and smiled at me. I followed behind, and the negroes hurried their steps and scowled. But I did not care. I felt a great curiosity come over me.

'At last they stopped at a square white house. There were no windows to it, only a little door like the door of a tomb. They set down the palanquin and knocked three times with a copper hammer. An Armenian in a caftan of green leather peered through the wicket, and when he saw them he opened, and spread a carpet on the ground, and the woman stepped out. As she went in, she turned round and smiled at me again. I had never seen any one so pale.

'When the moon rose I returned to the same place and sought for the house, but it was no longer there. When I saw that, I knew who the woman was, and wherefore she had smiled at me.

'Certainly thou shouldst have been with me. On the feast of the New Moon the young Emperor came forth from his palace and went into the mosque to pray. His hair and beard were dyed with rose-leaves, and his cheeks were powdered with a fine gold dust. The palms of his feet and hands were yellow with saffron.

'At sunrise he went forth from his palace in a robe of silver, and at sunset he returned to it again in a robe of gold. The people flung themselves on the ground and hid their faces, but I would not do so. I stood by the stall of a seller of dates and waited. When the Emperor saw me, he raised his painted eyebrows and stopped. I stood quite still, and made him no obeisance. The people marvelled at my boldness, and counselled me to flee from the city. I paid no heed to them, but went and sat with the sellers of strange gods, who by reason of their craft are abominated. When I told them what I had done, each of them gave me a god and prayed me to leave them.

'That night, as I lay on a cushion in the tea-house that is in the Street of

Pomegranates, the guards of the Emperor entered and led me to the palace. As I went in they closed each door behind me, and put a chain across it. Inside was a great court with an arcade running all round. The walls were of white alabaster, set here and there with blue and green tiles. The pillars were of green marble, and the pavement of a kind of peach-blossom marble. I had never seen anything like it before.

'As I passed across the court two veiled women looked down from a balcony and cursed me. The guards hastened on, and the butts of the lances rang upon the polished floor. They opened a gate of wrought ivory, and I found myself in a watered garden of seven terraces. It was planted with tulip-cups and moon-flowers, and silver-studded aloes. Like a slim reed of crystal a fountain hung in the dusky air. The cypress-trees were like burnt-out torches. From one of them a nightingale was singing.

'At the end of the garden stood a little pavilion. As we approached it two eunuchs came out to meet us. Their fat bodies swayed as they walked, and they glanced curiously at me with their yellow-lidded eyes. One of them drew aside the captain of the guard, and in a low voice whispered to him. The other kept munching scented pastilles, which he took with an affected gesture out of an oval box of lilac enamel.

'After a few moments the captain of the guard dismissed the soldiers. They went back to the palace, the eunuchs following slowly behind and plucking the sweet mulberries from the trees as they passed. Once the elder of the two turned round, and smiled at me with an evil smile.

'Then the captain of the guard motioned me towards the entrance of the pavilion. I walked on without trembling, and drawing the heavy curtain aside I entered in.

'The young Emperor was stretched on a couch of dyed lion skins, and a ger-falcon perched upon his wrist. Behind him stood a brass-turbaned Nubian, naked down to the waist, and with heavy ear-rings in his split ears. On a table by the side of the couch lay a mighty scimitar of steel.

'When the Emperor saw me he frowned, and said to me, "What is thy name? Knowest thou not that I am Emperor of this city?" But I made him no answer.

'He pointed with his finger at the scimitar, and the Nubian seized it, and rushing forward struck at me with great violence. The blade whizzed through me, and did me no hurt. The man fell sprawling on the floor, and when he rose up his teeth chattered with terror and he hid himself behind the couch.

'The Emperor leapt to his feet, and taking a lance from a stand of arms, he threw it at me. I caught it in its flight, and brake the shaft into two pieces. He shot at me with an arrow, but I held up my hands and it stopped in mid-air. Then he drew a dagger from a belt of white leather, and stabbed the Nubian in the throat lest the slave should tell of his dishonour. The man writhed like a trampled snake, and a red foam bubbled from his lips.

'As soon as he was dead the Emperor turned to me, and when he had wiped away the bright sweat from his brow with a little napkin of purfled and purple silk, he said to me, "Art thou a prophet, that I may not harm thee, or the son of a prophet, that I can do thee no hurt? I pray thee leave my city to-night, for while thou art in it I am no longer its lord."

'And I answered him, "I will go for half of thy treasure. Give me half of thy treasure, and I will go away."

'He took me by the hand, and led me out into the garden. When the captain of the guard saw me, he wondered. When the eunuchs saw me, their knees shook and they fell upon the ground in fear.

'There is a chamber in the palace that has eight walls of red porphyry, and a brass-scaled ceiling hung with lamps. The Emperor touched one of the walls and it opened, and we passed down a corridor that was lit with many torches. In niches upon each side stood great wine-jars filled to the brim with silver pieces. When we reached the centre of the corridor the Emperor spake the word that may not be spoken, and a granite door swung back on a secret spring, and he put his hands before his face lest his eyes should be dazzled.

'Thou couldst not believe how marvellous a place it was. There were huge tortoise-shells full of pearls, and hollowed moonstones of great size piled up with red rubies. The gold was stored in coffers of elephant-hide, and the gold-dust in leather bottles. There were opals and sapphires, the former in cups of crystal, and the latter in cups of jade. Round green emeralds were ranged in order upon thin plates of ivory, and in one corner were silk bags filled, some with turquoise-stones, and others with beryls. The ivory horns were heaped with purple amethysts, and the horns of brass with chalcedonies and sards. The pillars, which were of cedar, were hung with strings of yellow lynx-stones. In the flat oval shields there were carbuncles, both wine-coloured and coloured like grass. And yet I have told thee but a tithe of what was there.

'And when the Emperor had taken away his hands from before his face he said to me: "This is my house of treasure, and half that is in it is thine, even as I promised to thee. And I will give thee camels and camel drivers, and they shall do thy bidding and take thy share of the treasure to whatever part of the world thou desirest to go. And the thing shall be done to-night, for I would not that the Sun, who is my father, should see that there is in my city a man whom I cannot slay."

'But I answered him, "The gold that is here is thine, and the silver also is thine, and thine are the precious jewels and the things of price. As for me, I have no need of these. Nor shall I take aught from thee but that little ring that thou wearest on the finger of thy hand."

'And the Emperor frowned. "It is but a ring of lead" he cried, "nor has it any value. Therefore take thy half of the treasure and go from my city."

'"Nay," I answered, "but I will take nought but that leaden ring, for I know what is written within it, and for what purpose."

'And the Emperor trembled, and besought me and said, "Take all the treasure and go from my city. The half that is mine shall be thine also."

'And I did a strange thing, but what I did matters not, for in a cave that is but a day's journey from this place have I hidden the Ring of Riches. It is but a day's journey from this place, and it waits for thy coming. He who has this Ring is richer than all the kings of the world. Come therefore and take it, and the world's riches shall be thine.'

But the young Fisherman laughed. 'Love is better than Riches,' he cried, 'and the little Mermaid loves me.'

'Nay, but there is nothing better than Riches,' said the Soul.

'Love is better,' answered the young Fisherman, and he plunged into the deep, and the Soul went weeping away over the marshes.

And after the third year was over, the Soul came down to the shore of the sea, and called to the young Fisherman, and he rose out of the deep and said, 'Why dost thou call to me?'

And the Soul answered, 'Come nearer, that I may speak with thee, for I have seen marvellous things.'

So he came nearer, and couched in the shallow water, and leaned his head upon his hand and listened.

And the Soul said to him, 'In a city that I know of there is an inn that standeth by a river. I sat there with sailors who drank of two different-coloured wines, and ate bread made of barley, and little salt fish served in bay leaves with vinegar. And as we sat and made merry, there entered to us an old man bearing a leathern carpet and a lute that had two horns of amber. And when he had laid out the carpet on the floor, he struck with a quill on the wire strings of his lute, and a girl whose face was veiled ran in and began to dance before us. Her face was veiled with a veil of gauze, but her feet were naked. Naked were her feet, and they moved over the carpet like little white pigeons. Never have I seen anything so marvellous, and the city in which she dances is but a day's journey from this place.'

Now when the young Fisherman heard the words of his Soul, he remembered that the little Mermaid had no feet and could not dance. And a great desire came over him, and he said to himself, 'It is but a day's journey, and I can return to my love,' and he laughed and stood up in the shallow water, and strode towards the shore.

And when he had reached the dry shore he laughed again, and held out his arms to his Soul. And his Soul gave a great cry of joy and ran to meet him, and entered into him, and the young Fisherman saw stretched before him upon the sand that shadow of the body that is the body of the Soul.

And his Soul said to him, 'Let us not tarry, but get hence at once, for the Sea-gods are jealous, and have monsters that do their bidding.'

So they made haste, and all that night they journeyed beneath the moon, and all the next day they journeyed beneath the sun, and on the evening of the day they came to a city.

And the young Fisherman said to his Soul, 'Is this the city in which she dances of whom thou didst speak to me?'

And his Soul answered him, 'It is not this city, but another. Nevertheless let us enter in.'

So they entered in and passed through the streets, and as they passed through the Street of the Jewellers the young Fisherman saw a fair silver cup set forth in a booth. And his Soul said to him, 'Take that silver cup and hide it.'

So he took the cup and hid it in the fold of his tunic, and they went hurriedly out of the city.

And after that they had gone a league from the city, the young Fisherman frowned, and flung the cup away, and said to his Soul, 'Why didst thou tell me to take this cup and hide it, for it was an evil thing to do?'

But his Soul answered him, 'Be at peace, be at peace.'

And on the evening of the second day they came to a city, and the young Fisherman said to his Soul, 'Is this the city in which she dances of whom thou didst speak to me?'

And his Soul answered him, 'It is not this city, but another. Nevertheless let us enter in.'

So they entered in, and passed through the streets, and as they passed through the Street of the Sellers of Sandals, the young Fisherman saw a child standing by a jar of water. And his Soul said to him, 'Smite that child.' So he smote the child till it wept, and when he had done this they went hurriedly out of the city.

And after that they had gone a league from the city the young Fisherman grew wroth, and said to his Soul, 'Why didst thou tell me to smite the child, for it was an evil thing to do?'

But his Soul answered him, 'Be at peace, be at peace.'

And on the evening of the third day they came to a city, and the young Fisherman said to his Soul, 'Is this the city in which she dances of whom thou didst speak to me?'

And his Soul answered him, 'It may be that it is in this city, therefore let us enter in.'

So they entered in and passed through the streets, but nowhere could the young Fisherman find the river or the inn that stood by its side. And the people of the city looked curiously at him, and he grew afraid and said to his Soul, 'Let us go hence, for she who dances with white feet is not here.'

But his Soul answered, 'Nay, but let us tarry, for the night is dark and there will be robbers on the way.'

So he sat him down in the market-place and rested, and after a time there went by a hooded merchant who had a cloak of cloth of Tartary, and bare a lantern of pierced horn at the end of a jointed reed. And the merchant said to him, 'Why does thou sit in the market-place, seeing that the booths are closed and the bales corded?'

And the young Fisherman answered him, 'I can find no inn in this city, nor have I any kinsman who might give me shelter.'

'Are we not all kinsmen?' said the merchant. 'And did not one God make us? Therefore come with me, for I have a guest-chamber.'

So the young Fisherman rose up and followed the merchant to his house. And when he had passed through a garden of pomegranates and entered into the house, the merchant brought him rose-water in a copper dish that he might wash his hands, and ripe melons that he might quench his thirst, and set a bowl of rice and a piece of roasted kid before him.

And after that he had finished, the merchant led him to the guest-chamber, and bade him sleep and be at rest. And the young Fisherman gave him thanks, and kissed the ring that was on his hand, and flung himself down on the carpets of dyed goat's-hair. And when he had covered himself with a covering of black lamb's-wool he fell asleep.

And three hours before dawn, and while it was still night, his Soul waked him and said to him, 'Rise up and go to the room of the merchant, even to the room in which he sleepeth, and slay him, and take from him his gold, for we have need of it.'

And the young Fisherman rose up and crept towards the room of the merchant, and over the feet of the merchant there was lying a curved sword, and the tray by the side of the merchant held nine purses of gold. And he reached out his hand and touched the sword, and when he touched it the merchant started and awoke, and leaping up seized himself the sword and cried to the young Fisherman, 'Dost thou return evil for good, and pay with the shedding of blood for the kindness that I have shown thee?'

And his Soul said to the young Fisherman, 'Strike him,' and he struck him so that he swooned, and he seized then the nine purses of gold, and fled hastily through the garden of pomegranates, and set his face to the star that is the star of morning.

And when they had gone a league from the city, the young Fisherman beat his breast, and said to his Soul, 'Why didst thou bid me slay the merchant and take his gold? Surely thou art evil.'

But his Soul answered him, 'Be at peace, be at peace.'

'Nay,' cried the young Fisherman, 'I may not be at peace, for all that thou hast made me to do I hate. Thee also I hate, and I bid thee tell me wherefore thou hast wrought with me in this wise.'

And his Soul answered him, 'When thou didst send me forth into the world thou gavest me no heart, so I learned to do all these things and love them.'

'What sayest thou?' murmured the young Fisherman.

'Thou knowest,' answered his Soul, 'thou knowest it well. Hast thou forgotten that thou gavest me no heart? I trow not. And so trouble not thyself nor me, but be at peace, for there is no pain that thou shalt not give away, nor any pleasure that thou shalt not receive.'

And when the young Fisherman heard these words he trembled and said to his Soul, 'Nay, but thou art evil, and hast made me forget my love, and hast tempted me with temptations, and hast set my feet in the ways of sins.'

And his Soul answered him, 'Thou hast not forgotten that when thou didst send me forth into the world thou gavest me no heart. Come, let us go to another city, and make merry, for we have nine purses of gold.'

But the young Fisherman took the nine purses of gold, and flung them down, and trampled on them.

'Nay,' he cried, 'but I will have nought to do with thee, nor will I journey with thee anywhere, but even as I sent thee away before, so will I send thee away now, for thou hast wrought me no good.' And he turned his back to the moon, and with the little knife that had the handle of green viper's skin he strove to cut from his feet that shadow of the body which is the body of the Soul.

Yet his Soul stirred not from him, nor paid heed to his command, but said to him, 'The spell that the Witch told thee avails thee no more, for I may not leave thee, nor mayest thou drive me forth. Once in his life may a man send his Soul away, but he who receiveth back his Soul must keep it with him for ever, and this is his punishment and his reward.'

And the young Fisherman grew pale and clenched his hands and cried, 'She was a false Witch in that she told me not that.'

'Nay,' answered his Soul, 'but she was true to Him she worships, and whose servant she will be ever.'

And when the young Fisherman knew that he could no longer get rid of his Soul, and that it was an evil Soul, and would abide with him always, he fell upon the ground weeping bitterly.

And when it was day, the young Fisherman rose up and said to his Soul, 'I will bind my hands that I may not do thy bidding, and close my lips that I may not speak thy words, and I will return to the place where she whom I love has her dwelling. Even to the sea will I return, and to the little bay where she is wont to sing, and I will call to her and tell her the evil I have done and the evil thou hast wrought on me.'

And his Soul tempted him and said, 'Who is thy love, that thou shouldst return to her? The world has many fairer than she is. There are the dancing-girls of Samaris who dance in the manner of all kinds of birds and beasts. Their feet are painted with henna, and in their hands they have little copper bells. They laugh while they dance, and their laughter is as clear as the laughter of water. Come with me and I will show them to thee. For what is this trouble of thine about the things of sin? Is that which is pleasant to eat not made for the eater? Is there poison in that which is sweet to drink? Trouble not thyself, but come with me to another city. There is a little city hard by in which there is a garden of tulip-trees. And there dwell in this comely garden white peacocks and peacocks that have blue breasts. Their tails when they spread them to the sun are like disks of ivory and like gilt disks. And she who feeds them dances for pleasure, and sometimes she dances on her hands and at other times she dances with her feet. Her eyes are coloured with stibium, and her nostrils are shaped like the wings of a swallow. From a hook in one of her nostrils hangs a flower that is carved out of a pearl. She laughs while she dances, and the silver rings that are about her ankles tinkle like bells of silver. And so trouble not thyself any more, but come with me to this city.'

But the young Fisherman answered not his Soul, but closed his lips with the seal of silence and with a tight cord bound his hands, and journeyed back to the place from which he had come, even to the little bay where his love had been wont to sing. And ever did his Soul tempt him by the way, but he made it no answer, nor would he do any of the wickedness that it sought to make him do, so great was the power of the love that was within him.

And when he had reached the shore of the sea, he loosed the cord from his hands, and took the seal of silence from his lips, and called to the little Mermaid. But she came not to his call, though he called to her all day long and besought her.

And his Soul mocked him and said, 'Surely thou hast but little joy out of thy love. Thou art as one who in time of death pours water into a broken vessel. Thou gavest away what thou hast, and nought is given to thee in return. It were better for thee to come with me, for I know where the Valley of Pleasure lies, and what things are wrought there.'

But the young Fisherman answered not his Soul, but in a cleft of rock he built himself a house of wattles, and abode there for the space of a year. And every morning he called to the Mermaid, and every noon he called to her again, and at night-time he spake her name. Yet never did she rise out of the sea to meet him, nor in any place of the sea could he find her though he sought for her in the caves and in the green water, in the pools of the tide and in the wells that are at the bottom of the deep.

And ever did his Soul tempt him with evil, and whisper of terrible things. Yet did it not prevail against him, so great was the power of his love.

And after the year was over, the Soul thought within himself, 'I have tempted my master with evil, and his love is stronger than I am. I will tempt him now with good, and it may be that he will come with me.'

So he spake to the young Fisherman and said, 'I have told thee of the joy of the world, and thou hast turned a deaf ear to me. Suffer me now to tell thee of the world's pain, and it may be that thou wilt hearken. For of a truth pain is the Lord of this world, nor is there any one who escapes from its net. There be some who lack raiment, and others who lack bread. There be widows who sit in purple, and widows who sit in rags. To and fro over the fens go the lepers, and they are cruel to each other. The beggars go up and down on the highways, and their wallets are empty. Through the streets of the cities walks Famine, and the Plague sits at their gates. Come, let us go forth and mend these things, and make them not to be. Wherefore shouldst thou tarry here calling to thy love, seeing she comes not to thy call? And what is love, that thou shouldst set this high store upon it?'

But the young Fisherman answered it nought, so great was the power of his love. And every morning he called to the Mermaid, and every noon he called to her again, and at night-time he spake her name. Yet never did she rise out of the sea to meet him, nor in any place of the sea could he find her, though he sought for her in the rivers of the sea, and in the valleys that are under the waves, in the sea that the night makes purple, and in the sea that the dawn leaves grey.

And after the second year was over, the Soul said to the young Fisherman at night-time, and as he sat in the wattled house alone, 'Lo! now I have tempted thee with evil, and I have tempted thee with good, and thy love is stronger than I am. Wherefore will I tempt thee no longer, but I pray thee to suffer me to enter thy heart, that I may be one with thee even as before.'

'Surely thou mayest enter,' said the young Fisherman, 'for in the days when with no heart thou didst go through the world thou must have much suffered.'

'Alas!' cried his Soul, 'I can find no place of entrance, so compassed about with love is this heart of thine.'

'Yet I would that I could help thee,' said the young Fisherman.

And as he spake there came a great cry of mourning from the sea, even the cry that men hear when one of the Sea-folk is dead. And the young Fisherman leapt up, and left his wattled house, and ran down to the shore. And the black waves came hurrying to the shore, bearing with them a burden that was whiter than silver. White as the surf it was, and like a flower it tossed on the waves. And the surf took it from the waves, and the foam took it from the surf, and the shore received it, and lying at his feet the young Fisherman saw the body of the little Mermaid. Dead at his feet it was lying.

Weeping as one smitten with pain he flung himself down beside it, and he kissed the cold red of the mouth, and toyed with the wet amber of the hair. He flung himself down beside it on the sand, weeping as one trembling with joy, and in his brown arms he held it to his breast. Cold were the lips, yet he kissed them. Salt was the honey of the hair, yet he tasted it with a bitter joy. He kissed the closed eyelids, and the wild spray that lay upon their cups was less salt than his tears.

And to the dead thing he made confession. Into the shells of its ears he poured the harsh wine of his tale. He put the little hands round his neck, and with his fingers he touched the thin reed of the throat. Bitter, bitter was his joy, and full of strange gladness was his pain.

The black sea came nearer, and the white foam moaned like a leper. With white claws of foam the sea grabbled at the shore. From the palace of the Sea-King came the cry of mourning again, and far out upon the sea the great Tritons blew hoarsely upon their horns.

'Flee away,' said his Soul, 'for ever doth the sea come nigher, and if thou tarriest it will slay thee. Flee away, for I am afraid, seeing that thy heart is closed against me by reason of the greatness of thy love. Flee away to a place of safety. Surely thou wilt not send me without a heart into another world?'

But the young Fisherman listened not to his Soul, but called on the little Mermaid and said, 'Love is better than wisdom, and more precious than riches, and fairer than the feet of the daughters of men. The fires cannot destroy it, nor can the waters quench it. I called on thee at dawn, and thou didst come to my call. The moon heard thy name, yet hadst thou no heed of me. For evilly had I left thee, and to my own hurt had I wandered away. Yet ever did thy love abide with me, and ever was it strong, nor did aught prevail against it, though I have looked upon evil and looked upon good. And now that thou art dead, surely I will die with thee also.'

And his Soul besought him to depart, but he would not, so great was his love. And the sea came nearer, and sought to cover him with its waves, and when he knew that the end was at hand he kissed with mad lips the cold lips of the Mermaid, and the heart that was within him brake. And as through the fullness of his love his heart did break, the Soul found an entrance and entered in, and was one with him even as before. And the sea covered the young Fisherman with its waves.

And in the morning the Priest went forth to bless the sea, for it had been troubled. And with him went the monks and the musicians, and the candle-bearers, and the swingers of censers, and a great company.

And when the Priest reached the shore he saw the young Fisherman lying drowned in the surf, and clasped in his arms was the body of the little Mermaid. And he drew back frowning, and having made the sign of the Cross, he cried aloud and said, 'I will not bless the sea nor anything that is in it. Accursed be the Sea-folk, and accursed be all they who traffic with them. And as for him who for love's sake forsook God, and so lieth here with his leman slain by God's judgment, take up his body and the body of his leman, and bury them in the corner of the Field of the Fullers, and set no mark above them, nor sign of any kind, that none may know the place of their resting. For accursed were they in their lives, and accursed shall they be in their deaths also.'

And the people did as he commanded them, and in the corner of the Field of the Fullers, where no sweet herbs grew, they dug a deep pit, and laid the dead things within it.

And when the third year was over, and on a day that was a holy day, the Priest went up to the chapel, that he might show to the people the wounds of the Lord, and speak to them about the wrath of God.

And when he had robed himself with his robes, and entered in and bowed himself before the altar, he saw that the altar was covered with strange flowers that never had been seen before. Strange were they to look at, and of curious beauty, and their beauty troubled him, and their odour was sweet in his nostrils, and he felt glad, and understood not why he was glad.

And after that he had opened the tabernacle, and incensed the monstrance that was in it, and shown the fair wafer to the people, and hid it again behind the veil of veils, he began to speak to the people, desiring to speak to them of the wrath of God. But the beauty of the white flowers troubled him, and their odour was sweet in his nostrils, and there came another word into his lips, and he spake not of the wrath of God, but of the God whose name is Love. And why he so spake, he knew not.

And when he had finished his word the people wept, and the Priest went back to his sacristy, and his eyes were full of tears. And the deacons came in and began to unrobe him, and took from him the alb and the girdle, the maniple and the stole. And he stood as one in a dream.

And after that they had unrobed him, he looked at them and said, 'What are the flowers that stand on the altar, and whence do they come?'

And they answered him, 'What flowers they are we cannot tell, but they come from the corner of the Fullers' Field.' And the Priest trembled, and returned to his own house and prayed.

And in the morning, while it was still dawn, he went forth with the monks and the musicians, and the candle-bearers and the swingers of censers, and a great company, and came to the shore of the sea, and blessed the sea, and all the wild things that are in it. The Fauns also he blessed, and the little things that dance in the woodland, and the bright-eyed things that peer through the leaves. All the things in God's world he blessed, and the people were filled with joy and wonder. Yet never again in the corner of the Fullers' Field grew flowers of any kind, but the field remained barren even as before. Nor came the Sea-folk into the bay as they had been wont to do, for they went to another part of the sea.

THE STAR-CHILD

ONCE upon a time two poor Woodcutters were making their way home through a great pine-forest. It was winter, and a night of bitter cold. The snow lay thick upon the ground, and upon the branches of the trees: the frost kept snapping the little twigs on either side of them, as they passed: and when they came to the Mountain-Torrent she was hanging motionless in air, for the Ice-King had kissed her.

So cold was it that even the animals and the birds did not know what to make of it.

'Ugh!' snarled the Wolf, as he limped through the brushwood with his tail between his legs, 'this is perfectly monstrous weather. Why doesn't the Government look to it?'

'Weet! weet! weet!' twittered the green Linnets, 'the old Earth is dead, and they have laid her out in her white shroud.'

'The Earth is going to be married, and this is her bridal dress,' whispered the Turtle-doves to each other. Their little pink feet were quite frost-bitten, but they felt that it was their duty to take a romantic view of the situation.

'Nonsense!' growled the Wolf. 'I tell you that it is all the fault of the Government, and if you don't believe me I shall eat you.' The Wolf had a thoroughly practical mind, and was never at a loss for a good argument.

'Well, for my own part,' said the Woodpecker, who was a born philosopher, 'I don't care an atomic theory for explanations. If a thing is so, it is so, and at present it is terribly cold.'

Terribly cold it certainly was. The little Squirrels, who lived inside the tall fir-tree, kept rubbing each other's noses to keep themselves warm, and the Rabbits curled themselves up in their holes, and did not venture even to look out of doors. The only people who seemed to enjoy it were the great horned Owls. Their feathers were quite stiff with rime, but they did not mind, and they rolled their large yellow eyes, and called out to each other across the forest, 'Tu-whit! Tu-whoo! Tu-whit! Tu-whoo! what delightful weather we are having!'

On and on went the two Woodcutters, blowing lustily upon their fingers, and stamping with their huge iron-shod boots upon the caked snow. Once they sank into a deep drift, and came out as white as millers are, when the stones are grinding; and once they slipped on the hard smooth ice where the marsh-water was frozen, and their faggots fell out of their bundles, and they had to pick them up and bind them together again; and once they thought that they had lost their way, and a great terror seized on them, for they knew that the Snow is cruel to those who sleep in her arms. But they put their trust in the good Saint Martin, who watches over all travellers, and retraced their steps, and went warily, and at last they reached the outskirts of the forest, and saw, far down in the valley beneath them, the lights of the village in which they dwelt.

So overjoyed were they at their deliverance that they laughed aloud, and the Earth seemed to them like a flower of silver, and the Moon like a flower of gold.

Yet, after that they had laughed they became sad, for they remembered their poverty, and one of them said to the other, 'Why did we make merry, seeing that life is for the rich, and not for such as we are? Better that we had died of cold in the forest, or that some wild beast had fallen upon us and slain us.'

'Truly,' answered his companion, 'much is given to some, and little is given to others. Injustice has parcelled out the world, nor is there equal division of aught save of sorrow.'

But as they were bewailing their misery to each other this strange thing happened. There fell from heaven a very bright and beautiful star. It slipped down the side of the sky, passing by the other stars in its course, and, as they watched it wondering, it seemed to them to sink behind a clump of willow-trees that stood hard by a little sheepfold no more than a stone's-throw away.

'Why! there is a crock of gold for whoever finds it,' they cried, and they set to and ran, so eager were they for the gold.

And one of them ran faster than his mate, and outstripped him, and forced his way through the willows, and came out on the other side, and lo! there was indeed a thing of gold lying on the white snow. So he hastened towards it, and stooping down placed his hands upon it, and it was a cloak of golden tissue, curiously wrought with stars, and wrapped in many folds. And he cried out to his comrade that he had found the treasure that had fallen from the sky, and when his comrade had come up, they sat them down in the snow, and loosened the folds of the cloak that they might divide the pieces of gold. But, alas! no gold was in it, nor silver, nor, indeed, treasure of any kind, but only a little child who was asleep.

And one of them said to the other: 'This is a bitter ending to our hope, nor have we any good fortune, for what doth a child profit to a man? Let us leave it here, and go our way, seeing that we are poor men, and have children of our own whose bread we may not give to another.'

But his companion answered him: 'Nay, but it were an evil thing to leave the child to perish here in the snow, and though I am as poor as thou art, and have many mouths to feed, and but little in the pot, yet will I bring it home with me, and my wife shall have care of it.'

So very tenderly he took up the child, and wrapped the cloak around it to shield it from the harsh cold, and made his way down the hill to the village, his comrade marvelling much at his foolishness and softness of heart.

And when they came to the village, his comrade said to him, 'Thou hast the child, therefore give me the cloak, for it is meet that we should share.'

But he answered him: 'Nay, for the cloak is neither mine nor thine, but the child's only,' and he bade him Godspeed, and went to his own house and knocked.

And when his wife opened the door and saw that her husband had returned safe to her, she put her arms round his neck and kissed him, and took from his back the bundle of faggots, and brushed the snow off his boots, and bade him come in.

But he said to her, 'I have found something in the forest, and I have brought it to thee to have care of it,' and he stirred not from the threshold.

'What is it?' she cried. 'Show it to me, for the house is bare, and we have need of many things.' And he threw the cloak back, and showed her the sleeping child.

'Alack, goodman!' she murmured, 'have we not children enough of our own, that thou must needs bring a changeling to sit by the hearth? And who knows if it will not bring us bad fortune? And how shall we tend it?' And she was wroth against him.

'Nay, but it is a Star-Child,' he answered; and he told her the strange manner of the finding of it.

But she would not be appeased, but mocked at him, and spoke angrily, and cried; 'Our children lack bread, and shall we feed the child of another? Who is there who careth for us? And who giveth us food?'

'Nay, but God careth for the sparrows even, and feedeth them,' he answered.

'Do not the sparrows die of hunger in the winter?' she asked. 'And is it not winter now?' And the man answered nothing, but stirred not from the threshold.

And a bitter wind from the forest came in through the open door, and made her tremble, and she shivered, and said to him: 'Wilt thou not close the door? There cometh a bitter wind into the house, and I am cold.'

'Into a house where a heart is hard cometh there not always a bitter wind?' he asked. And the woman answered him nothing, but crept closer to the fire.

And after a time she turned round and looked at him, and her eyes were full of tears. And he came in swiftly, and placed the child in her arms, and she kissed it, and laid it in a little bed where the youngest of their own children was lying. And on the morrow the Woodcutter took the curious cloak of gold and placed it in a great chest, and a chain of amber that was round the child's neck his wife took and set it in the chest also.

So the Star-Child was brought up with the children of the Woodcutter, and sat at the same board with them, and was their playmate. And every year he became more beautiful to look at, so that all those who dwelt in the village were filled with wonder, for, while they were swarthy and black-haired, he was white and delicate as sawn ivory, and his curls were like the rings of the daffodil. His lips, also, were like the petals of a red flower, and his eyes were like violets by a river of pure water, and his body like the narcissus of a field where the mower comes not.

Yet did his beauty work him evil. For he grew proud, and cruel, and selfish. The children of the Woodcutter, and the other children of the village, he despised, saying that they were of mean parentage, while he was noble, being sprung from a Star, and he made himself master over them, and called them his servants. No pity had he for the poor, or for those who were blind or maimed or in any way afflicted, but would cast stones at them and drive them forth on to the highway, and bid them beg their bread elsewhere, so that none save the outlaws came twice to that village to ask for alms. Indeed, he was as one enamoured of beauty, and would mock at the weakly and ill-favoured, and make jest of them; and himself he loved, and in summer, when the winds were still, he would lie by the well in the priest's orchard and look down at the marvel of his own face, and laugh for the pleasure he had in his fairness.

Often did the Woodcutter and his wife chide him, and say: 'We did not deal with thee as thou dealest with those who are left desolate, and have none to succour them. Wherefore are thou so cruel to all who need pity?'

Often did the old priest send for him, and seek to teach him the love of living things, saying to him: 'The fly is thy brother. Do it no harm. The wild birds that roam through the forest have their freedom. Snare them not for thy pleasure. God made the blind-worm and the mole, and each has its place. Who art thou to bring pain into God's world? Even the cattle of the field praise Him.'

But the Star-Child heeded not their words, but would frown and flout, and go back to his companions, and lead them. And his companions followed him, for he was fair, and fleet of foot, and could dance, and pipe, and make music. And wherever the Star-Child led them they followed, and whatever the Star-Child bade them do, that did they.

And when he pierced with a sharp reed the dim eyes of the mole, they laughed, and when he cast stones at the leper they laughed also. And in all things he ruled them, and they became hard of heart even as he was.

Now there passed one day through the village a poor beggar-woman. Her garments were torn and ragged, and her feet were bleeding from the rough road on which she had travelled, and she was in very evil plight. And being weary she sat her down under a chestnut-tree to rest.

But when the Star-Child saw her, he said to his companions, 'See! There sitteth a foul beggar-woman under that fair and green-leaved tree. Come, let us drive her hence, for she is ugly and ill-favoured.'

So he came near and threw stones at her, and mocked her, and she looked at him with terror in her eyes, nor did she move her gaze from him. And when the Woodcutter, who was cleaving logs in a haggard hard by, saw what the Star-Child was doing, he ran up and rebuked him, and said to him: 'Surely thou art hard of heart and knowest no mercy, for what evil has this poor woman done to thee that thou shouldst treat her in this wise?'

And the Star-Child grew red with anger, and stamped his foot upon the ground, and said, 'Who art thou to question me what I do? I am no son of thine to do thy bidding.'

'Thou speakest truly,' answered the Woodcutter, 'yet did I show thee pity when I found thee in the forest.'

And when the woman heard these words she gave a loud cry and fell into a swoon. And the Woodcutter carried her to his own house, and his wife had care of her, and when she rose up from the swoon into which she had fallen, they set meat and drink before her, and bade her have comfort.

But she would neither eat nor drink, but said to the Woodcutter, 'Didst thou not say that the child was found in the forest? And was it not ten years from this day?'

And the Woodcutter answered, 'Yea, it was in the forest that I found him, and it is ten years from this day.'

'And what signs didst thou find with him?' she cried. 'Bare he not upon his neck a chain of amber? Was not round him a cloak of gold tissue broidered with stars?'

'Truly,' answered the Woodcutter, 'it was even as thou sayest.' And he took the cloak and the amber chain from the chest where they lay, and showed them to her.

And when she saw them she wept for joy, and said, 'He is my little son whom I lost in the forest. I pray thee send for him quickly, for in search of him have I wandered over the whole world.'

So the Woodcutter and his wife went out and called to the Star-Child, and said to him, 'Go into the house, and there shalt thou find thy mother, who is waiting for thee.'

So he ran in, filled with wonder and great gladness. But when he saw her who was waiting there, he laughed scornfully and said, 'Why, where is my mother? For I see none here but this vile beggar-woman.'

And the woman answered him, 'I am thy mother.'

'Thou art mad to say so,' cried the Star-Child angrily. 'I am no son of thine, for thou art a beggar, and ugly, and in rags. Therefore get thee hence, and let me see thy foul face no more.'

'Nay, but thou art indeed my little son, whom I bare in the forest,' she cried, and she fell on her knees, and held out her arms to him. 'The robbers stole thee from me, and left thee to die,' she murmured, 'but I recognised thee when I saw thee, and the signs also have I recognised, the cloak of golden tissue and the amber chain. Therefore, I pray thee come with me, for over the whole world have I wandered in search of thee. Come with me, my son, for I have need of thy love.'

But the Star-Child stirred not from his place, but shut the doors of his heart against her, nor was there any sound heard save the sound of the woman weeping for pain.

And at last he spoke to her, and his voice was hard and bitter. 'If in very truth thou art my mother,' he said, 'it had been better hadst thou stayed away, and not come here to bring me to shame, seeing that I thought I was the child of some Star, and not a beggar's child, as thou tellest me that I am. Therefore get thee hence, and let me see thee no more.'

'Alas! my son,' she cried, 'wilt thou not kiss me before I go? For I have suffered much to find thee.'

'Nay,' said the Star-Child, 'but thou art too foul to look at, and rather would I kiss the adder or the toad than thee.'

So the woman rose up, and went away into the forest weeping bitterly, and when the Star-Child saw that she had gone, he was glad, and ran back to his playmates that he might play with them.

But when they beheld him coming, they mocked him and said, 'Why, thou art as foul as the toad, and as loathsome as the adder. Get thee hence, for we will not suffer thee to play with us,' and they drave him out of the garden.

And the Star-Child frowned and said to himself, 'What is this that they say to me? I will go to the well of water and look into it, and it shall tell me of my beauty.'

So he went to the well of water and looked into it, and lo! his face was as the face of a toad, and his body was scaled like an adder. And he flung himself down on the grass and wept, and said to himself, 'Surely this has come upon me by reason of my sin. For I have denied my mother, and driven her away, and been proud, and cruel to her. Wherefore I will go and seek her through the whole world, nor will I rest till I have found her.'

And there came to him the little daughter of the Woodcutter, and she put her hand upon his shoulder and said, 'What doth it matter if thou hast lost thy comeliness? Stay with us, and I will not mock at thee.'

And he said to her, 'Nay, but I have been cruel to my mother, and as a punishment has this evil been sent to me. Wherefore I must go hence, and wander through the world till I find her, and she give me forgiveness.'

So he ran away into the forest and called out to his mother to come to him, but there was no answer. All day long he called to her, and when the sun set he lay down to sleep on a bed of leaves, and the birds and the animals fled from him, for they remembered his cruelty, and he was alone save for the toad that watched him, and the slow adder that crawled past.

And in the morning he rose up, and plucked some bitter berries from the trees and ate them, and took his way through the great wood, weeping sorely. And of everything that he met he made inquiry if perchance they had seen his mother.

He said to the Mole, 'Thou canst go beneath the earth. Tell me, is my mother there?'

And the Mole answered, 'Thou hast blinded mine eyes. How should I know?'

He said to the Linnet, 'Thou canst fly over the tops of the tall trees, and canst see the whole world. Tell me, canst thou see my mother?'

And the Linnet answered, 'Thou hast clipt my wings for thy pleasure. How should I fly?'

And to the little Squirrel who lived in the fir-tree, and was lonely, he said, 'Where is my mother?'

And the Squirrel answered, 'Thou hast slain mine. Dost thou seek to slay thine also?'

And the Star-Child wept and bowed his head, and prayed forgiveness of God's things, and went on through the forest, seeking for the beggar-woman. And on the third day he came to the other side of the forest and went down into the plain.

And when he passed through the villages the children mocked him, and threw stones at him, and the carlots would not suffer him even to sleep in the byres lest he might bring mildew on the stored corn, so foul was he to look at, and their hired men drave him away, and there was none who had pity on him. Nor could he hear anywhere of the beggar-woman who was his mother, though for the space of three years he wandered over the world, and often seemed to see her on the road in front of him, and would call to her, and run after her till the sharp flints made his feet to bleed. But overtake her he could not, and those who dwelt by the way did ever deny that they had seen her, or any like to her, and they made sport of his sorrow.

For the space of three years he wandered over the world, and in the world there was neither love nor loving-kindness nor charity for him, but it was even such a world as he had made for himself in the days of his great pride.

And one evening he came to the gate of a strong-walled city that stood by a river, and, weary and footsore though he was, he made to enter in. But the soldiers who stood on guard dropped their halberts across the entrance, and said roughly to him, 'What is thy business in the city?'

'I am seeking for my mother,' he answered, 'and I pray ye to suffer me to pass, for it may be that she is in this city.'

But they mocked at him, and one of them wagged a black beard, and set down his shield and cried, 'Of a truth, thy mother will not be merry when she sees thee, for thou art more ill-favoured than the toad of the marsh, or the adder that crawls in the fen. Get thee gone. Get thee gone. Thy mother dwells not in this city.'

And another, who held a yellow banner in his hand, said to him, 'Who is thy mother, and wherefore art thou seeking for her?'

And he answered, 'My mother is a beggar even as I am, and I have treated her evilly, and I pray ye to suffer me to pass that she may give me her forgiveness, if it be that she tarrieth in this city.' But they would not, and pricked him with their spears.

And, as he turned away weeping, one whose armour was inlaid with gilt flowers, and on whose helmet couched a lion that had wings, came up and made inquiry of the soldiers who it was who had sought entrance. And they said to him, 'It is a beggar and the child of a beggar, and we have driven him away.'

'Nay,' he cried, laughing, 'but we will sell the foul thing for a slave, and his price shall be the price of a bowl of sweet wine.'

And an old and evil-visaged man who was passing by called out, and said, 'I will buy him for that price,' and, when he had paid the price, he took the Star-Child by the hand and led him into the city.

And after that they had gone through many streets they came to a little door that was set in a wall that was covered with a pomegranate tree. And the old man touched the door with a ring of graved jasper and it opened, and they went down five steps of brass into a garden filled with black poppies and green jars of burnt clay. And the old man took then from his turban a scarf of figured silk, and bound with it the eyes of the Star-Child, and drave him in front of him. And when the scarf was taken off his eyes, the Star-Child found himself in a dungeon, that was lit by a lantern of horn.

And the old man set before him some mouldy bread on a trencher and said, 'Eat,' and some brackish water in a cup and said, 'Drink,' and when he had eaten and drunk, the old man went out, locking the door behind him and fastening it with an iron chain.

And on the morrow the old man, who was indeed the subtlest of the magicians of Libya and had learned his art from one who dwelt in the tombs of the Nile, came in to him and frowned at him, and said, 'In a wood that is nigh to the gate of this city of Giaours there are three pieces of gold. One is of white gold, and another is of yellow gold, and the gold of the third one is red. To-day thou shalt bring me the piece of white gold, and if thou bringest it not back, I will beat thee with a hundred stripes. Get thee away quickly, and at sunset I will be waiting for thee at the door of the garden. See that thou bringest the white gold, or it shall go ill with thee, for thou art my slave, and I have bought thee for the price of a bowl of sweet wine.' And he bound the eyes of the Star-Child with the scarf of figured silk, and led him through the house, and through the garden of poppies, and up the five steps of brass. And having opened the little door with his ring he set him in the street.

And the Star-Child went out of the gate of the city, and came to the wood of which the Magician had spoken to him.

Now this wood was very fair to look at from without, and seemed full of singing birds and of sweet-scented flowers, and the Star-Child entered it gladly. Yet did its beauty profit him little, for wherever he went harsh briars and thorns shot up from the ground and encompassed him, and evil nettles stung him, and the thistle pierced him with her daggers, so that he was in sore distress. Nor could he anywhere find the piece of white gold of which the Magician had spoken, though he sought for it from morn to noon, and from noon to sunset. And at sunset he set his face towards home, weeping bitterly, for he knew what fate was in store for him.

But when he had reached the outskirts of the wood, he heard from a thicket a cry as of some one in pain. And forgetting his own sorrow he ran back to the place, and saw there a little Hare caught in a trap that some hunter had set for it.

And the Star-Child had pity on it, and released it, and said to it, 'I am myself but a slave, yet may I give thee thy freedom.'

And the Hare answered him, and said: 'Surely thou hast given me freedom, and what shall I give thee in return?'

And the Star-Child said to it, 'I am seeking for a piece of white gold, nor can I anywhere find it, and if I bring it not to my master he will beat me.'

'Come thou with me,' said the Hare, 'and I will lead thee to it, for I know where it is hidden, and for what purpose.'

So the Star-Child went with the Hare, and lo! in the cleft of a great oak-tree he saw the piece of white gold that he was seeking. And he was filled with joy, and seized it, and said to the Hare, 'The service that I did to thee thou hast rendered back again many times over, and the kindness that I showed thee thou hast repaid a hundred-fold.'

'Nay,' answered the Hare, 'but as thou dealt with me, so I did deal with thee,' and it ran away swiftly, and the Star-Child went towards the city.

Now at the gate of the city there was seated one who was a leper. Over his face hung a cowl of grey linen, and through the eyelets his eyes gleamed like red coals. And when he saw the Star-Child coming, he struck upon a wooden bowl, and clattered his bell, and called out to him, and said, 'Give me a piece of money, or I must die of hunger. For they have thrust me out of the city, and there is no one who has pity on me.'

'Alas!' cried the Star-Child, 'I have but one piece of money in my wallet, and if I bring it not to my master he will beat me, for I am his slave.'

But the leper entreated him, and prayed of him, till the Star-Child had pity, and gave him the piece of white gold.

And when he came to the Magician's house, the Magician opened to him, and brought him in, and said to him, 'Hast thou the piece of white gold?' And the Star-Child answered, 'I have it not.' So the Magician fell upon him, and beat him, and set before him an empty trencher, and said, 'Eat,' and an empty cup, and said, 'Drink,' and flung him again into the dungeon.

And on the morrow the Magician came to him, and said, 'If to-day thou bringest me not the piece of yellow gold, I will surely keep thee as my slave, and give thee three hundred stripes.'

So the Star-Child went to the wood, and all day long he searched for the piece of yellow gold, but nowhere could he find it. And at sunset he sat him down and began to weep, and as he was weeping there came to him the little Hare that he had rescued from the trap.

And the Hare said to him, 'Why art thou weeping? And what dost thou seek in the wood?'

And the Star-Child answered, 'I am seeking for a piece of yellow gold that is hidden here, and if I find it not my master will beat me, and keep me as a slave.'

'Follow me,' cried the Hare, and it ran through the wood till it came to a pool of water. And at the bottom of the pool the piece of yellow gold was lying.

'How shall I thank thee?' said the Star-Child, 'for lo! this is the second time that you have succoured me.'

'Nay, but thou hadst pity on me first,' said the Hare, and it ran away swiftly.

And the Star-Child took the piece of yellow gold, and put it in his wallet, and hurried to the city. But the leper saw him coming, and ran to meet him, and knelt down and cried, 'Give me a piece of money or I shall die of hunger.'

And the Star-Child said to him, 'I have in my wallet but one piece of yellow gold, and if I bring it not to my master he will beat me and keep me as his slave.'

But the leper entreated him sore, so that the Star-Child had pity on him, and gave him the piece of yellow gold.

And when he came to the Magician's house, the Magician opened to him, and brought him in, and said to him, 'Hast thou the piece of yellow gold?' And the Star-Child said to him, 'I have not.' So the Magician fell upon him, and beat him, and loaded him with chains, and cast him again into the dungeon.

And on the morrow the Magician came to him, and said, 'If today thou bringest me the piece of red gold I will set thee free, but if thou bringest it not I will surely slay thee.'

So the Star-Child went to the wood, and all day long he searched for the piece of red gold, but nowhere could he find it. And at evening he sat him down and wept, and as he was weeping there came to him the little Hare.

And the Hare said to him, 'The piece of red gold that thou seekest is in the cavern that is behind thee. Therefore weep no more but be glad.'

'How shall I reward thee?' cried the Star-Child, 'for lo! this is the third time thou hast succoured me.'

'Nay, but thou hadst pity on me first,' said the Hare, and it ran away swiftly.

And the Star-Child entered the cavern, and in its farthest corner he found the piece of red gold. So he put it in his wallet, and hurried to the city. And the leper seeing him coming, stood in the centre of the road, and cried out, and said to him, 'Give me the piece of red money, or I must die,' and the Star-Child had pity on him again, and gave him the piece of red gold, saying 'Thy need is greater than mine.' Yet his heart was heavy, for he knew what evil fate awaited him.

But lo! as he passed through the gate of the city, the guards bowed down and made obeisance to him, saying, 'How beautiful is our lord!' and a crowd of citizens followed him, and cried out, 'Surely there is none so beautiful in the whole world!' so that the Star-Child wept, and said to himself, 'They are mocking me, and making light of my misery.' And so large was the concourse of the people, that he lost the threads of his way, and found himself at last in a great square, in which there was a palace of a King.

And the gate of the palace opened, and the priests and the high officers of the city ran forth to meet him, and they abased themselves before him, and said, 'Thou art our lord for whom we have been waiting, and the son of our King.'

And the Star-Child answered them and said, 'I am no king's son, but the child of a poor beggar-woman. And how say ye that I am beautiful, for I know that I am evil to look at?'

Then he, whose armour was inlaid with gilt flowers, and on whose helmet crouched a lion that had wings, held up a shield, and cried, 'How saith my lord that he is not beautiful?'

And the Star-Child looked, and lo! his face was even as it had been, and his comeliness had come back to him, and he saw that in his eyes which he had not seen there before.

And the priests and the high officers knelt down and said to him, 'It was prophesied of old that on this day should come he who was to rule over us.

Therefore, let our lord take this crown and this sceptre, and be in his justice and mercy our King over us.'

But he said to them, 'I am not worthy, for I have denied the mother who bare me, nor may I rest till I have found her, and known her forgiveness. Therefore, let me go, for I must wander again over the world, and may not tarry here, though ye bring me the crown and the sceptre.' And as he spake he turned his face from them towards the street that led to the gate of the city, and lo! amongst the crowd that pressed round the soldiers, he saw the beggar-woman who was his mother, and at her side stood the leper, who had sat by the road.

And a cry of joy broke from his lips, and he ran over, and kneeling down he kissed the wounds on his mother's feet, and wet them with his tears. He bowed his head in the dust, and sobbing, as one whose heart might break, he said to her: 'Mother, I denied thee in the hour of my pride. Accept me in the hour of my humility. Mother, I gave thee hatred. Do thou give me love. Mother, I rejected thee. Receive thy child now.' But the beggar-woman answered him not a word.

And he reached out his hands, and clasped the white feet of the leper, and said to him: 'Thrice did I give thee of my mercy. Bid my mother speak to me one.' But the leper answered him not a word.

And he sobbed again and said: 'Mother, my suffering is greater than I can bear. Give me thy forgiveness, and let me go back to the forest.' And the beggar-woman put her hand on his head, and said to him, 'Rise,' and the leper put his hand on his head, and said to him, 'Rise,' also.

And he rose up from his feet, and looked at them, and lo! they were a King and a Queen.

And the Queen said to him, 'This is thy father whom thou hast succoured.'

And the King said, 'This is thy mother whose feet thou hast washed with thy tears.'

And they fell on his neck and kissed him, and brought him into the palace and clothed him in fair raiment, and set the crown upon his head, and the sceptre in his hand, and over the city that stood by the river he ruled, and was its lord. Much justice and mercy did he show to all, and the evil Magician he banished, and to the Woodcutter and his wife he sent many rich gifts, and to their children he gave high honour. Nor would he suffer any to be cruel to bird or beast, but taught love and loving-kindness and charity, and to the poor he gave bread, and to the naked he gave raiment, and there was peace and plenty in the land.

Yet ruled he not long, so great had been his suffering, and so bitter the fire of his testing, for after the space of three years he died. And he who came after him ruled evilly.

THE HAPPY PRINCE

HIGH above the city, on a tall column, stood the statue of the Happy Prince. He was gilded all over with thin leaves of fine gold, for eyes he had two bright sapphires, and a large red ruby glowed on his sword-hilt.

He was very much admired indeed. 'He is as beautiful as a weathercock,' remarked one of the Town Councillors who wished to gain a reputation for having artistic tastes; 'only not quite so useful,' he added, fearing lest people should think him unpractical, which he really was not.

'Why can't you be like the Happy Prince?' asked a sensible mother of her little boy who was crying for the moon. 'The Happy Prince never dreams of crying for anything.'

'I am glad there is some one in the world who is quite happy,' muttered a disappointed man as he gazed at the wonderful statue.

'He looks just like an angel,' said the Charity Children as they came out of the cathedral in their bright scarlet cloaks and their clean white pinafores.

'How do you know?' said the Mathematical Master, 'you have never seen one.'

'Ah! but we have, in our dreams,' answered the children; and the Mathematical Master frowned and looked very severe, for he did not approve of children dreaming.

One night there flew over the city a little Swallow. His friends had gone away to Egypt six weeks before, but he had stayed behind, for he was in love with the most beautiful Reed. He had met her early in the spring as he was flying down the river after a big yellow moth, and had been so attracted by her slender waist that he had stopped to talk to her.

'Shall I love you?' said the Swallow, who liked to come to the point at once, and the Reed made him a low bow. So he flew round and round her, touching the water with his wings, and making silver ripples. This was his courtship, and it lasted all through the summer.

'It is a ridiculous attachment,' twittered the other Swallows; 'she has no money, and far too many relations;' and indeed the river was quite full of Reeds. Then, when the autumn came they all flew away.

After they had gone he felt lonely, and began to tire of his lady-love. 'She has no conversation,' he said, 'and I am afraid that she is a coquette, for she is always flirting with the wind.' And certainly, whenever the wind blew, the Reed made the most graceful curtseys. 'I admit that she is domestic,' he continued, 'but I love travelling, and my wife, consequently, should love travelling also.'

'Will you come away with me?' he said finally to her, but the Reed shook her head, she was so attached to her home.

'You have been trifling with me,' he cried. 'I am off to the Pyramids. Good-bye!' and he flew away.

All day long he flew, and at night-time he arrived at the city. 'Where shall I put up?' he said; 'I hope the town has made preparations.'

Then he saw the statue on the tall column.

'I will put up there,' he cried; 'it is a fine position, with plenty of fresh air.' So he alighted just between the feet of the Happy Prince.

'I have a golden bedroom,' he said softly to himself as he looked round, and he prepared to go to sleep; but just as he was putting his head under his wing a large drop of water fell on him. 'What a curious thing!' he cried; 'there is not a single cloud in the sky, the stars are quite clear and bright, and yet it is raining. The climate in the north of Europe is really dreadful. The Reed used to like the rain, but that was merely her selfishness.'

Then another drop fell.

'What is the use of a statue if it cannot keep the rain off?' he said; 'I must look for a good chimney-pot,' and he determined to fly away.

But before he had opened his wings, a third drop fell, and he looked up, and saw – Ah! what did he see?

The eyes of the Happy Prince were filled with tears, and tears were running down his golden cheeks. His face was so beautiful in the moonlight that the little Swallow was filled with pity.

'Who are you?' he said.

'I am the Happy Prince.'

'Why are you weeping then?' asked the Swallow; 'you have quite drenched me.'

'When I was alive and had a human heart,' answered the statue, 'I did not know what tears were, for I lived in the Palace of Sans-Souci, where sorrow is not allowed to enter. In the daytime I played with my companions in the garden, and in the evening I led the dance in the Great Hall. Round the garden ran a very lofty wall, but I never cared to ask what lay beyond it, everything about me was so beautiful. My courtiers called me the Happy Prince, and happy indeed I was, if pleasure be happiness. So I lived, and so I died. And now that I am dead they have set me up here so high that I can see all the ugliness and all the misery of my city, and though my heart is made of lead yet I cannot choose but weep.'

'What! is he not solid gold?' said the Swallow to himself. He was too polite to make any personal remarks out loud.

'Far away,' continued the statue in a low musical voice, 'far away in a little street there is a poor house. One of the windows is open, and through it I can see a woman seated at a table. Her face is thin and worn, and she has coarse, red hands, all pricked by the needle, for she is a seamstress. She is embroidering passion-flowers on a satin gown for the loveliest of the Queen's maids-of-honour to wear at the next Court-ball. In a bed in the corner of the room her little boy is lying ill. He has a fever, and is asking for oranges. His mother has nothing to give him but river water, so he is crying. Swallow, Swallow, little Swallow, will you not bring her the ruby out of my sword-hilt? My feet are fastened to this pedestal and I cannot move.'

'I am waited for in Egypt,' said the Swallow. 'My friends are flying up and down the Nile, and talking to the large lotus-flowers. Soon they will go to sleep in the tomb of the great King. The King is there himself in his painted coffin. He is wrapped in yellow linen, and embalmed with spices. Round his neck is a chain of pale green jade, and his hands are like withered leaves.'

'Swallow, Swallow, little Swallow,' said the Prince, 'will you not stay with me for one night, and be my messenger? The boy is so thirsty, and the mother so sad.'

'I don't think I like boys,' answered the Swallow. 'Last summer, when I was staying on the river, there were two rude boys, the miller's sons, who were always throwing stones at me. They never hit me, of course; we swallows fly far too well for that, and besides, I come of a family famous for its agility; but still, it was a mark of disrespect.'

But the Happy Prince looked so sad that the little Swallow was sorry. 'It is very cold here,' he said; 'but I will stay with you for one night, and be your messenger.'

'Thank you, little Swallow,' said the Prince.

So the Swallow picked out the great ruby from the Prince's sword, and flew away with it in his beak over the roofs of the town.

He passed by the cathedral tower, where the white marble angels were sculptured. He passed by the palace and heard the sound of dancing. A beautiful girl came out on the balcony with her lover. 'How wonderful the stars are,' he said to her, 'and how wonderful is the power of love!'

'I hope my dress will be ready in time for the State-ball,' she answered; 'I have ordered passion-flowers to be embroidered on it; but the seamstresses are so lazy.'

He passed over the river, and saw the lanterns hanging to the masts of the ships. He passed over the Ghetto, and saw the old Jews bargaining with each other, and weighing out money in copper scales. At last he came to the poor house and looked in. The boy was tossing feverishly on his bed, and the mother had fallen asleep, she was so tired. In he hopped, and laid the great ruby on the table beside the woman's thimble. Then he flew gently round the bed, fanning the boy's forehead with his wings. 'How cool I feel!' said the boy, 'I must be getting better:' and he sank into a delicious slumber.

Then the Swallow flew back to the Happy Prince, and told him what he had done. 'It is curious,' he remarked, 'but I feel quite warm now, although it is so cold.'

'That is because you have done a good action,' said the Prince. And the little Swallow began to think, and then he fell asleep. Thinking always made him sleepy.

When day broke he flew down to the river and had a bath. 'What a remarkable phenomenon!' said the Professor of Ornithology as he was passing over the bridge. 'A swallow in winter!' And he wrote a long letter about it to the local newspaper. Every one quoted it, it was full of so many words that they could not understand.

'To-night I go to Egypt,' said the Swallow, and he was in high spirits at the prospect. He visited all the public monuments, and sat a long time on top of the church steeple. Wherever he went the Sparrows chirruped, and said to each other, 'What a distinguished stranger!' so he enjoyed himself very much.

When the moon rose he flew back to the Happy Prince. 'Have you any commissions for Egypt?' he cried; 'I am just starting.'

'Swallow, Swallow, little Swallow,' said the Prince, 'will you not stay with me one night longer?'

'I am waited for in Egypt,' answered the Swallow. 'To-morrow my friends will fly up to the Second Cataract. The river-horse couches there among the bulrushes, and on a great granite house sits the God Memnon. All night long he watches the stars, and when the morning star shines he utters one cry of joy, and then he is silent. At noon the yellow lions come down to the water's edge to drink. They have eyes like green beryls, and their roar is louder than the roar of the cataract.'

'Swallow, Swallow, little Swallow,' said the Prince, 'far away across the city I see a young man in a garret. He is leaning over a desk covered with papers, and in a tumbler by his side there is a bunch of withered violets. His hair is brown and crisp, and his lips are red as a pomegranate, and he has large and dreamy eyes. He is trying to finish a play for the Director of the Theatre, but he is too cold to write any more. There is no fire in the grate, and hunger has made him faint.'

'I will wait with you one night longer,' said the Swallow, who really had a good heart. 'Shall I take him another ruby?'

'Alas! I have no ruby now,' said the Prince; 'my eyes are all that I have left. They are made of rare sapphires, which were brought out of India a thousand years ago. Pluck out one of them and take it to him. He will sell it to the jeweller, and buy firewood, and finish his play.'

'Dear Prince,' said the Swallow, 'I cannot do that'; and he began to weep.

'Swallow, Swallow, little Swallow,' said the Prince, 'do as I command you.'

So the Swallow plucked out the Prince's eye, and flew away to the student's garret. It was easy enough to get in, as there was a hole in the roof. Through this he darted, and came into the room. The young man had his head buried in his hands, so he did not hear the flutter of the bird's wings, and when he looked up he found the beautiful sapphire lying on the withered violets.

'I am beginning to be appreciated,' he cried; 'this is from some great admirer. Now I can finish my play,' and he looked quite happy.

The next day the Swallow flew down to the harbour. He sat on the mast of a large vessel and watched the sailors hauling big chests out of the hold with ropes. 'Heave a-hoy!' they shouted as each chest came up. 'I am going to Egypt!' cried the Swallow, but nobody minded, and when the moon rose he flew back to the Happy Prince.

'I am come to bid you good-bye,' he cried.

'Swallow, Swallow, little Swallow,' said the Prince, 'will you not stay with me one night longer?'

'It is winter,' answered the Swallow, 'and the chill snow will soon be here. In Egypt the sun is warm on the green palm-trees, and the crocodiles lie in the mud and look lazily about them. My companions are building a nest in the Temple of Baalbec, and the pink and white doves are watching them, and cooing to each other. Dear Prince, I must leave you, but I will never forget you, and next spring I will bring you back two beautiful jewels in place of those you have given away. The ruby shall be redder than a red rose, and the sapphire shall be as blue as the great sea.'

'In the square below,' said the Happy Prince, 'there stands a little match-girl. She has let her matches fall in the gutter, and they are all spoiled. Her father will beat her if she does not bring home some money, and she is crying. She has no shoes or stockings, and her little head is bare. Pluck out my other eye, and give it to her, and her father will not beat her.'

'I will stay with you one night longer,' said the Swallow, 'but I cannot pluck out your eye. You would be quite blind then.'

'Swallow, Swallow, little Swallow,' said the Prince, 'do as I command you.'

So he plucked out the Prince's other eye, and darted down with it. He swooped past the match-girl, and slipped the jewel into the palm of her hand. 'What a lovely bit of glass!' cried the little girl; and she ran home, laughing.

Then the Swallow came back to the Prince. 'You are blind now,' he said, 'so I will stay with you always.'

'No, little Swallow,' said the poor prince, 'you must go away to Egypt.'

'I will stay with you always,' said the Swallow, and he slept at the Prince's feet.

All the next day he sat on the Prince's shoulder, and told him stories of what he had seen in strange lands. He told him of the red ibises, who stand in long rows on the banks of the Nile, and catch goldfish in their beaks; of the Sphinx, who is as old as the world itself, and lives in the desert, and knows everything; of the merchants, who walk slowly by the side of their camels and carry amber beads in their hands; of the King of the Mountains of the Moon, who is as black as ebony, and worships a large crystal; of the great green snake that sleeps in a palm-tree, and has twenty priests to feed it with honey-cakes; and of the pygmies who sail over a big lake on large flat leaves, and are always at war with the butterflies.

'Dear little Swallow,' said the Prince, 'you tell me of marvellous things, but more marvellous than anything is the suffering of men and of women. There is no Mystery so great as Misery. Fly over my city, little Swallow, and tell me what you see there.'

So the Swallow flew over the great city, and saw the rich making merry in their beautiful houses, while the beggars were sitting at the gates. He flew into dark lanes, and saw the white faces of starving children looking out list-lessly at the black streets. Under the archway of a bridge two little boys were lying in one another's arms to try and keep themselves warm. 'How hungry we are!' they said. 'You must not lie here,' shouted the watchman, and they wandered out into the rain.

Then he flew back and told the Prince what he had seen.

'I am covered with fine gold,' said the Prince, 'you must take it off, leaf by leaf, and give it to my poor; the living always think that gold can make them happy.'

Leaf after leaf of the fine gold the Swallow picked off, till the Happy Prince looked quite dull and grey. Leaf after leaf of the fine gold he brought to the poor, and the children's faces grew rosier, and they laughed and played games in the street. 'We have bread now!' they cried.

Then the snow came, and after the snow came the frost. The streets looked as if they were made of silver, they were so bright and glistening; long icicles like crystal daggers hung down from the eaves of the houses, everybody went about in furs, and the little boys wore scarlet caps and skated on the ice.

The poor little Swallow grew colder and colder, but he would not leave the Prince, he loved him too well. He picked up crumbs outside the baker's door when the baker was not looking, and tried to keep himself warm by flapping his wings.

But at last he knew that he was going to die. He had just enough strength to fly up to the Prince's shoulder once more. 'Good-bye, dear Prince!' he murmured, 'will you let me kiss your hand?'

'I am glad that you are going to Egypt at last, little Swallow,' said the prince, 'you have stayed too long here; but you must kiss me on the lips, for I love you.'

'It is not to Egypt that I am going,' said the Swallow. 'I am going to the House of Death. Death is the brother of Sleep, is he not?'

And he kissed the Happy Prince on the lips, and fell down dead at his feet.

At that moment a curious crack sounded inside the statue, as if something had broken. The fact is that the leaden heart had snapped right in two. It certainly was a dreadfully hard frost.

Early the next morning the Mayor was walking in the square below in company with the Town Councillors. As they passed the column he looked up at the statue: 'Dear me! how shabby the Happy Prince looks!' he said.

'How shabby, indeed!' cried the Town Councillors, who always agreed with the Mayor; and they went up to look at it.

'The ruby has fallen out of his sword, his eyes are gone, and he is golden no longer,' said the Mayor; 'in fact, he is little better than a beggar!'

'Little better than a beggar,' said the Town Councillors.

'And here is actually a dead bird at his feet!' continued the Mayor. 'We must really issue a proclamation that birds are not to be allowed to die here.' And the Town Clerk made a note of the suggestion.

So they pulled down the statue of the Happy Prince. 'As he is no longer beautiful he is no longer useful,' said the Art Professor at the University.

Then they melted the statue in a furnace, and the Mayor held a meeting of the Corporation to decide what was to be done with the metal. 'We must have another statue, of course,' he said, 'and it shall be a statue of myself.'

'Of myself,' said each of the Town Councillors, and they quarrelled. When I last heard of them they were quarrelling still.

'What a strange thing!' said the overseer of the workmen at the foundry. 'This broken lead heart will not melt in the furnace. We must throw it away.' So they threw it on a dust-heap where the dead Swallow was also lying.

'Bring me the two most precious things in the city,' said God to one of His Angels; and the Angel brought Him the leaden heart and the dead bird.

'You have rightly chosen,' said God, 'for in my garden of Paradise this little bird shall sing for evermore, and in my city of gold the Happy Prince shall praise me.'

THE NIGHTINGALE AND THE ROSE

'SHE said that she would dance with me if I brought her red roses,' cried the young Student, 'but in all my garden there is no red rose.'

From her nest in the holm-oak tree the Nightingale heard him, and she looked out through the leaves and wondered.

'No red rose in all my garden!' he cried, and his beautiful eyes filled with tears. 'Ah, on what little things does happiness depend! I have read all that the wise men have written, and all the secrets of philosophy are mine, yet for want of a red rose is my life made wretched.'

'Here at last is a true lover,' said the Nightingale. 'Night after night have I sung of him, though I knew him not: night after night have I told his story to the stars and now I see him. His hair is dark as the hyacinth-blossom, and his lips are red as the rose of his desire; but passion has made his face like pale ivory, and sorrow has set her seal upon his brow.'

'The Prince gives a ball to-morrow night,' murmured the young student, 'and my love will be of the company. If I bring her a red rose she will dance with me till dawn. If I bring her a red rose, I shall hold her in my arms, and she will lean her head upon my shoulder, and her hand will be clasped in mine. But there is no red rose in my garden, so I shall sit lonely, and she will pass me by. She will have no heed of me, and my heart will break.'

'Here, indeed, is the true lover,' said the Nightingale. 'What I sing of, he suffers: what is joy to me, to him is pain. Surely love is a wonderful thing. It is more precious than emeralds, and dearer than fine opals. Pearls and pomegranates cannot buy it, nor is it set forth in the market-place. It may not be purchased of the merchants, nor can it be weighed out in the balance for gold.'

'The musicians will sit in their gallery,' said the young Student, 'and play upon their stringed instruments, and my love will dance to the sound of the harp and the violin. She will dance so lightly that her feet will not touch the floor, and the courtiers in their gay dresses will throng round her. But with me she will not dance, for I have no red rose to give her;' and he flung himself down on the grass, and buried his face in his hands, and wept.

'Why is he weeping?' asked a little Green Lizard, as he ran past him with his tail in the air.

'Why, indeed?' said a Butterfly, who was fluttering about after a sunbeam.

'Why, indeed?' whispered a Daisy to his neighbour, in a soft, low voice.

'He is weeping for a red rose,' said the Nightingale.

'For a red rose?' they cried; 'how very ridiculous!' and the little Lizard, who was something of a cynic, laughed outright.

But the Nightingale understood the secret of the Student's sorrow, and she sat silent in the oak-tree, and thought about the mystery of Love.

Suddenly she spread her brown wings for flight, and soared into the air. She passed through the grove like a shadow and like a shadow she sailed across the garden.

In the centre of the grass-plot was standing a beautiful Rose-tree, and when she saw it she flew over to it, and lit upon a spray.

'Give me a red rose,' she cried, 'and I will sing you my sweetest song.'

But the Tree shook its head.

'My roses are white,' it answered; 'as white as the foam of the sea, and whiter than the snow upon the mountain. But go to my brother who grows round the old sun-dial, and perhaps he will give you what you want.'

So the Nightingale flew over to the Rose-tree that was growing round the old sun-dial.

'Give me a red rose,' she cried, 'and I will sing you my sweetest song.'

But the Tree shook its head.

'My roses are yellow,' it answered; 'as yellow as the hair of the mermaiden who sits upon an amber throne, and yellower than the daffodil that blooms in the meadow before the mower comes with his scythe. But go to my brother who grows beneath the Student's window, and perhaps he will give you what you want.'

So the Nightingale flew over to the Rose-tree that was growing beneath the Student's window.

'Give me a red rose,' she cried, 'and I will sing you my sweetest song.'

But the Tree shook its head.

'My roses are red,' it answered, 'as red as the feet of the dove, and redder than the great fans of coral that wave and wave in the ocean-cavern. But the winter has chilled my veins, and the frost has nipped my buds, and the storm has broken my branches, and I shall have no roses at all this year.'

'One red rose is all I want,' cried the Nightingale, 'only one red rose! Is there no way by which I can get it?'

'There is a way,' answered the Tree; 'but it is so terrible that I dare not tell it to you.'

'Tell it to me,' said the Nightingale, 'I am not afraid.'

'If you want a red rose,' said the Tree, 'you must build it out of music by moonlight, and stain it with your own heart's-blood. You must sing to me with your breast against a thorn. All night long you must sing to me, and the thorn must pierce your heart, and your life-blood must flow into my veins, and become mine.'

'Death is a great price to pay for a red rose,' cried the Nightingale, 'and Life is very dear to all. It is pleasant to sit in the green'wood, and to watch the Sun in his chariot of gold, and the Moon in her chariot of pearl. Sweet is the scent of the hawthorn, and sweet are the bluebells that hide in the valley, and the heather that blows on the hill. Yet Love is better than Life, and what is the heart of a bird compared to the heart of a man?'

So she spread her brown wings for flight, and soared into the air. She swept over the garden like a shadow, and like a shadow she sailed through the grove.

The young Student was still lying on the grass, where she had left him, and the tears were not yet dry in his beautiful eyes.

'Be happy,' cried the Nightingale, 'be happy; you shall have your red rose. I will build it out of music by moonlight, and stain it with my own heart's-blood. All that I ask of you in return is that you will be a true lover, for Love is wiser than Philosophy, though he is wise, and mightier than Power, though he is mighty. Flame-coloured are his wings, and coloured like flame is his body. His lips are sweet as honey, and his breath is like frankincense.'

The Student looked up from the grass, and listened, but he could not understand what the Nightingale was saying to him, for he only knew the things that are written down in books.

But the Oak-tree understood, and felt sad, for he was very fond of the little Nightingale, who had built her nest in his branches.

'Sing me one last song,' he whispered; 'I shall feel lonely when you are gone.'

So the Nightingale sang to the Oak-tree, and her voice was like water bubbling from a silver jar.

When she had finished her song, the Student got up, and pulled a notebook and a lead-pencil out of his pocket.

'She has form,' he said to himself, as he walked away through the grove – 'that cannot be denied to her; but has she got feeling? I am afraid not. In fact, she is like most artists; she is all style without any sincerity. She would not sacrifice herself for others. She thinks merely of music, and everybody knows that the arts are selfish. Still, it must be admitted that she has some beautiful notes in her voice. What a pity it is that they do not mean anything, or do any practical good!' And he went into his room, and lay down on his little pallet-bed, and began to think of his love; and, after a time, he fell asleep.

And when the moon shone in the heavens the Nightingale flew to the Rose-tree, and set her breast against the thorn. All night long she sang, with her breast against the thorn, and the cold crystal Moon leaned down and listened. All night long she sang, and the thorn went deeper and deeper into her breast, and her life-blood ebbed away from her.

She sang first of the birth of love in the heart of a boy and a girl. And on the topmost spray of the Rose-tree there blossomed a marvellous rose, petal following petal, as song followed song. Pale was it, at first, as the mist that hangs over the river – pale as the feet of the morning, and silver as the wings of the dawn. As the shadow of a rose in a mirror of silver, as the shadow of a rose in a water-pool, so was the rose that blossomed on the topmost spray of the Tree.

But the Tree cried to the Nightingale to press closer against the thorn. 'Press closer, little Nightingale,' cried the Tree, 'or the Day will come before the rose is finished.'

So the Nightingale pressed closer against the thorn, and louder and louder grew her song, for she sang of the birth of passion in the soul of a man and a maid.

And a delicate flush of pink came into the leaves of the rose, like the flush in the face of the bridegroom when he kisses the lips of the bride. But the thorn had not yet reached her heart, so the rose's heart remained white, for only a Nightingale's heart's-blood can crimson the heart of a rose.

And the Tree cried to the Nightingale to press closer against the thorn. 'Press closer, little Nightingale,' cried the Tree, 'or the Day will come before the rose is finished.'

So the Nightingale pressed closer against the thorn, and the thorn touched her heart, and a fierce pang of pain shot through her. Bitter, bitter was the pain, and wilder and wilder grew her song, for she sang of the Love that is perfected by Death, of the Love that dies not in the tomb.

And the marvellous rose became crimson, like the rose of the eastern sky. Crimson was the girdle of petals, and crimson as a ruby was the heart.

But the Nightingale's voice grew fainter, and her little wings began to beat, and a film came over her eyes. Fainter and fainter grew her song, and she felt something choking her in her throat.

Then she gave one last burst of music. The white Moon heard it, and she forgot the dawn, and lingered on in the sky. The red rose heard it, and it trembled all over with ecstasy, and opened its petals to the cold morning air. Echo bore it to her purple cavern in the hills, and woke the sleeping shepherds from their dreams. It floated through the reeds of the river, and they carried its message to the sea.

'Look, look!' cried the Tree, 'the rose is finished now;' but the Nightingale made no answer, for she was lying dead in the long grass, with the thorn in her heart.

And at noon the Student opened his window and looked out.

'Why, what a wonderful piece of luck!' he cried; 'here is a red rose! I have never seen any rose like it in all my life. It is so beautiful that I am sure it has a long Latin name;' and he leaned down and plucked it.

Then he put on his hat, and ran up to the Professor's house with the rose in his hand.

The daughter of the Professor was sitting in the doorway winding blue silk on a reel, and her little dog was lying at her feet.

'You said that you would dance with me if I brought you a red rose,' cried the Student. 'Here is the reddest rose in all the world. You will wear it to-night next your heart, and as we dance together it will tell you how I love you.'

But the girl frowned.

'I am afraid it will not go with my dress,' she answered; 'and, besides, the Chamberlain's nephew has sent me some real jewels, and everybody knows that jewels cost far more than flowers.'

'Well, upon my word, you are very ungrateful,' said the Student angrily; and he threw the rose into the street, where it fell into the gutter, and a cart-wheel went over it.

'Ungrateful!' said the girl. 'I tell you what, you are very rude; and, after all, who are you? Only a Student. Why, I don't believe you have even got silver buckles to your shoes as the Chamberlain's nephew has;' and she got up from her chair and went into the house.

'What a silly thing Love is!' said the Student as he walked away. 'It is not half as useful as Logic, for it does not prove anything, and it is always telling one of things that are not going to happen, and making one believe things that are not true. In fact, it is quite unpractical, and, as in this age to be practical is everything, I shall go back to Philosophy and study Metaphysics.'

So he returned to his room and pulled out a great dusty book, and began to read.

THE SELFISH GIANT

EVERY afternoon, as they were coming from school, the children used to go and play in the Giant's garden.

It was a large lovely garden, with soft green grass. Here and there over the grass stood beautiful flowers like stars, and there were twelve peach-trees that in the spring-time broke out into delicate blossoms of pink and pearl, and in the autumn bore rich fruit. The birds sat on the trees and sang so sweetly that the children used to stop their games in order to listen to them. 'How happy we are here!' they cried to each other.

One day the Giant came back. He had been to visit his friend the Cornish ogre, and had stayed with him for seven years. After the seven years were over he had said all that he had to say, for his conversation was limited, and he determined to return to his own castle. When he arrived he saw the children playing in the garden.

'What are you doing here?' he cried in a very gruff voice, and the children ran away.

'My own garden is my own garden,' said the Giant; 'any one can understand that, and I will allow nobody to play in it but myself.' So he built a high wall all round it, and put up a notice-board.

> TRESPASSERS
> WILL BE
> PROSECUTED

He was a very selfish Giant.

The poor children had now nowhere to play. They tried to play on the road, but the road was very dusty and full of hard stones, and they did not like it. They used to wander round the high walls when their lessons were over, and talk about the beautiful garden inside. 'How happy we were there!' they said to each other.

Then the Spring came, and all over the country there were little blossoms and little birds. Only in the garden of the Selfish Giant it was still winter. The birds did not care to sing in it as there were no children, and the trees forgot to blossom. Once a beautiful flower put its head out from the grass, but when it saw the notice-board it was so sorry for the children that it slipped back into the ground again, and went off to sleep. The only people who were pleased were the Snow and the Frost. 'Spring has forgotten this garden,' they cried, 'so we will live here all the year round.' The Snow covered up the grass with her great white cloak, and the Frost painted all the trees silver. Then they invited the North Wind to stay with them, and he came. He was wrapped in furs, and he roared all day about the garden, and blew the chimney-pots down. 'This is a delightful spot,' he said, 'we must ask the Hail on a visit.' So the Hail came. Every day for three hours he rattled on the roof of the castle till he broke most of the slates, and then he ran round and round the garden as fast as he could go. He was dressed in grey, and his breath was like ice.

'I cannot understand why the Spring is so late in coming,' said the Selfish Giant, as he sat at the window and looked out at his cold, white garden; 'I hope there will be a change in the weather.'

But the Spring never came, nor the Summer. The Autumn gave golden fruit to every garden, but to the Giant's garden she gave none. 'He is too selfish,' she said. So it was always Winter there, and the North Wind and the Hail, and the Frost, and the Snow danced about through the trees.

One morning the Giant was lying awake in bed when he heard some lovely music. It sounded so sweet to his ears that he thought it must be the King's musicians passing by. It was really only a little linnet singing outside his window, but it was so long since he had heard a bird sing in his garden that it seemed to him to be the most beautiful music in the world. Then the Hail stopped dancing over his head, and the North Wind ceased roaring, and a delicious perfume came to him through the open casement. 'I believe the Spring has come at last,' said the Giant; and he jumped out of bed and looked out.

What did he see?

He saw a most wonderful sight. Through a little hole in the wall the children had crept in, and they were sitting in the branches of the trees. In every tree that he could see there was a little child. And the trees were so glad to have the children back again that they had covered themselves with blossoms, and were waving their arms gently above the children's heads. The birds were flying about and twittering with delight, and the flowers were looking up through the green grass and laughing. It was a lovely scene, only in one corner it was still winter. It was the farthest corner of the garden, and in it was standing a little boy. He was so small that he could not reach up to the branches of the tree, and he was wandering all round it, crying bitterly. The poor tree was still covered with frost and snow, and the North Wind was blowing and roaring above it. 'Climb up! little boy,' said the Tree, and it bent its branches down as low as it could; but the boy was too tiny.

And the Giant's heart melted as he looked out. 'How selfish I have been!' he said; 'now I know why the Spring would not come here. I will put that poor little boy on the top of the tree, and then I will knock down the wall, and my garden shall be the children's playground for ever and ever.' He was really very sorry for what he had done.

So he crept downstairs and opened the front door quite softly, and went out into the garden. But when the children saw him they were so frightened that they all ran away, and the garden became winter again. Only the little boy did not run, for his eyes were so full of tears that he did not see the Giant coming. And the Giant stole up behind him and took him gently in his hand, and put him up into the tree. And the tree broke at once into blossom, and the birds came and sang on it, and the little boy stretched out his two arms and flung them round the Giant's neck, and kissed him. And the other children when they saw that the Giant was not wicked any longer, came running back, and with them came the Spring. 'It is your garden now, little children,' said the Giant, and he took a great axe and knocked down the wall. And when the people were going to market at twelve o'clock they found the Giant playing with the children in the most beautiful garden they had ever seen.

All day long they played, and in the evening they came to the Giant to bid him good-bye.

'But where is your little companion?' he said: 'the boy I put into the tree.' The Giant loved him the best because he had kissed him.

'We don't know,' answered the children: 'he has gone away.'

'You must tell him to be sure and come to-morrow,' said the Giant. But the children said that they did not know where he lived, and had never seen him before; and the Giant felt very sad.

Every afternoon, when school was over, the children came and played with the Giant. But the little boy whom the Giant loved was never seen again. The Giant was very kind to all the children, yet he longed for his first little friend, and often spoke of him. 'How I would like to see him!' he used to say.

Years went over, and the Giant grew very old and feeble. He could not play about any more, so he sat in a huge arm-chair, and watched the children at their games, and admired his garden. 'I have many beautiful flowers,' he said; 'but the children are the most beautiful flowers of all.'

One winter morning he looked out of his window as he was dressing. He did not hate the Winter now, for he knew that it was merely the Spring asleep, and that the flowers were resting.

Suddenly he rubbed his eyes in wonder and looked and looked. It certainly was a marvellous sight. In the farthest corner of the garden was a tree quite covered with lovely white blossoms. Its branches were golden, and silver fruit hung down from them, and underneath it stood the little boy he had loved.

Downstairs ran the Giant in great joy, and out into the garden. He hastened across the grass, and came near to the child. And when he came quite close his face grew red with anger, and he said, 'Who hath dared to wound thee?' For on the palms of the child's hands were the prints of two nails, and the prints of two nails were on the little feet.

'Who hath dared to wound thee?' cried the Giant; 'tell me, that I may take my big sword and slay him.'

'Nay!' answered the child: 'but these are the wounds of Love.'

'Who art thou?' said the Giant, and a strange awe fell on him, and he knelt before the little child.

And the child smiled on the Giant, and said to him, 'You let me play once in your garden, to-day you shall come with me to my garden, which is Paradise.'

And when the children ran in that afternoon, they found the Giant lying dead under the tree, all covered with white blossoms.

THE DEVOTED FRIEND

ONE morning the old Water-rat put his head out of his hole. He had bright beady eyes and stiff grey whiskers, and his tail was like a long bit of black Indiarubber. The little ducks were swimming about in the pond, looking just like a lot of yellow canaries, and their mother, who was pure white with real red legs, was trying to teach them how to stand on their heads in the water.

'You will never be in the best society unless you can stand on your heads,' she kept saying to them; and every now and then she showed them how it was done. But the little ducks paid no attention to her. They were so young that they did not know what an advantage it is to be in society at all.

'What disobedient children!' cried the old Water-rat: 'they really deserve to be drowned.'

'Nothing of the kind,' answered the Duck, 'every one must make a beginning, and parents cannot be too patient.'

'Ah! I know nothing about the feelings of parents,' said the Water-rat; 'I am not a family man. In fact, I have never been married, and I never intend to be. Love is all very well in its way, but friendship is much higher. Indeed, I know of nothing in the world that is either nobler or rarer than a devoted friendship.'

'And what, pray, is your idea of the duties of a devoted friend?' asked a green Linnet, who was sitting on a willow-tree hard by, and had overheard the conversation.

'Yes, that is just what I want to know,' said the Duck; and she swam away to the end of the pond, and stood upon her head, in order to give her children a good example.

'What a silly question!' cried the Water-rat. 'I should expect my devoted friend to be devoted to me, of course.'

'And what would you do in return?' said the little bird, swinging upon a silver spray, and flapping his tiny wings.

'I don't understand you,' answered the Water-rat.

'Let me tell you a story on the subject,' said the Linnet.

'Is the story about me?' asked the Water-rat. 'If so, I will listen to it, for I am extremely fond of fiction.'

'It is applicable to you,' answered the Linnet; and he flew down, and alighting upon the bank, he told the story of The Devoted Friend.

'Once upon a time,' said the Linnet, 'there was an honest little fellow named Hans.'

'Was he very distinguished?' asked the Water-rat.

'No,' answered the Linnet, 'I don't think he was distinguished at all, except for his kind heart, and his funny, round, good-humoured face. He lived in a tiny cottage all by himself, and every day he worked in his garden. In all the country-side there was no garden so lovely as his. Sweet-Williams grew there, and Gilly-flowers, and Shepherds'-purses, and Fair-maids of France. There were damask Roses, and yellow Roses, lilac Crocuses and gold, purple Violets and white. Columbine and Ladysmock, Marjoram and Wild Basil, the Cowslip and the Flower-de-luce, the Daffodil and the Clove-Pink bloomed or blossomed in their proper order as the months went by, one flower taking another flower's place, so that there were always beautiful things to look at, and pleasant odours to smell.

'Little Hans had a great many friends, but the most devoted friend of all was big Hugh the Miller. Indeed, so devoted was the rich Miller to little Hans, that he would never go by his garden without leaning over the wall and plucking a large nosegay, or a handful of sweet herbs, or filling his pockets with plums and cherries if it was the fruit season.

' "Real friends should have everything in common," the Miller used to say, and little Hans nodded and smiled, and felt very proud of having a friend with such noble ideas.

'Sometimes, indeed, the neighbours thought it strange that the rich Miller never gave little Hans anything in return, though he had a hundred sacks of flour stored away in his mill, and six milch cows, and a large flock of woolly sheep; but Hans never troubled his head about these things, and nothing gave him greater pleasure than to listen to all the wonderful things the Miller used to say about the unselfishness of true friendship.

'So little Hans worked away in his garden. During the spring, the summer, and the autumn he was very happy, but when the winter came, and he had no fruit or flowers to bring to the market, he suffered a good deal from cold and hunger, and often had to go to bed without any supper but a few dried pears or some hard nuts. In the winter, also, he was extremely lonely, as the Miller never came to see him then.

' "There is no good in my going to see little Hans as long as the snow lasts," the Miller used to say to his wife, "for when people are in trouble they should be left alone and not be bothered by visitors. That at least is my idea about friendship, and I am sure I am right. So I shall wait till the spring comes, and then I shall pay him a visit, and he will be able to give me a large basket of primroses, and that will make him so happy."

' "You are certainly very thoughtful about others," answered the Wife, as she sat in her comfortable arm-chair by the big pinewood fire; "very thoughtful indeed. It is quite a treat to hear you talk about friendship. I am sure the clergyman himself could not say such beautiful things as you do, though he does live in a three-storied house, and wear a gold ring on his little finger."

' "But could we not ask little Hans up here?" said the Miller's youngest son. "If poor Hans is in trouble I will give him half my porridge, and show him my white rabbits."

' "What a silly boy you are!" cried the Miller; "I really don't know what is the use of sending you to school. You seem not to learn anything. Why, if little Hans came up here, and saw our warm fire, and our good supper, and our great cask of red wine, he might get envious, and envy is a most terrible thing, and would spoil anybody's nature. I certainly will not allow Hans' nature to be spoiled. I am his best friend, and I will always watch over him, and see that he is not led into any temptations. Besides, if Hans came here, he might ask me to let him have some flour on credit, and that I could not do. Flour is one thing, and friendship is another, and they should not be confused. Why, the words are spelt differently, and mean quite different things. Everybody can see that."

'"How well you talk!" said the Miller's Wife, pouring herself out a large glass of warm ale; "really I feel quite drowsy. It is just like being in church."

'"Lots of people act well," answered the Miller; "but very few people talk well, which shows that talking is much the more difficult thing of the two, and much the finer thing also;" and he looked sternly across the table at his little son, who felt so ashamed of himself that he hung his head down, and grew quite scarlet and began to cry into his tea. However, he was so young that you must excuse him.'

'Is that the end of the story?' asked the Water-rat.

'Certainly not,' answered the Linnet, 'that is the beginning.'

'Then you are quite behind the age,' said the Water-rat. 'Every good storyteller nowadays starts with the end, and then goes on to the beginning, and concludes with the middle. That is the new method. I heard all about it the other day from a critic who was walking round the pond with a young man. He spoke of the matter at great length, and I am sure he must have been right, for he had blue spectacles and a bald head, and whenever the young man made any remark, he always answered "Pooh!" But pray go on with your story. I like the Miller immensely. I have all kinds of beautiful sentiments myself, so there is a great sympathy between us.'

'Well,' said the Linnet, hopping now on one leg and now on the other, 'as soon as the winter was over, and the primroses began to open their pale yellow stars, the Miller said to his wife that he would go down and see little Hans.

'"Why, what a good heart you have!" cried his Wife; "you are always thinking of others. And mind you take the big basket with you for the flowers."

'So the Miller tied the sails of the windmill together with a strong iron chain, and went down the hill with the basket on his arm.

'"Good morning, little Hans," said the Miller.

'"Good morning," said Hans, leaning on his spade, and smiling from ear to ear.

'"And how have you been all the winter?" said the Miller.

'"Well, really," cried Hans, "it is very good of you to ask, very good indeed. I am afraid I had rather a hard time of it, but now the spring has come, and I am quite happy, and all my flowers are doing well."

'"We often talked of you during the winter, Hans," said the Miller, "and wondered how you were getting on."

' "That was kind of you," said Hans; "I was half afraid you had forgotten me."

' "Hans, I am surprised at you," said the Miller; "friendship never forgets. That is the wonderful thing about it, but I am afraid you don't understand the poetry of life. How lovely your primroses are looking, by-the-bye!"

' "They are certainly very lovely," said Hans, "and it is a most lucky thing for me that I have so many. I am going to bring them into the market and sell them to the Burgomaster's daughter, and buy back my wheelbarrow with the money."

' "Buy back your wheelbarrow? You don't mean to say you have sold it? What a very stupid thing to do!"

' "Well, the fact is," said Hans, "that I was obliged to. You see the winter was a very bad time for me, and I really had no money at all to buy bread with. So I first sold the silver buttons off my Sunday coat, and then I sold my silver chain, and then I sold my big pipe, and at last I sold my wheelbarrow. But I am going to buy them all back again now."

' "Hans," said the Miller, "I will give you my wheelbarrow. It is not in very good repair; indeed, one side is gone, and there is something wrong with the wheel-spokes; but in spite of that I will give it to you. I know it is very generous of me, and a great many people would think me extremely foolish for parting with it, but I am not like the rest of the world. I think that generosity is the essence of friendship, and, besides, I have got a new wheel-barrow for myself. Yes, you may set your mind at ease, I will give you my wheelbarrow."

' "Well, really, that is generous of you," said little Hans, and his funny round face glowed all over with pleasure. "I can easily put it in repair, as I have a plank of wood in the house."

' "A plank of wood!" said the Miller; "why, that is just what I want for the roof of my barn. There is a very large hole in it, and the corn will all get damp if I don't stop it up. How lucky you mentioned it! It is quite remarkable how one good action always breeds another. I have given you my wheelbarrow, and now you are going to give me your plank. Of course, the wheelbarrow is worth far more than the plank, but true friendship never notices things like that. Pray get it at once, and I will set to work at my barn this very day."

' "Certainly," cried little Hans, and he ran into the shed and dragged the plank out.

' "It is not a very big plank," said the Miller, looking at it, "and I am afraid that after I have mended my barn-roof there won't be any left for you to mend the wheelbarrow with; but, of course, that is not my fault. And now, as I have given you my wheelbarrow, I am sure you would like to give me some flowers in return. Here is the basket, and mind you fill it quite full."

' "Quite full?" said little Hans, rather sorrowfully, for it was really a very big basket, and he knew that if he filled it he would have no flowers left for the market, and he was very anxious to get his silver buttons back.

' "Well, really," answered the Miller, "as I have given you my wheelbarrow, I don't think that it is much to ask you for a few flowers. I may be wrong, but I should have thought that friendship, true friendship, was quite free from selfishness of any kind."

' "My dear friend, my best friend," cried little Hans, "you are welcome to all the flowers in my garden. I would much sooner have your good opinion than my silver buttons, any day;" and he ran and plucked all his pretty primroses, and filled the Miller's basket.

' "Good-bye, little Hans," said the Miller, and he went up the hill with the plank on his shoulder, and the big basket in his hand.

' "Good-bye," said little Hans, and he began to dig away quite merrily, he was so pleased about the wheelbarrow.

'The next day he was nailing up some honeysuckle against the porch, when he heard the Miller's voice calling to him from the road. So he jumped off the ladder, and ran down the garden, and looked over the wall.

'There was the Miller with a large sack of flour on his back.

' "Dear little Hans," said the Miller, "would you mind carrying this sack of flour for me to market?"

' "Oh, I am so sorry," said Hans, "but I am really very busy to-day. I have got all my creepers to nail up, and all my flowers to water, and all my grass to roll."

' "Well, really," said the Miller, "I think, that considering that I am going to give you my wheelbarrow it is rather unfriendly of you to refuse."

' "Oh, don't say that," cried little Hans, "I wouldn't be unfriendly for the whole world;" and he ran in for his cap, and trudged off with the big sack on his shoulders.

'It was a very hot day, and the road was terribly dusty, and before Hans had reached the sixth milestone he was so tired that he had to sit down and rest. However, he went on bravely, and at last he reached the market. After he had waited there for some time, he sold the sack of flour for a very good price, and then he returned home at once, for he was afraid that if he stopped too late he might meet some robbers on the way.

' "It has certainly been a hard day," said little Hans to himself as he was going to bed, "but I am glad I did not refuse the Miller, for he is my best friend and, besides, he is going to give me his wheelbarrow."

'Early the next morning the Miller came down to get the money for his sack of flour, but little Hans was so tired that he was still in bed.

' "Upon my word," said the Miller, "you are very lazy. Really, considering that I am going to give you my wheelbarrow, I think you might work harder. Idleness is a great sin, and I certainly don't like any of my friends to be idle or sluggish. You must not mind my speaking quite plainly to you. Of course I should not dream of doing so if I were not your friend. But what is the good of friendship if one cannot say exactly what one means? Anybody can say charming things and try to please and to flatter, but a true friend always says unpleasant things, and does not mind giving pain. Indeed, if he is a really true friend he prefers it, for he knows that then he is doing good."

' "I am very sorry," said little Hans, rubbing his eyes and pulling off his nightcap, "but I was so tired that I thought I would lie in bed for a little time, and listen to the birds singing. Do you know that I always work better after hearing the birds sing?"

'"Well, I am glad of that," said the Miller, clapping little Hans on the back, "for I want you to come up to the mill as soon as you are dressed and mend my barn-roof for me."

'Poor little Hans was very anxious to go and work in his garden, for his flowers had not been watered for two days, but he did not like to refuse the Miller, as he was such a good friend to him.

'"Do you think it would be unfriendly of me if I said I was busy?" he inquired in a shy and timid voice.

'"Well, really," answered the Miller, "I do not think it is much to ask of you, considering that I am going to give you my wheelbarrow; but, of course, if you refuse I will go and do it myself."

'"Oh! on no account," cried little Hans; and he jumped out of bed, and dressed himself, and went up to the barn.

'He worked there all day long, till sunset, and at sunset the Miller came to see how he was getting on.

'"Have you mended the hole in the roof yet, little Hans?" cried the Miller, in a cheery voice.

'"It is quite mended," answered little Hans, coming down the ladder.

'"Ah!" said the Miller, "there is no work so delightful as the work one does for others."

'"It is certainly a great privilege to hear you talk," answered little Hans, sitting down and wiping his forehead, "a very great privilege. But I am afraid I shall never have such beautiful ideas as you have."

'"Oh! they will come to you," said the Miller, "but you must take more pains. At present you have only the practice of friendship; some day you will have the theory also."

'"Do you really think I shall?" asked little Hans.

'"I have no doubt of it," answered the Miller, "but now that you have mended the roof, you had better go home and rest, for I want you to drive my sheep to the mountain to-morrow."

'Poor little Hans was afraid to say anything to this, and early next morning the Miller brought his sheep round to the cottage, and Hans started off with them to the mountain. It took him the whole day to get there and back; and when he returned he was so tired that he went off to sleep in his chair, and did not wake up till it was broad daylight.

'"What a delightful time I shall have in my garden!" he said, and he went to work at once.

'But somehow he was never able to look after his flowers at all, for his friend the Miller was always coming round and sending him off on long errands, or getting him to help at the mill. Little Hans was very much distressed at times, as he was afraid his flowers would think he had forgotten them, but he consoled himself by the reflection that the Miller was his best friend. "Besides," he used to say, "he is going to give me his wheelbarrow, and that is an act of pure generosity."

'So little Hans worked away for the Miller, and the Miller said all kinds of beautiful things about friendship, which Hans took down in a notebook, and used to read over at night, for he was a very good scholar.

'Now it happened that one evening little Hans was sitting by his fireside when a loud rap came at the door. It was a very wild night, and the wind was blowing and roaring round the house so terribly that at first he thought it was merely the storm. But a second rap came, and then a third, louder than any of the others.

' "It is some poor traveller," said little Hans to himself, and he ran to the door.

'There stood the Miller with a lantern in one hand and a big stick in the other.

' "Dear little Hans," cried the Miller, "I am in great trouble. My little boy has fallen off a ladder and hurt himself, and I am going for the Doctor. But he lives so far away, and it is such a bad night, that it has just occurred to me that it would be much better if you went instead of me. You know I am going to give you my wheelbarrow, and so it is only fair that you should do something for me in return."

' "Certainly," cried little Hans, "I take it quite as a compliment your coming to me, and I will start off at once. But you must lend me your lantern, as the night is so dark that I am afraid I might fall into the ditch."

' "I am very sorry," answered the Miller, "but it is my new lantern, and it would be a great loss to me if anything happened to it."

' "Well, never mind, I will do without it," cried little Hans, and he took down his great fur coat, and his warm scarlet cap, and tied a muffler round his throat, and started off.

'What a dreadful storm it was! The night was so black that little Hans could hardly see, and the wind was so strong that he could hardly stand. However, he was very courageous, and after he had been walking about three hours, he arrived at the Doctor's house, and knocked at the door.

' "Who is there?" cried the Doctor, putting his head out of his bedroom window.

' "Little Hans, Doctor."

' "What do you want, little Hans?"

' "The Miller's son has fallen from a ladder, and has hurt himself, and the Miller wants you to come at once."

' "All right!" said the Doctor; and he ordered his horse, and his big boots, and his lantern, and came downstairs, and rode off in the direction of the Miller's house, little Hans trudging behind him.

'But the storm grew worse and worse, and the rain fell in torrents, and little Hans could not see where he was going, or keep up with the horse. At last he lost his way, and wandered off on the moor, which was a very dangerous place, as it was full of deep holes, and there poor little Hans was drowned. His body was found the next day by some goatherds, floating in a great pool of water, and was brought back by them to the cottage.

'Everybody went to little Hans' funeral, as he was so popular, and the

Miller was the chief mourner.

' "As I was his best friend," said the Miller, "it is only fair that I should have the best place;" so he walked at the head of the procession in a long black cloak, and every now and then he wiped his eyes with a big pocket-handkerchief.

' "Little Hans is certainly a great loss to every one," said the Blacksmith, when the funeral was over, and they were all seated comfortably in the inn, drinking spiced wine and eating sweet cakes.

' "A great loss to me at any rate," answered the Miller; "why, I had as good as given him my wheelbarrow, and now I really don't know what to do with it. It is very much in my way at home, and it is in such bad repair that I could not get anything for it if I sold it. I will certainly take care not to give away anything again. One certainly suffers for being generous." '

'Well?' and the Water-rat, after a long pause.

'Well, that is the end,' said the Linnet.

'But what became of the Miller?' asked the Water-rat.

'Oh! I really don't know,' replied the Linnet; 'and I am sure that I don't care.'

'It is quite evident that you have no sympathy in your nature,' said the Water-rat.

'I am afraid you don't quite see the moral of the story,' remarked the Linnet.

'The what?' screamed the Water-rat.

'The moral.'

'Do you mean to say that the story has a moral?'

'Certainly,' said the Linnet.

'Well, really,' said the Water-rat, in a very angry manner, 'I think you should have told me that before you began. If you had done so, I certainly would not have listened to you; in fact, I should have said "Pooh, ' like the critic. However, I can say it now;' so he shouted out 'Pooh,' at the top of his voice, gave a whisk with his tail, and went back into his hole.

'And how do you like the Water-rat?' asked the Duck, who came paddling up some minutes afterwards. 'He has a great many good points, but for my own part I have a mother's feelings, and I can never look at a confirmed bachelor without the tears coming into my eyes.'

'I am rather afraid that I have annoyed him,' answered the Linnet. 'The fact is that I told him a story with a moral.'

'Ah! that is always a very dangerous thing to do,' said the Duck.

And I quite agree with her.

THE REMARKABLE ROCKET

THE King's son was going to be married, so there were general rejoicings. He had waited a whole year for his bride, and at last she had arrived. She was a Russian Princess, and had driven all the way from Finland in a sledge drawn by six reindeer. The sledge was shaped like a great golden swan, and between the swan's wings lay the little Princess herself. Her long ermine cloak reached right down to her feet, on her head was a tiny cap of silver tissue, and she was as pale as the Snow Palace in which she had always lived. So pale was she that as she drove through the streets all the people wondered. 'She is like a white rose!' they cried, and they threw down flowers on her from the balconies.

At the gate of the Castle the Prince was waiting to receive her. He had dreamy violet eyes, and his hair was like fine gold. When he saw her he sank upon one knee, and kissed her hand.

'Your picture was beautiful,' he murmured, 'but you are more beautiful than your picture;' and the little Princess blushed.

'She was like a white rose before,' said a young page to his neighbour, 'but she is like a red rose now;' and the whole Court was delighted.

For the next three days everybody went about saying, 'White rose, Red rose, Red rose, White rose,' and the King gave orders that the Page's salary was to be doubled. As he received no salary at all this was not of much use to him, but it was considered a great honour and was duly published in the Court Gazette.

When the three days were over the marriage was celebrated. It was a magnificent ceremony, and the bride and bridegroom walked hand in hand under a canopy of purple velvet embroidered with little pearls. Then there was a State Banquet, which lasted for five hours. The Prince and Princess sat at the top of the Great Hall and drank out of a cup of clear crystal. Only true lovers could drink out of this cup, for if false lips touched it, it grew grey and dull and cloudy.

'It is quite clear that they love each other,' said the little Page, 'as clear as crystal!' and the King doubled his salary a second time.

'What an honour!' cried all the courtiers.

After the banquet there was to be a Ball. The bride and bridegroom were to dance the Rose-dance together, and the King had promised to play the flute. He played very badly, but no one had ever dared to tell him so, because he was the King. Indeed, he knew only two airs, and was never quite certain which one he was playing; but it made no matter, for, whatever he did, everybody cried out, 'Charming! charming!'

The last item on the programme was a grand display of fireworks, to be let off exactly at midnight. The little Princess had never seen a firework in her life, so the King had given orders that the Royal Pyrotechnist should be in attendance on the day of her marriage.

'What are fireworks like?' she had asked the Prince, one morning, as she was walking on the terrace.

'They are like the Aurora Borealis,' said the King, who always answered questions that were addressed to other people, 'only much more natural. I prefer them to stars myself, as you always know when they are going to appear, and they are as delightful as my own flute-playing. You must certainly see them.'

So at the end of the King's garden a great stand had been set up, and as soon as the Royal Pyrotechnist had put everything in its proper place, the fireworks began to talk to each other.

'The world is certainly very beautiful,' cried a little Squib. 'Just look at those yellow tulips. Why! if they were real crackers they could not be lovelier. I am very glad I have travelled. Travel improves the mind wonderfully, and does away with all one's prejudices.'

'The King's garden is not the world, you foolish Squib,' said a big Roman Candle; 'the world is an enormous place, and it would take you three days to see it thoroughly.'

'Any place you love is the world to you,' exclaimed the pensive Catherine Wheel, who had been attached to an old deal box in early life, and prided herself on her broken heart; 'but love is not fashionable any more, the poets have killed it. They wrote so much about it that nobody believed them, and I am not surprised. True love suffers, and is silent. I remember myself once – But no matter now. Romance is a thing of the past.'

'Nonsense!' said the Roman Candle, 'Romance never dies. It is like the moon, and lives for ever. The bride and bridegroom, for instance, love each other very dearly. I heard all about them this morning from a brown-paper cartridge, who happened to be staying in the same drawer as myself, and he knew the latest Court news.'

But the Catherine Wheel shook her head. 'Romance is dead, Romance is dead, Romance is dead,' she murmured. She was one of those people who think that, if you say the same thing over and over a great many times, it becomes true in the end.

Suddenly, a sharp, dry cough was heard, and they all looked round.

It came from a tall, supercilious-looking Rocket, who was tied to the end of a long stick. He always coughed before he made any observations, so as to attract attention.

'Ahem! ahem!' he said, and everybody listened except the poor Catherine Wheel, who was still shaking her head, and murmuring, 'Romance is dead.'

'Order! order!' cried out a Cracker. He was something of a politician, and had always taken a prominent part in the local elections, so he knew the proper Parliamentary expressions to use.

'Quite dead,' whispered the Catherine Wheel, and she went off to sleep.

As soon as there was perfect silence, the Rocket coughed a third time and began. He spoke with a very slow, distinct voice, as if he were dictating his memoirs, and always looked over the shoulder of the person to whom he was talking. In fact, he had a most distinguished manner.

'How fortunate it is for the King's son,' he remarked, 'that he is to be married on the very day on which I am to be let off! Really, if it had not been arranged beforehand, it could not have turned out better for him; but Princes are always lucky.'

'Dear me!' said the little Squib, 'I thought it was quite the other way, and that we were to be let off in the Prince's honour.'

'It may be so with you,' he answered; 'indeed, I have no doubt that it is, but with me it is different. I am a very remarkable Rocket, and come of remarkable parents. My mother was the most celebrated Catherine Wheel of her day, and was renowned for her graceful dancing. When she made her great public appearance she spun round nineteen times before she went out, and each time that she did so she threw into the air seven pink stars. She was three feet and a half in diameter, and made of the very best gunpowder. My father was a Rocket like myself, and of French extraction. He flew so high that the people were afraid that he would never come down again. He did, though, for he was of a kindly disposition, and he made a most brilliant descent in a shower of golden rain. The newspapers wrote about his performance in very flattering terms. Indeed, the Court Gazette called him a triumph of Pylotechnic art.'

'Pyrotechnic, Pyrotechnic, you mean,' said a Bengal Light; 'I know it is Pyrotechnic, for I saw it written on my own canister.'

'Well, I said Pylotechnic,' answered the Rocket, in a severe tone of voice, and the Bengal Light felt so crushed that he began at once to bully the little squibs, in order to show that he was still a person of some importance.

'I was saying,' continued the Rocket, 'I was saying – What was I saying?'

'You were talking about yourself,' replied the Roman Candle.

'Of course; I knew I was discussing some interesting subject when I was so rudely interrupted. I hate rudeness and bad manners of every kind, for I am extremely sensitive. No one in the whole world is so sensitive as I am, I am quite sure of that.'

'What is a sensitive person?' said the Cracker to the Roman Candle.

'A person who, because he has corns himself, always treads on other people's toes,' answered the Roman Candle in a low whisper; and the Cracker nearly exploded with laughter.

'Pray, what are you laughing at?' inquired the Rocket; 'I am not laughing.'

'I am laughing because I am happy,' replied the Cracker.

'That is a very selfish reason,' said the Rocket angrily. 'What right have you to be happy? You should be thinking about others. In fact, you should be thinking about me. I am always thinking about myself, and I expect everybody else to do the same. That is what is called sympathy. It is a beautiful virtue, and I possess it in a high degree. Suppose, for instance, anything happened to me to-night, what a misfortune that would be for every one! The Prince and Princess would never be happy again, their whole married life would be spoiled; and as for the King, I know he would not get over it.

Really, when I begin to reflect on the importance of my position, I am almost moved to tears.'

'If you want to give pleasure to others,' cried the Roman Candle, 'you had better keep yourself dry.'

'Certainly,' exclaimed the Bengal Light, who was now in better spirits; 'that is only common sense.'

'Common sense, indeed!' said the Rocket indignantly; 'you forget that I am very uncommon, and very remarkable. Why, anybody can have common sense, provided that they have no imagination. But I have imagination, for I never think of things as they really are; I always think of them as being quite different. As for keeping myself dry, there is evidently no one here who can at all appreciate an emotional nature. Fortunately for myself, I don't care. The only thing that sustains one through life is the consciousness of the immense inferiority of everybody else, and this is a feeling I have always cultivated. But none of you have any hearts. Here you are laughing and making merry just as if the Prince and Princess had not just been married.'

'Well, really,' exclaimed a small Fire-balloon, 'why not? It is a most joyful occasion, and when I soar up into the air I intend to tell the stars all about it. You will see them twinkle when I talk to them about the pretty bride.'

'Ah! what a trivial view of life!' said the Rocket; 'but it is only what I expected. There is nothing in you; you are hollow and empty. Why, perhaps the Prince and Princess may go to live in a country where there is a deep river, and perhaps they may have one only son, a little fair-haired boy with violet eyes like the Prince himself; and perhaps some day he may go out to walk with his nurse; and perhaps the nurse may go to sleep under a great elder-tree; and perhaps the little boy may fall into the deep river and be drowned. What a terrible misfortune! Poor people, to lose their only son! It is really too dreadful! I shall never get over it.'

'But they have not lost their only son,' said the Roman Candle; 'no misfortune has happened to them at all.'

'I never said that they had,' replied the Rocket; 'I said that they might. If they had lost their only son there would be no use in saying any more about the matter. I hate people who cry over spilt milk. But when I think that they might lose their only son, I certainly am very much affected.'

'You certainly are!' cried the Bengal Light. 'In fact, you are the most affected person I ever met.'

'You are the rudest person I ever met,' said the Rocket, 'and you cannot understand my friendship for the Prince.'

'Why, you don't even know him,' growled the Roman Candle.

'I never said I knew him,' answered the Rocket. 'I dare say that if I knew him I should not be his friend at all. It is a very dangerous thing to know one's friends.'

'You had really better keep yourself dry,' said the Fire-balloon. 'That is the important thing.'

'Very important for you, I have no doubt,' answered the Rocket, 'but I shall weep if I choose;' and he actually burst into real tears, which flowed down his stick like raindrops, and nearly drowned two little beetles, who were just thinking of setting up house together, and were looking for a nice dry spot to live in.

'He must have a truly romantic nature,' said the Catherine Wheel, 'for he weeps when there is nothing at all to weep about;' and she heaved a deep sigh and thought about the deal box.

But the Roman Candle and the Bengal Light were quite indignant, and kept saying, 'Humbug! humbug!' at the top of their voices. They were extremely practical, and whenever they objected to anything they called it humbug.

Then the moon rose like a wonderful silver shield; and the stars began to shine, and a sound of music came from the palace.

The Prince and Princess were leading the dance. They danced so beautifully that the tall white lilies peeped in at the window and watched them, and the great red poppies nodded their heads and beat time.

Then ten o'clock struck, and then eleven, and then twelve, and at the last stroke of midnight every one came out on the terrace, and the King sent for the Royal Pyrotechnist.

'Let the fireworks begin,' said the King; and the Royal Pyrotechnist made a low bow, and marched down to the end of the garden. He had six attendants with him, each of whom carried a lighted torch at the end of a long pole.

It was certainly a magnificent display.

Whizz! Whizz! went the Catherine Wheel, as she spun round and round. Boom! Boom! went the Roman Candle. Then the Squibs danced all over the place, and the Bengal Lights made everything look scarlet. 'Good-bye,' cried the Fire-balloon, as he soared away, dropping tiny blue sparks. Bang! Bang! answered the Crackers, who were enjoying themselves immensely. Every one was a great success except the Remarkable Rocket. He was so damped with crying that he could not go off at all. The best thing in him was the gunpowder, and that was so wet with tears that it was of no use. All his poor relations, to whom he would never speak, except with a sneer, shot up into the sky like wonderful golden flowers with blossoms of fire. Huzza! Huzza! cried the Court; and the little Princess laughed with pleasure.

'I suppose they are reserving me for some grand occasion,' said the Rocket; 'no doubt that is what it means,' and he looked more supercilious than ever.

The next day the workmen came to put everything tidy. 'This is evidently a deputation,' said the Rocket; 'I will receive them with becoming dignity:' so he put his nose in the air, and began to frown severely, as if he were thinking about some very important subject. But they took no notice of him at all till they were just going away. Then one of them caught sight of him. 'Hallo!' he cried, 'what a bad rocket!' and he threw him over the wall into the ditch.

'BAD ROCKET? BAD ROCKET?' he said, as he whirled through the air; 'impossible! GRAND ROCKET, that is what the man said. BAD and GRAND sound very much the same, indeed they often are the same;' and he fell into the mud.

'It is not comfortable here,' he remarked, 'but no doubt it is some fashionable watering-place, and they have sent me away to recruit my health. My nerves are certainly very much shattered, and I require rest.'

Then a little Frog, with bright jewelled eyes, and a green mottled coat, swam up to him.

'A new arrival, I see!' said the Frog. 'Well, after all there is nothing like mud. Give me rainy weather and a ditch, and I am quite happy. Do you think it will be a wet afternoon? I am sure I hope so, but the sky is quite blue and cloudless. What a pity!'

'Ahem! ahem!' said the Rocket, and he began to cough.

'What a delightful voice you have!' cried the Frog. 'Really it is quite like a croak, and croaking is, of course, the most musical sound in the world. You will hear our glee-club this evening. We sit in the old duck-pond close by the farmer's house, and as soon as the moon rises we begin. It is so entrancing that everybody lies awake to listen to us. In fact, it was only yesterday that I heard the farmer's wife say to her mother that she could not get a wink of sleep at night on account of us. It is most gratifying to find oneself so popular.'

'Ahem! ahem!' said the Rocket angrily. He was very much annoyed that he could not get a word in.

'A delightful voice, certainly,' continued the Frog; 'I hope you will come over to the duck-pond. I am off to look for my daughters. I have six beautiful daughters, and I am so afraid the Pike may meet them. He is a perfect monster, and would have no hesitation in breakfasting off them. Well, good-bye; I have enjoyed our conversation very much, I assure you.'

'Conversation, indeed!' said the Rocket. 'You have talked the whole time yourself. That is not conversation.'

'Somebody must listen,' answered the Frog, 'and I like to do all the talking myself. It saves time, and prevents arguments.'

'But I like arguments,' said the Rocket.

'I hope not,' said the Frog complacently. 'Arguments are extremely vulgar, for everybody in good society holds exactly the same opinions. Good-bye a second time; I see my daughters in the distance;' and the little Frog swam away.

'You are a very irritating person,' said the Rocket, 'and very ill-bred. I hate people who talk about themselves, as you do, when one wants to talk about oneself, as I do. It is what I call selfishness, and selfishness is a most detestable thing, especially to any one of my temperament, for I am well known for my sympathetic nature. In fact, you should take example by me; you could not possibly have a better model. Now that you have the chance you had better avail yourself of it, for I am going back to Court almost immediately. I am a great favourite at Court; in fact, the Prince and Princess were married yesterday in my honour. Of course, you know nothing of these matters, for you are a provincial.'

'There is no good talking to him,' said a Dragonfly, who was sitting on the top of a large brown bulrush; 'no good at all, for he has gone away.'

'Well, that is his loss, not mine,' answered the Rocket. 'I am not going to stop talking to him merely because he pays no attention. I like hearing myself talk. It is one of my greatest pleasures. I often have long conversations all by myself, and I am so clever that sometimes I don't understand a single word of what I am saying.'

'Then you should certainly lecture on Philosophy,' said the Dragon-fly, and he spread a pair of lovely gauze wings and soared away into the sky.

'How very silly of him not to stay here!' said the Rocket. 'I am sure that he has not often got such a chance of improving his mind. However, I don't care a bit. Genius like mine is sure to be appreciated some day;' and he sank down a little deeper into the mud.

After some time a large White Duck swam up to him. She had yellow legs, and webbed feet, and was considered a great beauty on account of her waddle.

'Quack, quack, quack,' she said. 'What a curious shape you are! May I ask were you born like that, or is it the result of an accident?'

'It is quite evident that you have always lived in the country,' answered the Rocket, 'otherwise you would know who I am. However, I excuse your ignorance. It would be unfair to expect other people to be as remarkable as oneself. You will no doubt be surprised to hear that I can fly up into the sky, and come down in a shower of golden rain.'

'I don't think much of that,' said the Duck, 'as I cannot see what use it is to any one. Now, if you could plough the fields like the ox, or draw a cart like the horse, or look after the sheep like the collie-dog, that would be something.'

'My good creature,' cried the Rocket in a very haughty tone of voice, 'I see that you belong to the lower orders. A person of my position is never useful. We have certain accomplishments, and that is more than sufficient. I have no sympathy myself with industry of any kind, least of all with such industries as you seem to recommend. Indeed, I have always been of opinion that hard work is simply the refuge of people who have nothing whatever to do.'

'Well, well,' said the Duck, who was of a very peaceful disposition, and never quarrelled with any one, 'everybody has different tastes. I hope, at any rate, that you are going to take up your residence here.'

'Oh! dear no,' cried the Rocket. 'I am merely a visitor, a distinguished visitor. The fact is that I find this place rather tedious. There is neither society here, nor solitude. In fact, it is essentially suburban. I shall probably go back to Court, for I know that I am destined to make a sensation in the world.'

'I had thoughts of entering public life once myself,' remarked the Duck; 'there are so many things that need reforming. Indeed, I took the chair at a meeting some time ago, and we passed resolutions condemning everything that we did not like. However, they did not seem to have much effect. Now I go in for domesticity, and look after my family.'

'I am made for public life,' said the Rocket, 'and so are all my relations, even the humblest of them. Whenever we appear we excite great attention. I have not actually appeared myself, but when I do so it will be a magnificent sight. As for domesticity, it ages one rapidly, and distracts one's mind from higher things.'

'Ah! the higher things of life, how fine they are!' said the Duck; 'and that reminds me how hungry I feel:' and she swam away down the stream, saying, 'Quack, quack, quack.'

'Come back! come back!' screamed the Rocket, 'I have a great deal to say to you;' but the Duck paid no attention to him. 'I am glad that she has gone,' he said to himself, 'she has a decidedly middle-class mind;' and he sank a little deeper still into the mud, and began to think about the loneliness of genius, when suddenly two little boys in white smocks came running down the bank, with a kettle and some faggots.

'This must be the deputation,' said the Rocket, and he tried to look very dignified.

'Hallo!' cried one of the boys, 'look at this old stick; I wonder how it came here:' and he picked the Rocket out of the ditch.

'OLD STICK!' said the Rocket, 'impossible! GOLD STICK, that is what he said. Gold Stick is very complimentary. In fact, he mistakes me for one of the Court dignitaries!'

'Let us put it into the fire!' said the other boy, 'it will help to boil the kettle.'

So they piled the faggots together, and put the Rocket on top, and lit the fire.

'This is magnificent,' cried the Rocket, 'they are going to let me off in broad daylight, so that every one can see me.'

'We will go to sleep now,' they said, 'and when we wake up the kettle will be boiled;' and they lay down on the grass, and shut their eyes.

The Rocket was very damp, so he took a long time to burn. At last, however, the fire caught him.

'Now I am going off!' he cried, and he made himself very stiff and straight. 'I know I shall go much higher than the stars, much higher than the moon, much higher than the sun. In fact, I shall go so high that –'

Fizz! Fizz! Fizz! and he went straight up into the air.

'Delightful!' he cried, 'I shall go on like this for ever. What a success I am!' But nobody saw him.

Then he began to feel a curious tingling sensation all over him.

'Now I am going to explode,' he cried. 'I shall set the whole world on fire, and make such a noise that nobody will talk about anything else for a whole year.' And he certainly did explode. Bang! Bang! Bang! went the gunpowder. There was no doubt about it.

But nobody heard him, not even the two little boys, for they were sound asleep.

Then all that was left of him was the stick, and this fell down on the back of a Goose who was taking a walk by the side of the ditch.

'Good heavens!' cried the Goose. 'It is going to rain sticks;' and she rushed into the water.

'I knew I should create a great sensation,' gasped the Rocket, and he went out.

THE PORTRAIT OF MR. W. H.

1

I HAD been dining with Erskine in his pretty little house in Birdcage Walk, and we were sitting in the library over our coffee and cigarettes, when the question of literary forgeries happened to turn up in conversation. I cannot at present remember how it was that we struck upon this somewhat curious topic, as it was at that time, but I know we had a long discussion about Macpherson, Ireland, and Chatterton, and that with regard to the last I insisted that his so-called forgeries were merely the result of an artistic desire for perfect representation; that we had no right to quarrel with an artist for the conditions under which he chooses to present his work; and that all Art being to a certain degree a mode of acting, an attempt to realise one's own personality on some imaginative plane out of reach of the trammelling accidents and limitations of real life, to censure an artist for a forgery was to confuse an ethical with an aesthetical problem.

Erskine, who was a good deal older than I was, and had been listening to me with the amused deference of a man of forty, suddenly put his hand upon my shoulder and said to me, 'What would you say about a young man who had a strange theory about a certain work of art, believed in his theory, and committed a forgery in order to prove it?'

'Ah! That is quite a different matter,' I answered.

Erskine remained silent for a few moments, looking at the thin grey threads of smoke that were rising from his cigarette. 'Yes,' he said, after a pause, 'quite different.'

There was something in the tone of his voice, a slight touch of bitterness perhaps, that excited my curiosity. 'Did you ever know anybody who did that?' I cried.

'Yes,' he answered, throwing his cigarette into the fire – 'a great friend of mine, Cyril Graham. He was very fascinating, and very foolish, and very heartless. However, he left me the only legacy I ever received in my life.'

'What was that?' I exclaimed laughing. Erskine rose from his seat, and going over to a tall inlaid cabinet that stood between the two windows, unlocked it, and came back to where I was sitting, carrying a small panel picture set in an old and somewhat tarnished Elizabethan frame.

It was a full-length portrait of a young man in late sixteenth-century costume, standing by a table, with his right hand resting on an open book. He seemed about seventeen years of age, and was of quite extraordinary personal beauty, though evidently somewhat effeminate. Indeed, had it not been for the dress and the closely cropped hair, one would have said that the face, with its dreamy, wistful eyes and its delicate scarlet lips, was the face of a girl. In manner, and especially in the treatment of the hands, the picture reminded one of François Clouet's later work. The black velvet doublet with its fantastically gilded points, and the peacock-blue background against which it showed up so pleasantly, and from which it gained such luminous value of colour, were quite in Clouet's style; and the two masks of Tragedy and Comedy that hung somewhat formally from the marble pedestal had that hard severity of touch – so different from the facile grace of the Italians – which even at the Court of France the great Flemish master never completely lost, and which in itself has always been a characteristic of the northern temper.

'It is a charming thing,' I cried, 'but who is this wonderful young man whose beauty Art has so happily preserved for us?'

'This is the portrait of Mr. W. H.,' said Erskine, with a sad smile. It might have been a chance effect of light, but it seemed to me that his eyes were swimming with tears.

'Mr. W. H.!' I repeated; 'who was Mr. W. H.?'

'Don't you remember?' he answered; 'look at the book on which his hand is resting.'

'I see there is some writing there, but I cannot make it out,' I replied.

'Take this magnifying-glass and try,' said Erskine, with the same sad smile still playing about his mouth.

I took the glass, and moving the lamp a little nearer, I began to spell out the crabbed sixteenth-century handwriting. 'To The Onlie Begetter Of These Insuing Sonnets.' . . . 'Good heavens!' I cried, 'is this Shakespeare's Mr. W. H.?'

'Cyril Graham used to say so,' muttered Erskine.

'But it is not a bit like Lord Pembroke,' I rejoined. 'I know the Wilton portraits very well. I was staying near there a few weeks ago.'

'Do you really believe then that the Sonnets are addressed to Lord Pembroke?' he asked.

'I am sure of it,' I answered. 'Pembroke, Shakespeare, and Mrs. Mary Fitton are the three personages of the Sonnets; there is no doubt at all about it.'

'Well, I agree with you,' said Erskine, 'but I did not always think so. I used to believe – well, I suppose I used to believe in Cyril Graham and his theory.'

'And what was that?' I asked, looking at the wonderful portrait, which had already begun to have a strange fascination for me.

'It is a long story,' he murmured, taking the picture away from me – rather abruptly I thought at the time – 'a very long story; but if you care to hear it, I will tell it to you.'

'I love theories about the Sonnets,' I cried; 'but I don't think I am likely to be converted to any new idea. The matter has ceased to be a mystery to any one. Indeed, I wonder that it ever was a mystery.'

'As I don't believe in the theory, I am not likely to convert you to it,' said Erskine, laughing; 'but it may interest you.'

'Tell it to me, of course,' I answered. 'If it is half as delightful as the picture, I shall be more than satisfied.'

'Well,' said Erskine, lighting a cigarette, 'I must begin by telling you about Cyril Graham himself. He and I were at the same house at Eton. I was a year or two older than he was, but we were immense friends, and did all our work and all our play together. There was, of course, a good deal more play than work, but I cannot say that I am sorry for that. It is always an advantage not to have received a sound commercial education, and what I learned in the playing fields at Eton has been quite as useful to me as anything I was taught at Cambridge. I should tell you that Cyril's father and mother were both dead. They had been drowned in a horrible yachting accident off the Isle of Wight. His father had been in the diplomatic service, and had married a daughter, the only daughter, in fact, of old Lord Crediton, who became Cyril's guardian after the death of his parents. I don't think that Lord Crediton cared very much for Cyril. He had never really forgiven his daughter for marrying a man who had no title. He was extraordinary old aristocrat, who swore like a costermonger, and had the manners of a farmer. I remember seeing him once on Speech-day. He growled at me, gave me a sovereign, and told me not to grow up 'a damned Radical' like my father. Cyril had very little affection for him, and was only too glad to spend most of his holidays with us in Scotland. They never really got on together at all. Cyril thought him a bear, and he thought Cyril effeminate. He was effeminate, I suppose, in some things, though he was a capital rider and a capital fencer. In fact he got the foils before he left Eton. But he was very languid in his manner, and not a little vain of his good looks, and had a strong objection to football, which he used to say was a game only suitable for the sons of the middle classes. The two things that really gave him pleasure were poetry and acting. At Eton he was always dressing up and reciting Shakespeare, and when we went up to Trinity he became a member of the A.D.C. in his first term. I remember I was always very jealous of his acting. I was absurdly devoted to him; I suppose because we were so different in most things. I was a rather awkward, weakly lad, with huge feet, and horribly freckled. Freckles run in Scotch families just as gout does in English families. Cyril used to say that of the two he preferred the gout; but he always set an absurdly high value on personal appearance, and once read a paper before our Debating Society to prove that it was better to be good-looking than to be good. He certainly was wonderfully handsome. People who did not like him, philistines and college tutors, and young men reading for the Church, used to say that he was merely pretty; but there was a great deal more in his face than mere prettiness. I think he was the most splendid creature I ever saw, and nothing could exceed the grace of his movements, the charm of his manner. He fascinated everybody who was worth fascinating, and a great many people who were not. He was often wilful and petulant, and I used to think him dreadfully insincere. It was due, I think, chiefly to his inordinate desire to please. Poor Cyril! I told him once that he was contented with very cheap triumphs, but he only tossed his head, and smiled. He was horribly spoiled. All charming people, I fancy, are spoiled. It is the secret of their attraction.

'However, I must tell you about Cyril's acting. You know that no women are allowed to play at the A.D.C. At least they were not in my time. I don't know how it is now. Well, of course Cyril was always cast for the girls' parts, and when *As You Like It* was produced he played Rosalind. It was a marvellous performance. You will laugh at me, but I assure you that Cyril Graham was the only perfect Rosalind I have ever seen. It would be impossible to describe to you the beauty, the delicacy, the refinement of the whole thing. It made an immense sensation, and the horrid little theatre as it was then, was crowded every night. Even now when I read the play I can't help thinking of Cyril; the part might have been written for him, he played it with such extraordinary grace and distinction. The next term he took his degree, and came to London to read for the Diplomatic. But he never did any work. He spent his days in reading Shakespeare's Sonnets, and his evenings at the theatre. He was, of course, wild to go on the stage. It was all that Lord Crediton and I could do to prevent him. Perhaps, if he had gone on the stage he would be alive now. It is always a silly thing to give advice, but to give good advice is absolutely fatal. I hope you will never fall into that error. If you do, you will be sorry for it.

'Well, to come to the real point of the story, one afternoon I got a letter from Cyril asking me to come round to his rooms that evening. He had charming chambers in Piccadilly overlooking the Green Park, and as I used to go to see him almost every day, I was rather surprised at his taking the trouble to write. Of course I went, and when I arrived I found him in a state of great excitement. He told me that he had at last discovered the true secret of Shakespeare's Sonnets; that all the scholars and critics had been entirely on the wrong track; and that he was the first who, working purely by internal evidence, had found out who Mr. W. H. really was. He was perfectly wild with delight, and for a long time would not tell me his theory. Finally, he produced a bundle of notes, took his copy of the Sonnets off the mantelpiece, and sat down and gave me a long lecture on the whole subject.

'He began by pointing out that the young man to whom Shakespeare addressed these strangely passionate poems must have been somebody who was a really vital factor in the development of his dramatic art, and that this could not be said of either Lord Pembroke or Lord Southampton. Indeed, whoever he was, he could not have been anybody of high birth, as was shown very clearly by Sonnet xxv, in which Shakespeare contrasts himself with men who are "great princes' favourites"; says quite frankly –

> "Let those who are in favour with their stars
> Of public honour and proud titles boast,
> Whilst I, whom fortune of such triumph bars,
> Unlooked for joy in that I honour most;"

and ends the sonnet by congratulating himself on the mean state of him he so adored:

> "Then happy I, that love and am beloved

Where I may not remove nor be removed"

This sonnet Cyril declared would be quite unintelligible if we fancied that it
was addressed to either the Earl of Pembroke or the Earl of Southampton,
both of whom were men of the highest position in England and fully entitled
to be called "great princes"; he in corroboration of his view read me Sonnets
cxxiv and cxxv, in which Shakespeare tells us that his love is not "the child of
state," that it "suffers not in smiling pomp" but is "builded far from acci-
dent." I listened with a good deal of interest, for I don't think the point had
ever been made before; but what followed was still more curious, and seemed
to me at the time to dispose entirely of Pembroke's claim. We know from
Meres that the Sonnets had been written before 1598, and Sonnet civ in-
forms us that Shakespeare's friendship for Mr. W. H. been already in exist-
ence for three years. Now Lord Pembroke, who was born in 1580, did not
come to London till he was eighteen years of age, that is to say till 1598, and
Shakespeare's acquaintance with Mr. W. H. must have begun in 1594, or at
the latest in 1595. Shakespeare, accordingly, could not have known Lord
Pembroke until after the Sonnets had been written.

'Cyril pointed out also that Pembroke's father did not die until 1601;
whereas it was evident from the line,

"You had a father, let your son say so,"

that the father of Mr. W. H. was dead in 1598; and laid great stress on the
evidence afforded by the Wilton portraits which represent Lord Pembroke
as a swarthy dark-haired man, while Mr. W. H. was one whose hair was spun
like spun gold, and whose face the meeting-place for the "lily's white" and
the "deep vermilion in the rose"; being himself "fair," and "red," and
"white and red," and of beautiful aspect. Besides it was absurd to imagine
that any publisher of the time, and the preface is from the publisher's hand,
would have dreamed of addressing William Herbert, Earl of Pembroke, as
Mr. W. H.; the case of Lord Buckhurst being spoken of as Mr. Sackville be-
ing not really a parallel instance, as Lord Buckhurst, the first of that title, was
plain Mr. Sackville when he contributed to the "Mirror for Magistrates,"
while Pembroke, during his father's lifetime, was always known as Lord
Herbert. So far for Lord Pembroke, whose supposed claims Cyril easily de-
molished while I sat by in wonder. With Lord Southampton Cyril had even
less difficulty. Southampton became at a very early age the lover of Elizabeth
Vernon, so he needed no entreaties to marry; he was not beautiful; he did not
resemble his mother, as Mr. W. H. did –

"Thou art thy mother's glass, and she in thee
Calls back the lovely April of her prime;"

and, above all, his Christian name was Henry, whereas the punning sonnets
(CXXXV and CXLIII) show that the Christian name of Shakespeare's
friend was the same as his own – Will.

'As for the other suggestions of unfortunate commentators, that Mr.

W.H. is a misprint for Mr. W. S., meaning Mr. William Shakespeare; that "Mr. W. H. all" should read "Mr. W. Hall"; that Mr. W. H. is Mr. William Hathaway; that Mr. W. H. stands for Mr. Henry Willobie, the young Oxford poet, with the initials of his name reversed; and that a full stop should be placed after "wisheth," making Mr. W. H. the writer and not the subject of the dedication, – Cyril got rid of them in a very short time; and it is not worth while to mention his reasons, though I remember he sent me off into a fit of laughter by reading to me, I am glad to say not in the original, some extracts from a German commentator called Barnstorff, who insisted that Mr. W.H. was no less a person than "Mr. William Himself." Nor would he allow for a moment that the Sonnets are mere satires on the work of Drayton and John Davies of Hereford. To him, as indeed to me, they were poems of serious and tragic import, wrung out of the bitterness of Shakespeare's heart, and made sweet by the honey of his lips. Still less would he admit that they were merely a philosophical allegory, and that in them Shakespeare is addressing his Ideal Self, or Ideal Manhood, or the Spirit of Beauty, or the Reason, or the Divine Logos, or the Catholic Church. He felt, as indeed I think we all must feel, that the Sonnets are addressed to an individual, – to a particular young man whose personality for some reason seems to have filled the soul of Shakespeare with terrible joy and no less terrible despair.

'Having in this manner cleared the way, as it were, Cyril asked me to dismiss from my mind any preconceived ideas I might have formed on the subject, and to give a fair and unbiased hearing to his own theory. The problem he pointed out was this: Who was that young man of Shakespeare's day who, without being of noble birth or even of noble nature, was addressed by him in terms of such passionate adoration that we can but wonder at the strange worship, and are almost afraid to turn the key that unlocks the mystery of the poet's heart? Who was he whose physical beauty was such that it became the very corner-stone of Shakespeare's art; the very source of Shakespeare's inspiration; the very incarnation of Shakespeare's dreams? To look upon him as simply the object of certain love-poems was to miss the whole meaning of the poems: for the art of which Shakespeare talks in the Sonnets is not the art of the Sonnets themselves, which indeed were to him but slight and secret things – it is the art of the dramatist to which he is always alluding; and he to whom Shakespeare said –

> "Thou art all my art, and dost advance
> As high as learning my rude ignorance," –

he to whom he promised immortality,

> "Where breath most breathes, even in the mouths of men," –

he who was to him the tenth "muse" and

> "Ten times more in worth
> Than those old nine which rhymers invocate,"

was surely none other than the boy-actor for whom he created Viola and

Imogen, Juliet and Rosalind, Portia and Desdemona, and Cleopatra herself.'

'The boy-actor of Shakespeare's plays?' I cried.

'Yes,' said Erskine. 'This was Cyril Graham's theory, evolved as you see purely from the Sonnets themselves, and depending for its acceptance not so much on demonstrable proof or formal evidence, but on a kind of spiritual and artistic sense, by which alone he claimed could the true meaning of the poems be discerned. I remember his reading to me that fine sonnet –

> "How can my Muse want subject to invent,
> While thou dost breathe, that pour'st into my verse
> Thine own sweet argument, too excellent
> For every vulgar paper to rehearse
> O give thyself the thanks, if aught in me
> Worthy perusal stand against thy sight;
> For who's so dumb that cannot write to thee,
> When thou thyself dost give invention light?"

– and pointing out how completely it corroborated his view; and indeed he went through all the Sonnets carefully, and showed, or fancied that he showed, that, according to his new explanation of their meaning, things that had seemed obscure, or evil, or exaggerated, became clear and rational, and of high artistic import, illustrating Shakespeare's conception of the true relations between the art of the actor and the art of the dramatist.

'It is of course evident that there must have been in Shakespeare's company some wonderful boy-actor of great beauty, to whom he intrusted the presentation of his noble heroines; for Shakespeare was a practical theatrical manager as well as an imaginative poet, and Cyril Graham had actually discovered the boy-actor's name. He was Will, or as he preferred to call him, Willie Hughes. The Christian name he found of course in the punning sonnets, CXXXV and CXLIII; the surname was, according to him, hidden in the seventh line of Sonnet XX, where Mr. W. H. is described as –

> "A man in hew, all *Hews* in his controwling."

'In the original edition of the Sonnets "Hews" is printed with a capital letter and in italics, and this, he claimed, showed clearly that a play on words was intended, his view receiving a good deal of corroboration from those sonnets in which curious puns are made on the words "use" and "usury," and from such lines as –

> "Thou art as fair in knowledge as in hew."

Of course I was converted at once, and Willie Hughes became to me as real a person as Shakespeare. The only objection I made to the theory was that the name of Willie Hughes does not occur in the list of the actors of Shakespeare's company as it is printed in the first folio. Cyril, however, pointed out that the absence of Willie Hughes' name from this list really corroborated the theory, as it was evident from Sonnet LXXXVI, that he had abandoned Shakespeare's company to play at a rival theatre, probably in some of

Chapman's plays. It was in reference to this that in the great sonnet on Chapman Shakespeare said to Willie Hughes –

> "But when your countenance filled up his line,
> Then lacked I matter; that enfeebled mine"–

the expression "when your countenance filled up his line" referring clearly to the beauty of the young actor giving life and reality and added charm to Chapman's verse, the same idea being also put forward in Sonnet LXXIX:

> "Whilst I alone did call upon thy aid,
> My verse alone had all thy gentle grace,
> But now my gracious numbers are decayed,
> And my sick Muse doth give another place";

and in the immediately preceding sonnet, where Shakespeare says,

> "Every alien pen hath got my *use*
> And under thee their poesy disperse",

the play upon words (use = Hughes) being of course obvious, and the phrase "under thee their poesy disperse," meaning "by your assistance as an actor bring their plays before the people."

'It was a wonderful evening, and we sat up almost till dawn reading and re-reading the Sonnets. After some time, however, I began to see that before the theory could be placed before the world in a really perfected form, it was necessary to get some independent evidence about the existence of this young actor, Willie Hughes. If this could be once established, there could be no possible doubt about his identity with Mr. W. H.; but otherwise the theory would fall to the ground. I put this forward very strongly to Cyril, who was a good deal annoyed at what he called my philistine tone of mind, and indeed was rather bitter upon the subject. However, I made him promise that in his own interest he would not publish his discovery till he had put the whole matter beyond the reach of doubt; and for weeks and weeks we searched the registers of City Churches, the Alleyn MSS. at Dulwich, the Record Office, the books of the Lord Chamberlain – everything, in fact, that we thought might contain some allusion to Willie Hughes. We discovered nothing, of course, and each day the existence of Willie Hughes seemed to me to become more problematical. Cyril was in a dreadful state, and used to go over the whole question again and again, entreating me to believe; but I saw the one flaw in the theory, and I refused to be convinced till the actual existence of Willie Hughes, a boy-actor of the Elizabethan stage, had been placed beyond the reach of doubt or cavil.

'One day Cyril left town to stay with his grandfather, I thought at the time, but I afterwards heard from Lord Crediton that this was not the case; and about a fortnight afterwards I received a telegram from him, handed in at Warwick, asking me to be sure to come and dine with him in his chambers, that evening at eight o'clock. When I arrived, he said to me, "The only apostle who did not deserve proof was St. Thomas, and St. Thomas was the only apostle who got it." I asked him what he meant. He answered that he had been able not merely to establish the existence in the sixteenth century of a boy-actor of the name of Willie Hughes, but to prove by the most conclusive evidence that he was the Mr. W. H. of the Sonnets. He would not tell me anything more at the time; but after dinner he solemnly produced the picture I showed you, and told me that he had discovered it by the merest chance nailed to the side of an old chest that he had bought at a farmhouse in Warwickshire. The chest itself, which was a very fine example of Elizabethan work, and thoroughly authentic, he had, of course, brought with him, and in the centre of the front panel the initials W. H. were undoubtedly carved. It was this monogram that had attracted his attention, and he told me that it was not till he had had the chest in his possession for several days that he had thought of making any careful examination of the inside. One morning, however, he saw that the right-hand side of the chest was much thicker than the other, and looking more closely, he discovered that a framed panel was clamped against it. On taking it out, he found it was the picture that is now lying on the sofa. It was very dirty, and covered with mould; but he managed to clean it, and, to his great joy, saw that he had fallen by mere chance on the one thing for which he had been looking. Here was an authentic portrait of Mr. W. H. with his hand resting on the dedicatory page of the Sonnets, and on the corner of the picture could be faintly seen the name of the young man himself written in gold uncial letters on the faded *bleu de paon* ground, "Master Will Hews."

'Well, what was I to say? It is quite clear from Sonnet XLVII that Shakespeare had a portrait of Mr. W. H. in his possession, and it seemed to me more than probable that here we had the very "painted banquet" on which he invited his eye to feast; the actual picture that awoke his heart "to heart's and eye's delight." It never occurred to me for a moment that Cyril Graham was playing a trick on me, or that he was trying to prove his theory by means of a forgery.'

'But is it a forgery?' I asked.

'Of course it is,' said Erskine. 'It is a very good forgery; but it is a forgery none the less. I thought at the time that Cyril was rather calm about the whole matter; but I remember he kept telling me that he himself required no proof of the kind, and that he thought the theory complete without it. I laughed at him, and told him that without it the entire theory would fall to the ground, and I warmly congratulated him on his marvellous discovery. We then arranged that the picture should be etched or facsimiled, and placed as the frontispiece to Cyril's edition of the Sonnets; and for three months we did nothing but go over each poem line by line, till we had settled every difficulty of text or meaning. One unlucky day I was in a print-shop in Holborn, when I saw upon the counter some extremely beautiful drawings in silverpoint. I was so attracted by them that I bought them; and the proprietor of the place, a man called Rawlings, told me that they were done by a young painter of the name of Edward Merton, who was very clever, but as poor as a church mouse. I went to see Merton some days afterwards, having got his address from the print-seller, and found a pale, interesting young man, with a rather common-looking wife, – his model, as I subsequently learned. I told him how much I admired his drawings, at which he seemed very pleased, and I asked him if he would show me some of his other work. As we were looking over a portfolio, full of really very lovely things, – for Merton had a most delicate and delightful touch, – I suddenly caught sight of a drawing of the picture of Mr. W. H. There was no doubt whatever about it. It was almost a facsimile, – the only difference being that the two masks of Tragedy and Comedy were not suspended from the marble table as they are in the picture but were lying on the floor at the young man's feet. "Where on earth did you get that?" I asked. He grew rather confused, and said, – "Oh, that is nothing. I did not know it was in this portfolio. It is not a thing of any value." "It is what you did for Mr. Cyril Graham," exclaimed his wife; "and if this gentleman wishes to buy it, let him have it." "For Mr. Cyril Graham?" I repeated. "Did you paint the picture of Mr. W. H.?" "I don't understand what you mean," he answered, growing very red. Well, the whole thing was quite dreadful. The wife let it all out. I gave her five pounds when I was going away. I can't bear to think of it, now; but of course I was furious. I went off at once to Cyril's chambers, waited there for three hours before he came in, with that horried lie staring me in the face, and told him I had discovered his forgery. He grew very pale, and said, – "I did it purely for your sake. You would not be convinced in any other way. It does not affect the truth of the theory." "The truth of the theory!" I exclaimed; "the less we talk about that the better. You never even believed in it yourself. If you had, you would not have committed a forgery to prove it." High words passed between us; we had a fearful quarrel. I daresay I was unjust, and the next morning he was dead.'

'Dead!' I cried.

'Yes, he shot himself with a revolver. By the time I arrived, – his servant had sent for me at once, – the police were already there. He had left a letter for me, evidently written in the greatest agitation and distress of mind.'

'What was in it?' I asked.

'Oh, that he believed absolutely in Willie Hughes; that the forgery of the picture had been done simply as a concession to me, and did not in the slightest degree invalidate the truth of the theory; and that in order to show me how firm and flawless his faith in the whole thing was, he was going to offer his life as a sacrifice to the secret of the Sonnets. It was a foolish, mad letter. I remember he ended by saying that he intrusted to me the Willie Hughes theory, and that it was for me to present it to the world, and to unlock the secret of Shakespeare's heart.'

'It is a most tragic story,' I cried, 'but why have you not carried out his wishes?'

Erskine shrugged his shoulders. 'Because it is a perfectly unsound theory from beginning to end,' he answered.

'My dear Erskine,' I exclaimed, getting up from my seat, 'you are entirely wrong about the whole matter. It is the only perfect key to Shakespeare's

Sonnets that has ever been made. It is complete in every detail. I believe in Willie Hughes.'

'Don't say that,' said Erskine gravely; 'I believe there is something fatal about the idea, and intellectually there is nothing to be said for it. I have gone into the whole matter, and I assure you the theory is entirely fallacious. It is plausible up to a certain point. Then it stops. For heaven's sake, my dear boy, don't take up the subject of Willie Hughes. You will break your heart over it.'

'Erskine,' I answered, 'it is your duty to give this theory to the world. If you will not do it, I will. By keeping it back you wrong the memory of Cyril Graham, the youngest and the most splendid of all the martyrs of literature. I entreat you to do him this bare act of justice. He died for this thing, – don't let his death be in vain.'

Erskine looked at me in amazement. 'You are carried away by the sentiment of the whole story,' he said. 'You forget that a thing is not necessarily true because a man dies for it. I was devoted to Cyril Graham. His death was a horrible blow to me. I did not recover from it for years. I don't think I have ever recovered from it. But Willie Hughes! There is nothing in the idea of Willie Hughes. No such person ever existed. As for bringing the matter before the world, – the world thinks that Cyril Graham shot himself by accident. The only proof of his suicide was contained in the letter to me, and of this letter the public never heard anything. To the present day Lord Crediton is under the impression that the whole thing was accidental.'

'Cyril Graham sacrificed his life to a great idea,' I answered; 'and if you will not tell of his martyrdom, tell at least of his faith.'

'His faith,' said Erskine, 'was fixed in a thing that was false, in a thing that was unsound, in a thing that no Shakespearian scholar would accept for a moment. The theory would be laughed at. Don't make a fool of yourself, and don't follow a trail that leads nowhere. You start by assuming the existence of the very person whose existence is the thing to be proved. Besides, everybody knows that the Sonnets were addressed to Lord Pembroke. The matter is settled once for all.'

'The matter is not settled,' I exclaimed. 'I will take up the theory where Cyril Graham left it, and I will prove to the world that he was right.'

'Silly boy!' said Erskine. 'Go home, it is after three, and don't think about Willie Hughes any more. I am sorry I told you anything about it, and very sorry indeed that I should have converted you to a thing in which I don't believe.'

'You have given me the key to the greatest mystery of modern literature,' I answered; 'and I will not rest till I have made you recognise, till I have made everybody recognise, that Cyril Graham was the most subtle Shakespearean critic of our day.'

I was about to leave the room when Erskine called me back. 'My dear fellow,' he said, 'let me advise you not to waste your time over the Sonnets. I am quite serious. After all, what do they tell us about Shakespeare? Simply that he was the slave of beauty.'

'Well, that is the condition of being an artist!' I replied.

There was a strange silence for a few moments. Then Erskine got up, and looking at me with half closed eyes, said, 'Ah! How you remind me of Cyril! He used to say just that sort of thing to me.' He tried to smile, but there was a note of poignant pathos in his voice that I remember to the present day, as one remembers the tone of a particular violin that has charmed one, the touch of a particular woman's hand. The great events of life often leave one unmoved; they pass out of consciousness, and, when one thinks of them, become unreal. Even the scarlet flowers of passion seem to grow in the same meadow as the poppies of oblivion. We regret the burden of their memory, and have anodynes against them. But the little things, the things of no moment, remain with us. In some tiny ivory cell the brain stores the most delicate, and the most fleeting impressions.

As I walked home through St. James's Park, the dawn was just breaking over London. The swans were lying asleep on the smooth surface of the polished lake, like white feathers fallen upon a mirror of black steel. The gaunt Palace looked purple against the pale green sky, and in the garden of Stafford House the birds were just beginning to sing. I thought of Cyril Graham, and my eyes filled with tears.

2

IT was past twelve when I awoke, and the sun was streaming in through the curtains of my room in long dusty beams of tremulous gold. I told my servant that I would not be at home to anyone, and after I had discussed a cup of chocolate and a *petit-pain*, I took out of the library my copy of Shakespeare's Sonnets, and Mr. Tyler's facsimile edition of the Quarto, and began to go carefully through them. Each poem seemed to me to corroborate Cyril Graham's theory. I felt as if I had my hand upon Shakespeare's heart, and was counting each separate throb and pulse of passion. I thought of the wonderful boy-actor, and saw his face in every line.

Previous to this, in my Lord Pembroke days, if I may so term them, I must admit that it had always seemed to me very difficult to understand how the creator of Hamlet and Lear and Othello could have addressed in such extravagant terms of praise and passion one who was merely an ordinary young nobleman of the day. Along with most students of Shakespeare, I had found myself compelled to set the Sonnets apart as things quite alien to Shakespeare's development as a dramatist, as things possibly unworthy of the intellectual side of his nature. But now that I began to realise the truth of Cyril Graham's theory, I saw that the moods and passions they mirrored were absolutely essential to Shakespeare's perfection as an artist writing for the Elizabethan stage, and that it was in the curious theatric conditions of that stage that the poems themselves had their origin. I remember what joy I had in feeling that these wonderful Sonnets,

> 'Subtle as Sphinx; as sweet and musical
> As bright Apollo's lute, strung with his hair,'

were no longer isolated from the great aesthetic energies of Shakespeare's life but were an essential part of his dramatic activity, and revealed to us something of the secret of his method. To have discovered the true name of Mr. W. H. was comparatively nothing: others might have done that, had perhaps done it: but to have discovered his profession was a revolution in criticism.

Two sonnets, I remember, struck me particularly. In the first of these (LIII) Shakespeare, complimenting Willie Hughes on the versatility of his acting, on his wide range of parts, a range extending, as we know, from Rosalind to Juliet, from Beatrice to Ophelia, says to him: –

> 'What is your substance, whereof are you made,
> That millions of strange shadows on you tend?
> Since everyone hath, every one, one shade,
> And you, but one, can every shadow lend' –

lines that would be unintelligible if they were not addressed to an actor, for the word 'shadow' had in Shakespeare's day a technical meaning connected with the stage. 'The best in this kind are but shadows,' says Theseus of the actors in the *Midsummer Night's Dream*;

> 'Life's but a walking shadow, a poor player
> That struts and frets his hour upon the stage,'

cries Macbeth in the moment of his despair, and there are many similar allusions in the literature of the day. This sonnet evidently belonged to the series in which Shakespeare discusses the nature of the actor's art, and of the strange and rare temperament that is essential to the perfect stage-player. 'How is it,' says Shakespeare to Willie Hughes, 'that you have so many personalities?' and then he goes on to point out that his beauty is such that it seems to realise every form and phase of fancy, to embody each dream of the creative imagination, – an idea that is still further expanded in the sonnet that immediately follows, where, beginning with the fine thought,

> 'O, how much more doth beauty beauteous seem
> By that sweet ornament which *truth* doth give!'

Shakespeare invites us to notice how the truth of acting, the truth of visible presentation on the stage, adds to the wonder of poetry, giving life to its loveliness, and actual reality to its ideal form. And yet, in Sonnet LXVII, Shakespeare calls upon Willie Hughes to abandon the stage with its artificiality, its unreal life of painted face and mimic costume, its immoral influences and suggestions, its remoteness from the true world of noble action and sincere utterance.

> 'Ah! wherefore with infection should he live,
> And with his presence grace impiety,
> That sin by him advantage should receive,
> And lace itself with his society?
> Why should false painting imitate his cheek
> And steal dead seeing of his living hue?
> Why should poor beauty indirectly seek
> Roses of shadow, since his rose is true?'

It may seem strange that so great a dramatist as Shakespeare, who realised his own perfection as an artist and his full humanity as a man on the ideal plane of stage-writing and stage-playing, should have written in these terms about the theatre; but we must remember that in Sonnets CX and CXI, Shakespeare shows us that he too was wearied of the world of puppets, and full of shame at having made himself 'a motley to the view.' Sonnet CXI is especially bitter: –

> 'O, for my sake do you with Fortune chide,
> The guilty goddess of my harmful deeds,
> That did not better for my life provide
> Than public means which public manners breeds.
> Thence comes it that my name receives a brand,
> And almost thence my nature is subdued
> To what it works in, like the dyer's hand:
> Pity me, then, and wish I were renewed' –

and there are many signs of the same feeling elsewhere, signs familiar to all real students of Shakespeare.

One point puzzled me immensely as I read the Sonnets, and it was days before I struck on the true interpretation, which indeed Cyril Graham himself seemed to have missed. I could not understand how it was that Shakespeare set so high a value on his young friend marrying. He himself had married young and the result had been unhappiness, and it was not likely that he would have asked Willie Hughes to commit the same error. The boy-player of Rosalind had nothing to gain from marriage, or from the passions of real life. The early sonnets with their strange entreaties to have children seemed to be a jarring note.

The explanation of the mystery came on me quite suddenly, and I found it in the curious dedication. It will be remembered that this dedication was as follows: –

> 'TO . THE . ONLIE . BEGETTER . OF .
> THESE . INSUING . SONNETS .
> MR . W . H . ALL . HAPPINESSE .
> AND . THAT . ETERNITIE .
> PROMISED . BY .
> OUR . EVER-LIVING . POET .

WISHETH .
THE . WELL-WISHING .
ADVENTURER . IN .
SETTING .
FORTH
T. T.'

Some scholars have supposed that the word 'begetter' here means simply the procurer of the Sonnets for Thomas Thorpe the publisher; but this view is now generally abandoned, and the highest authorities are quite agreed that it is to be taken in the sense of inspirer, the metaphor being drawn from the analogy of physical life. Now I saw that the same metaphor was used by Shakespeare himself all through the poems, and this set me on the right track. Finally I made my great discovery. The marriage that Shakespeare proposes for Willie Hughes is the 'marriage with his Muse,' an expression which is definitely put forward in Sonnet LXXXII where, in the bitterness of his heart at the defection of the boy-actor for whom he had written his greatest parts, and whose beauty had indeed suggested them, he opens his complaint by saying –

'I grant thou wert not married to my Muse.'

The children he begs him to beget are no children of flesh and blood, but more immortal children of undying fame. The whole cycle of the early sonnets is simply Shakespeare's invitation to Willie Hughes to go upon the stage and become a player. How barren and profitless a thing, he says, is this beauty of yours if it be not used: –

'When forty winters shall besiege thy brow,
And dig deep trenches in thy beauty's field,
Thy youth's proud livery, so gazed on now,
Will be a tattered weed, of small worth held:
Then being asked where all thy beauty lies,
Where all the treasure of thy lusty days,
To say, within thine own deep-sunken eyes,
Were an all-eating shame and thriftless praise.'

You must create something in art: my verse 'is thine and *born* of thee'; only listen to me and, I will

'*bring forth* eternal numbers to outlive long date,'

and you shall people with forms of your own image the imaginary world of the stage. These children that you beget, he continues, will not wither away, as mortal children do, but you shall live in them and in my plays: do but –

'Make thee another self, for love of me,
That beauty still may live in thine or thee!'

Be not afraid to surrender your personality, to give your 'semblance to some other':

> 'To give away yourself keeps yourself still,
> And you must live, drawn by your own sweet skill.'

I may not be learned in astrology, and yet, in those 'constant stars' your eyes,

> 'I read such art
> As truth and beauty shall together thrive,
> If from thyself to store thou wouldst convert.'

What does it matter about others?

> 'Let those whom Nature hath not made for store,
> Harsh, featureless, and rude, barrenly perish':

With you it is different, Nature –

> 'carv'd thee for her seal, and meant thereby
> Thou shouldst print more, nor let that copy die.'

Remember, too, how soon Beauty forsakes itself. Its action is no stronger than a flower, and like a flower it lives and dies. Think of 'the stormy gusts of winter's day,' of the 'barren edge of Death's eternal cold,' and –

> 'ere thou be distilled,
> Make sweet some vial; treasure thou some place
> With beauty's treasure, ere it be self-killed.'

Why, even flowers do not altogether die. When roses wither,

> 'Of their sweet deaths are sweetest odours made':

and you who are 'my rose' should not pass away without leaving your form in Art. For Art has the very secret of joy.

> 'Ten times thyself were happier than thou art,
> If ten of thine ten times refigur'd thee.'

You do not require the 'bastard signs of fair,' the painted face, the fantastic disguises of other actors:

> '. . . the golden tresses of the dead,
> The right of sepulchres,'

need not be shorn away for you. In you –

> '. . . those holy antique hours are seen,
> Without all ornament, itself and true,
> Making no summer of another's green.'

All that is necessary is to 'copy what in you is writ'; to place you on the stage as you are in actual life. All those ancient poets who have written of 'ladies dead and lovely knights' have been dreaming of such a one as you, and:

> 'All their praises are but prophecies
> Of this our time, all you prefiguring.'

For your beauty seems to belong to all ages and to all lands. Your shade comes to visit me at night, but, I want to look upon your 'shadow' in the living day, I want to see you upon the stage. Mere description of you will not suffice:

> 'If I could write the beauty of your eyes,
> And in fresh numbers number all your graces,
> The age to come would say, "This poet lies;
> Such heavenly touches ne'er touched earthly faces."'

It is necessary that 'some child of yours,' some artistic creation that embodies you, and to which your imagination gives life, shall present you to the world's wondering eyes. Your own thoughts are your children, offspring of sense and spirit; give some expression to them, and you shall find –

> 'Those children nursed, delivered from thy brain,'

My thoughts, also, are my 'children.' They are of your begetting and my brain is:

> 'the womb wherein they grew.'

For this great friendship of ours is indeed a marriage, it is the 'marriage of true minds.'

I collected together all the passages that seemed to me to corroborate this view, and they produced a strong impression on me, and showed me how complete Cyril Graham's theory really was. I also saw that it was quite easy to separate those lines in which Shakespeare speaks of the Sonnets themselves from those in which he speaks of his great dramatic work. This was a point that had been entirely overlooked by all the critics up to Cyril Graham's day. And yet it was one of the most important in the whole series of poems. To the Sonnets Shakespeare was more or less indifferent. He did not wish to rest his fame on them. They were to him his 'slight Muse,' as he calls them, and intended, as Meres tells us, for private circulation only among a few, a very few, friends. Upon the other hand he was extremely conscious of the high artistic value of his plays, and shows a noble self-reliance upon his dramatic genius. When he says to Willie Hughes:

> 'But thy eternal summer shall not fade,
> Nor lose possession of that fair thou owest;
> Nor shall Death brag thou wander'st in his shade,
> When in *eternal lines* to time thou growest:
> So long as men can breathe or eyes can see,
> So long lives this and this gives life to thee'; –

the expression 'eternal lines' clearly alludes to one of his plays that he was sending him at the time, just as the concluding couplet points to his confidence in the probability of his plays being always acted. In his address to the Dramatic Muse (Sonnets C and CI) we find the same feeling.

> 'Where art thou, Muse, that thou forget'st so long
> To speak of that which gives thee all thy might?
> Spend'st thou thy fury on some worthless song,
> Darkening thy power to lend base subjects light?'

he cries, and he then proceeds to reproach the mistress of Tragedy and Comedy for her 'neglect of truth in beauty dyed,' and says:

> 'Because he needs no praise, wilt thou be dumb?
> Excuse not silence so; for 't lies in thee
> To make him much outlive a gilded tomb,
> And to be praised of ages yet to be.
>   Then do thy office, Muse, I teach thee how,
>   To make him seem long hence as he shows now.'

It is, however, perhaps in Sonnet LV that Shakespeare gives to this idea its fullest expression. To imagine that the 'powerful rhyme' of the second line refers to the sonnet itself was entirely to mistake Shakespeare's meaning. It seemed to me that it was extremely likely, from the general character of the sonnet, that a particular play was meant, and that the play was none other but *Romeo and Juliet*.

> 'Not marble, nor the gilded monuments
> Of princes shall outlive this powerful rhyme;
> But you shall shine more bright in these contents
> That unswept stone besmeared with sluttish time.
> When wasteful wars shall statues overturn,
> And broils root out the work of masonry,
> Not Mars his sword not war's quick fire shall burn
> The living record of your memory
> 'Gainst death and all-oblivious enmity
> Shall you pace forth; your praise shall still find room
> Even in the eyes of all posterity
> That wear this world out to the ending doom.
>   So, till the judgment that yourself arise,
>   You live in this, and dwell in lovers' eyes.'

It was also very suggestive to note how here as elsewhere Shakespeare promised Willie Hughes immortality in a form that appealed to men's eyes – that is to say, in a spectacular form, in a play that is to be looked at.

For two weeks I worked hard at the Sonnets, hardly ever going out, and refusing all invitations. Every day I seemed to be discovering something new, and Willie Hughes became to me a kind of spiritual presence, an ever-dominant personality. I could almost fancy that I saw him standing in the shadow of my room, so well had Shakespeare drawn him, with his golden hair, his tender flower-like grace, his dreamy deep-sunken eyes, his delicate mobile limbs, and his white lily hands. His very name fascinated me. Willie Hughes! Willie Hughes! How musically it sounded! Yes; who else but he could have been the master-mistress of Shakespeare's passion, the lord of his love to whom he was bound in vassalage, the delicate minion of pleasure, the rose of the whole world, the herald of the spring decked in the proud livery of youth, the lovely boy whom it was sweet music to hear, and whose beauty was the very raiment of Shakespeare's heart, as it was the keystone of his dramatic power? How bitter now seemed the whole tragedy of his desertion and his shame! – shame that he made sweet and lovely by the mere magic of his personality, but that was none the less shame. Yet as Shakespeare forgave him, should not we forgive him also? I did not care to pry into the mystery of his sin or of the sin, if such it was, of the great poet who had so dearly loved him. 'I am that I am,' said Shakespeare in a sonnet of noble scorn, –

> 'I am that I am, and they that level
> At my abuses reckon up their own;
> I may be straight, though they themselves be bevel;
> By their rank thoughts my deeds must not be shown.'

Willie Hughes's abandonment of Shakespeare's theatre was a different matter, and I investigated it at great length. Finally I came to the conclusion that Cyril Graham had been wrong in regarding the rival dramatist of Sonnet LXXX as Chapman. It was obviously Marlowe who was alluded to. At the time the Sonnets were written, which must have been between 1590 and 1595, such an expression as 'the proud full sail of his great verse' could not possibly have been used of Chapman's work, however applicable it might have been to the style of his later Jacobean plays. No; Marlowe was clearly the rival poet of whom Shakespeare spoke in such laudatory terms; the hymn he wrote in Willie Hughes' honour was the unfinished 'Hero and Leander,' and that

> 'Affable familiar ghost
> which nightly gulls him with intelligence,'

was the Mephistophiles of his Doctor Faustus. No doubt, Marlowe was fascinated by the beauty and grace of the boy-actor, and lured him away from the Blackfriars Theatre, that he might play the Gaveston of his *Edward II*. That Shakespeare had some legal right to retain Willie Hughes in his own company seems evident from Sonnet LXXXVII, where he says:

> 'Farewell! thou are too dear for my possessing,
> And like enough thou know'st thy estimate:
> The *charter of thy worth* gives thee releasing;
> My *bonds* in thee are all determinate.
> For how do I hold thee but by thy granting?
> And for that riches where is my deserving?
> The cause of this fair gift in me is wanting,
> *And so my patent back again is swerving*
> Thyself thou gav'st, thy own worth then not knowing,
> Or me, to whom thou gav'st it, else mistaking;

> So they great gift, upon misprision growing,
> Comes home again, on better judgment making.
> Thus have I had thee, as a dream doth flatter,
> In sleep a king, but waking no such matter.'

But whom he could not hold by love, he would not hold by force. Willie Hughes became a member of Lord Pembroke's company, and perhaps in the open yard of the Red Bull Tavern, played the part of King Edward's delicate minion. On Marlowe's death, he seems to have returned to Shakespeare, who, whatever his fellow-partners may have thought of the matter, was not slow to forgive the wilfulness and treachery of the young actor.

How well, too, had Shakespeare drawn the temperament of the stage-player! Willie Hughes was one of those –

> 'That do not do the thing they most do show,
> Who, moving others, are themselves as stone.'

He could act love, but could not feel it, could mimic passion without realising it.

> 'In many's looks the false heart's history
> Is writ in moods and frowns and wrinkles strange,'

but with Willie Hughes it was not so. 'Heaven,' says Shakespeare, in a sonnet of mad idolatry –

> 'Heaven in thy creation did decree
> That in thy face sweet love should ever dwell;
> Whate'er thy thoughts or thy heart's workings be,
> Thy looks should nothing thence but sweetness tell.'

In his 'inconstant mind' and his 'false heart' it was easy to recognise the insincerity and treachery that somehow seem inseparable from the artistic nature, as in his love of praise, that desire for immediate recognition that characterises all actors. And yet, more fortunate in this than other actors, Willie Hughes was to know something of immortality. Intimately connected with Shakespeare's plays, he was to live in them, and by their production.

> 'Your name from hence immortal life shall have,
> Though I, once gone, to all the world must die:
> The earth can yield me but a common grave,
> When you entombed in men's eyes shall lie.
> Your monument shall be my gentle verse,
> Which eyes not yet created shall o'er-read,
> And tongues to be your being shall rehearse,
> When all the breathers of this world are dead.'

Nash with his venomous tongue had railed against Shakespeare for 'reposing eternity in the mouth of a player,' the reference being obviously to the Sonnets.

But to Shakespeare, the actor was a deliberate and self-conscious fellow worker who gave form and substance to a poet's fancy, and brought into Drama the elements of a noble realism. His silence could be as eloquent as words, and his gestures as expressive, and in those terrible moments of Titan agony or of god-like pain, when thought outstrips utterance, when the soul sick with excess of anguish stammers or is dumb, and the very raiment of speech is rent and torn by passion in its storm, then the actor could become, though it were but for a moment, a creative artist, and touch by his mere presence and personality those springs of terror and of pity to which tragedy appeals. This full recognition of the actor's art, and of the actor's power, was one of the things that distinguished the Romantic from the Classical Drama, and one of the things, consequently, that we owed to Shakespeare, who, fortunate in much, was fortunate also in this, that he was able to find Richard Burbage and to fashion Willie Hughes.

With what pleasure he dwelt upon Willie Hughes' influence over his audience – the 'gazers' as he calls them; with what charm of fancy did he analyse the whole art! Even in the 'Lover's Complaint' he speaks of his acting, and tells us that he was a nature so impressionable to the quality of dramatic situations that he could assume 'all strange forms' –

> 'Of burning blushes, or of weeping water,
> Or swooning paleness':

explaining his meaning more fully later on where he tells us how Willie Hughes was able to deceive others by his wonderful power to –

> 'Blush at speeches rank, to weep at woes,
> Or to turn white and swoon at tragic shows.'

It had never been pointed out before that the shepherd of this lovely pastoral, whose 'youth in art and art in youth' are described with such subtlety of phrase and passion, was none other than the Mr. W. H. of the Sonnets. And yet there was no doubt that he was so. Not merely in personal appearance are the two lads the same, but their natures and temperaments are identical. When the false shepherd whispers to the fickle maid –

> 'All my offences that abroad you see
> Are errors of the blood, none of the mind;
> Love made them not':

when he says of his lovers,

> 'Harm have I done to them, but ne'er was harmed;
> Kept hearts in liveries, but mine own was free,
> And reigned, commanding in his monarchy':

when he tells us of the 'deep-brained sonnets' that one of them had sent him, and cries out in boyish pride –

> 'The broken bosoms that to me belong

Have emptied all their fountains in my well':

it is impossible not to feel that it is Willie Hughes who is speaking to us. 'Deep-brained sonnets,' indeed, had Shakespeare brought him, 'jewels' that to his careless eyes were but as 'trifles,' though –

> 'Each several stone,
> With wit well blazoned, smiled or made some moan';

and into the well of beauty he had emptied the sweet fountain of his song. That in both places it was an actor who was alluded to, was also clear. The betrayed nymph tells us of the 'false fire' in her lover's cheek, of the 'forced thunder' of his sighs, and of his 'borrowed motion': of whom, indeed, but of an actor could it be said that to him 'thought, characters, and words' were 'merely Art,' or that –

> 'To make the weeper laugh, the laugher weep,
> He had the dialect and different skill,
> Catching all passions in his craft of will'?

The play on words in the last line is the same as that used in the punning son-nets, and is continued in the following stanza of the poem, where we are told of the youth who –

> 'did in the general bosom reign
> Of young, of old; and sexes both enchanted',

that there were those who –

> '. . . dialogued for him what he would say,
> Asked their own wills, and made their Wills obey.'

Yes: the 'rose-cheeked Adonis' of the Venus poem, the false shepherd of the 'Lover's Complaint,' the 'tender churl,' the 'beauteous niggard' of the Son-nets, was none other but a young actor; and as I read through the various de-scriptions given of him, I saw that the love that Shakespeare bore him was as the love of a musician for some delicate instrument on which he delights to play, as a sculptor's love for some rare and exquisite material that suggests a new form of plastic beauty, a new mode of plastic expression. For all Art has its medium, its material, be it that of rhythmical words, or of pleasurable col-our, or of sweet and subtly-divided sound; and, as one of the most fascinat-ing critics of our day has pointed out, it is to the qualities inherent in each material, and special to it, that we owe the sensuous element in Art, and with it all that in Art is essentially artistic. What then shall we say of the material that the Drama requires for its perfect presentation? What of the Actor, who is the medium through which alone the Drama can truly reveal itself? Sure-ly, in that strange mimicry of life by the living which is the mode and method of theatric art, there are sensuous elements of beauty that none of the other arts possess. Looked at from one point of view, the common players of the saffron-strewn stage are Art's most complete, most satisfying instruments. There is no passion in bronze, nor motion in marble. The sculptor must surrender colour, and the painter fullness of form. The epos changes acts into words, and music changes words into tones. It is the Drama only that, to quote the fine saying of Gervinus, uses all means at once, and, appealing both to eye and ear, has at its disposal, and in its service, form and colour, tone, look, and word, the swiftness of motion, the intense realism of visible action.

It may be that in this very completeness of the instrument lies the secret of some weakness in the art. Those arts are happiest that employ a material remote from reality, and there is a danger in the absolute identity of medium and matter, the danger of ignoble realism and unimaginative imitation. Yet Shakespeare himself was a player, and wrote for players. He saw the possibilities that lay hidden in an art that up to his time had expressed itself but in bombast or in clowning. He has left us the most perfect rules for acting that have ever been written. He created parts that can be only truly revealed to us on the stage, wrote plays that need the theatre for their full realisation, and we cannot marvel that he so worshipped one who was the interpreter of his vision, as he was the incarnation of his dreams.

There was, however, more in his friendship than the mere delight of a dramatist in one who helps him to achieve his end. This was indeed a subtle element of pleasure, if not of passion, and a noble basis for an artistic comradeship. But it was not all that the Sonnets revealed to us. There was something beyond. There was the soul, as well as the language, of neo-Platonism.

'The fear of the Lord is the beginning of wisdom,' said the stern Hebrew prophet: 'The beginning of wisdom is Love,' was the gracious message of the Greek. And the spirit of the Renaissance, which already touched Hellenism at so many points, catching the inner meaning of this phrase and divining its secret, sought to elevate friendship to the high dignity of the antique ideal, to make it a vital factor in the new culture, and a mode of self-conscious intellectual development. In 1492 appeared Marsilio Ficino's translation of the 'Symposium' of Plato, and his wonderful dialogue, of all the Platonic dialogues perhaps the most perfect, as it is the most poetical, began to exercise a strange influence over men, and to colour their words and thoughts, and manner of living. In its subtle suggestions of sex in soul, in the curious analogies it draws between intellectual enthusiasm and the physical passion of love, in its dream of the incarnation of the Idea in a beautiful and living form, and of a real spiritual conception with a travail and a bringing to birth, there was something that fascinated the poets and scholars of the sixteenth century. Shakespeare, certainly, was fascinated by it, and had read the dialogue, if not in Ficino's translation, of which many copies found their way to England, perhaps in that French translation by Leroy to which Joachim du Bellay contributed so many graceful metrical versions. When he says to Willie Hughes,

> 'he that calls on thee, let him bring forth
> Eternal numbers to outlive long date,'

he is thinking of Diotima's theory that Beauty is the goddess who presides over birth, and draws into the light of day the dim conceptions of the soul: when he tells us of the 'marriage of true minds,' and exhorts his friend to beget children that time cannot destroy, he is but repeating the words in which the prophetess tells us that 'friends are married by a far nearer tie than those who beget mortal children, for fairer and more immortal are the children who are their common offspring.' So, also, Edward Blount in his dedication of 'Hero and Leander' talks of Marlowe's works as his 'right children,' being the 'issue of his brain'; and when Bacon claims that 'the best works and of greatest merit for the public have proceeded from the unmarried and childless men, which both in affection and means have married and endowed the public,' he is paraphrasing a passage in the 'Symposium.'

Friendship, indeed, could have desired no better warrant for its permanence or its ardours than the Platonic theory, or creed, as we might better call it, that the true world was the world of ideas, and that these ideas took visible form and became incarnate in man, and it is only when we realise the influence of neo-Platonism on the Renaissance that we can understand the true meaning of the amatory phrases and words with which friends were wont, at this time, to address each other. There was a kind of mystic transference of the expressions of the physical world to a sphere that was spiritual, that was removed from gross bodily appetite, and in which the soul was Lord. Love had, indeed, entered the olive garden of the new Academe, but he wore the same flame-coloured raiment, and had the same words of passion on his lips.

Michael Angelo, the 'haughtiest spirit in Italy' as he has been called, addresses the young Tommaso Cavalieri in such fervent and passionate terms that some have thought that the sonnets in question must have been intended for that noble lady, the widow of the Marchese di Pescara, whose white hand, when she was dying, the great sculptor's lips had stooped to kiss. But that it was to Cavalieri that they were written, and that the literal interpretation is the right one, is evident not merely from the fact that Michael Angelo plays with his name, as Shakespeare plays with the name of Willie Hughes, but from the direct evidence of Varchi, who was well acquainted with the young man, and who, indeed, tells us that he possessed 'besides incomparable personal beauty, so much charm of nature, such excellent abilities, and such a graceful manner, that he deserved, and still deserves, to be the better loved the more he is known.' Strange as these sonnets may seem to us now, when rightly interpreted they merely serve to show with what intense and religious fervour Michael Angelo addressed himself to the worship of intellectual beauty, and how, to borrow a fine phrase from Mr. Symonds, he pierced through the veil of flesh and sought the divine idea it imprisoned. In the sonnet written for Luigi del Riccio on the death of his friend, Cecchino Bracci, we can also trace, as Mr. Symonds points out, the Platonic conception of love as nothing if not spiritual, and of beauty as a form that finds its immortality within the lover's soul. Cecchino was a lad who died at the age of seventeen, and when Luigi asked Michael Angelo to make a portrait of him, Michael Angelo answered, 'I can only do so by drawing you in whom he still lives.'

> 'If the beloved in the lover shine,
> Since Art without him cannot work alone,
> Thee must I carve, to tell the world of him.'

The same idea is also put forward in Montaigne's noble essay on Friendship, a passion which he ranks higher than the love of brother for brother, or the love of man for woman. He tells us – I quote from Florio's translation, one of the books with which Shakespeare was familiar – how 'perfect amitie' is indivisible, how it 'possesseth the soule, and swaies it in all soveraigntie' and how 'by the inter-position of a spiritual beauty the desire of a spiritual conception is engendered in the beloved.' He writes of an 'internall beauty, of difficile knowledge, and abstruse discovery' that is revealed unto friends, and unto friends only. He mourns for the dead Etienne de la Boëtie, in accents of wild grief and inconsolable love. The learned Hubert Languet, the friend of Melanchthon and of the leaders of the reformed church, tells the young Philip Sidney how he kept his portrait by him some hours to feast his eyes upon it, and how his appetite was 'rather increased than diminished by the sight,' and Sidney writes to him, 'the chief hope of my life, next to the everlasting blessedness of heaven, will always be the enjoyment of true friendship, and there you shall have the chiefest place.' Later on there came to Sidney's house in London, one – some day to be burned at Rome, for the sin of seeing God in all things – Giordano Bruno, just fresh from his triumph before the University of Paris. 'A filosofia è necessario amore' were the words ever upon his lips, and there was something in his strange ardent personality that made men feel that he had discovered the new secret of life. Ben Jonson writing to one of his friends subscribes himself 'your true lover,' and dedicates his noble eulogy on Shakespeare 'To the memory of my Beloved.' Richard Barnfield in his 'Affectionate Shepherd' flutes on soft Virgilian reed the story of his attachment to some young Elizabethan of the day. Out of all the Eclogues, Abraham Fraunce selects the second for translation, and Fletcher's lines to Master W. C. show what fascination was hidden in the mere name of Alexis.

It was no wonder then that Shakespeare had been stirred by a spirit that so stirred his age. There had been critics, like Hallam, who had regretted that the Sonnets had ever been written, who had seen in them something dangerous, something unlawful even. To them it would have been sufficient to answer in Chapman's noble words:

> 'There is no danger to a man that knows
> What Life and Death is: there's not any law
> Exceeds his knowledge: neither is it lawful
> That he should stoop to any other law.'

But it was evident that the Sonnets needed no such defence as this, and that those who had talked of 'the folly of excessive and misplaced affection' had not been able to interpret either the language or the spirit of these great poems, so intimately connected with the philosophy and the art of their time.

It is no doubt true that to be filled with an absorbing passion is to surrender the security of one's lower life, and yet in such surrender there may be gain, certainly there was for Shakespeare. When Pico della Mirandola crossed the threshold of the villa of Careggi, and stood before Marsilio Ficino in all the grace and comeliness of his wonderful youth, the aged scholar seemed to see in him the realisation of the Greek ideal, and determined to devote his remaining years to the translation of Plotinus, that new Plato, in whom, as Mr. Pater reminds us, 'the mystical element in the Platonic philosophy had been worked out to the utmost limit of vision and ecstasy.' A romantic friendship with a young Roman of his day initiated Winckelmann into the secret of Greek art, taught him the mystery of its beauty and the meaning of its form. In Willie Hughes, Shakespeare found not merely a most delicate instrument for the presentation of his art, but the visible incarnation of his idea of beauty, and it is not too much to say that to this young actor, whose very name the dull writers of his age forgot to chronicle, the Romantic Movement of English Literature is largely indebted.

3

ONE evening I thought that I had really discovered Willie Hughes in Elizabethan literature. In a wonderfully graphic account of the last days of the great Earl of Essex, his chaplain Thomas Knell, tells us that the night before the Earl died, 'he called William Hewes, which was his musician, to play upon the virginals and to sing. "Play," said he, "my song, Will Hewes, and I will sing it myself." So he did it most joyfully, not as the howling swan, which, still·looking down, waileth her end, but as a sweet lark, lifting up his hands and casting up his eyes to his God, with this mounted the crystal skies, and reached with his unwearied tongue the top of highest heavens.' Surely the boy who played on the virginals to the dying father of Sidney's Stella was none other than the Will Hews to whom Shakespeare dedicated the Sonnets, and who he tells us was himself sweet 'music to hear.' Yet Lord Essex died in 1576, when Shakespeare was but twelve years of age. It was impossible that his musician could have been the Mr. W. H. of the Sonnets. Perhaps Shakespeare's young friend was the son of the player upon the virginals? It was at least something to have discovered that Will Hews was an Elizabethan name. Indeed the name Hews seemed to have been closely connected with music and the stage. The first English actress was the lovely Margaret Hews, whom Prince Rupert so madly adored. What more probable than that between her and Lord Essex' musician had come the boy-actor of Shakespeare's plays? In 1587 a certain Thomas Hews brought out at Gray's Inn a Euripidean tragedy entitled 'The Misfortunes of Arthur,' receiving much assistance in the arrangement of the dumb shows from one Francis Bacon, then a student of law. Surely he was some near kinsman of the lad to whom Shakespeare said –

'Take all my loves, my love, yea, take them all';

the 'profitless usurer?' of 'unused beauty,' as he describes him. But the proofs, the links – where were they? Alas! I could not find them. It seemed to me that I was always on the brink of absolute verification, but that I could never really attain to it. I thought it strange that no one had ever written a history of the English boy-actors of the sixteenth and seventeenth centuries, and determined to undertake the task myself, and to try to ascertain their true relations to the drama. The subject was, certainly, full of artistic interest. These lads had been the delicate reeds through which our poets had sounded their sweetest strains, the gracious vessels of honour into which they had poured the purple wine of their song. Foremost, naturally, among them all had been the youth to whom Shakespeare had intrusted the realisation of his most exquisite creations. Beauty had been his, such as our age has never, or but rarely seen, a beauty that seemed to combine the charm of both sexes, and to have wedded, as the Sonnets tell us, the grace of Adonis and the loveliness of Helen. He had been quick-witted, too, and eloquent, and from those finely curved lips that the satirist had mocked at had come the passionate cry of Juliet, and the bright laughter of Beatrice, Perdita's flower-like words, and Ophelia's wandering songs. Yet as Shakespeare himself had been but as a God among giants, so Willie Hughes had only been one out of many marvellous lads to whom our English Renaissance owed something of the secret of its joy, and it appeared to me that they also were worthy of some study and record.

In a little book with fine vellum leaves and damask silk cover – a fancy of mine in those fanciful days – I accordingly collected such information as I could about them, and even now there is something in the scanty record of their lives, in the mere mention of their names, that attracts me. I seemed to know them all: Robin Armin, the goldsmith's lad who was lured by Tarlton to go on the stage: Sandford, whose performance of the courtezan Flamantia Lord Burleigh witnessed at Gray's Inn: Cooke, who played Agrippina in the tragedy of 'Sejanus': Nat. Field, whose young and beardless portrait is still preserved for us at Dulwich, and who in 'Cynthia's Revels' played the 'Queen and Huntress chaste and fair': Gil Carie, who, attired as a mountain nymph, sang in the same lovely masque Echo's song of mourning for Narcissus: Parsons, the Salmacis of the strange pageant of 'Tamburlaine': Will. Ostler, who was one of 'The Children of the Queen's Chapel,' and accompanied King James to Scotland: George Vernon, to whom the king sent a cloak of scarlet, cloth, and a cape of crimson velvet: Alick Gough, who performed the part of Caenis, Vespasian's concubine, in Massinger's 'Roman Actor,' and three years later that of Acanthe, in the same dramatist's 'Picture': Barrett, the heroine of Richards' tragedy of 'Messalina': Dicky Robinson, 'a very pretty fellow,' Ben Jonson tells us, who was a member of Shakespeare's company, and was known for his exquisite taste in costume, as well as for his love of woman's apparel: Salathiel Pavy, whose early and tragic death Jonson mourned in one of the sweetest threnodies of our literature: Arthur Savile, who was one of 'the players of Prince Charles,' and took a girl's part in a comedy by Marmion: Stephen Hammerton, 'a most noted and beautiful woman actor,' whose pale oval face with its heavy-lidded eyes and somewhat sensuous mouth looks out at us from a curious miniature of the time: Hart, who made his first success by playing the Duchess in the tragedy of 'The Cardinal,' and who in a poem that is clearly modelled upon some of Shakespeare's Sonnets is described by one who had seen him as 'beauty to the eye, and music to the ear': and Kynaston, of whom Betterton said that 'it has been disputed among the judicious, whether any woman could have more sensibly touched the passions,' and whose white hands and amber-coloured hair seem to have retarded by some years the introduction of actresses upon our stage.

The Puritans, with their uncouth morals and ignoble minds had of course railed against them, and dwelt on the impropriety of boys disguising as women, and learning to affect the manners and passions of the female sex. Gosson, with his shrill voice, and Prynne, soon to be made earless for many shameful slanders, and others to whom the rare and subtle sense of abstract beauty was denied, had from the pulpit and through pamphlet said foul or foolish things to their dishonour. To Francis Lenton, writing in 1629, what he speaks of as –

> 'loose action, mimic gesture
> By a poor boy clad in a princely vesture,'

is but one of many –

> 'tempting baits of hell
> Which draw more youth unto the damned cell
> Of furious lust, than all the devil could do
> Since he obtained his first overthrow.'

Deuteronomy was quoted and the ill-digested learning of the period laid under contribution. Even our own time had not appreciated the artistic conditions of the Elizabethan and Jacobean drama. One of the most brilliant and intellectual actresses of this century had laughed at the idea of a lad of seventeen or eighteen playing Imogen, or Miranda, or Rosalind. 'How could any youth, however gifted and specially trained, even faintly suggest these fair and noble women to an audience? . . . One quite pities Shakespeare, who had to put up with seeing his brightest creations marred, misrepresented, and spoiled.' In his book on 'Shakespeare's Predecessors' Mr. John Addington Symonds also had talked of 'hobbledehoys' trying to represent the pathos of Desdemona and Juliet's passion. Were they right? Are they right? I did not think so then. I do not think so now. Those who remember the Oxford production of the 'Agamemnon,' the fine utterance and marble dignity of the Clytemnestra, the romantic and imaginative rendering of the prophetic madness of Cassandra, will not agree with Lady Martin or Mr. Symonds in their strictures on the conditions of the Elizabethan stage.

Of all the motives of dramatic curiosity used by our great playwrights, there is none more subtle or more fascinating than the ambiguity of the sexes. This idea, invented, as far as an artistic idea can be said to be invented, by Lyly, perfected and made exquisite for us by Shakespeare, seems to me to owe its origin, as it certainly owes it possibility of life-like presentation, to the circumstance that the Elizabethan stage, like the stage of the Greeks, admitted the appearance of no female performers. It is because Lyly was writing for the boy-actors of St. Paul's that we have the confused sexes and complicated loves of Phillida and Gallathea: it is because Shakespeare was writing for Willie Hughes that Rosalind dons doublet and hose, and calls herself Ganymede, that Viola and Julia put on pages' dress, that Imogen steals away in male attire. To say that only a woman can portray the passions of a woman, and that therefore no boy can play Rosalind, is to rob the art of acting of all claim to objectivity, and to assign to the mere accident of sex what properly belongs to imaginative insight and creative energy. Indeed, if sex be an element in artistic creation, it might rather be urged that the delightful combination of wit and romance which characterises so many of Shakespeare's heroines was at least occasioned if it was not actually caused by the fact that the players of these parts were lads and young men, whose passionate purity, quick mobile fancy, and healthy freedom from sentimentality can hardly fail to have suggested a new and delightful type of girlhood or of womanhood. The very difference of sex between the player and the part he represented must also, as Professor Ward points out, have constituted 'one more demand upon the imaginative capacities of the spectators,' and must have kept them from that over-realistic identification of the actor with his *rôle*, which is one of the weak points in modern theatrical criticism.

This, too, must be granted, that it was to these boy-actors that we owe the introduction of those lovely lyrics that star the plays of Shakespeare, Dekker, and so many of the dramatists of the period, those 'snatches of bird-like or god-like song,' as Mr. Swinburne calls them. For it was out of the choirs of the cathedrals and royal chapels of England that most of these lads came, and from their earliest years they had been trained in the singing of anthems and madrigals, and in all that concerns the subtle art of music. Chosen at first for the beauty of their voices, as well as for a certain comeliness and freshness of appearance, they were then instructed in gesture, dancing, and elocution, and taught to play both tragedies and comedies in the English as well as in the Latin language. Indeed, acting seems to have formed part of the ordinary education of the time, and to have been much studied not merely by the scholars of Eton and Westminster, but also by the students at the Universities of Oxford and Cambridge, some of whom went afterwards upon the public stage, as is becoming not uncommon in our own day. The great actors, too, had their pupils and apprentices, who were formally bound over to them by legal warrant, to whom they imparted the secrets of their craft, and who were so much valued that we read of Henslowe, one of the managers of the Rose Theatre, buying a trained boy of the name of James Bristowe for eight pieces of gold. The relations that existed between the masters and their pupils seem to have been of the most cordial and affectionate character. Robin Armin was looked upon by Tarlton as his adopted son, and in a will dated 'the fourth daie of Maie, anno Domini 1605,' Augustine Phillips, Shakespeare's dear friend and fellow actor, bequeathed to one of his apprentices his 'purple cloke, sword, and dagger,' his 'base viall,' and much rich apparel, and to another a sum of money and many beautiful instruments of music, 'to be delivered unto him at the expiration of his terme of yeres in his indenture of apprenticehood.' Now and then, when some daring actor kidnapped a boy for the stage, there was an outcry or an investigation. In 1600, for instance, a certain Norfolk gentleman of the name of Henry Clifton came to live in London in order that his son, then about thirteen years of age, might have the opportunity of attending the Bluecoat School, and from a petition which he presented to the Star Chamber, and which has been recently brought to light by Mr. Greenstreet, we learn that as the boy was walking quietly to Christ Church cloister one winter morning he was waylaid by James Robinson, Henry Evans, and Nathaniel Giles, and carried off to the Blackfriars Theatre, 'amongste a companie of lewde and dissolute mercenarie players,' as his father calls them, in order that he might be trained 'in acting of parts in base playes and enterludes.' Hearing of his son's misadventure, Mr. Clifton went down at once to the theatre, and demanded his surrender, but 'the sayd Nathaniel Giles, James Robinson and Henry Evans most arrogantlie then and there answered that they had authoritie sufficient soe to take any noble man's sonne in this land,' and handing the young schoolboy 'a scrolle of paper, conteyning parte of one of their said playes and enterludes,' commanded him to learn it by heart. Through a warrant issued by Sir John Fortescue, however, the boy was restored to his father the next day, and the Court of Star Chamber seems to have suspended or cancelled Evans' privileges.

The fact is that, following a precedent set by Richard III, Elizabeth had issued a commission authorising certain persons to impress into her service all boys who had beautiful voices that they might sing for her in her Chapel Royal, and Nathaniel Giles, her Chief Commissioner, finding that he could deal profitably with the managers of the Globe Theatre, agreed to supply them with personable and graceful lads for the playing of female parts, under colour of taking them for the Queen's service. The actors, accordingly, had a certain amount of legal warrant on their side, and it is interesting to note that many of the boys whom they carried off from their schools or homes, such as Salathiel Pavy, Nat. Field, and Alvery Trussell, became so fascinated by their new art that they attached themselves permanently to the theatre, and would not leave it.

Once it seemed as if girls were to take the place of boys upon the stage, and among the christenings chronicled in the registers of St. Giles', Crippelgate, occurs the following strange and suggestive entry: 'Comedia, base-born, daughter of Alice Bowker and William Johnson, one of the Queen's plaiers, 10 Feb. 1589.' But the child upon whom such high hopes had been built died at six years of age, and when, later on, some French actresses came over and played at Blackfriars, we learn that they were 'hissed, hooted, and pippin-pelted from the stage.' I think that, from what I have said above, we need not regret this in any way. The essentially male culture of the English Renaissance found its fullest and most perfect expression by its own method, and in its own manner.

I remember I used to wonder, at this time, what had been the social position and early life of Willie Hughes before Shakespeare had met him. My investigations into the history of the boy-actors had made me curious of every detail about him. Had he stood in the carved stall of some gilded choir, reading out of a great book painted with square scarlet notes and long black key lines? We know from the Sonnets how clear and pure his voice was, and what skill he had in the art of music. Noble gentlemen, such as the Earl of Leicester and Lord Oxford, had companies of boy-players in their service as part of their household. When Leicester went to the Netherlands in 1585 he brought with him a certain 'Will' described as a 'plaier'. Was this Willie Hughes? Had he acted for Leicester at Kenilworth, and was it there that Shakespeare had first known him? Or was he, like Robin Armin, simply a lad of low degree but possessing some strange beauty and marvellous fascination? It was evident from the early sonnets that when Shakespeare first came across him he had no connection whatsoever with the stage, and that he was not of high birth has already been shewn. I began to think of him not as the delicate chorister of a Royal Chapel, not as a petted minion trained to sing and dance in Leicester's stately masque, but as some fair-haired English lad whom in one of London's hurrying streets, or on Windsor's green silent meadows, Shakespeare had seen and followed, recognising the artistic possibilities that lay hidden in so comely and gracious a form, and divining by a quick and subtle instinct what an actor the lad would make could he be induced to go upon the stage. At this time Willie Hughes' father was dead, as we learn from Sonnet XIII, and his mother, whose remarkable beauty he is said to have inherited, may have been induced to allow him to become Shakespeare's apprentice by the fact that boys who played female characters were paid extremely large salaries, larger salaries, indeed, than were given to grown-up actors. Shakespeare's apprentice, at any rate, we know that he became, and we know what a vital factor he was in the development of Shakespeare's art. As a rule, a boy-actor's capacity for representing girlish parts on the stage lasted but for a few years at most. Such characters as Lady Macbeth, Queen Constance and Volumnia, remained of course always within the reach of those who had true dramatic genius and noble presence. Absolute youth was not necessary here, not desirable even. But with Imogen, and Perdita, and Juliet, it was different. 'Your beard has begun to grow, and I pray God your voice be not cracked,' says Hamlet mockingly to the boy-actor of the strolling company that came to visit him at Elsinore; and certainly when chins grew rough and voices harsh much of the charm and grace of the performance must have gone. Hence comes Shakespeare's passionate preoccupation with the youth of Willie Hughes, his terror of old age and wasting years, his wild appeal to time to spare the beauty of his friend:

> 'Make glad and sorry seasons as thou fleet'st,
> And do whate'er thou wilt, swift-footed time,
> To the wide world and all her fading sweets;
> But I forbid thee one most heinous crime:
> O carve not with the hours my Love's fair brow
> Nor draw no lines there with thine antique pen;
> Him in thy course untainted do allow
> For beauty's pattern to succeeding men.'

Time seems to have listened to Shakespeare's prayers, or perhaps Willie Hughes had the secret of perpetual youth. After three years he is quite unchanged:

> 'To me, fair friend, you never can be old,
> For as you were when first your eye I eyed,
> Such seems your beauty still. Three winters' cold
> Have from the forests shook three summers' pride,
> Three beauteous springs to yellow autumn turned,
> In process of the seasons have I seen,
> Three April perfumes in three hot Junes burned,
> Since first I saw you fresh which yet are green.'

More years pass over, and the bloom of his boyhood seems to be still with him. When, in 'The Tempest,' Shakespeare, through the lips of Prospero, flung away the wand of his imagination and gave his poetic sovereignty into the weak, graceful hands of Fletcher, it may be that the Miranda who stood wondering by was none other than Willie Hughes himself, and in the last sonnet that his friend addressed to him, the enemy that is feared is not Time but Death.

> 'O thou, my lovely boy, who in thy power
> Dost hold time's fickle glass, his sickle hour;
> Who hast by waning grown, and therein show'st
> Thy lovers withering as thy sweet self grow'st;
> If Nature, sovereign mistress over wrack,
> As thou goest onwards, still will pluck thee back,
> She keeps thee to this purpose, that her skill
> May Time disgrace and wretched minutes kill.
> Yet fear her, O thou minion of her pleasure!
> She may detain, but not still keep, her treasure.
> Her audit, though delay'd, answer'd must be,
> And her quietus is to render thee.'

4

IT was not for some weeks after I had begun my study of the subject that I ventured to approach the curious group of Sonnets (CXXVII–CLII) that deal with the dark woman who, like a shadow or thing of evil omen, came across Shakespeare's great romance, and for a season stood between him and Willie Hughes. They were obviously printed out of their proper place and should have been inserted between Sonnets XXXIII and XL. Psychological and artistic reasons necessitated this change, a change which I hope will be adopted by all future editors, as without it an entirely false impression is conveyed of the nature and final issue of this noble friendship.

Who was she, this black-browed, olive-skinned woman, with her amorous mouth 'that Love's own hand did make,' her 'cruel eye,' and her 'foul pride,' her strange skill on the virginals and her false, fascinating nature? An over-curious scholar of our day had seen in her a symbol of the Catholic Church, of that Bride of Christ who is 'black but comely.' Professor Minto, following in the footsteps of Henry Brown, had regarded the whole group of Sonnets as simply 'exercises of skill undertaken in a spirit of wanton defiance and derision of the commonplace.' Mr Gerald Massey, without any historical proof or probability, had insisted that they were addressed to the celebrated Lady Rich, the Stella of Sir Philip Sidney's sonnets, the Philoclea of his 'Arcadia,' and that they contained no personal revelation of Shakespeare's life and love, having been written in Lord Pembroke's name and at his request. Mr. Tyler had suggested that they referred to one of Queen Elizabeth's maids-of-honour, by name Mary Fitton. But none of these explanations satisfied the conditions of the problem. The woman that came between Shakespeare and Willie Hughes was a real woman, black-haired, and married, and of evil repute. Lady Rich's fame was evil enough, it is true, but her hair was of –

> 'fine threads of finest gold,
> In curled knots man's thought to hold',

and her shoulders like 'white doves perching.' She was, as King James said to her lover, Lord Mountjoy, 'a fair woman with a black soul.' As for Mary Fitton, we know that she was unmarried in 1601, the time when her amour with Lord Pembroke was discovered, and besides, any theories that connected Lord Pembroke with the Sonnets were, as Cyril Graham had shewn, put entirely out of court by the fact that Lord Pembroke did not come to London till they had been actually written and read by Shakespeare to his friends.

It was not, however, her name that interested me. I was content to hold with Professor Dowden that 'To the eyes of no diver among the wrecks of time will that curious talisman gleam.' What I wanted to discover was the nature of her influence over Shakespeare, as well as the characteristics of her personality. Two things were certain: she was much older than the poet, and the fascination that she exercised over him was at first purely intellectual. He began by feeling no physical passion for her. 'I do not love thee with mine eyes,' he says:

> 'Nor are mine ears with thy tongue's tune delighted;
> Nor tender feeling to base touches prone,
> Nor taste, nor smell, desire to be invited
> To any sensual feast with thee alone.'

He did not even think her beautiful:

> 'My mistress' eyes are nothing like the sun;
> Coral is far more red than her lips' red:
> If snow be white, why then her breasts are dun;
> If hairs be wires, black wires grow on her head.'

He had his moments of loathing for her, for, not content with enslaving the soul of Shakespeare, she seems to have sought to snare the senses of Willie Hughes. Then Shakespeare cries aloud, –

> 'Two loves I have of comfort and despair,
> Which like two spirits do suggest me still:
> The better angel is a man right fair,
> The worser spirit a woman colour'd ill.
> To win me soon to hell, my female evil
> Tempteth my better angel from my side,
> And would corrupt my saint to be a devil,
> Wooing his purity with her foul pride.'

Then he sees her as she really is, the 'bay where all men ride,' the 'wide world's common place,' the woman who is in the 'very refuse' of her evil deeds, and who is 'as black as hell, as dark as night.' Then it is that he pens that great sonnet upon Lust ('Th' expense of spirit in a waste of shame'), of which Mr Theodore Watts says rightly that it is the greatest sonnet ever written. And it is then, also, that he offers to mortgage his very life and genius to her if she will but restore to him that 'sweetest friend' of whom she had robbed him.

To compass this end he abandons himself to her, feigns to be full of an absorbing and sensuous passion of possession, forges false words of love, lies to her, and tells her that he lies.

> 'My thoughts and my discourse as madmen's are,
> At random from the truth vainly express'd;
> For I have sworn thee fair, and thought thee bright,
> Who art as black as hell, as dark as night.'

Rather than suffer his friend to be treacherous to him, he will himself be treacherous to his friend. To shield his purity, he will himself be vile. He knew the weakness of the boy-actor's nature, his susceptibility to praise, his inordinate love of admiration, and deliberately set himself to fascinate the woman who had come between them.

It is never with impunity that one's lips say Love's Litany. Words have their mystical power over the soul, and form can create the feeling from which it should have sprung. Sincerity itself, the ardent, momentary sincerity of the artist, is often the unconscious result of style, and in the case of those rare temperaments that are exquisitely susceptible to the influences of language, the use of certain phrases and modes of expression can stir the very pulse of passion, can send the red blood coursing through the veins, and can transform into a strange sensuous energy what in its origin had been mere aesthetic impulse, and desire of art. So, at least, it seems to have been with Shakespeare. He begins by pretending to love, wears a lover's apparel and has a lover's words upon his lips. What does it matter? It is only acting, only a comedy in real life. Suddenly he finds that what his tongue had spoken his soul had listened to, and that the raiment that he had put on for disguise is a plague-stricken and poisonous thing that eats into his flesh, and that he cannot throw away. Then comes Desire, with its many maladies, and Lust that makes one love all that one loathes, and Shame, with its ashen face and secret smile. He is enthralled by this dark woman, is for a season separated from his friend, and becomes the 'vassal-wretch' of one whom he knows to be evil and perverse and unworthy of his love, as of the love of Willie Hughes. 'O, from what power,' he says, –

> 'hast thou this powerful might,
> With insufficiency my heart to sway?
> To make me give the lie to my true sight,
> And swear that brightness does not grace the day?
> Whence has thou this becoming of things ill,
> That in the very refuse of thy deeds
> There is such strength and warrantise of skill
> That, in my mind, thy worst all best exceeds?'

He is keenly conscious of his own degradation, and finally, realising that his genius is nothing to her compared to the physical beauty of the young actor, he cuts with a quick knife the bond that binds him to her, and in this bitter sonnet bids her farewell: –

> 'In loving thee thou know'st I am forsworn,
> But thou art twice forsworn, to me love swearing:
> In act thy bed-vow broke, and new faith torn,
> In vowing new hate after new love bearing.
> But why of two oaths' breach do I accuse thee,
> When I break twenty? I am perjur'd most;
> For all my vows are oaths but to misuse thee,
> And all my honest faith in thee is lost:
> For I have sworn deep oaths of thy deep kindness,
> And, to enlighten thee, gave eyes to blindness,
> Or made them swear against the thing they see;
> For I have sworn thee fair; more perjur'd I,
> To swear against the truth so foul a lie!'

His attitude towards Willie Hughes in the whole matter shews at once the fervour and the self-abnegation of the great love he bore him. There is a poignant touch of pathos in the close of his sonnet:

> 'Those pretty wrongs that liberty commits,
> When I am sometime absent from thy heart,
> Thy beauty and thy years full well befits,
> For still temptation follows where thou art.
> Gentle thou art, and therefore to be won,
> Beauteous thou art, therefore to be assailed;
> And when a woman woos, what woman's son
> Will sourly leave her till she have prevailed?
> Ay me! but yet thou mightst my seat forbear,
> And chide thy beauty and thy straying youth,
> Who lead thee in their riot even there
> Where thou art forc'd to break a two-fold truth, –
> Hers, by thy beauty tempting her to thee,
> Thine, by thy beauty being false to me.'

But here he makes it manifest that his forgiveness was full and complete:

> 'No more be griev'd at that which thou hast done:
> Roses have thorns, and silver fountains mud;
> Clouds and eclipses stain both moon and sun,
> And loathsome canker lives in sweetest bud.
> All men make faults, and even I in this,
> Authorising thy trespass with compare,
> Myself corrupting, salving thy amiss,
> Excusing thy sins more than thy sins are;
> For to thy sensual fault I bring in sense, –
> The adverse party is thy advocate, –
> And 'gainst myself a lawful plea commence:
> Such civil war is in my love and hate,
> That I an accessary needs must be
> To that sweet thief which sourly robs from me.'

Shortly afterwards Shakespeare left London for Stratford (Sonnets XLIII–LII), and when he returned Willie Hughes seems to have grown tired of the woman who for a little time had fascinated him. Her name is never mentioned again in the Sonnets, nor is there any allusion made to her. She had passed out of their lives.

But who was she? And, even if her name has not come down to us, were there any allusions to her in contemporary literature? It seems to me that although better educated than most of the women of her time, she was not nobly born, but was probably the profligate wife of some old and wealthy citizen. We know that women of this class, which was then first rising into social prominence, were strangely fascinated by the new art of stage playing. They were to be found almost every afternoon at the theatre, when dramatic performances were being given, and 'The Actors' Remonstrance' is eloquent on the subject of their amours with the young actors.

Cranley in his 'Amanda' tells us of one who loved to mimic the actor's disguises, appearing one day 'embroidered, laced, perfumed, in glittering show ... as brave as any Countess,' and the next day, 'all in mourning, black and sad,' now in the grey cloak of a country wench, and now 'in the neat habit of a citizen.' She was a curious woman, 'more changeable and wavering than the moon,' and the books that she loved to read were Shakespeare's 'Venus and Adonis,' Beaumont's 'Salmacis and Hermaphroditus,' amorous pamphlets, and 'songs of love and sonnets exquisite.' These sonnets that were to her the 'bookes of her devotion,' were surely none other but Shakespeare's own, for the whole description reads like the portrait of the woman who fell in love with Willie Hughes, and, lest we should have any doubt on the subject, Cranley, borrowing Shakespeare's play on words, tells us that, in her 'proteus-like strange shapes,' she is one who –

'Changes hews with the chameleon.'

Manningham's Table-book, also, contains a clear allusion to the same story. Manningham was a student at the Middle Temple with Sir Thomas Overbury and Edmund Curle, whose chambers he seems to have shared; and his Diary is still preserved among the Harleian MSS. at the British Museum, a small duodecimo book written in a fair and tolerably legible hand, and containing many unpublished anecdotes about Shakespeare, Sir Walter Raleigh, Spenser, Ben Jonson and others. The dates, which are inserted with much care, extend from January 1600–1 to April 1603, and under the heading 'March 13, 1601,' Manningham tells us that he heard from a member of Shakespeare's company that a certain citizen's wife being at the Globe Theatre one afternoon, fell in love with one of the actors, and 'grew so farre in liking with him, that before shee went from the play shee appointed him to come that night unto hir,' but that Shakespeare 'overhearing their conclusion' anticipated his friend and came first to the lady's house, 'went before and was entertained,' as Manningham puts it, with some added looseness of speech which it is unnecessary to quote.

It seemed to me that we had here a common and distorted version of the story that is revealed to us in the Sonnets, the story of the dark woman's love for Willie Hughes, and Shakespeare's mad attempt to make her love him in his friend's stead. It was not, of course, necessary to accept it as absolutely true in every detail. According to Manningham's informant, for instance, the name of the actor in question was not Willie Hughes, but Richard Burbage. Tavern gossip, however, is proverbially inaccurate, and Burbage was, no doubt, dragged into the story to give point to the foolish jest about William the Conqueror and Richard the Third, with which the entry in Manningham's Diary ends. Burbage was our first great tragic actor, but it needed all his genius to counterbalance the physical defects of low stature and corpulent figure under which he laboured, and he was not the sort of man who would have fascinated the dark woman of the Sonnets, or would have cared to be fascinated by her. There was no doubt that Willie Hughes was referred to, and the private diary of a young law student of the time thus curiously corroborated Cyril Graham's wonderful guess at the secret of Shakespeare's great romance. Indeed, when taken in conjunction with 'Amanda,' Manningham's Table-book seemed to me to be an extremely strong link in the chain of evidence, and to place the new interpretation of the Sonnets on something like a secure historic basis, the fact that Cranley's poems were not published till after Shakespeare's death being really rather in favour of this view, as it was not likely that he would have ventured during the lifetime of the great dramatist to revive the memory of this tragic and bitter story.

This passion for the dark lady also enabled me to fix with still greater certainty the date of the Sonnets. From internal evidence, from the characteristics of language, style, and the like, it was evident that they belonged to Shakespeare's early period, the period of 'Love's Labour's Lost' and 'Venus and Adonis.' With the play, indeed, they are intimately connected. They display the same delicate euphuism, the same delight in fanciful phrase and curious expression, the artistic wilfulness and studied graces of the same 'fair tongue, conceit's expositor,' Rosaline, the –

> 'whitely wanton with a velvet brow,
> With two pitch-balls stuck in her face for eyes,'

who is born 'to make black fair,' and whose 'favour turns the fashion of the days,' is the dark lady of the Sonnets who makes black 'beauty's successive heir.' In the comedy as well as in the poems we have that half-sensuous philosophy that exalts the judgment of the senses 'above all slower, more toilsome means of knowledge,' and Berowne is perhaps, as Walter Pater suggests, a reflex of Shakespeare himself 'when he has just become able to stand aside from and estimate the first period of his poetry.'

Now though 'Love's Labour's Lost' was not published till 1598, when it was brought out 'newlie corrected and augmented' by Cuthbert Burby, there is no doubt that it was written and produced on the stage at a much earlier date, probably, as Professor Dowden points out, in 1588–9. If this be so, it is clear that Shakespeare's first meeting with Willie Hughes must have been in 1585, and it is just possible that this young actor may, after all, have been in his boyhood the musician of Lord Essex.

It is clear, at any rate, that Shakespeare's love for the dark lady must have passed away before 1594. In this year there appeared, under the editorship of Hadrian Dorell, that fascinating poem, or series of poems, 'Willobie his Avisa,' which is described by Mr. Swinburne as the one contemporary book which has been supposed to throw any direct or indirect light on the mystic matter of the Sonnets. In it we learn how a young gentleman of St. John's College, Oxford, by name Henry Willobie, fell in love with a woman so 'fair and chaste' that he called her Avisa, either because such beauty as hers had never been seen, or because she fled like a bird from the snare of his passion, and spread her wings for flight when he ventured but to touch her hand. Anxious to win his mistress, he consults his familiar friend W.S., 'who not

long before had tried the curtesy of the like passion, and was now newly re-
covered of the like infection.' Shakespeare encouraged him in the siege that
he is laying to the Castle of Beauty, telling him that every woman is to be
wooed, and every woman to be won; views this 'loving comedy' from far off,
in order to see 'whether it would sort to a happier end for this new actor than
it did for the old player,' and 'enlargeth the wound with the sharpe razor of a
willing conceit,' feeling the purely aesthetic interest of the artist in the
moods and emotions of others. It is unnecessary, however, to enter more
fully into this curious passage in Shakespeare's life, as all that I wanted to
point out was that in 1594 he had been cured of his infatuation for the dark
lady, and had already been acquainted for at least three years with Willie
Hughes.

My whole scheme of the Sonnets was now complete, and, by placing those
that refer to the dark lady in their proper order and position, I saw the perfect
unity and completeness of the whole. The drama – for indeed they formed a
drama and a soul's tragedy of fiery passion and of noble thought – is divided
into four scenes or acts. In the first of these (Sonnets I–XXXII) Shakespeare
invites Willie Hughes to go upon the stage as an actor, and to put to the ser-
vice of Art his wonderful physical beauty, and his exquisite grace of youth,
before passion has robbed him of the one, and time taken from him the other.
Willie Hughes, after a time, consents to be a player in Shakespeare's com-
pany, and soon becomes the very centre and keynote of his inspiration. Sud-
denly, in one red-rose July (Sonnets XXXIII–LII, LXI, and
CXXVII–CLII) there comes to the Globe Theatre a dark woman with won-
derful eyes, who falls passionately in love with Willie Hughes. Shakespeare,
sick with the malady of jealousy, and made mad by many doubts and fears,
tries to fascinate the woman who had come between him and his friend. The
love, that is at first feigned, becomes real, and he finds himself enthralled and
dominated by a woman whom he knows to be evil and unworthy. To her the
genius of a man is as nothing compared to a boy's beauty. Willie Hughes be-
comes for a time her slave and the toy of her fancy, and the second act ends
with Shakespeare's departure from London. In the third act her influence
has passed away. Shakespeare returns to London, and renews his friendship
with Willie Hughes, to whom he promises immortality in his plays. Mar-
lowe, hearing of the wonder and grace of the young actor, lures him away
from the Globe Theatre to play Gaveston in the tragedy of 'Edward II,' and
for the second time Shakespeare is separated from his friend. The last act
(Sonnets C–CXXVI) tells us of the return of Willie Hughes to Shake-
speare's company. Evil rumour has now stained the white purity of his
name, but Shakespeare's love still endures and is perfect. Of the mystery of
this love, and of the mystery of passion, we are told strange and marvellous
things, and the Sonnets conclude with an envoi of twelve lines whose motive
is the triumph of Beauty over Time, and of Death over Beauty.

And what had been the end of him who had been so dear to the soul of
Shakespeare, and who by his presence and passion had given reality to
Shakespeare's art? When the Civil War broke out, the English actors took

the side of their king, and many of them, like Robinson foully slain by Major Harrison at the taking of Basing House, laid down their lives in the king's service. Perhaps on the trampled heath of Marston, or on the bleak hills of Naseby, the dead body of Willie Hughes had been found by some of the rough peasants of the district, his gold hair 'dabbled with blood,' and his breast pierced with many wounds. Or it may be that the Plague, which was very frequent in London at the beginning of the seventeenth century and was indeed regarded by many of the Christians as a judgment sent on the city for its love of 'vaine plaies and idolatrous shewes,' had touched the lad while he was acting, and he had crept home to his lodgings to die there alone, Shakespeare being far away at Stratford, and those who had flocked in such numbers to see him, the 'gazers' whom, as the Sonnets tell us, he had 'led astray,' being too much afraid of contagion to come near him. A story of this kind was current at the time about a young actor, and was made use of by the Puritans in their attempts to stifle the free development of the English Renaissance. Yet, surely, had this actor been Willie Hughes, tidings of his tragic death would have been speedily brought to Shakespeare as he lay dreaming under the mulberry tree in his garden at New Place, and in an elegy as sweet as that written by Milton on Edward King, he would have mourned for the lad who had brought such joy and sorrow into his life, and whose connection with his art had been of so vital and intimate a character. Something made me feel certain that Willie Hughes had survived Shakespeare, and had fulfilled in some measure the high prophecies the poet had made about him, and one evening the true secret of his end flashed across me.

He had been one of those English actors who in 1611, the year of Shakespeare's retirement from the stage, went across sea to Germany and played before the great Duke Henry Julius of Brunswick, himself a dramatist of no mean order, and at the Court of that strange Elector of Brandenburg, who was so enamoured of beauty that he was said to have bought for his weight in amber the young son of a travelling Greek merchant, and to have given pageants in honour of his slave, all through that dreadful famine year of 1606-7, when the people died of hunger in the very streets of the town, and for the space of seven months there was no rain. The Library at Cassel contains to the present day a copy of the first edition of Marlowe's 'Edward II,' the only copy in existence, Mr. Bullen tells us. Who could have brought it to that town but he who had created the part of the king's minion, and for whom indeed it had been written? Those stained and yellow pages had once been touched by his white hands. We also know that 'Romeo and Juliet,' a play specially connected with Willie Hughes, was brought out at Dresden, in 1613, along with 'Hamlet' and 'King Lear,' and certain of Marlowe's plays, and it was surely to none other than Willie Hughes himself that in 1617 the death-mask of Shakespeare was brought by one of the suite of the English ambassador, pale token of the passing away of the great poet who had so dearly loved him. Indeed, there was something peculiarly fitting in the idea that the boy-actor, whose beauty had been so vital an element in the realism and romance of Shakespeare's art, had been the first to have brought to Germany the seed of the new culture, and was in his way the precursor of the *Aufklärung* or Illumination of the eighteenth century, that splendid movement which, though begun by Lessing and Herder, and brought to its full and perfect issue by Goethe was in no small part helped on by a young actor – Friedrich Schroeder – who awoke the popular consciousness, and by means of the feigned passions and mimetic methods of the stage showed the intimate, the vital, connection between life and literature. If this was so, – and there was certainly no evidence against it, – it was not improbable that Willie Hughes was one of those English comedians (*mimi quidam ex Britannia*, as the old chronicle calls them), who were slain at Nuremberg in a sudden uprising of the people, and were secretly buried in a little vineyard outside the city by some young men'who had found pleasure in their performances, and of whom some had sought to be instructed in the mysteries of the new art.' Certainly no more fitting place could there be for him to whom Shakespeare had said 'thou art all my art,' than this little vineyard outside the city walls. For was it not from the sorrows of Dionysos that Tragedy sprang? Was not the light laughter of Comedy, with its careless merriment and quick replies, first heard on the lips of the Sicilian vine-dressers? Nay, did not the purple and red stain of the wine-froth on face and limbs give the first suggestion of the charm and fascination of disguise? – the desire for self-concealment, the sense of the value of objectivity, thus showing itself in the rude beginnings of art. At any rate, wherever he lay – whether in the little vineyard at the gate of the Gothic town, or in some dim London churchyard amidst the roar and bustle of our great city – no gorgeous monument marked his resting place. His true tomb, as Shakespeare saw, was the poet's verse, his true monument the permanence of the drama. So had it been with others whose beauty had given a new creative impulse to their age. The ivory body of the Bithynian slave rots in the green ooze of the Nile, and on the yellow hills of the Cerameicus is strewn the dust of the young Athenian; but Antinous lives in sculpture, and Charmides in philosophy.

5

A young Elizabethan, who was enamoured of a girl so white that he named her Alba, has left on record the impression produced on him by one of the first performances of 'Love's Labour's Lost.' Admirable though the actors were, and they played 'in cunning wise,' he tells us, especially those who took the lovers' parts, he was conscious that everything was 'feigned,' that nothing came 'from the heart,' that though they appeared to grieve they 'felt no care,' and were merely presenting 'a show in jest.' Yet, suddenly, this fanciful comedy of unreal romance became to him, as he sat in the audience, the real tragedy of his life. The moods of his own soul seemed to have taken shape and substance, and to be moving before him. His grief had a mask that smiled, and his sorrow wore gay raiment. Behind the bright and quickly-changing pageant of the stage, he saw himself, as one sees one's image in a fantastic glass. The very words that came to the actors' lips were wrung out of his pain. Their false tears were of his shedding.

There are few of us who have not felt something akin to this. We become lovers when we see Romeo and Juliet, and Hamlet makes us students. The blood of Duncan is upon our hands, with Timon we rage against the world, and when Lear wanders out upon the heath the terror of madness touches us. Ours is the white sinlessness of Desdemona, and ours, also, the sin of Iago. Art, even the art of fullest scope and widest vision, can never really show us the external world. All that it shows us is our own soul, the one world of which we have any real cognizance. And the soul itself, the soul of each one of us, is to each one of us a mystery. It hides in the dark and broods, and consciousness cannot tell us of its workings. Consciousness, indeed, is quite inadequate to explain the contents of personality. It is Art, and Art only, that reveals us to ourselves.

We sit at the play with the woman we love, or listen to the music in some Oxford garden, or stroll with our friend through the cool galleries of the Pope's house at Rome, and suddenly we become aware that we have passions of which we have never dreamed, thoughts that make us afraid, pleasures whose secret has been denied to us, sorrows that have been hidden from our tears. The actor is unconscious of our presence: the musician is thinking of the subtlety of the fugue, of the tone of his instrument; the marble gods that smile so curiously at us are made of insensate stone. But they have given form and substance to what was within us; they have enabled us to realise our personality; and a sense of perilous joy, or some touch or thrill of pain, or that strange self-pity that man so often feels for himself, comes over us and leaves us different.

Some such impression the Sonnets of Shakespeare had certainly produced on me. As from opal dawns to sunsets of withered rose I read and re-read them in garden or chamber, it seemed to me that I was deciphering the story of a life that had once been mine, unrolling the record of a romance that, without my knowing it, had coloured the very texture of my nature, had dyed it with strange and subtle dyes. Art, as so often happens, had taken the place of personal experience. I felt as if I had been initiated into the secret of that passionate friendship, that love of beauty and beauty of love, of which Marsilio Ficino tells us, and of which the Sonnets in their noblest and purest significance, may be held to be the perfect expression.

Yes: I had lived it all. I had stood in the round theatre with its open roof and fluttering banners, had seen the stage draped with black for a tragedy, or set with gay garlands for some brighter show. The young gallants came out with their pages, and took their seats in front of the tawny curtain that hung from the satyr-carved pillars of the inner scene. They were insolent and debonair in their fantastic dresses. Some of them wore French lovelocks, and white doublets stiff with Italian embroidery of gold thread, and long hose of blue or pale yellow silk. Others were all in black, and carried huge plumed hats. These affected the Spanish fashion. As they played at cards, and blew thin wreaths of smoke from the tiny pipes that the pages lit for them, the truant prentices and idle schoolboys that thronged the yard mocked them. But they only smiled at each other. In the side boxes some masked women were sitting. One of them was waiting with hungry eyes and bitten lips for the drawing back of the curtain. As the trumpet sounded for the third time she leant forward, and I saw her olive skin and raven's-wing hair. I knew her. She had marred for a season the great friendship of my life. Yet there was something about her that fascinated me.

The play changed according to my mood. Sometimes it was 'Hamlet.' Taylor acted the Prince, and there were many who wept when Ophelia went mad. Sometimes it was 'Romeo and Juliet.' Burbage was Romeo. He hardly looked the part of the young Italian, but there was a rich music in his voice, and passionate beauty in every gesture. I saw 'As You Like It,' and 'Cymbeline,' and 'Twelfth Night,' and in each play there was some one whose life was bound up into mine, who realised for me every dream, and gave shape to every fancy. How gracefully he moved! The eyes of the audience were fixed on him.

And yet it was in this century that it had all happened. I had never seen my friend, but he had been with me for many years, and it was to his influence that I owed my passion for Greek thought and art, and indeed all my sympathy with the Hellenic spirit. (φιλοσοφεῖν μὲτ' ἐρῶτος!)[1] How that phrase had stirred me in my Oxford days! I did not understand then why it was so. But I knew now. There had been a presence beside me always. Its silver feet had trod night's shadowy meadows, and the white hands had moved aside the trembling curtains of the dawn. It had walked with me through the grey cloisters, and when I sat reading in my room, it was there also. What though I had been unconscious of it? The soul had a life of its own, and the brain its own sphere of action. There was something within us that knew nothing of sequence or extension, and yet, like the philosopher of the Ideal City, was the spectator of all time and of all existence. It had senses that quickened, passions that came to birth, spiritual ecstasies of contemplation, ardours of fiery-coloured love. It was we who were unreal, and our conscious life was the least important part of our development. The soul, the secret soul, was the only reality.

How curiously it had all been revealed to me! A book of Sonnets, published nearly three hundred years ago, written by a dead hand and in honour of a dead youth, had suddenly explained to me the whole story of my soul's romance. I remembered how once in Egypt I had been present at the opening of a frescoed coffin that had been found in one of the basalt tombs at Thebes. Inside there was the body of a young girl swathed in tight bands of linen, and with a gilt mask over her face. As I stooped down to look at it, I had seen that one of the little withered hands held a scroll of yellow papyrus covered with

---

[1] To become wise through love.

strange characters. How I wished now that I had it read to me! It might have told me something more about the soul that hid within me, and had its mysteries of passion of which I was kept in ignorance. Strange, that we knew so little about ourselves, and that our most intimate personality was concealed from us! Were we to look in tombs for our real life, and in art for the legend of our days?

Week after week, I pored over these poems, and each new form of knowledge seemed to me a mode of reminiscence. Finally, after two months had elapsed, I determined to make a strong appeal to Erskine to do justice to the memory of Cyril Graham, and to give to the world his marvellous interpretation of the Sonnets – the only interpretation that thoroughly explained the problem. I have not any copy of my letter, I regret to say, nor have I been able to lay my hand upon the original; but I remember that I went over the whole ground, and covered sheets of paper with passionate reiteration of the arguments and proofs that my study had suggested to me.

It seemed to me that I was not merely restoring Cyril Graham to his proper place in literary history, but rescuing the honour of Shakespeare himself from the tedious memory of a commonplace intrigue. I put into the letter all my enthusiasm. I put into the letter all my faith.

No sooner, in fact, had I sent it off than a curious reaction came over me. It seemed to me that I had given away my capacity for belief in the Willie Hughes theory of the Sonnets, that something had gone out of me, as it were, and that I was perfectly indifferent to the whole subject. What was it that had happened? It is difficult to say. Perhaps, by finding perfect expression for a passion, I had exhausted the passion itself. Emotional forces, like the forces of physical life, have their positive limitations. Perhaps the mere effort to convert any one to a theory involves some form of renunciation of the power of credence. Influence is simply a transference of personality, a mode of giving away what is most precious to one's self, and its exercise produces a sense, and, it may be, a reality of loss. Every disciple takes away something from his master. Or perhaps I had become tired of the whole thing, wearied of its fascination, and, my enthusiasm having burnt out, my reason was left to its own impassioned judgment. However it came about, I cannot pretend to explain it, there was no doubt that Willie Hughes suddenly became to me a mere myth, an idle dream, the boyish fancy of a young man who, like most ardent spirits, was more anxious to convince others than to be himself convinced.

I must admit that this was a bitter disappointment to me. I had gone through every phase of this great romance. I had lived with it, and it had become part of my nature. How was it that it had left me? Had I touched upon some secret that my soul desired to conceal? Or was there no permanence in personality? Did things come and go through the brain, silently, swiftly, and without footprints, like shadows through a mirror? Were we at the mercy of such impressions as Art or Life chose to give us? It seemed to me to be so.

It was at night-time that this feeling first came to me. I had sent my servant out to post the letter to Erskine, and was seated at the window looking out at the blue and gold city. The moon had not yet risen, and there was only one star in the sky, but the streets were full of quick-moving and flashing lights, and the windows of Devonshire House were illuminated for a great dinner to be given to some of the foreign princes then visiting London. I saw the scarlet liveries of the royal carriages, and the crowd hustling about the sombre gates of the courtyard.

Suddenly, I said to myself: 'I have been dreaming, and all my life for these two months has been unreal. There was no such person as Willie Hughes.' Something like a faint cry of pain came to my lips as I began to realise how I had deceived myself, and I buried my face in my hands, struck with a sorrow greater than any I had felt since boyhood. After a few moments I rose, and going into the library took up the Sonnets, and began to read them. But it was all to no avail. They gave me back nothing of the feeling that I had brought to them; they revealed to me nothing of what I had found hidden in their lines. Had I merely been influenced by the beauty of the forged portrait, charmed by that Shelley-like face into faith and credence? Or, as Erskine had suggested, was it the pathetic tragedy of Cyril Graham's death that had so deeply stirred me? I could not tell. To the present day I cannot understand the beginning or the end of this strange passage in my life.

However, as I had said some very unjust and bitter things to Erskine in my letter, I determined to go and see him as soon as possible, and make my apologies to him for my behaviour. Accordingly, the next morning I drove down to Birdcage Walk, where I found him sitting in his library, with the forged picture of Willie Hughes in front of him.

'My dear Erskine!' I cried, 'I have come to apologise to you.'

'To apologise to me?' he said. 'What for?'

'For my letter,' I answered.

'You have nothing to regret in your letter,' he said. 'On the contrary, you have done me the greatest service in your power. You have shown me that Cyril Graham's theory is perfectly sound.'

I stared at him in blank wonder.

'You don't mean to say that you believe in Willie Hughes?' I exclaimed.

'Why not?' he rejoined. 'You have proved the thing to me. Do you think I cannot estimate the value of evidence?'

'But there is no evidence at all,' I groaned, sinking into a chair. 'When I wrote to you I was under the influence of a perfectly silly enthusiasm. I had been touched by the story of Cyril Graham's death, fascinated by his artistic theory, enthralled by the wonder and novelty of the whole idea. I see now that the theory is based on a delusion. The only evidence for the existence of Willie Hughes is that picture in front of you, and that picture is a forgery. Don't be carried away by mere sentiment in this matter. Whatever romance may have to say about the Willie Hughes theory, reason is dead against it.'

'I don't understand you,' said Erskine, looking at me in amazement. 'You have convinced me by your letter that Willie Hughes is an absolute reality. Why have you changed your mind? Or is all that you have been saying to me merely a joke?'

'I cannot explain it to you,' I rejoined, 'but I see now that there is really nothing to be said in favour of Cyril Graham's interpretation. The Sonnets may not be addressed to Lord Pembroke. They probably are not. But for heaven's sake don't waste your time in a foolish attempt to discover a young Elizabethan actor who never existed, and to make a phantom puppet the centre of the great cycle of Shakespeare's Sonnets.'

'I see that you don't understand the theory,' he replied.

'My dear Erskine,' I cried, 'not understand it! Why, I feel as if I had invented it. Surely my letter shows you that I not merely went into the whole matter, but that I contributed proofs of every kind. The one flaw in the theory is that it presupposes the existence of the person whose existence is the subject of dispute. If we grant that there was in Shakespeare's company a young actor of the name of Willie Hughes, it is not difficult to make him the object of the Sonnets. But as we know that there was no actor of this name in the company of the Globe Theatre, it is idle to pursue the investigation further.'

'But that is exactly what we don't know,' said Erskine. 'It is quite true that his name does not occur in the list given in the first folio; but, as Cyril pointed out, that is rather a proof in favour of the existence of Willie Hughes than against it, if we remember his treacherous desertion of Shakespeare for a rival dramatist. Besides,' and here I must admit that Erskine made what seems to me now a rather good point, though, at the time, I laughed at it, 'there is no reason at all why Willie Hughes should not have gone upon the stage under an assumed name. In fact it is extremely probable that he did so. We know that there was a very strong prejudice against the theatre in his day, and nothing is more likely than that his family insisted upon his adopting some *nom de plume*. The editors of the first folio would naturally put him down under his stage name, the name by which he was best known to the public, but the Sonnets were of course an entirely different matter, and in the dedication to them the publisher very properly addresses him under his real initials. If this be so, and it seems to me the most simple and rational explanation of the matter, I regard Cyril Graham's theory as absolutely proved.'

'But what evidence have you?' I exclaimed, laying my hand on his. 'You have no evidence at all. It is mere hypothesis. And which of Shakespeare's actors do you think that Willie Hughes was? The "pretty fellow" Ben Jonson tells us of, who was so fond of dressing up in girls' clothes?'

'I don't know,' he answered rather irritably. 'I have not had time to investigate the point yet. But I feel quite sure that my theory is the true one. Of course it is a hypothesis, but then it is a hypothesis that explains everything, and if you had been sent to Cambridge to study science, instead of to Oxford to dawdle over literature, you would know that a hypothesis that explains everything is a certainty.'

'Yes, I am aware that Cambridge is a sort of educational institute,' I murmured. 'I am glad I was not there.'

'My dear fellow,' said Erskine, suddenly turning his keen grey eyes on me, 'you believe in Cyril Graham's theory, you believe in Willie Hughes, you know that the Sonnets are addressed to an actor, but for some reason or other you won't acknowledge it.'

'I wish I could believe it,' I rejoined. 'I would give anything to be able to do so. But I can't. It is a sort of moonbeam theory, very lovely, very fascinating, but intangible. When one thinks that one has got hold of it, it escapes one. No: Shakespeare's heart is still to us "a closet never pierc'd with crystal eyes, ' as he calls it in one of the sonnets. We shall never know the true secret of the passion of his life.'

Erskine sprang from the sofa, and paced up and down the room. 'We know it already,' he cried, 'and the world shall know it some day.'

I had never seen him so excited. He would not hear of my leaving him, and insisted on my stopping for the rest of the day.

We argued the matter over for hours, but nothing that I could say could make him surrender his faith in Cyril Graham's interpretation. He told me that he intended to devote his life to proving the theory, and that he was de-termined to do justice to Cyril Graham's memory. I entreated him, laughed at him, begged of him, but it was to no use. Finally we parted, not exactly in anger, but certainly with a shadow between us. He thought me shallow, I thought him foolish. When I called on him again, his servant told me that he had gone to Germany. The letters that I wrote to him remained unanswered.

Two years afterwards, as I was going into my club, the hall porter handed me a letter with a foreign postmark. It was from Erskine, and written at the Hôtel d'Angleterre, Cannes. When I had read it, I was filled with horror, though I did not quite believe that he would be so mad as to carry his resolve into execution. The gist of the letter was that he had tried in every way to verify the Willie Hughes theory, and had failed, and that as Cyril Graham had given his life for this theory, he himself had determined to give his own life also to the same cause. The concluding words of the letter were these: 'I still believe in Willie Hughes; and by the time you receive this I shall have died by my own hand for Willie Hughes' sake: for his sake, and for the sake of Cyril Graham, whom I drove to his death by my shallow scepticism and ig-norant lack of faith. The truth was once revealed to you, and you rejected it. It comes to you now, stained with the blood of two lives – do not turn away from it.'

It was a horrible moment. I felt sick with misery, and yet I could not be-lieve that he would carry out his intention. To die for one's theological opin-ions is the worst use a man can make of his life; but to die for a literary theory! It seemed impossible.

I looked at the date. The letter was a week old. Some unfortunate chance had prevented my going to the club for several days, or I might have got it in time to save him. Perhaps it was not too late. I drove off to my rooms, packed up my things, and started by the night mail from Charing Cross. The jour-ney was intolerable. I thought I would never arrive.

As soon as I did, I drove to the Hôtel d'Angleterre. It was quite true. Erskine was dead. They told me that he had been buried two days before in the English cemetery. There was something horribly grotesque about the whole tragedy. I said all kinds of wild things, and the people in the hall looked curiously at me.

Suddenly Lady Erskine, in deep mourning, passed across the vestibule. When she saw me she came up to me, murmured something about her poor son, and burst into tears. I led her into the sitting room. An elderly gentleman was there, reading a newspaper. It was the English doctor.

We talked a great deal about Erskine, but I said nothing about his motive for committing suicide. It was evident that he had not told his mother anything about the reason that had driven him to so fatal, so mad an act. Finally Lady Erskine rose and said, 'George left you something as a memento. It was a thing that he prized very much. I will get it for you.'

As soon as she had left the room I turned to the doctor and said, 'What a dreadful shock it must have been for Lady Erskine! I wonder that she bears it as well as she does.'

'Oh, she knew for months past that it was coming,' he answered.

'Knew it for months past!' I cried. 'But why didn't she stop him? Why didn't she have him watched? He must have been out of his mind.'

The doctor stared at me. 'I don't know what you mean,' he said.

'Well,' I cried, 'if a mother knows that her son is going to commit suicide –'

'Suicide!' he answered. 'Poor Erskine did not commit suicide. He died of consumption. He came here to die. The moment I saw him I knew that there was no chance. One lung was almost gone, and the other was very much affected. Three days before he died he asked me was there any hope. I told him frankly that there was none, and that he had only a few days to live. He wrote some letters, and was quite resigned, retaining his senses to the last.'

I got up from my seat, and going over to the open window I looked out on the crowded promenade. I remember that the brightly-coloured umbrellas and gay parasols seemed to me like huge fantastic butterflies fluttering by the shore of a blue-metal sea, and that the heavy odour of violets that came across the garden made me think of that wonderful sonnet in which Shakespeare tells us that the scent of these flowers always reminded him of his friend. What did it all mean? Why had Erskine written me that extraordinary letter? Why when standing at the very gate of death had he turned back to tell me what was not true? Was Hugo right? Is affectation the only thing that accompanies a man up the steps of the scaffold? Did Erskine merely want to produce a dramatic effect? That was not like him. It was more like something I might have done myself. No: he was simply actuated by a desire to reconvert me to Cyril Graham's theory, and he thought that if I could be made to believe that he too had given his life for it, I would be deceived by the pathetic fallacy of martyrdom. Poor Erskine! I had grown wiser since I had seen him. Martyrdom was to me merely a tragic form of scepticism, an attempt to realise by fire what one had failed to do by faith. No man dies for what he knows to be true. Men die for what they want to be true, for what some terror in their hearts tells them is not true. The very uselessness of Erskine's letter made me doubly sorry for him. I watched the people strolling in and out of the cafés, and wondered if any of them had known him. The white dust blew down the scorched sunlit road, and the feathery palms moved restlessly in the shaken air.

At that moment Lady Erskine returned to the room carrying the fatal portrait of Willie Hughes. 'When George was dying, he begged me to give you this,' she said. As I took it from her, her tears fell on my hand.

This curious work of art hangs now in my library, where it is very much admired by my artistic friends, one of whom has etched it for me. They have decided that it is not a Clouet, but an Ouvry. I have never cared to tell them its true history, but sometimes, when I look at it, I think there is really a great deal to be said for the Willie Hughes theory of Shakespeare's Sonnets.

THE PLAYS

Introduction by

TERENCE BROWN

W. B. Yeats, who as an impecunious young man in London, had the opportunity to observe his fellow Irishman and artist at the height of his conversational powers and at his most socially successful, astutely realised that the world Wilde explored so skilfully in his plays was one essentially alien to him. The upper classes and ruling elites of England, Yeats reckoned, to Wilde 'were as the nobles of Baghdad'. Coming as he did from the Dublin which combined professional, academic and bohemian ways of life in a rackety, even disreputable brilliance, the subtle gradations of the English class system offered him much to reflect upon in his inimitable, iconoclastic manner. The pyramidic solidity of its social structures, with a glittering apex in the gentleman's club, the Grosvenor Place town house and the country estate, was accordingly observed by Wilde with an eye that never took anything for granted, an eye acutely sensitive to the fact that a world which so manifestly took itself for granted had its foundations in the insecure, shifting sands of human need, ambition, power and passion. So plays that can seem simply clever, opportunistic exploitations of current theatrical fashions – for melodrama, for farce, for French *boulevard* comedy, for society plays that made everything of reversals, confusions, revelations, kleptodramatics – or simply vehicles for Wilde's epigrammatic wit, are amongst the most devastating of studies of the bases of English society at the moment when its masters ruled the world, when the sun which lightens the summery garden scenes of *The Importance of Being Earnest* never set upon a far-flung empire.

For Wilde does not flinch in the matter of money. Wealth is a given in the lavish interiors through which Wilde's elegant creations live, move and have their being. The opening passages of *An Ideal Husband*, for example, set in the octagon room of Sir Robert Chiltern's magnificent house can be seen as a tableau to be entitled 'The Ideal Home' with its chandelier, staircase, 18th century French tapestry, its music room to one side from which emerges the faint sound of a string quartet. We are in the apotheosis of the house beautiful into which guests are received as *objets d'art* in their own right. Yet it is clear from this play, as from the other social comedies, that such wealth depends on British imperial power, on the aggressive control of world trade which has opened a canal to the east at Suez and is now assessing similar, corrupt plans for the Argentine. Indeed, there is in the Faustian temptation to which Sir Robert has given way in this play, something of the eastern luxury and sumptuousness that makes Sir Robert a brother of Herod in *Salomé* in a shared knowledge of luxury as the proper, privileged background for power. For each the exoticism of strange beauty is the sign of a power over men which 'is the one pleasure worth knowing', though both learn to their cost that there are forces over which it cannot exercise mastery.

This then is a world of a ruling caste which has had its servants fly to India for gold and has ransacked the ocean for the orient pearl. Furthermore it quite unembarrassedly accepts that it needs to sustain its life by regular injections of energy and capital from the colonies. Its languid, exquisite mannerism is not so unworldly that it does not welcome a brash Australian to its midst, like Hopper in *Lady Windermere's Fan* because of, rather than despite the fact that, 'his father made a great fortune by selling some kind of food in circular tins'. He may take a daughter off one's hands and provide what the commercial and colonial classes are obliged to – the economic wherewithal for the ruling classes to continue their delightful lives. Indeed one senses that the impatience felt for the young American woman, Hester Worsley, in *A Woman Of No Importance* by the society *grandes dames* she offends by her puritanical outbursts is her disinclination to play a predestined part as the orphan of 'an American millionaire or philanthropist, or both' who will adapt to the conventions of that complex but adamantine artifice, the English class system. 'She is painfully natural, is she not?' says Lady Stutfield, sniffily.

It is of course Lady Bracknell who without sentimental compunction of any kind lets us see how money is the key to survival in the upper reaches of English society. In her famous interrogation of Jack Worthing, when she discovers the misfortunes that attended his birth, it is his fortune that she investigates with the surest touch. This is a woman who knows what's what in her world: 'What between the duties expected of one during one's lifetime, and the duties exacted from one after one's death, land has ceased to be either a profit or a pleasure. It gives one a position, and prevents one from keeping it up. That's all that can be said about land.' Lady Bracknell's hard-nosed financial acumen is so integral a part of her character that even when Wilde dramatises it in terms of farce in the final act ('A hundred and thirty thousand pounds! And in the funds! Miss Cardew seems to me a most attractive young lady now that I look at her') he seems merely to be highlighting a cruel truth about the mercenary exigencies of the social world he has come to know. And it is also in *The Importance of Being Earnest* (in the second act of the original four, printed here, which is not the more usually performed three-act version prepared at the behest of Wilde's actor manager) that Wilde lets us see for a moment the disasters that can strike when access to funds is not assured. A solicitor tracks down Algernon and serves him with a writ for Ernest's debts. Holloway prison beckons, like a premonitory warning of the dramatist's own fate, so shortly to unfold, in a society where ruin could be immediate and merciless. That among the various topics of the age that the characters address conversationally in the plays – the Married Women's Property Act, German philosophy – is bimetallism, should not then surprise, since we are eavesdropping on a social caste for whom money is a defining element.

In his plays Wilde subjects the hypocrisies and cruelties of the English establishment to a withering moral critique. Yet he does so without investing his plays with a wearying sense of self-importance or indeed with earnestness. They remain wonderfully theatrical, undeniably entertaining, even as they challenge the ethical assumptions of the world in which such entertainment is discovered. The question, for example, as to what constitutes virtue in a woman in both *Lady Windermere's Fan* and *A Woman of No Importance* is shown to have no ready answer in the moral values of the age with their simplistic, grotesquely hypocritical moral absolutes. In both a character is disturbed by the moral ambiguity of past lives as they effect their own and by the inadequacy of a black and white sense of right and wrong. Lady Windermere for all her puritanism finds herself trapped by circumstance and her own nature in a compromising position from which she has to be rescued by the woman 'with a past', Mrs Erlynne, who is in fact, though she never comes to know this, her own mother. Gerald in *A Woman of No Importance* must come to terms with the fact that his mother bore him illegitimately.

Both plays deal therefore in the kind of material that makes for melodrama and the revelations of *boulevard* theatre and comedy in general. They possess accordingly a dramatic atmosphere – with the concealments, intercepted letters, costume accessories which are vital to the plots, overheard and misinterpreted conversations, confusions of apparent motive – that would imply to an audience dramatic *dénouements* eagerly to be expected, in which all will be revealed in a comedic reassertion of harmonious order, the evil punished and the good rewarded. Wilde's achievement in such plays is therefore to maintain the dramatic impact of the conventions within which he worked but to deny the audience the kind of terminal gratifications implicitly promised in the form and theatrical style of his theatre. Instead he leaves his audiences with an altogether more problematic sense of things than the ostensible matter and mode would allow them to anticipate.

For the endings of Wilde's plays are profoundly equivocal. Lady Windermere has learnt something of herself by the conclusion of *Lady Windermere's Fan* but certainly not all, left as she is in the dark about her true mother. Mrs Erlynne rightly judges, we feel, that her daughter's future with her husband requires such ignorance. And Mrs Erlynne is to embark on a marriage with Lord Augustus founded on a necessary deception. Hester, Gerald and Mrs Arbuthnot have to leave England at the end of *A Woman of No Importance* since its social reality cannot accommodate their subversive, uncomfortably raw authenticity of feeling. The youthfully corrupted Sir Robert Chiltern in *An Ideal Husband* at the last is saved from the ruin which has pursued him in the person of an adventuress and blackmailer not because he defied her in refusing to make the speech in the House of Commons she demanded but because his tormentor has been hoist by her own petard. He and Lady Chiltern at the last share an oddly ambiguous kind of redemption in which they are permitted to continue to enjoy the fruits of a crime and the power it has made available, only as they respond to their extreme good fortune in a mature understanding of matrimonial love, though one in which women's freedom seems to be sacrificed.

As Kerry Powell has remarked about *Lady Windermere's Fan* in a comment that applies to the dramatist's social comedies in general: 'thus did Wilde work through the melodramatic formula, only to upset everything at the end by repudiating the categorical assumptions about right and wrong, sin and punishment, upon which this curious dramatic type was founded.'

A key figure in the Wildean dramatic universe is the dandy – the droll, epicene, epigrammatic commentator on the foibles of the age. And as dramatist Wilde invests a good deal of the moral authority of his plays in such figures. For in their languid, sardonic, worldly knowingness they create for themselves a position in their world that implies an observational, superior status to the other characters in the plays and to the social order in which they function as brilliantly self-possessed wits. Cecil Graham in *Lady Windermere's Fan* and Mrs Allonby in *A Woman of No Importance* are two such figures as is Lord Goring in *An Ideal Husband* who Wilde introduces in the following terms:'A well-bred, expressionless face. He is clever, but would not like to be thought so. A flawless dandy, he would be annoyed if he were considered romantic. He plays with life, and is on perfectly good terms with the world. He is fond of being misunderstood. It gives him a post of vantage.' At the beginning of the third act he is further glossed as one who 'stands in immediate relation to modern life, makes it indeed, and so masters it. He is the first well-dressed philosopher in the history of thought'. Such a figure can bear the moral weight that Wilde requires him to carry in the play (it is he who by a strategem rescues Sir Robert; who articulates the conviction that it is love 'that is the true explanation of this world') since he seems totally present to himself, wholly aware of and at ease with the complex realities of his own nature which he expresses in the guise of paradox.

Yet Wilde's expansive prose introductions of him do bespeak in the playwright uncertainty as to the dandy's exact role in the world in which he appears. He is at once an amused trifler, at a point of vantage, in direct relation to modern life and a maker and master of it. This spectrum of attributes may indeed reflect what Peter Raby has identified as the central critical problem of the Wildean dramaturgy when he writes 'The difficulty of placing the dandy satisfactorily within the dramatic context remained Wilde's most intractable aesthetic problem: it is the problem of "finding a world fit for the dandy to live in".' In the social comedies we are troubled by the undeniable fact that only the kind of world that the dandy inhabits, with its wealth-dependent elegance, could afford him or her the means (high fashion could not have come cheap in this moneyed world) and the manners which constitute the morally superior, self-conscious and therefore subversive identity dandyism represents. As Wilde's plays can seem complicit with the audiences for whom they were written even as they seek to subvert their assumptions, so the dandy as moral presence can seem fatally compromised by the world which he or she so knowingly, so self-possessedly, so superbly dominates by apparently invincible conversational style. As Raby points out, the dandy's mastery of all occasions cannot be sustained in the social comedies.

So the plays seem to acknowledge that the social context which the dandy apparently can occupy with impunity in fact threatens his integrity of being.

It is in Wilde's own master-work *The Importance of Being Earnest* or at least in some readings of it, some kinds of production, that this problem can perhaps be seen to undergo an ambiguous resolution. For in that work, the self-possession of the dandy in the social comedies becomes the wonderfully controlled, self-possessed artifice of the whole dramatic fabrication. It is a play that seems oddly transparent to itself, the actors playing parts that are manifestly in the control of a plot so patently absurd in its elaborate contrivance as to seem merely the occasion for a display of androgynous and therefore decadent mannerism. We enter a world where sexual roles are farcically reversed so as to drain the work of any credible erotic energy, where Gwendolin and even countrified Cecily display a masculine integrity of selfhood and purpose in the pursuit of matrimony while Jack and Algernon exhibit a vapid lack of secure personal identity and a willingness to be brought into being by circumstance, necessity and the sexual other, customarily reckoned to be the defining characteristics of the feminine gender. And the world in which this androgyne, asexual exchange takes place is one where paradox rules from an unassailable vantage point in the consistently epigrammatic scintillation of its dialogue. It is as if we enter a world of pure style – polished, glittering, glassy – the verbal equivalent of the ultimate, self-referential theatricality of Salomé's dance in her symbolically charged play. It is a world poised on the brink of modernist, Beckettian absurdity as the helter-skelter pace of the plot in performance renders ridiculous both the posed perfection of its various tableaux and the imperviousness of the players who must remain essentially unaffected by the lunacy they enact. For English *sang froid* it seems can take anything. We might equally be poised on the brink of a theatre of cruelty with Lady Bracknell as monstrous mistress of some Sadean madhouse where deed has been wholly disengaged from affect.

What we make of this unique theatrical creation is a matter for critical debate. A recent critic, Regenia Gagnier in her book *Idylls of the Marketplace: Oscar Wilde and the Victorian Public* (1986), reads the play as a consummate moment in a Wildean critique of the Victorian ruling classes. For her the play itself functioned in its primary context as a kind of fetished object, the heartlessness of which (about which Shaw originally complained) constituted an indictment of the world addressed in its cold, dispassionate brilliance. By contrast, for Camille Paglia in her *Art and Decadence From Nefertiti to Emily Dickinson* (1990) the play is that work in which Wilde sought to put the state of being of the androgyne of manners beyond the power of a philistine world. He does so by a ritual celebration of a hierarchical order in which the epigram of the epicene dandy is the basis of 'the most dazzling burst of Apollonian poetry in English literature'. Contemplating such critical division one is reminded, to conclude of two things. First, Owen Dudley Edwards has alerted us to the fact that the final apparently banal words of the play employ the word 'earnest' as a coterie joke in which that term is close in import to our own 'gay'. So perhaps we may never be able to pluck out the private mystery of a play that functions on so many levels and which may contain insider allusions lost to time. And secondly, one is reminded that Wilde himself in *The Truth of Masks* gave good warning to simple-minded critics who would seek to establish a unitary meaning for any work of art. For there he advised: 'A Truth in art is that whose contradiction is also true.'

NOTE

In preparing this introduction I was particularly indebted to the following:

Owen Dudley Edwards, ed. *The Fireworks of Oscar Wilde*, (1989).

Richard Ellmann, *Oscar Wilde*, (1988).

Richard Ellmann, ed. *Oscar Wilde: A Collection of Critical Essays*, (1969).

Regenia Gagnier, *Idylls of the Marketplace: Oscar Wilde and the Victorian Public*, (1986).

Camille Paglia, *Sexual Personae: Art and Decadence from Nefertiti to Emily Dickinson*, (1990).

Kerry Powell, *Oscar Wilde and the theatre of the 1890s*, (1990).

Peter Raby, *Oscar Wilde*, (1988).

Katherine Worth, *Oscar Wilde*, (1983).

THE IMPORTANCE OF BEING EARNEST

The persons of the play

JOHN WORTHING, J.P.
ALGERNON MONCRIEFF
REV. CANON CHASUBLE, D.D.
MR. GRIBSBY, Solicitor
MERRIMAN, Butler
LANE, Manservant

MOULTON, Gardener
LADY BRACKNELL
HON. GWENDOLEN FAIRFAX
CECILY CARDEW
MISS PRISM, Governess

ACT ONE

SCENE: *Morning-room in Algernon's flat in Half-Moon Street, London, W.* TIME: *The present. The room is luxuriously and artistically furnished. The sound of a piano is heard in the adjoining room.*

LANE *is arranging afternoon tea on the table, and after the music has ceased,* ALGERNON *enters.*

ALGERNON: Did you hear what I was playing, Lane?

LANE: I didn't think it polite to listen, sir.

ALGERNON: I'm sorry for that, for your sake. I don't play accurately – any one can play accurately – but I play with wonderful expression. As far as the piano is concerned, sentiment is my forte. I keep science for Life.

LANE: Yes, sir.

ALGERNON: And, speaking of the science of Life, have you got the cucumber sandwiches cut for Lady Bracknell?

LANE: Yes, sir.

ALGERNON: Ahem! Where are they?

LANE: Here, sir. (*Shows plate.*)

ALGERNON (*inspects them, takes two, and sits down on the sofa*): Oh! . . . by the way, Lane, I see from your book that on Thursday night, when Lord Shoreman and Mr. Worthing were dining with me, eight bottles of champagne are entered as having been consumed.

LANE: Yes, sir; eight bottles and a pint.

ALGERNON: Why is it that at a bachelor's establishment the servants invariably drink the champagne? I ask merely for information.

LANE: I attribute it to the superior quality of the wine, sir. I have often observed that in married households the champagne is rarely of a first-rate brand.

ALGERNON: Good heavens! Is marriage so demoralising as that?

LANE: I believe it *is* a very pleasant state, sir. I have had very little experience of it myself up to the present. I have only been married once. That was in consequence of a misunderstanding between myself and a young person.

ALGERNON (*languidly*): I don't know that I am much interested in your family life, Lane.

LANE: No, sir; it is not a very interesting subject. I never think of it myself.

ALGERNON: Very natural, I am sure. That will do, Lane, thank you.

LANE: Thank you, sir (LANE *moves to go out*.)

ALGERNON: Ah! . . . just give me another cucumber sandwich.

LANE: Yes, sir. (*Returns and hands plate.*)

LANE *goes out.*

ALGERNON: Lane's views on marriage seem somewhat lax. Really, if the lower orders don't set us a good example, what on earth is the use of them? They seem, as a class, to have absolutely no sense of moral responsibility.

Enter LANE.

LANE: Mr. Ernest Worthing.

Enter JACK. LANE *goes out.*

ALGERNON: How are you, my dear Ernest? What brings you up to town?

JACK: Oh, pleasure, pleasure! What else should bring one anywhere? Eating as usual, I see, Algy!

ALGERNON (*stiffly*): I believe it is customary in good society to take some slight refreshment at five o'clock. Where have you been since last Thursday?

JACK (*sitting down on the sofa*): Oh! in the country.

ALGERNON: What on earth do you do there?

JACK (*pulling off his gloves*): When one is in town one amuses oneself. When one is in the country one amuses other people. It is excessively boring.

ALGERNON: And who are the people you amuse?

JACK: (*airily*): Oh, neighbours, neighbours.

ALGERNON: Got nice neighbours in your part of Shropshire?

JACK: Perfectly horrid! Never speak to one of them.

ALGERNON: How immensely you must amuse them! (*Goes over and takes a sandwich*.) By the way, Shropshire is your county, is it not?

JACK: Eh? Shropshire? Yes, of course. Hallo! Why all these cups? Why cucumber sandwiches? Why such reckless extravagance in one so young? Who is coming to tea?

ALGERNON: Oh! merely Aunt Augusta and Gwendolen.

JACK: How perfectly delightful!

ALGERNON: Yes, that is all very well; but I am afraid Aunt Augusta won't quite approve of your being here.

JACK: May I ask why?

ALGERNON: My dear fellow, the way you flirt with Gwendolen is perfectly disgraceful. It is almost as bad as the way Gwendolen flirts with you.

JACK: I am in love with Gwendolen. I have come up to town expressly to propose to her.

ALGERNON: I thought you had come up for pleasure? ... I call that business.

JACK: How utterly unromantic you are!

ALGERNON: I really don't see anything romantic in proposing. It is very romantic to be in love. But there is nothing romantic about a definite proposal. Why, one may be accepted. One usually is, I believe. Then the excitement is all over. The very essence of romance is uncertainty. If ever I get married, I'll certainly try to forget the fact.

JACK: I have no doubt about that, dear Algy. The Divorce Court was specially invented for people whose memories are so curiously constituted.

ALGERNON: Oh! there is no use speculating on that subject. Divorces are made in heaven – (JACK *puts out his hand to take a sandwich.* ALGERNON *at once interferes.*) Please don't touch the cucumber sandwiches. They are ordered specially for Aunt Augusta. (*Takes one and eats it.*)

JACK: Well, you have been eating them all the time.

ALGERNON: That is quite a different matter. She is my aunt. (*Takes plate from below.*) Have some bread and butter. The bread and butter is for Gwendolen. Gwendolen is devoted to bread and butter.

JACK: (*advancing to table and helping himself.*): And very good bread and butter it is too.

ALGERNON: Well, my dear fellow, you need not eat as if you were going to eat it all. You behave as if you were married to her already. You are not married to her already, and I don't think you ever will be.

JACK: Why on earth do you say that?

ALGERNON: Well, in the first place girls never marry the men they flirt with. Girls don't think it right.

JACK: Oh, that is nonsense!

ALGERNON: It isn't. It is a great truth. It accounts for the extraordinary number of bachelors that one sees all over the place. In the second place, I don't give my consent.

JACK: Your consent! What utter nonsense you talk!

ALGERNON: My dear fellow, Gwendolen is my first cousin. And before I allow you to marry her, you will have to clear up the whole question of Cecily.

JACK: Cecily! What on earth do you mean? (ALGERNON *goes to the bell and rings it. Then returns to tea-table and eats another sandwich.*) What do you mean, Algy, by Cecily! I don't know any one of the name of Cecily ... as far as I remember.

Enter LANE.

ALGERNON: Bring me that cigarette case Mr. Worthing left in the smoking-room the last time he dined here.

LANE: Yes, sir.

LANE *goes out.*

JACK: Do you mean to say you have had my cigarette case all this time? I wish to goodness you had let me know. I have been writing frantic letters to Scotland Yard about it. I was very nearly offering a large reward.

ALGERNON: Well, I wish you would offer one. I happen to be more than usually hard up.

JACK: There is no good offering a large reward now that the thing is found.

Enter LANE *with the cigarette case on a salver.* ALGERNON *takes it at once.* LANE *goes out.*

ALGERNON: I think that is rather mean of you, Ernest, I must say. (*Opens case and examines it.*) However, it makes no matter, for, now that I look at the inscription inside, I find that the thing isn't yours after all.

JACK: Of course it's mine. (*Moving to him.*) You have seen me with it a hundred times, and you have no right whatsoever to read what is written inside. It is a very ungentlemanly thing to read a private cigarette case.

ALGERNON: Oh! it is absurd to have a hard and fast rule about what one should read and what one shouldn't. One should read everything. More than half of modern culture depends on what one shouldn't read.

JACK: I am quite aware of the fact, and I don't propose to discuss modern culture. It isn't the sort of thing one should talk of in private. I simply want my cigarette case back.

ALGERNON: Yes; but this isn't your cigarette case. This cigarette case is a present from some one of the name of Cecily, and you said you didn't know any one of that name.

JACK: Well, if you want to know, Cecily happens to be my aunt.

ALGERNON: Your aunt!

JACK: Yes. Charming old lady she is, too. Lives at Tunbridge Wells. Just give it back to me, Algy.

ALGERNON (*retreating to back of sofa*): But why does she call herself little Cecily if she is your aunt and lives at Tunbridge Wells? (*Reading.*) 'From little Cecily with her fondest love.'

JACK (*moving to sofa and kneeling upon it*): My dear fellow, what on earth is there in that? Some aunts are tall, some aunts are not tall. That is a matter that surely an aunt may be allowed to decide for herself. You seem to think that every aunt should be exactly like your aunt! That is absurd! For Heaven's sake give me back my cigarette case. (*Follows* ALGERNON *round the room.*)

ALGERNON: Yes. But why does your aunt call you her uncle? 'From little Cecily, with her fondest love to her dear Uncle Jack.' There is no objection, I admit, to an aunt being a small aunt, but why an aunt, no matter what her size may be, should call her own nephew her uncle, I can't quite make out. Besides, your name isn't Jack at all; it is Ernest.

JACK: It isn't Ernest; it's Jack.

ALGERNON: You have always told me it was Ernest. I have introduced you to every one as Ernest. You answer to the name of Ernest. You look as if your name was Ernest. You are the most earnest-looking person I ever saw in my life. It is perfectly absurd your saying that your name isn't Ernest. It's on your cards. Here is one of them. (*Taking it from case.*) 'Mr. Ernest Worthing, B.4, The Albany, W.' I'll keep this as a proof that your name is Ernest if ever you attempt to deny it to me, or to Gwendolen, or to any one else. (*Puts the card in his pocket.*)

JACK: Well, my name is Ernest in town and Jack in the country, and the cigarette case was given to me in the country.

ALGERNON: Yes, but that does not account for the fact that your small Aunt Cecily, who lives at Tunbridge Wells, calls you her dear Uncle. Come, old boy, you had much better have the thing out at once.

JACK: My dear Algy, you talk exactly as if you were a dentist. It is very vulgar to talk like a dentist when one isn't a dentist. It produces a false impression.

ALGERNON: Well, that is exactly what dentists always do. Now, go on! Tell me the whole thing. I may mention that I have always suspected you of being a confirmed and secret Bunburyist; and I am quite sure of it now.

JACK: Bunburyist? What on earth do you mean by a Bunburyist?

ALGERNON: I'll reveal to you the meaning of that incomparable expression as soon as you are kind enough to inform me why you are Ernest in town and Jack in the country.

JACK: Well, produce my cigarette case first.

ALGERNON: Here it is. (*Hands cigarette case.*) Now produce your explanation, and pray make it improbable. (*Sits on sofa.*)

JACK: My dear fellow, there is nothing improbable about my explanation at all. In fact, it's perfectly ordinary. Old Mr. Thomas Cardew, who adopted me when I was a little boy, under rather peculiar circumstances, and left me all the money I possess, made me in his will guardian to his grand-daughter, Miss Cecily Cardew. Cecily, who addresses me as her uncle from motives of respect that you could not possibly appreciate, lives at my place in the country under the charge of her admirable governess, Miss Prism.

ALGERNON: Where is that place in the country, by the way?

JACK: That is nothing to you, dear boy. You are not going to be invited. . . . I may tell you candidly that the place is not in Shropshire.

ALGERNON: I suspected that, my dear fellow! I have Bunburyed all over Shropshire on two separate occasions. Now, go on. Why are you Ernest in town and Jack in the country?

JACK: My dear Algy, I don't know whether you will be able to understand my real motives. You are hardly serious enough. When one is placed in the position of guardian, one has to adopt a very high moral tone on all subjects. It's one's duty to do so. And as a high moral tone can hardly be said to conduce very much to either one's health or one's happiness if carried to excess, in order to get up to town I have always pretended to have a younger brother of the name of Ernest, who lives in the Albany, and gets into the most dreadful scrapes. That, my dear Algy, is the whole truth pure and simple.

ALGERNON: The truth is rarely pure and never simple. Modern life would be very tedious if it were either, and modern literature a complete impossibility!

JACK: That wouldn't be at all a bad thing.

ALGERNON: Literary criticism is not your forte, my dear fellow. Don't try it. You should leave that to people who haven't been at a University. They do it so well in the daily papers. What you really are is a Bunburyist. I was quite right in saying you were a Bunburyist. You are one of the most advanced Bunburyists I know.

JACK: What on earth do you mean?

ALGERNON: You have invented a very useful younger brother called Ernest, in order that you may be able to come up to town as often as you like. I have invented an invaluable permanent invalid called Bunbury, in order that I may be able to go down into the country whenever I choose.

JACK: What nonsense.

ALGERNON: It isn't nonsense. Bunbury is perfectly invaluable. If it wasn't for Bunbury's extraordinary bad health, for instance, I wouldn't be able to dine with you at the Savoy to-night, for I have been really engaged to Aunt Augusta for more than a week.

JACK: I haven't asked you to dine with me anywhere to-night.

ALGERNON: I know. You are absurdly careless about sending out invitations. It is very foolish of you. Nothing annoys people so much as not receiving invitations.

JACK: Well, I can't dine at the Savoy. I owe them about £700. They are always getting judgments and things against me. They bother my life out.

ALGERNON: Why on earth don't you pay them? You have got heaps of money.

JACK: Yes, but Ernest hasn't, and I must keep up Ernest's reputation. Ernest is one of those chaps who never pays a bill. He gets writted about once a week.

ALGERNON: Well, let us dine at Willis's.

JACK: You had much better dine with your Aunt Augusta.

ALGERNON: I haven't the smallest intention of doing anything of the kind. To begin with, I dined there on Monday, and once a week is quite enough to dine with one's own relations. In the second place, whenever I do dine there I am always treated as a member of the family, and sent down with either no woman at all, or two. In the third place, I know perfectly well whom she will place me next to, to-night. She will place me next Mary Farquhar, who always flirts with her own husband across the dinner-table. That is not very pleasant. Indeed, it is not even decent . . . and that sort of thing is enormously on the increase. The amount of women in London who flirt with their own husbands is perfectly scandalous. It looks so bad. It is simply washing one's clean linen in public. Besides, now that I know you to be a confirmed Bunburyist I naturally want to talk to you about Bunburying. I want to tell you the rules.

JACK: I'm not a Bunburyist at all. If Gwendolen accepts me, I am going to kill my brother, indeed I think I'll kill him in any case. Cecily is a little too much interested in him. She is always asking me to forgive him, and that sort of thing. It is rather a bore. So I am going to get rid of Ernest. And I strongly advise you to do the same with Mr.... with your invalid friend who has the absurd name.

ALGERNON: Nothing will induce me to part with Bunbury, and if you ever get married, which seems to me extremely problematic, you will be very glad to know Bunbury. A man who marries without knowing Bunbury has a very tedious time of it.

JACK: That is nonsense. If I marry a charming girl like Gwendolen, and she is the only girl I ever saw in my life that I would marry, I certainly won't want to know Bunbury.

ALGERNON: Then your wife will. You don't seem to realise, that in married life three is company and two is none.

JACK (*sententiously*): That, my dear young friend, is the theory that the corrupt French Drama has been propounding for the last fifty years.

ALGERNON: Yes; and that the happy English home has proved in half the time.

JACK: For heaven's sake, don't try to be cynical. It's perfectly easy to be cynical.

ALGERNON: My dear fellow, it isn't easy to be anything nowadays. There's such a lot of beastly competition about. (*The sound of an electric bell is heard.*) Ah! that must be Aunt Augusta. Only relatives, or creditors, ever ring in that Wagnerian manner. Now, if I get her out of the way for ten minutes, so that you can have an opportunity for proposing to Gwendolen, may I dine with you to-night at Willis's?

JACK: I suppose so, if you want to.

ALGERNON: Yes, but you must be serious about it. I hate people who are not serious about meals. It is so shallow of them.

Enter LANE.

LANE: Lady Bracknell and Miss Fairfax.

ALGERNON *goes forward to meet them. Enter* LADY BRACKNELL *and* GWENDOLEN.

LADY BRACKNELL: Good-afternoon, dear Algernon, I hope you are behaving very well.

ALGERNON: I'm feeling very well, Aunt Augusta.

LADY BRACKNELL: That's not quite the same thing. In fact the two things rarely go together. (*Sees* JACK *and bows to him with icy coldness.*)

ALGERNON (*to* GWENDOLEN): Dear me, you are smart!

GWENDOLEN: I am always smart! Am I not, Mr. Worthing?

JACK: You're quite perfect, Miss Fairfax.

GWENDOLEN: Oh! I hope I am not that. It would leave no room for developments, and I intend to develop in many directions. (GWENDOLEN *and* JACK *sit down together in the corner.*)

LADY BRACKNELL: I'm sorry if we are a little late, Algernon, but I was obliged to call on dear Lady Harbury. I hadn't been there since her poor husband's death. I never saw a woman so altered; she looks quite twenty years younger. And now I'll have a cup of tea, and one of those nice cucumber sandwiches you promised me.

ALGERNON: Certainly, Aunt Augusta. (*Goes over to tea-table.*)

LADY BRACKNELL: Won't you come and sit here, Gwendolen?

GWENDOLEN: Thanks, mamma, I'm quite comfortable where I am.

ALGERNON (*picking up empty plate in horror*): Good heavens! Lane! Why are there no cucumber sandwiches? I ordered them specially.

LANE (*gravely*): There were no cucumbers in the market this morning, sir. I went down twice.

ALGERNON: No cucumbers!

LANE: No, sir. Not even for ready money.

ALGERNON: That will do, Lane, thank you.

LANE: Thank you, sir. (*Goes out.*)

ALGERNON: I am greatly distressed, Aunt Augusta, about there being no cucumbers, not even for ready money.

LADY BRACKNELL: It really makes no matter, Algernon. I had some crumpets with Lady Harbury, who seems to me to be living entirely for pleasure now.

ALGERNON: I hear her hair has turned quite gold from grief.

LADY BRACKNELL: It certainly has changed its colour. From what cause I, of course, cannot say. (ALGERNON *crosses and hands tea.*) Thank you. I've quite a treat for you to-night, Algernon. I am going to send you down with Mary Farquhar. She is such a nice woman, and so attentive to her husband. It's delightful to watch them.

ALGERNON: I am afraid, Aunt Augusta, I shall have to give up the pleasure of dining with you to-night after all.

LADY BRACKNELL: (*frowning*): I hope not, Algernon. It would put my table completely out. Your uncle would have to dine upstairs. Fortunately he is accustomed to that.

ALGERNON: It is a great bore, and, I need hardly say, a terrible disappointment to me, but the fact is I have just had a telegram to say that my poor friend Bunbury is very ill again. (*Exchanges glances with* JACK.) They seem to think I should be with him.

LADY BRACKNELL: It is very strange. This Mr. Bunbury seems to suffer from curiously bad health.

ALGERNON: Yes; poor Bunbury is a dreadful invalid.

LADY BRACKNELL: Well, I must say, Algernon, that I think it is high time that Mr. Bunbury made up his mind whether he was going to live or to die. This shilly-shallying with the question is absurd. Nor do I in any way approve of the modern sympathy with invalids. I consider it morbid. Illness of any kind is hardly a thing to be encouraged in others. Health is the primary duty of life. I am always telling that to your poor uncle, but he never seems to take much notice ... as far as any improvement in his ailments goes. Well, Algernon, of course if you are obliged to be beside the bedside of Mr. Bunbury, I have nothing more to say. But I would be much obliged if you would ask Mr. Bunbury, from me, to be kind enough not to have a relapse on Saturday, for I rely on you to arrange my music for me. It is my last reception, and one wants something that will encourage conversation, particularly at the end of the season when every one has practically said whatever they had to say, which, in most cases, was probably not much.

ALGERNON: I'll speak to Bunbury, Aunt Augusta, if he is still conscious, and I think I can promise you he'll be all right by Saturday. Of course the music is a great difficulty. You see, if one plays good music, people don't listen, and if one plays bad music people don't talk. But I'll run over the programme I've drawn out, if you will kindly come into the next room for a moment.

LADY BRACKNELL: Thank you, Algernon. It is very thoughtful of you. (*Rising and following* ALGERNON.) I'm sure the programme will be delightful, after a few expurgations. French songs I cannot possibly allow. People always seem to think that they are improper, and either look shocked, which is vulgar, or laugh, which is worse. But German sounds a thoroughly respectable language, and indeed, I believe is so. Gwendolen, you will accompany me.

GWENDOLEN: Certainly, mamma.

· LADY BRACKNELL *and* ALGERNON *go into the music-room*, GWENDOLEN *remains behind.*

JACK: Charming day it has been, Miss Fairfax.

GWENDOLEN: Pray don't talk to me about the weather, Mr. Worthing. Whenever people talk to me about the weather, I always feel quite certain that they mean something else. And that makes me so nervous.

JACK: I do mean something else.

GWENDOLEN: I thought so. In fact, I am never wrong.

JACK: And I would like to be allowed to take advantage of Lady Bracknell's temporary absence ...

GWENDOLEN: I would certainly advise you to do so. Mamma has a way of coming back suddenly into a room that I have often had to speak to her about.

JACK *nervously*: Miss Fairfax, ever since I met you I have admired you more than any girl ... I have ever met since ... I met you.

GWENDOLEN: Yes, I am quite well aware of the fact. And I often wish that in public, at any rate, you had been more demonstrative. For me you have always had an irresistible fascination. Even before I met you I was far from indifferent to you. (JACK *looks at her in amazement.*) We live, as I hope you know, Mr. Worthing, in an age of ideals. The fact is constantly mentioned in the more expensive monthly magazines, and has now reached the provincial pulpits, I am told; and my ideal has always been to love some one of the name of Ernest. There is something in that name that inspires absolute confidence. The moment Algernon first mentioned to me that he had a friend called Ernest, I knew I was destined to love you. The name, fortunately for my peace of mind, is, as far as my own experience goes, extremely rare.

JACK: You really love me, Gwendolen?

GWENDOLEN: Passionately!

JACK: Darling! You don't know how happy you've made me.

GWENDOLEN: My own Ernest! (*They embrace.*)

JACK: But you don't really mean to say that you couldn't love me if my name wasn't Ernest?

GWENDOLEN: But your name is Ernest.

JACK: Yes, I know it is. But supposing it was something else? Do you mean to say you couldn't love me then?

GWENDOLEN: (*glibly*): Ah! that is clearly a metaphysical speculation, and like most metaphysical speculations has very little reference at all to the actual facts of real life, as we know them.

JACK: Personally, darling, to speak quite candidly, I don't much care about the name of Ernest. . . . I don't think the name suits me at all.

GWENDOLEN: It suits you perfectly. It is a divine name. It has a music of its own. It produces vibrations.

JACK: Well, really, Gwendolen, I must say that I think there are lots of other much nicer names. I think Jack, for instance, a charming name.

GWENDOLEN: Jack? . . . No, there is very little music in the name Jack, if any at all, indeed. It does not thrill. It produces absolutely no vibrations. . . . I have known several Jacks, and they all, without exception, were more than usually plain. Besides, Jack is a notorious domesticity for John! And I pity any woman who is married to a man called John. She would have a very tedious life with him. She would probably never be allowed to know the entrancing pleasure of a single moment's solitude. The only really safe name is Ernest.

JACK: Gwendolen, I must get christened at once – I mean we must get married at once. There is no time to be lost.

GWENDOLEN: Married, Mr. Worthing?

JACK: (*astounded*): Well . . . surely. You know that I love you, and you led me to believe, Miss Fairfax, that you were not absolutely indifferent to me.

GWENDOLEN: I adore you. But you haven't proposed to me yet. Nothing has been said at all about marriage. The subject has not even been touched on.

JACK: Well . . . may I propose to you now?

GWENDOLEN: I think it would be an admirable opportunity. And to spare you any possible disappointment, Mr. Worthing, I think it only fair to tell you quite frankly beforehand that I am fully determined to accept you.

JACK: Gwendolen!

GWENDOLEN: Yes, Mr. Worthing, what have you got to say to me?

JACK: You know what I have got to say to you.

GWENDOLEN: Yes, but you don't say it.

JACK: Gwendolen, will you marry me? (*Goes on his knees.*)

GWENDOLEN: Of course I will, darling. How long you have been about it! I am afraid you have had very little experience in how to propose.

JACK: My own one, I have never loved anyone in the world but you.

GWENDOLEN: Yes, but men often propose for practice. I know my brother Gerald does. All my girl-friends tell me so. What wonderfully blue eyes you have, Ernest! They are quite, quite blue. I hope you will always look at me just like that, especially when there are other people present.

Enter LADY BRACKNELL.

LADY BRACKNELL: Mr. Worthing! Rise, sir, from this semi-recumbent posture. It is most indecorous.

GWENDOLEN: Mamma! (*He tries to rise; she restrains him.*) I must beg you to retire. This is no place for you. Besides, Mr. Worthing has not quite finished yet.

LADY BRACKNELL: Finished what, may I ask?

GWENDOLEN: I am engaged to Mr. Worthing, mamma. (*They rise together.*)

LADY BRACKNELL: Pardon me, you are not engaged to any one. When you do become engaged to some one, I, or your father, should his health permit him, will inform you of the fact. An engagement should come on a young girl as a surprise, pleasant or unpleasant, as the case may be. It is hardly a matter that she could be allowed to arrange for herself. . . . And now I have a few questions to put to you, Mr. Worthing!

JACK: I shall be charmed to reply to any questions, Lady Bracknell.

GWENDOLEN: You mean if you know the answers to them. Mamma's questions are sometimes peculiarly inquisitorial.

LADY BRACKNELL: I intend to make them very inquisitorial. And while I am making these inquiries, you, Gwendolen, will wait for me below in the carriage.

GWENDOLEN (*reproachfully*): Mamma!

LADY BRACKNELL: In the carriage, Gwendolen!

GWENDOLEN *goes to the door. She and* JACK *blow kisses to each other behind* LADY BRACKNELL'S *back.* LADY BRACKNELL *looks vaguely about as if she could not understand what the noise was. Finally turns round.*

Gwendolen, the carriage!

GWENDOLEN: Yes, mamma. (*goes out, looking back at* JACK.)

LADY BRACKNELL (*sitting down*): You can take a seat, Mr. Worthing.

Looks in her pocket for note-book and pencil.

JACK: Thank you, Lady Bracknell, I prefer standing.

LADY BRACKNELL (*pencil and note-book in hand*): I feel bound to tell you that you are not down on my list of eligible young men, although I have the same list as the dear Duchess of Bolton has. We work together, in fact. However, I am quite ready to enter your name, should your answers be what a really affectionate mother requires. Do you smoke?

JACK: Well, yes, I must admit I smoke.

LADY BRACKNELL: I am glad to hear it. A man should always have an occupation of some kind. There are far too many idle men in London as it is. How old are you?

JACK: Twenty-nine.

LADY BRACKNELL: A very good age to be married at. I have always been of opinion that a man who desires to get married should know either everything or nothing. Which do you know?

JACK: (*after some hesitation*): I know nothing, Lady Bracknell.

LADY BRACKNELL: I am pleased to hear it. I do not approve of anything that tampers with natural ignorance. Ignorance is like a delicate exotic fruit; touch it and the bloom is gone. The whole theory of modern education is radically unsound. Fortunately in England, at any rate, education produces no effect whatsoever. If it did, it would prove a serious danger to the upper classes, and probably lead to acts of violence in Grosvenor Square. What is your income?

JACK: Between seven and eight thousand a year.

LADY BRACKNELL: (*makes a note in her book*): In land, or in investments?

JACK: In investments, chiefly.

LADY BRACKNELL: That is satisfactory. What between the duties expected of one during one's lifetime, and the duties exacted from one after one's death, land has ceased to be either a profit or a pleasure. It gives one position, and prevents one from keeping it up. That's all that can be said about land.

JACK: I have a country house with some land, of course, attached to it, about fifteen hundred acres, I believe; but I don't depend on that for my real income. In fact, as far as I can make out, the poachers are the only people who make anything out of it.

LADY BRACKNELL: A country house! How many bedrooms? Well, that point can be cleared up afterwards. You have a town house, I hope? A girl with a simple, unspoiled nature, like Gwendolen, could hardly be expected to reside in the country.

JACK: Well, I own a house in Belgrave Square, but it is let by the year to Lady Bloxham. Of course, I can get it back whenever I like, at six months' notice.

LADY BRACKNELL: Lady Bloxham? I don't know her.

JACK: Oh, she goes about very little. She is a lady considerably advanced in years.

LADY BRACKNELL: Ah, nowadays that is no guarantee of respectability of character. What number in Belgrave Square?

JACK: 149.

LADY BRACKNELL: (*shaking her head*): The unfashionable side. I thought there was something. However, that could easily be altered.

JACK: Do you mean the fashion, or the side?

LADY BRACKNELL: (*sternly*): Both, if necessary, I presume. What are your politics?

JACK: Well, I am afraid I really have none. I am a Liberal Unionist.

LADY BRACKNELL: Oh, they count as Tories. They dine with us. Or come in the evening at any rate. You have, of course, no sympathy of any kind with the Radical Party?

JACK: Oh! I don't want to put the asses against the classes, if that is what you mean, Lady Bracknell.

LADY BRACKNELL: That is exactly what I do mean ... ahem! ... Are your parents living?

JACK: I have lost both my parents.

LADY BRACKNELL: Both? ... To lose one parent may be regarded as a misfortune ... to lose both seems like carelessness. Who was your father? He was evidently a man of some wealth. Was he born in what the Radical papers call the purple of commerce, or did he rise from the ranks of the aristocracy?

JACK: I am afraid I really don't know. The fact is, Lady Bracknell, I said I had lost my parents. It would be nearer the truth to say that my parents seem to have lost me. ... I don't actually know who I am by birth. I was ... well, I was found.

LADY BRACKNELL: Found!

JACK: The late Mr. Thomas Cardew, an old gentleman of a very charitable and kindly disposition, found me, and gave me the name of Worthing, because he happened to have a first-class ticket for Worthing in his pocket at the time. Worthing is a place in Sussex. It is a seaside resort.

LADY BRACKNELL: Where did the charitable gentleman who had a first-class ticket for this seaside resort find you?

JACK: (*gravely*): In a hand-bag.

LADY BRACKNELL: A hand-bag?

JACK: (*very seriously*): Yes, Lady Bracknell. I was in a hand-bag – a somewhat large, black leather hand-bag, with handles to it – an ordinary hand-bag in fact.

LADY BRACKNELL: In what locality did this Mr. James, or Thomas, Cardew come across this ordinary hand-bag?

JACK: In the cloak-room at Victoria Station. It was given to him in mistake for his own.

LADY BRACKNELL: The cloak-room at Victoria Station?

JACK: Yes. The Brighton line.

LADY BRACKNELL: The line is immaterial. Mr. Worthing, I confess I feel somewhat bewildered by what you have just told me. To be born, or at any rate bred, in a hand-bag, whether it had handles or not, seems to me to display a contempt for the ordinary decencies of family life that reminds one of the worst excesses of the French Revolution. And I presume you know what that unfortunate movement led to? As for the particular locality in which the hand-bag was found, a cloak-room at a railway station might serve to conceal a social indiscretion – has probably, indeed, been used for that purpose before now – but it could hardly be regarded as an assured basis for a recognised position in good society.

JACK: May I ask you then what you would advise me to do? I need hardly say I would do anything in the world to ensure Gwendolen's happiness.

LADY BRACKNELL: I would strongly advise you, Mr. Worthing, to try and acquire some relations as soon as possible, and to make a definite effort to produce at any rate one parent, of either sex, before the season is quite over.

JACK: Well, I don't see how I could possibly manage to do that. I can produce the hand-bag at any moment. It is in my dressing-room at home. I really think that should satisfy you, Lady Bracknell.

LADY BRACKNELL: Me, sir! What has it to do with me? You can hardly imagine that I and Lord Bracknell would dream of allowing our only daughter – a girl brought up with the utmost care – to marry into a cloak-room, and form an alliance with a parcel. (JACK *starts indignantly*.) Kindly open the door for me sir. You will of course understand that for the future there is to be no communication of any kind between you and Miss Fairfax.

LADY BRACKNELL *sweeps out in majestic indignation.* ALGERNON, *from the other room, strikes up the Wedding March.* JACK *looks perfectly furious, and goes to the door.*

JACK: For goodness' sake don't play that ghastly tune, Algy! How idiotic you are!

The music stops and ALGERNON *enters cheerily.*

ALGERNON: Didn't it go off all right, old boy? You don't mean to say Gwendolen refused you? I know it is a way she has. She is always refusing people. I think it is most ill-natured of her.

JACK: Oh, Gwendolen is as right as a trivet. As far as she is concerned, we are engaged. Her mother is perfectly unbearable. Never met such a Gorgon. . . . I don't really know what a Gorgon is like, but I am quite sure that Lady Bracknell is one. In any case, she is a monster, without being a myth, which is rather unfair. . . . I beg your pardon, Algy, I suppose I shouldn't talk about your own aunt in that way before you.

ALGERNON: My dear boy, I love hearing my relations abused. It is the only thing that makes me put up with them at all. Relations are simply a tedious pack of people, who haven't got the remotest knowledge of how to live, nor the smallest instinct about when to die.

JACK: Ah! I haven't got any relations. Don't know anything about relations.

ALGERNON: You are a lucky fellow. Relations never lend one any money, and won't give one credit, even for genius. They are a sort of aggravated form of the public.

JACK: And after all, what does it matter whether a man ever had a father and mother or not? Mothers, of course, are all right. They pay a chap's bills and don't bother him. But fathers bother a chap and never pay his bills. I don't know a single chap at the club who speaks to his father.

ALGERNON: Yes! Fathers are certainly not popular just at present.

(*Takes up the evening newspaper.*)

JACK: Popular! I bet you anything you like that there is not a single chap, of all the chaps that you and I know, who would be seen walking down St. James' Street with his own father. (*A pause.*) Anything in the papers?

ALGERNON: (*still reading.*) Nothing.

JACK: What a comfort.

ALGERNON: There is never anything in the papers, as far as I can see.

JACK: I think there is usually a great deal too much in them. They are always bothering one about people one doesn't know, one has never met, and one doesn't care twopence about. Brutes!

ALGERNON: I think people one hasn't met are charming. I'm very much interested at present in a girl I have never met; very much interested indeed.

JACK: Oh, that is nonsense!

ALGERNON: It isn't!

JACK: Well, I won't argue about the matter. You always want to argue about things.

ALGERNON: That is exactly what things were originally made for.

JACK: Upon my word, if I thought that, I'd shoot myself.... (*A pause.*) You don't think there is any chance of Gwendolen becoming like her mother in about a hundred and fifty years, do you, Algy?

ALGERNON: All women become like their mothers. That is their tragedy. No man does. That's his.

JACK: Is that clever?

ALGERNON: It is perfectly phrased! And quite as true as any observation in civilised life should be.

JACK: I am sick to death of cleverness. Everybody is clever nowadays. You can't go anywhere without meeting clever people. The thing has become an absolute public nuisance. I wish to goodness we had a few fools left.

ALGERNON: We have.

JACK: I should extremely like to meet them. What do they talk about?

ALGERNON: The fools? Oh! about the clever people of course.

JACK: What fools.

ALGERNON: By the way, did you tell Gwendolen the truth about your being Ernest in town, and Jack in the country?

JACK (*in a very patronising manner*): My dear fellow, the truth isn't quite the sort of think one tells to a nice, sweet, refined girl. What extraordinary ideas you have about the way to behave to a woman!

ALGERNON: The only way to behave to a woman is to make love to her, if she is pretty, and to some one else, if she is plain.

JACK: Oh, that is nonsense.

ALGERNON: What about the young lady whose guardian you are! Miss Cardew? What about your brother? What about the profligate Ernest?

JACK: Oh! Cecily is all right. Before the end of the week I shall have got rid of my brother . . . I think I'll probably kill him in Paris.

ALGERNON: Why Paris?

JACK: Oh! Less trouble: no nonsense about a funeral and that sort of thing – yes, I'll kill him in Paris. . . . Apoplexy will do perfectly well. Lots of people die of apoplexy, quite suddenly, don't they?

ALGERNON: Yes, but it's hereditary, my dear fellow. It's a sort of thing that runs in families.

JACK: Good heavens! Then I certainly won't choose that. What can I say?

ALGERNON: Oh! Say influenza.

JACK: Oh, no! that wouldn't sound probable at all. Far too many people have had it.

ALGERNON: Oh well! Say anything you choose. Say a severe chill. That's all right.

JACK: You are sure a severe chill isn't hereditary, or anything dreadful of that kind?

ALGERNON: Of course it isn't.

JACK: Very well then. That is settled.

ALGERNON: But I thought you said that . . . Miss Cardew was a little too much interested in your poor brother Ernest? Won't she feel his loss a good deal?

JACK: Oh! that is all right. Cecily is not a silly romantic girl, I am glad to say. She has got a capital appetite, goes long walks, and pays no attention at all to her lessons.

ALGERNON: I would rather like to see Cecily.

JACK: I will take very good care you never do. And you are not to speak of her as Cecily.

ALGERNON: Ah! I believe she is plain. Yes: I know perfectly well what she is like. She is one of those dull, intellectual girls one meets all over the place. Girls who have got large minds and large feet. I am sure she is more than usually plain, and I expect she is about thirty-nine, and looks it.

JACK: She happens to be excessively pretty, and she is only just eighteen.

ALGERNON: Have you told Gwendolen yet that you have an excessively pretty ward who is only eighteen?

JACK: Oh! one doesn't blurt these things out to people. Life is a question of tact. One leads up to the thing gradually. Cecily and Gwendolen are perfectly certain to be extremely great friends. I'll bet you anything you like that half an hour after they have met, they will be calling each other sister.

ALGERNON: Women only do that when they have called each other a lot of other things first. Now, my dear boy, if we want to get a good table at Willis's, we really must go and dress. Do you know it is nearly seven?

JACK: (irritably): Oh! it always is nearly seven.

ALGERNON: Well, I'm hungry.

JACK: I never knew you when you weren't. . . . However, all right. I'll go round to the Albany and meet you at Willis's at eight. You can call for me on your way, if you like.

ALGERNON: What shall we do after dinner? Go to a theatre?

JACK: Oh, no! I loathe listening.

ALGERNON: Well, let us go to the Club?

JACK: Oh, no! I hate talking.

ALGERNON: Well, we might trot round to the Empire at ten?

JACK: Oh, no! I can't bear looking at things. It is so silly.

ALGERNON: Well, what shall we do?

JACK: Nothing!

ALGERNON: It is awfully hard work doing nothing. However, I don't mind hard work where there is no definite object of any kind . . .

Enter Lane.

LANE: Miss Fairfax.

Enter GWENDOLEN. LANE *goes out.*

ALGERNON: Gwendolen, upon my word!

GWENDOLEN: Algy, kindly turn your back. I have something very particular to say to Mr. Worthing. As it is somewhat of a private matter, you will of course listen.

ALGERNON: Really, Gwendolen, I don't think I can allow this at all.

GWENDOLEN: Algy, you always adopt a strictly immoral attitude towards life. You are not quite old enough to do that. (ALGERNON *retires to the fireplace.*)

JACK: My own darling.

GWENDOLEN: Ernest, we may never be married. From the expression on mamma's face I fear we never shall. Few parents nowadays pay any regard to what their children say to them. The old-fashioned respect for the young is fast dying out. Whatever influence I ever had over mamma, I lost at the age of three. But although she may prevent us from becoming man and wife, and I may marry some one else, and marry often, nothing that she can possibly do can alter my eternal devotion to you.

JACK: Dear Gwendolen!

GWENDOLEN: The story of your romantic origin, as related to me by mamma, with unpleasing comments, has naturally stirred the deeper fibres of my nature. Your Christian name has an irresistible fascination. The simplicity of your character makes you exquisitely incomprehensible to me. Your town address at the Albany I have. What is your address in the country?

JACK: The Manor House, Woolton, Hertfordshire.

ALGERNON, *who has been carefully listening, smiles to himself, and writes the address on his shirt-cuff. Then picks up the Railway Guide.*

GWENDOLEN: There is a good postal service, I suppose? It may be necessary to do something desperate. That, of course, will require serious consideration. I will communicate with you daily.

JACK: My own one!

GWENDOLEN: How long do you remain in town?

JACK: Till Monday.

GWENDOLEN: Good! Algy, you may turn round now.

ALGERNON: Thanks, I've turned round already.

GWENDOLEN: You may also ring the bell.

JACK: You will let me see you to your carriage, my own darling?

GWENDOLEN: Certainly.

JACK: (to LANE, who now enters): I will see Miss Fairfax out.

LANE: Yes, sir.

JACK and GWENDOLEN go off.

LANE presents several letters on a salver to ALGERNON. It is to be surmised that they are bills, as ALGERNON, after looking at the envelopes, tears them up.

ALGERNON: A glass of sherry, Lane.

LANE: Yes, sir.

ALGERNON: To-morrow, Lane, I'm going Bunburying.

LANE: Yes, sir.

ALGERNON: I shall probably not be back till Monday. You can put up my dress clothes, my smoking jacket, and all the Bunbury suits....

LANE: Yes, sir. (*Handing sherry.*)

ALGERNON: I hope to-morrow will be a fine day, Lane.

LANE: It never is, sir.

ALGERNON: Lane, you're a perfect pessimist.

LANE: I do my best to give satisfaction, sir.

Enter JACK. LANE goes off.

JACK: There's a sensible, intellectual girl! the only girl I ever cared for in my life. (ALGERNON *is laughing immoderately.*) What on earth are you so amused at?

ALGERNON: Oh, I'm a little anxious about poor Bunbury, that is all.

JACK: If you don't take care, your friend Bunbury will get you into a serious scrape some day.

ALGERNON: I love scrapes. They are the only things that are never serious.

JACK: Oh, that's nonsense, Algy. You never talk anything but nonsense.

ALGERNON: Nobody ever does.

JACK looks indignantly at him and leaves the room. ALGERNON lights a cigarette, reads his shirt-cuff, and smiles.

ACT DROP

ACT TWO

SCENE: *Garden at the Manor House, Woolton. A flight of grey stone steps leads up to the house. The garden, an old-fashioned one, full of roses. Time of year, July. Basket chairs, and a table covered with books, are set under a large yew-tree.*

MISS PRISM *discovered seated at the table.* CECILY *is at the back watering flowers.*

MISS PRISM (*calling*): Cecily, Cecily! Surely such a utilitarian occupation as the watering of flowers is rather Moulton's duty than yours? Especially at a moment when intellectual pleasures await you. Your German grammar is on the table. Pray open it at page fifteen. We will repeat yesterday's lesson.

CECILY: Oh! I wish you would give Moulton the German lesson instead of me. Moulton!

MOULTON: (*looking out from behind a hedge, with a broad grin on his face*): Eh, Miss Cecily?

CECILY: Wouldn't you like to know German, Moulton? German is the language talked by people who live in Germany.

MOULTON (*shaking his head*): I don't hold with them furrin tongues, miss. (*Bowing to* MISS PRISM.) No offence to you, ma'am. (*Disappears behind hedge.*)

MISS PRISM: Cecily, this will never do. Pray open your Schiller at once.

CECILY (*coming over very slowly*): But I don't like German. It isn't at all a becoming language. I know perfectly well that I look quite plain after my German lesson.

MISS PRISM: Child, you know how anxious your guardian is that you should improve yourself in every way. He laid particular stress on your German, as he was leaving for town yesterday. Indeed, he always lays stress on your German when he is leaving for town.

CECILY: Dear Uncle Jack is so very serious! Sometimes he is so serious that I think he cannot be quite well.

MISS PRISM: (*drawing herself up*): Your guardian enjoys the best of health, and his gravity of demeanour is especially to be commended in one so comparatively young as he is. I know no one who has a higher sense of duty and responsibility.

CECILY: I suppose that is why he often looks a little bored when we three are together.

MISS PRISM: Cecily! I am surprised at you. Mr. Worthing has many troubles in his life. Idle merriment and triviality would be out of place in his conversation. You must remember his constant anxiety about that unfortunate young man his brother.

CECILY: I wish Uncle Jack would allow that unfortunate young man, his brother, to come down here sometimes. We might have a good influence over him, Miss Prism. I am sure you certainly would. You know German, and geology, and things of that kind influence a man very much.

CECILY *begins to write in her diary.*

MISS PRISM (*shaking her head*): I do not think that even I could produce any effect on a character that according to his own brother's admission is irretrievably weak and vacillating. Indeed I am not sure that I would desire to reclaim him. I am not in favour of this modern mania for turning bad people into good people at a moment's notice. As a man sows so let him reap.

CECILY: But men don't sew, Miss Prism.... And if they did, I don't see why they should be punished for it. There is a great deal too much punishment in the world. German is a punishment, certainly, and there is far too much German. You told me yourself yesterday that Germany was over-populated.

MISS PRISM: That is no reason why you should be writing your diary instead of translating 'William Tell'. You must put away your diary, Cecily. I really don't see why you should keep a diary at all.

CECILY: I keep a diary in order to enter the wonderful secrets of my life. If I didn't write them down, I should probably forget all about them.

MISS PRISM: Memory, my dear Cecily, is the diary that we all carry about with us.

CECILY: Yes, but it usually chronicles the things that have never happened, and couldn't possibly have happened. I believe that Memory is responsible for nearly all the three-volume novels that Mudie sends us.

MISS PRISM: Do not speak slightingly of the three-volume novel, Cecily. I wrote one myself in earlier days.

CECILY: Did you really, Miss Prism? How wonderfully clever you are! I hope it did not end happily? I don't like novels that end happily. They depress me so much.

MISS PRISM: The good ended happily, and the bad unhappily. That is what Fiction means.

CECILY: I suppose so. But it seems very unfair. And was your novel ever published?

MISS PRISM: Alas! no. The manuscript unfortunately was abandoned. (CECILY *starts.*) I use the word in the sense of lost or mislaid. To your work, child, these speculations are profitless.

CECILY (*smiling*): But I see Dr. Chasuble coming up through the garden.

MISS PRISM (*rising and advancing*): Dr. Chasuble! This is indeed a pleasure.

Enter CANON CHASUBLE.

CHASUBLE: And how are we this morning? Miss Prism, you are, I trust, well?

CECILY: Miss Prism has just been complaining of a slight headache. I think it would do her so much good to have a short stroll with you in the Park, Dr. Chasuble.

MISS PRISM: Cecily, I have not mentioned anything about a headache.

CECILY: No, dear Miss Prism, I know that, but I felt instinctively that you had a headache. Indeed I was thinking about that, and not about my German lesson, when the Rector came in.

CHASUBLE: I hope, Cecily, you are not inattentive.

CECILY: Oh, I am afraid I am.

CHASUBLE: That is strange. Were I fortunate enough to be Miss Prism's pupil, I would hang upon her lips (MISS PRISM *glares.*) I spoke metaphorically. My metaphor was drawn from bees. Ahem! Mr. Worthing, I suppose, has not returned from town yet?

MISS PRISM: We do not expect him till Monday afternoon.

CHASUBLE: Ah yes, he usually likes to spend his Sunday in London. He is not one of those whose sole aim is enjoyment, as, by all accounts, that unfortunate young man his brother seems to be. But I must not disturb Egeria and her pupil any longer.

MISS PRISM: Egeria? My name is Laetitia, Doctor.

CHASUBLE (*bowing*): A classical allusion merely, drawn from the Pagan authors. I shall see you both no doubt at Evensong?

MISS PRISM: I think, dear Doctor, I will have a stroll with you. I find I have a headache after all, and a walk might do it good.

CHASUBLE: With pleasure, Miss Prism, with pleasure. We might go as far as the schools and back.

MISS PRISM: That would be delightful. Cecily, you will read your Political Economy in my absence. The chapter on the Fall of the Rupee you may omit. It is somewhat too sensational for a young girl. Even these metallic problems have their melodramatic side.

CHASUBLE: Reading Political Economy, Cecily? It is wonderful how girls are educated nowadays. I suppose you know all about relations between Capital and Labour?

CECILY: I am afraid I am not learned at all. All I know is about the relations between Capital and Idleness – and that is merely from observation. So I don't suppose it is true.

MISS PRISM: Cecily, that sounds like Socialism! And I suppose you know where Socialism leads to?

CECILY: Oh, yes! That leads to Rational Dress, Miss Prism. And I suppose that when a woman is dressed rationally, she is treated rationally. She certainly deserves to be.

CHASUBLE: A wilful lamb! Dear child!

MISS PRISM (*smiling*): A sad trouble sometimes.

CHASUBLE: I envy you such tribulation.

Goes down the garden with MISS PRISM.

CECILY (*picks up books and throws them back on table*): Horrid Political Economy! Horrid Geography! Horrid, horrid German!

Enter MERRIMAN *with a card on a salver.*

MERRIMAN: Mr. Ernest Worthing has just driven over from the station. He has brought his luggage with him.

CECILY (*takes the card and reads it*): 'Mr. Ernest Worthing, B.4, The Albany, W.' Uncle Jack's brother! Did you tell him Mr. Worthing was in town?

MERRIMAN: Yes, Miss. He seemed very much disappointed. I mentioned that you and Miss Prism were in the garden. He said he was anxious to speak to you privately for a moment.

CECILY (*to herself*): I don't think Miss Prism would like my being alone with him. So I had better send for him at once, before she comes in. (*To* MERRIMAN.) Ask Mr. Ernest Worthing to come here. I suppose you had better talk to the housekeeper about a room for him.

MERRIMAN: I have already sent his luggage up to the Blue Room, Miss: next to Mr. Worthing's own room.

CECILY: Oh! That is all right.

MERRIMAN *goes off.*

I have never met any really wicked person before. I feel rather frightened. I am so afraid he will look just like everyone else.

Enter ALGERNON, *very gay and debonair.*

He does!

ALGERNON (*raising his hat*): You are my little cousin Cecily, I'm sure.

CECILY: You are under some strange mistake. I am not little. In fact, I believe I am more than usually tall for my age. (ALGERNON *is rather taken aback.*) But I am your cousin Cecily. You, I see from your card, are Uncle Jack's brother, my cousin Ernest, my wicked cousin Ernest.

ALGERNON: Oh! I am not really wicked at all, cousin Cecily. You mustn't think that I am wicked.

CECILY: If you are not, then you have certainly been deceiving us all in a very inexcusable manner. You have made Uncle Jack believe that you are very bad. I hope that you have not been leading a double life, pretending to be wicked and being really good all the time. That would be hypocrisy.

ALGERNON (*looks at her in amazement*): Oh! Of course I have been rather reckless.

CECILY: I am glad to hear it.

ALGERNON: In fact, now you mention the subject, I have been very bad in my own small way.

CECILY: I don't think you should be so proud of that, though I am sure it must have been very pleasant.

ALGERNON: It is much pleasanter being here with you.

CECILY: I can't understand how you are here at all. Uncle Jack telegraphed to you yesterday at the Albany that he would see you for the last time at six o'clock. He lets me read all the telegrams he sends you. I know some of them by heart.

ALGERNON: The fact is I didn't get the telegram till it was too late. Then I missed him at the Club, and the Hall Porter said he thought he had come down here. So, of course, I followed as I knew he wanted to see me.

CECILY: He won't be back till Monday afternoon.

ALGERNON: That is a great disappointment. I am obliged to go up by the first train on Monday morning. I have a business appointment that I am anxious... to miss!

CECILY: Couldn't you miss it anywhere but in London?

ALGERNON: No: the appointment is in London.

CECILY: Well, I know, of course, how important it is not to keep a business engagement, if one wants to retain any sense of the beauty of life, but still I think you had better wait till Uncle Jack arrives. I know he wants to speak to you about your emigrating.

ALGERNON: About my what?

CECILY: Your emigrating. He has gone up to buy your outfit.

ALGERNON: I certainly wouldn't let Jack buy my outfit. He has no taste in neckties at all.

CECILY: I don't think you will require neckties. Uncle Jack is sending you to Australia.

ALGERNON: Australia! I'd sooner die.

CECILY: Well, he said at dinner on Wednesday night, that you would have to choose between this world, the next world, and Australia.

ALGERNON: Oh, well! The accounts I have received of Australia and the next world, are not particularly encouraging. This world is good enough for me, cousin Cecily.

CECILY: Yes, but are you good enough for it?

ALGERNON: I'm afraid I'm not that. That is why I want you to reform me. You might make that your mission, if you don't mind, cousin Cecily.

CECILY: How dare you suggest that I have a mission?

ALGERNON: I beg your pardon: but I thought that every woman had a mission of some kind, nowadays.

CECILY: Every female has! No woman. Besides, I have no time to reform you this afternoon.

ALGERNON: Well, would you mind my reforming myself this afternoon?

CECILY: It is rather Quixotic of you. But I think you should try.

ALGERNON: I will. I feel better already.

CECILY: You are looking a little worse.

ALGERNON: That is because I am hungry.

CECILY: How thoughtless of me. I should have remembered that when one is going to lead an entirely new life, one requires regular and wholesome meals. Miss Prism and I lunch at two, off some roast mutton.

ALGERNON: I fear that would be too rich for me.

CECILY: Uncle Jack, whose health has been sadly undermined by the late hours you keep in town, has been ordered by his London doctor to have pâté de foie gras sandwiches and 1889 champagne at twelve. I don't know if such invalid fare would suit you.

ALGERNON: Oh! I will be quite content with '89 champagne.

CECILY: I am glad to see you have such simple tastes. This is the dining-room.

ALGERNON: Thank you. Might I have a buttonhole first? I never have any appetite unless I have a buttonhole first.

CECILY: A Maréchal Niel? (*Picks up scissors.*)

ALGERNON: No, I'd sooner have a pink rose.

CECILY: Why? (*Cuts a flower.*)

ALGERNON: Because you are like a pink rose, Cousin Cecily.

CECILY: I don't think it can be right for you to talk to me like that. Miss Prism never says such things to me.

ALGERNON: Then Miss Prism is a short-sighted old lady. (CECILY *puts the rose in his buttonhole.*) You are the prettiest girl I ever saw.

CECILY: Miss Prism says that all good looks are a snare.

ALGERNON: They are a snare that every sensible man would like to be caught in.

CECILY: Oh, I don't think I would care to catch a sensible man. I shouldn't know what to talk to him about.

They pass into the house. MISS PRISM *and* DR. CHASUBLE *return.*

MISS PRISM: You are too much alone, dear Dr. Chasuble. You should get married. A misanthrope I can understand – a womanthrope, never!

CHASUBLE (*with a scholar's shudder*): Believe me, I do not deserve so neol-ogistic a phrase. The precept as well as the practice of the Primitive Church was distinctly against matrimony.

MISS PRISM (*sententiously*): That is obviously the reason why the Primi-tive Church has not lasted up to the present day. And you do not seem to realise, dear Doctor, that by persistently remaining single, a man converts himself into a permanent public temptation. Men should be more careful; this very celibacy leads weaker vessels astray.

CHASUBLE: But is a man not equally attractive when married?

MISS PRISM: No married man is ever attractive except to his wife.

CHASUBLE: And often, I've been told, not even to her.

MISS PRISM: That depends on the intellectual sympathies of the woman. Maturity can always be depended on. Ripeness can be trusted. Young women are green. (DR. CHASUBLE *starts.*) I spoke horticulturally. My meta-phor was drawn from fruit. But where is Cecily?

CHASUBLE: Perhaps she followed us to the schools.

Enter JACK *slowly from the back of the garden. He is dressed in the deepest mourning, with crêpe hatband and black gloves.*

MISS PRISM: Mr. Worthing!

CHASUBLE: Mr. Worthing?

MISS PRISM: This is indeed a surprise. We did not look for you till Monday afternoon.

JACK (*shakes* MISS PRISM'S *hand in a tragic manner*): I have returned sooner than I expected. Dr. Chasuble, I hope you are well?

CHASUBLE: Dear Mr. Worthing, I trust this garb of woe does not betoken some terrible calamity?

JACK: My brother.

MISS PRISM: More shameful debts and extravagance?

CHASUBLE: Still leading his life of pleasure?

JACK (*shaking his head*): Dead!

CHASUBLE: Your brother Ernest dead?

JACK: Quite dead.

MISS PRISM: What a lesson for him! I trust he will profit by it.

CHASUBLE: Death is the inheritance of us all, Miss Prism. Nor should we look on it as a special judgment, but rather as a general providence. Life were incomplete without it . . . Mr. Worthing, I offer you my sincere condolence. You have at least the consolation of knowing that you were always the most generous and forgiving of brothers.

JACK: Poor Ernest! He had many faults, but it is a sad, sad blow.

CHASUBLE: Very sad indeed. Were you with him at the end?

JACK: No. He died abroad; in Paris, in fact. I had a telegram last night from the manager of the Grand Hotel.

CHASUBLE: Was the cause of death mentioned?

JACK: A severe chill, it seems.

MISS PRISM: As a man sows, so shall he reap.

CHASUBLE (*raising his hand*): Charity, dear Miss Prism, charity! None of us are perfect. I myself am peculiarly susceptible to draughts. Will the interment take place here?

JACK: No. He seems to have expressed a desire to be buried in Paris.

CHASUBLE: In Paris! (*Shakes his head.*) I fear that hardly points to any very serious state of mind at the last. You would no doubt wish me to make some slight allusion to this tragic domestic affliction next Sunday. (JACK *presses his hand convulsively.*) My sermon on the meaning of the manna in the wilderness can be adapted to almost any occasion, joyful, or, as in the present case, distressing. (*All sigh.*) I have preached it at harvest celebrations, christenings, confirmations, on days of humiliation and festal days. The last time I delivered it was in the Cathedral, as a charity sermon on behalf of the Society for the Prevention of Discontent among the Upper Orders. The Bishop, who was present, was much struck by some of the analogies I drew.

JACK: Ah! that reminds me, you mentioned christenings, I think, Dr. Chasuble? I suppose you know how to christen all right? (DR. CHASUBLE *looks astounded.*) I mean, of course, you are continually christening, aren't you?

MISS PRISM: It is, I regret to say, one of the Rector's most constant duties in this parish. I have often spoken to the poorer classes on the subject. But they don't seem to know what thrift is.

CHASUBLE: The Church rejects no babe, Miss Prism. In every child, there is the making of a saint. But is there any particular infant in whom you are interested, Mr. Worthing? Your brother was, I believe, unmarried, was he not?

JACK: Oh yes.

MISS PRISM (*bitterly*): People who live entirely for pleasure usually are.

JACK: But it is not for any child, dear Doctor. I am very fond of children. No! the fact is, I would like to be christened myself, this afternoon, if you have nothing better to do.

CHASUBLE: But surely, Mr. Worthing, you have been christened already?

JACK: I don't remember anything about it.

CHASUBLE: But have you any grave doubts on the subject?

JACK: I have the very gravest doubts. There are circumstances, unnecessary to mention at present, connected with my birth and early life that make me think I was a good deal neglected. I certainly wasn't properly looked after, at any rate. Of course I don't know if the thing would bother you in any way, or if you think I am a little too old now.

CHASUBLE: Oh! I am not by any means a bigoted Paedobaptist. The sprinkling and, indeed, the immersion of adults was a common practice of the Primitive Church.

JACK: Immersion! You don't mean to say that . . .

CHASUBLE: You need have no apprehensions. Sprinkling is all that is necessary, or indeed I think advisable. Our weather is so changeable. At what hour would you wish the ceremony performed?

JACK: Oh, I might trot round about five if that would suit you.

CHASUBLE: Perfectly, perfectly! In fact, I have two similar ceremonies to perform at that time. A case of twins that occurred recently in one of the outlying cottages on your own estate. Poor Jenkins the carter, a most hardworking man.

JACK: Oh! I don't see much fun in being christened along with other babies. It would be childish. Would half-past five do?

CHASUBLE: Admirably! Admirably! (*Takes out watch.*) And now, dear Mr. Worthing, I will not intrude any longer into a house of sorrow. I would merely beg you not to be too much bowed down by grief. What seem to us bitter trials are often blessings in disguise.

MISS PRISM: This seems to me a blessing of an extremely obvious kind.

Enter CECILY *from the house.*

CECILY: Uncle Jack! Oh, I am pleased to see you back. But what horrid clothes you have got on! Do go and change them.

MISS PRISM: Cecily!

CHASUBLE: My child! my child!

CECILY *goes towards* JACK; *he kisses her brow in a melancholy manner.*

CECILY: What is the matter, Uncle Jack? Do look happy! You look as if you had toothache, and I have got such a surprise for you. Who do you think is in the dining-room? Your brother!

JACK: Who?

CECILY: Your brother Ernest. He arrived about half an hour ago.

JACK: What nonsense! I haven't got a brother.

CECILY: Oh, don't say that. However badly he may have behaved to you in the past he is still your brother. You couldn't be so heartless as to disown him. I'll tell him to come out. And you will shake hands with him, won't you, Uncle Jack? (*Runs back into the house.*)

CHASUBLE: These are very joyful tidings. That telegram from Paris seems to have been a somewhat heartless jest by one who wished to play upon your feelings.

MISS PRISM: After we had all been resigned to his loss, his sudden return seems to me peculiarly distressing.

JACK: My brother is in the dining-room? I don't know what it all means. I think it is perfectly absurd.

Enter ALGERNON *and* CECILY *hand in hand. They come slowly up to* JACK.

JACK: Good heavens! (*Motions* ALGERNON *away.*)

ALGERNON: Brother John, I have come down from town to tell you that I am very sorry for all the trouble I have given you, and that I intend to lead a better life in the future. (JACK *glares at him and does not take his hand.*)

CHASUBLE: (*to* MISS PRISM): There is good in that young man. He seems to be sincerely repentant.

MISS PRISM: These sudden conversions do not please me. They belong to Dissent. They savour of the laxity of the Nonconformist.

CECILY: Uncle Jack, you are not going to refuse your own brother's hand?

JACK: Nothing will induce me to take his hand. I think his coming down here disgraceful. He knows perfectly well why.

CHASUBLE: Young man, you have had a very narrow escape of your life. I hope it will be a warning to you. We were mourning your demise when you entered.

ALGERNON: Yes, I see Jack has got a new suit of clothes. They don't fit him properly. His necktie is wrong.

CECILY: Uncle Jack, do be nice. There is some good in everyone. Ernest has just been telling me about his poor invalid friend Mr. Bunbury whom he goes to visit so often. And surely there must be some good in one who is kind to an invalid, and leaves the pleasures of London to sit by a bed of pain.

JACK: Oh! he has been talking about Bunbury has he?

CECILY: Yes, he has told me all about poor Mr. Bunbury, and his terrible state of health.

JACK: Bunbury! Well, I won't have him talk to you about Bunbury or about anything else. It is enough to drive one perfectly frantic.

CHASUBLE: Mr. Worthing, your brother has been unexpectedly restored to you by the mysterious dispensations of providence, who seems to desire your reconciliation. And indeed it is good for brothers to dwell together in amity.

ALGERNON: Of course I admit that the faults were all on my side. But I must say that I think that Brother John's coldness to me is peculiarly painful. I expected a warmer welcome, especially considering it is the first time I have come here.

CECILY: Uncle Jack, if you don't shake hands with Ernest I will never forgive you.

JACK: Never forgive me?

CECILY: Never, never, never!

JACK: I suppose I must then. (*Shakes hands and glares.*) You young scoundrel! You must get out of this place as soon as possible. I don't allow any Bunburying here.

CHASUBLE: It's pleasant, is it not, to see so perfect a reconciliation? You have done a beautiful action to–day, dear child.

MISS PRISM: We must not be premature in our judgments.

Enter MERRIMAN.

MERRIMAN: I have put Mr. Ernest's things in the room next to yours, sir. I suppose that is all right?

JACK: What?

MERRIMAN: Mr. Ernest's luggage, sir. I have unpacked it and put it in the room next to your own.

JACK: His luggage?

MERRIMAN: Yes, sir. Three portmanteaus, a dressing case, two hat-boxes, and a large luncheon-basket.

ALGERNON: I am afraid I can't stay more than a week this time.

MERRIMAN (*to* ALGERNON): I beg your pardon, sir, there is an elderly gentleman wishes to see you. He has just come in a cab from the station. (*Hands card on salver.*)

ALGERNON: To see me?

MERRIMAN: Yes, sir.

ALGERNON: (*reads card*): Parker and Gribsby, Solicitors. I don't know anything about them. Who are they?

JACK: (*takes card*): Parker and Gribsby. I wonder who they can be. I expect, Ernest, they have come about some business for your friend Bunbury. Perhaps Bunbury wants to make his will and wishes you to be executor. (*To* MERRIMAN.) Show the gentleman in at once.

MERRIMAN: Very good, sir.

MERRIMAN *goes out.*

JACK: I hope, Ernest, that I may rely on the statement you made to me last week when I finally settled all your bills for you. I hope you have no outstanding accounts of any kind.

ALGERNON: I haven't any debts at all, dear Jack. Thanks to your generosity I don't owe a penny, except for a few neckties, I believe.

JACK: I am sincerely glad to hear it.

Enter MERRIMAN.

MERRIMAN: Mr. Gribsby.

MERRIMAN *goes out. Enter* GRIBSBY.

GRIBSBY (*to* DR. CHASUBLE): Mr. Ernest Worthing?

MISS PRISM: This is Mr. Ernest Worthing.

GRIBSBY: Mr. Ernest Worthing?

ALGERNON: Yes.

GRIBSBY: Of B.4., The Albany?

ALGERNON: Yes, that is my address.

GRIBSBY: I am very sorry, sir, but we have a writ of attachment for twenty days against you at the suit of the Savoy Hotel Co. Limited for £762 14s. 2d.

ALGERNON: Against me?

GRIBSBY: Yes, sir.

ALGERNON: What perfect nonsense! I never dine at the Savoy at my own expense. I always dine at Willis's. It is far more expensive. I don't owe a penny to the Savoy.

GRIBSBY: The writ is marked as having been served on you personally at The Albany on May the 27th. Judgment was given in default against you on the fifth of June. Since then we have written to you no less than fifteen times, without receiving any reply. In the interest of our clients we had no option but to obtain an order for committal of your person.

ALGERNON: Committal! What on earth do you mean by committal? I haven't the smallest intention of going away. I am staying here for a week. I am staying with my brother. If you imagine I am going up to town the moment I arrive you are extremely mistaken.

GRIBSBY: I am merely a solicitor myself. I do not employ personal violence of any kind. The officer of the Court, whose function it is to seize the person of the debtor, is waiting in the fly outside. He has considerable experience in these matters. That is why we always employ him. But no doubt you will prefer to pay the bill.

ALGERNON: Pay it? How on earth am I going to do that? You don't suppose I have got any money? How perfectly silly you are. No gentleman ever has any money.

GRIBSBY: My experience is that it is usually relations who pay.

ALGERNON: Jack, you really must settle this bill.

JACK: Kindly allow me to see the particular items, Mr. Gribsby . . . (*turns over immense folio*) . . . £762 14s. 2d. since last October. I am bound to say I never saw such reckless extravagance in all my life. (*Hands it to* DR. CHASUBLE.)

MISS PRISM: £762 for eating! There can be little good in any young man who eats so much, and so often.

CHASUBLE: We are far away from Wordsworth's plain living and high thinking.

JACK: Now, Dr. Chasuble, do you consider that I am in any way called upon to pay this monstrous account for my brother.

CHASUBLE: I am bound to say that I do not think so. It would be encouraging his profligacy.

MISS PRISM: As a man sows, so let him reap. This proposed incarceration might be most salutary. It is to be regretted that it is only for twenty days.

JACK: I am quite of your opinion.

ALGERNON: My dear fellow, how ridiculous you are! You know perfectly well that the bill is really yours.

JACK: Mine?

ALGERNON: Yes, you know it is.

CHASUBLE: Mr. Worthing, if this is a jest, it is out of place.

MISS PRISM: It is gross effrontery. Just what I expected from him.

CECILY: And it is ingratitude. I didn't expect that.

JACK: Never mind what he says. This is the way he always goes on. You mean now to say that you are not Ernest Worthing, residing at B.4., The Albany. I wonder, as you are at it, that you don't deny being my brother at all. Why don't you?

ALGERNON: Oh! I am not going to do that, my dear fellow. It would be absurd. Of course I'm your brother. And that is why you should pay this bill for me.

JACK: I will tell you quite candidly that I have not the smallest intention of doing anything of the kind. Dr. Chasuble, the worthy Rector of this parish, and Miss Prism, in whose admirable and sound judgment I place great reliance, are both of the opinion that incarceration would do you a great deal of good. And I think so, too.

GRIBSBY (*pulls out watch*): I am sorry to disturb this pleasant family meeting, but time presses. We have to be at Holloway not later than four o'clock; otherwise it is difficult to obtain admission. The rules are very strict.

ALGERNON: Holloway!

GRIBSBY: It is at Holloway that detentions of this character take place always.

ALGERNON: Well, I really am not going to be imprisoned in the suburbs for having dined in the West End.

GRIBSBY: The bill is for suppers, not for dinners.

ALGERNON: I really don't care. All I say is that I am not going to be imprisoned in the suburbs.

GRIBSBY: The surroundings I admit are middle class; but the gaol itself is fashionable and well-aired; and there are ample opportunities of taking exercise at certain stated hours of the day. In the case of a medical certificate, which is always easy to obtain, the hours can be extended.

ALGERNON: Exercise! Good God! No gentleman ever takes exercise. You don't seem to understand what a gentleman is.

GRIBSBY: I have met so many of them, sir, that I am afraid I don't. There are the most curious varieties of them. The result of cultivation, no doubt. Will you kindly come now, sir, if it will not be inconvenient to you.

ALGERNON (*appealingly*): Jack!

MISS PRISM: Pray be firm, Mr. Worthing.

CHASUBLE: This is an occasion on which any weakness would be out of place. It would be a form of self-deception.

JACK: I am quite firm, and I don't know what weakness or deception of any kind is.

CECILY: Uncle Jack! I think you have a little money of mine, haven't you? Let me pay this bill. I wouldn't like your own brother to be in prison.

JACK: Oh! I couldn't possibly let you pay it, Cecily. That would be absurd.

CECILY: Then you will, won't you? I think you would be sorry if you thought your own brother was shut up. Of course, I am quite disappointed with him.

JACK: You won't speak to him again, Cecily, will you?

CECILY: Certainly not, unless, of course, he speaks to me first. It would be very rude not to answer him.

JACK: Well, I'll take care he doesn't speak to you. I'll take care he doesn't speak to anybody in this house. The man should be cut. Mr. Gribsby . . .

GRIBSBY: Yes, sir.

JACK: I'll pay this bill for my brother. It is the last bill I shall ever pay for him, too. How much is it?

GRIBSBY: £762 14*s*. 2*d*. Ah! The cab will be five-and-ninepence extra: hired for the convenience of the client.

JACK: All right.

MISS PRISM: I must say that I think such generosity quite foolish.

CHASUBLE (*with a wave of the hand*): The heart has its wisdom as well as the head, Miss Prism.

JACK: Payable to Parker and Gribsby, I suppose?

GRIBSBY: Yes, sir. Kindly don't cross the cheque. Thank you. (*To* DR. CHASUBLE) Good day. (DR. CHASUBLE *bows coldly*.) Good Day. (MISS PRISM *bows coldly*.) (*To* ALGERNON.) I hope I shall have the pleasure of meeting you again.

ALGERNON: I sincerely hope not. What ideas you have of the sort of society a gentleman wants to mix in. No gentleman ever wants to know a solicitor who wants to imprison one in the suburbs.

GRIBSBY: Quite so, quite so.

ALGERNON: By the way, Gribsby: Gribsby, you are not to go back to the station in that cab. That is my cab. It was taken for my convenience. You have got to walk to the station. And a very good thing, too. Solicitors don't walk nearly enough. I don't know any solicitor who takes sufficient exercise. As a rule they sit in stuffy offices all day long neglecting their business.

JACK: You can take the cab, Mr. Gribsby.

GRIBSBY Thank you, sir.

GRIBSBY *goes out.*

CECILY: The day is getting very sultry, isn't it, Dr. Chasuble?

CHASUBLE: There is thunder in the air.

MISS PRISM: The atmosphere requires to be cleared.

CHASUBLE: Have you read 'The Times' this morning, Mr. Worthing? There is a very interesting article on the growth of religious feeling among the laity.

JACK: I am keeping it for after dinner.

Enter MERRIMAN.

MERRIMAN: Luncheon is on the table, sir.

ALGERNON: Ah! That is good news. I am excessively hungry.

CECILY: (*interposing*): But you have lunched already.

JACK: Lunched already?

CECILY: Yes, Uncle Jack. He had some pâté de foie gras sandwiches, and a small bottle of that champagne that your doctor ordered for you.

JACK: My '89 champagne!

CECILY: Yes. I thought you would like him to have the same one as yourself.

JACK: Oh! Well, if he has lunched once, he can't be expected to lunch twice. It would be absurd.

MISS PRISM: To partake of two luncheons in one day would not be liberty. It would be licence.

CHASUBLE: Even the pagan philosophers condemned excess in eating. Aristotle speaks of it with severity. He uses the same terms about it as he does about usury.

JACK: Doctor, will you escort the ladies into luncheon?

CHASUBLE: With pleasure.

He goes into the house with MISS PRISM *and* CECILY.

JACK: Your Bunburying has not been a great success after all, Algy. I don't think it is a good day for Bunburying, myself.

ALGERNON: Oh! There are ups and downs in Bunburying, just as there are in everything else. I'd be all right if you would let me have some lunch. The main thing is that I have seen Cecily and she is a darling.

JACK: You are not to talk of Miss Cardew like that. I don't like it.

ALGERNON: Well, I don't like your clothes. You look perfectly ridiculous in them. Why on earth don't you go up and change? It is perfectly childish to be in deep mourning for a man who is actually staying for a whole week with you in your house as a guest. I call it grotesque.

JACK: You are certainly not staying with me for a whole week as a guest or anything else. You have got to leave . . . by the four-five train.

ALGERNON: I certainly won't leave you so long as you are in mourning. It would be most unfriendly. If I were in mourning you would stay with me, I suppose. I should think it very unkind if you didn't.

JACK: Well, will you go if I change my clothes?

ALGERNON: Yes, if you are not too long. I never saw anybody take so long to dress, and with such little result.

JACK: Well, at any rate, that is better than being always over-dressed as you are.

ALGERNON: If I am occasionally a little over-dressed, I make up for it by being always immensely over-educated.

JACK: Your vanity is ridiculous, your conduct an outrage, and your presence in my garden utterly absurd. However, you have got to catch the four-five, and I hope you will have a pleasant journey back to town. This Bunburying, as you call it, has not been a great success for you. (*Goes into the house.*)

ALGERNON: I think it has been a great success. I'm in love with Cecily, and that is everything. It is all very well, but one can't Bunbury when one is hungry. I think I'll join them at lunch. (*Goes towards door.*)

Enter CECILY.

CECILY: I promised Uncle Jack that I wouldn't speak to you again, unless you asked me a question. I can't understand why you don't ask me a question of some kind. I am afraid you are not quite so intellectual as I thought you were at first.

ALGERNON: Cecily, mayn't I come in to lunch?

CECILY: I wonder you can look me in the face after your conduct.

ALGERNON: I love looking you in the face.

CECILY: But why did you try to put your horrid bill on poor Uncle Jack? I think that was inexcusable of you.

ALGERNON: I know it was; but the fact is I have a most wretched memory. I quite forgot I owed the Savoy £762 14s. 2d.

CECILY: Well, I admit I am glad to hear that you have a bad memory. Good memories are not a quality that women admire much in men.

ALGERNON: Cecily, I am fearfully hungry.

CECILY: I can't understand your being so hungry, considering all you have had to eat since last October.

ALGERNON: Oh! Those suppers were for poor Bunbury. Late suppers are the only things his doctor allows him to eat.

CECILY: Well, I don't wonder then that Mr. Bunbury is always so ill, if he eats suppers for six or eight people every night of the week.

ALGERNON: That is what I always tell him. But he seems to think his doctors know best. He's perfectly silly about doctors.

CECILY: Of course I don't want you to starve, so I have told the butler to send you out some lunch.

ALGERNON: Cecily, what a perfect angel you are! May I not see you again before I go?

CECILY: Miss Prism and I will be here after lunch. I always have my afternoon lessons under the yew-tree.

ALGERNON: Can't you invent something to get Miss Prism out of the way?

CECILY: Do you mean invent a falsehood?

ALGERNON: Oh! Not a falsehood, of course. Simply something that is not quite true, but should be.

CECILY: I am afraid I couldn't possibly do that. I shouldn't know how. People never think of cultivating a young girl's imagination. It is the great defect of modern education. Of course, if you happened to mention that dear Dr. Chasuble was waiting somewhere to see Miss Prism, she would certainly go to meet him. She never likes to keep him waiting. And she has so few opportunities of doing so.

ALGERNON: What a capital suggestion!

CECILY: I didn't suggest anything, Cousin Ernest. Nothing would induce me to deceive Miss Prism in the smallest detail. I merely pointed out that if you adopted a certain line of conduct, a certain result would follow.

ALGERNON: Of course. I beg your pardon, Cousin Cecily. Then I shall come here at half-past three. I have something very serious to say to you.

CECILY: Serious?

ALGERNON: Yes: very serious.

CECILY: In that case I think we had better meet in the house. I don't like talking seriously in the open air. It looks so artificial.

ALGERNON: Then where shall we meet?

Enter JACK.

JACK: The dog-cart is at the door. You have got to go. Your place is by Bunbury. (*Sees* Cecily.) Cecily! Don't you think, Cecily, that you had better return to Miss Prism and Dr. Chasuble?

CECILY: Yes, Uncle Jack. Good-bye, Cousin Ernest. I am afraid I shan't see you again, as I shall be doing my lessons with Miss Prism in the drawing-room at half-past three.

ALGERNON: Good-bye, Cousin Cecily. You have been very kind to me.

CECILY *goes out.*

JACK: Now look here, Algy. You have got to go, and the sooner you go the better. Bunbury is extremely ill, and your place is by his side.

ALGERNON: I can't go at the present moment. I must first just have my second lunch. And you will be pleased to hear that Bunbury is very much better.

JACK: Well, you will have to go at three-fifty, at any rate. I ordered your things to be packed and the dog-cart to come round.

ACT DROP

ACT THREE

SCENE: *The drawing-room at the Manor House.* CECILY *and*
MISS PRISM *discovered; each writing at a separate table.*

MISS PRISM: Cecily! (CECILY *makes no answer.*) Cecily! You are again making entries in your diary. I think I have had occasion more than once to speak to you about that morbid habit of yours.

CECILY: I am merely, as I always do, taking you for my example, Miss Prism.

MISS PRISM: When one has thoroughly mastered the principles of Bimetallism one has the right to lead an introspective life. Hardly before. I must beg you to return to your Political Economy.

CECILY: In one moment, dear Miss Prism. The fact is I have only chronicled the events of to-day up till two-fifteen, and it was at two-thirty that the fearful catastrophe occurred.

MISS PRISM: Pardon me, Cecily, it was exactly at two-forty-five that Dr. Chasuble mentioned the very painful views held by the Primitive Church on Marriage.

CECILY: I was not referring to Dr. Chasuble at all. I was alluding to the tragic exposure of poor Mr. Ernest Worthing.

MISS PRISM: I highly disapprove of Mr. Ernest Worthing. He is a thoroughly bad young man.

CECILY: I fear he must be. It is the only explanation I can find of his strange attractiveness.

MISS PRISM (*rising*): Cecily, let me entreat of you not to be led away by whatever superficial qualities this unfortunate young man may possess.

CECILY: Ah! Believe me, dear Miss Prism, it is only the superficial qualities that last. Man's deeper nature is soon found out.

MISS PRISM: Child! I do not know where you get such ideas. They are certainly not to be found in any of the improving books that I have procured for you.

CECILY: Are there ever any ideas in improving books? I fear not. I get my ideas . . . in the garden.

MISS PRISM: Then you should certainly not be so much in the open air. The fact is, you have fallen lately, Cecily, into a bad habit of thinking for yourself. You should give it up. It is not quite womanly . . . Men don't like it.

Enter ALGERNON.

Mr. Worthing, I thought, I may say I was in hopes that you had already returned to town.

ALGERNON: My departure will not long be delayed. I have come to bid you good-bye, Miss Cardew. I am informed that a dog-cart has been already ordered for me. I have no option but to go back again into the cold world.

CECILY: I hardly know, Mr. Worthing, what you can mean by using such an expression. The day, even for the month of July, is unusually warm.

MISS PRISM: Profligacy is apt to dull the senses.

ALGERNON: No doubt. I am far from defending the weather. I think however that it is only my duty to mention to you, Miss Prism, that Dr. Chasuble is expecting you in the vestry.

MISS PRISM: In the vestry! That sounds serious. It can hardly be for any trivial purpose that the Rector selects for an interview a place of such peculiarly solemn associations. I do not think that it would be right to keep him waiting, Cecily?

CECILY: It would be very, very wrong. The vestry is, I am told, excessively damp.

MISS PRISM: True! I had not thought of that, and Dr. Chasuble is sadly rheumatic. Mr. Worthing, we shall probably not meet again. You will allow me, I trust, to express a sincere hope that you will now turn over a new leaf in life.

ALGERNON: I have already begun an entire volume, Miss Prism.

MISS PRISM: I am delighted to hear it. (*Puts on a large unbecoming hat.*) And do not forget that there is always hope even for the most depraved. Do not be idle, Cecily.

CECILY: I have no intention of being idle. I realise only too strongly that I have a great deal of serious work before me.

MISS PRISM: Ah! that is quite as it should be, dear.

MISS PRISM *goes out.*

ALGERNON: This parting, Miss Cardew, is very painful.

CECILY: It is always painful to part from people whom one has known for a very brief space of time. The absence of old friends one can endure with equanimity. But even a momentary separation from anyone to whom one has just been introduced is almost unbearable.

ALGERNON: Thank you.

Enter MERRIMAN.

MERRIMAN: The dog-cart is at the door, sir.

ALGERNON *looks appealing at* CECILY.

CECILY: It can wait, Merriman, for five minutes.

MERRIMAN: Yes, Miss.

Exit MERRIMAN.

ALGERNON: I hope, Cecily, I shall not offend you if I state quite frankly and openly that you seem to me to be in every way the visible personification of absolute perfection.

CECILY: I think your frankness does you great credit, Ernest. If you will allow me, I will copy your remarks into my diary. (*Goes over to table and begins writing in diary.*)

ALGERNON: Do you really keep a diary? I'd give anything to look at it. May I?

CECILY: Oh, no. (*Puts her hand over it.*) You see, it is simply a very young girl's record of her own thoughts and impressions, and consequently meant for publication. When it appears in volume form I hope you will order a copy. But pray, Ernest, don't stop. I delight in taking down from dictation. I have reached 'absolute perfection'. You can go on. I am quite ready for more.

ALGERNON: (*somewhat taken aback*): Ahem! Ahem!

CECILY: Oh, don't cough, Ernest. When one is dictating one should speak fluently and not cough. Besides, I don't know how to spell a cough. (*Writes as* ALGERNON *speaks.*)

ALGERNON: (*speaking very rapidly*): Miss Cardew, ever since half-past twelve this afternoon, when I first looked upon your wonderful and incomparable beauty, I have not merely been your abject slave and servant, but, soaring upon the pinions of a possibly monstrous ambition, I have dared to love you wildly, passionately, devotedly, hopelessly.

CECILY: (*laying down her pen*): Oh! please say that all over again. You speak far too fast and far too indistinctly. Kindly say it all over again.

ALGERNON: Miss Cardew, ever since you were half-past twelve – I mean ever since it was half-past twelve, this afternoon, when I first looked upon your wonderful and incomparable beauty ...

CECILY: Yes, I have got that, all right.

ALGERNON: (*stammering*): I – I –

CECILY *lays down her pen and looks reproachfully at him.*

(*Desperately.*) I have not merely been your abject slave and servant, but, soaring on the pinions of a possibly monstrous ambition, I have dared to love you wildly, passionately, devotedly, hopelessly. (*Takes out his watch and looks at it.*)

CECILY (*after writing for some time, looks up*): I have not taken down 'hopelessly'. It doesn't seem to make much sense, does it? (*A slight pause.*)

ALGERNON: (*starting back*): Cecily!

CECILY: Is that the beginning of an entirely new paragraph? Or should it be followed by a note of admiration?

ALGERNON: (*rapidly and romantically*): It is the beginning of an entirely new existence for me, and it shall be followed by such notes of admiration that my whole life shall be a subtle and sustained symphony of Love, Praise and Adoration combined.

CECILY: Oh, I don't think that makes any sense at all. The fact is that men should never try to dictate to women. They never know how to do it, and when they do do it, they always say something particularly foolish.

ALGERNON: I don't care whether what I say is foolish or not. All that I know is that I love you, Cecily. I love you, I want you. I can't live without you, Cecily! You know I love you. Will you marry me? Will you be my wife? (*Rushes over to her and puts his hand on hers.*)

CECILY: (*rising*): Oh, you have made me make a blot! And yours is the only real proposal I have ever had in all my life. I should like to have entered it neatly.

  Enter MERRIMAN.

MERRIMAN: The dog-cart is waiting, sir.

ALGERNON: Tell it to come round next week at the same hour.

MERRIMAN: (*looks at* CECILY *who makes no sign*): Yes, sir. (*Merriman retires*)

CECILY: Uncle Jack would be very much annoyed if he knew you were staying on till next week, at the same hour.

ALGERNON: Oh! I don't care about Jack! I don't care for anybody in the whole world but you. I love you. Cecily! you will marry me, won't you?

CECILY: You silly boy! Of course. Why, we have been engaged for the last three months.

ALGERNON: For the last three months?

CECILY: Three months all but a few days. (*Looks at diary, turns over page.*) Yes; it will be exactly three months on Thursday.

ALGERNON: I didn't know.

CECILY: Very few people nowadays ever realise the position in which they are placed. The age is, as Miss Prism often says, a thoughtless one.

ALGERNON: But how did we become engaged?

CECILY: Well, ever since dear Uncle Jack first confessed to us that he had a younger brother who was very wicked and bad, you of course have formed the chief topic of conversation between myself and Miss Prism. And of course a man who is much talked about is always very attractive. One feels there must be something in him, after all. I dare say it was foolish of me, but I fell in love with you, Ernest.

ALGERNON: Darling! And when was the engagement actually settled?

CECILY: On the 14th of February last. Worn out by your entire ignorance of my existence, I determined to end the matter one way or the other, and after a long struggle with myself I accepted you one evening in the garden. The next day I bought this little ring in your name. You see I always wear it, Ernest, and though it shows that you are sadly extravagant, still I have long ago forgiven you for that. Here in this drawer are all the little presents I have given you from time to time, neatly numbered and labelled. This is the pearl necklace you gave me on my birthday. And this is the box in which I keep all your letters. (*Opens box and produces letters tied up with blue ribbon.*)

ALGERNON: My letters! But my own sweet Cecily, I have never written you any letters.

CECILY: You need hardly remind me of that, Ernest. I remember it only too well. I grew tired of asking the postman every morning if he had a London letter for me. My health began to give way under the strain and anxiety.

So I wrote your letters for you, and had them posted to me in the village by my maid. I wrote always three times a week and sometimes oftener.

ALGERNON: Oh, do let me read them, Cecily.

CECILY: Oh, I couldn't possibly. They would make you far too conceited. The three you wrote me after I had broken off the engagement are so beautiful and so badly spelt that even now I can hardly read them without crying a little.

ALGERNON: But was our engagement ever broken off?

CECILY: Of course it was. On the 22nd of last March. You can see the entry if you like. (*Shows Diary*.) 'Today I broke off my engagement with Ernest. I feel it is better to do so. The weather still continues charming.'

ALGERNON: But why on earth did you break it off? What had I done? I had done nothing at all. Cecily, I am very much hurt indeed to hear you broke it off. Particularly when the weather was so charming.

CECILY: Men seem to forget very easily. I should have thought you would have remembered the violent letter you wrote to me because I danced with Lord Kelso at the county ball.

ALGERNON: But I did take it all back, Cecily, didn't I?

CECILY: Of course you did. Otherwise I wouldn't have forgiven you or accepted this little gold bangle with the turquoise and diamond heart, that you sent me the next day. (*Shows bangle*.)

ALGERNON: Did I give you this, Cecily? It's very pretty, isn't it?

CECILY: Yes. You have wonderfully good taste, Ernest. I have always said that of you. It's the excuse I've always given for your leading such a bad life.

ALGERNON: My own one! So we have been engaged for three months, Cecily!

CECILY: Yes; how the time has flown, hasn't it?

ALGERNON: I don't think so. I have found the days very long and very dreary without you.

CECILY: You dear romantic boy . . . (*puts her fingers through his hair*.) I hope your hair curls naturally. Does it?

ALGERNON: Yes darling, with a little help from others.

CECILY: I am so glad.

ALGERNON: You'll never break off our engagement again, Cecily?

CECILY: I don't think that I could break it off now that I have actually met you. Besides, of course, there is the question of your name.

ALGERNON: Yes, of course. (*Nervously*.)

CECILY: You must not laugh at me, darling, but it had always been a girlish dream of mine to love some one whose name was Ernest.

ALGERNON *rises*, CECILY *also*.

There is something in that name that seems to inspire absolute confidence. I pity any poor married woman whose husband is not called Ernest.

ALGERNON: But, my dear child, do you mean to say you could not love me if I had some other name?

CECILY: But what name?

ALGERNON: Oh, any name you like – Algernon – for instance. . . .

CECILY: But I don't like the name of Algernon.

ALGERNON: Well, my own dear, sweet, loving little darling, I really can't see why you should object to the name of Algernon. It is not at all a bad name. In fact, it is rather an aristocratic name. Half of the chaps who get into the Bankruptcy Court are called Algernon. But seriously, Cecily – (*moving to her*) – if my name was Algy, couldn't you love me?

CECILY: (*rising*): I might respect you, Ernest, I might admire your character, but I fear that I should not be able to give you my undivided attention.

ALGERNON: Ahem! Cecily! (*Picking up hat.*) Your Rector here is, I suppose, thoroughly experienced in the practice of all the rites and ceremonials of the Church?

CECILY: Oh, yes. Dr. Chasuble is a most learned man. He has never written a single book, so you can imagine how much he knows.

ALGERNON: I must see him at once on a most important christening – I mean on most important business.

CECILY: Oh!

ALGERNON: I shan't be away more than half an hour.

CECILY: Considering that we have been engaged since February the 14th, and that I only met you to–day for the first time, I think it is rather hard that you should leave me for so long a period as half an hour. Couldn't you make it twenty minutes?

ALGERNON: I'll be back in no time. (*Kisses her hand and rushes out.*)

CECILY: What an impetuous boy he is! I like his hair so much. I must enter his proposal in my diary.

Enter MERRIMAN.

MERRIMAN: A Miss Fairfax has just called to see Mr. Worthing. On very important business, Miss Fairfax states.

CECILY: Isn't Mr. Worthing in his library?

MERRIMAN: Mr. Worthing went over in the direction of the Rectory some time ago.

CECILY: Pray ask the lady to come in here; Mr. Worthing is sure to be back soon. And you can bring tea.

MERRIMAN: Yes, Miss. (*Goes out.*)

CECILY: Miss Fairfax! I suppose one of the many good elderly women who are associated with Uncle Jack in some of his Philanthropic work in London. I don't quite like women who are interested in Philanthropic work. I think it is so forward of them.

Enter MERRIMAN.

MERRIMAN: Miss Fairfax.

Enter GWENDOLEN. *Exit* MERRIMAN.

CECILY (*advancing to meet her*): Pray let me introduce myself to you. My name is Cecily Cardew.

GWENDOLEN: Cecily Cardew? (*Moving to her and shaking hands.*) What a very sweet name! Something tells me that we are going to be great friends. I like you already more than I can say. My first impressions of people are never wrong.

CECILY: How nice of you to like me so much after we have known each other such a comparatively short time. Pray sit down.

GWENDOLEN (*still standing up*): I may call you Cecily, may I not?

CECILY: With pleasure!

GWENDOLEN: And you will always call me Gwendolen, won't you?

CECILY: If you wish.

GWENDOLEN: Then that is all quite settled, is it not?

CECILY: I hope so.

A pause. They both sit down together.

GWENDOLEN: Perhaps this might be a favourable opportunity for my mentioning who I am. My father is Lord Bracknell. You have never heard of papa, I suppose?

CECILY: I don't think so.

GWENDOLEN: Outside the family circle, papa, I am glad to say, is entirely unknown. I think that is quite as it should be. The home seems to me to be the proper sphere for the man. And, certainly once a man begins to neglect his domestic duties he becomes painfully effeminate, does he not? And I don't like that. It makes men so very attractive. Cecily, mamma, whose views on education are remarkably strict, has brought me up to be extremely short-sighted; it is part of her system; so do you mind my looking at you through my glasses?

CECILY: Oh! not at all, Gwendolen. I am very fond of being looked at.

GWENDOLEN (*after examining* CECILY *carefully through a lorgnette*): You are here on a short visit, I suppose.

CECILY: Oh no! I live here.

GWENDOLEN (*severely*): Really? Your mother, no doubt, or some female relative of advanced years, resides here also?

CECILY: Oh no! I have no mother, nor, in fact, any relations.

GWENDOLEN: Indeed?

CECILY: My dear guardian, with the assistance, of Miss Prism, has the arduous task of looking after me.

GWENDOLEN: Your guardian?

CECILY: Yes, I am Mr. Worthing's ward.

GWENDOLEN: Oh! It is strange he never mentioned to me that he had a ward. How secretive of him! He grows more interesting hourly. I am not sure, however, that the news inspires me with feelings of unmixed delight.

(*Rising and going to her.*) I am very fond of you, Cecily; I have liked you ever since I met you! But I am bound to state that now that I know that you are Mr. Worthing's ward, I cannot help expressing a wish you were – well, just a little older than you seem to be – and not quite so very alluring in appearance. In fact, if I may speak candidly –

CECILY: Pray do! I think that whenever one has anything unpleasant to say, one should always be quite candid.

GWENDOLEN: Well, to speak with perfect candour, Cecily, I wish that you were fully forty-two, and more than unusually plain for your age. Ernest has a strong upright nature. He is the very soul of truth and honour. Disloyalty would be as impossible to him as deception. But even men of the noblest possible moral character are extremely susceptible to the influence of the physical charms of others. Modern, no less than Ancient History, supplies us with many most painful examples of what I refer to. If it were not so, indeed, History would be quite unreadable.

CECILY: I beg your pardon, Gwendolen, did you say Ernest?

GWENDOLEN: Yes.

CECILY: Oh, but it is not Mr. Ernest Worthing who is my guardian. It is his brother – his elder brother.

GWENDOLEN (*sitting down again*): Ernest never mentioned to me that he had a brother.

CECILY: I am sorry to say they have not been on good terms for a long time.

GWENDOLEN: Ah! that accounts for it. And now that I think of it I have never heard any man mention his brother. The subject seems distasteful to most men. Cecily, you have lifted a load from my mind. I was growing almost anxious. It would have been terrible if any cloud had come across a friendship like ours, would it not? Of course you are quite, quite sure that it is not Mr. Ernest Worthing who is your guardian?

CECILY: Quite sure. (*A pause.*) In fact, I am going to be his.

GWENDOLEN (*inquiringly*): I beg your pardon?

CECILY (*rather shy and confidingly*): Dearest Gwendolen, there is no reason why I should make a secret of it to you. Our little county newspaper is sure to chronicle the fact next week. Mr. Ernest Worthing and I are engaged to be married.

GWENDOLEN (*quite politely, rising*): My darling Cecily, I think there must be some slight error. Mr. Ernest Worthing is engaged to me. The announcement will appear in the *Morning Post* on Saturday at the latest.

CECILY (*very politely, rising*): I am afraid you must be under some misconception. Ernest proposed to me exactly ten minutes ago. (*Shows diary.*)

GWENDOLEN (*examines diary through her lorgnette carefully*): It is certainly very curious, for he asked me to be his wife yesterday afternoon at 5.30. If you would care to verify the incident, pray do so. (*Produces diary of her own.*) I never travel without my diary. One should always have something sensational to read in the train. I am so sorry, dear Cecily, if it is any disappointment to you, but I am afraid I have the prior claim.

CECILY: It would distress me more than I can tell you, dear Gwendolen, if it caused you any mental or physical anguish, but I feel bound to point out that since Ernest proposed to you he clearly changed his mind.

GWENDOLEN (*meditatively*): If the poor fellow has been entrapped into any foolish promise I shall consider it my duty to rescue him at once, and with a firm hand.

CECILY (*thoughtfully and sadly*): Whatever unfortunate entanglement my dear boy may have got into, I will never reproach him with it after we are married.

GWENDOLEN: Do you allude to me, Miss Cardew, as an entanglement? You are presumptuous. On an occasion of this kind it becomes more than a moral duty to speak one's mind. It becomes a pleasure.

CECILY: Do you suggest, Miss Fairfax, that I entrapped Ernest into an engagement? How dare you? This is no time for wearing the shallow mask of manners. When I see a spade I call it a spade.

GWENDOLEN (*satirically*): I am glad to say that I have never seen a spade. It is obvious that our social spheres have been widely different.

Enter MERRIMAN, *followed by the footman. He carries a salver, table cloth, and plate stand.* CECILY *is about to retort. The presence of the servants exercises a restraining influence, under which both girls chafe.*

MERRIMAN: Shall I lay the tea here as usual, Miss?

CECILY (*sternly, in a calm voice*): Yes, as usual.

MERRIMAN *begins to clear table and lay cloth. A long pause.* CECILY *and* GWENDOLEN *glare at each other.*

GWENDOLEN: Are there many interesting walks in the vicinity, Miss Cardew?

CECILY: Oh! yes! a great many. From the top of one of the hills quite close one can see five counties.

GWENDOLEN: Five counties! I don't think I should like that; I hate crowds.

CECILY (*sweetly*): I suppose that is why you live in town?

GWENDOLEN *bites her lip, and beats her foot nervously with her parasol.*

GWENDOLEN (*looking round*): Quite a charming room this is of yours, Miss Cardew.

CECILY: So glad you like it, Miss Fairfax.

GWENDOLEN: I had no idea there was anything approaching good taste in the more remote country districts. It is quite a surprise to me.

CECILY: I am afraid you judge of the country from what one sees in town. I believe most London houses are extremely vulgar.

GWENDOLEN: I suppose they do dazzle the rural mind. Personally I cannot understand how anybody manages to exist in the country – if anybody who is anybody does. The country always bores me to death.

CECILY: Ah! This is what the newspapers call agricultural depression, is it not? I believe the aristocracy are suffering very much from it just at present. It is almost an epidemic amongst them, I have been told. May I offer you some tea, Miss Fairfax?

GWENDOLEN (*with elaborate politeness*): Thank you. (*Aside.*) Detestable girl! But I require tea!

CECILY (*sweetly*): Sugar?

GWENDOLEN (*superciliously*): No, thank you. Sugar is not fashionable any more.

CECILY *looks angrily at her, takes up the tongs and puts four lumps of sugar into the cup.*

CECILY (*severely*): Cake or bread and butter?

GWENDOLEN (*in a bored manner*): Bread and butter, please. Cake is rarely seen at the best houses nowadays.

CECILY (*cuts a very large slice of cake and puts it on the tray*): Hand that to Miss Fairfax.

MERRIMAN *does so, and goes out with footman.* GWENDOLEN *drinks the tea and makes a grimace. Puts down cup at once, reaches out her hand to the bread and butter, looks at it, and finds it is cake. Rises in indignation.*

GWENDOLEN: You have filled my tea with lumps of sugar, and though I asked most distinctly for bread and butter, you have given me cake. I am known for the gentleness of my disposition, and the extraordinary sweetness of my nature, but I warn you, Miss Cardew, you may go too far.

CECILY (*rising*): To save my poor, innocent, trusting boy from the machinations of any other girl there are no lengths to which I would not go.

GWENDOLEN: From the moment I saw you I distrusted you. I felt that you were false and deceitful. I am never deceived in such matters. My first impressions of people are invariably right.

CECILY: It seems to me, Miss Fairfax, that I am trespassing on your valuable time. No doubt you have many other calls of a similar character to make in the neighbourhood.

Enter JACK.

GWENDOLEN (*catching sight of him*): Ernest! My own Ernest!

JACK: Gwendolen! Darling! (*Offers to kiss her.*)

GWENDOLEN (*drawing back*): A moment! May I ask if you are engaged to be married to this young lady? (*Points to* CECILY.)

JACK (*laughing*): To dear little Cecily! Of course not! What could have put such an idea into your pretty little head?

GWENDOLEN: Thank you. You may! (*Offers her cheek.*)

CECILY (*very sweetly*): I knew there must be some misunderstanding, Miss Fairfax. The gentleman whose arm is at present round your waist is my guardian, Mr. John Worthing.

GWENDOLEN: I beg your pardon?

CECILY: This is Uncle Jack.

GWENDOLEN: (*receding*): Jack! Oh!

    Enter ALGERNON.

CECILY: Here is Ernest.

ALGERNON (*goes over to* CECILY *without noticing anyone else*): My own love: (*Offers to kiss her.*)

CECILY (*drawing back*): A moment, Ernest! May I ask you – are you engaged to be married to this young lady?

ALGERNON (*looking round*): To what young lady? Good heavens! Gwendolen!

CECILY: Yes! to good heavens, Gwendolen, I mean to Gwendolen.

ALGERNON (*laughing*): Of course not! What could have put such an idea into your pretty little head?

CECILY: Thank you. (*Presenting her cheek to be kissed.*) You may. (ALGERNON (*kisses her.*)

GWENDOLEN: I felt there was some slight error, Miss Cardew. The gentleman who is now embracing you is my cousin, Mr. Algernon Moncrieff.

CECILY (*breaking away from* ALGERNON): Algernon Moncrieff! Oh!

    The two girls move towards each other and put their arms round each other's waists as if for protection.

CECILY: Are you called Algernon?

ALGERNON: I cannot deny it.

CECILY: Oh!

GWENDOLEN: Is your name really John?

JACK (*standing rather proudly*): I could deny it if I liked. I could deny anything if I liked. But my name certainly is John. It has been John for years.

CECILY (*to* GWENDOLEN): A gross deception has been practised on both of us.

GWENDOLEN: My poor wounded Cecily!

CECILY: My sweet wronged Gwendolen!

GWENDOLEN (*slowly and seriously*): You will call me sister, will you not?

    They embrace. JACK *and* ALGERNON *groan and walk up and down.*

CECILY (*rather brightly*): There is just one question I would like to be allowed to ask my guardian.

GWENDOLEN: An admirable idea! Mr. Worthing, there is just one question I would like to be permitted to put to you. Where is your brother Ernest? We are both engaged to be married to your brother Ernest, so it is a matter of some importance to us to know where your brother Ernest is at present.

JACK (*slowly and hesitatingly*): Gwendolen – Cecily – it is very painful for me to be forced to speak the truth. It is the first time in my life that I have ever been reduced to such a painful position, and I am really quite inexperienced in doing anything of the kind. However, I will tell you quite frankly that I have no brother Ernest. I have no brother at all. I never had a brother in my life, and I certainly have not the smallest intention of ever having one in the future.

CECILY (*surprised*): No brother at all?

JACK (*cheerily*): None!

GWENDOLEN (*severely*): Had you never a brother of any kind?

JACK (*pleasantly*): Never. Not even of any kind.

GWENDOLEN: I am afraid it is quite clear, Cecily, that neither of us is engaged to be married to any one.

CECILY: It is not a very pleasant position for a young girl suddenly to find herself in. Is it?

GWENDOLEN: Let us go into the garden. They will hardly venture to come after us there.

CECILY: No, men are so cowardly, aren't they?

They retire into the garden with scornful looks.

JACK: Pretty mess you have got me into.

ALGERNON *sits down at tea table and pours outs some tea. He seems quite unconcerned.*

What on earth do you mean by coming down here and pretending to be my brother? Perfectly monstrous of you!

ALGERNON (*eating muffin*): What on earth do you mean by pretending to have a brother! It was absolutely disgraceful! (*Eats another muffin.*)

JACK: I told you to go away by the three-fifty. I ordered the dog-cart for you. Why on earth didn't you take it?

ALGERNON: I hadn't had my tea.

JACK: This ghastly state of things is what you call Bunburying, I suppose?

ALGERNON: Yes, and a perfectly wonderful Bunbury it is. The most wonderful Bunbury I have ever had in my life.

JACK: Well, you've no right whatsoever to Bunbury here.

ALGERNON: That is absurd. One has a right to Bunbury anywhere one chooses. Every serious Bunburyist knows that.

JACK: Serious Bunburyist! Good heavens!

ALGERNON: Well, one must be serious about something, if one wants to have any amusement in life. I happen to be serious about Bunburying. What on earth you are serious about I haven't got the remotest idea. About everything, I should fancy. You have such an absolutely trivial nature.

JACK: Well, the only small satisfaction I have in the whole of this wretched business is that your friend Bunbury is quite exploded. You won't be able to run down to the country quite so often as you used to do, dear Algy. And a very good thing too.

ALGERNON: Your brother is a little off colour, isn't he, dear Jack? You won't be able to disappear to London quite so frequently as your wicked custom was. And not a bad thing either.

JACK: As for your conduct towards Miss Cardew, I must say that your taking in a sweet, simple, innocent girl like that is quite inexcusable. To say nothing of the fact that she is my ward.

ALGERNON: I can see no possible defence at all for your deceiving a brilliant, clever, thoroughly experienced young lady like Miss Fairfax. To say nothing of the fact that she is my cousin.

JACK: I wanted to be engaged to Gwendolen, that is all. I love her.

ALGERNON: Well, I simply wanted to be engaged to Cecily. I adore her.

JACK: There is certainly no chance of your marrying Miss Cardew.

ALGERNON: I don't think there is much likelihood, Jack, of you and Miss Fairfax being united.

JACK: Well, that is no business of yours.

ALGERNON: If it was my business, I wouldn't talk about it. It is very vulgar to talk about one's business. Only people like stockbrokers do that, and then merely at dinner parties.

JACK: How can you sit there, calmly eating muffins when we are in this horrible trouble, I can't make out. You seem to me to be perfectly heartless.

ALGERNON: Well, I can't eat muffins in an agitated manner. The butter would probably get on my cuffs. One should always eat muffins quite calmly. It is the only way to eat them.

JACK: I say it's perfectly heartless your eating muffins at all, under the circumstances.

ALGERNON: When I am in trouble, eating is the only thing that consoles me. Indeed, when I am in really great trouble, as any one who knows me intimately will tell you, I refuse everything except food and drink. At the present moment I am eating muffins because I am unhappy. Besides, I am particularly fond of muffins. (*Rising.*)

JACK (*rising*): Well, that is no reason why you should eat them all in that greedy way. (*Takes muffins from* ALGERNON.)

ALGERNON: (*offering tea-cake*): I wish you would have tea-cake instead. I don't like tea-cake.

JACK: Good heavens! I suppose a man may eat his own muffins in his own house!

ALGERNON: But you have just said it was perfectly heartless to eat muffins.

JACK: I said it was perfectly heartless of you, under the circumstances. That is a very different thing.

ALGERNON: That may be. But the muffins are the same. (*He seizes the muf-*

fin-dish from JACK.)

JACK: Algy, I wish to goodness you would go.

ALGERNON: You can't possibly ask me to go without having some dinner. It's absurd. I never go without my dinner. No one ever does, except vegetarians and people like that. Besides, I have just made arrangements with Dr. Chasuble to be christened at a quarter to six under the name of Ernest.

JACK: My dear fellow, the sooner you give up that nonsense the better. I made arrangements this morning with Dr. Chasuble to be christened myself at 5.30, and I naturally will take the name of Ernest. Gwendolen would wish it. We can't both be christened Ernest. It's absurd. Besides, I have a perfect right to be christened if I like. There is no evidence at all that I have ever been christened by anybody. I should think it extremely probable I never was, and so does Dr. Chasuble. It is entirely different in your case. You have been christened already.

ALGERNON: Yes, but I have not been christened for years.

JACK: Yes, but you have been christened. That is the important thing.

ALGERNON: Quite so. So I know my constitution can stand it. If you are not quite sure about your ever having been christened, I must say I think it rather dangerous your venturing on it now. It might make you very unwell. You can hardly have forgotten that some one very closely connected with you was very nearly carried off this week in Paris by a severe chill.

JACK: Yes; but you said yourself it was not hereditary, or anything of that kind.

ALGERNON: It usen't to be, I know – but I dare say it is now. Science is always making wonderful improvements in things.

JACK: May I ask, Algy, what on earth do you propose to do?

ALGERNON: Nothing. That is what I have been trying to do for the last ten minutes, and you have kept on doing everything in your power to distract my attention from my work.

JACK: Well, I shall go out into the garden, and see Gwendolen. I feel quite sure she expects me.

ALGERNON: I know from her extremely cold manner that Cecily expects me so I certainly shan't go out into the garden. When a man does exactly what a woman expects him to do she doesn't think much of him. One should always do what a woman doesn't expect, just as one should always say what she doesn't understand. The result is invariably perfect sympathy on both sides.

JACK: Oh, that is nonsense. You are always talking nonsense.

ALGERNON: It is much cleverer to talk nonsense than to listen to it, my dear fellow, and a much rarer thing too, in spite of all the public may say.

JACK: I don't listen to you. I can't listen to you.

ALGERNON: Oh, that is merely false modesty. You know perfectly well you could listen to me if you tried. You always under-rate yourself, an absurd thing to do nowadays when there are such a lot of conceited people about. Jack, you are eating the muffins again! I wish you wouldn't. There are only two left. (*Removes plate.*) I told you I was particularly fond of muffins.

JACK: But I hate tea-cake.

ALGERNON: Why on earth do you allow tea-cake to be served up to your guests, then? What ideas you have of hospitality!

JACK (*irritably*): Oh! That is not the point. We are not discussing tea-cakes. (*Crosses.*) Algy! you are perfectly maddening. You never can stick to the point in any conversation.

ALGERNON (*slowly*): No: it always hurts me.

JACK: Good heavens! What affectation! I loathe affectation.

ALGERNON: Well, my dear fellow, if you don't like affectation, I really don't see what you can like. Besides, it isn't affectation. The point always does hurt me, and I hate physical pain, of any kind.

JACK (*glares at* ALGERNON: *walks up and down stage. Finally comes up to table*): Algy! I have already told you to go. I don't want you here. Why don't you go?

ALGERNON: I haven't quite finished my tea yet. And there is still one muffin left. (*Takes the last muffin.*)

JACK *groans and sinks down in a chair and buries his face in his hands.*

ACT DROP

ACT FOUR

SCENE: *The same.* JACK *and* ALGERNON *discovered in the same position as at the close of Act* THREE. *Enter behind,* GWENDO-LEN *and* CECILY.

GWENDOLEN: The fact that they did not follow us at once into the garden, as any one else would have done, seems to me to show that they have some sense of shame left.

CECILY: They have been eating muffins. That looks like repentance.

GWENDOLEN (*after a pause*): They don't seem to notice us at all. Couldn't you cough?

CECILY: But I haven't got a cough.

GWENDOLEN: They're looking at us. What effrontery!

CECILY: They're approaching. That's very forward of them.

GWENDOLEN: Let us preserve a dignified silence.

CECILY: Certainly. It's the only thing to do now.

JACK *and* ALGERNON *whistle some dreadful popular air from a British Opera.*

GWENDOLEN: This dignified silence seems to produce an unpleasant effect.

CECILY: A most distasteful one.

GWENDOLEN: But we will not be the first to speak.

CECILY: Certainly not.

GWENDOLEN: Mr. Worthing, I have something very particular to ask you. Much depends on your reply.

CECILY: Gwendolen, your common sense is invaluable. Mr. Moncrieff, kindly answer me the following question. Why did you pretend to be my guardian's brother?

ALGERNON: In order that I might have an opportunity of meeting you.

CECILY (to GWENDOLEN): That certainly seems a satisfactory explanation, does it not?

GWENDOLEN: Yes, dear, if you can believe him.

CECILY: I don't. But that does not affect the wonderful beauty of his answer.

GWENDOLEN: True. In matters of grave importance, style, not sincerity, is the vital thing. Mr. Worthing, what explanation can you offer to me for pretending to have a brother? Was it in order that you might have an opportunity of coming up to town to see me as often as possible?

JACK: Can you doubt it, Miss Fairfax?

GWENDOLEN: I have the greatest doubts upon the subject. But I intend to crush them. This is not the moment for German scepticism. (Moving to CECILY.) Their explanations appear to be quite satisfactory, especially Mr. Worthing's. That seems to me to have the stamp of truth upon it.

CECILY: I am more than content with what Mr. Moncrieff said. His voice alone inspires one with absolute credulity.

GWENDOLEN: Then you think we should forgive them?

CECILY: Yes. I mean no.

GWENDOLEN: True! I had forgotten. There are principles at stake that one cannot surrender. Which of us should tell them? The task is not a pleasant one.

CECILY: Could we not both speak at the same time?

GWENDOLEN: An excellent idea! I always speak at the same time as other people. Will you take the time from me?

CECILY: Certainly.

GWENDOLEN *beats time with uplifted finger.*

GWENDOLEN *and* CECILY (*speaking together*): Your Christian names are still an insuperable barrier. That is all!

JACK *and* AGERNON (*speaking together*): Our Christian names! Is that all? But we are going to be christened this afternoon.

GWENDOLEN (*to* JACK): For my sake you are prepared to do this terrible thing?

JACK: I am.

CECILY (*to* ALGERNON): To please me you are ready to face this fearful ordeal?

ALGERNON: I am!

GWENDOLEN: How absurd to talk of the equality of the sexes! Where questions of self-sacrifice are concerned, men are infinitely beyond us.

JACK: We are. (*Clasps hands with* ALGERNON.)

CECILY: They have moments of physical courage of which we women know absolutely nothing.

GWENDOLEN (*to* JACK): Darling.

ALGERNON (*to* CECILY): Darling!

They fall into each other's arms.
Enter MERRIMAN. *When he enters he coughs loudly, seeing the situation.*

MERRIMAN: Ahem! Ahem! Lady Bracknell!

JACK: Good heavens!

Enter LADY BRACKNELL. *The couples separate in alarm. Exit* MERRIMAN.

LADY BRACKNELL: Gwendolen! What does this mean?

GWENDOLEN: Merely that I am engaged to be married to Mr. Worthing, mamma.

LADY BRACKNELL: Come here. Sit down. Sit down immediately. Hesitation of any kind is a sign of mental decay in the young, of physical weakness in the old. (*Turns to* JACK.) Apprised, sir, of my daughter's sudden flight by her trusty maid, whose confidence I purchased by means of a small coin, I followed her at once by a luggage train. Her unhappy father is, I am glad to say, under the impression that she is attending a more than usually lengthy lecture by the University Extension Scheme on the Influence of a permanent income on Thought. I do not propose to undeceive him. Indeed I have never undeceived him on any question. I would consider it wrong. But, of course, you will clearly understand that all communication between yourself and my daughter must cease immediately from this moment. On this point, as indeed on all points, I am firm.

JACK: I am engaged to be married to Gwendolen, Lady Bracknell!

LADY BRACKNELL: You are nothing of the kind, sir. And now, as regards Algernon!... Algernon!

ALGERNON: Yes, Aunt Augusta.

LADY BRACKNELL: May I ask if it is in this house that your invalid friend Mr. Bunbury resides?

ALGERNON (*stammering*): Oh! No! Bunbury doesn't live here. Bunbury is somewhere else at present. In fact, Bunbury is dead.

LADY BRACKNELL: Dead! When did Mr. Bunbury die? His death must have been extremely sudden.

ALGERNON (*airily*): Oh! I killed Bunbury this afternoon. I mean poor Bunbury died this afternoon.

LADY BRACKNELL: What did he die of?

ALGERNON: Bunbury? Oh, he was quite exploded.

LADY BRACKNELL: Exploded! Was he the victim of a revolutionary outrage? I was not aware that Mr. Bunbury was interested in social legislation. If so, he is well punished for his morbidity.

ALGERNON: My dear Aunt Augusta, I mean he was found out! The doctors found out that Bunbury could not live, that is what I mean – so Bunbury died.

LADY BRACKNELL: He seems to have had great confidence in the opinion of his physicians. I am glad, however, that he made up his mind at the last to some definite course of action, and acted under proper medical advice. And now that we have finally got rid of this Mr. Bunbury, may I ask, Mr. Worthing, who is that young person whose hand my nephew Algernon is now holding in what seems to me a peculiarly unnecessary manner?

JACK: That lady is Miss Cecily Cardew, my ward.

LADY BRACKNELL *bows coldly to* CECILY.

ALGERNON: I am engaged to be married to Cecily, Aunt Augusta.

LADY BRACKNELL: I beg your pardon?

CECILY: Mr. Moncrieff and I are engaged to be married, Lady Bracknell.

LADY BRACKNELL: (*with a shiver, crossing to the sofa and sitting down*): I do not know whether there is anything peculiarly exciting in the air of this particular part of Hertfordshire, but the number of engagements that go on seems to me considerably above the proper average that statistics have laid down for our guidance. I think some preliminary inquiry on my part would not be out of place. Mr. Worthing, is Miss Cardew at all connected with any of the larger railway stations in London? I merely desire information. Until yesterday I had no idea that there were any families or persons whose origin was a Terminus.

JACK *looks perfectly furious, but restrains himself.*

JACK (*in a clear, cold voice*): Miss Cardew is the grand-daughter of the late Mr. Thomas Cardew of 149 Belgrave Square, S.W. ; Gervase Park, Dorking, Surrey; and the Sporran, Fifeshire, N.B.

LADY BRACKNELL: That sounds not unsatisfactory. Three addresses always inspire confidence, even in tradesmen. But what proof have I of their authenticity?

JACK: I have carefully preserved the Court Guides of the period. They are open to your inspection, Lady Bracknell.

LADY BRACKNELL (*grimly*): I have known strange errors in that publication.

JACK: Miss Cardew's family solicitors are Messrs. Markby, Markby, and Markby of 149a Lincoln's Inn Fields, Western Central District, London. I have no doubt they will be happy to supply you with any further information. Their office hours are from ten till four.

LADY BRACKNELL: Markby, Markby and Markby? A firm of the very highest position in their profession. Indeed I am told that one of the Mr. Markbys is occasionally to be seen at dinner parties. So far I am satisfied.

JACK: (*very irritably*): How extremely kind of you, Lady Bracknell! I have also in my possession, you will be pleased to hear, certificates of Miss Cardew's birth, baptism, whooping cough, registration, vaccination, confirmation, and the measles; both the German and the English variety.

LADY BRACKNELL: Ah! A life crowded with incident, I see; though perhaps somewhat too exciting for a young girl. I am not myself in favour of premature experiences. (*Rises, looks at her watch.*) Gwendolen! the time approaches for our departure. We have not a moment to lose. As a matter of form, Mr. Worthing, I had better ask you if Miss Cardew has any little fortune?

JACK: Oh! About a hundred and thirty thousand pounds in the Funds. That is all. Good-bye, Lady Bracknell. So pleased to have seen you.

LADY BRACKNELL (*sitting down again*): A moment, Mr. Worthing. A hundred and thirty thousand pounds! And in the Funds! Miss Cardew seems to me a most attractive young lady, now that I look at her. Few girls of the present day have any really solid qualities, any of the qualities that last, and improve with time. We live, I regret to say, in an age of surfaces. (*To CECILY*): Come over here, dear. (CECILY *goes across.*) Pretty child! your dress is sadly simple, and your hair almost as Nature might have left it. But we can soon alter all that. A thoroughly experienced French maid produces a really marvellous result in a very brief space of time. I remember recommending one to young Lady Lancing, and after three months her own husband did not know her.

JACK: And after six months nobody knew her.

LADY BRACKNELL (*glares at JACK for a few moments. Then bends, with a practised smile, to CECILY*): Kindly turn round, sweet child. (CECILY *turns completely round.*) No, the side view is what I want. (CECILY *presents her profile.*) Yes, quite as I expected. There are distinct social possibilities in your profile. The two weak points in our age are its want of principle and its want of profile. The chin a little higher, dear. Style largely depends on the way the chin is worn. They are worn very high, just at present. Algernon!

ALGERNON: Yes, Aunt Augusta!

LADY BRACKNELL: There are distinct social possibilities in Miss Cardew's profile.

ALGERNON: Cecily is the sweetest, dearest, prettiest girl in the whole world. And I don't care twopence about social possibilities.

LADY BRACKNELL: Never speak disrespectfully of Society, Algernon. Only people who can't get into it do that. (*To CECILY*): Dear child, of course you know that Algernon has nothing but his debts to depend upon. But I do not approve of mercenary marriages. When I married Lord Bracknell I had no fortune of any kind. But I never dreamed for a moment of allowing that to stand in my way. Well, I suppose I must give my consent.

ALGERNON: Thank you, Aunt Augusta.

LADY BRACKNELL: Cecily, you may kiss me!

CECILY (*kisses her*): Thank you, Lady Bracknell.

LADY BRACKNELL: You may also address me as Aunt Augusta for the future.

CECILY: Thank you, Aunt Augusta.

LADY BRACKNELL: The marriage, I think, had better take place quite soon.

ALGERNON: Thank you, Aunt Augusta.

CECILY: Thank you, Aunt Augusta.

LADY BRACKNELL: To speak frankly, I am not in favour of long engagements. They give people the opportunity of finding out each other's character before marriage, which I think is never advisable.

JACK: I beg your pardon for interrupting you, Lady Bracknell, but this engagement is quite out of the question. I am Miss Cardew's guardian, and she cannot marry without my consent until she comes of age. That consent I absolutely decline to give.

LADY BRACKNELL: Upon what grounds, may I ask? Algernon is an extremely, I may almost say an ostentatiously, eligible young man. He has nothing, but he looks everything. What more can one desire?

JACK: It pains me very much to have to speak frankly to you, Lady Bracknell, about your nephew, but the fact is that I do not approve at all of his moral character. I suspect him of being untruthful.

ALGERNON *and* CECILY *look at him in indignant amazement.*

LADY BRACKNELL: Untruthful! My nephew Algernon? Impossible! He is an Oxonian.

JACK: I fear there can be no possible doubt about the matter. This afternoon during my temporary absence in London on an important question of romance, he obtained admission to my house by means of the false pretence of being my brother. Under an assumed name he drank, I've just been informed by my butler, an entire pint bottle of my Perrier-Jouet, Brut, '89; wine I was specially reserving for myself. Continuing his disgraceful deception, he succeeded in the course of the afternoon in alienating the affections of my only ward. He subsequently stayed to tea, and devoured every single muffin. And what makes his conduct all the more heartless is, that he was perfectly well aware from the first that I have no brother, that I never had a brother, and that I don't intend to have a brother, not even of any kind. I distinctly told him so myself yesterday afternoon.

CECILY: But, dear Uncle Jack, for the last year you have been telling us all that you had a brother. You dwelt continually on the subject. Algy merely corroborated your statement. It was noble of him.

JACK: Pardon me, Cecily, you are a little too young to understand these matters. To invent anything at all is an act of sheer genius, and, in a commercial age like ours, shows considerable physical courage. Few of our modern novelists dare to invent a single thing. It is an open secret that they don't know how to do it. Upon the other hand, to corroborate a falsehood is a distinctly cowardly action. I know it is a thing that the newspapers do one for the other, every day. But it is not the act of a gentleman. No gentleman ever corroborates anything.

ALGERNON (*furiously*): Upon my word Jack!

LADY BRACKNELL: Ahem! Mr. Worthing, after careful consideration I have decided entirely to overlook my nephew's conduct to you.

JACK: That is very generous of you, Lady Bracknell. My own decision, however, is unalterable. I decline to give my consent.

LADY BRACKNELL (*to* CECILY): Come here, sweet child. (CECILY *goes over*). How old are you, dear?

CECILY: Well, I am really only eighteen, but I always admit to twenty when I go to evening parties.

LADY BRACKNELL: You are perfectly right in making some slight alteration. Indeed, no woman should ever be quite accurate about her age. It looks so calculating.... (*In a meditative manner.*) Eighteen, but admitting to twenty at evening parties. Well, it will not be very long before you are of age and free from the restraints of tutelage. So I don't think your guardian's consent is, after all, a matter of any importance.

JACK: Pray excuse me, Lady Bracknell, for interrupting you again, but it is only fair to tell you that according to the terms of her grandfather's will Miss Cardew does not come legally of age till she is thirty-five.

LADY BRACKNELL: That does not seem to me to be a grave objection. Thirty-five is a very attractive age. London society is full of women of the very highest birth who have, of their own free choice, remained thirty-five for years. Lady Dumbleton is an instance in point. To my own knowledge she has been thirty-five ever since she arrived at the age of forty, which was many years ago now. I see no reason why our dear Cecily should not be even still more attractive at the age you mention than she is at present. There will be a large accumulation of property.

CECILY (*to* JACK): You are quite sure that I can't marry without your consent till I am thirty-five?

JACK: That is the wise provision of your grandfather's will, Cecily. He undoubtedly foresaw the sort of difficulty that would be likely to occur.

CECILY: Then grandpapa must have had a very extraordinary imagination. Algy ... could you wait for me till I was thirty-five? Don't speak hastily. It is a very serious question, and much of my future happiness, as well as all of yours, depends on your answer.

ALGERNON: Of course I could, Cecily. How can you ask me such a question? I could wait for ever for you. You know I could.

CECILY: Yes, I felt it instinctively, but I couldn't wait all that time. I hate waiting even five minutes for anybody. It always makes me rather cross. I am not punctual myself, I know, but I do like punctuality in others, and waiting, even to be married, is quite out of the question.

ALGERNON: Then what is to be done, Cecily?

CECILY: I don't know, Mr. Moncrieff.

LADY BRACKNELL: My dear Mr. Worthing, as Miss Cecily states positively that she cannot wait till she is thirty-five – a remark which I am bound to say seems to me to show a somewhat impatient nature – I would beg of you to reconsider your decision.

JACK: But my dear Lady Bracknell, the matter is entirely in your own hands. The moment you consent to my marriage with Gwendolen, I will most gladly allow your nephew to form an alliance with my ward.

LADY BRACKNELL (*rising and drawing herself up*): You must be quite aware that what you propose is out of the question.

JACK: Then a passionate celibacy is all that any of us can look forward to.

LADY BRACKNELL: That is not the destiny I propose for Gwendolen. Algernon, of course, can choose for himself. (*Pulls out her watch.*) Come, dear – (GWENDOLEN *rises*) – we have already missed five, if not six, trains. To miss any more might expose us to comment on the platform.

Enter DR. CHASUBLE.

CHASUBLE: Everything is quite ready for the christenings.

LADY BRACKNELL: The christenings, sir! Is not that somewhat premature?

CHASUBLE: (*looking rather puzzled, and pointing to* JACK *and* ALGERNON): Both these gentleman have expressed a desire for immediate baptism.

LADY BRACKNELL: At their age? The idea is grotesque and irreligious! Algernon, I forbid you to be baptized. I will not hear of such excess. Lord Bracknell would be highly displeased if he learned that that was the way in which you wasted your time and money.

CHASUBLE: Am I to understand then that there are to be no christenings at all this afternoon?

JACK: I don't think that, as things are now, it would be of much practical value to either of us, Dr. Chasuble.

CHASUBLE: I am grieved to hear such sentiments from you, Mr. Worthing. They savour of the heretical views of the Anabaptists, views that I have completely refuted in four of my unpublished sermons. Baptismal regeneration is not to be lightly spoken of. Indeed by the unanimous opinion of the fathers, baptism is a form of new birth. However, where adults are concerned, compulsory christening, except in the case of savage tribes, is, I regret to say, uncanonical, so I shall return to the church at once. Indeed, I have just been informed by the pew-opener that for the last hour and a half Miss Prism has been waiting for me in the vestry.

LADY BRACKNELL (*starting*): Miss Prism! Did I hear you mention a Miss Prism?

CHASUBLE: Yes, Lady Bracknell. I am on my way to join her.

LADY BRACKNELL: Pray allow me to detain you for a moment. This matter may prove to be one of vital importance to Lord Bracknell and myself. Is this Miss Prism a female of repellent aspect, remotely connected with education?

CHASUBLE (*somewhat indignantly*): She is the most cultivated of ladies, and the very picture of respectability.

LADY BRACKNELL: It is obviously the same person. May I ask what position she holds in your household?

CHASUBLE: (*severely*): I am a celibate, madam.

JACK (*interposing*): Miss Prism, Lady Bracknell has been for the last three years Miss Cardew's esteemed governess and valued companion.

LADY BRACKNELL: In spite of what I hear of her, I must see her at once. Let her be sent for.

CHASUBLE (*looking off*): She approaches; she is nigh.

Enter MISS PRISM *hurriedly.*

MISS PRISM: I was told you expected me in the vestry, dear Canon. I have been waiting for you there for an hour and three-quarters. (*Catches sight of* LADY BRACKNELL, *who has fixed her with a stony glare.* MISS PRISM *grows pale and quails. She looks anxiously round as if desirous to escape.*)

LADY BRACKNELL (*in a severe, judicial voice*): Prism! (MISS PRISM *bows her head in shame.*) Come here, Prism! (MISS PRISM *approaches in a humble manner.*) Prism! Where is that baby? (*General consternation. The* CANON *starts back in horror.* ALGERNON *and* JACK *pretend to be anxious to shield* CECILY *and* GWENDOLEN *from hearing the details of a terrible public scandal.*) Twenty-eight years ago, Prism, you left Lord Bracknell's house, Number 104, Upper Grosvenor Street, in charge of a perambulator that contained a baby of the male sex. You never returned. A few weeks later, through the elaborate investigations of the Metropolitan police, the perambulator was discovered at midnight standing by itself in a remote corner of Bayswater. It contained the manuscript of a three-volume novel of more than usually revolting sentimentality. (MISS PRISM *starts in involuntary indignation.*) But the baby was not there. (*Every one looks at* MISS PRISM.) Prism! Where is that baby? (*A pause.*)

MISS PRISM: Lady Bracknell, I admit with shame that I do not know. I only wish I did. The plain facts of the case are these. On the morning of the day you mention, a day that is for ever branded on my memory, I prepared as usual to take the baby out in its perambulator. I had also with me a somewhat old, capacious hand-bag in which I had intended to place the manuscript of a work of fiction that I had written during my few unoccupied hours. In a moment of mental abstraction, for which I never can forgive myself, I deposited the manuscript in the basinette, and placed the baby in the hand-bag.

JACK (*who has been listening attentively*): But where did you deposit the hand-bag?

MISS PRISM: Do not ask me, Mr. Worthing.

JACK: Miss Prism, this is a matter of no small importance to me. I insist on knowing where you deposited the hand-bag that contained that infant.

MISS PRISM: I left it in the cloak-room of one of the larger railway stations in London.

JACK: What railway station?

MISS PRISM (*quite crushed*): Victoria. The Brighton line. (*Sinks into a chair.*)

LADY BRACKNELL (*looking at* JACK): I sincerely hope nothing improbable is going to happen. The improbable is always in bad, or at any rate, questionable taste.

JACK: I must retire to my room for a moment.

CHASUBLE: This news seems to have upset you, Mr. Worthing. I trust your indisposition is merely temporary.

JACK: I will be back in a few moments, dear Canon. Gwendolen! Wait here for me!

GWENDOLEN: If you are not too long, I will wait here for you all my life.

Exit JACK *in great excitement.*

CHASUBLE: What do you think this means, Lady Bracknell?

LADY BRACKNELL: I dare not even suspect, Dr. Chasuble. I need hardly tell you that in families of high position strange coincidences are not supposed to occur. They are hardly considered the thing.

Noises heard overhead as if some one was throwing trunks about. Every one looks up.

CECILY: Uncle Jack seems strangely agitated.

CHASUBLE: Your guardian has a very emotional nature.

LADY BRACKNELL: This noise is extremely unpleasant. It sounds as if he was having an argument with the furniture. I dislike arguments of any kind. They are always vulgar, and often convincing.

CHASUBLE: (*looking up*): It has stopped now. (*The noise is re-doubled.*)

LADY BRACKNELL: I wish he would arrive at some conclusion.

GWENDOLEN: This suspense is terrible. I hope it will last.

Enter JACK *with a hand-bag of black leather in his hand.*

JACK (*rushing over* to MISS PRISM): Is this the hand-bag, Miss Prism? Examine it carefully before you speak. The happiness of more than one life depends on your answer.

MISS PRISM (*calmly*): It seems to be mine. Yes, here is the injury it received through the upsetting of a Gower Street omnibus in younger and happier days. Here is the stain on the lining caused by the explosion of a temperance beverage, an incident that occurred at Leamington. And here, on the lock, are my initials. I had forgotten that in an extravagant mood I had had them placed there. The bag is undoubtedly mine. I am delighted to have it so unexpectedly restored to me. It has been a great inconvenience being without it all these years.

JACK (*in a pathetic voice*): Miss Prism, more is restored to you than this hand-bag. I was the baby you placed in it.

MISS PRISM (*amazed*): You?

JACK (*embracing her*): Yes . . . mother!

MISS PRISM (*recoiling in indignant astonishment*): Mr. Worthing, I am unmarried!

JACK: Unmarried! I do not deny that is a serious blow. But after all, who has the right to cast a stone against one who has suffered? Cannot repentance wipe out an act of folly? Why should there be one law for men, and another for women? Mother, I forgive you. (*Tries to embrace her again.*)

MISS PRISM (*still more indignant*): But Mr. Worthing, there is some error. Maternity has never been an incident in my life. The suggestion, if it were not made before such a large number of people, would be almost indelicate. (*Pointing to* LADY BRACKNELL.) There stands the lady who can tell you who you really are. (*Retires to back of stage.*)

JACK (*after a pause*): Lady Bracknell, I hate to seem inquisitive, but would you kindly inform me who I am?

LADY BRACKNELL: I am afraid that the news I have to give you will not altogether please you. You are the son of my poor sister, Mrs. Moncrieff, and consequently Algernon's elder brother.

JACK: Algy's elder brother! Then I have a brother after all. I knew I had a brother! I always said I had a brother! Cecily, – how could you have ever doubted that I had a brother! (*Seizes hold of* ALGERNON.) Dr. Chasuble, my unfortunate brother. Miss Prism, my unfortunate brother. Gwendolen, my unfortunate brother. Algy, you young scoundrel, you will have to treat me with more respect in the future. You have never behaved to me like a brother in all your life.

ALGERNON: Well, not till to-day, old boy, I admit. (*Shakes hands.*) I did my best, however, though I was out of practice.

GWENDOLEN (*to* JACK): Darling!

JACK: Darling!

LADY BRACKNELL: Under these strange and unforeseen circumstances you can kiss your Aunt Augusta.

JACK (*staying where he is*): I am dazed with happiness. (*Kisses* GWENDO-LEN) I hardly know who I am kissing.

ALGERNON *takes the opportunity to kiss* CECILY.

GWENDOLEN: I hope that will be the last time I shall ever hear you make such an observation.

JACK: It will, darling.

MISS PRISM (*advancing, after coughing slightly*): Mr. Worthing, – Mr. Moncrieff as I should call you now – after what has just occurred I feel it my duty to resign my position in this household. Any inconvenience I may have caused you in your infancy through placing you inadvertently in this hand-bag I sincerely apologise for.

JACK: Don't mention it, dear Miss Prism. Don't mention anything. I am sure I had a very pleasant time in your nice hand-bag in spite of the slight damage it received through the overturning of an omnibus in your happier days. As for leaving us, the suggestion is absurd.

MISS PRISM: It is my duty to leave. I have really nothing more to teach dear Cecily. In the very difficult accomplishment of getting married I fear my sweet and clever pupil has far outstripped her teacher.

CHASUBLE: A moment – Laetitia!

MISS PRISM: Dr. Chasuble!

CHASUBLE: Laetitia, I have come to the conclusion that the Primitive Church was in error on certain points. Corrupt readings seem to have crept into the text. I beg to solicit the honour of your hand.

MISS PRISM: Frederick, at the present moment words fail me to express my feelings. But I will forward you, this evening, the three last volumes of my diary. In these you will be able to peruse a full account of the sentiments that I have entertained towards you for the last eighteen months.

Enter MERRIMAN.

MERRIMAN: Lady Bracknell's flyman says he cannot wait any longer.

LADY BRACKNELL (*rising*): True! I must return to town at once. (*Pulls out watch.*) I see I have now missed no less than nine trains. There is only one more.

MERRIMAN *goes out.* LADY BRACKNELL *moves towards the door.*

Prism, from your last observation to Dr. Chasuble, I learn with regret that you have not yet given up your passion for fiction in three volumes. And, if you really are going to enter into the state of matrimony which at your age seems to me, I feel bound to say, rather like flying in the face of an all-wise Providence, I trust you will be more careful of your husband than you were of your infant charge, and not leave poor Dr. Chasuble lying about at railway stations in hand-bags or receptacles of any kind. Cloak-rooms are notoriously draughty places. (MISS PRISM *bows her head meekly.*) Dr. Chasuble, you have my sincere good wishes, and if baptism be, as you say it is, a form of new birth, I would strongly advise you to have Miss Prism baptised without delay. To be born again would be of considerable advantage to her. Whether such a procedure be in accordance with the practice of the Primitive Church I do not know. But it is hardly probable, I should fancy, that they had to grapple with such extremely advanced problems. (*Turning sweetly to* CECILY *and patting her cheek.*) Sweet child! We will expect you at Upper Grosvenor Street in a few days.

CECILY: Thank you, Aunt Augusta!

LADY BRACKNELL: Come, Gwendolen.

GWENDOLEN (*to* JACK): My own! But what own are you? What is your Christian name, now that you have become some one else?

JACK: Good heavens! . . . I had quite forgotten that point. Your decision on the subject of my name is irrevocable, I suppose?

GWENDOLEN: I never change, except in my affections.

CECILY: What a noble nature you have, Gwendolen!

JACK: Then the question had better be cleared up at once. Aunt Augusta, a moment. At the time when Miss Prism left me in the hand-bag, had I been christened already? Pray be calm, Aunt Augusta. This is a terrible crisis and much depends on your answer.

LADY BRACKNELL (*quite calmly*): Every luxury that money could buy, including christening, had been lavished on you by your fond and doting parents.

JACK: Then I was christened! That is settled. Now, what name was I given? Let me know the worst.

LADY BRACKNELL (*after a pause*): Being the eldest son you were naturally christened after your father.

JACK (*irritably*): Yes, but what was my father's Christian name? Pray don't be so calm, Aunt Augusta. This is a terrible crisis and everything hangs on the nature of your reply. What was my father's Christian name?

LADY BRACKNELL (*meditatively*): I cannot at the present moment recall what the General's Christian name was. Your poor dear mother always addressed him as 'General'. That I remember perfectly. Indeed, I don't think she would have dared to have called him by his Christian name. But I have no doubt he had one. He was violent in his manner, but there was nothing eccentric about him in any way. That was rather the result of the Indian climate, and marriage, and indigestion, and other things of that kind. In fact he was rather a martinet about the little details of daily life. Too much so, I used to tell my sister.

JACK: Algy! Can't you recollect what our father's Christian name was?

ALGERNON: My dear boy, we were never even on speaking terms. He died before I was a year old.

JACK: His name would appear in the Army Lists of the period, I suppose, Aunt Augusta?

LADY BRACKNELL: The General was essentially a man of peace, except in his domestic life. But I have no doubt his name would appear in any military directory.

JACK: The Army Lists for the last forty years are here. (*Rushes to the bookcase and tears the books out. Distributes them rapidly.*) Here, Dr. Chasuble – Miss Prism, two for you – Cecily, Cecily, an Army List. Make a précis of it at once. Algernon, pray search English history for our father's Christian name if you have the smallest filial affection left. Aunt Augusta, I beg you to bring your masculine mind to bear on this subject. Gwendolen – no, it would agitate you too much. Leave these researches to less philosophic natures like ours.

GWENDOLEN (*heroically*): Give me six copies of any period, this century or the last. I do not care which!

JACK: Noble girl! Here are a dozen. More might be an inconvenience to you. (*Brings her a pile of Army Lists – rushes through them himself, taking each one from her hands as she tries to examine it.*) No, just let me look. No, allow me, dear. Darling, I think I can find it out sooner. Just allow me, my love.

CHASUBLE: What station, Mr. Moncrieff, did you say you wished to go to?

JACK (*pausing in despair*): Station! Who on earth is talking about a station? I merely want to find out my father's Christian name.

CHASUBLE: But you have handed me a Bradshaw. (*Looks at it.*) Of 1869, I observe. A book of considerable antiquarian interest: but not in any way bearing on the question of the names usually conferred on Generals at baptism.

CECILY: I am so sorry, Uncle Jack. But Generals don't seem to be even alluded to in the 'History of our own times', although it is the best edition. The one written in collaboration with the type-writing machine.

MISS PRISM: To me, Mr. Moncrieff, you have given two copies of the Price Lists of the Civil Service Stores. I do not find Generals marked anywhere. There seems to be either no demand or no supply.

LADY BRACKNELL: This treatise, 'The Green Carnation', as I see it is called, seems to be a book about the culture of exotics. It contains no reference to Generals in it. It seems a morbid and middle-class affair.

JACK (*very irritable indeed*): Good Heavens! And what nonsense are you reading, Algy? (*Takes book from him.*) The Army List? Well, I don't suppose you knew it was the Army List. And you have got it open at the wrong page. Besides, there is the thing staring you in the face. M. Generals . . . Malam – what ghastly names they have – Markby, Migsby, Mobbs, Moncrieff, Moncrieff! Lieutenant 1840, Captain, Lieutenant-Colonel, Colonel, General 1860. Christian names, Ernest John. (*Puts book quietly down and speaks quite calmly.*) I always told you Gwendolen, my name was Ernest, didn't I? Well, it is Ernest after all. I mean it naturally is Ernest.

LADY BRACKNELL: Yes, I remember now that the General was called Ernest. I knew I had some particular reason for disliking the name. Come, Gwendolen. (*Goes out.*)

GWENDOLEN: Ernest! My own Ernest! I felt from the first that you could have no other name!

JACK: Gwendolen, it is a terrible thing for a man to find out suddenly that all his life he has been speaking nothing but the truth. Can you forgive me?

GWENDOLEN: I can. For I feel that you are sure to change.

JACK: My own one!

CHASUBLE (*to* MISS PRISM): Laetitia! (*Embraces her.*)

MISS PRISM (*enthusiastically*): Frederick! At last!

ALGERNON: Cecily! (*Embraces her.*) At last!

JACK: Gwendolen! (*Embraces her.*) At last!

Enter LADY BRACKNELL.

LADY BRACKNELL: I have missed the last train! – My nephew, you seem to be displaying signs of triviality.

JACK: On the contrary, Aunt Augusta, I've now realised for the first time in my life the vital Importance of Being Earnest.

TABLEAU

CURTAIN

LADY WINDERMERE'S FAN

The persons of the play

LORD WINDERMERE.	THE DUCHESS OF BERWICK
LORD DARLINGTON	LADY AGATHA CARLISLE
LORD AUGUSTUS LORTON	LADY PLYMDALE
MR. DUMBY	LADY STUTFIELD
MR. CECIL GRAHAM	LADY JEDBURGH
MR. HOPPER	MRS. COWPER-COWPER
PARKER, Butler	MRS. ERLYNNE
LADY WINDERMERE	ROSALIE, Maid

ACT ONE

SCENE: *Morning-room of Lord Windermere's house in Carlton House Terrace, London. The action of the play takes place within twenty-four hours, beginning on a Tuesday afternoon at five o'clock, and ending the next day at 1.30 p.m.* TIME: *The present. Doors C. and R. Bureau with books and papers R. Sofa with small tea-table L. Window opening on to terrace L. Table R.*

LADY WINDERMERE *is at table R., arranging roses in a blue bowl.*

Enter PARKER.

PARKER: Is your ladyship at home this afternoon?
LADY WINDERMERE: Yes – who has called?
PARKER: Lord Darlington, my lady.
LADY WINDERMERE (*hesitates for a moment*): Show him up – and I'm at home to any one who calls.
PARKER: Yes, my lady. (*Exit C.*)
LADY WINDERMERE: It's best for me to see him before to-night. I'm glad he's come.

Enter PARKER *C.*

PARKER: Lord Darlington.

Enter LORD DARLINGTON *C. Exit* PARKER.

LORD DARLINGTON: How do you do, Lady Windermere?
LADY WINDERMERE: How do you do, Lord Darlington? No, I can't shake

hands with you. My hands are all wet with these roses. Aren't they lovely? They came up from Selby this morning.

LORD DARLINGTON: They are quite perfect. (*Sees a fan lying on the table.*) And what a wonderful fan! May I look at it?

LADY WINDERMERE: Do. Pretty, isn't it? It's got my name on it, and everything. I have only just seen it myself. It's my husband's birthday present to me. You know to-day is my birthday?

LORD DARLINGTON: No? Is it really?

LADY WINDERMERE: Yes, I'm of age to-day. Quite an important day in my life, isn't it? That is why I am giving this party to-night. Do sit down. (*Still arranging flowers.*)

LORD DARLINGTON: (*sitting down*): I wish I had known it was your birthday, Lady Windermere. I would have covered the whole street in front of your house with flowers for you to walk on. They are made for you. (*A short pause.*)

LADY WINDERMERE: Lord Darlington, you annoyed me last night at the Foreign Office. I am afraid you are going to annoy me again.

LORD DARLINGTON: I, Lady Windermere?

Enter PARKER *and* FOOTMAN *C., with tray and tea things.*

LADY WINDERMERE: Put it there, Parker. That will do. (*Wipes her hands with her pocket-handkerchief, goes to tea-table L., and sits down.*) Won't you come over, Lord Darlington?

Exit PARKER *C.*

LORD DARLINGTON (*takes chair and goes across L.C.*): I am quite miserable, Lady Windermere. You must tell me what I did. (*Sits down at table L.*)

LADY WINDERMERE: Well, you kept paying me elaborate compliments the whole evening.

LORD DARLINGTON (*smiling*): Ah, nowadays we are all of us so hard up, that the only pleasant things to pay *are* compliments. They're the only things we *can* pay.

LADY WINDERMERE (*shaking her head*): No, I am talking very seriously. You mustn't laugh, I am quite serious. I don't like compliments, and I don't see why a man should think he is pleasing a woman enormously when he says to her a whole heap of things that he doesn't mean.

LORD DARLINGTON: Ah, but I did mean them. (*Takes tea which she offers him.*)

LADY WINDERMERE (*gravely*): I hope not. I should be sorry to have to quarrel with you, Lord Darlington. I like you very much, you know that. But I shouldn't like you at all if I thought you were what most other men are. Believe me, you are better than most other men, and I sometimes think you pretend to be worse.

LORD DARLINGTON: We all have our little vanities, Lady Windermere.

LADY WINDERMERE: Why do you make that your special one? (*Still seated at table L.*)

LORD DARLINGTON (*still seated L.C.*): Oh, nowadays so many conceited people go about Society pretending to be good, that I think it shows rather a sweet and modest disposition to pretend to be bad. Besides, there is this to be said. If you pretend to be good, the world takes you very seriously. If you pretend to be bad, it doesn't. Such is the astounding stupidity of optimism.

LADY WINDERMERE: Don't you *want* the world to take you seriously then, Lord Darlington?

LORD DARLINGTON: No, not the world. Who are the people the world takes seriously? All the dull people one can think of, from the Bishops down to the bores. I should like *you* to take me very seriously, Lady Windermere, *you* more than any one else in life.

LADY WINDERMERE: Why – why me?

LORD DARLINGTON (*after a slight hesitation*): Because I think we might be great friends. Let us be great friends. You may want a friend some day.

LADY WINDERMERE: Why do you say that?

LORD DARLINGTON: Oh ! – we all want friends at times.

LADY WINDERMERE: I think we're very good friends already, Lord Darlington. We can always remain so as long as you don't –

LORD DARLINGTON: Don't what?

LADY WINDERMERE: Don't spoil it by saying extravagant silly things to me. You think I am a Puritan, I suppose? Well, I have something of the Puritan in me. I was brought up like that. I am glad of it. My mother died when I was a mere child. I lived always with Lady Julia, my father's elder sister, you know. She was stern to me, but she taught me what the world is forgetting, the difference that there is between what is right and what is wrong. *She* allowed of no compromise. *I* allow of none.

LORD DARLINGTON: My dear Lady Windermere!

LADY WINDERMERE (*leaning back on the sofa*): You look on me as being behind the age. Well, I am ! I should be sorry to be on the same level as an age like this.

LORD DARLINGTON: You think the age very bad?

LADY WINDERMERE: Yes. Nowadays people seem to look on life as a speculation. It is not a speculation. It is a sacrament. Its ideal is Love. Its purification is Sacrifice.

LORD DARLINGTON (*smiling*): Oh, anything is better than being sacrificed!

LADY WINDERMERE (*leaning forward*): Don't say that.

LORD DARLINGTON: I do say it. I felt it – I know it.

Enter PARKER *C.*

PARKER: The men want to know if they are to put the carpets on the terrace for to-night, my lady?

LADY WINDERMERE: You don't think it will rain, Lord Darlington, do you?

LORD DARLINGTON: I won't hear of its raining on your birthday.

LADY WINDERMERE: Tell them to do it at once, Parker.

Exit PARKER *C.*

LORD DARLINGTON (*still seated*): Do you think then – of course I am only putting an imaginary instance – do you think that in the case of a young married couple, say about two years married, if the husband suddenly becomes the intimate friend of a woman of – well, more than doubtful character – is always calling upon her, lunching with her, and probably paying her bills – do you think that the wife should not console herself?

LADY WINDERMERE (*frowning*): Console herself?

LORD DARLINGTON: Yes, I think she should – I think she has the right.

LADY WINDERMERE: Because the husband is vile – should the wife be vile also?

LORD DARLINGTON: Vileness is a terrible word, Lady Windermere.

LADY WINDERMERE: It is a terrible thing, Lord Darlington.

LORD DARLINGTON: Do you know I am afraid that good people do a great deal of harm in this world. Certainly the greatest harm they do is that they make badness of such extraordinary importance. It is absurd to divide people into good and bad. People are either charming or tedious. I take the side of the charming, and you, Lady Windermere, can't help belonging to them.

LADY WINDERMERE: Now, Lord Darlington. (*Rising and crossing R., front of him.*) Don't stir, I am merely going to finish my flowers. (*Goes to table R.C.*)

LORD DARLINGTON (*rising and moving chair*): And I must say I think you are very hard on modern life, Lady Windermere. Of course there is much against it, I admit. Most women, for instance, nowadays, are rather mercenary.

LADY WINDERMERE: Don't talk about such people.

LORD DARLINGTON: Well then, setting mercenary people aside, who, of course, are dreadful, do you think seriously that women who have committed what the world calls a fault should never be forgiven?

LADY WINDERMERE (*standing at table*): I think they should never be forgiven.

LORD DARLINGTON: And men? Do you think that there should be the same laws for men as there are for women?

LADY WINDERMERE: Certainly!

LORD DARLINGTON: I think life too complex a thing to be settled by these hard and fast rules.

LADY WINDERMERE: If we had 'these hard and fast rules,' we should find life much more simple.

LORD DARLINGTON: You allow of no exceptions?

LADY WINDERMERE: None!

LORD DARLINGTON: Ah, what a fascinating Puritan you are, Lady Windermere!

LADY WINDERMERE: The adjective was unnecessary, Lord Darlington.

LORD DARLINGTON: I couldn't help it. I can resist everything except temptation.

LADY WINDERMERE: You have the modern affectation of weakness.

LORD DARLINGTON: (*looking at her*): It's only an affectation, Lady Windermere.

Enter PARKER *C.*

PARKER: The Duchess of Berwick and Lady Agatha Carlisle.

Enter the DUCHESS OF BERWICK *and* LADY AGATHA CARLISLE *C.*

Exit PARKER *C.*

DUCHESS OF BERWICK (*coming down C. and shaking hands*): Dear Margaret, I am so pleased to see you. You remember Agatha, don't you? (*Crossing L.C.*) How do you do, Lord Darlington? I won't let you know my daughter, you are far too wicked.

LORD DARLINGTON: Don't say that, Duchess. As a wicked man I am a complete failure. Why, there are lots of people who say I have never really done anything wrong in the whole course of my life. Of course they only say it behind my back.

DUCHESS OF BERWICK: Isn't he dreadful? Agatha, this is Lord Darlington. Mind you don't believe a word he says. (LORD DARLINGTON *crosses R.C.*) No, no tea, thank you, dear. (*Crosses and sits on sofa.*) We have just had tea at Lady Markby's. Such bad tea, too. It was quite undrinkable. I wasn't at all surprised. Her own son-in-law supplies it. Agatha is looking forward so much to your ball to-night, dear Margaret.

LADY WINDERMERE (*seated L.C.*): Oh, you mustn't think it is going to be a ball, Duchess. It is only a dance in honour of my birthday. A small and early.

LORD DARLINGTON (*standing L.C.*): Very small, very early, and very select, Duchess.

DUCHESS OF BERWICK (*on sofa L.*): Of course it's going to be select. But we know *that*, dear Margaret, about *your* house. It is really one of the few houses in London where I can take Agatha, and where I feel perfectly secure about dear Berwick. I don't know what society is coming to. The most dreadful people seem to go everywhere. They certainly come to my parties – the men get furious if one doesn't ask them. Really, some one should make a stand against it.

LADY WINDERMERE: I will, Duchess. I will have no one in my house about whom there is any scandal.

LORD DARLINGTON (*R.C.*): Oh don't say that, Lady Windermere. I should never be admitted! (*Sitting*).

DUCHESS OF BERWICK: Oh, men don't matter. With women it is different. We're good. Some of us are, at least. But we are positively getting elbowed into the corner. Our husbands would really forget our existence if we didn't nag at them from time to time, just to remind them that we have a perfect legal right to do so.

LORD DARLINGTON: It's a curious thing, Duchess, about the game of marriage – a game, by the way, that is going out of fashion – the wives hold all the honours, and invariably lose the odd trick.

DUCHESS OF BERWICK: The odd trick? Is that the husband, Lord Darlington?

LORD DARLINGTON: It would be rather a good name for the modern husband.

DUCHESS OF BERWICK: Dear Lord Darlington, how thoroughly depraved you are!

LADY WINDERMERE: Lord Darlington is trivial.

LORD DARLINGTON: Ah, don't say that, Lady Windermere.

LADY WINDERMERE: Why do you *talk* so trivially about life, then?

LORD DARLINGTON: Because I think that life is far too important a thing ever to talk seriously about it. (*Moves up C.*)

DUCHESS OF BERWICK: What does he mean? Do, as a concession to my poor wits, Lord Darlington, just explain to me what you really mean.

LORD DARLINGTON (*coming down back of table*): I think I had better not, Duchess. Nowadays to be intelligible is to be found out. Good-bye! (*Shakes hands with* DUCHESS.) And now – (*goes up stage*) – Lady Windermere, good-bye. I may come to-night, mayn't I? Do let me come.

LADY WINDERMERE (*standing up stage with* LORD DARLINGTON): Yes, certainly. But you are not to say foolish, insincere things to people.

LORD DARLINGTON (*smiling*): Ah! You are beginning to reform me. It is a dangerous thing to reform any one, Lady Windermere. (*Bows, and exit C.*)

DUCHESS OF BERWICK (*who has risen, goes C.*): What a charming wicked creature! I like him so much. I'm quite delighted he's gone! How sweet you're looking! Where *do* you get your gowns? And now I must tell you how sorry I am for you, dear Margaret. (*Crosses to sofa and sits with* LADY WINDERMERE.) Agatha, darling!

LADY AGATHA: Yes, mamma. (*Rises.*)

DUCHESS OF BERWICK: Will you go and look over the photograph album that I see there?

LADY AGATHA: Yes, mamma. (*Goes to table up L.*)

DUCHESS OF BERWICK: Dear girl! She is so fond of photographs of Switzerland. Such a pure taste, I think. But I really am so sorry for you, Margaret.

LADY WINDERMERE (*smiling*): Why, Duchess?

DUCHESS OF BERWICK: Oh, on account of that horrid woman. She dresses so well, too, which makes it much worse, sets such a dreadful example. Augustus – you know my disreputable brother – such a trial to us all – well, Augustus is completely infatuated about her. It is quite scandalous, for she is absolutely inadmissible into society. Many a woman has a past, but I am told that she has at least a dozen, and that they all fit.

LADY WINDERMERE: Whom are you talking about, Duchess?

DUCHESS OF BERWICK: About Mrs. Erlynne.

LADY WINDERMERE: Mrs. Erlynne? I never heard of her, Duchess. And what *has* she to do with me?

DUCHESS OF BERWICK: My poor child! Agatha, darling!

LADY AGATHA: Yes, mamma.

DUCHESS OF BERWICK: Will you go out on the terrace and look at the sunset?

LADY AGATHA: Yes, mamma. (*Exit through window L.*)

DUCHESS OF BERWICK: Sweet girl! So devoted to sunsets! Shows such refinement of feeling, does it not? After all, there is nothing like Nature, is there?

LADY WINDERMERE: But what is it, Duchess? Why do you talk to me about this person?

DUCHESS OF BERWICK: Don't you really know? I assure you we're all so distressed about it. Only last night at dear Lady Jansen's every one was saying how extraordinary it was that, of all men in London, Windermere should behave in such a way.

LADY WINDERMERE: My husband – what has *he* got to do with any woman of that kind?

DUCHESS OF BERWICK: Ah, what indeed, dear? That is the point. He goes to see her continually, and stops for hours at a time, and while he is there she is not at home to any one. Not that many ladies call on her, dear, but she has a great many disreputable men friends – my own brother particularly, as I told you – and that is what makes it so dreadful about Windermere. We looked upon *him* as being such a model husband, but I am afraid there is no doubt about it. My dear nieces – you know the Saville girls, don't you? – such nice domestic creatures – plain, dreadfully plain, – but so good – well, they're always at the window doing fancy work, and making ugly things for the poor, which I think so useful of them in these dreadful socialistic days, and this terrible woman has taken a house in Curzon Street, right opposite them – such a respectable street, too! I don't know what we're coming to! And they tell me that Windermere goes there four and five times a week – they *see* him. They can't help it – and although they never talk scandal, they – well, of course – they remark on it to every one. And the worst of it all is that I have been told that this woman has got a great deal of money out of somebody, for it seems that she came to London six months ago without anything at all to speak of, and now she has this charming house in Mayfair, drives her ponies in the Park every afternoon and all – well, all – since she had known poor dear Windermere.

LADY WINDERMERE: Oh, I can't believe it!

DUCHESS OF BERWICK: But it's quite true, my dear. The whole of London knows it. That is why I felt it was better to come and talk to you, and advise you to take Windermere away at once to Homburg or to Aix, where he'll have something to amuse him, and where you can watch him all day long. I assure you, my dear, that on several occasions after I was first married, I had to pretend to be very ill, and was obliged to drink the most unpleasant mineral waters, merely to get Berwick out of town. He was so extremely susceptible. Though I am bound to say he never gave away any large sums of money to anybody. He is far too high-principled for that!

LADY WINDERMERE (*interrupting*): Duchess, Duchess, it's impossible! (*Rising and crossing stage to C.*): We are only married two years. Our child is but six months old. (*Sits in chair R. of L. table.*)

DUCHESS OF BERWICK: Ah, the dear pretty baby! How is the little darling? Is it a boy or a girl? I hope a girl – ah, no, I remember it's a boy! I'm so sorry. Boys are so wicked. My boy is excessively immoral. You wouldn't believe at what hours he comes home. And he's only left Oxford a few months – I really don't know what they teach them there.

LADY WINDERMERE: Are *all* men bad?

DUCHESS OF BERWICK: Oh, all of them, my dear, all of them, without any exception. And they never grow any better. Men become old, but they never become good.

LADY WINDERMERE: Windermere and I married for love.

DUCHESS OF BERWICK: Yes, we begin like that. It was only Berwick's brutal and incessant threats of suicide that made me accept him at all, and before the year was out, he was running after all kinds of petticoats, every colour, every shape, every material. In fact, before the honeymoon was over, I caught him winking at my maid, a most pretty, respectable girl. I dismissed her at once without a character. No, I remember I passed her on to my sister; poor dear Sir George is so short-sighted, I thought it wouldn't matter. But it did, though – it was most unfortunate. (*Rises.*) And now, my dear child, I must go, as we are dining out. And mind you don't take this little aberration of Windermere's too much to heart. Just take him abroad, and he'll come back to you all right.

LADY WINDERMERE: Come back to me? (*C.*)

DUCHESS OF BERWICK: (*L.C.*): Yes, dear, these wicked women get our husbands away from us, but they always come back, slightly damaged, of course. And don't make scenes, men hate them!

LADY WINDERMERE: It is very kind of you, Duchess, to come and tell all this. But I can't believe that my husband is untrue to me.

DUCHESS OF BERWICK: Pretty child! I was like that once. Now I know that all men are monsters. (LADY WINDERMERE *rings bell.*) The only thing to do is to feed the wretches well. A good cook does wonders, and that I know you have. My dear Margaret, you are not going to cry?

LADY WINDERMERE: You needn't be afraid, Duchess, I never cry.

DUCHESS OF BERWICK: That's quite right, dear. Crying is the refuge of plain women but the ruin of pretty ones. Agatha, darling!

LADY AGATHA (*entering L.*): Yes, mamma. (*Stands back of table L.C.*)

DUCHESS OF BERWICK: Come and bid good-bye to Lady Windermere, and thank her for your charming visit. (*Coming down again.*): And by the way, I must thank you for sending a card to Mr. Hopper – he's that rich young Australian people are taking such notice of just at present. His father made a great fortune by selling some kind of food in circular tins – most palatable, I believe – I fancy it is the thing the servants always refuse to eat. But the son is quite interesting. I think he's attracted by dear Agatha's clever talk. Of course, we should be very sorry to lose her, but I think that a mother who doesn't part with a daughter every season has no real affection. We're coming to-night, dear. (PARKER *opens C. doors.*) And remember my advice, take the poor fellow out of town at once, it is the only thing to do. Good-bye, once more; come, Agatha.

Exeunt DUCHESS *and* LADY AGATHA *C.*

LADY WINDERMERE: How horrible! I understand now what Lord Darlington meant by the imaginary instance of the couple not two years married. Oh! It can't be true – she spoke of enormous sums of money paid to this woman. I know where Arthur keeps his bank book – in one of the drawers of that desk. I might find out by that. I *will* find out. (*Opens drawer.*) No, it is some hideous mistake. (*Rises and goes C.*) Some silly scandal! He loves *me*! He loves *me*! But why should I not look? I am his wife, I have a right to look! (*Returns to bureau, takes out book and examines it page by page, smiles and gives a sigh of relief.*) I knew it! There is not a word of truth in this stupid story. (*Puts book back in drawer. As she does so, starts and takes out another book.*) A second book – private – locked! (*Tries to open it, but fails.*) Sees paper knife on bureau, and with it cuts cover from book. Begins to start at the first page.) 'Mrs. Erlynne – £600 – Mrs. Erlynne – £700 – Mrs. Erlynne – £400.' Oh! It is true! It is true! How horrible! (*Throws book on floor.*)

Enter LORD WINDERMERE *C.*

LORD WINDERMERE: Well, dear, has the fan been sent home yet? (*Going R.C. Sees book.*) Margaret, you have cut my bank book. You have no right to do such a thing!

LADY WINDERMERE: You think it wrong that you are found out, don't you?

LORD WINDERMERE: I think it wrong that a wife should spy on her husband.

LADY WINDERMERE: I did not spy on you. I never knew of this woman's existence till half an hour ago. Some one who pitied me was kind enough to tell me what every one in London knows already – your daily visits to Curzon Street, your mad infatuation, the monstrous sums of money you squander on this infamous woman! (*Crossing L.*)

LORD WINDERMERE: Margaret! Don't talk like that of Mrs. Erlynne, you don't know how unjust it is!

LADY WINDERMERE: (*turning to him*): You are very jealous of Mrs. Erlynne's honour. I wish you had been as jealous of mine.

LORD WINDERMERE: Your honour is untouched, Margaret. You don't think for a moment that – (*Puts book back into desk.*)

LADY WINDERMERE: I think that you spend your money strangely. That is all. Oh, don't imagine I mind about the money. As far as I am concerned, you may squander everything we have. But what I *do* mind is that you have loved me, you who have taught me to love you, should pass from the love that is given to the love that is bought. Oh, it's horrible! (*Sits on sofa.*) And it is I who feel degraded! *You* don't feel anything. I feel stained, utterly stained. You can't realise how hideous the last six months seems to me now – every kiss you have given me is tainted in my memory.

LORD WINDERMERE (*crossing to her*): Don't say that, Margaret. I never loved any one in the whole world but you.

LADY WINDERMERE (*rises*): Who is this woman, then? Why do you take a house for her?

LORD WINDERMERE: I did not take a house for her.

LADY WINDERMERE: You gave her the money to do it, which is the same thing.

LORD WINDERMERE: Margaret, as far as I have known Mrs. Erlynne –

LADY WINDERMERE: Is there a Mr. Erlynne – or is he a myth?

LORD WINDERMERE: Her husband died many years ago. She is alone in the world.

LADY WINDERMERE: No relations? (*A pause.*)

LORD WINDERMERE: None.

LADY WINDERMERE: Rather curious, isn't it? (*L.*)

LORD WINDERMERE (*L.C.*): Margaret, I was saying to you – and I beg you to listen to me – that as far as I have known Mrs. Erlynne, she has conducted herself well. If years ago –

LADY WINDERMERE: Oh! (*Crossing R.C.*) I don't want details about her life!

LORD WINDERMERE (*C.*): I am not going to give you any details about her life. I tell you simply this – Mrs. Erlynne was once honoured, loved, respected. She was well born, she had position – she lost everything – threw it away, if you like. That makes it all the more bitter. Misfortunes one can endure – they come from outside, they are accidents. But to suffer for one's own faults – ah! There is the sting of life. It was twenty years ago, too. She was little more than a girl then. She had been a wife for even less time than you have.

LADY WINDERMERE: I am not interested in her – and – you should not mention this woman and me in the same breath. It is an error of taste. (*Sitting R. at desk.*)

LORD WINDERMERE: Margaret, you could save this woman. She wants to get back into society, and she wants you to help her. (*Crossing to her.*)

LADY WINDERMERE: Me!

LORD WINDERMERE: Yes, you.

LADY WINDERMERE: How impertinent of her! (*A pause.*)

LORD WINDERMERE: Margaret, I came to ask you a great favour, and I still ask it of you, though you have discovered what I had intended you should never have known, that I have given Mrs. Erlynne a large sum of money. I want you to send her an invitation for our party to-night. (*Standing L. of her.*)

LADY WINDERMERE: You are mad! (*Rises.*)

LORD WINDERMERE: I entreat you. People may chatter about her, do chatter about her, of course, but they don't know anything definite against her. She has been to several houses – not to houses where you would go, I admit, but still to houses where women who are in what is called Society nowadays do go. That does not content her. She wants you to receive her once.

LADY WINDERMERE: As a triumph for her, I suppose?

LORD WINDERMERE: No; but because she knows that you are a good woman – and that if she comes here once she will have a chance of a happier, a surer life than she has had. She will make no further effort to know you. Won't you help a woman who is trying to get back?

LADY WINDERMERE: No! If a woman really repents, she never wishes to return to the society that has made or seen her ruin.

LORD WINDERMERE: I beg of you.

LADY WINDERMERE (*crossing to door R.*): I am going to dress for dinner, and don't mention the subject again this evening. Arthur – (*going to him C.*) – you fancy because I have no father or mother that I am alone in the world, and that you can treat me as you choose. You are wrong, I have friends, many friends.

LORD WINDERMERE (*L.C.*): Margaret, you are talking foolishly, recklessly. I won't argue with you, but I insist upon your asking Mrs. Erlynne to-night.

LADY WINDERMERE (*R.C.*): I shall do nothing of the kind. (*Crossing L.C.*)

LORD WINDERMERE: You refuse? (*C.*)

LADY WINDERMERE: Absolutely!

LORD WINDERMERE: Ah, Margaret, do this for my sake; it is her last chance.

LADY WINDERMERE: What has that to do with me?

LORD WINDERMERE: How hard good women are!

LADY WINDERMERE: How weak bad men are!

LORD WINDERMERE: Margaret, none of us men may be good enough for the women we marry – that is quite true – but you don't imagine I would ever – oh, the suggestion is monstrous!

LADY WINDERMERE: Why should *you* be different from other men? I am told that there is hardly a husband in London who does not waste his life over *some* shameful passion.

LORD WINDERMERE: I am not one of them.

LADY WINDERMERE: I am not sure of that!

LORD WINDERMERE: You are sure in your heart. But don't make chasm after chasm between us. God knows the last few minutes have thrust us wide enough apart. Sit down and write the card.

LADY WINDERMERE: Nothing in the whole world would induce me.

LORD WINDERMERE (*crossing to bureau*): Then I will! (*Rings electric bell, sits and writes card.*)

LADY WINDERMERE: You are going to invite this woman? (*Crossing to him.*)

LORD WINDERMERE: Yes.

Pause. Enter PARKER.

Parker!

PARKER: Yes, my lord. (*Comes down L.C.*)

LORD WINDERMERE: Have this note sent to Mrs. Erlynne at No. 84A Curzon Street. (*Crossing to L.C. and giving note to* PARKER.) There is no answer!

Exit PARKER *C.*

LADY WINDERMERE: Arthur, if that woman comes here, I shall insult her.

LORD WINDERMERE: Margaret, don't say that.

LADY WINDERMERE: I mean it.

LORD WINDERMERE: Child, if you did such a thing, there's not a woman in London who wouldn't pity you.

LADY WINDERMERE: There is not a *good* woman in London who would not applaud me. We have been too lax. We must make an example. I propose to begin to-night. (*Picking up fan.*) Yes, you gave me this fan to-day; it was your birthday present. If that woman crosses my threshold, I shall strike her across the face with it.

LORD WINDERMERE: Margaret, you couldn't do such a thing.

LADY WINDERMERE: You don't know me! (*Moves R.*)

Enter PARKER.

Parker!

PARKER: Yes, my lady.

LADY WINDERMERE: I shall dine in my own room. I don't want dinner, in fact. See that everything is ready by half-past ten. And, Parker, be sure you pronounce the names of the guests very distinctly to-night. Sometimes you speak so fast that I miss them. I am particularly anxious to hear the names quite clearly, so as to make no mistake. You understand, Parker?

PARKER: Yes, my lady.

LADY WINDERMERE: That will do!

Exit PARKER *C.*

(*Speaking to* LORD WINDERMERE): Arthur, if that woman comes here – I warn you –

LORD WINDERMERE: Margaret, you'll ruin us!

LADY WINDERMERE: Us! From this moment my life is separate from yours. But if you wish to avoid a public scandal, write at once to this woman, and tell her that I forbid her to come here!

LORD WINDERMERE: I will not – I cannot – she must come!

LADY WINDERMERE: Then I shall do exactly as I have said. (*Goes R.*) You leave me no choice. (*Exit R.*)

LORD WINDERMERE (*calling after her*): Margaret! Margaret! (*A pause.*) My God! What shall I do? I dare not tell her who this woman really is. The shame would kill her. (*Sinks down into a chair and buries his face in his hands.*)

ACT DROP

ACT TWO

SCENE: *Drawing-room in Lord Windermere's house. Door R.U. opening into ball-room, where band is playing. Door L. through which guests are entering. Door L.U. opens on to illuminated terrace. Palms, flowers, and brilliant lights. Room crowded with guests. Lady Windermere is receiving them.*

DUCHESS OF BERWICK (*up C.*): So strange Lord Windermere isn't here. Mr. Hopper is very late, too. You have kept those five dances for him, Agatha? (*Comes down.*)

LADY AGATHA: Yes, mamma.

DUCHESS OF BERWICK (*sitting on sofa*): Just let me see your card. I'm so glad Lady Windermere has revived cards. They're a mother's only safeguard. You dear simple little thing! (*Scratches out two names.*) No nice girl should ever waltz with such particularly younger sons! It looks so fast! The last two dances you might pass on the terrace with Mr. Hopper.

Enter MR. DUMBY *and* LADY PLYMDALE *from the ballroom.*

LADY AGATHA: Yes, mamma.

DUCHESS OF BERWICK (*fanning herself*): The air is so pleasant there.

PARKER: Mrs. Cowper-Cowper. Lady Stutfield. Sir James Royston. Mr. Guy Berkeley.

These people enter as announced.

DUMBY: Good evening, Lady Stutfield. I suppose this will be the last ball of the season?

LADY STUTFIELD: I suppose so, Mr. Dumby. It's been a delightful season, hasn't it?

DUMBY: Quite delightful! Good evening, Duchess. I suppose this will be the last ball of the season?

DUCHESS OF BERWICK: I suppose so, Mr. Dumby. It has been a very dull season, hasn't it?

DUMBY: Dreadfully dull! Dreadfully dull!

MRS. COWPER-COWPER: Good evening, Mr. Dumby. I suppose this will be the last ball of the season?

DUMBY: Oh, I think not. There'll probably be two more. (*Wanders back to* LADY PLYMDALE.)

PARKER: Mr. Rufford. Lady Jedburgh and Miss Graham. Mr. Hopper.

These people enter as announced.

HOPPER: How do you do, Lady Windermere? How do you do, Duchess? (*Bows to* LADY AGATHA.)

DUCHESS OF BERWICK: Dear Mr. Hopper, how nice of you to come so early. We all know how you are run after in London.

HOPPER: Capital place, London! They are not nearly so exclusive in London as they are in Sydney.

DUCHESS OF BERWICK: Ah! We know your value, Mr. Hopper. We wish there were more like you. It would make life so much easier. Do you know, Mr. Hopper, dear Agatha and I are so much interested in Australia. It must be so pretty with all the dear little kangaroos flying about. Agatha has found it on the map. What a curious shape it is! Just like a large packing case. However, it is a very young country, isn't it?

HOPPER: Wasn't it made at the same time as the others, Duchess?

DUCHESS OF BERWICK: How clever you are, Mr. Hopper. You have a cleverness quite of your own. Now I mustn't keep you.

HOPPER: But I should like to dance with Lady Agatha, Duchess.

DUCHESS OF BERWICK: Well, I *hope* she has a dance left. Have you a dance left, Agatha?

LADY AGATHA: Yes, mamma.

DUCHESS OF BERWICK: The next one?

LADY AGATHA: Yes, mamma.

HOPPER: May I have the pleasure? (LADY AGATHA *bows.*)

DUCHESS OF BERWICK: Mind you take great care of my little chatter-box, Mr. Hopper.

LADY AGATHA *and* MR. HOPPER *pass into the ballroom.*

Enter LORD WINDERMERE *L.*

LORD WINDERMERE: Margaret, I want to speak to you.

LADY WINDERMERE: In a moment. (*The music stops.*)

PARKER: Lord Augustus Lorton.

Enter LORD AUGUSTUS.

LORD AUGUSTUS: Good evening, Lady Windermere.

DUCHESS OF BERWICK: Sir James, will you take me into the ballroom?

Augustus has been dining with us to-night. I really have had quite enough of dear Augustus for the moment.

SIR JAMES ROYSTON *gives the* DUCHESS *his arm and escorts her into the ballroom.*

PARKER: Mr. and Mrs. Arthur Bowden. Lord and Lady Paisley. Lord Darlington.

These people enter as announced.

LORD AUGUSTUS (*coming up to* LORD WINDERMERE): Want to speak to you particularly, dear boy. I'm worn to a shadow. Know I don't look it. None of us men do look what we really are. Demmed good thing, too. What I want to know is this. Who is she? Where does she come from? Why hasn't she got any demmed relations! Demmed nuisance, relations! But they make one so demmed respectable.

LORD WINDERMERE: You are talking of Mrs. Erlynne, I suppose? I only met her six months ago. Till then, I never knew of her existence.

LORD AUGUSTUS: You have seen a good deal of her since then.

LORD WINDERMERE (*coldly*): Yes, I have seen a good deal of her since then. I have just seen her.

LORD AUGUSTUS: Egad! The women are very down on her. I have been dining with Arabella this evening! By Jove! You should have heard what she said about Mrs. Erlynne. She didn't leave a rag on her.... (*Aside.*) Berwick and I told her that didn't matter much, as the lady in question must have an extremely fine figure. You should have seen Arabella's expression.... But, look here, dear boy. I don't know what to do about Mrs. Erlynne. Egad! I might be married to her; she treats me with such demmed indifference. She's deuced clever, too! She explains everything. Egad! She explains you. She has got any amount of explanations for you – and all of them different.

LORD WINDERMERE: No explanations are necessary about my friendship with Mrs. Erlynne.

LORD AUGUSTUS: Hem! Well, look here, dear old fellow. Do you think she will ever get into this demmed thing called Society? Would you introduce her to your wife? No use beating about the confounded bush. Would you do that?

LORD WINDERMERE: Mrs. Erlynne is coming here to-night.

LORD AUGUSTUS: Your wife has sent her a card?

LORD WINDERMERE: Mrs. Erlynne has received a card.

LORD AUGUSTUS: Then she's all right, dear boy. But why didn't you tell me that before? It would have saved me a heap of worry and demmed misunderstandings!

LADY AGATHA *and* MR. HOPPER *cross and exit on terrace L.U.E.*

PARKER: Mr. Cecil Graham!

Enter MR. CECIL GRAHAM.

CECIL GRAHAM (*bows to* LADY WINDERMERE, *passes over and shakes hands with* LORD WINDERMERE): Good evening, Arthur. Why don't you ask me how I am? I like people to ask me how I am. It shows a wide-spread interest in my health. Now, to-night I am not at all well. Been dining with my people. Wonder why it is one's people are always so tedious? My father would talk morality after dinner. I told him he was old enough to know better. But my experience is that as soon as people are old enough to know better, they don't know anything at all. Hullo, Tuppy! Hear you're going to be married again; thought you were tired of that game.

LORD AUGUSTUS: You're excessively trivial, my dear boy, excessively trivial!

CECIL GRAHAM: By the way, Tuppy, which is it? Have you been twice married and once divorced, or twice divorced and once married? I say you've been twice divorced and once married. It seems so much more probable.

LORD AUGUSTUS: I have a very bad memory. I really don't remember which. (*Moves away R.*)

LADY PLYMDALE: Lord Windermere, I've something most particular to ask you.

LORD WINDERMERE: I am afraid – if you will excuse me – I must join my wife.

LADY PLYMDALE: Oh, you mustn't dream of such a thing. It's most dangerous nowadays for a husband to pay any attention to his wife in public. It always makes people think that he beats her when they're alone. The world has grown so suspicious of anything that looks like a happy married life. But I'll tell you what it is at supper. (*Moves towards door of ballroom.*)

LORD WINDERMERE (*C.*): Margaret! I must speak to you.

LADY WINDERMERE: Will you hold my fan for me, Lord Darlington? Thanks. (*Comes down to him.*)

LORD WINDERMERE (*crossing to her*): Margaret, what you said before dinner was, of course, impossible?

LADY WINDERMERE: That woman is not coming here to-night.

LORD WINDERMERE (*R.C.*): Mrs. Erlynne is coming here, and if you in any way annoy or wound her, you will bring shame and sorrow on us both. Remember that! Ah, Margaret, only trust me! A wife should trust her husband!

LADY WINDERMERE (*C.*): London is full of women who trust their husbands. One can always recognise them. They look so thoroughly unhappy. I am not going to be one of them (*Moves up.*) Lord Darlington, will you give me back my fan, please? Thanks.... A useful thing a fan, isn't it? ... I want a friend to-night, Lord Darlington; I didn't know I would want one so soon.

LORD DARLINGTON: Lady Windermere! I knew the time would come some day; but why to-night?

LORD WINDERMERE: I *will* tell her. I must. It would be terrible if there were any scene. Margaret . . .
PARKER: Mrs. Erlynne!

> LORD WINDERMERE *starts.* MRS. ERLYNNE *enters, very beautifully dressed and very dignified.* LADY WINDERMERE *clutches at her fan, then lets it drop on the floor. She bows coldly to* MRS. ERLYNNE, *who bows to her sweetly in turn, and sails into the room.*

LORD DARLINGTON: You have dropped your fan, Lady Windermere. (*Picks it up and hands it to her.*)
MRS. ERLYNNE (*C.*): How do you do, again, Lord Windermere? How charming your sweet wife looks! Quite a picture!
LORD WINDERMERE (*in a low voice*): It was terribly rash of you to come!
MRS. ERLYNNE (*smiling*): The wisest thing I ever did in my life. And, by the way, you must pay me a good deal of attention this evening. I am afraid of the women. You must introduce me to some of them. The men I can always manage. How do you do, Lord Augustus? You have quite neglected me lately. I have not seen you since yesterday. I am afraid you're faithless. Every one told me so.
LORD AUGUSTUS (*R.*): Now really, Mrs. Erlynne, allow me to explain.
MRS. ERLYNNE (*R.C.*): No, dear Lord Augustus, you can't explain anything. It is your chief charm.
LORD AUGUSTUS: Ah! If you find charms in me, Mrs. Erlynne –

> *They converse together.* LORD WINDERMERE *moves uneasily about the room watching* MRS. ERLYNNE.

LORD DARLINGTON (*to* LADY WINDERMERE): How pale you are!
LADY WINDERMERE: Cowards are always pale!
LORD DARLINGTON: You look faint. Come out on the terrace.
LADY WINDERMERE: Yes. (*To* PARKER): Parker, send my cloak out.
MRS. ERLYNNE (*crossing to her*): Lady Windermere, how beautifully your terrace is illuminated. Reminds me of Prince Doria's at Rome.

> LADY WINDERMERE *bows coldly, and goes off with* LORD DARLINGTON.

Oh, how do you do, Mr. Graham? Isn't that your aunt, Lady Jedburgh? I should so much like to know her.
CECIL GRAHAM (*after a moment's hesitation and embarrassment*): Oh, certainly, if you wish it. Aunt Caroline, allow me to introduce Mrs. Erlynne.
MRS. ERLYNNE: So pleased to meet you, Lady Jedburgh. (*Sits beside her on the sofa.*) Your nephew and I are great friends. I am so much interested in his political career. I think he's sure to be a wonderful success. He thinks like a Tory, and talks like a Radical, and that's so important nowadays. He's such a brilliant talker, too. But we all know from whom he inherits that. Lord

Allandale was saying to me only yesterday, in the Park, that Mr. Graham talks almost as well as his aunt.

LADY JEDBURGH (*R.*): Most kind of you to say these charming things to me! (MRS. ERLYNNE *smiles, and continues conversation.*)

DUMBY (*to* CECIL GRAHAM): Did you introduce Mrs. Erlynne to Lady Jedburgh?

CECIL GRAHAM: Had to, my dear fellow. Couldn't help it! That woman can make one do anything she wants. How, I don't know.

DUMBY: Hope to goodness she won't speak to me! (*Saunters towards* LADY PLYMDALE.)

MRS. ERLYNNE (*C. To* LADY JEDBURGH): On Thursday? With great pleasure. (*Rises, and speaks to* LORD WINDERMERE, *laughing.*) What a bore it is to have to be civil to these old dowagers! But they always insist on it!

LADY PLYMDALE (*to* MR.DUMBY): Who is that well-dressed woman talking to Windermere?

DUMBY: Haven't got the slightest idea! Looks like an *édition de luxe* of a wicked French novel, meant specially for the English market.

MRS. ERLYNNE: So that is poor Dumby with Lady Plymdale? I hear she is frightfully jealous of him. He doesn't seem anxious to speak to me to-night. I suppose he is afraid of her. Those straw-coloured women have dreadful tempers. Do you know, I think I'll dance with you first, Windermere. (LORD WINDERMERE *bites his lip and frowns.*) It will make Lord Augustus so jealous! Lord Augustus! (LORD AUGUSTUS *comes down.*) Lord Windermere insists on my dancing with him first; as it's his own house, I can't well refuse. You know I would much sooner dance with you.

LORD AUGUSTUS (*with a low bow*): I wish I could think so, Mrs. Erlynne.

MRS. ERLYNNE: You know it far too well. I can fancy a person dancing through life with you and finding it charming.

LORD AUGUSTUS (*placing his hand on his white waistcoat*): Oh, thank you, thank you. You are the most adorable of all ladies!

MRS. ERLYNNE: What a nice speech! So simple and so sincere! Just the sort of speech I like. Well, you shall hold my bouquet. (*Goes towards ballroom on* LORD WINDERMERE'S *arm.*) Ah, Mr. Dumby, how are you? I am so sorry I have been out the last three times you have called. Come and lunch on Friday.

DUMBY: (*with perfect nonchalance*): Delighted!

LADY PLYMDALE *glares with indignation at* MR. DUMBY. LORD AUGUSTUS *follows* MRS. ERLYNNE *and* LORD WINDERMERE *into the ballroom holding bouquet.*

LADY PLYMDALE (*to* MR. DUMBY): What an absolute brute you are! I never can believe a word you say! Why did you tell me you didn't know her? What do you mean by calling on her three times running? You are not to go to lunch there; of course you understand that?

DUMBY: My dear Laura, I wouldn't dream of going!

LADY PLYMDALE: You haven't told me her name yet! Who is she?

DUMBY (*coughs slightly and smooths his hair*): She's a Mrs. Erlynne.

LADY PLYMDALE: That woman!

DUMBY: Yes; that is what every one calls her.

LADY PLYMDALE: How very interesting! How intensely interesting! I really must have a good stare at her. (*Goes to door of ballroom and looks in.*) I have heard the most shocking things about her. They say she is ruining poor Windermere. And Lady Windermere, who goes in for being so proper, invites her! How extremely amusing! It takes a thoroughly good woman to do a thoroughly stupid thing. You are to lunch there on Friday!

DUMBY: Why?

LADY PLYMDALE: Because I want you to take my husband with you. He has been so attentive lately, that he has become a perfect nuisance. Now, this woman's just the thing for him. He'll dance attendance upon her as long as she lets him, and won't bother me. I assure you, women of that kind are most useful. They form the basis of other people's marriages.

DUMBY: What a mystery you are!

LADY PLYMDALE (*looking at him*): I wish *you* were!

DUMBY: I am – to myself. I am the only person in the world I should like to know thoroughly; but I don't see any chance of it just at present.

They pass into the ballroom, and LADY WINDERMERE *and* LORD DARLINGTON *enter from the terrace.*

LADY WINDERMERE: Yes. Yes. Her coming here is monstrous, unbearable. I know now what you meant to-day at tea time. Why didn't you tell me right out? You should have!

LORD DARLINGTON: I couldn't! A man can't tell these things about another man! But if I had known he was going to make you ask her here to-night, I think I would have told you. That insult, at any rate, you would have been spared.

LADY WINDERMERE: I did not ask her. He insisted on her coming – against my entreaties – against my commands. Oh! The house is tainted for me! I feel that every woman here sneers at me as she dances by with my husband. What have I done to deserve this? I gave him all my life. He took it – used it – spoiled it! I am degraded in my own eyes, and I lack courage – I am a coward! (*Sits down on sofa.*)

LORD DARLINGTON: If I know you at all, I know that you can't live with a man who treats you like this! What sort of life would you have with him? You would feel that he was lying to you every moment of the day. You would feel that the look in his eyes was false, his voice false, his touch false, his passion false. He would come to you when he was weary of others; you would have to comfort him. He would come to you when he was devoted to others; you would have to charm him. You would have to be to him the mask of his real life, the cloak to hide his secret.

LADY WINDERMERE: You are right – you are terribly right. But where am

I to turn? You said you would be my friend, Lord Darlington. Tell me, what am I to do? Be my friend now.

LORD DARLINGTON: Between men and women there is no friendship possible. There is passion, enmity, worship, love, but no friendship. I love you –

LADY WINDERMERE: No, no! (*Rises.*)

LORD DARLINGTON: Yes, I love you! You are more to me than anything in the whole world. What does your husband give you? Nothing. Whatever is in him he gives to this wretched woman, whom he has thrust into your society, into your home, to shame you before every one. I offer you my life –

LADY WINDERMERE: Lord Darlington!

LORD DARLINGTON: My life – my whole life. Take it, and do with it what you will. . . . I love you – love you as I have never loved any living thing. From the moment I met you I loved you, loved you blindly, adoringly, madly! You did not know it then – you know it now! Leave this house to-night. I won't tell you that the world matters nothing, or the world's voice, or the voice of society. They matter a great deal. They matter far too much. But there are moments when one has to choose between living one's own life, fully, entirely, completely – or dragging out some false, shallow, degrading existence that the world in its hypocrisy demands. You have that moment now. Choose! Oh, my love, choose.

LADY WINDERMERE (*moving slowly away from him, and looking at him with startled eyes*): I have not the courage.

LORD DARLINGTON (*following her*): Yes; you have the courage. There may be six months of pain, of disgrace even, but when you no longer bear his name, when you bear mine, all will be well. Margaret, my love, my wife that shall be some day – yes, my wife! You know it! What are you now? This woman has the place that belongs by right to you. Oh! Go – go out of this house, with head erect, with a smile upon your lips, with courage in your eyes. All London will know why you did it; and who will blame you? No one. If they do, what matter? Wrong? What is wrong? It's wrong for a man to abandon his wife for a shameless woman. It is wrong for a wife to remain with a man who so dishonours her. You said once you would make no compromise with things. Make none now. Be brave! Be yourself!

LADY WINDERMERE: I am afraid of being myself. Let me think. Let me wait! My husband may return to me. (*Sits down on sofa.*)

LORD DARLINGTON: And you would take him back! You are not what I thought you were. You are just the same as every other woman. You would stand anything rather than face the censure of a world whose praise you would despise. In a week you will be driving with this woman in the Park. She will be your constant guest – your dearest friend. You would endure anything rather than break with one blow this monstrous tie. You are right. You have no courage; none!

LADY WINDERMERE: Ah, give me time to think. I cannot answer you now. (*Passes her hand nervously over her brow.*)

LORD DARLINGTON: It must be now or not at all.

LADY WINDERMERE: (*rising from the sofa*): Then, not at all! (*A pause.*)

LORD DARLINGTON: You break my heart!

LADY WINDERMERE: Mine is already broken. (*A pause.*)

LORD DARLINGTON: To-morrow I leave England. This is the last time I shall ever look on you. You will never see me again. For one moment our lives met – our souls touched. They must never meet or touch again. Goodbye, Margaret. (*Exit.*)

LADY WINDERMERE: How alone I am in life. How terribly alone!

The music stops. Enter the DUCHESS OF BERWICK *and* LORD PAISLEY *laughing and talking. Other guests come in from ballroom.*

DUCHESS OF BERWICK: Dear Margaret, I've just been having such a delightful chat with Mrs. Erlynne. I am so sorry for what I said to you this afternoon about her. Of course, she must be all right if *you* invite her. A most attractive woman, and has such sensible views on life. Told me she entirely disapproved of people marrying more than once, so I feel quite safe about poor Augustus. Can't imagine why people speak against her. It's those horrid nieces of mine – the Saville girls – they're always talking scandal. Still, I should go to Homburg, dear, I really should. She is just a little too attractive. But where is Agatha? Oh, there she is. (LADY AGATHA *and* MR.HOPPER *enter from terrace L.U.E.*) Mr. Hopper, I am very, very angry with you. You have taken Agatha out on the terrace, and she is so delicate.

HOPPER (*L.C.*): Awfully sorry, Duchess. We went out for a moment and then got chatting together.

DUCHESS OF BERWICK (*C.*): Ah, about dear Australia, I suppose?

HOPPER: Yes!

DUCHESS OF BERWICK: Agatha, darling! (*Beckons her over.*)

LADY AGATHA: Yes, mamma!

DUCHESS OF BERWICK (*aside*): Did Mr.Hopper definitely –

LADY AGATHA: Yes, mamma.

DUCHESS OF BERWICK: And what answer did you give him, dear child?

LADY AGATHA: Yes, mamma.

DUCHESS OF BERWICK (*affectionately*): My dear one! You always say the right thing. Mr. Hopper! James! Agatha has told me everything. How cleverly you have both kept your secret.

HOPPER: You don't mind my taking Agatha off to Australia, then, Duchess?

DUCHESS OF BERWICK (*indignantly*): To Australia? Oh, don't mention that dreadful vulgar place.

HOPPER: But she said she'd like to come with me.

DUCHESS OF BERWICK (*severely*): Did you say that, Agatha?

LADY AGATHA: Yes, mamma.

DUCHESS OF BERWICK: Agatha, you say the most silly things possible. I think on the whole that Grosvenor Square would be a more healthy place to reside in. There are lots of vulgar people live in Grosvenor Square, but at any rate there are no horrid kangaroos crawling about. But we'll talk about that to-morrow. James, you can take Agatha down. You'll come to lunch, of course, James. At half-past one, instead of two. The Duke will wish to say a few words to you, I am sure.

HOPPER: I should like to have a chat with the Duke, Duchess. He has not said a single word to me yet.

DUCHESS OF BERWICK: I think you'll find he will have a great deal to say to you to-morrow. (*Exit* LADY AGATHA *with* MR. HOPPER.) And now good-night, Margaret. I'm afraid it's the old, old story, dear. Love – well, not love at first sight, but love at the end of the season, which is so much more satisfactory.

LADY WINDERMERE: Good-night, Duchess.

Exit the DUCHESS OF BERWICK *on* LORD PAISLEY'S *arm.*

LADY PLYMDALE: My dear Margaret, what a handsome woman your husband has been dancing with! I should be quite jealous if I were you! Is she a great friend of yours?

LADY WINDERMERE: No!

LADY PLYMDALE: Really? Good-night, dear. (*Looks at* MR.DUMBY *and exit.*)

DUMBY: Awful manners young Hopper has!

CECIL GRAHAM: Ah! Hopper is one of Nature's gentlemen, the worst type of gentleman I know.

DUMBY: Sensible woman, Lady Windermere. Lots of wives would have objected to Mrs. Erlynne coming. But Lady Windermere has that uncommon thing called common sense.

CECIL GRAHAM: And Windermere knows that nothing looks so like innocence as an indiscretion.

DUMBY: Yes; dear Windermere is becoming almost modern. Never thought he would. (*Bows to* LADY WINDERMERE *and exit.*)

LADY JEDBURGH: Good-night, Lady Windermere. What a fascinating woman Mrs. Erlynne is! She is coming to lunch on Thursday, won't you come too? I expect the Bishop and dear Lady Merton.

LADY WINDERMERE: I am afraid I am engaged, Lady Jedburgh.

LADY JEDBURGH: So sorry. Come, dear.

Exeunt LADY JEDBURGH *and* MISS GRAHAM.
Enter MRS. ERLYNNE *and* LORD WINDERMERE.

MRS. ERLYNNE: Charming ball it has been ! Quite reminds me of old days. (*Sits on sofa.*) And I see that there are just as many fools in society as there used to be. So pleased to find that nothing has altered! Except Margaret. She's grown quite pretty. The last time I saw her – twenty years ago, she was a fright in flannel. Positive fright, I assure you. The dear Duchess! And that sweet Lady Agatha! Just the type of girl I like! Well, really, Windermere, if I am to be the Duchess's sister-in-law –

LORD WINDERMERE (*sitting L. of her*): But are you –?

Exit MR. CECIL GRAHAM *with rest of guests.* LADY WINDERMERE *watches, with a look of scorn and pain,* MRS. ERLYNNE *and her husband. They are unconscious of her presence.*

MRS. ERLYNNE: Oh, yes! He's to call to-morrow at twelve o'clock. He wanted to propose to-night. In fact he did. He kept on proposing. Poor Augustus; you know how he repeats himself. Such a bad habit! But I told him I wouldn't give him an answer till to-morrow. Of course I am going to take him. And I dare say I'll make him an admirable wife, as wives go. And there is a great deal of good in Lord Augustus. Fortunately it is all on the surface. Just where good qualities should be. Of course you must help me in this matter.

LORD WINDERMERE: I am not called on to encourage Lord Augustus, I suppose?

MRS. ERLYNNE: Oh, no! I do the encouraging. But you will make me a handsome settlement, Windermere, won't you?

LORD WINDERMERE (*frowning*): Is that what you want to talk to me about to-night?

MRS. ERLYNNE: Yes.

LORD WINDERMERE (*with a gesture of impatience*): I will not talk of it here.

MRS. ERLYNNE (*laughing*): Then we will talk of it on the terrace. Even business should have a picturesque background. Should it not, Windermere? With a proper background women can do anything.

LORD WINDERMERE: Won't to-morrow do as well?

MRS. ERLYNNE: No; you see, to-morrow I am going to accept him. And I think it would be a good thing if I was able to tell him that I had – well, what shall I say? – £2000 a year left to me by a third cousin – or a second husband – or some distant relative of that kind. It would be an additional attraction, wouldn't it? You have a delightful opportunity now of paying me a compliment, Windermere. But you are not very clever at paying compliments. I am afraid Margaret doesn't encourage you in that excellent habit. It's a great mistake on her part. When men give up saying what is charming, they give up thinking what is charming. But seriously, what do you say to £2000? £2500, I think. In modern life margin is everything. Windermere, don't you think the world an intensely amusing place? I do!

Exit on terrace with LORD WINDERMERE. *Music strikes up in ballroom.*

LADY WINDERMERE: To stay in this house any longer is impossible. To-night a man who loves me offered me his whole life. I refused it. It was foolish of me. I will offer him mine now. I will give him mine. I will go to him! (*Puts on cloak and goes to the door, then turns back. Sits down at table and writes a letter, puts it into an envelope, and leaves it on table.*) Arthur has never understood me. When he reads this, he will. He may do as he chooses now with his life. I have done with mine as I think best, as I think right. It is he who has broken the bond of marriage – not I. I only break its bondage. (*Exit.*)

PARKER *enters L. and crosses towards the ballroom R. Enter* MRS. ERLYNNE.

MRS. ERLYNNE: Is Lady Windermere in the ballroom?

PARKER: Her ladyship has just gone out.

MRS. ERLYNNE: Gone out? She's not on the terrace?

PARKER: No, madam. Her ladyship has just gone out of the house.

MRS. ERLYNNE (*starts, and looks at the servant with a puzzled expression in her face.*): Out of the house?

PARKER: Yes, madam – her ladyship told me she had left a letter for his lordship on the table.

MRS. ERLYNNE: A letter for Lord Windermere?

PARKER: Yes, madam.

MRS. ERLYNNE: Thank you.

Exit PARKER. *The music in the ballroom stops.*

Gone out of her house! A letter addressed to her husband! (*Goes over to bureau and looks at letter. Takes it up and lays it down again with a shudder of fear.*) No, no! It would be impossible! Life doesn't repeat its tragedies like that! Oh, why does this horrible fancy come across me? Why do I remember now the one moment of my life I most wish to forget? Does life repeat its tragedies? (*Tears letter open and reads it, then sinks down into a chair with a gesture of anguish.*) Oh, how terrible! The same words that twenty years ago I wrote to her father! and how bitterly I have been punished for it! No; my punishment, my real punishment is to-night, is now! (*Still seated R.*)

Enter LORD WINDERMERE *L.U.E.*

LORD WINDERMERE: Have you said good-night to my wife? (*Comes C.*)

MRS. ERLYNNE (*crushing letter in her hand*): Yes.

LORD WINDERMERE: Where is she?

MRS. ERLYNNE: She is very tired. She has gone to bed. She said she had a headache.

LORD WINDERMERE: I must go to her. You'll excuse me?

MRS. ERLYNNE (*rising hurriedly*): Oh, no! It's nothing serious. She's only very tired, that is all. Besides, there are people still in the supper-room. She wants you to make her apologies to them. She said she didn't wish to be disturbed. (*Drops letter.*) She asked me to tell you!

LORD WINDERMERE (*picks up letter*): You have dropped something.

MRS. ERLYNNE: Oh yes, thank you, that is mine. (*Puts out her hand to take it.*)

LORD WINDERMERE (*still looking at letter*): But it's my wife's handwriting isn't it?

MRS. ERLYNNE (*takes the letter quickly*): Yes, it's – an address. Will you ask them to call my carriage, please?

LORD WINDERMERE: Certainly. (*Goes L. and Exit.*)

MRS. ERLYNNE: Thanks! What can I do? What can I do? I feel a passion awakening within me that I never felt before. What can it mean? The daughter must not be like the mother – that would be terrible. How can I save her? How can I save my child? A moment may ruin a life. Who knows that better than I? Windermere must be got out of the house; that is absolutely necessary. (*Goes L.*) But how shall I do it? It must be done somehow. Ah!

Enter LORD AUGUSTUS *R.U.E. carrying bouquet.*

LORD AUGUSTUS: Dear Lady, I am in such suspense! May I not have an answer to my request?

MRS. ERLYNNE: Lord Augustus, listen to me. You are to take Lord Windermere down to your club at once, and keep him there as long as possible. You understand?

LORD AUGUSTUS: But you said you wished me to keep early hours!

MRS. ERLYNNE (*nervously*): Do what I tell you. Do what I tell you.

LORD AUGUSTUS: And my reward?

MRS. ERLYNNE: Your reward? Your reward? Oh! Ask me that to-morrow. But don't let Windermere out of your sight to-night. If you do I will never forgive you. I will never speak to you again. I'll have nothing to do with you. Remember you are to keep Windermere at your club, and don't let him come back to-night. (*Exit L.*)

LORD AUGUSTUS: Well, really, I might be her husband already. Positively I might. (*Follows her in a bewildered manner.*)

ACT DROP

ACT THREE

SCENE: *Lord Darlington's rooms. A large sofa is in front of fireplace R. At the back of the stage a curtain is drawn across the window. Doors L. and R. Table R. with writing materials. Table C. with syphons, glasses, and Tantalus frame. Table L. with cigar and cigarette box. Lamps lit.*

LADY WINDERMERE (*standing by the fireplace*): Why doesn't he come? This waiting is horrible. He should be here. Why is he not here, to wake by passionate words some fire within me? I am cold – cold as a loveless thing. Arthur must have read my letter by this time. If he cared for me, he would have come after me, would have taken me back by force. But he doesn't care. He's entrammelled by this woman – fascinated by her – dominated by her. If a woman wants to hold a man, she has merely to appeal to what is worst in him. We make gods of men and they leave us. Other make brutes of them and they fawn and are faithful. How hideous life is! . . . Oh! It was mad of me to come here, horribly mad. And yet, which is the worst, I wonder, to be at the mercy of a man who loves one, or the wife of a man who in one's own house dishonours one? What woman knows? What woman in the whole world? But will he love me always, this man to whom I am giving my life? What do I bring him? Lips that have lost the note of joy, eyes that are blinded by tears, chill hands and icy heart. I bring him nothing. I must go back – no; I can't go back, my letter has put me in their power – Arthur would not take me back! That fatal letter! No! Lord Darlington leaves England to-morrow. I will go with him – I have no choice. (*Sits down for a few moments. Then starts up and puts on her cloak.*) No, no! I will go back, let Arthur do with me what he pleases. I can't wait here. It has been madness my coming. I must go at once. As for Lord Darlington. Oh! Here he is! What shall I do? What can I say to him? Will he let me go away at all? I have heard that men are brutal, horrible . . . Oh! (*Hides her face in her hands.*)

Enter MRS. ERLYNNE *L.*

MRS. ERLYNNE: Lady Windermere! (LADY WINDERMERE *starts and looks up. Then recoils in contempt.*) Thank Heaven I am in time. You must go back to your husband's house immediately.

LADY WINDERMERE: Must?

MRS. ERLYNNE (*authoritatively*): Yes, you must! There is not a second to be lost. Lord Darlington may return at any moment.

LADY WINDERMERE: Don't come near me!

MRS. ERLYNNE: Oh! You are on the brink of ruin, you are on the brink of a hideous precipice. You must leave this place at once; my carriage is waiting at the corner of the street. You must come with me and drive straight home.

LADY WINDERMERE *throws off her cloak and flings it on the sofa.*

What are you doing?

LADY WINDERMERE: Mrs. Erlynne – if you had not come here, I would have gone back. But now that I see you, I feel that nothing in the whole world would induce me to live under the same roof as Lord Windermere. You fill me with horror. There is something about you that stirs the wildest – rage within me. And I know why you are here. My husband sent you to lure me back that I might serve as a blind to whatever relations exist between you and him.

MRS. ERLYNNE: Oh! You don't think that – you can't.

LADY WINDERMERE: Go back to my husband, Mrs. Erlynne. He belongs to you and not to me. I suppose he is afraid of a scandal. Men are such cowards. They outrage every law of the world, and are afraid of the world's tongue. But he had better prepare himself. He shall have a scandal. He shall have the worst scandal there has been in London for years. He shall see his name in every vile paper, mine on every hideous placard.

MRS. ERLYNNE: No – no –

LADY WINDERMERE: Yes! He shall. Had he come himself, I admit I would have gone back to the life of degradation you and he had prepared for me – I was going back – but to stay himself at home, and to send you as his messenger – oh! It was infamous – infamous.

MRS. ERLYNNE (*C.*): Lady Windermere, you wrong me horribly – you wrong your husband horribly. He doesn't know you are here – he thinks you are safe in your own house. He thinks you are asleep in your own room. He never read the mad letter you wrote to him!

LADY WINDERMERE (*R.*): Never read it!

MRS. ERLYNNE: No – he knows nothing about it.

LADY WINDERMERE: How simple you think me! (*Going to her.*) You are lying to me!

MRS. ERLYNNE (*restraining herself*): I am not. I am telling you the truth.

LADY WINDERMERE: If my husband didn't read my letter, how is it that you are here? Who told you I had left the house you were shameless enough to enter? Who told you where I had gone to? My husband told you, and sent you to decoy me back. (*Crosses L.*)

MRS. ERLYNNE (*R.C.*): Your husband has never seen the letter. I – saw it, I opened it. I – read it.

LADY WINDERMERE (*turning to her*): You opened a letter of mine to my husband? You wouldn't dare!

MRS. ERLYNNE: Dare! Oh! To save you from the abyss into which you are falling, there is nothing in the world I would not dare, nothing in the whole world. Here is the letter. Your husband has never read it. He never shall read it. (*Going to fireplace.*) It should never have been written. (*Tears it and throws it into the fire.*)

LADY WINDERMERE (*with infinite contempt in her voice and look*): How do I know that that was my letter after all? You seem to think that commonest device can take me in!

MRS. ERLYNNE: Oh! Why do you disbelieve everything I tell you? What object do you think I have in coming here, except to save you from utter ruin, to save you from the consequence of a hideous mistake? That letter that is burnt now *was* your letter. I swear it to you!

LADY WINDERMERE (*slowly*): You took good care to burn it before I had examined it. I cannot trust you. You, whose whole life is a lie, how could you speak the truth about anything? (*Sits down.*)

MRS. ERLYNNE (*hurriedly*): Think as you like about me – say what you choose against me, but go back, go back to the husband you love.

LADY WINDERMERE (*sullenly*): I do *not* love him!

MRS. ERLYNNE: You do, and you know that he loves you.

LADY WINDERMERE: He does not understand what love is. He understands it as little as you do – but I see what you want. It would be a great advantage for you to get me back. Dear Heaven! What a life I would have then! Living at the mercy of a woman who has neither mercy nor pity in her, a woman whom it is an infamy to meet, a degradation to know, a vile woman, a woman who comes between husband and wife!

MRS. ERLYNNE (*with a gesture of despair*): Lady Windermere, Lady Windermere, don't say such terrible things. You don't know how terrible they are, how terrible and how unjust. Listen, you must listen! Only go back to your husband, and I promise you never to communicate with him again on any pretext – never to see him – never to have anything to do with his life or yours. The money that he gave me, he gave me not through love, but through hatred, not in worship, but in contempt. The hold I have over him –

LADY WINDERMERE (*rising*): Ah! You admit you have a hold!

MRS. ERLYNNE: Yes, and I will tell you what it is. It is his love for you, Lady Windermere.

LADY WINDERMERE: You expect me to believe that?

MRS. ERLYNNE: You must believe it! It is true. It is his love for you that has made him submit to – Oh! call it what you like, tyranny, threats, anything you choose. But it is his love for you. His desire to spare you – shame, yes, shame and disgrace.

LADY WINDERMERE: What do you mean? You are insolent! What have I to do with you?

MRS. ERLYNNE (*humbly*): Nothing. I know it – but I tell you that your husband loves you – that you may never meet with such love again in your whole life – that such love you will never meet – and that if you throw it away, the day may come when you will starve for love and it will not be given to you, beg for love and it will be denied you. Oh! Arthur loves you!

LADY WINDERMERE: Arthur? And you tell me there is nothing between you?

MRS. ERLYNNE: Lady Windermere, before Heaven your husband is guiltless of all offence towards you! And I – I tell you that had it ever occurred to me that such a monstrous suspicion would have entered your mind, I would have died rather than have crossed your life or his – oh! Died, gladly died! (*Moves away to sofa R.*)

LADY WINDERMERE: You talk as if you had a heart. Women like you have no hearts. Heart is not in you. You are bought and sold. (*Sits L.C.*)

MRS. ERLYNNE (*starts, with a gesture of pain. Then restrains herself, and comes over to where* LADY WINDERMERE *is sitting. As she speaks, she stretches out her hands towards her, but does not dare to touch her*): Believe what you choose about me. I am not worth a moment's sorrow. But don't spoil your beautiful young life on my account! You don't know what may be in store for you, unless you leave this house at once. You don't know what it is to fall into the pit, to be despised, mocked, abandoned, sneered at – to be an outcast! To find the door shut against one, to have to creep in by hideous byways, afraid every moment lest the mask should be stripped from one's face, and all the while to hear the laughter, the horrible laughter of the world, a thing more tragic than all the tears the world has ever shed. You don't know what it is. One pays for one's sin, and then one pays again, and all one's life one pays. You must never know that. As for me, if suffering be an expiation, then at this moment I have expiated all my faults, whatever they have been; for tonight you have made a heart in one who had it not, made it and broken it. But let that pass. I may have wrecked my own life, but I will not let you wreck yours. You – why, you are a mere girl, you would be lost. You haven't got the kind of brains that enables a woman to get back. You have neither the wit nor the courage. You couldn't stand dishonour! No! Go back, Lady Windermere, to the husband who loves you, whom you love. You have a child, Lady Windermere. Go back to that child who even now, in pain or in joy, may be calling to you. (LADY WINDERMERE *rises*.) God gave you that child. He will require from you that you make his life fine, that you watch over him. What answer will you make to God if his life is ruined through you? Back to your house, Lady Windermere – your husband loves you! He has never swerved for a moment from the love he bears you. But even if he had a thousand loves, you must stay with your child. If he was harsh to you, you must stay with your child. If he ill-treated you, you must stay with your child. If he abandoned you, your place is with your child.

LADY WINDERMERE *bursts into tears and buries her face in her hands.*

(*Rushing to her*): Lady Windermere!
    LADY WINDERMERE (*holding out her hands to her, helplessly, as a child might do*): Take me home. Take me home.
    MRS. ERLYNNE (*is about to embrace her. Then restrains herself. There is a look of wonderful joy in her face*): Come! Where is your cloak? (*Getting it from sofa*): Here. Put it on. Come at once!

    They go to the door.

LADY WINDERMERE: Stop! Don't you hear voices?
    MRS. ERLYNNE: No, no! There is no one!
    LADY WINDERMERE: Yes, there is! Listen! Oh! That is my husband's voice! He is coming in! Save me! Oh, it's some plot! You have sent for him.

    Voices outside.

MRS. ERLYNNE: Silence! I'm here to save you, if I can. But I fear it is too late! There! (*Points to the curtain across the window.*) The first chance you have slip out, if you ever get a chance!
    LADY WINDERMERE: But you?
    MRS. ERLYNNE: Oh! never mind me. I'll face them.

    LADY WINDERMERE *hides herself behind the curtain.*

LORD AUGUSTUS (*outside*): Nonsense, dear Windermere, you must not leave me!

MRS. ERLYNNE: Lord Augustus! Then it is I who am lost! (*Hesitates for a moment, then looks round and sees door R., and exit through it.*)

Enter LORD DARLINGTON, MR. DUMBY, LORD WINDERMERE, LORD AUGUSTUS LORTON, *and* MR. CECIL GRAHAM.

DUMBY: What a nuisance their turning us out of the club at this hour! It's only two o'clock. (*Sinks into a chair.*) The lively part of the evening is only just beginning. (*Yawns and closes his eyes.*)

LORD WINDERMERE: It is very good of you, Lord Darlington, allowing Augustus to force our company on you, but I'm afraid I can't stay long.

LORD DARLINGTON: Really! I am so sorry! You'll take a cigar, won't you?

LORD WINDERMERE: Thanks! (*Sits down.*)

LORD AUGUSTUS (*to* LORD WINDERMERE): My dear boy, you must not dream of going. I have a great deal to talk to you about, of demmed importance, too. (*Sits down with him at L. table.*)

CECIL GRAHAM: Oh! We all know what that is! Tuppy can't talk about anything but Mrs. Erlynne.

LORD WINDERMERE: Well, that is no business of yours, is it, Cecil?

CECIL GRAHAM: None! That is why it interests me. My own business always bores me to death. I prefer other people's.

LORD DARLINGTON: Have something to drink, you fellows. Cecil, you'll have a whisky and soda?

CECIL GRAHAM: Thanks. (*Goes to table with* LORD DARLINGTON): Mrs. Erlynne looked very handsome to-night, didn't she?

LORD DARLINGTON: I am not one of her admirers.

CECIL GRAHAM: I usen't to be, but I am now. Why! She actually made me introduce her to poor dear Aunt Caroline. I believe she is going to lunch there.

LORD DARLINGTON (*in surprise*): No?

CECIL GRAHAM: She is, really.

LORD DARLINGTON: Excuse me, you fellows. I'm going away to-morrow. And I have to write a few letters. (*Goes to writing-table and sits down.*)

DUMBY: Clever woman, Mrs. Erlynne.

CECIL GRAHAM: Hallo, Dumby! I thought you were asleep.

DUMBY: I am, I usually am!

LORD AUGUSTUS: A very clever woman. Knows perfectly well what a demmed fool I am – knows it as well as I do myself.

CECIL GRAHAM *comes towards him laughing.*

Ah, you may laugh, my boy, but it is a great thing to come across a woman who thoroughly understands one.

DUMBY: It is an awfully dangerous thing. They always end by marrying one.

CECIL GRAHAM: But I thought, Tuppy, you were never going to see her again! Yes! You told me so yesterday evening at the club. You said you'd heard –

Whispering to him.

LORD AUGUSTUS: Oh, she's explained that.
CECIL GRAHAM: And the Wiesbaden affair?
LORD AUGUSTUS: She's explained that too.
DUMBY: And her income, Tuppy? Has she explained that?
LORD AUGUSTUS (*in a very serious voice*): She's going to explain that to-morrow.

CECIL GRAHAM *goes back to C. table.*

DUMBY: Awfully commercial, women nowadays. Our grandmothers threw their caps over the mills, of course, but, by Jove, their grand-daughters only throw their caps over mills that can raise the wind for them.
LORD AUGUSTUS: You want to make her out a wicked woman. She is not!
CECIL GRAHAM: Oh! Wicked women bother one. Good women bore one. That is the only difference between them.
LORD AUGUSTUS (*puffing a cigar*): Mrs. Erlynne has a future before her.
DUMBY: Mrs. Erlynne has a past before her.
LORD AUGUSTUS: I prefer women with a past. They're always so demmed amusing to talk to.
CECIL GRAHAM: Well, you'll have lots of topics of conversation with *her*, Tuppy. (*Rising and going to him.*)
LORD AUGUSTUS: You're getting annoying, dear boy; you're getting demmed annoying.
CECIL GRAHAM (*puts his hands on his shoulders*): Now, Tuppy, you've lost your figure and you've lost your character. Don't lose your temper; you have only got one.
LORD AUGUSTUS: My dear boy, if I wasn't the most good-natured man in London –
CECIL GRAHAM: We'd treat you with more respect, wouldn't we, Tuppy? (*Strolls away.*)
DUMBY: The youth of the present day are quite monstrous. They have absolutely no respect for dyed hair.

LORD AUGUSTUS *looks round angrily.*

CECIL GRAHAM: Mrs. Erlynne has a very great respect for dear Tuppy.
DUMBY: Then Mrs. Erlynne sets an admirable example to the rest of her sex. It is perfectly brutal the way most women nowadays behave to men who are not their husbands.

LORD WINDERMERE: Dumby, you are ridiculous, and Cecil, you let your tongue run away with you. You must leave Mrs. Erlynne alone. You don't really know anything about her, and you're always talking scandal against her.

CECIL GRAHAM (*coming towards him L.C.*): My dear Arthur, I never talk scandal. *I* only talk gossip.

LORD WINDERMERE: What is the difference between scandal and gossip?

CECIL GRAHAM: Oh! Gossip is charming! History is merely gossip. But scandal is gossip made tedious by morality. Now, I never moralise. A man who moralises is usually a hypocrite, and a woman who moralises is invariably plain. There is nothing in the whole world so unbecoming to a woman as a Nonconformist conscience. And most women know it, I'm glad to say.

LORD AUGUSTUS: Just my sentiments, dear boy, just my sentiments.

CECIL GRAHAM: Sorry to hear it, Tuppy; whenever people agree with me, I always feel I must be wrong.

LORD AUGUSTUS: My dear boy, when I was your age –

CECIL GRAHAM: But you never were, Tuppy, and you never will be. (*Goes up to C.*) I say, Darlington, let us have some cards. You'll play, Arthur, won't you?

LORD WINDERMERE: No thanks, Cecil.

DUMBY (*with a sigh*): Good heavens! How marriage ruins a man! It's as demoralising as cigarettes, and far more expensive.

CECIL GRAHAM: You'll play, of course, Tuppy?

LORD AUGUSTUS (*pouring himself out a brandy and soda at table*): Can't, dear boy. Promised Mrs. Erlynne never to play or drink again.

CECIL GRAHAM: Now, my dear Tuppy, don't be led astray into the paths of virtue. Reformed, you would be perfectly tedious. That is the worst of women. They always want one to be good. And if we are good, when they meet us, they don't love us at all. They like to find us quite irretrievably bad, and to leave us quite unattractively good.

LORD DARLINGTON (*rising from R. Table, where he has been writing letters*): They always do find us bad!

DUMBY: I don't think we are bad. I think we are all good, except Tuppy.

LORD DARLINGTON: No, we are all in the gutter, but some of us are looking at the stars. (*Sits down at C. table.*)

DUMBY: We are all in the gutter, but some of us are looking at the stars? Upon my word, you are very romantic to-night, Darlington.

CECIL GRAHAM: Too romantic! You must be in love. Who is the girl?

LORD DARLINGTON: The woman I love is not free, or thinks she isn't. (*Glances instinctively at* LORD WINDERMERE *while he speaks.*)

CECIL GRAHAM: A married woman, then! Well, there's nothing in the world like the devotion of a married woman. It's a thing no married man knows anything about.

LORD DARLINGTON: Oh! She doesn't love me. She is a good woman. She is the only good woman I have ever met in my life.

CECIL GRAHAM: The only good woman you have ever met in your life?

LORD DARLINGTON: Yes!

CECIL GRAHAM (*lighting a cigarette*): Well, you are a lucky fellow! Why, I have met hundreds of good women. I never seem to meet any but good women. The world is perfectly packed with good women. To know them is a middle-class education.

LORD DARLINGTON: This woman has purity and innocence. She has everything we men have lost.

CECIL GRAHAM: My dear fellow, what on earth should we men do going about with purity and innocence? A carefully thought-out buttonhole is much more effective.

DUMBY: She doesn't really love you then?

LORD DARLINGTON: No, she does not!

DUMBY: I congratulate you, my dear fellow. In this world there are only two tragedies. One is not getting what one wants, and the other is getting it. The last is much the worst; the last is a real tragedy! But I am interested to hear she does not love you. How long could you love a woman who didn't love you, Cecil?

CECIL GRAHAM: A woman who didn't love me? Oh, all my life!

DUMBY: So could I. But it's so difficult to meet one.

LORD DARLINGTON: How can you be so conceited, Dumby?

DUMBY: I didn't say it as a matter of conceit. I said it as a matter of regret. I have been wildly, madly adored. I am sorry I have. It has been an immense nuisance. I should like to be allowed a little time to myself now and then.

LORD AUGUSTUS (*looking round*): Time to educate yourself, I suppose.

DUMBY: No, time to forget all I have learned. That is much more important, dear Tuppy.

LORD AUGUSTUS *moves uneasily in his chair.*

LORD DARLINGTON: What cynics you fellows are!

CECIL GRAHAM: What is a cynic? (*Sitting on the back of the sofa.*)

LORD DARLINGTON: A man who knows the price of everything and the value of nothing.

CECIL GRAHAM: And a sentimentalist, my dear Darlington, is a man who sees an absurd value in everything, and doesn't know the market price of any single thing.

LORD DARLINGTON: You always amuse me, Cecil. You talk as if you were a man of experience.

CECIL GRAHAM: I am. (*Moves up to front of fireplace.*)

LORD DARLINGTON: You are far too young!

CECIL GRAHAM: That is a great error. Experience is a question of instinct about life. I have got it. Tuppy hasn't. Experience is the name Tuppy gives to his mistakes. That is all.

LORD AUGUSTUS *looks round indignantly.*

DUMBY: Experience is the name every one gives to their mistakes.

CECIL GRAHAM (*standing with his back to the fireplace*): One shouldn't commit any. (*Sees* LADY WINDERMERE'S *fan on sofa.*)

DUMBY: Life would be very dull without them.

CECIL GRAHAM: Of course you are quite faithful to this woman you are in love with, Darlington, to this good woman?

LORD DARLINGTON: Cecil, if one really loves a woman, all other women in the world become absolutely meaningless to one. Love changes one – I am changed.

CECIL GRAHAM: Dear me! How very interesting! Tuppy, I want to talk to you.

LORD AUGUSTUS *takes no notice.*

DUMBY: It's no use talking to Tuppy. You might just as well talk to a brick wall.

CECIL GRAHAM: But I like talking to a brick wall – it's the only thing in the world that never contradicts me! Tuppy!

LORD AUGUSTUS: Well, what is it? What is it? (*Rising and going over to* CECIL GRAHAM.)

CECIL GRAHAM: Come over here. I want you particularly. (*Aside.*) Darlington has been moralising and talking about the purity of love, and that sort of thing, and he has got some woman in his rooms all the time.

LORD AUGUSTUS: No, really! Really!

CECIL GRAHAM (*in a low voice*): Yes, here is her fan. (*Points to the fan.*)

LORD AUGUSTUS (*chuckling*): By Jove! By Jove!

LORD WINDERMERE (*up by door*): I am really off now, Lord Darlington. I am sorry you are leaving England so soon. Pray call on us when you come back! My wife and I will be charmed to see you!

LORD DARLINGTON (*up stage with* LORD WINDERMERE): I am afraid I shall be away for many years. Good-night!

CECIL GRAHAM: Arthur!

LORD WINDERMERE: What?

CECIL GRAHAM: I want to speak to you for a moment. No, do come!

LORD WINDERMERE (*putting on his coat*): I can't – I'm off.

CECIL GRAHAM: It is something very particular. It will interest you enormously.

LORD WINDERMERE (*smiling*): It is some of your nonsense, Cecil.

CECIL GRAHAM: It isn't! It isn't really.

LORD AUGUSTUS (*going to him*): My dear fellow, you mustn't go yet. I have a lot to talk to you about. And Cecil has something to show you.

LORD WINDERMERE (*walking over*): Well, what is it?

CECIL GRAHAM: Darlington has got a woman here in his rooms. Here is her fan. Amusing, isn't it? (*A pause.*)

LORD WINDERMERE: Good God! (*Seizes the fan –* DUMBY *rises.*)

CECIL GRAHAM: What is the matter?

LORD WINDERMERE: Lord Darlington!

LORD DARLINGTON (*turning round*): Yes!

LORD WINDERMERE: What is my wife's fan doing here in your rooms? Hands off, Cecil. Don't touch me.

LORD DARLINGTON: Your wife's fan?

LORD WINDERMERE: Yes, here it is?

LORD DARLINGTON (*walking towards him*): I don't know!

LORD WINDERMERE: You must know. I demand an explanation. Don't hold me, you fool. (*To* CECIL GRAHAM.)

LORD DARLINGTON (*aside*): She is here after all!

LORD WINDERMERE: Speak, sir! Why is my wife's fan here? Answer me! By God! I'll search your rooms, and if my wife's here, I'll – (*Moves.*)

LORD DARLINGTON: You shall not search my rooms. You have no right to do so. I forbid you!

LORD WINDERMERE: You scoundrel! I'll not leave your room till I have searched every corner of it! What moves behind that curtain? (*Rushes forward towards the curtain C.*)

MRS. ERLYNNE (*enters behind R.*): Lord Windermere!

LORD WINDERMERE: Mrs. Erlynne!

Every one starts and turns round. LADY WINDERMERE *slips out from behind the curtain and glides from the room L.*

MRS. ERLYNNE: I am afraid I took your wife's fan in mistake for my own, when I was leaving your house to-night. I am so sorry. (*Takes fan from him.* LORD WINDERMERE *looks at her in contempt.* LORD DARLINGTON *in mingled astonishment and anger.* LORD AUGUSTUS *turns away. The other men smile at each other.*)

ACT DROP

ACT FOUR

SCENE: *Same as in Act One.*

LADY WINDERMERE (*lying on sofa*): How can I tell him? I can't tell him. It would kill me. I wonder what happened after I escaped from that horrible room. Perhaps she told them the true reason of her being there, and the real meaning of that – fatal fan of mine. Oh, if he knows – how can I look him in the face again? He would never forgive me. (*Touches bell.*) How securely one thinks one lives – out of reach of temptation, sin, folly. And then suddenly – Oh! Life is terrible. It rules us, we do not rule it.

Enter ROSALIE R.

ROSALIE: Did your ladyship ring for me?

LADY WINDERMERE: Yes. Have you found out at what time Lord Windermere came in last night?

ROSALIE: His lordship did not come in till five o'clock.

LADY WINDERMERE: Five o'clock? He knocked at my door this morning, didn't he?

ROSALIE: Yes, my lady – at half-past nine. I told him your ladyship was not awake yet.

LADY WINDERMERE: Did he say anything?

ROSALIE: Something about your ladyship's fan. I didn't quite catch what his lordship said. Has the fan been lost, my lady? I can't find it, and Parker says it was not left in any of the rooms. He has looked in all of them and on the terrace as well.

LADY WINDERMERE: It doesn't matter. Tell Parker not to trouble. That will do.

Exit ROSALIE.

LADY WINDERMERE (*rising*): She is sure to tell him. I can fancy a person doing a wonderful act of self-sacrifice, doing it spontaneously, recklessly, nobly – and afterwards finding out that it costs too much. Why should she hesitate between her ruin and mine? . . . How strange! I would have publicly disgraced her in my own house. She accepts public disgrace in the house of another to save me. . . . There is a bitter irony in things, a bitter irony in the way we talk of good and bad women. . . . Oh, what a lesson! And what a pity that in life we only get our lessons when they are of no use to us! For even if she doesn't tell, I must. Oh! The shame of it, the shame of it. To tell it is to live through it all again. Actions are the first tragedy in life, words are the second. Words are perhaps the worst. Words are merciless. . . . Oh! (*Starts as* LORD WINDERMERE *enters.*)

LORD WINDERMERE (*kisses her*): Margaret – how pale you look!

LADY WINDERMERE: I slept very badly.

LORD WINDERMERE (*sitting on sofa with her*): I am so sorry. I came in dreadfully late, and didn't like to wake you. You are crying, dear.

LADY WINDERMERE: Yes, I am crying, for I have something to tell you, Arthur.

LORD WINDERMERE: My dear child, you are not well. You've been doing too much. Let us go away to the country. You'll be all right at Selby. The season is almost over. There is no use staying on. Poor darling! We'll go away to-day, if you like. (*Rises.*) We can easily catch the 3.40. I'll send a wire to Fannen. (*Crosses and sits down at table to write a telegram.*)

LADY WINDERMERE: Yes; let us go away to-day. No; I can't go to-day, Arthur. There is some one I must see before I leave town – some one who has been kind to me.

LORD WINDERMERE (*rising and leaning over sofa*): Kind to you?

LADY WINDERMERE: Far more than that. (*Rises and goes to him.*) I will tell you, Arthur, but only love me, love me as you used to love me.

LORD WINDERMERE: Used to? You are not thinking of that wretched woman who came here last night? (*Coming round and sitting R. of her.*): You don't still imagine – no, you couldn't.

LADY WINDERMERE: I don't. I know now I was wrong and foolish.

LORD WINDERMERE: It was very good of you to receive her last night – but you are never to see her again.

LADY WINDERMERE: Why do you say that? (*A pause.*)

LORD WINDERMERE (*holding her hand*): Margaret, I thought Mrs. Erlynne was a woman more sinned against than sinning, as the phrase goes. I thought she wanted to be good, to get back into a place that she had lost by a moment's folly, to lead again a decent life. I believed what she told me – I was mistaken in her. She is bad – as bad as a woman can be.

LADY WINDERMERE: Arthur, Arthur, don't talk so bitterly about any woman. I don't think now that people can be divided into the good and the bad as though they were two separate races or creations. What are called good women may have terrible things in them, mad moods of recklessness, assertion, jealousy, sin. Bad women, as they are termed, may have in them sorrow, repentance, pity, sacrifice. And I don't think Mrs. Erlynne a bad woman – I know she's not.

LORD WINDERMERE: My dear child, the woman's impossible. No matter what harm she tries to do us, you must never see her again. She is inadmissible anywhere.

LADY WINDERMERE: But I want to see her. I want her to come here.

LORD WINDERMERE: Never!

LADY WINDERMERE: She came here once as *your* guest. She must come now as *mine*. That is but fair.

LORD WINDERMERE: She should never have come here.

LADY WINDERMERE (*rising*): It is too late, Arthur, to say that now. (*Moves away.*)

LORD WINDERMERE (*rising*): Margaret, if you knew where Mrs. Erlynne went last night, after she left this house, you would not sit in the same room with her. It was absolutely shameless, the whole thing.

LADY WINDERMERE: Arthur, I can't bear it any longer. I must tell you. Last night –

Enter PARKER *with a tray on which lie* LADY WINDERMERE'S *fan and a card.*

PARKER: Mrs. Erlynne has called to return your ladyship's fan which she took away by mistake last night. Mrs. Erlynne has written a message on the card.

LADY WINDERMERE: Oh, ask Mrs. Erlynne to be kind enough to come up. (*Reads card.*) Say I shall be very glad to see her.

Exit PARKER.

She wants to see me, Arthur.

LORD WINDERMERE (*takes card and looks at it*): Margaret, I *beg* you not to. Let me see her first, at any rate. She's a dangerous woman. She is the most dangerous woman I know. You don't realise what you're doing.

LADY WINDERMERE: It is right that I should see her.

LORD WINDERMERE: My child, you may be on the brink of a great sorrow. Don't go to meet it. It is absolutely necessary that I should see her before you do.

LADY WINDERMERE: Why should it be necessary?

Enter PARKER.

PARKER: Mrs. Erlynne.

Enter MRS. ERLYNNE. *Exit* PARKER.

MRS. ERLYNNE: How do you do, Lady Windermere? (*To* LORD WINDERMERE): How do you do? Do you know, Lady Windermere, I am so sorry about your fan. I can't imagine how I made such a silly mistake. Most stupid of me. And as I was driving in your direction, I thought I would take the opportunity of returning your property in person with many apologies for my carelessness, and of bidding you good-bye.

LADY WINDERMERE: Good-bye? (*Moves towards sofa with* MRS. ERLYNNE *and sits down beside her.*) Are you going away, then, Mrs. Erlynne?

MRS. ERLYNNE: Yes; I am going to live abroad again. The English climate doesn't suit me. My – heart is affected here, and that I don't like. I prefer living in the south. London is too full of fogs and – and serious people, Lord Windermere. Whether the fogs produce the serious people or whether the serious people produce the fogs, I don't know, but the whole thing rather gets on my nerves, and so I'm leaving this afternoon by the Club Train.

LADY WINDERMERE: This afternoon? But I wanted so much to come and see you.

MRS. ERLYNNE: How kind of you! But I am afraid I have to go.

LADY WINDERMERE: Shall I never see you again, Mrs. Erlynne?

MRS. ERLYNNE: I am afraid not. Our lives lie too far apart. But there is a little thing I would like you to do for me. I want a photograph of you, Lady Windermere – would you give me one? You don't know how gratified I should be.

LADY WINDERMERE: Oh, with pleasure. There is one on that table. I'll show it to you. (*Goes across to the table.*)

LORD WINDERMERE (*coming up to* MRS. ERLYNNE *and speaking in a low voice*): It is monstrous your intruding yourself here after your conduct last night.

MRS. ERLYNNE (*with an amused smile*): My dear Windermere, manners before morals!

LADY WINDERMERE (*returning*): I'm afraid it is very flattering – I am not so pretty as that. (*Showing photograph.*)

MRS. ERLYNNE: You are much prettier. But haven't you got one of yourself with your little boy?

LADY WINDERMERE: I have. Would you prefer one of those?

MRS. ERLYNNE: Yes.

LADY WINDERMERE: I'll go and get it for you, if you'll excuse me for a moment. I have one upstairs.

MRS. ERLYNNE: So sorry, Lady Windermere, to give you so much trouble.

LADY WINDERMERE (*moves to door R.*): No trouble at all, Mrs. Erlynne.

MRS. ERLYNNE: Thanks so much.

Exit LADY WINDERMERE *R.*

You seem rather out of temper this morning, Windermere. Why should you be? Margaret and I get on charmingly together.

LORD WINDERMERE: I can't bear to see you with her. Besides, you have not told me the truth, Mrs. Erlynne.

MRS. ERLYNNE: I have not told *her* the truth, you mean.

LORD WINDERMERE (*standing C.*): I sometimes wish you had. I should have been spared then the misery, the anxiety, the annoyance of the last six months. But rather than my wife should know – that the mother whom she was taught to consider as dead, the mother whom she has mourned as dead, is living – a divorced woman, going about under an assumed name, a bad woman preying upon life, as I know you now to be – rather than that, I was ready to supply you with money to pay bill after bill, extravagance after extravagance, to risk what occurred yesterday, the first quarrel I have ever had with my wife. You don't understand what that means to me. How could you? But I tell you that the only bitter words that ever came from those sweet lips of hers were on your account, and I hate to see you next her. You sully the innocence that is in her. (*Moves L.C.*) And then I used to think that with all your faults you were frank and honest. You are not.

MRS. ERLYNNE: Why do you say that?

LORD WINDERMERE: You made me get you an invitation to my wife's ball.

MRS. ERLYNNE: For my daughter's ball – yes.

LORD WINDERMERE: You came, and within an hour of your leaving the house you are found in a man's rooms – you are disgraced before every one. (*Goes up stage C.*)

MRS. ERLYNNE: Yes.

LORD WINDERMERE (*turning round on her*): Therefore I have a right to look upon you as what you are – a worthless, vicious woman. I have the right to tell you never to enter this house, never to attempt to come near my wife –

MRS. ERLYNNE (*coldly*): My daughter, you mean.

LORD WINDERMERE: You have no right to claim her as your daughter. You left her, abandoned her when she was but a child in the cradle, abandoned her for your lover, who abandoned you in turn.

MRS. ERLYNNE (*rising*): Do you count that to his credit, Lord Windermere – or to mine?

LORD WINDERMERE: To his, now that I know you.

MRS. ERLYNNE: Take care – you had better be careful.

LORD WINDERMERE: Oh, I am not going to mince words for you. I know you thoroughly.

MRS. ERLYNNE (*looking steadily at him*): I question that.

LORD WINDERMERE: I *do* know you. For twenty years of your life you lived without your child, without a thought of your child. One day you read in the papers that she had married a rich man. You saw your hideous chance. You knew that to spare her the ignominy of learning that a woman like you was her mother, I would endure anything. You began your blackmailing.

MRS. ERLYNNE (*shrugging her shoulders*): Don't use ugly words, Windermere. They are vulgar. I saw my chance, it is true, and took it.

LORD WINDERMERE: Yes, you took it – and spoiled it all last night by being found out.

MRS. ERLYNNE (*with a strange smile*): You are quite right, I spoiled it all last night.

LORD WINDERMERE: And as for your blunder in taking my wife's fan from here and then leaving it about in Darlington's rooms, it is unpardonable. I can't bear the sight of it now. I shall never let my wife use it again. The thing is soiled for me. You should have kept it and not brought it back.

MRS. ERLYNNE: I think I *shall* keep it. (*Goes up.*) It's extremely pretty. (*Takes up fan.*) I shall ask Margaret to give it to me.

LORD WINDERMERE: I hope my wife will give it to you.

MRS. ERLYNNE: Oh, I'm sure she will have no objection.

LORD WINDERMERE: I wish that at the same time she would give you a miniature she kisses every night before she prays. It's the miniature of a young innocent-looking girl with beautiful *dark* hair.

MRS. ERLYNNE: Ah, yes, I remember. How long ago that seems! (*Goes to sofa and sits down.*) It was done before I was married. Dark hair and an innocent expression were the fashion then, Windermere! (*A pause.*)

LORD WINDERMERE: What do you mean by coming here this morning? What is your object? (*Crossing L.C. and sitting.*)

MRS. ERLYNNE (*with a note of irony in her voice*): To bid good-bye to my dear daughter, of course.

> LORD WINDERMERE *bites his under lip in anger.* MRS. ERLYNNE *looks at him, and her voice and manner become serious. In her accents as she talks there is a note of deep tragedy. For a moment she reveals herself.*

Oh, don't imagine I am going to have a pathetic scene with her, weep on her neck and tell her who I am, and all that kind of thing. I have no ambition to play the part of a mother. Only once in my life have I known a mother's feelings. That was last night. They were terrible – they made me suffer – they made me suffer too much. For twenty years, as you say, I have lived childless

– I want to live childless still. (*Hiding her feelings with a trivial laugh.*) Besides, my dear Windermere, how on earth could I pose as a mother with a grown-up daughter? Margaret is twenty-one, and I have never admitted that I am more than twenty-nine, or thirty at the most. Twenty-nine when there are pink shades, thirty when there are not. So you see what difficulties it would involve. No, as far as I am concerned, let your wife cherish the memory of this dead, stainless mother. Why should I interfere with her illusions? I find it hard enough to keep my own. I lost one illusion last night. I thought I had no heart. I find I have, and a heart doesn't suit me, Windermere. Somehow it doesn't go with modern dress. It makes one look old. (*Takes up hand-mirror from table and looks into it.*) And it spoils one's career at critical moments.

LORD WINDERMERE: You fill me with horror – with absolute horror.

MRS. ERLYNNE (*rising*): I suppose, Windermere, you would like me to retire into a convent, or become a hospital nurse, or something of that kind, as people do in silly modern novels. That is stupid of you, Arthur; in real life we don't do such things – not as long as we have any good looks left, at any rate. No – what consoles one nowadays is not repentance, but pleasure. Repentance is quite out of date. And besides, if a woman really repents, she has to go to a bad dressmaker, otherwise no one believes in her. And nothing in the world would induce me to do that. No; I am going to pass entirely out of your two lives. My coming into them has been a mistake – I discovered that last night.

LORD WINDERMERE: A fatal mistake.

MRS. ERLYNNE (*smiling*): Almost fatal.

LORD WINDERMERE: I am sorry now I did not tell my wife the whole thing at once.

MRS. ERLYNNE: I regret my bad actions. You regret your good ones – that is the difference between us.

LORD WINDERMERE: I don't trust you. I *will* tell my wife. It's better for her to know, and from me. It will cause her infinite pain – it will humiliate her terribly, but it's right that she should know.

MRS. ERLYNNE: You propose to tell her?

LORD WINDERMERE: I am going to tell her.

MRS. ERLYNNE (*going up to him*): If you do, I will make my name so infamous that it will mar every moment of her life. It will ruin her, and make her wretched. If you dare to tell her, there is no depth of degradation I will not sink to, no pit of shame I will not enter. You shall not tell her – I forbid you.

LORD WINDERMERE: Why?

MRS. ERLYNNE (*after a pause*): If I said to you that I cared for her, perhaps loved her even – you would sneer at me, wouldn't you?

LORD WINDERMERE: I should feel it was not true. A mother's love means devotion, unselfishness, sacrifice. What could you know of such things?

MRS. ERLYNNE: You are right. What could I know of such things? Don't let us talk any more about it – as for telling my daughter who I am, that I do not allow. It is my secret, it is not yours. If I make up my mind to tell her, and

I think I will, I shall tell her before I leave the house – if not, I shall never tell her.

LORD WINDERMERE (*angrily*): Then let me beg of you to leave our house at once. I will make your excuses to Margaret.

Enter LADY WINDERMERE *R. She goes over to* MRS. ERLYNNE *with the photograph in her hand.* LORD WINDERMERE *moves to back of sofa, and anxiously watches* MRS. ERLYNNE *as the scene progresses.*

LADY WINDERMERE: I am so sorry, Mrs. Erlynne, to have kept you waiting. I couldn't find the photograph anywhere. At last I discovered it in my husband's dressing-room – he had stolen it.

MRS. ERLYNNE (*takes the photograph from her and looks at it*): I am not surprised – it is charming. (*Goes over to sofa with* LADY WINDERMERE, *and sits down beside her. Looks again at the photograph.*) And so that is your little boy! What is he called?

LADY WINDERMERE: Gerard, after my dear father.

MRS. ERLYNNE (*laying the photograph down*): Really?

LADY WINDERMERE: Yes. It if had been a girl, I would have called it after my mother. My mother had the same name as myself, Margaret.

MRS. ERLYNNE: My name is Margaret too.

LADY WINDERMERE: Indeed!

MRS. ERLYNNE: Yes. (*Pause.*) You are devoted to your mother's memory, Lady Windermere, your husband tells me.

LADY WINDERMERE: We all have ideals in life. At least we all should have. Mine is my mother.

MRS. ERLYNNE: Ideals are dangerous things. Realities are better. They wound, but they're better.

LADY WINDERMERE (*shaking her head*): If I lost my ideals, I should lose everything.

MRS. ERLYNNE: Everything?

LADY WINDERMERE: Yes. (*Pause.*)

MRS. ERLYNNE: Did your father often speak to you of your mother?

LADY WINDERMERE: No, it gave him too much pain. He told me how my mother had died a few months after I was born. His eyes filled with tears as he spoke. Then he begged me never to mention her name to him again. It made him suffer even to hear it. My father – my father really died of a broken heart. His was the most ruined life I know.

MRS. ERLYNNE (*rising*): I am afraid I must go now, Lady Windermere.

LADY WINDERMERE (*rising*): Oh no, don't.

MRS. ERLYNNE: I think I had better. My carriage must have come back by this time. I sent it to Lady Jedburgh's with a note.

LADY WINDERMERE: Arthur, would you mind seeing if Mrs. Erlynne's carriage has come back?

MRS. ERLYNNE: Pray don't trouble, Lord Windermere.

LADY WINDERMERE: Yes, Arthur, do go, please.

LORD WINDERMERE *hesitates for a moment and looks at* MRS. ERLYNNE. *She remains quite impassive. He leaves the room.*

(*To* MRS. ERLYNNE): Oh! What am I to say to you? You saved me last night. (*Goes towards her.*)

MRS. ERLYNNE: Hush – don't speak of it.

LADY WINDERMERE: I must speak of it. I can't let you think that I am going to accept this sacrifice. I am not. It is too great. I am going to tell my husband everything. It is my duty.

MRS. ERLYNNE: It is not your duty – at least you have duties to others besides him. You say you owe me something?

LADY WINDERMERE: I owe you everything.

MRS. ERLYNNE: Then pay your debt by silence. That is the only way in which it can be paid. Don't spoil the one good thing I have done in my life by telling it to any one. Promise me that what passed last night will remain a secret between us. You must not bring misery into your husband's life. Why spoil his love? You must not spoil it. Love is easily killed. Oh! How easily love is killed. Pledge me your word, Lady Windermere, that you will *never* tell him. I insist upon it.

LADY WINDERMERE (*with bowed head*): It is your will, not mine.

MRS. ERLYNNE: Yes, it is my will. And never forget your child – I like to think of you as a mother. I like you to think of yourself as one.

LADY WINDERMERE (*looking up*): I always will now. Only once in my life I have forgotten my own mother – that was last night. Oh, if I had remembered her I should not have been so foolish, so wicked.

MRS. ERLYNNE (*with a slight shudder*): Hush, last night is quite over.

Enter LORD WINDERMERE.

LORD WINDERMERE: Your carriage has not come back yet, Mrs. Erlynne.

MRS. ERLYNNE: It makes no matter. I'll take a hansom. There is nothing in the world so respectable as a good Shrewsbury and Talbot. And now, dear Lady Windermere, I am afraid it is really good-bye. (*Moves up C.*) Oh, I remember. You'll think me absurd, but do you know I've taken a great fancy to this fan that I was silly enough to run away with last night from your ball. Now, I wonder would you give it to me? Lord Windermere says you may. I know it is his present.

LADY WINDERMERE: Oh, certainly, if it will give you any pleasure. But it has my name on it. It has 'Margaret' on it.

MRS. ERLYNNE: But we have the same Christian name.

LADY WINDERMERE: Oh, I forgot. Of course, do have it. What a wonderful chance our names being the same!

MRS. ERLYNNE: Quite wonderful. Thanks – it will always remind me of you. (*Shakes hands with her.*)

Enter PARKER.

PARKER: Lord Augustus Lorton. Mrs. Erlynne's carriage has come.

Enter LORD AUGUSTUS.

LORD AUGUSTUS: Good-morning, dear boy. Good-morning, Lady Windermere. (*Sees* MRS. ERLYNNE.) Mrs. Erlynne!

MRS. ERLYNNE: How do you do, Lord Augustus? Are you quite well this morning?

LORD AUGUSTUS (*coldly*): Quite well, thank you, Mrs. Erlynne.

MRS. ERLYNNE: You don't look at all well, Lord Augustus. You stop up too late – it is so bad for you. You really should take more care of yourself. Good-bye, Lord Windermere. (*Goes towards door with a bow to* LORD AUGUSTUS. *Suddenly smiles and looks back at him.*) Lord Augustus! Won't you see me to my carriage? You might carry the fan.

LORD WINDERMERE: Allow me!

MRS. ERLYNNE: No; I want Lord Augustus. I have a special message for the dear Duchess. Won't you carry the fan, Lord Augustus?

LORD AUGUSTUS: If you really desire it, Mrs. Erlynne.

MRS. ERLYNNE (*laughing*): Of course I do. You'll carry it so gracefully. You would carry off anything gracefully, dear Lord Augustus. (*When she reaches the door she looks back for a moment at* LADY WINDERMERE. *Their eyes meet. Then she turns, and exit C. followed by* LORD AUGUSTUS.)

LADY WINDERMERE: You will never speak against Mrs. Erlynne again, Arthur, will you?

LORD WINDERMERE (*gravely*): She is better than one thought her.

LADY WINDERMERE: She is better than I am.

LORD WINDERMERE (*smiling as he strokes her hair*): Child, you and she belong to different worlds. Into your world evil has never entered.

LADY WINDERMERE: Don't say that, Arthur. There is the same world for all of us, and good and evil, sin and innocence, go through it hand in hand. To shut one's eyes to half of life that one may live securely is as though one blinded oneself that one might walk with more safety in a land of pit and precipice.

LORD WINDERMERE (*moves down with her*): Darling, why do you say that?

LADY WINDERMERE (*sits on sofa*): Because I, who had shut my eyes to life, came to the brink. And one who had separated us –

LORD WINDERMERE: We were never separated.

LADY WINDERMERE: We never must be again. O Arthur, don't love me less, and I will trust you more. I will trust you absolutely. Let us go to Selby. In the Rose Garden at Selby the roses are white and red.

Enter LORD AUGUSTUS *C.*

LORD AUGUSTUS: Arthur, she has explained everything!

LADY WINDERMERE *looks horribly frightened at this.* LORD WINDER-

MERE *starts*. LORD AUGUSTUS *takes* WINDERMERE *by the arm and brings him to front of stage. He talks rapidly and in a low voice.* LADY WINDER-MERE *stands watching them in terror.*

My dear fellow, she has explained every demmed thing. We all wronged her immensely. It was entirely for my sake she went to Darlington's rooms. Called first at the Club – fact is, wanted to put me out of suspense – and being told I had gone on – followed – naturally frightened when she heard a lot of us coming in – retired to another room – I assure you, most gratifying to me, the whole thing. We all behaved brutally to her. She is just the woman for me. Suits me down to the ground. All the conditions she makes are that we live entirely out of England. A very good thing too. Demmed clubs, demmed climate, demmed cooks, demmed everything. Sick of it all!

LADY WINDERMERE (*frightened*): Has Mrs. Erlynne –?

LORD AUGUSTUS (*advancing towards her with a low bow*): Yes, Lady Windermere – Mrs. Erlynne has done me the honour of accepting my hand.

LORD WINDERMERE: Well, you are certainly marrying a very clever woman!

LADY WINDERMERE (*taking her husband's hand*): Ah, you're marrying a very good woman!

CURTAIN

A WOMAN OF NO IMPORTANCE

The persons of the play

LORD ILLINGWORTH
SIR JOHN PONTEFRACT
LORD ALFRED RUFFORD
MR. KELVIL, M.P.
THE VEN. ARCHDEACON
  DAUBENY, D.D.
GERALD ARBUTHNOT
FARQUHAR, Butler

FRANCIS, Footman
LADY HUNSTANTON
LADY CAROLINE PONTEFRACT
LADY STUTFIELD
MRS. ALLONBY
MISS HESTER WORSLEY
ALICE, Maid
MRS. ARBUTHNOT

ACT ONE

SCENE: *Lawn in front of the terrace at Hunstanton Chase. The action of the play takes place within twenty-four hours.* TIME: *The present.*

SIR JOHN *and* LADY CAROLINE PONTEFRACT, MISS WORSELY, *on chairs under large yew tree.*

LADY CAROLINE: I believe this is the first English country house you have stayed at, Miss Worsley?

HESTER: Yes, Lady Caroline.

LADY CAROLINE: You have no country houses, I am told, in America?

HESTER: We have not many.

LADY CAROLINE: Have you any country? What we should call country?

HESTER (*smiling*): We have the largest country in the world, Lady Caroline. They used to tell us at school that some of our states are as big as France and England put together.

LADY CAROLINE: Ah! You must find it very draughty, I should fancy. (*To* SIR JOHN): John, you should have your muffler. What is the use of my always knitting mufflers for you if you won't wear them?

SIR JOHN: I am quite warm, Caroline, I assure you.

LADY CAROLINE: I think not, John. Well, you couldn't come to a more charming place than this, Miss Worsley, though the house is excessively damp, quite unpardonably damp, and dear Lady Hunstanton is sometimes a little lax about the people she asks down here. (*To* SIR JOHN): Jane mixes too much. Lord Illingworth, of course, is a man of high distinction. It is a privilege to meet him. And that member of Parliament, Mr. Kettle –

SIR JOHN: Kelvil, my love, Kelvil.

LADY CAROLINE: He must be quite respectable. One has never heard his name before in the whole course of one's life, which speaks volumes for a man, nowadays. But Mrs. Allonby is hardly a very suitable person.

HESTER: I dislike Mrs. Allonby. I dislike her more than I can say.

LADY CAROLINE: I am not sure, Miss Worsley, that foreigners like yourself should cultivate likes or dislikes about the people they are invited to meet. Mrs. Allonby is very well born. She is a niece of Lord Brancaster's. It is said, of course, that she ran away twice before she was married. But you know how unfair people often are. I myself don't believe she ran away more than once.

HESTER: Mr. Arbuthnot is very charming.

LADY CAROLINE: Ah, yes! The young man who has a post in a bank. Lady Hunstanton is most kind in asking him here, and Lord Illingworth seems to have taken quite a fancy to him. I am not sure, however, that Jane is right in taking him out of his position. In my young days, Miss Worsley, one never met any one in society who worked for their living. It was not considered the thing.

HESTER: In America those are the people we respect most.

LADY CAROLINE: I have no doubt of it.

HESTER: Mr. Arbuthnot has a beautiful nature! He is so simple, so sincere. He has one of the most beautiful natures I have ever come across. It is a privilege to meet *him*.

LADY CAROLINE: It is not customary in England, Miss Worsley, for a young lady to speak with such enthusiasm of any person of the opposite sex. English women conceal their feelings till after they are married. They show them then.

HESTER: Do you, in England, allow no friendship to exist between a young man and a young girl?

Enter LADY HUNSTANTON, *followed by* FOOTMAN *with shawls and a cushion.*

LADY CAROLINE: We think it very inadvisable. Jane, I was just saying what a pleasant party you have asked us to meet. You have a wonderful power of selection. It is quite a gift.

LADY HUNSTANTON: Dear Caroline, how kind of you! I think we all do fit in very nicely together. And I hope our charming American visitor will carry back pleasant recollections of our English country life. (*To Footman*): The cushion, there, Francis. And my shawl. The Shetland. Get the Shetland.

Exit Footman for shawl. Enter GERALD ARBUTHNOT.

GERALD: Lady Hunstanton, I have such good news to tell you. Lord Illingworth has just offered to make me his secretary.

LADY HUNSTANTON: His secretary? That is good news indeed, Gerald. It means a very brilliant future in store for you. Your dear mother will be delighted. I really must try and induce her to come up here to-night. Do you think she would, Gerald? I know how difficult it is to get her to go anywhere.

GERALD: Oh! I am sure she would, Lady Hunstanton, if she knew Lord

Illingworth had made me such an offer.

Enter Footman with shawl.

LADY HUNSTANTON: I will write and tell her about it, and ask her to come up and meet him. (*To Footman*): Just wait, Francis. (*Writes letter.*)

LADY CAROLINE: That is a very wonderful opening for so young a man as you are, Mr. Arbuthnot.

GERALD: It is indeed, Lady Caroline. I trust I shall be able to show myself worthy of it.

LADY CAROLINE: I trust so.

GERALD (*to* HESTER): *You* have not congratulated me yet, Miss Worsley.

HESTER: Are you very pleased about it?

GERALD: Of course I am. It means everything to me – things that were out of the reach of hope before may be within hope's reach now.

HESTER: Nothing should be out of the reach of hope. Life is a hope.

LADY HUNSTANTON: I fancy, Caroline, that Diplomacy is what Lord Illingworth is aiming at. I heard that he was offered Vienna. But that may not be true.

LADY CAROLINE: I don't think that England should be represented abroad by an unmarried man, Jane. It might lead to complications.

LADY HUNSTANTON: You are too nervous, Caroline. Believe me, you are too nervous. Besides, Lord Illingworth may marry any day. I was in hopes he would have married Lady Kelso. But I believe he said her family was too large. Or was it her feet? I forget which. I regret it very much. She was made to be an ambassador's wife.

LADY CAROLINE: She certainly has a wonderful faculty of remembering people's names, and forgetting their faces.

LADY HUNSTANTON: Well, that is very natural, Caroline, is it not? (*To Footman*): Tell Henry to wait for an answer. I have written a line to your dear mother, Gerald, to tell her your good news, and to say she really must come to dinner.

Exit Footman.

GERALD: That is awfully kind of you, Lady Hunstanton. (*To* HESTER): Will you come for a stroll, Miss Worsley?

HESTER: With pleasure. (*Exit with* GERALD.)

LADY HUNSTANTON: I am very much gratified at Gerald Arbuthnot's good fortune. He is quite a *protégé* of mine. And I am particularly pleased that Lord Illingworth should have made the offer of his own accord without my suggesting anything. Nobody likes to be asked favours. I remember poor Charlotte Pagden making herself quite unpopular one season, because she had a French governess she wanted to recommend to every one.

LADY CAROLINE: I saw the governess, Jane. Lady Pagden sent her to me. It was before Eleanor came out. She was far too good-looking to be in any respectable household. I don't wonder Lady Pagden was so anxious to get rid of her.

LADY HUNSTANTON: Ah, that explains it.

LADY CAROLINE: John, the grass is too damp for you. You had better go and put on your overshoes at once.

SIR JOHN: I am quite comfortable, Caroline, I assure you.

LADY CAROLINE: You must allow me to be the best judge of that, John. Pray do as I tell you.

SIR JOHN *gets up and goes off.*

LADY HUNSTANTON: You spoil him, Caroline, you do indeed!

Enter MRS. ALLONBY *and* LADY STUTFIELD.

(*To* MRS. ALLONBY): Well, dear, I hope you like the park. It is said to be well timbered.

MRS. ALLONBY: The trees are wonderful, Lady Hunstanton.

LADY STUTFIELD: Quite, quite wonderful.

MRS. ALLONBY: But somehow, I feel sure that if I lived in the country for six months, I should become so unsophisticated that no one would take the slightest notice of me.

LADY HUNSTANTON: I assure you, dear, that the country has not that effect at all. Why, it was from Melthorpe, which is only two miles from here, that Lady Belton eloped with Lord Fethersdale. I remember the occurrence perfectly. Poor Lord Belton died three days afterwards of joy, or gout. I forget which. We had a large party staying here at the time, so we were all very much interested in the whole affair.

MRS. ALLONBY: I think to elope is cowardly. It's running away from danger. And danger has become so rare in modern life.

LADY CAROLINE: As far as I can make out, the young women of the present day seem to make it the sole object of their lives to be always playing with fire.

MRS. ALLONBY: The one advantage of playing with fire, Lady Caroline, is that one never gets even singed. It is the people who don't know how to play with it who get burned up.

LADY STUTFIELD: Yes; I see that. It is very, very helpful.

LADY HUNSTANTON: I don't know how the world would get on with such a theory as that, dear Mrs. Allonby.

LADY STUTFIELD: Ah! The world was made for men and not for women.

MRS. ALLONBY: Oh, don't say that, Lady Stutfield. We have a much better time than they have. There are far more things forbidden to us than are forbidden to them.

LADY STUTFIELD: Yes; that is quite, quite true. I had not thought of that.

Enter SIR JOHN *and* MR. KELVIL.

LADY HUNSTANTON: Well, Mr. Kelvil, have you got through your work?

KELVIL: I have finished my writing for the day, Lady Hunstanton. It has been an arduous task. The demands on the time of a public man are very heavy nowadays, very heavy indeed. And I don't think they meet with adequate recognition.

LADY CAROLINE: John, have you got your overshoes on?

SIR JOHN: Yes, my love.

LADY CAROLINE: I think you had better come over here, John. It is more sheltered.

SIR JOHN: I am quite comfortable, Caroline.

LADY CAROLINE: I think not, John. You had better sit beside me.

SIR JOHN *rises and goes across.*

LADY STUTFIELD: And what have you been writing about this morning, Mr. Kelvil?

KELVIL: On the usual subject, Lady Stutfield. On Purity.

LADY STUTFIELD: That must be such a very, very interesting thing to write about.

KELVIL: It is the one subject of really national importance, nowadays, Lady Stutfield. I purpose addressing my constituents on the question before Parliament meets. I find that the poorer classes of this country display a marked desire for a higher ethical standard.

LADY STUTFIELD: How quite, quite nice of them.

LADY CAROLINE: Are you in favour of women taking part in politics, Mr. Kettle?

SIR JOHN: Kelvil, my love, Kelvil.

KELVIL: The growing influence of women is the one reassuring thing in our political life, Lady Caroline. Women are always on the side of morality, public and private.

LADY STUTFIELD: It is so very, very gratifying to hear you say that.

LADY HUNSTANTON: Ah, yes! The moral qualities in women – that is the important thing. I am afraid, Caroline, that dear Lord Illingworth doesn't value the moral qualities in women as much as he should.

Enter LORD ILLINGWORTH.

LADY STUTFIELD: The world says that Lord Illingworth is very, very wicked.

LORD ILLINGWORTH: But what world says that, Lady Stutfield? It must be the next world. This world and I are on excellent terms. (*Sits down beside* MRS. ALLONBY.)

LADY STUTFIELD: Every one *I* know says you are very, very wicked.

LORD ILLINGWORTH: It is perfectly monstrous the way people go about, nowadays, saying things against one behind one's back that are absolutely and entirely true.

LADY HUNSTANTON: Dear Lord Illingworth is quite hopeless, Lady Stutfield. I have given up trying to reform him. It would take a Public Company with a Board of Directors and a paid Secretary to do that. But you have the secretary already, Lord Illingworth, haven't you? Gerald Arbuthnot has told us of his good fortune; it is really most kind of you.

LORD ILLINGWORTH: Oh, don't say that, Lady Hunstanton. Kind is a dreadful word. I took a great fancy to young Arbuthnot the moment I met him, and he'll be of considerable use to me in something I am foolish enough to think of doing.

LADY HUNSTANTON: He is an admirable young man. And his mother is one of my dearest friends. He has just gone for a walk with our pretty American. She is very pretty, is she not?

LADY CAROLINE: Far too pretty. These American girls carry off all the good matches. Why can't they stay in their own country? They are always telling us it is the Paradise of women.

LORD ILLINGWORTH: It is, Lady Caroline. That is why, like Eve, they are so extremely anxious to get out of it.

LADY CAROLINE: Who are Miss Worsley's parents?

LORD ILLINGWORTH: American women are wonderfully clever in concealing their parents.

LADY HUNSTANTON: My dear Lord Illingworth, what do you mean? Miss Worsley, Caroline, is an orphan. Her father was a very wealthy millionaire or philanthropist, or both, I believe, who entertained my son quite hospitably, when he visited Boston. I don't know how he made his money, originally.

KELVIL: I fancy in American dry goods.

LADY HUNSTANTON: What are American dry goods?

LORD ILLINGWORTH: American novels.

LADY HUNSTANTON: How very singular! . . . Well, from whatever source her large fortune came, I have a great esteem for Miss Worsley. She dresses exceedingly well. All Americans do dress well. They get their clothes in Paris.

MRS. ALLONBY: They say, Lady Hunstanton, that when good Americans die they go to Paris.

LADY HUNSTANTON: Indeed? And when bad Americans die, where do they go to?

LORD ILLINGWORTH: Oh, they go to America.

KELVIL: I am afraid you don't appreciate America, Lord Illingworth. It is a very remarkable country, especially considering its youth.

LORD ILLINGWORTH: The youth of America is their oldest tradition. It has been going on now for three hundred years. To hear them talk one would imagine they were in their first childhood. As far as civilisation goes they are in their second.

KELVIL: There is undoubtedly a great deal of corruption in American politics. I suppose you allude to that?

LORD ILLINGWORTH: I wonder.

LADY HUNSTANTON: Politics are in a sad way, everywhere, I am told. They certainly are in England. Dear Mr. Cardew is ruining the country. I wonder Mrs. Cardew allows him. I am sure, Lord Illingworth, you don't think that uneducated people should be allowed to have votes?

LORD ILLINGWORTH: I think they are the only people who should.

KELVIL: Do you take no side then in modern politics, Lord Illingworth?

LORD ILLINGWORTH: One should never take sides in anything, Mr. Kelvil. Taking sides is the beginning of sincerity, and earnestness follows shortly afterwards, and the human being becomes a bore. However, the House of Commons really does very little harm. You can't make people good by Act of Parliament – that is something.

KELVIL: You cannot deny that the House of Commons has always shown great sympathy with the sufferings of the poor.

LORD ILLINGWORTH: That is its special vice. That is the special vice of the age. One should sympathise with the joy, the beauty, the colour of life. The less said about life's sores the better, Mr. Kelvil.

KELVIL: Still our East End is a very important problem.

LORD ILLINGWORTH: Quite so. It is the problem of slavery. And we are trying to solve it by amusing the slaves.

LADY HUNSTANTON: Certainly, a great deal may be done by means of cheap entertainments, as you say, Lord Illingworth. Dear Dr. Daubeny, our rector here, provides, with the assistance of his curates, really admirable recreations for the poor during the winter. And much good may be done by means of a magic lantern, or a missionary, or some popular amusement of that kind.

LADY CAROLINE: I am not at all in favour of amusements for the poor, Jane. Blankets and coals are sufficient. There is too much love of pleasure amongst the upper classes as it is. Health is what we want in modern life. The tone is not healthy, not healthy at all.

KELVIL: You are quite right, Lady Caroline.

LADY CAROLINE: I believe I am usually right.

MRS. ALLONBY: Horrid word 'health.'

LORD ILLINGWORTH: Silliest word in our language, and one knows so well the popular idea of health. The English country gentleman galloping after a fox – the unspeakable in full pursuit of the uneatable.

KELVIL: May I ask, Lord Illingworth, if you regard the House of Lords as a better institution than the House of Commons?

LORD ILLINGWORTH: A much better institution, of course. We in the House of Lords are never in touch with public opinion. That makes us a civilised body.

KELVIL: Are you serious in putting forward such a view?

LORD ILLINGWORTH: Quite serious, Mr. Kelvil. (*To* MRS. ALLONBY): Vulgar habit that is people have nowadays of asking one, after one has given them an idea, whether one is serious or not. Nothing is serious except passion. The intellect is not a serious thing, and never has been. It is an instrument on which one plays, that is all. The only serious form of intellect I know is the British intellect. And on the British intellect the illiterates play the drum.

LADY HUNSTANTON: What are you saying, Lord Illingworth, about the drum?

LORD ILLINGWORTH: I was merely talking to Mrs. Allonby about the leading articles in the London newspapers.

LADY HUNSTANTON: But do you believe all that is written in the newspapers?

LORD ILLINGWORTH: I do. Nowadays it is only the unreadable that occurs. (*Rises with* MRS. ALLONBY.)

LADY HUNSTANTON: Are you going, Mrs. Allonby?

MRS. ALLONBY: Just as far as the conservatory. Lord Illingworth told me this morning that there was an orchid there as beautiful as the seven deadly sins.

LADY HUNSTANTON: My dear, I hope there is nothing of the kind. I will certainly speak to the gardener.

Exit MRS. ALLONBY *and* LORD ILLINGWORTH.

LADY CAROLINE: Remarkable type, Mrs. Allonby.

LADY HUNSTANTON: She lets her clever tongue run away with her sometimes.

LADY CAROLINE: Is that the only thing, Jane, Mrs. Allonby allows to run away with her?

LADY HUNSTANTON: I hope so, Caroline, I am sure.

Enter LORD ALFRED.

Dear Lord Alfred, do join us.

LORD ALFRED *sits down beside* LADY STUTFIELD.

LADY CAROLINE: You believe good of every one, Jane. It is a great fault.

LADY STUTFIELD: Do you really, really think, Lady Caroline, that one should believe evil of every one?

LADY CAROLINE: I think it is much safer to do so, Lady Stutfield. Until, of course, people are found out to be good. But that requires a great deal of investigation nowadays.

LADY STUTFIELD: But there is so much unkind scandal in modern life.

LADY CAROLINE: Lord Illingworth remarked to me last night at dinner that the basis of every scandal is an absolutely immoral certainty.

KELVIL: Lord Illingworth is, of course, a very brilliant man, but he seems to me to be lacking in that fine faith in the nobility and purity of life which is so important in this century.

LADY STUTFIELD: Yes, quite, quite important, is it not?

KELVIL: He gives me the impression of a man who does not appreciate the beauty of our English home-life. I would say that he was tainted with foreign ideas on the subject.

LADY STUTFIELD: There is nothing, nothing like the beauty of home-life, is there?

KELVIL: It is the mainstay of our moral system in England, Lady Stutfield. Without it we would become like our neighbours.

LADY STUTFIELD: That would be so, so sad, would it not?

KELVIL: I am afraid, too, that Lord Illingworth regards woman simply as a toy. Now, I have never regarded woman as a toy. Woman is the intellectual helpmeet of man in public as in private life. Without her we should forget the true ideals. (*Sits down beside* LADY STUTFIELD.)

LADY STUTFIELD: I am so very, very glad to hear you say that.

LADY CAROLINE: You are a married man, Mr. Kettle?

SIR JOHN: Kelvil, dear, Kelvil.

KELVIL: I am married, Lady Caroline.

LADY CAROLINE: Family?

KELVIL: Yes.

LADY CAROLINE: How many?

KELVIL: Eight.

LADY STUTFIELD *turns her attention to* LORD ALFRED.

LADY CAROLINE: Mrs. Kettle and the children are, I suppose, at the sea-side?

SIR JOHN *shrugs his shoulders*.

KELVIL: My wife is at the seaside with the children, Lady Caroline.

LADY CAROLINE: You will join them later on, no doubt?

KELVIL: If my public engagements permit me.

LADY CAROLINE: Your public life must be a great source of gratification to Mrs. Kettle.

SIR JOHN: Kelvil, my love, Kelvil.

LADY STUTFIELD (*to* LORD ALFRED): How very, very charming those gold-tipped cigarettes of yours are, Lord Alfred.

LORD ALFRED: They are awfully expensive. I can only afford them when I'm in debt.

LADY STUTFIELD: It must be terribly, terribly distressing to be in debt.

LORD ALFRED: One must have some occupation nowadays. If I hadn't my debts I shouldn't have anything to think about. All the chaps I know are in debt.

LADY STUTFIELD: But don't the people to whom you owe the money give you a great, great deal of annoyance?

Enter Footman.

LORD ALFRED: Oh, no, they write; I don't.

LADY STUTFIELD: How very, very strange.

LADY HUNSTANTON: Ah, here is a letter, Caroline, from dear Mrs. Arbuthnot. She won't dine. I am so sorry. But she will come in the evening. I am very pleased, indeed. She is one of the sweetest of women. Writes a beautiful hand, too, so large, so firm. (*Hands letter to* LADY CAROLINE.)

LADY CAROLINE (*looking at it*): A little lacking in femininity, Jane. Femininity is the quality I admire most in women.

LADY HUNSTANTON (*taking back letter and leaving it on table*): Oh! She is very feminine, Caroline, and so good, too. You should hear what the Archdeacon says of her. He regards her as his right hand in the parish. (*Footman speaks to her.*) In the Yellow Drawing-room. Shall we all go in? Lady Stutfield, shall we go in to tea?

LADY STUTFIELD: With pleasure, Lady Hunstanton.

They rise and proceed to go off. SIR JOHN *offers to carry* LADY STUT-FIELD'S *cloak.*

LADY CAROLINE: John! If you would allow your nephew to look after Lady Stutfield's cloak, you might help me with my work-basket.

Enter LORD ILLINGWORTH *and* MRS. ALLONBY.

SIR JOHN: Certainly, my love.

Exeunt.

MRS. ALLONBY: Curious thing, plain women are always jealous of their husbands, beautiful women never are!

LORD ILLINGWORTH: Beautiful women never have time. They are always so occupied in being jealous of other people's husbands.

MRS. ALLONBY: I should have thought Lady Caroline would have grown tired of conjugal anxiety by this time! Sir John is her fourth!

LORD ILLINGWORTH: So much marriage is certainly not becoming. Twenty years of romance make a woman look like a ruin; but twenty years of marriage make her something like a public building.

MRS. ALLONBY: Twenty years of romance! Is there such a thing?

LORD ILLINGWORTH: Not in our day. Women have become too brilliant. Nothing spoils a romance so much as a sense of humour in the woman.

MRS. ALLONBY: Or the want of it in the man.

LORD ILLINGWORTH: You are quite right. In a Temple every one should be serious, except the thing that is worshipped.

MRS. ALLONBY: And that should be man?

LORD ILLINGWORTH: Women kneel so gracefully; men don't.

MRS. ALLONBY: You are thinking of Lady Stutfield!

LORD ILLINGWORTH: I assure you I have not thought of Lady Stutfield for the last quarter of an hour.

MRS. ALLONBY: Is she such a mystery?

LORD ILLINGWORTH: She is more than a mystery – she is a mood.

MRS. ALLONBY: Moods don't last.

LORD ILLINGWORTH: It is their chief charm.

Enter HESTER *and* GERALD.

GERALD: Lord Illingworth, every one has been congratulating me, Lady Hunstanton and Lady Caroline, and . . . every one. I hope I shall make a good secretary.

LORD ILLINGWORTH: You will be the pattern secretary, Gerald. (*Talks to him.*)

MRS. ALLONBY: You enjoy country life, Miss Worsley?

HESTER: Very much, indeed.

MRS. ALLONBY: Don't find yourself longing for a London dinner-party?

HESTER: I dislike London dinner-parties.

MRS. ALLONBY: I adore them. The clever people never listen, and the stupid people never talk.

HESTER: I think the stupid people talk a great deal.

MRS. ALLONBY: Ah, I never listen!

LORD ILLINGWORTH: My dear boy, if I didn't like you I wouldn't have made you the offer. It is because I like you so much that I want to have you with me.

Exit HESTER *with* GERALD.

Charming fellow, Gerald Arbuthnot!

MRS. ALLONBY: He is very nice; very nice indeed. But I can't stand the American young lady.

LORD ILLINGWORTH: Why?

MRS. ALLONBY: She told me yesterday, and in quite a loud voice too, that she was only eighteen. It was most annoying.

LORD ILLINGWORTH: One should never trust a woman who tells one her real age. A woman who would tell one that, would tell one anything.

MRS. ALLONBY: She is a Puritan besides –

LORD ILLINGWORTH: Ah, that is inexcusable. I don't mind plain women being Puritans. It is the only excuse they have for being plain. But she is decidedly pretty. I admire her immensely. (*Looks steadfastly at* MRS. ALLONBY.)

MRS. ALLONBY: What a thoroughly bad man you must be!

LORD ILLINGWORTH: What do you call a bad man?

MRS. ALLONBY: The sort of man who admires innocence.

LORD ILLINGWORTH: And a bad woman?

MRS. ALLONBY: Oh! The sort of woman a man never gets tired of.

LORD ILLINGWORTH: You are severe – on yourself.

MRS. ALLONBY: Define us as a sex.

LORD ILLINGWORTH: Sphinxes without secrets.

MRS. ALLONBY: Does that include the Puritan women?

LORD ILLINGWORTH: Do you know, I don't believe in the existence of Puritan women? I don't think there is a woman in the world who would not be a little flattered if one made love to her. It is that which makes women so irresistibly adorable.

MRS. ALLONBY: You think there is no woman in the world who would object to being kissed?

LORD ILLINGWORTH: Very few.

MRS. ALLONBY: Miss Worsley would not let you kiss her.

LORD ILLINGWORTH: Are you sure?

MRS. ALLONBY: Quite.

LORD ILLINGWORTH: What do you think she'd do if I kissed her?

MRS. ALLONBY: Either marry you, or strike you across the face with her glove. What would you do if she struck you across the face with her glove?

LORD ILLINGWORTH: Fall in love with her, probably.

MRS. ALLONBY: Then it is lucky you are not going to kiss her!

LORD ILLINGWORTH: Is that a challenge?

MRS. ALLONBY: It is an arrow shot into the air.

LORD ILLINGWORTH: Don't you know that I always succeed in whatever I try?

MRS. ALLONBY: I am sorry to hear it. We women adore failures. They lean on us.

LORD ILLINGWORTH: You worship successes. You cling to them.

MRS. ALLONBY: We are the laurels to hide their baldness.

LORD ILLINGWORTH: And they need you always, except at the moment of triumph.

MRS. ALLONBY: They are uninteresting then.

LORD ILLINGWORTH: How tantalising you are! (*A pause.*)

MRS. ALLONBY: Lord Illingworth, there is one thing I shall always like you for.

LORD ILLINGWORTH: Only one thing? And I have so many bad qualities.

MRS. ALLONBY: Ah, don't be too conceited about them. You may lose them as you grow old.

LORD ILLINGWORTH: I never intend to grow old. The soul is born old but grows young. That is the comedy of life.

MRS. ALLONBY: And the body is born young and grows old. That is life's tragedy.

LORD ILLINGWORTH: Its comedy also, sometimes. But what is the mysterious reason why you will always like me?

MRS. ALLONBY: It is that you have never made love to me.

LORD ILLINGWORTH: I have never done anything else.

MRS. ALLONBY: Really? I have not noticed it.

LORD ILLINGWORTH: How unfortunate! It might have been a tragedy for both of us.

MRS. ALLONBY: We should each have survived.

LORD ILLINGWORTH: One can survive everything nowadays, except death, and live down anything except a good reputation.

MRS. ALLONBY: Have you tried a good reputation?

LORD ILLINGWORTH: It is one of the many annoyances to which I have never been subjected.

MRS. ALLONBY: It may come.

LORD ILLINGWORTH: Why do you threaten me?

MRS. ALLONBY: I will tell you when you have kissed the Puritan.

Enter Footman.

FRANCIS: Tea is served in the Yellow Drawing-room, my lord.

LORD ILLINGWORTH: Tell her ladyship we are coming in.

FRANCIS: Yes, my lord. (*Exit.*)

LORD ILLINGWORTH: Shall we go in to tea?

MRS. ALLONBY: Do you like such simple pleasures?

LORD ILLINGWORTH: I adore simple pleasures. They are the last refuge of the complex. But, if you wish, let us stay here. Yes, let us stay here. The Book of Life begins with a man and a woman in a garden.

MRS. ALLONBY: It ends with Revelations.

LORD ILLINGWORTH: You fence divinely. But the button has come off your foil.

MRS. ALLONBY: I have still the mask.

LORD ILLINGWORTH: It makes your eyes lovelier.

MRS. ALLONBY: Thank you. Come.

LORD ILLINGWORTH (*sees* MRS. ARBUTHNOT'S *letter on table, and takes it up and looks at envelope*): What a curious handwriting! It reminds me of the handwriting of a woman I used to know years ago.

MRS. ALLONBY: Who?

LORD ILLINGWORTH: Oh! No one. No one in particular. A woman of no importance. (*Throws letter down, and passes up the steps of the terrace with* MRS. ALLONBY. *They smile at each other.*)

ACT DROP

ACT TWO

SCENE: *Drawing-room at Hunstanton Chase, after dinner, lamps lit. Door L.C. Door R.C.*
Ladies seated on sofa.

MRS. ALLONBY: What a comfort it is to have got rid of the men for a little!

LADY STUTFIELD: Yes; men persecute us dreadfully, don't they?

MRS. ALLONBY: Persecute us? I wish they did.

LADY HUNSTANTON: My dear!

MRS. ALLONBY: The annoying thing is that the wretches can be perfectly happy without us. That is why I think it is every woman's duty never to leave them alone for a single moment, except during this short breathing space after dinner; without which, I believe, we poor women would be absolutely worn to shadows.

Enter Servants with coffee.

LADY HUNSTANTON: Worn to shadows, dear?

MRS. ALLONBY: Yes, Lady Hunstanton. It is such a strain keeping men up to the mark. They are always trying to escape from us.

LADY STUTFIELD: It seems to me that it is we who are always trying to escape from them. Men are so very, very heartless. They know their power and use it.

LADY CAROLINE (*takes coffee from Servant*): What stuff and nonsense all this about men is! The thing to do is to keep men in their proper place.

MRS. ALLONBY: But what is their proper place, Lady Caroline.

LADY CAROLINE: Looking after their wives, Mrs. Allonby.

MRS. ALLONBY (*takes coffee from Servant*): Really? And if they're not married?

LADY CAROLINE: If they are not married, they would be looking after a wife. It's perfectly scandalous the amount of bachelors who are going about society. There should be a law passed to compel them all to marry within twelve months.

LADY STUTFIELD (*refuses coffee*): But if they're in love with some one who, perhaps, is tied to another?

LADY CAROLINE: In that case, Lady Stutfield, they would be married off in a week to some plain respectable girl, in order to teach them not to meddle with other people's property.

MRS. ALLONBY: I don't think that we should ever be spoken of as other people's property. All men are married women's property. That is the only true definition of what married women's property really is. But we don't belong to any one.

LADY STUTFIELD: Oh, I am so very, very glad to hear you say so.

LADY HUNSTANTON: But do you really think, dear Caroline, that legislation would improve matters in any way? I am told that, nowadays, all the married men live like bachelors, and all the bachelors like married men.

MRS. ALLONBY: I certainly never know one from the other.

LADY STUTFIELD: Oh, I think one can always know at once whether a man has home claims upon his life or not. I have noticed a very, very sad expression in the eyes of so many married men.

MRS. ALLONBY: Ah, all that I have noticed is that they are horribly tedious when they are good husbands, and abominably conceited when they are not.

LADY HUNSTANTON: Well, I suppose the type of husband has completely changed since my young days, but I'm bound to state that poor dear Hunstanton was the most delightful of creatures, and as good as gold.

MRS. ALLONBY: Ah, my husband is a sort of promissory note; I'm tired of meeting him.

LADY CAROLINE: But you renew him from time to time, don't you?

MRS. ALLONBY: Oh no, Lady Caroline. I have only had one husband as yet. I suppose you look upon me as quite an amateur.

LADY CAROLINE: With your views on life I wonder you married at all.

MRS. ALLONBY: So do I.

LADY HUNSTANTON: My dear child, I believe you are really very happy in your married life, but that you like to hide your happiness from others.

MRS. ALLONBY: I assure you I was horribly deceived in Ernest.

LADY HUNSTANTON: Oh, I hope not, dear. I knew his mother quite well. She was a Stratton, Caroline, one of Lord Crowland's daughters.

LADY CAROLINE: Victoria Stratton? I remember her perfectly. A silly, fair-haired woman with no chin.

MRS. ALLONBY: Ah, Ernest has a chin. He has a very strong chin, a square chin. Ernest's chin is far too square.

LADY STUTFIELD: But do you really think a man's chin can be too square? I think a man should look very, very strong, and that his chin should be quite, quite square.

MRS. ALLONBY: Then you should certainly know Ernest, Lady Stutfield. It is only fair to tell you beforehand he has got no conversation at all.

LADY STUTFIELD: I adore silent men.

MRS. ALLONBY: Oh, Ernest isn't silent. He talks the whole time. But he has got no conversation. What he talks about I don't know. I haven't listened to him for years.

LADY STUTFIELD: Have you never forgiven him then? How sad that seems! But all life is very, very sad, is it not?

MRS. ALLONBY: Life, Lady Stutfield, is simply a *mauvais quart d'heure* made up of exquisite moments.

LADY STUTFIELD: Yes, there are moments, certainly. But was it something very, very wrong that Mr. Allonby did? Did he become angry with you, and say anything that was unkind or true?

MRS. ALLONBY: Oh, dear, no. Ernest is invariably calm. That is one of the reasons he always gets on my nerves. Nothing is so aggravating as calmness. There is something positively brutal about the good temper of most modern men. I wonder we women stand it as well as we do.

LADY STUTFIELD: Yes; men's good temper shows they are not so sensitive as we are, not so finely strung. It makes a great barrier often between husband and wife, does it not? But I would so much like to know what was the wrong thing Mr. Allonby did.

MRS. ALLONBY: Well, I will tell you, if you solemnly promise to tell everybody else.

LADY STUTFIELD: Thank you, thank you. I will make a point of repeating it.

MRS. ALLONBY: When Ernest and I were engaged, he swore to me positively on his knees that he had never loved any one before in the whole course of his life. I was very young at the time, so I didn't believe him, I needn't tell you. Unfortunately, however, I made no inquires of any kind till after I had been actually married four or five months. I found out then that what he had told me was perfectly true. And that sort of thing makes a man so absolutely uninteresting.

LADY HUNSTANTON: My dear!

MRS. ALLONBY: Men always want to be a woman's first love. That is their clumsy vanity. We women have a more subtle instinct about things. What we like is to be a man's last romance.

LADY STUTFIELD: I see what you mean. It's very, very beautiful.

LADY HUNSTANTON: My dear child, you don't mean to tell me that you won't forgive your husband because he never loved any one else? Did you ever hear such a thing, Caroline? I am quite surprised.

LADY CAROLINE: Oh, women have become so highly educated, Jane, that nothing should surprise us nowadays, except happy marriages. They apparently are getting remarkably rare.

MRS. ALLONBY: Oh, they're quite out of date.

LADY STUTFIELD: Except amongst the middle classes, I have been told.

MRS. ALLONBY: How like the middle classes!

LADY STUTFIELD: Yes – is it not? – very, very like them.

LADY CAROLINE: If what you tell us about the middle classes is true, Lady Stutfield, it redounds greatly to their credit. It is much to be regretted that in our rank of life the wife should be so persistently frivolous, under the impression apparently that it is the proper thing to be. It is to that I attribute the unhappiness of so many marriages we all know of in society.

MRS. ALLONBY: Do you know, Lady Caroline, I don't think the frivolity of the wife has ever anything to do with it. More marriages are ruined nowadays by the common sense of the husband than by anything else. How can a woman be expected to be happy with a man who insists on treating her as if she was a perfectly rational being?

LADY HUNSTANTON: My dear!

MRS. ALLONBY: Man, poor, awkward, reliable, necessary man belongs to a sex that has been rational for millions and millions of years. He can't help himself. It is in his race. The History of Woman is very different. We have always been picturesque protests against the mere existence of common sense. We saw its dangers from the first.

LADY STUTFIELD: Yes, the common sense of husbands is certainly most, most trying. Do tell me your conception of the Ideal Husband. I think it would be so very, very helpful.

MRS. ALLONBY: The Ideal Husband? There couldn't be such a thing. The institution is wrong.

LADY STUTFIELD: The Ideal Man, then, in his relations to *us*.

LADY CAROLINE: He would probably be extremely realistic.

MRS. ALLONBY: The Ideal Man! Oh, the Ideal Man should talk to us as if we were goddesses, and treat us as if we were children. He should refuse all our serious requests, and gratify every one of our whims. He should encourage us to have caprices, and forbid us to have missions. He should always say much more than he means, and always mean much more than he says.

LADY HUNSTANTON: But how could he do both, dear?

MRS. ALLONBY: He should never run down other pretty women. That would show he had no taste, or make one suspect that he had too much. No; he should be nice about them all, but say that somehow they don't attract him.

LADY STUTFIELD: Yes, that is always very, very pleasant to hear about other women.

MRS. ALLONBY: If we ask him a question about anything, he should give us an answer all about ourselves. He should invariably praise us for whatever qualities he knows we haven't got. But he should be pitiless, quite pitiless, in reproaching us for the virtues that we have never dreamed of possessing. He should never believe that we know the use of useful things. That would be unforgivable. But he should shower on us everything we don't want.

LADY CAROLINE: As far as I can see, he is to do nothing but pay bills and compliments.

MRS. ALLONBY: He should persistently compromise us in public, and treat us with absolute respect when we are alone. And yet he should be always ready to have a perfectly terrible scene, whenever we want one, and to become miserable, absolutely miserable, at a moment's notice, and to overwhelm us with just reproaches in less than twenty minutes, and to be positively violent at the end of half an hour, and to leave us for ever at a quarter to eight, when we have to go and dress for dinner. And when, after that, one has seen him for really the last time, and he has refused to take back the little things he has given one, and promised never to communicate with one again, or to write one any foolish letters, he should be perfectly broken-hearted, and telegraph to one all day long, and send one little notes every half-hour by a private hansom, and dine quite alone at the club, so that every one should know how unhappy he was. And after a whole dreadful week, during which one has gone about everywhere with one's husband, just to show how absolutely lonely one was, he may be given a third last parting, in the evening, and then, if his conduct has been quite irreproachable, and one has behaved really badly to him, he should be allowed to admit that he has been entirely in the wrong, and when he has admitted that, it becomes a woman's duty to forgive, and one can do it all over again from the beginning, with variations.

LADY HUNSTANTON: How clever you are, my dear! You never mean a single word you say.

LADY STUTFIELD: Thank you, thank you. It has been quite, quite entrancing. I must try and remember it all. There are such a number of details that are so very, very important.

LADY CAROLINE: But you have not told us yet what the reward of the Ideal Man is to be.

MRS. ALLONBY: His reward? Oh, infinite expectation. That is quite enough for him.

LADY STUTFIELD: But men are so terribly, terribly exacting, are they not?

MRS. ALLONBY: That makes no matter. One should never surrender.

LADY STUTFIELD: Not even to the Ideal Man?

MRS. ALLONBY: Certainly not to him. Unless, of course, one wants to grow tired of him.

LADY STUTFIELD: Oh! ... Yes. I see that. It is very, very helpful. Do you think, Mrs. Allonby, I shall ever meet the Ideal Man? Or are there more than one?

MRS. ALLONBY: There are just four in London, Lady Stutfield.

LADY HUNSTANTON: Oh, my dear!

MRS. ALLONBY (*going over to her*): What has happened? Do tell me.

LADY HUNSTANTON (*in a low voice*): I had completely forgotten that the American young lady has been in the room all the time. I am afraid some of this clever talk may have shocked her a little.

MRS. ALLONBY: Ah, that will do her so much good!

LADY HUNSTANTON: Let us hope she didn't understand much. I think I had better go over and talk to her. (*Rises and goes across to* HESTER WORSLEY.) Well, dear Miss Worsley. (*Sitting down beside her.*) How quiet you have been in your nice little corner all this time! I suppose you have been reading a book? There are so many books here in the library.

HESTER: No, I have been listening to the conversation.

LADY HUNSTANTON: You mustn't believe everything that was said, you know, dear.

HESTER: I didn't believe any of it.

LADY HUNSTANTON: That is quite right, dear.

HESTER (*continuing*): I couldn't believe that any women could really hold such views of life as I have heard to-night from some of your guests. (*An awkward pause.*)

LADY HUNSTANTON: I hear you have such pleasant society in America. Quite like our own in places, my son wrote to me.

HESTER: There are cliques in America as elsewhere, Lady Hunstanton. But true American society consists simply of all the good women and good men we have in our country.

LADY HUNSTANTON: What a sensible system, and I dare say quite pleasant, too. I am afraid in England we have too many artificial social barriers. We don't see as much as we should of the middle and lower classes.

HESTER: In America we have no lower classes.

LADY HUNSTANTON: Really? What a very strange arrangement!

MRS. ALLONBY: What is that dreadful girl talking about?

LADY STUTFIELD: She is painfully natural, is she not?

LADY CAROLINE: There are a great many things you haven't got in America, I am told, Miss Worsley. They say you have no ruins, and no curiosities.

MRS. ALLONBY (*to* LADY STUTFIELD): What nonsense! They have their mothers and their manners.

HESTER: The English aristocracy supply us with our curiosities, Lady Caroline. They are sent over to us every summer, regularly, in the steamers, and propose to us the day after they land. As for ruins, we are trying to build up something that will last longer than brick or stone. (*Gets up to take her fan from table.*)

LADY HUNSTANTON: What is that, dear? Ah, yes, an iron Exhibition, is it not, at that place that has the curious name?

HESTER (*standing by table*): We are trying to build up life, Lady Hunstanton, on a better, truer, purer basis than life rests on here. This sounds strange to you all, no doubt. How could it sound other than strange? You rich people in England, you don't know how you are living. How could you know? You shut out from your society the gentle and the good. You laugh at the simple and the pure. Living, as you all do, on others and by them, you sneer at self-sacrifice, and if you throw bread to the poor, it is merely to keep them quiet for a season. With all your pomp and wealth and art you don't know how to live – you don't even know that. You love the beauty that you can see and touch and handle, the beauty that you can destroy, and do destroy, but of the unseen beauty of life, of the unseen beauty of a higher life, you know nothing. You have lost life's secret. Oh, your English society seems to me shallow, selfish, foolish. It has blinded its eyes, and stopped its ears. It lies like a leper in purple. It sits like a dead thing smeared with gold. It is all wrong, all wrong.

LADY STUTFIELD: I don't think one should know of these things. It is not very, very nice, is it?

LADY HUNSTANTON: My dear Miss Worsley, I thought you liked English society so much. You were such a success in it. And you were so much admired by the best people. I quite forget what Lord Henry Weston said of you – but it was most complimentary, and you know what an authority he is on beauty.

HESTER: Lord Henry Weston! I remember him, Lady Hunstanton. A man with a hideous smile and a hideous past. He is asked everywhere. No dinner-party is complete without him. What of those whose ruin is due to him? They are outcasts. They are nameless. If you met them in the street you would turn your head away. I don't complain of their punishment. Let all women who have sinned be punished.

MRS. ARBUTHNOT *enters from terrace behind in a cloak with a lace veil over her head. She hears the last words and starts.*

LADY HUNSTANTON: My dear young lady!

HESTER: It is right that they should be punished, but don't let them be the only ones to suffer. If a man and woman have sinned, let them both go forth into the desert to love or loathe each other there. Let them both be branded. Set a mark, if you wish, on each, but don't punish the one and let the other go free. Don't have one law for men and another for women. You are unjust to women in England. And till you count what is a shame in a woman to be infamy in a man, you will always be unjust, and Right, that pillar of fire, and Wrong, that pillar of cloud, will be made dim to your eyes, or be not seen at all, or if seen, not regarded.

LADY CAROLINE: Might I, dear Miss Worsley, as you are standing up, ask you for my cotton that is just behind you? Thank you.

LADY HUNSTANTON: My dear Mrs. Arbuthnot! I am so pleased you have come up. But I didn't hear you announced.

MRS. ARBUTHNOT: Oh, I came straight in from the terrace, Lady Hunstanton, just as I was. You didn't tell me you had a party.

LADY HUNSTANTON: Not a party. Only a few guests who are staying in the house, and whom you must know. Allow me. (*Tries to help her. Rings bell.*) Caroline, this is Mrs. Arbuthnot, one of my sweetest friends. Lady Caroline Pontefract, Lady Stutfield, Mrs. Allonby, and my young American friend, Miss Worsley, who has just been telling us all how wicked we are.

HESTER: I am afraid you think I spoke too strongly, Lady Hunstanton. But there are some things in England –

LADY HUNSTANTON: My dear young lady, there was a great deal of truth, I dare say, in what you said, and you looked very pretty while you said it, which is much more important, Lord Illingworth would tell us. The only point where I thought you were a little hard was about Lady Caroline's brother, about poor Lord Henry. He is really such good company.

Enter Footman.

Take Mrs. Arbuthnot's things.

Exit Footman with wraps.

HESTER: Lady Caroline, I had no idea it was your brother. I am sorry for the pain I must have caused you – I –

LADY CAROLINE: My dear Miss Worsley, the only part of your little speech, if I may so term it, with which I thoroughly agreed, was the part about my brother. Nothing that you could possibly say could be too bad for him. I regard Henry as infamous, absolutely infamous. But I am bound to state, as you were remarking, Jane, that he is excellent company, and he has one of the best cooks in London, and after a good dinner one can forgive anybody, even one's own relations.

LADY HUNSTANTON (*to* MISS WORSLEY): Now, do come, dear, and make friends with Mrs. Arbuthnot. She is one of the good, sweet, simple people you told us we never admitted into society. I am sorry to say Mrs. Arbuthnot comes very rarely to me. But that is not my fault.

MRS. ALLONBY: What a bore it is the men staying so long after dinner! I expect they are saying the most dreadful things about us.

LADY STUTFIELD: Do you really think so?.

MRS. ALLONBY: I am sure of it.

LADY STUTFIELD: How very, very horrid of them! Shall we go on to the terrace?

MRS. ALLONBY: Oh, anything to get away from the dowagers and the dowdies. (*Rises and goes with* LADY STUTFIELD *to door L.C.*) We are only going to look at the stars, Lady Hunstanton.

LADY HUNSTANTON: You will find a great many, dear, a great many. But don't catch cold. (*To* MRS. ARBUTHNOT): We shall all miss Gerald so much, dear Mrs. Arbuthnot.

MRS. ARBUTHNOT: But has Lord Illingworth really offered to make Gerald his secretary?

LADY HUNSTANTON: Oh, yes! He has been most charming about it. He has the highest possible opinion of your boy. You don't know Lord Illingworth, I believe, dear.

MRS. ARBUTHNOT: I have never met him.

LADY HUNSTANTON: You know him by name, no doubt?

MRS. ARBUTHNOT: I am afraid I don't. I live so much out of the world, and see so few people. I remember hearing years ago of an old Lord Illingworth who lived in Yorkshire, I think.

LADY HUNSTANTON: Ah, yes. That would be the last Earl but one. He was a very curious man. He wanted to marry beneath him. Or wouldn't, I believe. There was some scandal about it. The present Lord Illingworth is quite different. He is very distinguished. He does – well, he does nothing, which I am afraid our pretty American visitor here thinks very wrong of anybody, and I don't know that he cares much for the subjects in which you are so interested, dear Mrs. Arbuthnot. Do you think, Caroline, that Lord Illingworth is interested in the Housing of the Poor?

LADY CAROLINE: I should fancy not at all, Jane.

LADY HUNSTANTON: We all have our different tastes, have we not? But Lord Illingworth has a very high position, and there is nothing he couldn't get if he chose to ask for it. Of course, he is comparatively a young man still, and he has only come to his title within – how long exactly is it, Caroline, since Lord Illingworth succeeded?

LADY CAROLINE: About four years, I think, Jane. I know it was the same year in which my brother had his last exposure in the evening newspapers.

LADY HUNSTANTON: Ah, I remember. That would be about four years ago. Of course, there were a great many people between the present Lord Illingworth and the title, Mrs. Arbuthnot. There was – who was there, Caroline?

LADY CAROLINE: There was poor Margaret's baby. You remember how anxious she was to have a boy, and it was a boy, but it died, and her husband died shortly afterwards, and she married almost immediately, one of Lord Ascot's sons, who, I am told, beats her.

LADY HUNSTANTON: Ah, that is in the family, dear, that is in the family. And there was also, I remember, a clergyman who wanted to be a lunatic, or a lunatic who wanted to be a clergyman, I forget which, but I know the Court of Chancery investigated the matter, and decided that he was quite sane. And I saw him afterwards at poor Lord Plumstead's with straws in his hair, or something very odd about him. I can't recall what. I often regret, Lady Caroline, that dear Lady Cecilia never lived to see her son get the title.

MRS. ARBUTHNOT: Lady Cecilia?

LADY HUNSTANTON: Lord Illingworth's mother, dear Mrs. Arbuthnot, was one of the Duchess of Jerningham's pretty daughters, and she married Sir Thomas Harford, who wasn't considered a very good match for her at the time, though he was said to be the handsomest man in London. I knew them all quite intimately, and both the sons, Arthur and George.

MRS. ARBUTHNOT: It was the eldest son who succeeded, of course, Lady Hunstanton?

LADY HUNSTANTON: No, dear, he was killed in the hunting field. Or was it fishing, Caroline? I forget. But George came in for everything. I always tell him that no younger son has ever had such good luck as he has had.

MRS. ARBUTHNOT: Lady Hunstanton, I want to speak to Gerald at once. Might I see him? Can he be sent for?

LADY HUNSTANTON: Certainly, dear. I will send one of the servants into the dining-room to fetch him. I don't know what keeps the gentlemen so long. (*Rings bell.*) When I knew Lord Illingworth first as plain George Harford, he was simply a very brilliant young man about town, with not a penny of money except what poor dear Lady Cecilia gave him. She was quite devoted to him. Chiefly, I fancy, because he was on bad terms with his father. Oh, here is the dear Archdeacon. (*To Servant*): It doesn't matter.

Enter SIR JOHN *and* DOCTOR DAUBENY. SIR JOHN *goes over to* LADY STUTFIELD, DOCTOR DAUBENY *to* LADY HUNSTANTON.

THE ARCHDEACON: Lord Illingworth has been most entertaining. I have never enjoyed myself more. (*Sees* MRS. ARBUTHNOT.) Ah, Mrs. Arbuthnot.

LADY HUNSTANTON (*to* DOCTOR DAUBENY): You see I have got Mrs. Arbuthnot to come to me at last.

THE ARCHDEACON: That is a great honour, Lady Hunstanton. Mrs. Daubeny will be quite jealous of you.

LADY HUNSTANTON: Ah, I am so sorry Mrs. Daubeny could not come with you to-night. Headache as usual, I suppose.

THE ARCHDEACON: Yes, Lady Hunstanton; a perfect martyr. But she is happiest alone. She is happiest alone.

LADY CAROLINE (*to her husband*): John!

SIR JOHN *goes over to his wife.* DOCTOR DAUBENY *talks to* LADY HUNSTANTON *and* MRS. ARBUTHNOT.

MRS. ARBUTHNOT *watches* LORD ILLINGWORTH *the whole time. He has passed across the room without noticing her, and approaches* MRS. ALLONBY, *who with* LADY STUTFIELD *is standing by the door looking on to the terrace.*

LORD ILLINGWORTH: How is the most charming woman in the world?

MRS. ALLONBY (*taking* LADY STUTFIELD *by the hand*): We are both quite well, thank you, Lord Illingworth. But what a short time you have been in the dining-room! It seems as if we had only just left.

LORD ILLINGWORTH: I was bored to death. Never opened my lips the whole time. Absolutely longing to come in to you.

MRS. ALLONBY: You should have. The American girl has been giving us a lecture.

LORD ILLINGWORTH: Really? All Americans lecture, I believe. I suppose it is something in their climate. What did she lecture about?

MRS. ALLONBY: Oh, Puritanism, of course.

LORD ILLINGWORTH: I am going to convert her, am I not? How long do you give me?

MRS. ALLONBY: A week.

LORD ILLINGWORTH: A week is more than enough.

Enter GERALD *and* LORD ALFRED.

GERALD (*going to* MRS. ARBUTHNOT): Dear mother!

MRS. ARBUTHNOT: Gerald, I don't feel at all well. See me home, Gerald. I shouldn't have come.

GERALD: I am so sorry, mother. Certainly. But you must know Lord Illingworth first. (*Goes across room.*)

MRS. ARBUTHNOT: Not to-night, Gerald.

GERALD: Lord Illingworth, I want you so much to know my mother.

LORD ILLINGWORTH: With the greatest pleasure. (*To* MRS. ALLONBY): I'll be back in a moment. People's mothers always bore me to death. All women become like their mothers. That is their tragedy.

MRS. ALLONBY: No man does. That is his.

LORD ILLINGWORTH: What a delightful mood you are in to-night! (*Turns round and goes across with* GERALD *to* MRS. ARBUTHNOT. *When he sees her, he starts back in wonder. Then slowly his eyes turn towards* GERALD.)

GERALD: Mother, this is Lord Illingworth, who has offered to take me as his private secretary.

MRS. ARBUTHNOT *bows coldly.*

It is a wonderful opening for me, isn't it? I hope he won't be disappointed in me, that is all. You'll thank Lord Illingworth, mother, won't you?

MRS. ARBUTHNOT: Lord Illingworth is very good, I am sure, to interest himself in you for the moment.

LORD ILLINGWORTH (*putting his hand on* GERALD'S *shoulder*): Oh, Gerald and I are great friends already, Mrs. . . . . Arbuthnot.

MRS. ARBUTHNOT: There can be nothing in common between you and my son, Lord Illingworth.

GERALD: Dear mother, how can you say so? Of course, Lord Illingworth is awfully clever and that sort of thing. There is nothing Lord Illingworth doesn't know.

LORD ILLINGWORTH: My dear boy!

GERALD: He knows more about life than any one I have ever met. I feel an awful duffer when I am with you, Lord Illingworth. Of course, I have had so few advantages. I have not been to Eton or Oxford like other chaps. But Lord Illingworth doesn't seem to mind that. He has been awfully good to me, mother.

MRS. ARBUTHNOT: Lord Illingworth may change his mind. He may not really want you as his secretary.

GERALD: Mother!

MRS. ARBUTHNOT: You must remember, as you said yourself, you have had so few advantages.

MRS. ALLONBY: Lord Illingworth, I want to speak to you for a moment. Do come over.

LORD ILLINGWORTH: Will you excuse me, Mrs. Arbuthnot? Now, don't let your charming mother make any more difficulties, Gerald. The thing is quite settled, isn't it?

GERALD: I hope so.

LORD ILLINGWORTH *goes across to* MRS. ALLONBY.

MRS. ALLONBY: I thought you were never going to leave the lady in black velvet.

LORD ILLINGWORTH: She is excessively handsome. (*Looks at* MRS. ARBUTHNOT.)

LADY HUNSTANTON: Caroline, shall we all make a move to the music-room? Miss Worsley is going to play. You'll come too, dear Mrs. Arbuthnot, won't you? You don't know what a treat is in store for you. (*To* DOCTOR DAUBENY): I must really take Miss Worsley down some afternoon to the rectory. I should so much like dear Mrs. Daubeny to hear her on the violin. Ah, I forgot. Dear Mrs. Daubeny's hearing is a little defective, is it not?

THE ARCHDEACON: Her deafness is a great privation to her. She can't even hear my sermons now. She reads them at home. But she has many resources in herself, many resources.

LADY HUNSTANTON: She reads a good deal, I suppose?

THE ARCHDEACON: Just the very largest print. The eyesight is rapidly going. But she's never morbid, never morbid.

GERALD (*to* LORD ILLINGWORTH): Do speak to my mother, Lord Illingworth, before you go into the music-room. She seems to think, somehow, you don't mean what you said to me.

MRS. ALLONBY: Aren't you coming?

LORD ILLINGWORTH: In a few moments. Lady Hunstanton, if Mrs. Arbuthnot would allow me, I would like to say a few words to her, and we will join you later on.

LADY HUNSTANTON: Ah, of course. You will have a great deal to say to her, and she will have a great deal to thank you for. It is not every son who gets such an offer, Mrs. Arbuthnot. But I know you appreciate that, dear.

LADY CAROLINE: John!

LADY HUNSTANTON: Now, don't keep Mrs. Arbuthnot too long, Lord Illingworth. We can't spare her.

Exit following the other guests. Sound of violin heard from music-room.

LORD ILLINGWORTH: So that is our son, Rachel! Well, I am very proud of him. He is a Harford, every inch of him. By the way, why Arbuthnot, Rachel?

MRS. ARBUTHNOT: One name is as good as another, when one has no right to any name.

LORD ILLINGWORTH: I suppose so – but why Gerald?

MRS. ARBUTHNOT: After a man whose heart I broke – after my father.

LORD ILLINGWORTH: Well, Rachel, what is over is over. All I have got to say now is that I am very, very much pleased with our boy. The world will know him merely as my private secretary, but to me he will be something very near, and very dear. It is a curious thing, Rachel; my life seemed to be quite complete. It was not so. It lacked something, it lacked a son. I have found my son now. I am glad I have found him.

MRS. ARBUTHNOT: You have no right to claim him, or the smallest part of him. The boy is entirely mine, and shall remain mine.

LORD ILLINGWORTH: My dear Rachel, you have had him to yourself for over twenty years. Why not let me have him for a little now? He is quite as much mine as yours.

MRS. ARBUTHNOT: Are you talking of the child you abandoned? Of the child who, as far as you are concerned, might have died of hunger and of want?

LORD ILLINGWORTH: You forget, Rachel, it was you who left me. It was not I who left you.

MRS. ARBUTHNOT: I left you because you refused to give the child a name. Before my son was born, I implored you to marry me.

LORD ILLINGWORTH: I had no expectations then. And besides, Rachel, I wasn't much older than you were. I was only twenty-two. I was twenty-one, I believe, when the whole thing began in your father's garden.

MRS. ARBUTHNOT: When a man is old enough to do wrong he should be old enough to do right also.

LORD ILLINGWORTH: My dear Rachel, intellectual generalities are always interesting, but generalities in morals mean absolutely nothing. As for saying I left our child to starve, that, of course, is untrue and silly. My mother offered you six hundred a year. But you wouldn't take anything. You simply disappeared, and carried the child away with you.

MRS. ARBUTHNOT: I wouldn't have accepted a penny from her. Your father was different. He told you, in my presence, when we were in Paris, that it was your duty to marry me.

LORD ILLINGWORTH: Oh, duty is what one expects from others, it is not what one does oneself. Of course, I was influenced by my mother. Every man is when he is young.

MRS. ARBUTHNOT: I am glad to hear you say so. Gerald shall certainly not go away with you.

LORD ILLINGWORTH: What nonsense, Rachel!

MRS. ARBUTHNOT: Do you think I would allow my son –

LORD ILLINGWORTH: Our son.

MRS. ARBUTHNOT: My son – (LORD ILLINGWORTH *shrugs his shoulders*) – to go away with the man who spoiled my youth, who ruined my life, who has tainted every moment of my days? You don't realise what my past has been in suffering and in shame.

LORD ILLINGWORTH: My dear Rachel, I must candidly say that I think Gerald's future considerably more important than your past.

MRS. ARBUTHNOT: Gerald cannot separate his future from my past.

LORD ILLINGWORTH: That is exactly what he should do. That is exactly what you should help him to do. What a typical woman you are! You talk sentimentally and you are thoroughly selfish the whole time. But don't let us have a scene. Rachel, I want you to look at this matter from the common-sense point of view, from the point of view of what is best for our son, leaving you and me out of the question. What is our son at present? An underpaid clerk in a small Provincial Bank in a third-rate English town. If you imagine he is quite happy in such a position, you are mistaken. He is thoroughly discontented.

MRS. ARBUTHNOT: He was not discontented till he met you. You have made him so.

LORD ILLINGWORTH: Of course I made him so. Discontent is the first step in the progress of a man or a nation. But I did not leave him with a mere longing for things he could not get. No, I made him a charming offer. He jumped at it, I need hardly say. Any young man would. And now, simply because it turns out that I am the boy's own father and he my own son, you propose practically to ruin his career. That is to say, if I were a perfect stranger, you would allow Gerald to go away with me, but as he is my own flesh and blood you won't. How utterly illogical you are!

MRS. ARBUTHNOT: I will not allow him to go.

LORD ILLINGWORTH: How can you prevent it? What excuse can you give to him for making him decline such an offer as mine? I won't tell him in what relations I stand to him, I need hardly say. But you daren't tell him. You know that. Look how you have brought him up.

MRS. ARBUTHNOT: I have brought him up to be a good man.

LORD ILLINGWORTH: Quite so. And what is the result? You have educated him to be your judge if he ever finds you out. And a bitter, an unjust judge he will be to you. Don't be deceived, Rachel. Children begin by loving their parents. After a time they judge them. Rarely, if ever, do they forgive them.

MRS. ARBUTHNOT: George, don't take my son away from me. I have had twenty years of sorrow, and I have only had one thing to love me, only one thing to love. You have had a life of joy, and pleasure, and success. You have been quite happy, you have never thought of us. There was no reason, according to your views of life, why you should have remembered us at all. Your meeting us was a mere accident, a horrible accident. Forget it. Don't come now, and rob me of – of all I have in the whole world. You are so rich in other things. Leave me the little vineyard of my life; leave me the walled-in garden and the well of water; the ewe-lamb God sent me, in pity or in wrath, oh, leave me that. George, don't take Gerald from me.

LORD ILLINGWORTH: Rachel, at the present moment you are not necessary to Gerald's career; I am. There is nothing more to be said on the subject.

MRS. ARBUTHNOT: I will not let him go.

LORD ILLINGWORTH: Here is Gerald. He has a right to decide for himself.

Enter GERALD.

GERALD: Well, dear mother, I hope you have settled it all with Lord Illingworth?

MRS. ARBUTHNOT: I have not, Gerald.

LORD ILLINGWORTH: Your mother seems not to like your coming with me, for some reason.

GERALD: Why, mother?

MRS. ARBUTHNOT: I thought you were quite happy here with me, Gerald. I didn't know you were so anxious to leave me.

GERALD: Mother, how can you talk like that? Of course I have been quite happy with you. But a man can't stay always with his mother. No chap does. I want to make myself a position, to do something. I thought you would have been proud to see me Lord Illingworth's secretary.

MRS. ARBUTHNOT: I do not think you would be suitable as a private secretary to Lord Illingworth. You have no qualifications.

LORD ILLINGWORTH: I don't wish to seem to interfere for a moment, Mrs. Arbuthnot, but as far as your last objection is concerned, I surely am the best judge. And I can only tell you that your son has all the qualifications I had hoped for. He has more, in fact, than I had even thought of. Far more. (MRS. ARBUTHNOT *remains silent.*) Have you any other reason, Mrs. Arbuthnot, why you don't wish your son to accept this post?

GERALD: Have you, mother? Do answer.

LORD ILLINGWORTH: If you have, Mrs. Arbuthnot, pray, pray say it. We are quite by ourselves here. Whatever it is, I need not say I will not repeat it.

GERALD: Mother?

LORD ILLINGWORTH: If you would like to be alone with your son, I will leave you. You may have some other reason you don't wish me to hear.

MRS. ARBUTHNOT: I have no other reason.

LORD ILLINGWORTH: Then, my dear boy, we may look on the thing as settled. Come, you and I will smoke a cigarette on the terrace together. And Mrs. Arbuthnot, pray let me tell you, that I think you have acted very, very wisely.

Exit with GERALD. MRS. ARBUTHNOT *is left alone. She stands immobile with a look of unutterable sorrow on her face.*

ACT DROP

ACT THREE

SCENE: *The Picture Gallery at Hunstanton Chase. Door at back leading on to terrace.*

LORD ILLINGWORTH *and* GERALD, *R.C.* LORD ILLING-
WORTH *lolling on a sofa.* GERALD *in a chair.*

LORD ILLINGWORTH: Thoroughly sensible woman, your mother, Gerald. I knew she would come round in the end.

GERALD: My mother is awfully conscientious, Lord Illingworth, and I know she doesn't think I am educated enough to be your secretary. She is perfectly right, too. I was fearfully idle when I was at school, and I couldn't pass an examination now to save my life.

LORD ILLINGWORTH: My dear Gerald, examinations are of no value whatsoever. If a man is a gentleman, he knows quite enough, and if he is not a gentleman, whatever he knows is bad for him.

GERALD: But I am so ignorant of the world, Lord Illingworth.

LORD ILLINGWORTH: Don't be afraid, Gerald. Remember that you've got on your side the most wonderful thing in the world – youth! There is nothing like youth. The middle-aged are mortgaged to Life. The old are in life's lumber-room. But youth is the Lord of Life. Youth has a kingdom waiting for it. Every one is born a king, and most people die in exile, like most kings. To win back my youth, Gerald, there is nothing I wouldn't do – except take exercise, get up early, or be a useful member of the community.

GERALD: But you don't call yourself old, Lord Illingworth?

LORD ILLINGWORTH: I am old enough to be your father, Gerald.

GERALD: I don't remember my father; he died years ago.

LORD ILLINGWORTH: So Lady Hunstanton told me.

GERALD: It is very curious, my mother never talks to me about my father. I sometimes think she must have married beneath her.

LORD ILLINGWORTH (*winces slightly*): Really? (*Goes over and puts his hand on* GERALD'S *shoulder.*) You have missed not having a father, I suppose, Gerald?

GERALD: Oh, no; my mother has been so good to me. No one ever had such a mother as I have had.

LORD ILLINGWORTH: I am quite sure of that. Still I should imagine that most mothers don't quite understand their sons. Don't realise, I mean, that a son has ambitions, a desire to see life, to make himself a name. After all, Gerald, you couldn't be expected to pass all your life in such a hole as Wrockley, could you?

GERALD: Oh, no! It would be dreadful!

LORD ILLINGWORTH: A mother's love is very touching, of course, but it is often curiously selfish. I mean, there is a good deal of selfishness in it.

GERALD (*slowly*): I suppose there is.

LORD ILLINGWORTH: Your mother is a thoroughly good woman. But good women have such limited views of life, their horizon is so small, their interests are so petty, aren't they?

GERALD: They are awfully interested, certainly, in things we don't care much about.

LORD ILLINGWORTH: I suppose your mother is very religious, and that sort of thing.

GERALD: Oh, yes, she's always going to church.

LORD ILLINGWORTH: Ah! She is not modern, and to be modern is the only thing worth being nowadays. You want to be modern, don't you, Gerald? You want to know life as it really is. Not to be put off with any old-fashioned theories about life. Well, what you have to do at present is simply to fit yourself for the best society. A man who can dominate a London dinner-table can dominate the world. The future belongs to the dandy. It is the exquisites who are going to rule.

GERALD: I should like to wear nice things awfully, but I have always been told that a man should not think so much about his clothes.

LORD ILLINGWORTH: People nowadays are so absolutely superficial that they don't understand the philosophy of the superficial. By the way, Gerald, you should learn how to tie your tie better. Sentiment is all very well for the buttonhole. But the essential thing for a necktie is style. A well-tied tie is the first serious step in life.

GERALD (*laughing*): I might be able to learn how to tie a tie, Lord Illingworth, but I should never be able to talk as you do. I don't know how to talk.

LORD ILLINGWORTH: Oh! Talk to every woman as if you loved her, and to every man as if he bored you, and at the end of your first season you will have the reputation of possessing the most perfect social tact.

GERALD: But it is very difficult to get into society, isn't it?

LORD ILLINGWORTH: To get into the best society, nowadays, one has either to feed people, amuse people, or shock people – that is all!

GERALD: I suppose society is wonderfully delightful!

LORD ILLINGWORTH: To be in it is merely a bore. But to be out of it simply a tragedy. Society is a necessary thing. No man has any real success in this world unless he has got women to back him, and women rule society. If you have not got women on your side you are quite over. You might just as well be a barrister or a stockbroker, or a journalist at once.

GERALD: It is very difficult to understand women, is it not?

LORD ILLINGWORTH. You should never try to understand them. Women are pictures. Men are problems. If you want to know what a woman really means – which, by the way, is always a dangerous thing to do – look at her, don't listen to her.

GERALD: But women are awfully clever, aren't they?

LORD ILLINGWORTH: One should always tell them so. But, to the philosopher, my dear Gerald, women represent the triumph of matter over mind – just as men represent the triumph of mind over morals.

GERALD: How then can women have so much power as you say they have?

LORD ILLINGWORTH: The history of women is the history of the worst form of tyranny the world has ever known. The tyranny of the weak over the strong. It is the only tyranny that lasts.

GERALD: But haven't women got a refining influence?

LORD ILLINGWORTH: Nothing refines but the intellect.

GERALD: Still, there are many different kinds of women, aren't there?

LORD ILLINGWORTH: Only two kinds in society: the plain and the coloured.

GERALD: But there are good women in society, aren't there?

LORD ILLINGWORTH: Far too many.

GERALD: But do you think women shouldn't be good?

LORD ILLINGWORTH: One should never tell them so, they'd all become good at once. Women are a fascinatingly wilful sex. Every woman is a rebel, and usually in wild revolt against herself.

GERALD: You have never been married, Lord Illingworth, have you?

LORD ILLINGWORTH: Men marry because they are tired; women because they are curious. Both are disappointed.

GERALD: But don't you think one can be happy when one is married?

LORD ILLINGWORTH: Perfectly happy. But the happiness of a married man, my dear Gerald, depends on the people he has not married.

GERALD: But if one is in love?

LORD ILLINGWORTH: One should always be in love. That is the reason one should never marry.

GERALD: Love is a very wonderful thing, isn't it?

LORD ILLINGWORTH: When one is in love one begins by deceiving oneself. And one ends by deceiving others. That is what the world calls a romance. But a really *grande passion* is comparatively rare nowadays. It is the privilege of people who have nothing to do. That is the one use of the idle classes in a country, and the only possible explanation of us Harfords.

GERALD: Harfords, Lord Illingworth?

LORD ILLINGWORTH: That is my family name. You should study the Peerage, Gerald. It is the one book a young man about town should know thoroughly, and it is the best thing in fiction the English have ever done. And now, Gerald, you are going into a perfectly new life with me, and I want you to know how to live.

MRS. ARBUTHNOT *appears on terrace behind.*

For the world has been made by fools that wise men should live in it!

Enter L.C. LADY HUNSTANTON *and* DOCTOR DAUBENY.

LADY HUNSTANTON: Ah! Here you are, dear Lord Illingworth. Well, I suppose you have been telling our young friend, Gerald, what his new duties are to be, and giving him a great deal of good advice over a pleasant cigarette.

LORD ILLINGWORTH: I have been giving him the best of advice, Lady Hunstanton, and the best of cigarettes.

LADY HUNSTANTON: I am so sorry I was not here to listen to you, but I suppose I am too old now to learn. Except from you, dear Archdeacon, when you are in your nice pulpit. But then I always know what you are going to say, so I don't feel alarmed. (*Sees* MRS. ARBUTHNOT.) Ah! Dear Mrs. Arbuthnot, do come and join us. Come, dear.

Enter MRS. ARBUTHNOT.

Gerald has been having such a long talk with Lord Illingworth; I am sure you must feel very much flattered at the pleasant way in which everything has turned out for him. Let us sit down. (*They sit down.*) And how is your beautiful embroidery going on?

MRS. ARBUTHNOT: I am always at work, Lady Hunstanton.

LADY HUNSTANTON: Mrs. Daubeny embroiders a little, too, doesn't she?

THE ARCHDEACON: She was very deft with her needle once, quite a Dorcas. But the gout has crippled her fingers a good deal. She has not touched the tambour frame for nine or ten years. But she has many other amusements. She is very much interested in her own health.

LADY HUNSTANTON: Ah! That is always a nice distraction, is it not? Now, what are you talking about, Lord Illingworth? Do tell us.

LORD ILLINGWORTH: I was on the point of explaining to Gerald that the world has always laughed at its own tragedies, that being the only way in which it has been able to bear them. And that, consequently, whatever the world has treated seriously belongs to the comedy side of things.

LADY HUNSTANTON: Now I am quite out of my depth. I usually am when Lord Illingworth says anything. And the Humane Society is most careless. They never rescue me. I am left to sink. I have a dim idea, dear Lord Illingworth, that you are always on the side of the sinners, and I know I always try to be on the side of the saints, but that is as far as I get. And after all, it may be merely the fancy of a drowning person.

LORD ILLINGWORTH: The only difference between the saint and the sinner is that every saint has a past, and every sinner has a future.

LADY HUNSTANTON: Ah! That quite does for me. I haven't a word to say. You and I, dear Mrs. Arbuthnot, are behind the age. We can't follow Lord Illingworth. Too much care was taken with our education, I am afraid. To have been well brought up is a great drawback nowadays. It shuts one out from so much.

MRS. ARBUTHNOT: I should be sorry to follow Lord Illingworth in any of his opinions.

LADY HUNSTANTON: You are quite right, dear.

GERALD *shrugs his shoulders and looks irritably over at his mother. Enter* LADY CAROLINE.

LADY CAROLINE: Jane, have you seen John anywhere?

LADY HUNSTANTON: You needn't be anxious about him, dear. He is with Lady Stutfield; I saw them some time ago, in the Yellow Drawing-room. They seem quite happy together. You are not going, Caroline? Pray sit down.

LADY CAROLINE: I think I had better look after John.

Exit LADY CAROLINE.

LADY HUNSTANTON: It doesn't do to pay men so much attention. And Caroline has really nothing to be anxious about. Lady Stutfield is very sympathetic. She is just as sympathetic about one thing as she is about another. A beautiful nature.

Enter SIR JOHN *and* MRS. ALLONBY.

Ah! Here is Sir John! And with Mrs. Allonby too! I suppose it was Mrs. Allonby I saw him with. Sir John, Caroline has been looking everywhere for you.

MRS. ALLONBY: We have been waiting for her in the Music-room, dear Lady Hunstanton.

LADY HUNSTANTON: Ah! The Music-room, of course. I thought it was the Yellow Drawing-room, my memory is getting so defective. (*To the* ARCHDEACON) Mrs. Daubeny has a wonderful memory, hasn't she?

THE ARCHDEACON: She used to be quite remarkable for her memory, but since her last attack she recalls chiefly the events of her early childhood. But she finds great pleasure in such retrospections, great pleasure.

Enter LADY STUTFIELD *and* MR. KELVIL.

LADY HUNSTANTON: Ah! Dear Lady Stutfield! And what has Mr. Kelvil been talking to you about?

LADY STUTFIELD: About Bimetallism, as well as I remember.

LADY HUNSTANTON: Bimetallism! Is that quite a nice subject? However, I know people discuss everything very freely nowadays. What did Sir John talk to you about, dear Mrs. Allonby?

MRS. ALLONBY: About Patagonia.

LADY HUNSTANTON: Really? What a remote topic! But very improving, I have no doubt.

MRS. ALLONBY: He has been most interesting on the subject of Patagonia. Savages seem to have quite the same views as cultured people on almost all subjects. They are excessively advanced.

LADY HUNSTANTON: What do they do?

MRS. ALLONBY: Apparently everything.

LADY HUNSTANTON: Well, it is very gratifying, dear Archdeacon, is it not, to find that Human Nature is permanently one. On the whole, the world is the same world, is it not?

LORD ILLINGWORTH: The world is simply divided into two classes – those who believe the incredible, like the public – and those who do the improbable –

MRS. ALLONBY: Like yourself?

LORD ILLINGWORTH: Yes; I am always astonishing myself. It is the only thing that makes life worth living.

LADY STUTFIELD: And what have you been doing lately that astonishes you?

LORD ILLINGWORTH: I have been discovering all kinds of beautiful qualities in my own nature.

MRS. ALLONBY: Ah! Don't become quite perfect all at once. Do it gradually!

LORD ILLINGWORTH: I don't intend to grow perfect at all. At least, I hope I shan't. It would be most inconvenient. Women love us for our defects. If we have enough of them, they will forgive us everything, even our gigantic intellects.

MRS. ALLONBY: It is premature to ask us to forgive analysis. We forgive adoration; that is quite as much as should be expected from us.

Enter LORD ALFRED. *He joins* LADY STUTFIELD.

LADY HUNSTANTON: Ah! We women should forgive everything, shouldn't we, dear Mrs. Arbuthnot? I am sure you agree with me in that.

MRS. ARBUTHNOT: I do not, Lady Hunstanton. I think there are many things women should never forgive.

LADY HUNSTANTON: What sort of things?

MRS. ARBUTHNOT: The ruin of another woman's life. (*Moves slowly away to back of stage.*)

LADY HUNSTANTON: Ah! Those things are very sad, no doubt, but I believe there are admirable homes where people of that kind are looked after and reformed, and I think on the whole that the secret of life is to take things very, very easily.

MRS. ALLONBY: The secret of life is never to have an emotion that is unbecoming.

LADY STUTFIELD: The secret of life is to appreciate the pleasure of being terribly, terribly deceived.

KELVIL: The secret of life is to resist temptation, Lady Stutfield.

LORD ILLINGWORTH: There is no secret of life. Life's aim, if it has one, is simply to be always looking for temptations. There are not nearly enough. I sometimes pass a whole day without coming across a single one. It is quite dreadful. It makes one so nervous about the future.

LADY HUNSTANTON (*shakes her fan at him*): I don't know how it is, Lord

Illingworth, but everything you have said to-day seems to me excessively immoral. It has been most interesting, listening to you.

LORD ILLINGWORTH: All thought is immoral. Its very essence is destruction. If you think of anything, you kill it. Nothing survives being thought of.

LADY HUNSTANTON: I don't understand a word, Lord Illingworth. But I have no doubt it is all quite true. Personally, I have very little to reproach myself with, on the score of thinking. I don't believe in women thinking too much. Women should think in moderation, as they should do all things in moderation.

LORD ILLINGWORTH: Moderation is a fatal thing, Lady Hunstanton. Nothing succeeds like excess.

LADY HUNSTANTON: I hope I shall remember that. It sounds an admirable maxim. But I'm beginning to forget everything. It's a great misfortune.

LORD ILLINGWORTH: It is one of your most fascinating qualities, Lady Hunstanton. No woman should have a memory. Memory in a woman is the beginning of dowdiness. One can always tell from a woman's bonnet whether she has got a memory or not.

LADY HUNSTANTON: How charming you are, dear Lord Illingworth. You always find out that one's most glaring fault is one's important virtue. You have the most comforting view of life.

Enter FARQUHAR.

FARQUHAR: Doctor Daubeny's carriage!

Exit FARQUHAR.

LADY HUNSTANTON: My dear Archdeacon! It is only half-past ten.

THE ARCHDEACON (*rising*): I am afraid I must go, Lady Hunstanton. Tuesday is always one of Mrs. Daubeny's bad nights.

LADY HUNSTANTON (*rising*): Well, I won't keep you from her. (*Goes with him towards door.*) I have told Farquhar to put a brace of partridge into the carriage. Mrs. Daubeny may fancy them.

THE ARCHDEACON: It is very kind of you, but Mrs. Daubeny never touches solids now. Lives entirely on jellies. But she is wonderfully cheerful, wonderfully cheerful. She has nothing to complain of.

Exit with LADY HUNSTANTON.

MRS. ALLONBY (*goes over to* LORD ILLINGWORTH): There is a beautiful moon to-night.

LORD ILLINGWORTH: Let us go and look at it. To look at anything that is inconstant is charming nowadays.

MRS. ALLONBY: You have your looking-glass.

LORD ILLINGWORTH: It is unkind. It merely shows me my wrinkles.

MRS. ALLONBY: Mine is better behaved. It never tells me the truth.

LORD ILLINGWORTH: Then it is in love with you.

Exeunt SIR JOHN, LADY STUTFIELD, MR. KELVIL, *and* LORD ALFRED.

GERALD (*to* LORD ILLINGWORTH): May I come too?
LORD ILLINGWORTH: Do, my dear boy. (*Moves towards door with* MRS. ALLONBY *and* GERALD.)

LADY CAROLINE *enters, looks rapidly round and goes out in opposite direction to that taken by* SIR JOHN *and* LADY STUTFIELD.

MRS. ARBUTHNOT: Gerald!
GERALD: What, mother!

Exit LORD ILLINGWORTH *with* MRS. ALLONBY.

MRS. ARBUTHNOT: It is getting late. Let us go home.
GERALD: My dear mother. Do let us wait a little longer. Lord Illingworth is so delightful, and, by the way, mother, I have a great surprise for you. We are starting for India at the end of this month.
MRS. ARBUTHNOT: Let us go home.
GERALD: If you really want to, of course, mother, but I must bid good-bye to Lord Illingworth first. I'll be back in five minutes. (*Exit.*)
MRS. ARBUTHNOT: Let him leave me if he chooses, but not with him – not with him! I couldn't bear it. (*Walks up and down.*)

Enter HESTER.

HESTER: What a lovely night it is, Mrs. Arbuthnot.
MRS. ARBUTHNOT: Is it?
HESTER: Mrs. Arbuthnot, I wish you would let us be friends. You are so different from the other women here. When you came into the Drawing-room this evening, somehow you brought with you a sense of what is good and pure in life. I had been foolish. There are things that are right to say, but that may be said at the wrong time and to the wrong people.
MRS. ARBUTHNOT: I heard what you said. I agree with it, Miss Worsley.
HESTER: I didn't know you had heard it. But I knew you would agree with me. A woman who has sinned should be punished, shouldn't she?
MRS. ARBUTHNOT: Yes.
HESTER: She shouldn't be allowed to come into the society of good men and women?
MRS. ARBUTHNOT: She should not.
HESTER: And the man should be punished in the same way?
MRS. ARBUTHNOT: In the same way. And the children, if there are children, in the same way also?
HESTER: Yes, it is right that the sins of the parents should be visited on the

children. It is a just law. It is God's law.

MRS. ARBUTHNOT: It is one of God's terrible laws. (*Moves away to fireplace.*)

HESTER: You are distressed about your son leaving you, Mrs. Arbuthnot?

MRS. ARBUTHNOT: Yes.

HESTER: Do you like him going away with Lord Illingworth? Of course there is position, no doubt, and money, but position and money are not everything, are they?

MRS. ARBUTHNOT: They are nothing; they bring misery.

HESTER: Then why do you let your son go with him?

MRS. ARBUTHNOT: He wishes it himself.

HESTER: But if you asked him he would stay, would he not?

MRS. ARBUTHNOT: He has set his heart on going.

HESTER: He couldn't refuse you anything. He loves you too much. Ask him to stay. Let me send him to you. He is on the terrace at this moment with Lord Illingworth. I heard them laughing together as I passed through the Music-room.

MRS. ARBUTHNOT: Don't trouble, Miss Worsley, I can wait. It is of no consequence.

HESTER: No, I'll tell him you want him. Do – do ask him to stay.

Exit HESTER.

MRS. ARBUTHNOT: He won't come – I know he won't come.

Enter LADY CAROLINE. *She looks round anxiously. Enter* GERALD.

LADY CAROLINE: Mr. Arbuthnot, may I ask you is Sir John anywhere on the terrace?

GERALD: No, Lady Caroline, he is not on the terrace.

LADY CAROLINE: It is very curious. It is time for him to retire.

Exit LADY CAROLINE.

GERALD: Dear mother, I am afraid I kept you waiting. I forgot all about it. I am so happy to-night, mother; I have never been so happy.

MRS. ARBUTHNOT: At the prospect of going away?

GERALD: Don't put it like that, mother. Of course I am sorry to leave you. Why, you are the best mother in the whole world. But after all, as Lord Illingworth says, it is impossible to live in such a place as Wrockley. You don't mind it. But I'm ambitious; I want something more than that. I want to have a career. I want to do something that will make you proud of me, and Lord Illingworth is going to help me. He is going to do everything for me.

MRS. ARBUTHNOT: Gerald, don't go away with Lord Illingworth. I implore you not to. Gerald, I beg you!

GERALD: Mother, how changeable you are! You don't seem to know your own mind for a single moment. An hour and a half ago in the Drawing-room you agreed to the whole thing; now you turn round and make objections, and try to force me to give up my one chance in life. Yes, my one chance. You don't suppose that men like Lord Illingworth are to be found every day, do you, mother? It is very strange that when I have had such a wonderful piece of good luck, the one person to put difficulties in my way should be my own mother. Besides, you know, mother, I love Hester Worsley. Who could help loving her? I love her more than I ever have told you, far more. And if I had a position, if I had prospects, I could – I could ask her to . . . Don't you understand now, mother, what it means to me to be Lord Illingworth's secretary? To start like that is to find a career ready for one – before one – waiting for one. If I were Lord Illingworth's secretary I could ask Hester to be my wife. As a wretched bank clerk with a hundred a year it would be an impertinence.

MRS. ARBUTHNOT: I fear you need have no hopes of Miss Worsely. I know her views on life. She has just told them to me. (*A pause.*)

GERALD: Then I have my ambition left, at any rate. That is something – I am glad I have that! You have always tried to crush my ambition, mother – haven't you? You have told me that the world is a wicked place, that success is not worth having, that society is shallow, and all that sort of thing – well, I don't believe it, mother. I think the world must be delightful. I think society must be exquisite. I think success is a thing worth having. You have been wrong in all that you taught me, mother, quite wrong. Lord Illingworth is a successful man. He is a fashionable man. He is a man who lives in the world and for it. Well, I would give anything to be just like Lord Illingworth.

MRS. ARBUTHNOT: I would sooner see you dead.

GERALD: Mother, what is your objection to Lord Illingworth? Tell me – tell me right out. What is it?

MRS. ARBUTHNOT: He is a bad man.

GERALD: In what way bad? I don't understand what you mean.

MRS. ARBUTHNOT: I will tell you.

GERALD: I suppose you think him bad, because he doesn't believe the same things as you do. Well, men are different from women, mother. It is natural that they should have different views.

MRS. ARBUTHNOT: It is not what Lord Illingworth believes, or what he does not believe, that makes him bad. It is what he is.

GERALD: Mother, is it something you know of him? Something you actually know?

MRS. ARBUTHNOT: It is something I know.

GERALD: Something you are quite sure of?

MRS. ARBUTHNOT: Quite sure of.

GERALD: How long have you known it?

MRS. ARBUTHNOT: For twenty years.

GERALD: Is it fair to go back twenty years in any man's career? And what have you or I to do with Lord Illingworth's early life? What business is it of ours?

MRS. ARBUTHNOT: What this man has been, he is now, and will be always.

GERALD: Mother, tell me what Lord Illingworth did? If he did anything shameful, I will not go away with him. Surely you know me well enough for that?

MRS. ARBUTHNOT: Gerald, come near to me. Quite close to me, as you used to do when you were a little boy, when you were mother's own boy.

GERALD *sits down beside his mother. She runs her fingers through his hair, and strokes his hands.*

Gerald, there was a girl once, she was very young, she was little over eighteen at the time. George Harford – that was Lord Illingworth's name then – George Harford met her. She knew nothing about life. He – knew everything. He made this girl love him. He made her love so much that she left her father's house with him one morning. She loved him so much, and he had promised to marry her! He had solemnly promised to marry her, and she had believed him. She was very young, and – and ignorant of what life really is. But he put the marriage off from week to week, and month to month. She trusted in him all the while. She loved him. Before her child was born – for she had a child – she implored him for the child's sake to marry her, that the child might have a name, that her sin might not be visited on the child, who was innocent. He refused. After the child was born she left him, taking the child away, and her life was ruined, and her soul ruined, and all that was sweet, and good, and pure in her ruined also. She suffered terribly – she suffers now. She will always suffer. For her there is no joy, no peace, no atonement. She is a woman who drags a chain like a guilty thing. She is a woman who wears a mask, like a thing that is a leper. The fire cannot purify her. The waters cannot quench her anguish. Nothing can heal her! No anodyne can give her sleep! No poppies forgetfulness! She is lost! She is a lost soul! That is why I call Lord Illingworth a bad man. That is why I don't want my boy to be with him.

GERALD: My dear mother, it all sounds very tragic, of course. But I dare say the girl was just as much to blame as Lord Illingworth was. After all, would a really nice girl, a girl with any nice feelings at all, go away from her home with a man to whom she was not married, and live with him as his wife? No nice girl would.

MRS. ARBUTHNOT (*after a pause*): Gerald, I withdraw all my objections. You are at liberty to go away with Lord Illingworth, when and where you choose.

GERALD: Dear mother, I knew you wouldn't stand in my way. You are the best woman God ever made. And, as for Lord Illingworth, I don't believe he is capable of anything infamous or base. I can't believe it of him – I can't.

HESTER (*outside*): Let me go! Let me go!

Enter HESTER *in terror, and rushes over to* GERALD *and flings herself in his arms.*

HESTER: Oh! Save me – save me from him!

GERALD: From whom?

HESTER: He has insulted me! Horribly insulted me! Save me!

GERALD: Who? Who has dared – ?

LORD ILLINGWORTH *enters at back of stage.* HESTER *breaks from* GERALD'S *arms and points to him.*

GERALD (*he is quite beside himself with rage and indignation*): Lord Illingworth, you have insulted the purest thing on God's earth, a thing as pure as my own mother. You have insulted the woman I love most in the world with my own mother. As there is a God in Heaven, I will kill you!

MRS. ARBUTHNOT (*rushing across and catching hold of him*): No! no!

GERALD (*thrusting her back*): Don't hold me, mother. Don't hold me – I'll kill him!

MRS. ARBUTHNOT: Gerald!

GERALD: Let me go, I say!

MRS. ARBUTHNOT: Stop, Gerald, stop! He is your own father!

GERALD *clutches his mother's hands and looks into her face. She sinks slowly on the ground in shame.* HESTER *steals towards the door.* LORD ILLINGWORTH *frowns and bites his lip. After a time* GERALD *raises his mother up, puts his arm round her, and leads her from the room.*

ACT DROP

ACT FOUR

SCENE: *Sitting-room at Mrs. Arbuthnot's house at Wrockley. Large open French window at back, looking on to garden. Doors R.C. and L.C.*

GERALD ARBUTHNOT *writing at table.*

Enter ALICE *R.C. followed by* LADY HUNSTANTON *and* MRS. ALLONBY.

ALICE: Lady Hunstanton and Mrs. Allonby. (*Exit L.C.*)

LADY HUNSTANTON: Good-morning, Gerald.

GERALD (*rising*): Good-morning, Lady Hunstanton. Good-morning, Mrs. Allonby.

LADY HUNSTANTON (*sitting down*): We came to inquire for your dear mother, Gerald. I hope she is better?

GERALD: My mother has not come down yet, Lady Hunstanton.

LADY HUNSTANTON: Ah, I am afraid the heat was too much for her last night. I think there must have been thunder in the air. Or perhaps it was the music. Music makes one feel so romantic – at least it always gets on one's nerves.

MRS. ALLONBY: It's the same thing, nowadays.

LADY HUNSTANTON: I am so glad I don't know what you mean, dear. I am afraid you mean something wrong. Ah, I see you're examining Mrs. Arbuthnot's pretty room. Isn't it nice and old-fashioned?

MRS. ALLONBY (*surveying the room through her lorgnette*): It looks quite the happy English home.

LADY HUNSTANTON: That's just the word, dear; that just describes it. One feels your mother's good influence in everything she has about her, Gerald.

MRS. ALLONBY: Lord Illingworth says that all influence is bad, but that a good influence is the worst in the world.

LADY HUNSTANTON: When Lord Illingworth knows Mrs. Arbuthnot better he will change his mind. I must certainly bring him here.

MRS. ALLONBY: I should like to see Lord Illingworth in a happy English home.

LADY HUNSTANTON: It would do him a great deal of good, dear. Most women in London, nowadays, seem to furnish their rooms with nothing but orchids, foreigners, and French novels. But here we have the room of a sweet saint. Fresh natural flowers, books that don't shock one, pictures that one can look at without blushing.

MRS. ALLONBY: But I like blushing.

LADY HUNSTANTON: Well, there *is* a good deal to be said for blushing, if one can do it at the proper moment. Poor dear Hunstanton used to tell me I didn't blush nearly often enough. But then he was so very particular. He wouldn't let me know any of his men friends, except those who were over seventy, like poor Lord Ashton; who afterwards, by the way, was brought into the Divorce Court. A most unfortunate case.

MRS. ALLONBY: I delight in men over seventy. They always offer one the devotion of a lifetime. I think seventy an ideal age for a man.

LADY HUNSTANTON: She is quite incorrigible, Gerald, isn't she? By-the-by, Gerald, I hope your dear mother will come and see me more often now. You and Lord Illingworth start almost immediately, don't you?

GERALD: I have given up my intention of being Lord Illingworth's secretary.

LADY HUNSTANTON: Surely not, Gerald! It would be most unwise of you. What reason can you have?

GERALD: I don't think I should be suitable for the post.

MRS. ALLONBY: I wish Lord Illingworth would ask me to be his secretary. But he says I am not serious enough.

LADY HUNSTANTON: My dear, you really mustn't talk like that in this house. Mrs. Arbuthnot doesn't know anything about the wicked society in which we all live. She won't go into it. She is far too good. I consider it was a great honour her coming to me last night. It gave quite an atmosphere of respectability to the party.

MRS. ALLONBY: Ah, that must have been what you thought was thunder in the air.

LADY HUNTSTATON: My dear, how can you say that? There is no resemblance between the two things at all. But really, Gerald, what do you mean by not being suitable?

GERALD: Lord Illingworth's views of life and mine are too different.

LADY HUNSTANTON: But, my dear Gerald, at your age you shouldn't have any views of life. They are quite out of place. You must be guided by others in this matter. Lord Illingworth has made you the most flattering offer, and travelling with him you would see the world – as much of it, at least, as one should look at – under the best auspices possible, and stay with all the right people, which is so important at this solemn moment in your career.

GERALD: I don't want to see the world; I've seen enough of it.

MRS. ALLONBY: I hope you don't think you have exhausted life, Mr. Arbuthnot. When a man says that, one knows that life has exhausted him.

GERALD: I don't wish to leave my mother.

LADY HUNSTANTON: Now, Gerald, that is pure laziness on your part. Not leave your mother! If I were your mother I would insist on your going.

Enter ALICE *L.C.*

ALICE: Mrs. Arbuthnot's compliments, my lady, but she has a bad headache, and cannot see any one this morning. (*Exit R.C.*)

LADY HUNSTANTON (*rising*): A bad headache! I am so sorry! Perhaps you'll bring her up to Hunstanton this afternoon, if she is better, Gerald.

GERALD: I am afraid not this afternoon, Lady Hunstanton.

LADY HUNSTANTON: Well, to-morrow, then. Ah, if you had a father, Gerald, he wouldn't let you waste your life here. He would send you with Lord Illingworth at once. But mothers are so weak. They give up to their sons in everything. We are all heart, all heart. Come, dear, I must call at the rectory and inquire for Mrs. Daubeny, who, I am afraid, is far from well. It is wonderful how the Archdeacon bears up, quite wonderful. He is the most sympathetic of husbands. Quite a model. Good-bye, Gerald; give my fondest love to your mother.

MRS. ALLONBY: Good-bye, Mr. Arbuthnot.

GERALD: Good-bye.

Exit LADY HUNSTANTON *and* MRS. ALLONBY. GERALD *sits down and reads over his letter.*

GERALD: What name can I sign? I, who have no right to any name. (*Signs name, puts letter into envelope, addresses it, and is about to seal it, when door L.C. opens and* MRS. ARBUTHNOT *enters.* GERALD *lays down sealing-wax. Mother and son look at each other.*)

LADY HUNSTANTON: (*through French window at the back*): Good-bye again, Gerald. We are taking the short cut across your pretty garden. Now, remember my advice to you – start at once with Lord Illingworth.

MRS. ALLONBY: *Au revoir*, Mr. Arbuthnot. Mind you bring me back something nice from your travels – not an Indian shawl – on no account an Indian shawl. (*Exeunt.*)

GERALD: Mother, I have just written to him.

MRS. ARBUTHNOT: To whom?

GERALD: To my father. I have written to tell him to come here at four o'clock this afternoon.

MRS. ARBUTHNOT: He shall not come here. He shall not cross the threshold of my house.

GERALD: He must come.

MRS. ARBUTHNOT: Gerald, if you are going away with Lord Illingworth, go at once. Go before it kills me; but don't ask me to meet him.

GERALD: Mother, you don't understand. Nothing in the world would induce me to go away with Lord Illingworth, or to leave you. Surely you know me well enough for that. No; I have written to him to say –

MRS. ARBUTHNOT: What can you have to say to him?

GERALD: Can't you guess, mother, what I have written in this letter?

MRS. ARBUTHNOT: No.

GERALD: Mother, surely you can. Think, think what must be done, now, at once, within the next few days.

MRS. ARBUTHNOT: There is nothing to be done.

GERALD: I have written to Lord Illingworth to tell him that he must marry you.

MRS. ARBUTHNOT: Marry me?

GERALD: Mother, I will force him to do it. The wrong that has been done you must be repaired. Atonement must be made. Justice may be slow, mother, but it comes in the end. In a few days you shall be Lord Illingworth's lawful wife.

MRS. ARBUTHNOT: But, Gerald –

GERALD: I will insist upon his doing it. I will make him do it; he will not dare to refuse.

MRS. ARBUTHNOT: But, Gerald, it is I who refuse. I will not marry Lord Illingworth.

GERALD: Not marry him? Mother!

MRS. ARBUTHNOT: I will not marry him.

GERALD: But you don't understand: it is for your sake I am talking, not for mine. This marriage, this necessary marriage, this marriage which for obvious reasons must inevitably take place, will not help me, will not give me a name that will be really, rightly mine to bear. But surely it will be something for you, that you, my mother, should, however late, become the wife of the man who is my father. Will not that be something?

MRS. ARBUTHNOT: I will not marry him.

GERALD: Mother, you must.

MRS. ARBUTHNOT: I will not. You talk of atonement for a wrong done. What atonement can be made to me? There is no atonement possible. I am disgraced; he is not. That is all. It is the usual history of a man and a woman as it usually happens, as it always happens. And the ending is the ordinary ending. The woman suffers. The man goes free.

GERALD: I don't know if that is the ordinary ending, mother; I hope it is not. But your life, at any rate, shall not end like that. The man shall make whatever reparation is possible. It is not enough. It does not wipe out the past, I know that. But at least it makes the future better, better for you, mother.

MRS. ARBUTHNOT: I refuse to marry Lord Illingworth.

GERALD: If he came to you himself and asked you to be his wife you would give him a different answer. Remember, he is my father.

MRS. ARBUTHNOT: If he came himself, which he will not do, my answer would be the same. Remember, I am your mother.

GERALD: Mother, you make it terribly difficult for me by talking like that; and I can't understand why you won't look at this matter from the right, from the only proper standpoint. It is to take away the bitterness out of your life, to take away the shadow that lies on your name, that this marriage must take place. There is no alternative; and after the marriage you and I can go away together. But the marriage must take place first. It is a duty that you owe, not merely to yourself, but to all other women – yes; to all the other women in the world, lest he betray more.

MRS. ARBUTHNOT: I owe nothing to other women. There is not one of them to help me. There is not one woman in the world to whom I could go for pity, if I would take it, or for sympathy, if I could win it. Women are hard on each other. That girl, last night, good though she is, fled from the room as though I were a tainted thing. She was right. I am a tainted thing. But my wrongs are my own, and I will bear them alone. I must bear them alone. What have women who have not sinned to do with me, or I with them? We do not understand each other.

Enter HESTER *behind.*

GERALD: I implore you to do what I ask you.

MRS. ARBUTHNOT: What son has ever asked of his mother to make so hideous a sacrifice? None.

GERALD: What mother has ever refused to marry the father of her own child? None.

MRS. ARBUTHNOT: Let me be the first, then. I will not do it.

GERALD: Mother, you believe in religion, and you brought me up to believe in it also. Well, surely your religion, the religion that you taught me when I was a boy, mother, must tell you that I am right. You know it, you feel it.

MRS. ARBUTHNOT: I do not know it. I do not feel it, nor will I ever stand before God's altar and ask God's blessing on so hideous a mockery as a marriage between me and George Harford. I will not say the words the Church bids us to say. I will not say them. I dare not. How could I swear to love the man I loathe, to honour him who wrought you dishonour, to obey him who, in his mastery, made me to sin? No; marriage is a sacrament for those who love each other. It is not for such as him, or such as me. Gerald, to save you from the world's sneers and taunts I have lied to the world. For twenty years I have lied to the world. I could not tell the world the truth. Who can ever? But not for my own sake will I lie to God, and in God's presence. No, Gerald, no ceremony, Church-hallowed or State-made, shall ever bind me to George Harford. It may be that I am too bound to him already, who, robbing me, yet left me richer, so that in the mire of my life I found the pearl of price, or what I thought would be so.

GERALD: I don't understand you now.

MRS. ARBUTHNOT: Men don't understand what mothers are. I am no different from other women except in the wrong done me and the wrong I did, and my very heavy punishments and great disgrace. And yet, to bear you I had to look on death. To nurture you I had to wrestle with it. Death fought with me for you. All women have to fight with death to keep their children. Death, being childless, wants our children from us. Gerald, when you were naked I clothed you, when you were hungry I gave you food. Night and day all that long winter I tended you. No office is too mean, no care too lowly for the thing we women love – and oh! How *I* loved *you*. Not Hannah, Samuel more. And you needed love, for you were weakly, and only love could have kept you alive. Only love can keep any one alive. And boys are careless often, and without thinking give pain, and we always fancy that when they come to man's estate and know us better they will repay us. But it is not so. The world draws them from our side, and they make friends with whom they are happier than they are with us, and have amusements from which we are barred, and interests that are not ours; and they are unjust to us often, for when they find life bitter they blame us for it, and when they find it sweet we do not taste its sweetness with them. . . . You made many friends and went into their houses and were glad with them, and I, knowing my secret, did not dare to follow, but stayed at home and closed the door, shut out the sun and sat in darkness. My past was ever with me. . . . And you thought I didn't care for the pleasant things of life. I tell you I longed for them, but did not dare to touch them, feeling I had no right. You thought I was happier working amongst the poor. That was my mission, you imagined. It was not, but where else was I to go? The sick do not ask if the hand that smooths their pillow is pure, nor the dying care if the lips that touch their brow have known the kiss of sin. It was you I thought of all the time; I gave to them the love you did not need; lavished on them a love that was not theirs. . . . And you thought I spent too much of my time in going to Church, and in Church duties. But where else could I turn? God's house is the only house where sinners are made welcome, and you were always in my heart, Gerald, too much in my heart. For, though day after day, at morn or evensong, I have knelt in God's house, I have never repented of my sin. How could I repent of my sin when you, my love, were its fruit. Even now that you are bitter to me I cannot repent. I do not. You are more to me than innocence. I would rather be your mother – oh, much rather – than have been always pure.... Oh, don't you see? Don't you understand! It is my dishonour that has made you so dear to me. It is my disgrace that has bound you so closely to me. It is the price I paid for you – the price of soul and body – that makes me love you as I do. Oh, don't ask me to do this horrible thing. Child of my shame, be still the child of my shame!

GERALD: Mother, I didn't know you loved me so much as that. And I will be a better son to you than I have been. And you and I must never leave each other ... but, mother ... I can't help it ... you must become my father's wife. You must marry him. It is your duty.

HESTER (*running forward and embracing* MRS. ARBUTHNOT): No, no; you shall not. That would be real dishonour, the first you have ever known. That would be real disgrace: the first to touch you. Leave him and come with me. There are other countries than England.... Oh! Other countries over sea, better, wiser, and less unjust lands. The world is very wide and very big.

MRS. ARBUTHNOT: No, not for me. For me the world is shrivelled to a palm's breadth, and where I walk there are thorns.

HESTER: It shall not be so. We shall somewhere find green valleys and fresh waters, and if we weep, well, we shall weep together. Have we not both loved him?

GERALD: Hester!

HESTER (*waving him back*): Don't, don't! You cannot love me at all unless you love her also. You cannot honour me, unless she's holier to you. In her all womanhood is martyred. Not she alone, but all of us are stricken in her house.

GERALD: Hester, Hester, what shall I do?

HESTER: Do you respect the man who is your father?

GERALD: Respect him? I despise him! He is infamous.

HESTER: I thank you for saving me from him last night.

GERALD: Ah, that is nothing. I would die to save you. But you don't tell me what to do now!

HESTER: Have I not thanked you for saving *me*?

GERALD: But what should I do?

HESTER: Ask your own heart, not mine. I never had a mother to save, or shame.

MRS. ARBUTHNOT: He is hard – he is hard. Let me go away.

GERALD (*rushes over and kneels down beside his mother*): Mother, forgive me; I have been to blame.

MRS. ARBUTHNOT: Don't kiss my hands; they are cold. My heart is cold: something has broken it.

HESTER: Ah, don't say that. Hearts live by being wounded. Pleasure may turn a heart to stone, riches may make it callous, but sorrow – oh, sorrow, cannot break it. Besides, what sorrows have you now? Why, at this moment you are more dear to him than ever, *dear* though you have *been*, and oh, how dear you *have* been always. Ah! Be kind to him.

GERALD: You are my mother and my father all in one. I need no second parent. It was for you I spoke, for you alone. Oh, say something, mother. Have I but found one love to lose another? Don't tell me that. Oh, mother, you are cruel. (*Gets up and flings himself sobbing on a sofa.*)

MRS. ARBUTHNOT (*to* HESTER): But has he found indeed another love?

HESTER: You know I have loved him always.

MRS. ARBUTHNOT: But we are very poor.

HESTER: Who, being loved, is poor? Oh, no one. I hate my riches. They are a burden. Let him share it with me.

MRS. ARBUTHNOT: But we are disgraced. We rank among the outcasts. Gerald is nameless. The sins of the parents should be visited on the children. It is God's law.

HESTER: I was wrong. God's law is only Love.

MRS. ARBUTHNOT (*rises, and taking* HESTER *by the hand, goes slowly over to where* GERALD *is lying on the sofa with his head buried in his hands. She touches him and he looks up*): Gerald, I cannot give you a father, but I have brought you a wife.

GERALD: Mother, I am not worthy either of her or you.

MRS. ARBUTHNOT: So she comes first, you are worthy. And when you are away, Gerald . . . with . . . her – oh, think of me sometimes. Don't forget me. And when you pray, pray for me. We should pray when we are happiest, and you will be happy, Gerald.

HESTER: Oh, you don't think of leaving us?

GERALD: Mother, you won't leave us?

MRS. ARBUTHNOT: I might bring shame upon you!

GERALD: Mother!

MRS. ARBUTHNOT: For a little then; and if you let me, near you always.

HESTER (*to* MRS. ARBUTHNOT): Come out with us to the garden.

MRS. ARBUTHNOT: Later on, later on.

Exeunt HESTER *and* GERALD.

MRS. ARBUTHNOT *goes towards door L.C. Stops at looking-glass over mantelpiece and looks into it.*

Enter ALICE *R.C.*

ALICE: A gentleman to see you, ma'am.

MRS. ARBUTHNOT: Say I am not at home. Show me the card. (*Takes card from salver and looks at it.*) Say I will not see him.

LORD ILLINGWORTH *enters.* MRS. ARBUTHNOT *sees him in the glass and starts, but does not turn round. Exit* ALICE.

What can you have to say to me to-day, George Harford? You can have nothing to say to me. You must leave this house.

LORD ILLINGWORTH: Rachel, Gerald knows everything about you and me now, so some arrangement must be come to that will suit us all three. I assure you, he will find in me the most charming and generous of fathers.

MRS. ARBUTHNOT: My son may come in at any moment. I saved you last night. I may not be able to save you again. My son feels my dishonour strongly, terribly strongly. I beg you to go.

LORD ILLINGWORTH (*sitting down*): Last night was excessively unfortunate. That silly Puritan girl making a scene merely because I wanted to kiss her. What harm is there in a kiss?

MRS. ARBUTHNOT (*turning round*): A kiss may ruin a human life, George Harford. *I* know that. *I* know that too well.

LORD ILLINGWORTH: We won't discuss that at present. What is of importance to-day, as yesterday, is still our son. I am extremely fond of him, as you know, and odd though it may seem to you, I admired his conduct last night immensely. He took up the cudgels for that pretty prude with wonderful promptitude. He is just what I should have liked a son of mine to be. Except that no son of mine should ever take the side of the Puritans; that is always an error. Now, what I propose is this.

MRS. ARBUTHNOT: Lord Illingworth, no proposition of yours interests me.

LORD ILLINGWORTH: According to our ridiculous English laws, I can't legitimise Gerald. But I can leave him my property. Illingworth is entailed, of course, but it is a tedious barrack of a place. He can have Ashby, which is much prettier, Harborough, which has the best shooting in the north of England, and the house in St. James's Square. What more can a gentleman desire in this world?

MRS. ARBUTHNOT: Nothing more, I am quite sure.

LORD ILLINGWORTH: As for a title, a title is really rather a nuisance in these democratic days. As George Harford I had everything I wanted. Now I have merely everything that other people want, which isn't nearly so pleasant. Well, my proposal is this.

MRS. ARBUTHNOT: I told you I was not interested, and I beg you to go.

LORD ILLINGWORTH: The boy is to be with you for six months in the year, and with me for the other six. That is perfectly fair, is it not? You can have whatever allowance you like, and live where you choose. As for your past, no one knows anything about it except myself and Gerald. There is the Puritan, of course, the Puritan in white muslin, but she doesn't count. She couldn't tell the story without explaining that she objected to being kissed, could she? And all the women would think her a fool and the men think her a bore. And you need not be afraid that Gerald won't be my heir. I needn't tell you I have not the slightest intention of marrying.

MRS. ARBUTHNOT: You come too late. My son has no need of you. You are not necessary.

LORD ILLINGWORTH: What do you mean, Rachel?

MRS. ARBUTHNOT: That you are not necessary to Gerald's career. He does not require you.

LORD ILLINGWORTH: I do not understand you.

MRS. ARBUTHNOT: Look into the garden. (LORD ILLINGWORTH *rises and goes towards window*.) You had better not let them see you; you bring unpleasant memories. (LORD ILLINGWORTH *looks out and starts*.) She loves him. They love each other. We are safe from you, and we are going away.

LORD ILLINGWORTH: Where?

MRS. ARBUTHNOT: We will not tell you, and if you find us we will not know you. You seem surprised. What welcome would you get from the girl whose lips you tried to soil, from the boy whose life you have shamed, from the mother whose dishonour comes from you?

LORD ILLINGWORTH: You have grown hard, Rachel.

MRS. ARBUTHNOT: I was too weak once. It is well for me that I have changed.

LORD ILLINGWORTH: I was very young at the time. We men know life too early.

MRS. ARBUTHNOT: And we women know life too late. That is the difference between men and women. (*A pause*).

LORD ILLINGWORTH: Rachel, I want my son. My money may be of no use to him now. I may be of no use to him, but I want my son. Bring us together, Rachel. You can do it if you choose. (*Sees letter on table*).

MRS. ARBUTHNOT: There is no room in my boy's life for *you*. He is not interested in *you*.

LORD ILLINGWORTH: Then why does he write to me?

MRS. ARBUTHNOT: What do you mean?

LORD ILLINGWORTH: What letter is this? (*Takes up letter*.)

MRS. ARBUTHNOT: That – is nothing. Give it to me.

LORD ILLINGWORTH: It is addressed to *me*.

MRS. ARBUTHNOT: You are not to open it. I forbid you to open it.

LORD ILLINGWORTH: And in Gerald's handwriting.

MRS. ARBUTHNOT: It was not to have been sent. It is a letter he wrote to you this morning, before he saw me. But he is sorry now he wrote it, very sorry. You are not to open it. Give it to me.

LORD ILLINGWORTH: It belongs to me. (*Opens it, sits down and reads it slowly*. MRS. ARBUTHNOT *watches him all the time*.) You have read this letter, I suppose, Rachel?

MRS. ARBUTHNOT: No.

LORD ILLINGWORTH: You know what is in it?

MRS. ARBUTHNOT: Yes!

LORD ILLINGWORTH: I don't admit for a moment that the boy is right in what he says. I don't admit that it is any duty of mine to marry you. I deny it entirely. But to get my son back I am ready – yes, I am ready to marry you, Rachel – and to treat you always with the deference and respect due to my wife. I will marry you as soon as you choose. I give you my word of honour.

MRS. ARBUTHNOT: You made that promise to me once before and broke it.

LORD ILLINGWORTH: I will keep it now. And that will show you that I love my son, at least as much as you love him. For when I marry you, Rachel, there are some ambitions I shall have to surrender. High ambitions, too, if any ambition is high.

MRS. ARBUTHNOT: I decline to marry you, Lord Illingworth.

LORD ILLINGWORTH: Are you serious?

MRS. ARBUTHNOT: Yes.

LORD ILLINGWORTH: Do tell me your reasons. They would interest me enormously.

MRS. ARBUTHNOT: I have already explained them to my son.

LORD ILLINGWORTH: I suppose they were intensely sentimental, weren't they? You women live by your emotions and for them. You have no philosophy of life.

MRS. ARBUTHNOT: You are right. We women live by our emotions and for them. By our passions, and for them, if you will. I have two passions, Lord Illingworth: my love of him, my hate of you. You cannot kill those. They feed each other.

LORD ILLINGWORTH: What sort of love is that which needs to have hate as its brother?

MRS. ARBUTHNOT: It is the sort of love I have for Gerald. Do you think that terrible? Well, it is terrible. All love is terrible. All love is a tragedy. I loved you once, Lord Illingworth. Oh, what a tragedy for a woman to have loved you!

LORD ILLINGWORTH: So you really refuse to marry me?

MRS. ARBUTHNOT: Yes.

LORD ILLINGWORTH: Because you hate me?

MRS. ARBUTHNOT: Yes.

LORD ILLINGWORTH: And does my son hate me as you do?

MRS. ARBUTHNOT: No.

LORD ILLINGWORTH: I am glad of that, Rachel.

MRS. ARBUTHNOT: He merely despises you.

LORD ILLINGWORTH: What a pity! What a pity for him, I mean.

MRS. ARBUTHNOT: Don't be deceived, George. Children begin by loving their parents. After a time they judge them. Rarely if ever do they forgive them.

LORD ILLINGWORTH (*reads letter over again, very slowly*): May I ask by what arguments you made the boy who wrote this letter, this beautiful, passionate letter, believe that you should not marry his father, the father of your own child?

MRS. ARBUTHNOT: It was not I who made him see it. It was another.

LORD ILLINGWORTH: What *fin-de-siècle* person?

MRS. ARBUTHNOT: The Puritan, Lord Illingworth. (*A pause.*)

LORD ILLINGWORTH (*winces, then rises slowly and goes over to table where his hat and gloves are.* MRS. ARBUTHNOT *is standing close to the table. He picks up one of the gloves, and begins putting it on*): There is not much then for me to do here, Rachel?

MRS. ARBUTHNOT: Nothing.

LORD ILLINGWORTH: It is good-bye, is it?

MRS. ARBUTHNOT: For ever, I hope, this time, Lord Illingworth.

LORD ILLINGWORTH: How curious! At this moment you look exactly as you looked the night you left me twenty years ago. You have just the same expression in your mouth. Upon my word, Rachel, no woman ever loved me as you did. Why, you gave yourself to me like a flower, to do anything I liked with. You were the prettiest of playthings, the most fascinating of small romances. . . . (*Pulls out watch.*) Quarter to two! Must be strolling back to Hunstanton. Don't suppose I shall see you there again. I'm sorry, I am, really. It's been an amusing experience to have met amongst people of one's own rank, and treated quite seriously too, one's mistress and one's –

MRS. ARBUTHNOT *snatches up glove and strikes* LORD ILLINGWORTH *across the face with it.* LORD ILLINGWORTH *starts. He is dazed by the insult of his punishment. Then he controls himself and goes to window and looks out at his son. Sighs and leaves the room.*

MRS. ARBUTHNOT (*falls sobbing on the sofa*): He would have said it. He would have said it.

Enter GERALD *and* HESTER *from the garden.*

GERALD: Well, dear mother. You never came out after all. So we have come in to fetch you. Mother, you have not been crying? (*Kneels down beside her.*)

MRS. ARBUTHNOT: My boy! My boy! My boy! (*Running her fingers through his hair.*)

HESTER (*coming over*): But you have two children now. You'll let me be your daughter?

MRS. ARBUTHNOT (*looking up*): Would you choose me for a mother?

HESTER: You of all women I have ever known.

They move towards the door leading into garden with their arms round each other's waists. GERALD *goes to table L.C. for his hat. On turning round he sees* LORD ILLINGWORTH'S *glove lying on the floor, and picks it up.*

GERALD: Hallo, mother, whose glove is this? You have had a visitor. Who was it?

MRS. ARBUTHNOT (*turning round*): Oh, no one. No one in particular. A man of no importance.

CURTAIN

AN IDEAL HUSBAND

The persons of the play

THE EARL OF CAVERSHAM, K.G.
VISCOUNT GORING, his son
SIR ROBERT CHILTERN, Bart.,
  Under-Secretary for Foreign
  Affairs
VICOMTE DE NANJAC, Attaché
  at French Embassy in London
MR. MONTFORD
MASON, Butler to Sir Robert
  Chiltern

PHIPPS, Lord Goring's servant
JAMES and HAROLD, Footmen
LADY CHILTERN
LADY MARKBY
THE COUNTESS OF BASILDON
MRS. MARCHMONT
MISS MABEL CHILTERN, Sir Robert
  Chiltern's sister
MRS. CHEVELEY

ACT ONE

SCENE: *The octagon room at Sir Robert Chiltern's house in
Grosvenor Square, London. The action of the play is completed
within twenty-four hours.* TIME: *The present.*

The room is brilliantly lighted and full of guests.

At the top of the staircase stands LADY CHILTERN, *a woman
of grave Greek beauty, about twenty-seven years of age. She re-
ceives the guests as they come up. Over the well of the staircase
hangs a great chandelier with wax lights, which illumine a large
eighteenth-century French tapestry – representing the Triumph
of Love, from a design by Boucher – that is stretched on the stair-
case wall. On the right is the entrance to the music-room. The
sound of a string quartette is faintly heard. The entrance on the
left leads to other reception-rooms.* MRS. MARCHMONT *and*
LADY BASILDON, *two very pretty women, are seated together on
a Louis Seize sofa. They are types of exquisite fragility. Their
affectation of manner has a delicate charm. Watteau would have
loved to paint them.*

MRS. MARCHMONT: Going on to the Hartlocks' to-night, Margaret?
LADY BASILDON: I suppose so. Are you?
MRS. MARCHMONT: Yes. Horribly tedious parties they give, don't they?
LADY BASILDON: Horribly tedious! Never know why I go. Never know
why I go anywhere.
MRS. MARCHMONT: I come here to be educated.
LADY BASILDON: Ah! I hate being educated!

MRS. MARCHMONT: So do I. It puts one almost on a level with the commercial classes, doesn't it? But dear Gertrude Chiltern is always telling me that I should have some serious purpose in life. So I come here to try to find one.

LADY BASILDON (*looking round through her lorgnette*): I don't see anybody here to-night whom one could possibly call a serious purpose. The man who took me in to dinner talked to me about his wife the whole time.

MRS. MARCHMONT: How very trivial of him!

LADY BASILDON: Terribly trivial! What did your man talk about?

MRS. MARCHMONT: About myself.

LADY BASILDON (*languidly*): And were you interested?

MRS. MARCHMONT (*shaking her head*): Not in the smallest degree.

LADY BASILDON: What martyrs we are, dear Margaret!

MRS. MARCHMONT (*rising*): And how well it becomes us, Olivia!

They rise and go towards the music-room. The VICOMTE DE NANJAC, *a young attaché known for his neckties and his Anglomania, approaches with a low bow, and enters into conversation.*

MASON (*announcing guests from the top of the staircase*): Mr. and Lady Jane Barford. Lord Caversham.

Enter LORD CAVERSHAM, *an old gentleman of seventy, wearing the riband and star of the Garter. A fine Whig type. Rather like a portrait by Lawrence.*

LORD CAVERSHAM: Good-evening, Lady Chiltern! Has my good-for-nothing young son been here?

LADY CHILTERN (*smiling*): I don't think Lord Goring has arrived yet.

MABEL CHILTERN (*coming up to* LORD CAVERSHAM): Why do you call Lord Goring good-for-nothing?

MABEL CHILTERN is a perfect example of the English type of prettiness, the apple-blossom type. She has all the fragrance and freedom of a flower. There is ripple after ripple of sunlight in her hair, and the little mouth, with its parted lips, is expectant, like the mouth of a child. She has the fascinating tyranny of youth, and the astonishing courage of innocence. To sane people she is not reminiscent of any work of art. But she is really like a Tanagra statuette, and would be rather annoyed if she were told so.

LORD CAVERSHAM: Because he leads such an idle life.

MABEL CHILTERN: How can you say such a thing? Why, he rides in the Row at ten o'clock in the morning, goes to the Opera three times a week, changes his clothes at least five times a day, and dines out every night of the season. You don't call that leading an idle life, do you?

LORD CAVERSHAM (*looking at her with a kindly twinkle in his eyes*): You are a very charming young lady!

MABEL CHILTERN: How sweet of you to say that, Lord Caversham! Do come to us more often. You know we are always at home on Wednesdays, and you look so well with your star!

LORD CAVERSHAM: Never go anywhere now. Sick of London Society. Shouldn't mind being introduced to my own tailor; he always votes on the right side. But object strongly to being sent down to dinner with my wife's milliner. Never could stand Lady Caversham's bonnets.

MABEL CHILTERN: Oh, I love London Society! I think it has immensely improved. It is entirely composed now of beautiful idiots and brilliant lunatics. Just what Society should be?

LORD CAVERSHAM: Hum! Which is Goring? Beautiful idiot, or the other thing?

MABEL CHILTERN (gravely): I have been obliged for the present to put Lord Goring into a class quite by himself. But he is developing charmingly!

LORD CAVERSHAM: Into what?

MABEL CHILTERN (with a little curtsey): I hope to let you know very soon, Lord Caversham!

MASON (announcing guests): Lady Markby. Mrs. Cheveley.

Enter LADY MARKBY *and* MRS. CHEVELEY. LADY MARKBY *is a pleasant, kindly, popular woman, with grey hair à la marquise and good lace. MRS. CHEVELEY, who accompanies her, is tall and rather slight. Lips very thin and highly-coloured, a line of scarlet on a pallid face. Venetian red hair, aquiline nose, and long throat. Rouge accentuates the natural paleness of her complexion. Gray-green eyes that move restlessly. She is in heliotrope, with diamonds. She looks rather like an orchid, and makes great demands on one's curiosity. In all her movements she is extremely graceful. A work of art, on the whole, but showing the influence of too many schools.*

LADY MARKBY: Good-evening, dear Gertrude! So kind of you to let me bring my friend, Mrs. Cheveley. Two such charming women should know each other!

LADY CHILTERN (advances towards MRS. CHEVELEY with a sweet smile. Then suddenly stops, and bows rather distantly): I think Mrs. Cheveley and I have met before. I did not know she had married a second time.

LADY MARKBY (genially): Ah, nowadays people marry as often as they can, don't they? It is most fashionable. (To DUCHESS OF MARYBOROUGH): Dear Duchess, and how is the Duke? Brain still weak, I suppose? Well, that is only to be expected, is it not? His good father was just the same. There is nothing like race, is there?

MRS. CHEVELEY (playing with her fan): But have we really met before, Lady Chiltern? I can't remember where. I have been out of England for so long.

LADY CHILTERN: We were at school together, Mrs. Cheveley.

MRS. CHEVELEY (superciliously): Indeed? I have forgotten all about my schooldays. I have a vague impression that they were detestable.

LADY CHILTERN (*coldly*): I am not surprised!

MRS. CHEVELEY (*in her sweetest manner*): Do you know, I am quite looking forward to meeting your clever husband, Lady Chiltern. Since he has been at the Foreign Office, he has been so much talked of in Vienna. They actually succeed in spelling his name right in the newspapers. That in itself is fame, on the continent.

LADY CHILTERN: I hardly think there will be much in common between you and my husband, Mrs. Cheveley! (*Moves away.*)

VICOMTE DE NANJAC: Ah, chère Madame, quelle surprise! I have not seen you since Berlin!

MRS. CHEVELEY: Not since Berlin, Vicomte. Five years ago!

VICOMTE DE NANJAC: And you are younger and more beautiful than ever. How do you manage it?

MRS. CHEVELEY: By making it a rule only to talk to perfectly charming people like yourself.

VICOMTE DE NANJAC: Ah! You flatter me. You butter me, as they say here.

MRS. CHEVELEY: Do they say that here? How dreadful of them!

VICOMTE DE NANJAC: Yes, they have a wonderful language. It should be more widely known.

SIR ROBERT CHILTERN *enters. A man of forty, but looking somewhat younger. Clean-shaven, with finely-cut features, dark-haired and dark-eyed. A personality of mark. Not popular – few personalities are. But intensely admired by the few, and deeply respected by the many. The note of his manner is that of perfect distinction, with a slight touch of pride. One feels that he is conscious of the success he has made in life. A nervous temperament, with a tired look. The firmly-chiselled mouth and chin contrast strikingly with the romantic expression in the deep-set eyes. The variance is suggestive of an almost complete separation of passion and intellect, as though thought and emotion were each isolated in its own sphere through some violence of will-power. There is nervousness in the nostrils, and in the pale, thin, pointed hands. It would be inaccurate to call him picturesque. Picturesqueness cannot survive the House of Commons. But Vandyck would have liked to have painted his head.*

SIR ROBERT CHILTERN: Good-evening, Lady Markby. I hope you have brought Sir John with you?

LADY MARKBY: Oh! I have brought a much more charming person than Sir John. Sir John's temper since he has taken seriously to politics has become quite unbearable. Really, now that the House of Commons is trying to become useful, it does a great deal of harm.

SIR ROBERT CHILTERN: I hope not, Lady Markby. At any rate we do our best to waste the public time, don't we? But who is this charming person you have been kind enough to bring to us?

LADY MARKBY: Her name is Mrs. Cheveley! One of the Dorsetshire Cheveleys, I suppose. But I really don't know. Families are so mixed nowadays.

Indeed, as a rule, everybody turns out to be somebody else.

SIR ROBERT CHILTERN: Mrs. Cheveley? I seem to know the name.

LADY MARKBY: She has just arrived from Vienna.

SIR ROBERT CHILTERN: Ah! Yes. I think I know whom you mean.

LADY MARKBY: Oh! She goes everywhere there, and has such pleasant scandals about all her friends. I really must go to Vienna next winter. I hope there is a good chef at the Embassy.

SIR ROBERT CHILTERN: If there is not, the Ambassador will certainly have to be recalled. Pray point out Mrs. Cheveley to me. I should like to see her.

LADY MARKBY: Let me introduce you. (*To* MRS. CHEVELEY): My dear, Sir Robert Chiltern is dying to know you!

SIR ROBERT CHILTERN (*bowing*): Every one is dying to know the brilliant Mrs. Cheveley. Our attachés at Vienna write to us about nothing else.

MRS. CHEVELEY: Thank you, Sir Robert. An acquaintance that begins with a compliment is sure to develop into a real friendship. It starts in the right manner. And I find that I know Lady Chiltern already.

SIR ROBERT CHILTERN: Really?

MRS. CHEVELEY: Yes. She has just reminded me that we were at school together. I remember it perfectly now. She always got the good conduct prize. I have a distinct recollection of Lady Chiltern always getting the good conduct prize!

SIR ROBERT CHILTERN (*smiling*): And what prizes did you get, Mrs. Cheveley?

MRS. CHEVELEY: My prizes came a little later on in life. I don't think any of them were for good conduct. I forget!

SIR ROBERT CHILTERN: I am sure they were for something charming!

MRS. CHEVELEY: I don't know that women are always rewarded for being charming. I think they are usually punished for it! Certainly, more women grow old nowadays through the faithfulness of their admirers than through anything else! At least that is the only way I can account for the terribly haggard look of most of your pretty women in London!

SIR ROBERT CHILTERN: What an appalling philosophy that sounds! To attempt to classify you, Mrs. Cheveley, would be an impertinence. But may I ask, at heart, are you an optimist or a pessimist? Those seem to be the only two fashionable religions left to us nowadays.

MRS. CHEVELEY: Oh, I'm neither. Optimism begins in a broad grin, and Pessimism ends with blue spectacles. Besides, they are both of them merely poses.

SIR ROBERT CHILTERN: You prefer to be natural?

MRS. CHEVELEY: Sometimes. But it is such a very difficult pose to keep up.

SIR ROBERT CHILTERN: What would those modern psychological novelists, of whom we hear so much, say to such a theory as that?

MRS. CHEVELEY: Ah! The strength of women comes from the fact that psychology cannot explain us. Men can be analysed, women... merely adored.

SIR ROBERT CHILTERN: You think science cannot grapple with the problem of women?

MRS. CHEVELEY: Science can never grapple with the irrational. That is why it has no future before it, in this world.

SIR ROBERT CHILTERN: And women represent the irrational.

MRS. CHEVELEY: Well-dressed women do.

SIR ROBERT CHILTERN (*with a polite bow*): I fear I could hardly agree with you there. But do sit down. And now tell me, what makes you leave your brilliant Vienna for our gloomy London – or perhaps the question is indiscreet?

MRS. CHEVELEY: Questions are never indiscreet. Answers sometimes are.

SIR ROBERT CHILTERN: Well, at any rate, may I know if it is politics or pleasure?

MRS. CHEVELEY: Politics are my only pleasure. You see, nowadays it is not fashionable to flirt till one is forty, or to be romantic till one is forty-five, so we poor women who are under thirty, or say we are, have nothing open to us but politics or philanthropy. And philanthropy seems to me to have become simply the refuge of people who wish to annoy their fellow-creatures. I prefer politics. I think they are more . . . becoming!

SIR ROBERT CHILTERN: A political life is a noble career!

MRS. CHEVELEY: Sometimes. And sometimes it is a clever game, Sir Robert. And sometimes it is a great nuisance.

SIR ROBERT CHILTERN: Which do you find it?

MRS. CHEVELEY: A combination of all three. (*Drops her fan.*)

SIR ROBERT CHILTERN (*picks up fan*): Allow me!

MRS. CHEVELEY: Thanks.

SIR ROBERT CHILTERN: But you have not told me yet what makes you honour London so suddenly. Our season is almost over.

MRS. CHEVELEY: Oh! I don't care about the London season! It is too matrimonial. People are either hunting for husbands, or hiding from them. I wanted to meet you. It is quite true. You know what a woman's curiosity is. Almost as great as a man's! I wanted immensely to meet you, and . . . to ask you to do something for me.

SIR ROBERT CHILTERN: I hope it is not a little thing, Mrs. Cheveley. I find that little things are so very difficult to do.

MRS. CHEVELEY (*after a moment's reflection*): No, I don't think it is quite a little thing.

SIR ROBERT CHILTERN: I am so glad. Do tell me what it is.

MRS. CHEVELEY: Later on. (*Rises.*) And now may I walk through your beautiful house? I hear your pictures are charming. Poor Baron Arnheim – you remember the Baron? – used to tell me you had some wonderful Corots.

SIR ROBERT CHILTERN (*with an almost imperceptible start*): Did you know Baron Arnheim well?

MRS. CHEVELEY (*smiling*): Intimately. Did you?

SIR ROBERT CHILTERN: At one time.

MRS. CHEVELEY: Wonderful man, wasn't he?

SIR ROBERT CHILTERN (*after a pause*): He was very remarkable, in many ways.

MRS. CHEVELEY: I often think it such a pity he never wrote his memoirs. They would have been most interesting.

SIR ROBERT CHILTERN: Yes: he knew men and cities well, like the old Greek.

MRS. CHEVELEY: Without the dreadful disadvantage of having a Penelope waiting at home for him.

MASON: Lord Goring.

Enter LORD GORING. *Thirty-four, but always says he is younger. A well-bred, expressionless face. He is clever, but would not like to be thought so. A flawless dandy, he would be annoyed if he were considered romantic. He plays with life, and is on perfectly good terms with the world. He is fond of being misunderstood. It gives him a post of vantage.*

SIR ROBERT CHILTERN: Good-evening, my dear Arthur! Mrs. Cheveley, allow me to introduce to you Lord Goring, the idlest man in London.

MRS. CHEVELEY: I have met Lord Goring before.

LORD GORING (*bowing*): I did not think you would remember me, Mrs. Cheveley.

MRS. CHEVELEY: My memory is under admirable control. And are you still a bachelor?

LORD GORING: I . . . believe so.

MRS. CHEVELEY: How very romantic.

LORD GORING: Oh! I am not at all romantic. I am not old enough. I leave romance to my seniors.

SIR ROBERT CHILTERN: Lord Goring is the result of Boodle's Club, Mrs. Cheveley.

MRS. CHEVELEY: He reflects every credit on the institution.

LORD GORING: May I ask are you staying in London long?

MRS. CHEVELEY: That depends partly on the weather, partly on the cooking, and partly on Sir Robert.

SIR ROBERT CHILTERN: You are not going to plunge us into a European war, I hope?

MRS. CHEVELEY: There is no danger, at present!

She nods to LORD GORING, *with a look of amusement in her eyes, and goes out with* SIR ROBERT CHILTERN. LORD GORING *saunters over to* MABEL CHILTERN.

MABEL CHILTERN: You are very late!

LORD GORING: Have you missed me?

MABEL CHILTERN: Awfully!

LORD GORING: Then I am sorry I did not stay away longer. I like being missed.

MABEL CHILTERN: How very selfish of you!

LORD GORING: I am very selfish.

MABEL CHILTERN: You are always telling me of your bad qualities, Lord Goring.

LORD GORING: I have only told you half of them as yet, Miss Mabel!

MABEL CHILTERN: Are the others very bad?

LORD GORING: Quite dreadful! When I think of them at night I go to sleep at once.

MABEL CHILTERN: Well, I delight in your bad qualities. I wouldn't have you part with one of them.

LORD GORING: How very nice of you! But then you are always nice. By the way, I want to ask you a question, Miss Mabel. Who brought Mrs. Cheveley here? That woman in heliotrope, who has just gone out of the room with your brother?

MABEL CHILTERN: Oh, I think Lady Markby brought her. Why do you ask?

LORD GORING: I haven't seen her for years, that is all.

MABEL CHILTERN: What an absurd reason!

LORD GORING: All reasons are absurd.

MABEL CHILTERN: What sort of a woman is she?

LORD GORING: Oh! A genius in the daytime and a beauty at night!

MABEL CHILTERN: I dislike her already.

LORD GORING: That shows your admirable good taste.

VICOMTE DE NANJAC (*approaching*): Ah, the English young lady is the dragon of good taste, is she not? Quite the dragon of good taste.

LORD GORING: So the newspapers are always telling us.

VICOMTE DE NANJAC: I read all your English newspapers. I find them so amusing.

LORD GORING: Then, my dear Nanjac, you must certainly read between the lines.

VICOMTE DE NANJAC: I should like to, but my professor objects. (*To* MABEL CHILTERN): May I have the pleasure of escorting you to the music-room, Mademoiselle?

MABEL CHILTERN (*looking very disappointed*): Delighted, Vicomte, quite delighted! (*Turning to* LORD GORING): Aren't you coming to the music-room?

LORD GORING: Not if there is any music going on, Miss Mabel.

MABEL CHILTERN (*severely*): The music is in German. You would not understand it.

Goes out with the VICOMTE DE NANJAC. LORD CAVERSHAM *comes up to his son.*

LORD CAVERSHAM: Well, sir! What are you doing here? Wasting your life as usual! You should be in bed, sir. You keep too late hours! I heard of you the other night at Lady Rufford's dancing till four o'clock in the morning!

LORD GORING: Only a quarter to four, father.

LORD CAVERSHAM: Can't make out how you stand London Society. The thing has gone to the dogs, a lot of damned nobodies talking about nothing.

LORD GORING: I love talking about nothing, father. It is the only thing I know anything about.

LORD CAVERSHAM: You seem to me to be living entirely for pleasure.

LORD GORING: What else is there to live for, father? Nothing ages like happiness.

LORD CAVERSHAM: You are heartless, sir, very heartless.

LORD GORING: I hope not, father. Good-evening, Lady Basildon!

LADY BASILDON (*arching two pretty eyebrows*): Are you here? I had no idea you ever came to political parties.

LORD GORING: I adore political parties. They are the only place left to us where people don't talk politics.

LADY BASILDON: I delight in talking politics. I talk them all day long. But I can't bear listening to them. I don't know how the unfortunate men in the House stand these long debates.

LORD GORING: By never listening.

LADY BASILDON: Really?

LORD GORING (*in his most serious manner*): Of course. You see, it is a very dangerous thing to listen. If one listens one may be convinced; and a man who allows himself to be convinced by an argument is a thoroughly unreasonable person.

LADY BASILDON: Ah! That accounts for so much in men that I have never understood, and so much in women that their husbands never appreciate in them!

MRS. MARCHMONT (*with a sigh*): Our husbands never appreciate anything in us. We have to go to others for that!

LADY BASILDON (*emphatically*): Yes, always to others, have we not?

LORD GORING (*smiling*): And those are the views of the two ladies who are known to have the most admirable husbands in London.

MRS. MARCHMONT: That is exactly what we can't stand. My Reginald is quite hopelessly faultless. He is really unendurably so, at times! There is not the smallest element of excitement in knowing him.

LORD GORING: How terrible! Really, the thing should be more widely known!

LADY BASILDON: Basildon is quite as bad; he is as domestic as if he was a bachelor.

MRS. MARCHMONT (*pressing* LADY BASILDON'S *hand*): My poor Olivia! We have married perfect husbands, and we are well punished for it.

LORD GORING: I should have thought it was the husbands who were punished.

MRS. MARCHMONT: (*drawing herself up*): Oh, dear no! They are as happy as possible! And as for trusting us, it is tragic how much they trust us.

LADY BASILDON: Perfectly tragic!

LORD GORING: Or comic, Lady Basildon?

LADY BASILDON: Certainly not comic, Lord Goring. How unkind of you to suggest such a thing!

MRS. MARCHMONT: I am afraid Lord Goring is in the camp of the enemy, as usual, I saw him talking to that Mrs. Cheveley when he came in.

LORD GORING: Handsome woman, Mrs. Cheveley!

LADY BASILDON (*stiffly*): Please don't praise other women in our presence. You might wait for us to do that!

LORD GORING: I did wait.

MRS. MARCHMONT: Well, we are not going to praise her. I hear she went to the Opera on Monday night, and told Tommy Rufford at supper that, as far as she could see, London Society was entirely made up of dowdies and dandies.

LORD GORING: She is quite right, too. The men are all dowdies and the women are all dandies, aren't they?

MRS. MARCHMONT (*after a pause*): Oh! Do you really think that is what Mrs. Cheveley meant?

LORD GORING: Of course. And a very sensible remark for Mrs. Cheveley to make, too.

Enter MABEL CHILTERN. *She joins the group.*

MABEL CHILTERN: Why are you talking about Mrs. Cheveley? Everybody is talking about Mrs. Cheveley! Lord Goring says – what did you say, Lord Goring, about Mrs. Cheveley? Oh! I remember, that she was a genius in the daytime and a beauty at night.

LADY BASILDON: What a horrid combination! So very unnatural!

MRS. MARCHMONT (*in her most dreamy manner*): I like looking at geniuses, and listening to beautiful people!

LORD GORING: Ah! That is morbid of you, Mrs. Marchmont!

MRS. MARCHMONT (*brightening to a look of real pleasure*): I am so glad to hear you say that. Marchmont and I have been married for seven years, and he has never once told me that I was morbid. Men are so painfully unobservant.

LADY BASILDON (*turning to her*): I have always said, dear Margaret, that you were the most morbid person in London.

MRS. MARCHMONT: Ah! But you are always sympathetic, Olivia!

MABEL CHILTERN: Is it morbid to have a desire for food? I have a great desire for food. Lord Goring, will you give me some supper?

LORD GORING: With pleasure, Miss Mabel. (*Moves away with her.*)

MABEL CHILTERN: How horrid you have been! You have never talked to me the whole evening!

LORD GORING: How could I? You went away with the child-diplomatist.

MABEL CHILTERN: You might have followed us. Pursuit would have been only polite. I don't think I like you at all this evening!

LORD GORING: I like you immensely.

MABEL CHILTERN: Well, I wish you'd show it in a more marked way!

They go downstairs.

MRS. MARCHMONT: Olivia, I have a curious feeling of absolute faintness. I think I should like some supper very much. I know I should like some supper.

LADY BASILDON: I am positively dying for supper, Margaret!

MRS. MARCHMONT: Men are so horribly selfish, they never think of these things.

LADY BASILDON: Men are grossly material, grossly material!

The VICOMTE DE NANJAC *enters from the music-room with some other guests. After having carefully examined all the people present, he approaches* LADY BASILDON.

VICOMTE DE NANJAC: May I have the honour of taking you down to supper, Countess?

LADY BASILDON (*coldly*): I never take supper, thank you, Vicomte. (*The* VICOMTE *is about to retire.* LADY BASILDON, *seeing this, rises at once and takes his arm.*) But I will come down with you with pleasure.

VICOMTE DE NANJAC: I am so fond of eating! I am very English in all my tastes.

LADY BASILDON: You look quite English, Vicomte, quite English.

They pass out. MR. MONTFORD, *a perfectly groomed young dandy, approaches* MRS. MARCHMONT.

MR. MONTFORD: Like some supper, Mrs. Marchmont?

MRS. MARCHMONT (*languidly*): Thank you, Mr. Montford, I never touch supper. (*Rises hastily and takes his arm.*) But I will sit beside you, and watch you.

MR. MONTFORD: I don't know that I like being watched when I am eating!

MRS. MARCHMONT: Then I will watch some one else.

MR. MONTFORD: I don't know that I should like that either.

MRS. MARCHMONT (*severely*): Pray, Mr. Montford, do not make these painful scenes of jealousy in public!

They go downstairs with the other guests, passing SIR ROBERT CHILTERN *and* MRS. CHEVELEY, *who now enter.*

SIR ROBERT CHILTERN: And are you going to any of our country houses before you leave England, Mrs. Cheveley?

MRS. CHEVELEY: Oh, no! I can't stand your English house-parties. In England people actually try to be brilliant at breakfast. That is dreadful of them! Only dull people are brilliant at breakfast. And then the family skeleton is always reading family prayers. My stay in England really depends on you, Sir Robert. (*Sits down on the sofa.*)

SIR ROBERT CHILTERN (*taking a seat beside her*): Seriously?

MRS. CHEVELEY: Quite seriously. I want to talk to you about a great political and financial scheme, about this Argentine Canal Company, in fact.

SIR ROBERT CHILTERN: What a tedious, practical subject for you to talk about, Mrs. Cheveley!

MRS. CHEVELEY: Oh, I like tedious, practical subjects. What I don't like are tedious, practical people. There is a wide difference. Besides, you are interested, I know, in International Canal schemes. You were Lord Radley's secretary, weren't you, when the Government bought the Suez Canal shares?

SIR ROBERT CHILTERN: Yes. But the Suez Canal was a very great and splendid undertaking. It gave us our direct route to India. It had imperial value. It was necessary that we should have control. This Argentine scheme is a commonplace Stock Exchange swindle.

MRS. CHEVELEY: A speculation, Sir Robert! A brilliant, daring speculation.

SIR ROBERT CHILTERN: Believe me, Mrs. Cheveley, it is a swindle. Let us call things by their proper names. It makes matters simpler. We have all the information about it at the Foreign Office. In fact, I sent out a special Commission to inquire into the matter privately, and they report that the works are hardly begun, and as for the money already subscribed, no one seems to know what has become of it. The whole thing is a second Panama, and with not a quarter of the chance of success that miserable affair ever had. I hope you have not invested in it. I am sure you are far too clever to have done that.

MRS. CHEVELEY: I have invested very largely in it.

SIR ROBERT CHILTERN: Who could have advised you to do such a foolish thing?

MRS. CHEVELEY: Your old friend – and mine.

SIR ROBERT CHILTERN: Who?

MRS. CHEVELEY: Baron Arnheim.

SIR ROBERT CHILTERN (*frowning*): Ah! Yes. I remember hearing, at the time of his death, that he had been mixed up in the whole affair.

MRS. CHEVELEY: It was his last romance. His last but one, to do him justice.

SIR ROBERT CHILTERN (*rising*): But you have not seen my Corots yet. They are in the music-room. Corots seem to go with music, don't they? May I show them to you?

MRS. CHEVELEY (*shaking her head*): I am not in a mood to-night for silver twilights, or rose-pink dawns. I want to talk business. (*Motions to him with her fan to sit down again beside her.*)

SIR ROBERT CHILTERN: I fear I have no advice to give you, Mrs. Cheveley, except to interest yourself in something less dangerous. The success of the Canal depends, of course, on the attitude of England, and I am going to lay the report of the Commissioners before the House to-morrow night.

MRS. CHEVELEY: That you must not do. In your own interests, Sir

Robert, to say nothing of mine, you must not do that.

SIR ROBERT CHILTERN (*looking at her in wonder*): In my own interests? My dear Mrs. Cheveley, what do you mean? (*Sits down beside her.*)

MRS. CHEVELEY: Sir Robert, I will be quite frank with you. I want you to withdraw the report that you had intended to lay before the House, on the ground that you have reasons to believe that the Commissioners have been prejudiced or misinformed, or something. Then I want you to say a few words to the effect that the Government is going to reconsider the question, and that you have reason to believe that the Canal, if completed, will be of great international value. You know the sort of things ministers say in cases of this kind. A few ordinary platitudes will do. In modern life nothing produces such an effect as a good platitude. It makes the whole world kin. Will you do that for me?

SIR ROBERT CHILTERN: Mrs. Cheveley, you cannot be serious in making me such a proposition!

MRS. CHEVELEY: I am quite serious.

SIR ROBERT CHILTERN (*coldly*): Pray allow me to believe that you are not.

MRS. CHEVELEY (*speaking with great deliberation and emphasis*): Ah, but I am. And if you do what I ask you, I . . . will pay you very handsomely!

SIR ROBERT CHILTERN: Pay me!

MRS. CHEVELEY: Yes.

SIR ROBERT CHILTERN: I am afraid I don't quite understand what you mean.

MRS. CHEVELEY (*leaning back on the sofa and looking at him*): How very disappointing! And I have come all the way from Vienna in order that you should thoroughly understand me.

SIR ROBERT CHILTERN: I fear I don't.

MRS. CHEVELEY (*in her most nonchalant manner*): My dear Sir Robert, you are a man of the world, and you have your price, I suppose. Everybody has nowadays. The drawback is that most people are so dreadfully expensive. I know I am. I hope you will be more reasonable in your terms.

SIR ROBERT CHILTERN (*rises indignantly*): If you will allow me, I will call your carriage for you. You have lived so long abroad, Mrs. Cheveley, that you seem to be unable to realise that you are talking to an English gentleman.

MRS. CHEVELEY (*detains him by touching his arm with her fan, and keeping it there while she is talking*): I realise that I am talking to a man who laid the foundation of his fortune by selling to a Stock Exchange speculator a Cabinet secret.

SIR ROBERT CHILTERN (*biting his lip*): What do you mean?

MRS. CHEVELEY (*rising and facing him*): I mean that I know the real origin of your wealth and your career, and I have got your letter, too.

SIR ROBERT CHILTERN: What letter?

MRS. CHEVELEY (*contemptuously*): The letter you wrote to Baron Arnheim, when you were Lord Radley's secretary, telling the Baron to buy Suez Canal shares – a letter written three days before the Government announced its own purchase.

SIR ROBERT CHILTERN (*hoarsely*): It is not true.

MRS. CHEVELEY: You thought that letter had been destroyed. How foolish of you! It is in my possession.

SIR ROBERT CHILTERN: The affair to which you allude was no more than a speculation. The House of Commons had not yet passed the bill; it might have been rejected.

MRS. CHEVELEY: It was a swindle, Sir Robert. Let us call things by their proper names. It makes everything simpler. And now I am going to sell you that letter, and the price I ask for it is your public support of the Argentine scheme. You made your own fortune out of one canal. You must help me and my friends to make our fortunes out of another!

SIR ROBERT CHILTERN: It is infamous, what you propose – infamous!

MRS. CHEVELEY: Oh, no! This is the game of life as we all have to play it, Sir Robert, sooner or later!

SIR ROBERT CHILTERN: I cannot do what you ask me.

MRS. CHEVELEY: You mean you cannot help doing it. You know you are standing on the edge of a precipice. And it is not for you to make terms. It is for you to accept them. Supposing you refuse –

SIR ROBERT CHILTERN: What then?

MRS. CHEVELEY: My dear Sir Robert, what then? You are ruined, that is all! Remember to what a point your Puritanism in England has brought you. In old days nobody pretended to be a bit better than his neighbours. In fact, to be a bit better than one's neighbour was considered excessively vulgar and middle-class. Nowadays, with our modern mania for morality, every one has to pose as a paragon of purity, incorruptibility, and all the other seven deadly virtues – and what is the result? You all go over like ninepins – one after the other. Not a year passes in England without somebody disappearing. Scandals used to lend charm, or at least interest, to a man – now they crush him. And yours is a very nasty scandal. You couldn't survive it. If it were known that as a young man, secretary to a great and important minister, you sold a Cabinet secret for a large sum of money, and that was the origin of your wealth and career, you would be hounded out of public life, you would disappear completely. And after all, Sir Robert, why should you sacrifice your entire future rather than deal diplomatically with your enemy? For the moment I am your enemy. I admit it! And I am much stronger than you are. The big battalions are on my side. You have a splendid position, but it is your splendid position that makes you so vulnerable. You can't defend it! And I am in attack. Of course I have not talked morality to you. You must admit in fairness that I have spared you that. Years ago you did a clever, unscrupulous thing; it turned out a great success. You owe to it your fortune and position. And now you have got to pay for it. Sooner or later we have all to pay for what we do. You have to pay now. Before I leave you to-night, you have got to promise me to suppress your report, and to speak in the House in favour of this scheme.

SIR ROBERT CHILTERN: What you ask is impossible.

MRS. CHEVELEY: You must make it possible. You are going to make it possible. Sir Robert, you know what your English newspapers are like. Suppose that when I leave this house I drive down to some newspaper office, and give them this scandal and the proofs of it. Think of their loathsome joy, of the delight they would have in dragging you down, of the mud and mire they would plunge you in. Think of the hypocrite with his greasy smile penning his leading article, and arranging the foulness of the public placard.

SIR ROBERT CHILTERN: Stop! You want me to withdraw the report and to make a short speech stating that I believe there are possibilities in the scheme?

MRS. CHEVELEY (*sitting down on the sofa*): Those are my terms.

SIR ROBERT CHILTERN (*in a low voice*): I will give you any sum of money you want.

MRS. CHEVELEY: Even you are not rich enough, Sir Robert, to buy back your past. No man is.

SIR ROBERT CHILTERN: I will not do what you ask me. I will not.

MRS. CHEVELEY: You have to. If you don't . . . (*Rises from the sofa.*)

SIR ROBERT CHILTERN (*bewildered and unnerved*): Wait a moment! What did you propose? You said that you would give me back my letter, didn't you?

MRS. CHEVELEY: Yes. That is agreed. I will be in the Ladies' Gallery to-morrow night at half-past eleven. If by that time – and you will have had heaps of opportunity – you have made an announcement to the House in the terms I wish, I shall hand you back your letter with the prettiest thanks, and the best, or at any rate the most suitable, compliment I can think of. I intend to play quite fairly with you. One should always play fairly . . . when one has the winning cards. The Baron taught me that . . . amongst other things.

SIR ROBERT CHILTERN: You must let me have time to consider your proposal.

MRS. CHEVELEY: No; you must settle now!

SIR ROBERT CHILTERN: Give me a week – three days!

MRS. CHEVELEY: Impossible! I have got to telegraph to Vienna to-night.

SIR ROBERT CHILTERN: My God! What brought you into my life?

MRS. CHEVELEY: Circumstances. (*Moves towards the door.*)

SIR ROBERT CHILTERN: Don't go. I consent. The report shall be withdrawn. I will arrange for a question to be put to me on the subject.

MRS. CHEVELEY: Thank you. I knew we should come to an amicable agreement. I understood your nature from the first. I analysed you, though you did not adore me. And now you can get my carriage for me, Sir Robert. I see the people coming up from supper, and Englishmen always get romantic after a meal, and that bores me dreadfully. (*Exit* SIR ROBERT CHILTERN.)

Enter Guests, LADY CHILTERN, LADY MARKBY, LORD CAVERSHAM, LADY BASILDON, MRS. MARCHMONT, VICOMTE DE NANJAC, MR. MONTFORD.

LADY MARKBY: Well, dear Mrs. Cheveley, I hope you have enjoyed yourself. Sir Robert is very entertaining, is he not?

MRS. CHEVELEY: Most entertaining! I have enjoyed my talk with him immensely.

LADY MARKBY: He has had a very interesting and brilliant career. And he has married a most admirable wife. Lady Chiltern is a woman of the very highest principles, I am glad to say. I am a little too old now, myself, to trouble about setting a good example, but I always admire people who do. And Lady Chiltern has a very ennobling effect on life, though her dinner-parties are rather dull sometimes. But one can't have everything, can one? And now I must go, dear. Shall I call for you to-morrow?

MRS. CHEVELEY: Thanks.

LADY MARKBY: We might drive in the Park at five. Everything looks so fresh in the Park now!

MRS. CHEVELEY: Except the people!

LADY MARKBY: Perhaps the people are a little jaded. I have often observed that the Season as it goes on produces a kind of softening of the brain. However, I think anything is better than high intellectual pressure. That is the most unbecoming thing there is. It makes the noses of the young girls so particularly large. And there is nothing so difficult to marry as a large nose; men don't like them. Good-night, dear! (*To* LADY CHILTERN): Good-night, Gertrude! (*Goes out on* LORD CAVERSHAM'S *arm.*)

MRS. CHEVELEY: What a charming house you have, Lady Chiltern! I have spent a delightful evening. It has been so interesting getting to know your husband.

LADY CHILTERN: Why did you wish to meet my husband, Mrs. Cheveley?

MRS. CHEVELEY: Oh, I will tell you. I wanted to interest him in this Argentine Canal scheme, of which I dare say you have heard. And I found him most susceptible – susceptible to reason, I mean. A rare thing in a man. I converted him in ten minutes. He is going to make a speech in the House to-morrow night in favour of the idea. We must go to the Ladies' Gallery and hear him! It will be a great occasion!

LADY CHILTERN: There must be some mistake. That scheme could never have my husband's support.

MRS. CHEVELEY: Oh, I assure you it's all settled. I don't regret my tedious journey from Vienna now. It has been a great success. But, of course, for the next twenty-four hours the whole thing is a dead secret.

LADY CHILTERN (*gently*): A secret? Between whom?

MRS. CHEVELEY (*with a flash of amusement in her eyes*): Between your husband and myself.

SIR ROBERT CHILTERN (*entering*): Your carriage is here, Mrs. Cheveley!

MRS. CHEVELEY: Thanks! Good-evening, Lady Chiltern! Good-night, Lord Goring! I am at Claridge's. Don't you think you might leave a card?

LORD GORING: If you wish it, Mrs. Cheveley!

MRS. CHEVELEY: Oh, don't be so solemn about it, or I shall be obliged to leave a card on you. In England I suppose that would hardly be considered *en règle*.

Abroad, we are more civilised. Will you see me down, Sir Robert? Now that we have both the same interests at heart we shall be great friends, I hope!

Sails out on SIR ROBERT CHILTERN'S *arm.* LADY CHILTERN *goes to the top of the staircase and looks down at them as they descend. Her expression is troubled. After a little time she is joined by some of the guests, and passes with them into another reception-room.*

MABEL CHILTERN: What a horrid woman!

LORD GORING: You should go to bed, Miss Mabel.

MABEL CHILTERN: Lord Goring!

LORD GORING: My father told me to go to bed an hour ago. I don't see why I shouldn't give you the same advice. I always pass on good advice. It is the only thing to do with it. It is never of any use to oneself.

MABEL CHILTERN: Lord Goring, you are always ordering me out of the room. I think it most courageous of you. Especially as I am not going to bed for hours. (*Goes over to the sofa.*) You can come and sit down if you like, and talk about anything in the world, except the Royal Academy, Mrs. Cheveley, or novels in Scotch dialect. They are not improving subjects. (*Catches sight of something that is lying on the sofa half-hidden by the cushion.*) What is this? Some one has dropped a diamond brooch! Quite beautiful, isn't it? (*Shows it to him.*) I wish it was mine, but Gertrude won't let me wear anything but pearls, and I am thoroughly sick of pearls. They make one look so plain, so good and so intellectual. I wonder whom the brooch belongs to.

LORD GORING: I wonder who dropped it.

MABEL CHILTERN: It is a beautiful brooch.

LORD GORING: It is a handsome bracelet.

MABEL CHILTERN: It isn't a bracelet. It's a brooch.

LORD GORING: It can be used as a bracelet. (*Takes it from her and, pulling out a green letter-case, puts the ornament carefully in it, and replaces the whole thing in his breast-pocket with the most perfect sang froid.*)

MABEL CHILTERN: What are you doing?

LORD GORING: Miss Mabel, I am going to make a rather strange request to you.

MABEL CHILTERN (*eagerly*): Oh, pray do! I have been waiting for it all the evening.

LORD GORING (*is a little taken aback, but recovers himself*): Don't mention to anybody that I have taken charge of this brooch. Should any one write and claim it, let me know at once.

MABEL CHILTERN: That is a strange request.

LORD GORING: Well, you see I gave this brooch to somebody once, years ago.

MABEL CHILTERN: You did?

LORD GORING: Yes.

LADY CHILTERN *enters alone. The other guests have gone.*

MABEL CHILTERN: Then I shall certainly bid you good-night. Good-night, Gertrude! (*Exit.*)

LADY CHILTERN: Good-night, dear! (*To* LORD GORING): You saw whom Lady Markby brought here to-night?

LORD GORING: Yes. It was an unpleasant surprise. What did she come here for?

LADY CHILTERN: Apparently to try and lure Robert to uphold some fraudulent scheme in which she is interested. The Argentine Canal, in fact.

LORD GORING: She has mistaken her man, hasn't she?

LADY CHILTERN: She is incapable of understanding an upright nature like my husband's!

LORD GORING: Yes. I should fancy she came to grief if she tried to get Robert into her toils. It is extraordinary what astounding mistakes clever women make.

LADY CHILTERN: I don't call women of that kind clever. I call them stupid!

LORD GORING: Same thing often. Good-night, Lady Chiltern!

LADY CHILTERN: Good-night!

Enter SIR ROBERT CHILTERN.

SIR ROBERT CHILTERN: My dear Arthur, you are not going? Do stop a little!

LORD GORING: Afraid I can't, thanks. I have promised to look in at the Hartlocks'. I believe they have got a mauve Hungarian band that plays mauve Hungarian music. See you soon. Good-bye! (*Exit.*)

SIR ROBERT CHILTERN: How beautiful you look to-night, Gertrude!

LADY CHILTERN: Robert, it is not true, is it? You are not going to lend your support to this Argentine speculation? You couldn't!

SIR ROBERT CHILTERN (*starting*): Who told you I intended to do so?

LADY CHILTERN: That woman who has just gone out, Mrs. Cheveley, as she calls herself now. She seemed to taunt me with it. Robert, I know this woman. You don't. We were at school together. She was untruthful, dishonest, an evil influence on every one whose trust or friendship she could win. I hated, I despised her. She stole things, she was a thief. She was sent away for being a thief. Why do you let her influence you?

SIR ROBERT CHILTERN: Gertrude, what you tell me may be true, but it happened many years ago. It is best forgotten! Mrs. Cheveley may have changed since then. No one should be entirely judged by their past.

LADY CHILTERN (*sadly*): One's past is what one is. It is the only way by which people should be judged.

SIR ROBERT CHILTERN: That is hard saying, Gertrude!

LADY CHILTERN: It is a true saying, Robert. And what did she mean by boasting that she had got you to lend your support, your name, to a thing I have heard you describe as the most dishonest and fraudulent scheme there has ever been in political life?

SIR ROBERT CHILTERN (*biting his lip*): I was mistaken in the view I took. We all may make mistakes.

LADY CHILTERN: But you told me yesterday that you had received the report from the Commission, and that it entirely condemned the whole thing.

SIR ROBERT CHILTERN (*walking up and down*): I have reasons now to believe that the Commission was prejudiced, or, at any rate, misinformed. Besides, Gertrude, public and private life are different things. They have different laws, and move on different lines.

LADY CHILTERN: They should both represent man at his highest. I see no difference between them.

SIR ROBERT CHILTERN (*stopping*): In the present case, on a matter of practical politics, I have changed my mind. That is all.

LADY CHILTERN: All!

SIR ROBERT CHILTERN (*sternly*): Yes!

LADY CHILTERN: Robert! Oh! It is horrible that I should have to ask you such a question – Robert, are you telling me the whole truth?

SIR ROBERT CHILTERN: Why do you ask me such a question?

LADY CHILTERN (*after a pause*): Why do you not answer it?

SIR ROBERT CHILTERN (*sitting down*): Gertrude, truth is a very complex thing, and politics is a very complex business. There are wheels within wheels. One may be under certain obligations to people that one must pay. Sooner or later in political life one has to compromise. Every one does.

LADY CHILTERN: Compromise? Robert, why do you talk so differently to-night from the way I have always heard you talk? Why are you changed?

SIR ROBERT CHILTERN: I am not changed. But circumstances alter things.

LADY CHILTERN: Circumstances should never alter principles.

SIR ROBERT CHILTERN: But if I told you –

LADY CHILTERN: What?

SIR ROBERT CHILTERN: That it was necessary, vitally necessary?

LADY CHILTERN: It can never be necessary to do what is not honourable. Or if it be necessary, then what is it that I have loved! But it is not, Robert; tell me it is not. Why should it be? What gain would you get? Money? We have no need of that! And money that comes from a tainted source is a degradation. Power? But power is nothing in itself. It is power to do good that is fine – that, and that only. What is it, then? Robert, tell me why you are going to do this dishonourable thing!

SIR ROBERT CHILTERN: Gertrude, you have no right to use that word. I told you it was a question of rational compromise. It is no more than that.

LADY CHILTERN: Robert, that is all very well for other men, for men who treat life simply as a sordid speculation; but not for you, Robert, not for you. You are different. All your life you have stood apart from others. You have never let the world soil you. To the world, as to myself, you have been an ideal always. Oh! Be that ideal still. That great inheritance throw not away –

that tower of ivory do not destroy. Robert, men can love what is beneath them – things unworthy, stained, dishonoured. We women worship when we love; and when we lose our worship, we lose everything. Oh! Don't kill my love for you, don't kill that!

SIR ROBERT CHILTERN: Gertrude!

LADY CHILTERN: I know that there are men with horrible secrets in their lives – men who have done some shameful thing, and who in some critical moment have to pay for it, by doing some other act of shame – oh! Don't tell me you are such as they are! Robert, is there in your life any secret dishonour or disgrace? Tell me, tell me at once, that –

SIR ROBERT CHILTERN: That what?

LADY CHILTERN (*speaking very slowly*): That our lives may drift apart.

SIR ROBERT CHILTERN: Drift apart?

LADY CHILTERN: That they may entirely separate. It would be better for us both.

SIR ROBERT CHILTERN: Gertrude, there is nothing in my past life that you might not know.

LADY CHILTERN: I was sure of it, Robert, I was sure of it. But why did you say those dreadful things, things so unlike your real self? Don't let us ever talk about the subject again. You will write, won't you, to Mrs. Cheveley, and tell her that you cannot support this scandalous scheme of hers? If you have given her any promise you must take it back, that is all!

SIR ROBERT CHILTERN: Must I write and tell her that?

LADY CHILTERN: Surely, Robert! What else is there to do?

SIR ROBERT CHILTERN: I might see her personally. It would be better.

LADY CHILTERN: You must never see her again, Robert. She is not a woman you should ever speak to. She is not worthy to talk to a man like you. No; you must write to her at once, now, this moment, and let your letter show her that your decision is quite irrevocable!

SIR ROBERT CHILTERN: Write this moment!

LADY CHILTERN: Yes.

SIR ROBERT CHILTERN: But it is so late. It is close on twelve.

LADY CHILTERN: That makes no matter. She must know at once that she has been mistaken in you – and that you are not a man to do anything base or underhand or dishonourable. Write here, Robert. Write that you decline to support this scheme of hers, as you hold it to be a dishonest scheme. Yes – write the word dishonest. She knows what that word means. (SIR ROBERT CHILTERN *sits down and writes a letter. His wife takes it up and reads it.*) Yes; that will do. (*Rings bell.*) And now the envelope. (*He writes the envelope slowly. Enter* MASON.) Have this letter sent at once to Claridge's Hotel. There is no answer. (*Exit* MASON. LADY CHILTERN *kneels down beside her husband and puts her arms around him.*) Robert, love gives one an instinct to things. I feel to-night that I have saved you from something that might have been a danger to you, from something that might have made men honour you less than they do. I don't think you realise sufficiently, Robert, that you have brought into the political life of our time a nobler atmosphere, a finer attitude towards life, a freer air of purer aims and higher ideals – I know it, and for that I love you, Robert.

SIR ROBERT CHILTERN: Oh, love me always, Gertrude, love me always!

LADY CHILTERN: I will love you always, because you will always be worthy of love. We needs must love the highest when we see it! (*Kisses him and rises and goes out.*)

SIR ROBERT CHILTERN *walks up and down for a moment; then sits down and buries his face in his hands. The Servant enters and begins putting out the lights.* SIR ROBERT CHILTERN *looks up.*

SIR ROBERT CHILTERN: Put out the lights, Mason, put out the lights!

The Servant puts out the lights. The room becomes almost dark. The only light there is comes from the great chandelier that hangs over the staircase and illumines the tapestry of the Triumph of Love.

ACT DROP

ACT TWO

SCENE: *Morning-room at Sir Robert Chiltern's house.*

LORD GORING, *dressed in the height of fashion, is lounging in an arm-chair.* SIR ROBERT CHILTERN *is standing in front of the fireplace. He is evidently in a state of great mental excitement and distress. As the scene progresses he paces nervously up and down the room.*

LORD GORING: My dear Robert, it's a very awkward business, very awkward indeed. You should have told your wife the whole thing. Secrets from other people's wives are a necessary luxury in modern life. So, at least, I am always told at the club by people who are bald enough to know better. But no man should have a secret from his own wife. She invariably finds it out. Women have a wonderful instinct about things. They can discover everything except the obvious.

SIR ROBERT CHILTERN: Arthur, I couldn't tell my wife. When could I have told her? Not last night. It would have made a life-long separation between us, and I would have lost the love of the one woman in the world I worship, of the only woman who had ever stirred love within me. Last night it would have been quite impossible. She would have turned from me in horror... in horror and in contempt.

LORD GORING: Is Lady Chiltern as perfect as all that?

SIR ROBERT CHILTERN: Yes; my wife is as perfect as all that.

LORD GORING (*taking off his left-hand glove*): What a pity! I beg your pardon, my dear fellow, I didn't quite mean that. But if what you tell me is true, I should like to have a serious talk about life with Lady Chiltern.

SIR ROBERT CHILTERN: It would be quite useless.

LORD GORING: May I try?

SIR ROBERT CHILTERN: Yes; but nothing could make her alter her views.

LORD GORING: Well, at the worst it would simply be a psychological experiment.

SIR ROBERT CHILTERN: All such experiments are terribly dangerous.

LORD GORING: Everything is dangerous, my dear fellow. If it wasn't so, life wouldn't be worth living.... Well, I am bound to say that I think you should have told her years ago.

SIR ROBERT CHILTERN: When? When we were engaged? Do you think she would have married me if she had known that the origin of my fortune is such as it is, the basis of my career such as it is, and that I had done a thing that I suppose most men would call shameful and dishonourable?

LORD GORING (*slowly*): Yes; most men would call it ugly names. There is no doubt of that.

SIR ROBERT CHILTERN (*bitterly*): Men who every day do something of the same kind themselves. Men who, each one of them, have worse secrets in their own lives.

LORD GORING: That is the reason they are so pleased to find out other people's secrets. It distracts public attention from their own.

SIR ROBERT CHILTERN: And, after all, whom did I wrong by what I did? No one.

LORD GORING (*looking at him steadily*): Except yourself, Robert.

SIR ROBERT CHILTERN (*after a pause*): Of course I had private information about a certain transaction contemplated by the Government of the day, and I acted on it. Private information is practically the source of every large modern fortune.

LORD GORING (*tapping his boot with his cane*): And public scandal invariably the result.

SIR ROBERT CHILTERN (*pacing up and down the room*): Arthur, do you think that what I did nearly eighteen years ago should be brought up against me now? Do you think it fair that a man's whole career should be ruined for a fault done in one's boyhood almost? I was twenty-two at the time, and I had the double misfortune of being well-born and poor, two unforgivable things nowadays. Is it fair that the folly, the sin of one's youth, if men choose to call it a sin, should wreck a life like mine, should place me in the pillory, should shatter all that I have worked for, all that I have built up? Is it fair, Arthur?

LORD GORING: Life is never fair, Robert. And perhaps it is a good thing for most of us that it is not.

SIR ROBERT CHILTERN: Every man of ambition has to fight his century with its own weapons. What this century worships is wealth. The God of this century is wealth. To succeed one must have wealth. At all costs one must have wealth.

LORD GORING: You underrate yourself, Robert. Believe me, without your wealth you could have succeeded just as well.

SIR ROBERT CHILTERN: When I was old, perhaps. When I had lost my passion for power, or could not use it. When I was tired, worn out, disappointed. I wanted my success when I was young. Youth is the time for success. I couldn't wait.

LORD GORING: Well, you certainly have had your success while you are still young. No one in our day has had such a brilliant success. Under-Secretary for Foreign Affairs at the age of forty – that's good enough for any one, I should think.

SIR ROBERT CHILTERN: And if it is all taken away from me now? If I lose everything over a horrible scandal? If I am hounded from public life?

LORD GORING: Robert, how could you have sold yourself for money?

SIR ROBERT CHILTERN (*excitedly*): I did not sell myself for money. I bought success at a great price. That is all.

LORD GORING (*gravely*): Yes; you certainly paid a great price for it. But what first made you think of doing such a thing?

SIR ROBERT CHILTERN: Baron Arnheim.

LORD GORING: Damned scoundrel!

SIR ROBERT CHILTERN: No; he was a man of a most subtle and refined intellect. A man of culture, charm, and distinction. One of the most intellectual men I ever met.

LORD GORING: Ah! I prefer a gentlemanly fool any day. There is more to be said for stupidity than people imagine. Personally, I have a great admiration for stupidity. It is a sort of fellow-feeling, I suppose. But how did he do it? Tell me the whole thing.

SIR ROBERT CHILTERN (*throws himself into an arm-chair by the writing-table*): One night after dinner at Lord Radley's the Baron began talking about success in modern life as something that one could reduce to an absolutely definite science. With that wonderfully fascinating quiet voice of his he expounded to us the most terrible of all philosophies, the philosophy of power, preached to us the most marvellous of all gospels, the gospel of gold. I think he saw the effect he had produced on me, for some days afterwards he wrote and asked me to come and see him. He was living then in Park Lane, in the house Lord Woolcomb has now. I remember so well how, with a strange smile on his pale, curved lips, he led me through his wonderful picture gallery, showed me his tapestries, his enamels, his jewels, his carved ivories, made me wonder at the strange loveliness of the luxury in which he lived; and then told me that luxury was nothing but a background, a painted scene in a play, and that power, power over other men, power over the world, was the one thing worth having, the one supreme pleasure worth knowing, the one joy one never tired of, and that in our century only the rich possessed it.

LORD GORING (*with great deliberation*): A thoroughly shallow creed.

SIR ROBERT CHILTERN (*rising*): I didn't think so then. I don't think so now. Wealth has given me enormous power. It gave me at the very outset of my life freedom, and freedom is everything. You have never been poor, and never known what ambition is. You cannot understand what a wonderful chance the Baron gave me. Such a chance as few men get.

LORD GORING: Fortunately for them, if one is to judge by results. But tell me definitely, how did the Baron finally persuade you to – well, to do what you did?

SIR ROBERT CHILTERN: When I was going away he said to me that if I ever could give him any private information of real value he would make me a very rich man. I was dazed at the prospect he held out to me, and my ambition and my desire for power were at that time boundless. Six weeks later certain private documents passed through my hands.

LORD GORING (*keeping his eyes steadily fixed on the carpet*): State documents?

SIR ROBERT CHILTERN: Yes.

LORD GORING *sighs, then passes his hand across his forehead and looks up.*

LORD GORING: I had no idea that you, of all men in the world, could have been so weak, Robert, as to yield to such a temptation as Baron Arnheim held out to you.

SIR ROBERT CHILTERN: Weak? Oh, I am sick of hearing that phrase. Sick of using it about others. Weak! Do you really think, Arthur, that it is weakness that yields to temptation? I tell you that there are terrible temptations that it requires strength, strength and courage, to yield to. To stake all one's life on a single moment, to risk everything on one throw, whether the stake be power or pleasure, I care not – there is no weakness in that. There is a horrible, a terrible courage. I had that courage. I sat down the same afternoon and wrote Baron Arnheim the letter this woman now holds. He made three-quarters of a million over the transaction.

LORD GORING: And you?

SIR ROBERT CHILTERN: I received from the Baron £110, 000.

LORD GORING: You were worth more, Robert.

SIR ROBERT CHILTERN: No; that money gave me exactly what I wanted, power over others. I went into the House immediately. The Baron advised me in finance from time to time. Before five years I had almost trebled my fortune. Since then everything that I have touched has turned out a success. In all things connected with money I have had a luck so extraordinary that sometimes it has made me almost afraid. I remember having read somewhere, in some strange book, that when the gods wish to punish us they answer our prayers.

LORD GORING: But tell me, Robert, did you never suffer any regret for what you had done?

SIR ROBERT CHILTERN: No. I felt that I had fought the century with its own weapons, and won.

LORD GORING (*sadly*): You thought you had won.

SIR ROBERT CHILTERN: I thought so. (*After a long pause*): Arthur, do you despise me for what I have told you?

LORD GORING (*with deep feeling in his voice*): I am very sorry for you, Robert, very sorry indeed.

SIR ROBERT CHILTERN: I don't say that I suffered any remorse. I didn't. Not remorse in the ordinary, rather silly sense of the word. But I have paid conscience money many times. I had a wild hope that I might disarm destiny. The sum Baron Arnheim gave me I have distributed twice over in public charities since then.

LORD GORING (*looking up*): In public charities? Dear me! What a lot of harm you must have done, Robert!

SIR ROBERT CHILTERN: Oh, don't say that, Arthur; don't talk like that!

LORD GORING: Never mind what I say, Robert! I am always saying what I shouldn't say. In fact, I usually say what I really think. A great mistake nowadays. It makes one so liable to be understood. As regards this dreadful business, I will help you in whatever way I can. Of course you know that.

SIR ROBERT CHILTERN: Thank you, Arthur, thank you. But what is to be done? What can be done?

LORD GORING (*leaning back with his hands in his pockets*): Well, the English can't stand a man who is always saying he is in the right, but they are very fond of a man who admits that he has been in the wrong. It is one of the best things in them. However, in your case, Robert, a confession would not do. The money, if you will allow me to say so, is . . . awkward. Besides, if you did make a clean breast of the whole affair, you would never be able to talk morality again. And in England a man who can't talk morality twice a week to a large, popular, immoral audience is quite over as a serious politician. There would be nothing left for him as a profession except Botany or the Church. A confession would be of no use. It would ruin you.

SIR ROBERT CHILTERN: It would ruin me. Arthur, the only thing for me to do now is to fight the thing out.

LORD GORING (*rising from his chair*): I was waiting for you to say that, Robert. It is the only thing to do now. And you must begin by telling your wife the whole story.

SIR ROBERT CHILTERN: That I will not do.

LORD GORING: Robert, believe me, you are wrong.

SIR ROBERT CHILTERN: I couldn't do it. It would kill her love for me. And now about this woman, this Mrs. Cheveley. How can I defend myself against her? You knew her before, Arthur, apparently.

LORD GORING: Yes.

SIR ROBERT CHILTERN: Did you know her well?

LORD GORING (*arranging his necktie*): So little that I got engaged to be married to her once, when I was staying at the Tenbys'. The affair lasted for three days . . . nearly.

SIR ROBERT CHILTERN: Why was it broken off?

LORD GORING (*airily*): Oh, I forget. At least, it makes no matter. By the way, have you tried her with money? She used to be confoundedly fond of money.

SIR ROBERT CHILTERN: I offered her any sum she wanted. She refused.

LORD GORING: Then the marvellous gospel of gold breaks down sometimes. The rich can't do everything, after all.

SIR ROBERT CHILTERN: Not everything. I suppose you are right. Arthur, I feel that public disgrace is in store for me. I feel certain of it. I never knew what terror was before. I know it now. It is as if a hand of ice were laid upon one's heart. It is as if one's heart were beating itself to death in some empty hollow.

LORD GORING (*striking the table*): Robert, you must fight her. You must fight her.

SIR ROBERT CHILTERN: But how?

LORD GORING: I can't tell you how at present. I have not the smallest idea. But every one has some weak point. There is some flaw in each one of us. (*Strolls over to the fireplace and looks at himself in the glass.*) My father tells me that even I have faults. Perhaps I have. I don't know.

SIR ROBERT CHILTERN: In defending myself against Mrs. Cheveley I have a right to use any weapon I can find, have I not?

LORD GORING (*still looking in the glass*): In your place I don't think I should have the smallest scruple in doing so. She is thoroughly well able to take care of herself.

SIR ROBERT CHILTERN (*sits down at the table and takes a pen in his hand*): Well, I shall send a cipher telegram to the Embassy at Vienna, to inquire if there is anything known against her. There may be some secret scandal she might be afraid of.

LORD GORING (*settling his buttonhole*): Oh, I should fancy Mrs. Cheveley is one of those very modern women of our time who find a new scandal as becoming as a new bonnet, and air them both in the Park every afternoon at five-thirty. I am sure she adores scandals, and that the sorrow of her life at present is that she can't manage to have enough of them.

SIR ROBERT CHILTERN (*writing*): Why do you say that?

LORD GORING (*turning round*): Well, she wore far too much rouge last night, and not quite enough clothes. That is always a sign of despair in a woman.

SIR ROBERT CHILTERN (*striking a bell*): But it is worth while my wiring to Vienna, is it not?

LORD GORING: It is always worth while asking a question, though it is not always worth while answering one.

Enter MASON.

SIR ROBERT CHILTERN: Is Mr. Trafford in his room?

MASON: Yes, Sir Robert.

SIR ROBERT CHILTERN (*puts what he has written into an envelope, which he then carefully closes*): Tell him to have this sent off in cipher at once. There must not be a moment's delay.

MASON: Yes, Sir Robert.

SIR ROBERT CHILTERN: Oh! Just give that back to me again.

Writes something on the envelope. MASON *then goes out with the letter.*

SIR ROBERT CHILTERN: She must have had some curious hold over Baron Arnheim. I wonder what it was.

LORD GORING (*smiling*): I wonder.

SIR ROBERT CHILTERN: I will fight her to the death, as long as my wife knows nothing.

LORD GORING (*strongly*): Oh, fight in any case – in any case.

SIR ROBERT CHILTERN (*with a gesture of despair*): If my wife found out, there would be little left to fight for. Well, as soon as I hear from Vienna, I shall let you know the result. It is a chance, just a chance, but I believe in it. And as I fought the age with its own weapons, I will fight her with her weapons. It is only fair, and she looks like a woman with a past, doesn't she?

LORD GORING: Most pretty women do. But there is a fashion in pasts just as there is a fashion in frocks. Perhaps Mrs. Cheveley's past is merely a slightly *décolleté* one, and they are excessively popular nowadays. Besides, my dear Robert, I should not build too high hopes on frightening Mrs. Cheveley. I should not fancy Mrs. Cheveley is a woman who would be easily frightened. She has survived all her creditors, and she shows wonderful presence of mind.

SIR ROBERT CHILTERN: Oh! I live on hopes now. I clutch at every chance. I feel like a man on a ship that is sinking. The water is round my feet, and the very air is bitter with storm. Hush! I hear my wife's voice.

Enter LADY CHILTERN *in walking dress.*

LADY CHILTERN: Good-afternoon, Lord Goring.

LORD GORING: Good-afternoon, Lady Chiltern! Have you been in the Park?

LADY CHILTERN: No; I have just come from the Woman's Liberal Association, where, by the way, Robert, your name was received with loud applause, and now I have come in to have my tea. (*To* LORD GORING): You will wait and have some tea, won't you?

LORD GORING: I'll wait for a short time, thanks.

LADY CHILTERN: I will be back in a moment. I am only going to take my hat off.

LORD GORING (*in his most earnest manner*): Oh! Please don't. It is so pretty. One of the prettiest hats I ever saw. I hope the Woman's Liberal Association received it with loud applause.

LADY CHILTERN (*with a smile*): We have much more important work to do than look at each other's bonnets, Lord Goring.

LORD GORING: Really? What sort of work?

LADY CHILTERN: Oh! Dull, useful, delightful things, Factory Acts, Female Inspectors, the Eight Hours' Bill, the Parliamentary Franchise.... Everything, in fact, that you would find thoroughly uninteresting.

LORD GORING: And never bonnets?

LADY CHILTERN (*with mock indignation*): Never bonnets, never!

LADY CHILTERN *goes out through the door leading to her boudoir.*

SIR ROBERT CHILTERN (*takes* LORD GORING'S *hand*): You have been a good friend to me, Arthur, a thoroughly good friend.

LORD GORING: I don't know that I have been able to do much for you, Robert, as yet. In fact, I have not been able to do anything for you, as far as I can see. I am thoroughly disappointed with myself.

SIR ROBERT CHILTERN: You have enabled me to tell you the truth. That is something. The truth has always stifled me.

LORD GORING: Ah! The truth is a thing I get rid of as soon as possible! Bad habit, by the way. Makes one very unpopular at the club . . . with the older members. They call it being conceited. Perhaps it is.

SIR ROBERT CHILTERN: I would to God that I had been able to tell the truth . . . to live the truth. Ah! That is the great thing in life, to live the truth. (*Sighs, and goes towards the door.*) I'll see you soon again, Arthur, shan't I?

LORD GORING: Certainly. Whenever you like. I'm going to look in at the Bachelors' Ball to-night, unless I find something better to do. But I'll come round to-morrow morning. If you should want me to-night by any chance, send round a note to Curzon Street.

SIR ROBERT CHILTERN: Thank you.

As he reaches the door, LADY CHILTERN *enters from her boudoir.*

LADY CHILTERN: You are not going, Robert?

SIR ROBERT CHILTERN: I have some letters to write, dear.

LADY CHILTERN (*going to him*): You work too hard, Robert. You seem never to think of yourself, and you are looking so tired.

SIR ROBERT CHILTERN: It is nothing, dear, nothing. (*He kisses her and goes out.*)

LADY CHILTERN (*to* LORD GORING): Do sit down. I am so glad you have called. I want to talk to you about . . . well, not about bonnets, or the Woman's Liberal Association. You take far too much interest in the first subject, and not nearly enough in the second.

LORD GORING: You want to talk to me about Mrs. Cheveley?

LADY CHILTERN: Yes. You have guessed it. After you left last night I found out that what she had said was really true. Of course I made Robert write her a letter at once, withdrawing his promise.

LORD GORING: So he gave me to understand.

LADY CHILTERN: To have kept it would have been the first stain on a career that has been stainless always. Robert must be above reproach. He is not like other men. He cannot afford to do what other men do. (*She looks at* LORD GORING, *who remains silent.*) Don't you agree with me? You are Robert's greatest friend. You are our greatest friend, Lord Goring. No one, except myself, knows Robert better than you do. He has no secrets from me, and I don't think he has any from you.

LORD GORING: He certainly has no secrets from me. At least I don't think so.

LADY CHILTERN: Then am I not right in my estimate of him? I know I am right. But speak to me frankly.

LORD GORING (*looking straight at her*): Quite frankly?

LADY CHILTERN: Surely. You have nothing to conceal, have you?

LORD GORING: Nothing. But, my dear Lady Chiltern, I think, if you will allow me to say so, that in practical life –

LADY CHILTERN (*smiling*): Of which you know so little, Lord Goring –

LORD GORING: Of which I know nothing by experience, though I know something by observation. I think that in practical life there is something about success, actual success, that is a little unscrupulous, something about ambition that is unscrupulous always. Once a man has set his heart and soul on getting to a certain point, if he has to climb the crag, he climbs the crag; if he has to walk in the mire –

LADY CHILTERN: Well?

LORD GORING: He walks in the mire. Of course I am only talking generally about life.

LADY CHILTERN (*gravely*): I hope so. Why do you look at me so strangely, Lord Goring?

LORD GORING: Lady Chiltern, I have sometimes thought that . . . perhaps you are a little hard in some of your views on life. I think that . . . often you don't make sufficient allowances. In every nature there are elements of weakness, or worse than weakness. Supposing, for instance, that – that any public man, my father, or Lord Merton, or Robert, say, had, years ago, written some foolish letter to some one. . . .

LADY CHILTERN: What do you mean by a foolish letter?

LORD GORING: A letter gravely compromising one's position. I am only putting an imaginary case.

LADY CHILTERN: Robert is as incapable of doing a foolish thing as he is of doing a wrong thing.

LORD GORING (*after a long pause*): Nobody is incapable of doing a foolish thing. Nobody is incapable of doing a wrong thing.

LADY CHILTERN: Are you a Pessimist? What will the other dandies say? They will all have to go into mourning.

LORD GORING (*rising*): No, Lady Chiltern, I am not a Pessimist. Indeed I am not sure that I quite know what pessimism really means. All I do know is that life cannot be understood without much charity, cannot be lived without much charity. It is love, and not German philosophy, that is the true explanation of this world, whatever may be the explanation of the next. And if you are ever in trouble, Lady Chiltern, trust me absolutely, and I will help you in every way I can. If you ever want me, come to me for my assistance, and you shall have it. Come at once to me.

LADY CHILTERN (*looking at him in surprise*): Lord Goring, you are talking quite seriously. I don't think I ever heard you talk seriously before.

LORD GORING (*laughing*): You must excuse me, Lady Chiltern. It won't occur again, if I can help it.

LADY CHILTERN: But I like you to be serious.

Enter MABEL CHILTERN, *in the most ravishing frock.*

MABEL CHILTERN: Dear Gertrude, don't say such a dreadful thing to Lord Goring. Seriousness would be very unbecoming to him. Good-afternoon, Lord Goring! Pray be as trivial as you can.

LORD GORING: I should like to, Miss Mabel, but I am afraid I am ... a little out of practice this morning; and besides, I have to be going now.

MABEL CHILTERN: Just when I have come in! What dreadful manners you have! I am sure you were very badly brought up.

LORD GORING: I was.

MABEL CHILTERN: I wish I had brought you up!

LORD GORING: I am so sorry you didn't.

MABEL CHILTERN: It is too late now, I suppose?

LORD GORING (*smiling*): I am not so sure.

MABEL CHILTERN: Will you ride to-morrow morning?

LORD GORING: Yes, at ten.

MABEL CHILTERN: Don't forget.

LORD GORING: Of course I shan't. By the way, Lady Chiltern, there is no list of your guests in *The Morning Post* of to-day. It has apparently been crowded out by the County Council, or the Lambeth Conference, or something equally boring. Could you let me have a list? I have a particular reason for asking you.

LADY CHILTERN: I am sure Mr. Trafford will be able to give you one.

LORD GORING: Thanks, so much.

MABEL CHILTERN: Tommy is the most useful person in London.

LORD GORING (*turning to her*): And who is the most ornamental?

MABEL CHILTERN (*triumphantly*): I am.

LORD GORING: How clever of you to guess it! (*Takes up his hat and cane.*) Good-bye, Lady Chiltern! You will remember what I said to you, won't you?

LADY CHILTERN: Yes; but I don't know why you said it to me.

LORD GORING: I hardly know myself. Good-bye, Miss Mabel!

MABEL CHILTERN (*with a little moue of disappointment*): I wish you were not going. I have had four wonderful adventures this morning; four and a half, in fact. You might stop and listen to some of them.

LORD GORING: How very selfish of you to have four and a half! There won't be any left for me.

MABEL CHILTERN: I don't want you to have any. They would not be good for you.

LORD GORING: That is the first unkind thing you have ever said to me. How charmingly you said it! Ten to-morrow.

MABEL CHILTERN: Sharp.

LORD GORING: Quite sharp. But don't bring Mr. Trafford.

MABEL CHILTERN (*with a little toss of her head*): Of course I shan't bring Tommy Trafford. Tommy Trafford is in great disgrace.

LORD GORING: I am delighted to hear it. (*Bows and goes out.*)

MABEL CHILTERN: Gertrude, I wish you would speak to Tommy Trafford.

LADY CHILTERN: What has poor Mr. Trafford done this time? Robert says he is the best secretary he has ever had.

MABEL CHILTERN: Well, Tommy has proposed to me again. Tommy really does nothing but propose to me. He proposed to me last night in the music-room, when I was quite unprotected, as there was an elaborate trio going on. I didn't dare to make the smallest repartee, I need hardly tell you. If I had, it would have stopped the music at once. Musical people are so absurdly unreasonable. They always want one to be perfectly dumb at the very moment when one is longing to be absolutely deaf. Then he proposed to me in broad daylight this morning, in front of that dreadful statue of Achilles. Really, the things that go on in front of that work of art are quite appalling. The police should interfere. At luncheon I saw by the glare in his eye that he was going to propose again, and I just managed to check him in time by assuring him that I was a bimetallist. Fortunately I don't know what bimetallism means. And I don't believe anybody else does either. But the observation crushed Tommy for ten minutes. He looked quite shocked. And then Tommy is so annoying in the way he proposes. If he proposed at the top of his voice, I should not mind so much. That might produce some effect on the public. But he does it in a horrid confidential way. When Tommy wants to be romantic he talks to one just like a doctor. I am very fond of Tommy, but his methods of proposing are quite out of date. I wish, Gertrude, you would speak to him, and tell him that once a week is quite often enough to propose to any one, and that it should always be done in a manner that attracts some attention.

LADY CHILTERN: Dear Mabel, don't talk like that. Besides, Robert thinks very highly of Mr. Trafford. He believes he has a brilliant future before him.

MABEL CHILTERN: Oh! I wouldn't marry a man with a future before him for anything under the sun.

LADY CHILTERN: Mabel!

MABEL CHILTERN: I know, dear. You married a man with a future, didn't you! But then Robert was a genius, and you have a noble, self-sacrificing character. You can stand geniuses. I have no character at all, and Robert is the only genius I could ever bear. As a rule, I think they are quite impossible. Geniuses talk so much, don't they? Such a bad habit! And they are always thinking about themselves, when I want them to be thinking about me. I must go round now and rehearse at Lady Basildon's. You remember, we are having tableaux, don't you? The Triumph of something, I don't know what! I hope it will be triumph of me. Only triumph I am really interested in at present. (*Kisses* LADY CHILTERN *and goes out; then comes running back*). Oh, Gertrude, do you know who is coming to see you? That dreadful Mrs. Cheveley, in a most lovely gown. Did you ask her?

LADY CHILTERN (*rising*): Mrs. Cheveley! Coming to see me? Impossible!

MABEL CHILTERN: I assure you she is coming upstairs, as large as life and not nearly so natural.

LADY CHILTERN: You need not wait, Mabel. Remember, Lady Basildon is expecting you.

MABEL CHILTERN: Oh! I must shake hands with Lady Markby. She is delightful. I love being scolded by her.

Enter MASON.

MASON: Lady Markby. Mrs. Cheveley.

Enter LADY MARKBY *and* MRS. CHEVELEY.

LADY CHILTERN (*advancing to meet them*): Dear Lady Markby, how nice of you to come and see me! (*Shakes hands with her, and bows somewhat distantly to* MRS. CHEVELEY.) Won't you sit down, Mrs. Cheveley?

MRS. CHEVELEY: Thanks. Isn't that Miss Chiltern? I should like so much to know her.

LADY CHILTERN: Mabel, Mrs. Cheveley wishes to know you. (MABEL CHILTERN *gives a little nod.*)

MRS. CHEVELEY (*sitting down*): I thought your frock so charming, last night, Miss Chiltern. So simple and . . . suitable.

MABEL CHILTERN: Really? I must tell my dressmaker. It will be such a surprise to her. Good-bye, Lady Markby!

LADY MARKBY: Going already?

MABEL CHILTERN: I am so sorry but I am obliged to. I am just off to rehearsal. I have got to stand on my head in some tableaux.

LADY MARKBY: On your head, child? Oh! I hope not. I believe it is most unhealthy. (*Takes a seat on the sofa next* LADY CHILTERN.)

MABEL CHILTERN: But it is for an excellent charity; in aid of the Undeserving, the only people I am really interested in. I am the secretary, and Tommy Trafford is treasurer.

MRS. CHEVELEY: And what is Lord Goring?

MABEL CHILTERN: Oh! Lord Goring is president.

MRS. CHEVELEY: The post should suit him admirably, unless he has deteriorated since I knew him first.

LADY MARKBY (*reflecting*): You are remarkably modern, Mabel. A little too modern, perhaps. Nothing is so dangerous as being too modern. One is apt to grow old-fashioned quite suddenly. I have known many instances of it.

MABEL CHILTERN: What a dreadful prospect!

LADY MARKBY: Ah! My dear, you need not be nervous. You will always be as pretty as possible. That is the best fashion there is, and the only fashion that England succeeds in setting.

MABEL CHILTERN (*with a curtsey*): Thank you so much, Lady Markby, for England . . . and myself. (*Goes out.*)

LADY MARKBY (*turning to* LADY CHILTERN): Dear Gertrude, we just called to know if Mrs. Cheveley's diamond brooch has been found.

LADY CHILTERN: Here?

MRS. CHEVELEY: Yes. I missed it when I got back to Claridge's, and I thought I might possibly have dropped it here.

LADY CHILTERN: I have heard nothing about it. But I will send for the butler and ask. (*Touches the bell.*)

MRS. CHEVELEY: Oh, pray don't trouble, Lady Chiltern. I dare say I lost it at the Opera, before we came on here.

LADY MARKBY: Ah yes, I suppose it must have been at the Opera. The fact is, we all scramble and jostle so much nowadays that I wonder we have anything at all left on us at the end of an evening. I know myself that, when I am coming back from the Drawing room, I always feel as if I hadn't a shred on me, except a small shred of decent reputation, just enough to prevent the lower classes making painful observations through the windows of the carriage. The fact is that our Society is terribly over-populated. Really, some one should arrange a proper scheme of assisted emigration. It would do a great deal of good.

MRS. CHEVELEY: I quite agree with you, Lady Markby. It is nearly six years since I have been in London for the Season, and I must say Society has become dreadfully mixed. One sees the oddest people everywhere.

LADY MARKBY: That is quite true, dear. But one needn't know them. I'm sure I don't know half the people who come to my house. Indeed, from all I hear, I shouldn't like to.

Enter MASON.

LADY CHILTERN: What sort of brooch was it that you lost, Mrs. Cheveley?

MRS. CHEVELEY: A diamond snake-brooch with a ruby, a rather large ruby.

LADY MARKBY: I thought you said there was a sapphire on the head, dear?

MRS. CHEVELEY (*smiling*): No. Lady Markby – a ruby.

LADY MARKBY (*nodding her head*): And very becoming, I am quite sure.

LADY CHILTERN: Has a ruby and diamond brooch been found in any of the rooms this morning, Mason?

MASON: No, my lady.

MRS. CHEVELEY: It really is of no consequence, Lady Chiltern. I am so sorry to have put you to any inconvenience.

LADY CHILTERN (*coldly*): Oh, it has been no inconvenience. That will do, Mason. You can bring tea. (*Exit* MASON.)

LADY MARKBY: Well, I must say it is most annoying to lose anything. I remember once at Bath, years ago, losing in the Pump Room an exceedingly handsome cameo bracelet that Sir John had given me. I don't think he has ever given me anything since, I am sorry to say. He has sadly degenerated. Really, this horrid House of Commons quite ruins our husbands for us. I think the Lower House by far the greatest blow to a happy married life that there has been since that terrible thing called the Higher Education of Women was invented.

LADY CHILTERN: Ah! It is heresy to say that in this house, Lady Markby. Robert is a great champion of the Higher Education of Woman, and so, I am afraid, am I.

MRS. CHEVELEY: The higher education of men is what I should like to see. Men need it so sadly.

LADY MARKBY: They do, dear. But I am afraid such a scheme would be quite unpractical. I don't think man has much capacity for development. He has got as far as he can, and that is not far, is it? With regard to women, well, dear Gertrude, you belong to the younger generation, and I am sure it is all right if you approve of it. In my time, of course, we were taught not to understand anything. That was the old system, and wonderfully interesting it was. I assure you that the amount of things I and my poor dear sister were taught not to understand was quite extraordinary. But modern women understand everything, I am told.

MRS. CHEVELEY: Except their husbands. That is the one thing the modern woman never understands.

LADY MARKBY: And a very good thing too, dear, I dare say. It might break up many a happy home if they did. Not yours, I need hardly say, Gertrude. You have married a pattern husband. I wish I could say as much for myself. But since Sir John has taken to attending the debates regularly, which he never used to do in the good old days, his language has become quite impossible. He always seems to think that he is addressing the House, and consequently whenever he discusses the state of the agricultural labourer, or the Welsh Church, or something quite improper of that kind, I am obliged to send all the servants out of the room. It is not pleasant to see one's own butler, who has been with one for twenty-three years, actually blushing at the sideboard, and the footmen making contortions in corners like persons in circuses. I assure you my life will be quite ruined unless they send John at once to the Upper House. He won't take any interest in politics then, will he? The House of Lords is so sensible. An assembly of gentlemen. But in his present state, Sir John is really a great trial. Why, this morning before breakfast was half over, he stood up on the hearth-rug, put his hands in his pockets, and appealed to the country at the top of his voice. I left the table as soon as I had my second cup of tea, I need hardly say. But his violent language could be heard all over the house! I trust, Gertrude, that Sir Robert is not like that?

LADY CHILTERN: But I am very much interested in politics, Lady Markby. I love to hear Robert talk about them.

LADY MARKBY: Well, I hope he is not as devoted to Blue Books as Sir John is. I don't think they can be quite improving reading for any one.

MRS. CHEVELEY (languidly): I have never read a Blue Book. I prefer books... in yellow covers.

LADY MARKBY (genially unconscious): Yellow is a gayer colour, is it not? I used to wear yellow a good deal in my early days, and would do so now if Sir

John was not so painfully personal in his observations, and a man on the question of dress is always ridiculous, is he not?

MRS. CHEVELEY: Oh, no! I think men are the only authorities on dress.

LADY MARKBY: Really? One wouldn't say so from the sort of hats they wear? Would one?

The butler enters, followed by the footman. Tea is set on a small table close to LADY CHILTERN.

LADY CHILTERN: May I give you some tea, Mrs. Cheveley?

MRS. CHEVELEY: Thanks. (*The butler hands* MRS. CHEVELEY *a cup of tea on a salver.*)

LADY CHILTERN: Some tea, Lady Markby?

LADY MARKBY: No thanks, dear. (*The servants go out.*) The fact is, I have promised to go round for ten minutes to see poor Lady Brancaster, who is in very great trouble. Her daughter, quite a well-brought-up girl, too, has actually become engaged to be married to a curate in Shropshire. It is very sad, very sad indeed. I can't understand this modern mania for curates. In my time we girls saw them, of course, running about the place like rabbits. But we never took any notice of them, I need hardly say. But I am told that nowadays country society is quite honeycombed with them. I think it most irreligious. And then the eldest son has quarrelled with his father, and it is said that when they meet at the club Lord Brancaster always hides himself behind the money article in *The Times*. However, I believe that is quite a common occurrence nowadays and that they have to take in extra copies of *The Times* at all the clubs in St. James's Street; there are so many sons who won't have anything to do with their fathers, and so many fathers who won't speak to their sons. I think myself, it is very much to be regretted.

MRS. CHEVELEY: So do I. Fathers have so much to learn from their sons nowadays.

LADY MARKBY: Really, dear? What?

MRS. CHEVELEY: The art of living. The only really Fine Art we have produced in modern times.

LADY MARKBY (*shaking her head*): Ah! I am afraid Lord Brancaster knew a good deal about that. More than his poor wife ever did. (*Turning to* LADY CHILTERN): You know Lady Brancaster, don't you, dear?

LADY CHILTERN: Just slightly. She was staying at Langton last autumn, when we were there.

LADY MARKBY: Well, like all stout women, she looks the very picture of happiness, as no doubt you noticed. But there are many tragedies in her family, besides this affair of the curate. Her own sister, Mrs. Jekyll, had a most unhappy life; through no fault of her own, I am sorry to say. She ultimately was so broken-hearted that she went into a convent, or on to the operatic stage, I forget which. No; I think it was decorative art-needlework she took up. I know she had lost all sense of pleasure in life. (*Rising*): And now, Gertrude, if you will allow me, I shall leave Mrs. Cheveley in your charge and call back for her in a quarter of an hour. Or perhaps, dear Mrs. Cheveley, you wouldn't mind waiting in the carriage while I am with Lady Brancaster. As I intend it to be a visit of condolence, I shan't stay long.

MRS. CHEVELEY (*rising*): I don't mind waiting in the carriage at all, provided there is somebody to look at one.

LADY MARKBY: Well, I hear the curate is always prowling about the house.

MRS. CHEVELEY: I am afraid I am not fond of girl friends.

LADY CHILTERN (*rising*): Oh, I hope Mrs. Cheveley will stay here a little. I should like to have a few minutes' conversation with her.

MRS. CHEVELEY: How very kind of you, Lady Chiltern! Believe me, nothing would give me greater pleasure.

LADY MARKBY: Ah! no doubt you both have many pleasant reminiscences of your schooldays to talk over together. Good-bye, dear Gertrude! Shall I see you at Lady Bonar's to-night? She has discovered a wonderful new genius. He does . . . nothing at all, I believe. That is a great comfort, is it not?

LADY CHILTERN: Robert and I are dining at home by ourselves to-night, and I don't think I shall go anywhere afterwards. Robert, of course, will have to be in the House. But there is nothing interesting on.

LADY MARKBY: Dining at home by yourselves? Is that quite prudent? Ah, I forgot, your husband is an exception. Mine is the general rule, and nothing ages a woman so rapidly as having married the general rule.

Exit LADY MARKBY.

MRS. CHEVELEY: Wonderful woman, Lady Markby, isn't she? Talks more and says less than anybody I ever met. She is made to be a public speaker. Much more so than her husband, though he is a typical Englishman, always dull and usually violent.

LADY CHILTERN (*makes no answer, but remains standing. There is a pause. Then the eyes of the two women meet.* LADY CHILTERN *looks stern and pale.* MRS. CHEVELEY *seems rather amused*): Mrs. Cheveley, I think it is right to tell you quite frankly that, had I known who you really were, I should not have invited you to my house last night.

MRS. CHEVELEY (*with an impertinent smile*): Really?

LADY CHILTERN: I could not have done so.

MRS. CHEVELEY: I see that after all these years you have not changed a bit, Gertrude.

LADY CHILTERN: I never change.

MRS. CHEVELEY (*elevating her eyebrows*): Then life has taught you nothing?

LADY CHILTERN: It has taught me that a person who has once been guilty of a dishonest and dishonourable action may be guilty of it a second time, and should be shunned.

MRS. CHEVELEY: Would you apply that rule to every one?

LADY CHILTERN: Yes, to every one, without exception.

MRS. CHEVELEY: Then I am sorry for you, Gertrude, very sorry for you.

LADY CHILTERN: You see now, I am sure, that for many reasons any further acquaintance between us during your stay in London is quite impossible?

MRS. CHEVELEY (*leaning back in her chair*): Do you know, Gertrude, I don't mind your talking morality a bit. Morality is simply the attitude we adopt towards people whom we personally dislike. You dislike me. I am quite aware of that. And I have always detested you. And yet I have come here to do you a service.

LADY CHILTERN (*contemptuously*): Like the service you wished to render my husband last night, I suppose. Thank heaven, I saved him from that.

MRS. CHEVELEY (*starting to her feet*): It was you who made him write that insolent letter to me? It was you who made him break his promise?

LADY CHILTERN: Yes.

MRS. CHEVELEY: Then you must make him keep it. I give you till to-morrow morning – no more. If by that time your husband does not solemnly bind himself to help me in this great scheme in which I am interested –

LADY CHILTERN: This fraudulent speculation –

MRS. CHEVELEY: Call it what you choose. I hold your husband in the hollow of my hand, and if you are wise you will make him do what I tell him.

LADY CHILTERN (*rising and going towards her*): You are impertinent. What has my husband to do with you? With a woman like you?

MRS. CHEVELEY (*with a bitter laugh*): In this world like meets with like. It is because your husband is himself fraudulent and dishonest that we pair so well together. Between you and him there are chasms. He and I are closer than friends. We are enemies linked together. The same sin binds us.

LADY CHILTERN: How dare you class my husband with yourself? How dare you threaten him or me? Leave my house. You are unfit to enter it.

SIR ROBERT CHILTERN *enters from behind. He hears his wife's last words, and sees to whom they are addressed. He grows deadly pale.*

MRS. CHEVELEY: Your house! A house bought with the price of dishonour. A house, everything in which has been paid for by fraud. (*Turns round and sees* SIR ROBERT CHILTERN.) Ask him what the origin of his fortune is! Get him to tell you how he sold to a stockbroker a Cabinet secret. Learn from him to what you owe your position.

LADY CHILTERN: It is not true! Robert! It is not true!

MRS. CHEVELEY (*pointing at him with outstretched finger*): Look at him! Can he deny it! Does he dare to?

SIR ROBERT CHILTERN: Go! Go at once. You have done your worst now.

MRS. CHEVELEY: My worst? I have not yet finished with you, with either of you. I give you both till to-morrow at noon. If by then you don't do what I bid you to do, the whole world shall know the origin of Robert Chiltern.

SIR ROBERT CHILTERN *strikes the bell. Enter* MASON.

SIR ROBERT CHILTERN: Show Mrs. Cheveley out.

MRS. CHEVELEY *starts; then bows with somewhat exaggerated politeness to* LADY CHILTERN, *who makes no sign of response. As she passes by* SIR ROBERT CHILTERN, *who is standing close to the door, she pauses for a moment and looks him straight in the face. She then goes out, followed by the servant, who closes the door after him. The husband and wife are left alone.* LADY CHILTERN *stands like some one in a dreadful dream. Then she turns round and looks at her husband. She looks at him with strange eyes, as though she was seeing him for the first time.*

LADY CHILTERN: You sold a Cabinet secret for money! You began your life with fraud! You built up your career on dishonour! Oh, tell me it is not true! Lie to me! Lie to me! Tell me it is not true.

SIR ROBERT CHILTERN: What this woman said is quite true. But, Gertrude, listen to me. You don't realise how I was tempted. Let me tell you the whole thing. (*Goes towards her.*)

LADY CHILTERN: Don't come near me. Don't touch me. I feel as if you had soiled me for ever. Oh! What a mask you have been wearing all these years! A horrible painted mask! You sold yourself for money. Oh! A common thief were better. You put yourself up to sale to the highest bidder! You were bought in the market. You lied to the whole world. And yet you will not lie to me.

SIR ROBERT CHILTERN (*rushing towards her*): Gertrude! Gertrude!

LADY CHILTERN (*thrusting him back with outstretched hands*): No, don't speak! Say nothing! Your voice wakes terrible memories – memories of things that made me love you – memories of words that made me love you – memories that now are horrible to me. And how I worshipped you! You were to me something apart from common life, a thing pure, noble, honest, without stain. The world seemed to me finer because you were in it, and goodness more real because you lived. And now – oh, when I think that I made of a man like you my ideal! The ideal of my life!

SIR ROBERT CHILTERN: There was your mistake. There was your error. The error all women commit. Why can't you women love us, faults and all? Why do you place us on monstrous pedestals? We have all feet of clay, women as well as men; but when we men love women, we love them knowing their weaknesses, their follies, their imperfections, love them all the more, it may be, for that reason. It is not the perfect, but the imperfect, who have need of love. It is when we are wounded by our own hands, or by the hands of others, that love should come to cure us – else what use is love at all? All sins, except a sin against itself, Love should forgive. All lives, save loveless lives, true Love should pardon. A man's love is like that. It is wider, larger, more human than a woman's. Women think that they are making ideals of men. What they are making of us are false idols merely. You made your false idol of me, and I had not the courage to come down, show you my wounds, tell you my weaknesses. I was afraid that I might lose your love, as I have lost it now. And so, last night you ruined my life for me – yes, ruined it! What this woman asked of me was nothing compared to what she offered to me. She offered security, peace, stability. The sin of my youth, that I had thought was buried, rose up in front of me, hideous, horrible, with its hands at my throat. I could have killed it for ever, sent it back into its tomb, destroyed its record, burned the one witness against me. You prevented me. No one but you, you know it. And now what is there before me but public disgrace, ruin, terrible shame, the mockery of the world, a lonely dishonoured life, a lonely dishonoured death, it may be, some day? Let women make no more ideals of men! Let them not put them on altars and bow before them or they may ruin other lives as completely as you – you whom I have so wildly loved – have ruined mine!

He passes from the room. LADY CHILTERN *rushes towards him, but the door is closed when she reaches it. Pale with anguish, bewildered, helpless, she sways like a plant in the water. Her hands, outstretched, seem to tremble in the air like blossoms in the wind. Then she flings herself down beside a sofa and buries her face. Her sobs are like the sobs of a child.*

ACT DROP

ACT THREE

SCENE: *The Library in Lord Goring's house in Curzon Street, London. An Adam room. On the right is the door leading into the hall. On the left, the door of the smoking-room. A pair of folding doors at the back open into the drawing-room. The fire is lit. Phipps, the butler, is arranging some newspapers on the writing-table. The distinction of Phipps is his impassivity. He has been termed by enthusiasts the Ideal Butler. The Sphinx is not so incommunicable. He is a mask with a manner. Of his intellectual or emotional life, history knows nothing. He represents the dominance of form.*

Enter LORD GORING *in evening dress with a buttonhole. He is wearing a silk hat and Inverness cape. White-gloved, he carries a Louis Seize cane. His are all the delicate fopperies of Fashion. One sees that he stands in immediate relation to modern life, makes it indeed, and so masters it. He is the first well-dressed philosopher in the history of thought.*

LORD GORING: Got my second buttonhole for me, Phipps?
PHIPPS: Yes, my lord. (*Takes his hat, cane, and cape, and presents new buttonhole on salver.*)

LORD GORING: Rather distinguished thing, Phipps. I am the only person of the smallest importance in London at present who wears a buttonhole.

PHIPPS: Yes, my lord. I have observed that.

LORD GORING (*taking out old buttonhole*): You see, Phipps, Fashion is what one wears oneself. What is unfashionable is what other people wear.

PHIPPS: Yes, my lord.

LORD GORING: Just as vulgarity is simply the conduct of other people.

PHIPPS: Yes, my lord.

LORD GORING (*putting in new buttonhole*): And falsehoods the truths of other people.

PHIPPS: Yes, my lord.

LORD GORING: Other people are quite dreadful. The only possible society is oneself.

PHIPPS: Yes, my lord.

LORD GORING: To love oneself is the beginning of a lifelong romance, Phipps.

PHIPPS: Yes, my lord.

LORD GORING (*looking at himself in the glass*): Don't think I quite like this buttonhole, Phipps. Makes me look a little too old. Makes me almost in the prime of life, eh, Phipps?

PHIPPS: I don't observe any alteration in your lordship's appearance.

LORD GORING: You don't, Phipps?

PHIPPS: No, my lord.

LORD GORING: I am not quite sure. For the future a more trivial buttonhole, Phipps, on Thursday evenings.

PHIPPS: I will speak to the florist, my lord. She has had a loss in her family lately, which perhaps accounts for the lack of triviality your lordship complains of in the buttonhole.

LORD GORING: Extraordinary thing about the lower classes in England – they are always losing their relations.

PHIPPS: Yes, my lord! They are extremely fortunate in that respect.

LORD GORING (*turns round and looks at him.* PHIPPS *remains impassive*): Hum! Any letters, Phipps?

PHIPPS: Three, my lord. (*Hands letters on a salver.*)

LORD GORING (*takes letters*): Want my cab round in twenty minutes.

PHIPPS: Yes, my lord. (*Goes towards door.*)

LORD GORING (*holds up letter in pink envelope*): Ahem, Phipps, when did this letter arrive?

PHIPPS: It was brought by hand just after your lordship went to the club.

LORD GORING: That will do. (*Exit* PHIPPS.) Lady Chiltern's handwriting on Lady Chiltern's pink notepaper. That is rather curious. I thought Robert was to write. Wonder what Lady Chiltern has got to say to me? (*Sits at bureau and opens letter, and reads it.*) 'I want you. I trust you. I am coming to you. Gertrude.' (*Puts down the letter with a puzzled look. Then takes it up, and reads it again slowly.*) 'I want you. I trust you. I am coming to you.' She has found out everything! Poor woman! Poor woman! (*Pulls out watch and looks at it.*)

But what an hour to call! Ten o'clock! I shall have to give up going to the Berkshires. However, it is always nice to be expected, and not to arrive. I am not expected at the Bachelors', so I shall certainly go there. Well, I will make her stand by her husband. That is the only thing for any woman to do. It is the growth of the moral sense of women that makes marriage such a hopeless, one-sided institution. Ten o'clock. She should be here soon. I must tell Phipps I am not in to any one else. (*Goes towards bell.*)

Enter PHIPPS.

PHIPPS: Lord Caversham.

LORD GORING: Oh, why will parents always appear at the wrong time? Some extraordinary mistake in nature, I suppose. (*Enter* LORD CAVERSHAM.) Delighted to see you, my dear father. (*Goes to meet him.*)

LORD CAVERSHAM: Take my cloak off.

LORD GORING: Is it worth while, father?

LORD CAVERSHAM: Of course it is worth while, sir. Which is the most comfortable chair?

LORD GORING: This one, father. It is the chair I use myself, when I have visitors.

LORD CAVERSHAM: Thank ye. No draught, I hope, in this room?

LORD GORING: No, father.

LORD CAVERSHAM (*sitting down*): Glad to hear it. Can't stand draughts. No draughts at home.

LORD GORING: Good many breezes, father.

LORD CAVERSHAM: Eh? Eh? Don't understand what you mean. Want to have a serious conversation with you, sir.

LORD GORING: My dear father! At this hour?

LORD CAVERSHAM: Well, sir, it is only ten o'clock. What is your objection to the hour? I think the hour is an admirable hour!

LORD GORING: Well, the fact is, father, this is not my day for talking seriously. I am very sorry, but it is not my day.

LORD CAVERSHAM: What do you mean, sir?

LORD GORING: During the Season, father, I only talk seriously on the first Tuesday in every month, from four to seven.

LORD CAVERSHAM: Well, make it Tuesday, sir, make it Tuesday.

LORD GORING: But it is after seven, father, and my doctor says I must not have any serious conversation after seven. It makes me talk in my sleep.

LORD CAVERSHAM: Talk in your sleep, sir? What does that matter? You are not married.

LORD GORING: No, father, I am not married.

LORD CAVERSHAM: Hum! That is what I have come to talk to you about, sir. You have got to get married, and at once. Why, when I was your age, sir, I had been an inconsolable widower for three months, and was already paying my addresses to your admirable mother. Damme, sir, it is your duty to get married. You can't be always living for pleasure. Every man of position is married nowadays. Bachelors are not fashionable any more. They are a damaged lot. Too much is known about them. You must get a wife, sir. Look where your friend Robert Chiltern has got to by probity, hard work, and a sensible marriage with a good woman. Why don't you imitate him, sir? Why don't you take him for your model?

LORD GORING: I think I shall, father.

LORD CAVERSHAM: I wish you would, sir. Then I should be happy. At present I make your mother's life miserable on your account. You are heartless, sir, quite heartless.

LORD GORING: I hope not, father.

LORD CAVERSHAM: And it is high time for you to get married. You are thirty-four years of age, sir.

LORD GORING: Yes, father, but I only admit to thirty-two – thirty-one and a half when I have a really good buttonhole. This buttonhole is not . . . trivial enough.

LORD CAVERSHAM: I tell you you are thirty-four, sir. And there is a draught in your room, besides, which makes your conduct worse. Why did you tell me there was no draught, sir? I feel a draught, sir, I feel it distinctly.

LORD GORING: So do I, father. It is a dreadful draught. I will come and see you to-morrow, father. We can talk over anything you like. Let me help you on with your cloak, father.

LORD CAVERSHAM: No, sir; I have called this evening for a definite purpose, and I am going to see it through at all costs to my health or yours. Put down my cloak, sir.

LORD GORING: Certainly, father. But let us go into another room. (*Rings bell.*) There is a dreadful draught here. (*Enter* PHIPPS.) Phipps, is there a good fire in the smoking-room?

PHIPPS: Yes, my lord.

LORD GORING: Come in there, father. Your sneezes are quite heartrending.

LORD CAVERSHAM: Well, sir, I suppose I have a right to sneeze when I choose?

LORD GORING (*apologetically*): Quite so, father. I was merely expressing sympathy.

LORD CAVERSHAM: Oh, damn sympathy. There is a great deal too much of that sort of thing going on nowadays.

LORD GORING: I quite agree with you, father. If there was less sympathy in the world there would be less trouble in the world.

LORD CAVERSHAM (*going towards the smoking-room*): That is a paradox, sir. I hate paradoxes.

LORD GORING: So do I, father. Everybody one meets is a paradox nowadays. It is a great bore. It makes society so obvious.

LORD CAVERSHAM (*turning round, and looking at his son beneath his bushy eyebrows*): Do you always really understand what you say, sir?

LORD GORING (*after some hesitation*): Yes, father, if I listen attentively.

LORD CAVERSHAM (*indignantly*): If you listen attentively! . . . Conceited young puppy!

Goes off grumbling into the smoking-room. PHIPPS *enters.*

LORD GORING: Phipps, there is a lady coming to see me this evening on particular business. Show her into the drawing-room when she arrives. You understand?

PHIPPS: Yes, my lord.

LORD GORING: It is a matter of the gravest importance, Phipps.

PHIPPS: I understand, my lord.

LORD GORING: No one else is to be admitted, under any circumstances.

PHIPPS: I understand, my lord. (*Bell rings.*)

LORD GORING: Ah! That is probably the lady. I shall see her myself.

Just as he is going towards the door LORD CAVERSHAM *enters from the smoking-room.*

LORD CAVERSHAM: Well, sir? Am I to wait attendance on you?

LORD GORING (*considerably perplexed*): In a moment, father. Do excuse me. (LORD CAVERSHAM *goes back.*) Well, remember my instructions, Phipps – into that room.

PHIPPS: Yes, my lord.

LORD GORING *goes into the smoking-room.* HAROLD, *the footman, shows* MRS. CHEVELEY *in. Lamia-like, she is in green and silver. She has a cloak of black satin, lined with dead rose-leaf silk.*

HAROLD: What name, madam?

MRS. CHEVELEY (*to* PHIPPS, *who advances towards her*): Is Lord Goring not here? I was told he was at home?

PHIPPS: His lordship is engaged at present with Lord Caversham, madam.

Turns a cold, glassy eye on HAROLD, *who at once retires.*

MRS. CHEVELEY (*to herself*): How very filial!

PHIPPS: His lordship told me to ask you, madam, to be kind enough to wait in the drawing-room for him. His lordship will come to you there.

MRS. CHEVELEY (*with a look of surprise*): Lord Goring expects me?

PHIPPS: Yes, madam.

MRS. CHEVELEY: Are you quite sure?

PHIPPS: His lordship told me that if a lady called I was to ask her to wait in the drawing-room. (*Goes to the door of the drawing-room and opens it.*) His lordship's directions on the subject were very precise.

MRS. CHEVELEY (*to herself*): How thoughtful of him! To expect the unexpected shows a thoroughly modern intellect. (*Goes towards the drawing-room and looks in.*) Ugh! How dreary a bachelor's drawing-room always looks. I shall have to alter this. (PHIPPS *brings the lamp from the writing-table.*) No, I don't care for that lamp. It is far too glaring. Light some candles.

PHIPPS (*replaces lamp*): Certainly, madam.

MRS. CHEVELEY: I hope the candles have very becoming shades.

PHIPPS: We have had no complaints about them, madam, as yet.

Passes into the drawing-room and begins to light the candles.

MRS. CHEVELEY (*to herself*): I wonder what woman he is waiting for to-night. It will be delightful to catch him. Men always look so silly when they are caught. And they are always being caught. (*Looks about room and approaches the writing-table.*) What a very interesting room! What a very interesting picture! Wonder what his correspondence is like. (*Takes up letters.*) Oh, what a very uninteresting correspondence! Bills and cards, debts and dowagers! Who on earth writes to him on pink paper? How silly to write on pink paper! It looks like the beginning of a middle-class romance. Romance should never begin with sentiment. It should begin with science and end with a settlement. (*Puts letter down, then takes it up again.*) I know that handwriting. That is Gertrude Chiltern's. I remember it perfectly. The ten commandments in every stroke of the pen, and the moral law all over the page. Wonder what Gertrude is writing to him about? Something horrid about me, I suppose. How I detest that woman! (*Reads it.*) 'I trust you. I want you. I am coming to you. Gertrude.' 'I trust you. I want you. I am coming to you.'

A look of triumph comes over her face. She is just about to steal the letter, when PHIPPS *comes in.*

PHIPPS: The candles in the drawing-room are lit, madam, as you directed.

MRS. CHEVELEY: Thank you. (*Rises hastily and slips the letter under a large silver-cased blotting-book that is lying on the table.*)

PHIPPS: I trust the shades will be to your liking, madam. They are the most becoming we have. They are the same as his lordship uses himself when he is dressing for dinner.

MRS. CHEVELEY (*with a smile*): Then I am sure they will be perfectly right.

PHIPPS (*gravely*): Thank you, madam.

MRS. CHEVELEY *goes into the drawing-room.* PHIPPS *closes the door and retires. The door is then slowly opened, and* MRS. CHEVELEY *comes out and creeps stealthily towards the writing-table. Suddenly voices are heard from the smoking-room.* MRS. CHEVELEY *grows pale, and stops. The voices grow louder, and she goes back into the drawing-room biting her lip.*

Enter LORD GORING *and* LORD CAVERSHAM.

LORD GORING (*expostulating*): My dear father, if I am to get married, surely you will allow me to choose the time, place, and person? Particularly the person.

LORD CAVERSHAM (*testily*): That is a matter for me, sir. You would probably make a very poor choice. It is I who should be consulted, not you. There is property at stake. It is not a matter for affection. Affection comes later on in married life.

LORD GORING: Yes. In married life affection comes when people thoroughly dislike each other, father, doesn't it? (*Puts on* LORD CAVERSHAM'S *cloak for him.*)

LORD CAVERSHAM: Certainly, sir. I mean certainly not, sir. You are talking very foolishly to-night. What I say is that marriage is a matter for common sense.

LORD GORING: But women who have common sense are so curiously plain, father, aren't they? Of course I only speak from hearsay.

LORD CAVERSHAM: No woman, plain or pretty, has any common sense at all, sir. Common sense is the privilege of our sex.

LORD GORING: Quite so. And we men are so self-sacrificing that we never use it, do we, father?

LORD CAVERSHAM: I use it, sir. I use nothing else.

LORD GORING: So my mother tells me.

LORD CAVERSHAM: It is the secret of your mother's happiness. You are very heartless, sir, very heartless.

LORD GORING: I hope not, father.

Goes out for a moment. Then returns, looking rather put out, with SIR ROBERT CHILTERN.

SIR ROBERT CHILTERN: My dear Arthur, what a piece of good luck meeting you on the doorstep! Your servant had just told me you were not at home. How extraordinary!

LORD GORING: The fact is, I am horribly busy to-night, Robert, and I gave orders I was not at home to any one. Even my father had a comparatively cold reception. He complained of a draught the whole time.

SIR ROBERT CHILTERN: Ah! You must be at home to me, Arthur. You are my best friend. Perhaps by to-morrow you will be my only friend. My wife has discovered everything.

LORD GORING: Ah! I guessed as much!

SIR ROBERT CHILTERN (*looking at him*): Really! How!

LORD GORING (*after some hesitation*): Oh, merely by something in the expression of your face as you came in. Who told her?

SIR ROBERT CHILTERN: Mrs. Cheveley herself. And the woman I love knows that I began my career with an act of low dishonesty, that I built up my life upon sands of shame – that I sold, like a common huckster, the secret that had been intrusted to me as a man of honour. I thank heaven poor Lord Radley died without knowing that I betrayed him. I would to God I had died before I had been so horribly tempted, or had fallen so low. (*Burying his face in his hands.*)

LORD GORING (*after a pause*): You have heard nothing from Vienna yet, in answer to your wire?

SIR ROBERT CHILTERN (*looking up*): Yes; I got a telegram from the first secretary at eight o'clock to-night.

LORD GORING: Well?

SIR ROBERT CHILTERN: Nothing is absolutely known against her. On the contrary, she occupies a rather high position in society. It is a sort of open secret that Baron Arnheim left her the greater portion of his immense fortune. Beyond that I can learn nothing.

LORD GORING: She doesn't turn out to be a spy, then?

SIR ROBERT CHILTERN: Oh! Spies are of no use nowadays. Their profession is over. The newspapers do their work instead.

LORD GORING: And thunderingly well they do it.

SIR ROBERT CHILTERN: Arthur, I am parched with thirst. May I ring for something? Some hock and seltzer?

LORD GORING: Certainly. Let me. (*Rings the bell.*)

SIR ROBERT CHILTERN: Thanks! I don't know what to do, Arthur, I don't know what to do, and you are my only friend. But what a friend you are – the one friend I can trust. I can trust you absolutely, can't I?

Enter PHIPPS.

LORD GORING: My dear Robert, of course. (*To* PHIPPS): Bring some hock and seltzer.

PHIPPS: Yes, my lord.

LORD GORING: And Phipps!

PHIPPS: Yes, my lord.

LORD GORING: Will you excuse me for a moment, Robert? I want to give some directions to my servant.

SIR ROBERT CHILTERN: Certainly.

LORD GORING: When that lady calls, tell her that I am not expected home this evening. Tell her that I have been suddenly called out of town. You understand?

PHIPPS: The lady is in that room, my lord. You told me to show her into that room, my lord.

LORD GORING: You did perfectly right. (*Exit* PHIPPS.) What a mess I am in. No; I think I shall get through it. I'll give her a lecture through the door. Awkward thing to manage, though.

SIR ROBERT CHILTERN: Arthur, tell me what I should do. My life seems to have crumbled about me. I am a ship without a rudder in a night without a star.

LORD GORING: Robert, you love your wife, don't you?

SIR ROBERT CHILTERN: I love her more than anything in the world. I used to think ambition the great thing. It is not. Love is the great thing in the world. There is nothing but love, and I love her. But I am defamed in her eyes. I am ignoble in her eyes. There is a wide gulf between us now. She had found me out, Arthur, she has found me out.

LORD GORING: Has she never in her life done some folly – some indiscretion – that she should not forgive your sin?

SIR ROBERT CHILTERN: My wife! Never! She does not know what weakness or temptation is. I am of clay like other men. She stands apart as good women do – pitiless in her perfection – cold and stern and without mercy. But I love her, Arthur. We are childless, and I have no one else to love, no one else to love me. Perhaps if God had sent us children she might have been kinder to me. But God has given us a lonely house. And she has cut my heart in two. Don't let us talk of it. I was brutal to her this evening. But I suppose when sinners talk to saints they are brutal always. I said to her things that were hideously true, on my side, from my standpoint, from the standpoint of men. But don't let us talk of that.

LORD GORING: Your wife will forgive you. Perhaps at this moment she is forgiving you. She loves you, Robert. Why should she not forgive?

SIR ROBERT CHILTERN: God grant it! God grant it! (*Buries his face in his hands.*) But there is something more I have to tell you, Arthur.

Enter PHIPPS *with drinks.*

PHIPPS (*hands hock and seltzer to* SIR ROBERT CHILTERN): Hock and seltzer, sir.

SIR ROBERT CHILTERN: Thank you.

LORD GORING: Is your carriage here, Robert?

SIR ROBERT CHILTERN: No; I walked from the club.

LORD GORING: Sir Robert will take my cab, Phipps.

PHIPPS: Yes, my lord.

Exit.

LORD GORING: Robert, you don't mind my sending you away?

SIR ROBERT CHILTERN: Arthur, you must let me stay for five minutes. I have made up my mind what I am going to do to-night in the House. The debate on the Argentine Canal is to begin at eleven. (*A chair falls in the drawing-room.*) What is that!

LORD GORING: Nothing.

SIR ROBERT CHILTERN: I heard a chair fall in the next room. Some one has been listening.

LORD GORING: No, no; there is no one there.

SIR ROBERT CHILTERN: There is some one. There are lights in the room, and the door is ajar. Some one has been listening to every secret of my life. Arthur, what does this mean?

LORD GORING: Robert, you are excited, unnerved. I tell you there is no one in that room. Sit down, Robert.

SIR ROBERT CHILTERN: Do you give me your word that there is no one there?

LORD GORING: Yes.

SIR ROBERT CHILTERN: Your word of honour? (*Sits down.*)

LORD GORING: Yes.

SIR ROBERT CHILTERN (*rises*): Arthur, let me see for myself.

LORD GORING: No, no.

SIR ROBERT CHILTERN: If there is no one there why should I not look in that room? Arthur, you must let me go into that room and satisfy myself. Let me know that no eavesdropper has heard my life's secret. Arthur, you don't realise what I am going through.

LORD GORING: Robert, this must stop. I have told you that there is no one in that room – that is enough.

SIR ROBERT CHILTERN (*rushes to the door of the room*): It is not enough. I insist on going into this room. You have told me there is no one there, so what reason can you have for refusing me?

LORD GORING: For God's sake, don't! There is some one there. Some one whom you must not see.

SIR ROBERT CHILTERN: Ah, I thought so!

LORD GORING: I forbid you to enter that room.

SIR ROBERT CHILTERN: Stand back. My life is at stake. And I don't care who is there. I will know who it is to whom I have told my secret and my shame. (*Enters room.*)

LORD GORING: Great heavens! His own wife!

SIR ROBERT CHILTERN *comes back, with a look of scorn and anger on his face.*

SIR ROBERT CHILTERN: What explanation have you to give for the presence of that woman here?

LORD GORING: Robert, I swear to you on my honour that that lady is stainless and guiltless of all offence towards you.

SIR ROBERT CHILTERN: She is vile, an infamous thing!

LORD GORING: Don't say that, Robert! It was for your sake she came here. It was to try and save you she came here. She loves you and no one else.

SIR ROBERT CHILTERN: You are mad. What have I to do with her intrigues with you? Let her remain your mistress! You are well suited to each other. She, corrupt and shameful – you, false as a friend, treacherous as an enemy even –

LORD GORING: It is not true, Robert. Before heaven, it is not true. In her presence and in yours I will explain all.

SIR ROBERT CHILTERN: Let me pass, sir. You have lied enough upon your word of honour.

SIR ROBERT CHILTERN *goes out.* LORD GORING *rushes to the door of the drawing-room, when* MRS. CHEVELEY *comes out, looking radiant and much amused.*

MRS. CHEVELEY (*with a mock curtsey*): Good-evening, Lord Goring!

LORD GORING: Mrs. Cheveley! Great heavens ... May I ask what were you doing in my drawing-room?

MRS. CHEVELEY: Merely listening. I have a perfect passion for listening through keyholes. One always hears such wonderful things through them.

LORD GORING: Doesn't that sound rather like tempting Providence?

MRS. CHEVELEY: Oh! Surely Providence can resist temptation by this time. (*Makes a sign to him to take her cloak off, which he does.*)

LORD GORING: I am glad you have called. I am going to give you some good advice.

MRS. CHEVELEY: Oh! Pray don't. One should never give a woman anything that she can't wear in the evening.

LORD GORING: I see you are quite as wilful as you used to be.

MRS. CHEVELEY: Far more! I have greatly improved. I have had more experience.

LORD GORING: Too much experience is a dangerous thing. Pray have a cigarette. Half the pretty women in London smoke cigarettes. Personally I prefer the other half.

MRS. CHEVELEY: Thanks. I never smoke. My dressmaker wouldn't like it, and a woman's first duty in life is to her dressmaker, isn't it? What the second duty is, no one has as yet discovered.

LORD GORING: You have come here to sell me Robert Chiltern's letter, haven't you?

MRS. CHEVELEY: To offer it to you on conditions! How did you guess that?

LORD GORING: Because you haven't mentioned the subject. Have you got it with you?

MRS. CHEVELEY: (*sitting down*): Oh, no! A well-made dress has no pockets.

LORD GORING: What is your price for it?

MRS. CHEVELEY: How absurdly English you are! The English think that a cheque-book can solve every problem in life. Why, my dear Arthur, I have very much more money than you have, and quite as much as Robert Chiltern has got hold of. Money is not what I want.

LORD GORING: What do you want then, Mrs. Cheveley?

MRS. CHEVELEY: Why don't you call me Laura?

LORD GORING: I don't like the name.

MRS. CHEVELEY: You used to adore it.

LORD GORING: Yes; that's why. (MRS. CHEVELEY *motions to him to sit down beside her. He smiles, and does so.*)

MRS. CHEVELEY: Arthur, you loved me once.

LORD GORING: Yes.

MRS. CHEVELEY: And you asked me to be your wife.

LORD GORING: That was the natural result of my loving you.

MRS. CHEVELEY: And you threw me over because you saw, or said you saw, poor old Lord Mortlake trying to have a violent flirtation with me in the conservatory at Tenby.

LORD GORING: I am under the impression that my lawyer settled that matter with you on certain terms . . . dictated by yourself.

MRS. CHEVELEY: At that time I was poor; you were rich.

LORD GORING: Quite so. That is why you pretended to love me.

MRS. CHEVELEY (*shrugging her shoulders*): Poor old Lord Mortlake, who had only two topics of conversation, his gout and his wife! I never could quite make out which of the two he was talking about. He used the most horrible language about them both. Well, you were silly, Arthur. Why, Lord Mortlake was never anything more to me than an amusement. One of those utterly tedious amusements one only finds at an English country house on an English country Sunday. I don't think any one at all morally responsible for what he or she does at an English country house.

LORD GORING: Yes. I know lots of people think that.

MRS. CHEVELEY: I loved you, Arthur.

LORD GORING: My dear Mrs. Cheveley, you have always been far too clever to know anything about love.

MRS. CHEVELEY: I did love you. And you loved me. You know you loved me; and love is a very wonderful thing. I suppose that when a man has once loved a woman, he will do anything for her, except continue to love her? (*Puts her hand on his.*)

LORD GORING (*taking his hand away quietly*): Yes; except that.

MRS. CHEVELEY (*after a pause*): I am tired of living abroad. I want to come back to London. I want to have a charming house here. I want to have a salon. If one could only teach the English how to talk, and the Irish how to listen, society here would be quite civilised. Besides, I have arrived at the romantic stage. When I saw you last night at the Chilterns', I knew you were the only person I had ever cared for, if I ever have cared for anybody, Arthur. And so, on the morning of the day you marry me, I will give you Robert Chiltern's letter. That is my offer. I will give it to you now, if you promise to marry me.

LORD GORING: Now?

MRS. CHEVELEY (*smiling*): To-morrow.

LORD GORING: Are you really serious?

MRS. CHEVELEY: Yes, quite serious.

LORD GORING: I should make you a very bad husband.

MRS. CHEVELEY: I don't mind bad husbands. I have had two. They amused me immensely.

LORD GORING: You mean that you amused yourself immensely, don't you?

MRS. CHEVELEY: What do you know about my married life?

LORD GORING: Nothing; but I can read it like a book.

MRS. CHEVELEY: What book?

LORD GORING (*rising*): The Book of Numbers.

MRS. CHEVELEY: Do you think it is quite charming of you to be so rude to a woman in your own house?

LORD GORING: In the case of very fascinating women, sex is a challenge, not a defence.

MRS. CHEVELEY: I suppose that is meant for a compliment. My dear Arthur, women are never disarmed by compliments. Men always are. That is the difference between the two sexes.

LORD GORING: Women are never disarmed by anything, as far as I know them.

MRS. CHEVELEY (*after a pause*): Then you are going to allow your greatest friend, Robert Chiltern, to be ruined, rather than marry some one who really has considerable attractions left. I thought you would have risen to some great height of self-sacrifice, Arthur. I think you should. And the rest of your life you could spend in contemplating your own perfections.

LORD GORING: Oh! I do that as it is. And self-sacrifice is a thing that should be put down by law. It is so demoralising to the people for whom one sacrifices oneself. They always go to the bad.

MRS. CHEVELEY: As if anything could demoralise Robert Chiltern! You seem to forget that I know his real character.

LORD GORING: What you know about him is not his real character. It was an act of folly done in his youth, dishonourable, I admit, shameful, I admit, unworthy of him, I admit, and therefore . . . not his true character.

MRS. CHEVELEY: How you men stand up for each other!

LORD GORING: How you women war against each other!

MRS. CHEVELEY (*bitterly*): I only war against one woman, against Gertrude Chiltern. I hate her. I hate her now more than ever.

LORD GORING: Because you have brought a real tragedy into her life, I suppose.

MRS. CHEVELEY (*with a sneer*): Oh, there is only one real tragedy in a woman's life. The fact that her past is always her lover, and her future invariably her husband.

LORD GORING: Lady Chiltern knows nothing of the kind of life to which you are alluding.

MRS. CHEVELEY: A woman whose size in gloves is seven and three-quarters never knows much about anything. You know Gertrude has always worn seven and three-quarters? That is one of the reasons why there was never any moral sympathy between us. . . . Well, Arthur, I suppose this romantic interview may be regarded as at an end. You admit it was romantic, don't you? For the privilege of being your wife I was ready to surrender a great prize, the climax of my diplomatic career. You decline. Very well. If Sir Robert doesn't uphold my Argentine scheme, I expose him. *Voilà tout.*

LORD GORING: You mustn't do that. It would be vile, horrible, imfamous.

MRS. CHEVELEY (*shrugging her shoulders*): Oh, don't use big words. They mean so little. It is a commercial transaction. That is all. There is no good mixing up sentimentality in it. I offered to sell Robert Chiltern a certain thing. If he won't pay me my price, he will have to pay the world a greater price. There is no more to be said. I must go. Good-bye. Won't you shake hands?

LORD GORING: With you? No. Your transaction with Robert Chiltern may pass as a loathsome commercial transaction of a loathsome commercial age; but you seem to have forgotten that you came here to-night to talk of love, you whose lips desecrated the word love, you to whom the thing is a book closely sealed, went this afternoon to the house of one of the most noble and gentle women in the world to degrade her husband in her eyes, to try and kill her love for him, to put poison in her heart, and bitterness in her life, to break her idol, and, it may be, spoil her soul. That I cannot forgive you. That was horrible. For that there can be no forgiveness.

MRS. CHEVELEY: Arthur, you are unjust to me. Believe me, you are quite unjust to me. I didn't go to taunt Gertrude at all. I had no idea of doing anything of the kind when I entered. I called with Lady Markby simply to ask whether an ornament, a jewel, that I lost somewhere last night, had been found at the Chilterns'. If you don't believe me, you can ask Lady Markby. She will tell you it is true. The scene that occurred happened after Lady Markby had left, and was really forced on me by Gertrude's rudeness and sneers. I called, oh! – a little out of malice if you like – but really to ask if a diamond brooch of mine had been found. That was the origin of the whole thing.

LORD GORING: A diamond snake-brooch with a ruby?

MRS. CHEVELEY: Yes. How do you know?

LORD GORING: Because it is found. In point of fact, I found it myself, and stupidly forgot to tell the butler anything about it as I was leaving. (*Goes over to the writing-table and pulls out the drawers.*) It is in this drawer. No, that one. This is the brooch, isn't it? (*Holds up the brooch.*)

MRS. CHEVELEY: Yes. I am so glad to get it back. It was . . . a present.

LORD GORING: Won't you wear it?

MRS. CHEVELEY: Certainly, if you pin it in. (LORD GORING *suddenly clasps it on her arm.*) Why do you put it on as a bracelet? I never knew it could be worn as a bracelet.

LORD GORING: Really?

MRS. CHEVELEY (*holding out her handsome arm*): No; but it looks very well on me as a bracelet, doesn't it?

LORD GORING: Yes; much better than when I saw it last.

MRS. CHEVELEY: When did you see it last?

LORD GORING (*calmly*): Oh, ten years ago, on Lady Berkshire, from whom you stole it.

MRS. CHEVELEY (*starting*): What do you mean?

LORD GORING: I mean that you stole that ornament from my cousin, Mary Berkshire, to whom I gave it when she was married. Suspicion fell on a wretched servant, who was sent away in disgrace. I recognised it last night. I determined to say nothing about it till I had found the thief. I have found the thief now, and I have heard her own confession.

MRS. CHEVELEY (*tossing her head*): It is not true.

LORD GORING: You know it is true. Why, thief is written across your face at this moment.

MRS. CHEVELEY: I will deny the whole affair from beginning to end. I will say that I have never seen this wretched thing, that it was never in my possession.

MRS. CHEVELEY *tries to get the bracelet off her arm, but fails.* LORD GORING *looks on amused. Her thin fingers tear at the jewel to no purpose. A curse breaks from her.*

LORD GORING: The drawback of stealing a thing, Mrs. Cheveley, is that one never knows how wonderful the thing that one steals is. You can't get that bracelet off, unless you know where the spring is. And I see you don't know where the spring is. It is rather difficult to find.

MRS. CHEVELEY: You brute! You coward! (*She tries again to unclasp the bracelet, but fails.*)

LORD GORING: Oh! Don't use big words. They mean so little.

MRS. CHEVELEY (*again tears at the bracelet in a paroxysm of rage, with inarticulate sounds. Then stops, and looks at* LORD GORING): What are you going to do?

LORD GORING: I am going to ring for my servant. He is an admirable servant. Always comes in the moment one rings for him. When he comes I will tell him to fetch the police.

MRS. CHEVELEY (*trembling*): The police? What for?

LORD GORING: To-morrow the Berkshires will prosecute you. That is what the police are for.

MRS. CHEVELEY (*is now in an agony of physical terror. Her face is distorted. Her mouth awry. A mask has fallen from her. She is, for the moment, dreadful to look at*): Don't do that. I will do anything you want. Anything in the world you want.

LORD GORING: Give me Robert Chiltern's letter.

MRS. CHEVELEY: Stop! Stop! Let me have time to think.

LORD GORING: Give me Robert Chiltern's letter.

MRS. CHEVELEY: I have not got it with me. I will give it to you to-morrow.

LORD GORING: You know you are lying. Give it to me at once. (MRS. CHEVELEY *pulls the letter out, and hands it to him. She is horribly pale.*) This is it?

MRS. CHEVELEY (*in a hoarse voice*): Yes.

LORD GORING (*takes the letter, examines it, sighs, and burns it over the lamp*): For so-well dressed a woman, Mrs. Cheveley, you have moments of admirable common sense. I congratulate you.

MRS. CHEVELEY (*catches sight of* LADY CHILTERN'S *letter, the cover of which is just showing from under the blotting-book*): Please get me a glass of water.

LORD GORING: Certainly. (*Goes to the corner of the room and pours out a glass of water. While his back is turned* MRS. CHEVELEY *steals* LADY CHILTERN'S *letter. When* LORD GORING *returns with the glass she refuses it with a gesture.*)

MRS. CHEVELEY: Thank you. Will you help me on with my cloak?

LORD GORING: With pleasure. (*Puts her cloak on.*)

MRS. CHEVELEY: Thanks. I am never going to try to harm Robert Chiltern again.

LORD GORING: Fortunately you have not the chance, Mrs. Cheveley.

MRS. CHEVELEY: Well, if even I had the chance, I wouldn't. On the contrary, I am going to render him a great service.

LORD GORING: I am charmed to hear it. It is a reformation.

MRS. CHEVELEY: Yes. I can't bear so upright a gentleman, so honourable an English gentleman, being so shamefully deceived and so –

LORD GORING: Well?

MRS. CHEVELEY: I find that somehow Gertrude Chiltern's dying speech and confession has strayed into my pocket.

LORD GORING: What do you mean?

MRS. CHEVELEY (*with a bitter note of triumph in her voice*): I mean that I am going to send Robert Chiltern the love-letter his wife wrote to you to-night.

LORD GORING: Love-letter?

MRS. CHEVELEY (*laughing*): 'I want you. I trust you. I am coming to you. Gertrude.'

> LORD GORING *rushes to the bureau and takes up the envelope, finds it empty, and turns round.*

LORD GORING: You wretched woman, must you always be thieving? Give me back that letter. I'll take it from you by force. You shall not leave my room till I have got it.

> *He rushes towards her, but* MRS. CHEVELEY *at once puts her hand on the electric bell that is on the table. The bell sounds with shrill reverberations, and* PHIPPS *enters.*

MRS. CHEVELEY (*after a pause*): Lord Goring merely rang that you should show me out. Good-night, Lord Goring!

> *Goes out followed by* PHIPPS. *Her face is illuminated with evil triumph. There is joy in her eyes. Youth seems to have come back to her. Her last glance is like a swift arrow.* LORD GORING *bites his lip, and lights a cigarette.*

ACT DROP

ACT FOUR

SCENE: *Same as Act Two.*

> LORD GORING *is standing by the fireplace with his hands in his pockets. He is looking rather bored.*

LORD GORING (*pulls out his watch, inspects it, and rings the bell*): It is a great nuisance. I can't find any one in this house to talk to. And I am full of interesting information. I feel like the latest edition of something or other.

Enter servant.

JAMES: Sir Robert is still at the Foreign Office, my lord.

LORD GORING: Lady Chiltern not down yet?

JAMES: Her ladyship has not yet left her room. Miss Chiltern has just come in from riding.

LORD GORING (*to himself*): Ah! That is something.

JAMES: Lord Caversham has been waiting some time in the library for Sir Robert. I told him your lordship was here.

LORD GORING: Thank you. Would you kindly tell him I've gone?

JAMES (*bowing*): I shall do so, my lord.

Exit servant.

LORD GORING: Really, I don't want to meet my father three days running. It is a great deal too much excitement for any son. I hope to goodness he won't come up. Fathers should be neither seen nor heard. That is the only proper basis for family life. Mothers are different. Mothers are darlings. (*Throws himself down into a chair, picks up a paper and begins to read it.*)

Enter LORD CAVERSHAM.

LORD CAVERSHAM: Well, sir, what are you doing here? Wasting your time as usual, I suppose?

LORD GORING (*throws down paper and rises*): My dear father, when one pays a visit it is for the purpose of wasting other people's time, not one's own.

LORD CAVERSHAM: Have you been thinking over what I spoke to you about last night?

LORD GORING: I have been thinking about nothing else.

LORD CAVERSHAM: Engaged to be married yet?

LORD GORING (*genially*): Not yet; but I hope to be before lunch-time.

LORD CAVERSHAM (*caustically*): You can have till dinner-time if it would be of any convenience to you.

LORD GORING: Thanks awfully, but I think I'd sooner be engaged before lunch.

LORD CAVERSHAM: Humph! Never know when you are serious or not.

LORD GORING: Neither do I, father.

A pause.

LORD CAVERSHAM: I suppose you have read *The Times* this morning?

LORD GORING (*airily*): *The Times*? Certainly not. I only read *The Morning Post*. All that one should know about modern life is where the Duchesses are; anything else is quite demoralising.

LORD CAVERSHAM: Do you mean to say you have not read *The Times* leading article on Robert Chiltern's career?

LORD GORING: Good heavens! No. What does it say?

LORD CAVERSHAM: What should it say, sir? Everything complimentary, of course. Chiltern's speech last night on this Argentine Canal scheme was one of the finest pieces of oratory ever delivered in the House since Canning.

LORD GORING: Ah! Never heard of Canning. Never wanted to. And did ... did Chiltern uphold the scheme?

LORD CAVERSHAM: Uphold it, sir? How little you know him! Why, he denounced it roundly, and the whole system of modern political finance. This speech is the turning-point in his career, as *The Times* points out. You should read this article, sir. (*Opens* The Times.) 'Sir Robert Chiltern ... most rising of our young statesmen.... Brilliant orator.... Unblemished career.... Well-known integrity of character.... Represents what is best in English public life.... Noble contrast to the lax morality so common among foreign politicians.' They will never say that of you, sir.

LORD GORING: I sincerely hope not, father. However, I am delighted at what you tell me about Robert, thoroughly delighted. It shows he has got pluck.

LORD CAVERSHAM: He has got more than pluck, sir, he has got genius.

LORD GORING: Ah! I prefer pluck. It is not so common, nowadays, as genius is.

LORD CAVERSHAM: I wish you would go into Parliament.

LORD GORING: My dear father, only people who look dull ever get into the House of Commons, and only people who are dull ever succeed there.

LORD CAVERSHAM: Why don't you try to do something useful in life?

LORD GORING: I am far too young.

LORD CAVERSHAM (*testily*): I hate this affectation of youth, sir. It is a great deal too prevalent nowadays.

LORD GORING: Youth isn't an affectation. Youth is an art.

LORD CAVERSHAM: Why don't you propose to that pretty Miss Chiltern?

LORD GORING: I am of a very nervous disposition, especially in the morning.

LORD CAVERSHAM: I don't suppose there is the smallest chance of her accepting you.

LORD GORING: I don't know how the betting stands to-day.

LORD CAVERSHAM: If she did accept you she would be the prettiest fool in England.

LORD GORING: That is just what I should like to marry. A thoroughly sensible wife would reduce me to a condition of absolute idiocy in less than six months.

LORD CAVERSHAM: You don't deserve her, sir.

LORD GORING: My dear father, if we men married the women we deserved, we should have a very bad time of it.

Enter MABEL CHILTERN.

MABEL CHILTERN: Oh!.... How do you do, Lord Caversham? I hope

Lady Caversham is quite well?

LORD CAVERSHAM: Lady Caversham is as usual, as usual.

LORD GORING: Good-morning, Miss Mabel!

MABEL CHILTERN (*taking no notice at all of* LORD GORING, *and addressing herself exclusively to* LORD CAVERSHAM): And Lady Caversham's bonnets ... are they at all better?

LORD CAVERSHAM: They have had a serious relapse, I am sorry to say.

LORD GORING: Good-morning, Miss Mabel.

MABEL CHILTERN (*to* LORD CAVERSHAM): I hope an operation will not be necessary.

LORD CAVERSHAM (*smiling at her pertness*): If it is, we shall have to give Lady Caversham a narcotic. Otherwise she would never consent to have a feather touched.

LORD GORING (*with increased emphasis*): Good-morning, Miss Mabel!

MABEL CHILTERN (*turning round with feigned surprise*): Oh, are you here? Of course you understand that after your breaking your appointment I am never going to speak to you again.

LORD GORING: Oh, please don't say such a thing. You are the one person in London I really like to have to listen to me.

MABEL CHILTERN: Lord Goring, I never believe a single word that either you or I say to each other.

LORD CAVERSHAM: You are quite right, my dear, quite right as far as he is concerned, I mean.

MABEL CHILTERN: Do you think you could possibly make your son behave a little better occasionally? Just as a change.

LORD CAVERSHAM: I regret to say, Miss Chiltern, that I have no influence at all over my son. I wish I had. If I had, I know what I would make him do.

MABEL CHILTERN: I am afraid that he has one of those terribly weak natures that are not susceptible to influence.

LORD CAVERSHAM: He is very heartless, very heartless.

LORD GORING: It seems to me that I am a little in the way here.

MABEL CHILTERN: It is very good for you to be in the way, and to know what people say of you behind your back.

LORD GORING: I don't at all like knowing what people say of me behind my back. It makes me far too conceited.

LORD CAVERSHAM: After that, my dear, I really must bid you good-morning.

MABEL CHILTERN: Oh! I hope you are not going to leave me all alone with Lord Goring? Especially at such an early hour in the day.

LORD CAVERSHAM: I am afraid I can't take him with me to Downing Street. It is not the Prime Minister's day for seeing the unemployed.

Shakes hands with MABEL CHILTERN, *takes up his hat and stick, and goes out, with a parting glare of indignation at* LORD GORING.

MABEL CHILTERN (*takes up roses and begins to arrange them in a bowl on the table*): People who don't keep their appointments in the Park are horrid.

LORD GORING: Detestable.

MABEL CHILTERN: I am glad you admit it. But I wish you wouldn't look so pleased about it.

LORD GORING: I can't help it. I always look pleased when I am with you.

MABEL CHILTERN (*sadly*): Then I suppose it is my duty to remain with you?

LORD GORING: Of course it is.

MABEL CHILTERN: Well, my duty is a thing I never do, on principle. It always depresses me. So I am afraid I must leave you.

LORD GORING: Please don't, Miss Mabel. I have something very particular to say to you.

MABEL CHILTERN (*rapturously*): Oh! Is it a proposal?

LORD GORING (*somewhat taken aback*): Well, yes it is – I am bound to say it is.

MABEL CHILTERN (*with a sigh of pleasure*): I am so glad. That makes the second to-day.

LORD GORING (*indignantly*): The second to-day? What conceited ass has been impertinent enough to dare to propose to you before I had proposed to you?

MABEL CHILTERN: Tommy Trafford, of course. It is one of Tommy's days for proposing. He always proposes on Tuesdays and Thursdays, during the Season.

LORD GORING: You didn't accept him, I hope?

MABEL CHILTERN: I make it a rule never to accept Tommy. That is why he goes on proposing. Of course, as you didn't turn up this morning, I very nearly said yes. It would have been an excellent lesson both for him and for you if I had. It would have taught you both better manners.

LORD GORING: Oh! Bother Tommy Trafford. Tommy is a silly little ass. I love you.

MABEL CHILTERN: I know. And I think you might have mentioned it before. I am sure I have given you heaps of opportunities.

LORD GORING: Mabel, do be serious. Please be serious.

MABEL CHILTERN: Ah! That is the sort of thing a man always says to a girl before he has been married to her. He never says it afterwards.

LORD GORING (*taking hold of her hand*): Mabel, I have told you that I love you. Can't you love me a little in return?

MABEL CHILTERN: You silly Arthur! If you knew anything about . . . anything, which you don't, you would know that I adore you. Every one in London knows it except you. It is a public scandal the way I adore you. I have been going about for the last six months telling the whole of society that I adore you. I wonder you consent to have anything to say to me. I have no character left at all. At least, I feel so happy that I am quite sure I have no character left at all.

LORD GORING (*catches her in his arms and kisses her. Then there is a pause of bliss*): Dear! Do you know I was awfully afraid of being refused!

MABEL CHILTERN (*looking up at him*): But you never have been refused yet by anybody, have you, Arthur? I can't imagine any one refusing you.

LORD GORING (*after kissing her again*): Of course I'm not nearly good enough for you, Mabel.

MABEL CHILTERN (*nestling close to him*): I am so glad, darling. I was afraid you were.

LORD GORING (*after some hesitation*): And I'm . . . I'm a little over thirty.

MABEL CHILTERN: Dear, you look weeks younger than that.

LORD GORING (*enthusiastically*): How sweet of you to say so! . . . And it is only to fair to tell you frankly that I am fearfully extravagant.

MABEL CHILTERN: But so am I, Arthur. So we're sure to agree. And now I must go and see Gertrude.

LORD GORING: Must you really? (*Kisses her.*)

MABEL CHILTERN: Yes.

LORD GORING: Then do tell her I want to talk to her particularly. I have been waiting here all the morning to see either her or Robert.

MABEL CHILTERN: Do you mean to say you didn't come here expressly to propose to me?

LORD GORING (*triumphantly*): No; that was a flash of genius.

MABEL CHILTERN: Your first.

LORD GORING (*with determination*): My last.

MABEL CHILTERN: I am delighted to hear it. Now don't stir. I'll be back in five minutes. And don't fall into any temptations while I am away.

LORD GORING: Dear Mabel, while you are away, there are none. It makes me horribly dependent on you.

Enter LADY CHILTERN.

LADY CHILTERN: Good-morning, dear! How pretty you are looking!

MABEL CHILTERN: How pale you are looking, Gertrude! It is most becoming!

LADY CHILTERN: Good-morning, Lord Goring!

LORD GORING (*bowing*): Good-morning, Lady Chiltern!

MABEL CHILTERN (*aside to* LORD GORING): I shall be in the conservatory, under the second palm tree on the left.

LORD GORING: Second on the left?

MABEL CHILTERN (*with a look of mock surprise*): Yes; the usual palm tree.

Blows a kiss to him, unobserved by LADY CHILTERN, *and goes out.*

LORD GORING: Lady Chiltern, I have a certain amount of very good news to tell you. Mrs. Cheveley gave me up Robert's letter last night, and I burned it. Robert is safe.

LADY CHILTERN (*sinking on the sofa*): Safe! Oh! I am so glad of that. What a good friend you are to him – to us!

LORD GORING: There is only one person now that could be said to be in any danger.

LADY CHILTERN: Who is that?

LORD GORING (*sitting down beside her*): Yourself.

LADY CHILTERN: I! In danger? What do you mean?

LORD GORING: Danger is too great a word. It is a word I should not have used. But I admit I have something to tell you that may distress you, that terribly distresses me. Yesterday evening you wrote me a very beautiful, womanly letter, asking me for my help. You wrote to me as one of your oldest friends, one of your husband's oldest friends. Mrs. Cheveley stole that letter from my rooms.

LADY CHILTERN: Well, what use is it to her? Why should she not have it?

LORD GORING (*rising*): Lady Chiltern, I will be quite frank with you. Mrs. Cheveley puts a certain construction on that letter and proposes to send it to your husband.

LADY CHILTERN: But what construction could she put on it? ... Oh! Not that! Not that! If I in – in trouble, and wanting your help, trusting you, propose to come to you ... that you may advise me ... assist me. ... Oh! Are there women so horrible as that ... ? And she proposes to send it to my husband? Tell me what happened. Tell me all that happened.

LORD GORING: Mrs. Cheveley was concealed in a room adjoining my library, without my knowledge. I thought that the person who was waiting in that room to see me was yourself. Robert came in unexpectedly. A chair or something fell in the room. He forced his way in, and he discovered her. We had a terrible scene. I still thought it was you. He left me in anger. At the end of everything Mrs. Cheveley got possession of your letter – she stole it, when or how, I don't know.

LADY CHILTERN: At what hour did this happen?

LORD GORING: At half-past ten. And now I propose that we tell Robert the whole thing at once.

LADY CHILTERN (*looking at him with amazement that is almost terror*): You want me to tell Robert that the woman you expected was not Mrs. Cheveley, but myself? That it was I whom you thought was concealed in a room in your house, at half-past ten o'clock at night? You want me to tell him that?

LORD GORING: I think it is better that he should know the exact truth.

LADY CHILTERN (*rising*): Oh, I couldn't, I couldn't!

LORD GORING: May I do it?

LADY CHILTERN: No.

LORD GORING (*gravely*): You are wrong, Lady Chiltern.

LADY CHILTERN: No. The letter must be intercepted. That is all. But how can I do it? Letters arrive for him every moment of the day. His secretaries open them and hand them to him. I dare not ask the servants to bring me his letters. It would be impossible. Oh! Why don't you tell me what to do?

LORD GORING: Pray be calm, Lady Chiltern, and answer the questions I am going to put to you. You said his secretaries open his letters.

LADY CHILTERN: Yes.

LORD GORING: Who is with him to-day? Mr. Trafford, isn't it?

LADY CHILTERN: No, Mr. Montford, I think.

LORD GORING: You can trust him?

LADY CHILTERN (*with a gesture of despair*): Oh! How do I know?

LORD GORING: He would do what you asked him, wouldn't he?

LADY CHILTERN: I think so.

LORD GORING: Your letter was on pink paper. He could recognise it without reading it, couldn't he? By the colour?

LADY CHILTERN: I suppose so.

LORD GORING: Is he in the house now?

LADY CHILTERN: Yes.

LORD GORING: Then I will go and see him myself, and tell him that a certain letter, written on pink paper, is to be forwarded to Robert to-day, and that at all costs it must not reach him. (*Goes to the door, and opens it.*) Oh! Robert is coming upstairs with the letter in his hand. It has reached him already.

LADY CHILTERN (*with a cry of pain*): Oh! You have saved his life; what have you done with mine?

Enter SIR ROBERT CHILTERN. *He has the letter in his hand, and is reading it. He comes towards his wife, not noticing* LORD GORING'S *presence.*

SIR ROBERT CHILTERN: 'I want you. I trust you. I am coming to you. Gertrude.' Oh, my love! Is this true? Do you indeed trust me, and want me? If so, it was for me to come to you, not for you to write of coming to me. This letter of yours, Gertrude, makes me feel that nothing that the world may do can hurt me now. You want me, Gertrude.

LORD GORING, *unseen by* SIR ROBERT CHILTERN, *makes an imploring sign to* LADY CHILTERN *to accept the situation and* SIR ROBERT'S *error.*

LADY CHILTERN: Yes.

SIR ROBERT CHILTERN: You trust me, Gertrude?

LADY CHILTERN: Yes.

SIR ROBERT CHILTERN: Ah! Why did you not add you loved me?

LADY CHILTERN (*taking his hand*): Because I loved you.

LORD GORING *passes into the conservatory.*

SIR ROBERT CHILTERN (*kisses her*): Gertrude, you don't know what I feel. When Montford passed me your letter across the table – he had opened it by mistake, I suppose, without looking at the handwriting on the envelope – and I read it – oh! I did not care what disgrace or punishment was in store for me, I only thought you loved me still.

LADY CHILTERN: There is no disgrace in store for you, nor any public shame. Mrs. Cheveley has handed over to Lord Goring the document that was in her possession, and he has destroyed it.

SIR ROBERT CHILTERN: Are you sure of this, Gertrude?

LADY CHILTERN: Yes; Lord Goring has just told me.

SIR ROBERT CHILTERN: Then I am safe! Oh! What a wonderful thing to be safe! For two days I have been in terror. I am safe now. How did Arthur destroy my letter? Tell me.

LADY CHILTERN: He burned it.

SIR ROBERT CHILTERN: I wish I had seen that one sin of my youth burning to ashes. How many men there are in modern life who would like to see their past burning to white ashes before them! Is Arthur still here?

LADY CHILTERN: Yes; he is in the conservatory.

SIR ROBERT CHILTERN: I am so glad now I made that speech last night in the House, so glad. I made it thinking that public disgrace might be the result. But it has not been so.

LADY CHILTERN: Public honour has been the result.

SIR ROBERT CHILTERN: I think so. I fear so, almost. For although I am safe from detection, although every proof against me is destroyed, I suppose, Gertrude . . . I suppose I should retire from public life? (*He looks anxiously at his wife.*)

LADY CHILTERN (*eagerly*): Oh yes, Robert, you should do that. It is your duty to do that.

SIR ROBERT CHILTERN: It is much to surrender.

LADY CHILTERN: No; it will be much to gain.

SIR ROBERT CHILTERN *walks up and down the room with a troubled expression. Then comes over to his wife, and puts his hand on her shoulder.*

SIR ROBERT CHILTERN: And you would be happy living somewhere alone with me, abroad perhaps, or in the country away from London, away from public life? You would have no regrets?

LADY CHILTERN: Oh! None, Robert.

SIR ROBERT CHILTERN (*sadly*): And your ambition for me? You used to be ambitious for me.

LADY CHILTERN: Oh, my ambition! I have none now, but that we two may love each other. It was your ambition that led you astray. Let us not talk about ambition.

LORD GORING *returns from the conservatory, looking very pleased with himself, and with an entirely new buttonhole that some one has made for him.*

SIR ROBERT CHILTERN (*going towards him*): Arthur, I have to thank you for what you have done for me. I don't know how I can repay you. (*Shakes hands with him.*)

LORD GORING: My dear fellow, I'll tell you at once. At the present moment, under the usual palm tree . . . I mean in the conservatory . . .

Enter MASON.

MASON: Lord Caversham.

LORD GORING: That admirable father of mine really makes a habit of turning up at the wrong moment. It is very heartless of him, very heartless indeed.

Enter LORD CAVERSHAM. MASON *goes out.*

LORD CAVERSHAM: Good-morning, Lady Chiltern! Warmest congratulations to you, Chiltern, on your brilliant speech last night. I have just left the Prime Minister, and you are to have the vacant seat in the Cabinet.

SIR ROBERT CHILTERN (*with a look of joy and triumph*): A seat in the Cabinet?

LORD CAVERSHAM: Yes; here is the Prime Minister's letter. (*Hands letter.*)

SIR ROBERT CHILTERN (*takes letter and reads it*): A seat in the Cabinet!

LORD CAVERSHAM: Certainly, and you well deserve it too. You have got what we want so much in political life nowadays – high character, high moral tone, high principles. (*To* LORD GORING): Everything that you have not got, sir, and never will have.

LORD GORING: I don't like principles, father. I prefer prejudices.

SIR ROBERT CHILTERN *is on the brink of accepting the Prime Minister's offer, when he sees his wife looking at him with her clear candid eyes. He then realises that it is impossible.*

SIR ROBERT CHILTERN: I cannot accept this offer, Lord Caversham. I have made up my mind to decline it.

LORD CAVERSHAM: Decline it, sir?

SIR ROBERT CHILTERN: My intention is to retire at once from public life.

LORD CAVERSHAM (*angrily*): Decline a seat in the Cabinet, and retire from public life? Never heard such damned nonsense in the whole course of my existence. I beg your pardon, Lady Chiltern. Chiltern, I beg your pardon. (*To* LORD GORING.): Don't grin like that, sir.

LORD GORING: No, father.

LORD CAVERSHAM: Lady Chiltern, you are a sensible woman, the most sensible woman in London, the most sensible woman I know. Will you kindly prevent your husband from making such a ... from talking such.... Will you kindly do that, Lady Chiltern?

LADY CHILTERN: I think my husband is right in his determination, Lord Caversham. I approve of it.

LORD CAVERSHAM: You approve of it? Good heavens!

LADY CHILTERN (*taking her husband's hand*): I admire him for it. I admire him immensely for it. I have never admired him so much before. He is finer than even I thought him. (*To* SIR ROBERT CHILTERN): You will go and write your letter to the Prime Minister now, won't you? Don't hesitate about it, Robert.

SIR ROBERT CHILTERN (*with a touch of bitterness*): I suppose I had better write it at once. Such offers are not repeated. I will ask you to excuse me for a moment, Lord Caversham.

LADY CHILTERN: I may come with you, Robert, may I not?

SIR ROBERT CHILTERN: Yes, Gertrude.

LADY CHILTERN *goes with him*.

LORD CAVERSHAM: What is the matter with this family? Something wrong here, eh? (*Tapping his forehead.*) Idiocy? Hereditary, I suppose. Both of them, too. Wife as well as husband. Very sad. Very sad indeed! And they are not an old family. Can't understand it.

LORD GORING: It is not idiocy, father, I assure you.

LORD CAVERSHAM: What is it then, sir?

LORD GORING (*after some hesitation*): Well, it is what is called nowadays a high moral tone, father. That is all.

LORD CAVERSHAM: Hate these new-fangled names. Same thing as we used to call idiocy fifty years ago. Shan't stay in this house any longer.

LORD GORING (*taking his arm*): Oh! Just go in there for a moment, father. Third palm tree to the left, the usual palm tree.

LORD CAVERSHAM: What, sir?

LORD GORING: I beg your pardon, father, I forgot. The conservatory, father, the conservatory – there is some one there I want you to talk to.

LORD CAVERSHAM: What about, sir?

LORD GORING: About me, father.

LORD CAVERSHAM (*grimly*): Not a subject on which much eloquence is possible.

LORD GORING: No, father; but the lady is like me. She doesn't care much for eloquence in others. She thinks it a little loud.

LORD CAVERSHAM *goes into the conservatory*. LADY CHILTERN *enters*.

LORD GORING: Lady Chiltern, why are you playing Mrs. Cheveley's cards?

LADY CHILTERN (*startled*): I don't understand you.

LORD GORING: Mrs. Cheveley made an attempt to ruin your husband. Either to drive him from public life, or to make him adopt a dishonourable position. From the latter tragedy you saved him. The former you are now thrusting on him. Why should you do him the wrong Mrs. Cheveley tried to do and failed?

LADY CHILTERN: Lord Goring?

LORD GORING (*pulling himself together for a great effort, and showing the philosopher that underlies the dandy*): Lady Chiltern, allow me. You wrote me a letter last night in which you said you trusted me and wanted my help. Now is the moment when you really want my help, now is the time when you have got to trust me, to trust in my counsel and judgment. You love Robert.

Do you want to kill his love for you? What sort of existence will he have if you rob him of the fruits of his ambition, if you take him from the splendour of a great political career, if you close the doors of public life against him, if you condemn him to sterile failure, he who was made for triumph and success? Women are not meant to judge us, but to forgive us when we need forgiveness. Pardon, not punishment, is their mission. Why should you scourge him with rods for a sin done in his youth, before he knew you, before he knew himself? A man's life is of more value than a woman's. It has larger issues, wider scope, greater ambitions. A woman's life revolves in curves of emotions. It is upon lines of intellect that a man's life progresses. Don't make any terrible mistake, Lady Chiltern. A woman who can keep a man's love, and love him in return, has done all the world wants of women, or should want of them.

LADY CHILTERN (*troubled and hesitating*): But it is my husband himself who wishes to retire from public life. He feels it is his duty. It was he who first said so.

LORD GORING: Rather than lose your love, Robert would do anything, wreck his whole career, as he is on the brink of doing now. He is making for you a terrible sacrifice. Take my advice, Lady Chiltern, and do not accept a sacrifice so great. If you do, you will live to repent it bitterly. We men and women are not made to accept such sacrifices from each other. We are not worthy of them. Besides, Robert has been punished enough.

LADY CHILTERN: We have both been punished. I set him up too high.

LORD GORING (*with deep feeling in his voice*): Do not for that reason set him down now too low. If he has fallen from his altar, do not thrust him into the mire. Failure to Robert would be the very mire of shame. Power is his passion. He would lose everything, even his power to feel love. Your husband's life is at this moment in your hands, your husband's love is in your hands. Don't mar both for him.

Enter SIR ROBERT CHILTERN.

SIR ROBERT CHILTERN: Gertrude, here is the draft of my letter. Shall I read it to you?

LADY CHILTERN: Let me see it.

SIR ROBERT *hands her the letter. She reads it, and then, with a gesture of passion, tears it up.*

SIR ROBERT CHILTERN: What are you doing?

LADY CHILTERN: A man's life is of more value than a woman's. It has larger issues, wider scope, greater ambitions. Our lives revolve in curves of emotions. It is upon lines of intellect that a man's life progresses. I have just learnt this, and much else with it, from Lord Goring. And I will not spoil your life for you, nor see you spoil it as a sacrifice to me, a useless sacrifice!

SIR ROBERT CHILTERN: Gertrude! Gertrude!

LADY CHILTERN: You can forget. Men easily forget. And I forgive. That is how women help the world. I see that now.

SIR ROBERT CHILTERN (*deeply overcome by emotion, embraces her*): My wife! My wife! (*To* LORD GORING): Arthur, it seems that I am always to be in your debt.

LORD GORING: Oh dear no, Robert. Your debt is to Lady Chiltern, not to me!

SIR ROBERT CHILTERN: I owe you much. And now tell me what you were going to ask me just now as Lord Caversham came in.

LORD GORING: Robert, you are your sister's guardian, and I want your consent to my marriage with her. That is all.

LADY CHILTERN: Oh, I am so glad! I am so glad! (*Shakes hands with* LORD GORING.)

LORD GORING: Thank you, Lady Chiltern.

SIR ROBERT CHILTERN (*with a troubled look*): My sister to be your wife?

LORD GORING: Yes.

SIR ROBERT CHILTERN (*speaking with great firmness*): Arthur, I am very sorry, but the thing is quite out of the question. I have to think of Mabel's future happiness. And I don't think her happiness would be safe in your hands. And I cannot have her sacrificed!

LORD GORING: Sacrificed!

SIR ROBERT CHILTERN: Yes, utterly sacrificed. Loveless marriages are horrible. But there is one thing worse than an absolutely loveless marriage. A marriage in which there is love, but on one side only; faith, but on one side only; devotion, but on one side only and in which of the two hearts one is sure to be broken.

LORD GORING: But I love Mabel. No other woman has any place in my life.

LADY CHILTERN: Robert, if they love each other, why should they not be married?

SIR ROBERT CHILTERN: Arthur cannot bring Mabel the love that she deserves.

LORD GORING: What reason have you for saying that?

SIR ROBERT CHILTERN (*after a pause*): Do you really require me to tell you?

LORD GORING: Certainly I do.

SIR ROBERT CHILTERN: As you choose. When I called on you yesterday evening I found Mrs. Cheveley concealed in your rooms. It was between ten and eleven o'clock at night. I do not wish to say anything more. Your relations with Mrs. Cheveley have, as I said to you last night, nothing whatsoever to do with me. I know you were engaged to be married to her once. The fascination she exercised over you then seems to have returned. You spoke to me last night of her as a woman pure and stainless, a woman who you respected and honoured. That may be so. But I cannot give my sister's life into your hands. It would be wrong of me. It would be unjust, infamously unjust to her.

LORD GORING: I have nothing more to say.

LADY CHILTERN: Robert, it was not Mrs. Cheveley whom Lord Goring expected last night.

SIR ROBERT CHILTERN: Not Mrs. Cheveley! Who was it then?

LORD GORING: Lady Chiltern.

LADY CHILTERN: It was your own wife. Robert, yesterday afternoon Lord Goring told me that if ever I was in trouble I could come to him for help, as he was our oldest and best friend. Later on, after that terrible scene in this room, I wrote to him telling him that I trusted him, that I had need of him, that I was coming to him for help and advice. (SIR ROBERT CHILTERN *takes the letter out of his pocket.*) Yes, that letter. I didn't go to Lord Goring's, after all. I felt that it is from ourselves alone that help can come. Pride made me think that. Mrs. Cheveley went. She stole my letter and sent it anonymously to you this morning, that you should think.... Oh! Robert, I cannot tell you what she wished you to think....

SIR ROBERT CHILTERN: What! Had I fallen so low in your eyes that you thought that even for a moment I could have doubted your goodness? Gertrude, Gertrude, you are to me the white image of all good things, and sin can never touch you. Arthur, you can go to Mabel, and you have my best wishes! Oh! Stop a moment. There is no name at the beginning of this letter. The brilliant Mrs. Cheveley does not seem to have noticed that. There should be a name.

LADY CHILTERN: Let me write yours. It is you I trust and need. You and none else.

LORD GORING: Well, really, Lady Chiltern, I think I should have back my own letter.

LADY CHILTERN (*smiling*): No; you shall have Mabel. (*Takes the letter and writes her husband's name on it.*)

LORD GORING: Well, I hope she hasn't changed her mind. It's nearly twenty minutes since I saw her last.

Enter MABEL CHILTERN *and* LORD CAVERSHAM.

MABEL CHILTERN: Lord Goring, I think your father's conversation much more improving than yours. I am only going to talk to Lord Caversham in the future, and always under the usual palm tree.

LORD GORING: Darling! (*Kisses her.*)

LORD CAVERSHAM (*considerably taken aback*): What does this mean, sir? You don't mean to say that this charming, clever young lady has been so foolish as to accept you?

LORD GORING: Certainly, father! And Chiltern's been wise enough to accept the seat in the Cabinet.

LORD CAVERSHAM: I am very glad to hear that, Chiltern ... I congratulate you, sir. If the country doesn't go to the dogs or the Radicals, we shall have you Prime Minister, some day.

Enter MASON.

MASON: Luncheon is on the table, my Lady! (MASON *goes out*.)

MABEL CHILTERN: You'll stop to luncheon, Lord Caversham, won't you?

LORD CAVERSHAM: With pleasure, and I'll drive you down to Downing Street afterwards, Chiltern. You have a great future before you, a great future. (*To* LORD GORING): Wish I could say the same for you, sir. But your career will have to be entirely domestic.

LORD GORING: Yes, father, I prefer it domestic.

LORD CAVERSHAM: And if you don't make this young lady an ideal husband, I'll cut you off with a shilling.

MABEL CHILTERN: An ideal husband! Oh, I don't think I should like that. It sounds like something in the next world.

LORD CAVERSHAM: What do you want him to be then, dear?

MABEL CHILTERN: He can be what he chooses. All I want is to be ... to be ... oh! A real wife to him.

LORD CAVERSHAM: Upon my word, there is a good deal of common sense in that, Lady Chiltern.

They all go out except SIR ROBERT CHILTERN. *He sinks into a chair, wrapt in thought. After a little time* LADY CHILTERN *returns to look for him.*

LADY CHILTERN (*leaning over the back of the chair*): Aren't you coming in, Robert?

SIR ROBERT CHILTERN (*taking her hand*): Gertrude, is it love you feel for me, or is it pity merely?

LADY CHILTERN (*kisses him*): It is love, Robert. Love, and only love. For both of us a new life is beginning.

CURTAIN

SALOMÉ

A Tragedy in one Act.
Translated from the French of Oscar Wilde by
Lord Alfred Douglas

The persons of the play

HEROD ANTIPAS, Tetrarch of
   Judaea
JOKANAAN, The Prophet
THE YOUNG SYRIAN, Captain of
   the Guard
TIGELLINUS, A Young Roman
A CAPPADOCIAN
A NUBIAN
FIRST SOLDIER

SECOND SOLDIER
THE PAGE OF HERODIAS
JEWS, NAZARENES, ETC.
A SLAVE
NAAMAN, The Executioner
HERODIAS, Wife of the Tetrarch
SALOMÉ, Daughter of Herodias
THE SLAVES OF SALOMÉ

SCENE: *A great terrace in the Palace of* HEROD, *set above the
banqueting-hall. Some soldiers are leaning over the balcony. To
the right there is a gigantic staircase, to the left, at the back, an
old cistern surrounded by a wall of green bronze. Moonlight.*

THE YOUNG SYRIAN: How beautiful is the Princess Salomé to-night!

THE PAGE OF HERODIAS: Look at the moon! How strange the moon
seems! She is like a woman rising from a tomb. She is like a dead woman.
You would fancy she was looking for dead things.

THE YOUNG SYRIAN: She has a strange look. She is like a little princess
who wears a yellow veil, and whose feet are of silver. She is like a princess
who has little white doves for feet. You would fancy she was dancing.

THE PAGE OF HERODIAS: She is like a woman who is dead. She moves
very slowly.

Noise in the banqueting-hall.

FIRST SOLDIER: What an uproar! Who are those wild beasts howling!

SECOND SOLDIER: The Jews. They are always like that. They are dis-
puting about their religion.

FIRST SOLDIER: Why do they dispute about their religion?

SECOND SOLDIER: I cannot tell. They are always doing it. The Pharisees,
for instance, say that there are angels, and the Sadducees declare that angels
do not exist.

FIRST SOLDIER: I think it is ridiculous to dispute about such things.

THE YOUNG SYRIAN: How beautiful is the Princess Salomé tonight!

THE PAGE OF HERODIAS: You are always looking at her. You look at her too much. It is dangerous to look at people in such fashion. Something terrible may happen.

THE YOUNG SYRIAN: She is very beautiful to-night.

FIRST SOLDIER: The Tetrarch has a sombre look.

SECOND SOLDIER: Yes, he has a sombre look.

FIRST SOLDIER: He is looking at something.

SECOND SOLDIER: He is looking at some one.

FIRST SOLDIER: At whom is he looking?

SECOND SOLDIER: I cannot tell.

THE YOUNG SYRIAN: How pale the Princess is! Never have I seen her so pale. She is like the shadow of a white rose in a mirror of silver.

THE PAGE OF HERODIAS: You must not look at her. You look too much at her.

FIRST SOLDIER: Herodias has filled the cup of the Tetrarch.

THE CAPPADOCIAN: Is that the Queen Herodias, she who wears a black mitre sewn with pearls, and whose hair is powdered with blue dust?

FIRST SOLDIER: Yes, that is Herodias, the Tetrarch's wife.

SECOND SOLDIER: The Tetrarch is very fond of wine. He has wine of three sorts. One which is brought from the Island of Samothrace, and is purple like the cloak of Caesar.

THE CAPPADOCIAN: I have never seen Caesar.

SECOND SOLDIER: Another that comes from a town called Cyprus, and is yellow like gold.

THE CAPPADOCIAN: I love gold.

SECOND SOLDIER: And the third is a wine of Sicily. That wine is red like blood.

THE NUBIAN: The gods of my country are very fond of blood. Twice in the year we sacrifice to them young men and maidens; fifty young men and a hundred maidens. But it seems we never give them quite enough, for they are very harsh to us.

THE CAPPADOCIAN: In my country there are no gods left. The Romans have driven them out. There are some who say that they have hidden themselves in the mountains, but I do not believe it. Three nights I have been on the mountains seeking them everywhere. I did not find them. And at last I called them by their names, and they did not come. I think they are dead.

FIRST SOLDIER: The Jews worship a God that you cannot see.

THE CAPPADOCIAN: I cannot understand that.

FIRST SOLDIER: In fact, they only believe in things that you cannot see.

THE CAPPADOCIAN: That seems to me altogether ridiculous.

THE VOICE OF JOKANAAN: After me shall come another mightier than I. I am not worthy so much as to unloose the latchet of his shoes. When he cometh, the solitary places shall be glad. They shall blossom like the lily. The eyes of the blind shall see the day, and the ears of the deaf shall be opened.

The new-born child shall put his hand upon the dragon's lair, he shall lead the lions by their manes.

SECOND SOLDIER: Make him be silent. He is always saying ridiculous things.

FIRST SOLDIER: No, no. He is a holy man. He is very gentle, too. Every day, when I give him to eat he thanks me.

THE CAPPADOCIAN: Who is he?

FIRST SOLDIER: A prophet.

THE CAPPADOCIAN: What is his name?

FIRST SOLDIER: Jokanaan.

THE CAPPADOCIAN: Whence comes he?

FIRST SOLDIER: From the desert, where he fed on locusts and wild honey. He was clothed in camel's hair, and round his loins he had a leathern belt. He was very terrible to look upon. A great multitude used to follow him. He even had disciples.

THE CAPPADOCIAN: What is he talking of?

FIRST SOLDIER: We can never tell. Sometimes he says terrible things; but it is impossible to understand what he says.

THE CAPPADOCIAN: May one see him?

FIRST SOLDIER: No. The Tetrarch has forbidden it.

THE YOUNG SYRIAN: The Princess has hidden her face behind her fan! Her little white hands are fluttering like doves that fly to their dove-cots. They are like white butterflies. They are just like white butterflies.

THE PAGE OF HERODIAS: What is that to you? Why do you look at her? You must not look at her.... Something terrible may happen.

THE CAPPADOCIAN (*pointing to the cistern*): What a strange prison!

SECOND SOLDIER: It is an old cistern.

THE CAPPADOCIAN: An old cistern! It must be very unhealthy.

SECOND SOLDIER: Oh, no! For instance, the Tetrarch's brother, his elder brother, the first husband of Herodias the Queen, was imprisoned there for twelve years. It did not kill him. At the end of the twelve years he had to be strangled.

THE CAPPADOCIAN: Strangled? Who dared to do that?

SECOND SOLDIER (*pointing to the Executioner, a huge Negro*): That man yonder, Naaman.

THE CAPPADOCIAN: He was not afraid?

SECOND SOLDIER: Oh, no! The Tetrarch sent him the ring.

THE CAPPADOCIAN: What ring?

SECOND SOLDIER: The death-ring. So he was not afraid.

THE CAPPADOCIAN: Yet it is a terrible thing to strangle a king.

FIRST SOLDIER: Why? Kings have but one neck, like other folk.

THE CAPPADOCIAN: I think it terrible.

THE YOUNG SYRIAN: The Princess rises! She is leaving the table! She looks very troubled. Ah, she is coming this way. Yes, she is coming towards us. How pale she is! Never have I seen her so pale.

THE PAGE OF HERODIAS: Do not look at her. I pray you not to look at her.

THE YOUNG SYRIAN: She is like a dove that has strayed. . . . She is like a narcissus trembling in the wind. . . . She is like a silver flower.

Enter SALOMÉ.

SALOMÉ: I will not stay. I cannot stay. Why does the Tetrarch look at me all the while with his mole's eyes under his shaking eyelids? It is strange that the husband of my mother looks at me like that. I know not what it means. In truth, yes I know it.

THE YOUNG SYRIAN: You have just left the feast, Princess?

SALOMÉ: How sweet the air is here! I can breathe here! Within there are Jews from Jerusalem who are tearing each other in pieces over their foolish ceremonies, and barbarians who drink and drink, and spill their wine on the pavement, and Greeks from Smyrna with painted eyes and painted cheeks, and frizzed hair curled in twisted coils, and silent, subtle Egyptians, with long nails of jade and russett cloaks, and Romans brutal and coarse, with their uncouth jargon. Ah! How I loathe the Romans! They are rough and common, and they give themselves the airs of noble lords.

THE YOUNG SYRIAN: Will you be seated, Princess?

THE PAGE OF HERODIAS: Why do you speak to her? Why do you look at her? Oh! Something terrible will happen.

SALOMÉ: How good to see the moon. She is like a little piece of money, you would think she was a little silver flower. The moon is cold and chaste. I am sure she is a virgin, she has a virgin's beauty. Yes, she is a virgin. She has never defiled herself. She has never abandoned herself to men, like the other goddesses.

THE VOICE OF JOKANAAN: The Lord hath come. The son of man hath come. The centaurs have hidden themselves in the rivers, and the sirens have left the rivers, and are lying beneath the leaves of the forest.

SALOMÉ: Who was that who cried out?

SECOND SOLDIER: The prophet, Princess.

SALOMÉ: Ah, the prophet! He of whom the Tetrarch is afraid?

SECOND SOLDIER: We know nothing of that, Princess. It was the prophet Jokanaan who cried out.

THE YOUNG SYRIAN: Is it your pleasure that I bid them bring your litter, Princess? The night is fair in the garden.

SALOMÉ: He says terrible things about my mother, does he not!

SECOND SOLDIER: We never understand what he says, Princess.

SALOMÉ: Yes; he says terrible things about her.

Enter a SLAVE.

THE SLAVE: Princess, the Tetrarch prays you to return to the feast.

SALOMÉ: I will not go back.

THE YOUNG SYRIAN: Pardon me, Princess, but if you do not return some misfortune may happen.

SALOMÉ: Is he an old man, this prophet?

THE YOUNG SYRIAN: Princess, it were better to return. Suffer me to lead you in.

SALOMÉ: This prophet . . . is he an old man?

FIRST SOLDIER: No, Princess, he is quite a young man.

SECOND SOLDIER: You cannot be sure. There are those who say he is Elias.

SALOMÉ: Who is Elias?

SECOND SOLDIER: A very ancient prophet of this country, Princess.

THE SLAVE: What answer may I give the Tetrarch from the Princess?

THE VOICE OF JOKANAAN: Rejoice not thou, land of Palestine, because the rod of him who smote thee is broken. For from the seed of the serpent shall come forth a basilisk, and that which is born of it shall devour the birds.

SALOMÉ: What a strange voice! I would speak with him.

FIRST SOLDIER: I fear it is impossible, Princess. The Tetrarch does not wish any one to speak with him. He has even forbidden the high priest to speak with him.

SALOMÉ: I desire to speak with him.

FIRST SOLDIER: It is impossible, Princess.

SALOMÉ: I will speak with him.

THE YOUNG SYRIAN: Would it not be better to return to the banquet?

SALOMÉ: Bring forth this prophet.

Exit the SLAVE.

FIRST SOLDIER: We dare not, Princess.

SALOMÉ (*approaching the cistern and looking down into it*): How black it is down there! It must be terrible to be in so black a pit! It is like a tomb. . . . (*To the* SOLDIERS): Did you not hear me? Bring out the prophet. I wish to see him.

SECOND SOLDIER: Princess, I beg you do not require this of us.

SALOMÉ: You keep me waiting!

FIRST SOLDIER: Princess, our lives belong to you, but we cannot do what you have asked of us. And indeed, it is not of us that you should ask this thing.

SALOMÉ: (*looking at the* YOUNG SYRIAN): Ah!

THE PAGE OF HERODIAS: Oh! What is going to happen? I am sure that some misfortune will happen.

SALOMÉ (*going up to the* YOUNG SYRIAN): You will do this thing for me, will you not, Narraboth? You will do this thing for me. I have always been kind to you. You will do it for me. I would but look at this strange prophet. Men have talked so much of him. Often have I heard the Tetrarch talk of him. I think the Tetrarch is afraid of him. Are you, even you, also afraid of him, Narraboth?

THE YOUNG SYRIAN: I fear him not, Princess; there is no man I fear. But

the Tetrarch has formally forbidden that any man should raise the cover of
this well.

SALOMÉ: You will do this thing for me, Narraboth, and to–morrow when I
pass in my litter beneath the gateway of the idol-sellers I will let fall for you a
little flower, a little green flower.

THE YOUNG SYRIAN: Princess, I cannot, I cannot.

SALOMÉ (*smiling*): You will do this thing for me, Narraboth. You know
that you will do this thing for me. And to–morrow when I pass in my litter by
the bridge of the idol-buyers. I will look at you through the muslin veils, I
will look at you, Narraboth, it may be I will smile at you. Look at me, Narra–
both, look at me. Ah! You know that you will do what I ask of you. You know
it well. . . . I know that you will do this thing.

THE YOUNG SYRIAN (*signing to the third soldier*): Let the prophet come
forth. . . . The Princess Salomé desires to see him.

SALOMÉ: Ah!

THE PAGE OF HERODIAS: Oh! How strange the moon looks. You would
think it was the hand of a dead woman who is seeking to cover herself with a
shroud.

THE YOUNG SYRIAN: She has a strange look! She is like a little princess,
whose eyes are eyes of amber. Through the clouds of muslin she is smiling
like a little princess.

The prophet comes out of the cistern. SALOMÉ *looks at him and steps slowly
back.*

JOKANAAN: Where is he whose cup of abominations is now full? Where is
he, who in a robe of silver shall one day die in the face of all the people? Bid
him come forth, that he may hear the voice of him who had cried in the waste
places and in the houses of kings.

SALOMÉ: Of whom is he speaking?

THE YOUNG SYRIAN: You never can tell, Princess.

JOKANAAN: Where is she who, having seen the images of men painted on
the walls, the images of the Chaldeans limned in colours, gave herself up
unto the lust of her eyes, and sent ambassadors into Chaldea?

SALOMÉ: It is of my mother that he speaks.

THE YOUNG SYRIAN: Oh, no, Princess.

SALOMÉ: Yes, it is of my mother that he speaks.

JOKANAAN: Where is she who gave herself unto the Captains of Assyria,
who have baldricks on their loins, and tiaras of divers colours on their heads?
Where is she who hath given herself to the young men of Egypt, who are
clothed in fine linen and purple, whose shields are of gold, whose helmets are
of silver, whose bodies are mighty? Bid her rise up from the bed of her abom-
inations, from the bed of her incestuousness, that she may hear the words of
him who prepareth the way of the Lord, that she may repent her of her ini-
quities. Though she will never repent, but will stick fast in her abominations;
bid her come, for the fan of the Lord is in His hand.

SALOMÉ: But he is terrible, he is terrible!

THE YOUNG SYRIAN: Do not stay here, Princess, I beseech you.

SALOMÉ: It is his eyes above all that are terrible. They are like black holes burned by torches in a Tyrian tapestry. They are like black caverns where dragons dwell. They are like the black caverns of Egypt in which the dragons make their lairs. They are like black lakes troubled by fantastic moons.... Do you think he will speak again?

THE YOUNG SYRIAN: Do not stay here, Princess. I pray you do not stay here.

SALOMÉ: How wasted he is! He is like a thin ivory statue. He is like an image of silver. I am sure he is chaste as the moon is. He is like a moonbeam, like a shaft of silver. His flesh must be cool like ivory. I would look closer at him.

THE YOUNG SYRIAN: No, no, Princess.

SALOMÉ: I must look at him closer.

THE YOUNG SYRIAN: Princess! Princess!

JOKANAAN: Who is this woman who is looking at me? I will not have her look at me. Wherefore doth she look at me with her golden eyes, under her gilded eyelids? I know not who she is. I do not wish to know who she is. Bid her begone. It is not to her that I would speak.

SALOMÉ: I am Salomé, daughter of Herodias, Princess of Judaea.

JOKANAAN: Back! Daughter of Babylon! Come not near the chosen of the Lord. Thy mother hath filled the earth with the wine of her iniquities, and the cry of her sins hath come up to the ears of God.

SALOMÉ: Speak again, Jokanaan. Thy voice is wine to me.

THE YOUNG SYRIAN: Princess! Princess! Princess!

SALOMÉ: Speak again! Speak again, Jokanaan, and tell me what I must do.

JOKANAAN: Daughter of Sodom, come not near me! But cover thy face with a veil, and scatter ashes upon thine head, and get thee to the desert and seek out the Son of Man.

SALOMÉ: Who is he, the Son of Man? Is he as beautiful as thou art, Jokanaan?

JOKANAAN: Get thee behind me! I hear in the palace the beating of the wings of the angel of death.

THE YOUNG SYRIAN: Princess, I beseech thee to go within.

JOKANAAN: Angel of the Lord God, what dost thou here with thy sword? Whom seekest thou in this foul palace? The day of him who shall die in a robe of silver has not yet come.

SALOMÉ: Jokanaan!

JOKANAAN: Who speaketh?

SALOMÉ: Jokanaan, I am amorous of thy body! Thy body is white like the lilies of a field that the mower hath never mowed. Thy body is white like the snows that lie on the mountains, like the snows that lie on the mountains of Judaea, and come down into the valleys. The roses in the garden of the Queen of Arabia are not so white as thy body. Neither the roses in the garden of the Queen of Arabia, nor the feet of the dawn when they light on the leaves, nor the breast of the moon when she lies on the breast of the sea....

There is nothing in the world so white as thy body. Let me touch thy body.

JOKANAAN: Back! Daughter of Babylon! By woman came evil into the world. Speak not to me. I will not listen to thee. I listen but to the voice of the Lord God.

SALOMÉ: Thy body is hideous. It is like the body of a leper. It is like a plastered wall where vipers have crawled; like a plastered wall where the scorpions have made their nest. It is like a whitened sepulchre full of loathsome things. It is horrible, thy body is horrible. It is of thy hair that I am enamoured, Jokanaan. Thy hair is like clusters of grapes, like the clusters of black grapes that hang from the vine-trees of Edom in the land of the Edomites. Thy hair is like the cedars of Lebanon, like the great cedars of Lebanon that give their shade to the lions and to the robbers who would hide themselves by day. The long black nights, when the moon hides her face, when the stars are afraid, are not so black. The silence that dwells in the forest is not so black. There is nothing in the world so black as thy hair. . . . Let me touch thy hair.

JOKANAAN: Back, daughter of Sodom! Touch me not. Profane not the temple of the Lord God.

SALOMÉ: Thy hair is horrible. It is covered with mire and dust. It is like a crown of thorns which they have placed on thy forehead. It is like a knot of black serpents writhing round thy neck. I love not thy hair. . . . It is thy mouth that I desire, Jokanaan. Thy mouth is like a band of scarlet on a tower of ivory. It is like a pomegranate cut with a knife of ivory. The pomegranate-flowers that blossom in the garden of Tyre, and are redder than roses, are not so red. The red blasts of trumpets, that herald the approach of kings, and make afraid the enemy, are not so red. Thy mouth is redder than the feet of those who tread the wine in the wine-press. Thy mouth is redder than the feet of the doves who haunt the temples and are fed by the priests. It is redder than the feet of him who cometh from a forest where he hath slain a lion, and seen gilded tigers. Thy mouth is like a branch of coral that fishers have found in the twilight of the sea, the coral that they keep for the kings . . . ! It is like the vermilion that the Moabites find in the mines of Moab, the vermilion that the kings take from them. It is like the bow of the King of the Persians, that is painted with vermilion, and is tipped with coral. There is nothing in the world so red as thy mouth. . . . Let me kiss thy mouth.

JOKANAAN: Never, daughter of Babylon! Daughter of Sodom! Never.

SALOMÉ: I will kiss thy mouth, Jokanaan. I will kiss thy mouth.

THE YOUNG SYRIAN: Princess, Princess, thou who art like a garden of myrrh, thou who art the dove of all doves, look not at this man, look not at him! Do not speak such words to him. I cannot suffer them. . . . Princess, Princess, do not speak these things.

SALOMÉ: I will kiss thy mouth, Jokanaan.

THE YOUNG SYRIAN: Ah!

He kills himself and falls between SALOMÉ *and* JOKANAAN.

THE PAGE OF HERODIAS: The young Syrian has slain himself! The young captain has slain himself! He has slain himself who was my friend! I gave him a little box of perfumes and ear-rings wrought in silver, and now he has killed himself! Ah, did he not foretell that some misfortune would happen? I, too, foretold it, and it has happened. Well, I knew that the moon was seeking a dead thing, but I knew not that it was he whom she sought. Ah! Why did I not hide him from the moon? If I had hidden him in a cavern she would not have seen him.

FIRST SOLDIER: Princess, the young captain has just killed himself.

SALOMÉ: Let me kiss thy mouth, Jokanaan.

JOKANAAN: Art thou not afraid, daughter of Herodias? Did I not tell thee that I had heard in the palace the beatings of the wings of the angel of death, and hath he not come, the angel of death?

SALOMÉ: Let me kiss thy mouth.

JOKANAAN: Daughter of adultery, there is but one who can save thee, it is He of whom I spake. Go seek Him. He is in a boat on the sea of Galilee, and He talketh with His disciples. Kneel down on the shore of the sea, and call unto Him by His name. When He cometh to thee (and to all who call on Him He cometh) bow thyself at His feet and ask of Him the remission of thy sins.

SALOMÉ: Let me kiss thy mouth.

JOKANAAN: Cursed be thou! Daughter of an incestuous mother, be thou accursed!

SALOMÉ: I will kiss thy mouth, Jokanaan.

JOKANAAN: I do not wish to look at thee. I will not look at thee, thou art accursed, Salomé, thou art accursed.

He goes down into the cistern.

SALOMÉ: I will kiss thy mouth, Jokanaan. I will kiss thy mouth.

FIRST SOLDIER: We must bear away the body to another place. The Tetrarch does not care to see dead bodies, save the bodies of those whom he himself has slain.

THE PAGE OF HERODIAS: He was my brother, and nearer to me than a brother. I gave him a little box of perfumes, and a ring of agate that he wore always on his hand. In the evening we used to walk by the river, among the almond trees, and he would tell me of the things of his country. He spake ever very low. The sound of his voice was like the sound of the flute, of a flute player. Also he much loved to gaze at himself in the river. I used to reproach him for that.

SECOND SOLDIER: You are right; we must hide the body. The Tetrarch must not see it.

FIRST SOLDIER: The Tetrarch will not come to this place. He never comes on the terrace. He is too much afraid of the prophet.

Enter HEROD, HERODIAS, and all the COURT.

HEROD: Where is Salomé? Where is the Princess? Why did she not return to the banquet as I commanded her? Ah! There she is!

HERODIAS: You must not look at her! You are always looking at her!

HEROD: The moon has a strange look to-night. Has she not a strange look? She is like a mad woman, a mad woman who is seeking everywhere for lovers. She is naked, too. She is quite naked. The clouds are seeking to clothe her nakedness, but she will not let them. She shows herself naked in the sky. She reels through the clouds like a drunken woman. . . . I am sure she is looking for lovers. Does she not reel like a drunken woman? She is like a mad woman, is she not?

HERODIAS: No; the moon is like the moon, that is all. Let us go within. . . . You have nothing to do here.

HEROD: I will stay here! Manesseh, lay carpets there. Light torches, bring forth the ivory tables, and the tables of jasper. The air here is delicious. I will drink more wine with my guests. We must show all honours to the ambassadors of Caesar.

HERODIAS: It is not because of them that you remain.

HEROD: Yes; the air is delicious. Come, Herodias, our guests await us. Ah! I have slipped! I have slipped in blood! It is an ill omen. It is a very evil omen. Wherefore is there blood here . . . ? And this body, what does this body here? Think you that I am like the King of Egypt, who gives no feast to his guests but that he shows them a corpse? Whose is it? I will not look on it.

FIRST SOLDIER: It is our captain, sire. He is the young Syrian whom you made captain only three days ago.

HEROD: I gave no order that he should be slain.

SECOND SOLDIER: He killed himself, sire.

HEROD: For what reason? I had made him captain.

SECOND SOLDIER: We do not know, sire. But he killed himself.

HEROD: That seems strange to me. I thought it was only the Roman philosophers who killed themselves. Is it not true, Tigellinus, that the philosophers at Rome kill themselves?

TIGELLINUS: There are some who kill themselves, sire. They are the Stoics. The Stoics are coarse people. They are ridiculous people. I myself regard them as being perfectly ridiculous.

HEROD: I also. It is ridiculous to kill oneself.

TIGELLINUS: Everybody at Rome laughs at them. The Emperor has written a satire against them. It is recited everywhere.

HEROD: Ah! He has written a satire against them? Caesar is wonderful. He can do everything. . . . It is strange that the young Syrian has killed himself. I am sorry he has killed himself. I am very sorry, for he was fair to look upon. He was even very fair. He had very languorous eyes. I remember that I saw that he looked languorously at Salomé. Truly, I thought he looked too much at her.

HERODIAS: There are others who look at her too much.

HEROD: His father was a king. I drove him from his kingdom. And you made a slave of his mother, who was a queen, Herodias. So he was here as my guest, as it were, and for that reason I made him my captain. I am sorry he is dead. Ho! Why have you left the body here? I will not look at it – away with it. (*They take away the body*.) It is cold here. There is a wind blowing. Is there not a wind blowing?

HERODIAS: No, there is no wind.

HEROD: I tell you there is a wind that blows. . . . And I hear in the air something that is like the beating of wings, like the beating of vast wings. Do you not hear it?

HERODIAS: I hear nothing.

HEROD: I hear it no longer. But I heard it. It was the blowing of the wind, no doubt. It has passed away. But no, I hear it again. Do you not hear it? It is just like the beating of wings.

HERODIAS: I tell you there is nothing. You are ill. Let us go within.

HEROD: I am not ill. It is your daughter who is sick. She has the mien of a sick person. Never have I seen her so pale.

HERODIAS: I have told you not to look at her.

HEROD: Pour me forth wine. (*Wine is brought*.) Salomé, come drink a little wine with me. I have here a wine that is exquisite. Caesar himself sent it me. Dip into it thy little red lips, that I may drain the cup.

SALOMÉ: I am not thirsty, Tetrarch.

HEROD: You hear how she answers me, this daughter of yours?

HERODIAS: She does right. Why are you always gazing at her?

HEROD: Bring me ripe fruits. (*Fruits are brought*.) Salomé, come and eat fruit with me. I love to see in a fruit the mark of thy little teeth. Bite but a little of this fruit and then I will eat what is left.

SALOMÉ: I am not hungry, Tetrarch.

HEROD (*to* HERODIAS): You see how you have brought up this daughter of yours.

HERODIAS: My daughter and I come of a royal race. As for thee, thy father was a camel driver! He was also a robber!

HEROD: Thou liest!

HERODIAS: Thou knowest well that it is true.

HEROD: Salomé, come and sit next to me. I will give thee the throne of thy mother.

SALOMÉ: I am not tired, Tetrarch.

HERODIAS: You see what she thinks of you.

HEROD: Bring me – what is it that I desire? I forget. Ah! Ah! I remember.

THE VOICE OF JOKANAAN: Lo! The time is come! That which I foretold has come to pass, saith the Lord God. Lo! The day of which I spoke.

HERODIAS: Bid him be silent. I will not listen to his voice. This man is for ever vomiting insults against me.

HEROD: He has said nothing against you. Besides, he is a very great prophet.

HERODIAS: I do not believe in prophets. Can a man tell what will come to pass? No man knows it. Moreover, he is for ever insulting me. But I think you are afraid of him. . . . I know well that you are afraid of him.

HEROD: I am not afraid of him. I am afraid of no man.

HERODIAS: I tell you, you are afraid of him. If you are not afraid of him why do you not deliver him to the Jews, who for these six months past have been clamouring for him?

A JEW: Truly, my lord, it were better to deliver him into our hands.

HEROD: Enough on this subject. I have already given you my answer. I will not deliver him into your hands. He is a holy man. He is a man who has seen God.

A JEW: That cannot be. There is no man who hath seen God since the prophet Elias. He is the last man who saw God. In these days God doth not show Himself. He hideth Himself. Therefore great evils have come upon the land.

ANOTHER JEW: Verily, no man knoweth if Elias the prophet did indeed see God. Peradventure it was but the shadow of God that he saw.

A THIRD JEW: God is at no time hidden. He showeth Himself at all times and in everything. God is in what is evil, even as He is in what is good.

A FOURTH JEW: That must not be said. It is a very dangerous doctrine. It is a doctrine that cometh from the schools at Alexandria, where men teach the philosophy of the Greeks. And the Greeks are Gentiles. They are not even circumcised.

A FIFTH JEW: No one can tell how God worketh. His ways are very mysterious. It may be that the things which we call evil are good, and that the things which we call good are evil. There is no knowledge of anything. We must needs submit to everything, for God is very strong. He breaketh in pieces the strong together with the weak, for He regardeth not any man.

FIRST JEW: Thou speaketh truly. God is terrible. He breaketh the strong and the weak as a man brays corn in a mortar. But this man hath never seen God. No man hath seen God since the prophet Elias.

HERODIAS: Make them be silent. They weary me.

HEROD: But I have heard it said that Jokanaan himself is your prophet Elias.

THE JEW: That cannot be. It is more than three hundred years since the days of the prophet Elias.

HEROD: There be some who say that this man is the prophet Elias.

A NAZARENE: I am sure that he is the prophet Elias.

THE JEW: Nay, but he is not the prophet Elias.

THE VOICE OF JOKANAAN: So the day is come, the day of the Lord, and I hear upon the mountains the feet of Him who shall be the Saviour of the world.

HEROD: What does that mean? The Saviour of the world.

TIGELLINUS: It is a title that Caesar takes.

HEROD: But Caesar is not coming into Judaea. Only yesterday I received letters from Rome. They contained nothing concerning this matter. And you, Tigellinus, who were at Rome during the winter, you heard nothing concerning this matter, did you?

TIGELLINUS: Sire, I heard nothing concerning the matter. I was explaining the title. It is one of Caesar's titles.

HEROD: But Caesar cannot come. He is too gouty. They say that his feet are like the feet of an elephant. Also there are reasons of State. He who leaves Rome loses Rome. He will not come. Howbeit Caesar is lord, he will come if he wishes. Nevertheless, I do not think he will come.

FIRST NAZARENE: It was not concerning Caesar that the prophet spake these words, sire.

HEROD: Not of Caesar?

FIRST NAZARENE: No, sire.

HEROD: Concerning whom, then, did he speak?

FIRST NAZARENE: Concerning Messias who has come.

A JEW: Messias hath not come.

FIRST NAZARENE: He hath come, and everywhere He worketh miracles.

HERODIAS: Ho! Ho! Miracles! I do not believe in miracles. I have seen too many. (*To the Page*): My fan!

FIRST NAZARENE: This man worketh true miracles. Thus, at a marriage which took place in a little town of Galilee, a town of some importance, He changed water into wine. Certain persons who were present related it to me. Also, He healed two lepers that were seated before the Gate of Capernaum simply by touching them.

SECOND NAZARENE: Nay, it was blind men that He healed at Capernaum.

FIRST NAZARENE: Nay, they were lepers. But He hath healed blind people also, and He was seen on a mountain talking with angels.

A SADDUCEE: Angels do not exist.

A PHARISEE: Angels exist, but I do not believe that this Man has talked with them.

FIRST NAZARENE: He was seen by a great multitude of people talking with angels.

A SADDUCEE: Not with angels.

HERODIAS: How these men weary me! They are ridiculous! (*To the Page*): Well, my fan! (*The Page gives her the fan.*) You have a dreamer's look; you must not dream. It is only sick people who dream. (*She strikes the Page with her fan.*)

SECOND NAZARENE: There is also the miracle of the daughter of Jairus.

FIRST NAZARENE: Yes, that is sure. No man can gainsay it.

HERODIAS: These men are mad. They have looked too long on the moon. Command them to be silent.

HEROD: What is this miracle of the daughter of Jairus?

FIRST NAZARENE: The daughter of Jairus was dead. He raised her from the dead.

HEROD: He raises the dead?

FIRST NAZARENE: Yea, sire, He raiseth the dead.

HEROD: I do not wish Him to do that. I forbid Him to do that. I allow no man to raise the dead. This Man must be found and told that I forbid Him to raise the dead. Where is this Man at present?

SECOND NAZARENE: He is in every place, my lord, but it is hard to find Him.

FIRST NAZARENE: It is said that He is now in Samaria.

A JEW: It is easy to see that this is not Messias, if He is in Samaria. It is not to the Samaritans that Messias shall come. The Samaritans are accursed. They bring no offerings to the Temple.

SECOND NAZARENE: He left Samaria a few days since. I think that at the present moment He is in the neighbourhood of Jerusalem.

FIRST NAZARENE: No, He is not there. I have just come from Jerusalem. For two months they have had no tidings of Him.

HEROD: No matter! But let them find Him, and tell Him from me, I will not allow Him to raise the dead! To change water into wine, to heal the lepers and the blind.... He may do these things if He will. I say nothing against these things. In truth I hold it a good deed to heal a leper. But I allow no man to raise the dead. It would be terrible if the dead came back.

THE VOICE OF JOKANAAN: Ah, the wanton! The harlot! Ah! The daughter of Babylon with her golden eyes and her gilded eyelids! Thus saith the Lord God, Let there come against her a multitude of men. Let the people take stones and stone her....

HERODIAS: Command him to be silent.

THE VOICE OF JOKANAAN: Let the war captains pierce her with their swords, let them crush her beneath their shields.

HERODIAS: Nay, but it is infamous.

THE VOICE OF JAKANAAN: It is thus that I will wipe out all wickedness from the earth, and that all women shall learn not to imitate her abominations.

HERODIAS: You hear what he says against me? You allow him to revile your wife?

HEROD: He did not speak your name.

HERODIAS: What does that matter? You know well that it is I whom he seeks to revile. And I am your wife, am I not?

HEROD: Of a truth, dear and noble Herodias, you are my wife, and before that you were the wife of my brother.

HERODIAS: It was you who tore me from his arms.

HEROD: Of a truth I was stronger.... But let us not talk of that matter. I do not desire to talk of it. It is the cause of the terrible words that the prophet has spoken. Peradventure on account of it a misfortune will come. Let us not speak of this matter. Noble Herodias, we are not mindful of our guests. Fill thou my cup, my well-beloved. Fill with wine the great goblets of silver, and the great goblets of glass. I will drink to Caesar. There are Romans here; we must drink to Caesar.

ALL: Caesar! Caesar!

HEROD: Do you not see your daughter, how pale she is?

HERODIAS: What is it to you if she be pale or not?

HEROD: Never have I seen her so pale.

HERODIAS: You must not look at her.

THE VOICE OF JOKANAAN: In that day the sun shall become black like the sackcloth of hair, and the moon shall become like blood, and the stars of the heavens shall fall upon the earth like ripe figs that fall from the fig-tree, and the kings of the earth shall be afraid.

HERODIAS: Ah! Ah! I should like to see that day of which he speaks, when the moon shall become like blood, and when the stars shall fall upon the earth like ripe figs. This prophet talks like a drunken man . . . but I cannot suffer the sound of his voice. I hate his voice. Command him to be silent.

HEROD: I will not. I cannot understand what it is that he saith, but it may be an omen.

HERODIAS: I do not believe in omens. He speaks like a drunken man.

HEROD: It may be he is drunk with the wine of God.

HERODIAS: What wine is that, the wine of God? From what vineyards is it gathered? In what winepress may one find it?

HEROD (*from this point he looks all the while at Salomé*): Tigellinus, when you were at Rome of late, did the Emperor speak with you on the subject of . . . ?

TIGELLINUS: On what subject, sire?

HEROD: On what subject? Ah! I asked you a question, did I not? I have forgotten what I would have asked you.

HERODIAS: You are looking again at my daughter. You must not look at her. I have already said so.

HEROD: You say nothing else.

HERODIAS: I say it again.

HEROD: And that restoration of the Temple about which they have talked so much, will anything be done? They say the veil of the Sanctuary has disappeared, do they not?

HERODIAS: It was thyself didst steal it. Thou speakest at random. I will not stay here. Let us go within.

HEROD: Dance for me, Salomé.

HERODIAS: I will not have her dance.

SALOMÉ: I have no desire to dance, Tetrarch.

HEROD: Salomé, daughter of Herodias, dance for me.

HERODIAS: Let her alone.

HEROD: I command thee to dance, Salomé.

SALOMÉ: I will not dance, Tetrarch.

HERODIAS (*laughing*): You see how she obeys you.

HEROD: What is to me whether she dance or not? It is naught to me. To-night I am happy, I am exceeding happy. Never have I been so happy.

FIRST SOLDIER: The Tetrarch has a sombre look. Has he not a sombre look?

SECOND SOLDIER: Yes, he has a sombre look.

HEROD: Wherefore should I not be happy? Caesar, who is lord of the world, who is lord of all things, loves me well. He has just sent me most precious gifts. Also he has promised me to summon to Rome the King of Cappadocia, who is my enemy. It may be that at Rome he will crucify him, for he is able to do all things that he wishes. Verily, Caesar is lord. Thus you see I have a right to be happy. Indeed, I am happy. I have never been so happy. There is nothing in the world that can mar my happiness.

THE VOICE OF JOKANAAN: He shall be seated on this throne. He shall be clothed in scarlet and purple. In his hand he shall bear a golden cup full of his blasphemies. And the angel of the Lord shall smite him. He shall be eaten of worms.

HERODIAS: You hear what he says about you. He says that you will be eaten of worms.

HEROD: It is not of me that he speaks. He speaks never against me. It is of the King of Cappadocia that he speaks; the King of Cappadocia, who is mine enemy. It is he who shall be eaten of worms. It is not I. Never has he spoken word against me, this prophet, save that I sinned in taking to wife the wife of my brother. It may be he is right. For, of a truth, you are sterile.

HERODIAS: I am sterile, I? You say that, you that are ever looking at my daughter, you that would have her dance for your pleasure? It is absurd to say that. I have borne a child. You have gotten no child, no, not even from one of your slaves. It is you who are sterile, not I.

HEROD: Peace, woman! I say that you are sterile. You have borne me no child, and the prophet says that our marriage is not a true marriage. He says that it is an incestuous marriage, a marriage that will bring evils.... I fear he is right; I am sure that he is right. But it is not the moment to speak of such things. I would be happy at this moment. Of a truth, I am happy. There is nothing I lack.

HERODIAS: I am glad you are of so fair a humour to-night. It is not your custom. But it is late. Let us go within. Do not forget that we hunt at sunrise. All honours must be shown to Caesar's ambassadors, must they not?

SECOND SOLDIER: What a sombre look the Tetrarch wears.

FIRST SOLDIER: Yes, he wears a sombre look.

HEROD: Salomé, Salomé, dance for me. I pray thee dance for me. I am sad to-night. Yes, I am passing sad to-night. When I came hither I slipped in blood, which is an evil omen; and I heard, I am sure I heard in the air a beating of wings, a beating of giant wings. I cannot tell what they mean.... I am sad to-night. Therefore dance for me. Dance for me, Salomé, I beseech you. If you dance for me you may ask of me what you will, and I will give it you, even unto the half of my kingdom.

SALOMÉ (rising): Will you indeed give me whatsoever I shall ask, Tetrarch?

HERODIAS: Do not dance, my daughter.

HEROD: Everything, even the half of my kingdom.

SALOMÉ: You swear it, Tetrarch?

HEROD: I swear it, Salomé.

HERODIAS: Do not dance, my daughter.

SALOMÉ: By what will you swear, Tetrarch?

HEROD: By my life, by my crown, by my gods. Whatsoever you desire I will give it you, even to the half of my kingdom, if you will but dance for me. O, Salomé, Salomé, dance for me!

SALOMÉ: You have sworn, Tetrarch.

HEROD: I have sworn, Salomé.

SALOMÉ: All this I ask, even the half of your kingdom.

HERODIAS: My daughter, do not dance.

HEROD: Even to the half of my kingdom. Thou wilt be passing fair as a queen, Salomé, if it please thee to ask for the half of my kingdom. Will she not be fair as a queen? Ah! It is cold here! There is an icy wind, and I hear . . . wherefore do I hear in the air this beating of wings? Ah! One might fancy a bird, a huge black bird that hovers over the terrace. Why can I not see it, this bird? The beat of its wings is terrible. The breath of the wind of its wings is terrible. It is a chill wind. Nay, but it is not cold, it is hot. I am choking. Pour water on my hands. Give me snow to eat. Loosen my mantle. Quick, quick! Loosen my mantle. Nay, but leave it. It is my garland that hurts me, my garland of roses. The flowers are like fire. They have burned my forehead. (*He tears the wreath from his head and throws it on the table.*) Ah! I can breathe now. How red those petals are! They are like stains of blood on the cloth. That does not matter. You must not find symbols in everything you see. It makes life impossible. It were better to say that stains of blood are as lovely as rose petals. It were better far to say that. . . . But we will not speak of this. Now I am happy, I am passing happy. Have I not the right to be happy? Your daughter is going to dance for me. Will you not dance for me, Salomé? You have promised to dance for me.

HERODIAS: I will not have her dance.

SALOMÉ: I will dance for you, Tetrarch.

HEROD: You hear what your daughter says. She is going to dance for me. You do well to dance for me, Salomé. And when you have danced for me, forget not to ask of me whatsoever you wish. Whatsoever you wish I will give it you, even to the half of my kingdom. I have sworn it, have I not?

SALOMÉ: You have sworn it, Tetrarch.

HEROD: And I have never broken my word. I am not of those who break their oaths. I know not how to lie. I am the slave of my word, and my word is the word of a king. The King of Cappadocia always lies, but he is no true king. He is a coward. Also he owes me money that he will not repay. He has even insulted my ambassadors. He has spoken words that were wounding. But Caesar will crucify him when he comes to Rome. I am sure that Caesar will crucify him. And if not, yet will he die, being eaten of worms. The prophet has prophesied it. Well! Wherefore dost thou tarry, Salomé?

SALOMÉ: I am waiting until my slaves bring perfumes to me and the seven veils, and take off my sandals. (*Slaves bring perfumes and the seven veils, and take off the sandals of* SALOMÉ.)

HEROD: Ah, you are going to dance with naked feet. 'Tis well! 'Tis well. Your little feet will be like white doves. They will be like little white flowers that dance upon the trees. . . . No, no, she is going to dance on blood. There is blood spilt on the ground. She must not dance on blood. It were an evil omen.

HERODIAS: What is it to you if she dance on blood? Thou hast waded deep enough therein. . . .

HEROD: What is it to me? Ah! Look at the moon! She has become red. She has become red as blood. Ah! The prophet prophesied truly. He prophesied that the moon would become red as blood. Did he not prophesy it? All of you heard him. And now the moon has become red as blood. Do ye not see it?

HERODIAS: Oh, yes, I see it well, and the stars are falling like ripe figs, are they not? And the sun is becoming black like sackcloth of hair, and the kings of the earth are afraid. That at least one can see. The prophet, for once in his life, was right; the kings of the earth are afraid.... Let us go within. You are sick. They will say at Rome that you are mad. Let us go within, I tell you.

THE VOICE OF JOKANAAN: Who is this who cometh from Edom, who is this who cometh from Bozra, whose raiment is dyed with purple, who shineth in the beauty of his garments, who walketh mighty in his greatness? Wherefore is thy raiment stained with scarlet?

HERODIAS: Let us go within. The voice of that man maddens me. I will not have my daughter dance while he is continually crying out. I will not have her dance while you look at her in this fashion. In a word I will not have her dance.

HEROD: Do not rise, my wife, my queen, it will avail thee nothing. I will not go within till she hath danced. Dance, Salomé, dance for me.

HERODIAS: Do not dance, my daughter.

SALOMÉ: I am ready, Tetrarch. (SALOMÉ *dances the dance of the seven veils.*)

HEROD: Ah! Wonderful! Wonderful! You see that she has danced for me, your daughter. Come near, Salomé, come near, that I may give you your reward. Ah! I pay the dancers well. I will pay thee royally. I will give thee whatsoever thy soul desireth. What wouldst thou have? Speak.

SALOMÉ (*kneeling*): I would that they presently bring me in a silver charger...

HEROD (*laughing*): In a silver charger? Surely yes, in a silver charger. She is charming, is she not? What is it you would have in a silver charger, O sweet and fair Salomé, you who are fairer than all the daughters of Judaea? What would you have them bring thee in a silver charger? Tell me. Whatsoever it may be, they shall give it to you. My treasures belong to thee. What is it, Salomé?

SALOMÉ (*rising*): The head of Jokanaan.

HERODIAS: Ah! That is well said, my daughter.

HEROD: No, no!

HERODIAS: That is well said, my daughter.

HEROD: No, no, Salomé. You do not ask me that. Do not listen to your mother's voice. She is ever giving you evil counsel. Do not heed her.

SALOMÉ: I do not heed my mother. It is for mine own pleasure that I ask the head of Jokanaan in a silver charger. You have sworn, Herod. Forget not that you have sworn an oath.

HEROD: I know it. I have sworn by my gods. I know it well. But I pray you, Salomé, ask of me something else. Ask of me the half of my kingdom, and I will give it you. But ask not of me what you have asked.

SALOMÉ: I ask of you the head of Jokanaan.

HEROD: No, no, I do not wish it.

SALOMÉ: You have sworn, Herod.

HERODIAS: Yes, you have sworn. Everybody heard you. You swore it before everybody.

HEROD: Be silent! It is not to you I speak.

HERODIAS: My daughter has done well to ask the head of Jokanaan. He has covered me with insults. He has said monstrous things against me. One can see that she loves her mother well. Do not yield, my daughter. He has sworn, he has sworn.

HEROD: Be silent, speak not to me ...! Come, Salomé, be reasonable. I have never been hard to you. I have ever loved you. ... It may be that I have loved you too much. Therefore ask not this thing of me. This is a terrible thing, an awful thing to ask of me. Surely, I think you are jesting. The head of a man that is cut from his body is ill to look upon, is it not? It is not meet that the eyes of a virgin should look upon such a thing. What pleasure could you have in it? None. No, no, it is not what you desire. Hearken to me. I have an emerald, a great round emerald, which Caesar's minion sent me. If you look through this emerald you can see things which happen at a great distance. Caesar himself carries such an emerald when he goes to the circus. But my emerald is larger. I know well that it is larger. It is the largest emerald in the whole world. You would like that, would you not? Ask it of me and I will give it you.

SALOMÉ: I demand the head of Jokanaan.

HEROD: You are not listening. You are not listening. Suffer me to speak, Salomé.

SALOMÉ: The head of Jokanaan.

HEROD: No, no, you would not have that. You say that to trouble me, because I have looked at you all evening. It is true, I have looked at you all evening. Your beauty troubled me. Your beauty has grievously troubled me, and I have looked at you too much. But I will look at you no more. Neither at things, nor at people should one look. Only in mirrors should one look, for mirrors do but show us masks. Oh! Oh! bring wine! I thirst. ... Salomé, Salomé, let us be friends. Come now ...! Ah! What would I say? What was't? Ah! I remember ...! Salomé – nay, but come nearer to me; I fear you will not hear me – Salomé, you know my white peacocks, my beautiful white peacocks, that walk in the garden between the myrtles and the tall cypress trees. Their beaks are gilded with gold, and the grains that they eat are gilded with gold also, and their feet are stained with purple. When they cry out the rain comes, and the moon shows herself in the heavens when they spread their tails. Two by two they walk between the cypress trees and the black myrtles, and each has a slave to tend it. Sometimes they fly across the trees and anon they crouch in the grass, and round the lake. There are not in all the world birds so wonderful. There is no king in all the world who possesses such wonderful birds. I am sure that Caesar himself has no birds so fine as my birds. I will give you fifty of my peacocks. They will follow you whithersoever you go, and in the midst of them you will be like the moon in the midst of a great white cloud. . . . I will give them all to you. I have but a hundred, and in the whole world there is no king who has peacocks like unto my peacocks. But I will give them all to you. Only you must loose me from my oath, and must not ask of me that which you have asked of me.

He empties the cup of wine.

SALOMÉ: Give me the head of Jokanaan.

HERODIAS: Well said, my daughter! As for you, you are ridiculous with your peacocks.

HEROD: Be silent! You cry out always; you cry out like a beast of prey. You must not. Your voice wearies me. Be silent, I say. . . . Salomé, think of what you are doing. This man comes perchance from God. He is a holy man. The finger of God has touched him. God has put into his mouth terrible words. In the palace as in the desert God is always with him. . . . At least it is possible. One does not know. It is possible that God is for him and with him. Furthermore, if he died some misfortune might happen to me. In any case, he said that the day he dies a misfortune will happen to some one. That could only be to me. Remember, I slipped in blood when I entered. Also, I heard a beating of wings in the air, a beating of mighty wings. These are very evil omens, and there were others. I am sure there were others, though I did not see them. Well, Salomé, you do not wish a misfortune to happen to me? You do not wish that. Listen to me, then.

SALOMÉ: Give me the head of Jokanaan.

HEROD: Ah! You are not listening to me. Be calm. I – I am calm. I am quite calm. Listen. I have jewels hidden in this place – jewels that your mother even has never seen; jewels that are marvellous. I have a collar of pearls, set in four rows. They are like unto moons chained with rays of silver. They are like fifty moons caught in a golden net. On the ivory of her breast a queen has worn it. Thou shalt be as fair as a queen when thou wearest it. I have amethysts of two kinds, one that is black like wine, and one that is red like wine which has been coloured with water. I have topazes, yellow as are the eyes of tigers, and topazes that are pink as the eyes of a wood-pigeon, and green topazes that are as the eyes of cats. I have opals that burn always with an ice-like flame, opals that make sad men's minds, and are fearful of the shadows. I have onyxes like the eyeballs of a dead woman. I have moonstones that change when the moon changes, and are wan when they see the sun. I have sapphires big like eggs, and as blue as blue flowers. The sea wanders within them and the moon comes never to trouble the blue of their waves. I have chrysolites and beryls and chrysoprases and rubies. I have sardonyx and hyacinth stones, and stones of chalcedony, and I will give them all to you, all, and other things will I add to them. The King of the Indies has but even now sent me four fans fashioned from the feathers of parrots, and the King of Numidia a garment of ostrich feathers. I have a crystal, into which it is not lawful for a woman to look, nor may young men behold it until they have been beaten with rods. In a coffer of nacre I have three wondrous turquoises.

He who wears them on his forehead can imagine things which are not, and he who carries them in his hand can make women sterile. These are great treasures above all price. They are treasures without price. But this is not all. In an ebony coffer I have two cups of amber, that are like apples of gold. If an enemy pour poison into these cups, they become like an apple of silver. In a coffer incrusted with amber I have sandals incrusted with glass. I have mantles that have been brought from the land of the Seres, and bracelets decked about with carbuncles and with jade that come from the city of Euphrates.... What desirest thou more than this, Salomé? Tell me the thing that thou desirest, and I will give it thee. All that thou askest I will give thee save one thing. I will give thee all that is mine, save one life. I will give thee the mantle of the high priest. I will give thee the veil of the sanctuary.

THE JEWS: Oh! Oh!

SALOMÉ: Give me the head of Jokanaan.

HEROD (*sinking back in his seat*): Let her be given what she asks! Of a truth she is her mother's child! (*The* FIRST SOLDIER *approaches.* HERODIAS *draws from the hand of the* TETRARCH *the ring of death and gives it to the* SOLDIER, *who straightway bears it to the* EXECUTIONER. *The* EXECUTIONER *looks scared*.) Who has taken my ring? There was a ring on my right hand. Who has drunk my wine? There was wine in my cup. It was full of wine. Some one has drunk it? Oh! Surely some evil will befall some one. (*The* EXECUTIONER *goes down into the cistern*.) Ah! Wherefore did I give my oath? Kings ought never to pledge their word. If they keep it not, it is terrible, and if they keep it, it is terrible also.

HERODIAS: My daughter has done well.

HEROD: I am sure that some misfortune will happen.

SALOMÉ (*she leans over the cistern and listens*): There is no sound. I hear nothing. Why does he not cry out, this man? Ah! If any man sought to kill me, I would cry out, I would struggle, I would not suffer.... Strike, strike, Naaman, strike, I tell you.... No, I hear nothing. There is a silence, a terrible silence. Ah! Something has fallen upon the ground. I heard something fall. It is the sword of the headsman. He is afraid, this slave. He has let his sword fall. He dare not kill him. He is a coward, this slave! Let soldiers be sent. (*She sees the* PAGE OF HERODIAS *and addresses him*.) Come hither, thou wert the friend of him who is dead, is it not so? Well, I tell thee, there are not dead men enough. Go to the soldiers and bid them go down and bring me the thing I ask, the thing the Tetrarch has promised me, the thing that is mine. (*The* PAGE *recoils. She turns to the* SOLDIERS.) Hither, ye soldiers. Get ye down into this cistern and bring me the head of this man. (*The* SOLDIERS *recoil*.) Tetrarch, Tetrarch, command your soldiers that they bring me the head of Jokanaan.

A huge black arm, the arm of the EXECUTIONER, *comes forth from the cistern, bearing on a silver shield the head of* JOKANAAN. SALOMÉ *seizes it.* HEROD *hides his face with his cloak.* HERODIAS *smiles and fans herself. The* NAZARENES *fall on their knees and begin to pray.*

SALOMÉ: Ah! Thou wouldst not suffer me to kiss thy mouth, Jokanaan. Well! I will kiss it now. I will bite it with my teeth as one bites a ripe fruit. Yes, I will kiss thy mouth, Jokanaan. I said it. Did I not say it? I said it. Ah! I will kiss it now.... But wherefore dost thou not look at me, Jokanaan? Thine eyes that were so terrible, so full of rage and scorn, are shut now. Wherefore are they shut? Open thine eyes! Lift up thine eyelids, Jokanaan! Wherefore dost thou not look at me? Art thou afraid of me, Jokanaan, that thou wilt not look at me...? And thy tongue, that was like a red snake darting poison, it moves no more, it says nothing now, Jokanaan, that scarlet viper that spat its venom upon me. It is strange, is it not? How is it that the red viper stirs no longer...? Thou wouldst have none of me, Jokanaan. Thou didst reject me. Thou didst speak evil words against me. Thou didst treat me as a harlot, as a wanton, me, Salomé, daughter of Herodias, Princess of Judaea! Well, Jokanaan, I still live, but thou, thou art dead, and thy head belongs to me. I can do with it what I will. I can throw it to the dogs and to the birds of the air. That which the dogs leave, the birds of the air shall devour.... Ah, Jokanaan, Jokanaan, thou wert the only man that I have loved. All other men are hateful to me. But thou, thou wert beautiful! Thy body was a column of ivory set on a silver socket. It was a garden full of doves and of silver lilies. It was a tower of silver decked with shields of ivory. There was nothing in the world so white as thy body. There was nothing in the world so black as thy hair. In the whole world there was nothing so red as thy mouth. Thy voice was a censer that scattered strange perfumes, and when I looked on thee I heard a strange music. Ah! Wherefore didst thou not look at me, Jokanaan? Behind thine hands and thy curses thou didst hide thy face. Thou didst put upon thine eyes the covering of him who would see his God. Well, thou hast seen thy God, Jokanaan, but me, me, thou didst never see. If thou hadst seen me thou wouldst have loved me. I, I saw thee, Jokanaan, and I loved thee. Oh, how I loved thee! I loved thee yet, Jokanaan, I love thee only.... I am athirst for thy beauty; I am hungry for thy body; and neither wine nor fruits can appease my desire. What shall I do now, Jokanaan? Neither the floods nor the great waters can quench my passion. I was a princess, and thou didst scorn me. I was a virgin, and thou didst take my virginity from me. I was chaste, and thou didst fill my veins with fire.... Ah! ah! wherefore didst thou not look at me, Jokanaan? If thou hadst looked at me thou hadst loved me. Well I know that thou wouldst have loved me, and the mystery of love is greater than the mystery of death. Love only should one consider.

HEROD: She is monstrous, thy daughter, she is altogether monstrous. In truth, what she has done is a great crime. I am sure that it was a crime against an unknown God.

HERODIAS: I approve of what my daughter has done. And I will stay here now.

HEROD (rising): Ah! There speaks the incestuous wife! Come! I will not stay here. Come, I tell thee. Surely some terrible thing will befall. Manasseth, Issachar, Ozias, put out the torches. I will not look at things, I will not suffer things to look at me. Put out the torches! Hide the moon! Hide the stars! Let us hide ourselves in our palace, Herodias. I begin to be afraid.

The slaves put out the torches. The stars disappear. The great black cloud crosses the moon and conceals it completely. The stage becomes very dark. The TETRARCH *begins to climb the staircase.*

THE VOICE OF SALOMÉ: Ah! I have kissed thy mouth, Jokanaan. I have kissed thy mouth. There was a bitter taste on thy lips. Was it the taste of blood . . . ? But perchance it is the taste of love. . . . They say that love hath a bitter taste. . . . But what of that? What of that? I have kissed thy mouth, Jokanaan.

A moonbeam falls on SALOMÉ, *covering her with light.*

HEROD (*turning round and seeing* SALOMÉ): Kill that woman!

The soldiers rush forward and crush beneath their shields SALOMÉ, *daughter of* HERODIAS, *Princess of Judaea.*

CURTAIN

THE DUCHESS OF PADUA

The persons of the play

SIMONE GESSO, Duke of Padua
BEATRICE, his Wife
ANDREAS POLLAJUOLO, Cardinal of Padua
MAFFIO PETRUCCI,
JEPPO VITELLOZZO, } Gentlemen of the Duke's Household
TADDEO BARDI,
GUIDO FERRANTI, a Young Man
ASCANIO CRISTOFANO, his Friend
COUNT MORANZONE, an Old Man
BERNARDO CALVALCANTI, Lord Justice of Padua
HUGO, the Headsman
LUCY, a Tire Woman

SERVANTS, CITIZENS, SOLDIERS, MONKS, FALCONERS with their hawks and dogs, etc.

ACT ONE

> SCENE: *The Market Place of Padua at noon.* TIME: *The latter half of sixteenth century. In the background is the great Cathedral of Padua; the architecture is Romanesque, and wrought in black and white marbles; a flight of marble steps leads up to the Cathedral door; at the foot of the steps are two large stone lions; the houses on each side of the stage have coloured awnings from their windows, and are flanked by stone arcades; on the right of the stage is the public fountain, with a triton in green bronze blowing from a conch; around the fountain is a stone seat; the bell of the Cathedral is ringing, and the citizens, men, women and children, are passing into the Cathedral.*

Enter GUIDO FERRANTI *and* ASCANIO CRISTOFANO.

ASCANIO: Now by my life, Guido, I will go no farther; for if I walk another step I will have no life left to swear by; this wild-goose errand of yours! (*Sits down on the steps of the fountain.*)

GUIDO: I think it must be here. (*Goes up to passer-by and doffs his cap.*) Pray, sir, is this the market place, and that the church of Santa Croce? (*Citizen bows.*) I thank you, sir.

ASCANIO: Well?

GUIDO: Ay! It is here.

ASCANIO: I would it were somewhere else, for I see no wine-shop.

GUIDO (*taking a letter from his pocket and reading it*): 'The hour noon; the city, Padua; the place, the market; and the day, Saint Philip's Day.'

ASCANIO: And what of the man, how shall we know him?

GUIDO (*reading still*): 'I will wear a violet cloak with a silver falcon broidered on the shoulder.' A brave attire, Ascanio.

ASCANIO: I'd sooner have my leathern jerkin. And you think he will tell you of your father?

GUIDO: Why, yes! It is a month ago now, you remember; I was in the vineyard, just at the corner nearest the road, where the goats used to get in, a man rode up and asked me was my name Guido, and gave me this letter, signed 'Your Father's Friend,' bidding me be here to-day if I would know the secret of my birth, and telling me how to recognise the writer! I had always thought old Pedro was my uncle, but he told me that he was not, but that I had been left a child in his charge by some one he had never since seen.

ASCANIO: And you don't know who your father is?

GUIDO: No.

ASCANIO: No recollection of him even?

GUIDO: None, Ascanio, none.

ASCANIO (*laughing*): Then he could never have boxed your ears so often as my father did mine.

GUIDO (*smiling*): I am sure you never deserved it.

ASCANIO: Never; and that made it worse. I hadn't the consciousness of guilt to buoy me up. What hour did you say he fixed?

GUIDO: Noon. (*Clock in the Cathedral strikes.*)

ASCANIO: It is that now, and your man has not come. I don't believe in him, Guido. I think it is some wench who has set her eye at you; and, as I have followed you from Perugia to Padua, I swear you shall follow me to the nearest tavern. (*Rises.*) By the great gods of eating, Guido, I am as hungry as a widow is for a husband, as tired as a young maid is of good advice, and as dry as a monk's sermon. Come, Guido, you stand there looking at nothing, like the fool who tried to look into his own mind; your man will not come.

GUIDO: Well, I suppose you are right. Ah! (*Just as he is leaving the stage with* ASCANIO, *enter* LORD MORANZONE *in a violet cloak, with a silver falcon broidered on the shoulder; he passes across to the Cathedral, and just as he is going in* GUIDO *runs up and touches him.*)

MORANZONE: Guido Ferranti, thou hast come in time.

GUIDO: What! Does my father live?

MORANZONE: Ay! Lives in you.
Thou art the same in mould and lineament,
Carriage and form, and outward semblances;
I trust thou art in noble mind the same.

GUIDO: Oh, tell me of my father; I have lived
But for this moment.

MORANZONE: We must be alone.

GUIDO: This is my dearest friend, who out of love

Has followed me to Padua; as two brothers,
There is no secret which we do not share.

    MORANZONE: There is one secret which ye shall not share;
Bid him go hence.

    GUIDO (*To* ASCANIO): Come back within the hour.
He does not know that nothing in this world
Can dim the perfect mirror of our love.
Within the hour come.

    ASCANIO: Speak not to him,
There is a dreadful terror in his look.

    GUIDO (*laughing*): Nay, nay, I doubt not that he has come to tell,
That I am some great Lord of Italy,
And we will have long days of joy together.
Within the hour, dear Ascanio.

    Exit ASCANIO.

Now tell me of my father? (*Sits down on a stone seat.*) Stood he tall?
I warrant he looked tall upon his horse.
His hair was black? Or perhaps a reddish gold,
Like a red fire of gold? Was his voice low?
The very bravest men have voices sometimes
Full of low music; or a clarion was it
That brake with terror all his enemies?
Did he ride singly? Or with many squires
And valiant gentlemen to serve his taste?
For oftentimes methinks I feel my veins
Beat with the blood of kings. Was he a king?

    MORANZONE: Ay, of all men he was the kingliest.

    GUIDO (*proudly*): Then when you saw my noble father last
He was set high above the heads of men?

    MORANZONE: Ay, he was high above the heads of men,

    Walks over to GUIDO *and puts his hand upon his shoulder.*

On a red scaffold, with a butcher's block
Set for his neck.

    GUIDO (*leaping up*): What dreadful man art thou,
That like a raven, or the midnight owl,
Com'st with this awful message from the grave?

    MORANZONE: I am known here as the Count Moranzone,
Lord of a barren castle on a rock,
With a few acres of unkindly land
And six not thrifty servants. But I was one
Of Parma's noblest princes; more than that,
I was your father's friend.

GUIDO (*clasping his hand*): Tell me of him.

MORANZONE: You are the son of that great Duke Lorenzo,
Whose banner waved on many a well-fought field
Against the Saracen, and heretic Turk,
He was the Prince of Parma, and the Duke
Of all the fair domains of Lombardy
Down to the gates of Florence; nay, Florence even
Was wont to pay him tribute –

GUIDO: Come to his death.

MORANZONE: You will hear that soon enough. Being at war –
O noble lion of war, that would not suffer
Injustice done in Italy – he led
The very flower of chivalry against
That foul adulterous Lord of Rimini,
Giovanni Malatesta – whom God curse!
And was by him in treacherous ambush taken,
And was by him in common fetters bound,
And like a villain, or a low-born knave,
Was by him on the public scaffold murdered.

GUIDO (*clutching his dagger*): Doth Malatesta live?

MORANZONE: No, he is dead.

GUIDO: Did you say dead? O too swift runner, Death,
Couldst thou not wait for me a little space,
And I had done thy bidding!

MORANZONE (*clutching his wrist*): Thou canst do it!
The man who sold thy father is alive.

GUIDO: Sold! Was my father sold?

MORANZONE: Ay! Trafficked for,
Like a vile chattel, for a price betrayed,
Bartered and bargained for in privy market
By one whom he had held his perfect friend,
One he had trusted, one he had well loved,
One whom by ties of kindness he had bound –
Oh! To sow seeds of kindness in this world
Is but to reap ingratitude!

GUIDO: And he lives
Who sold my father.

MORANZONE: I will bring you to him.

GUIDO: So, Judas, thou art living! Well, I will make
This world thy field of blood, so buy it straightway,
For thou must hang there.

MORANZONE: Judas said you, boy?
Yes, Judas in his treachery, but still
He was more wise than Judas was, and held
Those thirty silver pieces not enough.

GUIDO: What got he for my father's blood?

MORANZONE: What got he?
Why cities, fiefs, and principalities,
Vineyards, and lands.
    GUIDO: Of which he shall but keep
Six feet of ground to rot in. Where is he,
This damned villain, this foul devil? Where?
Show me the man, and come he cased in steel,
In complete panoply and pride of war,
Ay, guarded by a thousand men-at-arms,
Yet I shall reach him through their spears, and feel
The last black drop of blood from his black heart
Crawl down my blade. Show me the man, I say,
And I will kill him.
    MORANZONE (*coldly*): Fool, what revenge is there?
Death is the common heritage of all,
And death comes best when it comes suddenly.

    Goes up close to GUIDO.

Thy father was betrayed, there is your cue;
For you shall sell the seller in his turn.
I will make you of his household, you will sit
At the same board with him, eat of his bread –
    GUIDO: O bitter bread!
    MORANZONE: Your palate is too nice,
Revenge will make it sweet. Thou shalt o' nights
Pledge him in wine, drink from his cup, and be
His intimate, so he will fawn on thee,
Love thee, and trust thee in all secret things.
If he bids thee be merry thou must laugh,
And if it be his humour to be sad
Thou shalt don sables. Then when the time is ripe –

    GUIDO *clutches his sword*.

Nay, nay, I trust thee not: your hot young blood,
Undisciplined nature, and too violent rage
Will never tarry for this great revenge,
But wreck itself on passion.
    GUIDO: Thou knowest me not.
Tell me the man, and I in everything
Will do thy bidding.
    MORANZONE: Well, when the time is ripe,
The victim trusting and the occasion sure,
I will by sudden secret messenger
Send thee a sign.

GUIDO: How shall I kill him, tell me?

MORANZONE: That night thou shalt creep into his private chamber;
That night remember.

GUIDO: I shall not forget.

MORANZONE: I do not know if guilty people sleep,
But if he sleeps see that you wake him first,
And hold your hand upon his throat, ay! That way,
Then having told him of what blood you are,
Sprung from what father, and for what revenge,
Bid him to pray for mercy; when he prays,
Bid him to set a price upon his life,
And when he strips himself of all his gold
Tell him thou needest not gold, and hast not mercy,
And do thy business straight away. Swear to me
You will not kill him till I bid you do it,
Or else I go to mine own house, and leave
You ignorant, and your father unavenged.

GUIDO: Now by my father's sword –

MORANZONE: The common hangman
Brake that in sunder in the public square.

GUIDO: Then by my father's grave –

MORANZONE: What grave! What grave?
Your noble father lieth in no grave,
I saw his dust strewn on the air, his ashes
Whirled through the windy streets like common straws
To plague a beggar's eyesight, and his head,
That gentle head, set on the prison spike,
Girt with the mockery of a paper crown
For the vile rabble in their insolence
To shoot their tongues at.

GUIDO: Was it so indeed?
Then by my father's spotless memory,
And by the shameful manner of his death,
And by the base betrayal by his friend,
For these at least remain, by these I swear
I will not lay my hand upon his life
Until you bid me, then – God help his soul,
For he shall die as never dog died yet,
And now, the sign, what is it?

MORANZONE: This dagger, boy;
It was your father's.

GUIDO: O, let me look at it!
I do remember now my reputed uncle,
That good old husbandman I left at home,
Told me a cloak wrapped round me when a babe
Bare too much yellow leopards wrought in gold;

I like them best in steel, as they are here,
They suit my purpose better. Tell me, sir,
Have you no message from my father to me?

    MORANZONE: Poor boy, you never saw that noble father,
For when by his false friend he had been sold,
Alone of all his gentlemen I escaped
To bear the news to Parma to the Duchess.

    GUIDO: Speak to me of my mother.

    MORANZONE: When your mother,
Than whom no saint in heaven was more pure,
Heard my black news, she fell into a swoon,
And, being with untimely travail seized –
Indeed, she was but seven months a bride –
Bare thee into the world before thy time,
And then her soul went heavenward, to wait
Thy father, at the gates of Paradise.

    GUIDO: A mother dead, a father sold and bartered!
I seem to stand on some beleaguered wall,
And messenger comes after messenger
With a new tale of terror; give me breath,
Mine ears are tired.

    MORANZONE: When thy mother died,
Fearing our enemies, I gave it out
Thou wert dead also, and then privily
Conveyed thee to an ancient servitor,
Who by Perugia lived; the rest thou knowest.

    GUIDO: Saw you my father afterwards?

    MORANZONE: Ay! Once;
In mean attire, like a vineyard dresser,
I stole to Rimini.

    GUIDO: (*taking his hand*): O generous heart!

    MORANZONE: One can buy everything in Rimini,
And so I bought the gaolers! When your father
Heard that a man child had been born to him,
His noble face lit up beneath his helm
Like a great fire seen far out at sea,
And taking my two hands, he bade me, Guido,
To rear you worthy of him, so I have reared you
To revenge his death upon the friend who sold him.

    GUIDO: Thou hast done well; I for my father thank you.
And now his name?

    MORANZONE: How you remind me of him,
You have each gesture that your father had.

    GUIDO: The traitor's name?

    MORANZONE: Thou wilt hear that anon;
The Duke and other nobles at the Court

Are coming hither.

GUIDO: What of that? his name?

MORANZONE: Do they not seem a valiant company
Of honourable, honest gentlemen?

GUIDO: His name, milord?

Enter the DUKE OF PADUA *with* COUNT BARDI, MAFFIO, PETRUCCI,
and other gentlemen of his Court.

MORANZONE (*quickly*):   The man to whom I kneel
Is he who sold your father! Mark me well.

GUIDO (*clutches his dagger*): The Duke!

MORANZONE: Leave off that fingering of thy knife.
Hast thou so soon forgotten?

Kneels to the DUKE.

                              My noble Lord.

DUKE: Welcome, Count Moranzone; 'tis some time
Since we have seen you here in Padua.
We hunted near your castle yesterday –
Call you it castle? That bleak house of yours
Wherein you sit a-mumbling o'er your beads,
Telling your vices like a good old man.
I trust I'll never be a good old man.
God would grow weary if I told my sins.

Catches sight of GUIDO *and starts back.*

Who is that?

MORANZONE: My sister's son, your Grace,
Who being now of age to carry arms,
Would for a season tarry at your Court.

DUKE (*still looking at* GUIDO): What is his name?

MORANZONE: Guido Ferranti, sir.

DUKE: His city?

MORANZONE: He is Mantuan by birth.

DUKE (*advancing towards* GUIDO): You have the eyes of one I used to
    know,
But he died childless. So, sir, you would serve me;
Well, we lack soldiers; are you honest, boy?
Then be not spendthrift of your honesty,
But keep it to yourself; in Padua
Men think that honesty is ostentatious, so
It is not of the fashion. Look at these lords
Smelling of civet and the pomander box. . . .

COUNT BARDI (*aside*): Here is some bitter arrow for us, sure.

DUKE: Why, every man among them has his price,
Although, to do them justice, some of them
Are quite expensive.

COUNT BARDI (*aside*): There it comes indeed.

DUKE: So be not honest: eccentricity
Is not a thing should ever be encouraged,
Although, in this dull stupid age of ours,
The most eccentric thing a man can do
Is to have brains, then the mob mocks at him;
And for the mob, despise it as I do,
I hold its bubble praise and windy favours
In such account, that popularity
Is the one insult I have never suffered.

MAFFIO (*aside*): He has enough of hate, if he needs that.

DUKE: Have prudence; in your dealings with the world
Be not too hasty; act on the second thought,
First impulses are generally good.

GUIDO (*aside*): Surely a toad sits on his lips, and spills its venom there.

DUKE: See thou hast enemies,
Else will the world think very little of thee,
It is its test of power; yet see you show
A smiling mask of friendship to all men,
Until you have them safely in your grip,
Then you can crush them.

GUIDO (*aside*):   O wise philosopher!
That for thyself dost dig so deep a grave.

MORANZONE (*to him*): Dost thou mark his words?

GUIDO: O, be thou sure I do.

DUKE: And be not over-scrupulous; clean hands
With nothing in them make a sorry show.
If you would have the lion's share of life
You must wear the fox's skin; Oh, it will fit you;
It is a coat which fitteth every man,
The fat, the lean, the tall man, and the short,
Whoever makes that coat, boy, is a tailor
That never lacks a customer.

GUIDO: Your Grace,
I shall remember.

DUKE: That is well, boy, well.
I would not have about me shallow fools,
Who with mean scruples weigh the gold of life,
And faltering, paltering, end by failure; failure,
The only crime which I have not committed:
I would have *men* about me. As for conscience,
Conscience is but the name which cowardice

Sir William Wilde in his regalia as Chevalier of the Swedish Order of the North Star bestowed on him in 1862.

Jane Francesa Wilde as 'Speranza of The National' around 1848. A later engraving from the portrait by Stephen Catterson Smith.

Oscar Wilde dressed in blue velvet photographed in Dublin aged about two.

Oscar as a fashionable undergraduate in 1876.

Oscar with a group of Magdalen friends, March 1876.

The self-appointed 'Professor of Aesthetics' in 1881.

MR. OSCAR WILDE.

QUITE TOO UTTERLY ECSTATIC.

Oscar, shortly before the publication of Poems *caricatured by Alfred Bryan
in* The Entr'acte, *26 March 1881.*

'The Bard of Beauty' by Alfred Thompson from Time *April 1880, one of the earliest caricatures of Oscar offering a sonnet to Ellen Terry and a triolet to Sarah Bernhardt.*

*Oscar photographed in New York by Napoleon Sarony on his American lecture
tour in 1882.*

Oscar photographed in New York by Napoleon Sarony on his American lecture tour in 1882.

Fleeing from battle scrawls upon its shield.
You understand me, boy?
    GUIDO: I do, your Grace,
And will in all things carry out the creed
Which you have taught me.
    MAFFIO: I never heard your Grace
So much in the vein for preaching; let the Cardinal
Look to his laurels, sir.
    DUKE: The Cardinal!
Men follow my creed, and they gabble his.
I do not think much of the Cardinal;
Although he is a holy churchman, and
I quite admit his dulness. Well, sir, from now
We count you of our household.

> *He holds out his hand for* GUIDO *to kiss.* GUIDO *starts back in horror, but at a gesture from* COUNT MORANZONE, *kneels and kisses it.*

We will see
That you are furnished with such equipage
As doth befit your honour and our state.
    GUIDO: I thank your Grace most heartily.
    DUKE: Tell me again
What is your name?
    GUIDO: Guido Ferranti, sir.
    DUKE: And you are Mantuan? Look to your wives, my lords,
When such a gallant comes to Padua.
Thou dost well to laugh, Count Bardi; I have noted
How merry is that husband by whose hearth
Sits an uncomely wife.
    MAFFIO: May it please your Grace,
The wives of Padua are above suspicion.
    DUKE: What, are they so ill-favoured! Let us go,
This Cardinal detains our pious Duchess;
His sermon and his beard want cutting both:
Will you come with us, sir, and hear a text
From holy Jerome?
    MORANZONE (*bowing*): My liege, there are some matters –
    DUKE (*interrupting*): Thou need'st make no excuse for missing mass.
Come, gentlemen.

> *Exit with his suite into Cathedral.*

    GUIDO (*after a pause*): So the Duke sold my father;
I kissed his hand.
    MORANZONE: Thou shalt do that many times.

GUIDO: Must it be so?

MORANZONE: Ay! Thou hast sworn an oath.

GUIDO: That oath shall make me marble.

MORANZONE: Farewell, boy,
Thou wilt not see me till the time is ripe.

GUIDO: I pray thou comest quickly.

MORANZONE: I will come
When it is time; be ready.

GUIDO: Fear me not.

MORANZONE: Here is your friend; see that you banish him
Both from your heart and Padua.

GUIDO: From Padua,
Not from my heart.

MORANZONE: Nay, from thy heart as well,
I will not leave thee till I see thee do it.

GUIDO: Can I have no friend?

MORANZONE: Revenge shall be thy friend,
Thou need'st no other.

GUIDO: Well, then be it so.

Enter ASCANIO CRISTOFANO.

ASCANIO: Come, Guido, I have been beforehand with you in everything,
for I have drunk a flagon of wine, eaten a pasty, and kissed the maid who
served it. Why, you look as melancholy as a schoolboy who cannot buy
apples, or a politician who cannot sell his vote. What news, Guido, what
news?

GUIDO: Why, that we two must part, Ascanio.

ASCANIO: That would be news indeed, but it is not true.

GUIDO: Too true it is, you must get hence, Ascanio,
And never look upon my face again.

ASCANIO: No, no; indeed you do not know me, Guido;
'Tis true I am a common yeoman's son,
Nor versed in fashions of much courtesy;
But, if you are nobly born, cannot I be
Your serving man? I will tend you with more love
Than any hired servant.

GUIDO (*clasping his hand*): Ascanio!

Sees MORANZONE *looking at him and drops* ASCANIO'S *hand*.

It cannot be.

ASCANIO: What, is it so with you?
I thought the friendship of the antique world
Was not yet dead, but that the Roman type
Might even in this poor and common age

Find counterparts of love; then by this love
Which beats between us like a summer sea,
Whatever lot has fallen to your hand
May I not share it?

GUIDO: Share it?

ASCANIO: Ay!

GUIDO: No, no.

ASCANIO: Have you then come to some inheritance
Of lordly castle, or of stored-up gold?

GUIDO (*bitterly*): Ay! I have come to my inheritance.
O bloody legacy! And O murderous dole!
Which, like the thrifty miser, must I hoard,
And to my own self keep; and so, I pray you,
Let us part here.

ASCANIO: What, shall we never more
Sit hand in hand, as we were wont to sit,
Over some book of ancient chivalry
Stealing a truant holiday from school,
Follow the huntsmen through the autumn woods,
And watch the falcons burst their tasselled jesses,
When the hare breaks from covert.

GUIDO: Never more.

ASCANIO: Must I go hence without a word of love?

GUIDO: You must go hence, and may love go with you.

ASCANIO: You are unknightly, and ungenerous.

GUIDO: Unknightly and ungenerous if you will.
Why should we waste more words about the matter!
Let us part now.

ASCANIO: Have you no message, Guido?

GUIDO: None; my whole past was but a schoolboy's dream,
To-day my life begins. Farewell.

ASCANIO: Farewell (*exit slowly*).

GUIDO: Now are you satisfied? Have you not seen
My dearest friend, and my most loved companion,
Thrust from me like a common kitchen knave!
Oh, that I did it! Are you not satisfied?

MORANZONE: Ay! I am satisfied. Now I go hence,
Back to my lonely castle on the hill.
Do not forget the sign, your father's dagger,
And do the business when I send it to you.

GUIDO: Be sure I shall.

Exit LORD MORANZONE.

GUIDO: O thou eternal heaven!
If there is aught of nature in my soul,

Of gentle pity, or fond kindliness,
Wither it up, blast it, bring it to nothing,
Or if thou wilt not, then will I myself
Cut pity with a sharp knife from my heart
And strangle mercy in her sleep at night
Lest she speak to me. Vengeance there I have it.
Be thou my comrade and my bedfellow,
Sit by my side, ride to the chase with me,
When I am weary sing me pretty songs,
When I am light o' heart, make jest with me,
And when I dream, whisper into my ear
The dreadful secret of a father's murder –
Did I say murder?

    Draws his dagger.

                Listen, thou terrible God!
Thou God that punishest all broken oaths,
And bid some angel write this oath in fire,
That from this hour, till my dear father's murder
In blood I have revenged, I do forswear
The noble ties of honourable friendship,
The noble joys of dear companionship,
Affection's bonds, and loyal gratitude,
Ay, more, from this same hour I do forswear
All love of women, and the barren thing
Which men call beauty –

    The organ peals in the Cathedral, and under a canopy of cloth of silver tissue, borne by four pages in scarlet, the DUCHESS OF PADUA *comes down the steps; as she passes across their eyes meet for a moment, and as she leaves the stage she looks back at* GUIDO, *and the dagger falls from his hand.*

Oh! Who is that?
    A CITIZEN: The Duchess of Padua!

                ACT DROP

ACT TWO

SCENE: *A state room in the Ducal Palace, hung with tapestries representing the Masque of Venus; a large door in the centre opens into a corridor of red marble, through which one can see a view of Padua; a large canopy is set (R.C.) with three thrones, one a little lower than the others; the ceiling is made of long gilded beams; furniture of the period, chairs covered with gilt leather, and buffets set with gold and silver plate, and chests painted with mythological scenes. A number of the courtiers are out on the corridor looking from it down into the street below; from the street comes the roar of a mob and cries of 'Death to the Duke': after a little interval enter the DUKE very calmly, he is leaning on the arm of GUIDO FERRANTI; with him enters also the LORD CARDINAL; the mob still shouting.*

DUKE: No, my Lord Cardinal, I weary of her!
Why, she is worse than ugly, she is good.
    MAFFIO (*excitedly*): Your Grace, there are two thousand people there
Who every moment grow more clamorous.
    DUKE: Tut, man, they waste their strength upon their lungs!
People who shout so loud, my lords, do nothing,
The only men I fear are silent men. (*A yell from the people.*)
You see, Lord Cardinal, how my people love me,
This is their serenade, I like it better
Than the soft murmurs of the amorous lute;
Is it not sweet to listen to? (*Another yell.*)
                                        I fear
They have become a little out of tune,
So I must tell my men to fire on them.
I cannot bear bad music! Go, Petrucci,
And tell the captain of the guard below
To clear the square. Do you not hear me, sir?
Do what I bid you.

    Exit PETRUCCI.

    CARDINAL: I beseech your Grace
To listen to their grievances.
    DUKE (*sitting on his throne*): Ay! The peaches
Are not so big this year as they were last.
I crave your pardon, my Lord Cardinal,
I thought you spake of peaches.

    A cheer from the people.

                    What is that?

GUIDO (*rushes to the window*): The Duchess has gone forth into the square,
And stands between the people and the guard,
And will not let them shoot.

DUKE: The devil take her!

GUIDO (*still at the window*): And followed by a dozen of the citizens
Has come into the Palace.

DUKE (*starting up*):   By Saint James,
Our Duchess waxes bold!

BARDI: Here comes the Duchess.

DUKE: Shut that door there; this morning air is cold.

They close the door on the corridor.
Enter the DUCHESS *followed by a crowd of meanly dressed Citizens.*

DUCHESS (*flinging herself upon her knees*): I do beseech your Grace to give
us audience.

DUKE: Am I a tailor, Madame, that you come
With such a ragged retinue before us?

DUCHESS: I think that their rags speak their grievances
With better eloquence than I can speak.

DUKE: What are these grievances?

DUCHESS: Alas, my Lord,
Such common things as neither you nor I,
Nor any of these noble gentlemen,
Have ever need at all to think about;
They say the bread, the very bread they eat,
Is made of sorry chaff.

FIRST CITIZEN: Ay! So it is,
Nothing but chaff.

DUKE: And very good food too,
I give it to my horses.

DUCHESS (*restraining herself*): They say the water,
Set in the public cisterns for their use,
Has, through the breaking of the aqueduct,
To stagnant pools and muddy puddles turned.

DUKE: They should drink wine; water is quite unwholesome.

SECOND CITIZEN: Alack, your Grace, the taxes which the customs
Take at the city gate are grown so high
We cannot buy wine.

DUKE: Then you should bless the taxes
Which make you temperate.

DUCHESS: Think, while we sit
In gorgeous pomp and state and nothing lack
Of all that wealth and luxury can give
And many servants have to wait upon us

And tend our meanest need, gaunt poverty
Creeps through their sunless lanes, and with sharp knives
Cuts the warm throats of children stealthily
And no word said.

THIRD CITIZEN: Ay! Marry, that is true,
My little son died yesternight from hunger,
He was but six years old; I am so poor,
I cannot bury him.

DUKE: If you are poor,
Are you not blessed in that? Why, poverty
Is one of the Christian virtues,

Turns to the CARDINAL.

                         Is it not?
I know, Lord Cardinal, you have great revenues,
Rich abbey-lands, and tithes, and large estates
For preaching voluntary poverty.

DUCHESS: Nay but, my lord the Duke, be generous;
While we sit here within a noble house
With shaded porticoes against the sun,
And walls and roofs to keep the winter out,
There are many citizens of Padua
Who in vile tenements live so full of holes,
That the chill rain, the snow, and the rude blast,
Are tenant also with them; others sleep
Under the arches of the public bridges
All through the autumn nights, till the wet mist
Stiffens their limbs, and fevers come, and so –

DUKE: And so they go to Abraham's bosom, Madam.
They should thank me for sending them to Heaven,
If they are wretched here.

To the CARDINAL.

                         Is it not said
Somewhere in Holy Writ, that every man
Should be contented with that state of life
God calls him to? Why should I change their state,
Or meddle with an all-wise providence,
Which has apportioned that some men should starve
And others surfeit? I did not make the world.

FIRST CITIZEN: He hath a hard heart.

SECOND CITIZEN: Nay, be silent, neighbour;
I think the Cardinal will speak for us.

CARDINAL: True, it is Christian to bear misery,

For out of misery God bringeth good,
Yet it is Christian also to be kind,
To feed the hungry, and to heal the sick,
And there seem many evils in this town,
Which in your wisdom might your Grace reform.

    FIRST CITIZEN: What is that word reform? What does it mean?

    SECOND CITIZEN: Marry, it means leaving things as they are; I like it not.

    DUKE: Reform, Lord Cardinal, did *you* say reform?
There is a man in Germany called Luther,
Who would reform the Holy Catholic Church.
Have you not made him heretic, and uttered
Anathema, maranatha, against him?

    CARDINAL (*rising from his seat*): He would have led the sheep out of the
      fold,
We do but ask of you to feed the sheep.

    DUKE: When I have shorn their fleeces I may feed them.
As for these rebels –

        DUCHESS *entreats him.*

    FIRST CITIZEN: That is a kind word,
He means to give us something.

    SECOND CITIZEN: Is that so?

    DUKE: These ragged knaves who come before us here,
With mouths chock-full of treason.

    THIRD CITIZEN: Good my Lord,
Fill up our mouths with bread; we'll hold our tongues.

    DUKE: Ye shall hold your tongues, whether you starve or not.
My lords, this age is so familiar grown,
That the low peasant hardly doffs his hat,
Unless you beat him; and the raw mechanic
Elbows the noble in the public streets,
As for this rabble here, I am their scourge,
And sent by God to lash them for their sins.

    DUCHESS: Hast thou the right? Art thou so free from sin?

    DUKE: When sin is lashed by virtue it is nothing,
But when sin lashes sin then is God glad.

    DUCHESS: Oh, are you not afraid?

    DUKE: What have I to fear?
Being man's enemy am I not God's friend?

    To the CITIZENS.

Well, my good loyal citizens of Padua,
Still as our gentle Duchess has so prayed us,
And to refuse so beautiful a beggar

Were to lack both courtesy and love,
Touching your grievances, I promise this –

FIRST CITIZEN: Marry, he will lighten the taxes!

SECOND CITIZEN: Or a dole of bread, think you, for each man?

DUKE: That, on next Sunday, the Lord Cardinal
Shall, after Holy Mass, preach you a sermon
Upon the Beauty of Obedience.

CITIZENS *murmur*.

FIRST CITIZEN: I' faith, that will not fill our stomachs!

SECOND CITIZEN: A sermon is but a sorry sauce, when
You have nothing to eat with it.

DUCHESS: Poor people,
You see I have no power with the Duke,
But if you go into the court without,
My almoner shall from my private purse,
Which is not ever too well stuffed with gold,
Divide a hundred ducats 'mongst you all.

ALMONER: Your grace has but a hundred ducats left.

DUCHESS: Give what I have.

FIRST CITIZEN: God save the Duchess, say I.

SECOND CITIZEN: God save her.

DUCHESS: And every Monday morn shall bread be set
For those who lack it.

CITIZENS *applaud and go out*.

FIRST CITIZEN (*going out*): Why, God save the Duchess again!

DUKE (*calling him back*): Come hither, fellow! What is your name?

FIRST CITIZEN: Dominick, sir.

DUKE: A good name! Why were you called Dominick?

FIRST CITIZEN (*scratching his head*): Marry, because I was born on Saint
George's day.

DUKE: A good reason! Here is a ducat for you!
Will you not cry for me God save the Duke?

FIRST CITIZEN (*feebly*): God save the Duke.

DUKE: Nay! Louder, fellow, louder.

FIRST CITIZEN (*a little louder*):   God save the Duke!

DUKE: More lustily, fellow, put more heart in it!
Here is another ducat for you.

FIRST CITIZEN (*enthusiastically*): God save the Duke!

DUKE (*mockingly*): Why, gentlemen, this simple fellow's love
Touches me much. *To the* CITIZEN, *harshly*. Go!

Exit CITIZEN, *bowing*.

                This is the way, my lords,
You can buy popularity nowadays.
Oh, we are nothing if not democratic!

    To the DUCHESS.

                    So. Well, Madam,
You spread rebellion 'midst our citizens
And by your doles and daily charities,
Have made the common people love you. Well,
I will not have you loved.
    DUCHESS (*looking at* GUIDO): Indeed, my lord,
I am not.
    DUKE: And I will not have you give
Bread to the poor merely because they are hungry.
    DUCHESS: My Lord, the poor have rights you cannot touch,
The right to pity, and the right to mercy.
    DUKE: So, so, you argue with me? This is she,
The gentle Duchess for whose hand I yielded
Three of the fairest towns in Italy,
Pisa, and Genoa, and Orvieto.
    DUCHESS: Promised, my Lord, not yielded: in that matter
Brake you your word as ever.
    DUKE: You wrong us, Madam,
There were state reasons.
    DUCHESS: What state reasons are there
For breaking holy promises to a state?
    DUKE: There are wild boars at Pisa in a forest
Close to the city: when I promised Pisa
Unto your noble and most trusting father,
I had forgotten there was hunting there.
    DUCHESS: Those who forget what honour is, forget
All things, my Lord.
    DUKE: At Genoa they say,
Indeed I doubt them not, that the red mullet
Runs larger in the harbour of that town
Than anywhere in Italy.

    Turning to one of the Court.

                You, my lord,
Whose gluttonous appetite is your only god,
Could satisfy our Duchess on that point.
    DUCHESS: And Orvieto?
    DUKE(*yawning*):   I cannot now recall
Why I did not surrender Orvieto

According to the word of my contract.
Maybe it was because I did not choose.

Goes over to the DUCHESS.

Why look you, Madam, you are here alone;
'Tis many a dusty league to your grey France,
And even there your father barely keeps
A hundred ragged squires for his Court.
What hope have you, I say? Which of these lords
And noble gentlemen of Padua
Stands by thy side.

DUCHESS: There is not one.

GUIDO *starts, but restrains himself.*

DUKE: Nor shall be.
While I am Duke in Padua: listen, Madam,
I am grown weary of your airs and graces,
Being mine own, you shall do as I will,
And if it be my will you keep the house,
Why then, this palace shall your prison be;
And if it be my will you walk abroad,
Why, you shall take the air from morn to night.

DUCHESS: Sir, by what right – ?
DUKE: Madam, my second Duchess
Asked the same question once: her monument
Lies in the chapel of Bartholomew.
Wrought in red marble; very beautiful.
Guido, your arm. Come, gentlemen, let us go
And spur our falcons for the mid-day chase.
Bethink you, Madam, you are here alone.

Exit the DUKE *leaning on* GUIDO, *with his Court.*

DUCHESS (*looking after them*): Is it not strange that one who seems so fair
Should thus affect the Duke, hang on each word
Which falls like poison from those cruel lips,
And never leave his side, as though he loved him?
Well, well, it makes no matter unto me,
I am alone, and out of reach of love.
The Duke said rightly that I was alone;
Deserted, and dishonoured, and defamed,
Stood ever woman so alone indeed?
Men when they woo us call us pretty children,
Tell us we have not wit to make our lives,

And so they mar them for us. Did I say woo?
We are their chattels, and their common slaves,
Less dear than the poor hound that licks their hand,
Less fondled than the hawk upon their wrist.
Woo, did I say? Bought rather, sold and bartered,
Our very bodies being merchandise.
I know it is the general lot of women,
Each miserably mated to some man
Wrecks her own life upon his selfishness:
That it is general makes it not less bitter.
I think I never heard a woman laugh,
Laugh for pure merriment, except one woman,
That was at night time, in the public streets.
Poor soul, she walked with painted lips, and wore
The mask of pleasure: I would not laugh like her;
No, death were better.

> *Enter* GUIDO *behind unobserved; the* DUCHESS *flings herself down before a picture of the Madonna.*

O, Mary mother, with your sweet pale face
Bending between the little angel heads
That hover round you, have you no help for me?
Mother of God, have you no help for me?
   GUIDO: I can endure no longer.
This is my love, and I will speak to her.
Lady, am I a stranger to your prayers?
   DUCHESS (*rising*): None but the wretched need my prayers, my lord.
   GUIDO: Then must I need them, lady.
   DUCHESS: How is that?
Does not the Duke show thee sufficient honour,
Or dost thou lack advancement at the Court?
Ah, sir, that lies not in my power to give you,
Being my own self held of no account.
   GUIDO: Your Grace, I lack no favours from the Duke,
Whom my soul loathes as I loathe wickedness,
But come to proffer on my bended knees,
My loyal service to thee unto death.
   DUCHESS: Alas! I am so fallen in estate
I can but give thee a poor meed of thanks.
   GUIDO (*seizing her hand*): Hast thou no love to give me?

> *The* DUCHESS *starts, and* GUIDO *falls at her feet.*

                                                    O dear saint,
If I have been too daring, pardon me!

Thy beauty sets my boyish blood aflame,
And, when my reverent lips touch thy white hand,
Each little nerve with such wild passion thrills
That there is nothing which I would not do
To gain thy love.

Leaps up.

                              Bid me reach forth and pluck
Perilous honour from the lion's jaws,
And I will wrestle with the Nemean beast
On the bare desert! Fling to the cave of War
A gaud, a ribbon, a dead flower, something
That once has touched thee, and I'll bring it back
Though all the hosts of Christendom were there,
Inviolate again! Ay, more than this,
Set me to scale the pallid white-faced cliffs
Of mighty England, and from that arrogant shield
Will I raze out the lilies of your France
Which England, that sea-lion of the sea,
Hath taken from her!
                              O dear Beatrice,
Drive me not from thy presence! Without thee
The heavy minutes crawl with feet of lead,
But, while I look upon thy loveliness,
The hours fly like winged Mercuries
And leave existence golden.
    DUCHESS: I did not think
I would be ever loved; do you indeed
Love me so much as now you say you do?
    GUIDO: Ask of the sea-bird if it loves the sea,
Ask of the roses if they love the rain,
Ask of the little lark, that will not sing
Till day break, if it loves to see the day: –
And yet, these are but empty images,
Mere shadows of my love, which is a fire
So great that all the waters of the main
Can not avail to quench it. Will you not speak?
    DUCHESS: I hardly know what I should say to you.
    GUIDO: Will you not say you love me?
    DUCHESS: Is that my lesson?
Must I say all at once? 'Twere a good lesson
If I did love you, sir; but, if I do not,
What shall I say then?
    GUIDO: If you do not love me,
Say, none the less, you do, for on your tongue

Falsehood for very shame would turn to truth.

DUCHESS: What if I do not speak at all? They say
Lovers are happiest when they are in doubt.

GUIDO: Nay, doubt would kill me, and if I must die,
Why, let me die for joy and not for doubt.
O tell me may I stay, or must I go?

DUCHESS: I would not have you either stay or go;
For if you stay you steal my love from me,
And if you go you take my love away.
Guido, though all the morning stars could sing
They could not tell the measures of my love.
I love you, Guido.

GUIDO (*stretching out his hands*): Oh, do not cease at all;
I thought the nightingale sang but at night;
Or if thou needst must cease, then let my lips
Touch the sweet lips that can such music make.

DUCHESS: To touch my lips is not to touch my heart.

GUIDO: Do you close that against me?

DUCHESS: Alas! My lord,
I have it not: the first day that I saw you
I let you take my heart away from me;
Unwilling thief, that without meaning it
Didst break into my fenced treasury
And filch my jewel from it! O strange theft,
Which made you richer though you knew it not,
And left me poorer, and yet glad of it!

GUIDO (*clasping her in his arms*): O love, love, love! Nay, sweet, lift up your
       head.
Let me unlock those little scarlet doors
That shut in music, let me dive for coral
In your red lips, and I'll bear back a prize
Richer than all the gold the Griffin guards
In rude Armenia.

DUCHESS: You are my lord,
And what I have is yours, and what I have not
Your fancy lends me, like a prodigal
Spending its wealth on what is nothing worth. (*Kisses him.*)

GUIDO: Methinks I am bold to look upon you thus:
The gentle violet hides beneath its leaf
And is afraid to look at the great sun
For fear of too much splendour, but my eyes,
O daring eyes! Are grown so venturous
That like fixed stars they stand, gazing at you,
And surfeit sense with beauty.

DUCHESS: Dear love, I would
You could look upon me for ever, for your eyes

Are polished mirrors, and when I peer
Into those mirrors I can see myself,
And so I know my image lives in you.

    GUIDO (*taking her in his arms*): Stand still, thou hurrying orb in the high
      heavens,
And make this hour immortal! (*A pause*).

    DUCHESS: Sit down here,
A little lower than me; yes, just so, sweet,
That I may run my fingers through your hair,
And see your face turn upwards like a flower
To meet my kiss.

                  Have you not sometimes noted,
When we unlock some long disusèd room
With heavy dust and soiling mildew filled,
Where never foot of man has come for years,
And from the windows take the rusty bar,
And fling the broken shutters to the air,
And let the bright sun in, how the good sun
Turns every grimy particle of dust
Into a little thing of dancing gold?
Guido, my heart is that long-empty room,
But you have let love in, and with its gold
Gilded all life. Do you not think that love
Fills up the sum of life?

    GUIDO: Ay! Without love
Life is no better than the unhewn stone
Which in the quarry lies, before the sculptor
Has set the God within it. Without love
Life is as silent as the common reeds
That through the marshes or by rivers grow,
And have no music in them.

    DUCHESS: Yet out of these
The singer, who is Love, will make a pipe
And from them he draws music; so I think
Love will bring music out of any life.
Is that not true?

    GUIDO: Sweet, women make it true.
There are men who paint pictures, and carve statues,
Paul of Verona and the dyer's son,
Or their great rival, who, by the sea at Venice,
Has set God's little maid upon the stair,
White as her own white lily, and as tall,
Or Raphael, whose Madonnas are divine
Because they are mothers merely; yet I think
Women are the best artists of the world,
For they can take the common lives of men

Soiled with the money-getting of our age,
And with love make them beautiful.
DUCHESS: Ah, dear,
I wish that you and I were very poor;
The poor, who love each other, are so rich.
GUIDO: Tell me again you love me, Beatrice.
DUCHESS (*fingering his collar*): How well this collar lies about your throat.

LORD MORANZONE *looks through the door from the corridor outside.*

GUIDO: Nay, tell me that you love me.
DUCHESS: I remember,
That when I was a child in my dear France,
Being at Court at Fontainebleau, the King
Wore such a collar.
GUIDO: Will you not say you love me?
DUCHESS (*smiling*): He was a very royal man, King Francis,
Yet he was not royal as you are.
Why need I tell you, Guido, that I love you?

Takes his head in her hands and turns his face up to her.

Do you not know that I am yours for ever,
Body and soul.

Kisses him, and then suddenly catches sight of MORANZONE *and leaps up.*

Oh, what is that?

MORANZONE *disappears.*

GUIDO: What, love?
DUCHESS: Methought I saw a face with eyes of flame
Look at us through the doorway.
GUIDO: Nay, 'twas nothing:
The passing shadow of the man on guard.

The DUCHESS *still stands looking at the window.*

'Twas nothing, sweet.
DUCHESS: Ay! What can harm us now,
Who are in Love's land? I do not think I'd care
Though the vile world should with its lackey Slander
Trample and tread upon my life; why should I?
They say the common field-flowers of the field
Have sweeter scent when they are trodden on

Than when they bloom alone, and that some herbs
Which have no perfume, on being bruised die
With all Arabia round them; so it is
With the young lives this dull world seeks to crush,
It does but bring the sweetness out of them,
And makes them lovelier often. And besides,
While we have love we have the best of life:
Is it not so?

GUIDO: Dear, shall we play or sing?
I think that I could sing now.

DUCHESS: Do not speak,
For there are times when all existences
Seem narrowed to one single ecstasy,
And Passion sets a seal upon the lips.

GUIDO: Oh, with mine own lips let me break that seal!
You love me, Beatrice?

DUCHESS: Ay! Is it not strange
I should so love mine enemy?

GUIDO: Who is he?

DUCHESS: Why, you: that with your shaft didst pierce my heart!
Poor heart, that lived its little lonely life
Until it met your arrow.

GUIDO: Ah, dear love,
I am so wounded by that bolt myself
That with untended wounds I lie a-dying,
Unless you cure me, dear Physician.

DUCHESS: I would not have you cured; for I am sick
With the same malady.

GUIDO: Oh how I love you!
See, I must steal the cuckoo's voice, and tell
The one tale over.

DUCHESS: Tell no other tale!
For, if that is the little cuckoo's song,
The nightingale is hoarse, and the loud lark
Has lost its music.

GUIDO: Kiss me, Beatrice!

*She takes his face in her hands and bends down and kisses him; a loud knock-
ing then comes at the door, and* GUIDO *leaps up; enter a* SERVANT.

SERVANT: A package for you, sir.
GUIDO (*carelessly*): Ah! Give it to me.

SERVANT *hands package wrapped in vermilion silk, and exit; as* GUIDO *is
about to open it the* DUCHESS *comes up behind, and in sport takes it from him.*

DUCHESS (*laughing*): Now I will wager it is from some girl
Who would have you wear her favour; I am so jealous
I will not give up the least part in you,
But like a miser keep you to myself,
And spoil you perhaps in keeping.
    GUIDO: It is nothing
    DUCHESS: Nay, it is from some girl.
    GUIDO: You know 'tis not.
    DUCHESS (*turns her back and opens it*): Now, traitor, tell me what does this
        sign mean,
A dagger with two leopards wrought in steel?
    GUIDO (*taking it from her*): O God!
    DUCHESS: I'll from the window look, and try
If I can'st see the porter's livery
Who left it at the gate? I will not rest
Till I have learned your secret.

    Runs laughing into the corridor.

    GUIDO: Oh, horrible!
Had I so soon forgot my father's death,
Did I so soon let love into my heart,
And must I banish love, and let in murder
That beats and clamours at the outer gate?
Ay, that I must! Have I not sworn an oath?
Yet not to-night; nay, it must be to-night.
Farewell then all the joy and light of life,
All dear recorded memories, farewell,
Farewell all love! Could I with bloody hands
Fondle and paddle with her innocent hands?
Could I with lips fresh from this butchery
Play with her lips? Could I with murderous eyes
Look in those violet eyes, whose purity
Would strike mine blind, and make each eyeball reel
In night perpetual? No, murder has set
A barrier between us far too high
For us to kiss across it.
    DUCHESS: Guido!
    GUIDO: Beatrice,
You must forget that name, and banish me
Out of your life for ever.
    DUCHESS (*going towards him*): O dear love!
    GUIDO (*stepping back*): There lies a barrier between us two
We dare not pass.
    DUCHESS: I dare do anything
So that you are beside me.

GUIDO: Ah! There it is,
I cannot be beside you, cannot breathe
The air you breathe; I cannot any more
Stand face to face with beauty, which unnerves
My shaking heart, and makes my desperate hand
Fail of its purpose. Let me go hence, I pray;
Forget you ever looked upon me.
  DUCHESS: What!
With your hot kisses fresh upon my lips
Forget the vows of love you made to me?
  GUIDO: I take them back!
  DUCHESS: Alas, you cannot, Guido,
For they are part of nature now; the air
Is tremulous with their music, and outside
The little birds sing sweeter for those vows.
  GUIDO: There lies a barrier between us now,
Which then I knew not, or I had forgot.
  DUCHESS: There is no barrier, Guido; why, I will go
In poor attire, and will follow you
Over the world.
  GUIDO (*wildly*): The world's not wide enough
To hold us two! Farewell, farewell for ever.
  DUCHESS (*calm, and controlling her passion*): Why did you come into my
      life at all, then,
Or in the desolate garden of my heart
Sow that white flower of love – ?
  GUIDO: O Beatrice!
  DUCHESS: Which now you would dig up, uproot, tear out,
Though each small fibre doth so hold my heart
That if you break one, my heart breaks with it?
Why did you come into my life? Why open
The secret wells of love I had sealed up?
Why did you open them – ?
  GUIDO: O God!
  DUCHESS (*clenching her hand*): And let
The floodgates of my passion swell and burst
Till, like the wave when rivers overflow
That sweeps the forest and the farm away,
Love in the splendid avalanche of its might
Swept my life with it? Must I drop by drop
Gather these waters back and seal them up?
Alas! Each drop will be a tear, and so
Will with its saltness make life very bitter.
  GUIDO: I pray you speak no more, for I must go
Forth from your life and love, and make a way
On which you cannot follow.

DUCHESS: I have heard
That sailors dying of thirst upon a raft,
Poor castaways upon a lonely sea,
Dream of green fields and pleasant water-courses,
And then wake up with red thirst in their throats,
And die more miserably because sleep
Has cheated them: so they die cursing sleep
For having sent them dreams; I will not curse you
Though I am cast away upon the sea
Which men call Desolation.
    GUIDO: O God, God!
    DUCHESS: But you will stay: listen, I love you, Guido.

    She waits a little.

Is echo dead, that when I say I love you
There is no answer?
    GUIDO: Everything is dead,
Save one thing only, which shall die to-night!
    DUCHESS: Then I must train my lips to say farewell,
And yet I think they will not learn that lesson,
For when I shape them for such utterance
They do but say I love you: must I chide them?
And if so, can my lips chide one another?
Alas, they both are guilty, and refuse
To say the word.
    GUIDO: Then I must say it for them,
Farewell, we two can never meet again.

    Rushes towards her.

    DUCHESS: If you are going, touch me not, but go.

    Exit GUIDO.

Never again, did he say never again?
Well, well, I know my business! I will change
The torch of love into a funeral torch,
And with the flowers of love will strew my bier,
And from love's songs will make a dirge, and so
Die, as the swan dies, singing.
                        O misery,
If thou wert so enamoured of my life,
Why couldst thou not some other form have borne?
The mask of pain, and not the mask of love,
The raven's voice, and not the nightingale's,

The blind mole's eyes, and not those agate eyes
Which, like the summer heavens, were so blue
That one could fancy one saw God in them,
So, misery, I had known thee.

                           Barrier! Barrier!
Why did he say there was a barrier?
There is no barrier between us two.
He lied to me, and shall I for that reason
Loathe what I love, and what I worshipped, hate?
I think we women do not love like that.
For if I cut his image from my heart,
My heart would, like a bleeding pilgrim, follow
That image through the world, and call it back
With little cries of love.

    Enter DUKE *equipped for the chase, with falconers and hounds.*

    DUKE: Madam, you keep us waiting;
You keep my dogs waiting.
    DUCHESS: I will not ride to–day.
    DUKE: How now, what's this?
    DUCHESS: My Lord, I cannot go.
    DUKE: What, pale face, do you dare to stand against me?
Why, I could set you on a sorry jade
And lead you through the town, till the low rabble
You feed toss up their hats and mock at you.
    DUCHESS: Have you no word of kindness ever for me?
    DUKE: Kind words are lime to snare our enemies!
I hold you in the hollow of my hand
And have no need on you to waste kind words.
    DUCHESS: Well, I will go.
    DUKE (*slapping his boot with his whip*): No, I have changed my mind,
You will stay here, and like a faithful wife
Watch from the window for our coming back.
Were it not dreadful if some accident
By chance should happen to your loving Lord?
Come, gentlemen, my hounds begin to chafe,
And I chafe too, having a patient wife.
Where is young Guido?
    MAFFIO: My liege, I have not seen him
For a full hour past.
    DUKE: It matters not,
I dare say I shall see him soon enough.
Well, Madam, you will sit at home and spin.
I do protest, sirs, the domestic virtues
Are often very beautiful in others.

Exit DUKE *with his Court*.

DUCHESS: The stars have fought against me, that is all,
And thus to-night when my Lord lieth asleep,
Will I fall upon my dagger, and so cease.
My heart is such a stone nothing can reach it
Except the dagger's edge: let it go there,
To find what name it carries: ay! To-night
Death will divorce the Duke; and yet to-night
He may die also, he is very old.
Why should he not die? Yesterday his hand
Shook with a palsy: men have died from palsy,
And why not he? Are there not fevers also,
Agues and chills, and other maladies
Most incident to old age?
No, no, he will not die, he is too sinful;
Honest men die before their proper time.
Good men will die: men by whose side the Duke
In all the sick pollution of his life
Seems like a leper: women and children die,
But the Duke will not die, he is too sinful.
Oh, can it be
There is some immortality in sin,
Which virtue has not? And does the wicked man
Draw life from what to other men were death,
Like poisonous plants that on corruption live?
No, no, I think God would not suffer that:
Yet the Duke will not die; he is too sinful.
But I will die alone, and on this night
Grim Death shall be my bridegroom, and the tomb
My secret house of pleasure: well, what of that?
The world's a graveyard, and we each, like coffins,
Within us bear a skeleton.

Enter LORD MORANZONE *all in black; he passes across the back of the stage
looking anxiously about*.

MORANZONE: Where is Guido?
I cannot find him anywhere.
    DUCHESS (*catches sight of him*): O God!
'Twas thou who took my love away from me.
    MORANZONE (*with a look of joy*): What, has he left you?
    DUCHESS: Nay, you know he has.
Oh, give him back to me, give him back, I say,
Or I will tear your body limb from limb,
And to the common gibbet nail your head

Until the carrion crows have stripped it bare.
Better you had crossed a hungry lioness
Before you came between me and my love.

With more pathos.

Nay, give him back, you know not how I love him,
Here by this chair he knelt a half hour since,
'Twas there he stood, and there he looked at me,
This is the hand he kissed, these are the lips
His lips made havoc of, and these the ears
Into whose open portals he did pour
A tale of love so musical that all
The birds stopped singing! Oh give him back to me.
    MORANZONE: He does not love you, Madam.
    DUCHESS: May the plague
Wither the tongue that says so! Give him back.
    MORANZONE: Madam, I tell you you will never see him.
Neither to-night, nor any other night.
    DUCHESS: What is your name?
    MORANZONE: My name? Revenge!

Exit

    DUCHESS: Revenge!
I think I never harmed a little child.
What should Revenge do coming to my door?
It matters not, for Death is there already,
Waiting with his dim torch to light my way.
'Tis true men hate thee, Death, and yet I think
Thou wilt be kinder to me than my lover,
And so dispatch the messengers at once,
Hurry the lazy steeds of lingering day,
And let the night, thy sister, come instead,
And drape the world in mourning; let the owl,
Who is thy minister, scream from his tower
And wake the toad with hooting, and the bat,
That is the slave of dim Persephone,
Wheel through the sombre air on wandering wing!
Tear up the shrieking mandrakes from the earth
And bid them make us music, and tell the mole
To dig deep down thy cold and narrow bed,
For I shall lie within thine arms to-night.

ACT DROP

ACT THREE

> SCENE: *A large corridor in the Ducal Palace: a window (L.C.)
> looks out on a view of Padua by moonlight: a staircase (R.C.)
> leads up to a door with a portière of crimson velvet, with the
> Duke's arms embroidered in gold on it: on the lowest step of the
> staircase a figure draped in black is sitting: the hall is lit by an
> iron cresset filled with burning tow: thunder and lightning out-
> side: the time is night.*

> *Enter* GUIDO *through the window.*

GUIDO: The wind is rising: how my ladder shook!
I thought that every gust would break the cords!

> *Looks out at the city.*

Christ! What a night:
Great thunder in the heavens, and wild lightnings
Striking from pinnacle to pinnacle
Across the city, till the dim houses seem
To shudder and to shake as each new glare
Dashes adown the street.

> *Passes across the stage to foot of staircase.*

                              Ah! Who art thou
That sittest on the stair, like unto Death
Waiting a guilty soul?

> *A pause.*

Canst thou not speak?
Or has this storm laid palsy on your tongue,
And chilled your utterance? Get from my path,
For I have certain business in yon chamber,
Which I must do alone.

> *The figure rises and takes off his mask.*

MORANZONE: Guido Ferranti,
Thy murdered father laughs for joy to-night.
GUIDO (*confusedly*): What, art thou here?
MORANZONE: Ay, waiting for your coming.
GUIDO (*looking away from him*): I did not think to see you, but am glad,
That thou mayest know the very thing I mean to do.

MORANZONE: First, I would have you know my well-laid plans;
Listen: I have set horses at the gate
Which leads to Parma: when thou hast done thy business
We will ride hence, and by to-morrow night
If our good horses fail not by the way?
Parma will see us coming; I have advised
Many old friends of your great father there,
Who have prepared the citizens for revolt.
With money, and with golden promises,
The which we need not keep, I have bought over
Many that stand by this usurping Duke.
As for the soldiers, they, the Duke being dead,
Will fling allegiance to the winds, so thou
Shalt sit again within thy father's palace,
As Parma's rightful lord.

GUIDO: It cannot be.

MORANZONE: Nay, but it shall.

GUIDO: Listen, Lord Moranzone,
I am resolved not to kill this man.

MORANZONE: Surely my ears are traitors, speak again:
It cannot be but age has dulled my powers,
I am an old man now: what did you say?
You said that with that dagger in your belt
You would avenge your father's bloody murder;
Did you not say that?

GUIDO: No, my lord, I said
I was resolved not to kill the Duke.

MORANZONE: You said not that; it is my senses mock me;
Or else this midnight air o'ercharged with storm
Alters your message in the giving it.

GUIDO: Nay, you heard rightly; I'll not kill this man.

MORANZONE: What of thine oath, thou traitor, what of thine oath?

GUIDO: I am resolved not to keep that oath.

MORANZONE: What of thy murdered father?

GUIDO: Dost thou think
My father would be glad to see me coming,
This old man's blood still hot upon mine hands?

MORANZONE: Ay! He would laugh for joy.

GUIDO: I do not think so,
There is better knowledge in the other world;
Vengeance is God's, let God himself revenge.

MORANZONE: Thou art God's minister of vengeance.

GUIDO: No!
God hath no minister but his own hand.
I will not kill this man.

MORANZONE: Why are you here,

If not to kill him, then?

GUIDO: Lord Moranzone,
I purpose to ascend to the Duke's chamber,
And as he lies asleep lay on his breast
The dagger and this writing; when he awakes
Then he will know who held him in his power
And slew him not: this is the noblest vengeance
Which I can take.

MORANZONE: You will not slay him?

GUIDO: No.

MORANZONE: Ignoble son of a noble father,
Who sufferest this man who sold that father
To live an hour.

GUIDO: 'Twas thou that hindered me;
I would have killed him in the open square,
The day I saw him first.

MORANZONE: It was not yet time;
Now it is time, and, like some green-faced girl,
Thou pratest of forgiveness.

GUIDO: No! revenge:
The right revenge my father's son should take.

MORANZONE: O wretched father, thus again betrayed,
And by thine own son too! You are a coward,
Take out the knife, get to the Duke's chamber,
And bring me back his heart upon the blade.
When he is dead, then you can talk to me
Of noble vengeances.

GUIDO: Upon thine honour,
And by the love thou bearest my father's name,
Dost thou think my father, that great gentleman,
That generous soldier, that most chivalrous lord,
Would have crept at night-time, like a common thief,
And stabbed an old man sleeping in his bed,
However he had wronged him: tell me that.

MORANZONE (*after some hesitation*): You have sworn an oath, see that you
     keep that oath.
Boy, do you think I do not know your secret,
Your traffic with the Duchess?

GUIDO: Silence, liar!
The very moon in heaven is not more chaste,
Nor the white stars so pure.

MORANZONE: And yet, you love her;
Weak fool, to let love in upon your life,
Save as a plaything.

GUIDO: You do well to talk:
Within your veins, old man, the pulse of youth

Throbs with no ardour. Your eyes full of rheum
Have against Beauty closed their filmy doors,
And your clogged ears, losing their natural sense,
Have shut you from the music of the world.
You talk of love! You know not what it is.

   MORANZONE: Oh, in my time, boy, I have walked i' the moon.
Swore I would live on kisses and on blisses,
Swore I would die for love, and did not die,
Wrote love bad verses; ay, and sung them badly,
Like all true lovers: Oh, I have done the tricks!
I know the partings and the chamberings;
We are all animals at best, and love
Is merely passion with a holy name.

   GUIDO: Now then I know you have not loved at all.
Love is the sacrament of life; it sets
Virtue where virtue was not; cleanses men
Of all the vile pollutions of this world;
It is the fire which purges gold from dross,
It is the fan which winnows wheat from chaff,
It is the spring which in some wintry soil
Makes innocence to blossom like a rose.
The days are over when God walked with men,
But Love, which is His image, holds His place.
When a man loves a woman, then he knows
God's secret, and the secret of the world.
There is no house so lowly or so mean,
Which, if their hearts be pure who live in it,
Love will not enter; but if bloody murder
Knock at the Palace gate and is let in,
Love like a wounded thing creeps out and dies.
This is the punishment God sets on sin.
The wicked cannot love.

A groan comes from the DUKE'S *chamber.*

                                  Ah! What is that?
Do you not hear? 'Twas nothing.
                                     So I think
That it is woman's mission by their love
To save the souls of men: and loving her,
My Lady, my white Beatrice, I begin
To see a nobler and a holier vengeance
In letting this man live, than doth reside
In bloody deeds o' night, stabs in the dark,
And young hands clutching at a palsied throat.
It was, I think, for love's sake that Lord Christ,

Who was indeed himself incarnate Love,
Bade every man forgive his enemy.

MORANZONE (*sneeringly*): That was in Palestine, not Padua;
And said for saints: I have to do with men.

GUIDO: It was for all time said.

MORANZONE: And your white Duchess,
What will she do to thank you? Will she not come,
And put her cheek to yours, and fondle you,
For having left her lord to plague her life?

GUIDO: Alas, I will not see her face again.
'Tis but twelve hours since I parted from her,
So suddenly, and with such violent passion,
That she has shut her heart against me now;
No, I will never see her.

MORANZONE: What will you do?

GUIDO: After that I have laid the dagger there,
Get hence to–night from Padua.

MORANZONE: ·   And then?

GUIDO: I will take service with the Doge at Venice,
And bid him pack me straightway to the wars,
In Holy Land against the Infidel;
And there I will, being now sick of life,
Throw that poor life against some desperate spear.

A groan from the DUKE'S *chamber again.*

Did you not hear a voice?

MORANZONE: I always hear,
From the dim confines of some sepulchre,
A voice that cries for vengeance: We waste time,
It will be morning soon; are you resolved
You will not kill the Duke?

GUIDO: I am resolved.

MORANZONE: Guido Ferranti, in that chamber yonder
There lies the man who sold your father's life,
And gave him to the hangman's murderous hands.
There does he sleep: you have your father's dagger;
Will you not kill him?

GUIDO: No, I will not kill him.

MORANZONE: O wretched father, lying unavenged.

GUIDO: More wretched were thy son a murderer.

MORANZONE: Why, what is life?

GUIDO: I do not know, my lord,
I did not give it, and I dare not take it.

MORANZONE: I do not thank God often; but I think
I thank him now that I have got no son!

And you, what bastard blood flows in your veins
That when you have your enemy in your grasp
You let him go! I would that I had left you
With the dull hinds that reared you.

GUIDO: Better perhaps
That you had done so! May be better still
I'd not been born to this distressful world.

MORANZONE: Farewell!

GUIDO: Farewell! Some day, Lord Moranzone,
You will understand my vengeance.

MORANZONE: Never, boy.

Gets out of window and exit by rope ladder.

GUIDO: Father, I think thou knowest my resolve,
And with this nobler vengeance are content.
Father, I think in letting this man live
That I am doing what you would have done.
Father, I know not if a human voice
Can pierce the iron gateway of the dead,
Or if the dead are set in ignorance
Of what we do, or do not, for their sakes.
And yet I feel a presence in the air,
There is a shadow standing at my side,
And ghostly kisses seem to touch my lips,
And leave them holier.

Kneels down.

                    O father, if 'tis thou,
Canst thou not burst through the decrees of death,
And if corporeal semblance show thyself,
That I may touch thy hand!

                              No, there is nothing.

Rises.

'Tis the night that cheats us with its phantoms,
And, like a puppet-master, makes us think
That things are real which are not. It grows late.
Now must I do my business.

Pulls out a letter from his doublet and reads it.

                              When he wakes,
And sees this letter, and the dagger with it,
Will he not have some loathing for his life,
Repent, perchance, and lead a better life,

Or will he mock because a young man spared
His natural enemy? I do not care,
Father, it is your bidding that I do,
Your bidding, and the bidding of my love
Which teaches me to know you as you are.

*Ascends staircase stealthily, and just as he reaches out his hand to draw back
the curtain the* DUCHESS *appears all in white.* GUIDO *starts back.*

DUCHESS: Guido! What do you here so late?
GUIDO: O white and spotless angel of my life,
Sure thou hast come from Heaven with a message
That mercy is more noble than revenge?
DUCHESS: Ay! I do pray for mercy earnestly.
GUIDO: O father, now I know I do your bidding,
For hand in hand with Mercy, like a God,
Has Love come forth to meet me on the way.
DUCHESS: I felt you would come back to me again,
Although you left me very cruelly:
Why did you leave me? Nay, that matters not,
For I can hold you now, and feel your heart
Beat against mine with little throbs of love:
Our hearts are two caged birds, trying to kiss
Across their cages' bars: but the time goes,
It will be morning in an hour or so;
Let us get horses: I must post to Venice,
They will not think of looking for me there.
   GUIDO: Love, I will follow you across the world.
   DUCHESS: But are you sure you love me?
   GUIDO: Is the lark
Sure that it loves the dawn that bids it sing?
   DUCHESS: Could nothing ever change you?
   GUIDO: Nothing ever:
The shipman's needle is not set more sure
Than I am to the lodestone of your love.
   DUCHESS: There is no barrier between us now.
   GUIDO: None, love, nor shall be.
   DUCHESS: I have seen to that.
   GUIDO: Tarry here for me.
   DUCHESS: No, you are not going?
You will not leave me as you did before?
   GUIDO: I will return within a moment's space,
But first I must repair to the Duke's chamber,
And leave this letter and this dagger there,
That when he wakes –
   DUCHESS: When who wakes?

GUIDO: Why, the Duke.

DUCHESS: He will not wake again.

GUIDO: What, is he dead?

DUCHESS: Ay! He is dead.

GUIDO: O God! How wonderful

Are all thy secret ways! Who would have said
That on this very night, when I had yielded
Into thy hands the vengeance that is Thine,
Thou with thy finger should have touched the man,
And bade him come before thy judgment seat.

   DUCHESS: I have just killed him.

   GUIDO (*in horror*):   Oh!

   DUCHESS: He was asleep;
Come closer, love, and I will tell you all.
Kiss me upon the mouth, and I will tell you.
You will not kiss me now? – well, you will kiss me
When I have told you how I killed the Duke.
After you left me with such bitter words,
Feeling my life went lame without your love,
I had resolved to kill myself to-night.
About an hour ago I waked from sleep,
And took my dagger from beneath my pillow,
Where I had hidden it to serve my need,
And drew it from the sheath, and felt the edge,
And thought of you, and how I loved you, Guido,
And turned to fall upon it, when I marked
The old man sleeping, full of years and sin;
There lay he muttering curses in his sleep.
And as I looked upon his evil face
Suddenly like a flame there flashed across me,
There is the barrier which Guido spoke of:
You said there lay a barrier between us,
What barrier but he? –
                     I hardly know
What happened, but a steaming mist of blood
Rose up between us two.

   GUIDO: O horrible!

DUCHESS: You would have said so had you seen that mist:
And then the air rained blood and then he groaned,
And then he groaned no more! I only heard
The dripping of the blood upon the floor.

   GUIDO: Enough, enough.

   DUCHESS: Will you not kiss me now?
Do you remember saying that women's love
Turns men to angels? Well, the love of man
Turns women into martyrs; for its sake

We do or suffer anything.

GUIDO: O God!

DUCHESS: Will you not speak?

GUIDO: I cannot speak at all.

DUCHESS: This is the knife with which I killed the Duke.
I did not think he would have bled so much,
But I can wash my hands in water after;
Can I not wash my hands? Ay, but my soul?
Let us not talk of this! Let us go hence:
Is not the barrier broken down between us?
What would you more? Come, it is almost morning.

Puts her hand on GUIDO'S

GUIDO (*breaking from her*): O damned saint! O angel fresh from Hell!
What bloody devil tempted thee to this!
That thou hast killed thy husband, that is nothing –
Hell was already gaping for his soul –
But thou hast murdered Love, and in its place
Has set a horrible and bloodstained thing,
Whose very breath breeds pestilence and plague,
And strangles Love.

DUCHESS (*in amazed wonder*): I did it all for you
I would not have you do it, had you willed it,
For I would keep you without blot or stain,
A thing unblemished, unassailed, untarnished.
Men do not know what women do for love.
Have I not wrecked my soul for your dear sake,
Here and hereafter?

                          Oh be kind to me,
I did it all for you.

GUIDO: No, do not touch me,
Between us lies a thin red stream of blood,
I dare not look across it: when you stabbed him
You stabbed Love with a sharp knife to the heart.
We cannot meet again.

DUCHESS: (*wringing her hands*): For you! For you!
I did it all for you: have you forgotten?
You said there was a barrier between us;
That barrier lies now i' the upper chamber
Upset, overthrown, beaten, and battered down,
And will not part us ever.

GUIDO: No, you mistook:
Sin was the barrier, you have raised it up;
Crime was the barrier, you have set it there.
The barrier was murder, and your hand

Oscar photographed in New York by Napoleon Sarony on his American lecture tour in 1882.

SOCIETY'S HOPES AND FEARS.

HOPE No. 2.—Mr. OSCAR WILDE.

"Let me play the lion too: I will roar, that I will do any man's heart good to hear me."
Scene II., Act I, *Midsummer Night's Dream.*

Oscar, armed with his Poems in one hand, hopes to storm America.

*Constance Lloyd painted by
Louis Desange in 1882, two
years before she became
Oscar's wife.*

Vyvyan and Cyril, Wilde's children, in aesthetic dress about 1891.

Constance Wilde with her eldest son Cyril in 1889.

Oscar, man about town, in 1889.

Oscar Wilde and Lord Alfred 'Bosie' Douglas taken in Oxford probably in the Spring of 1893.

Oscar in exile. A photograph probably taken with his own camera in Rome 1900.

The Hotel d'Alsace in Paris where Oscar Wilde lived for the last year of his life and died on 30 November 1900.

Oscar Wilde's tomb in Paris's Père-Lachaise cemetery sculpted by Jacob Epstein.

Has builded it so high it shuts out heaven,
It shuts out God.

DUCHESS: I did it all for you;
You dare not leave me now: nay, Guido, listen.
Get horses ready, we will fly to-night.
The past is a bad dream, we will forget it:
Before us lies the future: will we not have
Sweet days of love beneath our vines and laugh? —
No, no, we will not laugh, but, when we weep,
Well, we will weep together; I will serve you
Like a poor housewife, like a common slave;
I will be very meek and very gentle:
You do not know me.

GUIDO: Nay, I know you now;
Get hence, I say, out of my sight.

DUCHESS (*pacing up and down*): O God,
How I have loved this man!

GUIDO: You never loved me.
Had it been so, Love would have stopped your hand,
Nor suffered you to stain his holy shrine,
Where none can enter but the innocent.

DUCHESS: These are but words, words, words.

GUIDO: Get hence, I pray:
How could we sit together at Love's table?
You have poured poison in the sacred wine,
And Murder dips his fingers in the sop.
Rather than this I had died a thousand deaths.

DUCHESS: I having done it, die a thousand deaths.

GUIDO: It is not death but life that you should fear.

DUCHESS (*throws herself on her knees*): Then slay me now! I have spilt
    blood to-night,
You shall spill more, so we go hand in hand
To heaven or to hell. Draw your sword, Guido,
And traffic quickly for my life with Death,
Who is grown greedy of such merchandize.
Quick, let your soul go chambering in my heart,
It will but find its master's image there.
Nay, if you will not slay me with your sword,
Bid me to fall upon this reeking knife,
And I will do it.

GUIDO (*wresting knife from her*): Give it to me, I say.
O God, your very hands are wet with blood!
This place is Hell, I cannot tarry here.

DUCHESS: Will you not raise me up before you go,
Or must I like a beggar keep my knees.

GUIDO: I pray you let me see your face no more.

DUCHESS: Better for me I had not seen your face.
O think it was for you I killed this man.

GUIDO *recoils: she seizes his hands as she kneels.*

Nay, Guido, listen for a while:
Until you came to Padua I lived
Wretched indeed, but with no murderous thought,
Very submissive to a cruel Lord,
Very obedient to unjust commands,
As pure I think as any gentle girl
Who now would turn in horror from my hands –
You came: ah! Guido, the first kindly words
I ever heard since I had come from France
Were from your lips: well, well, that is no matter.
You came, and in the passion of your eyes
I read love's meaning, everything you said
Touched my dumb soul to music, and you seemed
Fair as that young Saint Michael on the wall
In Santa Croce, where we go and pray.
I wonder will I ever pray again?
Well, you were fair, and in your boyish face
The morning seemed to lighten, so I loved you.
And yet I did not tell you of my love.
'Twas you who sought me out, knelt at my feet
As I kneel now at yours, and with sweet vows,

Kneels.

Whose music seems to linger in my ears,
Swore that you loved me, and I trusted you.
I think there are many women in the world
Who had they been unto this vile Duke mated,
Chained to his side, as the poor galley slave
Is to a leper chained, – ay! Many women
Who would have tempted you to kill the man.
I did not.
            Yet I know that had I done so,
I had not been thus humbled in the dust.

Stands up.

But you have loved me very faithfully.

After a pause approaches him timidly.

I do not think you understand me, Guido:
It was for your sake that I wrought this deed
Whose horror now chills my young blood to ice,
For your sake only.

Stretching out her arm.

                     Will you not speak to me?
Love me a little: in my girlish life
I have been starved for love, and kindliness
Has passed me by.
    GUIDO: I dare not look at you:
You come to me with too pronounced a favour,
Get to your tirewomen.
    DUCHESS: Ay, there it is!
There speaks the man! Yet had you come to me
With any heavy sin upon your soul,
Some murder done for hire, not for love,
Why, I had sat and watched at your bedside
All through the night-time, lest Remorse might come
And pour his poisons in your ear, and so
Keep you from sleeping! Sure it is the guilty,
Who, being very wretched, need love most.
    GUIDO: There is no love where there is any guilt,
    DUCHESS: No love where there is any guilt! O God,
How differently do we love from men!
There is many a woman here in Padua,
Some workman's wife, or ruder artisan's,
Whose husband spends the wages of the week
In a coarse revel, or a tavern brawl,
And reeling home late on the Saturday night,
Finds his wife sitting by a fireless hearth,
Trying to hush the child who cries for hunger,
And then sets to and beats his wife because
The child is hungry, and the fire black.
Yet the wife loves him! And will rise next day
With some red bruise across a careworn face,
And sweep the house, and do the common service,
And try and smile, and only be too glad
If he does not beat her a second time
Before her child! – that is how women love.

A pause: GUIDO *says nothing.*

Do you say nothing? Oh be kind to me
While yet I know the summer of my days.

I think you will not drive me from your side.
Where have I got to go if you reject me? –
You for whose sake this hand has murdered life,
You for whose sake my soul has wrecked itself
Beyond all hope of pardon.

GUIDO: Get thee gone:
The dead man is a ghost, and our love too,
Flits like a ghost about its desolate tomb,
And wanders through this charnel house, and weeps
That when you slew your lord you slew it also.
Do you not see?

DUCHESS: I see when men love women
They give them but a little of their lives,
But women when they love give everything;
I see that, Guido, now.

GUIDO: Away, away,
And come not back till you have waked your dead.

DUCHESS: I would to God that I could wake the dead,
Put vision in the glazèd eyes, and give
The tongue its natural utterance, and bid
The heart to beat again; that cannot be:
For what is done, is done: and what is dead
Is dead for ever: the fire cannot warm him:
The winter cannot hurt him with its snows;
Something has gone from him; if you call him now,
He will not answer; if you mock him now,
He will not laugh; and if you stab him now
He will not bleed.

                    I would that I could wake him!
O God, put back the sun a little space,
And from the roll of time blot out to-night,
And bid it not have been! Put back the sun,
And make me what I was an hour ago!
No, no, time will not stop for anything,
Nor the sun stay its courses, though Repentance
Calling it back grow hoarse; but you, my love,
Have you no word of pity even for me?
O Guido, Guido, will you not kiss me once?
Drive me not to some desperate resolve:
Women grow mad when they are treated thus:
Will you not kiss me once?

GUIDO (holding up knife): I will not kiss you
Until the blood grows dry upon this knife,
And not even then.

DUCHESS: Dear Christ! How little pity
We women get in this untimely world;

Men lure us to some dreadful precipice,
And, when we fall, they leave us.

GUIDO (*wildly*):   Back to your dead!

DUCHESS (*going up the stairs*): Why, then I will be gone! And may you find
More mercy than you showed to me to-night!

GUIDO: Let me find mercy when I go at night
And do foul murder.

DUCHESS (*coming down a few steps*): Murder did you say?
Murder is hungry, and still cries for more,
And Death, his brother, is not satisfied,
But walks the house, and will not go away,
Unless he has a comrade! Tarry, Death,
For I will give thee a most faithful lackey
To travel with thee! Murder, call no more,
For thou shalt eat thy fill.

                              There is a storm
Will break upon this house before the morning,
So horrible, that the white moon already
Turns grey and sick with terror, the low wind
Goes moaning round the house, and the high stars
Run madly through the vaulted firmament,
As through the night wept tears of liquid fire
For what the day shall look upon. O weep,
Thou lamentable heaven! Weep thy fill!
Though sorrow like a cataract drench the fields,
And make the earth one bitter lake of tears,
It would not be enough.

A peal of thunder.

                              Do you not hear,
There is artillery in the Heaven to-night.
Vengeance is wakened up, and has unloosed
His dogs upon the world, and in this matter
Which lies between us two, let him who draws
The thunder on his head beware the ruin
Which the forked flame brings after.

A flash of lightning followed by a peal of thunder.

GUIDO: Away! Away!

Exit the DUCHESS, *who as she lifts the crimson curtain looks back for a moment at* GUIDO, *but he makes no sign. More thunder.*

Now is life fallen in ashes at my feet.

And noble self-slain; and in its place
Crept murder with its silent bloody feet.
And she who wrought it – Oh! And yet she loved me,
And for my sake did do this dreadful thing.
I have been cruel to her: Beatrice!
Beatrice, I say, come back.

Begins to ascend staircase, when the noise of Soldiers is heard.

                    Ah! What is that?
Torches ablaze, and noise of hurrying feet.
Pray God they have not seized her.

Noise grows louder.

                    Beatrice!
There is yet time to escape. Come down, come out!

The voice of the DUCHESS *outside.*

This way went he, the man who slew my lord.

Down the staircase come hurrying a confused body of Soldiers; GUIDO *is no
seen at first, till the* DUCHESS *surrounded by Servants carrying torches ap
pears at the top of the staircase, and points to* GUIDO, *who is seized at once
one of the Soldiers dragging the knife from his hand and showing it to the Cap
tain of the Guard in sight of the audience.*

TABLEAU.

ACT DROP

ACT FOUR

SCENE: *The Court of Justice: the walls are hung with stamped
grey velvet: above the hangings the wall is red, and gilt symbol-
ical figures bear up the roof, which is made of red beams with sof-
fits and grey moulding: a canopy of white satin flowered with
gold is set for the Duchess: below it a long bench with red cloth for
the Judges: below that a table for the clerks of the Court. Two
soldiers stand on each side of the canopy, and two soldiers guard
the door; the citizens have some of them collected in the Court,
others are coming in greeting one another; two tipstaffs in violet
keep order with long white wands.*

FIRST CITIZEN: Good morrow, neighbour Anthony.
SECOND CITIZEN: Good morrow, neighbour Dominick.

FIRST CITIZEN: This is a strange day for Padua, is it not? – the Duke being dead.

SECOND CITIZEN: I tell you, neighbour Dominick, I have not known such a day since the last Duke died: and if you believe me not, I am no true man.

FIRST CITIZEN: They will try him first, and sentence him afterwards, will they not, neighbour Anthony?

SECOND CITIZEN: Nay, for he might 'scape his punishment then; but they will condemn him first so that he gets his deserts, and give him trial afterwards so that no injustice is done.

FIRST CITIZEN: Well, well, it will go hard with him I doubt not.

SECOND CITIZEN: Surely it is a grievous thing to shed a Duke's blood.

THIRD CITIZEN: They say a Duke has blue blood.

SECOND CITIZEN: I think our Duke's blood was black like his soul.

FIRST CITIZEN: Have a watch, neighbour Anthony, the officer is looking at thee.

SECOND CITIZEN: I care not if he does but look at me; he cannot whip me with the lashes of his eye.

THIRD CITIZEN: What think you of this young man who stuck the knife into the Duke?

SECOND CITIZEN: Why, that he is a well-behaved, and a well-meaning, and a well-favoured lad, and yet wicked in that he killed the Duke.

THIRD CITIZEN: 'Twas the first time he did it: may be the law will not be hard on him, as he did not do it before.

SECOND CITIZEN: True.

TIPSTAFF: Silence, knave.

SECOND CITIZEN: Am I thy looking-glass, Master Tipstaff, that thou callest me knave?

FIRST CITIZEN: Here be one of the household coming. Well, Dame Lucy, thou art of the Court, how does thy poor mistress the Duchess, with her sweet face?

MISTRESS LUCY: O well-a-day! O miserable day! O day! O misery! Why it is just nineteen years last June, at Michaelmas, since I was married to my husband, and it is August now, and here is the Duke murdered; there is a co-incidence for you!

SECOND CITIZEN: Why, if it is coincidence, they may not kill the young man: there is no law against coincidences.

FIRST CITIZEN: But how does the Duchess?

MISTRESS LUCY: Well, well, I knew some harm would happen to the house: six weeks ago the cakes were all burned on one side, and last Saint Martin even as ever was, there flew into the candle a big moth that had wings, and almost scared me.

FIRST CITIZEN: But come to the Duchess, good gossip: what of her?

MISTRESS LUCY: Marry, it is time you should ask after her, poor lady; she is distraught almost. Why, she has not slept, but paced the chamber all night long. I prayed her to have a posset, or some *aquavitæ*, and to get to bed and sleep a little for her health's sake, but she answered me she was afraid she might dream. That was a strange answer, was it not?

SECOND CITIZEN: These great folk have not much sense, so Providence makes it up to them in fine clothes.

MISTRESS LUCY: Well, well, God keep murder from us, I say, as long as we are alive.

Enter LORD MORANZONE *hurriedly.*

MORANZONE: Is the Duke dead?

SECOND CITIZEN: He has a knife in his heart, which they say is not healthy for any man.

MORANZONE: Who is accused of having killed him?

SECOND CITIZEN: Why, the prisoner, sir.

MORANZONE: But who is the prisoner?

SECOND CITIZEN: Why, he that is accused of the Duke's murder.

MORANZONE: I mean, what is his name?

SECOND CITIZEN: Faith, the same which his godfathers gave him: what else should it be?

TIPSTAFF: Guido Ferranti is his name, my lord.

MORANZONE: I almost knew thine answer ere you gave it.

Aside.

Yet it is strange he should have killed the Duke,
Seeing he left me in such different mood.
It is most likely when he saw the man,
This devil who had sold his father's life,
That passion from their seat within his heart
Thrust all his boyish theories of love,
And in their place set vengeance; yet I marvel
That he escaped not.

Turning again to the crowd.

How was he taken, tell me.

THIRD CITIZEN: Marry, sir, he was taken by the heels.

MORANZONE: But who seized him?

THIRD CITIZEN: Why, those that did lay hold of him.

MORANZONE: How was the alarm given?

THIRD CITIZEN: That I cannot tell you, sir.

MISTRESS LUCY: It was the Duchess herself who pointed him out.

MORANZONE (*aside*): The Duchess! There is something strange in this.

MISTRESS LUCY: Ay! And the dagger was in his hand – the Duchess's own dagger.

MORANZONE: What did you say?

MISTRESS LUCY: Why, marry, that it was with the Duchess's dagger that the Duke was killed.

MORANZONE (*aside*): There is some mystery about this: I cannot understand it.

SECOND CITIZEN: They be very long a-coming.

FIRST CITIZEN: I warrant they will come soon enough for the prisoner.

TIPSTAFF: Silence in the Court!

FIRST CITIZEN: Thou dost break silence in bidding us keep it, Master Tipstaff.

Enter the LORD JUSTICE *and the other Judges.*

SECOND CITIZEN: Who is he in scarlet? Is he the headsman?

THIRD CITIZEN: Nay, he is the Lord Justice.

Enter GUIDO *guarded.*

SECOND CITIZEN: There be the prisoner surely.

THIRD CITIZEN: He looks honest.

FIRST CITIZEN: That be his villainy: knaves nowadays do look so honest that honest folk are forced to look like knaves so as to be different.

Enter the Headsman, who takes his stand behind GUIDO.

SECOND CITIZEN: Yon be the headsman then! O Lord! Is the axe sharp, think you?

FIRST CITIZEN: Ay! Sharper than thy wits are; but the edge is not towards him, mark you.

SECOND CITIZEN (*scratching his neck*): I' faith, I like it not so near.

FIRST CITIZEN: Tut, thou need'st not be afraid; they never cut the heads of common folk: they do but hang us.

Trumpets outside.

THIRD CITIZEN: What are the trumpets for? Is the trial over?

FIRST CITIZEN: Nay, 'tis for the Duchess.

Enter the DUCHESS *in black velvet; her train of flowered black velvet is carried by two pages in violet; with her is the* CARDINAL *in scarlet, and the gentlemen of the Court in black; she takes her seat on the throne above the Judges, who rise and take their caps off as she enters; the* CARDINAL *sits next to her a little lower; the Courtiers group themselves about the throne.*

SECOND CITIZEN: O poor lady, how pale she is! Will she sit there?

FIRST CITIZEN: Ay! She is in the Duke's place now.

SECOND CITIZEN: That is a good thing for Padua; the Duchess is a very kind and merciful Duchess; why, she cured my child of the ague once.

THIRD CITIZEN: Ay, and has given us bread: do not forget the bread.
A SOLDIER: Stand back, good people.
SECOND CITIZEN: If we be good, why should we stand back?
TIPSTAFF: Silence in the Court!
LORD JUSTICE: May it please your Grace,
Is it your pleasure we proceed to trial
of the Duke's murder?

> DUCHESS *bows*.

                          Set the prisoner forth.
What is thy name?
GUIDO: It matters not, my lord.
LORD JUSTICE: Guido Ferranti is thy name in Padua.
GUIDO: A man may die as well under that name as any other.
LORD JUSTICE: Thou art not ignorant
What dreadful charge men lay against thee here,
Namely, the treacherous murder of thy Lord,
Simone Gesso, Duke of Padua;
What dost thou say in answer?
GUIDO: I say nothing.
LORD JUSTICE: Dost thou admit this accusation, then?
GUIDO: I admit naught, and yet I naught deny.
I pray thee, my Lord Justice, be as brief
As the Court's custom and the laws allow.
I will not speak.
LORD JUSTICE: Why, then, it cannot be
That of this murder thou art innocent,
But rather that thy stony obstinate heart
Hath shut its doors against the voice of justice.
Think not thy silence will avail thee aught,
'Twill rather aggravate thy desperate guilt,
Of which indeed we are most well assured;
Again I bid thee speak.
GUIDO: I will say nothing.
LORD JUSTICE: Then naught remains for me but to pronounce
Upon thy head the sentence of swift Death.
GUIDO: I pray thee give thy message speedily.
Thou couldst not bring me anything more dear.
LORD JUSTICE (*rising*): Guido Ferranti –
MORANZONE (*stepping from the crowd*): Tarry, my Lord Justice.
LORD JUSTICE: Who art thou that bid'st justice tarry, sir?
MORANZONE: So be it justice it can go its way;
But if it be not justice –
LORD JUSTICE: Who is this?
COUNT BARDI: A very noble gentleman, and well known
To the late Duke.

LORD JUSTICE: Sir, thou art come in time
To see the murder of the Duke avenged.
There stands the man who did this heinous thing.

MORANZONE: Has merely blind suspicion fixed on him,
Or have ye any proof he did the deed?

LORD JUSTICE: Thrice has the Court entreated him to speak,
But surely guilt weighs heavy on the tongue,
For he says nothing in defence, nor tries
To purge himself of this most dread account,
Which innocence would surely do.

MORANZONE: My lord,
I ask again what proof have ye?

LORD JUSTICE (*holding up the dagger*): This dagger,
Which from his blood-stained hands, itself all blood,
Last night the soldiers seized: what further proof
Need we indeed?

MORANZONE (*takes the dagger and approaches the* DUCHESS): Saw I not
    such a dagger
Hang from your Grace's girdle yesterday?

The DUCHESS *shudders and makes no answer.*

Ah! my Lord Justice, may I speak a moment
With this young man, who in such peril stands?

LORD JUSTICE: Ay, willingly, my lord, and may you turn him
To make a full avowal of his guilt.

LORD MORANZONE *goes over to* GUIDO, *who stands R. and clutches him
    by the hand.*

MORANZONE (*in a low voice*): She did it! Nay, I saw it in her eyes.
Boy, dost thou think I'll let thy father's son
Be by this woman butchered to his death?
Her husband sold your father, and the wife
Would sell the son in turn.

GUIDO: Lord Moranzone,
I alone did this thing: be satisfied,
My father is avenged.

MORANZONE: Enough, enough,
I know you did not kill him; had it been you,
Your father's dagger, not this woman's toy,
Had done the business: see how she glares at us!
By heaven, I will tear off that marble mask,
And tax her with this murder before all.

GUIDO: You shall not do it.

MORANZONE: Nay, be sure I shall.

GUIDO: My lord, you must not dare to speak.

MORANZONE: Why not?

If she is innocent she can prove it so;
If guilty, let her die.

GUIDO: What shall I do?

MORANZONE: Or thou or I shall tell the truth in Court.

GUIDO: The truth is that I did it.

MORANZONE: Sayest thou so?
Well, I will see what the good Duchess says.

GUIDO: No, no, I'll tell the tale.

MORANZONE: That is well, Guido.
Her sins be on her head and not on thine.
Did she not give you to the guard?

GUIDO: She did.

MORANZONE: Then upon her revenge thy father's death:
She was the wife of Judas.

GUIDO: Ay, she was.

MORANZONE: I think you need no prompting now to do it,
Though you were weak and like a boy last night.

GUIDO: Weak like a boy, was I indeed last night?
Be sure I will not be like that to-day.

LORD JUSTICE: Doth he confess?

GUIDO: My lord, I do confess.
That foul unnatural murder has been done.

FIRST CITIZEN: Why, look at that: he has a pitiful heart, and does not like
murder; they will let him go for that.

LORD JUSTICE: Say you no more?

GUIDO: My lord, I say this also,
That to spill human blood is deadly sin.

SECOND CITIZEN: Marry, he should tell that to the headsman: 'tis a good
sentiment.

GUIDO: Lastly, my lord, I do entreat the Court
To give me leave to utter openly
The dreadful secret of this mystery,
And to point out the very guilty one
Who with this dagger last night slew the Duke.

LORD JUSTICE: Thou hast leave to speak.

DUCHESS (*rising*):   I say he shall not speak:
What need have we of further evidence?
Was he not taken in the house at night
In Guilt's own bloody livery.

LORD JUSTICE (*showing her the statute*): Your Grace
Can read the law.

DUCHESS (*waiving book aside*): Bethink you, my Lord Justice,
Is it not very like that such a one
May, in the presence of the people here,
Utter some slanderous word against my Lord,
Against the city, or the city's honour,

Perchance against myself.

LORD JUSTICE: My liege, the law.

DUCHESS: He shall not speak, but, with gags in his mouth,
Shall climb the ladder to the bloody block.

LORD JUSTICE: The law, my liege.

DUCHESS: We are not bound by law,
But with it we bind others.

MORANZONE: My Lord Justice,
Thou wilt not suffer this injustice here.

LORD JUSTICE: The Court needs not thy voice, Lord Moranzone.
Madam, it were a precedent most evil
To wrest the law from its appointed course,
For, though the cause be just, yet anarchy
Might on this licence touch these golden scales
And unjust causes unjust victories gain.

COUNT BARDI: I do not think your Grace can stay the law.

DUCHESS: Ay, it is well to preach and prate of law:
Methinks, my haughty lords of Padua,
If ye are hurt in pocket or estate,
So much as makes your monstrous revenues
Less by the value of one ferry toll,
Ye do not wait the tedious law's delay
With such sweet patience as ye counsel me.

COUNT BARDI: Madam, I think you wrong our nobles here.

DUCHESS: I think I wrong them not. Which of ye all
Finding a thief within his house at night,
With some poor chattel thrust into his rags,
Will stop and parley with him? Do ye not
Give him unto the officer and his hook
To be dragged gaolwards straightway? And so now,
Had ye been men, finding this fellow here,
With my Lord's life still hot upon his hands,
Ye would have haled him out into the court,
And struck his head off with an axe.

GUIDO: O God!

DUCHESS: Speak, my Lord Justice.

LORD JUSTICE: Your Grace, it cannot be:
The laws of Padua are most certain here:
And by those laws the common murderer even
May with his own lips plead, and make defence.

DUCHESS: Tarry a little with thy righteousness.
This is no common murderer, Lord Justice,
But a great outlaw, and a most vile traitor,
Taken in open arms against the state.
For he who slays the man who rules a state
Slays the state also, widows every wife,

And makes each child an orphan, and no less
Is to be held a public enemy,
Than if he came with mighty ordonnance,
And all the spears of Venice at his back,
To beat and batter at our city gates –
Nay, is more dangerous to our commonwealth
Than gleaming spears and thundering ordonnance,
For walls and gates, bastions and forts, and things
Whose common elements are wood and stone
May be raised up, but who can raise again
The ruined body of my murdered lord,
And bid it live and laugh?

   MAFFIO: Now by Saint Paul
I do not think that they will let him speak.

   JEPPO VITELLOZZO: There is much in this, listen.

   DUCHESS: Wherefore now,
Throw ashes on the head of Padua,
With sable banners hang each silent street,
Let every man be clad in solemn black,
But ere we turn to these sad rites of mourning
Let us bethink us of the desperate hand
Which wrought and brought this ruin on our state,
And straightway pack him to that narrow house,
Where no voice is, but with a little dust
Death fills up the lying mouths of men.

   GUIDO: Unhand me, knaves! I tell thee, my Lord Justice,
Thou mightest as well bid the untrammeled ocean,
The winter whirlwind, or the Alpine storm,
Nor roar their will, as bid me hold my peace!
Ay! Though ye put your knives into my throat,
Each grim and gaping wound shall find a tongue,
And cry against you.

   LORD JUSTICE: Sir, this violence
Avails you nothing; for save the tribunal
Give thee a lawful right to open speech,
Naught that thou sayest can be credited.

   The DUCHESS *smiles and* GUIDO *falls back with a gesture of despair.*

Madam, myself, and these wise Justices,
Will with your Grace's sanction now retire
Into another chamber, to decide
And search the statutes and the precedents.

   DUCHESS: Go, my Lord Justice, search the statutes well,
Nor let this brawling traitor have his way.

   MORANZONE: Go, my Lord Justice, search thy conscience well,

Nor let a man be sent to death unheard.

Exit the LORD JUSTICE *and the Judges.*

DUCHESS: Silence, thou evil genius of my life!
Thou com'st between us two a second time;
This time, my lord, I think the turn is mine.
    GUIDO: I shall not die till I have uttered voice.
    DUCHESS: Thou shalt die silent, and thy secret with thee.
    GUIDO: Art thou that Beatrice, Duchess of Padua?
    DUCHESS: I am what thou hast made me; look at me well,
I am thy handiwork.
    MAFFIO: See, is she not
Like that white tigress which we saw at Venice,
Sent by some Indian soldan to the Doge.
    JEPPO: Hush! She may hear thy chatter.
    HEADSMAN: My young fellow,
I do not know why thou shouldst care to speak,
Seeing my axe is close upon thy neck,
And words of thine will never blunt its edge.
But if thou art so bent upon it, why
Thou mightest plead unto the Churchman yonder:
The common people call him kindly here,
Indeed I know he has a kindly soul.
    GUIDO: This man, whose trade is death, hath courtesies
More than the others.
    HEADSMAN: Why, God love you, sir,
I'll do you your last service on this earth.
    GUIDO: My good Lord Cardinal, in a Christian land,
With Lord Christ's face of mercy looking down
From the high seat of Judgment, shall a man
Die unabsolved, unshrived? And if not so
May I not tell this dreadful tale of sin,
If any sin there be upon my soul.
    DUCHESS: Thou dost but waste thy time.
    CARDINAL: Alack, my son,
I have no power with the secular arm.
My task begins when justice has been done,
To urge the wavering sinner to repent
And to confess to Holy Church's ear
The dreadful secrets of a sinful mind.
    DUCHESS: Thou mayest speak to the confessional
Until thy lips grow weary of their tale,
But here thou shalt not speak.
    GUIDO: My reverend father,
You bring me but cold comfort.

CARDINAL: Nay, my son,
For the great power of our mother Church,
Ends not with this poor bubble of a world,
Of which we are but dust, as Jerome saith,
For if the sinner doth repentant die,
Our prayers and holy masses much avail
To bring the guilty soul from purgatory.

DUCHESS: And when in purgatory thou seest my Lord
With that red star of blood upon his heart,
Tell him I sent thee hither.

GUIDO: O dear God!

MORANZONE: This is the woman, is it, whom you loved?

CARDINAL: Your Grace is very cruel to this man.

DUCHESS: No more than he was cruel to her Grace.

CARDINAL: Ay! He did slay your husband.

DUCHESS: Ay! He did.

CARDINAL: Yet mercy is the sovereign right of princes.

DUCHESS: I got no mercy, and I give it not.
He hath changed my heart into a heart of stone,
He hath sown rank nettles in a goodly field,
He hath poisoned the wells of pity in my breast,
He hath withered up all kindness at the root;
My life is as some famine-murdered land,
Whence all good things have perished utterly:
I am what he hath made me.

The DUCHESS *weeps.*

JEPPO: Is it not strange
That she should so have loved the wicked Duke?

MAFFIO: It is most strange when women love their lords,
And when they love them not it is most strange.

JEPPO: What a philosopher thou art, Petrucci!

MAFFIO: Ay! I can bear the ills of other men,
Which is philosophy.

DUCHESS: They tarry long,
These greybeards and their council; bid them come;
Bid them come quickly, else I think my heart
Will beat itself to bursting: not indeed, that I here care to live:
God knows my life
Is not so full of joy, yet, for all that,
I would not die companionless, or go
Lonely to Hell.

                    Look, my Lord Cardinal,
Canst thou not see across my forehead here,
In scarlet letters writ, the word Revenge?

Fetch me some water, I will wash it off:
'Twas branded there last night, but in the daytime
I need not wear it, need I, my Lord Cardinal?
Oh how it sears and burns into my brain:
Give me a knife; not that one, but another,
And I will cut it out.

CARDINAL: It is most natural
To be incensed against the murderous hand
That treacherously stabbed your sleeping lord.

DUCHESS: I would, old Cardinal, I could burn that hand;
But it will burn hereafter.

CARDINAL: Nay, the Church
Ordains us to forgive our enemies.

DUCHESS: Forgiveness? What is that? I never got it.
They come at last: well, my Lord Justice, well.

Enter the LORD JUSTICE.

LORD JUSTICE: Most gracious Lady, and our sovereign Liege,
We have long pondered on the point at issue,
And much considered of your Grace's wisdom,
And never wisdom spake from fairer lips –

DUCHESS: Proceed, sir, without compliment.

LORD JUSTICE: We find,
As your own Grace did rightly signify,
That any citizen, who by force or craft
Conspires against the person of the Liege,
Is *ipso facto* outlaw, void of rights
Such as pertain to other citizens,
Is traitor, and a public enemy,
Who may by any casual sword be slain
Without the slayer's danger, nay if brought
Into the presence of the tribunal,
Must with dumb lips and silence reverent
Listen unto his well-deserved doom,
Nor has the privilege of open speech.

DUCHESS: I thank thee, my Lord Justice, heartily;
I like your law: and now I pray dispatch
This public outlaw to his righteous doom;
For I am weary, and the headsman weary,
What is there more?

LORD JUSTICE: Ay, there is more, your Grace.
This man being alien born, not Paduan,
Nor by allegiance bound unto the Duke,
Save such as common nature doth lay down,
Hath, though accused of treasons manifold,

Whose slightest penalty is certain death,
Yet still the right of public utterance
Before the people and the open Court,
Nay, shall be much entreated by the Court,
To make some formal pleading for his life,
Lest his own city, righteously incensed,
Should with an unjust trial tax our state,
And wars spring up against the commonwealth:
So merciful are the laws of Padua
Unto the stranger living in her gates.

    DUCHESS: Being of my Lord's household, is he stranger here?
    LORD JUSTICE: Ay, until seven years of service spent
He cannot be a Paduan citizen.
    GUIDO: I thank thee, my Lord Justice, heartily;
I like your law.
    SECOND CITIZEN: I like no law at all:
Were there no law there'd be no law-breakers,
So all men would be virtuous.
    FIRST CITIZEN: So they would;
'Tis a wise saying that, and brings you far.
    TIPSTAFF: Ay! To the gallows, knave.
    DUCHESS: Is this the law?
    LORD JUSTICE: It is the law most certainly, my liege.
    DUCHESS: Show me the book: 'tis written in blood-red.
    JEPPO: Look at the Duchess.
    DUCHESS: Thou accursed law,
I would that I could tear thee from the state
As easy as I tear thee from this book.

    Tears out the page.

Come here, Count Bardi: are you honourable?
Get a horse ready for me at my house,
For I must ride to Venice instantly.
    BARDI: To Venice, Madam?
    DUCHESS: Not a word of this.
Go, go at once.

    Exit COUNT BARDI.

                A moment, my Lord Justice.
If, as thou sayest it, this is the law –
Nay, nay, I doubt not that thou sayest right,
Though right be wrong in such a case as this –
May I not by virtue of mine office
Adjourn this Court until another day?

LORD JUSTICE: Madam, you cannot stay a trial for blood.

DUCHESS: I will not tarry then to hear this man
Rail with rude tongue against our sacred person.
I have some business also in my house
Which I must do: Come, gentlemen.

LORD JUSTICE: My liege,
You cannot leave this court until the prisoner
Be purged or guilty of this dread offence.

DUCHESS: Cannot, Lord Justice? By what right do you
Set barriers in my path where I should go?
Am I not Duchess here in Padua,
And the state's regent?

LORD JUSTICE: For that reason, Madam,
Being the fountain-head of life and death
Whence, like a mighty river, justice flows,
Without thy presence justice is dried up
And fails of purpose: thou must tarry here.

DUCHESS: What, wilt thou keep me here against my will?

LORD JUSTICE: We pray thy will be not against the law.

DUCHESS: What if I force my way out of the Court?

LORD JUSTICE: Thou canst not force the Court to give thee way.

DUCHESS: I will not tarry. (*Rises from her seat.*)

LORD JUSTICE: Is the usher here?
Let him stand forth. (*Usher comes forward.*)
                    Thou knowest thy business, sir.

The Usher closes the doors of the Court, which are L., and when the DUCH-
ESS *and her retinue approach, kneels down.*

USHER: In all humility I beseech your Grace
Turn not my duty to discourtesy,
Nor make my unwelcome office an offence.
The self-same laws which make your Grace the Regent
Bid me watch here: my Liege, to break those laws
Is but to break thine office and not mine.

DUCHESS: Is there no gentleman amongst you all
To prick this prating fellow from our way?

MAFFIO (*drawing his sword*): Ay ! That will I.

LORD JUSTICE: Count Maffio, have a care,
And you, sir. (*To* JEPPO.)
                    The first man who draws his sword
Upon the meanest officer of this Court,
Dies before nightfall.

DUCHESS: Sirs, put up your swords:
It is most meet that I should hear this man. (*Goes back to throne.*)

MORANZONE: Now has thou got thy enemy in thy hand.

LORD JUSTICE (*taking the time-glass up*): Guido Ferranti, while the crumbling sand
Falls through this time-glass, thou hast leave to speak.
This and no more.

GUIDO: It is enough, my lord.

LORD JUSTICE: Thou standest on the extreme verge of death;
See that thou speakest nothing but the truth,
Naught else will serve thee.

GUIDO: If I speak it not,
Then give my body to the headsman there.

LORD JUSTICE (*turns the time-glass*): Let there be silence while the prisoner speaks.

TIPSTAFF: Silence in the Court there.

GUIDO: My Lords Justices.
And reverent judges of this worthy court,
I hardly know where to begin my tale,
So strangely dreadful is this history.
First, let me tell you of what birth I am.
I am the son of that good Duke Lorenzo
Who was with damned treachery done to death
By a most wicked villain, lately Duke
Of this good town of Padua.

LORD JUSTICE: Have a care,
It will avail thee nought to mock this prince
Who now lies in his coffin.

MAFFIO: By Saint James,
This is the Duke of Parma's rightful heir.

JEPPO: I always thought him noble.

GUIDO: I confess
That with the purport of a just revenge,
A most just vengeance on a man of blood,
I entered the Duke's household, served his will,
Sat at his board, drank of his wine, and was
His intimate: so much I will confess,
And this too, that I waited till he grew
To give the fondest secrets of his life
Into my keeping, till he fawned on me,
And trusted me in every private matter
Even as my noble father trusted him;
That for this thing I waited.   (*To the Headsman.*)
                          Thou man of blood!
Turn not thine axe on me before the time:
Who knows if it be time for me to die?
Is there no other neck in court but mine?

LORD JUSTICE: The sand within the time-glass flows apace.
Come quickly to the murder of the Duke.

GUIDO: I will be brief: Last night at twelve o' the clock,
By a strong rope I scaled the palace wall,
With purport to revenge my father's murder –
Ay! With that purport I confess, my lord.
This much I will acknowledge, and this also,
That as with stealthy feet I climbed the stair
Which led unto the chamber of the Duke,
And reached my hand out for the scarlet cloth
Which shook and shivered in the gusty door,
Lo! The white moon that sailed in the great heaven
Flooded with silver light the darkened room,
Night lit her candles for me, and I saw
The man I hated, cursing in his sleep,
And thinking of a most dear father murdered,
Sold to the scaffold, bartered to the block,
I smote the treacherous villain to the heart
With this same dagger, which by chance I found
Within the chamber.

    DUCHESS (*rising from her seat*): Oh!

    GUIDO (*hurriedly*):   I killed the Duke.
Now, my Lord Justice, if I may crave a boon,
Suffer me not to see another sun
Light up the misery of this loathsome world.

    LORD JUSTICE: Thy boon is granted, thou shalt die to-night.
Lead him away: Come, Madam.

    GUIDO *is led off; as he goes the* DUCHESS *stretches out her arms and rushes down the stage.*

    DUCHESS: Guido! Guido! (*Faints.*)

                TABLEAU

               ACT DROP

ACT FIVE

SCENE: *A dungeon in the public prison of Padua; Guido lies asleep on a pallet (L.C.); a table with a goblet on it is set (L.C.); five soldiers are drinking and playing dice in the corner on a stone table; one of them has a lantern hung to his halbert; a torch is set in the wall over Guido's head. Two grated windows behind, one on each side of the door which is (C.), look out into a passage; the stage is rather dark.*

    FIRST SOLDIER (*throws dice*): Sixes again! Good Pietro.

    SECOND SOLDIER: I' faith, lieutenant, I will play with thee no more. I will lose everything.

THIRD SOLDIER: Except thy wits; thou art safe there!

SECOND SOLDIER: Ay, ay, he cannot take them from me.

THIRD SOLDIER: No; for thou hast no wits to give him.

THE SOLDIERS (*loudly*): Ha! Ha! Ha!

FIRST SOLDIER: Silence! You will wake the prisoner; he is asleep.

SECOND SOLDIER: What matter? He will get sleep enough when he is buried. I warrant he'd be glad if we could wake him when he's in the grave.

THIRD SOLDIER: Nay! For when he wakes there it will be judgment day.

SECOND SOLDIER: Ay, and he has done a grievous thing; for, look you, to murder one of us who are but flesh and blood is a sin and to kill a Duke goes being near against the law.

FIRST SOLDIER: Well, well, he was a wicked Duke.

SECOND SOLDIER: And so he should not have touched him; if one meddles with wicked people, one is like to be tainted with their wickedness.

THIRD SOLDIER: Ay, that is true. How old is the prisoner?

SECOND SOLDIER: Old enough to do wrong, and not old enough to be wise.

FIRST SOLDIER: Why, then, he might be any age.

SECOND SOLDIER: They say the Duchess wanted to pardon him.

FIRST SOLDIER: Is that so?

SECOND SOLDIER: Ay, and did much entreat the Lord Justice, but he would not.

FIRST SOLDIER: I had thought, Pietro, that the Duchess was omnipotent.

SECOND SOLDIER: True, she is well-favoured; I know none so comely.

THE SOLDIERS: Ha! Ha! Ha!

FIRST SOLDIER: I meant I had thought our Duchess could do anything.

SECOND SOLDIER: Nay, for he is now given over to the Justices, and they will see that justice be done; they and stout Hugh the headsman; but when his head is off, why then the Duchess can pardon him if she like; there is no law against that.

FIRST SOLDIER: I do not think that stout Hugh, as you call him, will do the business for him after all. This Guido is of gentle birth, and so by the law can drink poison first, if it so be his pleasure.

THIRD SOLDIER: Faith, to drink poison is a poor pleasure.

SECOND SOLDIER: What kind of poison is it?

FIRST SOLDIER: Why, of the kind that kills.

SECOND SOLDIER: What sort of a thing is poison?

FIRST SOLDIER: It is a drink, like water, only not so healthy: if you would taste it there is some in the cup there.

SECOND SOLDIER: By Saint James, if it be not healthy, I will have none of it!

THIRD SOLDIER: And if he does not drink it?

FIRST SOLDIER: Why, then, they will kill him.

THIRD SOLDIER: And if he does drink it?

FIRST SOLDIER: Why, then, he will die.

SECOND SOLDIER: He has a grave choice to make. I trust he will choose wisely.

Knocking comes at the door.

FIRST SOLDIER: See who that is.

THIRD SOLDIER *goes over and looks through the wicket.*

THIRD SOLDIER: It is a woman, sir.
FIRST SOLDIER: Is she pretty?
THIRD SOLDIER: I can't tell. She is masked, lieutenant.
FIRST SOLDIER: It is only very ugly or very beautiful women who ever hide their faces. Let her in.

Soldier opens the door, and the DUCHESS *masked and cloaked enters.*

DUCHESS (*to* THIRD SOLDIER): Are you the officer on guard?
FIRST SOLDIER (*coming forward*): I am, madam.
DUCHESS: I must see the prisoner alone.
FIRST SOLDIER: I am afraid that is impossible. (*The* DUCHESS *hands him a ring, he looks at it and returns it to her with a bow and makes a sign to the* SOLDIERS.) Stand without there.

Exeunt the SOLDIERS.

DUCHESS: Officer, your men are somewhat rough.
FIRST SOLDIER: They mean no harm.
DUCHESS: I will be going back in a few minutes. As I pass through the corridor do not let them try and lift my mask.
FIRST SOLDIER: You need not be afraid, madam.
DUCHESS: I have a particular reason for wishing my face not to be seen.
FIRST SOLDIER: Madam, with this ring you can go in and out as you please; it is the Duchess's own ring.
DUCHESS: Leave us. (*The* SOLDIER *turns to go out.*) A moment sir. For what hour is . . .
FIRST SOLDIER: At twelve o'clock, madam, we have orders to lead him out; but I dare say he won't wait for us; he's more like to take a drink out of that poison yonder. Men are afraid of the headsman.
DUCHESS: Is that poison?
FIRST SOLDIER: Ay, madam, and very sure poison too.
DUCHESS: You may go, sir.
FIRST SOLDIER: By Saint James, a pretty hand! I wonder who she is. Some woman who loved him, perhaps.

Exit.

DUCHESS (*taking her mask off*): At last!
He can escape now in this cloak and vizard,
We are of a height almost: they will not know him;
As for myself what matter?
So that he does not curse me as he goes,
I care but little; I wonder will he curse me,
He has the right. It is eleven now.
They will not come till twelve. What will they say
When they find the bird has flown?

> *Goes over to the table.*

                                   So this is poison.
Is it not strange that in this liquor here
There lies the key to all philosophies?

> *Takes the cup up.*

It smells of poppies. I remember well
That, when I was a child in Sicily,
I took the scarlet poppies from the corn,
And made a little wreath, and my grave uncle,
Don John of Naples, laughed: I did not know
That they had power to stay the springs of life,
To make the pulse cease beating, and to chill
The blood in its own vessels, till men come
And with a hook hale the poor body out,
And throw it in a ditch: the body, ay, –
What of the soul? That goes to heaven or hell.
Where will mine go?

> *Takes the torch from the wall, and goes over to the bed.*

                              How peacefully here he sleeps,
Like a young schoolboy tired out with play:
I would that I could sleep so peacefully,
But I have dreams.

> *Bending over him.*

Poor boy: what if I kissed him?
No, no, my lips would burn him like a fire.
He has had enough of Love. Still that white neck
Will 'scape the headsman: I have seen to that:
He will get hence from Padua to-night,
And that is well. You are very wise. Lord Justices,

And yet you are not half so wise as I am,
And that is well.

      O God! how I have loved you,
And what a bloody flower did Love bear!

  Comes back to the table.

What if I drank these juices, and so ceased?
Were it not better than to wait till Death
Come to my bed with all his serving men,
Remorse, disease, old age, and misery?
I wonder does one suffer much: I think
That I am very young to die like this,
But so it must be. Why, why should I die?
He will escape to-night, and so his blood
Will not be on my head. No, I must die:
I have been guilty, therefore I must die:
He loves me not, and therefore I must die:
I would die happier if he would kiss me,
But he will not do that. I did not know him,
I thought he meant to sell me to the judge;
That is not strange; we women never know
Our lovers till they leave us.

  Bell begins to toll.

      Thou vile bell,
That like a bloodhound from thy brazen throat
Call'st for this man's life, cease! Thou shalt not get it.
He stirs – I must be quick:

  Takes up cup.

      O Love, Love, Love,
I did not think that I would pledge thee thus!

  *Drinks poison, and sets the cup down on the table behind her: the noise
wakens* GUIDO, *who starts up, and does not see what she has done. There is si-
lence for a minute, each looking at the other.*

I do not come to ask your pardon now,
Seeing I know I stand beyond all pardon,
A very guilty, very wicked woman;
Enough of that: I have already, sir,
Confessed my sin to the Lords Justices;
They would not listen to me: and some said

I did invent a tale to save your life,
You having trafficked with me; others said
That women played with pity as with men;
Others that grief for my slain Lord and husband
Had robbed me of my wits: they would not hear me,
And, when I sware it on the holy book,
They bade the doctor cure me. They are ten,
Ten against one, and they possess your life.
They call me Duchess here in Padua.
I do not know, sir; if I be the Duchess,
I wrote your pardon, and they would not take it;
They call it treason, say I taught them that;
Maybe I did. Within an hour, Guido,
They will be here, and drag you from the cell,
And bind your hands behind your back, and bid you
Kneel at the block: I am before them there;
Here is the signet ring of Padua,
'Twill bring you safely through the men on guard,
There is my cloak and vizard; they have orders
Not to be curious; when you pass the gate
Turn to the left, and at the second bridge
You will find horses waiting: by to-morrow
You will be at Venice, safe.

    A pause.

                             Do you not speak?
Will you not even curse me ere you go? –
You have the right.

    A pause.

                           You do not understand
There lies between you and the headsman's axe
Hardly so much sand in the hour-glass
As a child's palm could carry: here is the ring:
I have washed my hand: there is no blood upon it:
You need not fear. Will you not take the ring?
    GUIDO (*takes ring and kisses it*): Ay! gladly, Madam.
    DUCHESS: And leave Padua.
    GUIDO: Leave Padua.
    DUCHESS: But it must be to-night.
    GUIDO: To-night it shall be.
    DUCHESS: Oh, thank God for that!
    GUIDO: So I can live; life never seemed so sweet
As at this moment.

DUCHESS: Do not tarry, Guido,
There is my cloak: the horse is at the bridge,
The second bridge below the ferry house:
Why do you tarry? Can your ears not hear
This dreadful bell, whose every ringing stroke
Robs one brief minute from your boyish life.
Go quickly.

    GUIDO: Ay! He will come soon enough.

    DUCHESS: Who?

    GUIDO (*calmly*): Why, the headsman.

    DUCHESS: No, no.

    GUIDO: Only he
Can bring me out of Padua.

    DUCHESS: You dare not!
You dare not burden my o'erburdened soul
With two dead men! I think one is enough.
For when I stand before God, face to face,
I would not have you, with a scarlet thread
Around your white throat, coming up behind
To say I did it: Why, the very devils
Who howl away in hell would pity me:
You will not be more cruel than the devils
Who are shut out from God.

    GUIDO: Madam, I wait.

    DUCHESS: No, no, you cannot: you do not understand,
I have less power in Padua to-night
Than any common woman; they will kill you.
I saw the scaffold as I crossed the square,
Already the low rabble throng about it,
With fearful jests, and horrid merriment,
As though it were a morris-dancer's platform,
And not Death's sable throne. O Guido, Guido,
You must escape!

    GUIDO: Ay, by the hand of death,
Not by your hand.

    DUCHESS.   Oh, you are merciless,
Merciless now as ever: No, no, Guido,
You must go hence.

    GUIDO: Madam, I tarry here.

    DUCHESS: Guido, you shall not: it would be a thing
So terrible that the amazed stars
Would fall from heaven, and the palsied moon
Be in her sphere eclipsed, and the great sun
Refuse to shine upon the unjust earth
Which saw thee die.

    GUIDO: Be sure I shall not stir.

DUCHESS (*wringing her hands*): You do not know: once that the judges come
I have no power to keep you from the axe;
You cannot wait: have I not sinned enough?
Is one sin not enough, but must it breed
A second sin more horrible again
Than was the one that bare it? O God, God,
Seal up sin's teeming womb, and make it barren,
I will not have more blood upon my hand
Than I have now.

    GUIDO (*seizing her hand*): What! Am I fallen so low
That I may not have leave to die for you?

    DUCHESS (*tearing her hand away*): Die for me? – no, my life is a vile thing,
Thrown to the miry highways of this world;
You shall not die for me, you shall not, Guido,
I am a guilty woman.

    GUIDO: Guilty? – let those
Who know what a thing temptation is,
In the red fire of passion, those whose lives
Are dull and colourless, in a word let those,
If any such there be, who have not loved,
Cast stones against you. As for me —

    DUCHESS: Alas!

    GUIDO (*falling at her feet*): You are my lady, and you are my love!
O hair of gold, O crimson lips, O face
Made for the luring and the love of man!
Incarnate image of pure loveliness!
Worshipping thee I do forget the past,
Worshipping thee my soul comes close to thine,
Worshipping thee I seem to be a god,
And though they give my body to the block,
Yet is my love eternal !

    DUCHESS *puts her hands over her face*: GUIDO *draws them down.*

                Sweet, lift up
The trailing curtains that overhang thine eyes
That I may look into those eyes, and tell you
I love you, never more than now when Death
Thrusts his cold lips between us: Beatrice,
I love you: have you no word left to say?
Oh, I can bear the executioner,
But not this silence: will you not say you love me?
Speak but that word and Death shall lose his sting,
But speak it not, and fifty thousand deaths
Are, in comparison, mercy. Oh you are cruel,

And do not love me.

DUCHESS: Alas! I have no right.
For I have stained the innocent hands of love
With spilt-out blood: there is blood on the ground,
I set it there.

GUIDO: Sweet, it was not yourself,
It was some devil tempted you. No, no,

DUCHESS (*rising suddenly*):
We are each our own devil, and we make
This world our hell.

GUIDO: Then let high Paradise
Fall into Tartarus! For I shall make
This world my heaven for a little space.
I love you, Beatrice.

DUCHESS: I am not worthy,
Being a thing of sin.

GUIDO: No, my Lord Christ,
The sin was mine, if any sin there was.
'Twas I who nurtured murder in my heart,
Sweetened my meats, seasoned my wine with it,
And in my fancy slew the accursed Duke
A hundred times a day. Why, had this man
Died half so often as I wished him to,
Death had been stalking ever through the house,
And murder had not slept.

                        But you, fond heart,
Whose little eyes grew tender over a whipt hound,
You whom the little children laughed to see
Because you brought the sunlight where you passed,
You the white angel of God's purity,
This which men call your sin, what was it?

DUCHESS: Ay!
What was it? There are times it seems a dream,
An evil dream sent by an evil god,
And then I see the dead face in the coffin
And know it is no dream, but that my hand
Is red with blood, and that my desperate soul
Striving to find some haven for its love
From the wild tempest of this raging world,
Has wrecked its bark upon the rocks of sin.
What was it, said you? – murder merely? Nothing
But murder, horrible murder.

GUIDO: Nay, nay, nay,
'Twas but the passion-flower of your love
That in one moment leapt to terrible life,
And in one moment bare this gory fruit,

Which I had plucked in thought a thousand times.
My soul was murderous, but my hand refused;
Your hand wrought murder, but your soul was pure.
And so I love you, Beatrice, and let him
Who has no mercy for your stricken head,
Lack mercy up in heaven! Kiss me, sweet.

Tries to kiss her.

DUCHESS: No, no, your lips are pure, and mine are soiled,
For Guilt has been my paramour, and Sin
Lain in my bed: O Guido, if you love me
Get hence, for every moment is a worm
Which gnaws your life away: nay, sweet, get hence,
And if in after time you think of me,
Think of me as of one who loved you more
Than anything on earth; think of me, Guido,
As of a woman merely, one who tried
To make her life a sacrifice to love,
And slew love in the trial: Oh, what is that?
The bell has stopped from ringing, and I hear
The feet of armed men upon the stair.
    GUIDO (*aside*): That is the signal for the guard to come.
    DUCHESS: Why has the bell stopped ringing?
    GUIDO: If you must know,
That stops my life on this side of the grave,
But on the other we shall meet again.
    DUCHESS: No, no, 'tis not too late: you must get hence;
The horse is by the bridge, there is still time.
Away, away, you must not tarry here!

    Noise of SOLDIERS *in the passage.*

A VOICE OUTSIDE: Room for the Lord Justice of Padua!

    The LORD JUSTICE *is seen through the grated window passing down the corridor preceded by men bearing torches.*

DUCHESS: It is too late.
A VOICE OUTSIDE: Room for the headsman.
DUCHESS (*sinks down*):   Oh!

    The HEADSMAN *with his axe on his shoulder is seen passing the corridor, followed by Monks bearing candles.*

GUIDO: Farewell, dear love, for I must drink this poison.

I do not fear the headsman, but I would die
Not on the lonely scaffold.

DUCHESS: Oh!

GUIDO: But here,
Here in thine arms, kissing thy mouth: farewell!

Goes to the table and takes the goblet up.

What, art thou empty?

Throws it to the ground.

                              O thou churlish gaoler,
Even of poisons niggard!

DUCHESS (*faintly*):   Blame him not.

GUIDO: O God! You have not drunk it, Beatrice?
Tell me you have not?

DUCHESS: Were I to deny it,
There is a fire eating at my heart
Which would find utterance.

GUIDO: O treacherous love,
Why have you not left a drop for me?

DUCHESS: No, no, it held but death enough for one.

GUIDO: Is there no poison still upon your lips,
That I may draw it from them?

DUCHESS: Why should you die?
You have not spilt blood, and so need not die:
I have spilt blood, and therefore I must die.
Was it not said blood should be spilt for blood?
Who said that? I forget.

GUIDO: Tarry for me,
Our souls will go together.

DUCHESS: Nay, you must live.
There are many other women in the world
Who will love you, and not murder for your sake.

GUIDO: I love you only.

DUCHESS: You need not die for that.

GUIDO: Ah, if we die together, love, why then
Can we not lie together in one grave.

DUCHESS: A grave is but a narrow wedding-bed.

GUIDO: It is enough for us.

DUCHESS: And they will strew it
With a stark winding-sheet, and bitter herbs;
I think there are no roses in the grave,
Or if there are, they all are withered now
Since my Lord went there.

GUIDO: Ah! Dear Beatrice,
Your lips are roses that death cannot wither.
    DUCHESS: Nay, if we lie together, will not my lips
Fall into dust, and your enamoured eyes
Shrivel to sightless sockets, and the worms,
Which are our groomsmen, eat away your heart?
    GUIDO: I do not care: Death has no power on love,
And so by Love's immortal sovereignty
I will die with you.
    DUCHESS: But the grave is black,
And the pit black, so I must go before
To light the candles for your coming hither.
No, no, I will not die, I will not die.
Love, you are strong, and young, and very brave,
Stand between me and the angel of death,
And wrestle with him for me.

    Thrusts GUIDO *in front of her with his back to the audience.*

                              I will kiss you,
When you have thrown him. Oh, have you no cordial,
To stay the workings of this poison in me?
Are there no rivers left in Italy
That you will not fetch me one cup of water
To quench this fire?
    GUIDO: O God!
    DUCHESS: You did not tell me
There was a drought in Italy, and no water,
Nothing but fire.
    GUIDO: O Love!
    DUCHESS: Send for a leech,
Not him who stanched my husband, but another,
We have no time: send for a leech, I say:
There is an antidote against each poison,
And he will sell it if we give him money.
Tell him that I will give him Padua,
For one short hour of life: I will not die.
Oh, I am sick to death; no, do not touch me,
This poison gnaws my heart: I did not know
It was such pain to die: I thought that life
Had taken all the agonies to itself;
It seems it is not so.
    GUIDO: O damnéd stars,
Quench your vile cresset-lights in tears, and bid
The moon, your mistress, shine no more to-night.
    DUCHESS: Guido, why are we here? I think this room

Is poorly furnished for a marriage chamber.
Let us go hence at once. Where are the horses?
We should be on our way to Venice now.
How cold the night is! We must ride faster.
That is our wedding-bell, is it not, Guido?

The Monks begin to chant outside.

Music! It should be merrier; but grief
Is of the fashion now – I know not why.
You must not weep: do we not love each other? –
That is enough. Death, what do you here?
You were not bidden to this table, sir;
Away, we have no need of you: I tell you
It was in wine I pledged you, not in poison.
They lied who told you that I drank your poison.
It was spilt upon the ground, like my Lord's blood;
You came too late.

GUIDO: Sweet, there is nothing there:
These things are only unreal shadows.

DUCHESS: Death,
Why do you tarry, get to the upper chamber;
The cold meats of my husband's funeral feast
Are set for you; this is a wedding feast.
You are out of place, sir; and, besides, 'tis summer.
We do not need these heavy fires now,
You scorch us. Guido, bid that grave-digger
Stop digging in the earth that empty grave.
I will not lie there. Oh, I am burned up,
Burned up and blasted by these fires within me.
Can you do nothing? Water, give me water,
Or else more poison. No: I feel no pain –
Is it not curious I should feel no pain? –
And Death has gone away, I am glad of that.
I thought he meant to part us. Tell me, Guido,
Are you not sorry that you ever saw me?

GUIDO: I swear I would not have lived otherwise.
Why, in this dull and common world of ours
Men have died looking for such moments as this
And have not found them.

DUCHESS: Then you are not sorry?
How strange that seems.

GUIDO: What, Beatrice, have I not
Stood face to face with beauty; that is enough
For one man's life. Why, love, I could be merry;
I have been often sadder at a feast,

But who were sad at such a feast as this
When Love and Death are both our cup-bearers;
We love and die together.

DUCHESS: Oh, I have been
Guilty beyond all women, and indeed
Beyond all women punished. Do you think –
No, that could not be – oh, do you think that love
Can wipe the bloody stain from off my hands,
Pour balm into my wounds, heal up my hurts,
And wash my scarlet sins as white as snow? –
For I have sinned.

GUIDO: They do not sin at all
Who sin for love.

DUCHESS: No, I have sinned, and yet
Perchance my sin will be forgiven me.
I have loved much.

> *They kiss each other now for the first time in this Act, when suddenly the*
> DUCHESS *leaps up in the dreadful spasm of death, tears in agony at her dress,*
> *and finally, with face twisted and distorted with pain, falls back dead in a*
> *chair.* GUIDO *seizing her dagger from her belt, kills himself; and, as he falls*
> *across her knees, clutches at the cloak which is on the back of the chair. There is*
> *a little pause. Then down the passage comes the tramp of Soldiers; the door is*
> *opened, and the* LORD JUSTICE, *the Headsman, and the Guard enter and see*
> *this figure shrouded in black, and* GUIDO *lying dead across her. The* LORD
> JUSTICE *rushes forward and drags the cloak off the* DUCHESS, *whose face is*
> *now the marble image of peace, the sign of God's forgiveness.*

TABLEAU

CURTAIN

VERA, *or* THE NIHILISTS

A Drama in a Prologue, and Four Acts

Persons in the Prologue

PETER SABOUROFF (an Innkeeper)
VERA SABOUROFF (his Daughter)
MICHAEL (a Peasant)

DMITRI SABOUROFF
NICOLAS
COLONEL KOTEMKIN

Persons in the play

IVAN THE CZAR
PRINCE PAUL MARALOFFSKI
(Prime Minister of Russia)
PRINCE PETROVITCH
COUNT ROUVALOFF

MARQUIS DE POIVRARD
BARON RAFF
GENERAL KOTEMKIN
A PAGE
COLONEL OF THE GUARD

Nihilists

PETER TCHERNAVITCH, President
of the Nihilists
MICHAEL
ALEXIS IVANACIEVITCH, known as
a Student of Medicine

PROFESSOR MARFA
VERA SABOUROFF
SOLDIERS, CONSPIRATORS,
Etc.

PROLOGUE

SCENE: *A Russian inn. Large door opening on snowy landscape at back of stage.* PETER SABOUROFF *and* MICHAEL.

PETER (*warming his hands at a stove*): Has Vera not come back yet, Michael?

MICHAEL: No, Father Peter, not yet; 'tis a good three miles to the post office, and she has to milk the cows besides, and that dun one is a rare plaguey creature for a wench to handle.

PETER: Why didn't you go with her, you young fool? She'll never love you unless you are always at her heels; women like to be bothered.

MICHAEL: She says I bother her too much already, Father Peter, and I fear she'll never love me after all.

PETER: Tut, tut, boy, why shouldn't she? You're young, and wouldn't be ill-favoured either, had God or thy mother given thee another face. Aren't you one of Prince Maraloffski's gamekeepers; and haven't you got a good grass farm, and the best cow in the village? What more does a girl want?

MICHAEL: But Vera, Father Peter –

PETER: Vera, my lad, has got too many ideas; I don't think much of ideas myself; I've got on well enough in life without 'em; why shouldn't my children? There's Dmitri! Could have stayed here and kept the inn; many a young lad would have jumped at the offer in these hard times; but he, scatter-brained featherhead of a boy, must needs go off to Moscow to study the law! What does he want knowing about the law? Let a man do his duty, say I, and no one will trouble him.

MICHAEL: Ay! But, Father Peter, they say a good lawyer can break the law as often as he likes, and no one can say him nay. If a man knows the law he knows his duty.

PETER: True, Michael, if a man knows the law there is nothing illegal he cannot do when he likes: that is why folk become lawyers. That is about all they are good for; and there he stays, and has not written a line to us for four months now – a good son that, eh?

MICHAEL: Come, come, Father Peter, Dmitri's letters must have gone astray – perhaps the new postman can't read; he looks stupid enough, and Dmitri, why, he was the best fellow in the village. Do you remember how he shot the bear at the barn in the great winter?

PETER: Ay, it was a good shot; I never did a better myself.

MICHAEL: And as for dancing, he tired out three fiddlers Christmas come two years.

PETER: Ay, ay, he was a merry lad. It is the girl that has the seriousness – she goes about as solemn as a priest for days at a time.

MICHAEL: Vera is always thinking of others.

PETER: There is her mistake, boy. Let God and our little Father the Czar look to the world. It is none of my work to mend my neighbour's thatch. Why, last winter old Michael was frozen to death in his sleigh in the snow-storm, and his wife and children starved afterwards when the hard times came; but what business was it of mine? I didn't make the world. Let God and the Czar look to it. And then the blight came, and the black plague with it, and the priests couldn't bury the people fast enough, and they lay dead on the roads – men and women both. But what business was it of mine? I didn't make the world. Let God and the Czar look to it. Or two autumns ago, when the river overflowed on a sudden, and the children's school was carried away and drowned every girl and boy in it. I didn't make the world – let God or the Czar look to it.

MICHAEL: But, Father Peter –

PETER: No, no, boy; no man could live if he took his neighbour's pack on his shoulder. (*Enter* VERA *in peasant's dress.*) Well, my girl, you've been long enough away – where is the letter?

VERA: There is none to-day, Father.

PETER: I knew it.

VERA: But there will be one to-morrow, Father.

PETER: Curse him, for an ungrateful son.

VERA: O Father, don't say that; he must be sick.

PETER: Ay! Sick of Profligacy, perhaps.

VERA: How dare you say that of him, Father? You know that is not true.

PETER: Where does the money go, then? Michael, listen. I gave Dmitri half his mother's fortune to bring with him to pay the lawyer folk at Moscow. He has only written three times, and every time for more money. He got it, not at my wish, but at hers (*pointing to* VERA), and now for five months, close on six almost, we have heard nothing from him.

VERA: Father, he will come back.

PETER: Ay! The prodigals always return; but let him never darken my doors again.

VERA (*sitting down pensive*): Some evil has come on him; he must be dead! Oh! Michael, I am so wretched about Dmitri.

MICHAEL: Will you never love any one but him, Vera?

VERA (*smiling*): I don't know; there is so much else to do in the world but love.

MICHAEL: Nothing else worth doing, Vera.

PETER: What noise is that, Vera? (*A metallic clink is heard.*)

VERA (*rising and going to the door*): I don't know, Father; it is not like the cattle bells, or I would think Nicholas had come from the fair. Oh, Father! It is soldiers coming down the hill – there is one of them on horseback. How pretty they look! But there are some men with them, with chains on! They must be robbers. Oh! Don't let them in, Father; I couldn't look at them.

PETER: Men in chains! Why, we are in luck, my child! I heard this was to be the new road to Siberia, to bring the prisoners to the mines; but I didn't believe it. My fortune is made! Bustle, Vera, bustle! I'll die a rich man after all. There will be no lack of good customers now. An honest man should have the chance of making his living out of rascals now and then.

VERA: Are these men rascals, Father? What have they done?

PETER: I reckon they're some of those Nihilists the priest warns us against. Don't stand there idle, my girl.

VERA: I suppose, then, they are all wicked men.

Sound of soldiers outside; cry of 'Halt!' Enter Russian officer with a body of soldiers and eight men in chains, raggedly dressed; one of them on entering, hurriedly puts his coat above his ears and hides his face; some soldiers guard the door, others sit down; the prisoners stand.

COLONEL: Innkeeper!

PETER: Yes, Colonel.

COLONEL (*pointing to Nihilists*): Give these men some bread and water.

PETER (*to himself*): I shan't make much out of that order.

COLONEL: As for myself, what have you got fit to eat?

PETER: Some good dried venison, your Excellency – and some rye whisky.

COLONEL: Nothing else?

PETER: Why, more whisky, your Excellency.

COLONEL: What clods these peasants are! You have a better room than this?

PETER: Yes, sir.

COLONEL: Bring me there. Sergeant, post your picket outside, and see that these scoundrels do not communicate with any one. No letter writing, you dogs, or you'll be flogged for it. Now for the venison. (*To* PETER *bowing before him.*) Get out of the way, you fool! Who is that girl? (*Sees* VERA.)

PETER: My daughter, your Highness.

COLONEL: Can she read and write?

PETER: Ay, that she can, sir.

COLONEL: Then she is a dangerous woman. No peasant should be allowed to do anything of the kind. Till your fields, store your harvests, pay your taxes, and obey your masters – that is your duty.

VERA: Who are our masters?

COLONEL: Young woman, these men are going to the mines for life for asking the same foolish question.

VERA: Then they have been unjustly condemned.

PETER: Vera, keep your tongue quiet. She is a foolish girl, sir, who talks too much.

COLONEL: Every woman does talk too much. Come, where is this venison? Count, I am waiting for you. How can you see anything in a girl with coarse hands? (*He passes with* PETER *and his aide-de-camp into an inner room.*)

VERA (*to one of the Nihilists*): Won't you sit down? You must be tired.

SERGEANT: Come now, young woman, no talking to my prisoners.

VERA: I shall speak to them. How much do you want?

SERGEANT: How much have you?

VERA: Will you let these men sit down if I give you this? (*Takes off her peasant's necklace.*) It is all I have; it was my mother's.

SERGEANT: Well, it looks pretty enough, and is heavy too. What do you want with these men?

VERA: They are hungry and wretched. Let me go to them?

ONE OF THE SOLDIERS: Let the wench be, if she pays us.

SERGEANT: Well, have your way. If the Colonel sees you, you may have to come with us, my pretty one.

VERA (*advances to the Nihilists*): Sit down; you must be tired. (*Serves them food.*) What are you?

A PRISONER: Nihilists.

VERA: Who put you in chains?

PRISONER: Our Father the Czar.

VERA: Why?

PRISONER: For loving liberty too well.

VERA (*to the prisoner who hides his face*): What did you want to do?

DMITRI: To give liberty to thirty millions of people enslaved to one man.

VERA (*startled at the voice*): What is your name?

DMITRI: I have no name.

VERA: Where are your friends?

DMITRI: I have no friends.

VERA: Let me see your face!

DMITRI: You will see nothing but suffering in it. They have tortured me.

VERA (*tears his cloak from his face*): O God! Dmitri! My brother!

DMITRI: Hush! Vera; be calm. You must not let my father know; it would kill him. I thought I could free Russia. I heard men talk of Liberty one night in a café. I had never heard the word before. It seemed to be a new God they spoke of. I joined them. It was there all the money went. Five months ago they seized us. They found me printing the paper. I am going to the mines for life. I could not write. I thought it would be better to let you think I was dead; for they are bringing us to a living tomb.

VERA (*looking round*): You must escape, Dmitri. I will take your place.

DMITRI: Impossible! You can only revenge us.

VERA: I shall revenge you.

DMITRI: Listen! There is a house in Moscow –

SERGEANT: Prisoners, attention! The Colonel is coming – young woman, your time is up.

Enter COLONEL, AIDE-DE-CAMP, *and* PETER.

PETER: I hope your Highness is pleased with the venison. I shot it myself.

COLONEL: It had been better had you talked less about it. Sergeant, get ready. (*Gives purse to* PETER.) Here, you cheating rascal!

PETER: My fortune is made! Long live your Highness. I hope your Highness will come often this way.

COLONEL: By St. Nicholas, I hope not. It is too cold here for me. (*To* VERA): Young girl, don't ask questions again about what does not concern you. I will not forget your face.

VERA: Nor I yours, or what you are doing.

COLONEL: You peasants are getting too saucy since you ceased to be serfs, and the knout is the best school for you to learn politics in. Sergeant, proceed.

The COLONEL *turns and goes to the top of stage. The prisoners pass out double file; as* DMITRI *passes* VERA *he lets a piece of paper fall on the ground; she puts her foot on it and remains immobile.*

PETER (*who has been counting the money the* COLONEL *gave him*): Long life to your Highness. I will hope to see another batch soon. (*Suddenly catches sight of* DMITRI *as he is going out of the door, and screams and rushes up.*) Dmitri! Dmitri! My God! What brings you here? He is innocent, I tell you. I'll pay for him. Take your money (*flings money on the ground*), take all I have, give me my son. Villains! Villains! Where are you bringing him?

COLONEL: To Siberia, old man.

PETER: No, no; take me instead.

COLONEL: He is a Nihilist.

PETER: You lie! You lie! He is innocent. (*The soldiers force him back with their guns and shut the door against him. He beats with his fists against it.*) Dmitri! Dmitri! A Nihilist! A Nihilist! (*Falls down on floor.*)

VERA (*who has remained motionless, picks up paper now from under her foot and reads*): '99 Rue Tchernavaya, Moscow. To strangle whatever nature is in me; neither to love nor to be loved; neither to pity nor to be pitied; neither to marry nor to be given in marriage, till the end is come.' My brother, I shall keep the oath. (*Kisses the paper.*) You shall be revenged!

VERA *stands immobile, holding paper in her lifted hand.* PETER *is lying on the floor.* MICHAEL, *who has just come in, is bending over him.*

END OF PROLOGUE

ACT ONE

SCENE: *99 Tchernavaya, Moscow. A large garret lit by oil lamps hung from the ceiling. Some masked men standing silent and apart from one another. A man in a scarlet mask is writing at a table. Door at back. Man in yellow with drawn sword at it. Knocks heard. Figures in cloaks and masks enter.*

Password. Per crucem ad lucem.[1]
Answer. Per sanguinem ad libertatem.[2]

Clock strikes. CONSPIRATORS *form a semi-circle in the middle of the stage.*

PRESIDENT: What is the word?
FIRST CONSPIRATOR: Nabat.
PRESIDENT: The answer?
SECOND CONSPIRATOR: Kalit.
PRESIDENT: What hour is it?
THIRD CONSPIRATOR: The hour to suffer.
PRESIDENT: What day?
FOURTH CONSPIRATOR: The day of oppression.
PRESIDENT: What year?
FIFTH CONSPIRATOR: The year of hope.
PRESIDENT: How many are we in number?
SIXTH CONSPIRATOR: Ten, nine, and three.
PRESIDENT: The Galilaean had less to conquer the world; but what is our mission?
SEVENTH CONSPIRATOR: To give freedom.
PRESIDENT: Our creed?
EIGHTH CONSPIRATOR: To annihilate.

---

[1] Through the cross to the light.
[2] Through blood to liberty.

PRESIDENT: Our duty?

NINTH CONSPIRATOR: To obey.

PRESIDENT: Brothers, the questions have been answered well. There are none but Nihilists present. Let us see each other's faces.

THE CONSPIRATORS *unmask*. Michael, recite the oath.

MICHAEL: To strangle whatever nature is in us; neither to love nor to be loved, neither to pity nor to be pitied, neither to marry nor to be given in marriage, till the end is come; to stab secretly by night; to drop poison in the glass; to set father against son, and husband against wife; without fear, without hope, without future, to suffer, to annihilate, to revenge.

PRESIDENT: Are we all agreed?

CONSPIRATORS: We are all agreed. (*They disperse in various directions about the stage.*)

PRESIDENT: 'Tis after the hour, Michael, and she is not yet here.

MICHAEL: Would that she were! We can do little without her.

ALEXIS: She cannot have been seized, President? But the police are on her track, I know.

MICHAEL: You always do seem to know a good deal about the movements of the police in Moscow – too much for an honest conspirator.

PRESIDENT: If those dogs have caught her, the red flag of the people will float on a barricade in every street till we find her! It was foolish of her to go to the Grand Duke's ball. I told her so, but she said she wanted to see the Czar and all his cursed brood face to face for once.

ALEXIS: Gone to the State ball!

MICHAEL: I have no fear. She is as hard to capture as a she-wolf is, and twice as dangerous; besides, she is well disguised. To-night it is a masked ball. But is there any news from the Palace, President? What is that bloody despot doing now besides torturing his only son? What sort of whelp is this Czarevitch, by the way? Have any of you seen him? One hears strange stories about him. They say he loves the people; but a king's son never does that. You cannot breed them like that.

PRESIDENT: Since he came back from abroad a year ago his father has kept him in close prison in his palace.

MICHAEL: An excellent training to make him a tyrant in his turn; but is there any news, I say?

PRESIDENT: A council is to be held to-morrow, at four o'clock, on some secret business the committee cannot find out.

MICHAEL: A council in a king's palace is sure to be about some bloody work or other. But in what room is it to be held?

PRESIDENT (*reading from letter*): In the yellow tapestry room called after the Empress Catherine.

MICHAEL: I care not for such long-sounding names. I would know where it is.

PRESIDENT: I cannot tell, Michael. I know more about the inside of prisons than of palaces.

MICHAEL (*speaking suddenly to* ALEXIS): Where is this room, Alexis?

ALEXIS: It is on the first floor, looking out on to the inner courtyard. But why do you ask, Michael?

MICHAEL: Nothing, nothing, boy! I merely take a great interest in the Czar's life and movements, and I knew you could tell me all about the palace. Every poor student of medicine in Moscow knows all about kings' houses. It is their duty, is it not?

ALEXIS (*aside*): Can Michael suspect me? There is something strange in his manner to-night. Why doesn't she come? The whole fire of revolution seems fallen into dull ashes when she is not here.

MICHAEL: Have you cured many patients, lately, at your hospital, boy?

ALEXIS: There is one who lies sick to death I would fain cure, but cannot.

MICHAEL: Ay! And who is that?

ALEXIS: Russia, our mother.

MICHAEL: The curing of Russia is surgeon's business, and must be done by the knife. I like not your method of medicine.

PRESIDENT: Professor, we have read the proofs of your last article; it is very good indeed.

MICHAEL: What is it about, Professor?

PROFESSOR: The subject, my good brother, is assassination considered as a method of political reform.

MICHAEL: I think little of pen and ink in revolutions. One dagger will do more than a hundred epigrams. Still, let us read this scholar's last production. Give it to me. I will read it myself.

PROFESSOR: Brother, you never mind your stops; let Alexis read it.

MICHAEL: Ay! He is as tripping of speech as if he were some young aristocrat; but for my own part I care not for the stops so that the sense be plain.

ALEXIS (*reading*): 'The past has belonged to the tyrant, and he has defiled it; ours is the future, and we shall make it holy.' Ay! Let us make the future holy; let there be one revolution at least which is not bred in crime, nurtured in murder!

MICHAEL: They have spoken to us by the sword, and by the sword we shall answer! You are too delicate for us, Alexis. There should be none here but men whose hands are rough with labour or red with blood.

PRESIDENT: Peace, Michael, peace! He is the bravest heart amongst us.

MICHAEL (*aside*): He will need to be brave to-night.

The sound of sleigh bells is heard outside.

VOICE (*outside*): Per crucem ad lucem. (*Answer of man on guard*): Per sanguinem ad libertatem.

MICHAEL: Who is that?

Enter VERA in a cloak, which she throws off, appearing in full ball dress.

VERA: God save the people!

PRESIDENT: Welcome, Vera, welcome! We have been sick at heart till we saw you; but now methinks the star of freedom has come to wake us from the night.

VERA: It is night, indeed, brother! Night without moon or star! Russia is smitten to the heart! The man Ivan whom men called the Czar strikes now at our mother with a dagger deadlier than any ever forged by tyranny against a people's life!

MICHAEL: What has the tyrant done now?

VERA: To-morrow martial law is to be proclaimed over all Russia.

OMNES: Martial law! We are lost! We are lost!

ALEXIS: Martial law! Impossible!

MICHAEL: Fool, nothing is impossible in Russia but reform.

VERA: Ay, martial law. The last right to which the people clung has been taken from them. Without trial, without appeal, without accuser even, our brothers will be taken from their houses, shot in the streets like dogs, sent away to die in the snow, to starve in the dungeon, to rot in the mine. Do you know what martial law means? It means the strangling of a whole nation. The streets will be filled with soldiers night and day; there will be sentinels at every door. No man dare walk abroad now but the spy or the traitor. Cooped up in the dens we hide in, meeting by stealth, speaking with bated breath; what good can we do now for Russia?

PRESIDENT: We can suffer at least.

VERA: We have done that too much already. The hour is now come to annihilate and to revenge.

PRESIDENT: Up to this the people have borne everything.

VERA: Because they have understood nothing. But now we, the Nihilists, have given them the tree of knowledge to eat of, and the day of silent suffering is over for Russia.

MICHAEL: Martial law, Vera! This is fearful tidings you bring.

PRESIDENT: It is the death-warrant of liberty in Russia.

VERA: Or the signal for revolution.

MICHAEL: Are you sure it is true?

VERA: Here is the proclamation. I stole it myself at the ball to-night from a young fool, one of Prince Paul's secretaries, who had been given it to copy. It was that which made me so late.

VERA *hands proclamation to* MICHAEL, *who reads it.*

MICHAEL: 'To ensure the public safety – martial law. By order of the Czar, father of his people.' The father of his people!

VERA: Ay! A father whose name shall not be hallowed, whose kingdom shall change to a republic, whose trespasses shall not be forgiven him, because he has robbed us of our daily bread; with whom is neither might, nor right, nor glory, now or for ever.

PRESIDENT: It must be about this time that the council meet to-morrow. It has not yet been signed.

ALEXIS: It shall not be while I have a tongue to plead with.

MICHAEL: Or while I have hands to smite with.

VERA: Martial law! O God, how easy it is for a king to kill his people by thousands, but we cannot rid ourselves of one crowned man in Europe! What is there of awful majesty in these men which makes the hand unsteady, the dagger treacherous, the pistol-shot harmless? Are they not men of like passions with ourselves, vulnerable to the same diseases, of flesh and blood not different from our own? What made Olgiati tremble at the supreme crisis of that Roman life, and Guido's nerve fail him when he should have been of iron and of steel? A plague, I say, on these fools of Naples, Berlin, and Spain! Methinks that if I stood face to face with one of the crowned men my eye would see more clearly, my aim be more sure, my whole body gain a strength and power that was not my own! Oh, to think what stands between us and freedom in Europe! A few old men, wrinkled, feeble, tottering dotards whom a boy could strangle for a ducat, or a woman stab in a night-time. These are the things that keep us from liberty. But now methinks the brood of men is dead and the dull earth grown sick of childbearing, else would no crowned dog pollute God's air by living.

OMNES: Try us! Try us! Try us!

MICHAEL: We shall try thee, too, some day, Vera.

VERA: I pray God thou mayest! Have I not strangled whatever nature is in me, and shall I not keep my oath?

MICHAEL (*to* PRESIDENT): Martial law, President! Come, there is no time to be lost. We have twelve hours yet before us till the council meet. Twelve hours! One can overthrow a dynasty in less than that.

PRESIDENT: Ay! Or lose one's own head.

MICHAEL *and the* PRESIDENT *retire to one corner of the stage and sit whispering.* VERA *takes up the proclamation, and reads it to herself.* ALEXIS *watches and suddenly rushes up to her.*

ALEXIS: Vera!

VERA: Alexis, you here! Foolish boy, have I not prayed you to stay away? All of us here are doomed to die before our time, fated to expiate by suffering whatever good we do; but you, with your bright boyish face, you are too young to die yet.

ALEXIS: One is never too young to die for one's country!

VERA: Why do you come here night after night?

ALEXIS: Because I love the people.

VERA: But your fellow-students must miss you. Are there no traitors among them? You know what spies there are in the University here. O Alexis, you must go! You see how desperate suffering has made us. There is no room here for a nature like yours. You must not come again.

ALEXIS: Why do you think so poorly of me? Why should I live while my brothers suffer?

VERA: You spake to me of your mother once. You said you loved her. Oh, think of her!

ALEXIS: I have no mother now but Russia, my life is hers to take or give away; but to-night I am here to see you. They tell me you are leaving for Novgorod to-morrow.

VERA: I must. They are getting faint-hearted there, and I would fan the flame of this revolution into such a blaze that the eyes of all kings in Europe shall be blinded. If martial law is passed they will need me all the more there. There is no limit, it seems, to the tyranny of one man; but to the suffering of a whole people there shall be a limit. Too many of us have died on block and barricade: it is their turn to be victims now.

ALEXIS: God knows it, I am with you. But you must not go. The police are watching every train for you. When you are seized they have orders to place you without trial in the lowest dungeon of the palace. I know it – no matter how. Oh, think how without you the sun goes from our life, how the people will lose their leader and liberty her priestess. Vera, you must not go!

VERA: You are right: I will stay. I would live a little longer for freedom, a little longer for Russia.

ALEXIS: When you die then Russia is smitten indeed; when you die then I shall lose all hope – all. . . . Vera, this is fearful news you bring – martial law – it is too terrible. I knew it not, by my soul, I knew it not!

VERA: How could you have known it? It is too well laid a plot for that. This great White Czar, whose hands are red with the blood of the people he has murdered, whose soul is black with this iniquity, is the cleverest conspirator of us all. Oh, how could Russia bear two hearts like yours and his!

ALEXIS: Vera, the Emperor was not always like this. There was a time when he loved the people. It is that devil, whom God curse, Prince Paul Maraloffski, who has brought him to this. To-morrow, I swear it, I shall plead for the people to the Emperor.

VERA: Plead to the Czar! Foolish boy, it is only those who are sentenced to death that ever see our Czar. Besides, what should he care for a voice that pleads for mercy? The cry of a strong nation in its agony has not moved that heart of stone.

ALEXIS (*aside*): Yet shall I plead to him. They can but kill me.

PROFESSOR: Here are the proclamations, Vera. Do you think they will do?

VERA: I shall read them. How fair he looks! Methinks he never seemed so noble as to-night. Liberty is blessed in having such a lover.

ALEXIS: Well, President, what are you deep in?

MICHAEL: We are thinking of the best way of killing bears. (*Whispers to* PRESIDENT *and leads him aside.*)

PROFESSOR (*to* VERA): And the letters from our brothers at Paris and Berlin. What answer shall we send to them?

VERA (*takes them mechanically*): Had I not strangled nature, sworn neither to love nor to be loved, methinks I might have loved him. Oh, I am a fool, a traitor myself, a traitor myself! But why did he come amongst us with his bright young face, his heart aflame for liberty, his pure white soul? Why does he make me feel at times as if I would have him as my king, Republican though I be? Oh, fool, fool, fool! False to your oath! Weak as water! Have done! Remember what you are – a Nihilist, a Nihilist!

PRESIDENT (*to* MICHAEL): But you will be seized, Michael.

MICHAEL: I think not. I will wear the uniform of the Imperial Guard, and the Colonel on duty is one of us. It is on the first floor, you remember; so I can take a long shot.

PRESIDENT: Shall I not tell the brethren?

MICHAEL: Not a word, not a word! There is a traitor amongst us.

VERA: Come, are these the proclamations? Yes, they will do; yes, they will do. Send five hundred to Kiev and Odessa and Novgorod, five hundred to Warsaw, and have twice the number distributed among the Southern provinces, though these dull Russian peasants care little for our proclamations, and less for our martyrdoms. When the blow is struck, it must be from the town, not from the country.

MICHAEL: Ay, and by the sword, not by the goose quill.

VERA: Where are the letters from Poland?

PROFESSOR: Here.

VERA: Unhappy Poland! The eagles of Russia have fed on her heart. We must not forget our brothers there.

PRESIDENT: Is it true, Michael?

MICHAEL: Ay, I stake my life on it.

PRESIDENT: Let the doors be locked, then. Alexis Ivanacievitch entered on our roll of the brothers as a student of the School of Medicine at Moscow. Why did you not tell us of this bloody scheme of martial law?

ALEXIS: I, President?

MICHAEL: Ay, you! You knew it, none better. Such weapons as these are not forged in a day. Why did you not tell us of it? A week ago there had been time to lay the mine, to raise the barricade, to strike one blow at least for liberty. But now the hour is past! It is too late, it is too late! Why did you keep it a secret from us. I say?

ALEXIS: Now by the hand of freedom, Michael, my brother, you wrong me. I knew nothing of this hideous law. By my soul, my brothers, I knew not of it! How should I know?

MICHAEL: Because you are a traitor! Where did you go when you left us the night of our last meeting here?

ALEXIS: To mine own house, Michael.

MICHAEL: Liar! I was on your track. You left here an hour after midnight. Wrapped in a large cloak, you crossed the river by a boat a mile below the second bridge, and gave the ferryman a gold piece, you, the poor student of medicine! You doubled back twice, and hid in an archway so long that I had almost made up my mind to stab you at once, only that I am fond of hunting. So! You thought you had baffled all pursuit, did you? Fool! I am a bloodhound that never loses the scent. I followed you from street to street. At last I saw you pass swiftly across the Place St. Isaac, whisper to the guards some secret password, enter the palace by a private door with your own key.

CONSPIRATORS: The palace!

VERA: Alexis!

MICHAEL: I waited. All through the dreary watches of our long Russian night I waited, that I might kill you with your Judas hire still hot in your hand. But you never came back; you never left that palace. I saw the blood-red sun rise through the yellow fog over the murky town; I saw a new day of oppression dawn on Russia; but you never came back. So you pass nights in the palace, do you? You know the password for the guards; you have a key to a secret door. You are a spy – I never trusted you, with your soft white hands, your curled hair, your pretty graces. You have no mark of suffering about you; you cannot be of the people. You are a spy – a spy – traitor!

OMNES: Kill him! Kill him! (*Draw their knives.*)

VERA: (*rushing in front of* ALEXIS): Stand back, I say, Michael! Stand back all! Do not dare lay a hand upon him! He is the noblest heart amongst us.

OMNES: Kill him! Kill him! He is a spy!

VERA: Dare to lay a finger on him, and I leave you all to yourselves.

PRESIDENT: Vera, did you not hear what Michael said of him? He stayed all night in the Czar's palace. He has a password and a private key. What else should he be but a spy?

VERA: Bah! I do not believe Michael. It is a lie! It is a lie! Alexis, say it is a lie!

ALEXIS: It is true. Michael has told what he saw. I did pass that night in the Czar's palace. Michael has spoken the truth.

VERA: Stand back, I say; stand back! Alexis, I do not care. I trust you; you would not betray us; you would not sell the people for money. You are honest, true! Oh, say you are no spy!

ALEXIS: Spy? You know I am not. I am with you, my brothers, to the death.

MICHAEL: Ay, to your own death.

ALEXIS: Vera, you know I am true.

VERA: I know it well.

PRESIDENT: Why are you here, traitor?

ALEXIS: Because I love the people.

MICHAEL: Then you can be a martyr for them?

VERA: You must kill me first, Michael, before you lay a finger on him.

PRESIDENT: Michael, we dare not lose Vera. It is her whim to let this boy live. We can keep him here to-night. Up to this he has not betrayed us.

Tramp of soldiers outside, knocking at door.

VOICE: Open, in the name of the Emperor!

MICHAEL: He *has* betrayed us. This is your doing, spy!

PRESIDENT: Come, Michael, come. We have no time to cut one another's throats while we have our own heads to save.

VOICE: Open, in the name of the Emperor!

PRESIDENT: Brothers, be masked, all of you. Michael, open the door. It is our only chance.

Enter GENERAL KOTEMKIN *and soldiers.*

GENERAL: All honest citizens should be in their own houses an hour be

fore midnight, and not more than five people have a right to meet privately.
Have you not noticed the proclamation, fellows?

MICHAEL: Ay, you have spoiled every honest wall in Moscow with it.

VERA: Peace, Michael, peace. Nay, Sir, we know it not. We are a company
of strolling players travelling from Samara to Moscow to amuse his Imperial
Majesty the Czar.

GENERAL: But I heard loud voices before I entered. What was that?

VERA: We were rehearsing a new tragedy.

GENERAL: Your answers are too *honest* to be true. Come, let me see who
you are. Take off those players' masks. By St. Nicholas, my beauty, if your
face matches your figure, you must be a choice morsel! Come, I say, pretty
one; I would sooner see your face than those of all the others.

PRESIDENT: O God! If he sees it is Vera, we are all lost!

GENERAL: No coquetting, my girl. Come, unmask, I say, or I shall tell my
guards to do it for you.

ALEXIS: Stand back, I say, General Kotemkin!

GENERAL: Who are you, fellow, that talk with such a tripping tongue to
your betters? (ALEXIS *takes his mask off.*) His Imperial Highness the
Czarevitch!

OMNES: The Czarevitch! It is all over!

PRESIDENT: I knew he was a spy. He will give us up to the soldiers.

MICHAEL (*to* VERA): Why did you not let me kill him? Come, we must
fight to the death for it.

VERA: Peace! He will not betray us.

ALEXIS: A whim of mine, General! You know how my father keeps me
from the world and imprisons me in the palace. I should really be bored to
death if I could not get out at night in disguise sometimes, and have some ro-
mantic adventure in town. I fell in with these honest folks a few hours ago.

GENERAL: Actors, are they, Prince?

ALEXIS: Ay, and very ambitious actors, too. They only care to play before
kings.

GENERAL: I' faith, your Highness, I was in hopes I had made a good haul
of Nihilists.

ALEXIS: Nihilists in Moscow, General! With you as head of the police!
Impossible!

GENERAL: So I always tell your Imperial father. But I heard at the council
to-day that that woman Vera Sabouroff, the head of them, had been seen in
this very city. The Emperor's face turned as white as the snow outside. I
think I never saw such terror in any man before.

ALEXIS: She is a dangerous woman, then, this Vera Sabouroff?

GENERAL: The most dangerous in all Europe.

ALEXIS: Did you ever see her, General?

GENERAL: Why, five years ago, when I was a plain Colonel, I remember
her, your Highness, a common waiting-girl in an inn. If I had known then
what she was going to turn out, I would have flogged her to death on the
roadside. She is not a woman at all; she is a sort of devil! For the last eighteen

months I have been hunting her, and caught sight of her once last September outside Odessa.

ALEXIS: How did you let her go, General?

GENERAL: I was by myself, and she shot one of my horses just as I was gaining on her. If I see her again I shan't miss my chance. The Emperor has put twenty thousand roubles on her head.

ALEXIS: I hope you will get it, General; but meanwhile you are frightening these honest folk out of their wits, and disturbing the tragedy. Good-night, General.

GENERAL: Yes; but I should like to see their faces, your Highness.

ALEXIS: No, General; you must not ask that; you know how these gypsies hate to be stared at.

GENERAL: Yes. But, your Highness –

ALEXIS (*haughtily*): General, they are my friends, that is enough. Good-night. And, General, not a word of my little adventure here, you understand.

GENERAL: But shall we not see you back to the palace? The State ball is almost over and you are expected.

ALEXIS: I shall be there; but I shall return alone. Remember, not a word.

GENERAL: Or your pretty gipsy, eh, Prince? Your pretty gipsy! I' faith, I should like to see her before I go; she has such fine eyes through her mask. Well, good night, your Highness; good night.

ALEXIS: Good night, General.

Exeunt GENERAL *and the soldiers.*

VERA (*throwing off her mask*): Saved! And by you!

ALEXIS (*clasping her hand*): Brothers, you trust me now?

Exit.

TABLEAU

ACT DROP

ACT TWO

SCENE: *Council Chamber in the Emperor's Palace, hung with yellow tapestry. Table, with chair of State, set for the Czar; window behind, opening on to a balcony. As the scene progresses the light outside gets darker.*

Present: PRINCE PAUL MARALOFFSKI, PRINCE PETRO-VITCH, COUNT ROUVALOFF, BARON RAFF, COUNT PETOUCHOF.

PRINCE PETROVITCH: So our young scatter-brained Czarevitch has been forgiven at last, and is to take his seat here again.

PRINCE PAUL: Yes; if that is not meant as an extra punishment. For my own part, at least, I find these Cabinet Councils extremely tiring.

PRINCE PETROVITCH: Naturally, you are always speaking.

PRINCE PAUL: No; I think it must be that I have to listen sometimes. It is so exhausting not to talk.

COUNT ROUVALOFF: Still, anything is better than being kept in a sort of prison, like he was – never allowed to go out into the world.

PRINCE PAUL: My dear Count, for romantic young people like he is the world always looks best at a distance; and a prison where one's allowed to order one's own dinner is not at all a bad place. (*Enter the* CZAREVITCH. *The courtiers rise.*) Ah! Good afternoon, Prince. Your Highness is looking a little pale to-day.

CZAREVITCH (*slowly, after a pause*): I want change of air.

PRINCE PAUL (*smiling*): A most revolutionary sentiment! Your Imperial father would highly disapprove of any reforms even with the thermometer in Russia.

CZAREVITCH (*bitterly*): My Imperial father had kept me for six months in this dungeon of a palace. This morning he has me suddenly woke up to see some wretched Nihilists hung; it sickened me, the bloody butchery, though it was a noble thing to see how well these men can die.

PRINCE PAUL: When you are as old as I am, Prince, you will understand that there are few things easier than to live badly and to die well.

CZAREVITCH: Easy to die well! A lesson experience cannot have taught you, much as you know of a bad life.

PRINCE PAUL (*shrugging his shoulders*): Experience, the name men give to their mistakes. I never commit any.

CZAREVITCH (*bitterly*): No; crimes are more in your line.

PRINCE PETROVITCH (*to the* CZAREVITCH): The Emperor was a good deal agitated about your late appearance at the ball last night, Prince.

COUNT ROUVALOFF (*laughing*): I believe he thought the Nihilists had broken into the palace and carried you off.

BARON RAFF: If they had you would have missed a charming dance.

PRINCE PAUL: And an excellent supper. Gringoire really excelled himself in his salad. Ah! You may laugh, Baron; but to cook a good salad is a much more difficult thing than cooking accounts. To make a good salad is to be a brilliant diplomatist – the problem is entirely the same in both cases. To know exactly how much oil one must put with one's vinegar.

BARON RAFF: A cook and a diplomatist! An excellent parallel. If I had a son who was a fool I'd make him one or the other.

PRINCE PAUL: I see your father did not hold the same opinion, Baron. But, believe me, you are wrong to run down cookery. Culture depends on cookery. For myself, the only immortality I desire is to invent a new sauce. I have never had time enough to think seriously about it, but I feel it is in me, I feel it is in me.

CZAREVITCH: You have certainly missed your *métier*, Prince Paul; the *cordon bleu* of the kitchen would have suited you much better than the Grand

Cross of Honour. But you know you could never have worn your white apron well; you would have soiled it too soon, your hands are not clean enough.

PRINCE PAUL (*bowing*): You forget – or, how could they be? I manage your father's business.

CZAREVITCH (*bitterly*): You mismanage my father's business, you mean! Evil genius of his life that you are! Before you came there was some love left in him. It is you who have embittered his nature, poured into his ear the poison of treacherous council, made him hated by the whole people, made him what he is – a tyrant!

The courtiers look significantly at each other.

PRINCE PAUL (*calmly*): I see your Highness does want change of air. But I have been an eldest son myself. (*Lights a cigarette.*) I know what it is when a father won't die to please one.

The CZAREVITCH *goes to the top of the stage, and leans against the window, looking out.*

PRINCE PETROVITCH (*to* BARON RAFF): Foolish boy! He will be sent into exile, or worse, if he is not careful.

BARON RAFF: Yes. What a mistake it is to be sincere!

PRINCE PETROVITCH: The only folly you never committed, Baron.

BARON RAFF: One has only one head, you know, Prince.

PRINCE PAUL: My dear Baron, your head is the last thing any one would wish to take from you. (*Pulls out snuff-box and offers it to* PRINCE PETROVITCH.)

PRINCE PETROVITCH: Thanks, Prince! Thanks!

PRINCE PAUL: Very delicate, isn't it? I get it direct from Paris. But under this vulgar Republic everything has degenerated over there. *Côtelettes à l'impériale* vanished of course with the Bonaparte, and omelettes went out with the Orleanists. La belle France is entirely ruined, Prince, through bad morals and worse cookery. (*Enter the* MARQUIS DE POIVRARD.) Ah! Marquis. I trust Madame la Marquise is well.

MARQUIS DE POIVRARD: You ought to know better than I do, Prince Paul; you see more *of* her.

PRINCE PAUL (*bowing*): Perhaps I see more *in* her, Marquis. Your wife is really a charming woman, so full of *esprit*, and so satirical too; she talks continually of you when we are together.

PRINCE PETROVITCH (*looking at the clock*): His Majesty is a little late today, is he not?

PRINCE PAUL: What has happened to you, my dear Petrovitch? You seem quite out of sorts. You haven't quarrelled with your cook, I hope? What a tragedy that would be for you; you would lose all your friends.

PRINCE PETROVITCH: I fear I wouldn't be so fortunate as that. You forget I would still have my purse. But you are wrong for once; my chef and I are on excellent terms.

PRINCE PAUL: Then your creditors or Mademoiselle Vera Sabouroff have been writing to you? They compose more than half of my correspondents. But really you needn't be alarmed. I find the most violent proclamations from the Executive Committee, as they call it, left all over my house. I never read them; they are so badly spelt as a rule.

PRINCE PETROVITCH: Wrong again, Prince; the Nihilists leave me alone for some reason or other.

PRINCE PAUL (aside): True! Indifference is the revenge the world takes on mediocrities.

PRINCE PETROVITCH: I am bored with life, Prince. Since the opera season ended I have been a perpetual martyr to *ennui*.

PRINCE PAUL: The *maladie du siècle!* You want a new excitement, Prince. Let me see – you have been married twice already; suppose you try – falling in love for once.

BARON RAFF: I cannot understand your nature.

PRINCE PAUL (smiling): If my nature had been made to suit your comprehension rather than my own requirements, I am afraid I would have made a very poor figure in the world.

COUNT ROUVALOFF: There seems to be nothing in life about which you would not jest.

PRINCE PAUL: Ah! My dear Count, life is much too important a thing ever to talk seriously about it.

CZAREVITCH (coming back from window): I don't think Prince Paul's nature is such a mystery. He would stab his best friend for the sake of writing an epigram on his tombstone.

PRINCE PAUL: *Parbleu!* I would sooner lose my best friend than my worst enemy. To have friends, you know, one need only be good-natured; but when a man has no enemy left there must be something mean about him.

CZAREVITCH (bitterly): If to have enemies is a measure of greatness, then you must be a Colossus, indeed, Prince.

PRINCE PAUL: Yes, your Highness, I know I'm the most hated man in Russia, except your father, except your father of course. He doesn't seem to like it much, by the way; but I do, I assure you. (Bitterly.) I love to drive through the streets and see how the rabble scowl at me from every corner. It makes me feel I am a power in Russia; one man against millions! Besides, I have no ambition to be a popular hero, to be crowned with laurels one year and pelted with stones the next; I prefer dying peaceably in my own bed.

CZAREVITCH: And after death?

PRINCE PAUL (shrugging his shoulders): Heaven is a despotism. I shall be at home there.

CZAREVITCH: Do you ever think of the people and their rights?

PRINCE PAUL: The people and their rights bore me. I am sick of both. In these modern days to be vulgar, illiterate, common and vicious, seems to give a man a marvellous infinity of rights that his honest fathers never dreamed of. Believe me, Prince, in good democracy, every man should be an aristocrat; but these people in Russia who seek to thrust us out are no better than the animals in one's preserves, and made to be shot at, most of them.

CZAREVITCH (*excitedly*): If they *are* common, illiterate, vulgar, no better than the beasts of the field, who made them so? (*Enter* AIDE-DE-CAMP.)

AIDE-DE-CAMP: His Imperial Majesty, the Emperor! (PRINCE PAUL *looks at the* CZAREVITCH, *and smiles.*)

Enter the CZAR, *surrounded by his guard.*

CZAREVITCH (*rushing forward to meet him*): Sire!

CZAR (*nervous and frightened*): Don't come too near me, boy! Don't come too near me, I say! There is always something about an heir to a crown unwholesome to his father. Who is that man over there? I don't know him. What is he doing? Is he a conspirator? Have you searched him? Give him till to-morrow to confess, then hang him! Hang him!

PRINCE PAUL: Sire, you are anticipating history. This is Count Petouchof, your new Ambassador to Berlin. He is come to kiss hands on his appointment.

CZAR: To kiss my hand? There is some plot in it. He wants to poison me. There, kiss my son's hand; it will do quite as well.

PRINCE PAUL *signs to* COUNT PETOUCHOF *to leave the room. Exeunt* PETOUCHOF *and the guards.* CZAR *sinks down into his chair. The courtiers remain silent.*

PRINCE PAUL (*approaching*): Sire! Will your Majesty –

CZAR: What do you startle me for like that? No, I won't. (*Watches the courtiers nervously.*) Why are you clattering your sword, sir? (*To* COUNT ROUVALOFF): Take it off. I shall have no man wear a sword in my presence (*looking at* CZAREVITCH), least of all my son. (*To* PRINCE PAUL): You are not angry with me, Prince? You won't desert me, will you? Say you won't desert me. What do you want? You can have anything – anything.

PRINCE PAUL (*bowing very low*): Sire, 'tis enough for me to have your confidence. (*Aside*): I was afraid he was going to revenge himself, and give me another decoration.

CZAR (*returning to his chair*): Well, gentlemen.

MARQUIS DE POIVRARD: Sire, I have the honour to present to you a loyal address from your subjects in the Province of Archangel, expressing their horror at the last attempt on your Majesty's life.

PRINCE PAUL: The last attempt but two, you ought to have said, Marquis. Don't you see it is dated three weeks back?

CZAR: They are good people in the Province of Archangel – honest, loyal people. They love me very much – simple, loyal people; give them a new saint, it costs nothing. Well, Alexis (*turning to the* CZAREVITCH) – how many traitors were hung this morning?

CZAREVITCH: There were three men strangled, Sire.

CZAR: There should have been three thousand. I would to God that this people had but one neck that I might strangle them with one noose! Did they tell anything? Whom did they implicate? What did they confess?

CZAREVITCH: Nothing, Sire.

CZAR: They should have been tortured then; why weren't they tortured? Must I always be fighting in the dark? Am I never to know from what root these traitors spring?

CZAREVITCH: What root should there be of discontent among the people but tyranny and injustice amongst their rulers?

CZAR: What did you say, boy? Tyranny! Tyranny! Am I a tyrant? I'm not. I love the people. I'm their father. I'm called so in every official proclamation. Have a care, boy; have a care. You don't seem to be cured yet of your foolish tongue. (*Goes over to* PRINCE PAUL *and puts his hand on his shoulder.*) Prince Paul, tell me, were there many people there this morning to see the Nihilists hung?

PRINCE PAUL: Hanging is of course a good deal less of a novelty in Russia now, Sire, than it was three or four years ago; and you know how easily the people get tired even of their best amusements. But the square and the tops of the houses were really quite crowded, were they not, Prince? (*To the* CZAREVITCH, *who takes no notice.*)

CZAR: That's right; all loyal citizens should be there. It shows them what to look forward to. Did you arrest any one in the crowd?

PRINCE PAUL: Yes, Sire; a woman, for cursing your name. (*The* CZAREVITCH *starts anxiously.*) She was the mother of two of the criminals.

CZAR (*looking at* CZAREVITCH): She should have blessed me for having rid her of her children. Send her to prison.

CZAREVITCH: The prisons of Russia are too full already, Sire. There is no room in them for any more victims.

CZAR: They don't die fast enough, then. You should put more of them into one cell at once. You don't keep them long enough in the mines. If you do they're sure to die; but you're all too merciful. I'm too merciful myself. Send her to Siberia. She is sure to die on the way. (*Enter an* AIDE-DE-CAMP.) Who's that? Who's that?

AIDE-DE-CAMP: A letter for his Imperial Majesty.

CZAR (*to* PRINCE PAUL): I won't open it. There may be something in it.

PRINCE PAUL: It would be a very disappointing letter, Sire, if there wasn't. (*Takes letter himself, and reads it.*)

PRINCE PETROVITCH (*to* COUNT ROUVALOFF): It must be some sad news. I know that smile too well.

PRINCE PAUL: From the Chief of the Police at Archangel, Sire. 'The Governor of the province was shot this morning by a woman as he was entering the courtyard of his own house. The assassin has been seized.'

CZAR: I never trusted the people in Archangel. It's a nest of Nihilists and conspirators. Take away their saints; they don't deserve them.

PRINCE PAUL: Your Highness would punish them more severely by giving them an extra one. Three governors shot in two months! (*Smiles to him-*

self.) Sire, permit me to recommend your loyal subject, the Marquis de Poivrard, as the new governor of your Province of Archangel.

MARQUIS DE POIVRARD (*hurriedly*): Sire, I am unfit for this post.

PRINCE PAUL: Marquis, you are too modest. Believe me, there is no man in Russia I would sooner see Governor of Archangel than yourself. (*Whispers to* CZAR.)

CZAR: Quite right, Prince Paul; you are always right. See that the Marquis's letters are made out at once.

PRINCE PAUL: He can start to-night, Sire. I shall really miss you very much, Marquis. I always liked your taste in wine and wives extremely.

MARQUIS DE POIVRARD (*to the* CZAR): Start to-night, Sire?

(PRINCE PAUL *whispers to the* CZAR.)

CZAR: Yes, Marquis, to-night; it is better to go at once.

PRINCE PAUL: I shall see that Madame la Marquise is not too lonely while you are away; so you need not be alarmed for her.

COUNT ROUVALOFF (*to* PRINCE PETROVITCH): I should be more alarmed for myself.

CZAR: The Governor of Archangel shot in his own courtyard by a woman! I'm not safe here. I'm not safe anywhere, with that she-devil of the revolution, Vera Sabouroff, here in Moscow. Prince Paul, is that woman still here?

PRINCE PAUL: They tell me she was at the Grand Duke's ball last night. I can hardly believe that; but she certainly had intended to leave for Novgorod to-day, Sire. The police were watching every train for her; but, for some reason or other, she did not go. Some traitor must have warned her. But I shall catch her yet. A chase after a beautiful woman is always exciting.

CZAR: You must hunt her down with bloodhounds, and when she is taken I shall hew her limb from limb. I shall stretch her on the rack till her pale white body is twisted and curled like paper in the fire.

PRINCE PAUL: Oh, we shall have another hunt immediately, for her, Sire! Prince Alexis will assist us, I am sure.

CZAREVITCH: You never require any assistance to ruin a woman, Prince Paul.

CZAR: Vera, the Nihilist, in Moscow! O God, were it not better to die at once the dog's death they plot for me than to live as I live now! Never to sleep, or, if I do, to dream such horrid dreams that hell itself were peace when matched with them. To trust none but those I have bought, to buy none worth trusting! To see a traitor in every smile, poison in every dish, a dagger in every hand! To lie awake at night, listening from hour to hour for the stealthy creeping of the murderer, for the laying of the damned mine! You are all spies! You are all spies! You worst of all – you, my own son! Which of you is it who hides these bloody proclamations under my own pillow, or at the table where I sit? Which of ye all is the Judas who betrays me? O God! O God! Methinks there was a time once, in our war with England, when nothing could make me afraid. (*This with more calm and pathos.*) I have ridden into the crimson heart of war, and borne back an eagle which those wild islanders had taken from us. Men said I was brave then. My father gave me the Iron Cross of Valour. Oh, could he see me now, with this coward's livery ever in my cheek! (*Sinks into his chair.*) I never knew any love when I was a boy. I was ruled by terror myself, how else should I rule now? (*Starts up.*) But I will have revenge; I will have revenge. For every hour I have lain awake at night, waiting for the noose or the dagger, they shall pass years in Siberia, centuries in the mines! Ay! I shall have revenge.

CZAREVITCH: Father! Have mercy on the people. Give them what they ask.

PRINCE PAUL: And begin, Sire, with your own head; they have a particular liking for that.

CZAR: The people! The people! A tiger which I have let loose on myself; but I will fight with it to the death. I am done with half measures. I shall crush these Nihilists at a blow. There shall not be a man of them, no, nor a woman either, left alive in Russia. Am I Emperor for nothing, that a woman should hold me at bay? Vera Sabouroff shall be in my power, I swear it, before a week is ended, though I burn my whole city to find her. She shall be flogged by the knout, stifled in the fortress, strangled in the square!

CZAREVITCH: O God!

CZAR: For two years her hands have been clutching at my throat; for two years she has made my life a hell; but I shall have revenge. Martial law, Prince, martial law over the whole Empire; that will give me revenge. A good measure, Prince, eh? A good measure.

PRINCE PAUL: And an economical one too, Sire. It will carry off your surplus population in six months, and save you any expense in courts of justice; they will not be needed now.

CZAR: Quite right. There are too many people in Russia, too much money spent on them, too much money on courts of justice. I'll shut them up.

CZAREVITCH: Sire, reflect before –

CZAR: When can you have the proclamations ready, Prince Paul?

PRINCE PAUL: They have been printed for the last six months, Sire. I knew you would need them.

CZAR: That's good! That's very good! Let us begin at once. Ah, Prince, if every king in Europe had a minister like you –

CZAREVITCH: There would be less kings in Europe than there are.

CZAR (*in frightened whisper, to* PRINCE PAUL): What does he mean? Do you trust him? His prison hasn't cured him yet. Shall I banish him? Shall I (*whispers*) . . . ? The Emperor Paul did it. The Empress Catherine there (*points to picture on the wall*) did it. Why shouldn't I?

PRINCE PAUL: Your Majesty, there is no need for alarm. The Prince is a very ingenuous young man. He pretends to be devoted to the people, and lives in a palace; preaches socialism, and draws a salary that would support a province. Some day he'll find out that the best cure for Republicism is the Imperial crown, and will cut up the red cap of liberty to make decorations for his Prime Minister.

CZAR: You are right. If he really loved the people, he could not be my son.

PRINCE PAUL: If he lived with the people for a fortnight, their bad dinners would soon cure him of his democracy. Shall we begin, Sire?

CZAR: At once. Read the proclamation. Gentlemen, be seated. Alexis, Alexis, I say, come and hear it! It will be good practice for you; you will be doing it yourself some day.

CZAREVITCH: I have heard too much of it already. (*Takes his seat at the table.* COUNT ROUVALOFF *whispers to him.*)

CZAR: What are you whispering about there, Count Rouvaloff?

COUNT ROUVALOFF: I was giving his Royal Highness some good advice, your Majesty.

PRINCE PAUL: Count Rouvaloff is the typical spendthrift, Sire; he is always giving away what he needs most. (*Lays papers before the* CZAR.) I think, Sire, you will approve of this: 'Love of the people, ' 'Father of his people, ' 'Martial law, ' and the usual allusions to Providence in the last line. All it requires now is your Imperial Majesty's signature.

CZAREVITCH: Sire!

PRINCE PAUL (*hurriedly*): I promise your Majesty to crush every Nihilist in Russia in six months if you sign this proclamation; every Nihilist in Russia.

CZAR: Say that again! To crush every Nihilist in Russia; to crush this woman, their leader, who makes war upon me in my own city. Prince Paul Maraloffski, I create you Maréchal of the whole Russian Empire to help you to carry out martial law. Give me the proclamation. I will sign it at once.

PRINCE PAUL (*points on paper*): Here, Sire.

CZAREVITCH (*starts up and puts his hands on the paper*): Stay! I tell you, stay! The priests have taken heaven from the people, and you would take away the earth away too.

PRINCE PAUL (*hurriedly*): We have no time, Prince, now. This boy will ruin everything. The pen, Sire.

CZAREVITCH: What! Is it so small a thing to strangle a nation, to murder a kingdom, to wreck an empire? Who are we who dare lay this ban of terror on a people? Have we less vices than they have, that we bring them to the bar of judgment before us?

PRINCE PAUL: What a Communist the Prince is! He would have an equal distribution of sin as well as of property.

CZAREVITCH: Warmed by the same sun, nurtured by the same air, fashioned of flesh and blood like to our own, wherein are they different to us, save that they starve while we surfeit, that they toil while we idle, that they sicken while we poison, that they die while we –

CZAR: How dare –?

CZAREVITCH: I dare all for the people; but you would rob them of common rights of men.

CZAR: The people have no rights.

CZAREVITCH: Then they have great wrongs. Father, they have won your battles for you; from the pine forests of the Baltic to the palms of India they have ridden on victory's mighty wings! Boy as I am in years, I have seen wave after wave of living men sweep up the heights of battle to their death; ay, and snatch perilous conquest from the scales of war when the bloody crescent seemed to shake above our eagles.

CZAR (*somewhat moved*): Those men are dead. What have I to do with them?

CZAREVITCH: Nothing! The dead are safe; you cannot harm them now. They sleep their last long sleep. Some in Turkish waters, others by the wind-swept heights of Norway and the Dane! But these, the living, our brothers, what have you done for them? They asked you for bread, you gave them a stone. They sought for freedom, you scourged them with scorpions. You have sown the seeds of this revolution yourself – !

PRINCE PAUL: And are we not cutting down the harvest?

CZAREVITCH: Oh, my brothers! Better far that ye had died in the iron hail and screaming shell of battle than to come back to such a doom as this! The beasts of the forest have their lairs, and the wild beasts their caverns, but the people of Russia, conquerors of the world, have no where to lay their heads.

PRINCE PAUL: They have the headsman's block.

CZAREVITCH: The block! Ay! You have killed their souls at your pleasure, you would kill their bodies now.

CZAR: Insolent boy! Have you forgotten who is Emperor of Russia?

CZAREVITCH: No! The people reign now, by the grace of God. You should have been their shepherd; you have fled away like the hireling, and let the wolves in upon them.

CZAR: Take him away! Take him away, Prince Paul!

CZAREVITCH: God hath given his people tongues to speak with; you would cut them out that they may be dumb in their agony, silent in their tor-ture! But, He hath given them hands to smite with, and they shall smite! Ay! From the sick and labouring womb of this unhappy land some revolution, like a bloody child, may rise up and slay you.

CZAR (*leaping up*): Devil! Assassin! Why do you beard me thus to my face?

CZAREVITCH: Because I am a Nihilist! (*The ministers start to their feet; there is a dead silence for a few minutes.*)

CZAR: A Nihilist! A Nihilist! Viper whom I have nurtured, traitor whom I have fondled, is this your bloody secret? Prince Paul Maraloffski, Maréchal of the Russian Empire, arrest the Czarevitch!

MINISTERS: Arrest the Czarevitch!

CZAR: A Nihilist! If you have sown with them, you shall reap with them! If you have talked with them, you shall rot with them! If you have lived with them, with them you shall die!

PRINCE PETROVITCH: Die!

CZAR: A plague on all sons, I say! There should be no more marriages in Russia when one can breed such Serpents as you are! Arrest the Czarevitch, I say!

PRINCE PAUL: Czarevitch! By order of the Emperor, I demand your sword. (CZAREVITCH *gives up sword*; PRINCE PAUL *places it on the table.*)

CZAREVITCH: You will find it unstained by blood.

PRINCE PAUL: Foolish boy! You are not made for a conspirator; you have not learned to hold your tongue. Heroics are out of place in a palace.

CZAR (*sinks into his chair with his eyes fixed on the* CZAREVITCH): O God! My own son against me, my own flesh and blood against me; but I am rid of them all now.

CZAREVITCH: The mighty brotherhood to which I belong has a thousand such as I am, ten thousand better still! (*The* CZAR *starts in his seat.*) The star of freedom is risen already, and far off I hear the mighty wave Democracy break on these cursed shores.

PRINCE PAUL (*to* PRINCE PETROVITCH): In that case you and I must learn how to swim.

CZAREVITCH: Father, Emperor, Imperial Master, I plead not for my own life, but for the lives of my brothers, the people.

PRINCE PAUL (*bitterly*): Your brothers, the people, Prince, are not content with their own lives, they always want to take their neighbours' too.

CZAR (*standing up*): I am tired of being afraid. I have done with terror now. From this day I proclaim war against the people – war to their annihilation. As they have dealt with me, so shall I deal with them. I shall grind them to powder, and strew their dust upon the air. There shall be a spy in every man's house, a traitor on every hearth, a hangman in every village, a gibbet in every square. Plague, leprosy, or fever shall be less deadly than my wrath; I will make every frontier a graveyard, every province a lazar-house, and cure the sick by the sword. I shall have peace in Russia, though it be the peace of the dead. Who said I was a coward? Who said I was afraid? See, thus shall I crush this people beneath my feet! (*Takes up sword of* CZAREVITCH *off table and tramples on it.*)

CZAREVITCH: Father, beware, the sword you tread on may turn and wound you. The people suffer long, but vengeance comes at last, vengeance with red hands and silent feet.

PRINCE PAUL: Bah! The people are bad shots; they always miss one.

CZAREVITCH: There are times when the people are the instruments of God.

CZAR: Ay! And when kings are God's scourges for the people. Take him away! Take him away! Bring in my guards. (*Enter the Imperial Guard.* CZAR *points to* CZAREVITCH, *who stands alone at the side of the stage.*) We will bring him to prison ourselves: prison! I trust no prison. He would escape and kill me. I will have him shot here, here in the open square by the soldiers. Let me never see his face again. (CZAREVITCH *is being led out.*) No, no, leave him! I don't trust guards. They are all Nihilists! (*To* PRINCE PAUL): I trust you, you have no mercy. (*Throws window open and goes out on balcony.*)

CZAREVITCH: If I am to die for the people I am ready. One Nihilist more or less in Russia, what does that matter?

PRINCE PAUL (*looking at his watch*): The dinner is sure to be spoiled. How annoying politics are; and eldest sons!

VOICE (*outside, in the street*): God save the people! (CZAR *is shot, and staggers back into the room.*)

CZAREVITCH (*breaking from the guards, and rushing over*): Father!

CZAR: Murderer! Murderer! You did it! Murderer! (*Dies.*)

TABLEAU

ACT DROP

ACT THREE

SCENE: *same and business as Act One. Man in yellow dress, with drawn sword, at the door.*

Password outside. Væ tyrannis.[1]
Answer. Væ victis[2] (*repeated three times*).

Enter CONSPIRATORS, *who form a semicircle, masked and cloaked.*

PRESIDENT: What hour is it?
FIRST CONSPIRATOR: The hour to strike.
PRESIDENT: What day?
SECOND CONSPIRATOR: The day of Marat.
PRESIDENT: In what month?
THIRD CONSPIRATOR: The months of liberty.
PRESIDENT: What is our duty?
FOURTH CONSPIRATOR: To obey.
PRESIDENT: Our creed?
FIFTH CONSPIRATOR: *Parbleu*, Monsieur le President, I never knew you had one.
CONSPIRATORS: A spy! A spy! Unmask! Unmask! A spy!
PRESIDENT: Let the doors be shut. There are others but Nihilists present.
CONSPIRATORS: Unmask! Unmask! Kill him! kill him! (*Masked Conspirator unmasks.*) Prince Paul!
VERA: Devil! Who lured you into the lion's den?
CONSPIRATORS: Kill him! Kill him!
PRINCE PAUL: *En vérité*, Messieurs, you are not over-hospitable in your welcome.
VERA: Welcome! What welcome should we give you but the dagger or the noose?
PRINCE PAUL: I had no idea really that the Nihilists were so exclusive. Let me assure you that if I had not always had an *entrée* to the very best society,

---

[1] Woe to tyrants.
[2] Woe to the conquered.

and the very worst conspiracies, I could never have been Prime Minister in Russia.

VERA: The tiger cannot change its nature, nor the snake lose its venom; but are you turned a lover of the people?

PRINCE PAUL: Mon Dieu, non, Mademoiselle! I would much sooner talk scandal in a drawing-room than treason in a cellar. Besides, I hate the common mob, who smell of garlic, smoke bad tobacco, get up early, and dine off one dish.

PRESIDENT: What have you to gain, then, by a revolution?

PRINCE PAUL: Mon ami, I have nothing left to lose. That scatter-brained boy, this new Czar, has banished me.

VERA: To Siberia?

PRINCE PAUL: No, to Paris. He has confiscated my estates, robbed me of my office and my cook. I have nothing left but my decorations. I am here for revenge.

PRESIDENT: Then you have a right to be one of us. We also meet daily for revenge.

PRINCE PAUL: You want money of course. No one ever joins a conspiracy who has any. Here. (*Throws money on table.*) You have so many spies that I should think you want information. Well, you will find me the best-informed man in Russia on the abuses of our Government. I made them nearly all myself.

VERA: President, I don't trust this man. He has done us too much harm in Russia to let him go in safety.

PRINCE PAUL: Believe me, Mademoiselle, you are wrong. I will be a most valuable addition to your circle; and as for you, gentlemen, if I had not thought that you would be useful to me I shouldn't have risked my neck among you, or dined an hour earlier than usual so as to be in time.

PRESIDENT: Ay, if he had wanted to spy on us, Vera, he wouldn't have come himself.

PRINCE PAUL (*aside*): No; I should have sent my best friend.

PRESIDENT: Besides, Vera, he is just the man to give us the information we want about some business we have in hand to-night.

VERA: Be it so if you wish it.

PRESIDENT: Brothers, is it your will that Prince Paul Maraloffski be admitted, and take the oath of the Nihilist?

CONSPIRATORS: It is! It is!

PRESIDENT (*holding out dagger and a paper*): Prince Paul, the dagger or the oath?

PRINCE PAUL (*smiles sardonically*): I would sooner annihilate than be annihilated. (*Takes paper.*)

PRESIDENT: Remember: Betray us, and as long as earth holds poison or steel, as long as men can strike or women betray, you shall not escape vengeance. The Nihilists never forget their friends, or forgive their enemies.

PRINCE PAUL: Really? I did not think you were so civilised.

VERA (*pacing up and down behind*): Why is he not here? He will not keep the crown. I know him well.

PRESIDENT: Sign. (PRINCE PAUL *signs*.) You said you thought we had no creed. You were wrong. Read it!

VERA: This is a dangerous thing, President. What can we do with this man?

PRESIDENT: We can use him. He is of value to us to-night and to-morrow.

VERA: Perhaps there will be no morrow for any of us; but we have given him our word: he is safer here than ever he was in his palace.

PRINCE PAUL (*reading*): 'The rights of humanity'! In the old times men carried out their rights for themselves as they lived, but nowadays every baby seems born with a social manifesto in its mouth much bigger than itself. 'Nature is not a temple, but a workshop: we demand the right to labour.' Ah, I shall surrender my own rights in that respect.

VERA (*pacing up and down behind*): Oh, will he never come? Will he never come?

PRINCE PAUL: 'The family as subversive of true socialistic and communal unity is to be annihilated.' Yes, President, I agree completely with Article 5. A family is a terrible incumbrance, especially when one is not married. (*Three knocks at the door.*)

VERA: Alexis at last!

Password: Væ tyrannis!

Answer: Væ victis! (*Enter* MICHAEL STROGANOFF.)

PRESIDENT: Michael, the regicide! Brothers, let us do honour to a man who has killed a king.

VERA (*aside*): Oh, he will come yet!

PRESIDENT: Michael, you have saved Russia.

MICHAEL: Ay, Russia was free for a moment when the tyrant fell, but the sun of liberty has set again like that false dawn which cheats our eyes in autumn.

PRESIDENT: The dread night of tyranny is not yet past for Russia.

MICHAEL (*clutching his knife*): One more blow, and the end is come indeed.

VERA (*aside*): One more blow! What does he mean? Oh, impossible! But why is he not with us? Alexis! Alexis! Why are you not here?

PRESIDENT: But how did you escape, Michael? They said you had been seized.

MICHAEL: I was dressed in the uniform of the Imperial Guard. The Colonel on duty was a brother, and gave me the password. I drove through the troops in safety with it, and, thanks to my good horse, reached the walls before the gates were closed.

PRESIDENT: What a chance his coming out on the balcony was!

MICHAEL: A chance? There is no such thing as chance. It was God's finger led him there.

PRESIDENT: And where have you been these three days?

MICHAEL: Hiding in the house of the priest Nicholas at the cross-roads.

PRESIDENT: Nicholas is an honest man.

MICHAEL: Ay, honest enough for a priest. I am here now for vengeance on a traitor!

VERA (*aside*): O God, will he never come? Alexis! Why are you not here? You cannot have turned traitor!

MICHAEL (*seeing* PRINCE PAUL): Prince Paul Maraloffski here! By St. George, a lucky capture! This must have been Vera's doing. She is the only one who could have lured that serpent into the trap.

PRESIDENT: Prince Paul has just taken the oath.

VERA: Alexis, the Czar, has banished him from Russia.

MICHAEL: Bah! A blind to cheat us. We will keep Prince Paul here, and find some office for him in our reign of terror. He is well accustomed by this time to bloody work.

PRINCE PAUL (*approaching* MICHAEL): That was a long shot of yours, *mon camarade*.

MICHAEL: I have had a good deal of practice shooting, since I have been a boy, off your Highness's wild boars.

PRINCE PAUL: Are my gamekeepers like moles, then, always asleep?

MICHAEL: No, Prince. I am one of them; but, like you, I am fond of robbing what I am put to watch.

PRESIDENT: This must be a new atmosphere for you, Prince Paul. We speak the truth to one another here.

PRINCE PAUL: How misleading you must find it! You have an odd medley here, President.

PRESIDENT: You recognise a good many friends, I dare say?

PRINCE PAUL: Yes, there is always more brass than brains in an aristocracy.

PRESIDENT: But you are here yourself?

PRINCE PAUL: I? As I cannot be a Prime Minister, I must be a Nihilist. There is no alternative.

VERA: O God, will he never come? The hand is on the stroke of the hour. Will he never come?

MICHAEL (*aside*): President, you know what we have to do? 'Tis but a sorry hunter who leaves the wolf cub alive to avenge his father. How are we to get at this boy? It must be to-night. To-morrow he will be throwing some sop of reform to the people, and it will be too late for à republic.

PRINCE PAUL: You are quite right. Good kings are the only dangerous enemies that modern democracy has and when he has begun by banishing me you may be sure he intends to be a patriot.

MICHAEL: I am sick of patriot kings; what Russia needs is a Republic.

PRINCE PAUL: Messieurs, I have brought you two documents which I think will interest you – the proclamation this young Czar intends publishing to-morrow, and a plan of the Winter Palace, where he sleeps to-night. (*Hands papers.*)

VERA: I dare not ask them what they are plotting about. Oh, why is Alexis not here?

PRESIDENT: Prince, this is most valuable information. Michael, you were right. If it is not to-night it will be too late. Read that.

MICHAEL: Ah! A loaf of bread flung to a starving nation. A lie to cheat the people. (*Tears it up*.) It must be to-night. I do not believe him. Would he have kept his crown had he loved the people? But how are we to get at him, and shall we who could not bear the scorpions of the father suffer the whips of the son? No; whatever is, must be destroyed: whatever is, is wrong.

PRINCE PAUL: The key of the private door in the street. (*Hands key*.)

PRESIDENT: Prince, we are in your debt.

PRINCE PAUL (*smiling*): The normal condition of the Nihilists.

MICHAEL: Ay, but we are paying our debts off with interest now. Two Emperors in one week. That will make the balance straight. We would have thrown in a Prime Minister if you had not come.

PRINCE PAUL: Ah, I am sorry you told me. It robs my visit of all its picturesqueness and adventure. I thought I was perilling my head by coming here, and you tell me I have saved it. One is sure to be disappointed if one tries to get romance out of modern life.

MICHAEL: It is not so romantic a thing to lose one's head, Prince Paul.

PRINCE PAUL: No, but it must often be very dull to keep it. Don't you find that sometimes? (*Clock strikes six*.)

VERA (*sinking into a seat*): Oh, it is past the hour! It is past the hour!

MICHAEL (*to* PRESIDENT): Remember to-morrow will be too late.

PRESIDENT: Brothers, it is full time. Which of us is absent?

CONSPIRATORS: Alexis! Alexis!

PRESIDENT: Michael, read Rule 7.

MICHAEL: 'When any brother shall have disobeyed a summons to be present, the president shall inquire if there is anything alleged against him.'

PRESIDENT: Is there anything against our brother Alexis?

CONSPIRATORS: He wears a crown! He wears a crown!

PRESIDENT: Michael, read Article 7 of the Code of Revolution.

MICHAEL: 'Between the Nihilists and all men who wear crowns above their fellows, there is war to the death.'

PRESIDENT: Brothers, what say you? Is Alexis, the Czar, guilty or not?

OMNES: He is guilty!

PRESIDENT: What shall the penalty be?

OMNES: Death!

PRESIDENT: Let the lots be prepared; it shall be to-night.

PRINCE PAUL: Ah, this is really interesting! I was getting afraid conspiracies were as dull as courts are.

PROFESSOR MARFA: My forte is more in writing pamphlets than in taking shots. Still a regicide has always a place in history.

MICHAEL: If your pistol is as harmless as your pen, this young tyrant will have a long life.

PRINCE PAUL: You ought to remember, too, Professor, that if you were seized, as you probably would be, and hung, as you certainly would be, there would be nobody left to read your own articles.

PRESIDENT: Brothers, are you ready?

VERA (*starting up*): Not yet! Not yet! I have a word to say.

MICHAEL (*aside*): Plague take her! I knew it would come to this.

VERA: This boy has been our brother. Night after night he has perilled his own life to come here. Night after night, when every street was filled with spies, every house with traitors. Delicately nurtured like a king's son, he has dwelt among us.

PRESIDENT: Ay! Under a false name. He lied to us at the beginning. He lies to us now at the end.

VERA: I swear he is true. There is not a man here who does not owe him his life a thousand times. When the bloodhounds were on us that night, who saved us from arrest, torture, flogging, death, but he ye seek to kill? –

MICHAEL: To kill all tyrants is our mission!

VERA: He is no tyrant. I know him well! He loves the people.

PRESIDENT: We know him too; he is a traitor.

VERA: A traitor! Three days ago he could have betrayed every man of you here, and the gibbet would have been your doom. He gave you all your lives once. Give him a little time – a week, a month, a few days; but now! O God, not now!

CONSPIRATORS (*brandishing daggers*): To-night! To-night! To-night!

VERA: Peace, you gorged adders! Peace!

MICHAEL: What, are we not here to annihilate? Shall we not keep our oath?

VERA: Your oath! Your oath! Greedy that you are of gain, every man's hand lusting for his neighbour's pelf, every heart set on pillage and rapine; who, of ye all, if the crown were set on his head, would give an empire up for the mob to scramble for? The people are not yet fit for a republic in Russia.

PRESIDENT: Every nation is fit for a republic.

MICHAEL: The man is a tyrant.

VERA: A tyrant! Hath he not dismissed his evil counsellors. That ill-omened raven of his father's life hath had his wings clipped and his claws pared, and comes to us croaking for revenge. Oh, have mercy on him! Give him a week to live!

PRESIDENT: Vera, pleading for a king!

VERA (*proudly*): I plead not for a king, but for a brother.

MICHAEL: For a traitor to his oath, a coward who should have flung the purple back to the fools that gave it him. No, Vera, no. The brood of men is not yet dead, nor the dull earth grown sick of child-bearing. No crowned man in Russia shall pollute God's air by living.

PRESIDENT: You bade us try you once. We have tried you, and you are found wanting.

MICHAEL: Vera, I am not blind; I know your secret. You love this boy, this young prince with his pretty face, his curled hair, his soft white hands. Fool that you are, dupe of a lying tongue, do you know what he would have done to you, this boy you think loved you? He would have made you his mistress, used your body at his pleasure, thrown you away when he was wearied of you; you, the priestess of liberty, the flame of revolution, the torch of democracy.

VERA: What he would have done to me matters little. To the people, at least, he will be true. He loves the people; at least, he loves liberty.

PRESIDENT: So, he would' play the citizen-king, would he, while we starve? Would flatter us with sweet speeches, would cheat us with promises like his father, would lie to us as his whole race have lied.

MICHAEL: And you whose very name made every despot tremble for his life, you, Vera Sabouroff, you would betray liberty for a lover and the people for a paramour!

CONSPIRATORS: Traitress! Draw the lots; draw the lots!

VERA: In thy throat thou liest, Michael! I love him not. He loves me not.

MICHAEL: You love him not? Shall he not die then?

VERA (*with an effort, clenching her hands*): Ay, it is right that he should die. He hath broken his oath. There should be no crowned man in Europe. Have I not sworn it? To be strong, our new republic should be drunk with the blood of kings. He hath broken his oath. As the father died so let the son die too. Yet not to-night, not to-night. Russia, that hath borne her centuries of wrong, can wait a week for liberty. Give him a week.

PRESIDENT: We will have none of you! Begone from us to this boy you love.

MICHAEL: Though I find him in your arms I shall kill him.

CONSPIRATORS: To-night! To-night! To-night!

MICHAEL (*holding up his hand*): A moment! I have something to say. (*Approaches* VERA; *speaks very slowly.*) Vera Sabouroff, have you forgotten your brother? (*Pauses to see effect;* VERA *starts.*) Have you forgotten that young face, pale with famine; those young limbs twisted with torture; the iron chains they made him walk in? What week of liberty did they give him? What pity did they show him for a day? (VERA *falls in a chair.*) Oh! You could talk glibly enough then of vengeance, glibly enough of liberty. When you said you would come to Moscow, your old father caught you by the knees and begged you not to leave him to die childless and alone. I seem to hear his cries still ringing in my ears, but you were as deaf to him as the rocks on the roadside. You left your father that night, and three weeks after he died of a broken heart. You wrote to me to follow you here. I did so; first because I loved you; but you soon cured me of that; whatever gentle feeling, whatever pity, whatever love, whatever humanity, was in my heart you withered up and destroyed, as the canker worm eats the corn. You bade me cast out love from my breast as a vile thing, you turned my hand to iron, and my heart to stone; you told me to live for freedom and revenge. I have done so. But you, what have you done?

VERA: Let the lots be drawn! (CONSPIRATORS *applaud.*)

PRINCE PAUL (*aside*): Ah, the Grand Duke will come to the throne sooner than he expected. He is sure to make a good king under my guidance. He is so cruel to animals, and never keeps his word.

MICHAEL: Now you are yourself at last, Vera.

VERA (*standing motionless in the middle*): The lots, I say, the lots! I am no woman now. My blood seems turned to gall; my heart is as cold as steel is; my hand shall be more deadly. From the desert and the tomb the voice of my prisoned brother cries aloud, and bids me strike one blow for liberty. The lots, I say, the lots!

PRESIDENT: Are ready. Michael, you have the right to draw first: you are a regicide.

VERA: O God, into my hands! Into my hands! (*They draw the lots from a bowl surmounted by a skull.*)

PRESIDENT: Open your lots.

VERA (*opening her lot*): The lot is mine! See, the bloody sign upon it! Dmitri, my brother, you shall have your revenge now.

PRESIDENT: Vera Sabouroff, you are chosen to be a regicide. God has been good to you. The dagger or the poison? (*Offers her dagger and vial.*)

VERA: I can trust my hand better with the dagger; it never fails. (*Takes dagger.*) I shall stab him to the heart, as he has stabbed me. Traitor, to leave us for a ribbon, a gaud, a bauble, to lie to me every day he came here, to forget us in an hour. Michael was right, he loved me not, nor the people either. Methinks that if I was a mother and bore a man-child, I would poison my breast against him, lest he might grow to a traitor or to a king. (PRINCE PAUL *whispers to the* PRESIDENT.)

PRESIDENT: Ay, Prince Paul, that is the best way. Vera, the Czar sleeps tonight in his own room in the north wing of the palace. Here is a key of the private door in the street. The password of the guards will be given to you. His own servants will be drugged. You will find him alone.

VERA: It is well. I shall not fail.

PRESIDENT: We will wait outside in the Place Saint Isaac, under the window. As the clock strikes twelve from the tower of St. Nicholas you will give us the sign that the dog is dead.

VERA: And what shall the sign be?

PRESIDENT: You are to throw us out the bloody dagger.

MICHAEL: Dripping with the traitor's life.

PRESIDENT: Else we shall know that you have been seized, and we will burst our way in, drag you from his guards.

MICHAEL: And kill him in the midst of them.

PRESIDENT: Michael, you will lead us?

MICHAEL: Ay, I shall lead you. See that your hand fails you not, Vera Sabouroff.

VERA: Fool, is it so hard a thing to kill one's enemy?

PRINCE PAUL (*aside*): This is the ninth conspiracy I have been in in Russia. They always end in a *voyage en Siberie* for my friends and a new decoration for myself.

MICHAEL: It is your last conspiracy, Prince.

PRESIDENT: At twelve o'clock, the bloody dagger.

VERA: Ay, red with the blood of that false heart. I shall not forget it. (*Standing in middle of stage.*) To strangle whatever nature is in me, neither to love nor to be loved, neither to pity nor to be pitied. Ay! It is an oath, an oath. Methinks the spirit of Charlotte Corday has entered my soul now. I shall

carve my name on the world, and be ranked among the great heroines. Ay!
The spirit of Charlotte Corday beats in each petty vein, and nerves my wo-
man's hand to strike, as I have nerved my woman's heart to hate. Though he
laugh in his dreams I shall not falter. Though he sleep peacefully I shall not
miss my blow. Be glad, my brother, in your stifled cell; be glad and laugh to-
night. To-night this new-fledged Czar shall post with bloody feet to hell, and
greet his father there! This Czar! O traitor, liar, false to his oath, false to me!
To play the patriot among us, and now to wear a crown; to sell us, like Judas,
for thirty silver pieces, to betray us with a kiss! (*With more passion*.) O Lib-
erty, O mighty mother of eternal time, thy robe is purple with the blood of
those who have died for thee! Thy throne is the Calvary of the people, thy
crown the crown of thorns. O crucified mother, the despot has driven a nail
through thy right hand, and the tyrant through thy left! Thy feet are pierced
with their iron. When thou wert athirst thou calledst on the priests for water,
and they gave thee bitter drink. They thrust a sword into thy side. They
mocked thee in thine agony of age on age. Here, on thy altar, O Liberty, do I
dedicate myself to thy service; do with me as thou wilt! (*Brandishing the dag-
ger*.) The end has come now, and by thy sacred wounds, O crucified mother,
O Liberty, I swear that Russia shall be saved!

ACT DROP

ACT FOUR

SCENE: *Antechamber of the Czar's private room. Large win-
dows at the back, with drawn curtains over it.*
    Present: PRINCE PETROVITCH, BARON RAFF, MARQUIS
DE POIVRARD, COUNT ROUVALOFF.

PRINCE PETROVITCH: He is beginning well, this young Czar.

BARON RAFF (*shrugs his shoulders*): All young Czars do begin well.

COUNT ROUVALOFF: And end badly.

MARQUIS DE POIVRARD: Well, I have no right to complain. He has done
me one good service, at any rate.

PRINCE PETROVITCH: Cancelled your appointment to Archangel, I
suppose?

MARQUIS DE POIVRARD: Yes; my head wouldn't have been safe there for
an hour.

Enter GENERAL KOTEMKIN.

BARON RAFF: Ah! General, any more news of our romantic young
Emperor?

GENERAL KOTEMKIN: You are quite right to call him romantic, Baron; a
week ago I found him amusing himself in a garret with a company of strolling

players; to-day his whim is all the convicts in Siberia are to be recalled, and the political prisoners, as he calls them, amnestied.

PRINCE PETROVITCH: Political prisoners! Why, half of them are no better than common murderers!

COUNT ROUVALOFF: And the other half much worse?

BARON RAFF: Oh, you wrong them, surely, Count. Wholesale trade has always been more respectable than retail.

COUNT ROUVALOFF: But he is really too romantic. He objected yesterday to my having the monopoly of the salt tax. He said the people had a right to have cheap salt.

MARQUIS DE POIVRARD: Oh, that's nothing; but he actually disapproved of a State banquet every night because there is a famine in the Southern provinces. (*The young* CZAR *enters unobserved, and overhears the rest.*)

PRINCE PETROVITCH: *Quelle bêtise!*

The more starvation there is among the people the better. It teaches them self-denial, an excellent virtue, Baron.

BARON RAFF: I have often heard so.

GENERAL KOTEMKIN: He talked of a Parliament, too, in Russia, and said the people should have deputies to represent them.

BARON RAFF: As if there was not enough brawling in the streets already, but we must give the people a room to do it in. But, Messieurs, the worst is yet to come. He threatens a complete reform of the public service on the ground that the people are too heavily taxed.

MARQUIS DE POIVRARD: He can't be serious there. What is the use of the people except for us to get money out of? But talking of the taxes, my dear Baron you must really let me have forty thousand roubles to-morrow; my wife says she must have a new diamond bracelet.

COUNT ROUVALOFF (*aside to* BARON RAFF): Ah, to match the one Prince Paul gave her last week, I suppose.

PRINCE PETROVITCH: I must have sixty thousand roubles at once, Baron. My son is overwhelmed with debts of honour which he can't pay.

BARON RAFF: What an excellent son to imitate his father so carefully!

GENERAL KOTEMKIN: You are always getting money. I never get a single kopeck I have not got a right to. It's unbearable; it's ridiculous! My nephew is going to be married. I must get his dowry for him.

PRINCE PETROVITCH: My dear General, your nephew must be a perfect Turk. He seems to get married three times a week regularly.

GENERAL KOTEMKIN: Well, he wants a dowry to console him.

COUNT ROUVALOFF: I am sick of town. I want a house in the country.

MARQUIS DE POIVRARD: I am sick of the country. I want a house in town.

BARON RAFF: Gentlemen, I am extremely sorry for you. It is out of the question.

PRINCE PETROVITCH: But my son, Baron?

GENERAL KOTEMKIN: But my nephew?

MARQUIS DE POIVRARD: But my house in town?

COUNT ROUVALOFF: But my house in the country?

MARQUIS DE POIVRARD: But my wife's diamond bracelet?

BARON RAFF: Gentlemen, impossible! The old régime in Russia is dead; the funeral begins to-day.

COUNT ROUVALOFF: Then I shall wait for the resurrection.

PRINCE PETROVITCH: Yes; but, *en attendant*, what are we to do?

BARON RAFF: What have we always done in Russia when a Czar suggests reform? Nothing. You forget we are diplomatists. Men of thought should have nothing to do with action. Reforms in Russia are very tragic, but they always end in a farce.

COUNT ROUVALOFF: I wish Prince Paul were here. By the by, I think this boy is rather ungrateful to him. If that clever old Prince had not proclaimed him Emperor at once without giving him time to think about it, he would have given up his crown, I believe, to the first cobbler he met in the street.

PRINCE PETROVITCH: But do you think, Baron, that Prince Paul is really going?

BARON RAFF: He is exiled.

PRINCE PETROVITCH: Yes; but is he going?

BARON RAFF: I am sure of it; at least he told me he had sent two telegrams already to Paris about his dinner.

COUNT ROUVALOFF: Ah! That settles the matter.

CZAR (*coming forward*): Prince Paul had better send a third telegram and order (*counting them*) six extra places.

BARON RAFF: The devil!

CZAR: No, Baron, the Czar. Traitors! There would be no bad kings in the world if there were no bad ministers like you. It is men such as you are who wreck mighty empires on the rock of their own greatness. Our mother, Russia, hath no need of such unnatural sons. You can make no atonement now; it is too late for that. The grave cannot give back your dead, nor the gibbet your martyrs, but I shall be more merciful to you. I give you your lives! That is the curse I would lay on you. But if there is a man of you found in Moscow by to-morrow night your heads will be off your shoulders.

BARON RAFF: You remind us wonderfully, Sire, of your Imperial father.

CZAR: I banish you all from Russia. Your estates are confiscated to the people. You may carry your titles with you. Reforms in Russia, Baron, always end in a farce. You will have a good opportunity, Prince Petrovitch, of practising self-denial, that excellent virtue! That excellent virtue! So, Baron, you think a Parliament in Russia would be merely a place for brawling. Well, I will see that the reports of each session are sent to you regularly.

BARON RAFF: Sire, you are adding another horror to exile.

CZAR: But you will have such time for literature now. You forget you are diplomatists. Men of thought should have nothing to do with action.

PRINCE PETROVITCH: Sire, we did but jest.

CZAR: Then I banish you for your bad jokes. *Bon voyage* Messieurs. If you value your lives you will catch the first train for Paris. (*Exeunt Ministers.*) Russia is well rid of such men as these. They are the jackals that follow in the lion's track. They have no courage themselves except to pillage and rob. But for these men and for Prince Paul my father would have been a good king, would not have died so horribly as he did die. How strange it is, the most real parts of one's life always seem to be a dream! The council, the fearful law which was to kill the people, the arrest, the cry in the court-yard, the pistol-shot, my father's bloody hands, and then the crown! One can live for years sometimes without living at all, and then all life comes crowding into one single hour. I had no time to think. Before my father's hideous shriek of death had died in my ears I found this crown on my head, the purple robe around me, and heard myself called a king. I would have given it up all then; it seemed nothing to me then; but now, can I give it up now? Well, Colonel, well? (*Enter* COLONEL OF THE GUARD.)

COLONEL: What password does your Imperial Majesty desire should be given to-night?

CZAR: Password?

COLONEL: For the cordon of guards, Sire, on night duty around the palace.

CZAR: You can dismiss them. I have no need of them. (*Exit* COLONEL). (*Goes to the crown lying on the table.*) What subtle potency lies hidden in this gaudy bauble, the crown, that makes one feel like a god when one wears it? To hold in one's hand this little fiery-coloured world, to reach out one's arm to earth's uttermost limit, to girdle the seas with one's galley; to make the land a highway for one's hosts; this is to wear a crown! To wear a crown! The meanest serf in Russia who is loved is better crowned than I. How love out-weighs the balance! How poor appears the widest empire of this golden world when matched with love! Pent up in this palace, with spies dogging every step, I have heard nothing of her; I have not seen her once since that fearful hour, three days ago, when I found myself suddenly the Czar of this wide waste, Russia. Oh, could I see her for a moment; tell her now the secret of my life I have never dared to utter before; tell her why I wear this crown, when I have sworn eternal war against all crowned men! There was a meeting to-night. I received my summons by an unknown hand; but how could I go? I, who have broken my oath! Who have broken my oath!

Enter PAGE.

PAGE: It is after eleven, Sire. Shall I take the first watch in your room to-night?

CZAR: Why should you watch me, boy? The stars are my best sentinels.

PAGE: It was your Imperial father's wish, Sire, never to be left alone while he slept.

CZAR: My father was troubled with bad dreams. Go, get to your bed, boy; it is nigh on midnight, and these late hours will spoil those red cheeks. (PAGE *tries to kiss his hand.*) Nay, nay; we have played together too often for that. Oh, to breathe the same air as her, and not to see her! The light seems to have gone from my life, the sun vanished from my day.

PAGE: Sire – Alexis – let me stay with you to-night! There is some danger over you; I feel there is.

CZAR: What should I fear? I have banished all my enemies from Russia. Set the brazier here, by me; it is very cold, and I would sit by it for a time. Go, boy, go; I have much to think about to-night. (*Goes to back of stage, draws aside a curtain. View of Moscow by moonlight.*) The snow has fallen heavily since sunset. How white and cold my city looks under this pale moon! And yet what hot and fiery hearts beat in this icy Russia, for all its frost and snow. Oh, to see her for a moment; to tell her all; to tell her why I am a king! But she does not doubt me; she said she would trust in me. Though I have broken my oath, she will have trust. It is very cold. Where is my cloak? I shall sleep for an hour. Then I have ordered my sledge, and, though I die for it, I shall see Vera to-night. Did I not bid thee go, boy? What! Must I play the tyrant so soon? Go, go! I cannot live without seeing her. My horses will be here in an hour; one hour between me and love! How heavy this charcoal fire smells. (*Exit the* PAGE. *Lies down on a couch beside brazier.*)

Enter VERA, *in a black cloak.*

VERA: Asleep! God, thou art good! Who shall deliver him from my hands now? This is he! The democrat who would make himself a king, the republican who hath worn a crown, the traitor who hath lied to us. Michael was right. He loved not the people. He loved me not. (*Bends over him.*) Oh, why should such deadly poison lie in such sweet lips? Was there not gold enough in his hair before, but he should tarnish it with this crown? But my day has come now; the day of the people, of liberty, has come! Your day, my brother, has come! Though I have strangled whatever nature is in me, I did not think it had been so easy to kill. One blow and it is over, and I can wash my hands in water afterwards, I can wash my hands afterwards. Come, I shall save Russia. I have sworn it. (*Raises the dagger to strike.*)

CZAR (*starting up, seizes her by both hands*): Vera, you here! My dream was no dream at all. Why have you left me three days alone, when I most needed you? O God, you think I am a traitor, a liar, a king? I am, for love of you. Vera, it was for you I broke my oath and wear my father's crown. I would lay at your feet this mighty Russia, which you and I have loved so well; would give you this earth as your footstool; set this crown on your head. The people will love us. We will rule them by love, as a father rules his children. There shall be liberty in Russia for every man to think as his heart bids him; liberty for men to speak as they think. I have banished the wolves that preyed on us; I have brought back your brother from Siberia; I have opened the blackened jaws of the mine. The courier is already on his way; within a week Dmitri and all those with him will be back in their own land. The people shall be free – are free now. When they gave me this crown first, I would have flung it back to them, had it not been for you, Vera. O God! It is men's custom in Russia to bring gifts to those they love. I said, I will bring to the woman I love a people, an empire, a world! Vera, it is for you, for you alone, I kept this crown; for you alone I am a king. Oh, I have loved you better than my oath! Why will you not speak to me? You love me not! You love me not! You have come to warn me of some plot against my life. What is life worth to me without you? (CONSPIRATORS *murmur outside*.)

VERA: Oh, lost! Lost! Lost!

CZAR: Nay, you are safe here. It wants five hours still of dawn. To-morrow, I will lead you forth to the whole people –

VERA: To-morrow –

CZAR: Will crown you with my own hands as Empress in that great cathedral which my fathers built.

VERA (*loosens her hand violently from him, and starts up*): I am a Nihilist! I cannot wear a crown!

CZAR (*falls at her feet*): I am no king now. I am only a boy who has loved you better than his honour, better than his oath. For love of the people I would have been a patriot. For love of you I have been a traitor. Let us go forth together, we will live amongst the common people. I am no king. I will toil for you like the peasant or the serf. Oh, love me a little too! (CONSPIRATORS *murmur outside*.)

VERA (*clutching dagger*): To strangle whatever nature is in me, neither to love nor to be loved, neither to pity nor – oh, I am a woman! God help me, I am a woman! O Alexis! I too have broken my oath; I am a traitor. I love. Oh, do not speak, do not speak – (*kisses his lips*) – the first, the last time. (*He clasps her in his arms; they sit on the couch together*.)

CZAR: I could die now.

VERA: What does death do in thy lips? Thy life, thy love are enemies of death. Speak not of death. Not yet, not yet.

CZAR: I know not why death came into my heart. Perchance the cup of life is filled too full of pleasure to endure. This is our wedding night.

VERA: Our wedding night!

CZAR: And if death came himself, methinks that I could kiss his pallid mouth, and such sweet poison from it.

VERA: Our wedding night! Nay, nay. Death should not sit at the feast. There is no such thing as death.

CZAR: There shall not be for us. (CONSPIRATORS *murmur outside*.)

VERA: What is that? Did you not hear something?

CZAR: Only your voice, that fowler's note which lures my heart away like a poor bird upon the limed twig.

VERA: Methought that someone laughed.

CZAR: It was but the wind and rain; the night is full of storm. (CONSPIRATORS *murmur outside*.)

VERA: It should be so, indeed. Oh, where are your guards? Where are your guards?

CZAR: Where should they be but at home? I shall not live pent round by sword and steel. The love of a people is a king's best bodyguard.

VERA: The love of a people!

CZAR: Sweet, you are safe here. Nothing can harm you here. O love, I knew you trusted me! You said you would have trust.

VERA: I have had trust. O love, the past seems but some dull, grey dream from which our souls have wakened. This is life at last.

CZAR: Ay, life at last.

VERA: Our wedding night! Oh, let me drink my fill of love to-night! Nay, sweet, not yet, not yet. How still it is, and yet methinks the air is full of music. It is some nightingale who, wearying of the south, has come to sing in this bleak north to lovers such as we. It is the nightingale. Dost thou not hear it?

CZAR: O sweet, mine ears are clogged to all sweet sounds save thine own voice, and mine eyes blinded to all sights but thee, else had I heard that nightingale, and seen the golden-vestured morning sun itself steal from its sombre east before its time, for jealousy that thou art twice as fair.

VERA: Yet would that thou hadst heard the nightingale. Methinks that bird will never sing again.

CZAR: It is no nightingale. 'Tis love himself singing for very ecstasy of joy that thou art changed into his votaress. (*Clock begins striking twelve.*) Oh, listen, sweet, it is the lovers' hour. Come, let us stand without, and hear the midnight answered from tower to tower over the wide white town. Our wedding night! What is that? What is that? (*Loud murmurs of* CONSPIRATORS *in the street.*)

VERA (*breaks from him and rushes across the stage*): The wedding guests are here already! Ay! You shall have your sign! (*Stabs herself.*) You shall have your sign! (*Rushes to the window.*)

CZAR (*intercepts her by rushing between her and window, and snatches dagger out of her hand*): Vera!

VERA (*clinging to him*): Give me back the dagger! Give me back the dagger! There are men in the street who seek your life! Your guards have betrayed you! This bloody dagger is the signal that you are dead. (CONSPIRATORS *begin to shout below in the street.*) Oh, there is not a moment to be lost! Throw it out! Throw it out! Nothing can save me now; this dagger is poisoned! I feel death already in my heart. There was no other way but this.

CZAR (*holding dagger out of her reach*): Death is in my heart too; we shall die together!

VERA: Oh, love! Love! Love! Be merciful to me! The wolves are hot upon you! – you must live for liberty, for Russia, for me! Oh, you do not love me! You offered me an empire once! Give me this dagger, now! Oh, you are cruel! My life for yours! What does it matter? (*Loud shout in the street,* 'VERA! VERA! *To the rescue! To the rescue!*')

CZAR: The bitterness of death is past for me.

VERA: Oh, they are breaking in below! See! The bloody man behind you! (CZAR *turns round for an instant.*) Ah! (VERA *snatches dagger and flings it out of window.*)

CONSPIRATORS (*below*): Long live the people!

CZAR: What have you done?

VERA: I have saved Russia! (*Dies*).

TABLEAU

CURTAIN

A FLORENTINE TRAGEDY[1]

Enter THE HUSBAND

SIMONE: My good wife, you come slowly, were it not better
To run to meet your lord? Here, take my cloak.
Take this pack first. 'Tis heavy. I have sold nothing:
Save a furred robe unto the Cardinal's son,
Who hopes to wear it when his father dies,
And hopes that will be soon.

                         But who is this?
Why you have here some friend. Some kinsman doubtless,
Newly returned from foreign lands and fallen
Upon a house without a host to greet him?
I crave your pardon, kinsman. For a house
Lacking a host is but an empty thing
And void of honour; a cup without its wine,
A scabbard without steel to keep it straight,
A flowerless garden widowed of the sun.
Again I crave your pardon, my sweet cousin.

BIANCA: This is no kinsman and no cousin neither.

SIMONE: No kinsman, and no cousin! You amaze me.
Who is it then who with such courtly grace
Deigns to accept our hospitalities?

GUIDO: My name is Guido Bardi.

SIMONE:
                           What! The son
Of that great Lord of Florence whose dim towers
Like shadows silvered by the wandering moon
I see from out my casement every night!
Sir Guido Bardi, you are welcome here,
Twice welcome. For I trust my honest wife,
Most honest if uncomely to the eye,
Hath not with foolish chatterings wearied you,
As is the wont of women.

GUIDO:
                       Your gracious lady,
Whose beauty is a lamp that pales the stars
And robs Diana's quiver of her beams
Has welcomed me with such sweet courtesies
That if it be her pleasure, and your own,
I will come often to your simple house.
And when your business bids you walk abroad

---

[1] This play is only a fragment and was never completed. The poet, T. Sturge Moore, wrote an opening scene for the purpose of presentation, but only Oscar Wilde's work is given here.

I will sit here and charm her loneliness
Lest she might sorrow for you overmuch.
What say you, good Simone?

SIMONE: My noble Lord,
You bring me such high honour that my tongue
Like a slave's tongue is tied, and cannot say
The word it would. Yet not to give you thanks
Were to be too unmannerly. So, I thank you,
From my heart's core.

                    It is such things as these
That knit a state together, when a Prince
So nobly born and of such fair address,
Forgetting unjust Fortune's differences,
Comes to an honest burgher's honest home
As a most honest friend.

                    And yet, my Lord,
I fear I am too bold. Some other night
We trust that you will come here as a friend,
To-night you come to buy my merchandise.
Is it not so? Silks, velvets, what you will,
I doubt not but I have some dainty wares
Will woo your fancy. True, the hour is late,
But we poor merchants toil both night and day
To make our scanty gains. The tolls are high,
And every city levies its own toll,
And prentices are unskilful, and wives even
Lack sense and cunning, though Bianca here
Has brought me a rich customer to-night.
Is it not so, Bianca? But I waste time.
Where is my pack? Where is my pack, I say?
Open it, my good wife. Unloose the cords.
Kneel down upon the floor. You are better so.
Nay not that one, the other. Despatch, despatch!
Buyers will grow impatient oftentimes.
We dare not keep them waiting. Ay! 'tis that,
Give it to me; with care. It is most costly.
Touch it with care. And now, my noble Lord –
Nay, pardon, I have here a Lucca damask,
The very web of silver and the roses
So cunningly wrought that they lack perfume merely
To cheat the wanton sense. Touch it, my Lord.
Is it not soft as water, strong as steel?
And then the roses! Are they not finely woven?
I think the hillsides that best love the rose,
At Bellosguardo or at Fiesole,
Throw no such blossoms on the lap of spring,

Or if they do their blossoms droop and die.
Such is the fate of all the dainty things
That dance in wind and water. Nature herself
Makes war on her own loveliness and slays
Her children like Medea. Nay but, my Lord,
Look closer still. Why in this damask here
It is summer always, and no winter's tooth
Will ever blight these blossoms. For every ell
I paid a piece of gold. Red gold, and good,
The fruit of careful thrift.

GUIDO: Honest Simone,
Enough, I pray you. I am well content,
To-morrow I will send my servant to you,
Who will pay twice your price.

SIMONE: My generous Prince!
I kiss your hands. And now I do remember
Another treasure hidden in my house
Which you must see. It is a robe of state:
Woven by a Venetian: the stuff, cut-velvet:
The pattern, pomegranates: each separate seed
Wrought of a pearl: the collar all of pearls,
As thick as moths in summer streets at night,
And whiter than the moons that madmen see
Through prison bars at morning. A male ruby
Burns like a lighted coal within the clasp.
The Holy Father has not such a stone,
Nor could the Indies show a brother to it
The brooch itself is of most curious art,
Cellini never made a fairer thing
To please the great Lorenzo. You must wear it.
There is none worthier in our city here,
And it will suit you well. Upon one side
A slim and horned satyr leaps in gold
To catch some nymph of silver. Upon the other
Stands Silence with a crystal in her hand,
No bigger than the smallest ear of corn,
That wavers at the passing of a bird,
And yet so cunningly wrought that one would say
It breathed, or held its breath.

                              Worthy Bianca,
Would not this noble and most costly robe
Suit young Lord Guido well?

                              Nay, but entreat him;
He will refuse you nothing, though the price
Be as a prince's ransom. And your profit
Shall not be less than mine.

BIANCA:　　　　　　　Am I your prentice?
Why should I chaffer for your velvet robe?

GUIDO: Nay, fair Bianca, I will buy your robe,
And all things that the honest merchant has
I will buy also. Princes must be ransomed,
And fortunate are all high lords who fall
Into the white hands of so fair a foe.

SIMONE: I stand rebuked. But you will buy my wares?
Will you not buy them? Fifty thousand crowns
Would scarce repay me. But you, my Lord, shall have them
For forty thousand. Is that price too high?
Name your own price. I have a curious fancy
To see you in this wonder of the loom
Amidst the noble ladies of the court,
A flower among flowers.

　　　　　　　　　They say, my lord,
These highborn dames do so affect your Grace
That where you go they throng like flies around you,
Each seeking for your favour.

　　　　　　　　　I have heard also
Of husbands that wear horns, and wear them bravely,
A fashion most fantastical.

GUIDO:　　　　　　　Simone,
Your reckless tongue needs curbing; and besides,
You do forget this gracious lady here
Whose delicate ears are surely not attuned
To such coarse music.

SIMONE:　　　　　　True: I had forgotten,
Nor will offend again. Yet, my sweet Lord,
You'll buy the robe of state. Will you not buy it?
But forty thousand crowns. 'Tis but a trifle,
To one who is Giovanni Bardi's heir.

GUIDO: Settle this thing to-morrow with my steward
Antonio Costa. He will come to you.
And you will have a hundred thousand crowns
If that will serve your purpose.

SIMONE:　　　　　　A hundred thousand!
Said you a hundred thousand? Oh! Be sure
That will for all time, and in everything
Make me your debtor. Ay! From this time forth
My house, with everything my house contains
Is yours, and only yours.

　　　　　　　　　A hundred thousand!
My brain is dazed. I will be richer far
Than all the other merchants. I will buy
Vineyards, and lands, and gardens. Every loom

From Milan down to Sicily shall be mine,
And mine the pearls that the Arabian seas
Store in their silent caverns.
                              Generous Prince,
This night shall prove the herald of my love,
Which is so great that whatsoe'er you ask
It will not be denied you.

SIMONE: What if I asked
For white Bianca here?

GUIDO: You jest, my Lord,
She is not worthy of so great a Prince.
She is but made to keep the house and spin.
Is it not so, good wife? It is so. Look!
Your distaff waits for you. Sit down and spin.
Women should not be idle in their homes.
For idle fingers make a thoughtless heart.
Sit down, I say.

BIANCA: What shall I spin?

SIMONE: Oh! Spin
Some robe which, dyed in purple, sorrow might wear
For her own comforting: or some long-fringed cloth
In which a new-born and unwelcome babe
Might wail unheeded; or a dainty sheet
Which, delicately perfumed with sweet herbs,
Might serve to wrap a dead man. Spin what you will;
I care not, I.

BIANCA: The brittle thread is broken,
The dull wheel wearies of its ceaseless round,
The duller distaff sickens of its load;
I will not spin to-night.

SIMONE: It matters not.
To-morrow you shall spin, and every day
Shall find you at your distaff. So, Lucretia
Was found by Tarquin. So, perchance, Lucretia
Waited for Tarquin. Who knows? I have heard
Strange things about men's wives. And now, my lord,
What news abroad? I heard to-day at Pisa
That certain of the English merchants there
Would sell their woollens at a lower rate
Than the just laws allow, and have entreated
The Signory to hear them.
                          Is this well?
Should merchant be to merchant as a wolf?
And should the stranger living in our land
Seek by enforced privilege or craft
To rob us of our profits?

GUIDO: What should I do
With merchants or their profits? Shall I go
And wrangle with the Signory on your count?
And wear the gown in which you buy from fools,
Or sell to sillier bidders? Honest Simone,
Wool-selling or wool-gathering is for you.
My wits have other quarries.

BIANCA: Noble Lord,
I pray you pardon my good husband here,
His soul stands ever in the market-place,
And his heart beats but at the price of wool.
Yet he is honest in his common way.

To SIMONE.

And you, have you no shame? A gracious Prince
Comes to our house, and you must weary him
With most misplaced assurance. Ask his pardon.

SIMONE: I ask it humbly. We will talk to-night
Of other things. I hear the Holy Father
Has sent a letter to the King of France
Bidding him cross that shield of snow, the Alps,
And make a peace in Italy, which will be
Worse than war of brothers, and more bloody
Than civil rapine or intestine feuds.

GUIDO: Oh! We are weary of that King of France,
Who never comes, but ever talks of coming.
What are these things to me? There are other things
Closer, and of more import, good Simone.

BIANCA (*to* SIMONE): I think you tire our most gracious guest.
What is the King of France to us? As much
As are your English merchants with their wool.

.   .   .

SIMONE: Is it so then? Is all this mighty world
Narrowed into the confines of this room
With but three souls for poor inhabitants?
Ay! There are times when the great universe,
Like cloth in some unskilful dyer's vat,
Shrivels into a handsbreadth, and perchance
That time is now! Well! Let that time be now.
Let this mean room be as that mighty stage
Whereon kings die, and our ignoble lives
Become the stakes God plays for.

                                        I do not know

Why I speak thus. My ride has wearied me.
And my horse stumbled thrice, which is an omen
That bodes not good to any.

                       Alas! My lord,
How poor a bargain is this life of man,
And in how mean a market are we sold!
When we are born our mothers weep, but when
We die there is none weep for us. No, not one. (*Passes to back of stage.*)

    BIANCA: How like a common chapman does he speak!
I hate him, soul and body. Cowardice
Has set her pale seal on his brow. His hands
Whiter than poplar leaves in windy springs,
Shake with some palsy; and his stammering mouth
Blurts out a foolish froth of empty words
Like water from a conduit.

    GUIDO: Sweet Bianca,
He is not worthy of your thought or mine.
The man is but a very honest knave
Full of fine phrases for life's merchandise,
Selling most dear what he must hold most cheap,
A windy brawler in a world of words.
I never met so eloquent a fool.

    BIANCA: Oh, would that Death might take him where he stands!

    SIMONE (*turning round*): Who spake of Death? Let no one speak of Death.
What should Death do in such a merry house,
With but a wife, a husband, and a friend
To give it greeting? Let Death go to houses
Where there are vile, adulterous things, chaste wives
Who grow weary of their noble lords
Draw back the curtains of their marriage beds,
And in polluted and dishonoured sheets
Feed some unlawful lust. Ay! 'Tis so
Strange, and yet so. *You* do not know the world.
You are too single and too honourable.
I know it well. And would it were not so,
But wisdom comes with winters. My hair grows grey,
And youth has left my body. Enough of that.
To-night is ripe for pleasure, and indeed,
I would be merry, as beseems a host
Who finds a gracious and unlooked-for guest
Waiting to greet him. (*Takes up a lute.*)
                   But what is this, my lord?
Why, you have brought a lute to play to us.
Oh! Play, sweet Prince. And, if I am bold,
Pardon, but play.

    GUIDO: I will not play to-night.

Some other night, Simone.

        (*To* BIANCA) You and I
Together, with no listeners but the stars,
Or the more jealous moon.

  SIMONE: Nay, but my lord!
Nay, but I do beseech you. For I have heard
That by the simple fingering of a string,
Or delicate breath breathed along hollowed reeds,
Or blown into cold mouths of cunning bronze,
Those who are curious in this art can draw
Poor souls from prison-houses. I have heard also
How such strange magic lurks within these shells
And innocence puts vine-leaves in her hair,
And wantons like a maenad. Let that pass.
Your lute I know is chaste. And therefore play:
Ravish my ears with some sweet melody;
My soul is in a prison-house, and needs
Music to cure its madness. Good Bianca,
Entreat our guest to play.

  BIANCA: Be not afraid,
Our well-loved guest will choose his place and moment:
That moment is not now. You weary him
With your uncouth insistence.

  GUIDO: Honest Simone,
Some other night. To-night I am content
With the low music of Bianca's voice,
Who, when she speaks, charms the too amorous air.
And makes the reeling earth stand still, or fix
His cycle round her beauty.

  SIMONE: You flatter her.
She has her virtues as most women have,
But beauty is a gem she may not wear.
It is better so, perchance.

               Well, my dear lord,
If you will not draw melodies from your lute
To charm my moody and o'er-troubled soul
You'll drink with me at least? (*Sees table.*)

               Your place is laid.
Fetch me a stool, Bianca. Close the shutters.
Set the great bar across. I would not have
The curious world with its small prying eyes
To peer upon our pleasure.

             Now, my lord,
Give us a toast from a full brimming cup. (*Starts back.*)
What is this stain upon the cloth? It looks
As purple as a wound upon Christ's side.

Wine merely is it? I have heard it said
When wine is spilt blood is spilt also,
But that's a foolish tale.

               My lord, I trust
My grape is to your liking? The wine of Naples
Is fiery like its mountains. Our Tuscan vineyards
Yield a more wholesome juice.

GUIDO: I like it well,
Honest Simone; and, with your good leave,
Will toast the fair Bianca when her lips
Have like red rose-leaves floated on this cup
And left its vintage sweeter. Taste, Bianca. (BIANCA *drinks*.)
Oh, all the honey of Hyblean bees,
Matched with this draught were bitter!

                    Good Simone,
You do not share the feast.

SIMONE: It is strange, my lord,
I cannot eat or drink with you to-night.
Some humour, or some fever in my blood,
At other seasons temperate, or some thought
That like an adder creeps from point to point,
That like a madman crawls from cell to cell,
Poisons my palate and makes appetite
A loathing, not a longing. (*Goes aside*.)

GUIDO: Sweet Bianca,
This common chapman wearies me with words.
I must go hence. To-morrow I will come.
Tell me the hour.

BIANCA: Come with the youngest dawn!
Until I see you all my life is vain.

GUIDO: Ah! Loose the falling midnight of your hair,
And in those stars, your eyes, let me behold
Mine image, as in mirrors. Dear Bianca,
Though it be but a shadow, keep me there,
Nor gaze at anything that does not show
Some symbol of my semblance. I am jealous
Of what your vision feasts on.

BIANCA: Oh! Be sure
Your image will be with me always. Dear,
Love can translate the very meanest thing
Into a sign of sweet remembrances.
But come before the lark with its shrill song
Has waked a world of dreamers. I will stand
Upon the balcony.

GUIDO: And by a ladder
Wrought out of scarlet silk and sewn with pearls

Will come to meet me. White foot after foot,
Like snow upon a rose-tree.

BIANCA: As you will.
You know that I am yours for love or Death.

GUIDO: Simone, I must go to mine house.

SIMONE: So soon? Why should you? the great Duomo's bell
Has not yet tolled its midnight, and the watchmen
Who with their hollow horns mock the pale moon,
Lie drowsy in their towers. Stay awhile.
I fear we may not see you here again,
And that fear saddens my too simple heart.

GUIDO: Be not afraid, Simone. I will stand
Most constant in my friendship. But to-night
I go to mine own home, and that at once.
To-morrow, sweet Bianca.

SIMONE: Well, well, so be it.
I would have wished for fuller converse with you,
My new friend, my honourable guest,
But that it seems may not be.

                              And besides,
I do not doubt your father waits for you,
Wearying for voice or footstep. You, I think,
Are his one child? He has no other child.
You are the gracious pillar of his house,
The flower of a garden full of weeds.
Your father's nephews do not love him well.
So run folk's tongues in Florence. I meant but that;
Men say they envy your inheritance
And look upon your vineyard with fierce eyes
As Ahab looked on Naboth's goodly field.
But that is but the chatter of a town
Where women talk too much.

                              Good night, my lord.
Fetch a pine torch, Bianca. The old staircase
Is full of pitfalls, and the churlish moon
Grows, like a miser, niggard of her beams,
And hides her face behind a muslin mask
As harlots do when they go forth to snare
Some wretched soul in sin. Now, I will get
Your cloak and sword. Nay, pardon, my good Lord,
It is but meet that I should wait on you
Who have so honoured my poor burgher's house,
Drunk of my wine, and broken bread, and made
Yourself a sweet familiar. Oftentimes
My wife and I will talk of this fair night
And its great issues.

Why, what a sword is this!
Ferrara's temper, pliant as a snake,
And deadlier, I doubt not. With such steel
One need fear nothing in the moil of life.
I never touched so delicate a blade.
I have a sword too, somewhat rusted now.
We men of peace are taught humility,
And to bear many burdens on our backs,
And not to murmur at an unjust world,
And to endure unjust indignities.
We are taught that, and like the patient Jew
Find profit in our pain.

                   Yet I remember
How once upon the road to Padua
A robber sought to take my pack-horse from me,
I slit his throat and left him. I can bear
Dishonour, public insult, many shames,
Shrill scorn, and open contumely, but he
Who filches from me something that is mine,
Ay! Though it be the meanest trencher-plate
From which I feed mine appetite – oh! He
Perils his soul and body in the theft
And dies for his small sin. From what strange clay
We men are moulded!

    GUIDO: Why do you speak like this?

    SIMONE: I wonder, my Lord Guido, if my sword
Is better tempered than this steel of yours?
Shall we make trial? Or is my state too low
For you to cross your rapier against mine,
In jest, or earnest?

    GUIDO: Naught would please me better
Than to stand fronting you with naked blade
In jest, or earnest. Give me mine own sword.
Fetch yours. To-night will settle the great issue
Whether the Prince's or the merchant's steel
Is better tempered. Was not that your word?
Fetch your own sword. Why do you tarry, sir?

    SIMONE: My lord, of all the gracious courtesies
That you have showered on my barren house
This is the highest.

              Bianca, fetch my sword.
Thrust back that stool and table. We must have
An open circle for our match at arms,
And good Bianca here shall hold the torch
Lest what is but a jest grow serious.

    BIANCA (*to* GUIDO): Oh! Kill him, kill him!

SIMONE: Hold the torch, Bianca. (*They begin to fight.*)
Have at you! Ah! Ha! Would you?

(*He is wounded by* GUIDO.)

A scratch, no more. The torch was in mine eyes.
Do not look sad, Bianca. It is nothing.
Your husband bleeds, 'tis nothing. Take a cloth,
Bind it about mine arm. Nay, not so tight.
More softly, my good wife. And be not sad,
I pray you be not sad. No: take it off.
What matter if I bleed? (*Tears bandage off.*)
                  Again! Again!

(SIMONE *disarms* GUIDO.)

My gentle Lord, you see that I was right.
My sword is better tempered, finer steel,
But let us match our daggers.
    BIANCA (*to* GUIDO): Kill him! Kill him!
    SIMONE: Put out the torch, Bianca. (BIANCA *puts out torch.*)
                  Now, my good Lord,
Now to the death of one, or both of us,
Or all the three it may be. (*They fight.*)
                There and there.
Ah, devil! Do I hold thee in my grip?

(SIMONE *overpowers* GUIDO *and throws him down over table.*)

    GUIDO: Fool! take your strangling fingers from my throat.
I am my father's only son; the State
Has but one heir, and that false enemy France
Waits for the ending of my father's line
To fall upon our city.
    SIMONE: Hush! Your father
When he is childless will be happier.
As for the State, I think our state of Florence
Needs no adulterous pilot at its helm.
Your life would soil its lilies.
    GUIDO: Take off your hands.
Take off your damned hands. Loose me, I say!
    SIMONE: Nay, you are caught in such a cunning vice
That nothing will avail you, and your life
Narrowed into a single point of shame
Ends with that shame and ends most shamefully.
    GUIDO: Oh! Let me have a priest before I die!

SIMONE: What wouldst thou have a priest for? Tell thy sins
To God, whom thou shalt see this very night
And then no more for ever. Tell thy sins
To Him who is most just, being pitiless,
Most pitiful being just. As for myself...
　　GUIDO: Oh! Help me, sweet Bianca! Help me, Bianca,
Thou knowest I am innocent of harm.
　　SIMONE: What, is there life yet in those lying lips?
Die like a dog with lolling tongue! Die! Die!
And the dumb river shall receive your corse
And wash it all unheeded to the sea.
　　GUIDO: Lord Christ receive my wretched soul to-night!
　　SIMONE: Amen to that. Now for the other.

He dies. SIMONE *rises and looks at* BIANCA. *She comes towards him as one
dazed with wonder and with outstretched arms.*

BIANCA: Why
Did you not tell me you were so strong?
　　SIMONE: Why
Did you not tell me you were beautiful? (*He kisses her on the mouth.*)

CURTAIN

LA SAINTE COURTISANE
or
THE WOMAN COVERED WITH JEWELS

The scene represents a corner of a valley in the Thebaid. On the right hand of the stage is a cavern. In front of the cavern stands a great crucifix.

On the left, sand dunes.

The sky is blue like the inside of a cup of lapis lazuli. The hills are of red sand. Here and there on the hills there are clumps of thorns.

FIRST MAN: Who is she? She makes me afraid. She has a purple cloak and her hair is like threads of gold. I think she must be the daughter of the Emperor. I have heard the boatmen say that the Emperor has a daughter who wears a cloak of purple.

SECOND MAN: She has birds' wings upon her sandals, and her tunic is the colour of green corn. It is like corn in spring when she stands still. It is like young corn troubled by the shadows of hawks when she moves. The pearls on her tunic are like many moons.

FIRST MAN: They are like the moons one sees in the water when the wind blows from the hills.

SECOND MAN: I think she is one of the gods. I think she comes from Nubia.

FIRST MAN: I am sure she is the daughter of the Emperor. Her nails are stained with henna. They are like the petals of a rose. She has come here to weep for Adonis.

SECOND MAN: She is one of the gods. I do not know why she has left her temple. The gods should not leave their temples. If she speaks to us let us not answer and she will pass by.

FIRST MAN: She will not speak to us. She is the daughter of the Emperor.

MYRRHINA: Dwells he not here, the beautiful young hermit, he who will not look on the face of woman?

FIRST MAN: Of a truth it is here the hermit dwells.

MYRRHINA: Why will he not look on the face of woman?

SECOND MAN: We do not know.

MYRRHINA: Why do ye yourselves not look at me?

FIRST MAN: You are covered with bright stones, and you dazzle our eyes.

SECOND MAN: He who looks at the sun becomes blind. You are too bright to look at. It is not wise to look at things that are very bright. Many of the priests in the temples are blind, and have slaves to lead them.

MYRRHINA: Where does he dwell, the beautiful young hermit who will not look on the face of woman? Has he a house of reeds or a house of burnt clay or does he lie on the hillside? Or does he make his bed in the rushes?

FIRST MAN: He dwells in that cavern yonder.

MYRRHINA: What a curious place to dwell in.

FIRST MAN: Of old a centaur lived there. When the hermit came the centaur gave a shrill cry, wept and lamented, and galloped away.

SECOND MAN: No. It was a white unicorn who lived in the cave. When it saw the hermit coming the unicorn knelt down and worshipped him. Many people saw it worshipping him.

FIRST MAN: I have talked with people who saw it.

SECOND MAN: Some say he was a hewer of wood and worked for hire. But that may not be true.

MYRRHINA: What gods then do ye worship? Or do ye worship any gods? There are those who have no gods to worship. The philosophers who wear long beards and brown cloaks have no gods to worship. They wrangle with each other in the porticoes. The [manuscript illegible] laugh at them.

FIRST MAN: We worship seven gods. We may not tell their names. It is a very dangerous thing to tell the names of the gods. No one should ever tell the name of his god. Even the priests who praise the gods all day long, and eat of their food with them, do not call them by their right names.

MYRRHINA: Where are these gods ye worship?

FIRST MAN: We hide them in the folds of our tunics. We do not show them to any one. If we showed them to any one they might leave us.

MYRRHINA: Where did ye meet with them?

FIRST MAN: They were given to us by an embalmer of the dead who had found them in a tomb. We served him for seven years.

MYRRHINA: The dead are terrible. I am afraid of Death.

FIRST MAN: Death is not a god. He is only the servant of the gods.

MYRRHINA: He is the only god I am afraid of. Ye have seen many of the gods?

FIRST MAN: We have seen many of them. One sees them chiefly at night time. They pass one by very swiftly. Once we saw some of the gods at daybreak. They were walking across a plain.

MYRRHINA: Once as I was passing through the market place I heard a sophist from Gilicia say that there is only one God. He said it before many people.

FIRST MAN: That cannot be true. We have ourselves seen many, though we are but common men and of no account. When I saw them I hid myself in a bush. They did me no harm.

MYRRHINA: Tell me more about the beautiful young hermit. Talk to me about the beautiful young hermit who will not look on the face of woman. What is the story of his days? What mode of life has he?

FIRST MAN: We do not understand you.

MYRRHINA: What does he do, the beautiful young hermit? Does he sow or reap? Does he plant a garden or catch fish in a net? Does he weave linen on a loom? Does he set his hand to the wooden plough and walk behind the oxen?

SECOND MAN: He being a very holy man does nothing. We are common men and of no account. We toil all day long in the sun. Sometimes the ground is very hard.

MYRRHINA: Do the birds of the air feed him? Do the jackals share their booty with him?

FIRST MAN: Every evening we bring him food. We do not think that the birds of the air feed him.

MYRRHINA: Why do ye feed him? What profit have ye in so doing?

SECOND MAN: He is a very holy man. One of the gods whom he has offended has made him mad. We think he has offended the moon.

MYRRHINA: Go and tell him that one who has come from Alexandria desires to speak with him.

FIRST MAN: We dare not tell him. This hour he is praying to his God. We pray thee to pardon us for not doing thy bidding.

MYRRHINA: Are ye afraid of him?

FIRST MAN: We are afraid of him.

MYRRHINA: Why are ye afraid of him?

FIRST MAN: We do not know.

MYRRHINA: What is his name?

FIRST MAN: The voice that speaks to him at night time in the cavern calls to him by the name of Honorius. It was also by the name of Honorius that the three lepers who passed by once called to him. We think that his name is Honorius.

MYRRHINA: Why did the three lepers call to him?

FIRST MAN: That he might heal them.

MYRRHINA: Did he heal them?

SECOND MAN: No. They had committed some sin: it was for that reason they were lepers. Their hands and faces were like salt. One of them wore a mask of linen. He was a king's son.

MYRRHINA: What is the voice that speaks to him at night time in his cave?

FIRST MAN: We do not know whose voice it is. We think it is the voice of his God. For we have seen no man enter his cavern nor any come forth from it.

MYRRHINA: Honorius.

HONORIUS (*from within*): Who calls Honorius?

MYRRHINA: Come forth, Honorius.

My chamber is ceiled with cedar and odorous with myrrh. The pillars of my bed are of cedar and the hangings are of purple. My bed is strewn with purple and the steps are of silver. The hangings are sewn with silver pomegranates and the steps that are of silver are strewn with saffron and with myrrh. My lovers hang garlands round the pillars of my house. At night time they come with the flute players and the players of the harp. They woo me with apples and on the pavement of my courtyard they write my name in wine.

From the uttermost parts of the world my lovers come to me. The kings of the earth come to me and bring me presents.

When the Emperor of Byzantium heard of me he left his porphyry chamber and set sail in his galleys. His slaves bare no torches that none might know of his coming. When the King of Cyprus heard of me he sent me ambassadors. The two Kings of Libya who are brothers brought me gifts of amber.

I took the minion of Caesar from Caesar and made him my play-fellow. He came to me at night in a litter. He was pale as a narcissus, and his body was like honey.

The son of the Praefect slew himself in my honour, and the Tetrarch of Cilicia scourged himself for my pleasure before my slaves.

The King of Hierapolis who is a priest and a robber set carpets for me to walk on.

Sometimes I sit in the circus and the gladiators fight beneath me. Once a Thracian who was my lover was caught in the net. I gave the signal for him to die and the whole theatre applauded. Sometimes I pass through the gymnasium and watch the young men wrestling or in the race. Their bodies are bright with oil and their brows are wreathed with willow sprays and with myrtle. They stamp their feet on the sand when they wrestle and when they run the sand follows them like a little cloud. He at whom I smile leaves his companions and follows me to my home. At other times I go down to the harbour and watch the merchants unloading their vessels. Those that come from Tyre have cloaks of silk and earrings of emerald. Those that come from Massilia have cloaks of fine wool and earrings of brass. When they see me coming they stand on the prows of their ships and call to me, but I do not answer them. I go to the little taverns where the sailors lie all day long drinking black wine and playing with dice and I sit down with them.

I made the Prince my slave, and his slave who was a Tyrian I made my Lord for the space of a moon.

I put a figured ring on his finger and brought him to my house. I have wonderful things in my house.

The dust of the desert lies on your hair and your feet are scratched with thorns and your body is scorched by the sun. Come with me, Honorius, and I will clothe you in a tunic of silk. I will smear your body with myrrh and pour spikenard on your hair. I will clothe you in hyacinth and put honey in your mouth. Love –

HONORIUS: There is no love but the love of God.

MYRRHINA: Who is He whose love is greater than that of mortal men?

HONORIUS: It is He whom thou seest on the cross, Myrrhina. He is the Son of God and was born of a virgin. Three wise men who were kings brought Him offerings, and the shepherds who were lying on the hills were wakened by a great light.

The Sibyls knew of His coming. The groves and the oracles spake of Him. David and the prophets announced Him. There is no love like the love of God nor any love that can be compared to it.

The body is vile, Myrrhina. God will raise thee up with a new body which will not know corruption, and thou wilt dwell in the Courts of the Lord and see Him whose hair is like fine wool and whose feet are of brass.

MYRRHINA: The beauty . . .

HONORIUS: The beauty of the soul increases till it can see God. Therefore, Myrrhina, repent of thy sins. The robber who was crucified beside Him He brought into Paradise. (*Exit.*)

MYRRHINA: How strangely he spake to me. And with what scorn he did regard me. I wonder why he spake to me so strangely.

HONORIUS: Myrrhina, the scales have fallen from my eyes and I see now clearly what I did not see before. Take me to Alexandria and let me taste of the seven sins.

MYRRHINA: Do not mock me, Honorius, nor speak to me with such bitter words. For I have repented of my sins and I am seeking a cavern in this desert where I too may dwell so that my soul may become worthy to see God.

HONORIUS: The sun is setting, Myrrhina. Come with me to Alexandria.

MYRRHINA: I will not go to Alexandria.

HONORIUS: Farewell, Myrrhina.

MYRRHINA: Honorius, farewell. No, no, do not go.

.　　　.　　　.　　　.　　　.　　　.　　　.　　　.

I have cursed my beauty for what it has done, and cursed the wonder of my body for the evil that it has brought upon you.

Lord, this man brought me to Thy feet. He told me of Thy coming upon earth, and of the wonder of Thy birth and the great wonder of Thy death also. By him, O Lord, Thou wast revealed to me.

HONORIUS: You talk as a child, Myrrhina, and without knowledge. Loosen your hands. Why didst thou come to this valley in thy beauty?

MYRRHINA: The God whom thou worshipped led me here that I might repent of my iniquities and know Him as the Lord.

HONORIUS: Why didst thou tempt me with words?

MYRRHINA: That thou shouldst see Sin in its painted mask and look on Death in its robe of Shame.

THE POEMS

Introduction by

DECLAN KIBERD

'We Irish are too poetical to be poets,' lamented Wilde, who tended to see his life as the real poem and his writings as no more than marginal commentaries on it. 'But,' he modestly added, 'we are the greatest talkers since the Greeks.'

Behind the mask of flippancy, he was making, as always, a very serious point: that the romantic notion of the poet, as a colourful and intense character, was not necessarily conducive to great poetry. The true artist possessed not so much a fixed and ready-made identity as a capacity to empathise at different moments with all moods, persons and things. The poet might turn out to be the most *un*poetical thing in God's creation. Wilde's own chosen model, John Keats, had said no less when he remarked that men of genius were great as certain chemicals operating on the mass of neutral intellect, but 'they have not any individuality, any determined character'. What they had instead was Negative Capability, the capacity to become this or that thing as the occasion demanded. The surest way for such an artist to strengthen intellect was to let the mind become a thoroughfare for all possible thoughts, to suspend a final judgement for as long as could be.

The traces of Keats – his sensuous classicism, his word-music, his tragic sense of doom – are pervasive in Wilde's own poems: but even more potent is the influence of Keats's aesthetic principles, the chief of which was that the artist must compartmentalise personality for the purpose of literary utterance. Although Keats has a reputation as the quintessential romantic, he was also the forerunner of those modernists who saw the progress of the poet as an escape from personality into a more classical objectivity. The massive pressure under which romantic authors like Wordsworth had placed the first person singular was bound to lead to eventual exhaustion: Keats himself had wittily mocked it as 'the Wordsworthian or egotistical sublime'. Half a century later, Wilde developed this insight in his delightful assertion that 'all bad poetry springs from genuine feeling'. The best way to intensify a personality was not to make it singular, but to multiply it: otherwise, in being true to a single self, a person might be simultaneously false to half a dozen others. When Victorian headmasters praised a boy as having 'character', what they really meant was that he was stable and predictable in his devotion to a single self-image – in other words, earnest and safe. Such stable selves might be well-fitted to running an industry or an empire, but they were not good for art. The price for rejecting the possibilities of multiple selfhood had been paid by an England which had produced no great play in the nineteenth century until the advent of Wilde and Shaw: but it could also be measured in the increasing banality of a poetry which overworked the buzz-word 'I'.

Art was art because of its delight in the play of ideas and feelings: a truth in art was that whose opposite might also be true. So Wilde invented the idea of the mask, which would prove so useful to Yeats and others. It would be more accurate to say, however, that Wilde *discovered* the uses of the mask when he moved from Ireland to England. His undergraduate career at Oxford proved that the Irishman only discovers himself as such when he goes abroad: at home in Dublin, Wilde had been seen as an Anglo-Irish youth, but in Oxford he appeared to his friends as a flashy, if fastidious, Paddy with 'a suspicion of brogue' and 'an unfamiliar turn to his phrasing'. The university helped him to shape his belief that 'man is least himself when he talks in his own person', but 'give him a mask and he will tell you the truth'.

Anglo-Saxonist theorists of the later nineteenth century held that the Celts were doomed by their multiple selfhood. It was said that Celts could see so many options in a situation that they were invariably immobilised, unlike English specialists who might have simplified themselves, but who did not succumb to pitfalls which they had not the imagination to discern. Wilde, however, contended that in this Celtic psychology lay the shape of things to come. He has been described as the first major artist to discredit the romantic idea of 'sincerity' and to replace it with the darker modern imperative of 'authenticity'. He wrote from the perspective of one who sees that the only real fool on earth is the conventionally 'sincere' man who fails to see that he, also, is wearing a mask, the mask of his own sincerity. If all good art must somehow contain the essential criticisms of its prevailing codes, an authentic life must also recognise all that is most opposed to it.

This rich and revolutionary philosophy was applied most fully in Wilde's plays, which in a sense complete the paradox – for, if the artist wished for a poetry emptied of all personal feeling, he could nonetheless boast of having made the drama as personal as the lyric poem. It may well be that there is a great deal more of Wilde's autobiography concealed in his plays than in any of his poems, and a great deal more poetry too. This element was noted by W. H. Auden when he shrewdly described the plays as 'verbal opera'. He was thinking, perhaps, of the wonderful iambic pentameters and the cunning alliteration with which, for instance, Lady Harbury's mourning after the death of a troublesome husband is evoked:

'I hear her hair has turned quite gold from grief.'

As one could know the poet by his music, said Wilde in his essay on 'The Decay of Dying', so one could tell the liar by his rhythmic utterance. The line about Lady Harbury is worthy of Alexander Pope.

It was, however, in the early poems that such skills were honed and the theory of multiple selfhood put to the initial test. In these lyrics, the tone varies form the sensuous to the strict, from the cavalier to the puritanical. If one lyric celebrates Keats as 'poet-painter of our English land'. another

excoriates that same land with Miltonic austerity as a fallen place guilty of
the sins of empire. Sometimes these two seemingly opposed movements are
rehearsed within a single poem. 'Ave Imperatrix' by its very title promises a
celebration of Britain's global rule, only to become at its half-way point a ter-
rified accounting of its human costs, to rulers as well as to ruled:

> What profit now that we have bound
> 　The whole world round with nets of gold,
> If hidden in our heart is found
> 　The care that groweth never old?

The only hope is that 'the young Republic' of Wilde's dreams will 'rise from
these crimson seas of war'.

Milton, Blake and Shelley were the presiding exemplars of this radical aes-
thetic, with Oliver Cromwell featuring in a surprising number of references
as emblematic of the country's lost radicalism. Long before T. S. Eliot de-
fined the canon of English literature as royalist, Wilde had pointed to an
equally illustrious tradition of republican dissidence: in his commonplace
book, kept while at Oxford, he averred that it was to dissenters like Bunyan
and Milton that most of the progress of England was owed and he berated
Matthew Arnold for giving such writers less than their deserts. A cavalier in
his prose, Wilde proved something of a puritan in his poetry ... though in
'Sonnet to Liberty' he was honest enough to admit that his own radicalism
was motivated more by the idea of apocalyptic change than by a deep fellow-
feeling with the victims of poverty and oppression. His refusal to senti-
mentalise such victims, or to stake a claim to such empathy, would be a cor-
nerstone of his essay 'The Soul of Man under Socialism'. There, as in many
of these poems, against the exacting Christian ideal of living for others, he
posits what he sees as the truly Christ-like principle of the person who pre-
fers to live for him- or herself. Wilde's Jesus is, in this respect, very like
Kierkegaard's: a man who, on the Day of Judgement, will not ask penitents
why they failed to be more like him, but instead why they refused to become
themselves.

Many of these early lyrics chronicle the young Wilde's conflicting re-
sponses to the experience of Rome, always a supreme test of English Protes-
tant nerve in nineteenth century writing. 'Easter Day' shows a man at once
fascinated and repelled by Popish opulence, though the final note is a
Miltonic disapproval of a false and garish priesthood which betrays the true
simplicity of Christ, who, even then, appeared to Wilde in the guise of artist-
martyr. 'On the Sale by Auction of Keats's Love Letters' develops this im-
age by likening the poet's fate to that of the crucified Jesus, for whose gar-
ments the squalid Roman soldiers cast lots. Such a complex of ideas,
conflating artistry and sacrifice, combining pagan energy with Christlike
suffering, had a huge effect in Ireland, and would be invoked to devastating
effect by Patrick Pearse and the rebel poets of the 1916 Rising.

Again and again in the poems, Wilde's breath is taken away by the baroque
magnificence of Rome, against which he usually sets the more chastely pro-

portioned symmetries of ancient Greece. If Greece tends to win out in the contrast, that is because so often Wilde's Greece is no more than a version of his own ideal England. 'This English Thames is holier far than Rome', not just because it is the river which nurtured his radical heroes, but also because England too has its own sense of artistic form and ethical decorum. Wilde's reputation as an art-for-art's-sake bohemian is one of the great misrepresentations of modern journalism, connived in, of course, by himself. These poems demonstrate what many have long suspected, that the dandy was at heart a moralist who wished to preach his parables to people in some acceptably sugared form. If so many of his disciples licked off the sugar and disdained the pill underneath, that was not completely his fault.

When the *Poems* were published in 1881, the more astute readers sensed that the visible swagger with which Wilde denounced the enemies of beauty could not completely conceal the rather conventional style and morality beneath. *Punch* magazine announced rather patronisingly that they were but 'Swinburne and water'. Oliver Elton detected chronic plagiarism and counselled the Oxford Union not to accept a gift of the poems which its members had solicited of Wilde for their library: 'They are in fact by William Shakespeare, by Philip Sidney, by John Donne, by Lord Byron, by William Morris, by Algernon Swinburne, and by sixty more, whose words have furnished the list of passages which I hold in my hand at this moment. The Union Library already contains better and fuller editions of all these poets . . .' On the other side, J. A. Symonds praised the book, and especially 'Humanitad', as producing 'strains which, if properly developed, might be trumpets in our time'.

Why did Wilde not blossom into one of the age's foremost poets? One answer has already been hinted at: he simply transferred his poetry-making impulse to the plays and prose. Another may lie in the fact that, by the later nineteenth century, poetry no longer enjoyed the prestige which it had had in the days of Wordsworth and Keats: indeed, the tradition in which they had worked seemed in terminal decline. 'Why do you not write prose?' Walter Pater had asked: 'Prose is so much more difficult.' In that context, Rodney Shewan's post-mortem on *Poems* is acute indeed: 'the volume reads like a personal anthology through which the poet, as nostalgic critic of some five centuries of verse, attempts to define his relationship to a tradition which had disintegrated before he has had the chance to contribute to it.'

Wilde did, however, make a final and very memorable contribution to English poetry. 'The Ballad of Reading Gaol', first published by Prisoner No. C.3.3, carried his theories of poetic impersonality into a new dimension (though many people guessed all too easily who the author was). Despite its intermittent bathos and too-obvious looting of Coleridge's 'Rime of the Ancient Mariner', the ballad does not fail to live, being if not exactly a great poem, then at least one which has the whiff of greatness about some of its stanzas. In it, Wilde finally rejects Greek ideas of self-creation through joy and instead resigns himself to a Christian notion of purgation through pain. Though born a Protestant, Wilde died a Catholic: and, in fact, even his sparkling comedies are informed by the morality of *felix culpa*, the happy fault or fortunate fall, according to which a person is educated by sin into a deeper self-knowledge. If, in its comic mode, this notion is expressed in aphorisms about experience being the name a man gives to his mistakes, its tragic corollary was summed up by a fellow-Irishman, James Joyce. He said that, for all its Greek colourings, the Wildean personality was finally placed in service to a theory of beauty which 'at its very base is the truth inherent in the soul of Catholicism: that man cannot reach the divine except through that sense of separation and loss called sin'. Even those early poems which seem most dismissive of Catholicism will be found to contain that undertow of fascination and awe which would draw their author to it.

POEMS

EDITORIAL NOTE

The order of the poetry which follows is chronological by date of composition or of publication. The reasons for this change are given in the 1994 introduction. The texts were taken from the 1882 edition wherever possible. Poems not included in that edition are taken from vol. IX of the 1908 *Collected Works* or, in the case of 'Pan' and 'Désespoir', from later editions. Of the fifteen additional poems not before included in the Collins *Complete Works* (see Appendix D), all but two have been taken from manuscript sources. For Wilde's own thematic grouping of the poems for the 1882 edition, see Appendix B.

YE SHALL BE GODS

Before the dividing of days
   Or the singing of summer or spring
God from the dust did raise
   A splendid and goodly thing:
Man – from the womb of the land,
   Man – from the sterile sod
Torn by a terrible hand –
   Formed in the image of God.
But the life of man is a sorrow
   And death a relief from pain,
For love only lasts till tomorrow
   And life without love is vain.

ΣΤΡΟΦΗ[1]
And your strength will wither like grass
   Scorched by a pitiless sun,
And the might of your hands will pass
   And the sands of your life will run.
O gods not of saving but sorrow
   Whose joy is in weeping of men,
Who shall lend thee their life, or who borrow
   From others to give thee again?
O gods ever wrathful and tearless,
   O gods not of night but of day,
Though your faces be frowning and fearless
   Thy kingdom shall pass – men say.

---

[1] Strophe.

ΑΝΤΙΣΤΡΟΦΗ[1]

The spirit of man is arisen
   And crowned as a mighty King.
The people have broken from prison
   And the voices once voiceless now sing.
Cry aloud, O dethroned and defeated,
   Cry aloud for the fading of might,
Too long were ye feared and entreated,
   Too long did men worship thy light.

Aye, weep for your crimes without number,
   The loving and luring of men,
For your greatness is sunken in slumber,
   Your light will n'er lighten again.

ΣΤΡΟΦΗ Β

But as many a lovely flower
   Is born of a sterile seed,
In a fatal and fearful hour
   There grew from this creedless breed
Love – fostered in flame and in fire
   That dies but to blossom again,
Love – ever distilling desire
   Like wine with the eyelids of men.
We kneel to the great Iapygian,
   We bow to the Lampsacene's shrine,
For hers is the only religion,
   And hers to entice and entwine –

ΑΝΤΙΣΤΡΟΦΗ Β

There once was another, men tell us,
   The giver and taker of life,
A lovingless God and a jealous
   Whose joy was in weeping and strife.
He is gone; and his temple 'tis sunken
   In ashes and fallen in dust,
For the souls of the people are drunken
   With dreams of the Lady of Lust –
We kneel to the Cyprian Mother,
   We take up our lyres and sing,
'Thou are crowned with the crown of another,
   Thou are throned where another was King.'

---

[1] Antistrophe. The strophe was chanted as the chorus proceeded in one direction. As they returned they chanted its exact counterpart, the antistrophe, in reply.

Chorus of Cloud Maidens

'Αριστοφάνους Νεφέλαι, 275–290, 298–313[1]

ΣΤΡΟΦΗ[2]
    Cloud maidens that float on for ever,
        Dew-sprinkled, fleet bodies, and fair,
    Let us rise from our Sire's loud river,
        Great Ocean, and soar through the air
    To the peaks of the pine-covered mountains where the
            pines hang as tresses of hair.
    Let us seek the watch-towers undaunted,
        Where the well-watered corn-fields abound,
    And through murmurs of rivers nymph-haunted
        The songs of the sea-waves resound;
    And the sun in the sky never wearies of spreading his
            radiance around.
        Let us cast off the haze
        Of the mists from our band,
        Till with far-seeing gaze
        We may look on the land.

ΑΝΤΙΣΤΡΟΦΗ[3]
Cloud maidens that bring the rain-shower,
    To the Pallas-loved land let us wing,
To the land of stout heroes and Power,
    Where Kekrops was hero and king,
Where honour and silence is given
    To the mysteries that none may declare,
Where are gifts to the high gods in heaven
    When the house of the gods is laid bare,
Where are lofty roofed temples, and statues well carven
        and fair
    Where are feasts to the happy immortals
When the sacred procession draws near,
    Where garlands make bright the bright portals
At all seasons and months in the year;
    And when spring days are here,
Then we tread to the wine-god a measure,
    In Bacchanal dance and in pleasure,

---

[1] From the *Clouds* of Aristophanes.
[2] Strophe.
[3] Antistrophe. (*See footnote on page 746*).

'Mid the contests of sweet singing choirs,
　And the crash of loud lyres.

Oxford, 1874

From Spring Days to Winter

(*For Music*)

In the glad springtime when leaves were green,
　O merrily the throstle sings!
I sought, amid the tangled sheen,
Love whom mine eyes had never seen,
　O the glad dove has golden wings!

Between the blossoms red and white,
　O merrily the throstle sings!
My love first came into my sight,
O perfect vision of delight,
　O the glad dove has golden wings!

The yellow apples glowed like fire,
　O merrily the throstle sings!
O Love too great for lip or lyre,
Blown rose of love and of desire,
　O the glad dove has golden wings!

But now with snow the tree is grey,
　Ah, sadly now the throstle sings!
My love is dead: ah! Well-a-day,
See at her silent feet I lay
　A dove with broken wings!
　Ah, Love! Ah, Love! That thou wert slain –
Fond Dove, fond Dove return again!

Requiescat

Tread lightly, she is near
　Under the snow,
Speak gently, she can hear
　The daisies grow.

All her bright golden hair
　Tarnished with rust,
She that was young and fair
　Fallen to dust.

Lily-like, white as snow,
　　She hardly knew
She was a woman, so
　　Sweetly she grew.

Coffin-board, heavy stone,
　　Lie on her breast,
I vex my heart alone,
　　She is at rest.

Peace, Peace, she cannot hear
　　Lyre or sonnet,
All my life's buried here,
　　Heap earth upon it.

Avignon

SAN MINIATO

See, I have climbed the mountain side
　　Up to this holy house of God,
　　Where once that Angel-Painter trod
Who saw the heavens opened wide,

　　And throned upon the crescent moon
　　The Virginal white Queen of Grace, –
　　Mary! could I but see thy face
Death could not come at all too soon.

　　O crowned by God with thorns and pain!
　　Mother of Christ! O mystic wife!
　　My heart is weary of this life
And over-sad to sing again.

　　O crowned by God with love and flame!
　　O crowned by Christ the Holy One!
　　O listen ere the searching sun
Show to the world my sin and shame.

BY THE ARNO

　　The oleander on the wall
　　Grows crimson in the dawning light,
　　Though the grey shadows of the night
Lie yet on Florence like a pall.

The dew is bright upon the hill,
   And bright the blossoms overhead,
   But ah! the grasshoppers have fled,
The little Attic song is still.

Only the leaves are gently stirred
   By the soft breathing of the gale,
   And in the almond-scented vale
The lonely nightingale is heard.

The day will make thee silent soon,
   O nightingale sing on for love!
   While yet upon the shadowy grove
Splinter the arrows of the moon.

Before across the silent lawn
   In sea-green vest the morning steals,
   And to love's frightened eyes reveals
The long white fingers of the dawn

Fast climbing up the eastern sky
   To grasp and slay the shuddering night,
   All careless of my heart's delight,
Or if the nightingale should die.

ROME UNVISITED

1

The corn has turned from grey to red,
   Since first my spirit wandered forth,
   From the drear cities of the north,
And to Italia's mountains fled.

And here I set my face towards home,
   For all my pilgrimage is done,
   Although, methinks, yon blood-red sun
Marshals the way to Holy Rome.

O Blessed Lady, who dost hold
   Upon the seven hills thy reign!
   O Mother without blot or stain,
Crowned with bright crowns of triple gold!

O Roma, Roma, at thy feet
  I lay this barren gift of song!
  For, ah! the way is steep and long
That leads unto thy sacred street.

2

And yet what joy it were for me
  To turn my feet unto the south,
  And journeying towards the Tiber mouth
To kneel again at Fiesole!

And wandering through the tangled pines
  That break the gold of Arno's stream,
  To see the purple mist and gleam
Of morning on the Apennines.

By many a vineyard-hidden home,
  Orchard and olive-garden grey,
  Till from the drear Campagna's way
The seven hills bear up the dome!

3

A pilgrim from the northern seas –
  What joy for me to seek alone
  The wondrous Temple and the throne
Of Him who holds the awful keys!

When, bright with purple and with gold,
  Come priest and holy Cardinal,
  And borne above the heads of all
The gentle Shepherd of the Fold.

O joy to see before I die
  The only God-anointed King,
  And hear the silver trumpets ring
A triumph as He passes by!

Or at the brazen-pillared shrine
  Holds high the mystic sacrifice,
  And shows his God to human eyes
Beneath the veil of bread and wine.

4

For lo, what changes time can bring!
   The cycles of revolving years
    May free my heart from all its fears,
And teach my lips a song to sing.

Before yon field of trembling gold
   Is garnered into dusty sheaves,
    Or ere the autumn's scarlet leaves
Flutter as birds adown the wold,

I may have run the glorious race,
   And caught the torch while yet aflame,
    And called upon the holy name
Of Him who now doth hide His face.

Arona

LA BELLA DONNA DELLA MIA MENTE[1]

My limbs are wasted with a flame,
   My feet are sore with travelling,
For, calling on my Lady's name,
   My lips have now forgot to sing.

O Linnet in the wild-rose brake
   Strain for my Love thy melody,
O Lark sing louder for love's sake,
   My gentle Lady passeth by.

She is too fair for any man
   To see or hold his heart's delight,
Fairer than Queen or courtesan
   Or moonlit water in the night.

Her hair is bound with myrtle leaves,
   (Green leaves upon her golden hair!)
Green grasses through the yellow sheaves
   Of autumn corn are not more fair.

Her little lips, more made to kiss
   Than to cry bitterly for pain,
Are tremulous as brook-water is,
   Or roses after evening rain.

---

[1] Lovely lady of my memory.

Her neck is like white melilote
    Flushing for pleasure of the sun,
The throbbing of the linnet's throat
    Is not so sweet to look upon.

As a pomegranate, cut in twain,
    White-seeded, is her crimson mouth,
Her cheeks are as the fading stain
    Where the peach reddens to the south.

O twining hands! O delicate
    White body made for love and pain!
O House of love! O desolate
    Pale flower beaten by the rain!

CHANSON

A ring of gold and a milk-white dove
    Are goodly gifts for thee,
And a hempen rope for your own love
    To hang upon a tree.

For you a House of Ivory,
    (Roses are white in the rose-bower)!
A narrow bed for me to lie,
    (White, O white, is the hemlock flower)!

Myrtle and jessamine for you,
    (O the red rose is fair to see)!
For me the cypress and the rue,
    (Finest of all is rosemary)!

For you three lovers of your hand,
    (Green grass where a man lies dead)!
For me three paces on the sand,
    (Plant lilies at my head)!

UNTITLED

See! the gold sun has risen,
    (Ah God! how very fair)
Too soon he has broken from prison –
    Ah Sweet! it is only my hair.

Nay, for I see the snow-white day
   Come from his rosy bower,
And I know that the night has fled away,
   Ah Sweet! 'tis my breast flower.

Nay, but the night has surely fled,
   For crimson grows the south,
And the gates of dawn are opening red,
   Ah Sweet, it is only my mouth.

Then why do I see the sky so blue,
   Flecked where the linnet flies,
Ah love lie nearer, and tell me true
   Is it only the light in thine eyes?

Nay but the sun doth o'er us pass
   Turning my blood to wine,
As we lie by a stream and the warm soft grass
   Ah Sweet! 'tis my body and thine.

UNTITLED

She stole behind him where he lay
   All tossed and tired from the dance.
He turned his curly head away
   With pretty boyish petulance.

She said, 'I loved you all the while,
   Rough Colin is a clumsy clout.'
He twirled his crook, and would not smile
   His cross lips from their rosy pout.

She said, 'You are more dear to me
   Than are the fat lambs of my flock.'
He would not speak, but sulkily
   Smoothed down his crumpled linen smock.

She said, 'I love you best of all,'
   And put her little hand in his.
Her voice was sweeter than the call
   At evening of the pigeon is.

He shook her clinging fingers off:
   (But little maids have little wiles)
She said, 'I heard your white ewe cough,
   Just as I passed beyond the stiles.'

He rose and seized his polished crook;
  She hid her face in birdlike laughter;
He raced along the sedgy brook
  And she – alas, she followed after.

She followed, and he ran before,
  Carelessly whistling to the wind,
But ere he closed the sheepfold door
  The gold-haired child crept in behind.

There rose a little undertune
  Of singing in the wattled fold,
And through its latticed cloud the moon
  Leaned down with naked arms of gold.

THE DOLE OF THE KING'S DAUGHTER

(Breton)

Seven stars in the still water,
  And seven in the sky;
Seven sins on the King's daughter,
  Deep in her soul to lie.

Red roses are at her feet,
  (Roses are red in her red-gold hair)
And O where her bosom and girdle meet
  Red roses are hidden there.

Fair is the knight who lieth slain
  Amid the rush and reed,
See the lean fishes that are fain
  Upon dead men to feed.

Sweet is the page that lieth there,
  (Cloth of gold is goodly prey,)
See the black ravens in the air,
  Black, O black as the night are they.

What do they there so stark and dead?
  (There is blood upon her hand)
Why are the lilies flecked with red?
  (There is blood on the river sand.)

There are two that ride from the south and east,
  And two from the north and west,
For the black raven a goodly feast,
  For the King's daughter rest.

There is one man who loves her true,
    (Red, O red, is the stain of gore!)
He hath duggen a grave by the darksome yew,
    (One grave will do for four.)

No moon in the still heaven,
    In the black water none,
The sins on her soul are seven,
    The sin upon his is one.

LOVE SONG

Though the wind shakes lintel and rafter,
    And the priest sits mourning alone,
For the ruin that comes hereafter
    When the world shall be overthrown,
What matter the wind and weather
    To those that live for a day?
When my Love and I are together,
    What matter what men may say?

I and my love where the wild red rose is,
    When hands grow weary and eyes are bright,
Kisses are sweet as the evening closes,
    Lips are reddest before the night,
And what matter if Death be an endless slumber
    And thorns the commonest crown for the head,
What matter if sorrow like wild weeds cumber,
    When kisses are sweetest, and lips are red?

I that am only the idlest singer
    That ever sang by a desolate sea,
A goodlier gift than song can bring her,
    Sweeter than sound of minstrelsy,
For singers grow weary, and lips will tire,
    And winds will scatter the pipe and reed,
And even the sound of the silver lyre
    Sickens my heart in the days of need,
But never at all do I fail or falter
    For I know that Love is a god, and fair,
And if death and derision follow after,
    The only god worth a sin and a prayer.

And She and I are as Queen and Master,
    Why should we care if a people groan

'Neath a despot's feet, or some red disaster
Shatter the fool on his barren throne?
What matter if prisons and palaces crumble,
And the red flag floats in the piled-up street,
When over the sound of the cannon's rumble
The voice of my Lady is clear and sweet?
For the worlds are many and we are single,
And sweeter to me when my Lady sings,
Than the cry when the East and the West world mingle,
For clamour of battle, and the fall of Kings.

So out of the reach of tears and sorrow
Under the wild-rose let us play,
And if death and severing come tomorrow,
I have your kisses, sweet heart, today.

Magdalen College, Oxford

TRISTITIAE

Αἴλινον, αἴλινον εἰπέ, τὸ δ' εὖ νικάτω.[1]

O well for him who lives at ease
With garnered gold in wide domain,
Nor heeds the splashing of the rain,
The crashing down of forest trees.

O well for him who ne'er hath known
The travail of the hungry years,
A father grey with grief and tears,
A mother weeping all alone.

But well for him whose foot hath trod
The weary road of toil and strife,
Yet from the sorrows of his life
Builds ladders to be nearer God.

---

[1] Cry woe, woe and let the good prevail.

THE TRUE KNOWLEDGE

.. ἀναγκαίως δ' ἔχει
βίον θερίζειν ὥστε κάρπιμον στάχυν,
καὶ τὸν μὲν εἶναι τὸν δὲ μή.[1]

Thou knowest all; I seek in vain
What lands to till or sow with seed –
The land is black with briar and weed,
Nor cares for falling tears or rain.

Thou knowest all; I sit and wait
With blinded eyes and hands that fail,
Till the last lifting of the veil
And the first opening of the gate.

Thou knowest all; I cannot see.
I trust I shall not live in vain,
I know that we shall meet again
In some divine eternity.

HEART'S YEARNINGS

Ἔρως τῶν ἀδυνάτων[2]

Surely to me the world is all too drear,
To shape my sorrow to a tuneful strain,
It is enough for wearied ears to hear
The Passion-Music of a fevered brain,
Or low complainings of a heart's pain.

My saddened soul is out of tune with time,
Nor have I care to set the crooked straight,
Or win green laurels for some pleasant rhyme,
Only with tired eyes I sit and wait,
Until the opening of the Future's Mystic Gate.

I am so tired of all the busy throng
That chirp and chatter in the noisy street,
That I would sit alone and sing no song
But listen for the coming of Love's feet.
Love is a pleasant messenger to greet.

---

[1] It is inevitable that life should be harvested like a crop that is ripe, and one man should die while another lives. (Euripides, *Hypsipile*.)
[2] Love of the impossible.

O Love come close before the hateful day,
   And tarry not until the night is dead,
O Love come quickly, for although one pray,
   What has God ever given in thy stead
   But dust and ashes for the head?

Strain, strain O longing eyes till Love is near;
   O Heart be ready for his entering thee,
O Breaking Heart be free from doubt and fear,
   For when Love comes he cometh gloriously,
   And entering love is very fair to see.

Peace, Peace O breaking heart, Love comes apace,
   And surely great delight and gladness brings,
Now look at last upon his shining face,
   And listen to the flying of his wings
   And the sweet voice of Love that sings.

O pale moon shining fair and clear
   Between the apple-blossoms white,
That cluster round my window here,
   Why does Love tarry in his flight
   And not come near for my heart's delight –

I only hear the sighing of the breeze
   That makes complaint in a sweet undertune,
I only see the blossom-laden trees
   Splintering the arrows of the golden moon,
   That turns black night into the burnished noon.

Magdalen College, Oxford

THE LITTLE SHIP

Have your forgotten the ship love
   I made as a childish toy,
When you were a little girl love,
   And I was a little boy?

Ah! never in all the fleet love
   Such a beautiful ship was seen,
For the sides were painted blue love
   And the deck was yellow and green.

I carved a wonderful mast love
   From my Father's Sunday stick,
You cut up your one good dress love
   That the sail should be of silk.

And I launched it on the pond love
    And I called it after you,
And for the want of the bottle of wine love
    We christened it with the dew.

And we put your doll on board love
    With a cargo of chocolate cream,
But the little ship struck on a cork love
    And the doll went down with a scream!

It is forty years since then love
    And your hair is silver grey,
And we sit in our old armchairs love
    And we watch our children play.

And I have a wooden leg love
    And the title of K. C. B.
For bringing Her Majesty's Fleet love
    Over the stormy sea.

But I've never forgotten the ship love
    I made as a childish toy
When you were a little girl love
    And I was a sailor boy.

ΘΡΗΝΩΙΔΙΑ[1]

Song sung by the captive women of Troy on the beach at Aulis, while the Achaeans were there storm-bound through the wrath of dishonoured Achilles, and waiting for a fair wind to bring them home.[2]

ΣΤΡΟΦΗ[3]

O fair wind blowing from the sea!
    Who through the dark and mist dost guide
    The ships that on the billows ride,
Unto what land, ah, misery!
Shall I be borne, across what stormy wave,
Or to whose house a purchased slave?

---

[1] A Song of Lamentation
[2] Euripides, *Hecuba*, 444–83
[3] Strophe.

O sea-wind blowing fair and fast
  Is it unto the Dorian strand,
    Or to those far and fabled shore,
      Where great Apidanus outpours
His streams upon the fertile land,
Or shall I tread the Phthian sand,
Borne by the swift breath of the blast?

ΑΝΤΙΣΤΡΟΦΗ[1]

O blowing wind! You bring my sorrow near,
  For surely borne with splashing of the oar,
And hidden in some galley-prison drear
  I shall be led unto that distant shore
    Where the tall palm-tree first took root, and made,
    With clustering laurel leaves, a pleasant shade
For Leto when with travail great she bore
A god and goddess in Love's bitter fight
Her body's anguish, and her soul's delight.

      It may be in Delos,
        Encircled of seas,
      I shall sing with some maids
        From the Cyclades,

      Or Artemis goddess
        And queen and maiden,
      Sing of the gold
        In her hair heavy-laden.

      Sing of her hunting,
        Her arrows and bow,
      And in singing find solace
        From weeping and woe.

ΣΤΡΟΦΗ Β

      Or it may be my bitter doom
      To stand a handmaid at the loom,
In distant Athens of supreme renown;
        And weave some wondrous tapestry,
        Or work in bright embroidery,
Upon the crocus flowered robe and saffron-coloured
              gown,

        The flying horses wrought in gold,
        The silver chariot onward rolled
That bears Athena through the Town;

---

[1] Antistrophe. *(See footnote on page 746.)*

Or the warring giants that strove to climb
    From earth to heaven to reign as kings,
And Zeus the conquering son of Time
    Borne on the hurricane's eagle wings;
And the lightning flame and the bolts that fell
    From the risen cloud at the god's behest,
And hurled the rebels to darkness of hell,
    To a sleep without slumber or waking or rest.

ΑΝΤΙΣΤΡΟΦΗ Β

Alas! Our children's sorrow, and their pain
        In slavery.
Alas! Our warrior sires nobly slain
        For liberty.
Alas! Our country's glory, and the name
        Of Troy's fair town;
By the lances and the fighting and the flame
        Tall Troy is down.

I shall pass with my soul over-laden,
    To a land far away and unseen,
For Asia is slave and handmaiden,
    Europa is Mistress and Queen.
Without love, or love's holiest treasure,
    I shall pass into Hades abhorred,
To the grave as my chamber of pleasure,
    To death as my Lover and Lord.

LOTUS LAND

The sultry noon is amorous for rain;
    The golden bee, the lily's paramour,
    Sleeps in the lily-bell, which doth allure
And bind its lovers with a honied chain;
How still it is! no passionate note of pain
    Comes from the tawny songstress of the brake,
    And in the polished mirror of the lake
My purple mountains see themselves again.

O sad, and sweet, and silent! surely here
A man might dwell apart from troublous fear,
    Watching the bounteous seasons as they go
From lusty spring to winter; – Yet you say
That there is War in Europe on this day?
    Red War and Ravenous? Can this be so!

Illaunroe

DÉSESPOIR

The seasons send their ruin as they go,
For in the spring the narciss shows its head
Nor withers till the rose has flamed to red,
And in the autumn purple violets blow,
And the slim crocus stirs the winter snow;
Wherefore yon leafless trees will bloom again
And this grey land grow green with summer rain
And send up cowslips for some boy to mow.

But what of life whose bitter hungry sea
Flows at our heels, and gloom of sunless night
Covers the days which never more return?
Ambition, love and all the thoughts that burn
We lose too soon, and only find delight
In withered husks of some dead memory.

LOTUS LEAVES

νεμεσσῶμαί γε μὲν οὐδέν
κλαίειν ὅς κε θάνῃσι βροτῶν καὶ πότμον ἐπίσπῃ,
τοῦτό νυ καὶ γέρας οἶον ὀϊζυροῖσι βροτοῖσι
κείρασθαί τε κόμην βαλέειν τ' ἀπὸ δάκρυ παρειῶν.[1]

There is no peace beneath the noon.
  Ah! In those meadows is there peace
  Where, girdled with a silver fleece,
As a bright shepherd, strays the moon?

Queen of the gardens of the sky,
  Where stars like lilies, white and fair,
  Shine through the mists of frosty air,
Oh, tarry, for the dawn is nigh!

Oh, tarry, for the envious day
  Stretches long hands to catch thy feet,
  Alas! But thou art over-fleet,
Alas! I know thou wilt not stay.

---

[1] For my part I am not in the least ashamed to weep for any man who has died and met his fate. Indeed to cut our hair and let a tear fall from our cheeks is the only tribute we can pay to unlucky mortals. (Homer, *Odyssey*, IV 195–198.)

Up sprang the sun to run his race,
 The breeze blew fair on meadow and lea;
 But in the west I seemed to see
The likeness of a human face.

A linnet on the hawthorn spray
 Sang of the glories of the spring,
 And made the flow'ring copses ring
With gladness for the new-born day.

A lark from out the grass I trod
 Flew wildly, and was lost to view
 In the great seamless veil of blue
That hangs before the face of God.

The willow whispered overhead
 That death is but a newer life,
 And that with idle words of strife
We bring dishonour on the dead.

I took a branch from off the tree,
 And hawthorn-blossoms drenched with dew,
 I bound them with a sprig of yew,
And made a garland fair to see.

I laid the flowers where He lies,
 (Warm leaves and flowers on the stone);
 What joy I had to sit alone
Till evening broke on tired eyes:

Till all the shifting clouds had spun
 A robe of gold for God to wear,
 And into seas of purple air
Sank the bright galley of the sun.

Shall I be gladdened for the day,
 And let my inner heart be stirred
 By murmuring tree or song of bird,
And sorrow at the wild wind's play?

Not so: such idle dreams belong
 To souls of lesser depth than mine;
 I feel that I am half divine;
I know that I am great and strong.

I know that every forest tree
 By labour rises from the root;
 I know that none shall gather fruit
By sailing on the barren sea.

UNTITLED

1

O loved one lying far away
   Beyond the reach of human moan,
   Can coffin board and heavy stone
Turn godlike man to senseless clay?

Or hast thou eyes to see the light
   And feeling quick with joy and pain?
   Alas! I think a lesser gain
Is mine, if thou can'st see me right.

Alas! how mean we must appear
   When looked on by the holy dead!
   I trust the glory round thy head
Hast kept thine eyes from seeing clear.

2

For in my heart these fancies rise
   That I the singer of this song
   Am weak where thou didst think me strong
And foolish where you feigned me wise.

Now that I lack thy helping hand
   I shift with every changing creed,
   No better than a broken reed
Less stable than the shifting sand.

Less stable than the changing sea,
   At every setting of the sun
   I cry in vain, 'What have I done
This day for immortality?'

A Fragment from The Agamemnon of Aeschylos

(Lines 1140–1173)

The scene is the court-yard of the Palace at Argos. Agamemnon has already entered the House of Doom, and Clytemnestra has followed close on his heels. Cassandra is left alone upon the stage. The conscious terror of death and the burden of prophecy lie heavy upon her; terrible signs and visions greet her approach. She sees blood upon the lintel, and the smell of blood scares her, as some bird, from the door. The ghosts of the murdered children come to mourn with her. Her second sight pierces the Palace walls; she sees the fatal bath, the tramelling net, and the axe sharpened for her own ruin and her lord's.

But not even in the hour of her last anguish is Apollo merciful; her warnings are unheeded, her prophetic utterances made mock of.

The orchestra is filled with a chorus of old men weak, foolish, irresolute. They do not believe the weird woman of mystery till the hour for help is past, and the cry of Agamemnon echoes from the house, 'Oh me! I am stricken with a stroke of death.'

Chorus
Thy prophecies are but a lying tale,
    For cruel gods have brought thee to this state,
    And of thyself and thine own wretched fate
Sing you this song and these unhallowed lays,
    Like the brown bird of grief insatiate
Crying for sorrow of its dreary days;
    Crying for Itys, Itys, in the vale –
    The nightingale! The nightingale!

Cassandra
Yet I would that to me they had given
    The fate of that singer so clear,
Fleet wings to fly up unto heaven,
    Away from all mourning and fear;
For ruin and slaughter await me – the cleaving with
    sword and the spear.

Chorus
Whence come these crowding fancies on thy brain,
    Sent by some god it may be, yet for naught?
Why dost thou sing with evil-tongued refrain,
Moulding thy terrors to this hideous strain
    With shrill, sad cries, as if by death distraught?
Why dost thou tread that path of prophecy,

Where, upon either hand,
Landmarks for ever stand
With horrid legend for all men to see?

Cassandra

O bitter bridegroom who didst bear
  Ruin to those that loved thee true!
O holy stream Scamander, where
  With gentle nurturement I grew
  In the first days, when life and love were new.
And now – and now – it seems that I must lie
  In the dark land that never sees the sun;
Sing my sad songs of fruitless prophecy
  By the black stream Cokytos that doth run
  Through long, low hills of dreary Acheron.

Chorus

Ah, but thy word is clear!
Even a child among men,
Even a child might see
What is lying hidden here.
Ah! I am smitten deep
To the heart with a deadly blow
At the evil fate of the maid,
At the cry of her song of woe!
Sorrows for her to bear!
Wonders for me to hear!

Cassandra

O my poor land laid waste with flame and fire!
  O ruined city overthrown by fate!
Ah, what availed the offerings of my Sire
  To keep the foreign foemen from the gate!
Ah, what availed the herds of pasturing kine
To save my country from the wrath divine!
Ah, neither prayer nor priest availèd aught,
Nor the strong captains that so stoutly fought,
  For the tall town lies desolate and low.
  And I, the singer of this song of woe,
Know, by the fires burning in my brain,
That Death, the healer of all earthly pain,
  Is close at hand! I will not shirk the blow.

A Vision

Two crownèd Kings, and One that stood alone
  With no green weight of laurels round his head,
  But with sad eyes as one uncomforted,
And wearied with man's never-ceasing moan
For sins no bleating victim can atone,
  And sweet long lips with tears and kisses fed.
  Girt was he in a garment black and red,
And at his feet I marked a broken stone
  Which sent up lilies, dove-like, to his knees.
Now at their sight, my heart being lit with flame
  I cried to Beatricé, 'Who are these?'
And she made answer, knowing well each name,
  'Aeschylos first, the second Sophokles,
  And last (wide stream of tears!) Euripides.'

Sonnet on Approaching Italy

I reached the Alps: the soul within me burned,
  Italia, my Italia, at thy name:
  And when from out the mountain's heart I came
And saw the land for which my life had yearned,
I laughed as one who some great prize had earned:
  And musing on the marvel of thy fame
  I watched the day, till marked with wounds of flame
The turquoise sky to burnished gold was turned.
The pine-trees waved as waves a woman's hair,
  And in the orchards every twining spray
  Was breaking into flakes of blossoming foam:
But when I knew that far away at Rome
  In evil bonds a second Peter lay,
  I wept to see the land so very fair.

Turin

SONNET

Written in Holy Week at Genoa

I wandered in Scoglietto's far retreat,
  The oranges on each o'erhanging spray
  Burned as bright lamps of gold to shame the day;
Some startled bird with fluttering wings and fleet
Made snow of all the blossoms; at my feet
  Like silver moons the pale narcissi lay:
  And the curved waves that streaked the great, green bay
Laughed i' the sun, and life seemed very sweet.
Outside the young boy-priest passed singing clear,
  'Jesus the son of Mary has been slain,
  O come and fill his sepulchre with flowers.'
Ah, God! Ah, God! those dear Hellenic hours
  Had drowned all memory of Thy bitter pain,
  The Cross, the Crown, the Soldiers and the Spear.

IMPRESSION DE VOYAGE

The sea was sapphire coloured, and the sky
  Burned like a heated opal through the air;
  We hoisted sail; the wind was blowing fair
For the blue lands that to the eastward lie.
From the steep prow I marked with quickening eye
  Zakynthos, every olive grove and creek,
  Ithaca's cliff, Lycaon's snowy peak,
And all the flower-strewn hills of Arcady.
The flapping of the sail against the mast,
  The ripple of the water on the side,
  The ripple of girls' laughter at the stern,
The only sounds: – when 'gan the West to burn,
  And a red sun upon the seas to ride,
  I stood upon the soil of Greece at last!

Katakolo

THE THEATRE AT ARGOS

Nettles and poppy mar each rock-hewn seat:
  No poet crowned with olive deathlessly
  Chants his glad song, nor clamorous Tragedy

Startles the air; green corn is waving sweet
Where once the Chorus danced to measures fleet;
  Far to the East a purple stretch of sea,
  The cliffs of gold that prisoned Danae;
And desecrated Argos at my feet.

No season now to mourn the days of old,
A nation's shipwreck on the rocks of Time,
  Or the dread storms of all-devouring Fate,
  For now the peoples clamour at our gate,
The world is full of plague and sin and crime,
And God Himself is half-dethroned for Gold!

Argos, 1877

URBS SACRA AETERNA[1]

Rome! what a scroll of History thine has been;
  In the first days thy sword republican
  Ruled the whole world for many an age's span:
Then of the peoples wert thou royal Queen,
Till in thy streets the bearded Goth was seen;
  And now upon thy walls the breezes fan
  (Ah, city crowned by God, discrowned by man!)
The hated flag of red and white and green.
When was thy glory! when in search for power
  Thine eagles flew to greet the double sun,
  And the wild nations shuddered at thy rod?
Nay, but thy glory tarried for this hour,
  When pilgrims kneel before the Holy One,
  The prisoned shepherd of the Church of God.

Monte Mario

THE GRAVE OF KEATS

Rid of the world's injustice, and his pain,
  He rests at last beneath God's veil of blue:
  Taken from life when life and love were new
The youngest of the martyrs here is lain,
Fair as Sebastian, and as early slain.
  No cypress shades his grave, no funeral yew,
  But gentle violets weeping with the dew

---

[1] Sacred and Eternal City.

Weave on his bones an ever-blossoming chain.
O proudest heart that broke for misery!
   O sweetest lips since those of Mitylene!
   O poet-painter of our English Land!
Thy name was writ in water – it shall stand:
   And tears like mine will keep thy memory green,
   As Isabella did her Basil-tree.

Rome

SONNET

On the Massacre of the Christians in Bulgaria

Christ, dost thou live indeed? Or are thy bones
Still straitened in their rock-hewn sepulchre?
And was thy Rising only dreamed by Her
Whose love of thee for all her sin atones?
For here the air is horrid with men's groans,
The priests who call upon thy name are slain,
Dost thou not hear the bitter wail of pain
From those whose children lie upon the stones?
Come down, O Son of God! Incestuous gloom
Curtains the land, and through the starless night
Over thy Cross a Crescent moon I see!
If thou in very truth didst burst the tomb
Come down, O Son of Man! And show thy might,
Lest Mahomet be crowned instead of Thee!

EASTER DAY

The silver trumpets rang across the Dome:
   The people knelt upon the ground with awe:
   And borne upon the necks of men I saw,
Like some great God, the Holy Lord of Rome.
Priest-like, he wore a robe more white than foam,
   And, king-like, swathed himself in royal red,
   Three crowns of gold rose high upon his head:
In splendour and in light the Pope passed home.
My heart stole back across wide wastes of years
   To One who wandered by a lonely sea,
   And sought in vain for any place of rest:
   'Foxes have holes, and every bird its nest.
I, only I, must wander wearily,
And bruise my feet, and drink wine salt with tears.'

SONNET

On Hearing the Dies Irae Sung in the Sistine Chapel

Nay, Lord, not thus! white lilies in the spring,
   Sad olive-groves, or silver-breasted dove,
   Teach me more clearly of Thy life and love
Than terrors of red flame and thundering.
The hillside vines dear memories of Thee bring:
   A bird at evening flying to its nest
   Tells me of One who had no place of rest:
I think it is of Thee the sparrows sing.
Come rather on some autumn afternoon,
   When red and brown are burnished on the leaves,
   And the fields echo to the gleaner's song.
Come when the splendid fulness of the moon
   Looks down upon the rows of golden sheaves,
   And reap Thy harvest: we have waited long.

ITALIA

Italia! thou art fallen, though with sheen
   Of battle-spears thy clamorous armies stride
   From the north Alps to the Sicilian tide!
Ay! fallen, though the nations hail thee Queen
Because rich gold in every town is seen,
   And on thy sapphire-lake in tossing pride
   Of wind-filled vans thy myriad galleys ride
Beneath one flag of red and white and green.
O Fair and Strong! O Strong and Fair in vain!
   Look southward where Rome's desecrated town
   Lies mourning for her God-anointed King!
Look heaven-ward! shall God allow this thing?
   Nay! but some flame-girt Raphael shall come down,
   And smite the Spoiler with the sword of pain.

Venice

Vita Nuova

I stood by the unvintageable sea
   Till the wet waves drenched face and hair with spray;
   The long red fires of the dying day
Burned in the west; the wind piped drearily;
And to the land the clamorous gulls did flee:
   'Alas!' I cried, 'My life is full of pain,
   And who can garner fruit or golden grain
From these waste fields which travel ceaselessly!'
My nets gaped wide with many a break and flaw,
   Nathless I threw them as my final cast
   Into the sea, and waited for the end.
When lo! a sudden glory! and I saw
   The argent splendour of white limbs ascend,
   And in that joy forgot my tortured past.

E Tenebris[1]

Come down, O Christ, and help me! reach thy hand,
   For I am drowning in a stormier sea
   Than Simon on thy lake of Galilee:
The wine of life is spilt upon the sand,
My heart is as some famine-murdered land
   Whence all good things have perished utterly,
   And well I know my soul in Hell must lie
If I this night before God's throne should stand.
'He sleeps perchance, or rideth to the chase,
   Like Baal, when his prophets howled that name
   From morn to noon on Carmel's smitten height.'
Nay, peace, I shall behold, before the night,
   The feet of brass, the robe more white than flame,
   The wounded hands, the weary human face.

Quantum Mutata[2]

There was a time in Europe long ago
   When no man died for freedom anywhere,
   But England's lion leaping from its lair

---

[1] Out of darkness.
[2] How much changed.

Laid hands on the oppressor! It was so
While England could a great Republic show.
    Witness the men of Piedmont, chiefest care
    Of Cromwell, when with impotent despair
The Pontiff in his painted portico
Trembled before our stern ambassadors.
    How comes it then that from such high estate
    We have thus fallen, save that Luxury
With barren merchandise piles up the gate
    Where noble thoughts and deeds should enter by:
    Else might we still be Milton's heritors.

TO MILTON

Milton! I think thy spirit hath passed away
From these white cliffs and high-embattled towers;
    This gorgeous fiery-coloured world of ours
Seems fallen into ashes dull and grey,
And the age changed unto a mimic play
    Wherein we waste our else too-crowded hours:
    For all our pomp and pageantry and powers
We are but fit to delve the common clay,
Seeing this little isle on which we stand,
    This England, this sea-lion of the sea,
    By ignorant demagogues is held in fee,
Who love her not: Dear God! is this the land
    Which bare a triple empire in her hand
    When Cromwell spake the word Democracy!

AVE MARIA GRATIA PLENA[1]

Was this His coming! I had hoped to see
    A scene of wondrous glory, as was told
    Of some great God who in a rain of gold
Broke open bars and fell on Danae:
Or a dread vision as when Semele
    Sickening for love and unappeased desire
    Prayed to see God's clear body, and the fire
Caught her brown limbs and slew her utterly:
With such glad dreams I sought this holy place,

---

[1] Hail Mary, full of grace.

And now with wondering eyes and heart I stand
Before this supreme mystery of Love:
A kneeling girl with passionless pale face,
    An angel with a lily in his hand,
    And over both the white wings of a Dove.

Florence

WASTED DAYS[1]

From a picture painted by Miss V. T.[2]

A fair slim boy not made for this world's pain,
    With hair of gold thick clustering round his ears,
    And longing eyes half veiled by foolish tears
Like bluest water seen through mists of rain;
Pale cheeks whereon no kiss hath left its stain,
    Red under-lip drawn in for fear of Love,
    And white throat whiter than the breast of dove –
Alas! Alas! If all should be in vain.
Corn-fields behind, and reapers all a-row
    In weariest labour, toiling wearily,
    To no sweet sound of laughter, or of lute;
And careless of the crimson sunset-glow,
    The boy still dreams; nor knows that night is nigh,
    And in the night-time no man gathers fruit.

THE GRAVE OF SHELLEY

Like burnt-out torches by a sick man's bed
    Gaunt cypress-trees stand round the sun-bleached stone;
    Here doth the little night-owl make her throne,
And the slight lizard show his jewelled head.
And, where the chaliced poppies flame to red,
    In the still chamber of yon pyramid
    Surely some Old-World Sphinx lurks darkly hid,
Grim warder of this pleasaunce of the dead.

Ah! sweet indeed to rest within the womb
    Of Earth, great mother of eternal sleep,
But sweeter far for thee a restless tomb
    In the blue cavern of an echoing deep,

---

[1] The first seven lines were re-written and used in 'Madonna Mia' for *Poems* 1881.
[2] Violet Troubridge.

Or where the tall ships founder in the gloom
    Against the rocks of some wave-shattered steep.

Rome

SANTA DECCA

The Gods are dead: no longer do we bring
    To grey-eyed Pallas crowns of olive-leaves!
    Demeter's child no more hath tithe of sheaves,
And in the noon the careless shepherds sing,
For Pan is dead, and all the wantoning
    By secret glade and devious haunt is o'er:
    Young Hylas seeks the water-springs no more;
Great Pan is dead, and Mary's son is King.

And yet – perchance in this sea-trancèd isle,
    Chewing the bitter fruit of memory,
    Some God lies hidden in the asphodel.
Ah Love! If such there be, then it were well
    For us to fly his anger: nay, but see,
    The leaves are stirring: let us watch awhile.

Corfu

THEORETIKOS[1]

This mighty empire hath but feet of clay
    Of all its ancient chivalry and might
    Our little island is forsaken quite:
Some enemy hath stolen its crown of bay,
And from its hills that voice hath passed away
    Which spake of Freedom: O come out of it,
    Come out of it, my Soul, thou art not fit
For this vile traffic-house, where day by day
    Wisdom and reverence are sold at mart,
    And the rude people rage with ignorant cries
Against an heritage of centuries.
    It mars my calm: wherefore in dreams of Art
    And loftiest culture I would stand apart,
Neither for God, nor for his enemies.

---

[1] The contemplative.

AMOR INTELLECTUALIS[1]

Oft have we trod the vales of Castaly
   And heard sweet notes of sylvan music blown
From antique reeds to common folk unknown:
   And often launched our bark upon that sea
Which the nine Muses hold in empery,
   And ploughed free furrows through the wave and foam,
   Nor spread reluctant sail for more safe home
Till we had freighted well our argosy.
Of which despoilèd treasures these remain,
   Sordello's passion, and the honied line
Of young Endymion, lordly Tamburlaine
   Driving his pampered jades, and, more than these,
The seven-fold vision of the Florentine,
   And grave-browed Milton's solemn harmonies.

AT VERONA

How steep the stairs within Kings' houses are
   For exile-wearied feet as mine to tread,
   And O how salt and bitter is the bread
Which falls from this Hound's table, – better far
That I had died in the red ways of war,
   Or that the gate of Florence bare my head,
   Than to live thus, by all things comraded
Which seek the essence of my soul to mar.

'Curse God and die: what better hope than this?
   He hath forgotten thee in all the bliss
   Of his gold city, and eternal day' –
Nay peace: behind my prison's blinded bars
   I do possess what none can take away
   My love, and all the glory of the stars.

---

[1] The love of minds.

RAVENNA

(Newdigate Prize Poem)

1

A year ago I breathed the Italian air, –
And yet, methinks this northern Spring is fair, –
These fields made golden with the flower of March,
The throstle singing on the feathered larch,
The cawing rooks, the wood-doves fluttering by,
The little clouds that race across the sky;
And fair the violet's gentle drooping head,
The primrose, pale for love uncomforted,
The rose that burgeons on the climbing briar,
The crocus-bed, (that seems a moon of fire
Round-girdled with a purple marriage-ring);
And all the flowers of our English Spring,
Fond snowdrops, and the bright-starred daffodil.
Up starts the lark beside the murmuring mill,
And breaks the gossamer-threads of early dew;
And down the river, like a flame of blue,
Keen as an arrow flies the water-king,
While the brown linnets in the greenwood sing.
A year ago! – It seems a little time
Since last I saw that lordly southern clime,
Where flower and fruit to purple radiance blow,
And like bright lamps the fabled apples glow.
Full Spring it was – and by rich flowering vines,
Dark olive-groves and noble forest-pines,
I rode at will; the moist glad air was sweet,
The white road rang beneath my horse's feet,
And musing on Ravenna's ancient name,
I watched the day till, marked with wounds of flame,
The turquoise sky to burnished gold was turned.

O how my heart with boyish passion burned,
When far away across the sedge and mere
I saw that Holy City rising clear,
Crowned with her crown of towers! On and on
I galloped, racing with the setting sun,
And ere the crimson after-glow was passed,
I stood within Ravenna's walls at last!

2

How strangely still! No sound of life or joy
Startles the air; no laughing shepherd-boy
Pipes on his reed, nor ever through the day
Comes the glad sound of children at their play:
O sad, and sweet, and silent! Surely here
A man might dwell apart from troublous fear,
Watching the tide of seasons as they flow
From amorous Spring to Winter's rain and snow,
And have no thought of sorrow; here, indeed,
Are Lethe's waters, and that fatal weed
Which makes a man forget his fatherland.

Ay! Amid lotus-meadows dost thou stand,
Like Proserpine, with poppy-laden head,
Guarding the holy ashes of the dead.
For though thy brood of warrior sons hath ceased,
Thy noble dead are with thee! they at least
Are faithful to thine honour: guard them well,
O childless city! For a mighty spell,
To wake men's hearts to dreams of things sublime,
Are the lone tombs where rest the Great of Time.

3

Yon lonely pillar, rising on the plain,
Marks where the bravest knight of France was slain, –
The Prince of chivalry, the Lord of war,
Gaston de Foix: for some untimely star
Led him against thy city, and he fell,
As falls some forest-lion fighting well.
Taken from life while life and love were new,
He lies beneath God's seamless veil of blue;
Tall lance-like reeds wave sadly o'er his head,
And oleanders bloom to deeper red,
Where his bright youth flowed crimson on the ground.

Look farther north unto that broken mound –
There, prisoned now within a lordly tomb
Raised by a daughter's hand, in lonely gloom,
Huge-limbed Theodoric, the Gothic king,
Sleeps after all his weary conquering.
Time hath not spared his ruin, – wind and rain
Have broken down his stronghold, and again
We see that Death is mighty lord of all,

And king and clown to ashen dust must fall.

Mighty indeed *their* glory! yet to me
Barbaric king, or knight of chivalry,
Or the great queen herself, were poor and vain,
Beside the grave where Dante rests from pain.
His gilded shrine lies open to the air;
And cunning sculptor's hands have carven there
The calm white brow, as calm as earliest morn,
The eyes that flashed with passionate love and scorn,
The lips that sang of Heaven and of Hell,
The almond-face which Giotto drew so well,
The weary face of Dante; – to this day,
Here in his place of resting, far away
From Arno's yellow waters, rushing down
Through the wide bridges of that fairy town,
Where the tall tower of Giotto seems to rise
A marble lily under sapphire skies!
Alas! My Dante! thou hast known the pain
Of meaner lives, – the exile's galling chain,
How steep the stairs within kings' houses are,
And all the petty miseries which mar
Man's nobler nature with the sense of wrong.
Yet this dull world is grateful for thy song;
Our nations do thee homage, – even she,
That cruel queen of vine-clad Tuscany,
Who bound with crown of thorns thy living brow,
Hath decked thine empty tomb with laurels now,
And begs in vain the ashes of her son.

O mightiest exile! All thy grief is done:
Thy soul walks now beside thy Beatrice;
Ravenna guards thine ashes: sleep in peace.

4

How lone this palace is; how grey the walls!
No minstrel now wakes echoes in these halls.
The broken chain lies rusting on the door,
And noisome weeds have split the marble floor:
Here lurks the snake, and here the lizards run
By the stone lions blinking in the sun.
Byron dwelt here in love and revelry
For two long years – a second Anthony,
Who of the world another Actium made!
Yet suffered not his royal soul to fade,

Or lyre to break, or lance to grow less keen,
'Neath any wiles of an Egyptian queen.
For from the East there came a mighty cry,
And Greece stood up to fight for Liberty,
And called him from Ravenna: never knight
Rode forth more nobly to wild scenes of fight!
None fell more bravely on ensanguined field,
Borne like a Spartan back upon his shield!
O Hellas! Hellas! in thine hour of pride,
Thy day of might, remember him who died
To wrest from off thy limbs the trammelling chain:
O Salamis! O lone Plataean plain!
O tossing waves of wild Euboean sea!
O wind-swept heights of lone Thermopylae!
He loved you well – ay, not alone in word,
Who freely gave to thee his lyre and sword,
Like Aeschylos at well-fought Marathon:

And England, too, shall glory in her son,
Her warrior-poet, first in song and fight.
No longer now shall Slander's venomed spite
Crawl like a snake across his perfect name,
Or mar the lordly scutcheon of his fame.

For as the olive-garland of the race,
Which lights with joy each eager runner's face,
As the red cross which saveth men in war,
As a flame-bearded beacon seen from far
By mariners upon a storm-tossed sea, –
Such was his love for Greece and Liberty!

Byron, thy crowns are ever fresh and green:
Red leaves of rose from Sapphic Mitylene
Shall bind thy brows; the myrtle blooms for thee,
In hidden glades by lonely Castaly;
The laurels wait thy coming: all are thine,
And round thy head one perfect wreath will twine.

5

The pine-tops rocked before the evening breeze
With the hoarse murmur of the wintry seas,
And the tall stems were streaked with amber bright; –
I wandered through the wood in wild delight,
Some startled bird, with fluttering wings and fleet,
Made snow of all the blossoms; at my feet,

Like silver crowns, the pale narcissi lay,
And small birds sang on every twining spray.
O waving trees, O forest liberty!
Within your haunts at least a man is free,
And half forgets the weary world of strife:
The blood flows hotter, and a sense of life
Wakes i' the quickening veins, while once again
The woods are filled with gods we fancied slain.
Long time I watched, and surely hoped to see
Some goat-foot Pan make merry minstrelsy
Amid the reeds! some startled Dryad-maid
In girlish flight! or lurking in the glade,
The soft brown limbs, the wanton treacherous face
Of woodland god! Queen Dian in the chase,
White-limbed and terrible, with look of pride,
And leash of boar-hounds leaping at her side!
Or Hylas mirrored in the perfect stream.

O idle heart! O fond Hellenic dream!
Ere long, with melancholy rise and swell,
The evening chimes, the convent's vesper bell,
Struck on mine ears amid the amorous flowers.
Alas! Alas! these sweet and honied hours
Had whelmed my heart like some encroaching sea,
And drowned all thoughts of black Gethsemane.

6

O lone Ravenna! many a tale is told
Of thy great glories in the days of old:
Two thousand years have passed since thou didst see
Caesar ride forth to royal victory.
Mighty thy name when Rome's lean eagles flew
From Britain's isles to far Euphrates blue;
And of the peoples thou wast noble queen,
Till in thy streets the Goth and Hun were seen.
Discrowned by man, deserted by the sea,
Thou sleepest, rocked in lonely misery!
No longer now upon thy swelling tide,
Pine-forest-like, thy myriad galleys ride!
For where the brass-beaked ships were wont to float,
The weary shepherd pipes his mournful note;
And the white sheep are free to come and go
Where Adria's purple waters used to flow.

O fair! O sad! O Queen uncomforted!

In ruined loveliness thou liest dead,
Alone of all thy sisters; for at last
Italia's royal warrior hath passed
Rome's lordliest entrance, and hath worn his crown
In the high temples of the Eternal Town!
The Palatine hath welcomed back her king,
And with his name the seven mountains ring!

And Naples hath outlived her dream of pain,
And mocks her tyrant! Venice lives again,
New risen from the waters! and the cry
Of Light and Truth, of Love and Liberty,
Is heard in lordly Genoa, and where
The marble spires of Milan wound the air,
Rings from the Alps to the Sicilian shore,
And Dante's dream is now a dream no more.

But thou, Ravenna, better loved than all,
Thy ruined palaces are but a pall
That hides thy fallen greatness! and thy name
Burns like a grey and flickering candle-flame
Beneath the noonday splendour of the sun
Of new Italia! For the night is done,
The night of dark oppression, and the day
Hath dawned in passionate splendour: far away
The Austrian hounds are hunted from the land,
Beyond those ice-crowned citadels which stand
Girdling the plain of royal Lombardy,
From the far West unto the Eastern sea.

I know, indeed, that sons of thine have died
In Lissa's waters, by the mountain-side
Of Aspromonte, on Novara's plain, –
Nor have thy children died for thee in vain:
And yet, methinks, thou hast not drunk this wine
From grapes new-crushed of Liberty divine,
Thou hast not followed that immortal Star
Which leads the people forth to deeds of war.
Weary of life, thou liest in silent sleep,
As one who marks the lengthening shadows creep,
Careless of all the hurrying hours that run,
Mourning some day of glory, for the sun
Of Freedom hath not shewn to thee his face,
And thou hast caught no flambeau in the race.

Yet wake not from thy slumbers, – rest thee well,
Amidst thy fields of amber asphodel,
Thy lily-sprinkled meadows, – rest thee there,

To mock all human greatness: who would dare
To vent the paltry sorrows of his life
Before thy ruins, or to praise the strife
Of kings' ambition, and the barren pride
Of warring nations! wert not thou the Bride
Of the wild Lord of Adria's stormy sea!
The Queen of double Empires! and to thee
Were not the nations given as thy prey!
And now – thy gates lie open night and day,
The grass grows green on every tower and hall,
The ghastly fig hath cleft thy bastioned wall;
And where thy mailèd warriors stood at rest
The midnight owl hath made her secret nest.
O fallen! Fallen! from thy high estate,
O city trammelled in the toils of Fate,
Doth nought remain of all thy glorious days,
But a dull shield, a crown of withered bays!

Yet who beneath this night of wars and fears,
From tranquil tower can watch the coming years;
Who can foretell what joys the day shall bring,
Or why before the dawn the linnets sing?
Thou, even thou, mayst wake, as wakes the rose
To crimson splendour from its grave of snows;
As the rich corn-fields rise to red and gold
From these brown lands, now stiff with Winter's cold;
As from the storm-rack comes a perfect star!

O much-loved city! I have wandered far
From the wave-circled islands of my home;
Have seen the gloomy mystery of the Dome
Rise slowly from the drear Campagna's way,
Clothed in the royal purple of the day:
I from the city of the violet crown
Have watched the sun by Corinth's hill go down,
And marked the 'myriad laughter' of the sea
From starlit hills of flower-starred Arcady;
Yet back to thee returns my perfect love,
As to its forest-nest the evening dove.

O poet's city! one who scarce has seen
Some twenty summers cast their doublets green
For Autumn's livery, would seek in vain
To wake his lyre to sing a louder strain,
Or tell thy days of glory; – poor indeed
Is the low murmur of the shepherd's reed,
Where the loud clarion's blast should shake the sky,

And flame across the heavens! and to try
Such lofty themes were folly: yet I know
That never felt my heart a nobler glow
Than when I woke the silence of thy street
With clamorous trampling of my horse's feet,
And saw the city which now I try to sing,
After long days of weary travelling.

7

   Adieu, Ravenna! but a year ago,
I stood and watched the crimson sunset glow
From the lone chapel on thy marshy plain:
The sky was as a shield that caught the stain
Of blood and battle from the dying sun,
And in the west the circling clouds had spun
A royal robe, which some great God might wear,
While into ocean-seas of purple air
Sank the gold galley of the Lord of Light.

   Yet here the gentle stillness of the night
Brings back the swelling tide of memory,
And wakes again my passionate love for thee:
Now is the Spring of Love, yet soon will come
On meadow and tree the Summer's lordly bloom;
And soon the grass with brighter flowers will blow,
And send up lilies for some boy to mow.
Then before long the Summer's conqueror,
Rich Autumn-time, the season's usurer,
Will lend his hoarded gold to all the trees,
And see it scattered by the spendthrift breeze;
And after that the Winter cold and drear.
So runs the perfect cycle of the year.
And so from youth to manhood do we go,
And fall to weary days and locks of snow.
Love only knows no winter; never dies:
Nor cares for frowning storms or leaden skies,
And mine for thee shall never pass away,
Though my weak lips may falter in my lay.

   Adieu! Adieu! yon silent evening star,
The night's ambassador, doth gleam afar,
And bid the shepherd bring his flocks to fold.
Perchance before our inland seas of gold
Are garnered by the reapers into sheaves,
Perchance before I see the Autumn leaves,

I may behold thy city; and lay down
Low at thy feet the poet's laurel crown.

Adieu! Adieu! yon silver lamp, the moon,
Which turns our midnight into perfect noon,
Doth surely light thy towers, guarding well
Where Dante sleeps, where Byron loved to dwell.

MAGDALEN WALKS

The little white clouds are racing over the sky,
    And the fields are strewn with the gold of the flower of March,
    The daffodil breaks under foot, and the tasselled larch
Sways and swings as the thrush goes hurrying by.

A delicate odour is borne on the wings of the morning breeze,
    The odour of deep wet grass, and of brown new-furrowed earth,
    The birds are singing for joy of the Spring's glad birth,
Hopping from branch to branch on the rocking trees.

And all the woods are alive with the murmur and sound of Spring,
    And the rose-bud breaks into pink on the climbing briar,
    And the crocus-bed is a quivering moon of fire
Girdled round with the belt of an amethyst ring.

And the plane to the pine-tree is whispering some tale of love
    Till it rustles with laughter and tosses its mantle of green,
    And the gloom of the wych-elm's hollow is lit with the iris sheen
Of the burnished rainbow throat and the silver breast of a dove.

See! The lark starts up from his bed in the meadow there,
    Breaking the gossamer threads and the nets of dew,
    And flashing adown the river, a flame of blue!
The kingfisher flies like an arrow, and wounds the air.

THE BURDEN OF ITYS

This English Thames is holier far than Rome,
    Those harebells like a sudden flush of sea
Breaking across the woodland, with the foam
    Of meadow-sweet and white anemone
To fleck their blue waves, – God likelier there
Than hidden in that crystal-hearted star the pale monks bear!

Those violet-gleaming butterflies that take
   Yon creamy lily for their pavilion
Are monsignores, and where the rushes shake
   A lazy pike lies basking in the sun,
His eyes half shut, – he is some mitred old
Bishop *in partibus*! Look at those gaudy scales all green and gold.

The wind the restless prisoner of the trees
   Does well for Palestrina, one would say
The mighty master's hands were on the keys
   Of the Maria organ, which they play
When early on some sapphire Easter morn
In a high litter red as blood or sin the Pope is borne

From his dark House out to the Balcony
   Above the bronze gates and the crowded square,
Whose very fountains seem for ecstasy
   To toss their silver lances in the air,
And stretching out weak hands to East and West
In vain sends peace to peaceless lands, to restless nations rest.

Is not yon lingering orange after-glow
   That stays to vex the moon more fair than all
Rome's lordliest pageants! strange, a year ago
   I knelt before some crimson Cardinal
Who bare the Host across the Esquiline,
And now – those common poppies in the wheat seem twice as fine.

The blue-green beanfields yonder, tremulous
   With the last shower, sweeter perfume bring
Through this cool evening than the odorous
   Flame-jewelled censers the young deacons swing,
When the grey priest unlocks the curtained shrine,
And makes God's body from the common fruit of corn and vine.

Poor Fra Giovanni bawling at the mass
   Were out of tune now, for a small brown bird
Sings overhead, and through the long cool grass
   I see that throbbing throat which once I heard
On starlit hills of flower-starred Arcady,
Once where the white and crescent sand of Salamis meets sea.

Sweet is the swallow twittering on the eaves
   At daybreak, when the mower whets his scythe,
And stock-doves murmur, and the milkmaid leaves
   Her little lonely bed, and carols blithe
To see the heavy-lowing cattle wait
Stretching their huge and dripping mouths across the farmyard gate.

And sweet the hops upon the Kentish leas,
   And sweet the wind that lifts the new-mown hay,
And sweet the fretful swarms of grumbling bees
   That round and round the linden blossoms play;
And sweet the heifer breathing in the stall,
And the green bursting figs that hang upon the red-brick wall.

And sweet to hear the cuckoo mock the spring
   While the last violet loiters by the well,
And sweet to hear the shepherd Daphnis sing
   The song of Linus through a sunny dell
Of warm Arcadia where the corn is gold
And the slight lithe-limbed reapers dance about the wattled fold.

And sweet with young Lycoris to recline
   In some Illyrian valley far away,
Where canopied on herbs amaracine
   We too might waste the summer-trancèd day
Matching our reeds in sportive rivalry,
While far beneath us frets the troubled purple of the sea.

But sweeter far if silver-sandalled foot
   Of some long-hidden God should ever tread
The Nuneham meadows, if with reeded flute
   Pressed to his lips some Faun might raise his head
By the green water-flags, ah! sweet indeed
To see the heavenly herdsman call his white-fleeced flock to feed.

Then sing to me thou tuneful chorister,
   Though what thou sing'st be thine own requiem!
Tell me thy tale thou hapless chronicler
   Of thine own tragedies! do not contemn
These unfamiliar haunts, this English field,
For many a lovely coronal our northern isle can yield

Which Grecian meadows know not, many a rose
   Which all day long in vales Aeolian
A lad might seek in vain for over-grows
   Our hedges like a wanton courtesan
Unthrifty of its beauty; lilies too
Ilissos never mirrored star our streams, and cockles blue

Dot the green wheat which, though they are the signs
   For swallows going south, would never spread
Their azure tents between the Attic vines;
   Even that little weed of ragged red,
Which bids the robin pipe, in Arcady
Would be a trespasser, and many an unsung elegy

Sleeps in the reeds that fringe our winding Thames
    Which to awake were sweeter ravishment
Than ever Syrinx wept for, diadems
    Of brown bee-studded orchids which were meant
For Cytheraea's brows are hidden here
Unknown to Cytheraea, and by yonder pasturing steer

There is a tiny yellow daffodil,
    The butterfly can see it from afar,
Although one summer evening's dew could fill
    Its little cup twice over ere the star
Had called the lazy shepherd to his fold
And be no prodigal; each leaf is flecked with spotted gold

As if Jove's gorgeous leman Danae
    Hot from his gilded arms had stooped to kiss
The trembling petals, or young Mercury
    Low-flying to the dusky ford of Dis
Had with one feather of his pinions
Just brushed them! the slight stem which bears the burden of its suns

Is hardly thicker than the gossamer,
    Or poor Arachne's silver tapestry,
Men say it bloomed upon the sepulchre
    Of One I sometime worshipped, but to me
It seems to bring diviner memories
Of faun-loved Heliconian glades and blue nymph-haunted seas,

Of an untrodden vale at Tempe where
    On the clear river's marge Narcissus lies,
The tangle of the forest in his hair,
    The silence of the woodland in his eyes,
Wooing that drifting imagery which is
No sooner kissed than broken; memories of Salmacis

Who is not boy nor girl and yet is both,
    Fed by two fires and unsatisfied
Through their excess, each passion being loth
    For love's own sake to leave the other's side
Yet killing love by staying; memories
Of Oreads peeping through the leaves of silent moonlit trees,

Of lonely Ariadne on the wharf
    At Naxos, when she saw the treacherous crew
Far out at sea, and waved her crimson scarf
    And called false Theseus back again nor knew
That Dionysos on an amber pard
Was close behind her; memories of what Maeonia's bard

With sightless eyes beheld, the wall of Troy,
    Queen Helen lying in the Ivory room,
And at her side an amorous red-lipped boy
    Trimming with dainty hand his helmet's plume,
And far away the moil, the shout, the groan,
As Hector shielded off the spear and Ajax hurled the stone;

Of wingèd Perseus with his flawless sword
    Cleaving the snaky tresses of the witch,
And all those tales imperishably stored
    In little Grecian urns, freightage more rich
Than any gaudy galleon of Spain
Bare from the Indies ever! these at least bring back again,

For well I know they are not dead at all,
    The ancient Gods of Grecian poesy;
They are asleep, and when they hear thee call
    Will wake and think 'tis very Thessaly,
This Thames and Daulian waters, this cool glade
The yellow-irised mead where once young Itys laughed and played.

If it was thou dear jasmine-cradled bird
    Who from the leafy stillness of thy throne
Sang to the wondrous boy, until he heard
    The horn of Atalanta faintly blown
Across the Cumnor hills, and wandering
Through Bagley wood at evening found the Attic poets' spring, –

Ah! tiny sober-suited advocate
    That pleadest for the moon against the day!
If thou didst make the shepherd seek his mate
    On that sweet questing, when Proserpina
Forgot it was not Sicily and leant
Across the mossy Sandford stile in ravished wonderment, –

Light-winged and bright-eyed miracle of the wood!
    If ever thou didst soothe with melody
One of that little clan, that brotherhood
    Which loved the morning-star of Tuscany
More than the perfect sun of Raphael
And is immortal, sing to me! for I too love thee well.

Sing on! Sing on! Let the dull world grow young,
    Let elemental things take form again,
And the old shapes of Beauty walk among
    The simple garths and open crofts, as when
The son of Leto bare the willow rod,
And the soft sheep and shaggy goats followed the boyish God.

Sing on! Sing on! and Bacchus will be here
   Astride upon his gorgeous Indian throne,
And over whimpering tigers shake the spear
   With yellow ivy crowned and gummy cone,
While at his side the wanton Bassarid
Will throw the lion by the mane and catch the mountain kid!

Sing on! And I will wear the leopard skin,
   And steal the moonèd wings of Ashtaroth,
Upon whose icy chariot we could win
   Cithaeron in an hour ere the froth
Has over-brimmed the wine-vat or the Faun
Ceased from the treading! Ay, before the flickering lamp of dawn

Has scared the hooting owlet to its nest,
   And warned the bat to close its filmy vans,
Some Maenad girl with vine-leaves on her breast
   Will filch their beech-nuts from the sleeping Pans
So softly that the little nested thrush
Will never wake, and then with shrilly laugh and leap will rush

Down the green valley where the fallen dew
   Lies thick beneath the elm and count her store,
Till the brown Satyrs in a jolly crew
   Trample the loosestrife down along the shore,
And where their hornèd master sits in state
Bring strawberries and bloomy plums upon a wicker crate!

Sing on! and soon with passion-wearied face
   Through the cool leaves Apollo's lad will come,
The Tyrian prince his bristled boar will chase
   Adown the chestnut-copses all abloom,
And ivory-limbed, grey-eyed, with look of pride,
After yon velvet-coated deer the virgin maid will ride.

Sing on! and I the dying boy will see
   Stain with his purple blood the waxen bell
That overweighs the jacinth, and to me
   The wretched Cyprian her woe will tell,
And I will kiss her mouth and streaming eyes,
And lead her to the myrtle-hidden grove where Adon lies!

Cry out aloud on Itys! memory
   That foster-brother of remorse and pain
Drops poison in mine ear, – O to be free,
   To burn one's old ships! and to launch again
Into the white-plumed battle of the waves
And fight old Proteus for the spoil of coral-flowered caves!

O for Medea with her poppied spell!
  O for the secret of the Colchian shrine!
O for one leaf of that pale asphodel
  Which binds the tired brows of Proserpine,
And sheds such wondrous dews at eve that she
Dreams of the fields of Enna, by the far Sicilian sea,

Where oft the golden-girdled bee she chased
  From lily to lily on the level mead,
Ere yet her sombre Lord had bid her taste
  The deadly fruit of that pomegranate seed,
Ere the black steeds had harried her away
Down to the faint and flowerless land, the sick and sunless day.

O for one midnight and as paramour
  The Venus of the little Melian farm!
O that some antique statue for one hour
  Might wake to passion, and that I could charm
The Dawn at Florence from its dumb despair,
Mix with those mighty limbs and make that giant breast my lair!

Sing on! Sing on! I would be drunk with life,
  Drunk with the trampled vintage of my youth,
I would forget the wearying wasted strife,
  The riven veil, the Gorgon eyes of Truth,
The prayerless vigil and the cry for prayer,
The barren gifts, the lifted arms, the dull insensate air!

Sing on! Sing on! O feathered Niobe,
  Thou canst make sorrow beautiful, and steal
From joy its sweetest music, not as we
  Who by dead voiceless silence strive to heal
Our too untended wounds, and do but keep
Pain barricadoed in our hearts, and murder pillowed sleep.

Sing louder yet, why must I still behold
  The wan white face of that deserted Christ,
Whose bleeding hands my hands did once enfold,
  Whose smitten lips my lips so oft have kissed,
And now in mute and marble misery
Sits in his lone dishonoured House and weeps, perchance for me?

O Memory cast down thy wreathèd shell!
  Break thy hoarse lute O sad Melpomene!
O Sorrow, Sorrow keep thy cloistered cell
  Nor dim with tears this limpid Castaly!
Cease, Philomel thou dost the forest wrong
To vex its sylvan quiet with such wild impassioned song!

Cease, cease, or if 'tis anguish to be dumb
 Take from the pastoral thrush her simpler air,
Whose jocund carelessness doth more become
 This English woodland than they keen despair,
Ah! cease and let the north wind bear thy lay
Back to the rocky hills of Thrace, the stormy Daulian bay.

A moment more, the startled leaves had stirred,
 Endymion would have passed across the mead
Moonstruck with love, and this still Thames had heard
 Pan plash and paddle groping for some reed
To lure from her blue cave that Naiad maid
Who for such piping listens half in joy and half afraid.

A moment more, the waking dove had cooed,
 The silver daughter of the silver sea
With the fond gyves of clinging hands had wooed
 Her wanton from the chase, and Dryope
Had thrust aside the branches of her oak
To see the lusty gold-haired lad rein in his snorting yoke.

A moment more, the trees had stooped to kiss
 Pale Daphne just awakening from the swoon
Of tremulous laurels, lonely Salmacis
 Had bared his barren beauty to the moon,
And through the vale with sad voluptuous smile
Antinous had wandered, the red lotus of the Nile

Down leaning from his black and clustering hair,
 To shade those slumberous eyelids' caverned bliss,
Or else on yonder grassy slope with bare
 High-tuniced limbs unravished Artemis
Had bade her hounds give tongue, and roused the deer
From his green ambuscade with shrill halloo and pricking spear.

Lie still, lie still, O passionate heart, lie still!
 O Melancholy, fold thy raven wing!
O sobbing Dryad, from thy hollow hill
 Come not with such despondent answering
No more thou wingèd Marsyas complain,
Apollo loveth not to hear such troubled songs of pain!

It was a dream, the glade is tenantless,
 No soft Ionian laughter moves the air,
The Thames creeps on in sluggish leadenness,
 And from the copse left desolate and bare
Fled is young Bacchus with his revelry,
Yet still from Nuneham wood there comes that thrilling melody

So sad, that one might think a human heart
    Brake in each separate note, a quality
Which music sometimes has, being the Art
    Which is most nigh to tears and memory;
Poor mourning Philomel, what dost thou fear?
Thy sister doth not haunt these fields, Pandion is not here.

Here is no cruel Lord with murderous blade,
    No woven web of bloody heraldries,
But mossy dells for roving comrades made,
    Warm valleys where the tired student lies
With half-shut book, and many a winding walk
Where rustic lovers stray at eve in happy simple talk.

The harmless rabbit gambols with its young
    Across the trampled towing-path, where late
A troop of laughing boys in jostling throng
    Cheered with their noisy cries the racing eight;
The gossamer, with ravelled silver threads,
Works at its little loom, and from the dusky red-eaved sheds

Of the lone Farm a flickering light shines out
    Where the swinked shepherd drives his bleating flock
Back to their wattled sheep-cotes, a faint shout
    Comes from some Oxford boat at Sandford lock,
And starts the moor-hen from the sedgy rill,
And the dim lengthening shadows flit like swallows up the hill.

The heron passes homeward to the mere,
    The blue mist creeps among the shivering trees,
Gold world by world the silent stars appear
    And like a blossom blown before the breeze
A white moon drifts across the shimmering sky,
Mute arbitress of all thy sad, thy rapturous threnody.

She does not heed thee, wherefore should she heed,
    She knows Endymion is not far away;
'Tis I, 'tis I, whose soul is as the reed
    Which has no message of its own to play,
So pipes another's bidding, it is I,
Drifting with every wind on the wide sea of misery.

Ah! the brown bird has ceased: one exquisite trill
    About the sombre woodland seems to cling
Dying in music, else the air is still,
    So still that one might hear the bat's small wing
Wander and wheel above the pines, or tell
Each tiny dew-drop dripping from the bluebell's brimming cell.

And far away across the lengthening wold,
  Across the willowy flats and thickets brown,
Magdalen's tall tower tipped with tremulous gold
  Marks the long High Street of the little town,
And warns me to return; I must not wait,
Hark! 'Tis the curfew booming from the bell at Christ Church gate.

THEOCRITUS

A Villanelle

O singer of Persephone!
  In the dim meadows desolate
Dost thou remember Sicily?

Still through the ivy flits the bee
  Where Amaryllis lies in state;
O Singer of Persephone!

Simaetha calls on Hecate
  And hears the wild dogs at the gate;
Dost thou remember Sicily?

Still by the light and laughing sea
  Poor Polypheme bemoans his fate;
O Singer of Persephone!

And still in boyish rivalry
  Young Daphnis challenges his mate;
Dost thou remember Sicily?

Slim Lacon keeps a goat for thee,
  For thee the jocund shepherds wait;
O Singer of Persephone!
Dost thou remember Sicily?

NOCTURNE

The moon hath spread a pavilion
    Of silver and of amethyst:
But where is young Endymion,
Where are the lips that should be kissed?

The roof of fleecy cloud is spun,
    Of silken light the ropes are trist:
But where is young Endymion,
Where are the lips that should be kissed?

To spite her jealous Lord the Sun
    She wears a veil of seagreen mist:
But where is young Endymion,
Where are the lips that should be kissed?

All through the weary hours that run
    She keeps the lingering lover's tryst:
But where is young Endymion,
Where are the lips that should be kissed?

Her gold torch-bearers one by one
    Pass from her side and are not missed:
But where is young Endymion,
Where are the lips that should be kissed?

Ah down in moonless Acheron
    Pale Prosperine is glad, I wist:
For there is young Endymion,
There are the lips that should be kissed.

Verona

ENDYMION

(*For music*)

The apple trees are hung with gold,
    And birds are loud in Arcady,
The sheep lie bleating in the fold,
The wild goat runs across the wold,
But yesterday his love he told,
    I know he will come back to me.
O rising moon! O Lady moon!
    Be you my lover's sentinel,
    You cannot choose but know him well,

For he is shod with purple shoon,
You cannot choose but know my love,
  For he a shepherd's crook doth bear,
And he is soft as any dove,
  And brown and curly is his hair.

The turtle now has ceased to call
  Upon her crimson-footed groom,
The grey wolf prowls about the stall,
The lily's singing seneschal
Sleeps in the lily-bell, and all
  The violet hills are lost in gloom.
O risen moon! O holy moon!
  Stand on the top of Helice,
  And if my own true love you see,
Ah! if you see the purple shoon,
The hazel crook, the lad's brown hair,
  The goat-skin wrapped about his arm,
Tell him that I am waiting where
  The rushlight glimmers in the Farm.

The falling dew is cold and chill,
  And no bird sings in Arcady,
The little fauns have left the hill,
Even the tired daffodil
Has closed its gilded doors, and still
  My lover comes not back to me.
False moon! False moon! O waning moon!
  Where is my own true lover gone,
  Where are the lips vermilion,
The shepherd's crook, the purple shoon?
Why spread that silver pavilion,
  Why wear that veil of drifting mist?
Ah! thou hast young Endymion,
  Thou hast the lips that should be kissed!

CHARMIDES

1

He was a Grecian lad, who coming home
  With pulpy figs and wine from Sicily
Stood at his galley's prow, and let the foam
  Blow through his crisp brown curls unconsciously,
And holding wave and wind in boy's despite
Peered from his dripping seat across the wet and stormy night.

Till with the dawn he saw a burnished spear
   Like a thin thread of gold against the sky,
And hoisted sail, and strained the creaking gear,
   And bade the pilot head her lustily
Against the nor'west gale, and all day long
Held on his way, and marked the rowers' time with measured song,

And when the faint Corinthian hills were red
   Dropped anchor in a little sandy bay,
And with fresh boughs of olive crowned his head,
   And brushed from cheek and throat the hoary spray,
And washed his limbs with oil, and from the hold
Brought out his linen tunic and his sandals brazen-soled,

And a rich robe stained with the fishes' juice
   Which of some swarthy trader he had bought
Upon the sunny quay at Syracuse,
   And was with Tyrian broideries inwrought,
And by the questioning merchants made his way
Up through the soft and silver woods, and when the labouring day

Had spun its tangled web of crimson cloud,
   Clomb the high hill, and with swift silent feet
Crept to the fane unnoticed by the crowd
   Of busy priests, and from some dark retreat
Watched the young swains his frolic playmates bring
The firstling of their little flock, and the shy shepherd fling

The crackling salt upon the flame, or hang
   His studded crook against the temple wall
To Her who keeps away the ravenous fang
   Of the base wolf from homestead and from stall;
And then the clear-voiced maidens 'gan to sing,
And to the altar each man brought some goodly offering,

A beechen cup brimming with milky foam,
   A fair cloth wrought with cunning imagery
Of hounds in chase, a waxen honey-comb
   Dripping with oozy gold which scarce the bee
Had ceased from building, a black skin of oil
Meet for the wrestlers, a great boar the fierce and white-tusked spoil

Stolen from Artemis that jealous maid
   To please Athena, and the dappled hide
Of a tall stag who in some mountain glade
   Had met the shaft; and then the herald cried,
And from the pillared precinct one by one
Went the glad Greeks well pleased that they their simple vows had done.

And the old priest put out the waning fires
    Save that one lamp whose restless ruby glowed
For ever in the cell, and the shrill lyres
    Came fainter on the wind, as down the road
In joyous dance these country folk did pass,
And with stout hands the warder closed the gates of polished brass.

Long time he lay and hardly dared to breathe,
    And heard the cadenced drip of spilt-out wine,
And the rose-petals falling from the wreath
    As the night breezes wandered through the shrine,
And seemed to be in some entrancèd swoon
Till through the open roof above the full and brimming moon

Flooded with sheeny waves the marble floor,
    When from his nook up leapt the venturous lad,
And flinging wide the cedar-carven door
    Beheld an awful image saffron-clad
And armed for battle! the gaunt Griffin glared
From the huge helm, and the long lance of wreck and ruin flared

Like a red rod of flame, stony and steeled,
    The Gorgon's head its leaden eyeballs rolled,
And writhed its snaky horrors through the shield,
    And gaped aghast with bloodless lips and cold
In passion impotent, while with blind gaze
The blinking owl between the feet hooted in shrill amaze.

The lonely fisher as he trimmed his lamp
    Far out at sea off Sunium, or cast
The net for tunnies, heard a brazen tramp
    Of horses smite the waves, and a wild blast
Divide the folded curtains of the night,
And knelt upon the little poop, and prayed in holy fright.

And guilty lovers in their venery
    Forgat a little while their stolen sweets,
Deeming they heard dread Dian's bitter cry;
    And the grim watchmen on their lofty seats
Ran to their shields in haste precipitate,
Or strained black-bearded throats across the dusky parapet.

For round the temple rolled the clang of arms,
    And the twelve Gods leapt up in marble fear,
And the air quaked with dissonant alarums
    Till huge Poseidon shook his mighty spear,
And on the frieze the prancing horses neighed,
And the low tread of hurrying feet rang from the cavalcade.

Ready for death with parted lips he stood,
   And well content at such a price to see
That calm wide brow, that terrible maidenhood,
   The marvel of that pitiless chastity,
Ah! well content indeed, for never wight
Since Troy's young shepherd prince had seen so wonderful a sight.

Ready for death he stood, but lo! the air
   Grew silent, and the horses ceased to neigh,
And off his brow he tossed the clustering hair,
   And from his limbs he threw the cloak away;
For whom would not such love make desperate,
And nigher came, and touched her throat, and with hands violate

Undid the cuirass, and the crocus gown,
   And bared the breasts of polished ivory,
Till from the waist the peplos falling down
   Left visible the secret mystery
Which to no lover will Athena show,
The grand cool flanks, the crescent thighs, the bossy hills of snow.

Those who have never known a lover's sin
   Let them not read my ditty, it will be
To their dull ears so musicless and thin
   That they will have no joy of it, but ye
To whose wan cheeks now creeps the lingering smile,
Ye who have learned who Eros is, – O listen yet awhile.

A little space he let his greedy eyes
   Rest on the burnished image, till mere sight
Half swooned for surfeit of such luxuries,
   And then his lips in hungering delight
Fed on her lips, and round the towered neck
He flung his arms, nor cared at all his passion's will to check.

Never I ween did lover hold such tryst,
   For all night long he murmured honeyed word,
And saw her sweet unravished limbs, and kissed
   Her pale and argent body undisturbed,
And paddled with the polished throat, and pressed
His hot and beating heart upon her chill and icy breast.

It was as if Numidian javelins
   Pierced through and through his wild and whirling brain,
And his nerves thrilled like throbbing violins
   In exquisite pulsation, and the pain
Was such sweet anguish that he never drew
His lips from hers till overhead the lark of warning flew.

They who have never seen the daylight peer
   Into a darkened room, and drawn the curtain,
And with dull eyes and wearied from some dear
   And worshipped body risen, they for certain
Will never know of what I try to sing,
How long the last kiss was, how fond and late his lingering.

The moon was girdled with a crystal rim,
   The sign which shipmen say is ominous
Of wrath in heaven, the wan stars were dim,
   And the low lightening east was tremulous
With the faint fluttering wings of flying dawn,
Ere from the silent sombre shrine his lover had withdrawn.

Down the steep rock with hurried feet and fast
   Clomb the brave lad, and reached the cave of Pan,
And heard the goat-foot snoring as he passed,
   And leapt upon a grassy knoll and ran
Like a young fawn unto an olive wood
Which in a shady valley by the well-built city stood;

And sought a little stream, which well he knew,
   For oftentimes with boyish careless shout
The green and crested grebe he would pursue,
   Or snare in woven net the silver trout,
And down amid the startled reeds he lay
Panting in breathless sweet affright, and waited for the day.

On the green bank he lay, and let one hand
   Dip in the cool dark eddies listlessly,
And soon the breath of morning came and fanned
   His hot flushed cheeks, or lifted wantonly
The tangled curls from off his forehead, while
He on the running water gazed with strange and secret smile.

And soon the shepherd in rough woollen cloak
   With his long crook undid the wattled cotes,
And from the stack a thin blue wreath of smoke
   Curled through the air across the ripening oats,
And on the hill the yellow house-dog bayed
As through the crisp and rustling fern the heavy cattle strayed.

And when the light-foot mower went afield
   Across the meadows laced with threaded dew,
And the sheep bleated on the misty weald,
   And from its nest the waking corncrake flew,
Some woodmen saw him lying by the stream
And marvelled much that any lad so beautiful could seem,

Nor deemed him born of mortals, and one said,
   'It is young Hylas, that false runaway
Who with a Naiad now would make his bed
   Forgetting Herakles,' but others, 'Nay,
It is Narcissus, his own paramour,
Those are the fond and crimson lips no woman can allure.'

And when they nearer came a third one cried,
   'It is young Dionysos who has hid
His spear and fawnskin by the river side
   Weary of hunting with the Bassarid,
And wise indeed were we away to fly:
They live not long who on the gods immortal come to spy.'

So turned they back, and feared to look behind,
   And told the timid swain how they had seen
Amid the reeds some woodland God reclined,
   And no man dared to cross the open green,
And on that day no olive-tree was slain,
Nor rushes cut, but all deserted was the fair domain,

Save when the neat-herd's lad, his empty pail
   Well slung upon his back, with leap and bound
Raced on the other side, and stopped to hail,
   Hoping that he some comrade new had found,
And got no answer, and then half afraid
Passed on his simple way, or down the still and silent glade

A little girl ran laughing from the farm,
   Not thinking of love's secret mysteries,
And when she saw the white and gleaming arm
   And all his manlihood, with longing eyes
Whose passion mocked her sweet virginity
Watched him awhile, and then stole back sadly and wearily.

Far off he heard the city's hum and noise,
   And now and then the shriller laughter where
The passionate purity of brown-limbed boys
   Wrestled or raced in the clear healthful air,
And now and then a little tinkling bell
As the shorn wether led the sheep down to the mossy well.

Through the grey willows danced the fretful gnat,
   The grasshopper chirped idly from the tree,
In sleek and oily coat the water-rat
   Breasting the little ripples manfully
Made for the wild-duck's nest, from bough to bough
Hopped the shy finch, and the huge tortoise crept across the slough.

On the faint wind floated the silky seeds
  As the bright scythe swept through the waving grass,
The ousel-cock splashed circles in the reeds
  And flecked with silver whorls the forest's glass,
Which scarce had caught again its imagery
Ere from its bed the dusky tench leapt at the dragon-fly.

But little care had he for any thing
  Though up and down the beech the squirrel played,
And from the copse the linnet 'gan to sing
  To her brown mate her sweetest serenade;
Ah! little care indeed, for he had seen
The breasts of Pallas and the naked wonder of the Queen.

But when the herdsmen called his straggling goats
  With whistling pipe across the rocky road,
And the shard-beetle with its trumpet-notes
  Boomed through the darkening woods, and seemed to bode
Of coming storm, and the belated crane
Passed homeward like a shadow, and the dull big drops of rain

Fell on the pattering fig-leaves, up he rose,
  And from the gloomy forest went his way
Past sombre homestead and wet orchard-close,
  And came at last unto a little quay,
And called his mates aboard, and took his seat
On the high poop, and pushed from land, and loosed the dripping sheet,

And steered across the bay, and when nine suns
  Passed down the long and laddered way of gold,
And nine pale moons had breathed their orisons
  To the chaste stars their confessors, or told
Their dearest secret to the downy moth
That will not fly at noonday, through the foam and surging froth

Came a great owl with yellow sulphurous eyes
  And lit upon the ship, whose timbers creaked
As though the lading of three argosies
  Were in the hold, and flapped its wings and shrieked,
And darkness straightway stole across the deep,
Sheathed was Orion's sword, dread Mars himself fled down the steep,

And the moon hid behind a tawny mask
  Of drifting cloud, and from the ocean's marge
Rose the red plume, the huge and hornèd casque,
  The seven-cubit spear, the brazen targe!
And clad in bright and burnished panoply
Athena strode across the stretch of sick and shivering sea!

To the dull sailors' sight her loosened locks
   Seemed like the jagged storm-rack, and her feet
Only the spume that floats on hidden rocks,
   And, marking how the rising waters beat
Against the rolling ship, the pilot cried
To the young helmsman at the stern to luff to windward side.

But he, the overbold adulterer,
   A dear profaner of great mysteries,
An ardent amorous idolater,
   When he beheld those grand relentless eyes
Laughed loud for joy, and crying out 'I come'
Leapt from the lofty poop into the chill and churning foam.

Then fell from the high heaven one bright star,
   One dancer left the circling galaxy,
And back to Athens on her clattering car
   In all the pride of venged divinity
Pale Pallas swept with shrill and steely clank,
And a few gurgling bubbles rose where her boy lover sank.

And the mast shuddered as the gaunt owl flew
   With mocking hoots after the wrathful Queen,
And the old pilot bade the trembling crew
   Hoist the big sail, and told how he had seen
Close to the stern a dim and giant form,
And like a dipping swallow the stout ship dashed through the storm.

And no man dared to speak of Charmides
   Deeming that he some evil thing had wrought,
And when they reached the strait Symplegades
   They beached their galley on the shore, and sought
The toll-gate of the city hastily,
And in the market showed their brown and pictured pottery.

2

But some good Triton-god had ruth, and bare
   The boy's drowned body back to Grecian land,
And mermaids combed his dank and dripping hair
   And smoothed his brow, and loosed his clenching hand,
Some brought sweet spices from far Araby,
And others bade the halcyon sing her softest lullaby.

And when he neared his old Athenian home,
   A mighty billow rose up suddenly

Upon whose oily back the clotted foam
    Lay diapered in some strange fantasy,
And clasping him unto its glassy breast
Swept landward, like a white-maned steed upon a venturous quest!

Now where Colonos leans unto the sea
    There lies a long and level stretch of lawn;
The rabbit knows it, and the mountain bee
    For it deserts Hymettus, and the Faun
Is not afraid, for never through the day
Comes a cry ruder than the shout of shepherd lads at play.

But often from the thorny labyrinth
    And tangled branches of the circling wood
The stealthy hunter sees young Hyacinth
    Hurling the polished disk, and draws his hood
Over his guilty gaze, and creeps away,
Nor dares to wind his horn, or – else at the first break of day

The Dryads come and throw the leathern ball
    Along the reedy shore, and circumvent
Some goat-eared Pan to be their seneschal
    For fear of bold Poseidon's ravishment,
And loose their girdles, with shy timorous eyes,
Lest from the surf his azure arms and purple beard should rise.

On this side and on that a rocky cave,
    Hung with the yellow-belled laburnum, stands;
Smooth is the beach, save where some ebbing wave
    Leaves its faint outline etched upon the sands,
As though it feared to be too soon forgot
By the green rush, its playfellow, – and yet, it is a spot

So small, that the inconstant butterfly
    Could steal the hoarded money from each flower
Ere it was noon, and still not satisfy
    Its over-greedy love, – within an hour
A sailor boy, were he but rude enow
To land and pluck a garland for his galley's painted prow,

Would almost leave the little meadow bare,
    For it knows nothing of great pageantry,
Only a few narcissi here and there
    Stand separate in sweet austerity,
Dotting the un-mown grass with silver stars,
And here and there a daffodil waves tiny scimitars.

Hither the billow brought him, and was glad
    Of such dear servitude, and where the land

Was virgin of all waters laid the lad
   Upon the golden margent of the strand,
And like a lingering lover oft returned
To kiss those pallid limbs which once with intense fire burned,

Ere the wet seas had quenched that holocaust,
   That self-fed flame, that passionate lustihead,
Ere grisly death with chill and nipping frost
   Had withered up those lilies white and red
Which, while the boy would through the forest range,
Answered each other in a sweet antiphonal counter-change.

And when at dawn the wood-nymphs, hand-in-hand,
   Threaded the bosky dell, their satyr spied
The boy's pale body stretched upon the sand,
   And feared Poseidon's treachery, and cried,
And like bright sunbeams flitting through a glade
Each startled Dryad sought some safe and leafy ambuscade,

Save one white girl, who deemed it would not be
   So dread a thing to feel a sea-god's arms
Crushing her breasts in amorous tyranny,
   And longed to listen to those subtle charms
Insidious lovers weave when they would win
Some fencèd fortress, and stole back again, nor thought it sin

To yield her treasure unto one so fair,
   And lay beside him, thirsty with love's drouth,
Called him soft names, played with his tangled hair,
   And with hot lips made havoc of his mouth
Afraid he might not wake, and then afraid
Lest he might wake too soon, fled back, and then, fond renegade,

Returned to fresh assault, and all day long
   Sat at his side, and laughed at her new toy,
And held his hand, and sang her sweetest song,
   Then frowned to see how froward was the boy
Who would not with her maidenhood entwine,
Nor knew that three days since his eyes had looked on Proserpine,

Nor knew what sacrilege his lips had done,
   But said, 'He will awake, I know him well,
He will awake at evening when the sun
   Hangs his red shield on Corinth's citadel;
This sleep is but a cruel treachery
To make me love him more, and in some cavern of the sea

Deeper than ever falls the fisher's line
   Already a huge Triton blows his horn,

And weaves a garland from the crystalline
   And drifting ocean-tendrils to adorn
The emerald pillars of our bridal bed,
For sphered in foaming silver, and with coral-crownèd head,

We two will sit upon a throne of pearl,
   And a blue wave will be our canopy,
And at our feet the water-snakes will curl
   In all their amethystine panoply
Of diamonded mail, and we will mark
The mullets swimming by the mast of some storm-foundered bark,

Vermilion-finned with eyes of bossy gold
   Like flakes of crimson light, and the great deep
His glassy-portaled chamber will unfold,
   And we will see the painted dolphins sleep
Cradled by murmuring halcyons on the rocks
Where Proteus in quaint suit of green pastures his monstrous flocks.

And tremulous opal-hued anemones
   Will wave their purple fringes where we tread
Upon the mirrored floor, and argosies
   Of fishes flecked with tawny scales will thread
The drifting cordage of the shattered wreck,
And honey-coloured amber beads our twining limbs will deck.'

But when that baffled Lord of War the Sun
   With gaudy pennon flying passed away
Into his brazen House, and one by one
   The little yellow stars began to stray
Across the field of heaven, ah! then indeed
She feared his lips upon her lips would never care to feed,

And cried, 'Awake, already the pale moon
   Washes the trees with silver, and the wave
Creeps grey and chilly up this sandy dune,
   The croaking frogs are out, and from the cave
The night-jar shrieks, the fluttering bats repass,
And the brown stoat with hollow flanks creeps through the dusky grass.

Nay, though thou art a God, be not so coy,
   For in yon stream there is a little reed
That often whispers how a lovely boy
   Lay with her once upon a grassy mead,
Who when his cruel pleasure he had done
Spread wings of rustling gold and soared aloft into the sun.

Be not so coy, the laurel trembles still
   With great Apollo's kisses, and the fir

Whose clustering sisters fringe the seaward hill
    Hath many a tale of that bold ravisher
Whom men call Boreas, and I have seen
The mocking eyes of Hermes through the poplar's silvery sheen.

Even the jealous Naiads call me fair,
    And every morn a young and ruddy swain
Woos me with apples and with locks of hair,
    And seeks to soothe my virginal disdain
By all the gifts the gentle wood-nymphs love;
But yesterday he brought to me an iris-plumaged dove

With little crimson feet, which with its store
    Of seven spotted eggs the cruel lad
Had stolen from the lofty sycamore
    At daybreak, when her amorous comrade had
Flown off in search of berried juniper
Which most they love; the fretful wasp, that earliest vintager

Of the blue grapes, hath not persistency
    So constant as this simple shepherd-boy
For my poor lips, his joyous purity
    And laughing sunny eyes might well decoy
A Dryad from her oath to Artemis;
For very beautiful is he, his mouth was made to kiss;

His argent forehead, like a rising moon
    Over the dusky hills of meeting brows,
Is crescent shaped, the hot and Tyrian noon
    Leads from the myrtle-grove no goodlier spouse
For Cytheraea, the first silky down
Fringes his blushing cheeks, and his young limbs are strong and brown:

And he is rich, and fat and fleecy herds
    Of bleating sheep upon his meadows lie,
And many an earthen bowl of yellow curds
    Is in his homestead for the thievish fly
To swim and drown in, the pink clover mead
Keeps its sweet store for him, and he can pipe on oaten reed.

And yet I love him not; it was for thee
    I kept my love; I knew that thou would'st come
To rid me of this pallid chastity;
    Thou fairest flower of the flowerless foam
Of all the wide Aegean, brightest star
Of ocean's azure heavens where the mirrored planets are!

I knew that thou would'st come, for when at first
    The dry wood burgeoned, and the sap of Spring

Swelled in my green and tender bark or burst
  To myriad multitudinous blossoming
Which mocked the midnight with its mimic moons
That did not dread the dawn, and first the thrushes' rapturous tunes

Startled the squirrel from its granary,
  And cuckoo flowers fringed the narrow lane,
Through my young leaves a sensuous ecstasy
  Crept like new wine, and every mossy vein
Throbbed with the fitful pulse of amorous blood,
And the wild winds of passion shook my slim stem's maidenhood.

The trooping fawns at evening came and laid
  Their cool black noses on my lowest boughs,
And on my topmost branch the blackbird made
  A little nest of grasses for his spouse,
And now and then a twittering wren would light
On a thin twig which hardly bare the weight of such delight.

I was the Attic shepherd's trysting place,
  Beneath my shadow Amaryllis lay,
And round my trunk would laughing Daphnis chase
  The timorous girl, till tired out with play
She felt his hot breath stir her tangled hair,
And turned, and looked, and fled no more from such delightful snare.

Then come away into my ambuscade
  Where clustering woodbine weaves a canopy
For amorous pleasaunce, and the rustling shade
  Of Paphian myrtles seems to sanctify
The dearest rites of love, there in the cool;
And green recesses of its farthest depth there is a pool,

The ouzel's haunt, the wild bee's pasturage,
  For round its rim great creamy lilies float
Through their flat leaves in verdant anchorage,
  Each cup a white-sailed golden-laden boat
Steered by a dragon-fly, – be not afraid;
To leave this wan and wave-kissed shore, surely the place was made

For lovers such as we: the Cyprian Queen,
  One arm around her boyish paramour,
Strays often there at eve, and I have seen
  The moon strip off her misty vestiture
For young Endymion's eyes, be not afraid;
The panther feet of Dian never tread that secret glade.

Nay if thou will'st, back to the beating brine,
  Back to the boisterous billow let us go,

And walk all day beneath the hyaline
    Huge vault of Neptune's watery portico,
And watch the purple monsters of the deep
Sport in ungainly play, and from his lair keen Xiphias leap.

For if my mistress find me lying here
    She will not ruth or gentle pity show,
But lay her boar-spear down, and with austere
    Relentless fingers string the cornel bow,
And draw the feathered notch against her breast,
And loose the archèd cord, ay, even now upon the quest

I hear her hurrying feet, – awake, awake,
    Thou laggard in love's battle! once at least
Let me drink deep of passion's wine, and slake
    My parchèd being with the nectarous feast
Which even Gods affect! O come, Love, come,
Still we have time to reach the cavern of thine azure home.'

Scare had she spoken when the shuddering trees
    Shook, and the leaves divided, and the air
Grew conscious of a God, and the grey seas
    Crawled backward, and a long and dismal blare
Blew from some tasselled horn, a sleuth-hound bayed,
And like a flame a barbèd reed flew whizzing down the glade.

And where the little flowers of her breast
    Just brake into their milky blossoming,
This murderous paramour, this unbidden guest,
    Pierced and struck deep in horrid chambering,
And ploughed a bloody furrow with its dart,
And dug a long red road, and cleft with wingèd death her heart.

Sobbing her life out with a bitter cry
    On the boy's body fell the Dryad maid,
Sobbing for incomplete virginity,
    And raptures unenjoyed, and pleasures dead,
And all the pain of things unsatisfied,
And the bright drops of crimson youth crept down her throbbing side.

Ah! Pitiful it was to hear her moan,
    And very pitful to see her die
Ere she had yielded up her sweets, or known
    The joy of passion, that dread mystery
Which not to know is not to live at all,
And yet to know is to be held in death's most deadly thrall.

But as it hapt the Queen of Cythere,
    Who with Adonis all night long had lain

Within some shepherd's hut in Arcady,
  On team of silver doves and gilded wain
Was journeying Paphos-ward, high up afar
From mortal ken between the mountains and the morning star,

And when low down she spied the hapless pair,
  And heard the Oread's faint despairing cry,
Whose cadence seemed to play upon the air
  As though it were a viol, hastily
She bade her pigeons fold each straining plume,
And dropt to earth, and reached the strand, and saw their dolorous doom.

For as a gardener turning back his head
  To catch the last notes of the linnet, mows
With careless scythe too near some flower bed,
  And cuts the thorny pillar of the rose,
And with the flower's loosened loveliness
Strews the brown mould, or as some shepherd lad in wantonness;

Driving his little flock along the mead
  Treads down two daffodils, which side by side
Have lured the lady-bird with yellow brede
  And made the gaudy moth forget its pride,
Treads down their brimming golden chalices
Under light feet which were not made for such rude ravages;

Or as a schoolboy tired of his book
  Flings himself down upon the reedy grass
And plucks two water-lilies from the brook,
  And for a time forgets the hour glass,
Then wearies of their sweets, and goes his way,
And lets the hot sun kill them, even so these lovers lay.

And Venus cried, 'It is dread Artemis
  Whose bitter hand hath wrought this cruelty,
Or else that mightier maid whose care it is
  To guard her strong and stainless majesty
Upon the hill Athenian, – alas!
That they who loved so well unloved into Death's house should pass.'

So with soft hands she laid the boy and girl
  In the great golden waggon tenderly,
Her white throat whiter than a moony pearl
  Just threaded with a blue vein's tapestry
Had not yet ceased to throb, and still her breast
Swayed like a wind-stirred lily in ambiguous unrest.

And then each pigeon spread its milky van,
  The bright car soared into the dawning sky,

And like a cloud the aerial caravan
   Passed over the Aegean silently,
Till the faint air was troubled with the song
From the wan mouths that call on bleeding Thammuz all night long.

But when the doves had reached their wonted goal
   Where the wide stair of orbèd marble dips
Its snows into the sea, her fluttering soul
   Just shook the trembling petals of her lips
And passed into the void, and Venus knew
That one fair maid the less would walk amid her retinue,

And bade her servants carve a cedar chest
   With all the wonder of this history,
Within whose scented womb their limbs should rest
   Where olive-trees make tender the blue sky
On the low hills of Paphos, and the Faun
Pipes in the noonday, and the nightingale sings on till dawn.

Nor failed they to obey her hest, and ere
   The morning bee had stung the daffodil
With tiny fretful spear, or from its lair
   The waking stag had leapt across the rill
And roused the ouzel, or the lizard crept
Athwart the sunny rock, beneath the grass their bodies slept.

And when day brake, within that silver shrine
   Fed by the flames of cressets tremulous,
Queen Venus knelt and prayed to Proserpine
   That she whose beauty made Death amorous
Should beg a guerdon from her pallid Lord,
And let Desire pass across dread Charon's icy ford.

3

In melancholy moonless Acheron,
   Far from the goodly earth and joyous day,
Where no spring ever buds, nor ripening sun
   Weighs down the apple trees, nor flowery May
Chequers with chestnut blooms the grassy floor,
Where thrushes never sing, and piping linnets mate no more,

There by a dim and dark Lethaean well
   Young Charmides was lying; wearily
He plucked the blossoms from the asphodel,
   And with its little rifled treasury
Strewed the dull waters of the dusky stream,
And watched the white stars founder, and the land was like a dream,

When as he gazed into the watery glass
   And through his brown hair's curly tangles scanned
His own wan face, a shadow seemed to pass
   Across the mirror, and a little hand
Stole into his, and warm lips timidly
Brushed his pale cheeks, and breathed their secret forth into a sigh.

Then turned he round his weary eyes and saw,
   And ever nigher still their faces came,
And nigher ever did their young mouths draw
   Until they seemed one perfect rose of flame,
And longing arms around her neck he cast,
And felt her throbbing bosom, and his breath came hot and fast,

And all his hoarded sweets were hers to kiss,
   And all her maidenhood was his to slay,
And limb to limb in long and rapturous bliss
   Their passion waxed and waned, – O why essay
To pipe again of love, too venturous reed!
Enough, enough that Eros laughed upon that flowerless mead.

Too venturous poesy, O why essay
   To pipe again of passion! Fold thy wings
O'er daring Icarus and bid thy lay
   Sleep hidden in the lyre's silent strings
Till thou hast found the old Castalian rill,
Or from the Lesbian waters plucked drowned Sappho's golden quill!

Enough, enough that he whose life had been
   A fiery pulse of sin, a splendid shame,
Could in the loveless land of Hades glean
   One scorching harvest from those fields of flame
Where passion walks with naked unshod feet
And is not wounded – ah! Enough that once their lips could meet

In that wild throb when all existences
   Seemed narrowed to one single ecstasy
Which dies through its own sweetness and the stress
   Of too much pleasure, ere Persephone
Had bade them serve her by the ebon throne
Of the pale God who in the fields of Enna' loosed her zone.

BALLADE DE MARGUERITE

(*Normande*)

I am weary of lying within the chase
When the knights are meeting in market-place.

Nay, go not thou to the red-roofed town
Lest the hooves of the war-horse tread thee down.

But I would not go where the Squires ride,
I would only walk by my Lady's side.

Alack! And alack! thou art overbold,
A Forester's son may not eat off gold.

Will she love me the less that my Father is seen
Each Martinmas day in a doublet green?

Perchance she is sewing at tapestrie,
Spindle and loom are not meet for thee.

Ah, if she is working the arras bright
I might ravel the threads by the fire-light.

Perchance she is hunting of the deer,
How could you follow o'er hill and mere?

Ah, if she is riding with the court,
I might run beside her and wind the morte.

Perchance she is kneeling in St. Denys,
(On her soul may our Lady have gramercy!)

Ah, if she is praying in lone chapelle,
I might swing the censer and ring the bell.

Come in, my son, for you look sae pale,
Thy father shall fill thee a stoup of ale.

But who are these knights in bright array?
Is it a pageant the rich folks play?

'Tis the King of England from over sea,
Who has come unto visit our fair countrie.

But why does the curfew toll sae low?
And why do the mourners walk a-row?

O 'tis Hugh of Amiens my sister's son
Who is lying stark, for his day is done.

Nay, nay, for I see white lilies clear,
It is no strong man who lies on the bier.

O 'tis old Dame Jeannette that kept the hall,
I knew she would die at the autumn fall.

Dame Jeannette had not that gold-brown hair,
Old Jeannette was not a maiden fair.

O 'tis none of our kith and none of our kin,
(Her soul may our Lady assoil from sin!)

But I hear the boy's voice chaunting sweet,
'Elle est morte, la Marguerite.'

Come in, my son, and lie on the bed,
And let the dead folk bury their dead.

O mother, you know I loved her true:
O mother, hath one grave room for two?

LA BELLE GABRIELLE

(*From the French*)

Ah! could I charm the silver-breasted moon
    To lie with me upon the Latmian hill
Through the hot hours of the purple noon
    Till of strange joys my lips had drunk their fill.

Love could I change wan water into wine
    To make more glad some heavy-lidded bride
Whose soul is sick with passion to entwine
    The crimson-caftaned lover at her side.

Love could I make the lily-petals part
    And filch the treasures of its golden seed,
Or swoon for passion in the rose's heart
    Till its red leaves with redder pain did bleed.

Love could I see Narcissus lean to kiss
    His laughing double in the glassy stream,
Or hear the smitten lips of Salmacis
    Laugh low for pleasure of some unreal dream.

Ah what to me were silver-breasted moon,
    Or all the sweets young Narciss' could unfold,
Or wondering lovers, or rose-chaliced swoon,
    Or hair made golden with the lily's gold.

HUMANITAD

It is full winter now: the trees are bare,
    Save where the cattle huddle from the cold
Beneath the pine, for it doth never wear
    The Autumn's gaudy livery whose gold
Her jealous brother pilfers, but is true
To the green doublet; bitter is the wind, as though it blew

From Saturn's cave; a few thin wisps of hay
    Lie on the sharp black hedges, where the wain
Dragged the sweet pillage of a summer's day
    From the low meadows up the narrow lane;
Upon the half-thawed snow the bleating sheep
Press close against the hurdles, and the shivering house-dogs creep

From the shut stable to the frozen stream
    And back again disconsolate, and miss
The bawling shepherds and the noisy team ;
    And overhead in circling listlessness
The cawing rooks whirl round the frosted stack,
Or crowd the dripping boughs; and in the fen the icepools crack

Where the gaunt bittern stalks among the reeds
    And flaps his wings, and stretches back his neck,
And hoots to see the moon; across the meads
    Limps the poor frightened hare, a little speck;
And a stray seamew with its fretful cry
Flits like a sudden drift of snow against the dull grey sky.

Full winter: and the lusty goodman brings
    His load of faggots from the chilly byre,
And stamps his feet upon the hearth, and flings
    The sappy billets on the waning fire,
And laughs to see the sudden lightening scare
His children at their play; and yet, – the Spring is in the air,

Already the slim crocus stirs the snow,
    And soon yon blanchèd fields will bloom again
With nodding cowslips for some lad to mow,
    For with the first warm kisses of the rain
The winter's icy sorrow breaks to tears,
And the brown thrushes mate, and with bright eyes the rabbit peers

From the dark warren where the fir-cones lie,
    And treads one snowdrop under foot, and runs
Over the mossy knoll, and blackbirds fly
    Across our path at evening, and the suns
Stay longer with us; ah! how good to see
Grass-girdled Spring in all her joy of laughing greenery

Dance through the hedges till the early rose,
    (That sweet repentance of the thorny briar!)
Burst from its sheathèd emerald and disclose
    The little quivering disk of golden fire
Which the bees know so well, for with it come
Pale boy's-love, sops-in-wine, and daffodillies all in bloom.

Then up and down the field the sower goes,
    While close behind the laughing younker scares
With shrilly whoop the black and thievish crows,
    And then the chestnut-tree its glory wears,
And on the grass the creamy blossom falls
In odorous excess, and faint half-whispered madrigals

Steal from the bluebells' nodding carillons
    Each breezy morn, and then white jessamine,
That star of its own heaven, snap-dragons
    With lolling crimson tongues, and eglantine
In dusty velvets clad usurp the bed
And woodland empery, and when the lingering rose hath shed

Red leaf by leaf its folded panoply,
    And pansies closed their purple-lidded eyes,
Chrysanthemums from gilded argosy
    Unload their gaudy scentless merchandise,
And violets getting overbold withdraw
From their shy nooks, and scarlet berries dot the leafless haw.

O happy field! and O thrice happy tree!
    Soon will your Queen in daisy-flowered smock
And crown of flower-de-luce trip down the lea,
    Soon will the lazy shepherds drive their flock
Back to the pasture by the pool, and soon
Through the green leaves will float the hum of murmuring bees at noon.

Soon will the glade be bright with bellamour,
    The flower which wantons love, and those sweet nuns
Vale-lilies in their snowy vesture
    Will tell their beaded pearls, and carnations
With mitred dusky leaves will scent the wind,
And straggling traveller's-joy each hedge with yellow stars will bind.

Dear Bride of Nature and most bounteous Spring!
    That canst give increase to the sweet-breath'd kine,
And to the kid its little horns, and bring
    The soft and silky blossoms to the vine,
Where is that old nepenthe which of yore
Man got from poppy root and glossy-berried mandragore!

There was a time when any common bird
　　Could make me sing in unison, a time
When all the strings of boyish life were stirred
　　To quick response or more melodious rhyme
By every forest idyll; – do I change?
Or rather doth some evil thing through thy fair pleasaunce range?

Nay, nay, thou art the same: 'tis I who seek
　　To vex with sighs thy simple solitude,
And because fruitless tears bedew my cheek
　　Would have thee weep with me in brotherhood;
Fool! Shall each wronged and restless spirit dare
To taint such wine with the salt poison of his own despair!

Thou art the same: 'tis I whose wretched soul
　　Takes discontent to be its paramour,
And gives its kingdom to the rude control
　　Of what should be its servitor, – for sure
Wisdom is somewhere, though the stormy sea
Contain it not, and the huge deep answer ' 'Tis not in me.'

To burn with one clear flame, to stand erect
　　In natural honour, not to bend the knee
In profitless prostrations whose effect
　　Is by itself condemned, what alchemy
Can teach me this? what herb Medea brewed
Will bring the unexultant peace of essence not subdued.

The minor chord which ends the harmony,
　　And for its answering brother waits in vain
Sobbing for incompleted melody,
　　Dies a Swan's death; but I the heir of pain,
A silent Memnon with blank lidless eyes,
Wait for the light and music of those suns which never rise.

The quenched-out torch, the lonely cypress-gloom,
　　The little dust stored in the narrow urn,
The gentle XAIPE[1] of the Attic tomb, –
　　Were not these better far than to return
To my old fitful restless malady,
Or spend my days within the voiceless cave of misery?

---

[1] Farewell.

Nay! For perchance that poppy crownèd God
    Is like the watcher by a sick man's bed
Who talks of sleep but gives it not; his rod
    Hath lost its virtue, and, when all is said,
Death is too rude, too obvious a key
To solve one single secret in a life's philosophy.

And Love! That noble madness, whose august
    And inextinguishable might can slay
The soul with honeyed drugs, – alas! I must
    From such sweet ruin play the runaway,
Although too constant memory never can
Forget the archèd splendour of those brows Olympian

Which for a little season made my youth
    So soft a swoon of exquisite indolence
That all the chiding of more prudent Truth
    Seemed the thin voice of jealousy, – O Hence
Thou huntress deadlier than Artemis!
Go seek some other quarry! for of thy too perilous bliss

My lips have drunk enough, – no more, no more, –
    Though Love himself should turn his gilded prow
Back to the troubled waters of this shore
    Where I am wrecked and stranded, even now
The chariot wheels of passion sweep too near,
Hence! Hence! I pass unto a life more barren, more austere.

More barren – ay, those arms will never lean
    Down through the trellised vines and draw my soul
In sweet reluctance through the tangled green;
    Some other head must wear that aureole,
For I am Hers who loves not any man
Whose white and stainless bosom bears the sign Gorgonian.

Let Venus go and chuck her dainty page,
    And kiss his mouth, and toss his curly hair,
With net and spear and hunting equipage
    Let young Adonis to his tryst repair,
But me her fond and subtle-fashioned spell
Delights no more, though I could win her dearest citadel.

Ay, though I were that laughing shepherd boy
    Who from Mount Ida saw the little cloud
Pass over Tenedos and lofty Troy
    And knew the coming of the Queen, and bowed
In wonder at her feet, not for the sake
Of a new Helen would I bid her hand the apple take.

Then rise supreme Athena argent-limbed!
   And, if my lips be music-less, inspire
At least my life: was not thy glory hymned
   By One who gave to thee his sword and lyre
Like Aeschylos at well-fought Marathon,
And died to show that Milton's England still could bear a son!

And yet I cannot tread the Portico
   And live without desire, fear and pain,
Or nurture that wise calm which long ago
   The grave Athenian master taught to men,
Self-poised, self-centred, and self-comforted,
To watch the world's vain phantasies go by with unbowed head.

Alas! that serene brow, those eloquent lips,
   Those eyes that mirrored all eternity,
Rest in their own Colonos, an eclipse
   Hath come on Wisdom, and Mnemosyne
Is childless; in the night which she had made
For lofty secure flight Athena's owl itself hath strayed.

Nor much with Science do I care to climb,
   Although by strange and subtle witchery
She draw the moon from heaven; the Muse of Time
   Unrolls her gorgeous-coloured tapestry
To no less eager eyes; often indeed
In the great epic of Polymnia's scroll I love to read

How Asia sent her myriad hosts to war
   Against a little town, and panoplied
In gilded mail with jewelled scimitar,
   White-shielded, purple-crested, rode the Mede
Between the waving poplars and the sea
Which men call Artemisium, till he saw Thermopylae

Its steep ravine spanned by a narrow wall,
   And on the nearer side a little brood
Of careless lions holding festival!
   And stood amazèd at such hardihood,
And pitched his tent upon the reedy shore,
And stayed two days to wonder, and then crept at midnight o'er

Some unfrequented height, and coming down
   The autumn forests treacherously slew
What Sparta held most dear and was the crown
   Of far Eurotas, and passed on, nor knew
How God had staked an evil net for him
In the small bay at Salamis, – and yet, the page grows dim,

Its cadenced Greek delights me not, I feel
    With such a goodly time too out of tune
To love it much: for like the Dial's wheel
    That from its blinded darkness strikes the noon
Yet never sees the sun, so do my eyes
Restlessly follow that which from my cheated vision flies.

O for one grand unselfish simple life
    To teach us what is Wisdom! speak ye hills
Of lone Helvellyn, for this note of strife
    Shunned your untroubled crags and crystal rills,
Where is that Spirit which living blamelessly
Yet dared to kiss the smitten mouth of his own century!

Speak ye Rydalian laurels! Where is He
    Whose gentle head ye sheltered, that pure soul
Whose gracious days of uncrowned majesty
    Through lowliest conduct touched the lofty goal
Where Love and Duty mingle! him at least
The most high Laws were glad of, He had sat at Wisdom's feast,

But we are Learning's changelings, know by rote
    The clarion watchword of each Grecian school
And follow none, the flawless sword which smote
    The pagan Hydra is an effete tool
Which we ourselves have blunted, what man now
Shall scale the august ancient heights and to old Reverence bow?

One such indeed I saw, but, Ichabod!
    Gone is that last dear son of Italy,
Who being man died for the sake of God,
    And whose un-risen bones sleep peacefully,
O guard him, guard him well, my Giotto's tower,
Thou marble lily of the lily town! Let not the lour

Of the rude tempest vex his slumber, or
    The Arno with its tawny troubled gold
O'er-leap its marge, no mightier conqueror
    Clomb the high Capitol in the days of old
When Rome was indeed Rome, for Liberty
Walked like a Bride beside him, at which sight pale Mystery

Fled shrieking to her farthest sombrest cell
    With an old man who grabbled rusty keys,
Fled shuddering, for that immemorial knell
    With which oblivion buries dynasties
Swept like a wounded eagle on the blast,
As to the holy heart of Rome the great triumvir passed.

He knew the holiest heart and heights of Rome.,
   He drave the base wolf from the lion's lair,
And now lies dead by that empyreal dome
   Which overtops Valdarno hung in air
By Brunelleschi – O Melpomene
Breathe through thy melancholy pipe thy sweetest threnody!

Breathe through the tragic stops such melodies
   That Joy's self may grow jealous, and the Nine
Forget awhile their discreet emperies,
   Mourning for him who on Rome's lordliest shrine
Lit for men's lives the light of Marathon,
And bare to sun-forgotten fields the fire of the sun!

O guard him, guard him well, my Giotto's tower,
   Let some young Florentine each eventide
Bring coronals of that enchanted flower
   Which the dim woods of Vallombrosa hide,
And deck the marble tomb wherein he lies
Whose soul is as some mighty orb unseen of mortal eyes.

Some mighty orb whose cycled wanderings,
   Being tempest-driven to the farthest rim
Where Chaos meets Creation and the wings
   Of the eternal chanting Cherubim
Are pavilioned on Nothing, passed away
Into a moonless void, – and yet, though he is dust and clay,

He is not dead, the immemorial Fates
   Forbid it, and the closing shears refrain,
Lift up your heads ye everlasting gates!
   Ye argent clarions, sound a loftier strain!
For the vile thing he hated lurks within
Its sombre house, alone with God and memories of sin.

Still what avails it that she sought her cave
   That murderous mother of red harlotries?
At Munich on the marble architrave
   The Grecian boys die smiling, but the seas
Which wash Aegina fret in loneliness
Not mirroring their beauty, so our lives grow colourless

For lack of our ideals, if one star
   Flame torch-like in the heavens the unjust
Swift daylight kills it, and no trump of war
   Can wake to passionate voice the silent dust
Which was Mazzini once! Rich Niobe
For all her stony sorrows hath her sons, but Italy!

What Easter Day shall make her children rise,
  Who were not Gods yet suffered? what sure feet
Shall find their grave-clothes folded? what clear eyes
  Shall see them bodily? O it were meet
To roll the stone from off the sepulchre
And kiss the bleeding roses of their wounds, in love of Her

Our Italy! our mother visible!
  Most blessed among nations and most sad,
For whose dear sake the young Calabrian fell
  That day at Aspromonte and was glad
That in an age when God was bought and sold
One man could die for Liberty! but we, burnt out and cold,

See Honour smitten on the cheek and gyves
  Bind the sweet feet of Mercy: Poverty
Creeps through our sunless lanes and with sharp knives
  Cuts the warm throats of children stealthily,
And no word said: – O we are wretched men
Unworthy of our great inheritance! where is the pen

Of austere Milton? where the mighty sword
  Which slew its master righteously? the years
Have lost their ancient leader, and no word
  Breaks from the voiceless tripod on our ears:
While as a ruined mother in some spasm
Bears a base child and loathes it, so our best enthusiasm

Genders unlawful children, Anarchy
  Freedom's own Judas, the vile prodigal
Licence who steals the gold of Liberty
  And yet has nothing, Ignorance the real
One Fratricide since Cain, Envy the asp
That stings itself to anguish, Avarice whose palsied grasp

Is in its extent stiffened, moneyed Greed
  For whose dull appetite men waste away
Amid the whirr of wheels and are the seed
  Of things which slay their sower, these each day
Sees rife in England, and the gentle feet
Of Beauty tread no more the stones of each unlovely street.

What even Cromwell spared is desecrated
  By the weed and worm, left to the stormy play
Of wind and beating snow, or renovated
  By more destructful hands: Time's worst decay
Will wreathe its ruins with some loveliness,
But these new Vandals can but make a rainproof barrenness.

Where is that Art which bade the Angels sing
   Through Lincoln's lofty choir, till the air
Seems from such marble harmonies to ring
   With sweeter song than common lips can dare
To draw from actual reed? Ah! where is now
The cunning hand which made the flowering hawthorn branches bow

For Southwell's arch, and carved the House of One
   Who loved the lilies of the field with all
Our dearest English flowers? the same sun
   Rises for us: the seasons natural
Weave the same tapestry of green and grey:
The unchanged hills are with us: but that Spirit hath passed away.

And yet perchance it may be better so,
   For Tyranny is an incestuous Queen,
Murder her brother is her bedfellow,
   And the Plague chambers with her: in obscene
And bloody paths her treacherous feet are set;
Better the empty desert and a soul inviolate!

For gentle brotherhood, the harmony
   Of living in the healthful air, the swift
Clean beauty of strong limbs when men are free
   And women chaste, these are the things which lift
Our souls up more than even Agnolo's
Gaunt blinded Sibyl poring o'er the scroll of human woes,

Or Titian's little maiden on the stair
   White as her own sweet lily and as tall,
Or Mona Lisa smiling through her hair, –
   Ah! Somehow life is bigger after all
Than any painted Angel, could we see
The God that is within us! the old Greek serenity

Which curbs the passion of that level line
   Of marble youths, who with untroubled eyes
And chastened limbs ride round Athena's shrine
   And mirror her divine economies,
And balanced symmetry of what in man
Would else wage ceaseless warfare, – this at least within the span

Between our mother's kisses and the grave
   Might so inform our lives, that we could win
Such mighty empires that from her cave
   Temptation would grow hoarse, and pallid Sin
Would walk ashamed of his adulteries,
And Passion creep from out the House of Lust with startled eyes.

To make the Body and the Spirit one
   With all right things, till no thing live in vain
From morn to noon, but in sweet unison
   With every pulse of flesh and throb of brain
The soul in flawless essence high enthroned,
Against all outer vain attack invincibly bastioned,

Mark with serene impartiality
   The strife of things, and yet be comforted,
Knowing that by the chain causality
   All separate existences are wed
Into one supreme whole, whose utterance
Is joy, or holier praise! Ah! surely this were governance

Of Life in most august omnipresence,
   Through which the rational intellect would find
In passion its expression, and mere sense,
   Ignoble else, lend fire to the mind,
And being joined with it in harmony
More mystical than that which binds the stars planetary,

Strike form their several tones one octave chord
   Whose cadence being measureless would fly
Through all the circling spheres, then to its Lord
   Return refreshed with its new empery
And more exultant power, – this indeed
Could we but reach it were to find the last, the perfect creed

Ah! it was easy when the world was young
   To keep one's life free and inviolate,
From our sad lips another song is rung,
   By our hands our heads are desecrate,
Wanderers in drear exile, and dispossessed
Of what should be our own, we can but feed on wild unrest.

Somehow the grace, the bloom of things has flown,
   And of all men we are most wretched who
Must live each other's lives and not our own
   For very pity's sake and then undo
All that we lived for – it was otherwise
When soul and body seemed to blend in mystic symphonies.

But we have left those gentle haunts to pass
   With weary feet to the new Calvary,
Where we behold, as one who in a glass
   Sees his own face, self-slain Humanity,
And in the dumb reproach of that sad gaze
Learn what an awful phantom the red hand of man can raise.

O smitten mouth! O forehead crowned with thorn!
    O chalice of all common miseries!
Thou for our sakes that loved thee not hast borne
    An agony of endless centuries,
And we were vain and ignorant nor knew
That when we stabbed thy heart it was our own real hearts we slew.

Being ourselves the sowers and the seeds,
    The night that covers and the lights that fade,
The spear that pierces and the side that bleeds,
    The lips betraying and the life betrayed;
The deep hath calm: the moon hath rest: but we
Lords of the natural world are yet our own dread enemy.

Is this the end of all that primal force
    Which, in its changes being still the same,
From eyeless Chaos cleft its upward course,
    Through ravenous seas and whirling rocks and flame,
Till the suns met in heaven and began
Their cycles, and the morning stars sang, and the Word was Man!

Nay, nay, we are but crucified, and though
    The bloody sweat falls from our brows like rain,
Loosen the nails – we shall come down I know,
    Staunch the red wounds – we shall be whole again,
No need have we of hyssop-laden rod,
That which is purely human, that is Godlike, that is God.

ATHANASIA

To that gaunt House of Art which lacks for naught
    Of all the great things men have saved from Time,
The withered body of a girl was brought
    Dead ere the world's glad youth had touched its prime,
And seen by lonely Arabs lying hid
In the dim womb of some black pyramid.

But when they had unloosed the lined band
    Which swathed the Egyptian's body, – lo! was found
Closed in the wasted hollow of her hand
    A little seed, which sown in English ground
Did wondrous snow of starry blossoms bear
And spread rich odours through our spring-tide air.

With such strange arts this flower did allure
  That all forgotten was the asphodel,
And the brown bee, the lily's paramour,
  Forsook the cup where he was wont to dwell,
For not a thing of earth it seemed to be,
But stolen from some heavenly Arcady.

In vain the sad narcissus, wan and white
  At its own beauty, hung across the stream,
The purple dragon-fly had no delight
  With its gold dust to make his wings a-gleam,
Ah! no delight the jasmine-bloom to kiss,
  Or brush the rain-pearls from the eucharis.

For love of it the passionate nightingale
  Forgot the hills of Thrace, the cruel king,
And the pale dove no longer cared to sail
  Through the wet woods at time of blossoming,
But round this flower of Egypt sought to float,
With silvered wing and amethystine throat.

While the hot sun blazed in his tower of blue
  A cooling wind crept from the land of snows,
And the warm south with tender tears of dew
  Drenched its white leaves when Hesperos up-rose
Amid those sea-green meadows of the sky
On which the scarlet bars of sunset lie.

But when o'er wastes of lily-haunted field
  The tired birds had stayed their amorous tune,
And broad and glittering like an argent shield
  High in the sapphire heavens hung the moon,
Did no strange dream or evil memory make
Each tremulous petal of its blossoms shake?

Ah no! to this bright flower a thousand years
  Seemed but the lingering of a summer's day,
It never knew the tide of cankering fears
  Which turn a boy's gold hair to withered grey,
The dread desire of death it never knew,
Or how all folk that they were born must rue.

For we to death with pipe and dancing go,
  Now would we pass the ivory gate again,
As some sad river wearied of its flow
  Through the dull plains, the haunts of common men,
Leaps lover-like into the terrible sea!
And counts it gain to die so gloriously.

We mar our lordly strength in barren strife
　　With the world's legions led by clamorous care,
It never feels decay but gathers life
　　From the pure sunlight and the supreme air,
We live beneath Time's wasting sovereignty,
It is the child of all eternity.

THE NEW HELEN

Where hast thou been since round the walls of Troy
The sons of God fought in that great emprise?
Why dost thou walk our common earth again?
Hast thou forgotten that impassioned boy,
His purple galley and his Tyrian men
And treacherous Aphrodite's mocking eyes?
For surely it was thou, who, like a star
　　Hung in the silver silence of the night,
　　Didst lure the Old World's chivalry and might
Into the clamorous crimson waves of war!

Or didst thou rule the fire-laden moon?
In amorous Sidon was thy temple built
Over the light and laughter of the sea
　　Where, behind lattice scarlet-wrought and gilt,
　　Some brown-limbed girl did weave thee tapestry
All through the waste and wearied hours of noon;
Till her wan cheek with flame of passion burned,
　　And she rose up the sea-washed lips to kiss
Of some glad Cyprian sailor, safe returned
　　From Calpé and the cliffs of Herakles!

No! Thou art Helen, and none other one!
It was for thee that young Sarpedôn died,
And Memnôn's manhood was untimely spent;
It was for thee gold-crested Hector tried
With Thetis' child that evil race to run,
In the last year of thy beleaguerment;
Ay! Even now the glory of thy fame
　　Burns in those fields of trampled asphodel,
　　Where the high lords whom Ilion knew so well
Clash ghostly shields, and call upon thy name.

Where hast thou been? In that enchanted land
Whose slumbering vales forlorn Calypso knew,
Where never mower rose at break of day

But all unswathed the trammelling grasses grew,
And the sad shepherd saw the tall corn stand
Till summer's red had changed to withered grey?
Didst thou lie there by some Lethaean stream
  Deep brooding on thine ancient memory,
The crash of broken spears, the fiery gleam
  From shivered helm, the Grecian battle-cry?

Nay, thou wert hidden in that hollow hill
With one who is forgotten utterly,
That discrowned Queen men call the Erycine;
Hidden away that never mightst thou see
The face of Her, before whose mouldering shrine
To-day at Rome the silent nations kneel;
Who gat from Love no joyous gladdening,
But only Love's intolerable pain,
Only a sword to pierce her heart in twain,
Only the bitterness of child-bearing.

The lotus-leaves which heal the wounds of Death
Lie in thy hand; O, be thou kind to me,
While yet I know the summer of my days;
For hardly can my tremulous lips draw breath
To fill the silver trumpet with thy praise,
So bowed am I before thy mystery;
So bowed and broken on Love's terrible wheel,
  That I have lost all hope and heart to sing,
  Yet care I not what ruin time may bring
If in thy temple thou wilt let me kneel.

Alas, alas, thou wilt not tarry here,
But, like that bird, the servant of the sun,
Who flies before the north wind and the night,
So wilt thou fly our evil land and drear,
Back to the tower of thine old delight,
And the red lips of young Euphorion;
Nor shall I ever see thy face again,
  But in this poisonous garden – close must stay,
Crowning my brows with the thorn-crown of pain,
  Till all my loveless life shall pass away.

O Helen! Helen! Helen! yet a while,
Yet for a little while, O, tarry here,
Till the dawn cometh and the shadows flee!
For in the gladsome sunlight of thy smile
Of heaven or hell I have no thought or fear,
Seeing I know no other god but thee:
No other god save him, before whose feet

In nets of gold the tired planets move,
    The incarnate spirit of spiritual love
Who in thy body holds his joyous seat.

Thou wert not born as common women are!
But, girt with silver splendour of the foam,
Didst from the depths of sapphire seas arise!
And at thy coming some immortal star,
Bearded with flame, blazed in the Eastern skies,
And waked the shepherds on thine island-home.
Thou shalt not die: no asps of Egypt creep
    Close at thy heels to taint the delicate air;
    No sullen-blooming poppies stain thy hair,
Those scarlet heralds of eternal sleep.

Lily of love, pure and inviolate!
Tower of ivory! Red rose of fire!
Thou hast come down our darkness to illume:
For we, close-caught in the wide nets of Fate,
Wearied with waiting for the World's Desire,
Aimlessly wandered in the house of gloom,
Aimlessly sought some slumberous anodyne
    For wasted lives, for lingering wretchedness,
Till we beheld thy re-arisen shrine,
    And the white glory of thy loveliness.

PANTHEA

Nay, let us walk from fire unto fire,
    From passionate pain to deadlier delight, –
I am too young to live without desire,
    Too young art thou to waste this summer night
Asking those idle questions which of old
Man sought of seer and oracle, and no reply was told.

For, sweet, to feel is better than to know,
    And wisdom is a childless heritage,
One pulse of passion – youth's first fiery glow, –
    Are worth the hoarded proverbs of the sage:
Vex not thy soul with dead philosophy,
Have we not lips to kiss with, hearts to love and eyes to see!

Dost thou not hear the murmuring nightingale,
    Like water bubbling from a silver jar,
So soft she sings the envious moon is pale,
    That high in heaven she is hung so far

She cannot hear that love-enraptured tune, –
Mark how she wreathes each horn with mist, yon late and labouring moon.

White lilies, in whose cups the gold bees dream,
  The fallen snow of petals where the breeze
Scatters the chestnut blossom, or the gleam
  Of boyish limbs in water, – are not these
Enough for thee, dost thou desire more?
Alas! the Gods will give nought else from their eternal store.

For our high Gods have sick and wearied grown
  Of all our endless sins, our vain endeavour
For wasted days of youth to make atone
  By pain or prayer or priest, and never, never,
Hearken they now to either good or ill,
But send their rain upon the just and the unjust at will.

They sit at ease, our Gods they sit at ease,
  Strewing with leaves of rose their scented wine,
They sleep, they sleep, beneath the rocking trees
  Where asphodel and yellow lotus twine,
Mourning the old glad days before they knew
What evil things the heart of man could dream, and dreaming do.

And far beneath the brazen floor they see
  Like swarming flies the crowd of little men,
The bustle of small lives, then wearily
  Back to their lotus-haunts they turn again
Kissing each others' mouths, and mix more deep
The poppy-seeded draught which brings soft purple-lidded sleep.

There all day long the golden-vestured sun,
  Their torch-bearer, stands with his torch ablaze,
And, when the gaudy web of noon is spun
  By its twelve maidens, through the crimson haze
Fresh from Endymion's arms comes forth the moon,
And the immortal Gods in toils of mortal passions swoon.

There walks Queen Juno through some dewy mead,
  Her grand white feet flecked with the saffron dust
Of wind-stirred lilies, while young Ganymede
  Leaps in the hot and amber-foaming must,
His curls all tossed, as when the eagle bare
The frightened boy from Ida through the blue Ionian air.

There in the green heart of some garden close
  Queen Venus with the shepherd at her side,
Her warm soft body like the briar rose
  Which would be white yet blushes at its pride,

Laughs low for love, till jealous Salmacis
Peers through the myrtle-leaves and sighs for pain of lonely bliss.

There never does that dreary north-wind blow
　　Which leaves our English forests bleak and bare,
Nor ever falls the swift white-feathered snow,
　　Nor ever doth the red-toothed lightning dare
To wake them in the silver-fretted night
When we lie weeping for some sweet sad sin, some dead delight.

Alas! they know the far Lethaean spring,
　　The violet-hidden waters well they know,
Where one whose feet with tired wandering
　　Are faint and broken may take heart and go,
And from those dark depths cool and crystalline
Drink, and draw balm, and sleep for sleepless souls, and anodyne.

But we oppress our natures, God or Fate
　　Is our enemy, we starve and feed
On vain repentance – O we are born too late!
　　What balm for us in bruisèd poppy seed
Who crowd into one finite pulse of time
The joy of infinite love and the fierce pain of infinite crime.

O we are wearied of this sense of guilt,
　　Wearied of pleasure's paramour despair,
Wearied of every temple we have built,
　　Wearied of every right, unanswered prayer,
For man is weak; God sleeps: and heaven is high:
One fiery-coloured moment: one great love; and lo! we die.

Ah! but no ferry-man with labouring pole
　　Nears his black shallop to the flowerless strand,
No little coin of bronze can bring the soul
　　Over Death's river to the sunless land,
Victim and wine and vow are all in vain,
The tomb is sealed; the soldiers watch; the dead rise not again.

We are resolved into the supreme air,
　　We are made one with what we touch and see,
With our heart's blood each crimson sun is fair,
　　With our young lives each spring-impassioned tree
Flames into green, the wildest beasts that range
The moor our kinsmen are, all life is one, and all is change.

With beat of systole and of diastole
　　One grand great life throbs through earth's giant heart,
And mighty waves of single Being roll
　　From nerveless germ to man, for we are part

Of every rock and bird and beast and hill,
One with the things that prey on us, and one with what we kill.

From lower cells of waking life we pass
  To full perfection; thus the world grows old:
We who are godlike now were once a mass
  Of quivering purple flecked with bars of gold,
Unsentient or of joy or misery,
And tossed in terrible tangles of some wild and wind-swept sea.

This hot hard flame with which our bodies burn
  Will make some meadow blaze with daffodil,
Ay! and those argent breasts of thine will turn
  To water-lilies; the brown fields men till
Will be more fruitful for our love to-night,
Nothing is lost in nature, all things live in Death's despite.

The boy's first kiss, the hyacinth's first bell,
  The man's last passion, and the last red spear
That from the lily leaps, the asphodel
  Which will not let its blossoms blow for fear
Of too much beauty, and the timid shame
Of the young bridegroom at his lover's eyes, – these with the same

One sacrament are consecrate, the earth
  Not we alone hath passions hymeneal,
The yellow buttercups that shake for mirth
  At daybreak know a pleasure not less real
Than we do, when in some fresh-blossoming wood,
We draw the spring into our hearts, and feel that life is good.

So when men bury us beneath the yew
  Thy crimson-stainèd mouth a rose will be,
And thy soft eyes lush bluebells dimmed with dew,
  And when the white narcissus wantonly
Kisses the wind its playmate some faint joy
Will thrill our dust, and we will be again fond maid and boy.

And thus without life's conscious torturing pain
  In some sweet flower we will feel the sun,
And from the linnet's throat will sing again,
  And as two gorgeous-mailèd snakes will run
Over our graves, or as two tigers creep
Through the hot jungle where the yellow-eyed huge lions sleep

And give them battle! how my heart leaps up
  To think of that grand living after death
In beast and bird and flower, when this cup,
  Being filled too full of spirit, bursts for breath,

And with the pale leaves of some autumn day
The soul earth's earliest conqueror becomes earth's last great prey.

O think of it! we shall inform ourselves
   Into all sensuous life, the goat-foot Faun,
The Centaur, or the merry bright-eyed Elves
   That leave their dancing rings to spite the dawn
Upon the meadows, shall not be more near
Than you and I to nature's mysteries, for we shall hear

The thrush's heart beat, and the daisies grow,
   And the wan snowdrop sighing for the sun
On sunless days in winter, we shall know
   By whom the silver gossamer is spun,
Who paints the diapered fritillaries,
On what wide wings from shivering pine to pine the eagle flies.

Ay! had we never loved at all, who knows
   If yonder daffodil had lured the bee
Into its gilded womb, or any rose
   Had hung with crimson lamps its little tree!
Methinks no leaf would ever bud in spring,
But for lovers' lips that kiss, the poets' lips that sing.

Is the light vanished from our golden sun,
   Or is this daedal-fashioned earth less fair,
That we are nature's heritors, and one
   With every pulse of life that beats the air?
Rather new suns across the sky shall pass,
New splendour come unto the flower, new glory to the grass.

And we two lovers shall not sit afar,
   Critics of nature, but the joyous sea
Shall be our raiment, and the bearded star
   Shoot arrows at our pleasure! We shall be
Part of the mighty universal whole,
And through all aeons mix and mingle with the Kosmic Soul!

We shall be notes in that great Symphony
   Whose cadence circles through the rhythmic spheres,
And all the live World's throbbing heart shall be
   One with our heart; the stealthy creeping years
Have lost their terrors now, we shall not die,
The Universe itself shall be our Immortality.

PHÈDRE

To Sarah Bernhardt

How vain and dull this common world must seem
　　To such a One as thou, who should'st have talked
　　At Florence with Mirandola, or walked
Through the cool olives of the Academe:
Thou should'st have gathered reeds from a green stream
　　For Goat-foot Pan's shrill piping, and have played
　　With the white girls in that Phaeacian glade
Where grave Odysseus wakened from his dream.

Ah! Surely once some urn of Attic clay
　　Held thy wan dust, and thou hast come again
　　Back to this common world so dull and vain,
For thou wert weary of the sunless day,
　　The heavy fields of scentless asphodel,
　　The loveless lips with which men kiss in Hell.

QUEEN HENRIETTA MARIA

To Ellen Terry

In the lone tent, waiting for victory,
　　She stands with eyes marred by the mists of pain,
　　Like some wan lily overdrenched with rain:
The clamorous clang of arms, the ensanguined sky,
War's ruin, and the wreck of chivalry
　　To her proud soul no common fear can bring:
　　Bravely she tarrieth for her Lord the King,
Her soul a-flame with passionate ecstasy.
O Hair of Gold! O Crimson Lips! O Face
　　Made for the luring and the love of man!
　　With thee I do forget the toil and stress,
The loveless road that knows no resting place,
　　Time's straitened pulse, the soul's dread weariness,
　　My freedom, and my life republican!

LOUIS NAPOLEON

Eagle of Austerlitz! where were thy wings
　　When far away upon a barbarous strand,
　　In fight unequal, by an obscure hand,
Fell the last scion of thy brood of Kings!

Poor boy! thou shalt not flaunt thy cloak of red,
　　Or ride in state through Paris in the van
　　Of thy returning legions, but instead
Thy mother France, free and republican,

Shall on thy dead and crownless forehead place
　　The better laurels of a soldier's crown,
　　That not dishonoured should thy soul go down
To tell the mighty Sire of thy race

That France hath kissed the mouth of Liberty,
　　And found it sweeter than his honied bees,
　　And that the giant wave Democracy
Breaks on the shores where Kings lay couched at ease.

MADONNA MIA

A lily-girl, not made for this world's pain,
　　With brown, soft hair close braided by her ears,
　　And longing eyes half veiled by slumberous tears
Like bluest water seen through mists of rain:
Pale cheeks whereon no love hath left its stain,
　　Red underlip drawn in for fear of love,
　　And white throat, whiter than the silvered dove,
Through whose wan marble creeps one purple vein.
Yet, though my lips shall praise her without cease,
　　Even to kiss her feet I am not bold,
　　Being o'ershadowed by the wings of awe,
Like Dante, when he stood with Beatrice
　　Beneath the flaming Lion's breast, and saw
　　The seventh Crystal, and the Stair of Gold.

Roses and Rue

To L.L.[1]

Could we dig up this long-buried treasure,
    Were it worth the pleasure,
We never could learn love's song,
    We are parted too long.

Could the passionate past that is fled
    Call back its dead,
Could we live it all over again,
    Were it worth the pain!

I remember we used to meet
    By an ivied seat,
And you warbled each pretty word
    With the air of a bird;

And your voice had a quaver in it,
    Just like a linnet,
And shook, as the blackbird's throat
    With its last big note;

And your eyes, they were green and grey
    Like an April day,
But lit into amethyst
    When I stooped and kissed;

And your mouth, it would never smile
    For a long, long while,
Then it rippled all over with laughter
    Five minutes after.

You were always afraid of a shower,
    Just like a flower:
I remember you started and ran
    When the rain began.

I remember I never could catch you,
    For no one could match you,
You had wonderful, luminous, fleet
    Little wings to your feet.

I remember your hair – did I tie it?
    For it always ran riot –
Like a tangled sunbeam of gold:
    These things are old.

---

[1] Lillie Langtry.

I remember so well the room,
   And the lilac bloom
That beat at the dripping pane
   In the warm June rain;

And the colour of your gown,
   It was amber-brown,
And two yellow satin bows
   From your shoulders rose.

And the handkerchief of French lace
   Which you held to your face –
Had a small tear left a stain?
   Or was it the rain?

On your hand as it waved adieu
   There were veins of blue;
In your voice as it said good-bye
   Was a petulant cry,

'You have only wasted your life'
   (Ah, that was the knife!)
When I rushed through the garden gate
   It was all too late.

Could we live it over again,
   Were it worth the pain,
Could the passionate past that is fled
   Call back its dead!

Well, if my heart must break,
   Dear love, for your sake,
It will break in music, I know,
   Poets' hearts break so.

But strange that I was not told
   That the brain can hold
In a tiny ivory cell,
   God's heaven and hell.

PORTIA

To Ellen Terry

I marvel not Bassanio was so bold
    To peril all he had upon the lead,
    Or that proud Aragon bent low his head
Or that Morocco's fiery heart grew cold:
For in that gorgeous dress of beaten gold
    Which is more golden than the golden sun
    No woman Veronesé looked upon
Was half so fair as thou whom I behold.
Yet fairer when with wisdom as your shield
    The sober-suited lawyer's gown you donned,
And would not let the laws of Venice yield
    Antonio's heart to that accursèd Jew —
    O Portia! Take my heart: it is thy due:
I think I will not quarrel with the Bond.

APOLOGIA

Is it thy will that I should wax and wane,
    Barter my cloth of gold for hodden grey,
And at thy pleasure weave that web of pain
    Whose brightest threads are each a wasted day?

Is it thy will — Love that I love so well —
    That my Soul's House should be a tortured spot
Wherein, like evil paramours, must dwell
    The quenchless flame, the worm that dieth not?

Nay, if it be thy will I shall endure,
    And sell ambition at the common mart,
And let dull failure be my vesture,
    And sorrow dig its grave within my heart.

Perchance it may be better so — at least
    I have not made my heart a heart of stone,
Nor starved my boyhood of its goodly feast,
    Nor walked where Beauty is a thing unknown.

Many a man hath done so; sought to fence
    In straitened bonds the soul that should be free,
Trodden the dusty road of common sense,
    While all the forest sang of liberty,

Not marking how the spotted hawk in flight
   Passed on wide pinion through the lofty air,
To where some steep untrodden mountain height
   Caught the last tresses of the Sun God's hair.

Or how the little flower be trod upon,
   The daisy, that white-feathered shield of gold,
Followed with wistful eyes the wandering sun
   Content if once its leaves were aureoled.

But surely it is something to have been
   The best belovèd for a little while,
To have walked hand in hand with Love, and seen
   His purple wings flit once across thy smile.

Ay! though the gorgèd asp of passion feed
   On my boy's heart, yet have I burst the bars,
Stood face to face with Beauty, known indeed
   The Love which moves the Sun and all the stars!

QUIA MULTUM AMAVI[1]

Dear Heart, I think the young impassioned priest
   When first he takes from out the hidden shrine
His God imprisoned in the Eucharist,
   And eats the bread, and drinks the dreadful wine,

Feels not such awful wonder as I felt
   When first my smitten eyes beat full on thee,
And all night long before thy feet I knelt
   Till thou wert wearied of Idolatry.

Ah! Hadst thou liked me less and loved me more,
   Through all those summer days of joy and rain,
I had not now been sorrow's heritor,
   Or stood a lackey in the House of Pain.

Yet, though remorse, youth's white-faced seneschal,
   Tread on my heels with all his retinue,
I am most glad I loved thee – think of all
   The suns that go to make one speedwell blue!

---

[1] Because I have loved much.

Silentium Amoris[1]

As often-times the too resplendent sun
  Hurries the pallid and reluctant moon
Back to her sombre cave, ere she hath won
  A single ballad from the nightingale,
  So doth thy Beauty make my lips to fail,
And all my sweetest singing out of tune.

And as at dawn across the level mead
  On wings impetuous some wind will come,
And with its too harsh kisses break the reed
  Which was its only instrument of song,
  So me too stormy passions work my wrong,
And for excess of Love my Love is dumb.

But surely unto Thee mine eyes did show
  Why I am silent, and my lute unstrung;
Else it were better we should part, and go,
  Thou to some lips of sweeter melody,
  And I to nurse the barren memory
Of unkissed kisses, and songs never sung.

Her Voice

The wild bee reels from bough to bough
  With his furry coat and his gauzy wing,
Now in a lily-cup, and now
    Setting a jacinth bell a-swing,
        In his wandering;
  Sit closer love: it was here I trow
      I made that vow,

Swore that two lives should be like one
  As long as the sea-gull loved the sea,
As long as the sunflower sought the sun, –
    It shall be, I said, for eternity
        'Twixt you and me!
  Dear friend, those times are over and done;
      Love's web is spun.

Look upward where the poplar trees
  Sway and sway in the summer air,
Here in the valley never a breeze

---

[1] The silence of love.

Scatters the thistledown, but there
                Great winds blow fair
From the mighty murmuring mystical seas,
                And the wave–lashed leas.

Look upward where the white gull screams,
        What does it see that we do not see?
Is that a star? or the lamp that gleams
        On some outward voyaging argosy,
                Ah! can it be
We have lived our lives in a land of dreams!
                How sad it seems.

Sweet, there is nothing left to say
        But this, that love is never lost,
Keen winter stabs the breasts of May
        Whose crimson roses burst his frost,
                Ships tempest-tossed
Will find a harbour in some bay,
                And so we may.

And there is nothing left to do
        But to kiss once again, and part,
Nay, there is nothing we should rue,
        I have my beauty, – you your Art,
                Nay, do not start,
One world was not enough for two
                Like me and you.

MY VOICE

Within this restless, hurried, modern world
        We took our hearts' full pleasure – You and I,
And now the white sails of our ship are furled,
        And spent the lading of our argosy.

Wherefore my cheeks before their time are wan,
        For very weeping is my gladness fled,
Sorrow has paled my young mouth's vermilion,
        And Ruin draws the curtains of my bed.

But all this crowded life has been to thee
        No more than lyre, or lute, or subtle spell
Of viols, or the music of the sea
        That sleeps, a mimic echo, in the shell.

ΓΛΥΚΥΠΙΚΡΟΣ ΕΡΩΣ[1]

Sweet, I blame you not, for mine the fault was, had
    I not been made of common clay
I had climbed the higher heights unclimbed yet,
    seen the fuller air, the larger day.

From the wildness of my wasted passion I had
    struck a better, clearer song,
Lit some lighter light of freer freedom, battled
    with some Hydra-headed wrong.

Had my lips been smitten into music by the kisses
    that but made them bleed,
You had walked with Bice and the angels on that
    verdant and enamelled mead.

I had trod the road which Dante treading saw the
    suns of seven circles shine,
Ay! perchance had seen the heavens opening, as
    they opened to the Florentine.

And the mighty nations would have crowned me,
    who am crownless now and without name,
And some orient dawn had found me kneeling on
    the threshold of the House of Fame.

I had sat within that marble circle where the
    oldest bard is as the young,
And the pipe is ever dropping honey, and the lyre's
    strings are ever strung.

Keats had lifted up his hymeneal curls from out
    the poppy-seeded wine,
With ambrosial mouth had kissed my forehead,
    clasped the hand of noble love in mine.

And at springtide, when the apple-blossoms brush
    the burnished bosom of the dove,
Two young lovers lying in an orchard would have
    read the story of our love.

Would have read the legend of my passion, known
    the bitter secret of my heart,
Kissed as we have kissed, but never parted as we
    two are fated now to part.

---

[1] Bittersweet love.

For the crimson flower of our life is eaten by the
   cankerworm of truth
And no hand can gather up the fallen withered
   petals of the rose of youth.

Yet I am not sorry that I loved you – ah! what
   else had I a boy to do, –
For the hungry teeth of time devour, and the
   silent-footed years pursue.

Rudderless, we drift athwart a tempest, and when
   once the storm of youth is past,
Without lyre, without lute or chorus, Death the
   silent pilot comes at last.

And within the grave there is no pleasure, for the
   blindworm battens on the root,
And Desire shudders into ashes, and the tree of
   Passion bears no fruit.

Ah! what else had I to do but love you, God's
   own mother was less dear to me,
And less dear the Cytheraean rising like an argent
   lily from the sea.

I have made my choice, have lived my poems, and
   though youth is gone in wasted days,
I have found the lover's crown of myrtle better
   that the poet's crown of bays.

THE GARDEN OF EROS

It is full summer now, the heart of June;
   Not yet the sunburnt reapers are astir
Upon the upland meadow where too soon
   Rich autumn time, the season's usurer,
Will lend his hoarded gold to all the trees,
And see his treasure scattered by the wild and spendthrift breeze.

Too soon indeed! yet here the daffodil,
   That love-child of the Spring, has lingered on
To vex the rose with jealousy, and still
   The harebell spreads her azure pavilion,
And like a strayed and wandering reveller
Abandoned of its brothers, whom long since June's messenger

The missel-thrush has frighted from the glade,
  One pale narcissus loiters fearfully
Close to a shadowy nook, where half afraid
  Of their own loveliness some violets lie
That will not look the gold sun in the face
For fear of too much splendour, – ah! methinks it is a place

Which should be trodden by Persephone
  When wearied of the flowerless fields of Dis!
Or danced on by the lads of Arcady!
  The hidden secret of eternal bliss
Known to the Grecian here a man might find,
Ah! you and I may find it now if Love and Sleep be kind.

There are the flowers which mourning Herakles
  Strewed on the tomb of Hylas, columbine,
Its white doves all a-flutter where the breeze
  Kissed them too harshly, the small celandine,
That yellow-kirtled chorister of eve,
And lilac lady's-smock, – but let them bloom alone, and leave

Yon spirèd hollyhock red-crocketed
  To sway its silent chimes, else must the bee,
Its little bellringer, go seek instead
  Some other pleasaunce; the anemone
That weeps at daybreak, like a silly girl
Before her love, and hardly lets the butterflies unfurl

Their painted wings beside it, – bid it pine
  In pale virginity; the winter snow
Will suit it better than those lips of thine
  Whose fires would but scorch it, rather go
And pluck that amorous flower which blooms alone,
Fed by the pander wind with dust of kisses not its own.

The trumpet-mouths of red convolvulus
  So dear to maidens, creamy meadow-sweet,
Whiter than Juno's throat and odorous
  As all Arabia, hyacinths the feet
Of Huntress Dian would be loth to mar
For any dappled fawn, – pluck these, and those fond flowers which are

Fairer than what Queen Venus trod upon
  Beneath the pines of Ida, eucharis,
That morning star which does not dread the sun,
  And budding marjoram which but to kiss
Would sweeten Cytheraea's lips and make
Adonis jealous, – these for thy head, – and for thy girdle take

Yon curving spray of purple clematis
   Whose gorgeous dye outflames the Tyrian King,
And foxgloves with their nodding chalices,
   But that one narciss which the startled Spring
Let from her kirtle fall when first she heard
In her own woods the wild tempestuous song of summer's bird,

Ah! Leave it for a subtle memory
   Of those sweet tremulous days of rain and sun,
When April laughed between her tears to see
   The early primrose with shy footsteps run
From the gnarled oak-tree roots till all the wold,
Spite of its brown and trampled leaves, grew bright with shimmering gold.

Nay, pluck it too, it is not half so sweet
   As thou thyself, my soul's idolatry!
And when thou art a-wearied at thy feet
   Shall oxlips weave their brightest tapestry,
For thee the woodbine shall forget its pride
And veil its tangled whorls, and thou shalt walk on daisies pied.

And I will cut a reed by yonder spring
   And make the wood-gods jealous, and old Pan
Wonder what young intruder dares to sing
   In these still haunts, where never foot of man
Should tread at evening, lest he chance to spy
The marble limbs of Artemis and all her company.

And I will tell thee why the jacinth wears
   Such dread embroidery of dolorous moan,
And why the hapless nightingale forbears
   To sing her song at noon, but weeps alone
When the fleet swallow sleeps, and rich men feast,
And why the laurel trembles when she sees the lightening east.

And I will sing how sad Proserpina
   Unto a grave and gloomy Lord was wed,
And lure the silver-breasted Helena
   Back from the lotus meadows of the dead,
So shalt thou see that awful loveliness
For which two mighty Hosts met fearfully in war's abyss!

And then I'll pipe to thee that Grecian tale
   How Cynthia loves the lad Endymion,
And hidden in a grey and misty veil
   Hies to the cliffs of Latmos once the Sun
Leaps from his ocean bed in fruitless chase
Of those pale flying feet which fade away in his embrace.

And if my flute can breathe sweet melody,
　　We may behold Her face who long ago
Dwelt among men by the Aegean sea,
　　And whose sad house with pillaged portico
And friezeless wall and columns toppled down
Looms o'er the ruins of that fair and violet-cinctured town.

Spirit of Beauty! tarry still awhile,
　　They are not dead, thine ancient votaries;
Some few there are to whom thy radiant smile
　　Is better than a thousand victories,
Though all the nobly slain of Waterloo
Rise up in wrath against them! Tarry still, there are a few

Who for thy sake would give their manlihood
　　And consecrate their being; I at least
Have done so, made thy lips my daily food,
　　And in thy temples found a goodlier feast
Than this starved age can give me, spite of all
Its new-found creeds so sceptical and so dogmatical.

Here not Cephissos, not Ilissos flows,
　　The woods of white Colonos are not here,
On our bleak hills the olive never blows,
　　No simple priest conducts his lowing steer
Up the steep marble way, nor through the town
Do laughing maidens bear to thee the crocus-flowered gown.

Yet tarry! for the boy who loved thee best,
　　Whose very name should be a memory
To make thee linger, sleeps in silent rest
　　Beneath the Roman walls, and melody,
Still mourns her sweetest lyre; none can play
The lute of Adonais: with his lips Song passed away.

Nay, when Keats died the Muses still had left
　　One silver voice to sing his threnody,
But ah! too soon of it we were bereft
　　When on that riven night and stormy sea
Panthea claimed her singer as her own,
And slew the mouth that praised her; since which time we walk alone,

Save for that fiery heart, that morning star
　　Of re-arisen England, whose clear eye
Saw from our tottering throne and waste of war
　　The grand Greek limbs of young Democracy
Rise mightily like Hesperus and bring
The great Republic! him at least thy love hath taught to sing,

And he hath been with thee at Thessaly,
   And seen white Atalanta fleet of foot
In passionless and fierce virginity
   Hunting the tuskèd boar, his honied lute
Hath pierced the cavern of the hollow hill,
And Venus laughs to know one knee will bow before her still.

And he hath kissed the lips of Proserpine,
   And sung the Galilean's requiem,
That wounded forehead dashed with blood and wine
   He hath discrowned, the Ancient Gods in him
Have found their last, most ardent worshipper,
And the new Sign grows grey and dim before its conqueror.

Spirit of Beauty! tarry with us still,
   It is not quenched the torch of poesy,
The star that shook above the Eastern hill
   Holds unassailed its argent armoury
From all the gathering gloom and fretful fight –
O tarry with us still! for through the long and common night,

Morris, our sweet and simple Chaucer's child,
   Dear heritor of Spenser's tuneful reed,
With soft and sylvan pipe has oft beguiled
   The weary soul of man in troublous need,
And from the far and flowerless fields of ice
Has brought fair flowers to make an earthly paradise.

We know them all, Gudrun the strong men's bride,
   Aslaug and Olafson we know them all,
How giant Grettir fought and Sigurd died,
   And what enchantment held the king in thrall
When lonely Brynhild wrestled with the powers
That war against all passion, ah! how oft through summer hours,

Long listless summer hours when the noon
   Being enamoured of a damask rose
Forgets to journey westward, till the moon
   The pale usurper of its tribute grows
From a thin sickle to a silver shield
And chides its loitering car – how oft, in some cool grassy field

Far from the cricket-ground and noisy eight,
   At Bagley, where the rustling bluebells come
Almost before the blackbird finds a mate
   And overstay the swallow, and the hum
Of many murmuring bees flits through the leaves,
Have I lain poring on the dreamy tales his fancy weaves,

And through their unreal woes and mimic pain
   Wept for myself, and so was purified,
And in their simple mirth grew glad again;
   For as I sailed upon that pictured tide
The strength and splendour of the storm was mine
Without the storm's red ruin, for the singer is divine;

The little laugh of water falling down
   Is not so musical, the clammy gold
Close hoarded in the tiny waxen town
   Has less of sweetness in it, and the old
Half-withered reeds that waved in Arcady
Touched by his lips break forth again to fresher harmony.

Spirit of Beauty, tarry yet awhile!
   Although the cheating merchants of the mart
With iron roads profane our lovely isle,
   And break on whirling wheels the limbs of Art,
Ay! though the crowded factories beget
The blindworm Ignorance that slays the soul, O tarry yet!

For One at least there is, – He bears his name
   From Dante and the seraph Gabriel, –
Whose double laurels burn with deathless flame
   To light thine altar; He too loves thee well,
Who saw old Merlin lured in Vivien's snare,
And the white feet of angels coming down the golden stair,

Loves thee so well, that all the World for him
   A gorgeous-coloured vestiture must wear,
And Sorrow take a purple diadem,
   Or else be no more Sorrow, and Despair
Gild its own thorns, and Pain, like Adon, be
Even in anguish beautiful; – such is the empery

Which Painters hold, and such the heritage
   This gentle solemn Spirit doth possess,
Being a better mirror of his age
   In all his pity, love, and weariness,
Than those who can but copy common things,
And leave the Soul unpainted with its mighty questionings.

But they are few, and all romance has flown,
   And men can prophesy about the sun,
And lecture on his arrows – how, alone,
   Through a waste void the soulless atoms run,
How from each tree its weeping nymph has fled,
And that no more 'mid English reeds a Naiad shows her head.

Methinks these new Actaeons boast too soon
   That they have spied on beauty; what if we
Have analysed the rainbow, robbed the moon
   Of her most ancient, chastest mystery,
Shall I, the last Endymion, lose all hope
Because rude eyes peer at my mistress through a telescope!

What profit if this scientific age
   Burst through our gates with all its retinue
Of modern miracles! Can it assuage
   One lover's breaking heart? What can it do
To make one life more beautiful, one day
More godlike in its period? But now the age of Clay

Returns in horrid cycle, and the earth
   Hath borne again a noisy progeny
Of ignorant Titans, whose ungodly birth
   Hurls them against the august hierarchy
Which sat upon Olympus, to the Dust
They have appealed, and to that barren arbiter they must

Repair for judgment; let them, if they can,
   From Natural Warfare and insensate Chance,
Create the new Ideal rule for man!
   Methinks that was not my inheritance;
For I was nurtured otherwise, my soul
Passes from higher heights of life to a more supreme goal.

Lo! while we spake the earth did turn away
   Her visage from the God, and Hecate's boat
Rose silver-laden, till the jealous day
   Blew all its torches out: I did not note
The waning hours, to young Endymions
Time's palsied fingers count in vain his rosary of suns!

Mark how the yellow iris wearily
   Leans back its throat, as though it would be kissed
By its false chamberer, the dragon-fly,
   Who, like a blue vein on a girl's white wrist,
Sleeps on that snowy primrose of the night,
Which 'gins to flush with crimson shame, and die beneath the light.

Come let us go, against the pallid shield
   Of the wan sky the almond blossoms gleam,
The corncrake nested in the unmown field
   Answers its mate, across the misty stream
On fitful wing the startled curlews fly,
And in his sedgy bed the lark, for joy that Day is nigh,

Scatters the pearlèd dew from off the grass,
    In tremulous ecstasy to greet the sun,
Who soon in gilded panoply will pass
    Forth from yon orange-curtained pavilion
Hung in the burning east: see, the red rim
O'ertops the expectant hills! It is the God! for love of him

Already the shrill lark is out of sight,
    Flooding with waves of song this silent dell, –
Ah! There is something more in that bird's flight
    Than could be tested in a crucible!
But the air freshens, let us go, why soon
The woodmen will be here; how we have lived this night of June!

AVE IMPERATRIX

Set in this stormy Northern sea,
    Queen of these restless fields of tide,
England! What shall men say of thee,
    Before whose feet the worlds divide?

The earth, a brittle globe of glass,
    Lies in the hollow of thy hand,
And through its heart of crystal pass,
    Like shadows through a twilight land,

The spears of crimson-suited war,
    The long white-crested waves of fight,
And all the deadly fires which are
    The torches of the lords of Night.

The yellow leopards, strained and lean,
    The treacherous Russian knows so well,
With gaping blackened jaws are seen
    Leap through the hail of screaming shell.

The strong sea-lion of England's wars
    Hath left his sapphire cave of sea,
To battle with the storm that mars
    The star of England's chivalry.

The brazen-throated clarion blows
    Across the Pathan's reedy fen,
And the high steeps of Indian snows
    Shake to the tread of armèd men.

And many an Afghan chief, who lies
    Beneath his cool pomegranate-trees,
Clutches his sword in fierce surmise
    When on the mountain-side he sees

The fleet-foot Marri scout, who comes
    To tell how he hath heard afar
The measured roll of English drums
    Beat at the gates of Kandahar.

For southern wind and east wind meet
    Where, girt and crowned by sword and fire,
England with bare and bloody feet
    Climbs the steep road of wide empire.

O lonely Himalayan height,
    Grey pillar of the Indian sky,
Where saw'st thou last in clanging flight
    Our wingèd dogs of Victory?

The almond-groves of Samarcand,
    Bokhara, where red lilies blow,
And Oxus, by whose yellow sand
    The grave white-turbaned merchants go:

And on from thence to Ispahan,
    The gilded garden of the sun,
Whence the long dusty caravan
    Brings cedar wood and vermilion;

And that dread city of Cabool
    Set at the mountain's scarpèd feet,
Whose marble tanks are ever full
    With water for the noonday heat:

Where through the narrow straight Bazaar
    A little maid Circassian
Is led, a present from the Czar
    Unto some old and bearded khan, –

Here have our wild war-eagles flown,
    And flapped wide wings in fiery fight;
But the sad dove, that sits alone
    In England – she hath no delight.

In vain the laughing girl will lean
    To greet her love with love-lit eyes:
Down in some treacherous black ravine,
    Clutching his flag, the dead boy lies.

And many a moon and sun will see
    The lingering wistful children wait
To climb upon their father's knee;
    And in each house made desolate

Pale women who have lost their lord
    Will kiss the relics of the slain –
Some tarnished epaulette – some sword –
    Poor toys to soothe such anguished pain.

For not in quiet English fields
    Are these, our brothers, lain to rest,
Where we might deck their broken shields
    With all the flowers the dead love best.

For some are by the Delhi walls,
    And many in the Afghan land,
And many where the Ganges falls
    Through seven mouths of shifting sand.

And some in Russian waters lie,
    And others in the seas which are
The portals to the East, or by
    The wind-swept heights of Trafalgar.

O wandering graves! O restless sleep!
    O silence of the sunless day!
O still ravine! O stormy deep!
    Give up your prey! Give up your prey!

And thou whose wounds are never healed,
    Whose weary race is never won,
O Cromwell's England! must thou yield
    For every inch of ground a son?

Go! Crown with thorns thy gold-crowned head,
    Change thy glad song to song of pain;
Wind and wild wave have got thy dead,
    And will not yield them back again.

Wave and wild wind and foreign shore
    Possess the flower of English land –
Lips that thy lips shall kiss no more,
    Hands that shall never clasp thy hand.

What profit now that we have bound
    The whole round world with nets of gold,
If hidden in our heart is found
    The care that groweth never old?

What profit that our galleys ride,
   Pine-forest-like, on every main?
Ruin and wreck are at our side,
   Grim warders of the House of Pain.

Where are the brave, the strong, the fleet?
   Where is our English chivalry?
Wild grasses are their burial-sheet,
   And sobbing waves their threnody.

O loved ones lying far away,
   What word of love can dead lips send!
O wasted dust! O senseless clay!
   Is this the end! is this the end!

Peace, peace! we wrong the noble dead
   To vex their solemn slumber so;
Though childless, and with thorn-crowned head,
   Up the steep road must England go.

Yet when this fiery web is spun,
   Her watchmen shall descry from far
The young Republic like a sun
   Rise from these crimson seas of war.

PAN

Double Villanelle

1

O goat-foot God of Arcady!
This modern world is grey and old,
And what remains to us of thee?

No more the shepherd lads in glee
Throw apples at thy wattled fold,
O goat-foot God of Arcady!

Nor through the laurels can one see
Thy soft brown limbs, thy beard of gold,
And what remains to us of thee?

And dull and dead our Thames would be,
For here the winds are chill and cold,
O goat-foot God of Arcady!

Then keep the tomb of Helice,
Thine olive-woods, thy vine-clad wold,
And what remains to us of thee?

Though many an unsung elegy
Sleeps in the reeds our rivers hold,
O goat-foot God of Arcady!
Ah, what remains to us of thee?

2

Ah, leave the hills of Arcady,
Thy satyrs and their wanton play,
This modern world hath need of thee.

No nymph or Faun indeed have we,
For Faun and nymph are old and grey,
Ah, leave the hills of Arcady!

This is the land where liberty
Lit grave-browed Milton on his way,
This modern world hath need of thee!

A land of ancient chivalry
Where gentle Sidney saw the day,
Ah, leave the hills of Arcady.

This fierce sea-lion of the sea,
This England lacks some stronger lay,
This modern world hath need of thee!

Then blow some trumpet loud and free,
And give thine oaten pipe away,
Ah, leave the hills of Arcady!
This modern world hath need of thee!

THE ARTIST'S DREAM OR SEN ARTYSTY

From the Polish of Madame Helena Modjeska

I too have had my dreams: ay, known indeed
The crowded visions of a fiery youth
Which haunt me still.

                  Methought that once I lay
Within some garden close, what time the Spring
Breaks like a bird from Winter, and the sky
Is sapphire-vaulted. The pure air was soft,
And the deep grass I lay on soft as air.
The strange and secret life of the young trees
Swelled in the green and tender bark, or burst
To buds of sheathèd emerald; violets
Peered from their nooks of hiding, half afraid
Of their own loveliness; the vermeil rose
Opened its heart, and the bright star-flower
Shone like a star of morning. Butterflies,
In painted liveries of brown and gold,
Took the shy bluebells as their pavilions
And seats of pleasaunce; overhead a bird
Made snow of all the blossoms as it flew
To charm the woods with singing: the whole world
Seemed waking to delight!
                And yet – and yet –
My soul was filled with leaden heaviness:
I had no joy in Nature; what to me,
Ambition's slave, was crimson-stainèd rose
Or the gold-sceptred crocus? The bright bird
Sang out of tune for me, and the sweet flowers
Seemed but a pageant, and an unreal show
That mocked my heart; for, like the fabled snake
That stings itself to anguish, so I lay
Self-tortured, self-tormented.
                 The day crept
Unheeded on the dial, till the sun
Dropt, purple-sailed, into the gorgeous East,
When, from the fiery heart of that great orb,
Came One whose shape of beauty far outshone
The most bright vision of this common earth.
Girt was she in a robe more white than flame
Or furnace-heated brass; upon her head
She bare a laurel crown, and, like a star
That falls from the high heaven suddenly,
Passed to my side.

Then kneeling low, I cried
'O much-desired! O long-waited for!
Immortal Glory! Great world-conqueror!
Oh, let me not die crownless; once, at least,
Let thine imperial laurels bind my brows,
Ignoble else. Once let the clarion note
And trump of loud ambition sound my name
And for the rest I care not.'

Then to me,
In gentle voice, the angel made reply:
'Child, ignorant of the true happiness,
Nor knowing life's best wisdom, thou wert made
For light and love and laughter, not to waste
Thy youth in shooting arrows at the sun,
Or nurturing that ambition in thy soul
Whose deadly poison will infect thy heart,
Marring all joy and gladness! Tarry here
In the sweet confines of this garden-close
Whose level meads and glades delectable
Invite for pleasure; the wild bird that wakes
These silent dells with sudden melody,
Shall be thy playmate; and each flower that blows
Shall twine itself unbidden in thy hair –
Garland more meet for thee than the dread weight
Of Glory's laurel wreath.'

'Ah! fruitless gifts,'
I cried, unheeding of her prudent word,
'Are all such mortal flowers, whose brief lives
Are bounded by the dawn and setting sun.
The anger of the noon can wound the rose,
And the rain rob the crocus of its gold;
But thine immortal coronal of Fame,
Thy crown of deathless laurel, this alone
Age cannot harm, nor winter's icy tooth
Pierce to its hurt, nor common things profane.'
No answer made the angel, but her face
Dimmed with the mists of pity.

Then methought
That from mine eyes, wherein ambition's torch
Burned with its latest and most ardent flame,
Flashed forth two level beams of straitened light,
Beneath whose fulgent fires the laurel crown
Twisted and curled, as when the Sirian star
Withers the ripening corn, and one pale leaf
Fell on my brow; and I leapt up and felt
The mighty pulse of Fame, and heard far off

The sound of many nations praising me!

One fiery-coloured moment of great life!
And then – how barren was the nation's praise!
How vain the trump of Glory! Bitter thorns
Were in that laurel leaf, whose toothed barbs
Burned and bit deep till fire and red flame
Seemed to feed full upon my brain, and make
The garden a bare desert.
                                        With wild hands
I strove to tear it from my bleeding brow,
But all in vain; and with a dolorous cry
That paled the lingering stars before their time,
I waked at last, and saw the timorous dawn
Peer with grey face into my darkened room,
And would have deemed it a mere idle dream
But for this restless pain that gnaws my heart,
And the red wounds of thorns upon my brow.

LIBERTATIS SACRA FAMES[1]

Albeit nurtured in democracy,
    And liking best that state republican
    Where every man is Kinglike and no man
Is crowned above his fellows, yet I see,
Spite of this modern fret for Liberty,
    Better the rule of One, whom all obey,
    Than to let clamorous demagogues betray
Our freedom with the kiss of anarchy.
Wherefore I love them not whose hands profane
    Plant the red flag upon the piled-up street
    For no right cause, beneath whose ignorant reign
Arts, Culture, Reverence, Honour, all things fade,
    Save Treason and the dagger of her trade,
    And Murder with his silent bloody feet.

---

[1] Sacred hunger for liberty.

Sonnet To Liberty

Not that I love thy children, whose dull eyes
See nothing save their own unlovely woe,
Whose minds know nothing, nothing care to know,
But that the roar of thy Democracies,
Thy reigns of Terror, thy great Anarchies,
Mirror my wildest passions like the sea
And give my rage a brother ——! Liberty!
For this sake only do thy dissonant cries
Delight my discreet soul, else might all kings
By bloody knout or treacherous cannonades
Rob nations of their rights inviolate
And I remain unmoved – and yet, and yet,
These Christs that die upon the barricades,
God knows it I am with them, in some things.

Taedium Vitae[1]

To stab my youth with desperate knives, to wear
This paltry age's gaudy livery,
To let each base hand filch my treasury,
To mesh my soul within a woman's hair,
And to be mere Fortune's lackeyed groom, – I swear
I love it not! These things are less to me
Than the thin foam that frets upon the sea,
Less than the thistledown of summer air
Which hath no seed: better to stand aloof
Far from these slanderous fools who mock my life
Knowing me not, better the lowliest roof
Fit for the meanest hind to sojourn in,
Than to go back to that hoarse cave of strife
Where my white soul first kissed the mouth of sin.

---

[1] Weariness of life.

FABIEN DEI FRANCHI

To my friend Henry Irving

The silent room, the heavy creeping shade,
    The dead that travel fast, the opening door,
    The murdered brother rising through the floor,
The ghost's white fingers on thy shoulders laid,
And then the lonely duel in the glade,
    The broken swords, the stifled scream, the gore,
    Thy grand revengeful eyes when all is o'er, –
These things are well enough, – but thou wert made
    For more august creation! Frenzied Lear
    Should at thy bidding wander on the heath
    With the shrill fool to mock him, Romeo
For thee should lure his love, and desperate fear
Pluck Richard's recreant dagger from its sheath –
    Thou trumpet set for Shakespeare's lips to blow!

SERENADE

(For Music)

The western wind is blowing fair
    Across the dark Aegean sea,
And at the secret marble stair
    My Tyrian galley waits for thee.
Come down! the purple sail is spread,
    The watchman sleeps within the town,
O leave thy lily-flowered bed,
    O Lady mine come down, come down!

She will not come, I know her well,
    Of lover's vows she hath no care,
And little good a man can tell
    Of one so cruel and so fair.
True love is but a woman's toy,
    They never know the lover's pain,
And I who loved as loves a boy
    Must love in vain, must love in vain.

O noble pilot, tell me true,
    Is that the sheen of golden hair?
Or is it but the tangled dew
    That binds the passion-flowers there?

Good sailor come and tell me now
    Is that my Lady's lily hand?
Or is it but the gleaming prow,
    Or is it but the silver sand?

No! No! 'tis not the tangled dew,
    'Tis not the silver-fretted sand,
It is my own dear Lady true
    With golden hair and lily hand!
O noble pilot, steer for Troy,
    Good sailor, ply the labouring oar,
This is the Queen of life and joy
    Whom we must bear from Grecian shore!

The waning sky grows faint and blue,
    It wants an hour still of day,
Aboard! Aboard! my gallant crew,
    O lady mine, away! Away!
O noble pilot, steer for Troy,
    Good sailor, ply the labouring oar,
O loved as only loves a boy!
    O loved for ever evermore!

CAMMA

To Ellen Terry

As one who poring on a Grecian urn
    Scans the fair shapes some Attic hand hath made,
    God with slim goddess, goodly man with maid,
And for their beauty's sake is loth to turn
And face the obvious day, must I not yearn
    For many a secret moon of indolent bliss,
    When in the midmost shrine of Artemis
I see thee standing, antique-limbed, and stern?

And yet – methinks I'd rather see thee play
    That serpent of old Nile, whose witchery
    Made Emperors drunken, – come, great Egypt, shake
Our stage with all thy mimic pageants! Nay,
    I am grown sick of unreal passions, make
    The world thine Actium, me thine Antony!

IMPRESSION DU MATIN

The Thames nocturne of blue and gold
   Changed to a Harmony in grey:
   A barge with ochre-coloured hay
Dropt from the wharf: and chill and cold

The yellow fog came creeping down
   The bridges, till the houses' walls
   Seemed changed to shadows and St. Paul's
Loomed like a bubble o'er the town.

Then suddenly arose the clang
   Of waking life; the streets were stirred
   With country waggons: and a bird
Flew to the glistening roofs and sang.

But one pale woman all alone,
   The daylight kissing her wan hair,
   Loitered beneath the gas lamps' flare,
With lips of flame and heart of stone.

IN THE GOLD ROOM

A Harmony

Her ivory hands on the ivory keys
   Strayed in a fitful fantasy,
Like the silver gleam when the poplar trees
   Rustle their pale leaves listlessly,
   Or the drifting foam of a restless sea
When the waves show their teeth in the flying breeze.

Her gold hair fell on the wall of gold
   Like the delicate gossamer tangles spun
On the burnished disk of the marigold,
   Or the sunflower turning to meet the sun
   When the gloom of the dark blue night is done,
And the spear of the lily is aureoled.

And her sweet red lips on these lips of mine
   Burned like the ruby fire set
In the swinging lamp of a crimson shrine,
   Or the bleeding wounds of the pomegranate,
   Or the heart of the lotus drenched and wet
With the spilt-out blood of the rose-red wine.

IMPRESSIONS

1

Les Silhouettes

The sea is flecked with bars of grey,
The dull dead wind is out of tune,
And like a withered leaf the moon
Is blown across the stormy bay.

Etched clear upon the pallid sand
Lies the black boat: a sailor boy
Clambers aboard in careless joy
With laughing face and gleaming hand.

And overhead the curlews cry,
Where through the dusky upland grass
The young brown-throated reapers pass,
Like silhouettes against the sky.

2

La Fuite de la Lune

To outer senses there is peace,
A dreamy peace on either hand,
Deep silence in the shadowy land,
Deep silence where the shadows cease.

Save for a cry that echoes shrill
From some lone bird disconsolate;
A corncrake calling to its mate;
The answer from the misty hill.

And suddenly the moon withdraws
Her sickle from the lightening skies,
And to her sombre cavern flies,
Wrapped in a veil of yellow gauze.

IMPRESSION

Le Réveillon

The sky is laced with fitful red,
The circling mists and shadows flee,
The dawn is rising from the sea,
Like a white lady from her bed.

And jagged brazen arrows fall
Athwart the feathers of the night,
And a long wave of yellow light
Breaks silently on tower and hall,

And spreading wide across the wold,
Wakes into flight some fluttering bird,
And all the chestnut tops are stirred,
And all the branches streaked with gold.

HÉLAS!

To drift with every passion till my soul
Is a stringed lute on which all winds can play,
Is it for this that I have given away
Mine ancient wisdom, and austere control?
Methinks my life is a twice-written scroll
Scrawled over on some boyish holiday
With idle songs for pipe and virelay,
Which do but mar the secret of the whole.
Surely there was a time I might have trod
The sunlit heights, and from life's dissonance
Struck one clear chord to reach the ears of God:
Is that time dead? Lo! with a little rod
I did but touch the honey of romance —
And must I lose a soul's inheritance?

TO V. F.[1]

Through many loveless songless days
We have to seek the golden shrine,
But Venus taught you how to twine
Love's violets with Apollo's bays.

---

[1] 'Violet Fane', the pen–name of Mary Singleton.

To M. B. J.[1]

Green are the summer meadows,
    Blue is the summer sky,
And the swallows like flickering shadows
    Over the tall corn fly.

And the red rose flames on the thicket,
    And the red breast sings on the spray,
And the drowsy hum of the cricket
    Comes from the new mown hay.

And the morning dewdrops glisten,
    And the lark is on the wing,
Ah! how can you stop and listen
    To what I have to sing.

IMPRESSIONS

1

Le Jardin

The lily's withered chalice falls
    Around its rod of dusty gold,
    And from the beech-trees on the wold
The last wood-pigeon coos and calls.

The gaudy leonine sunflower
    Hangs black and barren on its stalk,
    And down the windy garden walk
The dead leaves scatter, – hour by hour.

Pale privet-petals white as milk
    Are blown into a snowy mass:
    The roses lie upon the grass
Like little shreds of crimson silk.

---

[1] Margaret Burne-Jones.

2

La Mer

A white mist drifts across the shrouds,
  A wild moon in this wintry sky
  Gleams like an angry lion's eye
Out of a mane of tawny clouds.

The muffled steersman at the wheel
  Is but a shadow in the gloom; –
  And in the throbbing engine-room
Leap the long rods of polished steel.

The shattered storm has left its trace
  Upon this huge and heaving dome,
  For the thin threads of yellow foam
Float on the waves like ravelled lace.

LE JARDIN DES TUILERIES

This winter air is keen and cold,
  And keen and cold this winter sun,
  But round my chair the children run
Like little things of dancing gold.

Sometimes about the painted kiosk
  The mimic soldiers strut and stride,
  Sometimes the blue-eyed brigands hide
In the bleak tangles of the bosk.

And sometimes, while the old nurse cons
  Her book, they steal across the square,
  And launch their paper navies where
Hugh Triton writhes in greenish bronze.

And now in mimic flight they flee,
  And now they rush, a boisterous band –
  And, tiny hand on tiny hand,
Climb up the black and leafless tree.

Ah! cruel tree! if I were you,
  And children climbed me, for their sake
  Though it be winter I would break
Into spring blossoms white and blue!

The Harlot's House

We caught the tread of dancing feet,
We loitered down the moonlit street,
And stopped beneath the harlot's house.

Inside, above the din and fray,
We heard the loud musicians play
The 'Treues Liebes Herz' of Strauss.

Like strange mechanical grotesques,
Making fantastic arabesques,
The shadows raced across the blind.

We watched the ghostly dancers spin
To sound of horn and violin,
Like black leaves wheeling in the wind.

Like wire-pulled automatons,
Slim silhouetted skeletons
Went sidling through the slow quadrille.

They took each other by the hand,
And danced a stately saraband;
Their laughter echoed thin and shrill.

Sometimes a clockwork puppet pressed
A phantom lover to her breast,
Sometimes they seemed to try to sing.

Sometimes a horrible marionette
Came out, and smoked its cigarette
Upon the steps like a live thing.

Then, turning to my love, I said,
'The dead are dancing with the dead,
The dust is whirling with the dust.'

But she – she heard the violin,
And left my side, and entered in:
Love passed into the house of lust.

Then suddenly the tune went false,
The dancers wearied of the waltz,
The shadows ceased to wheel and whirl.

And down the long and silent street,
The dawn, with silver-sandalled feet,
Crept like a frightened girl.

FANTAISIES DÉCORATIVES

I

Le Panneau

Under the rose-tree's dancing shade
  There stands a little ivory girl,
  Pulling the leaves of pink and pearl
With pale green nails of polished jade.

The red leaves fall upon the mould,
  The white leaves flutter, one by one,
  Down to a blue bowl where the sun,
Like a great dragon, writhes in gold.

The white leaves float upon the air,
  The red leaves flutter idly down,
  Some fall upon her yellow gown,
And some upon her raven hair.

She takes an amber lute and sings,
  And as she sings a silver crane
  Begins his scarlet neck to strain,
And flap his burnished metal wings.

She takes a lute of amber bright,
  And from the thicket where he lies
  Her lover, with his almond eyes,
Watches her movements in delight.

And now she gives a cry of fear,
  And tiny tears begin to start;
  A thorn has wounded with its dart
The pink-veined sea-shell of her ear.

And now she laughs a merry note:
  There has fallen a petal of the rose
  Just where the yellow satin shows
The blue-veined flower of her throat.

With pale green nails of polished jade,
  Pulling the leaves of pink and pearl,
  There stands a little ivory girl
Under the rose-tree's dancing shade.

2

Les Ballons

Against these turbid turquoise skies
    The light and luminous balloons
    Dip and drift like satin moons,
Drift like silken butterflies;

Reel with every windy gust,
    Rise and reel like dancing girls,
    Float like strange transparent pearls,
Fall and float like silver dust.

Now to the low leaves they cling,
    Each with coy fantastic pose,
    Each a petal of a rose
Straining at a gossamer string.

Then to the tall trees they climb,
    Like thin globes of amethyst,
    Wandering opals keeping tryst
With the rubies of the lime.

UNDER THE BALCONY

O beautiful star with the crimson mouth!
    O moon with the brows of gold!
Rise up, rise up, from the odorous south!
            And light for my love her way,
            Lest her little feet should stray
On the windy hill and the wold!
O beautiful star with the crimson mouth!
    O moon with the brows of gold!

O ship that shakes on the desolate sea!
    O ship with the wet, white sail!
Put in, put in, to the port to me!
            For my love and I would go
            To the land where the daffodils blow
In the heart of a violet dale!
O ship that shakes on the desolate sea!
    O ship with the wet, white sail!

O rapturous bird with the low, sweet note!
    O bird that sits on the spray!

Sing on, sing on, from your soft brown throat!
And my love in her little bed
Will listen, and lift her head
From the pillow, and come my way!
O rapturous bird with the low, sweet note!
O bird that sits on the spray!

O blossom that hangs in the tremulous air!
O blossom with lips of snow!
Come down, come down, for my love to wear!
You will die on her head in a crown,
You will die in a fold of her gown,
To her little light heart you will go!
O blossom that hangs in the tremulous air!
O blossom with lips of snow!

To My Wife

With a copy of my poems

I can write no stately proem
As a prelude to my lay;
From a poet to a poem
I would dare to say.

For if of these fallen petals
One to you seem fair,
Love will waft it till it settles
On your hair.

And when wind and winter harden
All the loveless land,
It will whisper of the garden,
You will understand.

On the sale by Auction of Keats' Love Letters

These are the letters which Endymion wrote
To one he loved in secret, and apart.
And now the brawlers of the auction mart
Bargain and bid for each poor blotted note,
Ay! for each separate pulse of passion quote

The merchant's price. I think they love not art
  Who break the crystal of a poet's heart
That small and sickly eyes may glare and gloat.

Is it not said that many years ago,
  In a far Eastern town, some soldiers ran
  With torches through the midnight, and began
To wrangle for mean raiment, and to throw
  Dice for the garments of a wretched man,
Not knowing the God's wonder, or His woe?

THE NEW REMORSE

The sin was mine; I did not understand.
  So now is music prisoned in her cave,
  Save where some ebbing desultory wave
Frets with its restless whirls this meagre strand.
And in the withered hollow of this land
  Hath Summer dug herself so deep a grave,
  That hardly can the leaden willow crave
One silver blossom from keen Winter's hand.

But who is this who cometh by the shore?
  (Nay, love, look up and wonder!) Who is this
  Who cometh in dyed garments from the South?
It is thy new-found Lord, and he shall kiss
  The yet unravished roses of thy mouth,
  And I shall weep and worship, as before.

CANZONET

I have no store
Of gryphon-guarded gold;
  Now, as before,
Bare is the shepherd's fold.
  Rubies nor pearls
Have I to gem thy throat;
  Yet woodland girls
Have loved the shepherd's note.

  Then, pluck a reed
And bid me sing to thee,
  For I would feed
Thine ears with melody,

> Who art more fair
>   Than fairest fleur-de-lys,
>   More sweet and rare
>   Than sweetest ambergris.
>
>   What dost thou fear?
> Young Hyacinth is slain,
>   Pan is not here,
> And will not come again.
>   No hornèd Faun
> Treads down the yellow leas,
>   No God at dawn
> Steals through the olive trees.
>
>   Hylas is dead,
> Nor will he e'er divine
>   Those little red
> Rose-petalled lips of thine.
>   On the high hill
> No ivory dryads play,
>   Silver and still
> Sinks the sad autumn day.

WITH A COPY OF 'A HOUSE OF POMEGRANATES'

Go, little book,
To him who, on a lute with horns of pearl,
Sang of the white feet of the Golden Girl:
And bid him look
Into thy pages: it may hap that he
May find that golden maidens dance through thee.

SYMPHONY IN YELLOW

An omnibus across the bridge
  Crawls like a yellow butterfly,
  And, here and there, a passer-by
Shows like a little restless midge.

Big barges full of yellow hay
  Are moored against the shadowy wharf,
  And, like a yellow silken scarf,
The thick fog hangs along the quay.

The yellow leaves begin to fade
  And flutter from the Temple elms,
  And at my feet the pale green Thames
Lies like a rod of rippled jade.

LA DAME JAUNE

She took the curious amber charms
  From off her neck, and laid them down,
  She loosed her jonquil-coloured gown,
And shook the bracelets from her arms.

She loosed her lemon-satin stays,
  She took a carven ivory comb,
  Her hair crawled down like yellow foam,
And flickered in the candle's rays.

I watched her thick locks, like a mass
  Of honey, dripping from the pin;
  Each separate hair was as the thin
Gold thread within a Venice glass.

REMORSE

(*A Study in Saffron*)

I love your topaz-coloured eyes
  That light with blame these midnight streets,
I love your body when it lies
  Like amber on the silken sheets.

I love the honey-coloured hair
  That ripples to your ivory hips;
I love the languid listless air
  With which you kiss my boyish lips.

I love the bows that bend above
  Those eyelids of chalcedony:
But most of all, my love! I love
  Your beautiful fierce chastity!

10 Nov. 89

11 Ryder Street

IN THE FOREST

Out of the mid-wood's twilight
   Into the meadow's dawn,
Ivory limbed and brown-eyed,
   Flashes my Faun!

He skips through the copses singing,
   And his shadow dances along,
And I know not which I should follow,
   Shadow or song!

O Hunter, snare me his shadow!
   O Nightingale, catch me his strain!
Else moonstruck with music and madness
   I track him in vain!

THE SPHINX

In a dim corner of my room for longer than my
   fancy thinks
A beautiful and silent Sphinx has watched me
   through the shifting gloom.

Inviolate and immobile she does not rise she does
   not stir
For silver moons are naught to her and naught to
   her the suns that reel.

Red follows grey across the air, the waves of moon-
   light ebb and flow
But with the Dawn she does not go and in the
   night-time she is there.

Dawn follows Dawn and Nights grow old and all
   the while this curious cat
Lies couching on the Chinese mat with eyes of satin
   rimmed with gold.

Upon the mat she lies and leers and on the tawny
   throat of her
Flutters the soft and silky fur or ripples to her
   pointed ears.

Come forth, my lovely seneschal! so somnolent, so
   statuesque!
Come forth you exquisite grotesque! half woman
   and half animal!

Come forth my lovely languorous Sphinx! And
    put your head upon my knee!
And let me stroke your throat and see your body
    spotted like the Lynx!

And let me touch those curving claws of yellow
    ivory and grasp
The tail that like a monstrous Asp coils round your
    heavy velvet paws!

A thousand weary centuries are thine while I have
    hardly seen
Some twenty summers cast their green for Autumn's
    gaudy liveries.

But you can read the Hieroglyphs on the great
    sandstone obelisks,
And you have talked with Basilisks, and you have
    looked on Hippogriffs.

O tell me, were you standing by when Isis to Osiris
    knelt?
And did you watch the Egyptian melt her union
    for Antony

And drink the jewel-drunken wine and bend her
    head in mimic awe
To see the huge proconsul draw the salted tunny
    from the brine?

And did you mark the Cyprian kiss white Adon on
    his catafalque?
And did you follow Amenalk, the God of
    Heliopolis?

And did you talk with Thoth, and did you hear
    the moon-horned Io weep?
And know the painted kings who sleep beneath
    the wedge-shaped Pyramid?

Lift up your large black satin eyes which are like
    cushions where one sinks!
Fawn at my feet, fantastic Sphinx! and sing me
    all your memories!

Sing to me of the Jewish maid who wandered with
    the Holy Child,
And how you led them through the wild, and how
    they slept beneath your shade.

Sing to me of that odorous green eve when crouching
by the marge
You heard from Adrian's gilded barge the laughter
of Antinous

And lapped the stream and fed your drouth and
watched with hot and hungry stare
The ivory body of that rare young slave with his
pomegranate mouth!

Sing to me of the Labyrinth in which the twi-
formed bull was stalled!
Sing to me of the night you crawled across the
temple's granite plinth

When through the purple corridors the screaming
scarlet Ibis flew
In terror, and a horrid dew dripped from the
moaning Mandragores,

And the great torpid crocodile within the tank shed
slimy tears,
And tare the jewels from his ears and staggered
back into the Nile,

And the priests cursed you with shrill psalms as
in your claws you seized their snake
And crept away with it to slake your passion by the
shuddering palms.

Who were your lovers? who were they who wrestled
for you in the dust?
Which was the vessel of your Lust? what Leman
had you, every day?

Did giant Lizards come and crouch before you on
the reedy banks?
Did Gryphons with great metal flanks leap on you
in your trampled couch?

Did monstrous hippopotami come sliding toward
you in the mist?
Did gilt-scaled dragons writhe and twist with passion
as you passed them by?

And from the brick-built Lycian tomb what horrible
Chimera came
With fearful heads and fearful flame to breed new
wonders from your womb?

Or had you shameful secret quests and did you
    harry to your home
Some Nereid coiled in amber foam with curious
    rock crystal breasts?

Or did you treading through the froth call to the
    brown Sidonian
For tidings of Leviathan, Leviathan or Be-
    hemoth?

Or did you when the sun was set climb up the
    cactus-covered slope
To meet your Ethiop whose body was of
    polished jet?

Or did you while the earthen skiffs dropped down
    the grey Nilotic flats
At twilight and the flickering bats flew round the
    temple's triple glyphs

Steal to the border of the bar and swim across the
    silent lake
And slink into the vault and make the Pyramid
    your lúpanar

Till from each black sarcophagus rose up the
    painted swathèd dead?
Or did you lure unto your bed the ivory-horned
    Tragelaphos?

Or did you love the god of flies who plagued the
    Hebrews and was splashed
With wine unto the waist? or Pasht, who had
    green beryls for her eyes?

Or that young god, the Tyrian, who was more
    amorous than the dove
Of Ashtaroth? or did you love the god of the
    Assyrian

Whose wings, like strange transparent talc, rose
    high above his hawk-faced head,
Painted with silver and with red and ribbed
    with rods of Oreichalch?

Or did huge Apis from his car leap down and lay
    before your feet
Big blossoms of the honey-sweet and honey-coloured
    nenuphar?

How subtle-secret is your smile! did you love
    none then? Nay, I know
Great Ammon was your bedfellow! he lay with
    you beside the Nile!

The river-horses in the slime trumpeted when
    they saw him come
Odorous with Syrian galbanum and smeared with
    spikenard and with thyme.

He came along the river bank like some tall galley
    argent-sailed,
He strode across the waters, mailed in beauty, and
    the waters sank.

He strode across the desert sand: he reached the
    valley where you lay:
He waited till the dawn of day: then touched
    your black breasts with his hand.

You kissed his mouth with mouths of flame: you
    made the hornèd god your own:
You stood behind him on his throne: you called
    him by his secret name.

You whispered monstrous oracles into the caverns
    of his ears:
With blood of goats and blood of steers you taught
    him monstrous miracles.

White Ammon was your bedfellow! your chamber
    was the steaming Nile!
And with your curved archaic smile you watched
    his passion come and go.

With Syrian oils his brows were bright: and wide-
    spread as a tent at noon
His marble limbs made pale the moon and lent the
    day a larger light.

His long hair was nine cubits' span and coloured
    like that yellow gem
Which hidden in their garment's hem the merchants bring
    from Kurdistan.

His face was as the must that lies upon a vat of
    new-made wine:
The seas could not insapphirine the perfect azure
    of his eyes.

His thick soft throat was white as milk and threaded
    with thin veins of blue:
And curious pearls like frozen dew were broidered
    on his flowing silk.

On pearl and porphyry pedestalled he was too
    bright to look upon:
For on his ivory breast there shone the wondrous
    ocean-emerald,

That mystic moonlit jewel which some diver of the
    Colchian caves
Had found beneath the blackening waves and
    carried to the Colchian witch.

Before his gilded galiot ran naked vine-wreathed
    corybants,
And lines of swaying elephants knelt down to draw
    his chariot,

And lines of swarthy Nubians bare up his litter as
    he rode
Down the great granite-paven road between the
    nodding peacock fans.

The merchants brought him steatite from Sidon in
    their painted ships:
The meanest cup that touched his lips was fashioned
    from a chrysolite.

The merchants brought him cedar chests of rich
    apparel bound with cords;
His train was borne by Memphian lords: young
    kings were glad to be his guests.

Ten hundred shaven priests did bow to Ammon's
    altar day and night,
Ten hundred lamps did wave their light through
    Ammon's carven house – and now

Foul snake and speckled adder with their young
    ones crawl from stone to stone
For ruined is the house and prone the great rose-
    marble monolith!

Wild ass or trotting jackal comes and couches in the
    mouldering gates:
Wild satyrs call unto their mates across the fallen
    fluted drums.

And on the summit of the pile the blue-faced ape
    of Horus sits
And gibbers while the fig-tree splits the pillars of
    the peristyle.

The god is scattered here and there: deep hidden
    in the windy sand
I saw his giant hand still clenched in im-
    potent despair.

And many a wandering caravan of stately negroes
    silken-shawled,
Crossing the desert, halts appalled before the neck
    that none can span.

And many a bearded Bedouin draws back his
    yellow-striped burnous
To gaze upon the Titan thews of him who was thy
    paladin.

Go, seek his fragments on the moor and wash
    them in the evening dew,
And from their pieces make anew thy mutilated
    paramour!

Go, seek them where they lie alone and from their
    broken pieces make
Thy bruisèd bedfellow! and wake mad passions in
    the senseless stone!

Charm his dull ear with Syrian hymns! he loved
    your body! Oh, be kind,
Pour spikenard on his hair, and wind soft rolls of
    linen round his limbs!

Wind round his head the figured coins! stain with
    red fruits those pallid lips!
Weave purple for his shrunken hips! and purple
    for his barren loins!

Away to Egypt! have no fear. Only one God has
    ever died.
Only one God has left His side be wounded by a
    soldier's spear.

But these, thy lovers, are not dead. Still by the
    hundred-cubit gate
Dog-faced Anubis sits in state with lotus-lilies
    for thy head.

Still from his chair of porphyry gaunt Memnon
    strains his lidless eyes
Across the empty land, and cries each yellow
    morning unto thee.

And Nilus with his broken horn lies in his black
    and oozy bed
And till thy coming will not spread his waters
    on the withering corn.

Your lovers are not dead, I know. Thy will rise
    up and hear your voice
And clash their cymbals and rejoice and run to
    kiss your mouth! and so,

Set wings upon your argosies! Set horses to your
    ebon car!
Back to your Nile! or if you are grown sick of
    dead divinities

Follow some roving lion's spoor across the copper-
    coloured plain,
Reach out and hale him by the mane and bid him
    be your paramour!

Couch by his side upon the grass and set your white
    teeth in his throat
And when you hear his dying note lash your long
    flanks of polished brass

And take a tiger for your mate, whose amber sides
    are flecked with black,
And ride upon his gilded back in triumph through
    the Theban gate,

And toy with him in amorous jests, and when he
    turns, and snarls, and gnaws,
O smite him with your jasper claws! and bruise
    him with your agate breasts!

Why are you tarrying? get hence! I weary of
    your sullen ways,
I weary of your steadfast gaze, your somnolent
    magnificence.

Your horrible and heavy breath makes the light
    flicker in the lamp,
And of my brow I feel the damp and dreadful dews
    of night and death.

Your eyes are like fantastic moons that shiver in
    some stagnant lake,
Your tongue is like a scarlet snake that dances to
    fantastic tunes,

Your pulse makes poisonous melodies, and your
    black throat is like the hole
Left by some torch or burning coal on Saracenic
    tapestries.

Away! the sulphur-coloured stars are hurrying
    through the Western gate!
Away! or it may be too late to climb their silent
    silver cars!

See, the dawn shivers round the grey gilt-dialled
    towers, and the rain
Streams down each diamonded pane and blurs with
    tears the wannish day.

What snake-tressed fury fresh from Hell, with un-
    couth gestures and unclean,
Stole from the poppy-drowsy queen and led you to
    a student's cell?

What songless tongueless ghost of sin crept through
    the curtains of the night,
And saw my taper turning bright, and knocked,
    and bade you enter in?

Are there not others more accursed, whiter with
    leprosies than I?
Are Abana and Pharphar dry that you come here to
    slake your thirst?

Get hence, you loathsome mystery! hideous
    animal, get hence!
You wake in me each bestial sense, you make me
    what I would not be.

You make my creed a barren sham, you wake foul
    dreams of sensual life,
And Atys with his blood-stained knife were better
    than the thing I am.

False Sphinx! false Sphinx! by reedy Styx old
    Charon, leaning on his oar,
Waits for my coin. Go thou before, and leave
    me to my crucifix,

Whose pallid burden, sick with pain, watches the
    world with wearied eyes,
And weeps for every soul that dies, and weeps for
    every soul in vain.

THE BALLAD OF READING GAOL

1

He did not wear his scarlet coat,
  For blood and wine are red,
And blood and wine were on his hands
  When they found him with the dead,
The poor dead woman whom he loved,
  And murdered in her bed.

He walked amongst the Trial Men
  In a suit of shabby grey;
A cricket cap was on his head,
  And his step seemed light and gay;
But I never saw a man who looked
  So wistfully at the day.

I never saw a man who looked
  With such a wistful eye
Upon that little tent of blue
  Which prisoners call the sky,
And at every drifting cloud that went
  With sails of silver by.

I walked, with other souls in pain,
  Within another ring,
And was wondering if the man had done
  A great or little thing,
When a voice behind me whispered low,
  'That fellow's got to swing.'

Dear Christ! the very prison walls
  Suddenly seemed to reel,
And the sky above my head became
  Like a casque of scorching steel;
And, though I was a soul in pain,
  My pain I could not feel.

I only knew what hunted thought
  Quickened his step, and why
He looked upon the garish day
  With such a wistful eye;
The man had killed the thing he loved,
  And so he had to die.

*

Yet each man kills the thing he loves,
  By each let this be heard,
Some do it with a bitter look,
  Some with a flattering word.
The coward does it with a kiss,
  The brave man with a sword!

Some kill their love when they are young,
  And some when they are old;
Some strangle with the hands of Lust,
  Some with the hands of Gold:
The kindest use a knife, because
  The dead so soon grow cold.

Some love too little, some too long,
  Some sell, and others buy;
Some do the deed with many tears,
  And some without a sigh:
For each man kills the thing he loves,
  Yet each man does not die.

He does not die a death of shame
  On a day of dark disgrace,
Nor have a noose about his neck,
  Nor a cloth upon his face,
Nor drop feet foremost through the floor
  Into an empty space.

He does not sit with silent men
  Who watch him night and day;
Who watch him when he tries to weep,
  And when he tries to pray;
Who watch him lest himself should rob
  The prison of its prey.

He does not wake at dawn to see
  Dread figures throng his room,
The shivering Chaplain robed in white,
  The Sheriff stern with gloom,
And the Governor all in shiny black,
  With the yellow face of Doom.

He does not rise in piteous haste
  To put on convict-clothes,
While some coarse-mouthed Doctor gloats, and notes
  Each new and nerve-twitched pose,
Fingering a watch whose little ticks
  Are like horrible hammer-blows.

He does not know that sickening thirst
  That sands one's throat, before
The hangman with his gardener's gloves
  Slips through the padded door,
And binds one with three leathern thongs,
  That the throat may thirst no more.

He does not bend his head to hear
  The Burial Office read,
Nor, while the terror of his soul
  Tells him he is not dead,
Cross his own coffin, as he moves
  Into the hideous shed.

He does not stare upon the air
  Through a little roof of glass:
He does not pray with lips of clay
  For his agony to pass;
Nor feel upon his shuddering cheek
  The kiss of Caiaphas.

2

Six weeks our guardsman walked the yard,
  In the suit of shabby grey:
His cricket cap was on his head,
  And his step seemed light and gay,
But I never saw a man who looked
  So wistfully at the day.

I never saw a man who looked
  With such a wistful eye
Upon that little tent of blue
  Which prisoners call the sky,
And at every wandering cloud that trailed
  Its ravelled fleeces by.

He did not wring his hands, as do
  Those witless men who dare
To try to rear the changeling Hope
  In the cave of black Despair:
He only looked upon the sun,
  And drank the morning air.

He did not wring his hands nor weep,
  Nor did he peek or pine,

But he drank the air as though it held
    Some healthful anodyne;
With open mouth he drank the sun
    As though it had been wine!

And I and all the souls in pain,
    Who tramped the other ring,
Forgot if we ourselves had done
    A great or little thing,
And watched with gaze of dull amaze
    The man who had to swing.

And strange it was to see him pass
    With a step so light and gay,
And strange it was to see him look
    So wistfully at the day,
And strange it was to think that he
    Had such a debt to pay.

*

For oak and elm have pleasant leaves
    That in the spring-time shoot;
But grim to see is the gallows-tree,
    With its adder-bitten root,
And, green or dry, a man must die
    Before it bears its fruit!

The loftiest place is that seat of grace
    For which all worldlings try:
But who would stand in hempen band
    Upon a scaffold high,
And through a murderer's collar take
    His last look at the sky?

It is sweet to dance to violins
    When Love and Life are fair:
To dance to flutes, to dance to lutes
    Is delicate and rare:
But it is not sweet with nimble feet
    To dance upon the air!

So with curious eyes and sick surmise
    We watched him day by day,
And wondered if each one of us
    Would end the self-same way,
For none can tell to what red Hell
    His sightless soul may stray.

At last the dead man walked no more
   Amongst the Trial Men,
And I knew that he was standing up
   In the black dock's dreadful pen,
And that never would I see his face
   In God's sweet world again.

Like two doomed ships that pass in storm
   We had crossed each other's way:
But we made no sign, we said no word,
   We had no word to say;
For we did not meet in the holy night,
   But in the shameful day.

A prison wall was round us born,
   Two outcast men we were:
The world had thrust us from its heart,
   And God from out His care:
And the iron gin that waits for Sin
   Had caught us in its snare.

3

In Debtor's Yard the stones are hard,
   And the dripping wall is high,
So it was there he took the air
   Beneath the leaden sky,
And by each side a Warder walked,
   For fear the man might die.

Or else he sat with those who watched
   His anguish night and day;
Who watched him when he rose to weep,
   And when he crouched to pray;
Who watched him lest himself should rob
   Their scaffold of its prey.

The Governor was strong upon
   The Regulations Act:
The Doctor said that Death was but
   A scientific fact:
And twice a day the Chaplain called,
   And left a little tract.

And twice a day he smoked his pipe,
   And drank his quart of beer:
His soul was resolute, and held
   No hiding-place for fear;

He often said that he was glad
   The hangman's hands were near.

But why he said so strange a thing
   No Warder dared to ask:
For he to whom a watcher's doom
   Is given as his task,
Must set a lock upon his lips,
   And make his face a mask.

Or else he might be moved, and try
   To comfort or console:
And what should Human Pity do
   Pent up in Murderers' Hole?
What word of grace in such a place
   Could help a brother's soul?

With slouch and swing around the ring
   We trod the Fools' Parade!
We did not care: we knew we were
   The Devil's Own Brigade:
And shaven head and feet of lead
   Make a merry masquerade.

We tore the tarry rope to shreds
   With blunt and bleeding nails;
We rubbed the doors, and scrubbed the floors,
   And cleaned the shining rails:
And, rank by rank, we soaped the plank,
   And clattered with the pails.

We sewed the sacks, we broke the stones,
   We turned the dusty drill:
We banged the tins, and bawled the hymns,
   And sweated on the mill:
But in the heart of every man
   Terror was lying still.

So still it lay that every day
   Crawled like a weed-clogged wave:
And we forgot the bitter lot
   That waits for fool and knave,
Till once, as we tramped in from work,
   We passed an open grave.

With yawning mouth the yellow hole
   Gaped for a living thing;
The very mud cried out for blood
   To the thirsty asphalte ring:

And we knew that ere one dawn grew fair
  Some prisoner had to swing.

Right in we went, with soul intent
  On Death and Dread and Doom:
The hangman, with his little bag,
  Went shuffling through the gloom:
And each man trembled as he crept
  Into his numbered tomb.

*

That night the empty corridors
  Were full of forms of Fear,
And up and down the iron town
  Stole feet we could not hear,
And through the bars that hide the stars
  White faces seemed to peer.

He lay as one who lies and dreams
  In a pleasant meadow-land,
The watchers watched him as he slept,
  And could not understand
How one could sleep so sweet a sleep
  With a hangman close at hand.

But there is no sleep when men must weep
  Who never yet have wept:
So we – the fool, the fraud, the knave –
  That endless vigil kept,
And through each brain on hands of pain
  Another's terror crept.

Alas! it is a fearful thing
  To feel another's guilt!
For, right within, the Sword of Sin
  Pierced to its poisoned hilt,
And as molten lead were the tears we shed
  For the blood we had not spilt.

The Warders with their shoes of felt
  Crept by each padlocked door,
And peeped and saw, with eyes of awe,
  Grey figures on the floor,
And wondered why men knelt to pray
  Who never prayed before.

All through the night we knelt and prayed,
    Mad mourners of a corse!
The troubled plumes of midnight were
    The plumes upon a hearse:
And bitter wine upon a sponge
    Was the savour of Remorse.

*

The grey cock crew, the red cock crew,
    But never came the day:
And crooked shapes of Terror crouched,
    In the corners where we lay:
And each evil sprite that walks by night
    Before us seemed to play.

They glided past, they glided fast,
    Like travellers through a mist:
They mocked the moon in a rigadoon
    Of delicate turn and twist,
And with formal pace and loathsome grace
    The phantoms kept their tryst.

With mop and mow, we saw them go,
    Slim shadows hand in hand:
About, about, in ghostly rout
    They trod a saraband:
And the damned grotesques made arabesques;
    Like the wind upon the sand!

With the pirouettes of marionettes,
    They tripped on pointed tread:
But with flutes of Fear they filled the ear,
    As their grisly masque they led,
And loud they sang, and long they sang.
    For they sang to wake the dead.

'Oho!' they cried, '*The world is wide
But fettered limbs go lame!
And once, or twice, to throw the dice
    Is a gentlemanly game,
But he does not win who plays with Sin
    In the secret House of Shame.*'

No things of air these antics were,
    That frolicked with such glee:
To men whose lives were held in gyves,
    And whose feet might not go free,

Ah! wounds of Christ! they were living things
  Most terrible to see.

Around, around, they waltzed and wound;
  Some wheeled in smirking pairs;
With the mincing step of a demirep
  Some sidled up the stairs:
And with subtle sneer, and fawning leer,
  Each helped us at our prayers.

The morning wind began to moan,
  But still the night went on:
Through its giant loom the web of gloom
  Crept till each thread was spun:
And, as we prayed, we grew afraid
  Of the Justice of the Sun.

The moaning wind went wandering round
  The weeping prison-wall:
Till like a wheel of turning steel
  We felt the minutes crawl:
O moaning wind! what had we done
  To have such a seneschal?

At last I saw the shadowed bars,
  Like a lattice wrought in lead,
Move right across the whitewashed wall
  That faced my three-plank bed,
And I knew that somewhere in the world
  God's dreadful dawn was red.

At six o'clock we cleaned our cells,
  At seven all was still,
But the sough and swing of a mighty wing
  The prison seemed to fill,
For the Lord of Death with icy breath
  Had entered in to kill.

He did not pass in purple pomp,
  Nor ride a moon-white steed.
Three yards of cord and a sliding board
  Are all the gallows' need:
So with rope of shame the Herald came
  To do the secret deed.

We were as men who through a fen
  Of filthy darkness grope:
We did not dare to breathe a prayer,
  Or to give our anguish scope:

Something was dead in each of us,
  And what was dead was Hope.

For Man's grim Justice goes its way,
  And will not swerve aside:
It slays the weak, it slays the strong,
  It has a deadly stride:
With iron heel it slays the strong,
  The monstrous parricide!

We waited for the stroke of eight:
  Each tongue was thick with thirst:
For the stroke of eight is the stroke of Fate
  That makes a man accursed,
And Fate will use a running noose
  For the best man and the worst.

We had no other thing to do,
  Save to wait for the sign to come:
So, like things of stone in a valley lone,
  Quiet we sat and dumb:
But each man's heart beat thick and quick,
  Like a madman on a drum!

With sudden shock the prison-clock
  Smote on the shivering air,
And from all the gaol rose up a wail
  Of impotent despair,
Like the sound that frightened marshes hear
  From some leper in his lair.

And as one sees most fearful things
  In the crystal of a dream,
We saw the greasy hempen rope
  Hooked to the blackened beam,
And heard the prayer the hangman's snare
  Strangled into a scream.

And all the woe that moved him so
  That he gave that bitter cry,
And the wild regrets, and the bloody sweats,
  None knew so well as I:
For he who lives more lives than one
  More deaths than one must die.

4

There is no chapel on the day
  On which they hang a man:
The Chaplain's heart is far too sick,
  Or his face is far too wan,
Or there is that written in his eyes
  Which none should look upon.

So they kept us close till nigh on noon,
  And then they rang the bell,
And the Warders with their jingling keys
  Opened each listening cell,
And down the iron stair we tramped,
  Each from his separate Hell.

Out into God's sweet air we went,
  But not in wonted way,
For this man's face was white with fear,
  And that man's face was grey,
And I never saw sad men who looked
  So wistfully at the day.

I never saw sad men who looked
  With such a wistful eye
Upon that little tent of blue
  We prisoners called the sky,
And at every careless cloud that passed
  In happy freedom by.

But there were those amongst us all
  ·Who walked with downcast head,
And knew that, had each got his due,
  They should have died instead:
He had but killed a thing that lived,
  Whilst they had killed the dead.

For he who sins a second time
  Wakes a dead soul to pain,
And draws it from its spotted shroud,
  And makes it bleed again,
And makes it bleed great gouts of blood,
  And makes it bleed in vain!

*

Like ape or clown, in monstrous garb
    With crooked arrows starred,
Silently we went round and round
    The slippery asphalte yard;
Silently we went round and round,
    And no man spoke a word.

Silently we went round and round,
    And through each hollow mind
The Memory of dreadful things
    Rushed like a dreadful wind,
And Horror stalked before each man,
    And Terror crept behind.

*

The Warders strutted up and down,
    And kept their herd of brutes,
Their uniforms were spick and span,
    And they wore their Sunday suits,
But we knew the work they had been at,
    By the quicklime on their boots.

For where a grave had opened wide,
    There was no grave at all:
Only a stretch of mud and sand
    By the hideous prison-wall,
And a little heap of burning lime,
    That the man should have his pall.

For he has a pall, this wretched man,
    Such as few men can claim:
Deep down below a prison-yard,
    Naked for greater shame,
He lies, with fetters on each foot,
    Wrapt in a sheet of flame!

And all the while the burning lime
    Eats flesh and bone away,
It eats the brittle bone by night,
    And the soft flesh by day,
It eats the flesh and bone by turns,
    But it eats the heart alway.

*

For three long years they will not sow
    Or root or seedling there:
For three long years the unblessed spot
    Will sterile be and bare,
And look upon the wondering sky
    With unreproachful stare.

They think a murderer's heart would taint
    Each simple seed they sow.
It is not true! God's kindly earth
    Is kindlier than men know,
And the red rose would but blow more red,
    The white rose whiter blow.

Out of his mouth a red, red rose!
    Out of his heart a white!
For who can say by what strange way,
    Christ brings His will to light,
Since the barren staff the pilgrim bore
    Bloomed in the great Pope's sight?

But neither milk-white rose nor red
    May bloom in prison-air;
The shard, the pebble, and the flint,
    Are what they give us there:
For flowers have been known to heal
    A common man's despair.

So never will wine-red rose or white,
    Petal by petal, fall
On that stretch of mud and sand that lies
    By the hideous prison-wall,
To tell the men who tramp the yard
    That God's Son died for all.

Yet though the hideous prison-wall
    Still hems him round and round,
And a spirit may not walk by night
    That is with fetters bound,
And a spirit may but weep that lies
    In such unholy ground,

He is at peace – this wretched man –
    At peace, or will be soon:
There is no thing to make him mad,
    Nor does Terror walk at noon,

For the lampless Earth in which he lies
   Has neither Sun nor Moon.

They hanged him as a beast is hanged!
   They did not even toll
A requiem that might have brought
   Rest to his startled soul,
But hurriedly they took him out,
   And hid him in a hole.

They stripped him of his canvas clothes,
   And gave him to the flies:
They mocked the swollen purple throat,
   And the stark and staring eyes:
And with laughter loud they heaped the shroud
   In which their convict lies.

The Chaplain would not kneel to pray
   By his dishonoured grave:
Nor mark it with that blessed Cross
   That Christ for sinners gave,
Because the man was one of those
   Whom Christ came down to save.

Yet all is well; he has but passed
   To Life's appointed bourne:
And alien tears will fill for him
   Pity's long-broken urn,
For his mourners will be outcast men,
   And outcasts always mourn

5

I know not whether Laws be right,
   Or whether Laws be wrong;
All that we know who lie in gaol
   Is that the wall is strong;
And that each day is like a year,
   A year whose days are long.

But this I know, that every Law
   That men hath made for Man,
Since first Man took his brother's life,
   And the sad world began,
But straws the wheat and saves the chaff
   With a most evil fan.

This too I know – and wise it were
  If each could know the same –
That every prison that men build
  Is built with bricks of shame,
And bound with bars lest Christ should see
  How men their brothers maim.

With bars they blur the gracious moon,
  And blind the goodly sun;
And they do well to hide their Hell,
  For in it things are done
That Son of God nor son of Man
  Ever should look upon!

*

The vilest deeds like poison weeds,
  Bloom well in prison-air;
It is only what is good in Man
  That wastes and withers there:
Pale Anguish keeps the heavy gate,
  And the Warder is Despair.

For they starve the little frightened child
  Till it weeps both night and day:
And they scourge the weak, and flog the fool,
  And gibe the old and grey,
And some grow mad, and all grow bad,
  And none a word may say.

Each narrow cell in which we dwell
  Is a foul and dark latrine,
And the fetid breath of living Death
  Chokes up each grated screen,
And all, but Lust, is turned to dust
  In Humanity's machine.

The brackish water that we drink
  Creeps with a loathsome slime,
And the bitter bread they weigh in scales
  Is full of chalk and lime,
And Sleep will not lie down, but walks
  Wild-eyed, and cries to Time.

*

But though lean Hunger and green Thirst
   Like asp with adder fight,
We have little care of prison fare,
   For what chills and kills outright
Is that every stone one lifts by day
   Becomes one's heart by night.

With midnight always in one's heart,
   And twilight in one's cell,
We turn the crank, or tear the rope,
   Each in his separate Hell,
And the silence is more awful far
   Than the sound of a brazen bell.

And never a human voice comes near
   To speak a gentle word:
And the eye that watches through the door
   Is pitiless and hard:
And by all forgot, we rot and rot,
   With soul and body marred.

And thus we rust Life's iron chain
   Degraded and alone:
And some men curse, and some men weep,
   And some men make no moan:
But God's eternal Laws are kind
   And break the heart of stone.

*

And every human heart that breaks,
   In prison-cell or yard,
Is as that broken box that gave
   Its treasure to the Lord,
And filled the unclean leper's house
   With the scent of costliest nard.

Ah! Happy they whose hearts can break
   And peace of pardon win!
How else may man make straight his plan
   And cleanse his soul from Sin?
How else but through a broken heart
   May Lord Christ enter in?

*

And he of the swollen purple throat,
    And the stark and staring eyes,
Waits for the holy hands that took
    The Thief to Paradise;
And a broken and a contrite heart
    The Lord will not despise.

The man in red who reads the Law
    Gave him three weeks of life,
Three little weeks in which to heal
    His soul of his soul's strife,
And cleanse from every blot of blood
    The hand that held the knife.

And with tears of blood he cleansed the hand,
    The hand that held the steel:
For only blood can wipe out blood,
    And only tears can heal:
And the crimson stain that was of Cain
    Became Christ's snow-white seal.

6

In Reading gaol by Reading town
    There is a pit of shame,
And in it lies a wretched man
    Eaten by teeth of flame,
In a burning winding-sheet he lies,
    And his grave has got no name.

And there, till Christ call forth the dead,
    In silence let him lie:
No need to waste the foolish tear,
    Or heave the windy sigh:
The man had killed the thing he loved,
    And so he had to die.

And all men kill the thing they love,
    By all let this be heard,
Some do it with a bitter look,
    Some with a flattering word,
The coward does it with a kiss,
    The brave man with a sword!

POEMS IN PROSE

THE ARTIST

One evening there came into his soul the desire to fashion an image of *The Pleasure that abideth for a Moment*. And he went forth into the world to look for bronze. For he could only think in bronze.

But all the bronze of the whole world had disappeared, nor anywhere in the whole world was there any bronze to be found, save only the bronze of the image of *The Sorrow that endureth for Ever*.

Now this image he had himself, and with his own hands, fashioned, and had set it on the tomb of the one thing he had loved in life. On the tomb of the dead thing he had most loved had he set this image of his own fashioning, that it might serve as a sign of the love of man that dieth not, and a symbol of the sorrow of man that endureth for ever. And in the whole world there was no other bronze save the bronze of this image.

And he took the image he had fashioned, and set it in a great furnace, and gave it to the fire.

And out of the bronze of the image of *The Sorrow that endureth for Ever* he fashioned an image of *The Pleasure that abideth for a Moment*.

THE DOER OF GOOD

It was night-time and He was alone.

And He saw afar-off the walls of a round city and went towards the city.

And when He came near He heard within the city the tread of the feet of joy, and the laughter of the mouth of gladness and the loud noise of many lutes. And He knocked at the gate and certain of the gate-keepers opened to Him.

And He beheld a house that was of marble and had fair pillars of marble before it. The pillars were hung with garlands, and within and without there were torches of cedar. And He entered the house.

And when He had passed through the hall of chalcedony and the hall of jasper, and reached the long hall of feasting, He saw lying on a couch of sea-purple one whose hair was crowned with red roses and whose lips were red with wine.

And He went behind him and touched him on the shoulder and said to him, 'Why do you live like this?'

And the young man turned round and recognised Him, and made answer and said, 'But I was a leper once, and you healed me. How else should I live?'

And He passed out of the house and went again into the street.

And after a little while He saw one whose face and raiment were painted and whose feet were shod with pearls. And behind her came, slowly as a hunter, a young man who wore a cloak of two colours. Now the face of the woman was as the fair face of an idol, and the eyes of the young man were bright with lust.

And He followed swiftly and touched the hand of the young man and said to him, 'Why do you look at this woman and in such wise?'

And the young man turned round and recognised Him and said, 'But I was blind once, and you gave me sight. At what else should I look?'

And He ran forward and touched the painted raiment of the woman and said to her, 'Is there no other way in which to walk save the way of sin?'

And the woman turned round and recognised Him, and laughed and said, 'But you forgave me my sins, and the way is a pleasant way.'

And He passed out of the city.

And when He had passed out of the city He saw seated by the roadside a young man who was weeping.

And He went towards him and touched the long locks of his hair and said to him, 'Why are you weeping?'

And the young man looked up and recognised Him and made answer, 'But I was dead once and you raised me from the dead. What else should I do but weep?'

THE DISCIPLE

When Narcissus died the pool of his pleasure changed from a cup of sweet waters into a cup of salt tears, and the Oreads came weeping through the woodland that they might sing to the pool and give it comfort.

And when they saw that the pool had changed from a cup of sweet waters into a cup of salt tears, they loosened the green tresses of their hair and cried to the pool and said, 'We do not wonder that you should mourn in this manner for Narcissus, so beautiful was he.'

'But was Narcissus beautiful?' said the pool.

'Who should know that better than you?' answered the Oreads. 'Us did he ever pass by, but you he sought for, and would lie on your banks and look down at you, and in the mirror of your waters he would mirror his own beauty.'

And the pool answered, 'But I loved Narcissus because, as he lay on my banks and looked down at me, in the mirror of his eyes I saw ever my own beauty mirrored.'

THE MASTER

Now when the darkness came over the earth Joseph of Arimathea, having lighted a torch of pinewood, passed down from the hill into the valley. For he had business in his own home.

And kneeling on the flint stones of the Valley of Desolation he saw a young man who was naked and weeping. His hair was the colour of honey, and his body was as a white flower, but he had wounded his body with thorns and on his hair had he set ashes as a crown.

And he who had great possessions said to the young man who was naked and weeping, 'I do not wonder that your sorrow is so great, for surely He was a just man.'

And the young man answered, 'It is not for Him that I am weeping, but for myself. I too have changed water into wine, and I have healed the leper and given sight to the blind. I have walked upon the waters, and from the dwellers in the tombs I have cast out devils. I have fed the hungry in the desert where there was no food, and I have raised the dead from their narrow houses, and at my bidding, and before a great multitude of people, a barren fig-tree withered away. All things that this man has done I have done also. And yet they have not crucified me.'

THE HOUSE OF JUDGMENT

And there was silence in the House of Judgment, and the Man came naked before God.

And God opened the Book of the Life of the Man.

And God said to the Man, 'Thy life hath been evil, and thou hast shown cruelty to those who were in need of succour, and to those who lacked help thou hast been bitter and hard of heart. The poor called to thee and thou didst not hearken, and thine ears were closed to the cry of My afflicted. The inheritance of the fatherless thou didst take unto thyself, and thou didst send the foxes into the vineyard of they neighbour's field. Thou didst take the bread of the children and give it to the dogs to eat, and My lepers who lived in the marshes, and were at peace and praised Me, thou didst drive forth on to the highways, and on Mine earth out of which I made thee thou didst spill innocent blood.'

And the Man made answer and said, 'Even so did I.'

And again God opened the Book of the Life of the Man.

And God said to the Man, 'Thy life hath been evil, and the Beauty I have shown thou hast sought for, and the Good I have hidden thou didst pass by. The walls of thy chamber were painted with images, and from the bed of thine abominations thou didst rise up to the sound of flutes. Thou didst build seven altars to the sins I have suffered, and didst eat of the thing that may not be eaten, and the purple of thy raiment was broidered with the three signs of shame. Thine idols were neither of gold nor of silver that endure, but of flesh that dieth. Thou didst stain their hair with perfumes and put pomegranates in their hands. Thou didst stain their feet with saffron and spread carpets before them. With antimony thou didst stain their eyelids and their bodies thou didst smear with myrrh. Thou didst bow thyself to the ground before them, and the thrones of thine idols were set in the sun. Thou didst show to the sun thy shame and to the moon thy madness.'

And the Man made answer and said, 'Even so did I.'

And a third time God opened the Book of the Life of the Man.

And God said to the Man, 'Evil hath been thy life, and with evil didst thou requite good, and with wrongdoing kindness. The hands that fed thee thou didst wound, and the breasts that gave thee suck thou didst despise. He who came to thee with water went away thirsting, and the outlawed men who hid thee in their tents at night thou didst betray before dawn. Thine enemy who spared thee thou didst snare in an ambush, and the friend who walked with thee thou didst sell for a price, and to those who brought thee Love thou didst ever give Lust in thy turn.'

And the Man made answer and said, 'Even so did I.'

And God closed the Book of the Life of the Man, and said, 'Surely I will send thee into Hell. Even into Hell will I send thee.'

And the Man cried out, 'Thou canst not.'

And God said to the Man, 'Wherefore can I not send thee to Hell, and for what reason?'

'Because in Hell have I always lived,' answered the Man.

And there was silence in the House of Judgment.

And after a space God spake, and said to the Man, 'Seeing that I may not send thee into Hell, surely I will send thee unto Heaven. Even unto Heaven will I send thee.'

And the Man cried out, 'Thou canst not.'

And God said to the Man, 'Wherefore can I not send thee unto Heaven, and for what reason?'

'Because never, and in no place, have I been able to imagine it,' answered the Man.

And there was silence in the House of Judgment.

THE TEACHER OF WISDOM

From his childhood he had been as one filled with the perfect knowledge of God, and even while he was yet but a lad many of the saints, as well as certain holy women who dwelt in the free city of his birth, had been stirred to much wonder by the grave wisdom of his answers.

And when his parents had given him the robe and the ring of manhood he kissed them, and left them and went out into the world, that he might speak to the world about God. For there were at that time many in the world who either knew not God at all, or had but an incomplete knowledge of Him, or worshipped the false gods who dwell in groves and have no care of their worshippers.

And he set his face to the sun and journeyed, walking without sandals, as he had seen the saints walk, and carrying at his girdle a leathern wallet and a little water-bottle of burnt clay.

And as he walked along the highway he was full of the joy that comes from the perfect knowledge of God, and he sang praises unto God without ceasing; and after a time he reached a strange land in which there were many cities.

And he passed through eleven cities. And some of these cities were in valleys, and others were by the banks of great rivers, and others were set on hills. And in each city he found a disciple who loved him and followed him, and a great multitude also of people followed him from each city, and the knowledge of God spread in the whole land, and many of the rulers were converted, and the priests of the temples in which there were idols found that half of their gain was gone, and when they beat upon their drums at noon none, or but a few, came with peacocks and with offerings of flesh as had been the custom of the land before his coming.

Yet the more the people followed him, and the greater the number of his disciples, the greater became his sorrow. And he knew not why his sorrow was so great. For he spake ever about God, and out of the fulness of that perfect knowledge of God which God had Himself given to him.

And one evening he passed out of the eleventh city, which was a city of Armenia, and his disciples and a great crowd of people followed after him; and he went up on to a mountain and sat down on a rock that was on the mountain, and his disciples stood round him, and the multitude knelt in the valley.

And he bowed his head on his hands and wept, and said to his Soul, 'Why is it that I am full of sorrow and fear, and that each of my disciples is as an enemy that walks in the noonday?'

And his Soul answered him and said, 'God filled thee with the perfect knowledge of Himself, and thou hast given this knowledge away to others. The pearl of great price thou hast divided, and the vesture without seam thou hast parted asunder. He who giveth away wisdom robbeth himself. He is as one who giveth his treasure to a robber. Is not God wiser than thou art? Who art thou to give away the secret that God hath told thee? I was rich once, and thou hast made me poor. Once I saw God, and now thou hast hidden Him from me.'

And he wept again, for he knew that his Soul spake truth to him, and that he had given to others the perfect knowledge of God, and that he was as one clinging to the skirts of God, and that his faith was leaving him by reason of the number of those who believed in him.

And he said to himself, 'I will talk no more about God. He who giveth away wisdom robbeth himself.'

And after the space of some hours his disciples came near him and bowed themselves to the ground and said, 'Master, talk to us about God, for thou hast the perfect knowledge of God, and no man save thee hath this knowledge.'

And he answered them and said, 'I will talk to you about all other things that are in heaven and on earth, but about God I will not talk to you. Neither now, nor at any time, will I talk to you about God.'

And they were wroth with him and said to him, 'Thou hast led us into the desert that we might hearken to thee. Wilt thou send us away hungry, and the great multitude that thou hast made to follow thee?'

And he answered them and said, 'I will not talk to you about God.'

And the multitude murmured against him and said to him, 'Thou hast led us into the desert, and hast given us no food to eat. Talk to us about God and it will suffice us.'

But he answered them not a word. For he knew that if he spake to them about God he would give away his treasure.

And his disciples went away sadly, and the multitude of people returned to their own homes. And many died on the way.

And when he was alone he rose up and set his face to the moon, and journeyed for seven moons, speaking to no man nor making any answer. And when the seventh moon had waned he reached that desert which is the desert of the Great River. And having found a cavern in which a Centaur had once dwelt, he took it for his place of dwelling, and made himself a mat of reeds on which to lie, and became a hermit. And every hour the Hermit praised God that He had suffered him to keep some knowledge of Him and of His wonderful greatness.

Now, one evening, as the Hermit was seated before the cavern in which he had made his place of dwelling, he beheld a young man of evil and beautiful face who passed by in mean apparel and with empty hands. Every evening with empty hands the young man passed by, and every morning he returned with his hands full of purple and pearls. For he was a Robber and robbed the caravans of the merchants.

And the Hermit looked at him and pitied him. But he spake not a word. For he knew that he who speaks a word loses his faith.

And one morning, as the young man returned with his hands full of purple and pearls, he stopped and frowned and stamped his foot upon the sand, and said to the Hermit: 'Why do you look at me ever in this manner as I pass by? What is it that I see in your eyes? For no man has looked at me before in this manner. And the thing is a thorn and a trouble to me.'

And the Hermit answered him and said, 'What you see in my eyes is pity. Pity is what looks out at you from my eyes.'

And the young man laughed with scorn, and cried to the Hermit in a bitter voice, and said to him, 'I have purple and pearls in my hands, and you have but a mat of reeds on which to lie. What pity should you have for me? And for what reason have you this pity?'

'I have pity for you,' said the Hermit, 'because you have no knowledge of God.'

'Is this knowledge of God a precious thing?' asked the young man, and he came close to the mouth of the cavern.

'It is more precious than all the purple and the pearls of the world,' answered the Hermit.

'And have you got it?' said the young Robber, and he came closer still.

'Once, indeed,' answered the Hermit, 'I possessed the perfect knowledge of God. But in my foolishness I parted with it, and divided it amongst others. Yet even now is such knowledge as remains to me more precious than purple or pearls.'

And when the young Robber heard this he threw away the purple and the pearls that he was bearing in his hands, and drawing a sharp sword of curved steel he said to the Hermit, 'Give me, forthwith, this knowledge of God that you possess, or I will surely slay you. Wherefore should I not slay him who has a treasure greater than my treasure?'

And the Hermit spread out his arms and said, 'Were it not better for me to go unto the uttermost courts of God and praise Him, than to live in the world and have no knowledge of Him? Slay me if that be your desire. But I will not give away my knowledge of God.'

And the young Robber knelt down and besought him, but the Hermit would not talk to him about God, nor give him his Treasure, and the young Robber rose up and said to the Hermit, 'Be it as you will. As for myself, I will go to the City of the Seven Sins, that is but three days' journey from this place, and for my purple they will give me pleasure, and for my pearls they will sell me joy.' And he took up the purple and the pearls and went swiftly away.

And the Hermit cried out and followed him and besought him. For the space of three days he followed the young Robber on the road and entreated him to return, nor to enter into the City of the Seven Sins.

And ever and anon the young Robber looked back at the Hermit and called to him, and said, 'Will you give me this knowledge of God which is more precious than purple and pearls? If you will give me that, I will not enter the city.'

And ever did the Hermit answer, 'All things that I have I will give thee, save that one thing only. For that thing it is not lawful for me to give away.'

And in the twilight of the third day they came nigh to the great scarlet gates of the City of the Seven Sins. And from the city there came the sound of much laughter.

And the young Robber laughed in answer, and sought to knock at the gate. And as he did so the Hermit ran forward and caught him by the skirts of his raiment, and said to him: 'Stretch forth your hands, and set your arms around my neck, and put your ear close to my lips, and I will give you what remains to me of the knowledge of God.' And the young Robber stopped.

And when the Hermit had given away his knowledge of God, he fell upon the ground and wept, and a great darkness hid from him the city and the young Robber, so that he saw them no more.

And as he lay there weeping he was aware of One who was standing beside him; and He who was standing beside him had feet of brass and hair like fine wool. And He raised the Hermit up, and said to him: 'Before this time thou hadst the perfect knowledge of God. Now thou shalt have the perfect love of God. Wherefore art thou weeping?' And He kissed him.

ESSAYS, SELECTED JOURNALISM, LECTURES AND LETTERS

Introduction by

MERLIN HOLLAND

There is a perfectly understandable tradition in Collected Works of putting all the miscellaneous writings in a heterogeneous bundle at the end. They take on that forlorn air of the indigestible bits left on the side of a plate after a good meal – a necessary part of the whole but an acquired taste if consumed at all. To appreciate a more serious Oscar Wilde, though, we need to forget the conventional view (as one does in most things to do with Wilde) and see what many regard as leftovers with the eyes of the child, who invariably leaves the tastiest pieces until last.

Seriousness and Wilde for most of his non-academic readers are laughably incompatible. The popular view of the flamboyant, witty homosexual with his legacy of society comedies and a few children's stories (he hated the idea and said they were 'written, not for children, but for childlike people from eighteen to eighty') is still alive and in rude health. *De Profundis* and *The Ballad of Reading Gaol* are explained away as post-prison writings of a largely autobiographical nature; the poetry is, for the most part, seen as derivative and slight; *The Picture of Dorian Gray* qualifies for inclusion in the canon of lightweight Wilde on account of its sparkling dialogue and Gothic theme; and the rest of the writings tend to be ignored. This may seem a harsh judgement but I am afraid that a bibliography of Wilde's writings in print over the last thirty years would prove my point. Publishers have pandered to public taste in Wilde, and Wilde at his most thought-provoking has not been in demand. Richard Ellmann edited a single-volume edition of Wilde's critical writings twenty-five years ago and, apart from collected works, they have not been seen between two covers since. Isobel Murray's editions for Oxford University Press have included some of the essays together with an eloquent plea in her introductions that we look at him in greater depth, but there is little evidence of it outside the academic world.

When Robert Ross, his literary executor, first had the Collected Works published in 1908, more than a third of its pages were taken up with Wilde's essays, lectures and reviews. Including *De Profundis* they span the whole of his writing life from 1879 to 1897 and serve as a remarkable key to his intellectual development. This may sound an extravagant claim, but there is more of the unadorned Wilde to be found in them than anywhere else in his work; it was even said that Wilde himself had a higher opinion of his best essays than the rest of his writings. Of 'The Decay of Lying' he wrote to Violet Fane: 'It is meant to bewilder the masses by its fantastic form; *au fond* it is of course serious'. For one who spent most of his time mocking the dull solemnity of the English, (in this essay in particular) it was, on the face of it an odd admission. In fact it is perfectly illustrative of the distinction he drew between the serious subject handled earnestly and the same treated with a lightness of touch, which turns it from a dumpling into a soufflé. By 1891 when *Intentions* was published his soufflés were superb.

'The Rise of Historical Criticism', it has to be said, is something of a dumpling. It was written in 1879 for the Chancellor's Essay Prize at Oxford which, in the event, was never awarded. Long-winded and academic in style, it draws clearly on Wilde's classical reading for his degree, though the breadth of his reading and his knowledge of modern historians was already impressive. While appearing to side with the rationality of historical criticism against primitive superstition and myth, there is a point at which one senses a sneaking admiration for the fictitious speeches which find their way into the narratives of Herodotus, Thucydides and Tacitus. The seeds are already sown for Vivian's opening speech in 'The Decay of Lying' ten years on.

Similarly uncharacteristic of the later Wilde was the first lecture which he gave on his American tour in 1882. Entitled 'The English Renaissance', in its first form it was over-long and over-theoretical. He had borrowed heavily from Ruskin, Morris and Pater, often verbatim, and attempted some kind of synthesis between the Whistler/Rossetti school of creative art and the more down-to-earth applications of the decorative arts movement as championed by Morris and Ruskin. The subtleties were lost on many in his American audiences who were often bored and showed it. Within a month the lecture had undergone a radical transformation to become 'The Decorative Arts' – shorter, simpler and altogether more appealing – which he fine-tuned, adding appropriate anecdotes as he travelled around the country. Kevin O'Brien (see bibliography) points out the disservice done by Robert Ross in reproducing his own edition of 'The English Renaissance' in the 1908 *Collected Works* when the final version of 'The Decorative Arts' (reproduced here) was the main lecture for his American tour from mid-February onwards. His second lecture, 'The House Beautiful', reserved for towns in which he had two engagements, was written during a week's break from lecturing in Chicago. Engagingly colloquial and passably witty, it is much more along the stylistic lines of later Wilde but the content suffers from its reliance on the established opinions of others: the iconoclastic, individual Wilde has still to emerge.

Apart from providing him with a lifelong supply of gentle jibes at the Americans and their country and a perceptive and amusing lecture on his return, this baptism by fire seems to have confirmed for Wilde the importance of two stylistic principles which remain characteristic of nearly all his published work from then on. The power of humour to engage his audience, no matter how serious the subject matter, becomes a Wildean trademark. Writing to Marie Prescott early in 1883 about the comedy lines in *Vera* he says: 'Never be afraid that by raising a laugh you destroy tragedy. On the contrary you intensify it. Drama appeals to human nature and must have as its ulti-mate basis the science of psychology and physiology. Now one of the facts of physiology is the desire of any very intensified emotion to be relieved by some emotion that is its opposite. So I cannot cut out my comedy lines. Be-sides, the essence of good dialogue is interruption.'

The play itself, incidentally, was a flop but the juxtaposition of humour and seriousness, of wit and erudition he later developed through his book re-views and journalism to culminate with superb effect in the dialogues of *In-tentions*. The other matter of style was probably more of a reversion than an adoption. His lectures, which had started formal and stilted, took on a more relaxed almost conversational tone by the end of the tour and as they did, so the reviews became more favourable. Wilde, from the earliest days, was never more relaxed than in the drawing-room. His mother's *salon* in Mer-rion Square had been famous for its conversation as had been his former classics tutor at Trinity, J.P. Mahaffy, whose book on the subject he re-viewed (see 'Aristotle at Afternoon Tea'), lamenting the fact that Mahaffy did not write as he talked. For Wilde it is a style which runs easily through the journalism, feels slightly restricted by the formality of those essays not in dialogue form, and by the time of *Dorian Gray* is almost pure theatre with chunks of Lord Henry's and Dorian's exchanges finding a second life in *A Woman of No Importance*. The logical conclusion, as Owen Dudley Edwards has pointed out in his introduction to the Stories, was for this master of con-versation to burst the constraints of prose and finish up nightly addressing the largest drawing-room in London – the West End stage.

Of Wilde's journalism there is but a selection reproduced here, a cross-section of book-reviews, short essays and theatre notices, no more than a tiny percentage of his total output. Over the years it has provided a fertile hunt-ing-ground for critics chasing literary sources for Wilde's work but not enough has been done to evaluate some of the subjective opinions so fre-quently voiced there. Researchers may well have been reluctant to take him at face value given the inherent irony of some of the articles. Can we trust the printed opinions of a man who says at the end of 'The Truth of Masks': ' Not that I agree with everything I have said in this essay. There is much with which I entirely disagree. The essay simply represents an artistic standpoint. For in art there is no such thing as a universal truth. A Truth in art is that whose contradictory is also true'? Nevertheless there are odd pieces which seem to have a place in the Wildean puzzle even if they do not have a reliable significance in their own right. At the end of the first paragraph of his 1885 notice of 'A Handbook to Marriage', he expresses firmly egalitarian views on marriage and women's education. It is one of many instances. Another taken almost at random is from his regular column 'Literary and Other Notes' for *The Woman's World* in December 1887 where he remarks on the success of two young women at university which 'shows how worthy women are of that higher culture and education which has been so tardily and, in some in-stances, so grudgingly granted to them'. In isolation such remarks might be seen as condescending, but in their context, and taken together with other evidence throughout his writings of Wilde's interest in women's position in society, they are unusually advanced for the time. In the same article on the subject of educating the poor he wrote: 'In these cold crowded cities of the North, the proper basis for morals, using the word in its wide Hellenic signification, is to be found in architecture not in books.' In the light of current debate on the depersonalising effect of cheap inner city housing and its effect on crime, Wilde was surprisingly close to the mark.

Intentions is an uneven collection. 'The Truth of Masks' which had been published six years before as 'Shakespeare and Stage Costume' seems to have been added in as a make-weight piece. Wilde incorporated one or two changes into the original, together with a new conclusion which sounds as much of an afterthought as it indeed was. The title is changed to appear less pedestrian but promises more than it delivers. A short while after publication when approached for the French translation rights to the four essays, Wilde sensibly suggested substituting 'The Soul of Man'.

His fascination with the artist and crime in 'Pen, Pencil and Poison' has an uncomfortable premonitory ring about it. Some years before he had prepared a lecture on the Bristol forger Thomas Chatterton who clearly exercised a similar fascination on him. 'One can fancy an intense personality being created out of sin,' he says. 'The fact of a man being a poisoner is nothing against his prose. The domestic virtues are not the true basis of art.' Surprising perhaps that Wilde's prosecutor, Ned Carson, didn't bring that one up in court as well. It raises the interesting conjecture as to what extent his own excursions into the Victorian homosexual underworld were prompted by a Baudelairean *nostalgie de la boue'* – 'feasting with panthers' as he later called it in *De Profundis*.

'The Critic as Artist' and 'The Decay of Lying' are probably Wilde at his intellectually most sparkling. There is a deliciously subversive quality about both of them and presented in dialogue form he is able to take as many stances as he wishes, to argue with himself and still remain unaligned. The first, as Ellmann has pointed out, was an attempt to tweak Matthew Arnold's nose over a famous lecture given in 1864 on 'The Function of Criticism' in which he stated that 'the aim of criticism is to see the object as in itself it really is'. Wilde's view is that the critic should see the object as it really is not. The critic should be freed from his subordinate role and eventually through knowledge become more creative than the creative artist himself, finally assuming a sort of Christ-like suffering through the burden of omniscience. 'The Decay of Lying', less ambitious in scope, argues against the contemporary trend towards realism, even naturalism in art – 'our monstrous worship of facts' as Wilde puts it. Throughout both essays there is a strong sense of his championing of the individual, the artist set apart by his beliefs and convictions which finds its ultimate expression in *De Profundis*.

The fanciful flights of ideas in the dialogues 'iridescent with fancy and winged with paradox' give way in 'The Soul of Man' to an entirely different approach. Wilde admits that his solution to encouraging the individual in a socialist society is Utopian, but as he says: 'A map of the world that does not include Utopia is not worth even glancing at, for it leaves out the one country at which Humanity is always landing.' Shaw recalled years later being told that Wilde had attended a socialist meeting in Westminster at which he had been speaking and how it had prompted Wilde to try his hand at an essay on socialism. The result, it is said, was ridiculed by the Fabians. It has never been difficult to raise objections to some of the arguments but it is increasingly clear almost exactly 100 years after it was written, that the tyranny of communism in Eastern Europe has been forced to give way to the acceptance of the individual even if not entirely on Wilde's Utopian terms. More interesting still was Robert Ross's discovery on going to Russia in 1911 that 'The Soul of Man' had become a best-selling tract and had gone through dozens of editions since Wilde's death.

The story of *De Profundis*, Wilde's letter from Reading Goal to Alfred Douglas, is as eventful in its own small way, as the life of its author, including a posthumous trial and a fifty-year spell under lock and key. It was not until Wilde had been in prison for fourteen months, until he had passed from Pentonville to Wandsworth to Reading that he was finally allowed writing materials in his cell. This privilege was granted exceptionally by the Chairman of the Prison Commissioners, Sir Evelyn Ruggles-Brise, subject to certain conditions, principally that pen and paper were to be removed each night at locking-up and anything written was to be submitted to the governor. At first Wilde only had a coarsely bound notebook, but as he wrote to a friend in September 1896: 'I take notes of books I read, and copy lines and phrases in poets: the mere handling of pen and ink helps me . . . I cling to my notebook: before I had it my brain was going in very evil circles.' Then early in 1897 he started on his letter to Douglas. Within three months it was complete and his intention was to send it to Robert Ross, who was to have two typed copies made and send the original to Douglas. However the Prison Commissioners flatly refused to allow the letter to be sent out and instructed Major Nelson, the governor, to keep it and give it to the prisoner on his release. Wilde finally handed Ross the manuscript when they met in Dieppe on 20 May, but because of its length the typing was not complete until August. Ross, so he later testified, then kept the original and sent one of the copies to Douglas and from that moment – silence. By October, after an emotional reunion, Wilde and Douglas had set up house in Naples, the potentially explosive recriminations in the letter ignored or more probably unread. In later years Douglas initially admitted receiving a long document from Ross and throwing it into the river Marne after reading the first few pages; later he denied ever having received it at all. Wilde never mentions it again.

In 1905, five years after his friend's death, Robert Ross felt that the time was right to give the world an expurgated version of the letter. About one third was published by Methuen to generally good press reviews including one by Douglas, oblivious that he was the intended recipient. In 1909 after publishing a slightly enlarged version in the *Collected Works*, Ross deposited the manuscript in the British Museum with the proviso that it was to be sealed for fifty years. And there it would have remained had Arthur Ransome not referred to it in his 1912 biography of Wilde as being 'addressed . . . to a man to whom Wilde felt that he owed some, at least, of the circumstances of his public disgrace'. Douglas immediately sued author, publisher and the Times book-club distributing the book, and when the case came to court, the manuscript had to be produced from the British Museum to support Ransome's plea of justification. Some of the unpublished portions, fiercely critical of Douglas's character, were read out. At one stage Douglas was nearly held in contempt of court for refusing to be present at the readings. In the end the jury decided that the libel was justified and he lost his case.

In 1927 my father decided to sell a large collection of Wilde's letters which had been left to him on Ross's death in 1918. Among them was the letter instructing Ross to make copies of *De Profundis* and to send Douglas the original. It prompted Douglas to press his claim to the Museum for ownership of the manuscript. The Trustees refused to hand it over. Had they done so, given Douglas's attitude at the time, it would almost certainly have been destroyed. It was not until 1949, four years after Douglas's death, that my father was finally able to publish the work from the single typescript copy which Ross had kept and bequeathed to him. Even that was littered with errors and omissions and it was not until 1962, once the manuscript was open to the public, that the first complete and accurate version was published in *The Letters of Oscar Wilde*.

It is difficult to read *De Profundis* without conflicting emotions. The compassion for a man of Wilde's sensibilities being broken in prison for what today is not even an offence; the astonishment at his arrogance, his ego, the extraordinary projection of himself into the figure of the suffering artist, crucified Christ-like by society; the touches of genuine humility. Above all, it is a record of those last two years spent with Douglas before he lost his reason and allowed himself (willingly) to be used as a pawn in the game between Douglas and his father. Douglas always maintained that it was nothing but lies, which was hard to believe then, and is now seen to be false from the corroborative evidence elsewhere. It is made all the more poignant when one realises that within three and a half years of writing it he was dead and had never seen his wife and children again.

Now, long after his death Wilde still manages to put up his mask of clever superficiality, designed, one feels, to conceal any great seriousness of thought, while revealing just enough to counter accusations of banality. The world is expected to view him as an enigma, Sphinx-like, countering question with paradox, always one step ahead and just out of reach of the critic's scalpel. 'Be warned in time, James, and remain, as I do, incomprehensible,' he wrote to Whistler in 1885. 'To be great is to be misunderstood.' But in this collection of miscellaneous pieces he has left the reader just enough clues to look behind the scenes from where, in the end, an even greater man may emerge by being that much better understood.

THE HOUSE BEAUTIFUL

The decorative arts have flourished most when the position of women was highly honoured, when woman occupied that place on the social scale which she ever ought to do. One of the most striking facts of history is that art was never so fine, never so delicate as where women were highly honoured, while there has been no good decorative work done in any age or any country where women have not occupied a high social position. It has been from the desire of women to beautify their households that decorative art has always received its impulse and encouragement. Women have natural art instincts, which men usually acquire only after long special training and study; and it may be the mission of the women in this country to revive decorative art into honest, healthy life.

In asking you to build and decorate your houses more beautifully, I do not ask you to spend large sums, as art does not depend in the slightest degree upon extravagance or luxury, but rather the procuring of articles which, however cheaply purchased and unpretending, are beautiful and fitted to impart pleasure to the observer as they did to the maker. And so I do not address those millionaires who can pillage Europe for their pleasure, but those of moderate means who can, if they will, have designs of worth and beauty before them always and at little cost.

Nothing that is made is too trivial or too poor for art to ennoble, for genius can glorify stone, metal, and wood by the manner in which these simple materials are fashioned and shaped. Why, the most valuable curio in an art museum is, perhaps, a little urn out of which a Greek girl drew water from a well over two thousand years ago and made of the clay on which we walk, yet more artistic than all the dreadful silver centre-pieces of modern times, with their distorted camels and electroplated palm-trees.

Today even a man of taste and wealth cannot always get his ideas embodied in art; he cannot escape the ugly surroundings of the age or procure any but the shoddy articles which are usually made. Nor will your art improve until you seek your workmen and educate them to higher views of their relation to art, and reveal to them the possibilities of their callings, for the great difficulty that stands in the way of your artistic development is not a lack of interest in art, not a lack of love for art, but that you do not honour the handi-craftsman sufficiently, and do not recognise him as you should; all art must begin with the handicraftsman, and you must reinstate him into his rightful position, and thus make labour, which is always honourable, noble also.

And you must have here a school of decorative art where the principles of good taste and the simpler truths about design would be taught, for the workman's technical knowledge of his craft makes it easy to teach him the practice of art principles. And this school should be in direct relation with manufacture and commerce. If a manufacturer wanted a new pattern for a carpet, or a new design for wallpaper, he could go to this school, and offer a prize for the best design for the purpose he required. In this way everyone will learn that it is more practical to build and decorate in an artistic manner.

In the question of decoration the first necessity is that any system of art should bear the impress of a distinct individuality; it is difficult to lay down rules as to the decoration of dwellings because every home should wear an individual air in all its furnishings and decorations. This individuality in most cases up to the present has been left to the upholsterers, with the consequence of a general sameness about many dwellings which is not worth looking at, for the decorations of a house should express the feeling of those who live in it. There are, however, certain broad principles of art which should be generally observed, and within which there is plenty of room for the play of individual tastes. Have nothing in your house that has not given pleasure to the man who made it and is not a pleasure to those who use it. Have nothing in your house that is not useful or beautiful; if such a rule were followed out, you would be astonished at the amount of rubbish you would get rid of. Let there be no sham imitation of one material in another, such as paper representing marble, or wood painted to resemble stone, and have no machine-made ornaments. Let us have everything perfectly bare of ornament rather than have any machine-made ornament; ornament should represent the feeling in a man's life, as of course nothing machine-made can do; and, by the way, a man who works with his hands alone is only a machine.

As regards materials for houses: if rich enough, you will probably have marble. I would not object to this, but don't treat it as if it were ordinary stone, and build a house of mere blocks of it, like those great plain, staring, white structures so common in this country. I hope you will employ workmen competent to beautify it with delicate tracings and that you will have it beautifully inlaid with coloured marbles, as at Venice, to lend it colour and warmth. And next – stone. The use of the natural hues of stone is one of the real signs of proper architecture. This country affords unusual facilities for using different varieties of stones, in every variety of hue, from pale yellow to purple, red to orange, green to grey and white, and beautiful harmonies may be achieved in ingraining them. Let the painter's work be reserved for the inner chambers.

If one cannot build in marble or coloured stones, there remains red brick or wood. Red brick is warm and delightful to look at and is the most beautiful and simple form of those who have not much to spend. In England we build of red brick, and the stately homes from the reign of the Tudors down to that of George II give good designs for brick houses. Cut brick gives you the opportunity of working in terracotta ornamentation, the most beautiful of all exterior decorations – the old Lombard's special prize, and an art we are trying to revive in England.

Wood is the universal material. Wood buildings I like, but wish to see them painted in a better way. You must have warmer colours: there is far too much white and that cold grey colour used; they never look well in large bodies and are dreary in wet weather and glaring in fine weather; imitate rather the rich browns and olive-greens found in nature. The frame house could be made more joyous to look upon with the air of the carver. Every child should be taught woodcarving, and I recommend the establishment in this city of a school of design for the sole purpose of teaching woodcarving. Even the poor Swiss shepherd boy spends his leisure time doing beautiful carving instead of reading detestable novels. Americans might carve as well, and I am sadly disappointed that you do not develop this art more.

All ornaments should be carved, and have no cast-iron ornaments, nor any of those ugly things made by machinery. You should not have cast-iron railings fixed outside the house, which boys are always knocking down, and very rightly too, for they always look cheap and shabby. If possible have beaten ironwork; of all the metal works in this country, so far as it relates to cast iron, it is a shame that none are nobly or beautifully wrought like the beaten globes of even the poorest Italian cities. The old iron ornaments of Verona that were worked by hand out of the noble metal into beautiful figures are as beautiful and strong now as when wrought three or four hundred years ago by artistic handicraftsmen. Finally, your black-leaded knocker should give way to a bright brass one.

Within the house: the hall should not be papered, since the walls are exposed more or less to the elements by the frequent opening and closing of the door; it could be wainscoted with some of America's beautiful woods, such as the maple, or distempered with ordinary paint. Wainscoting makes the house warm, it is easily done by any carpenter, and it will admit of fine work in panel painting, which is a style of decoration most desirable, and one that is growing greatly in favour.

Don't carpet the floor: ordinary red brick tiles make a warm and beautiful floor, and I prefer it to the geometrically arranged tiles of the present day. There should be no pictures in the hall, for it is no place for a good picture, and a poor one should be put nowhere. It is a mere passageway, except in stately mansions, and no picture should be placed where you have not time to sit down and reverence and admire and study it.

Hat racks are, I suppose, necessary. I have never seen a really nice hat rack; the ordinary one is more like some horrible instrument of torture than anything useful or graceful, and it is perhaps the ugliest thing in the house. A large painted oak chest is the best stand for cloaks; for hats, a pretty rack in wood to hang on the wall in light wood or bamboo would be best. A few large chairs would complete the furniture in the hallway. Have none of those gloomy horrors, stuffed animals or stuffed birds, in the hall, or anywhere else under glass cases. Plain marble tables, such as I have seen in America in such number, should not be tolerated unless the marble is beautifully inlaid and the wood carved.

As regards rooms generally: in America the great fault in decoration is the entire want of harmony or a definite scheme in colour; there is generally a collection of a great many things individually pretty but which do not combine to make a harmonious whole. Colours resemble musical notes: a single false colour or false note destroys the whole. Therefore, in decorating a room one keynote of colour should predominate; it must be decided before hand what scheme of colour is desired and have all else adapted to it, like the answering calls in a symphony of music; otherwise, your room will be a museum of colours. With regard to choice of colour, the disciples of the new school of decorative art are said to be very fond of gloomy colours. Well, we set great value on toned or secondary colours, because all decoration means gradually ascending colours, while bright colours should be kept for ornament. On the walls secondary colours should be used, and the ceiling should never be painted in bright colours; the best Eastern embroidery, for instance, is filled with light colours. Start with a low tone as the keynote, and then you get the real value of primary colours by having little bits of colour, beautiful embroidery, and artwork set like precious gems in the more sombre colours. If you have the whole room and things generally in bright colours, the capabilities of the room are exhausted for all other colour effects, and you would have to have fireworks for ornaments to set it off. All depends upon the graduation of colour; look at the rose and see how all its beauty depends upon its exquisite gradations of colour, one answering to the other.

Mr Whistler has recently done two rooms in London which are marvels of beauty. One is the famous Peacock Room, which I regard as the finest thing in colour and art decoration that the world has ever known since Correggio painted that wonderful room in Italy where the little children are dancing on the walls; everything is of the colours in peacocks' feathers, and each part so coloured with regard to the whole that the room, when lighted up, seems like a great peacock tail spread out. It cost £3,000. Mr Whistler finished the other room just before I came away – a breakfast room in blue and yellow, and costing only £30. The walls are distempered in blue, the ceiling is a light and warm yellow; the floor is laid with a richly painted matting in light yellow, with a light line or leaf here and there of blue. The woodwork is all cane-yellow, and the shelves are filled with blue and white china; the curtains of white serge have a yellow border tastefully worked in, and hang in careless but graceful folds. When the breakfast-table is laid in this apartment, with its light cloth and its dainty blue and white china, with a cluster of red and yellow chrysanthemums in an old Nankin vase in the centre, it is a charming room, catching all the warm light and taking on of all surrounding beauty, and giving to the guest a sense of joyousness, comfort, and rest. Nothing could be simpler, it costs little, and it shows what a great effect might be realised with a little and simple colour.

A designer must imagine in colour, must think in colour, must see in colour. Your workmen should be taught to work more freely in colours, and this can only be done by accustoming them to beautiful ones. Even in imaginative art predominance must now be given to colour: a picture is primarily a flat surface coloured to produce a delightful effect upon the beholder, and if it fails of that, it is surely a bad picture. The aim of all art is simply to make life more joyous.

You should have such men as Whistler among you to teach you the beauty and joy of colour. When he paints a picture, he paints by reference not to the subject, which is merely intellectual, but to colour. I was speaking to Mr Whistler once, before a great critic, of what could be done with one colour. The critic chose white as the colour offering fewest tones; Mr Whistler painted his beautiful *Symphony in White*, which you no doubt have imagined to be something quite bizarre. It is nothing of the sort. Think of a cool grey sky with white clouds, a grey sea flecked with the crests of white-capped waves; a grey balcony on which are two little girls clad in pure white leaning over the railing; an almond tree covered in white blossoms is by the side of the balcony, from which one of the girls is idly plucking with white hands the petals which flutter across the picture. Such pictures as this one are of infinitely more value than horrible pictures of historical scenes; here are no extensive intellectual schemes to trouble you and no metaphysics, of which we have had quite enough in art. If the simple and unaided colour strikes the right keynote, the whole conception is made clear. I doubt not that our Aesthetic movement has given to the world an increased sense of the value of colour, and that in time a new science of the art of dealing in colour will be evolved.

But to return to our room. If there is much, or heavy furniture, the design on the walls should be rich; if the furniture is limited, or light, the design should be light and simple. The walls cannot often in this country be hung with tapestry; therefore, they should be papered. However, do not use white and gold paper; divide the wall into two uneven parts, either with a dado and paper from it to the cornice, or with a frieze and paper from it downwards; I do not advise the use of both unless the walls are very high. You will want a joyous paper on the wall, full of flowers and pleasing designs, but the dado should not be of paper, but either of woods or some of the beautiful Japanese mattings which come to this country, so as to carry out the principles of utility, that is, to protect the lower and more exposed part of the wall from being scratched or marred by the furniture coming in contact with it. Nor should the frieze be of paper; it should be painted, and the remainder of the wall papered.

About the ceiling: the ceiling is a great problem always – what to do with that great expanse of white plaster. Don't paper it; that gives one the sensation of living in a paper box, which is not pleasant. The ceiling should be broken up in texture, so that the light may constantly play upon it, and not lie in a dead way. If you are having a house built, contract with the builder to leave the main rafters of the ceiling exposed in outline; this conveys a sense of solidity and support, and there may be worked out the most delightful effects in finishing between the rafters, as is done in panel work or plaster decorations. For ceiling decoration, the old style of plaster may be used, but not the modern plaster – it dries almost immediately and is a glaring glossy white; the beautiful old plaster of the Queen Anne period, often so beautifully designed, was of a finer, more plastic texture, it took a long time to dry, and one had time to mould it. If you cannot use plaster, the ceiling might be panelled in wood, with paintings or stamped leather in the centres. If you cannot have the cross-beams or woodwork, then have it painted in a colour which predominates in the room, but do not in any event paper it; on papered ceilings the light falls dull and lifeless and sodden.

Have no great flaring gas-chandelier in the middle of the room; if you have, it does not make much difference how you adorn and beautify the room, or whether it is done at all, for in six months' time the gas will discolour and ruin all you do. Also, no light should shine directly in one's eyes; the room shall be lit by reflection of the light rather than by direct light. If you must have gas, let the room be lighted from side-brackets on the wall, and each jet of flame should be covered with delicate shades or hidden by screens so that the light may be reflected from the walls and ceiling. Lamps and wax candles are still better as they give a softer light, are best to read by, do not destroy any other decoration, and are very much prettier and healthier than gas.

As regards the floor: don't carpet it all over, as nothing is more unhealthy or inartistic than modern carpets; carpets absorb the dust, and it is impossible to keep them as perfectly clean as anything about us should be. In this, as in all things, art and sanitary regulations go hand in hand. It is better to use a parquetry flooring around the sides and rugs in the centre; if inlaid or stained floors are not practical, have them laid with pretty matting and strewn with those very handsome and economical rugs from China, Persia, and Japan.

As regards windows: builders do not realise that there is a difference between light and glare; most modern windows are much too large and glaring, and are made as if you only wanted them to look out of; they annihilate light and let in a glare that is destructive to all sense of repose, and by which one cannot write or work or enjoy any comfort; you are obliged to pull down the shutters whenever you enter a room. The small, old windows just let in light enough. If you have big windows in your house, let a portion of them be filled with stained glass – of course, I do not mean such stained glass representations as are seen in churches and cathedrals – I advise merely the use of toned green or grey glass with little bright spots of pure colour which give a more subdued light, a pleasing blending of colours, and a sense of quiet and repose.

As regards style of furniture: avoid the 'early English' or Gothic furniture; the Gothic, now so much thought of in this country, though honestly made and better than modern styles, is really so heavy and massive that it is out of place when surrounded with the pretty things which we of this age love to gather around us; it is very well for those who lived in castles and who needed occasionally to use it as a means of defence or as a weapon of war. A lighter and more graceful style of furniture is more suitable for our peaceful times. Eastlake furniture is more rational than much that is modern: it is economical, substantial, and enduring, and carried out Mr Eastlake's idea of showing the work of the craftsman. However, it is a little bare and cold, has no delicate lines, and does not look like refined work for refined people; Eastlake furniture is Gothic without the joyous colour of the Gothic, and pretty ornaments of glass are out of place in a Gothic room for they would be an anachronism. The furniture of the Italian Renaissance is too costly, and French furniture, gilt and gaudy, is very vulgar, monstrous, and unserviceable.

The style most liked in England, and the one which is the most suitable in every way for you, is that known as Queen Anne furniture. Why it goes by the name of Queen Anne I do not know; it was designed and used one hundred years before the reign of that monarch, but there is no reason why we should not use that name as well as any other, so long as we are not deceived as to its meaning. This furniture is beautiful without being gaudy, so delicate in appearance and yet so strong. It is good furniture made by refined people for refined people, and is so well adapted to our styles of crockery, to our light decorations, and our system of ornamentation, and it is as beautiful as any that can be found in Italy. It is a furniture which will last a very long time; pieces of very old furniture of this kind are to be seen in a great many houses in England and which are still as sound as they ever were. It is most comfortable too: what seem to be stiff and straight lines are really very delicately curved lines, exquisite in their symmetry, and while the cushion of the modern chair is a monster of iron springs, that of the Queen Anne period slopes back and is made to fit the figure, which gives great ease and thereby combines comfort and beauty. It is most beautiful, too, in colour: the rich colour of the mahogany and the bright brass catches all the warm lights, and is the most cheerful of all designs. Modern furniture should be better than the old, with all our improved machinery and our great variety of woods to choose from, but it is not.

When I advise you to have Queen Anne furniture, I do not want you to send to Chippendale in England for it; it could be made here, and to that end a good school of design should be established. In your school of design let the pupils, instead of painting pictures, work at decoration and designs, and their work will soon be in all your houses. Young designers should begin by painting on furniture, which they could really learn to do well in six months and soon be able to give delight by their work. In Bavaria the furniture is beautiful because of the colour alone. The people of Switzerland adorn their own houses, and there is no reason why as great excellence in making all these things should not be reached by the people of this country as by any other part of the world. But pottery takes more knowledge to secure good results; you have to know a great deal about the potters' wheel: you have to understand practically the results of burning, of overglazing and underglazing, and other processes.

An invaluable school of art would be a museum, which, instead of showing stuffed giraffes and other horrible objects which scientific men wish to see gathered together, would contain all kinds of simple decorative work, different styles of furniture, dress, etc., made in different periods, and especially in the periods when English artists made beautiful things, and where local artisans and handicraftsmen could go and study the styles and patterns of the noble designers and artisans who worked before them. Such efforts at cultivation would be appreciated by the working people, as witnessed by the scene in the South Kensington museum in London on Saturday night, where artisans are to be seen, notebook in hand, gathering ideas to be used in their next week's work. A good museum would teach your artisans more in one year than they would learn by means of books or lectures in ten years.

You are probably provided with a mantelpiece, about which you were not consulted; it is probably dreary, and cold white marble with machine-made ornamentation that is always so coarse and heavy. In that case there is nothing for it but to hide it as you best can: you might do it with matting, or you might cover it with carved wood and build your mantel up to the ceiling with little shelves on which you may place your rare china or ornaments; at the back of the shelves Spanish leather may be placed, or panels which you can paint yourself; in the centre of the shelves a space might be left for a little circular mirror. The great gilt mirrors of today are not only costly, but destroy all attempts at decoration; mirrors were meant to concentrate light in a room, which is the beauty of the little circular mirrors.

Your fireplace should not be of highly polished steel, nor should there ever be a cast-iron grate which, as a rule, is heavy and coarse. The porcelain stoves used in Holland are beautiful, and I am glad always to see the healthy, old-English open fireplace; but you should have red tiles, an iron basket, and bright brass tongs and shovel. The amount of colour which one can get into a fireplace is simply incalculable: the fire, the red tiles, the brass work – everything is full of colour.

The pictures hung up in most of the houses I have visited in America were dull, commonplace and tawdry. Poor pictures are worse than none. If there are good pictures in the house make the decoration subordinate; if you have not good pictures confine yourself entirely to decorative art for wall ornaments. For instance, sconces of beaten brass light up the wall. It is foolish to hang small plates on the wall, for small plates should be on a shelf and not stuck about. Large pieces of china, or large, noble Japanese dishes could be suspended on the wall and arranged with an idea of taste, and their beauty should be enhanced at night by the light of candles instead of gas.

Embroidery you will have, of course, but don't, I pray you, have everything covered with embroidery as if it were washing day. Don't do little things with embroidery, but cover large surfaces with delicate designs; good embroidery must be done on a larger scale than you do it: cushions, curtains, covers, and every large surface should be covered with delicate embroidery patterns, but don't use silk – it is too iridescent.

One must have a piano I suppose, but it is a melancholy thing, and more like a dreadful, funereal packing-case in form than anything else. Some people cover it up with embroidery, which is well enough if the piano is out of tune, or one plays badly, or if one does not love music: the cloth cover entirely spoils the tone, and no one who really loves music would think of using one. Some people put china and books on it, as if it were a table, but this is clearly wrong. The best form for pianos, the upright grand, gives grand opportunities for inlaying or for painting; the first school of decorative art in America which decorates pianos successfully will create an era in decorative art. It should not be made of rosewood, nor be highly polished, nor should manufacturers put any machine-made ornaments upon them, but should give us them perfectly plain, and then we could beautify them with colour. It must not be supposed that I am so impractical as to object to machinery, but none of us want to hear even the choicest lines ground out by a music box, and it is the same with other arts; machinery's mission is to lighten men's labour. The revolving stool should be sent to the museum of horrors, and a seat large enough for two players be substituted.

Flowers you will have, of course, about your room, but don't have all kinds of flowers vaguely arranged or crowded together in great bouquets. Some flowers, such as roses or violets whose greatest beauty is their colour, are made to be seen in masses, but flowers which are perfect in form, like the narcissus, daffodil, or lily, should be placed singly in a small Venetian glass so that they can hang naturally as they are seen upon their stem.

Speaking of glass: never have cut glass; it is too common for use, and is so hard and sharp, and without grace in its lines. Have delicate blown glass. I dislike very much the American dinner service: plain white china is too cold, and modern designs in silver are of vulgar design. People of taste cannot help expressing their indignation, upon going into the modern jewellery establishment, at the sight of the great amount of costly material that is ruined in the manufacture of centre-pieces. The beauty of the table depends upon the quality and appearance of the china and glass; for a good permanent dinner set have Japanese or blue and white china, and have old silverware until your artisans learn to make it. There should be flowers on the table too.

Those of you who have old china use it I hope. There is nothing so absurd as having good china stuck up in a cabinet merely for show while the family drink from delft; if you can't use good old china without breaking it, then you don't deserve to have it. Whatever you have that is beautiful if for use, then you should use it, or part with it to someone who will. The handling of coarse things begets coarse handling: in a restaurant in San Francisco I saw a Chinese navvy drinking his tea out of a most beautiful cup as delicate as the petal of a flower, while I had to drink, at one of the first-class hotels in which thousands were spent on gaudy colours and gilding, out of a cup which was an inch-and-a-half thick; these navvies do not break these delicate cups, because they are accustomed to handling them. You have to use delicate things to accustom your servants to handle them securely; it will be a martyrdom for a long time at first, but you may be content to suffer in so good a cause. I bought Venetian glass when I was at college, and for the first term my servant broke one glass every day, and a decanter on Sunday, but I persevered in buying them, and during the succeeding terms of my whole stay at college he did not break a single piece.

About pictures: I have to see the ruining of so many fine pictures in the framing, by reason of the frame being out of all keeping with the picture. I don't like to see the great, glaring, pretentious gold frames for fine pictures; use gold frames only where the picture can plainly bear it, and in all other cases picture frames should be tinted a middle tone between the picture and the wall. Oil paintings in gold frames should be richly hung with velvet bands, while water-colours and etchings should be suspended by cords.

Nothing is more saddening, nothing more melancholy, than having to look upon pictures hung in lines; you might as well set ten or twenty young girls on a platform playing one tune on pianos at the same time. Two pictures should not be hung side by side – they will either kill one another, or else commit artistic suicide; to stick them in rows makes me wonder why people like pictures at all. Your pictures may be hung with good effect upon a chocolate shade of paper, but not having geometrical figures, which distract the attention. They should be hung from a ledge under the frieze and should be hung also on the eye-line; the habit in America of hanging them up near the cornices struck me as irrational at first; it was not until I saw how bad the pictures were that I realised the advantage of the custom.

Put no photographs of paintings on your walls – they are libels on great masters; there is no way to get a worse idea of a painter than by a photograph of his work; I don't think I ever saw a photograph that was a decoration, for the first thing you should see is its beauty of colour, and there is no colour of worth for decorative purposes in photographs. They are ridiculous pretences, and should be kept in portfolios to show to friends whose friendship is not treacherous. As a painting should be an exquisite arrangement of colours, so an engraving should be an exquisite arrangement of black and white, which the photograph never is. Most modern engravings are not good; they may be hung on walls, or framed in plain wood and placed on a shelf; woodcuts of masters like Doré may be framed in wood and hung on the walls.

Every house should have some good casts of old Greek work if possible. There can be no nobler influence in a room than a marble Venus of Milo: in the presence of an image so pure, no tongue would date to talk scandal. There should be casts of good men in the library.

And now books: an old library is one of the most beautifully coloured things imaginable; the old colours are toned down and they are so well bound, for whatever is beautiful is well made. Modern bookbinding is one of the greatest drawbacks to the beauty of many libraries – books are bound in all manner of gaudy colours. The best binding is white vellum, which in a few years looks like ivory, or calf, and with age takes on the tints of gold. You can't have all your books rebound. The only thing left is to have curtains to hide them out of sight until a more tasteful style than the modern one of binding prevails. When I landed in Boston I found my old publisher, who had moved from London, binding my poems in all those dreadful colours which I had spent my youth trying to abolish; he might have spared me, I thought.

As regards dress: the true nobility of dress is an important part of education, but there is much in the dress of modern times to discourage us. If it were not for the lovely dressing of the thirteenth and fourteenth centuries, the excellence of Venetian art would never have existed; but there is nothing in the styles of the present to give such models to the artists; I hardly dare suggest what must be the thought of the true sculptor when asked to work out the statue of a modern – his thought must be suicidal. There is nothing more indicative of moral decline than squalor and an indifference to dress: the money spent on modern dress is an extravagant waste.

People should not mar beautiful surroundings by gloomy dress; dress nowadays is altogether too sombre, and we should accustom ourselves to the use of more colour and brightness; there should always be a beautifully arranged composition of well-balanced light and shade. There would be more joy in life if we would accustom ourselves to use all the beautiful colours we can in fashioning our own clothes. The dress of the future, I think, will use drapery to a great extent and will abound with joyous colour.

One should have nothing on one's dress that has not some meaning or that is not useful; beauty in dress consists in its simplicity – all useless and encumbering bows, flounces, knots, and other such meaningless things so fashionable today are nothing but the foolish inventions of the milliner. All the evil of modern dressing has come from the failure to recognise that the right people to construct our apparel are artists, and not modern milliners, whose chief aim is to swell their bills.

Nothing is beautiful, such as tight corsets, which is destructive of health; all dress follows out the lines of the figure – it should be free to move about in, showing the figure. Anything that disfigures the form or blots out the beauty of the natural lines is ugly, and so a knowledge of anatomy as well as art is necessary in correct dressmaking. If one could fancy the Medicean Venus taken from her pedestal in the Louvre to Mr Worth's establishment in the Palais Royal to be dressed in modern French millinery, every single beautiful line would be destroyed, and no one would look at her a second time.

Go through a book of costumes, and you will find that when dress was most simple, it was most beautiful: one of the earliest forms is the ancient Greek drapery, which is most simple and so exquisite for your girls, but I must warn you that it is most difficult to design. And then I think we may be pardoned a little enthusiasm over the dress of the time of Charles II, so beautiful, indeed, that in spite of its invention being with the Cavaliers, it was copied by the Puritans. And the dress for the children at that time must not be passed over: it was a very golden age for the little ones; I don't think that they have ever looked so lovely as they do in the pictures of that time. And the ladies might study the costumes of the old Venetian ladies and pattern after them. If something more modern is desired, the dress of the last century in England was also particularly generous and graceful: it can be found in the style of dress painted by Sir Joshua Reynolds and by Gainsborough; there is nothing bizarre about it, and it is full of harmony and beauty. There should be nothing *outré* in dress; a man or woman of taste can so conform their dress that it will not merit disapproval but receive the praise of those who have an artistic eye.

Of all ugly things, nothing can exceed in ugliness artificial flowers, which, I am sure, none of you wear; and it is better not to wear any modern jewellery, since none of the designs are good. It is difficult to speak of the modern bonnet – there are no limits to indignation, but there are limits to language –

for the modern bonnet is an irrational monstrosity not affording the wearer the slightest use: it does not keep the sun off in summer nor the rain off in winter. The large hat of the last century was more sensible and useful, and nothing is more graceful in the world than a broad-brimmed hat. We have lost the art of draping the human form and have even discarded the graceful cloak with its deep folds for the unnatural and ungraceful jacket; the cloak, on the other hand, is always graceful, and is the simplest and most beautiful drapery ever devised.

The uncomfortable character of our present dress is shown by our willingness to adopt a new fashion every three months. All really beautiful dress is durable too, and if the beautiful is obtained, economy would be secured also. In these days, when we have suffered so dreadfully from the incursions of the modern milliners, we hear ladies boast that they do not wear a dress more than once; in the old days, when the dresses were decorated with beautiful designs and worked with exquisite embroidery, ladies rather took a pride in bringing out the garment and wearing it many times, and handing it down to their daughters, as something precious and beautiful for them to wear – a process which I think would be quite appreciated by modern husbands and fathers when called upon to settle the bills.

And how shall men dress? Men say they don't particularly care how they dress, and that it is little matter. I am bound to reply that I don't believe them and don't think that you do either. They dress in black and sober greys and browns because that is the custom, and their dress is not beautiful, either, in design, being careless and without harmony of style. In all my journeys through the country, the only well-dressed men I have seen in America were the miners of the Rocky Mountains; they wore a wide-brimmed hat which shaded their faces from the sun and protected them from the rain, and their flowing cloak, which is by far the most beautiful piece of drapery ever invented, may well be dwelt upon with admiration. Their high boots too were sensible and practical. These miners dressed for comfort and of course attained the beautiful. As I looked at them, I could not help thinking with regret of the time when these picturesque miners should have made their fortunes and would go West to assume again all the abomination of modern fashionable attire. Indeed, I made some of them promise that when they again appeared in the more crowded scenes of Eastern civilisation, they would still continue to wear their lovely costume, but I don't believe they will.

The dress of the men of the last century was graceful; the gentlemen might study for their pattern the noble and beautiful attire of George Washington; that brave and great man dressed with taste, as did other American gentlemen of his day. Men should dress more in velvet – grey or brown or black – as it catches the light and shade, while broadcloth is ugly as it does not absorb the light. Trousers become dirty in the street; knee-breeches are more comfortable and convenient – prettier to look at, too, and easier to keep out of the mud; high boots in the streets keep the mud off, but low shoes and silk stockings should be used in the drawing room. Finally, cloaks should be worn instead of coats.

In conclusion, what is the relation of art to morals? It is sometimes said that our art is opposed to good morals; but on the contrary, it fosters morality. Wars and the clash of arms and the meeting of men in battle must be always, but I think that art, by creating a common intellectual atmosphere between all countries might, if it could not overshadow the world with the silvery wings of peace, at least make men such brothers that they would not go out to slay one another for the whim or folly of some king or minister as they do in Europe; for national hatreds are always strongest where culture is lowest. And hence the enormous importance given to all the decorative arts in our English renaissance; we want children to grow up in England in the simple atmosphere of all fair things; the refining influence of art, begun in childhood, will be of the highest value to all of us in teaching our children to love what is beautiful and good, and hate what is evil and ugly. Then when a child grows up he learns that industrious we must be, but industry without art is simply barbarism.

For there never was an age that so much needed the spiritual ministry of art as the present. Today more than ever the artist and a love of the beautiful are needed to temper and counteract the sordid materialism of the age. In an age when science has undertaken to declaim against the soul and spiritual nature of man, and when commerce is ruining beautiful rivers and magnificent woodlands and the glorious skies in its greed for gain, the artist comes forward as a priest and prophet of nature to protest, and even to work against the prostitution or the perversion of what is lofty and noble in humanity and beautiful in the physical world, and his religion in its benefits to mankind is as broad and shining as the sun. There are grand truths and beauty in the Catholic pictorial art, and in the Protestant religious music, which no sectarian prejudices and no narrow-minded bigotry can keep the world from acknowledging and admiring. I urge you all not to become discouraged because ridicule is thrown upon those who have the boldness to run counter to popular prejudice; in time the true aesthetic principles will prevail. Throughout the world, in all times and in all ages, there have been those who have had the courage to advocate opinions that were for the time abhorred by the public. But if those who hold those opinions have the courage to maintain and defend them, it is absolutely certain that in the end the truth will prevail.

And so let it be for you to create an art that is made with the hands of the people, for the joy of the people too, an art that will be a democratic art, entering into the houses of the people, making beautiful the simplest vessels they contain, for there is nothing in common life too mean, in common things too trivial, to be ennobled by your touch, nothing in life that art cannot raise and sanctify.

THE DECORATIVE ARTS

In my lecture tonight I do not wish to give you any abstract definition of beauty; you can get along very well without philosophy if you surround yourselves with beautiful things; but I wish to tell you of what we have done and are doing in England to search out those men and women who have knowledge and power of design, of the schools of art provided for them, and the noble use we are making of art in the improvement of the handicraft of our country. I believe that every city produces every year a certain amount of artistic knowledge and artistic intellect, and it is our purpose to develop that intellect and use it for the creation of beautiful things.

Few people will deny that they are doing injury to themselves and their children by living outside the beauty of life, which we call art, for art is no mere accident of existence which men may take or leave, but a very necessity of human life, if we are to live as nature intended us to live, that is, unless we are content to be something less than men.

Now, one of the first questions you will ask me is, 'what art should we devote ourselves to in this country?' It seems to me that what you want most here is not that higher order of imaginative art of the poet and the painter, because they will take care of themselves, nothing will make or mar them, but there is an art that you can make or mar, and that is decorative art, the art that will hallow the vessels of everyday use, exerting its influence in the simplest and humblest of homes. If you develop art culture by beautifying the things around you, you may be certain that other arts will follow in the course of time. The art I speak of will be a democratic art made by the hands of the people and for the benefit of the people, for the real basis of all art is to be found in the application of the beautiful in things common to all and in the cultivation and development of this among the artisans of the day.

And what is the meaning of the term 'decorative art?' In the first place, it means the value the workman places on his work, it is the pleasure that he must take in making a beautiful thing. To progress in the decorative arts, to make chaste and elegant patterns of carpet or wall paper, even the little wreath of leaf or vine traced around the margin of cups we drink out of, requires more than mere machine work: it requires delicacy of hand, cultivated taste, and nobility of character. For the mark of all good art is not that the thing is done exactly or finely, for machinery may do as much, but that it is worked out with the tender, appealing vitality of the workman's heart and head.

No one takes any pleasure in doing bad or fraudulent work; the craving for the artistic finds a place in every heart, and the fair decorations with which we love to surround ourselves, and which we call art, bear a deeper, holier meaning that the mere money value of the workmanship, a meaning that places them far above the usual price, since in them we recognize those heart-throbs of joy, and keen thrills of intellectual pleasure known only to the maker of beautiful things. And so wherever good work and good decoration is found, it is a certain sign that the workman has laboured not only with his hands, but with his heart and his head also.

But one cannot get good work done unless the handicraftsman is furnished with rational and beautiful designs; if you have commonplace design, you must have commonplace work, and if you have commonplace work, you must have commonplace workmen; but really good design will produce thoroughly good workmen whose work is beautiful at the moment and for all time. Give the workman noble designs, dignify and ennoble his work, and through this, his life. I suppose that the poet will sing or the artist will paint regardless whether the world praises or blames; he has his own world and is independent of his fellow men, but the ordinary handicraftsman is almost entirely dependent upon your pleasure and opinion and upon the influences which surround him for his knowledge of form and colour. And so it is of the utmost importance that he be supplied with the noble productions of original minds so that he may acquire that artistic temperament without which there is no creation of art, there is no understanding of art, there is not even an understanding of life.

How necessary, then, when the artist and the poet have supplied the handicraftsman with beautiful designs, thoughts, and ideas, that in working them out he should be honoured with a loving encouragement and satisfied with fair surroundings. For the great difficulty that stands in the way of your artistic development is not a lack of interest in art, nor a lack of love for art, but that you do not honour the handicraftsman sufficiently, and do not recognize him as you should; all art must begin with the handicraftsman, and you must reinstate him into his rightful position. Until you do art will be confined to the few, for if art is not a luxury for the rich and idle, then it should be made beautiful for us to appear in the beautification of our houses. Nor will you honour the handicraftsman sufficiently until you can see that there is no nobler profession for your son to learn than the creation of the beautiful; we must be prepared to give to these crafts the best of our young men and young women, and when you have noble designs, you will attract these men and women of real refinement and knowledge to work for you.

You ask me to name the most practical advance in art in the last five years in England? It is this: of the young men with me at Oxford, men of position, taste, and high mental culture, one is now designing furniture, a second is working metal, a third is trying to revive the lost art of tapestry-making, and so on. Indeed, such progress has been made in England during the last five years in all branches of the decorative arts that I expect to see her take her place once again as the foremost of all nations in the cultivation and development of art and the encouragement of those who love to perpetuate in their handiwork the beauties about them.

But we are told that this is a practical age, and in the rush of business men have no time to think of delicate ornaments, that in the rush to catch a train a man cannot stop to examine the pattern of the carpet he is stepping over. We are told that if articles in everyday use are only honestly made, we are satisfied if they are not ornamental.

Indeed, honesty of work is essential to progress in a practical age, yet is this an honest age? This century has been marked by more dishonest workmanship and has produced more rubbish than any that preceded it. Every householder who furnishes a new residence discovers this in his carpets, which are badly designed, badly woven and dyed with cheap aniline dyes, and which become faded and shabby with one summer's sun; furniture is machine-made, and much of it is not even honestly joined, but simply glued, and becomes split and twisted in less than five years' time. The wonder is that we do not live out-of-doors. We must not be deceived by the attempt to draw the fine line of distinction between what is beautiful and what is useful. Utility is always on the side of the beautifully decorated article and the skill of the workman.

There is one article of furniture which has confronted me wherever I have gone on this continent, and that for absolutely horrid ugliness surpasses anything I have seen—the cast-iron American stove. If it had been left in its natural ugliness it might be endured as a necessary nuisance, like a dull relation or a rainy day, but manufacturers persist in decorating it with wreaths of black-leaded and grimy roses at the base and surmounting it with a dismal funereal urn—or, where they are more extravagant than usual, with two.

Thus it is that the dishonesty of the age has coined the most perfectly dreadful word at present forming our language—'second-hand'—the meaning of which is that the moment you begin to use anything it begins to decrease in value until after six months it is worth nothing. I hope that the word will fall into such complete disuse that when philologists in the future try to discover what it means they shall not be able.

For it must always be remembered that what is well and carefully made by an honest workman after a rational design increases in beauty and value as the years go on, like the walls of Gothic cathedrals, which contain old marbles still as beautiful as when the chisels of the old workmen first rang upon them, carved woods as lovely and durable as when the plane first smoothed their sides, and they are now more firmly set in the earth and more beautiful than when first built. And the old furniture brought over from Europe or made by the Pilgrims two hundred years ago, and which I saw in New England, is just as strong and as beautiful today as it was on the day it came from the hands of its artificers. Simple of design, yet honestly made, it does not depreciate in value as does our modern furniture, and you have the satisfaction of knowing that your grandparents used that furniture before you, and your grandchildren will use it after you are gone. So always will good work thrive, and so should it. If this term 'second-hand' is to be understood as it now is, then have your handicrafts fallen indeed.

Why, then, this dishonesty and hypocrisy in our workmanship, this exceeding hollowness of modern handicraft, of articles of furniture which tell a lie every moment of their existence, of so-called works of art that are unpunished crimes? It is because they are made by artisans who no longer love their work. The old furniture, so massive, strong and honest, was made by workmen who were familiar with the principles of beautiful design in an age when manual labour was considered noble and honourable.

Your art will not improve until you seek out your workman and give him as far as possible the right surroundings; for remember that the real test and virtue of a workman is not his earnestness, nor his industry even, but his power of design only; and that design is no offspring of idle fancy; it is the result of accumulative observation and delightful habit. All the teaching in the world is of no avail in art unless you surround your workman with happy influences and with delightful things; it is impossible for him to have right ideas about colour unless he sees the lovely colours of nature unspoiled about him, impossible for him to supply beautiful incident and action in his work unless he sees beautiful incident and action in the world about him, for to cultivate sympathy, you must be among living things and thinking about them, and to cultivate admiration you must be among beautiful things and looking at them. And so your houses and streets should be living schools of art where your workman may see beautiful forms as he goes to his work in the morning and returns to his home at eventide.

Go back to the eras of the highest decorative art and you will find it a time when the workman had beautiful surroundings; for the best periods of the decorative arts have been the ages of costume, when men and women wore noble attire and walked in beauty that could pass at once into marble and stone to be the admiration of all succeeding ages.

Think of what was the scene which presented itself in his afternoon walk to a designer of the Gothic school of Pisa: Nino Pisano or any of his men: on each side of a bright river saw rise a line of brighter palaces, arched and pillared and inlaid with deep red porphyry and with serpentine; along the quays before their gates were riding troops of knights, noble in face and form, dazzling in crest and shield; horse and man one labyrinth of quaint colour and gleaming light; the purple and silver and scarlet fringes flowing over the strong limbs and clashing mail like sea waves over rocks at sunset; opening each side of the river were gardens, courts, and cloisters, long successions of white pillars among reeds of vine, leaping of fountains through buds of pomegranate and orange; and still along the garden paths, and under and through the crimson of the pomegranate shadows, moving slowly, groups of the fairest women that Italy ever saw: fairest, purest, and thoughtfullest, trained in all high knowledge as in all courteous art, in dance, in song, in sweet wit, in lofty learning, in loftier courage, in loftiest love, able alike to cheer, to enchant, or save the souls of men.

Above all this scenery of perfect human life rose dome and bell-tower burning with white alabaster and gold; beyond dome and bell-tower the slopes of mighty hills, hoary with olive; far in the north above a purple sea of peaks of solemn Apennine, the clear, sharp-cloven Carrara mountains sent up their steadfast flames of marble summits into amber sky; and over all these, ever present, near or far, seen through the leaves of vine, or imaged with all its march of clouds in the Arno's stream, or set with its depth of blue close against the golden hair and burning cheek of lady and knight, that untroubled and sacred heaven in which every cloud that passed was literally the chariot of an angel, and every ray of its evening and morning streamed from the throne of God.

What think you of that for a school of design? And then contrast that with the depressing monotonous appearance of any modern commercial city—the sombre dress of men and women, the meaningless and barren architecture, the vulgar and glaring advertisements that desecrate not merely your eye and ear, but every rock and river and hill that I have seen yet in America. I do not say anything against commercial people, for it is not commerce that destroys art; Genoa was built by its traders, Florence by its bankers, and Venice, loveliest of them all, by her noble and honest merchants. I do not regard the commercial spirit of the present age as being opposed to the development of art, and I look to our merchants to support the changes we seek to make.

Look at the ignoble character of modern dress. I do not know a greater heroism than that which opposes the conventionalities of dress; the sombre dress of the age is robbing life of its beauty and is ruinous to art. Not a deed of heroism done on either continent in this century is fitly portrayed on canvas, and yet the history of a country should live on canvas and in marble as well as in dreary volumes; the history of Italy, of Holland, and, for a time, that of our own England, was told in speaking marble and living paintings.

Healthy art is that which realizes that beauty of the age in which we live, while art is unhealthy that is obliged to go back to old romantic ages for its themes. Well, the sombre and ignoble character of dress at present in fashion has brought art into a very unhealthy state by driving artists back to past ages for their subjects, although there is no more romantic age than our own. Instead of this servile imitation of romantic ages, we should strive to make our own age a romantic age, and art should reproduce for us the faces and forms we love and revere. But modern dress prevents the production of a picture or a statue in which may be embodied the element of that beauty and true nobility of form and feature pleasing to the eyes of those qualified to appreciate a work of art; it has almost annihilated sculpture, which has become all but extinct in England, and in looking around at the figures which adorn our parks, one could almost wish that we had killed the noble art completely: to see the statues of our departed statesmen in marble frock-coats and bronze, double-breasted waistcoats adds a new horror to death.

It is not that the flawless serenity of marble cannot bear the burden of the modern intellectual spirit or become instinct with the fire of romantic passion; the tomb of Duke Lorenzo and the chapel of the Medici show us that, in great cathedrals, such as that of Chartres, or in the decorations of any building in Europe erected between the eleventh and sixteenth centuries, is to be seen wrought in stone the whole history of the olden time, the representation of what the people most loved and took pleasure in. We look at the capitals of the pillars and the tracery of the arches and see the picture of the century before us, joining hands with it across the waste of years; you have simply to use your eyes and you can read more in an hour than you can in a week out of a book. Contrast these with our public buildings: a workman is given a design stolen from a Greek temple and does it because he is paid for doing it—the worst reason for doing anything; no modern stonecutter could leave the stamp of this age upon his work as the ancient workmen did.

The problem is how to restore to the modern workman these right conditions, without which it is impossible to work freely or to work well. If we want to do real service to art we must alter the external forms of dress; the dress of the future, I think, will use drapery to a great extent and will abound with joyous colour. True art in dress will make our attire an instructor, an educator.

Give then, as I said, to your American workmen of today the bright and noble surroundings that you can yourself create. Stately and simple architecture for your city, bright and simple dress for your men and women—those are the conditions of a real artistic movement; for the artist is not concerned primarily with any theory of life but with life itself, with the joy and loveliness that should come daily on eye and ear from a beautiful external world.

But this is not enough. You must give your workman a school of art wherein he can learn rational design. There are many schools of art in America, but they should place themselves in a more immediate relation with trade, commerce, and manufacture and devote more time than they do now to making the common things of life beautiful. Then art in America would not lag behind the old world, but be quickened into loftier powers.

And you must attach to each school a museum—I do not mean the dreadful modern museum where you find a stuffed and very dusty giraffe face to face with a case or two of fossils—but where the workman can see clay, marble, wood, or glass specimens of the best decorative art to be found in Europe and Asia so that he may come to know what is simple and true and beautiful.

Such a place is the South Kensington Museum in London, whereon we build greater hopes for the future than on any other one thing, for it is a rational museum, a museum of decorative art. There I go every Saturday night, when the Museum is opened later than usual, to see the workmen whom we so much want to reach, and whom it is often so difficult to reach, the weaver, the glass-blower, the woodcarver, the embroiderer, and others with their notebooks open, and I feel certain that the week after such a visit their work is better for their observance. And it is here that the man of refinement and culture comes face to face with the workman who ministers to his joy; he comes to know more of the nobility of the workman, and the workman, feeling the appreciation, goes away with a heightened sense of the nobility of his calling.

Again, your artists must decorate what is more simple and useful. In your art schools I found no attempt to decorate such things as the common vessels for water. There is no excuse for the ugly water jugs or pitchers of today, for you might readily have more delicate and beautiful forms for them. A museum could be filled with the different kinds used in hot countries: in the olden times in Eastern countries when water was precious and when the daughters of men in the highest rank could go to the well to draw water, there was beauty and variety of form and design in nothing so much as in common water vessels. Yet we continue to submit to the depressing jugs with the handle all on one side.

There is one thing much worse than no art, and that is bad art. A wrong principle is often employed, and an inappropriateness of design in many of the schools of decorative art, arising from a want of instruction in the difference between imaginative and decorative art. I have seen young ladies painting moonlights upon dinner plates and sunsets on soup plates. I don't think it adds anything to the pleasure of canvas-back duck to take it out of such glories. Such scenes should be kept to be hung on the walls, for we should leave to the painter the art of giving undying beauty to the beauty that dies away and fades; besides, we do not want a soup plate whose bottom seems to vanish into the misty hollow of a distant hill; one neither feels safe nor comfortable under such conditions.

You must encourage and support art in your own city instead of sending to New York or to other places, paying heavily for such things by way of freight; you should make by your own workmen beautiful art for the enjoyment of your citizens: weave your own carpets, design your own furniture, make your own pottery and other things from approved designs instead of submitting to be charged heavily for goods which do not suit you and which do not really represent your feeling and good taste, for you have here the primary elements of a great artistic movement.

Believe me, the conditions of art are much simpler than people imagine: for the noblest art one requires a clear, healthy atmosphere, not polluted as the air of our English cities is by the smoke and grime and horridness which comes from open furnace and from factory chimney. You must have a strong and healthy physique among your men and women; sickly or idle or melancholy people don't do much in art, believe me; and lastly you require a sense of individualism about each man and woman, because that, the very keynote of life, is also the essence of art—a desire on the part of man to express the noblest side of his nature in the noblest way, to show the world how many things he can reverence, love and understand.

For, the motives of art lie about you in all directions as they were around about the ancients. If the modern sculptor were to ask me where he should go for a model, I would tell him that he might, if he would, find in everyday life subjects in the nobility of labour entirely worthy of his attention—the depicting of men in their daily work; there is not a worker in mine or ditch, in the shop or at the furnace, who is not at some moment of his work in graceful attitude. Such scenes of beauty lie at the scientific basis of aesthetics, which is not mere dainty ornament and luxury, but the expression of strength, utility, and health. Who ever saw an ungraceful smith at his anvil or an ungraceful carpenter at his bench? The most graceful thing I ever beheld was a miner in a Colorado silver mine driving a new shaft with a hammer; at any moment he might have been transformed into marble or bronze and become noble in art forever. Work is man's great prerogative and the real essential of art; it is only the loafer and the idle saunterer who is as useless and uninteresting to the artist as he is to himself.

Or I would ask the sculptor to go with me to any of your schools or universities, to the running ground and gymnasium, to watch the young men start for a race, hurling quoit or curb, kneeling to tie their shoes before leaping, stepping from the boat, or bending to the oar, and to carve them. The Greek sculptor asked for no higher subject for art than could be found on the running ground or in the gymnasium, and I recommend that plaster casts of the best Greek statuary be placed in all gymnasiums as models to correct that foolish impression that mental culture and athletics are always divorced.

There is and has been in Europe one school of painters and sculptors whose favourite subjects in their work are kings and queens, and another whose talent and genius are employed in the reproduction of faces and forms on canvas and in marble of saints and kindred subjects in reality and ideality. Now, the Greeks sculptured gods and goddesses because they loved them, and the Middle Ages, saints and kings because they believed in them. But the saint is now hardly prominent enough a feature to become a motive for high art, and the day of kings and queens is gone; and so art should now sculpture the men who cover the world with a network of iron and the sea with ships. Thus a universal deference to the dignity of the kingdom of industry would do much to reconcile the workman with his lot, and end the strife and bridge the now-widening chasm between capital and labour.

And so, as I said, find your subjects in everyday life: your own men and women, your own flowers and fields, your own hills and mountains; these are what your art should represent to you, for every nation can represent with prudence or with success only those things in which it delights, what you have with you and before you daily, dearest to your sight and to your heart, by the magic of your hand or the music of your lips you can gloriously express to others. All these commend themselves to the thoughtful student and artist.

Not merely has nature given you the noblest motives for a new school of decoration, but to you above all other countries has she given the materials to work in. The noble Titan forests out of which you build your houses should be an incentive to woodcarving, because the beautiful in art can be built only of wood well-carved. I wish to say little about your wooden houses, which are painted in the most oppressive colours I have ever seen, but it does seem to me that the adoption of the prevailing colour, white, with which you cover them, making the white walls appear as a sheet of white flame in the noonday sun, is a gross mistake when the barrenness of the houses is overcome so easily by woodcarving, which is the simplest of the decorative arts and the one in which the artist is least likely to go astray. In Switzerland, the little barefooted shepherd boy that blows a horn all day on the hills after some stray goats will return home and there carve in wood over his father's door the figures of the birds and flowers he has seen, and beautifies the house with his art. What a Swiss boy can do well, an American boy can do twice as well, if he is properly taught to do it.

There is nothing to my mind more coarse in conception, nothing more vulgar in execution, than modern jewellery. How easy for you to change all that, and to produce goldsmith's work that would be a joy to all of us. In Europe we have not the quantity of gold and of silver that lies around you in your mountain hollows or strewn along your river beds, and our jewellers have not the opportunities of those of America as artificers of these metals; yet when I was in Leadville, the richest city for silver in the world, and heard of the most incredible quantity of silver taken from its mountains, I thought how sad it was that the silver should be made into flat, ugly dollars, useful perhaps to the artist—for dollars are very good in their way—but which should not be the end and aim of life. There should be some better record of it left in your history than the merchant's panic and the ruined home. We discover, remember, often enough, how constantly the history of a great nation will live in and by its art; only a few thin wreaths of beaten gold are all that remain to tell us of the stately empire of Etruria; and while from the streets of Florence the noble knight and haughty duke have long since passed away, the gates which the simple goldsmith, Ghiberti, made for their pleasure still guard their lovely house of baptism, worthy still of the praise of Michelangelo, who called them worthy to be the Gates of Paradise.

Be sure of one thing: we shall get no good work done unless we come face to face with the designer and dispense with all middlemen. We should not be content to have the salesman stand between us, who knows nothing of what he is selling save that he is charging a great deal too much for it. We shall know the workmen and they us, and they will understand the requirements of our state. When this is accomplished we shall then understand the nobility of all rational workmanship, and in this way we shall surround ourselves with beautiful things; for the good we get from art is not what we derive directly, but what improvement is made in us by being accustomed to the sight of all comely and gracious things.

And art will do more than make our lives joyous and beautiful; it will become part of the new history of the world and a part of the brotherhood of man; for art, by creating a common intellectual atmosphere between all countries might, if it could not overshadow the world with the silvery wings of peace, at least make men such brothers that they would not go out to slay one another for the whim or folly of some king or minister as they do in Europe, for national hatreds are always strongest where culture is lowest.

Thinking this, what place can I ascribe to art in our education? Consider how susceptible children are to the influence of beauty, for they are easily impressed and are pretty much what their surroundings make them. How can you expect them, then, to tell the truth if everything about them is telling lies, like the paper in the hall declaring itself marble? Why, I have seen wall-paper which must lead a boy brought up under its influence to a career of crime; you should not have such incentives to sin lying about your drawing-rooms.

And hence the enormous importance given to all the decorative arts in our English renaissance; we want children to grow up in England in the simple atmosphere of all fair things so that they will love what is beautiful and good, and hate what is evil and ugly, long before they know the reason why. If you go into a house where everything is coarse and you find the common cups chipped and the saucers cracked, it will often be because the children have an utter contempt for them, but if everything is dainty and delicate, you teach them practically what beauty is, and gentleness and refinement of manner are unconsciously acquired.

But you will say, these things get broken. When I was in San Francisco, I used to visit the Chinese theatres for their rich dresses, and the Chinese restaurants on account of the beautiful tea they made there. I saw rough Chinese navvies, who did work that the ordinary Californian rightly might be disgusted with and refuse to do, sitting there drinking their tea out of tiny porcelain cups, which might be mistaken for the petals of a white rose, and handling them with care, fully appreciating the influence of their beauty; whereas in all the grand hotels of the land, where thousands of dollars have been lavished on great gilt mirrors and gaudy columns, I have been given my chocolate in the morning and my coffee in the evening in common delft cups about an inch-and-a-half thick. I think I have deserved something nicer. If these men could use cups with that tenderness, your children will learn by the influence of beauty and example to act in a like manner. The great need in America is for good decoration; art is not given to the people by costly foreign paintings in private galleries; people can learn more by a well-shaped vessel for ordinary use.

Most of you will agree that there is an education independent of books that is of far greater service in life. The art systems of the past have been devised by philosophers who look upon human beings as obstructions, and they have tried to educate boys' minds before they had any. Most of us remember the dreary hours we have spent at our books, and then what we have learned in the woods by watching the work of the artisan in his shop as we passed the door.

In the false education of our present system, minds too young to grapple with the subjects in the right sense are burdened with those bloody slaughters and barbarous brawls of the French and English wars and that calendar of infamy, European history. How much better would it be in these early years to teach children in the useful branches of art, to use their hands in the rational service of mankind. Bring a boy up in the atmosphere of art, give him a mind before trying to teach him, develop his soul before trying to save it.

In every school I would have a workshop, and I would have an hour a day set apart when boys could learn something practically of art: turning a potter's wheel, beating a leaf of gold, carving wood, working metal, or other such things as could give him an insight into the various decorative arts. This would be a golden hour to the children, and they would enjoy that hour most, learn more of the lessons of life and of the morality of art than in years of book study. And you would soon raise up a race of handicraftsmen who would transform the face of your country.

It is a great mistake of the age not to honour working men and their pursuits as they should be honoured. These men have been educated to use their hands and are useful members of society, a class ever productive of good to all, while in contrast may be found the great army of useless idlers whose costly education tends only to cultivate their memories for a time and is now, in the broad sea of practical life, nearly, if not quite completely, useless to them. For instance, I have seen an example of the uselessness of modern education among well-educated young men in Colorado, among others that of Eton students, men of fine physique and high mental cultivation, but whose knowledge of the names of all the kings of the Saxon Heptarchy, and all the incidents of the second Punic War, was of no use to them in Leadville and Denver.

How much better it would have been if those young men had been taught to use their hands, to make furniture and other things useful to those miners. The best people of all classes should be given to the pursuits of artistic industry, and everyone should be taught to use his hands; the human hand is the most beautiful and delicate piece of mechanism in the world, although many people seem to have no other use for their hands than to squeeze them into gloves that are far too small for them.

The most practical school of morals in the world, the best educator, is true art: it never lies, never misleads, and never corrupts, for all good art, all high art, is founded on honesty, sincerity, and truth. Under its influence children learn to abhor the liar and cheat in art—the man who paints wood to represent marble, or iron to look like stone—and to him retribution comes immediately, and he never succeeds. And if you teach a boy art, the beauty of form and colour will find its way into his heart, and he will love nature more; for there is no better way to learn to love nature than to understand art—it dignifies every flower of the field. He will have more pleasure and joy in nature when he sees how no flower by the wayside is too lowly, no little blade of grass too common, but some great designer has seen it and loved it and made noble use of it in decoration.

And art culture will do more to train children to be kind to animals and all living things than all our harrowing moral tales, for when he sees how lovely the little leaping squirrel is on the beaten brass or the bird arrested in flight on carven marble, he will not throw the customary stone. The boy will learn too to wonder and worship at God's works more, for all art is perfect praise of God, the duplication of His handiwork. He will look on art and on nature as the craftsman looks on the carving round the arch of a Gothic cathedral, with all its marvels of the animal and vegetable world being a *Te Deum* in God's honour, quite as beautiful and far more lasting than that chanted *Te Deum* sung within its sacred walls, which dies in music at evensong; for art is the one thing that death cannot harm.

The victories of art can give more than heroes yield or the sword demands, for what we want is something spiritual added to life. And if you wish for art you must revolt against the luxury of riches and the tyranny of materialism, for you may lay up treasures by your railways, or open your ports to the galleys of the world, but you will find the independence of art is the perfect expression of freedom. The steel of Toledo and the silk of Genoa did but give strength to oppression and add lustre to pride. Let it be for you to create an art that is made with the hands of the people, for the joy of the people, too, an art that will be an expression of your delight in life. There is nothing in common life too mean, in common things too trivial to be ennobled by your touch; nothing in life that art cannot sanctify.

And when artisans are among you, don't dishonour them or leave them in necessity; I hardly think people know how much a word of sympathy means to young artists, who often are sustained and inspired by a word; search out your young artists, cheer them in their race through the asphodel meadows of youth, and bring once more into their faces the proud bright scarlet with your encouragement; and in return there will be no flower in your meadows that does not wreathe its tendrils around your pillows, no little leaf in your Titan forests that does not lend its form to design, no curving spray of wild rose or briar that does not live forever in carven arch or window of marble, no bird in your air that is not giving the iridescent wonder of its colour, the exquisite curves of its wings in flight, to make more precious the preciousness of simple adornment. For the voices that have their dwelling in sea and mountain are not alone the chosen music of liberty only; other messages are there in the wonder of windswept height and the majesty of silent deep, messages that, if you will listen to them, will give you the wonder of all new imagination, the treasure of all new beauty.

PERSONAL IMPRESSIONS OF AMERICA

I fear I cannot picture America as altogether an Elysium – perhaps, from the ordinary standpoint I know but little about the country. I cannot give its latitude or longitude; I cannot compute the value of its dry goods, and I have no very close acquaintance with its politics. These are matters which may not interest you, and they certainly are not interesting to me.

The first thing that struck me on landing in America was that if the Americans are not the most well-dressed people in the world, they are the most comfortably dressed. Men are seen there with the dreadful chimney-pot hat, but there are very few hatless men; men wear the shocking swallow-tail coat, but few are to be seen with no coat at all. There is an air of comfort in the appearance of the people which is a marked contrast to that seen in this country, where, too often, people are seen in close contact with rags.

The next thing particularly noticeable is that everybody seems in a hurry to catch a train. This is a state of things which is not favourable to poetry or romance. Had Romeo or Juliet been in a constant state of anxiety about trains, or had their minds been agitated by the question of return-tickets, Shakespeare could not have given us those lovely balcony scenes which are so full of poetry and pathos.

America is the noisiest country that ever existed. One is waked up in the morning, not by the singing of the nightingale, but by the steam whistle. It is surprising that the sound practical sense of the Americans does not reduce this intolerable noise. All art depends upon exquisite and delicate sensibility, and such continual turmoil must ultimately be destructive of the musical facility.

There is not so much beauty to be found in American cities as in Oxford, Cambridge, Salisbury or Winchester, where are lovely relics of a beautiful age; but still there is a good deal of beauty to be seen in them now and then, but only where the American has not attempted to create it. Where the Americans have attempted to produce beauty they have signally failed. A remarkable characteristic of the Americans is the manner in which they have applied science to modern life.

This is apparent in the most cursory stroll through New York. In England an inventor is regarded almost as a crazy man, and in too many instances invention ends in disappointment and poverty. In America an inventor is honoured, help is forthcoming, and the exercise of ingenuity, the application of science to the work of man, is there the shortest road to wealth. There is no country in the world where machinery is so lovely as in America.

I have always wished to believe that the line of strength and the line of beauty are one. That wish was realised when I contemplated American machinery. It was not until I had seen the waterworks at Chicago that I realised the wonders of machinery; the rise and fall of the steel rods, the symmetrical motion of the great wheels is the most beautifully rhythmic thing I have ever seen. One is impressed in America, but not favourably impressed, by the inordinate size of everything. The country seems to try to bully one into a belief in its power by its impressive bigness.

I was disappointed with Niagara – most people must be disappointed with Niagara. Every American bride is taken there, and the sight of the stupendous waterfall must be one of the earliest, if not the keenest, disappointments in American married life. One sees it under bad conditions, very far away, the point of view not showing the splendour of the water. To appreciate it really one has to see it from underneath the fall, and to do that it is necessary to be dressed in a yellow oil-skin, which is as ugly as a mackintosh – and I hope none of you ever wears one. It is a consolation to know, however, that such an artist as Madame Bernhardt has not only worn that yellow, ugly dress, but has been photographed in it.

Perhaps the most beautiful part of America is the West, to reach which, however, involves a journey by rail of six days, racing along tied to an ugly tin-kettle of a steam engine. I found but poor consolation for this journey in the fact that the boys who infest the cars and sell everything that one can eat – or should not eat – were selling editions of my poems vilely printed on a kind of grey blotting paper, for the low price of ten cents. Calling these boys on one side I told them that though poets like to be popular they desire to be paid, and selling editions of my poems without giving me a profit is dealing a blow at literature which must have a disastrous effect on poetical aspirations. The invariable reply that they made was that they themselves made a profit out of the transaction and that was all they cared about.

It is a popular superstition that in America a visitor is invariably addressed as 'stranger'. When I went to Texas I was called 'Captain'; when I got to the centre of the country I was addressed as 'Colonel'. On the whole, however, 'Sir', the old English method of addressing people, is the most common.

It is, perhaps, worth while to note that what many people call Americanisms are really old English expressions which have lingered in our colonies while they have been lost in our own country. Many people imagine that the term 'I guess', which is so common in America, is purely an American expression, but it was used by John Locke in his work on the *Understanding*, just as we now use 'I think'.

It is in the colonies, and not in the mother country, that the old life of the country really exists. If one wants to realise what English Puritanism is – not at its worst (when it is very bad), but at its best, and then it is not very good – I do not think one can find much of it in England, but much can be found about Boston and Massachusetts. We have got rid of it. America still preserves it, to be, I hope, a short-lived curiosity.

San Francisco is a really beautiful city. China Town, peopled by Chinese labourers, is the most artistic town I have ever come across. The people – strange, melancholy Orientals, whom many people would call common, and they are certainly very poor – have determined that they will have nothing about them that is not beautiful. In the Chinese restaurants, where these navvies meet to have supper in the evening, I found them drinking out of china cups as delicate as the petals of a rose-leaf, whereas at the gaudy hotels

I was supplied with a delft cup an inch and a half thick. When the Chinese bill was presented it was made out on rice paper, the account being done in indian ink as fantastically as if an artist had been etching little birds on a fan.

Salt Lake City contains only two buildings of note, the chief being the Tabernacle, which is in the shape of a soup-kettle. It is decorated by the only native artist, and he has treated religious subjects in the naïve spirit of the early Florentine painters, representing people of our own day in the dress of the period side by side with people of biblical history who are clothed in some romantic costume.

The building next in importance is called the Amelia Palace, in honour of one of Brigham Young's wives. When he died the present president of the Mormons stood up in the Tabernacle and said that it had been revealed to him that he was to have the Amelia Palace, and that on this subject there were to be no more revelations of any kind!

From Salt Lake City one travels over the great plains of Colorado and up the Rocky Mountains, on the top of which is Leadville, the richest city in the world. It has also got the reputation of being the roughest, and every man carries a revolver. I was told that if I went there they would be sure to shoot me or my travelling manager. I wrote and told them that nothing that they could do to my travelling manager would intimidate me. They are miners – men working in metals, so I lectured to them on the Ethics of Art. I read them passages from the autobiography of Benvenuto Cellini and they seemed much delighted. I was reproved by my hearers for not having brought him with me. I explained that he had been dead for some little time which elicited the enquiry 'Who shot him'. They afterwards took me to a dancing-saloon where I saw the only rational method of art criticism I have ever come across. Over the piano was printed a notice:

> PLEASE DO NOT SHOOT
> THE PIANIST.
> HE IS DOING HIS BEST.

The mortality among pianists in that place is marvellous. Then they asked me to supper, and having accepted, I had to descend a mine in a rickety bucket in which it was impossible to be graceful. Having got into the heart of the mountain I had supper, the first course being whisky, the second whisky and the third whisky.

I went to the theatre to lecture and I was informed that just before I went there two men had been seized for committing a murder, and in that theatre they had been brought on to the stage at eight o'clock in the evening, and then and there tried and executed before a crowded audience. But I found these miners very charming and not at all rough.

Among the more elderly inhabitants of the South I found a melancholy tendency to date every event of importance by the late war. 'How beautiful the moon is tonight,' I once remarked to a gentleman who was standing next to me. 'Yes,' was his reply, 'but you should have seen it before the war.'

So infinitesimal did I find the knowledge of Art, west of the Rocky Mountains, that an art patron – one who in his day had been a miner – actually sued the railroad company for damages because the plaster cast of Venus of Milo, which he had imported from Paris, had been delivered minus the arms. And, what is more surprising still, he gained his case and the damages.

Pennsylvania, with its rocky gorges and woodland scenery, reminded me of Switzerland. The prairie reminded me of a piece of blotting-paper.

The Spanish and French have left behind them memorials in the beauty of their names. All the cities that have beautiful names derive from the Spanish or the French. The English people give intensely ugly names to places. One place had such an ugly name that I refused to lecture there. It was called Grigsville. Supposing I had founded a School of Art there – fancy 'Early Grigsville'. Imagine a School of Art teaching 'Grigsville Renaissance'.

As for slang I did not hear much of it, though a young lady who had changed her clothes after an afternoon dance did say that 'after the heel kicks she shifted her day goods'.

American youths are pale and precocious, or sallow and supercilious, but American girls are pretty and charming – little oases of pretty unreasonableness in a vast desert of practical common sense.

Every American girl is entitled to have twelve young men devoted to her. They remain her slaves and she rules them with charming nonchalance.

The men are entirely given to business; they have, as they say, their brains in front of their heads. They are also exceedingly acceptive of new ideas. Their education is practical. We base the education of children entirely on books, but we must give a child a mind before we can instruct the mind. Children have a natural antipathy to books – handicraft should be the basis of education. Boys and girls should be taught to use their hands to make something, and they would be less apt to destroy and be mischievous.

In going to America one learns that poverty is not a necessary accompaniment to civilisation. There at any rate is a country that has no trappings, no pageants and no gorgeous ceremonies. I saw only two processions – one was the fire brigade preceded by the police, the other was the police preceded by the fire brigade.

Every man when he gets to the age of twenty-one is allowed a vote, and thereby immediately acquires his political education. The Americans are the best politically educated people in the world. It is well worth one's while to go to a country which can teach us the beauty of the word FREEDOM and the value of the thing LIBERTY.

MRS LANGTRY AS HESTER GRAZEBROOK

New York World, 7 November 1882

It is only in the best Greek gems, on the silver coins of Syracuse, or among the marble figures of the Parthenon frieze, that one can find the ideal representation of the marvellous beauty of that face which laughed through the leaves last night as Hester Grazebrook.

Pure Greek it is, with the grave low forehead, the exquisitely arched brow; the noble chiselling of the mouth, shaped as if it were the mouthpiece of an instrument of music; the supreme and splendid curve of the cheek; the augustly pillared throat which bears it all: it is Greek, because the lines which compose it are so definite and so strong, and yet so exquisitely harmonised that the effect is one of simple loveliness purely: Greek, because its essence and its quality, as is the quality of music and of architecture, is that of beauty based on absolutely mathematical laws.

But while art remains dumb and immobile in its passionless serenity, with the beauty of this face it is different: the grey eyes lighten into blue or deepen into violet as fancy succeeds fancy; the lips become flower-like in laughter or, tremulous as a bird's wing, mould themselves at last into the strong and bitter moulds of pain or scorn. And then motion comes, and the statue wakes into life. But the life is not an ordinary life of common days; it is life with a new value given to it, the value of art: and the charm to me of Hester Grazebrook's acting in the first scene of the play[1] last night was that mingling of classic grace with absolute reality which is the secret of all beautiful art, of the plastic work of the Greeks and of the pictures of Jean François Millet equally.

I do not think that the sovereignty and empire of women's beauty has at all passed away, though we may no longer go to war with them as the Greeks did for the daughter of Leda. The greatest empire still remains for them – the empire of art. And, indeed, this wonderful face, seen last night for the first time in America, has filled and permeated with the pervading image of its type the whole of our modern art in England. Last century it was the romantic type which dominated in art, the type loved by Reynolds and Gainsborough, of wonderful contrasts of colour, of exquisite and varying charm of expression, but without that definite plastic feeling which divides classic from romantic work. This type degenerated into mere facile prettiness in the hands of lesser masters, and, in protest against it, was created by the hands of the Pre-Raphaelites a new type, with its rare combination of Greek form with Florentine mysticism. But this mysticism becomes overstrained and a

---

[1] *An Unequal Match*, by Tom Taylor, at Wallack's Theatre, New York, 6 November 1882

burden, rather than an aid to expression, and a desire for the pure Hellenic joy and serenity came in its place; and in all our modern work, in the paintings of such men as Albert Moore and Leighton and Whistler, we can trace the influence of this single face giving fresh life and inspiration in the form of a new artistic ideal.

As regards Hester Grazebrook's dresses, the first was a dress whose grace depended entirely on the grace of the person who wore it. It was merely the simple dress of a village girl in England. The second was a lovely combination of blue and creamy lace. But the masterpiece was undoubtedly the last, a symphony in silver-grey and pink, a pure melody of colour which I feel sure Whistler would call a *Scherzo*, and take as its visible motive the moonlight wandering in silver mist through a rose-garden; unless indeed he saw this dress, in which case he would paint it and nothing else, for it is a dress such as Velasquez only could paint, and Whistler very wisely always paints those things which are within reach of Velasquez only.

The scenery was, of course, prepared in a hurry. Still, much of it was very good indeed: the first scene especially, with its graceful trees and open forge and cottage porch, though the roses were dreadfully out of tone and, besides their crudity of colour, were curiously badly grouped. The last scene was exceedingly clever and true to nature as well, being that combination of lovely scenery and execrable architecture which is so specially characteristic of a German spa. As for the drawing room scene, I cannot regard it as in any way a success. The heavy ebony doors are entirely out of keeping with the satin panels; the silk hangings and festoons of black and yellow are quite meaningless in their position and consequently quite ugly; the carpet is out of all colour relation with the rest of the room, and the table-cover is mauve. Still, to have decorated even so bad a room in six days must, I suppose, be a subject of respectful wonder, though I should have fancied that Mr Wallack had many very much better sets in his own stock.

But I am beginning to quarrel generally with most modern scene-painting. A scene is primarily a decorative background for the actors, and should always be kept subordinate, first to the players, their dress, gesture, and action; and secondly, to the fundamental principle of decorative art, which is not to imitate but to suggest nature. If the landscape is given its full realistic value, the value of the figures to which it serves as a background is impaired and often lost, and so the painted hangings of the Elizabethan age were a far more artistic, and so a far more rational form of scenery than most modern scene-painting is. From the same master-hand which designed the curtain of Madison Square Theatre I should like very much to see a good decorative landscape in scene-painting; for I have seen no open-air scene in any theatre which did not really mar the value of the actors. One must either, like Titian, make the landscape subordinate to the figures, or, like Claude, the figures subordinate to the landscape; for if we desire realistic acting we cannot have realistic scene-painting.

I need not describe, however, how the beauty of Hester Grazebrook survived the crude roses and the mauve tablecloth triumphantly. That it is a beauty that will be appreciated to the full in America I do not doubt for a moment, for it is only countries which possess great beauty that can appreciate beauty at all. It may also influence the art of America as it has influenced the art of England, for of the rare Greek type it is the most absolutely perfect example.

The Philistine may, of course, object that to be absolutely perfect is impossible. Well, that is so: but then it is only the impossible things that are worth doing nowadays!

WOMAN'S DRESS

Pall Mall Gazette, 14 October 1884

MR OSCAR WILDE, *who asks us to permit him 'that most charming of all pleasures, the pleasure of answering one's critics', sends us the following remarks*:

The 'Girl Graduate' must of course have precedence, not merely for her sex but for her sanity: her letter is extremely sensible. She makes two points: that high-heels are a necessity for any lady who wishes to keep her dress clean from the Stygian mud of our streets, and that without a tight corset 'the ordinary number of petticoats and etceteras' cannot be properly or conveniently held up. Now, it is quite true that as long as the lower garments are suspended from the hips a corset is an absolute necessity; the mistake lies in not suspending all apparel from the shoulders. In the latter case a corset becomes useless, the body is left free and unconfined for respiration and motion, there is more health, and consequently more beauty. Indeed all the most ungainly and uncomfortable articles of dress that fashion has ever in her folly prescribed, not the tight corset merely, but the farthingale, the vertugadin, the hoop, the crinoline, and that modern monstrosity the so-called 'dress improver' also, all of them have owed their origin to the same error, the error of not seeing that it is from the shoulders, and from the shoulders only, that all garments should be hung.

And as regards high-heels, I quite admit that some additional height to the shoe or boot is necessary if long gowns are to be worn in the street; but what I object to is that the height should be given to the heel only, and not to the sole of the foot also. The modern high-heeled boot is, in fact, merely the clog of the time of Henry VI, with the front prop left out, and its inevitable effect is to throw the body forward, to shorten the steps, and consequently to produce that want of grace which always follows want of freedom.

Why should clogs be despised? Much art has been expended on clogs. They have been made of lovely woods, and delicately inlaid with ivory, and with mother-of-pearl. A clog might be a dream of beauty, and, if not too high or too heavy, most comfortable also. But if there be any who do not like clogs, let them try some adaptation of the trouser of the Turkish lady, which is loose round the limb and tight at the ankle.

The 'Girl Graduate', with a pathos to which I am not insensible, entreats me not to apotheosise 'that awful, befringed, beflounced, and bekilted divided skirt'. Well, I will acknowledge that the fringes, the flounces, and the kilting do certainly defeat the whole object of the dress, which is that of ease and liberty; but I regard these things as mere wicked superfluities, tragic proofs that the divided skirt is ashamed of its own division. The principle of the dress is good, and, though it is not by any means perfection, it is a step towards it.

Here I leave the 'Girl Graduate', with much regret, for Mr Wentworth Huyshe. Mr Huyshe makes the old criticism that Greek dress is unsuited to our climate, and, to me the somewhat new assertion, that the men's dress of a hundred years ago was preferable to that of the second part of the seventeenth century, which I consider to have been the exquisite period of English costume.

Now, as regards the first of these two statements, I will say, to begin with, that the warmth of apparel does not depend really on the number of garments worn, but on the material of which they are made. One of the chief faults of modern dress is that it is composed of far too many articles of clothing, most of which are of the wrong substance but over a substratum of pure wool, such as is supplied by Dr Jaeger under the modern German system, some modification of Greek costume is perfectly applicable to our climate, our country and our century. This important fact has already been pointed out by Mr E. W. Godwin in his excellent, though too brief, handbook on Dress, contributed to the Health Exhibition. I call it an important fact because it makes almost any form of lovely costume perfectly practicable in our cold climate. Mr Godwin, it is true, points out that the English ladies of the thirteenth century abandoned after some time the flowing garments of the early Renaissance in favour of a tighter mode, such as Northern Europe seems to demand. This I quite admit, and its significance; but what I contend, and what I am sure Mr Godwin would agree with me in, is that the principles, the laws of Greek dress may be perfectly realised, even in a moderately tight gown with sleeves: I mean the principle of suspending all apparel from the shoulders, and of relying for beauty of effect not on the stiff ready-ornaments of the modern milliner – the bows where there should be no bows, and the flounces where there should be no flounces – but on the exquisite play of light and line that one gets from rich and rippling folds. I am not proposing any antiquarian revival of an ancient costume, but trying merely to point out the right laws of dress, laws which are dictated by art and not by archaeology, by science and not by fashion; and just as the best work of art in our days is that which combines classic grace with absolute reality, so from a continuation of the Greek principles of beauty with the German principles of health will come, I feel certain, the costume of the future.

And now to the question of men's dress, or rather to Mr Huyshe's claim of the superiority, in point of costume, of the last quarter of the eighteenth century over the second quarter of the seventeenth. The broad-brimmed hat of 1640 kept the rain of winter and the glare of summer from the face; the same cannot be said of the hat of one hundred years ago, which, with its comparatively narrow brim and high crown, was the precursor of the modern 'chimney-pot': a wide turned-down collar is a much healthier thing than a strangling stock, and a short cloak much more comfortable than a sleeved overcoat, even though the latter may have had 'three capes'; a cloak is easier to put on and off, lies lightly on the shoulder in summer, and wrapped round one in winter keeps one perfectly warm. A doublet, again, is simpler than a coat and waistcoat; instead of two garments one has one; by not being open it also protects the chest better.

Short loose trousers are in every way to be preferred to the tight knee-breeches which often impede the proper circulation of the blood; and finally, the soft leather boots which could be worn above or below the knee, are more supple, and give consequently more freedom, than the stiff Hessian which Mr Huyshe so praises. I say nothing about the question of grace and pictur-esqueness, for I suppose that no one, not even Mr Huyshe, would prefer a macaroni to a cavalier, a Lawrence to a Vandyke, or the third George to the first Charles; but for ease, warmth and comfort this seventeenth-century dress is infinitely superior to anything that came after it, and I do not think it is excelled by any preceding form of costume. I sincerely trust that we may soon see in England some national revival of it.

Mr Whistler's Ten o'Clock

Pall Mall Gazette, 21 February 1885

Last night, at Prince's Hall, Mr Whistler made his first public appearance as a lecturer on art, and spoke for more than an hour with really marvellous eloquence on the absolute uselessness of all lectures of the kind. Mr Whistler began his lecture with a very pretty *aria* on prehistoric history, describing how in earlier times hunter and warrior would go forth to chase and foray, while the artist sat at home making cup and bowl for their service. Rude imitations of nature they were first, like the gourd bottle, till the sense of beauty and form developed and, in all its exquisite proportions, the first vase was fashioned. Then came a higher civilisation of architecture and armchairs, and with exquisite design, and dainty diaper, the useful things of life were made lovely; and the hunter and the warrior lay on the couch when they were tired, and, when they were thirsty, drank from the bowl, and never cared to lose the exquisite proportion of the one, or the delightful ornament of the other; and this attitude of the primitive anthropophagous Philistine formed the text of the lecture and was the attitude which Mr Whistler entreated his audience to adopt towards art. Remembering, no doubt, many charming invitations to wonderful private views, this fashionable assemblage seemed somewhat aghast, and not a little amused, at being told that the slightest appearance among a civilised people of any joy in beautiful things is a grave impertinence to all painters; but Mr Whistler was relentless, and, with charming ease and much grace of manner, explained to the public that the only thing they should cultivate was ugliness, and that on their permanent stupidity rested all the hopes of art in the future.

The scene was in every way delightful; he stood there, a miniature Mephistopheles, mocking the majority! He was like a brilliant surgeon lecturing to a class composed of subjects destined ultimately for dissection, and solemnly assuring them how valuable to science their maladies were, and how absolutely uninteresting the slightest symptoms of health on their part would be. In fairness to the audience, however, I must say that they seemed extremely gratified at being rid of the dreadful responsibility of admiring anything, and nothing could have exceeded their enthusiasm when they were told by Mr Whistler that no matter how vulgar their dresses were, or how hideous their surroundings at home, still it was possible that a great painter, if there was such a thing, could, by contemplating them in the twilight and half closing his eyes, see them under really picturesque conditions, and produce a picture which they were not to attempt to understand, much less dare to enjoy. Then there were some arrows, barbed, and brilliant, shot off, with all the speed and splendour of fireworks, at the archaeologists, who spend their lives in verifying the birthplaces of nobodies, and estimate the value of a work of art by its dates or its decay; at the art-critics who always treat a picture as if it were a novel, and try to find out the plot; at dilettanti in general and amateurs in particular; and (*O mea culpa*!) at dress reformers most of all. 'Did not Velasquez paint crinolines? What more do you want?'

Having thus made a holocaust of humanity, Mr Whistler turned to Nature, and in a few moments convicted her of the Crystal Palace, Bank holidays, and a general overcrowding of detail, both in omnibuses and in landscapes, and then, in a passage of singular beauty, not unlike one that occurs in Corot's letters, spoke of the artistic value of dim dawns and dusks, when the mean facts of life are lost in exquisite and evanescent effects, when common things are touched with mystery and transfigured with beauty, when the warehouses become as palaces and the tall chimneys of the factory seem like campaniles in the silver air.

Finally, after making a strong protest against anybody but a painter judging of painting, and a pathetic appeal to the audience not to be lured by the aesthetic movement into having beautiful things about them, Mr Whistler concluded his lecture with a pretty passage about Fusiyama on a fan, and made his bow to an audience which he had succeeded in completely fascinating by his wit, his brilliant paradoxes, and, at times, his real eloquence. Of course, with regard to the value of beautiful surroundings I differ entirely from Mr Whistler. An artist is not an isolated fact; he is the resultant of a certain *milieu* and a certain *entourage*, and can no more be born of a nation that is devoid of any sense of beauty than a fig can grow from a thorn or a rose blossom from a thistle. That an artist will find beauty in ugliness, *le beau dans l'horrible*, is now a commonplace of the schools, the *argot* of the atelier, but I strongly deny that charming people should be condemned to live with magenta ottomans and Albert-blue curtains in their rooms in order that some painter may observe the side-lights on the one and the values of the other. Nor do I accept the dictum that only a painter is a judge of painting. I say that only an artist is a judge of art; there is a wide difference. As long as a painter is a painter merely, he should not be allowed to talk of anything but mediums and megilp, and on those subjects should be compelled to hold his tongue; it is only when he becomes an artist that the secret laws of artistic creation are revealed to him. For there are not many arts, but one art merely – poem, picture and Parthenon, sonnet and statue – all are in their essence the same, and he who knows one knows all. But the poet is the supreme artist, for he is the master of colour and of form, and the real musician besides, and is lord over all life and all arts; and so to the poet beyond all others are these mysteries known; to Edgar Allan Poe and to Baudelaire, not to Benjamin West and Paul Delaroche. However, I should not enjoy anybody else's lectures unless in a few points I disagreed with them, and Mr Whistler's lecture last night was, like everything that he does, a masterpiece. Not merely for its clever satire and amusing jests will it be remembered, but for the pure and perfect beauty of many of its passages – passages delivered with an earnestness which seemed to amaze those who had looked on Mr Whistler as a master of persiflage merely, and had not known him as we do, as a master of painting also. For that he is indeed one of the very greatest masters of painting is my opinion. And I may add that in this opinion Mr Whistler himself entirely concurs.

DINNERS AND DISHES

Pall Mall Gazette, 7 March 1885

A man can live for three days without bread, but no man can live for one day without poetry, was an aphorism of Baudelaire. You can live without pictures and music but you cannot live without eating, says the author of *Dinners and Dishes*; and this latter view is, no doubt, the more popular. Who, indeed, in these degenerate days would hesitate between an ode and an omelette, a sonnet and a salmis? Yet the position is not entirely Philistine; cookery is an art; are not its principles the subject of South Kensington lectures, and does not the Royal Academy give a banquet once a year? Besides, as the coming democracy will, no doubt, insist on feeding us all on penny dinners, it is well that the laws of cookery should be explained: for were the national meal burned, or badly seasoned, or served up with the wrong sauce a dreadful revolution might follow.

Under these circumstances we strongly recommend *Dinners and Dishes* to everyone: it is brief and concise and makes no attempt at eloquence, which is extremely fortunate. For even on ortolans who could endure oratory? It also has the advantage of not being illustrated. The subject of a work of art has, of course, nothing to do with its beauty, but still there is always something depressing about the coloured lithograph of a leg of mutton.

As regards the author's particular views, we entirely agree with him on the important question of macaroni. 'Never,' he says, 'ask me to back a bill for a man who has given me a macaroni pudding.' Macaroni is essentially a savoury dish and may be served with cheese or tomatoes but never with sugar and milk. There is also a useful description of how to cook risotto – a delightful dish too rarely seen in England; an excellent chapter on the different kinds of salads, which should be carefully studied by those many hostesses whose imaginations never pass beyond lettuce and beetroot; and actually a recipe for making Brussels sprouts eatable. The last is, of course, a masterpiece.

The real difficulty that we all have to face in life is not so much the science of cookery as the stupidity of cooks. And in this little handbook to practical epicureanism the tyrant of the English kitchen is shown in her proper light. Her entire ignorance of herbs, her passion for extracts and essences, her total inability to make a soup which is anything more than a combination of pepper and gravy, her inveterate habit of sending up bread poultices with pheasants – all these sins and many others are ruthlessly unmasked by the author. Ruthlessly and rightly. For the British cook is a foolish woman who should be turned for her iniquities into a pillar of salt which she never knows how to use.

But our author is not local merely. He has been in many lands; he has eaten back-hendl at Vienna and kulibatch at St Petersburg; he has had the courage to face the buffalo veal of Roumania and to dine with a German family at one o'clock; he has serious views on the right method of cooking those famous white truffles of Turin of which Alexandre Dumas was so fond; and, in the face of the Oriental Club, declares that Bombay curry is better than the curry of Bengal. In fact he seems to have had experience of almost every kind of meal except the 'square meal' of the Americans. This he should study at once; there is a great field for the philosophic epicure in the United States. Boston beans may be dismissed at once as delusions, but soft-shell crabs, terrapin, canvas-back ducks, blue fish and the pompono of New Orleans are all wonderful delicacies, particularly when one gets them at Delmonico's. Indeed, the two most remarkable bits of scenery in the States are undoubtedly Delmonico's and the Yosemité Valley; and the former place has done more to promote a good feeling between England and America than anything else has in this century.

We hope the 'Wanderer' will go there soon and add a chapter to *Dinners and Dishes*, and that his book will have in England the influence it deserves. There are twenty ways of cooking a potato and three hundred and sixty-five ways of cooking an egg, yet the British cook, up to the present moment, knows only three methods of sending up either one or the other.

Dinners and Dishes by 'Wanderer' (Simpkin and Marshall)

HAMLET AT THE LYCEUM

Dramatic Review, 9 May 1885

It sometimes happens that at a *première* in London the least enjoyable part of the performance is the play. I have seen many audiences more interesting than the actors, and have often heard better dialogue in the foyer than I have on the stage. At the Lyceum, however, this is rarely the case, and when the play is a play of Shakespeare's, and among its exponents are Mr Irving and Miss Ellen Terry, we turn from the gods in the gallery and from the goddesses in the stalls, to enjoy the charm of the production, and to take delight in the art. The lions are behind the footlights and not in front of them when we have a noble tragedy nobly acted. And I have rarely witnessed such enthusiasm as that which greeted on last Saturday night the two artists I have mentioned. I would like, in fact, to use the word ovation, but a pedantic professor has recently informed us, with the Batavian buoyancy of misapplied learning, that this expression is not to be employed except when a sheep is sacrificed. At the Lyceum last week I need hardly say nothing so dreadful occurred. The only inartistic incident of the evening was the hurling of a bouquet from a box at Mr Irving while he was engaged in portraying the agony of Hamlet's death, and the pathos of his parting with Horatio. The Dramatic College might take up the education of spectators as well as that of players, and teach people that there is a proper moment for the throwing of flowers as well as a proper method.

As regards Mr Irving's own performance, it has been already so elaborately criticised and described, from his business with the supposed pictures in the closet scene down to his use of 'peacock' for 'paddock', that little remains to be said; nor, indeed, does a Lyceum audience require the interposition of the dramatic critic in order to understand or to appreciate the Hamlet of this great actor. I call him a great actor because he brings to the interpretation of a work of art two qualities which we in this century so much desire, the qualities of personality and of perfection. A few years ago it seemed to many, and perhaps rightly, that the personality overshadowed the art. No such criticism would be fair now. The somewhat harsh angularity of movement and faulty pronunciation have been replaced by exquisite grace of gesture and clear precision of word, where such precision is necessary. For delightful as good elocution is, few things are so depressing as to hear a passionate passage recited instead of being acted. The quality of a fine performance is its life more than its learning, and every word in a play has a musical as well as an intellectual value, and must be made expressive of a certain emotion. So it does not seem to me that in all parts of a play perfect pronunciation is necessarily dramatic. When the words are 'wild and whirling', the expression of them must be wild and whirling also. Mr Irving, I think, manages his voice with singular art; it was impossible to discern a false note or wrong intonation in his dialogue or his soliloquies, and his strong dramatic power, his realistic power as an actor, is as effective as ever. A great critic at the beginning of this century said that Hamlet is the most difficult part to personate on a stage, that it is like the attempt to 'embody a shadow'. I cannot say that I agree with this idea. Hamlet seems to me essentially a good acting part, and in Mr Irving's performance of it there is that combination of poetic grace with absolute reality which is so eternally delightful. Indeed, if the words easy and difficult have any meaning at all in matters of art, I would be inclined to say that Ophelia is the more difficult part. She has, I mean, less material by which to produce her effects. She is the occasion of the tragedy, but she is neither its heroine nor its chief victim. She is swept away by circumstances, and gives the opportunity for situation, of which she is not herself the climax, and which she does not herself command. And of all the parts which Miss Terry has acted in her brilliant career, there is none in which her infinite powers of pathos and her imaginative and creative faculty are more shown than in her Ophelia. Miss Terry is one of those rare artists who needs for her dramatic effect no elaborate dialogue, and for whom the simplest words are sufficient. 'I love you not,' says Hamlet, and all that Ophelia answers is, 'I was the more deceived.' These are not very grand words to read, but as Miss Terry gave them in acting they seemed to be the highest possible expression of Ophelia's character. Beautiful, too, was the quick remorse she conveyed by her face and gesture the moment she had lied to Hamlet and told him her father was at home. This I thought a masterpiece of good acting, and her mad scene was wonderful beyond all description. The secrets of Melpomene are known to Miss Terry as well as the secrets of Thalia. As regards the rest of the company there is always a high standard at the Lyceum, but some particular mention should be made of Mr Alexander's brilliant performance of Laertes. Mr Alexander has a most effective presence, a charming voice, and a capacity for wearing lovely costumes with ease and elegance. Indeed, in the latter respect, his only rival was Mr Norman Forbes, who played either Guildenstern or Rosencrantz very gracefully. I believe one of our budding Hazlitts is preparing a volume to be entitled 'Great Guildensterns and Remarkable Rosencrantzes', but I have never been able myself to discern any difference between these two characters. They are, I think, the only characters Shakespeare has not cared to individualise. Whichever of the two, however, Mr Forbes acted, he acted it well. Only one point in Mr Alexander's performance seemed to me open to question, that was his kneeling during the whole of Polonius's speech. For this I see no necessity at all, and it makes the scene look less natural than it should – gives it, I mean, too formal an air. However, the performance was most spirited and gave great pleasure to everyone. Mr Alexander is an artist from whom much will be expected, and I have no doubt he will give us much that is fine and noble. He seems to have all the qualifications for a good actor.

There is just one other character I should like to notice. The First Player seemed to me to act far too well. He should act very badly. The First Player, besides his position in the dramatic evolution of the tragedy, is Shakespeare's caricature of the ranting actor of his day, just as the passage he recites is Shakespeare's own parody on the dull plays of some of his rivals. The whole point of Hamlet's advice to the players seems to me to be lost unless the Player himself has been guilty of the fault which Hamlet reprehends, unless he has sawn the air with his hand, mouthed his lines, torn his passion to tatters, and out-Heroded Herod. The very sensibility which Hamlet notices in the actor, such as his real tears and the like, is not the quality of a good artist. The part should be played after the manner of a provincial tragedian. It is meant to be a satire, and to play it well is to play it badly. The scenery and costumes were excellent with the exception of the King's dress, which was coarse in colour and tawdry in effect. And the Player Queen should have come in boy's attire to Elsinore.

However, last Saturday night was not a night for criticism. The theatre was filled with those who desired to welcome Mr Irving back to his own theatre, and we were all delighted at his re-appearance among us. I hope that some time will elapse before he and Miss Terry cross again that disappointing Atlantic Ocean.

OLIVIA AT THE LYCEUM

Dramatic Review, 30 May 1885

Whether or not it is an advantage for a novel to be produced in a dramatic form is, I think, open to question. The psychological analysis of such work as that of Mr George Meredith, for instance, would probably lose by being transmuted into the passionate action of the stage, nor does M. Zola's *formule scientifique* gain anything at all by theatrical presentation. With Goldsmith it is somewhat different. In *The Vicar of Wakefield* he seeks simply to please his readers, and desires not to prove a theory; he looks on life rather as a picture to be painted than as a problem to be solved; his aim is to create men and women more than to vivisect them; his dialogue is essentially dramatic, and his novel seems to pass naturally into the dramatic form. And to me there is something very pleasurable in seeing and studying the same subject under different conditions of art. For life remains eternally unchanged; it is art which, by presenting it to us under various forms, enables us to realise its many-sided mysteries, and to catch the quality of its most fiery-coloured moments. The originality, I mean, which we ask from the artist, is originality of treatment, not of subject. It is only the unimaginative who ever invents. The true artist is known by the use he makes of what he annexes, and he annexes everything.

Looking in this light at Mr Wills's *Olivia*, it seems to me a very exquisite work of art. Indeed, I know no other dramatist who could have re-told this beautiful English tale with such tenderness and such power, neither losing the charm of the old story nor forgetting the conditions of the new form. The sentiment of the poet and the science of the playwright are exquisitely balanced in it. For though in prose it is a poem, and while a poem it is also a play.

But fortunate as Mr Wills has been in the selection of his subject and in his treatment of it, he is no less fortunate in the actors who interpret his work. To whatever character Miss Terry plays she brings the infinite charm of her beauty, and the marvellous grace of her movements and gestures. It is impossible to escape from the sweet tyranny of her personality. She dominates her audience by the secret of Cleopatra. In her Olivia, however, it is not merely her personality that fascinates us but her power also, her power over pathos, and her command of situation. The scene in which she bade goodbye to her family was touching beyond any scene I remember in any modern play, yet no harsh or violent note was sounded; and when in the succeeding act she struck, in natural and noble indignation, the libertine who had betrayed her, there was, I think, no one in the theatre who did not recognise that in Miss Terry our stage possesses a really great artist, who can thrill an audience without harrowing it, and by means that seem simple and easy can produce the finest dramatic effect. Mr Irving, as Dr Primrose, intensified the beautiful and blind idolatry of the old pastor for his daughter till his own tragedy seems almost greater than hers; the scene in the third act, where he breaks down in his attempt to reprove the lamb that has strayed from the fold, was a masterpiece of fine acting; and the whole performance, while carefully elaborate in detail, was full of breadth and dignity. I acknowledge that I liked him least at the close of the second act. It seems to me that here we should be made to feel not merely the passionate rage of the father, but the powerlessness of the old man. The taking down of the pistols, and the attempt to follow the young duellist, are pathetic because they are useless, and I hardly think that Mr Irving conveyed this idea. As regards the rest of the characters, Mr Terriss's Squire Thornhill was an admirable picture of a fascinating young rake. Indeed, it was so fascinating that the moral equilibrium of the audience was quite disturbed, and nobody seemed to care very much for the virtuous Mr Burchell. I was not sorry to see this triumph of the artistic over the ethical sympathy. Perfect heroes are the monsters of melodramas, and have no place in dramatic art. Life possibly contains them, but Parnassus often rejects what Peckham may welcome. I look forward to a reaction in favour of the cultured criminal. Mr Norman Forbes was a very pleasing Moses, and gave his Latin quotations charmingly, Miss Emery's Sophy was most winning, and, indeed, every part seemed to me well acted except that of the virtuous Mr Burchell. This fact, however, rather pleased me than otherwise, as it increased the charm of his attractive nephew.

The scenery and costumes were excellent, as indeed they always are at the Lyceum when the piece is produced under Mr Irving's direction. The first scene was really very beautiful, and quite as good as the famous cherry orchard of the Théâtre Français. A critic who posed as an authority on field sports assured me that no one ever went out hunting when roses were in full bloom. Personally, that is exactly the season I would select for the chase, but then I know more about flowers than I do about foxes, and like them much better. If the critic was right, either the roses must wither or Squire Thornhill must change his coat. A more serious objection may be brought against the division of the last act into three scenes. There, I think, there was a distinct dramatic loss. The room to which Olivia returns should have been exactly the same room she had left. As a picture of the eighteenth century, however, the whole production was admirable, and the details, both of acting and of *mise-en-scène*, wonderfully perfect. I wish Olivia would take off her pretty mittens when her fortune is being told. Chiromancy is a science which deals almost entirely with the lines on the palm of the hand, and mittens would seriously interfere with its mysticism. Still, when all is said, how easily does this lovely play, this artistic presentation, survive criticisms founded on chiromancy and cub-hunting! The Lyceum under Mr Irving's management has become a centre of art. We are all of us in his debt. I trust that we may see some more plays by living dramatists produced at his theatre, for *Olivia* has been exquisitely mounted and exquisitely played.

A HANDBOOK TO MARRIAGE

Pall Mall Gazette, 18 November 1885

In spite of its somewhat alarming title this book may be highly recommended to everyone. As for the authorities the author quotes, they are almost numberless, and range from Socrates down to Artemus Ward. He tells us of the wicked bachelor who spoke of marriage as 'a very harmless amusement' and advised a young friend of his to 'marry early and marry often'; of Dr Johnson who proposed that marriage should be arranged by the Lord Chancellor, without the parties concerned having any choice in the matter; of the Sussex labourer who asked, 'Why should I give a woman half my victuals for cooking the other half?' and of Lord Verulam who thought that unmarried men did the best public work. And, indeed, marriage is the one subject on which all women agree and all men disagree. Our author, however, is clearly of the same opinion as the Scotch lassie who, on her father warning her what a solemn thing it was to get married, answered, 'I ken that, father, but it's a great deal solemner to be single.' He may be regarded as the champion of married life. Indeed, he has a most interesting chapter on marriage-made men, and though he dissents, and we think rightly, from the view recently put forward by a lady or two on the Women's Rights platform that Solomon owed all his wisdom to the number of his wives, still he appeals to Bismarck, John Stuart Mill, Mahommed and Lord Beaconsfield, as instances of men whose success can be traced to the influence of the women they married. Archbishop Whately once defined woman as 'a creature that does not reason and pokes the fire from the top', but since his day the higher education of women has considerably altered their position. Women have always had an emotional sympathy with those they love; Girton and Newnham have rendered intellectual sympathy also possible. In our day it is best for a man to be married, and men must give up the tyranny in married life which was once so dear to them, and which, we are afraid, lingers still, here and there.

'Do you wish to be my wife, Mabel?' said a little boy. 'Yes,' incautiously answered Mabel. 'Then pull off my boots.'

On marriage vows our author has, too, very sensible views and very amusing stories. He tells us of a nervous bridegroom who, confusing the baptismal and marriage ceremonies, replied when asked if he consented to take the bride for his wife: 'I renounce them all'; of a Hampshire rustic who, when giving the ring, said solemnly to the bride: 'With my body I thee wash up, and with all my hurdle goods I thee and thou'; of another who, when asked whether he would take his partner to be his wedded wife, replied with shameful indecision: 'Yes, I'm willin'; but I'd a sight rather have her sister'; and of a Scotch lady who, on the occasion of her daughter's wedding, was asked by an old friend whether she might congratulate her on the event, and answered: 'Yes, yes, upon the whole it is very satisfactory; it is true Jeannie hates her gudeman, but then there's always a something!' Indeed, the good stories contained in this book are quite endless and make it very pleasant reading, while the good advice is on all points admirable.

Most young married people nowadays start in life with a dreadful collection of ormolu inkstands covered with sham onyxes, or with a perfect museum of salt-cellars. We strongly recommend this book as one of the best of wedding presents. It is a complete handbook to an earthly Paradise, and its author may be regarded as the Murray of matrimony and the Baedeker of bliss.

How to be Happy though Married: Being a Handbook to Marriage. By a Graduate in the University of Matrimony. [E. J. Hardy] (T. Fisher Unwin.)

BALZAC IN ENGLISH

Pall Mall Gazette, 13 September 1886

Many years ago, in a number of *All the Year Round*, Charles Dickens complained that Balzac was very little read in England, and although since then the public has become more familiar with the great masterpieces of French fiction, still it may be doubted whether the *Comédie humaine* is at all appreciated or understood by the general run of novel readers. It is really the greatest monument that literature has produced in our century, and M. Taine hardly exaggerates when he says that, after Shakespeare, Balzac is our most important magazine of documents on human nature. Balzac's aim, in fact, was to do for humanity what Buffon had done for the animal creation. As the naturalist studied lions and tigers, so the novelist studied men and women. Yet he was no mere reporter. Photography and *procès verbal* were not the essentials of his method. Observation gave him the facts of life, but his genius converted facts into truths, and truths into truth. He was, in a word, a marvellous combination of the artistic temperament with the scientific spirit. The latter he bequeathed to his disciples; the former was entirely his own. The distinction between such a book as M. Zola's *L'Assommoir* and such a book as Balzac's *Illusions perdues* is the distinction between unimaginative realism and imaginative reality. 'All Balzac's characters,' said Baudelaire, 'are gifted with the same ardour of life that animated himself. All his fictions are as deeply coloured as dreams. Every mind is a weapon loaded to the muzzle with will. The very scullions have genius.' He was, of course, accused of being immoral. Few writers who deal directly with life escape that charge. His answer to the accusation was characteristic and conclusive. 'Whoever contributes his stone to the edifice of ideas,' he wrote, 'whoever proclaims an abuse, whoever sets his mark upon an evil to be abolished, always passes for immortal. If you are true in your portraits, if, by dint of daily and nightly toil, you succeed in writing the most difficult language in the world, the word immoral is thrown in your face.' The morals of the personages of the *Comédie humaine* are simply the morals of the world around us. They are part of the artist's subject-matter; they are not part of his method. If there be any need of censure it is to life, not to literature, that it should be given. Balzac, besides, is essentially universal. He sees life from every point of view. He has no preferences and no prejudices. He does not try to prove anything. He feels that the spectacle of life contains its own secret. '*Il crée un monde et se tait.*'

And what a world it is! What a panorama of passions! What a pell-mell of men and women! It was said of Trollope that he increased the number of our acquaintances without adding to our visiting list; but after the *Comédie humaine* one begins to believe that the only real people are the people who have never existed. Lucien de Rubempré, Le Père Goriot, Ursule Mirouët, Marguerite Claës, the Baron Hulot, Madame Marneffe, le Cousin Pons, de

Marsay – all bring with them a kind of contagious illusion of life. They have a fierce vitality about them: their existence is fervent and fiery-coloured; we not merely feel for them but we see them – they dominate our fancy and defy scepticism. A steady course of Balzac reduces our living friends to shadows, and our acquaintances to the shadows of shades. Who would care to go out to an evening party to meet Tomkins, the friend of one's boyhood, when one can sit at home with Lucien de Rubempré? It is pleasanter to have the entrée to Balzac's society than to receive cards from all the duchesses in Mayfair.

In spite of this, there are many people who have declared the *Comédie humaine* to be indigestible. Perhaps it is: but then what about truffles? Balzac's publisher refused to be disturbed by any such criticism as that. 'Indigestible, is it?' he exclaimed with what, for a publisher, was rare good sense. 'Well, I should hope so; who ever thinks of a dinner that isn't?' And our English publisher, Mr Routledge, clearly agrees with M. Poulet-Malassis, as he is occupied in producing a complete translation of the *Comédie humaine*. The two volumes that at present lie before us contain *César Birotteau*, that terrible tragedy of finance, and *L'Illustre Gaudissart*, the apotheosis of the commercial traveller, the *Duchesse de Langeais*, most marvellous of modern love stories, *Le Chef d'œuvre inconnu*, from which Mr Henry James took his *Madonna of the Future*, and that extraordinary romance *Une Passion dans le désert*. The choice of stories is quite excellent, but the translations are very unequal, and some of them are positively bad. *L'Illustre Gaudissart*, for instance, is full of the most grotesque mistakes, mistakes that would disgrace a schoolboy. '*Bon conseil vaut un oeil dans la main*' is translated as 'Good advice is an egg in the hand'! '*Ecus rebelles*' is rendered 'rebellious lucre', and such common expressions as '*faire la barbe*', '*attendre la vente*', '*n'entendre rien*', '*pâlir sur une affaire*', are all mistranslated. '*Des bois de quoi se faire un cure-dent*' is not 'a few trees to slice into toothpicks', but 'as much timber as would make a toothpick'; '*son horloge enfermée dans une grande armoire oblongue*' is not 'a clock which he kept shut up on a long oblong closet' but simply 'a clock in a tall clock-case'; '*journal viager*' is not 'an annuity', '*garce*' is not the same as 'farce', and '*dessins des Indes*' are not 'drawings of the Indies'. On the whole, nothing can be worse than this translation, and if Mr Routledge wishes the public to read his version of the *Comédie humaine*, he should engage translators who have some slight knowledge of French.

César Birotteau is better, though it is not by any means free from mistakes. 'To suffer under the Maximum' is an absurd rendering of '*subir le maximum*'; '*perse*' is 'chintz', not 'Persian chintz'; '*rendre le pain bénit*' is not 'to take the wafer'; '*rivière*' is hardly a 'fillet of diamonds'; and to translate '*son coeur avait un calus à l'endroit du loyer*' by 'his heart was a callus in the direction of the lease' is an insult to two languages. On the whole, the best version is that of the *Duchesse de Langeais*, though even this leaves much to be desired. Such a sentence as 'to imitate the rough logician who marched before the Pyrrhonians *while denying his own movement*' entirely misses the point of Balzac's '*imiter le rude logicien qui marchait devant les pyrrhoniens, qui niaient le mouvement*.'

We fear Mr Routledge's edition will not do. It is well printed and nicely bound; but his translators do not understand French. It is a great pity, for *La Comédie humaine* is one of the masterpieces of the age.

Balzac's Novels in English. *The Duchesse de Langeais and Other Stories*; *César Birotteau*. (Routledge and Sons.)

A RIDE THROUGH MOROCCO

Pall Mall Gazette, 8 October 1886

Morocco is a sort of paradox among countries, for though it lies westward of Piccadilly yet it is purely oriental in character, and though it is but three hours' sail from Europe yet it makes you feel (to use the forcible expression of an American writer) as if you had been 'taken up by the scruff of the neck and set down in the Old Testament'. Mr Hugh Stutfield has ridden twelve hundred miles through it, penetrated to Fez and Wazan, seen the lovely gate at Mequinez and the Hassen Tower by Rabat, feasted with sheikhs and fought with robbers, lived in an atmosphere of Moors, mosques and mirages, visited the city of the lepers and the slave-market of Sus, and played loo under the shadow of the Atlas Mountains. He is not an Herodotus nor a Sir John Mandeville, but he tells his stories very pleasantly. His book, on the whole, is delightful reading, for though Morocco is picturesque he does not weary us with word-painting; though it is poor he does not bore us with platitudes. Now and then he indulges in a traveller's licence and thrills the simple reader with statements as amazing as they are amusing. The Moorish coinage, he tells us, is so cumbersome that if a man gives you change for half-a-crown you have to hire a donkey to carry it away; the Moorish language is so guttural that no one can ever hope to pronounce it aright who has not been brought up within hearing of the grunting of camels, a steady course of sneezing being, consequently, the only way by which a European can acquire anything like the proper accent; the sultan does not know how much he is married, but he unquestionably is so to a very large extent; on the principle that you cannot have too much of a good thing a woman is valued in proportion to her stoutness, and so far from there being any reduction made in the marriage-market for taking a quantity, you must pay so much per pound; the Arabs believe the Shereef of Wazan to be such a holy man that, if he is guilty of taking champagne, the forbidden wine is turned into milk as he quaffs it, and if he gets extremely drunk he is merely in a mystical trance.

Mr Stutfield, however, has his serious moments, and his account of the commerce, government and social life of the Moors is extremely interesting. It must be confessed that the picture he draws is in many respects a very tragic one. The Moors are the masters of a beautiful country and of many beautiful arts, but they are paralysed by their fatalism and pillaged by their rulers. Few races, indeed, have had a more terrible fall than these Moors. Of the great intellectual civilisation of the Arabs no trace remains. The names of Averroes and Almaimón, of Al Abbas and Ben Husa are quite unknown. Fez, once the Athens of Africa, the cradle of the sciences, is now a mere commercial caravansary. Its universities have vanished, its library is almost empty. Freedom of thought has been killed by the Koran, freedom of living by bad government. But Mr Stutfield is not without hopes for the future. So far from agreeing with Lord Salisbury that 'Morocco may go her own way', he strongly supports Captain Warren's proposition that we should give up Gibraltar to Spain in exchange for Ceuta, and thereby prevent the Mediterranean from becoming a French lake, and give England a new granary for corn. The Moorish empire, he warns us, is rapidly breaking up, and if in the 'general scramble for Africa' that has already begun, the French gain possession of Morocco, he points out that our supremacy over the Straits will be lost. Whatever may be thought of Mr Stutfield's political views, and his suggestions for 'multiple control' and 'collective European action', there is no doubt that in Morocco England has interests to defend and a mission to pursue, and this part of the book should be carefully studied. As for the general reader who, we fear, is not as a rule interested in the question of 'multiple control', if he is a sportsman, he will find in *El Magreb* a capital account of pig-sticking; if he is artistic, he will be delighted to know that the importation of magenta into Morocco is strictly prohibited; if criminal jurisprudence has any charms for him, he can examine a code that punishes slander by rubbing cayenne paper into the lips of the offender; and if he is merely lazy, he can take a pleasant ride of twelve hundred miles in Mr Stutfield's company without stirring out of his armchair.

El Magreb: Twelve Hundred Miles' Ride through Morocco. By Hugh Stutfield. (Sampson Low, Marston and Co.)

THE AMERICAN INVASION

Court and Society Review, 23 March 1887

A terrible danger is hanging over the Americans in London. Their future and their reputation this season depend entirely on the success of Buffalo Bill and Mrs Brown-Potter. The former is certain to draw; for English people are far more interested in American barbarism than they are in American civilisation. When they sight Sandy Hook they look to their rifles and ammunition; and, after dining once at Delmonico's, start off for Colorado or California, for Montana or the Yellow Stone Park. Rocky Mountains charm them more than riotous millionaires; they have been known to prefer buffaloes to Boston. Why should they not? The cities of America are inexpressibly tedious. The Bostonians take their learning too sadly; culture with them is an accomplishment rather than an atmosphere; their 'Hub', as they call it, is a paradise of prigs. Chicago is a sort of monster-shop, full of bustle and bores. Political life at Washington is like political life in a suburban vestry. Baltimore is amusing for a week, but Philadelphia is dreadfully provincial; and though one can dine in New York one could not dwell there. Better the Far West with its grizzly bears and its untamed cowboys, its free open-air life and its free open-air manners, its boundless prairies and its boundless mendacity! This is what Buffalo Bill is going to bring to London; and we have no doubt that London will fully appreciate his show.

With regard to Mrs Brown-Potter, as acting is no longer considered absolutely essential for success on the English stage, there is really no reason why the pretty bright-eyed lady who charmed us all last June by her merry laugh and her nonchalant ways, should not – to borrow an expression from her native language – made a big boom and paint the town red. We sincerely hope she will; for, on the whole, the American invasion has done English Society a great deal of good. American women are bright, clever, and wonderfully cosmopolitan. Their patriotic feelings are limited to an admiration for Niagara and a regret for the Elevated Railway; and, unlike the men, they never bore us with Bunker Hill. They take their dresses from Paris and their manners from Piccadilly, and wear both charmingly. They have a quaint pertness, a delightful conceit, a native self-assertion. They insist on being paid compliments and have almost succeeded in making Englishmen eloquent. For our aristocracy they have an ardent admiration; they adore titles and are a permanent blow to Republican principles. In the art of amusing men they are adepts, both by nature and education, and can actually tell a story without forgetting the point – an accomplishment that is extremely rare among the women of other countries. It is true that they lack repose and that their voices are somewhat harsh and strident when they land first at Liverpool; but after a time one gets to love these pretty whirlwinds in petticoats that sweep so recklessly through Society and are so agitating to all duchesses who have daughters. There is something fascinating in their funny, exaggerated gestures and their petulant way of tossing the head. Their eyes have no magic nor mystery in them, but they challenge us for combat; and when we engage we are always worsted. Their lips seem made for laughter and yet they never grimace. As for their voices, they soon get them into tune. Some of them have been known to acquire a fashionable drawl in two Seasons; and after they have been presented to Royalty they all roll their 'r's as vigorously as a young equerry or an old lady-in-waiting. Still, they never really lose their accent; it keeps peeping out here and there, and when they chatter together they are like a bevy of peacocks. Nothing is more amusing than to watch two American girls greeting each other in a drawing-room or in the Row. They are like children with their shrill staccato cries of wonder, their odd little exclamations. Their conversation sounds like a series of exploding crackers; they are exquisitely incoherent and use a sort of primitive, emotional language. After five minutes they are left beautifully breathless and look at each other half in amusement and half in affection. If a stolid young Englishman is fortunate enough to be introduced to them he is amazed at their extraordinary vivacity, their electric quickness of repartee, their inexhaustible store of curious catchwords. He never really understands them, for their thoughts flutter about with the sweet irresponsibility of butterflies; but he is pleased and amused and feels as if he were in an aviary. On the whole, American girls have a wonderful charm and, perhaps, the chief secret of their charm is that they never talk seriously except about amusements. They have, however, one grave fault – their mothers. Dreary as were those old Pilgrim Fathers who left our shores more than two centuries ago to found New England beyond seas, the Pilgrim Mothers who have returned to us in the nineteenth century are drearier still.

Here and there, of course, there are exceptions, but as a class they are either dull, dowdy or dyspeptic. It is only fair to the rising generation of America to state that they are not to blame for this. Indeed, they spare no pains at all to bring up their parents properly and give them a suitable, if somewhat late, education. From its earliest years every American child spends most of its time correcting the faults of its father and mother; and no one who has had the opportunity of watching an American family on the deck of an Atlantic steamer, or in the refined seclusion of a New York boarding-house, can fail to have been struck by this characteristic of their civilisation. In America the young are always ready to give to those who are older than themselves the full benefits of their inexperience. A boy of only eleven or twelve years of age will firmly but kindly point out to his father his defects of manner or temper; will never weary of warning him against extravagance, idleness, late hours, unpunctuality, and the other temptations to which the aged are so particularly exposed; and sometimes, should he fancy that he is monopolising too much of the conversation at dinner, will remind him, across the table, of the new child's adage, 'Parents should be seen, not heard.' Nor does any mistaken idea of kindness prevent the little American girl from censuring her mother whenever it is necessary. Often, indeed, feeling that a rebuke conveyed in the presence of others is more truly efficacious than one merely whispered in the quiet of the nursery, she will call the attention of perfect strangers to her mother's general untidiness, her want of intellectual Boston conversation, immoderate love of iced water and green corn, stinginess in the matter of candy, ignorance of the uses of the best Baltimore society, bodily ailments and the like. In fact, it may be truly said that no American child is ever blind to the deficiencies of its parents, no matter how much it may love them.

Yet, somehow, this educational system has not been so successful as it deserved. In many cases, no doubt, the material with which the children had to deal was crude and incapable of real development; but the fact remains that the American mother is a tedious person. The American father is better, for he is never seen in London. He passes his life entirely in Wall Street and communicates with his family once a month by means of a telegram in cipher. The mother, however, is always with us, and, lacking the quick imitative faculty of the younger generation, remains uninteresting and provincial to the last. In spite of her, however, the American girl is always welcome. She brightens our dull dinner-parties for us and makes life go pleasantly by for a season. In the race for coronets she often carries off the prize; but, once she has gained the victory, she is generous and forgives her English rivals everything, even their beauty.

Warned by the example of her mother that American women do not grow old gracefully, she tries not to grow old at all and often succeeds. She has exquisite feet and hands, is always *bien chaussée et bien gantée* and can talk brilliantly upon any subject, provided that she knows nothing about it.

Her sense of humour keeps her from the tragedy of a *grande passion*, and, as there is neither romance nor humility in her love, she makes an excellent wife. What her ultimate influence on English life will be it is difficult to estimate at present; but there can be no doubt that, of all the factors that have contributed to the social revolution of London, there are few more important, and none more delightful, than the American Invasion.

TWO BIOGRAPHIES OF KEATS

Pall Mall Gazette, 27 September 1887

A poet, said Keats once, 'is the most unpoetical of all God's creatures', and whether the aphorism be universally true of not, this is certainly the impression produced by the two last biographies that have appeared of Keats himself. It cannot be said that either Mr Colvin or Mr William Rossetti makes us love Keats more or understand him better. In both these books there is much that is like 'chaff in the mouth', and in Mr Rossetti's there is not a little that is like 'brass on the palate'. To a certain degree this is, no doubt, inevitable nowadays. Everybody pays a penalty for peeping through keyholes, and the keyhole and the backstairs are essential parts of the method of the modern biographers. It is only fair, however, to state at the outset that Mr Colvin has done his work much better than Mr Rossetti. The account Mr Colvin gives of Keats's boyhood, for instance, is very pleasing, and so is the sketch of Keats's circle of friends, both Leigh Hunt and Haydon being admirably drawn. Here and there, trivial family details are introduced without much regard to proportion, and the posthumous panegyrics of devoted friends are not really of so much value, in helping us to form any true estimate of Keats's actual character, as Mr Colvin seems to imagine. We have no doubt that when Bailey wrote to Lord Houghton that common sense and gentleness were Keats's two special characteristics the worthy Archdeacon meant extremely well, but we prefer the real Keats, with his passionate wilfulness, his fantastic moods and his fine inconsistence. Part of Keats's charm as a man is his fascinating incompleteness. We do not want him reduced to a sand-paper smoothness or made perfect by the addition of popular virtues. Still, if Mr Colvin has not given us a very true picture of Keats's character, he has certainly told the story of his life in a pleasant and readable manner. He may not write with the ease and grace of a man of letters, but he is never pretentious and not often pedantic.

Mr Rossetti's book is a great failure. To begin with, Mr Rossetti commits the great mistake of separating the man from the artist. The facts of Keats's life are interesting only when they are shown in their relation to his creative activity. The moment they are isolated they are either uninteresting or painful. Mr Rossetti complains that the early part of Keats's life is uneventful and the latter part depressing, but the fault lies with the biographer, not with the subject.

The book opens with a detailed account of Keats's life, in which he spares us nothing, from what he calls the 'sexual misadventure at Oxford' down to the six weeks' dissipation after the appearance of the *Blackwood* article and the hysterical and morbid ravings of the dying man. No doubt, most if not all of the things Mr Rossetti tells us are facts; but there is neither tact shown in the selection that is made of the facts nor sympathy in the use to which they are put. When Mr Rossetti writes of the man he forgets the poet, and when he criticises the poet he shows that he does not understand the man. His first error, as we have said, is isolating the life from the work; his second error is his treatment of the work itself. Take, for instance, his criticism of that wonderful 'Ode to a Nightingale', with all its marvellous magic of music, colour and form. He begins by saying that 'the first point of weakness' in the poem is the 'surfeit of mythological allusions', a statement which is absolutely untrue, as out of the eight stanzas of the poem only three contain any mythological allusions at all, and of these not one is either forced or remote. Then coming to the second verse,

> Oh for a draught of vintage, that hath been
> Cool'd a long age in the deep-delvèd earth,
> Tasting of Flora and the country-green,
> Dance, and Provençal song, and sunburnt mirth!

Mr Rossetti exclaims in a fine fit of 'Blue Ribbon' enthusiasm: 'Surely nobody wants wine as a preparation for enjoying a nightingale's music, whether in a literal or in a fanciful relation'! 'To call wine "the true, the blushful Hippocrene" ... seems' to him 'both stilted and repulsive'; 'the phrase "with beaded bubbles winking at the brim" is (though picturesque) trivial'; 'the succeeding image, "Not charioted by Bacchus and his pards"' is 'far worse'; while such an expression as 'light-wingèd Dryad of the trees' is an obvious pleonasm, for Dryad really means Oak-nymph! As for that superb burst of passion,

> Thou wast not born, for death, immortal Bird!
> No hungry generations tread thee down:
> The voice I hear this passing night was heard
> In ancient days by emperor and clown:

Mr Rossetti tells us that it is a palpable, or rather 'palpaple (sic) fact that this address ... is a logical solecism', as men live longer than nightingales. As Mr Colvin makes very much the same criticism, talking of 'a breach of logic which is also ... a flaw in the poetry', it may be worth while to point out to these two last critics of Keats's work that what Keats meant to convey was the contrast between the permanence of beauty and the change and decay of human life, an idea which receives its fullest expression in the 'Ode to a Grecian Urn'. Nor do the other poems fare much better at Mr Rossetti's hands. The fine invocation in 'Isabella' –

> Moan hither, all ye syllables of woe,
> From the deep throat of sad Melpomene!
> Through bronzèd lyre in tragic order go,
> And touch the strings into a mystery.

seems to him 'a fadeur'; the Indian Bacchante of the fourth book of Endymion he calls a 'sentimental and beguiling wine-bibber', and, as for Endymion himself, he declares that he cannot understand 'how his human organism, with respirative and digestive processes, continues to exist', and gives us his own idea of how Keats should have treated the subject. An eminent French critic once exclaimed in despair, '*Je trouve des physiologistes partout!*'; but it has been reserved for Mr Rossetti to speculate on Endymion's digestion, and we readily accord to him all the distinction of the position. Even where Mr Rossetti seeks to praise, he spoils what he praises. To speak of *Hyperion* as 'a monument of Cyclopean architecture in verse' is bad enough, but to call it 'a Stonehenge of reverberance' is absolutely detestable; nor do we learn much about 'The Eve of St Mark' by being told that its 'simplicity is full-blooded as well as quaint'. What is the meaning, also, of stating that Keats's 'Notes on Shakespeare' are 'somewhat strained and *bloated*'? And is there nothing better to be said of Madeline in 'The Eve of St Agnes' than that 'she is made a very charming and loveable figure, *although she does nothing very particular except to undress without looking behind her, and to elope*'? There is no necessity to follow Mr Rossetti any further as he flounders about through the quagmire that he has made for his own feet. A critic who can say that 'not many of Keats's poems are highly admirable' need not be too seriously treated. Mr Rossetti is an industrious man and a painstaking writer, but he entirely lacks the temper necessary for the interpretation of such poetry as was written by John Keats.

It is pleasant to turn again to Mr Colvin, who criticises always with modesty and often with acumen. We do not agree with him when he accepts Mrs Owens's theory of a symbolic and allegoric meaning underlying *Endymion*, his final judgment on Keats as 'the most Shaksperean spirit that has lived since Shakspere' is not very fortunate, and we are surprised to find him suggesting, on the evidence of a rather silly story of Severn's, that Sir Walter Scott was privy to the *Blackwood* article. There is nothing, however, about his estimate of the poet's work that is harsh, irritating or uncouth. The true Marcellus of English song has not yet found his Virgil, but Mr Colvin makes a tolerable Statius.

Keats. By Sidney Colvin. 'English Men of Letters' Series. (Macmillan and Co.)
Life of John Keats. By William Michael Rossetti. 'Great Writers' Series. (Walter Scott.)

ARISTOTLE AT AFTERNOON TEA

Pall Mall Gazette, 16 December 1887

In Society, says Mr Mahaffy, every civilised man and woman ought to feel it their duty to say something, even when there is hardly anything to be said, and, in order to encourage this delightful art of brilliant chatter, he has published a social guide without which no *débutante* or dandy should ever dream of going out to dine. Not that Mr Mahaffy's book can be said to be, in any sense of the word, popular. In discussing this important subject of conversation, he has not merely followed the scientific method of Aristotle which is, perhaps, excusable, but he has adopted the literary style of Aristotle for which no excuse is possible. There is, also, hardly a single anecdote, hardly a single illustration, and the reader is left to put the Professor's abstract rules into practice, without either the examples or the warnings of history to encourage or to dissuade him in his reckless career. Still, the book can be warmly recommended to all who propose to substitute the vice of verbosity for the stupidity of silence. It fascinates in spite of its form and pleases in spite of its pedantry, and is the nearest approach, that we know of, in modern literature to meeting Aristotle at an afternoon tea.

As regards physical conditions, the only one that is considered by Mr Mahaffy as being absolutely essential to a good conversationalist, is the possession of a musical voice. Some learned writers have been of opinion that a slight stammer often gives peculiar zest to conversation, but Mr Mahaffy rejects this view and is extremely severe on every eccentricity from a native brogue to an artificial catchword. With his remarks on the latter point, the meaningless repetition of phrases, we entirely agree. Nothing can be more irritating than the scientific person who is always saying '*Exactly so*,' or the common-place person who ends every sentence with '*Don't you know?*' or the pseudo-artistic person who murmurs '*Charming, charming*,' on the smallest provocation. It is, however, with the mental and moral qualifications for conversation that Mr Mahaffy specially deals. Knowledge he, naturally, regards as an absolute essential, for, as he most justly observes, 'an ignorant man is seldom agreeable, except as a butt'. Upon the other hand, strict accuracy should be avoided. 'Even a consummate liar,' says Mr Mahaffy, is a better ingredient in a company than 'the scrupulously truthful man, who weighs every statement, questions every fact, and corrects every inaccuracy.' The liar at any rate recognises that recreation, not instruction, is the aim of conversation, and is a far more civilised being than the blockhead who loudly expresses his disbelief in a story which is told simply for the amusement of the company. Mr Mahaffy, however, makes an exception in favour of the eminent specialist and tells us that intelligent questions addressed to an astronomer, or a pure mathematician, will elicit many curious facts which will pleasantly beguile the time. Here, in the interest of Society, we feel bound to enter a formal protest. Nobody, even in the provinces, should ever be allowed to ask an intelligent question about pure mathematics across a dinner-table. A question of this kind is quite as bad as enquiring suddenly about the state of a man's soul, a sort of *coup* which, as Mr Mahaffy remarks elsewhere, 'many pious people have actually thought a decent introduction to a conversation'.

As for the moral qualifications of a good talker, Mr Mahaffy, following the example of his great master, warns us against any disproportionate excess of virtue. Modesty, for instance, may easily become a social vice, and to be continually apologising for one's ignorance or stupidity is a grave injury to conversation, for 'what we want to learn from each member is his free opinion on the subject in hand, not his own estimate of the value of that opinion'. Simplicity, too, is not without its dangers. The *enfant terrible*, with his shameless love of truth, the raw country-bred girl who always says what she means, and the plain, blunt man who makes a point of speaking his mind on every possible occasion, without ever considering whether he has a mind at all, are the fatal examples of what simplicity leads to. Shyness may be a form of vanity, and reserve a development of pride, and as for sympathy, what can be more detestable than the man, or woman, who insists on agreeing with everybody, and so makes 'a discussion, which implies differences in opinion', absolutely impossible? Even the unselfish listener is apt to become a bore. 'These silent people,' says Mr Mahaffy, 'not only take all they can get in Society for nothing, but they take it without the smallest gratitude, and have the audacity afterwards to censure those who have laboured for their amusement.' Tact, which is an exquisite sense of the symmetry of things, is, according to Mr Mahaffy, the highest and best of all the moral conditions for conversation. The man of tact, he most wisely remarks, 'will instinctively avoid jokes about Blue Beard' in the company of a woman who is a man's third wife; he will never be guilty of talking like a book, but will rather avoid too careful an attention to grammar and the rounding of periods; he will cultivate the art of graceful interruption, so as to prevent a subject being worn threadbare by the aged or the inexperienced; and should he be desirous of telling a story, he will look round and consider each member of the party, and if there be a single stranger present will forgo the pleasure of anecdotage rather than make the social mistake of hurting even one of the guests. As for prepared or premeditated art, Mr Mahaffy has a great contempt for it and tells us of a certain college don (let us hope not at Oxford or Cambridge) who always carried a jest-book in his pocket and had to refer to it when he wished to make a repartee. Great wits, too, are often very cruel, and great humorists often very vulgar, so it will be better to try and 'make good conversation without any large help from these brilliant but dangerous gifts'.

In a *tête-à-tête* one should talk about persons, and in general Society about things. The state of the weather is always an excusable exordium, but it is convenient to have a paradox or heresy on the subject always ready so as to direct the conversation into other channels. Really domestic people are almost invariably bad talkers as their very virtues in home life have dulled their interest in outer things. The very best mothers will insist on chattering of their babies and prattling about infant education. In fact, most women do not take sufficient interest in politics, just as most men are deficient in general reading. Still, anybody can be made to talk, except the very obstinate, and even a commercial traveller may be drawn out and become quite interesting. As for Society small-talk, it is impossible, Mr Mahaffy tells us, for any sound theory of conversation to depreciate gossip, 'which is perhaps the main factor in agreeable talk throughout Society'. The retailing of small personal points about great people always gives pleasure, and if one is not fortunate enough to be an Arctic traveller or an escaped Nihilist, the best thing one can do is to relate some anecdote of 'Prince Bismarck, or King Victor Emmanuel, or Mr Gladstone'. In the case of meeting a genius and a Duke at dinner, the good talker will try to raise himself to the level of the former and to bring the latter down to his own level. To succeed among one's social superiors one must have no hesitation in contradicting them. Indeed, one should make bold criticisms and introduce a bright and free tone into a Society whose grandeur and extreme respectability make it, Mr Mahaffy remarks, as pathetically as inaccurately, 'perhaps somewhat dull'. The best conversationalists are those whose ancestors have been bilingual, like the French and Irish, but the art of conversation is really within the reach of almost everyone, except those who are morbidly truthful, or whose high moral worth requires to be sustained by a permanent gravity of demeanour and a general dulness of mind.

These are the broad principles contained in Mr Mahaffy's clever little book, and many of them will, no doubt, commend themselves to our readers. The maxim, 'If you find the company dull, blame yourself,' seems to us somewhat optimistic, and we have no sympathy at all with the professional story-teller who is really a great bore at a dinner-table; but Mr Mahaffy is quite right in insisting that no bright social intercourse is possible without equality, and it is no objection to his book to say that it will not teach people how to talk cleverly. It is not logic that makes men reasonable, not the science of ethics that makes men good, but it is always useful to analyse, to for-mularise and to investigate. The only thing to be regretted in the volume is the arid and jejune character of the style. If Mr Mahaffy would only write as he talks, his book would be much pleasanter reading.

The Principles of the Art of Conversation: A Social Essay. By J. P. Mahaffy. (Macmillan and Co.)

MR MORRIS ON TAPESTRY

Pall Mall Gazette, 2 November 1888

Yesterday evening Mr William Morris delivered a most interesting and fascinating lecture on Carpet and Tapestry Weaving at the Arts and Crafts Exhibition now held at the New Gallery. Mr Morris had small practical models of the two looms used, the carpet loom where the weaver sits in front of his work; the more elaborate tapestry loom where the weaver sits behind, at the back of the stuff, has his design outlined on the upright threads and sees in a mirror the shadow of the pattern and picture as it grows gradually to perfection. He spoke at much length on the question of dyes – praising madder and kermes for reds, precipitate of iron or ochre for yellows, and for blue either indigo or woad. At the back of the platform hung a lovely Flemish tapestry of the fourteenth century and a superb Persian carpet about two hundred and fifty years old. Mr Morris pointed out the loveliness of the carpet – its delicate suggestion of hawthorn-blossom, iris and rose, its rejection of imitation and shading; and showed how it combined the great quality of decorative design – being at once clear and well defined in form: each outline exquisitely traced, each line deliberate in its intention and its beauty, and the whole effect being one of unity, of harmony, almost of mystery, the colours being so perfectly harmonised together and the little bright notes of colour being so cunningly placed either for tone or brilliancy.

Tapestries, he said, were to the North of Europe what fresco was to the South – our climate, amongst other reasons, guiding us in our choice of material for wall-covering. England, France, and Flanders were the three great tapestry countries – Flanders with its great wool trade being the first in splendid colours and superb Gothic design. The keynote of tapestry, the secret of its loveliness, was, he told the audience, the complete filling up of every corner and square inch of surface with lovely and fanciful and suggestive design. Hence the wonder of those great Gothic tapestries where the forest trees rise in different places, one over the other, each leaf perfect in its shape and colour and decorative value, while in simple raiment of beautiful design knights and ladies wandered in rich flower gardens, and rode with hawk on wrist through long green arcades, and sat listening to lute and viol in blossom-starred bowers or by cool gracious water springs. Upon the other hand, when the Gothic feeling died away, and Boucher and others began to design, they gave us wide expanses of waste sky, elaborate perspective, posing nymphs and shallow artificial treatment. Indeed, Boucher met with scant mercy at Mr Morris's vigorous hands and was roundly abused, and modern Gobelins, with M. Bougereau's cartoons, fared no better.

Mr Morris told some delightful stories about old tapestry-work from the days when in the Egyptian tombs the dead were laid wrapped in picture cloths, some of which are now in the South Kensington museum, to the time of the great Turk Bajazet who, having captured some Christian knights, would accept nothing for their ransom but the 'storied tapestries of France' and gerfalcons. As regards the use of tapestry in modern days, he pointed out that we were richer than the Middle Ages, and so should be better able to afford this form of lovely wall-covering, which for artistic tone is absolutely without rival. He said that the very limitation of material and form forced the imaginative designer into giving us something really beautiful and decorative. 'What is the use of setting an artist in a twelve-acre field and telling him to design a house? Give him a limited space and he is forced by its limitation to concentrate, and to fill with pure loveliness the narrow surface at his disposal.' The worker also gives to the original design a very perfect richness of detail, and the threads with their varying colours and delicate reflections convey into the work a new source of delight. Here, he said, we found perfect unity between the imaginative artist and the handicraftsman. The one was not too free, the other was not a slave. The eye of the artist saw, his brain conceived, his imagination created, but the hand of the weaver had also its opportunity for wonderful work, and did not copy what was already made, but recreated and put into a new and delightful form a design that for its perfection needed the loom to aid, and had to pass into a fresh and marvellous material before its beauty came to its real flower and blossom of absolutely right expression and artistic effect. But, said Mr Morris in conclusion, to have great work we must be worthy of it. Commercialism, with its vile god cheapness, its callous indifference to the worker, its innate vulgarity of temper, is our enemy. To gain anything good we must sacrifice something of our luxury – must think more of others, more of the State, the commonweal: 'We cannot have riches and wealth both,' he said; we must choose between them.

The lecture was listened to with great attention by a very large and distinguished audience, and Mr Morris was loudly applauded.

The next lecture will be on Sculpture by Mr George Simonds, and if it is half so good as Mr Morris it will well repay a visit to the lecture-room. Mr Crane deserves great credit for his exertions in making this exhibition what it should be, and there is no doubt but that it will exercise an important and a good influence on all the handicrafts of our country.

LONDON MODELS

English Illustrated Magazine, January 1889

Professional models are a purely human invention. To the Greeks, for instance, they were quite unknown. Mr Mahaffy, it is true, tell us that Pericles used to present peacocks to the great ladies of Athenian society in order to induce them to sit to his friend Phidias, and we know that Polygnotus introduced into his picture of the Trojan women the face of Elpinice, the celebrated sister of the great Conservative leader of the day, but these *grandes dames* clearly do not come under our category. As for the old masters, they undoubtedly made constant studies from their pupils and apprentices, and even their religious pictures are full of the portraits of their friends and relations, but they do not seem to have had the inestimable advantage of the existence of a class of people whose sole profession is to pose. In fact the model, in our sense of the word, is a direct creation of Academic Schools.

Every country now has its own models, except America. In New York, and even in Boston, a good model is so great a rarity that most of the artists are reduced to painting Niagara and millionaires. In Europe, however, it is different. Here we have plenty of models, and of every nationality. The Italian models are the best. The natural grace of their attitudes, as well as the wonderful picturesqueness of their colouring, makes them facile – often too facile – subjects for the painter's brush. The French models, though not so beautiful as the Italian, possess a quickness of intellectual sympathy, a capacity, in fact, of understanding the artist, which is quite remarkable. They have also a great command over the varieties of facial expression, are peculiarly dramatic, and can chatter the *argot* of the *atelier* as cleverly as the critic of the *Gil Blas*. The English models form a class entirely by themselves. They are not so picturesque as the Italian, nor so clever as the French, and they have absolutely no tradition, so to speak, of their order. Now and then some old veteran knocks at a studio door, and proposes to sit as Ajax defying the lightning, or as King Lear upon the blasted heath. One of them some time ago called on a popular painter who, happening at the moment to require his services, engaged him, and told him to begin by kneeling down in the attitude of prayer. 'Shall I be Biblical or Shakespearean, sir?' asked the veteran. 'Well – Shakespearean,' answered the artist, wondering by what subtle *nuance* of expression the model would convey the difference. 'All right, sir,' said the professor of posing, and he solemnly knelt down and began to wink with his left eye! This class, however, is dying out. As a rule the model, nowadays, is a pretty girl, from about twelve to twenty-five years of age, who knows nothing about art, cares less, and is merely anxious to earn seven or eight shillings a day without much trouble. English models rarely look at a picture, and never venture on any aesthetic theories. In fact, they realise very completely Mr Whistler's idea of the function of an art critic, for they pass no criticisms at all. They accept all schools of art with the grand catholicity of the auctioneer, and sit to a fantastic young impressionist as readily as to a learned and laborious academician. They are neither for the Whistlerites nor against them; the quarrel between the school of facts and the school of effects touches them not; idealistic and naturalistic are words that convey no meaning to their ears; they merely desire that the studio shall be warm, and the lunch hot, for all charming artists give their models lunch.

As to what they are asked to do they are equally indifferent. On Monday they will don the rags of a beggar-girl for Mr Pumper, whose pathetic pictures of modern life draw such tears from the public, and on Tuesday they will pose in a peplum, for Mr Phoebus, who thinks that all really artistic subjects are necessarily BC. They career gaily through all centuries and through all costumes, and, like actors, are interesting only when they are not themselves. They are extremely good-natured, and very accommodating. 'What do you sit for?' said a young artist to a model who had sent him in her card (all models, by the way, have cards and a small black bag). 'Oh, for anything you like, sir,' said the girl, 'landscape if necessary!'

Intellectually, it must be acknowledged, they are Philistines, but physically they are perfect – at least some are. Though none of them can talk Greek, many can look Greek, which to a nineteenth-century painter is naturally of great importance. If they are allowed, they chatter a great deal, but they never say anything. Their observations are the only *banalités* heard in Bohemia. However, though they cannot appreciate the artist as artist, they are quite ready to appreciate the artist as a man. They are very sensitive to kindness, respect and generosity. A beautiful model who had sat for two years to one of our most distinguished English painters, got engaged to a street-vendor of penny-ices. On her marriage the painter sent her a pretty wedding present, and received in return a nice letter of thanks with the following remarkable postscript: 'Never eat the green ices!'

When they are tired a wise artist gives them a rest. Then they sit in a chair and read penny dreadfuls, till they are roused from the tragedy of literature to take their place again in the tragedy of art. A few of them smoke cigarettes. This, however, is regarded by the other models as showing a want of seriousness, and is not generally approved of. They are engaged by the day and by the half-day. The tariff is a shilling an hour, to which great artists usually add an omnibus fare. The two best things about them are their extraordinary prettiness, and their extreme respectability. As a class they are very well-behaved, particularly those who sit for the figure, a fact which is curious or natural according to the view one takes of human nature. They usually marry well, and sometimes they marry the artist. For an artist to marry his model is as fatal as for a *gourmet* to marry his cook: the one gets no sittings, and the other gets no dinners.

On the whole the English female models are very naïve, very natural, and very good-humoured. The virtues which the artist values most in them are prettiness and punctuality. Every sensible model consequently keeps a diary of her engagements, and dresses neatly. The bad season is, of course, the summer, when the artists are out of town. However, of late years some artists have engaged their models to follow them, and the wife of one of our most charming painters has often had three or four models under her charge in the country, so that the work of her husband and his friends should not be interrupted. In France the models migrate *en masse* to the little seaport villages or forest hamlets where the painters congregate. The English models, however, wait patiently in London, as a rule, till the artists come back. Nearly all of them live with their parents, and help to support the house. They have every qualification for being immortalised in art except that of beautiful hands. The hands of the English model are nearly always coarse and red.

As for the male models, there is the veteran whom we have mentioned above. He has all the traditions of the grand style, and is rapidly disappearing with the school he represents. An old man who talks about Fuseli is, of course, unendurable, and, besides, patriarchs have ceased to be fashionable subjects. Then there is the true Academy model. He is usually a man of thirty, rarely good-looking, but a perfect miracle of muscles. In fact he is the apotheosis of anatomy, and is so conscious of his own splendour that he tells you of his tibia and his thorax, as if no one else had anything of the kind. Then come the Oriental models. The supply of these is limited, but there are always about a dozen in London. They are very much sought after as they can remain immobile for hours, and generally possess lovely costumes. However, they have a very poor opinion of English art, which they regard as something between a vulgar personality and a commonplace photograph. Next we have the Italian youth who has come over specially to be a model, or takes to it when his organ is out of repair. He is often quite charming with his large melancholy eyes, his crisp hair, and his slim brown figure. It is true he eats garlic, but then he can stand like a faun and couch like a leopard, so he is forgiven. He is always full of pretty compliments, and has been known to have kind words of encouragement for even our greatest artists. As for the English lad of the same age, he never sits at all. Apparently he does not regard the career of a model as a serious profession. In any case he is rarely, if ever, to be got hold of. English boys, too, are difficult to find. Sometimes an ex-model who has a son will curl his hair, and wash his face, and bring him the round of the studios, all soap and shininess. The young school don't like him, but the older school do, and when he appears on the walls of the Royal Academy he is called *The Infant Samuel*. Occasionally also an artist catches a couple of *gamins* in the gutter and asks them to come to his studio. The first time they always appear, but after that they don't keep their appointments. They dislike sitting still, and have a strong and perhaps natural objection to looking pathetic. Besides, they are always under the impression that the artist is laughing at them. It is a sad fact, but there is no doubt that the poor are completely unconscious of their own picturesqueness. Those of them who can be induced to sit do so with the idea that the artist is merely a benevolent philanthropist who has chosen an eccentric method of distributing alms to the undeserving. Perhaps the School Board will teach the London *gamin* his own artistic value, and then they will be better models than they are now. One remarkable privilege belongs to the Academy model, that of extorting a sovereign from any newly elected Associate or R.A. They wait at Burlington House till the announcement is made, and then race to the hapless artist's house. The one who arrives first receives the money. They have of late been much troubled at the long distances they have had to run, and they look with disfavour on the election of artists who live at Hampstead or at Bedford Park, for it is considered a point of honour not to employ the underground railway, omnibuses, or any artificial means of locomotion. The race is to the swift.

Besides the professional posers of the studio there are posers of the Row, the posers at afternoon teas, the posers in politics and the circus posers. All four classes are delightful, but only the last class is ever really decorative. Acrobats and gymnasts can give the young painter infinite suggestions, for they bring into their art an element of swiftness of motion and of constant change that the studio model necessarily lacks. What is interesting in these 'slaves of the ring' is that with them Beauty is an unconscious result not of conscious aim, the result in fact of the mathematical calculation of curves and distances, of absolute precision of eye, of the scientific knowledge of the equilibrium of forces, and of perfect physical training. A good acrobat is always graceful, though grace is never his object; he is graceful because he does what he has to do in the best way in which it can be done – graceful because he is natural. If an ancient Greek were to come to life now, which considering the probable severity of his criticisms would be rather trying to our conceit, he would be found far oftener at the circus than at the theatre. A good circus is an oasis of Hellenism in a world that reads too much to be wise, and thinks too much to be beautiful. If it were not for the running-ground at Eton, the towing-path at Oxford, the Thames swimming-baths, and the yearly circuses, humanity would forget the plastic perfection of its own form, and degenerate into a race of short-sighted professors and spectacled *précieuses*. Not that the circus proprietors are, as a rule, conscious of their high mission. Do they not bore us with the *haute école*, and weary us with Shakespearean clowns? Still, at least, they give us acrobats, and the acrobat is an artist. The mere fact that he never speaks to the audience shows how well he appreciates the great truth that the aim of art is not to reveal personality but to please. The clown may be blatant, but the acrobat is always beautiful. He is an interesting combination of the spirit of Greek sculpture with the spangles of the modern costumier. He has even had his niche in the novels of our age, and if *Manette Salomon* be the unmasking of the model, *Les Frères Zemganno* is the apotheosis of the acrobat.

As regards the influence of the ordinary model on our English school of painting, it cannot be said that it is altogether good. It is, of course, an advantage for the young artist sitting in his studio to be able to isolate 'a little corner of life', as the French say, from disturbing surroundings, and to study it under certain effects of light and shade. But this very isolation leads often to mere mannerism in the painter, and robs him of that broad acceptance of the general facts of life which is the very essence of art. Model-painting, in a word, while it may be the condition of art, is not by any means its aim. It is simply practice, not perfection. Its use trains the eye and the hand of the

painter, its abuse produces in his work an effect of mere posing and pretti-
ness. It is the secret of much of the artificiality of modern art, this constant
posing of pretty people, and when art becomes artificial it becomes mono-
tonous. Outside the little world of the studio, with its draperies and its *bric-
à-brac*, lies the world of life with its infinite, its Shakespearean variety. We
must, however, distinguish between the two kinds of models, those who sit
for the figure and those who sit for the costume. The study of the first is al-
ways excellent, but the costume-model is becoming rather wearisome in
modern pictures. It is really of very little use to dress up a London girl in
Greek draperies and to paint her as a goddess. The robe may be the robe of
Athens, but the face is usually the face of Brompton. Now and then, it is true,
one comes across a model whose face is an exquisite anachronism, and who
looks lovely and natural in the dress of any century but her own. This, how-
ever, is rather rare. As a rule models are absolutely *de notre siècle*, and should
be painted as such. Unfortunately they are not, and, as a consequence, we are
shown every year a series of scenes from fancy dress balls which are called
historical pictures, but are little more than mediocre representations of mod-
ern people masquerading. In France they are wiser. The French painter uses
the model simply for study; for the finished picture he goes direct to life.

However, we must not blame the sitters for the shortcomings of the artists.
The English models are a well-behaved and hard-working class, and if they
are more interested in artists than in art, a large section of the public is in the
same condition, and most of our modern exhibitions seem to justify its
choice.

DE PROFUNDIS

"Epistola: In Carcere et Vinculis"

H.M. Prison
Reading
[January–March 1897]

DEAR BOSIE, After long and fruitless waiting I have determined to write to you myself, as much for your sake as for mine, as I would not like to think that I had passed through two long years of imprisonment without ever having received a single line from you, or any news or message even, except such as gave me pain.

Our ill-fated and most lamentable friendship has ended in ruin and public infamy for me, yet the memory of our ancient affection is often with me, and the thought that loathing, bitterness and contempt should for ever take that place in my heart once held by love is very sad to me: and you yourself will, I think, feel in your heart that to write to me as I lie in the loneliness of prison-life is better than to publish my letters without my permission or to dedicate poems to me unasked, though the world will know nothing of whatever words of grief or passion, of remorse or indifference you may choose to send as your answer or your appeal.

I have no doubt that in this letter in which I have to write of your life and of mine, of the past and of the future, of sweet things changed to bitterness and of bitter things that may be turned into joy, there will be much that will wound your vanity to the quick. If it prove so, read the letter over and over again till it kills your vanity. If you find in it something of which you feel that you are unjustly accused, remember that one should be thankful that there is any fault of which one can be unjustly accused. If there be in it one single passage that brings tears to your eyes, weep as we weep in prison where the day no less than the night is set apart for tears. It is the only thing that can save you. If you go complaining to your mother, as you did with reference to the scorn of you I displayed in my letter to Robbie, so that she may flatter and soothe you back into self-complacency or conceit, you will be completely lost. If you find one false excuse for yourself, you will soon find a hundred, and be just what you were before. Do you still say, as you said to Robbie in your answer, that I '*attribute unworthy motives*' to you? Ah! You had no motives in life. You had appetites merely. A motive is an intellectual aim. That you were '*very young*' when our friendship began? Your defect was not that you knew so little about life, but that you knew so much. The morning dawn of boyhood with its delicate bloom, its clear pure light, its joy of innocence and expectation you had left far behind. With very swift and running feet you had passed from Romance to Realism. The gutter and the things that live in it had begun to fascinate you. That was the origin of the trouble in which you sought my aid, and I, so unwisely according to the wisdom of this world, out of pity and kindness gave it to you. You must read this letter right through, though each word may become to you as the fire or knife of the surgeon that makes the delicate flesh burn or bleed. Remember that the fool in the eyes of the gods and the fool in the eyes of man are very different. One who is entirely ignorant of the modes of Art in its revolution or the moods of thought in its progress, of the pomp of the Latin line or the richer music of the vowelled Greek, of Tuscan sculpture or Elizabethan song may yet be full of the very sweetest wisdom. The real fool, such as the gods mock or mar, is he who does not know himself. I was such a one too long. You have been such a one too long. Be so no more. Do not be afraid. The supreme vice is shallowness. Everything that is realised is right. Remember also that whatever is misery to you to read, is still greater misery to me to set down. To you the Unseen Powers have been very good. They have permitted you to see the strange and tragic shapes of Life as one sees shadows in a crystal. The head of Medusa that turns living men to stone, you have been allowed to look at in a mirror merely. You yourself have walked free among the flowers. From me the beautiful world of colour and motion has been taken away.

I will begin by telling you that I blame myself terribly. As I sit here in this dark cell in convict clothes, a disgraced and ruined man, I blame myself. In the perturbed and fitful nights of anguish, in the long monotonous days of pain, it is myself I blame. I blame myself for allowing an unintellectual friendship, a friendship whose primary aim was not the creation and contemplation of beautiful things, to entirely dominate my life. From the very first there was too wide a gap between us. You had been idle at your school, worse than idle at your university. You did not realise that an artist, and especially such an artist as I am, one, that is to say, the quality of whose work depends on the intensification of personality, requires for the development of his art the companionship of ideas, an intellectual atmosphere, quiet, peace, and solitude. You admired my work when it was finished: you enjoyed the brilliant successes of my first nights, and the brilliant banquets that followed them: you were proud, and quite naturally so, of being the intimate friend of an artist so distinguished: but you could not understand the conditions requisite for the production of artistic work. I am not speaking in phrases of rhetorical exaggeration but in terms of absolute truth to actual fact when I remind you that during the whole time we were together I never wrote one single line. Whether at Torquay, Goring, London, Florence, or elsewhere, my life, as long as you were by my side, was entirely sterile and uncreative. And with but few intervals you were, I regret to say, by my side always.

I remember, for instance, in September '93, to select merely one instance out of many, taking a set of chambers, purely in order to work undisturbed, as I had broken my contract with John Hare for whom I had promised to write a play, and who was pressing me on the subject. During the first week you kept away. We had, not unnaturally indeed, differed on the question of the artistic value of your translation of *Salomé*, so you contented yourself with sending me foolish letters on the subject. In that week I wrote and completed in every detail, as it was ultimately performed, the first act of *An Ideal Husband*. The second week you returned and my work practically had to be given up. I arrived at St James's Place every morning at 11.30, in order to have the opportunity of thinking and writing without the interruptions inseparable from my own household, quiet and peaceful as that household was. But the attempt was vain. At twelve o'clock you drove up, and stayed smoking cigarettes and chattering till 1.30, when I had to take you out to luncheon at the Café Royal or the Berkeley. Luncheon with its *liqueurs* lasted usually till 3.30. For an hour you retired to White's. At tea-time you appeared again, and stayed till it was time to dress for dinner. You dined with me either at the Savoy or at Tite Street. We did not separate as a rule till after midnight, as supper at Willis's had to wind up the entrancing day. That was my life for those three months, every single day, except during the four days when you went abroad. I then, of course, had to go over to Calais to fetch you back. For one of my nature and temperament it was a position at once grotesque and tragic.

You surely must realise that now? You must see now that your incapacity of being alone: your nature so exigent in its persistent claim on the attention and time of others: your lack of any power of sustained intellectual concentration: the unfortunate accident – for I like to think it was no more – that you had not yet been able to acquire the 'Oxford temper' in intellectual matters, never, I mean, been one who could play gracefully with ideas but had arrived at violence of opinion merely – that all these things, combined with the fact that your desires and interests were in Life not in Art, were as destructive to your own progress in culture as they were to my work as an artist? When I compare my friendship with you to my friendship with such still younger men as John Gray and Pierre Louÿs I feel ashamed. My real life, my higher life was with them and such as they.

Of the appalling results of my friendship with you I don't speak at present. I am thinking merely of its quality while it lasted. It was intellectually degrading to me. You had the rudiments of an artistic temperament in its germ. But I met you either too late or too soon, I don't know which. When you were away I was all right. The moment, in the early December of the year to which I have been alluding, I had succeeded in inducing your mother to send you out of England, I collected again the torn and ravelled web of my imagination, got my life back into my own hands, and not merely finished the three remaining acts of *An Ideal Husband*, but conceived and had almost completed two other plays of a completely different type, the *Florentine Tragedy* and *La Sainte Courtisane*, when suddenly, unbidden, unwelcome, and under circumstances fatal to my happiness you returned. The two works left then imperfect I was unable to take up again. The mood that created them I could never recover. You now, having yourself published a volume of verse, will be able to recognise the truth of everything I have said here. Whether you can or not it remains as a hideous truth in the very heart of our friendship. While you were with me you were the absolute ruin of my Art, and in allowing you to stand persistently between Art and myself I give to myself shame and blame in the fullest degree. You couldn't know, you couldn't understand, you couldn't appreciate. I had no right to expect it of you at all. Your interests were merely in your meals and moods. Your desires were simply for amusements, for ordinary or less ordinary pleasures. They were what your temperament needed, or thought it needed for the moment. I should have forbidden you my house and my chambers except when I specially invited you. I blame myself without reserve for my weakness. It was merely weakness. One half-hour with Art was always more to me than a cycle with you. Nothing really at any period of my life was ever of the smallest importance to me compared with Art. But in the case of an artist, weakness is nothing less than a crime, when it is a weakness that paralyses the imagination.

I blame myself again for having allowed you to bring me to utter and discreditable financial ruin. I remember one morning in the early October of '92 sitting in the yellowing woods at Bracknell with your mother. At that time I knew very little of your real nature. I had stayed from a Saturday to Monday with you at Oxford. You had stayed with me at Cromer for ten days and played golf. The conversation turned on you, and your mother began to speak to me about your character. She told me of your two chief faults, your vanity, and your being, as she termed it, '*all wrong about money*.' I have a distinct recollection of how I laughed. I had no idea that the first would bring me to prison, and the second to bankruptcy. I thought vanity a sort of graceful flower for a young man to wear; as for extravagance – for I thought she meant no more than extravagance – the virtues of prudence and thrift were not in my own nature or my own race. But before our friendship was one month older I began to see what your mother really meant. Your insistence on a life of reckless profusion: your incessant demands for money: your claim that all your pleasures should be paid for by me whether I was with you or not: brought me after some time into serious monetary difficulties, and what made the extravagances to me at any rate so monotonously uninteresting, as your persistent grasp on my life grew stronger and stronger, was that the money was really spent on little more than the pleasures of eating, drinking, and the like. Now and then it is a joy to have one's table red with wine and roses, but you outstripped all taste and temperance. You demanded without grace and received without thanks. You grew to think that you had a sort of right to live at my expense and in a profuse luxury to which you had never been accustomed, and which for that reason made your appetites all the more keen, and at the end if you lost money gambling in some Algiers Casino you simply telegraphed next morning to me in London to lodge the amount of your losses to your account at your bank, and gave the matter no further thought of any kind.

When I tell you that between the autumn of 1892 and the date of my imprisonment I spent with you and on you more than £5000 in actual money, irrespective of the bills I incurred, you will have some idea of the sort of life on which you insisted. Do you think I exaggerate? My ordinary expenses with you for an ordinary day in London – for luncheon, dinner, supper, amusements, hansoms and the rest of it – ranged from £12 to £20, and the week's expenses were naturally in proportion and ranged from £80 to £130. For our three months at Goring my expenses (rent of course included) were £1340. Step by step with the Bankruptcy Receiver I had to go over every item of my life. It was horrible. '*Plain living and high thinking*' was, of course, an ideal you could not at that time have appreciated, but such extravagance was a disgrace to both of us. One of the most delightful dinners I remember ever having had is one Robbie and I had together in a little Soho café, which cost about as many shillings as my dinners to you used to cost pounds. Out of my dinner with Robbie came the first and best of all my dialogues. Idea, title, treatment, mode, everything was struck out at a 3 franc 50 c. *table-d'hôte*. Out of the reckless dinners with you nothing remains but the memory that too much was eaten and too much was drunk. And my yielding to your demands was bad for you. You know that now. It made you grasping often: at times not a little unscrupulous: ungracious always. There was on far too many occasions too little joy or privilege in being your host. You forgot – I will not say the formal courtesy of thanks, for formal courtesies will strain a close friendship – but simply the grace of sweet companionship, the charm of pleasant conversation, that τερπνὸν κακόν as the Greeks called it, and all those gentle humanities that make life lovely, and are an accompaniment to life as music might be, keeping things in tune and filling with melody the harsh or silent places. And though it may seem strange to you that one in the terrible position in which I am situated should find a difference between one disgrace and another, still I frankly admit that the folly of throwing away all this money on you, and letting you squander my fortune to your own hurt as well as to mine, gives to me and in my eyes a note of common profligacy to my Bankruptcy that makes me doubly ashamed of it. I was made for other things.

But most of all I blame myself for the entire ethical degradation I allowed you to bring on me. The basis of character is will-power, and my will-power became absolutely subject to yours. It sounds a grotesque thing to say, but it is none the less true. Those incessant scenes that seemed to be almost physically necessary to you, and in which your mind and body grew distorted and you became a thing as terrible to look at as to listen to: that dreadful mania you inherit from your father, the mania for writing revolting and loathsome letters: your entire lack of any control over your emotions as displayed in your long resentful moods of sullen silence, no less than in the sudden fits of almost epileptic rage: all these things in reference to which one of my letters to you, left by you lying about at the Savoy or some other hotel and so produced in Court by your father's Counsel, contained an entreaty not devoid of pathos, had you at that time been able to recognise pathos either in its elements or its expression: – these, I say, were the origin and causes of my fatal yielding to you in your daily increasing demands. You wore one out. It was the triumph of the smaller over the bigger nature. It was the case of that tyranny of the weak over the strong which somewhere in one of my plays I describe as being 'the only tyranny that lasts.'

And it was inevitable. In every relation of life with others one has to find some *moyen de vivre*. In your case, one had either to give up to you or to give you up. There was no other alternative. Through deep if misplaced affection for you: through great pity for your defects of temper and temperament: through my own proverbial good-nature and Celtic laziness: through an artistic aversion to coarse scenes and ugly words: through that incapacity to bear resentment of any kind which at that time characterised me: through my dislike of seeing life made bitter and uncomely by what to me, with my eyes really fixed on other things, seemed to be mere trifles too petty for more than a moment's thought or interest – through these reasons, simple as they may sound, I gave up to you always. As a natural result, your claims, your efforts at domination, your exactions grew more and more unreasonable. Your meanest motive, your lowest appetite, your most common passion, became to you laws by which the lives of others were to be guided always, and to which, if necessary, they were to be without scruple sacrificed. Knowing that by making a scene you could always have your way, it was but natural that you should proceed, almost unconsciously I have no doubt, to every excess of vulgar violence. At the end you did not know to what goal you were hurrying, or with what aim in view. Having made your own of my genius, my will-power, and my fortune, you required, in the blindness of an inexhaustible greed, my entire existence. You took it. At the one supremely and tragically critical moment of all my life, just before my lamentable step of beginning my absurd action, on the one side there was your father attacking me with hideous cards left at my club, on the other side there was you attacking me with no less loathsome letters. The letter I received from you on the morning of the day I let you take me down to the Police Court to apply for the ridiculous warrant for your father's arrest was one of the worst you ever wrote, and for the most shameful reason. Between you both I lost my head. My judgment forsook me. Terror took its place. I saw no possible escape, I may say frankly, from either of you. Blindly I staggered as an ox into the shambles. I had made a gigantic psychological error. I had always thought that my giving up to you in small things meant nothing: that when a great moment arrived I could reassert my will-power in its natural superiority. It was not so. At the great moment my will-power completely failed me. In life there is really no small or great thing. All things are of equal value and of equal size. My habit – due to indifference chiefly at first – of giving up to you in everything had become insensibly a real part of my nature. Without my knowing it, it had stereotyped my temperament to one permanent and fatal mood. That is why, in the subtle epilogue to the first edition of his essays, Pater says that 'Failure is to form habits.' When he said it the dull Oxford people thought the phrase a mere wilful inversion of the somewhat wearisome text of Aristotelian *Ethics*, but there is a wonderful, a terrible truth hidden in it. I had allowed you to sap my strength of character, and to me the formation of a habit had proved to be not Failure merely but Ruin. Ethically you had been even still more destructive to me than you had been artistically.

The warrant once granted, your will of course directed everything. At a time when I should have been in London taking wise counsel, and calmly considering the hideous trap in which I had allowed myself to be caught – the booby-trap as your father calls it to the present day – you insisted on my taking you to Monte Carlo, of all revolting places on God's earth, that all day, and all night as well, you might gamble as long as the Casino remained open. As for me – baccarat having no charms for me – I was left alone outside to myself. You refused to discuss even for five minutes the position to which you and your father had brought me. My business was merely to pay your hotel expenses and your losses. The slightest allusion to the ordeal awaiting me was regarded as a bore. A new brand of champagne that was recommended to us had more interest for you.

On our return to London those of my friends who really desired my welfare implored me to retire abroad, and not to face an impossible trial. You imputed mean motives to them for giving such advice, and cowardice to me for listening to it. You forced me tò stay to brazen it out, if possible, in the box by absurd and silly perjuries. At the end, I was of course arrested and your father became the hero of the hour: more indeed than the hero of the hour merely: your family now ranks, strangely enough, with the Immortals: for with that grotesqueness of effect that is as it were a Gothic element in history, and makes Clio the least serious of all the Muses, your father will always live among the kind pure-minded parents of Sunday-school literature, your place is with the Infant Samuel, and in the lowest mire of Malebolge I sit between Gilles de Retz and the Marquis de Sade.

Of course I should have got rid of you, I should have shaken you out of my life as a man shakes from his raiment a thing that has stung him. In the most wonderful of all his plays Aeschylus tells us of the great Lord who brings up in his house the lion-cub, the λέοντος ἷνιν, and loves it because it comes bright-eyed to his call and fawns on him for its food: φαιδρωπὸς ποτὶ χεῖρα, σαίνων τε γαστρὸς ἀνάγκαις. And the thing grows up and shows the nature of its race, ἦθος τὸ πρόσθε τοκήων, and destroys the lord and his house and all that he possesses. I feel that I was such a one as he. But my fault was, not that I did not part from you, but that I parted from you far too often. As far as I can make out I ended my friendship with you every three months regularly, and each time that I did so you managed by means of entreaties, telegrams, letters, the interposition of your friends, the interposition of mine, and the like to induce me to allow you back. When at the end of March '93 you left my house at Torquay I had determined never to speak to you again, or to allow you under any circumstances to be with me, so revolting had been the scene you had made the night before your departure. You wrote and telegraphed from Bristol to beg me to forgive you and meet you. Your tutor, who had stayed behind, told me that he thought that at times you were quite irresponsible for what you said and did, and that most, if not all, of the men at Magdalen were of the same opinion. I consented to meet you, and of course I forgave you. On the way up to town you begged me to take you to the Savoy. That was indeed a visit fatal to me.

Three months later, in June, we are at Goring. Some of your Oxford friends come to stay from a Saturday to Monday. The morning of the day they went away you made a scene so dreadful, so distressing that I told you that we must part. I remember quite well, as we stood on the level croquet-ground with the pretty lawn all round us, pointing out to you that we were spoiling each other's lives, that you were absolutely ruining mine and that I evidently was not making you really happy, and that an irrevocable parting, a complete separation was the one wise philosophic thing to do. You went sullenly after luncheon, leaving one of your most offensive letters behind with the butler to be handed to me after your departure. Before three days had elapsed you were telegraphing from London to beg to be forgiven and allowed to return. I had taken the place to please you. I had engaged your own servants at your request. I was always terribly sorry for the hideous temper to which you were really a prey. I was fond of you. So I let you come back and forgave you. Three months later still, in September, new scenes occurred, the occasion of them being my pointing out to you the schoolboy faults of your attempted translation of *Salomé*. You must by this time be a fair enough French scholar to know that the translation was as unworthy of you, as an ordinary Oxonian, as it was of the work it sought to render. You did not of course know it then, and in one of the violent letters you wrote to me on the point you said that you were under '*no intellectual obligation of any kind*' to me. I remember that when I read that statement, I felt that it was the one really true thing you had written to me in the whole course of our friendship. I saw that a less cultivated nature would really have suited you much better. I am not saying this in bitterness at all, but simply as a fact of companionship. Ultimately the bond of all companionship, whether in marriage or in friendship, is conversation, and conversation must have a common basis, and between two people of widely different culture the only common basis possible is the lowest level. The trivial in thought and action is charming. I had made it the keystone of a very brilliant philosophy expressed in plays and paradoxes. But the froth and folly of our life grew often very wearisome to me: it was only in the mire that we met: and fascinating, terribly fascinating though the one topic round which your talk invariably centred was, still at the end it became quite monotonous to me. I was often bored to death by it, and accepted it as I accepted your passion for going to music-halls, or your mania for absurd extravagances in eating and drinking, or any other of your, to me, less attractive characteristics, as a thing, that is to say, that one simply had to put up with, a part of the high price one paid for knowing you. When after leaving Goring I went to Dinard for a fortnight you were extremely angry with me for not taking you with me, and, before my departure there, made some very unpleasant scenes on the subject at the Albemarle Hotel, and sent me some equally unpleasant telegrams to a country house I was staying at for a few days. I told you, I remember, that I thought it was your duty to be with your own people for a little, as you had passed the whole season away from them. But in reality, to be perfectly frank with you, I could not under any circumstances have let you be with me. We had been together for nearly twelve weeks. I required rest and freedom from the terrible strain of your companionship. It was necessary for me to be a little by myself. It was intellectually necessary. And so I confess I saw in your letter, from which I have quoted, a very good opportunity for ending the fatal friendship that had sprung up between us, and ending it without bitterness, as I had indeed tried to do on that bright June morning at Goring, three months before. It was however represented to me – I am bound to say candidly by one of my own friends to whom you had gone in your difficulty – that you would be much hurt, perhaps almost humiliated at having your work sent back to you like a schoolboy's exercise; that I was expecting far too much intellectually from you; and that, no matter what you wrote or did, you were absolutely and entirely devoted to me. I did not want to be the first to check or discourage you in your beginnings in literature: I knew quite well that no translation, unless one done by a poet, could render the colour and cadence of my work in any adequate measure: devotion seemed to me, seems to me still, a wonderful thing, not to be lightly thrown away: so I took the translation and you back. Exactly three months later, after a series of scenes culminating in one more than usually revolting, when you came one Monday evening to my rooms accompanied by two of your friends, I found myself actually flying abroad next morning to escape from you, giving my family some absurd reason for my sudden departure, and leaving a false address with my servant for fear you might follow me by the next train. And I remember that afternoon, as I was in the railway-carriage whirling up to Paris, thinking what an impossible, terrible, utterly wrong state my life had got into, when I, a man of world-wide reputation, was actually forced to run away from England, in order to try and get rid of a friendship that was entirely destructive of everything fine in me either from the intellectual or ethical point of view: the person from whom I was flying being no terrible creature sprung from sewer or mire into modern life with whom I had entangled my days, but you yourself, a young man of my own social rank and position, who had been at my own College at Oxford, and was an incessant guest at my house. The usual telegrams of entreaty and remorse followed: I disregarded them. Finally you threatened that unless I consented to meet you, you would under no circumstances consent to proceed to Egypt. I had myself, with your knowledge and concurrence, begged your mother to send you to Egypt away from England, as you were wrecking your life in London. I knew that if you did not go it would be a terrible disappointment to her, and for her sake I did meet you, and under the influence of great emotion, which even you cannot have forgotten, I forgave the past; though I said nothing at all about the future.

On my return to London next day I remember sitting in my room and sadly and seriously trying to make up my mind whether or not you really were what you seemed to me to be, so full of terrible defects, so utterly ruinous both to yourself and to others, so fatal a one to know even or to be with. For a whole week I thought about it, and wondered if after all I was not unjust and mistaken in my estimate of you. At the end of the week a letter from your mother is handed in. It expressed to the full every feeling I myself had about you. In it she spoke of your blind exaggerated vanity which made you despise your home, and treat your elder brother – that *candidissima anima*[1] – 'as a Philistine:' of your temper which made her afraid to speak to you about your life, the life she felt, she knew, you were leading: about your conduct in money matters, so distressing to her in more ways than one: of the degeneration and change that had taken place in you. She saw, of course, that heredity had burdened you with a terrible legacy, and frankly admitted it, admitted it with terror: he is 'the one of my children who has inherited the fatal Douglas temperament,' she wrote of you. At the end she stated that she felt bound to declare that your friendship with me, in her opinion, had so intensified your vanity that it had become the source of all your faults, and earnestly begged me not to meet you abroad. I wrote to her at once, in reply, and told her that I agreed entirely with every word she had said. I added much more. I went as far as I could possibly go. I told her that the origin of our friendship was you in your undergraduate days at Oxford coming to beg me to help you in very serious trouble of a very particular character. I told her that your life had been continually in the same manner troubled. The reason of your going to Belgium you had placed to the fault of your companion in that journey, and your mother had reproached me with having introduced you to him. I replaced the fault on the right shoulders, on yours. I assured her at the end that I had not the smallest intention of meeting you abroad, and begged her to try to keep you there, either as an honorary *attaché*, if that were possible, or to learn modern languages, if it were not; or for any reason she chose, at least during two or three years, and for your sake as well as for mine.

In the meantime you are writing to me by every post from Egypt. I took not the smallest notice of any of your communications. I read them, and tore them up. I had quite settled to have no more to do with you. My mind was made up, and I gladly devoted myself to the Art whose progress I had allowed you to interrupt. At the end of three months, your mother, with that unfortunate weakness of will that characterises her, and that in the tragedy of my life has been an element no less fatal than your father's violence, actually writes to me herself – I have no doubt, of course, at your instigation – tells me that you are extremely anxious to hear from me, and in order that I should have no excuse for not communicating with you, sends me your address in Athens, which, of course, I knew perfectly well. I confess I was absolutely astounded at her letter. I could not understand how, after what she had written to me in December, and what I in answer had written to her, she could in any way try to repair or to renew my unfortunate friendship with you. I acknowledged her letter, of course, and again urged her to try and get you connected with some Embassy abroad, so as to prevent your returning to England, but I did not write to you, or take any more notice of your telegrams than I did before your mother had written to me. Finally, you actually telegraphed to my wife begging her to use her influence with me to get me to write to you. Our friendship had always been a source of distress to her: not

[1] Shining soul.

merely because she had never liked you personally, but because she saw how your continual companionship altered me, and not for the better: still, just as she had always been most gracious and hospitable to you, so she could not bear the idea of my being in any way unkind – for so it seemed to her – to any of my friends. She thought, knew indeed, that it was a thing alien to my character. At her request I did communicate with you. I remember the wording of my telegram quite well. I said that time healed every wound but that for many months to come I would neither write to you nor see you. You started without delay for Paris, sending me passionate telegrams on the road to beg me to see you once, at any rate. I declined. You arrived in Paris late on a Saturday night, and found a brief letter from me waiting for you at your hotel stating that I would not see you. Next morning I received in Tite Street a telegram of some ten or eleven pages in length from you. You stated in it that no matter what you had done to me you could not believe that I would absolutely decline to see you: you reminded me that for the sake of seeing me even for one hour you had travelled six days and nights across Europe without stopping once on the way: you made what I must admit was a most pathetic appeal, and ended with what seemed to me a threat of suicide, and one not thinly veiled. You had yourself often told me how many of your race there had been who had stained their hands in their own blood; your uncle certainly, your grandfather possibly; many others in the mad, bad line from which you come. Pity, my old affection for you, regard for your mother to whom your death under such dreadful circumstances would have been a blow almost too great for her to bear, the horror of the idea that so young a life, and one that amidst all its ugly faults had still promise of beauty in it, should come to so revolting an end, mere humanity itself – all these, if excuses be necessary, must serve as my excuse for consenting to accord you one last interview. When I arrived in Paris, your tears, breaking out again and again all through the evening, and falling over your cheeks like rain as we sat, at dinner first at Voisin's, at supper at Paillard's afterwards: the unfeigned joy you evinced at seeing me, holding my hand whenever you could, as though you were a gentle and penitent child: your contrition, so simple and sincere, at the moment: made me consent to renew our friendship. Two days after we had returned to London, your father saw you having luncheon with me at the Café Royal, joined my table, drank of my wine, and that afternoon, through a letter addressed to you, began his first attack on me.

It may be strange, but I had once again, I will not say the chance, but the duty of separating from you forced on me. I need hardly remind you that I refer to your conduct to me at Brighton from October 10th to 13th, 1894. Three years ago is a long time for you to go back. But we who live in prison, and in whose lives there is no event but sorrow, have to measure time by throbs of pain, and the record of bitter moments. We have nothing else to think of. Suffering – curious as it may sound to you – is the means by which we exist, because it is the only means by which we become conscious of existing; and the remembrance of suffering in the past is necessary to us as the warrant, the evidence, of our continued identity. Between myself and the memory of joy lies a gulf no less deep than that between myself and joy in its actuality. Had our life together been as the world fancied it to be, one simply of pleasure, profligacy and laughter, I would not be able to recall a single passage in it. It is because it was full of moments and days tragic, bitter, sinister in their warnings, dull or dreadful in their monotonous scenes and unseemly violences, that I can see or hear each separate incident in its detail, can indeed see or hear little else. So much in this place do men live by pain that my friendship with you, in the way through which I am forced to remember it, appears to me always as a prelude consonant with those varying modes of anguish which each day I have to realise; nay more, to necessitate them even; as though my life, whatever it had seemed to myself and others, had all the while been a real Symphony of Sorrow, passing through its rhythmically-linked movements to its certain resolution, with that inevitableness that in Art characterises the treatment of every great theme.

I spoke of your conduct to me on three successive days, three years ago, did I not? I was trying to finish my last play at Worthing by myself. The two visits you had paid to me had ended. You suddenly appeared a third time bringing with you a companion whom you actually proposed should stay in my house. I (you must admit now quite properly) absolutely declined. I entertained you, of course; I had no option in the matter: but elsewhere, and not in my own home. The next day, a Monday, your companion returned to the duties of his profession, and you stayed with me. Bored with Worthing, and still more, I have no doubt, with my fruitless efforts to concentrate my attention on my play, the only thing that really interested me at the moment, you insist on being taken to the Grand Hotel at Brighton. The night we arrive you fall ill with that dreadful low fever that is foolishly called the influenza, your second, if not third attack. I need not remind you how I waited on you, and tended you, not merely with every luxury of fruit, flowers, presents, books, and the like that money can procure, but with that affection, tenderness and love that, whatever you may think, is not to be procured for money. Except for an hour's walk in the morning, an hour's drive in the afternoon, I never left the hotel. I got special grapes from London for you, as you did not care for those the hotel supplied, invented things to please you, remained either with you or in the room next to yours, sat with you every evening to quiet or amuse you. After four or five days you recover, and I take lodgings in order to try and finish my play. You, of course, accompany me. The morning after the day on which we were installed I feel extremely ill. You have to go to London on business, but promise to return in the afternoon. In London you meet a friend, and do not come back to Brighton till late the next day, by which time I am in a terrible fever, and the doctor finds I have caught the influenza from you. Nothing could have been more uncomfortable for anyone ill than the lodgings turn out to be. My sitting-room is on the first floor, my bedroom on the third. There is no manservant to wait on one, not even anyone to send out on a message, or to get what the doctor orders. But you are there. I feel no alarm. The next two days you leave me entirely alone without care, without attendance, without anything. It was not a

question of grapes, flowers, and charming gifts: it was a question of mere ne-
cessaries: I could not even get the milk the doctor had ordered for me: lem-
onade was pronounced an impossibility: and when I begged you to procure
me a book at the bookseller's, or if they had not got whatever I had fixed on to
choose something else, you never even take the trouble to go there. And
when I was left all day without anything to read in consequence, you calmly
tell me that you bought me the book and that they promised to send it down,
a statement which I found out by chance afterwards to have been entirely un-
true from beginning to end. All the while you are of course living at my ex-
pense, driving about, dining at the Grand Hotel, and indeed only appearing
in my room for money. On Saturday night, you having left me completely
unattended and alone since the morning, I asked you to come back after din-
ner, and sit with me for a little. With irritable voice and ungracious manner
you promise to do so. I wait till eleven o'clock and you never appear. I then
left a note for you in your room just reminding you of the promise you had
made me, and how you had kept it. At three in the morning, unable to sleep,
and tortured with thirst, I made my way, in the dark and cold, down to the
sitting-room in the hopes of finding some water there. I found *you*. You fell
on me with every hideous word an intemperate mood, an undisciplined and
untutored nature could suggest. By the terrible alchemy of egotism you con-
verted your remorse into rage. You accused me of selfishness in expecting
you to be with me when I was ill; of standing between you and your amuse-
ments; of trying to deprive you of your pleasures. You told me, and I know it
was quite true, that you had come back at midnight simply in order to change
your dress-clothes, and go out again to where you hoped new pleasures were
waiting for you, but that by leaving for you a letter in which I had reminded
you that you had neglected me the whole day and the whole evening, I had
really robbed you of your desire for more enjoyments, and diminished your
actual capacity for fresh delights. I went back upstairs in disgust, and re-
mained sleepless till dawn, nor till long after dawn was I able to get anything
to quench the thirst of the fever that was on me. At eleven o'clock you came
into my room. In the previous scene I could not help observing that by my
letter I had, at any rate, checked you in a night of more than usual excess. In
the morning you were quite yourself. I waited naturally to hear what excuses
you had to make, and in what way you were going to ask for the forgiveness
that you knew in your heart was invariably waiting for you, no matter what
you did; your absolute trust that I would always forgive you being the thing
in you that I always really liked the best, perhaps the best thing in you to like.
So far from doing that, you began to repeat the same scene with renewed em-
phasis and more violent assertion. I told you at length to leave the room: you
pretended to do so, but when I lifted up my head from the pillow in which I
had buried it, you were still there, and with brutality of laughter and hysteria
of rage you moved suddenly towards me. A sense of horror came over me, for
what exact reason I could not make out; but I got out of my bed at once, and
bare-footed and just as I was, made my way down the two flights of stairs to
the sitting-room, which I did not leave till the owner of the lodgings – whom

I had rung for – had assured me that you had left my bedroom, and promised to remain within call, in case of necessity. After an interval of an hour, during which time the doctor had come and found me, of course, in a state of absolute nervous prostration, as well as in a worse condition of fever than I had been at the outset, you returned silently, for money: took what you could find on the dressing-table and mantlepiece, and left the house with your luggage. Need I tell you what I thought of you during the two wretched lonely days of illness that followed? Is it necessary for me to state that I saw clearly that it would be a dishonour to myself to continue even an acquaintance with such a one as you had showed yourself to be? That I recognised that the ultimate moment had come, and recognised it as being really a great relief? And that I knew that for the future my Art and Life would be freer and better and more beautiful in every possible way? Ill as I was, I felt at ease. The fact that the separation was irrevocable gave me peace. By Tuesday the fever had left me, and for the first time I dined downstairs. Wednesday was my birthday. Amongst the telegrams and communications on my table was a letter in your handwriting. I opened it with a sense of sadness over me. I knew that the time had gone by when a pretty phrase, an expression of affection, a word of sorrow would make me take you back. But I was entirely deceived. I had underrated you. The letter you sent to me on my birthday was an elaborate repetition of the two scenes, set cunningly and carefully down in black and white! You mocked me with common jests. Your one satisfaction in the whole affair was, you said, that you retired to the Grand Hotel, and entered your luncheon to my account before you left for town. You congratulated me on my prudence in leaving my sickbed, on my sudden flight downstairs. '*It was an ugly moment for you*,' you said, '*uglier than you imagine.*' Ah! I felt it but too well. What it had really meant I did not know: whether you had with you the pistol you had bought to try and frighten your father with, and that, thinking it to be unloaded, you had once fired off in a public restaurant in my company: whether your hand was moving towards a common dinner-knife that by chance was lying on the table between us: whether, forgetting in your rage your low stature and inferior strength, you had thought of some specially personal insult, or attack even, as I lay ill there: I could not tell. I do not know to the present moment. All I know is that a feeling of utter horror had come over me, and that I had felt that unless I left the room at once, and got away, you would have done, or tried to do, something that would have been, even to you, a source of lifelong shame. Only once before in my life had I experienced such a feeling of horror at any human being. It was when in my library at Tite Street, waving his small hands in the air in epileptic fury, your father, with his bully, or his friend, between us, had stood uttering every foul word his foul mind could think of, and screaming the loathsome threats he afterwards with such cunning carried out. In the latter case he, of course, was the one who had to leave the room first. I drove him out. In your case I went. It was not the first time I had been obliged to save you from yourself.

You concluded your letter by saying: '*When you are not on your pedestal you are not interesting. The next time you are ill I will go away at once.*' Ah! What coarseness of fibre does that reveal! What an entire lack of imagination! How callous, how common had the temperament by that time become! '*When you are not on your pedestal you are not interesting. The next time you are ill I will go away at once.*' How often have those words come back to me in the wretched solitary cell of the various prisons I have been sent to. I have said them to myself over and over again, and seen in them, I hope unjustly, some of the secret of your strange silence. For you to write thus to me, when the very illness and fever from which I was suffering I had caught from tending you, was of course revolting in its coarseness and crudity; but for any human being in the whole world to write thus to another would be a sin for which there is no pardon, were there any sin for which there is none.

I confess that when I had finished your letter I felt almost polluted, as if by associating with one of such a nature I had soiled and shamed my life irretrievably. I had, it is true, done so, but I was not to learn how fully till just six months later on in life. I settled with myself to go back to London on the Friday, and see Sir George Lewis personally and request him to write to your father to state that I had determined never under any circumstances to allow you to enter my house, to sit at my board, to talk to me, walk with me, or anywhere and at any time to be my companion at all. This done I would have written to you just to inform you of the course of action I had adopted; the reasons you would inevitably have realised for yourself. I had everything arranged on Thursday night, when on Friday morning, as I was sitting at breakfast before starting, I happened to open the newspaper and saw in it a telegram stating that your elder brother, the real head of the family, the heir to the title, the pillar of the house, had been found dead in a ditch with his gun lying discharged beside him. The horror of the circumstances of the tragedy, now known to have been an accident, but then stained with a darker suggestion; the pathos of the sudden death of one so loved by all who knew him, and almost on the eve, as it were, of his marriage; my idea of what your own sorrow would, or should be; my consciousness of the misery awaiting your mother at the loss of the one to whom she clung for comfort and joy in life, and who, as she told me once herself, had from the very day of his birth never caused her to shed a single tear; my consciousness of your own isolation, both your other brothers being out of Europe, and you consequently the only one to whom your mother and sister could look, not merely for companionship in their sorrow, but also for those dreary responsibilities of dreadful detail that Death always brings with it; the mere sense of the *lacrimae rerum*, of the tears of which the world is made, and of the sadness of all human things – out of the confluence of these thoughts and emotions crowding into my brain came infinite pity for you and your family. My own griefs and bitternesses against you I forgot. What you had been to me in my sickness, I could not be to you in your bereavement. I telegraphed at once to you my deepest sympathy, and in the letter that followed invited you to come to my house as soon as you were able. I felt that to abandon you at that particular moment, and formally through a solicitor, would have been too terrible for you.

On your return to town from the actual scene of the tragedy to which you had been summoned, you came at once to me very sweetly and very simply, in your suit of woe, and with your eyes dim with tears. You sought consolation and help, as a child might seek it. I opened to you my house, my home, my heart. I made your sorrow mine also, that you might have help in bearing it. Never, even by one word, did I allude to your conduct towards me, to the revolting scenes, and the revolting letter. Your grief, which was real, seemed to me to bring you nearer to me than you had ever been. The flowers you took from me to put on your brother's grave were to be a symbol not merely of the beauty of his life, but of the beauty that in all lives lies dormant and may be brought to light.

The gods are strange. It is not of our vices only they make instruments to scourge us. They bring us to ruin through what in us is good, gentle, humane, loving. But for my pity and affection for you and yours, I would not now be weeping in this terrible place.

Of course I discern in all our relations, not Destiny merely, but Doom: Doom that walks always swiftly, because she goes to the shedding of blood. Through your father you come of a race, marriage with whom is horrible, friendship fatal, and that lays violent hands either on its own life or on the lives of others. In every little circumstance in which the ways of our lives met; in every point of great, or seemingly trivial import in which you came to me for pleasure or for help; in the small chances, the slight accidents that look, in their relation to life, to be no more than the dust that dances in a beam, or the leaf that flutters from a tree, Ruin followed, like the echo of a bitter cry, or the shadow that hunts with the beast of prey. Our friendship really begins with your begging me in a most pathetic and charming letter to assist you in a position appalling to anyone, doubly so to a young man at Oxford: I do so, and ultimately through your using my name as your friend with Sir George Lewis, I begin to lose his esteem and friendship, a friendship of fifteen years' standing. When I was deprived of his advice and help and regard I was deprived of the one great safeguard of my life.

You send me a very nice poem, of the undergraduate school of verse, for my approval: I reply by a letter of fantastic literary conceits: I compare you to Hylas, or Hyacinth, Jonquil or Narcisse, or someone whom the great god of Poetry favoured, and honoured with his love. The letter is like a passage from one of Shakespeare's sonnets, transposed to a minor key. It can only be understood by those who have read the *Symposium* of Plato, or caught the spirit of a certain grave mood made beautiful for us in Greek marbles. It was, let me say frankly, the sort of letter I would, in a happy if wilful moment, have written to any graceful young man of either University who had sent me a poem of his own making, certain that he would have sufficient wit or culture to interpret rightly its fantastic phrases. Look at the history of that letter! It passes from you into the hands of a loathsome companion: from him to a gang of blackmailers: copies of it are sent about London to my friends, and to the manager of the theatre where my work is being performed: every construction but the right one is put on it: Society is thrilled with the absurd rumours that I have had to pay a huge sum of money for having written an infamous letter to you: this forms the basis of your father's worst attack: I produce the original letter myself in Court to show what it really is: it is denounced by your father's Counsel as a revolting and insidious attempt to corrupt Innocence: ultimately it forms part of a criminal charge: the Crown takes it up: the Judge sums up on it with little learning and much morality: I go to prison for it at last. That is the result of writing you a charming letter.

While I am staying with you at Salisbury you are terribly alarmed at a threatening communication from a former companion of yours: you beg me to see the writer and help you: I do so: the result is Ruin to me. I am forced to take everything you have done on my own shoulders and answer for it. When, having failed to take your degree, you have to go down from Oxford, you telegraph to me in London to beg me to come to you. I do so at once: you ask me to take you to Goring, as you did not like, under the circumstances, to go home: at Goring you see a house that charms you: I take it for you: the result from every point of view is Ruin to me. One day you come to me and ask me, as a personal favour to you, to write something for an Oxford undergraduate magazine, about to be started by some friend of yours, whom I had never heard of in all my life, and knew nothing at all about. To please you – what did I not do always to please you? – I sent him a page of paradoxes destined originally for the *Saturday Review*. A few months later I find myself standing in the dock of the Old Bailey on account of the character of the magazine. It forms part of the Crown charge against me. I am called upon to defend your friend's prose and your own verse. The former I cannot palliate; the latter I, loyal to the bitter extreme, to your youthful literature as to your youthful life, do very strongly defend, and will not hear of your being a writer of indecencies. But I go to prison, all the same, for your friend's undergraduate magazine, and 'the Love that dares not tell its name.' At Christmas I give you a 'very pretty present,' as you described it in your letter of thanks, on which I knew you had set your heart, worth some £40 or £50 at most. When the crash of my life comes, and I am ruined, the bailiff who seizes my library, and has it sold, does so to pay for the 'very pretty present.' It was for that the execution was put into my house. At the ultimate and terrible moment when I am taunted, and spurred-on by your taunts, to take an action against your father and have him arrested, the last straw to which I clutch in my wretched efforts to escape is the terrible expense. I tell the solicitor in your presence that I have no funds, that I cannot possibly afford the appalling costs, that I have no money at my disposal. What I said was, as you know, perfectly true. On that fatal Friday instead of being in Humphreys's office weakly consenting to my own ruin, I would have been happy and free in France, away from you and your father, unconscious of his loathsome card, and indifferent to your letters, if I had been able to leave the Avondale Hotel. But the hotel people absolutely refused to allow me to go. You had been staying with me for ten days: indeed you had ultimately, to my great and, you will admit, rightful indignation, brought a companion of yours to stay with me also: my bill for the ten days was nearly £140. The proprietor said he could not allow my luggage to be removed from the hotel till I had paid the account in full. That is what kept me in London. Had it not been for the hotel bill I would have gone to Paris on Thursday morning.

When I told the solicitor I had no money to face the gigantic expense, you interposed at once. You said that your own family would be only too delighted to pay all the necessary costs: that your father had been an incubus to them all: that they had often discussed the possibility of getting him put into a lunatic asylum so as to keep him out of the way: that he was a daily source of annoyance and distress to your mother and to everyone else: that if I would only come forward to have him shut up I would be regarded by the family as their champion and their benefactor: and that your mother's rich relations themselves would look on it as a real delight to be allowed to pay all costs and expenses that might be incurred in any such effort. The solicitor closed at once, and I was hurried to the Police Court. I had no excuse left for not going. I was forced into it. Of course your family don't pay the costs, and, when I am made bankrupt, it is by your father, and *for* the costs – the meagre balance of them – some £700. At the present moment my wife, estranged from me over the important question of whether I should have £3 or £3.10 a week to live on, is preparing a divorce suit, for which, of course, entirely new evidence and an entirely new trial, to be followed perhaps by more serious proceedings, will be necessary. I, naturally, know nothing of the details. I merely know the name of the witness on whose evidence my wife's solicitors rely. It is your own Oxford servant, whom at your special request I took into my service for our summer at Goring.

But, indeed, I need not go on further with more instances of the strange Doom you seem to have brought on me in all things big or little. It makes me feel sometimes as if you yourself had been merely a puppet worked by some secret and unseen hand to bring terrible events to a terrible issue. But puppets themselves have passions. They will bring a new plot into what they are presenting, and twist the ordered issue of vicissitude to suit some whim or appetite of their own. To be entirely free, and at the same time entirely dominated by law, is the eternal paradox of human life that we realise at every moment; and this, I often think, is the only explanation possible of your nature, if indeed for the profound and terrible mysteries of a human soul there is any explanation at all, except one that makes the mystery more marvellous still.

Of course you had your illusions, lived in them indeed, and through their shifting mists and coloured veils saw all things changed. You thought, I remember quite well, that your devoting yourself to me, to the entire exclusion of your family and family life, was a proof of your wonderful appreciation of me, and your great affection. No doubt to you it seemed so. But recollect that with me was luxury, high living, unlimited pleasure, money without stint. Your family life bored you. The 'cold cheap wine of Salisbury,' to use a phrase of your own making, was distasteful to you. On my side, and along with my intellectual attractions, were the fleshpots of Egypt. When you could not find me to be with, the companions whom you chose as substitutes were not flattering.

You thought again that in sending a lawyer's letter to your father to say that, rather than sever your eternal friendship with me, you would give up the allowance of £250 a year which, with I believe deductions for your Oxford debts, he was then making you, you were realising the very chivalry of friendship, touching the noblest note of self-denial. But your surrender of your little allowance did not mean that you were ready to give up even one of your most superfluous luxuries, or most unnecessary extravagances. On the contrary. Your appetite for luxurious living was never so keen. My expenses for eight days in Paris for myself, you, and your Italian servant were nearly £150: Paillard alone absorbing £85. At the rate at which you wished to live, your entire income for a whole year, if you had taken your meals alone, and had been especially economical in your selection of the cheaper form of pleasures, would hardly have lasted you for three weeks. The fact that in what was merely a pretence of bravado you had surrendered your allowance, such as it was, gave you at last a plausible reason for your claim to live at my expense, or what you thought a plausible reason: and on many occasions you seriously availed yourself of it, and gave the very fullest expression to it: and the continued drain, principally of course on me, but also to a certain extent, I know, on your mother, was never so distressing, because in my case at any rate, never so completely unaccompanied by the smallest word of thanks, or sense of limit.

You thought again that in attacking your own father with dreadful letters, abusive telegrams, and insulting postcards you were really fighting your mother's battles, coming forward as her champion, and avenging the no doubt terrible wrongs and sufferings of her married life. It was quite an illusion on your part; one of your worst indeed. The way for you to have avenged your mother's wrongs on your father, if you considered it part of a son's duty to do so, was by being a better son to your mother than you had been: by not making her afraid to speak to you on serious things: by not signing bills the payment of which devolved on her: by being gentler to her, and not bringing sorrow into her days. Your brother Francis made great amends to her for what she had suffered, by his sweetness and goodness to her through the brief years of his flower-like life. You should have taken him as your model. You were wrong even in fancying that it would have been an absolute delight and joy to your mother if you *had* managed through me to get your father put into prison. I feel sure you were wrong. And if you want to know what a woman really feels when her husband, and the father of her children, is in prison dress, in a prison cell, write to my wife and ask her. She will tell you.

I also had my illusions. I thought life was going to be a brilliant comedy, and that you were to be one of many graceful figures in it. I found it to be a revolting and repellent tragedy, and that the sinister occasion of the great catastrophe, sinister in its concentration of aim and intensity of narrowed will-power, was yourself, stripped of that mask of joy and pleasure by which you, no less than I, had been deceived and led astray.

You can now understand – can you not? – a little of what I am suffering. Some paper, the *Pall Mall Gazette* I think, describing the dress-rehearsal of one of my plays, spoke of you as following me about like my shadow: the memory of our friendship is the shadow that walks with me here: that seems never to leave me: that wakes me up at night to tell me the same story over and over till its wearisome iteration makes all sleep abandon me till dawn: at dawn it begins again: it follows me into the prison-yard and makes me talk to myself as I tramp round: each detail that accompanied each dreadful moment I am forced to recall: there is nothing that happened in those ill-starred years that I cannot recreate in that chamber of the brain which is set apart for grief or for despair: every strained note of your voice, every twitch and gesture of your nervous hands, every bitter word, every poisonous phrase comes back to me: I remember the street or river down which we passed, the wall or woodland that surrounded us, at what figure on the dial stood the hands of the clock, which way went the wings of the wind, the shape and colour of the moon.

There is, I know, one answer to all that I have said to you, and that is that you loved me: that all through those two and a half years during which the Fates were weaving into one scarlet pattern the threads of our divided lives you really loved me. Yes: I know you did. No matter what your conduct to me was I always felt that at heart you really did love me. Though I saw quite clearly that my position in the world of Art, the interest my personality had always excited, my money, the luxury in which I lived, the thousand and one things that went to make up a life so charmingly, and so wonderfully improbable as mine was, were, each and all of them, elements that fascinated you and made you cling to me: yet besides all this there was something more, some strange attraction for you: you loved me far better than you loved anybody else. But you, like myself, have had a terrible tragedy in your life, though one of an entirely opposite character to mine. Do you want to learn what it was? It was this. In you Hate was always stronger than Love. Your hatred of your father was of such stature that it entirely outstripped, o'erthrew, and overshadowed your love of me. There was no struggle between them at all, or but little; of such dimensions was your Hatred and of such monstrous growth. You did not realise that there is no room for both passions in the same soul. They cannot live together in that fair carven house. Love is fed by the imagination, by which we become wiser than we know, better than we feel, nobler than we are: by which we can see Life as a whole: by which, and by which alone, we can understand others in their real as in their ideal relations. Only what is fine, and finely conceived, can feed Love. But anything will feed Hate. There was not a glass of champagne you drank, not a rich dish you ate of in all those years, that did not feed your Hate and make it fat. So to gratify it, you gambled with my life, as you gambled with my money, carelessly, recklessly, indifferent to the consequence. If you lost, the loss would not, you fancied, be yours. If you won, yours, you knew, would be the exultation, and the advantages of victory.

Hate blinds people. You were not aware of that. Love can read the writing on the remotest star, but Hate so blinded you that you could see no further than the narrow, walled-in, and already lust-withered garden of your common desires. Your terrible lack of imagination, the one really fatal defect of your character, was entirely the result of the Hate that lived in you. Subtly, silently, and in secret, Hate gnawed at your nature, as the lichen bites at the root of some sallow plant, till you grew to see nothing but the most meagre interests and the most petty aims. That faculty in you which Love would have fostered, Hate poisoned and paralysed. When your father first began to attack me it was as your private friend, and in a private letter to you. As soon as I had read the letter, with its obscene threats and coarse violences, I saw at once that a terrible danger was looming on the horizon of my troubled days: I told you I would not be the catspaw between you both in your ancient hatred of each other: that I in London was naturally much bigger game for him than a Secretary for Foreign Affairs at Homburg: that it would be unfair to me to place me even for a moment in such a position: and that I had something better to do with my life than to have scenes with a man drunken, *déclassé*, and half-witted as he was. You could not be made to see this. Hate blinded you. You insisted that the quarrel had really nothing to do with me: that you would not allow your father to dictate to you in your private friendships: that it would be most unfair of me to interfere. You had already, before you saw me on the subject, sent your father a foolish and vulgar telegram, as your answer. That of course committed you to a foolish and vulgar course of action to follow. The fatal errors of life are not due to man's being unreasonable: an unreasonable moment may be one's finest moment. They are due to man's being logical. There is a wide difference. That telegram conditioned the whole of your subsequent relations with your father, and consequently the whole of my life. And the grotesque thing about it is that it was a telegram of which the commonest street-boy would have been ashamed. From pert telegrams to priggish lawyers' letters was a natural progress, and the result of your lawyer's letters to your father was, of course, to urge him on still further. You left him no option but to go on. You forced it on him as a point of honour, or of dishonour rather, that your appeal should have the more effect. So the next time he attacks me, no longer in a private letter and as your private friend, but in public and as a public man. I have to expel him from my house. He goes from restaurant to restaurant looking for me, in order to insult me before the whole world, and in such a manner that if I retaliated I would be ruined, and if I did not retaliate I would be ruined also. *Then* surely was the time when *you* should have come forward, and said that you would not expose me to such hideous attacks, such infamous persecution, on your account, but would, readily and at once, resign any claim you had to my friendship? You feel that now, I suppose. But it never even occurred to you then. Hate blinded you. All you could think of (besides of course writing to him insulting letters and telegrams) was to buy a ridiculous pistol that goes off in the Berkeley, under circumstances that create a worse scandal than ever came to *your* ears. Indeed the idea of your being the object of a terrible quarrel between your father and a man of my position seemed to delight you.

It, I suppose very naturally, pleased your vanity, and flattered your self-importance. That your father might have had your body, which did not interest me, and left me your soul, which did not interest him, would have been to you a distressing solution of the question. You scented the chance of a public scandal and flew to it. The prospect of a battle in which you would be safe delighted you. I never remember you in higher spirits than you were for the rest of that season. Your only disappointment seemed to be that nothing actually happened, and that no further meeting or fracas had taken place between us. You consoled yourself by sending him telegrams of such a character that at last the wretched man wrote to you and said that he had given orders to his servants that no telegram was to be brought to him under any pretence whatsoever. That did not daunt you. You saw the immense opportunities afforded by the open postcard, and availed yourself of them to the full. You hounded him on in the chase still more. I do not suppose he would ever really have given it up. Family instincts were strong in him. His hatred of you was just as persistent as your hatred of him, and I was the stalking-horse for both of you, and a mode of attack as well as a mode of shelter. His very passion for notoriety was not merely individual but racial. Still, if his interest had flagged for a moment your letters and postcards would soon have quickened it to its ancient flame. They did so. And he naturally went on further still. Having assailed me as a private gentleman and in private, as a public man and in public, he ultimately determines to make his final and great attack on me as an artist, and in the place where my Art is being represented. He secures by fraud a seat for the first night of one of my plays, and contrives a plot to interrupt the performance, to make a foul speech about me to the audience, to insult my actors, to throw offensive or indecent missiles at me when I am called before the curtain at the close, utterly in some hideous way to ruin me through my work. By the merest chance, in the brief and accidental sincerity of a more than usually intoxicated mood, he boasts of his intention before others. Information is given to the police, and he is kept out of the theatre. You had your chance then. Then was your opportunity. Don't you realise now that you should have seen it, and come forward and said that you would not have my Art, at any rate, ruined for your sake? You knew what my Art was to me, the great primal note by which I had revealed, first myself to myself, and then myself to the world; the real passion of my life; the love to which all other loves were as marsh-water to red wine, or the glow-worm of the marsh to the magic mirror of the moon. Don't you understand now that your lack of imagination was the one really fatal defect of your character? What you had to do was quite simple, and quite clear before you, but Hate blinded you, and you could see nothing. I could not apologise to your father for his having insulted me and persecuted me in the most loathsome manner for nearly nine months. I could not get rid of you out of my life. I had tried it again and again. I had gone so far as actually leaving England and going abroad in the hope of escaping from you. It had all been of no use. You were the only person who could have done anything.

The key of the situation rested entirely with yourself. It was the one great opportunity you had of making some slight return to me for all the love and affection and kindness and generosity and care I had shown you. Had you appreciated me even at a tenth of my value as an artist you would have done so. But Hate blinded you. The faculty 'by which, and by which alone, we can understand others in their real as in their ideal relations' was dead in you. You thought simply of how to get your father into prison. To see him 'in the dock,' as you used to say: that was your one idea. The phrase became one of the many *scies* of your daily conversation. One heard it at every meal. Well, you had your desire gratified. hate granted you every single thing you wished for. It was an indulgent Master to you. It is so, indeed, to all who serve it. For two days you sat on a high seat with the Sheriffs, and feasted your eyes with the spectacle of your father standing in the dock of the Central Criminal Court. And on the third day I took his place. What had occurred? In your hideous game of hate together, you had both thrown dice for my soul, and you happened to have lost. That was all.

You see that I have to write your life to you, and you have to realise it. We have known each other now for more than four years. Half of the time we have been together: the other half I have had to spend in prison as the result of our friendship. Where you will receive this letter, if indeed it ever reaches you, I don't know. Rome, Naples, Paris, Venice, some beautiful city on sea or river, I have no doubt, holds you. You are surrounded, if not with all the useless luxury you had with me, at any rate with everything that is pleasurable to eye, ear, and taste. Life is quite lovely to you. And yet, if you are wise, and wish to find Life much lovelier still, and in a different manner, you will let the reading of this terrible letter – for such I know it is – prove to you as important a crisis and turning-point of your life as the writing of it is to me. Your pale face used to flush easily with wine or pleasure. If, as you read what is here written, it from time to time becomes scorched, as though by a furnace-blast, with shame, it will be all the better for you. The supreme vice is shallowness. Whatever is realised is right.

I have now got as far as the House of Detention, have I not? After a night passed in the Police Cells I am sent there in the van. You were most attentive and kind. Almost every afternoon, if not actually every afternoon till you go abroad, you took the trouble to drive up to Holloway to see me. You also wrote very sweet and nice letters. But that it was not your father but you who had put me into prison, that from beginning to end you were the responsible person, that it was through you, for you, and by you that I was there, never for one instant dawned upon you. Even the spectacle of me behind the bars of a wooden cage could not quicken that dead unimaginative nature. You had the sympathy and the sentimentality of the spectator of a rather pathetic play. That you were the true author of the hideous tragedy did not occur to you. I saw that you realised nothing of what you had done. I did not desire to be the one to tell you what your own heart should have told you, what it indeed would have told you if you had not let Hate harden it and make it insensate. Everything must come to one out of one's own nature. There is no use in telling a person a thing that they don't feel and can't understand. If I write to you now as I do it is because your own silence and conduct during my long imprisonment have made it necessary. Besides, as things had turned out, the blow had fallen upon me alone. That was a source of pleasure to me. I was content for many reasons to suffer, though there was always to my eyes, as I watched you, something not a little contemptible in your complete and wilful blindness. I remember your producing with absolute pride a letter you had published in one of the halfpenny newspapers about me. It was a very prudent, temperate, indeed commonplace production. You appealed to the '*English sense of fair play,* ' or something very dreary of that kind, on behalf of '*a man who was down.*' It was the sort of letter you might have written had a painful charge been brought against some respectable person with whom personally you had been quite unacquainted. But you thought it a wonderful letter. You looked on it as a proof of almost quixotic chivalry. I am aware that you wrote other letters to other newspapers that they did not publish. But then they were simply to say that you hated your father. Nobody cared if you did or not. Hate, you have yet to learn, is, intellectually considered, the Eternal Negation. Considered from the point of view of the emotions it is a form of Atrophy, and kills everything but itself. To write to the papers to say that one hates someone else is as if one were to write to the papers to say that one had some secret and shameful malady: the fact that the man you hated was your own father, and that the feeling was thoroughly reciprocated, did not make your Hate noble or fine in any way. If it showed anything it was simply that it was an hereditary disease.

I remember again, when an execution was put into my house, and my books and furniture were seized and advertised to be sold, and Bankruptcy was impending, I naturally wrote to tell you about it. I did not mention that it was to pay for some gifts of mine to you that the bailiffs had entered the home where you had so often dined. I thought, rightly or wrongly, that such news might pain you a little. I merely told you the bare facts. I thought it proper that you should know them. You wrote back from Boulogne in a strain of almost lyrical exultation. You said that you knew your father was 'hard up for money,' and had been obliged to raise £1500 for the expenses of the trial, and that my going bankrupt was really a 'splendid score' off him as he would not then be able to get any of his costs out of me! Do you realise now what Hate blinding a person is? Do you recognise now that when I described it as an Atrophy destructive of everything but itself, I was scientifically describing a real psychological fact? That all my charming things were to be sold: my Burne-Jones drawings: my Whistler drawings: my Monticelli: my Simeon Solomons: my china: my Library with its collection of presentation volumes from almost every poet of my time, from Hugo to Whitman, from Swinburne to Mallarmé, from Morris to Verlaine; with its beautifully bound editions of my father's and mother's works; its wonderful array of college and school prizes, its *éditions de luxe*, and the like; was absolutely nothing to you. You said it was a great bore: that was all. What you really saw in it was the possibility that your father might ultimately lose a few hundred pounds, and that paltry consideration filled you with ecstatic joy. As for the costs of the trial, you may be interested to know that your father openly said in the Orleans Club that if it had cost him £20,000 he would have considered the money thoroughly well spent, he had extracted such enjoyment, and delight, and triumph out of it all. The fact that he was able not merely to put me into prison for two years, but to take me out for an afternoon and make me a public bankrupt was an extra-refinement of pleasure that he had not expected. It was the crowning-point of my humiliation, and of his complete and perfect victory. Had your father had no claim for his costs on me, you, I know perfectly well, would, as far as words go, at any rate have been most sympathetic about the entire loss of my library, a loss irreparable to a man of letters, the one of all my material losses the most distressing to me. You might even, remembering the sums of money I had lavishly spent on you and how you had lived on me for years, have taken the trouble to buy in some of my books for me. The best all went for less than £150: about as much as I would spend on you in an ordinary week. But the mean small pleasure of thinking that your father was going to be a few pence out of pocket made you forget all about trying to make me a little return, so slight, so easy, so inexpensive, so obvious, and so enormously welcome to me, had you brought it about. Am I right in saying that Hate blinds people? Do you see it now? If you don't, try to see it.

How clearly I saw it then, as now, I need not tell you. But I said to myself: *'At all costs I must keep Love in my heart. If I go into prison without Love what will become of my Soul?'* The letters I wrote to you at that time from Holloway were my efforts to keep Love as the dominant note of my own nature. I could if I had chosen have torn you to pieces with bitter reproaches. I could have rent you with maledictions. I could have held up a mirror to you, and shown you such an image of yourself that you would not have recognised it as your own till you found it mimicking back your gestures of horror, and then you would have known whose shape it was, and hated it and yourself for ever. More than that indeed. The sins of another were being placed to my account. Had I so chosen, I could on either trial have saved myself at his expense, not from shame indeed but from imprisonment. Had I cared to show that the Crown witnesses – the three most important – had been carefully coached by your father and his solicitors, not in reticences merely, but in assertions, in the absolute transference, deliberate, plotted, and rehearsed, of the actions and doings of someone else on to me, I could have had each one of them dismissed from the box by the Judge, more summarily than even wretched perjured Atkins was. I could have walked out of Court with my tongue in my cheek, and my hands in my pockets, a free man. The strongest pressure was put upon me to do so. I was earnestly advised, begged, entreated to do so by people whose sole interest was my welfare, and the welfare of my house. But I refused. I did not choose to do so. I have never regretted my decision for a single moment, even in the most bitter periods of my imprisonment. Such a course of action would have been beneath me. Sins of the flesh are nothing. They are maladies for physicians to cure, if they should be cured. Sins of the soul alone are shameful. To have secured my acquittal by such means would have been a life-long torture to me. But do you really think that you were worthy of the love I was showing you then, or that for a single moment I thought you were? Do you really think that at any period in our friendship you were worthy of the love I showed you, or that for a single moment I thought you were? I knew you were not. But Love does not traffic in a marketplace, nor use a huckster's scales. Its joy, like the joy of the intellect, is to feel itself alive. The aim of Love is to love: no more, and no less. You were my enemy: such an enemy as no man ever had. I had given you my life, and to gratify the lowest and most contemptible of all human passions, Hatred and Vanity and Greed, you had thrown it away. In less than three years you had entirely ruined me from every point of view. For my own sake there was nothing for me to do but to love you. I knew, if I allowed myself to hate you, that in the dry desert of existence over which I had to travel, and am travelling still, every rock would lose its shadow, every palm tree be withered, every well of water prove poisoned at its source. Are you beginning now to understand a little? Is your imagination wakening from the long lethargy in which it has lain? You know already what Hate is. Is it beginning to dawn on you what Love is, and what is the nature of Love? It is not too late for you to learn, though to teach it to you I may have had to go to a convict's cell.

After my terrible sentence, when the prison-dress was on me, and the prison-house closed, I sat amidst the ruins of my wonderful life, crushed by anguish, bewildered with terror, dazed through pain. But I would not hate you. Every day I said to myself, '*I must keep Love in my heart today, else how shall I live through the day*'. I reminded myself that you meant no evil, to me at any rate: I set myself to think that you had but drawn a bow at a venture, and that the arrow had pierced a King between the joints of the harness. To have weighed you against the smallest of my sorrows, the meanest of my losses, would have been, I felt, unfair. I determined I would regard you as one suffering too. I forced myself to believe that at last the scales had fallen from your long-blinded eyes. I used to fancy, and with pain, what your horror must have been when you contemplated your terrible handiwork. There were times, even in those dark days, the darkest of all my life, when I actually longed to console you. So sure was I that at last you had realised what you had done.

It did not occur to me then that you could have the supreme vice, shallowness. Indeed, it was a real grief to me when I had to let you know that I was obliged to reserve for family business my first opportunity of receiving a letter: but my brother-in-law had written to me to say that if I would only write once to my wife she would, for my own sake and for our children's sake, take no action for divorce. I felt my duty was to do so. Setting aside other reasons, I could not bear the idea of being separated from Cyril, that beautiful, loving, loveable child of mine, my friend of all friends, my companion beyond all companions, one single hair of whose little golden head should have been dearer and of more value to me than, I will not merely say you from top to toe, but the entire chrysolite of the whole world: was so indeed to me always, though I failed to understand it till too late.

Two weeks after your application, I get news of you. Robert Sherard, that bravest and most chivalrous of all brilliant beings, comes to see me, and among other things tells me that in that ridiculous *Mercure de France*, with its absurd affectation of being the true centre of literary corruption, you are about to publish an article on me with specimens of my letters. He asks me if it really was by my wish. I was greatly taken aback, and much annoyed, and gave orders that the thing was to be stopped at once. You had left my letters lying about for blackmailing companions to steal, for hotel servants to pilfer, for housemaids to sell. That was simply your careless want of appreciation of what I had written to you. But that you should seriously propose to publish selections from the balance was almost incredible to me. And which of my letters were they? I could get no information. That was my first news of you. It displeased me.

The second piece of news followed shortly afterwards. Your father's solicitors had appeared in the prison, and served me personally with a Bankruptcy notice, for a paltry £700, the amount of their taxed costs. I was adjudged a public insolvent, and ordered to be produced in Court. I felt most strongly, and feel still, and will revert to the subject again, that these costs should have been paid by your family. You had taken personally on yourself the responsibility of stating that your family would do so. It was that which had made the solicitor take up the case in the way he did. You were absolutely responsible. Even irrespective of your engagement on your family's behalf you should have felt that as you had brought the whole ruin on me, the least that could have been done was to spare me the additional ignominy of bankruptcy for an absolutely contemptible sum of money, less than half of what I spent on you in three brief summer months at Goring. Of that, however, no more here. I did through the solicitor's clerk, I fully admit, receive a message from you on the subject, or at any rate in connection with the occasion. The day he came to receive my depositions and statements, he leant across the table – the prison warder being present – and having consulted a piece of paper which he pulled from his pocket, said to me in a low voice: 'Prince Fleur-de-Lys wishes to be remembered to you.' I stared at him. He repeated the message again. I did not know what he meant. 'The gentleman is abroad at present,' he added mysteriously. It all flashed across me, and I remember that, for the first and last time in my entire prison-life, I laughed. In that laugh was all the scorn of all the world. Prince Fleur-de-Lys! I saw – and subsequent events showed me that I rightly saw – that nothing that had happened had made you realise a single thing. You were in your own eyes still the graceful prince of a trivial comedy, not the sombre figure of a tragic show. All that had occurred was but as a feather for the cap that gilds a narrow head, a flower to pink the doublet that hides a heart that Hate, and Hate alone, can warm, that Love, and Love alone, finds cold. Prince Fleur-de-Lys! You were, no doubt, quite right to communicate with me under an assumed name. I myself, at that time, had no name at all. In the great prison where I was then incarcerated I was merely the figure and letter of a little cell in a long gallery, one of a thousand lifeless numbers, as of a thousand lifeless lives. But surely there were many real names in real history which would have suited you much better, and by which I would have had no difficulty at all in recognising you at once? I did not look for you behind the spangles of a tinsel vizard only suitable for an amusing masquerade. Ah! Had your soul been, as for its own perfection even it should have been, wounded with sorrow, bowed with remorse, and humble with grief, such was not the disguise it would have chosen beneath whose shadow to seek entrance to the House of Pain! The great things of life are what they seem to be, and for that reason, strange as it may sound to you, are often difficult to interpret. But the little things of life are symbols. We receive our bitter lessons most easily through them. Your seemingly casual choice of a feigned name was, and will remain, symbolic. It reveals you.

Six weeks later a third piece of news arrives. I am called out of the Hospital Ward, where I was lying wretchedly ill, to receive a special message from you through the Governor of the Prison. He reads me out a letter you had addressed to him in which you stated that you proposed to publish an article 'on the case of Mr Oscar Wilde,' in the *Mercure de France* ('a magazine,' you added for some extraordinary reason, 'corresponding to our English *Fortnightly Review*') and were anxious to obtain my permission to publish extracts and selections from – what letters? The letters I had written you from Holloway Prison! The letters that should have been to you things sacred and secret beyond anything in the whole world! These actually were the letters you proposed to publish for the jaded *décadent* to wonder at, for the greedy *feuilletoniste*[1] to chronicle, for the little lions of the *Quartier Latin* to gape and mouth at! Had there been nothing in your own heart to cry out against so vulgar a sacrilege you might at least have remembered the sonnet he wrote who saw with such sorrow and scorn the letters of John Keats sold by public auction in London and have understood at last the real meaning of my lines

> I think they love not Art
> Who break the crystal of a poet's heart
> That small and sickly eyes may glare or gloat.

For what was your article to show? That I had been too fond of you? The Paris *gamin* was quite aware of the fact. They all read the newspapers, and most of them write for them. That I was a man of genius? The French understood that, and the peculiar quality of my genius, much better than you did, or could have been expected to do. That along with genius goes often a curious perversity of passion and desire? Admirable: but the subject belongs to Lombroso rather than to you. Besides, the pathological phenomenon in question is also found amongst those who have not genius. That in your war of hate with your father I was at once shield and weapon to each of you? Nay more, that in that hideous hunt for my life, that took place when the war was over, he never could have reached me had not your nets been already about my feet? Quite true: but I am told that Henri Bauër had already done it ex-

---

[1] Lightweight journalist.

tremely well. Besides, to corroborate his view, had such been your intention, you did not require to publish my letters; at any rate those written from Holloway Prison.

Will you say, in answer to my questions, that in one of my Holloway letters I had myself asked you to try, as far as you were able, to set me a little right with some small portion of the world? Certainly, I did so. Remember how and why I am here, at this very moment. Do you think I am here on account of my relations with the witnesses on my trial? My relations, real or supposed, with people of that kind were matters of no interest to either the Government or Society. They knew nothing of them, and cared less. I am here for having tried to put your father into prison. My attempt failed of course. My own Counsel threw up their briefs. Your father completely turned the tables on me, and had *me* in prison, has me there still. That is why there is contempt felt for me. That is why people despise me. That is why I have to serve out every day, every hour, ever minute of my dreadful imprisonment. That is why my petitions have been refused.

You were the only person who, and without in any way exposing yourself to scorn or danger or blame, could have given another colour to the whole affair: have put the matter in a different light: have shown to a certain degree how things really stood. I would not of course have expected, nor indeed wished you to have stated how and for what purpose you had sought my assistance in your trouble at Oxford: or how, and for what purpose, if you had a purpose at all, you had practically never left my side for nearly three years. My incessant attempts to break off a friendship that was so ruinous to me as an artist, as a man of position, as a member of society even, need not have been chronicled with the accuracy with which they have been set down here. Nor would I have desired you to have described the scenes you used to make with such almost monotonous recurrence: nor to have reprinted your wonderful series of telegrams to me with their strange mixture of romance and finance; nor to have quoted from your letters the more revolting or heartless passages, as I have been forced to do. Still, I thought it would have been good, as well for you as for me, if you had made some protest against your father's version of our friendship, one no less grotesque than venomous, and as absurd in its reference to you as it was dishonouring in its reference to me. That version has now actually passed into serious history: it is quoted, believed, and chronicled: the preacher has taken it for his text, and the moralist for his barren theme: and I who appealed to all the ages have had to accept my verdict from one who is an ape and a buffoon. I have said, and with some bitterness, I admit, in this letter that such was the irony of things that your father would live to be the hero of a Sunday-school tract: that you would rank with the infant Samuel: and that my place be between Gilles de Retz and the Marquis de Sade. I dare say it is best so. I have no desire to complain. One of the many lessons that one learns in prison is that things are what they are, and will be what they will be. Nor have I any doubt that the leper of mediævalism, and the author of *Justine*, will prove better company than *Sandford and Merton*.

But at the time I wrote to you I felt that for both our sakes it would be a good thing, a proper thing, a right thing *not* to accept the account your father had put forward through his Counsel for the edification of a Philistine world, and that is why I asked you to think out and write something that would be nearer the truth. It would at least have been better for you than scribbling to the French papers about the domestic life of your parents. What did the French care whether or not your parents had led a happy domestic life? One cannot conceive a subject more entirely uninteresting to them. What did interest them was how an artist of my distinction, one who by the school and movement of which he was the incarnation had exercised a marked influence on the direction of French thought, could, having led such a life, have brought such an action. Had you proposed for your article to publish the letters, endless I fear in number, in which I had spoken to you of the ruin you were bringing on my life, of the madness of moods of rage that you were allowing to master you to your own hurt as well as to mine, and of my desire, nay, my determination to end a friendship so fatal to me in every way, I could have understood it, though I would not have allowed such letters to be published: when your father's Counsel desiring to catch me in a contradiction suddenly produced in Court a letter of mine, written to you in March '93, in which I stated that, rather than endure a repetition of the hideous scenes you seemed to take such a terrible pleasure in making, I would readily consent to be 'blackmailed by every renter in London,' it was a very real grief to me that that side of my friendship with you should incidentally be revealed to the common gaze: but that you should have been so slow to see, so lacking in all sensitiveness, and so dull in apprehension of what is rare, delicate and beautiful, as to propose yourself to publish the letters in which, and through which, I was trying to keep alive the very spirit and soul of Love, that it might dwell in my body through the long years of that body's humiliation – this was, and still is to me, a source of the very deepest pain, the most poignant disappointment. Why you did so, I fear I know but too well. If Hate blinded your eyes, Vanity sewed your eyelids together with threads of iron. The faculty 'by which, and by which alone, one can understand others in their real as in their ideal relations,' your narrow egotism had blunted, and long disuse had made of no avail. The imagination was as much in prison as I was. Vanity had barred up the windows, and the name of the warder was Hate.

All this took place in the early part of November of the year before last. A great river of life flows between you and a date so distant. Hardly, if at all, can you see across so wide a waste, But to me it seems to have occurred, I will not say yesterday, but today. Suffering is one long moment. We cannot divide it by seasons. We can only record its moods, and chronicle their return. With us time itself does not progress. It revolves. It seems to circle round one centre of pain. The paralysing immobility of a life, every circumstance of which is regulated after an unchangeable pattern, so that we eat and drink and walk and lie down and pray, or kneel at least for prayer, according to the inflexible laws of an iron formula: this immobile quality, that makes each dreadful day in the very minutest detail like its brother, seems to communicate itself to those external forces the very essence of whose existence is ceaseless change. Of seed-time or harvest, of the reapers bending over the corn, or the grape-gatherers threading through the vines, of the grass in the orchard made white with broken blossoms, or strewn with fallen fruit, we know nothing, and can know nothing. For us there is only one season, the season of Sorrow. The very sun and moon seem taken from us. Outside, the day may be blue and gold, but the light that creeps down through the thickly-muffled glass of the small iron-barred window beneath which one sits is grey and niggard. It is always twilight in one's cell, as it is always midnight in one's heart. And in the sphere of thought, no less than in the sphere of time, motion is no more. The thing that you personally have long ago forgotten, or can easily forget, is happening to me now, and will happen to me again to-morrow. Remember this, and you will be able to understand a little of why I am writing to you, and in this manner writing.

A week later, I am transferred here. Three more months go over and my mother dies. You knew, none better, how deeply I loved and honoured her. Her death was so terrible to me that I, once a lord of language, have no words in which to express my anguish and my shame. Never, even in the most perfect days of my development as an artist, could I have had words fit to bear so august a burden, or to move with sufficient stateliness of music through the purple pageant of my incommunicable woe. She and my father had bequeathed me a name they had made noble and honoured not merely in Literature, Art, Archaeology and Science, but in the public history of my own country in its evolution as a nation. I had disgraced that name eternally. I had made it a low byword among low people. I had dragged it through the very mire. I had given it to brutes that they might make it brutal, and to fools that they might turn it into a synonym for folly. What I suffered then, and still suffer, is not for pen to write or paper to record. My wife, at that time kind and gentle to me, rather than that I should hear the news from indifferent or alien lips, travelled, ill as she was, all the way from Genoa to England to break to me herself the tidings of so irreparable, so irredeemable a loss. Messages of sympathy reached me from all who had still affection for me. Even people who had not known me personally, hearing what a new sorrow had come into my broken life, wrote to ask that some expression of their condolence should be conveyed to me. You alone stood aloof, sent me no message, and wrote me no letter. Of such actions, it is best to say what Virgil says to Dante of those whose lives have been barren in noble impulse and shallow of intention: '*Non ragioniam di lor, ma guarda, e passa*[1].'

Three more months go over. The calendar of my daily conduct and labour that hangs on the outside of my cell-door, with my name and sentence written upon it, tells me that it is Maytime. My friends come to see me again. I enquire, as I always do, after you. I am told that you are in your villa at Naples, and are bringing out a volume of poems. At the close of the interview

---

[1] Let us not speak of them, but look, and pass on.

it is mentioned casually that you are dedicating them to me. The tidings seemed to give me a sort of nausea of life. I said nothing, but silently went back to my cell with contempt and scorn in my heart. How could you dream of dedicating a volume of poems to me without first asking my permission? Dream, do I say? How could you dare to do such a thing? Will you give as your answer that in the days of my greatness and fame I had consented to receive the dedication of your early work? Certainly, I did so; just as I would have accepted the homage of any other young man beginning the difficult and beautiful art of literature. All homage is delightful to an artist, and doubly sweet when youth brings it. Laurel and bay leaf wither when aged hands pluck them. Only youth has a right to crown an artist. That is the real privilege of being young, if youth only knew it. But the days of abasement and infamy are different from those of greatness and of fame. You have yet to learn that Prosperity, Pleasure and Success may be rough of grain and common in fibre, but that sorrow is the most sensitive of all created things. There is nothing that stirs in the whole world of thought or motion to which Sorrow does not vibrate in terrible if exquisite pulsation. The thin beaten-out leaf of tremulous gold that chronicles the direction of forces that the eye cannot see is in comparison coarse. It is a wound that bleeds when any hand but that of Love touches it and even then must bleed again, though not for pain.

You could write to the Governor of Wandsworth Prison to ask my permission to publish my letters in the *Mercure de France*, '*corresponding to our* English *Fortnightly Review*.' Why not have written to the Governor of the Prison at Reading, to ask my permission to dedicate your poems to me, whatever fantastic description you may have chosen to give of them? Was it because in the one case the magazine in question had been prohibited by me from publishing the letters, the legal copyright of which, as you are of course perfectly well aware, was and is vested entirely in me, and in the other you thought that you could enjoy the wilfulness of your own way without my knowing anything about it till it was too late to interfere? The mere fact that I was a man disgraced, ruined, and in prison should have made you, if you desired to write my name on the fore-page of your work, beg it of me as a favour, an honour, a privilege. That is the way in which one should approach those who are in distress and sit in shame.

Where there is Sorrow there is holy ground. Some day you will realise what that means. You will know nothing of life till you do. Robbie, and natures like his, can realise it. When I was brought down from my prison to the Court of Bankruptcy between two policemen, Robbie waited in the long dreary corridor, that before the whole crowd, whom an action so sweet and simple hushed into silence, he might gravely raise his hat to me, as handcuffed and with bowed head I passed him by. Men have gone to heaven for smaller things than that. It was in this spirit, and with this mode of love that the saints knelt down to wash the feet of the poor, or stooped to kiss the leper on the cheek. I have never said one single word to him about what he did. I do not know to the present moment whether he is aware that I was even conscious of his action. It is not a thing for which one can render formal thanks in formal words. I store it in the treasury-house of my heart. I keep it there as a secret debt that I am glad to think I can never possibly repay. It is embalmed and kept sweet by the myrrh and cassia of many tears. When Wisdom has been profitless to me, and Philosophy barren, and the proverbs and phrases of those who have sought to give me consolation as dust and ashes in my mouth, the memory of that little lowly silent act of Love has unsealed for me all the wells of pity, made the desert blossom like a rose, and brought me out of the bitterness of lonely exile into harmony with the wounded, broken and great heart of the world. When you are able to understand, not merely how beautiful Robbie's action was, but why it meant so much to me, and always will mean so much, then, perhaps, you will realise how and in what spirit you should have approached me for permission to dedicate to me your verses.

It is only right to state that in any case I would not have accepted the dedication. Though, possibly, it would under other circumstances have pleased me to have been asked, I would have refused the request for *your* sake, irrespective of any feelings of my own. The first volume of poems that in the very springtime of his manhood a young man sends forth to the world should be like a blossom or flower of spring, like the white thorn in the meadow at Magdalen, or the cowslips in the Cumnor fields. It should not be burdened by the weight of a terrible, a revolting tragedy, a terrible, a revolting scandal. If I had allowed my name to serve as herald to the book it would have been a grave artistic error. It would have brought a wrong atmosphere round the whole work, and in modern art atmosphere counts for so much. Modern life is complex and relative. Those are its two distinguishing notes. To render the first we require atmosphere with its subtlety of *nuances*, of suggestion, of strange perspectives: as for the second we require background. That is why Sculpture has ceased to be a representative art; and why Music *is* a representative art; and why Literature is, and has been, and always will remain the supreme representative art.

Your little book should have brought with it Sicilian and Arcadian airs, not the pestilent foulness of the criminal dock or the close breath of the convict cell. Nor would such a dedication as you proposed have been merely an error of taste in Art; it would from other points of view have been entirely unseemly. It would have looked like a continuance of your conduct before and after my arrest. It would have given people the impression of being an attempt at foolish bravado: an example of that kind of courage that is sold cheap and bought cheap in the streets of shame. As far as our friendship is concerned Nemesis has crushed us both like flies. The dedication of verses to me when I was in prison would have seemed a sort of silly effort at smart repartee, an accomplishment on which in your old days of dreadful letter-writing – days never, I sincerely hope for your sake, to return – you used openly to pride yourself and about which it was your joy to boast. It would not have produced the serious, the beautiful effect which I trust – I believe indeed – you had intended. Had you consulted me, I would have advised you to delay the publication of your verses for a little; or, if that proved displeasing to you, to publish anonymously at first, and then when you had won lovers by your song – the only sort of lovers really worth the winning – you might have turned round and said to the world 'These flowers that you admire are of my sowing, and now I offer them to one whom you regard as a pariah and an outcast, as my tribute to what I love and reverence and admire in him.' But you chose the wrong method and the wrong moment. There is a tact in love, and a tact in literature: you were not sensitive to either.

I have spoken to you at length on this point in order that you should grasp its full bearings, and understand why I wrote at once to Robbie in terms of such scorn and contempt of you, and absolutely prohibited the dedication, and desired that the words I had written of you should be copied out carefully and sent to you. I felt that at last the time had come when you should be made to see, to recognise, to realise a little of what you had done. Blindness may be carried so far that it becomes grotesque, and an unimaginative nature, if something be not done to rouse it, will become petrified into absolute insensibility, so that while the body may eat, and drink, and have its pleasures, the soul, whose house it is, may, like the soul of Branca d'Oria in Dante, be dead absolutely. My letter seems to have arrived not a moment too soon. It fell on you, as far as I can judge, like a thunderbolt. You describe yourself, in your answer to Robbie, as being 'deprived of all power of thought and expression.' Indeed, apparently, you can think of nothing better than to write to your mother to complain. Of course, she, with that blindness to your real good that has been her ill-starred fortune and yours, gives you every comfort she can think of, and lulls you back, I suppose, into your former unhappy, unworthy condition; while as far as I am concerned, she lets my friends know that she is 'very much annoyed' at the severity of my remarks about you. Indeed it is not merely to my friends that she conveys her sentiments of annoyance, but also to those – a very much larger number, I need hardly remind you – who are not my friends: and I am informed now, and through channels very kindly-disposed to you and yours, that in consequence of this a great deal of the sympathy that, by reason of my distinguished genius and terrible sufferings, had been gradually but surely growing up for me, has been entirely taken away. People say 'Ah! He first tried to get the kind father put into prison and failed: now he turns round and blames the innocent son for his failure. How right we were to despise him! How worthy of contempt he is!' It seems to me that, when my name is mentioned in your mother's presence, if she has no word of sorrow or regret for her share – no slight one – in the ruin of my house, it would be more seemly if she remained silent. And as for you – don't you think now that, instead of writing to *her* to complain, it would have been better for you, in every way, to have written to *me* directly, and to have had the courage to say to me whatever you had or fancied you had to say? It is nearly a year ago now since I wrote that letter. You cannot have remained during that entire time 'deprived of all power of thought and expression.' Why did you not write to me? You saw by my letter how deeply wounded, how outraged I was by your whole conduct. More than that; you saw your entire friendship with me set before you, at last, in its true light, and by a mode not to be mistaken. Often in old days I had told you that you were ruining my life. You had always laughed. When Edwin Levy at the very beginning of our friendship, seeing your manner of putting me forward to bear the brunt, and annoyance, and expense even of that unfortunate Oxford mishap of yours, if we must so term it, in reference to which his advice and help had been sought, warned me for the space of a whole hour against knowing you, you laughed, as at Bracknell I described to you my long and impressive interview with him. When I told you how even that unfortunate young man who ultimately stood beside me in the Dock had warned me more than once that you would prove far more fatal in bringing me to utter destruction than any even of the common lads whom I was foolish enough to know, you laughed, though not with such sense of amusement. When my more prudent or less well-disposed friends either warned me or left me, on account of my friendship with you, you laughed with scorn. You laughed immoderately when, on the occasion of your father writing his first abusive letter to you about me, I told you that I knew I would be the mere catspaw of your dreadful quarrel and come to some evil between you. But every single thing had happened as I had said it would happen, as far as the result goes. You had no excuse for not seeing how all things had come to pass. Why did you not write to me? Was it cowardice? Was it callousness? What was it? The fact that I was outraged with you, and had expressed my sense of outrage, was all the more reason for writing. If you thought my letter just, you should have written. If you thought it in the smallest point unjust, you should have written. I waited for a letter. I felt sure that at last you would see that, if old affection, much-protested love, the thousand acts of ill-requited kindness I had showered on you, the thousand unpaid debts of gratitude you owed me – that if all these were nothing to you, mere duty itself, most barren of all bonds between man and man, should have made you write. You cannot say that you seriously thought I was obliged to receive none but business communications from members of my family. You knew perfectly well that every twelve weeks Robbie was writing to me a little budget of literary news. Nothing can be more charming than his letters, in their wit, their clever concentrated criticism, their light touch: they are real letters: they are like a person talking to one: they have the quality of a French *causerie intime*: and in his delicate modes of deference to me, appealing at one time to my judgment, at another to my sense of humour, at another to my instinct for beauty or to my culture, and reminding me in a hundred subtle ways that once I was to many an arbiter of style in Art, the supreme arbiter to some, he shows how he has the tact of love as well as the tact of literature. His letters have been the little messengers between me and that beautiful unreal world of Art where once I was King, and would have remained King, indeed, had I not let myself be lured into the imperfect world of coarse uncompleted passions, of appetite without distinction, desire without limit, and formless greed. Yet, when all is said, surely you might have been able to understand, or conceive, at any rate, in your own mind, that, even on the ordinary grounds of mere psychological curiosity, it would have been more interesting to me to hear from you than to learn that Alfred Austin was trying to bring out a volume of poems, or that Street was writing dramatic criticisms for the *Daily Chronicle*, or that by one who cannot speak a panegyric without stammering Mrs Meynell had been pronounced to be the new Sibyl of Style.

Ah! Had *you* been in prison – I will not say through any fault of mine, for that would be a thought too terrible for me to bear – but through fault of your own, error of your own, faith in some unworthy friend, slip in sensual mire, trust misapplied, or love ill-bestowed, or none, or all of these – do you think that I would have allowed you to eat your heart away in darkness and solitude without trying in some way, however slight, to help you to bear the bitter burden of your disgrace? Do you think that I would not have let you know that if you suffered, I was suffering too: that if you wept, there were tears in my eyes also: and that if you lay in the house of bondage and were despised of men, I out of my griefs had built a house in which to dwell until your coming, a treasury in which all that men had denied to you would be laid up for your healing, one hundredfold in increase? If bitter necessity, or prudence, to *me* more bitter still, had prevented my being near you, and robbed me of the joy of your presence, though seen through prison-bars and in a shape of shame, I would have written to you in season and out of season in the hope that some mere phrase, some single word, some broken echo even of Love might reach you. If you had refused to receive my letters, I would have written none the less, so that you should have known that at any rate there were always letters waiting for you. Many have done so to me. Every three months people write to me, or propose to write to me. Their letters and communications are kept. They will be handed to me when I go out of prison. I know that they are there. I know the names of the people who have written them. I know that they are full of sympathy, and affection, and kindness. That is sufficient for me. I need to know no more. Your silence has been horrible. Nor has it been a silence of weeks and months merely, but of years; of years even as they have to count them who, like yourself, live swiftly in happiness, and can hardly catch the gilt feet of the days as they dance by, and are out of breath in the chase after pleasure. It is a silence without excuse; a silence without palliation. I knew you had feet of clay. Who knew it better? When I wrote, among my aphorisms, that it was simply the feet of clay that made the gold of the image precious, it was of you I was thinking. But it is no gold image with clay feet that you have made of yourself. Out of the very dust of the common highway that the hooves of horned things pash into mire you have moulded your perfect semblance for me to look at, so that, whatever my secret desire might have been, it would be impossible for me now to have for you any feeling other than that of contempt and scorn, for myself any feeling other than that of contempt and scorn either. And setting aside all other reasons, your indifference, your worldly wisdom, your callousness, your prudence, whatever you may choose to call it, has been made doubly bitter to me by the peculiar circumstances that either accompanied or followed my fall.

Other miserable men, when they are thrown into prison, if they are robbed of the beauty of the world, are at least safe, in some measure, from the world's most deadly slings, most awful arrows. They can hide in the darkness of their cells, and of their very disgrace make a mode of sanctuary. The world, having had its will, goes its way, and they are left to suffer undisturbed. With me it has been different. Sorrow after sorrow has come beating at the prison doors in search of me. They have opened the gates wide and let them in. Hardly, if at all, have my friends been suffered to see me. But my enemies have had full access to me always. Twice in my public appearances at the Bankruptcy Court, twice again in my public transferences from one prison to another, have I been shown under conditions of unspeakable humiliation to the gaze and mockery of men. The messenger of Death has brought me his tidings and gone his way, and in entire solitude, and isolated from all that could give me comfort, or suggest relief, I have had to bear the intolerable burden of misery and remorse that the memory of my mother placed upon me, and places on me still. Hardly has that wound been dulled, not healed, by time, when violent and bitter and harsh letters come to me from my wife through her solicitor. I am, at once, taunted and threatened with poverty. That I can bear. I can school myself to worse than that. But my two children are taken from me by legal procedure. That is and will remain to me a source of infinite distress, of infinite pain, of grief without end or limit. That the law should decide, and take upon itself to decide, that I am one unfit to be with my own children is something quite horrible to me. The disgrace of prison is as nothing compared to it. I envy the other men who tread the yard along with me. I am sure that their children wait for them, look for their coming, will be sweet to them.

The poor are wiser, more charitable, more kind, more sensitive than we are. In their eyes prison is a tragedy in a man's life, a misfortune, a casualty, something that calls for sympathy in others. They speak of one who is in prison as of one who is '*in trouble*' simply. It is the phrase they always use, and the expression has the perfect wisdom of Love in it. With people of our rank it is different. With us prison makes a man a pariah. I, and such as I am, have hardly any right to air and sun. Our presence taints the pleasures of others. We are unwelcome when we reappear. To revisit the glimpses of the moon is not for us. Our very children are taken away. Those lovely links with humanity are broken. We are doomed to be solitary, while our sons still live. We are denied the one thing that might heal us and help us, that might bring balm to the bruised heart, and peace to the soul in pain.

And to all this has been added the hard, small fact that by your actions and by your silence, by what you have done and by what you have left undone, you have made every day of my long imprisonment still more difficult for me to live through. The very bread and water of prison fare you have by your conduct changed. You have rendered the one bitter and the other brackish to me. The sorrow you should have shared you have doubled, the pain you should have sought to lighten you have quickened to anguish. I have no doubt that you did not mean to do so. I know that you did not mean to do so. It was simply that 'one really fatal defect of your character, your entire lack of imagination.'

And the end of it all is that I have got to forgive you. I must do so. I don't write this letter to put bitterness into your heart, but to pluck it out of mine. For my own sake I must forgive you. One cannot always keep an adder in one's breast to feed on one, nor rise up every night to sow thorns in the garden of one's soul. It will not be difficult at all for me to do so, if you help me a little. Whatever you did to me in old days I always readily forgave. It did you no good then. Only one whose life is without stain of any kind can forgive sins. But now when I sit in humiliation and disgrace it is different. My forgiveness should mean a great deal to you now. Some day you will realise it. Whether you do so early or late, soon or not at all, my way is clear before me. I cannot allow you to go through life bearing in your heart the burden of having ruined a man like me. The thought might make you callously indifferent, or morbidly sad. I must take the burden from you and put it on my own shoulders.

I must say to myself that neither you nor your father, multiplied a thousand times over, could possibly have ruined a man like me: that I ruined myself: and that nobody, great or small, can be ruined except by his own hand. I am quite ready to do so. I am trying to do so, though you may not think it at the present moment. If I have brought this pitiless indictment against you, think what an indictment I bring without pity against myself. Terrible as what you did to me was, what I did to myself was far more terrible still.

I was a man who stood in symbolic relations to the art and culture of my age. I had realised this for myself at the very dawn of my manhood, and had forced my age to realise it afterwards. Few men hold such a position in their own lifetime and have it so acknowledged. It is usually discerned, if discerned at all, by the historian, or the critic, long after both the man and his age have passed away. With me it was different. I felt it myself, and made others feel it. Byron was a symbolic figure, but his relations were to the passion of his age and its weariness of passion. Mine were to something more noble, more permanent, of more vital issue, of larger scope.

The gods had given me almost everything. I had genius, a distinguished name, high social position, brilliancy, intellectual daring: I made art a philosophy, and philosophy an art: I altered the minds of men and the colours of things: there was nothing I said or did that did not make people wonder: I took the drama, the most objective form known to art, and made it as personal a mode of expression as the lyric or the sonnet, at the same time that I widened its range and enriched its characterisation: drama, novel, poem in rhyme, poem in prose, subtle or fantastic dialogue, whatever I touched I made beautiful in a new mode of beauty: to truth itself I gave what is false no less than what is true as its rightful province, and showed that the false and the true are merely forms of intellectual existence. I treated Art as the supreme reality, and life as a mere mode of fiction: I awoke the imagination of my century so that it created myth and legend around me: I summed up all systems in a phrase, and all existence in an epigram.

Along with these things, I had things that were different. I let myself be lured into long spells of senseless and sensual ease. I amused myself with being a *flâneur*, a dandy, a man of fashion. I surrounded myself with the smaller natures and the meaner minds. I became the spendthrift of my own genius, and to waste an eternal youth gave me a curious joy. Tired of being on the heights I deliberately went to the depths in the search for new sensations. What the paradox was to me in the sphere of thought, perversity became to me in the sphere of passion. Desire, at the end, was a malady, or a madness, or both. I grew careless of the lives of others. I took pleasure where it pleased me and passed on. I forgot that every little action of the common day makes or unmakes character, and that therefore what one has done in the secret chamber one has some day to cry aloud on the housetops. I ceased to be Lord over myself. I was no longer the Captain of my Soul, and did not know it. I allowed you to dominate me, and your father to frighten me. I ended in horrible disgrace. There is only one thing for me now, absolute Humility: just as there is only one thing for you, absolute Humility also. You had better come down into the dust and learn it beside me.

I have lain in prison for nearly two years. Out of my nature has come wild despair; an abandonment to grief that was piteous even to look at: terrible and impotent rage: bitterness and scorn: anguish that wept aloud: misery that could find no voice: sorrow that was dumb. I have passed through every possible mood of suffering. Better than Wordsworth himself I know what Wordsworth meant when he said:

> Suffering is permanent, obscure, and dark
> And has the nature of Infinity.

But while there were times when I rejoiced in the idea that my sufferings were to be endless, I could not bear them to be without meaning. Now I find hidden away in my nature something that tells me that nothing in the whole world is meaningless, and suffering least of all. That something hidden away in my nature, like a treasure in a field, is Humility.

It is the last thing left in me, and the best: the ultimate discovery at which I have arrived: the starting-point for a fresh development. It has come to me right out of myself, so I know that it has come at the proper time. It could not have come before, nor later. Had anyone told me of it, I would have rejected it. Had it been brought to me, I would have refused it. As I found it, I want to keep it. I must do so. It is the one thing that has in it the elements of life, of a new life, a *Vita Nuova* for me. Of all things it is the strangest. One cannot give it away, and another may not give it to one. One cannot acquire it, except by surrendering everything that one has. It is only when one has lost all things, that one knows that one possesses it.

Now that I realise that it is in me, I see quite clearly what I have got to do, what, in fact, I must do. And when I use such a phrase as that, I need not tell you that I am not alluding to any external sanction or command. I admit none. I am far more of an individualist than I ever was. Nothing seems to me of the smallest value except what one gets out of oneself. My nature is seeking a fresh mode of self-realisation. That is all I am concerned with. And the first thing that I have got to do is to free myself from any possible bitterness of feeling against you.

I am completely penniless, and absolutely homeless. Yet there are worse things in the world than that. I am quite candid when I tell you that rather than go out from this prison with bitterness in my heart against you or against the world I would gladly and readily beg my bread from door to door. If I got nothing from the house of the rich, I would get something at the house of the poor. Those who have much are often greedy. Those who have little always share. I would not a bit mind sleeping in the cool grass in summer, and when winter came on sheltering myself by the warm close-thatched rick, or under the penthouse of a great barn, provided I had love in my heart. The external things of life seem to me now of no importance at all. You can see to what intensity of individualism I have arrived, or am arriving rather, for the journey is long, and 'where I walk there are thorns.'

Of course I know that to ask for alms on the highway is not to be my lot, and that if ever I lie in the cool grass at night-time it will be to write sonnets to the Moon. When I go out of prison, Robbie will be waiting for me on the other side of the big iron-studded gate, and he is the symbol not merely of his own affection, but of the affection of many others besides. I believe I am to have enough to live on for about eighteen months at any rate, so that, if I may not write beautiful books, I may at least read beautiful books, and what joy can be greater? After that, I hope to be able to recreate my creative faculty. But were things different: had I not a friend left in the world: were there not a single house open to me even in pity: had I to accept the wallet and ragged cloak of sheer penury: still as long as I remained free from all resentment, hardness, and scorn, I would be able to face life with much more calm and confidence than I would were my body in purple and fine linen, and the soul within it sick with hate. And I shall really have no difficulty in forgiving you. But to make it a pleasure for me you must feel that you want it. When you really want it you will find it waiting for you.

I need not say that my task does not end there. It would be comparatively easy if it did. There is much more before me. I have hills far steeper to climb, valleys much darker to pass through. And I have to get it all out of myself. Neither Religion, Morality, nor Reason can help me at all.

Morality does not help me. I am a born antinomian. I am one of those who are made for exceptions, not for laws. But while I see that there is nothing wrong in what one does, I see that there is something wrong in what one becomes. It is well to have learned that.

Religion does not help me. The faith that others give to what is unseen, I give to what one can touch, and look at. My Gods dwell in temples made with hands, and within the circle of actual experience is my creed made perfect and complete: too complete it may be, for like many or all of those who have placed their Heaven in this earth, I have found in it not merely the beauty of Heaven, but the horror of Hell also. When I think about Religion at all, I feel as if I would like to found an order for those who cannot believe: the Confraternity of the Fatherless one might call it, where on an altar, on which no taper burned, a priest, in whose heart peace had no dwelling, might celebrate with unblessed bread and a chalice empty of wine. Everything to be true must become a religion. And agnosticism should have its ritual no less than faith. It has sown its martyrs, it should reap its saints, and praise God daily for having hidden Himself from man. But whether it be faith or agnosticism, it must be nothing external to me. Its symbols must be of my own creating. Only that is spiritual which makes its own form. If I may not find its secret within myself, I shall never find it. If I have not got it already, it will never come to me.

Reason does not help me. It tells me that the laws under which I am convicted are wrong and unjust laws, and the system under which I have suffered a wrong and unjust system. But, somehow, I have got to make both of these things just and right to me. And exactly as in Art one is only concerned with what a particular thing is at a particular moment to oneself, so it is also in the ethical evolution of one's character. I have got to make everything that has happened to me good for me. The plank-bed, the loathsome food, the hard ropes shredded into oakum till one's finger-tips grow dull with pain, the menial offices with which each day begins and finishes, the harsh orders that routine seems to necessitate, the dreadful dress that makes sorrow grotesque to look at, the silence, the solitude, the shame – each and all of these things I have to transform into a spiritual experience. There is not a single degradation of the body which I must not try and make into a spiritualising of the soul.

I want to get to the point when I shall be able to say, quite simply and without affectation, that the two great turning-points of my life were when my father sent me to Oxford, and when society sent me to prison. I will not say that it is the best thing that could have happened to me, for that phrase would savour of too great bitterness towards myself. I would sooner say, or hear it said of me, that I was so typical a child of my age that in my perversity, and for that perversity's sake, I turned the good things of my life to evil, and the evil things of my life to good. What is said, however, by myself or by others matters little. The important thing, the thing that lies before me, the thing that I have to do, or be for the brief remainder of my days one maimed, marred, and incomplete, is to absorb into my nature all that has been done to me, to make it part of me, to accept it without complaint, fear, or reluctance. The supreme vice is shallowness. Whatever is realised is right.

When first I was put into prison some people advised me to try and forget who I was. It was ruinous advice. It is only by realising what I am that I have found comfort of any kind. Now I am advised by others to try on my release to forget that I have ever been in a prison at all. I know that would be equally fatal. It would mean that I would be always haunted by an intolerable sense of disgrace, and that those things that are meant as much for me as for anyone else – the beauty of the sun and moon, the pageant of the seasons, the music of daybreak and the silence of great nights, the rain falling through the leaves, or the dew creeping over the grass and making it silver – would all be tainted for me, and lose their healing power and their power of communicating joy. To reject one's own experiences is to arrest one's own development. To deny one's own experiences is to put a lie into the lips of one's own life. It is no less than a denial of the Soul. For just as the body absorbs things of all kinds, things common and unclean no less than those that the priest or a vision has cleansed, and converts them into swiftness or strength, into the play of beautiful muscles and the moulding of fair flesh, into the curves and colours of the hair, the lips, the eye: so the Soul, in its turn, has its nutritive functions also, and can transform into noble moods of thought, and passions of high import, what in itself is base, cruel, and degrading: nay more, may find in these its most august modes of assertion, and can often reveal itself most perfectly through what was intended to desecrate or destroy.

The fact of my having been the common prisoner of a common gaol I must frankly accept, and, curious as it may seem to you, one of the things I shall have to teach myself is not to be ashamed of it. I must accept it as a punishment, and if one is ashamed of having been punished, one might just as well never have been punished at all. Of course there are many things of which I was convicted that I had not done, but then there are many things of which I was convicted that I had done, and a still greater number of things in my life for which I was never indicted at all. And as for what I have said in this letter, that the gods are strange, and punish us for what is good and humane in us as much as for what is evil and perverse, I must accept the fact that one is punished for the good as well as for the evil that one does. I have no doubt that it is quite right one should be. It helps one, or should help one, to realise both, and not to be too conceited about either. And if I then am not ashamed of my punishment, as I hope not to be, I shall be able to think, and walk, and live with freedom.

Many men on their release carry their prison along with them into the air, hide it as a secret disgrace in their hearts, and at length like poor poisoned things creep into some hole and die. It is wretched that they should have to do so, and it is wrong, terribly wrong, of Society that it should force them to do so. Society takes upon itself the right to inflict appalling punishments on the individual, but it also has the supreme vice of shallowness, and fails to realise what it has done. When the man's punishment is over, it leaves him to himself: that is to say it abandons him at the very moment when its highest duty towards him begins. It is really ashamed of its own actions, and shuns those whom it has punished, as people shun a creditor whose debt they cannot pay, or one on whom they have inflicted an irreparable, an irredeemable wrong. I claim on my side that if I realise what I have suffered, Society should realise what it has inflicted on me: and that there should be no bitterness or hate on either side.

Of course I know that from one point of view things will be made more difficult for me than for others; must indeed, by the very nature of the case, be made so. The poor thieves and outcasts who are imprisoned here with me are in many respects more fortunate than I am. The little way in grey city or green field that saw their sin is small: to find those who know nothing of what they have done they need go no further than a bird might fly between the twilight before dawn and dawn itself: but for me 'the world is shrivelled to a hands-breadth,' and everywhere I turn my name is written on the rocks in lead. For I have come, not from obscurity into the momentary notoriety of crime, but from a sort of eternity of fame to a sort of eternity of infamy, and sometimes seem to myself to have shown, if indeed it required showing, that between the famous and the infamous there is but one step, if so much as one.

Still, in the very fact that people will recognise me wherever I go, and know all about my life, as far as its follies go, I can discern something good for me. It will force on me the necessity of again asserting myself as an artist, and as soon as I possibly can. If I can produce one more beautiful work of art I shall be able to rob malice of its venom, and cowardice of its sneer, and to pluck out the tongue of scorn by the roots. And if life be, as it surely is, a problem to me, I am no less a problem to Life. People must adopt some attitude towards me, and so pass judgment both on themselves and me. I need not say I am not talking of particular individuals. The only people I would care to be with now are artists and people who have suffered: those who know what Beauty is, and those who know what Sorrow is: nobody else interests me. Nor am I making any demands on Life. In all that I have said I am simply concerned with my own mental attitude towards life as a whole: and I feel that not to be ashamed of having been punished is one of the first points I must attain to, for the sake of my own perfection, and because I am so imperfect.

Then I must learn how to be happy. Once I knew it, or thought I knew it, by instinct. It was always springtime once in my heart. My temperament was akin to joy. I filled my life to the very brim with pleasure, as one might fill a cup to the very brim with wine. Now I am approaching life from a completely new standpoint, and even to conceive happiness is often extremely difficult for me. I remember during my first term at Oxford reading in Pater's *Renaissance* – that book which has had such a strange influence over my life – how Dante places low in the Inferno those who wilfully live in sadness, and going to the College Library and turning to the passage in the *Divine Comedy* where beneath the dreary marsh lie those who were 'sullen in the sweet air,' saying for ever through their sighs:

> *Tristi fummo*
> *nell'aer dolce che dal sol s'allegra.*[1]

I knew the church condemned *accidia*,[2] but the whole idea seemed to me quite fantastic, just the sort of sin, I fancied, a priest who knew nothing about real life would invent. Nor could I understand how Dante, who says that 'sorrow remarries us to God,' could have been so harsh to those who were enamoured of melancholy, if any such there really were. I had no idea that some day this would become to me one of the greatest temptations of my life.

While I was in Wandsworth Prison I longed to die. It was my one desire.

---

[1] We were sullen in the sweet air which rejoiceth in the sunlight.
[2] Sloth (one of the seven deadly sins).

When after two months in the Infirmary I was transferred here, and found myself growing gradually better in physical health, I was filled with rage. I determined to commit suicide on the very day on which I left prison. After a time that evil mood passed away, and I made up my mind to live, but to wear gloom as a King wears purple: never to smile again: to turn whatever house I entered into a house of mourning: to make my friends walk slowly in sadness with me: to teach them that melancholy is the true secret of life: to maim them with an alien sorrow: to mar them with my own pain. Now I feel quite differently. I see it would be both ungrateful and unkind of me to pull so long a face that when my friends came to see me they would have to make their faces still longer in order to show their sympathy, or, if I desired to entertain them, to invite them to sit down silently to bitter herbs and funeral baked meats. I must learn how to be cheerful and happy.

The last two occasions on which I was allowed to see my friends here I tried to be as cheerful as possible, and to show my cheerfulness in order to make them some slight return for their trouble in coming all the way from town to visit me. It is only a slight return, I know, but it is the one, I feel certain, that pleases them most. I saw Robbie for an hour on Saturday week, and I tried to give the fullest possible expression to the delight I really felt at our meeting. And that, in the views and ideas I am here shaping for myself, I am quite right is shown to me by the fact that now for the first time since my imprisonment I have a real desire to live.

There is before me so much to do that I would regard it as a terrible tragedy if I died before I was allowed to complete at any rate a little of it. I see new developments in Art and Life, each one of which is a fresh mode of perfection. I long to live so that I can explore what is no less than a new world to me. Do you want to know what this new world is? I think you can guess what it is. It is the world in which I have been living.

Sorrow, then, and all that it teaches one, is my new world. I used to live entirely for pleasure. I shunned sorrow and suffering of every kind. I hated both. I resolved to ignore them as far as possible, to treat them, that is to say, as modes of imperfection. They were not part of my scheme of life. They had no place in my philosophy. My mother, who knew life as a whole, used often to quote to me Goethe's lines – written by Carlyle in a book he had given her years ago – and translated, I fancy, by him also:

> Who never ate his bread in sorrow,
> Who never spent the midnight hours
> Weeping and waiting for the morrow,
> He knows you not, ye Heavenly Powers.

They were the lines that noble Queen of Prussia, whom Napoleon treated with such coarse brutality, used to quote in her humiliation and exile: they were lines my mother often quoted in the troubles of her later life: I absolutely declined to accept or admit the enormous truth hidden in them. I could not understand it. I remember quite well how I used to tell her that I did not want to eat my bread in sorrow, or to pass any night weeping and watching for a more bitter dawn. I had no idea that it was one of the special things that the Fates had in store for me; that for a whole year of my life, indeed, I was to do little else. But so has my portion been meted out to me; and during the last few months I have, after terrible struggles and difficulties, been able to comprehend some of the lessons hidden in the heart of pain. Clergymen, and people who use phrases without wisdom, sometimes talk of suffering as a mystery. It is really a revelation. One discerns things that one never discerned before. One approaches the whole of history from a different standpoint. What one had felt dimly through instinct, about Art, is intellectually and emotionally realised with perfect clearness of vision and absolute intensity of apprehension.

I now see that sorrow, being the supreme emotion of which man is capable, is at once the type and test of all great Art. What the artist is always looking for is that mode of existence in which soul and body are one and indivisible: in which the outward is expressive of the inward: in which Form reveals. Of such modes of existence there are not a few: youth and the arts preoccupied with youth may serve as a model for us at one moment: at another, we may like to think that, in its subtlety and sensitiveness of impression, its suggestion of a spirit dwelling in external things and making its raiment of earth and air, of mist and city alike, and in the morbid sympathy of its moods, and tones and colours, modern landscape art is realising for us pictorially what was realised in such plastic perfection by the Greeks. Music, in which all subject is absorbed in expression and cannot be separated from it, is a complex example, and a flower or a child a simple example of what I mean: but Sorrow is the ultimate type both in Life and Art.

Behind Joy and Laughter there may be a temperament, coarse, hard and callous. But behind Sorrow there is always Sorrow. Pain, unlike Pleasure, wears no mask. Truth in Art is not any correspondence between the essential idea and the accidental existence; it is not the resemblance of shape to shadow, or of the form mirrored in the crystal to the form itself: it is no Echo coming from a hollow hill, any more than it is the well of silver water in the valley that shows the Moon to the Moon and Narcissus to Narcissus. Truth in Art is the unity of a thing with itself: the outward rendered expressive of the inward: the soul made incarnate: the body instinct with spirit. For this reason there is no truth comparable to Sorrow. There are times when Sorrow seems to me to be the only truth. Other things may be illusions of the eye or the appetite, made to blind the one and cloy the other, but out of Sorrow have the worlds been built, and at the birth of a child or a star there is pain.

More than this, there is about Sorrow an intense, an extraordinary reality. I have said of myself that I was one who stood in symbolic relations to the art and culture of my age. There is not a single wretched man in this wretched place along with me who does not stand in symbolic relations to the very secret of life. For the secret of life is suffering. It is what is hidden behind everything. When we begin to live, what is sweet is so sweet to us, and what is bitter so bitter, that we inevitably direct all our desires towards pleasure, and seek not merely for 'a month or twain to feed on honeycomb,' but for all our years to taste no other food, ignorant the while that we may be really starving the soul.

I remember talking once on this subject to one of the most beautiful personalities I have ever known: a woman, whose sympathy and noble kindness to me both before and since the tragedy of my imprisonment have been beyond power of description: one who has really assisted me, though she does not know it, to bear the burden of my troubles more than anyone else in the whole world has: and all through the mere fact of her existence: through her being what she is, partly an ideal and partly an influence, a suggestion of what one might become, as well as a real help towards becoming it, a soul that renders the common air sweet, and makes what is spiritual seem as simple and natural as sunlight or the sea, one for whom Beauty and Sorrow walk hand in hand and have the same message. On the occasion of which I am thinking I recall distinctly how I said to her that there was enough suffering in one narrow London lane to show that God did not love man, and that wherever there was any sorrow, though but that of a child in some little garden weeping over a fault that it had or had not committed, the whole face of creation was completely marred. I was entirely wrong. She told me so, but I could not believe her. I was not in the sphere in which such belief was to be attained to. Now it seems to me that Love of some kind is the only possible explanation of the extraordinary amount of suffering that there is in the world. I cannot conceive any other explanation. I am convinced that there is no other, and that if the worlds have indeed, as I have said, been built out of Sorrow, it has been by the hands of Love, because in no other way could the Soul of man for whom the worlds are made reach the full stature of its perfection. Pleasure for the beautiful body, but Pain for the beautiful Soul.

When I say that I am convinced of these things I speak with too much pride. Far off, like a perfect pearl, one can see the city of God. It is so wonderful that it seems as if a child could reach it in a summer's day. And so a child could. But with me and such as I am it is different. One can realise a thing in a single moment, but one loses it in the long hours that follow with leaden feet. It is so difficult to keep 'heights that the soul is competent to gain.' We think in Eternity, but we move slowly through Time: and how slowly time goes with us who lie in prison I need not speak again, nor of the weariness and despair that creep back into one's cell, and into the cell of one's heart, with such strange insistence that one has, as it were, to garnish and sweep one's house for their coming, as for an unwelcome guest, or a bitter master, or a slave whose slave it is one's chance or choice to be. And, though at present you may find it a thing hard to believe, it is true none the less that for you, living in freedom and idleness and comfort, it is more easy to learn the lessons of Humility than it is for me, who begin the day by going down on my knees and washing the floor of my cell. For prison-life, with its endless privations and restrictions, makes one rebellious. The most terrible thing about it is not that it breaks one's heart – hearts are made to be broken – but that it turns one's heart to stone. One sometimes feels that it is only with a front of brass and a lip of scorn that one can get through the day at all. And he who is in a state of rebellion cannot receive grace, to use the phrase of which the Church is so fond – so rightly fond, I dare say – for in life, as in Art, the mood of rebellion closes up the channels of the soul, and shuts out the airs of heaven. Yet I must learn these lessons here, if I am to learn them anywhere, and must be filled with joy if my feet are on the right road, and my face set towards the 'gate which is called Beautiful,' though I may fall many times in the mire, and often in the mist go astray.

This new life, as through my love of Dante I like sometimes to call it, is, of course, no new life at all, but simply the continuance, by means of development, and evolution, of my former life. I remember when I was at Oxford saying to one of my friends – as we were strolling round Magdalen's narrow bird-haunted walks one morning in the June before I took my degree – that I wanted to eat of the fruit of all the trees in the garden of the world, and that I was going out into the world with that passion in my soul. And so, indeed, I went out, and so I lived. My only mistake was that I confined myself so exclusively to the trees of what seemed to me the sungilt side of the garden, and shunned the other side for its shadow and its gloom. Failure, disgrace, poverty, sorrow, despair, suffering, tears even, the broken words that come from the lips of pain, remorse that makes one walk in thorns, conscience that condemns, self-abasement that punishes, the misery that puts ashes on its head, the anguish that chooses sackcloth for its raiment and into its own drink puts gall – all these were things of which I was afraid. And as I had determined to know nothing of them, I was forced to taste each one of them in turn, to feed on them, to have for a season, indeed, no other food at all.

I don't regret for a single moment having lived for pleasure. I did it to the full, as one should do everything that one does to the full. There was no pleasure I did not experience. I threw the pearl of my soul into a cup of wine. I went down the primrose path to the sound of flutes. I lived on honeycomb. But to have continued the same life would have been wrong because it would have been limiting. I had to pass on. The other half of the garden had its secrets for me also. Of course all this is foreshadowed and prefigured in my art. Some of it is in 'The Happy Prince': some of it in 'The Young King,' notably in the passage where the Bishop says to the kneeling boy, 'Is not He who made misery wiser than thou art?' a phrase which when I wrote it seemed to me little more than a phrase: a great deal of it is hidden away in the note of Doom that like a purple thread runs through the gold cloth of *Dorian Gray*: in 'The Critic as Artist' it is set forth in many colours: in *The Soul of Man* it is written down simply and in letters too easy to read: it is one of the refrains whose recurring *motifs* make *Salomé* so like a piece of music and bind it together as a ballad: in the prose-poem of the man who from the bronze of the image of the 'Sorrow that abideth for Ever' it is incarnate. It could not have been otherwise. At every single moment of one's life one is what one is going to be no less than what one has been. Art is a symbol, because man is a symbol.

It is, if I can fully attain to it, the ultimate realisation of the artistic life. For the artistic life is simple self-development. Humility in the artist is his frank acceptance of all experiences, just as Love in the artist is simply that sense of Beauty that reveals to the world its body and its soul. In *Marius the Epicurean* Pater seeks to reconcile the artistic life with the life of religion in the deep, sweet and austere sense of the word. But Marius is little more than a spectator: an ideal spectator indeed, and one to whom it is given 'to contemplate the spectacle of life with appropriate emotions,' which Wordsworth defines as the poet's true aim: yet a spectator merely, and perhaps a little too much occupied with the comeliness of the vessels of the Sanctuary to notice that it is the Sanctuary of Sorrow that he is gazing at.

I see a far more intimate and immediate connection between the true life of Christ and the true life of the artist, and I take a keen pleasure in the reflection that long before Sorrow had made my days her own and bound me to her wheel I had written in *The Soul of Man* that he who would lead a Christ-like life must be entirely and absolutely himself, and had taken as my types not merely the shepherd on the hillside and the prisoner in his cell but also the painter to whom the world is a pageant and the poet for whom the world is a song. I remember saying once to André Gide, as we sat together in some Paris café, that while Metaphysics had but little real interest for me, and Morality absolutely none, there was nothing that either Plato or Christ had said that could not be transferred immediately into the sphere of Art, and there find its complete fulfilment. It was a generalisation as profound as it was novel.

Nor is it merely that we can discern in Christ that close union of personality with perfection which forms the real distinction between classical and romantic Art and makes Christ the true precursor of the romantic movement in life, but the very basis of his nature was the same as that of the nature of the artist, an intense and flamelike imagination. He realised in the entire sphere of human relations that imaginative sympathy which in the sphere of Art is the sole secret of creation. He understood the leprosy of the leper, the darkness of the blind, the fierce misery of those who live for pleasure, the strange poverty of the rich. You can see now – can you not? – that when you wrote to me in my trouble, 'When you are not on your pedestal you are not interesting. The next time you are ill I will go away at once,' you were as remote from the true temper of the artist as you were from what Matthew Arnold calls 'the secret of Jesus.' Either would have taught you that whatever happens to another happens to oneself, and if you want an inscription to read at dawn and at night-time and for pleasure or for pain, write up on the wall of your house in letters for the sun to gild and the moon to silver '*Whatever happens to another happens to oneself*,' and should anyone ask you what such an inscription can possibly mean you can answer that it means 'Lord Christ's heart and Shakespeare's brain.'

Christ's place indeed is with the poets. His whole conception of Humanity sprang right out of the imagination and can only be realised by it. What God was to the Pantheist, man was to him. He was the first to conceive the divided races as a unity. Before his time there had been gods and men. He alone saw that on the hills of life there were but God and Man, and, feeling through the mysticism of sympathy that in himself each had been made incarnate, he calls himself the Son of the One or the son of the other, according to his mood. More than anyone else in history he wakes in us that temper of wonder to which Romance always appeals. There is still something to me almost incredible in the idea of a young Galilean peasant imagining that he could bear on his own shoulders the burden of the entire world: all that had been already done and suffered, and all that was yet to be done and suffered: the sins of Nero, of Caesar Borgia, of Alexander VI., and of him who was Emperor of Rome and Priest of the Sun: the sufferings of those whose name is Legion and whose dwelling is among the tombs, oppressed nationalities, factory children, thieves, people in prison, outcasts, those who are dumb under oppression and whose silence is heard only of God: and not merely imagining this but actually achieving it, so that at the present moment all who come in contact with his personality, even though they may neither bow to his altar nor kneel before his priest, yet somehow find that the ugliness of their sins is taken away and the beauty of their sorrow revealed to them.

I have said of him that he ranks with the poets. That is true. Shelley and Sophocles are of his company. But his entire life also is the most wonderful of poems. For 'pity and terror' there is nothing in the entire cycle of Greek Tragedy to touch it. The absolute purity of the protagonist raises the entire scheme to a height of romantic art from which the sufferings of 'Thebes and Pelops' line' are by their very horror excluded, and shows how wrong Aristotle was when he said in his treatise on the Drama that it would be impossible to bear the spectacle of one blameless in pain. Nor in Aeschylus nor Dante, those stern masters of tenderness, in Shakespeare, the most purely human of all the great artists, in the whole of Celtic myth and legend where the loveliness of the world is shown through a mist of tears, and the life of a man is no more than the life of a flower, is there anything that for sheer simplicity of pathos wedded and made one with sublimity of tragic effect can be said to equal or approach even the last act of Christ's Passion. The little supper with his companions, one of whom had already sold him for a price: the anguish in the quiet moonlit olive-garden: the false friend coming close to him so as to betray him with a kiss: the friend who still believed in him and on whom as on a rock he had hoped to build a House of Refuge for Man denying him as the bird cried to the dawn: his own utter loneliness, his submission, his acceptance of everything: and along with it all such scenes as the high priest of Orthodoxy rending his raiment in wrath, and the Magistrate of Civil Justice calling for water in the vain hope of cleansing himself of that stain of innocent blood that makes him the scarlet figure of History: the coronation-ceremony of Sorrow, one of the most wonderful things in the whole of recorded time: the crucifixion of the Innocent One before the eyes of his mother and of the disciple whom he loved: the soldiers gambling and throwing dice for his clothes: the terrible death by which he gave the world its most eternal symbol: and his final burial in the tomb of the rich man, his body swathed in Egyptian linen with costly spices and perfumes as though he had been a King's son – when one contemplates all this from the point of view of

Art alone one cannot but be grateful that the supreme office of the Church should be the playing of the tragedy without the shedding of blood, the mystical presentation by means of dialogue and costume and gesture even of the Passion of her Lord, and it is always a source of pleasure and awe to me to remember that the ultimate survival of the Greek Chorus, lost elsewhere to art, is to be found in the servitor answering the priest at Mass.

Yet the whole life of Christ – so entirely may Sorrow and Beauty be made one in their meaning and manifestation – is really an idyll, though it ends with the veil of the temple being rent, and the darkness coming over the face of the earth, and the stone rolled to the door of the sepulchre. One always thinks of him as a young bridegroom with his companions, as indeed he somewhere describes himself, or as a shepherd straying through a valley with his sheep in search of green meadow or cool stream, or as a singer trying to build out of music the walls of the city of God, or as a lover for whose love the whole world was too small. His miracles seem to me as exquisite as the coming of Spring, and quite as natural. I see no difficulty at all in believing that such was the charm of his personality that his mere presence could bring peace to souls in anguish, and that those who touched his garments or his hands forgot their pain: or that as he passed by on the highway of life people who had seen nothing of life's mysteries saw them clearly, and others who had been deaf to every voice but that of Pleasure heard for the first time the voice of Love and found it as 'musical as is Apollo's lute': or that evil passions fled at his approach, and men whose dull unimaginative lives had been but a mode of death rose as it were from the grave when he called them: or that when he taught on the hillside the multitude forgot their hunger and thirst and the cares of this world, and that to his friends who listened to him as he sat at meat the coarse food seemed delicate, and the water had the taste of good wine, and the whole house became full of the odour and sweetness of nard.

Renan in his *Vie de Jésus* – that gracious Fifth Gospel, the Gospel according to St Thomas one might call it – says somewhere that Christ's great achievement was that he made himself as much loved after his death as he had been during his lifetime. And certainly, if his place is among the poets, he is the leader of all the lovers. He saw that love was that lost secret of the world for which the wise men had been looking, and that it was only through love that one could approach either the heart of the leper or the Feet of God.

And, above all, Christ is the most supreme of Individualists. Humility, like the artistic acceptance of all experiences, is merely a mode of manifestation. It is man's soul that Christ is always looking for. He calls it 'God's Kingdom' – ἡ βασιλεία τοῦ θεοῦ – and finds it in everyone. He compares it to little things, to a tiny seed, to a handful of leaven, to a pearl. That is because one only realises one's soul by getting rid of all alien passions, all acquired culture, and all external possessions be they good or evil.

I bore up against everything with some stubbornness of will and much rebellion of nature till I had absolutely nothing left in the world but Cyril. I had lost my name, my position, my happiness, my freedom, my wealth. I was a prisoner and a pauper. But I had still one beautiful thing left, my own eldest son. Suddenly he was taken away from me by the law. It was a blow so appalling that I did not know what to do, so I flung myself on my knees, and bowed my head, and wept and said 'The body of a child is as the body of the Lord: I am not worthy of either.' That moment seemed to save me. I saw then that the only thing for me was to accept everything. Since then – curious as it will no doubt sound to you – I have been happier. It was of course my soul in its ultimate essence that I had reached. In many ways I had been its enemy, but I found it waiting for me as a friend. When one comes in contact with the soul it makes one simple as a child, as Christ said one should be.

It is tragic how few people ever 'possess their souls' before they die. 'Nothing is more rare in any man,' says Emerson, 'than an act of his own.' It is quite true. Most people are other people. Their thoughts are someone else's opinions, their life a mimicry, their passions a quotation. Christ was not merely the supreme Individualist, but he was the first in History. People have tried to make him out an ordinary Philanthropist, like the dreadful philanthropists of the nineteenth century, or ranked him as an Altruist with the unscientific and sentimental. But he was really neither one nor the other. Pity he has, of course, for the poor, for those who are shut up in prisons, for the lowly, for the wretched, but he has far more pity for the rich, for the hard Hedonists, for those who waste their freedom in becoming slaves to things, for those who wear soft raiment and live in Kings' houses. Riches and Pleasure seemed to him to be really greater tragedies than Poverty and Sorrow. And as for Altruism, who knew better than he that it is vocation not volition that determines us, and that one cannot gather grapes off thorns or figs from thistles?

To live for others as a definite self-conscious aim was not his creed. It was not the basis of his creed. When he says 'Forgive your enemies,' it is not for the sake of the enemy but for one's own sake that he says so, and because Love is more beautiful than Hate. In his entreaty to the young man whom when he looked on he loved, 'Sell all that thou hast and give it to the poor,' it is not of the state of the poor that he is thinking but of the soul of the young man, the lovely soul that wealth was marring. In his view of life he is one with the artist who knows that by the inevitable law of self-perfection the poet must sing, and the sculptor think in bronze, and the painter make the world a mirror for his moods, as surely and as certainly as the hawthorn must blossom in Spring, and the corn burn to gold at harvest-time, and the Moon in her ordered wanderings change from shield to sickle, and from sickle to shield.

But while Christ did not say to men, 'Live for others,' he pointed out that there was no difference at all between the lives of others and one's own life. By this means he gave to man an extended, a Titan personality. Since his coming the history of each separate individual is, or can be made, the history of the world. Of course Culture has intensified the personality of man. Art has made us myriad-minded. Those who have the artistic temperament go into exile with Dante and learn how salt is the bread of others and how steep their stairs: they catch for a moment the serenity and calm of Goethe, and yet know but too well why Baudelaire cried to God:

> O Seigneur, donnez-moi la force et le courage
> De contempler mon corps et mon coeur sans dégoût.[1]

Out of Shakespeare's sonnets they draw, to their own hurt it may be, the secret of his love and make it their own: they look with new eyes on modern life because they have listened to one of Chopin's nocturnes, or handled Greek things, or read the story of the passion of some dead man for some dead woman whose hair was like threads of fine gold and whose mouth was as a pomegranate. But the sympathy of the artistic temperament is necessarily with what has found expression. In words or in colour, in music or in marble, behind the painted masks of an AEschylean play or through some Sicilian shepherd's pierced and jointed reeds the man and his message must have been revealed.

To the artist, expression is the only mode under which he can conceive life at all. To him what is dumb is dead. But to Christ it was not so. With a width and wonder of imagination, that fills one almost with awe, he took the entire world of the inarticulate, the voiceless world of pain, as his kingdom, and made of himself its eternal mouthpiece. Those of whom I have spoken, who are dumb under oppression and 'whose silence is heard only of God,' he chose as his brothers. He sought to become eyes to the blind, ears to the deaf, and a cry on the lips of those whose tongue had been tied. His desire was to be to the myriads who had found no utterance a very trumpet through which they might call to Heaven. And feeling, with the artistic nature of one to whom Sorrow and Suffering were modes through which he could realise his conception of the Beautiful, that an idea is of no value till it becomes incarnate and is made an image, he makes of himself the image of the Man of Sorrows, and as such has fascinated and dominated Art as no Greek god ever succeeded in doing.

For the Greek gods, in spite of the white and red of their fair fleet limbs, were not really what they appeared to be. The curved brow of Apollo was like the sun's disk crescent over a hill at dawn, and his feet were as the wings of the morning, but he himself had been cruel to Marsyas and had made Niobe childless: in the steel shields of the eyes of Pallas there had been no pity for Arachne: the pomp and peacocks of Hera were all that was really noble about her: and the Father of the Gods himself had been too fond of the daughters of men. The two deep suggestive figures of Greek mythology were, for religion, Demeter, an earth-goddess, not one of the Olympians, and, for art, Dionysus, the son of a mortal woman to whom the moment of his birth had proved the moment of her death also.

But Life itself from its lowliest and most humble sphere produced one far more marvellous than the mother of Proserpina or the son of Semele. Out of

---

[1] O Lord give me the strength and the courage to look at my body and my heart without disgust.

the carpenter's shop at Nazareth had come a personality infinitely greater than any made by myth or legend, and one, strangely enough, destined to reveal to the world the mystical meaning of wine and the real beauty of the lilies of the field as none, either on Cithaeron or at Enna, had ever done it.

The song of Isaiah, '*He is despised and rejected of men, a man of sorrows and acquainted with grief: and we hid as it were our faces from him,*' had seemed to him to be a prefiguring of himself, and in him the prophecy was fulfilled. We must not be afraid of such a phrase. Every single work of art is the fulfilment of a prophecy. For every work of art is the conversion of an idea into an image. Every single human being should be the fulfilment of a prophecy. For every human being should be the realisation of some ideal, either in the mind of God or in the mind of man. Christ found the type, and fixed it, and the dream of a Virgilian poet, either at Jerusalem or at Babylon, became in the long progress of the centuries incarnate in him for whom the world was waiting. '*His visage was marred more than any man's, and his form more than the sons of men,*' are among the signs noted by Isaiah as distinguishing the new ideal, and as soon as Art understood what was meant it opened like a flower at the presence of one in whom truth in Art was set forth as it had never been before. For is not truth in Art, as I have said, 'that in which the outward is expressive of the inward; in which the soul is made flesh, and the body instinct with spirit: in which Form reveals'?

To me one of the things in history the most to be regretted is that the Christ's own renaissance which had produced the Cathedral of Chartres, the Arthurian cycle of legends, the life of St Francis of Assisi, the art of Giotto, and Dante's *Divine Comedy*, was not allowed to develop on its own lines but was interrupted and spoiled by the dreary classical Renaissance that gave us Petrarch, and Raphael's frescoes, and Palladian architecture, and formal French tragedy, and St Paul's Cathedral, and Pope's poetry, and everything that is made from without and by dead rules, and does not spring from within through some spirit informing it. But wherever there is a romantic movement in Art, there somehow, and under some form, is Christ, or the soul of Christ. He is in *Romeo and Juliet*, in the *Winter's Tale*, in Provençal poetry, in 'The Ancient Mariner,' in 'La Belle Dame sans Merci,' and in Chatterton's 'Ballad of Charity.'

We owe to him the most diverse things and people. Hugo's *Les Misérables*, Baudelaire's *Fleurs du Mal*, the note of pity in Russian novels, the stained glass and tapestries and quattrocento work of Burne-Jones and Morris, Verlaine and Verlaine's poems, belong to him no less than the Tower of Giotto, Lancelot and Guinevere, Tannhäuser, the troubled romantic marbles of Michael Angelo, pointed architecture, and the love of children and flowers – for both of whom, indeed, in classical art there was but little place, hardly enough for them to grow or play in, but who from the twelfth century down to our own day have been continually making their appearance in art, under various modes and at various times, coming fitfully and wilfully as children and flowers are apt to do. Spring always seeming to one as if the flowers had been hiding, and only came out into the sun because they were afraid that grown-up people would grow tired of looking for them and give up the search, and the life of a child being no more than an April day on which there is both rain and sun for the narcissus.

And it is the imaginative quality of Christ's own nature that makes him this palpitating centre of romance. The strange figures of poetic drama and ballad are made by the imagination of others, but out of his own imagination entirely did Jesus of Nazareth create himself. The cry of Isaiah had really no more to do with his coming than the song of the nightingale has to do with the rising of the moon – no more, though perhaps no less. He was the denial as well as the affirmation of prophecy. For every expectation that he fulfilled, there was another that he destroyed. In all beauty, says Bacon, there is 'some strangeness of proportion,' and of those who are born of the spirit, of those, that is to say, who like himself are dynamic forces, Christ says that they are like the wind that 'bloweth where it listeth and no man can tell whence it cometh or whither it goeth.' That is why he is so fascinating to artists. He has all the colour-elements of life: mystery, strangeness, pathos, suggestion, ecstasy, love. He appeals to the temper of wonder, and creates that mood by which alone he can be understood.

And it is to me a joy to remember that if he is 'of imagination all compact,' the world itself is of the same substance. I said in *Dorian Gray* that the great sins of the world take place in the brain, but it is in the brain that everything takes place. We know now that we do not see with the eye or hear with the ear. They are merely channels for the transmission, adequate or inadequate, of sense-impressions. It is in the brain that the poppy is red, that the apple is odorous, that the skylark sings.

Of late I have been studying the four prose-poems about Christ with some diligence. At Christmas I managed to get hold of a Greek Testament, and every morning, after I have cleaned my cell and polished my tins, I read a little of the Gospels, a dozen verses taken by chance anywhere. It is a delightful way of opening the day. To you, in your turbulent, ill-disciplined life, it would be a capital thing if you would do the same. It would do you no end of good, and the Greek is quite simple. Endless repetition, in and out of season, has spoiled for us the *naïveté*, the freshness, the simple romantic charm of the Gospels. We hear them read far too often, and far too badly, and all repetition is anti-spiritual. When one returns to the Greek it is like going into a garden of lilies out of some narrow and dark house.

And to me the pleasure is doubled by the reflection that it is extremely probable that we have the actual terms, the *ipsissima verba*,[1] used by Christ. It was always supposed that Christ talked in Aramaic. Even Renan thought so. But now we know that the Galilean peasants, like the Irish peasants of our own day, were bilingual, and that Greek was the ordinary language of intercourse all over Palestine, as indeed all over the Eastern world. I never liked the idea that we only knew of Christ's own words through a translation of a translation. It is a delight to me to think that as far as his conversation was

[1] Very words.

concerned, Charmides might have listened to him, and Socrates reasoned with him, and Plato understood him: that he really said ἐγώ εἰμι ὁ ποιμὴν ὁ καλός:[1] that when he thought of the lilies of the field, and how they neither toil nor spin, his absolute expression was καταμάθετε τὰ κρίνα τοῦ ἀγροῦ, πῶς αὐξάνει · οὐ κοπιᾷ οὐδὲ νήθει,[2] and that his last word when he cried out 'My life has been completed, has reached its fulfilment, has been perfected,' was exactly as St John tells us it was: τετέλεσται:[3] no more.

And while in reading the Gospels – particularly that of St John himself, or whatever early Gnostic took his name and mantle – I see this continual assertion of the imagination as the basis of all spiritual and material life, I see also that to Christ imagination was simply a form of Love, and that to him Love was Lord in the fullest meaning of the phrase. Some six weeks ago I was allowed by the Doctor to have white bread to eat instead of the coarse black or brown bread of ordinary prison fare. It is a great delicacy. To you it will sound strange that dry bread could possibly be a delicacy to anyone. I assure you that to me it is so much so that at the close of each meal I carefully eat whatever crumbs may be left on my tin plate, or have fallen on the rough towel that one uses as a cloth so as not to soil one's table: and do so not from hunger – I get now quite sufficient food – but simply in order that nothing should be wasted of what is given to me. So one should look on love.

Christ, like all fascinating personalities, had the power not merely of saying beautiful things himself, but of making other people say beautiful things to him; and I love the story St Mark tells us about the Greek woman – the γυνὴ Ἑλληνίς – who, when as a trial of her faith he said to her that he could not give her the bread of the children of Israel, answered him that the little dogs – κυνάρια, 'little dogs' it should be rendered – who are under the table eat of the crumbs that the children let fall. Most people live *for* love and admiration. But it is *by* love and admiration that we should live. If any love is shown us we should recognise that we are quite unworthy of it. Nobody is worthy to be loved. The fact that God loves man shows that in the divine order of ideal things it is written that eternal love is to be given to what is eternally unworthy. Or if that phrase seems to you a bitter one to hear, let us say that everyone is worthy of love, except he who thinks that he is. Love is a sacrament that should be taken kneeling, and *Domine, non sum dignus*[4] should be on the lips and hearts in the hearts of those who receive it. I wish you would sometimes think of that. You need it so much.

If I ever write again, in the sense of producing artistic work, there are just two subjects on which and through which I desire to express myself: one is 'Christ, as the precursor of the Romantic movement in life': the other is 'the Artistic life considered in its relation to Conduct.' The first is, of course, intensely fascinating, for I see in Christ not merely the essentials of the su-

---

[1] I am the good shepherd.
[2] Consider the lilies of the field how they grow, they toil not, neither do they spin.
[3] It is finished.
[4] Lord, I am unworthy.

preme romantic type, but all the accidents, the wilfulnesses even, of the romantic temperament also. He was the first person who ever said to people that they should live 'flower-like' lives. He fixed the phrase. He took children as the type of what people should try to become. He held them up as examples to their elders, which I myself have always thought the chief use of children, if what is perfect should have a use. Dante describes the soul of a man as coming from the hand of God 'weeping and laughing like a little child,' and Christ also saw that the soul of each one should be '*a guisa di fanciulla, che piangendo e ridendo pargoleggia.*'[1] He felt that life was changeful, fluid, active, and that to allow it to be stereotyped into any form was death. He saw that people should not be too serious over material, common interests: that to be unpractical was a great thing: that one should not bother too much over affairs. 'The birds didn't, why should man?' He is charming when he says, 'Take no thought for the morrow. Is not the *soul* more than meat? Is not the *body* more than raiment?' A Greek might have said the latter phrase. It is full of Greek feeling. But only Christ could have said both, and so summed up life perfectly for us.

His morality is all sympathy, just what morality should be. If the only thing he had ever said had been 'Her sins are forgiven her because she loved much,' it would have been worth while dying to have said it. His justice is all poetical justice, exactly what justice should be. The beggar goes to heaven because he had been unhappy. I can't conceive a better reason for his being sent there. The people who work for an hour in the vineyard in the cool of the evening receive just as much reward as those who had toiled there all day long in the hot sun. Why shouldn't they? Probably no one deserved anything. Or perhaps they were a different kind of people. Christ had no patience with the dull lifeless mechanical systems that treat people as if they were things, and so treat everybody alike: as if anybody, or anything for that matter, was like aught else in the world. For him there were no laws: there were exceptions merely.

That which is the very keynote of romantic art was to him the proper basis of actual life. He saw no other basis. And when they brought him one taken in the very act of sin and showed him her sentence written in the law and asked him what was to be done, he wrote with his finger on the ground as though he did not hear them, and finally, when they pressed him again and again, looked up and said 'Let him of you who has never sinned be the first to throw the stone at her.' It was worth while living to have said that.

Like all poetical natures, he loved ignorant people. He knew that in the soul of one who is ignorant there is always room for a great idea. But he could not stand stupid people, especially those who are made stupid by education – people who are full of opinions not one of which they can understand, a peculiarly modern type, and one summed up by Christ when he describes it as the type of one who has the key of knowledge, can't use it himself, and won't allow other people to use it, though it may be made to open the gate of God's

---

[1] Like a little girl who lies around weeping and laughing.

Kingdom. His chief war was against the Philistines. That is the war every child of light has to wage. Philistinism was the note of the age and community in which he lived. In their heavy inaccessibility to ideas, their dull respectability, their tedious orthodoxy, their worship of vulgar success, their entire preoccupation with the gross materialistic side of life, and their ridiculous estimate of themselves and their importance, the Jew of Jerusalem in Christ's day was the exact counterpart of the British Philistine of our own. Christ mocked at the 'whited sepulchres' of respectability, and fixed that phrase for ever. He treated worldly success as a thing to be absolutely despised. He saw nothing in it at all. He looked on wealth as an encumbrance to a man. He would not hear of life being sacrificed to any system of thought or morals. He pointed out that forms and ceremonies were made for man, not man for forms and ceremonies. He took Sabbatarianism as a type of the things that should be set at nought. The cold philanthropies, the ostentatious public charities, the tedious formalisms so dear to the middle-class mind, he exposed with utter and relentless scorn. To us, what is termed Orthodoxy is merely a facile unintelligent acquiescence, but to them, and in their hands, it was a terrible and paralysing tyranny. Christ swept it aside. He showed that the spirit alone was of value. He took a keen pleasure in pointing out to them that though they were always reading the Law and the Prophets they had not really the smallest idea of what either of them meant. In opposition to their tithing of each separate day into its fixed routine of prescribed duties, as they tithed mint and rue, he preached the enormous importance of living completely for the moment.

Those whom he saved from their sins are saved simply for beautiful moments in their lives. Mary Magdalen, when she sees Christ, breaks the rich vase of alabaster that one of her seven lovers had given her and spills the odorous spices over his tired, dusty feet, and for that one moment's sake sits for ever with Ruth and Beatrice in the tresses of the snow-white Rose of Paradise. All that Christ says to us by way of a little warning is that *every* moment should be beautiful, that the soul should *always* be ready for the coming of the Bridegroom, *always* waiting for the voice of the Lover. Philistinism being simply that side of man's nature that is not illumined by the imagination, he sees all the lovely influences of life as modes of Light: the imagination itself is the world-light, τὸ φῶς τοῦ κοσμοῦ: the world is made by it, and yet the world cannot understand it: that is because the imagination is simply a manifestation of Love, and it is love, and the capacity for it, that distinguishes one human being from another.

But it is when he deals with the Sinner that he is most romantic, in the sense of most real. The world had always loved the Saint as being the nearest possible approach to the perfection of God. Christ, through some divine instinct in him, seems to have always loved the sinner as being the nearest possible approach to the perfection of man. His primary desire was not to reform people, any more than his primary desire was to relieve suffering. To turn an interesting thief into a tedious honest man was not his aim. He would have thought little of the Prisoners' Aid Society and other modern movements of the kind. The conversion of a Publican into a Pharisee would not have seemed to him a great achievement by any means. But in a manner not yet understood of the world he regarded sin and suffering as being in themselves beautiful, holy things, and modes of perfection. It *sounds* a very dangerous idea. It is so. All great ideas *are* dangerous. That it was Christ's creed admits of no doubt. That it is the true creed I don't doubt myself.

Of course the sinner must repent. But why? Simply because otherwise he would be unable to realise what he had done. The moment of repentance is the moment of initiation. More than that. It is the means by which one alters one's past. The Greeks thought that impossible. They often say in their gnomic aphorisms 'Even the Gods cannot alter the past.' Christ showed that the commonest sinner could do it. That it was the one thing he could do. Christ, had he been asked, would have said – I feel quite certain about it – that the moment the prodigal son fell on his knees and wept he really made his having wasted his substance with harlots, and then kept swine and hungered for the husks they ate, beautiful and holy incidents in his life. It is difficult for most people to grasp the idea. I dare say one has to go to prison to understand it. If so, it may be worth while going to prison.

There is something so unique about Christ. Of course, just as there are false dawns before the dawn itself, and winter-days so full of sudden sunlight that they will cheat the wise crocus into squandering its gold before its time, and make some foolish bird call to its mate to build on barren boughs, so there were Christians before Christ. For that we should be grateful. The unfortunate thing is that there have been none since. I make one exception, St Francis of Assisi. But then God had given him at his birth the soul of a poet, as he himself when quite young had in mystical marriage taken Poverty as his bride; and with the soul of a poet and the body of a beggar he found the way to perfection not difficult. He understood Christ, and so he became like him. We do not require the *Liber Conformitatum* to teach us that the life of St Francis was the true *Imitatio Christi*: a poem compared to which the book that bears that name is merely prose. Indeed, that is the charm about Christ, when all is said. He is just like a work of art himself. He does not really teach one anything, but by being brought into his presence one becomes something. And everybody is predestined to his presence. Once at least in his life each man walks with Christ to Emmaus.

As regards the other subject, the relation of the artistic life to conduct, it will no doubt seem strange to you that I should select it. People point to Reading Gaol, and say 'There is where the artistic life leads a man.' Well, it might lead one to worse places. The more mechanical people, to whom life is a shrewd speculation dependent on a careful calculation of ways and means, always know where they are going, and go there. They start with the desire of being the Parish Beadle, and, in whatever sphere they are placed, they succeed in being the Parish Beadle and no more. A man whose desire is to be something separate from himself, to be a Member of Parliament, or a successful grocer, or a prominent solicitor, or a judge, or something equally tedious, invariably succeeds in being what he wants to be. That is his punishment. Those who want a mask have to wear it.

But with the dynamic forces of life, and those in whom those dynamic forces become incarnate, it is different. People whose desire is solely for self-realisation never know where they are going. They can't know. In one sense of the word it is, of course, necessary, as the Greek oracle said, to know oneself. That is the first achievement of knowledge. But to recognise that the soul of a man is unknowable is the ultimate achievement of Wisdom. The final mystery is oneself. When one has weighed the sun in a balance, and measured the steps of the moon, and mapped out the seven heavens star by star, there still remains oneself. Who can calculate the orbit of his own soul? When the son of Kish went out to look for his father's asses, he did not know that a man of God was waiting for him with the very chrism of coronation, and that his own soul was already the Soul of a King.

I hope to live long enough, and to produce work of such a character, that I shall be able at the end of my days to say, 'Yes: this is just where the artistic life leads a man.' Two of the most perfect lives I have come across in my own experience are the lives of Verlaine and of Prince Kropotkin: both of them men who passed years in prison: the first, the one Christian poet since Dante, the other a man with the soul of that beautiful white Christ that seems coming out of Russia. And for the last seven or eight months, in spite of a succession of great troubles reaching me from the outside world almost without intermission, I have been placed in direct contact with a new spirit working in this prison through men and things, that has helped me beyond any possibility of expression in words; so that while for the first year of my imprisonment I did nothing else, and can remember doing nothing else, but wring my hands in impotent despair, and say 'What an ending! What an appalling ending!'; now I try to say to myself, and sometimes when I am not torturing myself do really and sincerely say, 'What a beginning! What a wonderful beginning!' It may really be so. It may become so. If it does, I shall owe much to this new personality that has altered every man's life in this place.

Things in themselves are of little importance, have indeed – let us for once thank Metaphysics for something that she has taught us – no real existence. The spirit alone is of importance. Punishment may be inflicted in such a way that it will heal, not make a wound, just as alms may be given in such a manner that the bread changes to a stone in the hands of the giver. What a change there is – not in the regulations, for they are fixed by iron rule, but in the spirit that uses them as its expression – you can realise when I tell you that had I been released last May, as I tried to be, I would have left this place loathing it and every official in it with a bitterness of hatred that would have poisoned my life. I have had a year longer of imprisonment, but Humanity has been in the prison along with us all, and now when I go out I shall always remember great kindnesses that I have received here from almost everybody, and on the day of my release will give my thanks to many people and ask to be remembered by them in turn.

The prison-system is absolutely and entirely wrong. I would give anything to be able to alter it when I go out. I intend to try. But there is nothing in the world so wrong but that the spirit of Humanity, which is the spirit of Love, the spirit of the Christ who is not in Churches, may make it, if not right, at least possible to be borne without too much bitterness of heart.

I know also that much is waiting for me outside that is very delightful, from what St Francis of Assisi calls '*my brother the wind*' and '*my sister the rain*,' lovely things both of them, down to the shop-windows and sunsets of great cities. If I made a list of all that still remains to me, I don't know where I should stop: for, indeed, God made the world just as much for me as for any-one else. Perhaps I may go out with something I had not got before. I need not tell you that to me Reformations in Morals are as meaningless and vulgar as Reformations in Theology. But while to propose to be a better man is a piece of unscientific cant, to have become a *deeper* man is the privilege of those who have suffered. And such I think I have become. You can judge for yourself.

If after I go out a friend of mine gave a feast, and did not invite me to it, I shouldn't mind a bit. I can be perfectly happy by myself. With freedom, books, flowers, and the moon, who could not be happy? Besides, feasts are not for me any more. I have given too many to care about them. That side of life is over for me, very fortunately I dare say. But if, after I go out, a friend of mine had a sorrow, and refused to allow me to share it, I should feel it most bitterly. If he shut the doors of the house of mourning against me I would come back again and again and beg to be admitted, so that I might share in what I was entitled to share in. If he thought me unworthy, unfit to weep with him, I should feel it as the most poignant humiliation, as the most ter-rible mode in which disgrace could be inflicted on me. But that could not be. I have a right to share in Sorrow, and he who can look at the loveliness of the world, and share its sorrow, and realise something of the wonder of both, is in immediate contact with divine things, and has got as near to God's secret as anyone can get.

Perhaps there may come into my art also, no less than into my life, a still deeper note, one of greater unity of passion, and directness of impulse. Not width but intensity is the true aim of modern Art. We are no longer in Art concerned with the type. It is with the exception we have to do. I cannot put my sufferings into any form they took, I need hardly say. Art only begins where Imitation ends. But something must come into my work, of fuller har-mony of words perhaps, of richer cadences, of more curious colour-effects, of simpler architectural-order, of some aesthetic quality at any rate.

When Marsyas was 'torn from the scabbard of his limbs' – *dalla vagina delle membre sue*, to use one of Dante's most terrible, most Tacitean phrases – he had no more song, the Greeks said. Apollo had been victor. The lyre had vanquished the reed. But perhaps the Greeks were mistaken. I hear in much modern Art the cry of Marsyas. It is bitter in Baudelaire, sweet and plaintive in Lamartine, mystic in Verlaine. It is in the deferred resolutions of Chopin's music. It is in the discontent that haunts the recurrent faces of Burne-Jones's women. Even Matthew Arnold, whose song of Callicles tells of 'the triumph of the sweet persuasive lyre,' and the 'famous final victory,' in such a clear note of lyrical beauty – even he, in the troubled undertone of doubt and distress that haunts his verse, had not a little of it. Neither Goethe nor Wordsworth could heal him, though he followed each in turn, and when he seeks to mourn for 'Thyrsis' or to sing of 'the Scholar Gipsy,' it is the reed that he has to take for the rendering of his strain. But whether or not the Phrygian Faun was silent, I cannot be. Expression is as necessary to me as leaf and blossom are to the black branches of the trees that show themselves above the prison wall and are so restless in the wind. Between my art and the world there is now a wide gulf, but between Art and myself there is none. I hope at least that there is none.

To each of us different fates have been meted out. Freedom, pleasure, amusements, a life of ease have been your lot, and you are not worthy of it. My lot has been one of public infamy, of long imprisonment, of misery, of ruin, of disgrace, and I am not worthy of it either – not yet, at any rate. I remember I used to say that I thought I could bear a real tragedy if it came to me with purple pall and a mask of noble sorrow, but that the dreadful thing about modernity was that it put Tragedy into the raiment of Comedy, so that the great realities seemed commonplace or grotesque or lacking in style. It is quite true about modernity. It has probably always been true about actual life. It is said that all martyrdoms seemed mean to the looker-on. The nineteenth century is no exception to the general rule.

Everything about my tragedy has been hideous, mean, repellent, lacking in style. Our very dress makes us grotesques. We are the zanies of sorrow. We are clowns whose hearts are broken. We are specially designed to appeal to the sense of humour. On November 13th 1895 I was brought down here from London. From two o'clock till half-past two on that day I had to stand on the centre platform of Clapham Junction in convict dress and handcuffed, for the world to look at. I had been taken out of the Hospital Ward without a moment's notice being given to me. Of all possible objects I was the most grotesque. When people saw me they laughed. Each train as it came up swelled the audience. Nothing could exceed their amusement. That was of course before they knew who I was. As soon as they had been informed, they laughed still more. For half an hour I stood there in the grey November rain surrounded by a jeering mob.

For a year after that was done to me I wept every day at the same hour and for the same space of time. That is not such a tragic thing as possibly it sounds to you. To those who are in prison, tears are a part of every day's experience. A day in prison on which one does not weep is a day on which one's heart is hard, not a day on which one's heart is happy.

Well, now I am really beginning to feel more regret for the people who laughed than for myself. Of course when they saw me I was not on my pedestal. I was in the pillory. But it is a very unimaginative nature that only cares for people on their pedestals. A pedestal may be a very unreal thing. A pillory is a terrific reality. They should have known also how to interpret sorrow better. I have said that behind Sorrow there is always Sorrow. It were still wiser to say that behind sorrow there is always a soul. And to mock at a soul in pain is a dreadful thing. Unbeautiful are their lives who do it. In the strangely simple economy of the world people only get what they give, and to those who have not enough imagination to penetrate the mere outward of things and feel pity, what pity can be given save that of scorn?

I have told you this account of the mode of my being conveyed here simply that you should realise how hard it has been for me to get anything out of my punishment but bitterness and despair. I have however to do it, and now and then I have moments of submission and acceptance. All the spring may be hidden in a single bud, and the low ground-nest of the lark may hold the joy that is to herald the feet of many rose-red dawns, and so perhaps whatever beauty of life still remains to me is contained in some moment of surrender, abasement and humiliation. I can, at any rate, merely proceed on the lines of my own development, and by accepting all that has happened to me make myself worthy of it.

People used to say of me that I was too individualistic. I must be far more of an individualist than I ever was. I must get far more out of myself than I ever got, and ask far less of the world than I ever asked. Indeed my ruin came, not from too great individualism of life, but from too little. The one disgraceful, unpardonable, and to all time contemptible action of my life was my allowing myself to be forced into appealing to Society for help and protection against your father. To have made such an appeal against anyone would have been from the individualistic point of view bad enough, but what excuse can there ever be put forward for having made it against one of such nature and aspect?

Of course once I had put into motion the forces of Society, Society turned on me and said, 'Have you been living all this time in defiance of my laws, and do you now appeal to those laws for protection? You shall have those laws exercised to the full. You shall abide by what you have appealed to.' The result is I am in gaol. And I used to feel bitterly the irony and ignominy of my position when in the course of my three trials, beginning at the Police Court, I used to see your father bustling in and out in the hopes of attracting public attention, as if anyone could fail to note or remember the stableman's gait and dress, the bowed legs, the twitching hands, the hanging lower lip, the bestial and half-witted grin. Even when he was not there, or was out of sight, I used to feel conscious of his presence, and the blank dreary walls of the great Court-room, the very air itself, seemed to me at times to be hung with multitudinous masks of that apelike face. Certainly no man ever fell so ignobly, and by such ignoble instruments, as I did. I say, in *Dorian Gray* somewhere, that 'a man cannot be too careful in the choice of his enemies.' I little thought that it was by a pariah that I was to be made a pariah myself.

This urging me, forcing me to appeal to Society for help, is one of the things that makes me despise you so much, that makes me despise myself so much for having yielded to you. Your not appreciating me as an artist was quite excusable. It was temperamental. You couldn't help it. But you might have appreciated me as an Individualist. For that no culture was required. But you didn't, and so you brought the element of Philistinism into a life that had been a complete protest against it, and from some points of view a complete annihilation of it. The Philistine element in life is not the failure to understand Art. Charming people such as fishermen, shepherds, ploughboys, peasants and the like know nothing about Art, and are the very salt of the earth. He is the Philistine who upholds and aids the heavy, cumbrous, blind mechanical forces of Society, and who does not recognise the dynamic force when he meets it either in a man or a movement.

People thought it dreadful of me to have entertained at dinner the evil things of life, and to have found pleasure in their company. But they, from the point of view through which I, as an artist in life, approached them, were delightfully suggestive and stimulating. It was like feasting with panthers. The danger was half the excitement. I used to feel as the snake-charmer must feel when he lures the cobra to stir from the painted cloth or reed-basket that holds it, and makes it spread its hood at his bidding, and sway to and fro in the air as a plant sways restfully in a stream. They were to me the brightest of gilded snakes. Their poison was part of their perfection. I did not know that when they were to strike at me it was to be at your piping and for your father's pay. I don't feel at all ashamed of having known them. They were intensely interesting. What I do feel ashamed of is the horrible Philistine atmosphere into which you brought me. My business as an artist was with Ariel. You set me to wrestle with Caliban. Instead of making beautiful coloured, musical things such as *Salomé*, and the *Florentine Tragedy*, and *La Sainte Courtisane*, I found myself forced to send long lawyer's letters to your father and constrained to appeal to the very things against which I had always protested. Clibborn and Atkins were wonderful in their infamous war against life. To entertain them was an astounding adventure. Dumas *père*, Cellini, Goya, Edgar Allan Poe, or Baudelaire, would have done just the same. What is loathsome to me is the memory of interminable visits paid by me to the solicitor Humphreys in your company, when in the ghastly glare of a bleak room you and I would sit with serious faces telling serious lies to a bald man, till I really groaned and yawned with *ennui*. *There* is where I found myself after two years' friendship with you, right in the centre of Philistia, away from everything that was beautiful, or brilliant, or wonderful, or daring. At the end I had to come forward, on your behalf, as the champion of Respectability in conduct, of Puritanism, in life, and of Morality in Art. *Voilà où mènent les mauvais chemins!*[1]

And the curious thing to me is that you should have tried to imitate your father in his chief characteristics. I cannot understand why he was to you an exemplar, where he should have been a warning, except that whenever there is hatred between two people there is bond or brotherhood of some kind. I suppose that, by some strange law of the antipathy of similars, you loathed each other, not because in so many points you were so different, but because in some you were so like. In June 1893 when you left Oxford, without a degree and with debts, petty in themselves, but considerable to a man of your

---

[1] That's where evil ways lead.

father's income, your father wrote you a very vulgar, violent and abusive letter. The letter you sent him in reply was in every way worse, and of course far less excusable, and consequently you were extremely proud of it. I remember quite well your saying to me with your most conceited air that you could beat your father 'at his own trade.' Quite true. But what a trade! What a competition! You used to laugh and sneer at your father for retiring from your cousin's house where he was living in order to write filthy letters to him from a neighbouring hotel. You used to do just the same to me. You constantly lunched with me at some public restaurant, sulked or made a scene during luncheon, and then retired to White's Club and wrote me a letter of the very foulest character. The only difference between you and your father was that after you had dispatched your letter to me by special messenger, you would arrive yourself at my rooms some hours later, not to apologise, but to know if I had ordered dinner at the Savoy, and if not, why not. Sometimes you would actually arrive before the offensive letter had been read. I remember on one occasion you had asked me to invite to luncheon at the Café Royal two of your friends, one of whom I had never seen in my life. I did so, and at your special request ordered beforehand a specially luxurious luncheon to be prepared. The *chef*, I remember, was sent for, and particular instructions given about the wines. Instead of coming to luncheon you sent me at the Café an abusive letter, timed so as to reach me after we had been waiting half an hour for you. I read the first line, and saw what it was, and putting the letter in my pocket, explained to your friends that you were suddenly taken ill, and that the rest of the letter referred to your symptoms. In point of fact I did not read the letter till I was dressing for dinner at Tite Street that evening. As I was in the middle of its mire, wondering with infinite sadness how you could write letters that were really like the froth and foam on the lips of an epileptic, my servant came in to tell me that you were in the hall and were very anxious to see me for five minutes. I at once sent down and asked you to come up. You arrived, looking I admit very frightened and pale, to beg my advice and assistance, as you had been told that a man from Lumley, the solicitor, had been enquiring for you at Cadogan Place, and you were afraid that your Oxford trouble or some new danger was threatening you. I consoled you, and told you, what proved to be the case, that it was merely a tradesman's bill probably, and let you stay to dinner, and pass your evening with me. You never mentioned a single word about your hideous letter, nor did I. I treated it as simply an unhappy symptom of an unhappy temperament. The subject was never alluded to. To write to me a loathsome letter at 2.30, and fly to me for help and sympathy at 7.15 the same afternoon, was a perfectly ordinary occurrence in your life. You went quite beyond your father in such habits, as you did in others. When his revolting letters to you were read in open Court he naturally felt ashamed and pretended to weep. Had your letters to him been read by his own Counsel still more horror and repugnance would have been felt by everyone. Nor was it merely in style that you 'beat him at his own trade,' but in mode of attack you distanced him completely. You availed yourself of the public telegram, and the open postcard. I think you might have left such modes of annoyance to people like Alfred Wood whose sole source of income it is. Don't you? What was a profession to him and his class was a pleasure to you, and a very evil one. Nor have you given up your horrible habit of writing offensive letters, after all that has happened to me through them and for them. You still regard it as one of your accomplishments, and you exercise it on my friends, on those who have been kind to me in prison like Robert Sherard and others. That is disgraceful of you. When Robert Sherard heard from me that I did not wish you to publish any article on me in the *Mercure de France*, with or without letters, you should have been grateful to him for having ascertained my wishes on the point, and for having saved you from, without intending it, inflicting more pain on me than you had done already. You must remember that a patronising and Philistine letter about 'fair play' for a 'man who is down' is all right for an English newspaper. It carried on the old traditions of English journalism in regard to their attitude towards artists. But in France such a tone would have exposed me to ridicule and you to contempt. I could not have allowed any article till I had known its aim, temper, mode of approach and the like. In art good intentions are not of the smallest value. All bad art is the result of good intentions.

Nor is Robert Sherard the only one of my friends to whom you have addressed acrimonious and bitter letters because they sought that my wishes and my feelings should be consulted in matters concerning myself, the publication of articles on me, the dedication of your verses, the surrender of my letters and presents, and such like. You have annoyed or sought to annoy others also.

Does it ever occur to you what an awful position I would have been in if for the last two years, during my appalling sentence, I had been dependent on you as a friend? Do you ever think of that? Do you ever feel any gratitude to those who by kindness without stint, devotion without limit, cheerfulness and joy in giving, have lightened my black burden for me, have visited me again and again, have written to me beautiful and sympathetic letters, have managed my affairs for me, have arranged my future life for me, have stood by me in the teeth of obloquy, taunt, open sneer or insult even? I thank God every day that he gave me friends other than you. I owe everything to them. The very books in my cell are paid for by Robbie out of his pocket-money. From the same source are to come clothes for me, when I am released. I am not ashamed of taking a thing that is given by love and affection. I am proud of it. But do you ever think of what my friends such as More Adey, Robbie, Robert Sherard, Frank Harris, and Arthur Clifton, have been to me in giving me comfort, help, affection, sympathy and the like? I suppose that has never dawned on you. And yet – if you had any imagination in you – you would know that there is not a single person who has been kind to me in my prison-life, down to the warder who may give me a good-morning or a good-night that is not one of his prescribed duties – down to the common policemen who in their homely rough way strove to comfort me on my journeys to and fro from the Bankruptcy Court under conditions of terrible mental distress – down to the poor thief who, recognising me as we tramped round the yard at

Wandsworth, whispered to me in the hoarse prison-voice men get from long and compulsory silence: '*I am sorry for you: it is harder for the likes of you than it is for the likes of us*' – not one of them all, I say, the very mire from whose shoes you should not be proud to be allowed to kneel down and clean.

Have you imagination enough to see what a fearful tragedy it was for me to have come across your family? What a tragedy it would have been for anyone at all, who had a great position, and great name, anything of importance to lose? There is hardly one of the elders of your family – with the exception of Percy, who is really a good fellow – who did not in some way contribute to my ruin.

I have spoken of your mother to you with some bitterness, and I strongly advise you to let her see this letter, for your own sake chiefly. If it is painful to her to read such an indictment against one of her sons, let her remember that *my* mother, who intellectually ranks with Elizabeth Barrett Browning, and historically with Madame Roland, died broken-hearted because the son of whose genius and art she had been so proud, and whom she had regarded always as a worthy continuer of a distinguished name, had been condemned to the treadmill for two years. You will ask me in what way your mother contributed to my destruction. I will tell you. Just as you strove to shift on to me all your immoral responsibilities, so your mother strove to shift on to me all her moral responsibilities with regard to you. Instead of speaking directly to you about your life, as a mother should, she always wrote privately to me with earnest, frightened entreaties not to let you know that she was writing to me. You see the position in which I was placed between you and your mother. It was one as false, as absurd, and as tragic as the one in which I was placed between you and your father. In August 1892, and on the 8th November in the same year, I had two long interviews with your mother about you. On both occasions I asked her why she did not speak directly to you herself. On both occasions she gave me the same answer: '*I am afraid to: he gets so angry when he is spoken to.*' The first time, I knew you so slightly that I did not understand what she meant. The second time, I knew you so well that I understood perfectly. (During the interval you had had an attack of jaundice and been ordered by the doctor to go for a week to Bournemouth, and had induced me to accompany you as you hated being alone.) But the first duty of a mother is not to be afraid of speaking seriously to her son. Had your mother spoken seriously to you about the trouble she saw you were in in July 1892 and made you confide in her it would have been much better, and much happier ultimately for both of you. All the underhand and secret communications with me were wrong. What was the use of your mother sending me endless little notes, marked 'Private' on the envelope, begging me not to ask you so often to dinner, and not to give you any money, each note ending with an earnest postscript '*On no account let Alfred know that I have written to you*'? What good could come of such a correspondence? Did you ever wait to be asked to dinner? Never. You took all your meals as a matter of course with me. If I remonstrated, you always had one observation: '*If I don't dine with you, where am I to dine? You don't suppose that I am going to dine at home.*' It was unanswerable. And if I absolutely refused to let you dine with me, you always threatened that you would do something foolish, and always did it. What possible result could there be from letters such as your mother used to send me, except that which did occur, a foolish and fatal shifting of the moral responsibility on to my shoulders? Of the various details in which your mother's weakness and lack of courage proved so ruinous to herself, to you, and to me, I don't want to speak any more, but surely, when she heard of your father coming down to my house to make a loathsome scene and create a serious scandal, she might then have seen that a serious crisis was impending, and taken some serious steps to try and avoid it? But all she could think of doing was to send down plausible George Wyndham with his pliant tongue to propose to me – what? That I should 'gradually drop you'!

As if it had been possible for me to gradually drop you! I had tried to end our friendship in every possible way, going so far as actually to leave England and give a false address abroad in the hopes of breaking at one blow a bond that had become irksome, hateful, and ruinous to me. Do you think that I *could* have 'gradually dropped' you? Do you think that would have satisfied your father? You know it would not. What your father wanted, indeed, was not the cessation of our friendship, but a public scandal. That is what he was striving for. His name had not been in the papers for years. He saw the opportunity of appearing before the British public in an entirely new character, that of the affectionate father. His sense of humour was roused. Had I severed my friendship with you it would have been a terrible disappointment to him, and the small notoriety of a second divorce suit, however revolting its details and origin, would have proved but little consolation to him. For what he was aiming at was popularity, and to pose as a champion of purity, as it is termed, is, in the present condition of the British public, the surest mode of becoming for the nonce a heroic figure. Of this public I have said in one of my plays that if it is Caliban for one half of the year, it is Tartuffe for the other, and your father, in whom both characters may be said to have become incarnate, was in this way marked out as the proper representative of Puritanism in its aggressive and most characteristic form. No gradual dropping of you would have been of any avail, even had it been practicable. Don't you feel now that the only thing for your mother to have done was to have asked me to come to see her, and had you and your brother present, and said definitely that the friendship must absolutely cease? She would have found in me her warmest seconder, and with Drumlanrig and myself in the room she need not have been afraid of speaking to you. She did not do so. She was afraid of her responsibilities, and tried to shift them on to me. One letter she did certainly write to me. It was a brief one, to ask me not to send the lawyer's letter to your father warning him to desist. She was quite right. It was ridiculous my consulting lawyers and seeking their protection. But she nullified any effect her letter might have produced by her usual postscript: '*On no account let Alfred know that I have written to you.*' You were entranced at the idea of my sending lawyers' letters to your father, as well as yourself. It was your suggestion. I could not tell you that your mother was strongly against the idea, for she had bound me with the most solemn promises never to tell you about her letters to me, and I foolishly kept my promise to her. Don't you see that it was wrong of her not to speak directly to you? That all the backstairs-interviews with me, and the area-gate correspondence were wrong? Nobody can shift their responsibilities on anyone else. They always return ultimately to the proper owner. Your one idea of life, your one philosophy, if you are to be credited with a philosophy, was that whatever you did was to be paid for by someone else: I don't mean merely in the financial sense – that was simply the practical application of your philosophy to everyday life – but in the broadest, fullest sense of transferred responsibility. You made that your creed. It was very successful as far as it went. You forced me into taking the action because you knew that your father would not attack your life or yourself in any way, and that I would defend both to the utmost, and take on my own shoulders whatever would be thrust on me. You were quite right. Your father and I, each from different motives of course, did exactly as you counted on our doing. But somehow, in spite of everything, you have not really escaped. The 'infant Samuel theory,' as for brevity's sake one may term it, is all very well as far as the general world goes. It may be a good deal scorned in London, and a little sneered at in Oxford, but that is merely because there are a few people who know you in each place, and because in each place you left traces of your passage. Outside of a small set in those two cities, the world looks on you as the good young man who was very nearly tempted into wrong-doing by the wicked and immoral artist, but was rescued just in time by his kind and loving father. It sounds all right. And yet, you know you have not escaped. I am not referring to a silly question asked by a silly juryman, which was of course treated with contempt by the Crown and by the Judge. No one cared about that. I am referring perhaps principally to yourself. In your own eyes, and some day you will have to think of your conduct, you are not, cannot be quite satisfied at the way in which things have turned out. Secretly you must think of yourself with a good deal of shame. A brazen face is a capital thing to show the world, but now and then when you are alone, and have no audience, you have, I suppose, to take the mask off for mere breathing purposes. Else, indeed, you would be stifled.

And in the same manner your mother must at times regret that she tried to shift her grave responsibilities on someone else, who already had enough of a burden to carry. She occupied the position of both parents to you. Did she really fulfil the duties of either? If I bore with your bad temper and your rudeness and your scenes, she might have borne with them too. When last I saw my wife – fourteen months ago now – I told her that she would have to be to Cyril a father as well as a mother. I told her everything about your mother's mode of dealing with you in every detail as I have set it down in this letter, only of course far more fully. I told her the reason of the endless notes with 'Private' on the envelope that used to come to Tite Street from your mother, so constantly that my wife used to laugh and say that we must be collaborating in a society novel or something of that kind. I implored her not to be to Cyril what your mother was to you. I told her that she should bring him up so that if he shed innocent blood he would come and tell her, that she might cleanse his hands for him first, and then teach him how by penance or expiation to cleanse his soul afterwards. I told her that if she was frightened of facing the responsibility of the life of another, though her own child, she should get a guardian to help her. That she has, I am glad to say, done. She has chosen Adrian Hope, a man of high birth and culture and fine character, her own cousin, whom you met once at Tite Street, and with him Cyril and Vyvyan have a good chance of a beautiful future. Your mother, if she was afraid of talking seriously to you, should have chosen someone amongst her own relatives to whom you might have listened. But she should not have been afraid. She should have had it out with you and faced it. At any rate, look at the result. Is she satisfied and pleased?

I know she puts the blame on me. I hear of it, not from people who know you, but from people who do not know you, and do not desire to know you. I hear of it often. She talks of the influence of an elder over a younger man, for instance. It is one of her favourite attitudes towards the question, and it is always a successful appeal to popular prejudice and ignorance. I need not ask you what influence I had over you. You know I had none. It was one of your frequent boasts that I had none, and the only one indeed that was well-founded. What was there, as a mere matter of fact, in you that I could influence? Your brain? It was undeveloped. Your imagination? It was dead. Your heart? It was not yet born. Of all the people who have ever crossed my life you were the one, and the only one, I was unable in any way to influence in any direction. When I lay ill and helpless in a fever caught from tending on you, I had not sufficient influence over you to induce you to get me even a cup of milk to drink, or to see that I had the ordinary necessaries of a sick-room, or to take the trouble to drive a couple of hundred yards to a bookseller's to get me a book at my own expense. When I was actually engaged in writing, and penning comedies that were to beat Congreve for brilliancy, and Dumas *fils* for philosophy, and I suppose everybody else for every other quality, I had not sufficient influence with you to get you to leave me undisturbed as an artist should be left. Wherever my writing room was, it was to you an ordinary lounge, a place to smoke and drink hock-and-seltzer in, and chatter about absurdities. The 'influence of an elder over a younger man' is an excellent theory till it comes to my ears. Then it becomes grotesque. When it comes to your ears, I suppose you smile – to yourself. You are certainly entitled to do so. I hear also much of what she says about money. She states, and with perfect justice, that she was ceaseless in her entreaties to me not to supply you with money. I admit it. Her letters were endless, and the postscript '*Pray do not let Alfred know that I have written to you*' appears in them all. But it was no pleasure to me to have to pay every single thing for you from your morning shave to your midnight hansom. It was a horrible bore. I used to complain to you again and again about it. I used to tell you – you remember, don't you? – how I loathed your regarding me as a '*useful*' person, how no artist wishes to be so regarded or so treated; artists, like art itself, being of their very essence quite useless. You used to get very angry when I said it to you. The truth always made you angry. Truth, indeed, is a thing that is most painful to listen to and most painful to utter. But it did not make you alter your views or your mode of life. Every day I had to pay for every single thing you did all day long. Only a person of absurd good nature or of indescribable folly would have done so. I unfortunately was a complete combination of both. When I used to suggest that your mother should supply you with the money you wanted, you always had a very pretty and graceful answer. You said that the income allowed her by your father – some £1500 a year I believe – was quite inadequate to the wants of a lady of her position, and that you could not go to her for more money than you were getting already. You were quite right about her income being one absolutely unsuitable to a lady of her position and tastes, but you should not have made that an excuse for living in luxury on me: it should on the contrary have been a suggestion to you for economy in your own life. The fact is that you were, and are I suppose still, a typical sentimentalist. For a sentimentalist is simply one who desires to have the luxury of an emotion without paying for it. To propose to spare your mother's pocket was beautiful. To do so at my expense was ugly. You think that one can have one's emotions for nothing. One cannot. Even the finest and the most self-sacrificing emotions have to be paid for. Strangely enough, that is what makes them fine. The intellectual and emotional life of ordinary people is a very contemptible affair. Just as they borrow their ideas from a sort of circulating library of thought – the *Zeitgeist* of an age that has no soul – and send them back soiled at the end of each week, so they always try to get their emotions on credit, and refuse to pay the bill when it comes in. You should pass out of that conception of life. As soon as you have to pay for an emotion you will know its quality, and be the better for such knowledge. And remember that the sentimentalist is always a cynic at heart. Indeed sentimentality is merely the bank holiday of cynicism. And delightful as cynicism is from its intellectual side, now that it has left the Tub for the Club, it never can be more than the perfect philosophy for a man who has no soul. It has its social value, and to an artist all modes of expression are interesting, but in itself it is a poor affair, for to the true cynic nothing is ever revealed.

I think that if you look back now to your mother's income, and your attitude towards my income, you will not feel proud of yourself, and perhaps you may some day, if you don't show your mother this letter, explain to her that your living on me was a matter in which my wishes were not consulted for a moment. It was simply a peculiar, and to me personally most distressing, form that your devotion to me took. To make yourself dependent on me for the smallest as well as the largest sums lent you in your own eyes all the charm of childhood, and in the insisting on my paying for every one of your pleasures you thought that you had found the secret of eternal youth. I confess that it pains me when I hear of your mother's remarks about me, and I am sure that on reflection you will agree with me that if she has no word of regret or sorrow for the ruin your race has brought on mine it would be better if she remained silent. Of course there is no reason she should see any portion of this letter that refers to any mental development I have been going through, or to any point of departure I hope to attain to. It would not be interesting to her. But the parts concerned purely with your life I should show her if I were you.

If I were you, in fact, I would not care about being loved on false pretences. There is no reason why a man should show his life to the world. The world does not understand things. But with people whose affection one desires to have it is different. A great friend of mine – a friend of ten years' standing – came to see me some time ago and told me that he did not believe a single word of what was said against me, and wished me to know that he considered me quite innocent, and the victim of a hideous plot concocted by your father. I burst into tears at what he said, and told him that while there was much amongst your father's definite charges that was quite untrue and transferred to me by revolting malice, still that my life had been full of perverse pleasures and strange passions, and that unless he accepted that fact as a fact about me and realised it to the full, I could not possibly be friends with him any more, or ever be in his company. It was a terrible shock to him, but we are friends, and I have not got his friendship on false pretences. I have said to you that to speak the truth is a painful thing. To be forced to tell lies is much worse.

I remember as I was sitting in the dock on the occasion of my last trial listening to Lockwood's appalling denunciation of me – like a thing out of Tacitus, like a passage in Dante, like one of Savonarola's indictments of the Popes at Rome – and being sickened with horror at what I heard. Suddenly it occurred to me, '*How splendid it would be, if I was saying all this about myself!*' I saw then at once that what is said of a man is nothing. The point is, who says it. A man's very highest moment is, I have no doubt at all, when he kneels in the dust, and beats his breast, and tells all the sins of his life. So with you. You would be much happier if you let your mother know a little at any rate of your life from yourself. I told her a good deal about it in December 1893, but of course I was forced into reticences and generalities. It did not seem to give her any more courage in her relations with you. On the contrary. She avoided looking at the truth more persistently than ever. If you told her yourself it would be different. My words may perhaps be often too bitter to you. But the facts you cannot deny. Things were as I have said they were, and if you have read this letter as carefully as you should have done you have met yourself face to face.

I have now written, and at great length, to you in order that you should realise what you were to me before my imprisonment, during those three years' fatal friendship: what you have been to me during my imprisonment, already within two moons of its completion almost: and what I hope to be to myself and to others when my imprisonment is over. I cannot reconstruct my letter, or rewrite it. You must take it as it stands, blotted in many places with tears, in some with the signs of passion or pain, and make it out as best you can, blots, corrections and all. As for the corrections and *errata*, I have made them in order that my words should be an absolute expression of my thoughts, and err neither through surplusage nor through being inadequate. Language requires to be tuned, like a violin: and just as too many or too few vibrations in the voice of the singer or the trembling of the string will make the note false, so too much or too little in words will spoil the message. As it stands, at any rate, my letter has its definite meaning behind every phrase. There is in it nothing of rhetoric. Wherever there is erasion or substitution, however slight, however elaborate, it is because I am seeking to render my real impression, to find for my mood its exact equivalent. Whatever is first in feeling comes always last in form.

I will admit that it is a severe letter. I have not spared you. Indeed you may say that, after admitting that to weigh you against the smallest of my sorrows, the meanest of my losses, would be really unfair to you, I have actually done so, and made scruple by scruple the most careful assay of your nature. That is true. But you must remember that you put yourself into the scales.

You must remember that, if when matched with one mere moment of my imprisonment the balance in which you lie kicks the beam, Vanity made you choose the balance, and Vanity made you cling to it. *There* was the one great psychological error of our friendship, its entire want of proportion. You forced your way into a life too large for you, one whose orbit transcended your power of vision no less than your power of cyclic motion, one whose thoughts, passions and actions were of intense import, of wide interest, and fraught, too heavily indeed, with wonderful or awful consequence. Your little life of little whims and moods was admirable in its own little sphere. It was admirable at Oxford, where the worst that could happen to you was a reprimand from the Dean or a lecture from the President, and where the highest excitement was Magdalen becoming head of the river, and the lighting of a bonfire in the quad as a celebration of the august event. It should have continued in its own sphere after you left Oxford. In yourself, you were all right. You were a very complete specimen of a very modern type. It was simply in reference to me that you were wrong. Your reckless extravagance was not a crime. Youth is always extravagant. It was your forcing me to pay for your extravagances that was disgraceful. Your desire to have a friend with whom you could pass your time from morning to night was charming. It was almost idyllic. But the friend you fastened on should not have been a man of letters, an artist, one to whom your continual presence was as utterly destructive of all beautiful work as it was actually paralysing to the creative faculty. There was no harm in your seriously considering that the most perfect way of passing an evening was to have a champagne dinner at the Savoy, a box at a Music-Hall to follow, and a champagne supper at Willis's as a *bonne-bouche* for the end. Heaps of delightful young men in London are of the same opinion. It is not even an eccentricity. It is the qualification for becoming a member of White's. But you had no right to require of me that I should become the purveyor of such pleasures for you. It showed your lack of any real appreciation of my genius. Your quarrel with your father, again, whatever one may think about its character, should obviously have remained a question entirely between the two of you. It should have been carried on in a back yard. Such quarrels, I believe, usually are. Your mistake was in insisting on its being played as a tragi-comedy on a high stage in History, with the whole world as the audience, and myself as the prize for the victor in the contemptible contest. The fact that your father loathed you, and that you loathed your father, was not a matter of any interest to the English public. Such feelings are very common in English domestic life, and should be confined to the place they characterise: the home. Away from the home-circle they are quite out of place. To translate them is an offence. Family-life is not to be treated as a red flag to be flaunted in the streets, or a horn to be blown hoarsely on the housetops. You took Domesticity out of its proper sphere, just as you took yourself out of your proper sphere.

And those who quit their proper sphere change their surroundings merely, not their natures. They do not acquire the thoughts or passions appropriate to the sphere they enter. It is not in their power to do so. Emotional forces, as I say somewhere in *Intentions*, are as limited in extent and duration as the forces of physical energy. The little cup that is made to hold so much can hold so much and no more, though all the purple vats of Burgundy be filled with wine to the brim, and the treaders stand knee-deep in the gathered grapes of the stony vineyards of Spain. There is no error more common than that of thinking that those who are the causes or occasions of great tragedies share in the feelings suitable to the tragic mood: no error more fatal than expecting it of them. The martyr in his 'shirt of flame' may be looking on the face of God, but to him who is piling the faggots or loosening the logs for the blast the whole scene is no more than the slaying of an ox is to the butcher, or the felling of a tree to the charcoal-burner in the forest, or the fall of a flower to one who is mowing down the grass with a scythe. Great passions are for the great of soul, and great events can be seen only by those who are on a level with them.

I know of nothing in all Drama more incomparable from the point of view of Art, or more suggestive in its subtlety of observation, than Shakespeare's drawing of Rosencrantz and Guildenstern. They are Hamlet's college friends. They have been his companions. They bring with them memories of pleasant days together. At the moment when they come across him in the play he is staggering under the weight of a burden intolerable to one of his temperament. The dead have come armed out of the grave to impose on him a mission at once too great and too mean for him. He is a dreamer, and he is called upon to act. He has the nature of the poet and he is asked to grapple with the common complexities of cause and effect, with life in its practical realisation, of which he knows nothing, not with life in its ideal essence, of which he knows much. He has no conception of what to do, and his folly is to feign folly. Brutus used madness as a cloak to conceal the sword of his purpose, the dagger of his will, but to Hamlet madness is a mere mask for the hiding of weakness. In the making of mows and jests he sees a chance of delay. He keeps playing with action, as an artist plays with a theory. He makes himself the spy of his proper actions, and listening to his own words knows them to be but 'words, words, words.' Instead of trying to be the hero of his own history, he seeks to be the spectator of his own tragedy. He disbelieves in everything, including himself, and yet his doubt helps him not, as it comes not from scepticism but from a divided will.

Of all this, Guildenstern and Rosencrantz realise nothing. They bow and smirk and smile, and what the one says the other echoes with sicklier iteration. When at last, by means of the play within the play and the puppets in their dalliance, Hamlet 'catches the conscience' of the King, and drives the wretched man in terror from his throne, Guildenstern and Rosencrantz see no more in his conduct than a rather painful breach of court-etiquette. That is as far as they can attain to in 'the contemplation of the spectacle of life with appropriate emotions.' They are close to his very secret and know nothing of it. Nor would there be any use in telling them. They are the little cups that can hold so much and no more. Towards the close it is suggested that, caught in a cunning springe set for another, they have met, or may meet with a violent and sudden death. But a tragic ending of this kind, though touched by Hamlet's humour with something of the surprise and justice of comedy, is really not for such as they. They never die. Horatio, who in order to 'report Hamlet and his cause aright to the unsatisfied,'

> Absents him from felicity a while,
> And in this harsh world draws his breath in pain,

dies, though not before an audience, and leaves no brother. But Guildenstern and Rosencrantz are as immortal as Angelo and Tartuffe, and should rank with them. They are what modern life has contributed to the antique ideal of friendship. He who writes a new De Amicitia must find a niche for them and praise them in Tusculan prose. They are types fixed for all time. To censure them would show a lack of appreciation. They are merely out of their sphere: that is all. In sublimity of soul there is no contagion. High thoughts and high emotions are by their very existence isolated. What Ophelia herself could not understand was not to be realised by 'Guildenstern and gentle Rosencrantz,' by 'Rosencrantz and gentle Guildenstern.' Of course I do not propose to compare you. There is a wide difference between you. What with them was chance, with you was choice. Deliberately and by me uninvited you thrust yourself into my sphere, usurped there a place for which you had neither right nor qualifications, and having by curious persistence, and by the rendering of your very presence a part of each separate day, succeeded in absorbing my entire life, could do no better with that life than break it in pieces. Strange as it may sound to you, it was but natural that you should do so. If one gives to a child a toy too wonderful for its little mind, or too beautiful for its but half-awakened eyes, it breaks the toy, if it is wilful; if it is listless it lets it fall and goes its way to its own companions. So it was with you. Having got hold of my life, you did not know what to do with it. You couldn't have known. It was too wonderful a thing to be in your grasp. You should have let it slip from your hands and gone back to your own companions at their play. But unfortunately you were wilful, and so you broke it. That, when everything is said, is perhaps the ultimate secret of all that has happened. For secrets are always smaller than their manifestations. By the displacement of an atom a world may be shaken. And that I may not spare myself any more than you I will add this: that dangerous to me as my meeting with you was, it was rendered fatal to me by the particular moment in which we met. For you were at that time of life when all that one does is no more than the sowing of the seed, and I was at that time of life when all that one does is no less than the reaping of the harvest.

There are some few things more about which I must write to you. The first is about my Bankruptcy. I heard some days ago, with great disappointment I admit, that it is too late now for your family to pay your father off, that it would be illegal, and that I must remain in my present painful position for some considerable time to come. It is bitter to me because I am assured on legal authority that I cannot even publish a book without the permission of the Receiver to whom all the accounts must be submitted. I cannot enter into a contract with the manager of a theatre, or produce a play without the receipts passing to your father and my few other creditors. I think that even you will admit now that the scheme of 'scoring off' your father by allowing him to make me a bankrupt has not really been the brilliant all-round success you imagined it was going to turn out. It has not been so to me at any rate, and my feelings of pain and humiliation at my pauperism should have been consulted rather than your own sense of humour, however caustic or unexpected. In point of actual fact, in permitting my Bankruptcy, as in urging me on to the original trial, you really were playing right into your father's hands, and doing just what he wanted. Alone, and unassisted, he would from the very outset have been powerless. In you – though you did not mean to hold such a horrible office – he has always found his chief ally.

I am told by More Adey in his letter that last summer you really did express on more than one occasion your desire to repay me 'a little of what I spent' on you. As I said to him in my answer, unfortunately I spent on you my art, my life, my name, my place in history, and if your family had all the marvellous things in the world at their command, of what the world holds as marvellous, genius, beauty, wealth, high position and the like, and laid them all at my feet, it would not repay me for one tithe of the smallest things that have been taken from me, or one tear of the least tears that I have shed. However, of course everything one does has to be paid for. Even to the Bankrupt it is so. You seem to be under the impression that Bankruptcy is a convenient means by which a man can avoid paying his debts, a 'score off his creditors' in fact. It is quite the other way. It is the method by which a man's creditors 'score off' him, if we are to continue your favourite phrase, and by which the Law by the confiscation of all his property forces him to pay every one of his debts, and if he fails to do so leaves him as penniless as the commonest mendicant who stands in an archway, or creeps down a road, holding out his hand for the alms for which, in England at any rate, he is afraid to ask. The Law has taken from me not merely all that I have, my books, furniture, pictures, my copyright in my published works, my copyright in my plays, everything in fact from *The Happy Prince* and *Lady Windermere's Fan* down to the stair-carpets and door-scraper of my house, but also all that I am ever going to have. My interest in my marriage-settlement, for instance, was sold. Fortunately I was able to buy it in through my friends. Otherwise, in case my wife died, my two children during my lifetime would be as penniless as myself. My interest in our Irish estate, entailed on me by my own father, will I suppose have to go next. I feel very bitterly about its being sold, but I must submit.

Your father's seven hundred pence – or pounds is it? – stand in the way, and must be refunded. Even when I am stripped of all I have, and am ever to have, and am granted a discharge as a hopeless Insolvent, I have still got to pay my debts. The Savoy dinners – the clear turtle soup, the luscious ortolans wrapped in their crinkled Sicilian vine-leaves, the heavy amber-coloured, indeed almost amber-scented champagne – Dagonet 1880, I think, was your favourite wine? – all have still to be paid for. The suppers at Willis's, the special *cuvée* of Perrier-Jouet reserved always for us, the wonderful *pâtés* procured directly from Strasburg, the marvellous *fine champagne* served always at the bottom of great bell-shaped glasses that its bouquet might be the better savoured by the true epicures of what was really exquisite in life – these cannot be left unpaid, as bad debts of a dishonest *client*. Even the dainty sleeve-links – four heart-shaped moonstones of silver mist, girdled by alternate ruby and diamond for their setting – that I designed, and had made at Henry Lewis's as a special little present to you, to celebrate the success of my second comedy – these even – though I believe you sold them for a song a few months afterwards – have to be paid for. I cannot leave the jeweller out of pocket for the presents I gave you, no matter what you did with them. So, even if I get my discharge, you see I have still my debts to pay.

And what is true of a bankrupt is true of everyone else in life. For every single thing that is done someone has to pay. Even you yourself – with all your desire for absolute freedom from all duties, your insistence on having everything supplied to you by others, your attempts to reject any claim on your affection, or regard, or gratitude – even you will have some day to reflect seriously on what you have done, and try, however unavailingly, to make some attempt at atonement. The fact that you will not be able to do so will be part of your punishment. You can't wash your hands of all responsibility, and propose with a shrug or a smile to pass on to a new friend and a freshly spread feast. You can't treat all that you have brought upon me as a sentimental reminiscence to be served up occasionally with the cigarettes and *liqueurs*, a picturesque background to a modern life of pleasure like an old tapestry hung in a common inn. It may for the moment have the charm of a new sauce or a fresh vintage, but the scraps of a banquet grow stale, and the dregs of a bottle are bitter. Either today, or tomorrow, or some day you have got to realise it. Otherwise you may die without having done so, and then what a mean, starved, unimaginative life you would have had. In my letter to More I have suggested one point of view from which you had better approach the subject as soon as possible. He will tell you what it is. To understand it you will have to cultivate your imagination. Remember that imagination is the quality that enables one to see things and people in their real as in their ideal relations. If you cannot realise it by yourself, talk to others on the subject. I have had to look at my past face to face. Look at your past face to face. Sit down quietly and consider it. The supreme vice is shallowness. Whatever is realised is right. Talk to your brother about it. Indeed the proper person to talk to *is* Percy. Let him read this letter, and know all the circumstances of our friendship. When things are clearly put before him, no judgment is better. Had we told him the truth, what a lot would have been saved to me of suffering and disgrace! You remember I proposed to do so, the night you arrived in London from Algiers. You absolutely refused. So when he came in after dinner we had to play the comedy of your father being an insane man subject to absurd and unaccountable delusions. It was a capital comedy while it lasted, none the less so because Percy took it all quite seriously. Unfortunately it ended in a very revolting manner. The subject on which I write now is one of its results, and if it be a trouble to you, pray do not forget that it is the deepest of my humiliations, and one I must go through. I have no option. You have none either.

The second thing about which I have to speak to you is with regard to the conditions, circumstances, and the place of our meeting when my term of imprisonment is over. From extracts from your letter to Robbie written in the early summer of last year I understand that you have sealed up in two packages my letters and my presents to you – such at least as remain of either – and are anxious to hand them personally to me. It is, of course, necessary that they should be given up. You did not understand why I wrote beautiful letters to you, any more than you understood why I gave you beautiful presents. You failed to see that the former were not meant to be published, any more than the latter were meant to be pawned. Besides, they belong to a side of life that is long over, to a friendship that somehow you were unable to appreciate at its proper value. You must look back with wonder now to the days when you had my entire life in your hands. I too look back to them with wonder, and with other, far different, emotions.

I am to be released, if all goes well with me, towards the end of May, and hope to go at once to some little seaside village abroad with Robbie and More Adey. The sea, as Euripides says in one of his plays about Iphigenia, washes away the stains and wounds of the world. Θάλασσα κλύζει πάντα τ' ἀνθρώπων κακά.

I hope to be at least a month with my friends, and to gain, in their healthful and affectionate company, peace, and balance, and a less troubled heart, and a sweeter mood. I have a strange longing for the great simple primeval things, such as the Sea, to me no less of a mother than the Earth. It seems to me that we all look at Nature too much, and live with her too little. I discern great sanity in the Greek attitude. They never chattered about sunsets, or discussed whether the shadows on the grass were really mauve or not. But they saw that the sea was for the swimmer, and the sand for the feet of the runner. They loved the trees for the shadow that they cast, and the forest for its silence at noon. The vineyard-dresser wreathed his hair with ivy that he might keep off the rays of the sun as he stooped over the young shoots, and for the artist and the athlete, the two types that Greece gave us, they plaited into garlands the leaves of the bitter laurel and of the wild parsley which else had been of no service to man.

We call ourselves a utilitarian age, and we do not know the uses of any single thing. We have forgotten that Water can cleanse, and Fire purify, and that the Earth is mother to us all. As a consequence our Art is of the Moon and plays with shadows, while Greek art is of the Sun and deals directly with things. I feel sure that in elemental forces there is purification, and I want to go back to them and live in their presence. Of course, to one so modern as I am, *enfant de mon siècle,* merely to look at the world will be always lovely. I tremble with pleasure when I think that on the very day of my leaving prison both the laburnum and the lilac will be blooming in the gardens, and that I shall see the wind stir into restless beauty the swaying gold of the one, and make the other toss the pale purple of its plumes so that all the air shall be Arabia for me. Linnaeus fell on his knees and wept for joy when he saw for the first time the long heath of some English upland made yellow with the tawny aromatic blossoms of the common furze, and I know that for me, to whom flowers are part of desire, there are tears waiting in the petals of some rose. It has always been so with me from my boyhood. There is not a single colour hidden away in the chalice of a flower, or the curve of a shell, to which by some subtle sympathy with the very soul of things, my nature does not answer. Like Gautier I have always been one of those *pour qui le monde visible existe*.

Still, I am conscious now that behind all this Beauty, satisfying though it be, there is some Spirit hidden of which the painted forms and shapes are but modes of manifestation, and it is with this Spirit that I desire to become in harmony. I have grown tired of the articulate utterances of men and things. The Mystical in Art, the Mystical in Life, the Mystical in Nature – this is what I am looking for and in the great symphonies of Music, in the initiation of Sorrow, in the depths of the Sea I may find it. It is absolutely necessary for me to find it somewhere.

All trials are trials for one's life, just as all sentences are sentences of death, and three times have I been tried. The first time I left the box to be arrested, the second time to be led back to the House of Detention, the third time to pass into a prison for two years. Society, as we have constituted it, will have no place for me, has none to offer; but Nature, whose sweet rains fall on unjust and just alike, will have clefts in the rocks where I may hide, and secret valleys in whose silence I may weep undisturbed. She will hang the night with stars so that I may walk abroad in the darkness without stumbling, and send the wind over my footprints so that none may track me to my hurt: she will cleanse me in great waters, and with bitter herbs make me whole.

At the end of a month, when the June roses are in all their wanton opulence, I will, if I feel able, arrange through Robbie to meet you in some quiet foreign town like Bruges, whose grey houses and green canals and cool still ways had a charm for me, years ago. For the moment you will have to change your name. The little title of which you were so vain – and indeed it made your name sound like the name of a flower – you will have to surrender, if you wish to see *me*; just as *my* name, once so musical in the mouth of Fame, will have to be abandoned by me, in turn. How narrow, and mean, and inadequate to its burdens is this century of ours! It can give to Success its palace of porphyry, but for Sorrow and Shame it does not keep even a wattled house in which they may dwell: all it can do for *me* is to bid me alter my name into some other name, where even mediaevalism would have given me the cowl of the monk or the face-cloth of the leper behind which I might be at peace.

I hope that our meeting will be what a meeting between you and me should be, after everything that has occurred. In old days there was always a wide chasm between us, the chasm of achieved Art and acquired culture: there is a still wider chasm between us now, the chasm of Sorrow: but to Humility there is nothing that is impossible, and to Love all things are easy.

As regards your letter to me in answer to this, it may be as long or as short as you choose. Address the envelope to 'The Governor, H.M. Prison, Reading.' Inside, in another, and an open envelope, place your own letter to me: if your paper is very thin do not write on both sides, as it makes it hard for others to read. I have written to you with perfect freedom. You can write to me with the same. What I must know from you is why you have never made any attempt to write to me, since the August of the year before last, more especially after, in the May of last year, eleven months ago now, you knew, and admitted to others that you knew, how you made me suffer, and how I realised it. I waited month after month to hear from you. Even if I had not been waiting but had shut the doors against you, you should have remembered that no one can possibly shut the doors against Love for ever. The unjust judge in the Gospels rises up at length to give a just decision because Justice comes knocking daily at his door; and at night-time the friend, in whose heart there is no real friendship, yields at length to his friend 'because of his importunity.' There is no prison in any world into which Love cannot force an entrance. If you did not understand that, you did not understand anything about Love at all. Then, let me know all about your article on me for the *Mercure de France*. I know something of it. You had better quote from it. It is set up in type. Also, let me know the exact terms of your Dedication of your poems. If it is in prose, quote the prose; if in verse, quote the verse. I have no doubt that there will be beauty in it. Write to me with full frankness about yourself: about your life: your friends: your occupations: your books. Tell me about your volume and its reception. Whatever you have to say for yourself, say it without fear. Don't write what you don't mean: that is all. If anything in your letter is false or counterfeit I shall detect it by the ring at once.

It is not for nothing, or to no purpose, that in my lifelong cult of literature I have made myself

> Miser of sound and syllable, no less
> Than Midas of his coinage.

Remember also that I have yet to know you. Perhaps we have yet to know each other.

For yourself, I have but this last thing to say. Do not be afraid of the past. If people tell you that it is irrevocable, do not believe them. The past, the present and the future are but one moment in the sight of God, in whose sight we should try to live. Time and space, succession and extension, are merely accidental conditions of Thought. The Imagination can transcend them, and move in a free sphere of ideal existences. Things, also, are in their essence what we choose to make them. A thing *is*, according to the mode in which one looks at it. 'Where others,' says Blake, 'see but the Dawn coming over the hill, I see the sons of God shouting for joy.' What seemed to the world and to myself my future I lost irretrievably when I let myself be taunted into taking the action against your father: had, I dare say, lost it really long before that. What lies before me is my past. I have got to make myself look on that with different eyes, to make the world look on it with different eyes, to make God look on it with different eyes. This I cannot do by ignoring it, or slighting it, or praising it, or denying it. It is only to be done fully by accepting it as an inevitable part of the evolution of my life and character: by bowing my head to everything that I have suffered. How far I am away from the true temper of soul, this letter in its changing, uncertain moods, its scorn and bitterness, its aspirations and its failure to realise those aspirations, shows you quite clearly. But do not forget in what a terrible school I am sitting at my task. And incomplete, imperfect, as I am, yet from me you may have still much to gain. You came to me to learn the Pleasure of Life and the Pleasure of Art. Perhaps I am chosen to teach you something much more wonderful, the meaning of Sorrow, and its beauty. Your affectionate friend

OSCAR WILDE

TWO LETTERS TO THE DAILY CHRONICLE

This letter appeared in the *Daily Chronicle*, under the heading THE CASE OF WARDER MARTIN, SOME CRUELTIES OF PRISON LIFE, on 28 May, but it was presumably begun on or soon after the 24th, when the *Daily Chronicle* printed a letter from Warder Martin recounting the circumstances of his dismissal and added an editorial comment: "We are, of course, unable to verify our correspondent's statement, but we print his letter."

On the 28th Wilde's letter was backed up by two leading articles, and another letter from Martin, discussing the Home Secretary's denial (in reply to a question from Michael Davitt) that the facts were as Martin had stated them.

To the Editor of the 'Daily Chronicle' [Published 28 May 1897]

SIR, – I learn with great regret, through the columns of your paper, that the warder Martin, of Reading Prison, has been dismissed by the Prison Commissioners for having given some sweet biscuits to a little hungry child. I saw the three children myself on the Monday preceding my release. They had just been convicted, and were standing in a row in the central hall in their prison dress, carrying their sheets under their arms previous to their being sent to the cells allotted to them. I happened to be passing along one of the galleries on my way to the reception room, where I was to have an interview with a friend. They were quite small children, the youngest – the one to whom the warder gave the biscuits – being a tiny little chap, for whom they had evidently been unable to find clothes small enough to fit. I had, of course, seen many children in prison during the two years during which I was myself confined. Wandsworth Prison especially contained always a large number of children. But the little child I saw on the afternoon of Monday the 17th, at Reading, was tinier than any one of them. I need not say how utterly distressed I was to see these children at Reading, for I knew the treatment in store for them. The cruelty that is practised by day and night on children in English prisons is incredible, except to those that have witnessed it and are aware of the brutality of the system.

People nowadays do not understand what cruelty is. They regard it as a sort of terrible mediaeval passion, and connect it with the race of men like Eccelin da Romano, and others, to whom the deliberate infliction of pain gave a real madness of pleasure. But men of the stamp of Eccelin are merely abnormal types of perverted individualism. Ordinary cruelty is simply stupidity. It is the entire want of imagination. It is the result in our days of stereotyped systems, of hard-and-fast rules, and of stupidity. Wherever there is centralisation there is stupidity. What is inhuman in modern life is officialism. Authority is as destructive to those who exercise it as it is to those on whom it is exercised. It is the Prison Board, and the system that it carries out, that is the primary source of the cruelty that is exercised on a child in prison. The people who uphold the system have excellent intentions. Those who carry it out are humane in intention also. Responsibility is shifted on to the disciplinary regulations. It is supposed that because a thing is the rule it is right.

The present treatment of children is terrible, primarily from people not understanding the peculiar psychology of a child's nature. A child can understand a punishment inflicted by an individual, such as a parent or guardian, and bear it with a certain amount of acquiescence. What it cannot understand is a punishment inflicted by society. It cannot realise what society is. With grown people it is, of course, the reverse. Those of us who are either in prison or have been sent there, can understand, and do understand, what that collective force called society means, and whatever we may think of its methods or claims, we can force ourselves to accept it. Punishment inflicted on us by an individual, on the other hand, is a thing that no grown person endures, or is expected to endure.

The child consequently, being taken away from its parents by people whom it has never seen, and of whom it knows nothing, and finding itself in a lonely and unfamiliar cell, waited on by strange faces, and ordered about and punished by the representatives of a system that it cannot understand, becomes an immediate prey to the first and most prominent emotion produced by modern prison life – the emotion of terror. The terror of a child in prison is quite limitless. I remember once in Reading, as I was going out to exercise, seeing in the dimly lit cell right opposite my own a small boy. Two warders – not unkindly men – were talking to him, with some sternness apparently, or perhaps giving him some useful advice about his conduct. One was in the cell with him, the other was standing outside. The child's face was like a white wedge of sheer terror. There was in his eyes the terror of a hunted animal. The next morning I heard him at breakfast-time crying, and calling to be let out. His cry was for his parents. From time to time I could hear the deep voice of the warder on duty telling him to keep quiet. Yet he was not even convicted of whatever little offence he had been charged with. He was simply on remand. That I knew by his wearing his own clothes, which seemed neat enough. He was, however, wearing prison socks and shoes. This showed that he was a very poor boy, whose own shoes, if he had any, were in a bad state. Justices and magistrates, an entirely ignorant class as a rule, often remand children for a week, and then perhaps remit whatever sentence they are entitled to pass. They call this 'not sending a child to prison.' It is, of course, a stupid view on their part. To a little child, whether he is in prison on remand or after conviction, is not a subtlety of social position he can comprehend. To him the horrible thing is to be there at all. In the eyes of humanity it should be a horrible thing for him to be there at all.

This terror that seizes and dominates the child, as it seizes the grown man also, is of course intensified beyond power of expression by the solitary cellular system of our prisons. Every child is confined to its cell for twenty-three hours out of the twenty-four. This is the appalling thing. To shut up a child in a dimly lit cell, for twenty-three hours out of the twenty-four, is an example of the cruelty of stupidity. If an individual, parent or guardian, did this to a child, he would be severely punished. The Society for the Prevention of Cruelty to Children would take the matter up at once. There would be on all hands the utmost detestation of whomsoever had been guilty of such cruelty. A heavy sentence would, undoubtedly, follow conviction. But our own actual society does worse itself, and to the child to be so treated by a strange abstract force, of whose claims it has no cognisance, is much worse than it would be to receive the same treatment from its father or mother, or some one it knew. The inhuman treatment of a child is always inhuman, by whomsoever it is inflicted. But inhuman treatment by society is to the child the more terrible because there is no appeal. A parent or guardian can be moved, and let out a child from the dark lonely room in which it is confined. But a warder cannot. Most warders are very fond of children. But the system prohibits them from rendering the child any assistance. Should they do so, as Warder Martin did, they are dismissed.

The second thing from which a child suffers in prison is hunger. The food that is given to it consists of a piece of usually badly-baked prison bread and a tin of water for breakfast at half-past seven. At twelve o'clock it gets dinner, composed of a tin of coarse Indian meal stirabout; and at half-past five it gets a piece of dry bread and a tin of water for its supper. This diet in the case of a strong grown man is always productive of illness of some kind, chiefly, of course, diarrhoea, with its attendant weakness. In fact, in a big prison astringent medicines are served out regularly by the warders as a matter of course. In the case of a child, the child is, as a rule, incapable of eating the food at all. Any one who knows anything about children knows how easily a child's digestion is upset by a fit of crying, or trouble and mental distress of any kind. A child who has been crying all day long, and perhaps half the night, in a lonely dimly lit cell, and is preyed upon by terror, simply cannot eat food of this coarse, horrible kind. In the case of the little child to whom Warder Martin gave the biscuits, the child was crying with hunger on Tuesday morning, and utterly unable to eat the bread and water served to it for its breakfast. Martin went out after the breakfasts had been served, and bought the few sweet biscuits for the child rather than see it starving. It was a beautiful action on his part, and was so recognised by the child, who, utterly unconscious of the regulation of the Prison Board, told one of the senior warders how kind this junior warder had been to him. The result was, of course, a report and a dismissal.

I know Martin extremely well, and I was under his charge for the last seven weeks of my imprisonment. On his appointment at Reading he had charge of Gallery C, in which I was confined, so I saw him constantly. I was struck by the singular kindness and humanity of the way in which he spoke to me and to the other prisoners. Kind words are much in prison, and a pleasant 'Good-morning' or 'Good-evening' will make one as happy as one can be in a prison. He was always gentle and considerate. I happen to know another case in which he showed great kindness to one of the prisoners, and I have no hesitation in mentioning it. One of the most horrible things in prison is the badness of the sanitary arrangements. No prisoner is allowed, under any circumstances, to leave his cell after half-past five p.m. If, consequently, he is suffering from diarrhœa, he has to use his cell as a latrine, and pass the night in a most fetid and unwholesome atmosphere. Some days before my release, Martin was going the rounds at half-past seven with one of the senior warders for the purpose of collecting the oakum and tools of the prisoners. A man just convicted, and suffering from violent diarrhoea in consequence of the food, as is always the case, asked the senior warder to allow him to empty the slops in his cell on account of the horrible odour of the cell and the possibility of illness again in the night. The senior warder refused absolutely; it was against the rules. The man had to pass the night in this dreadful condition. Martin, however, rather than see this wretched man in such a loathsome predicament, said he would empty the man's slops himself, and did so. A warder emptying a prisoner's slops, is of course, against the rules, but Martin did this act of kindness to the man out of the simple humanity of his nature, and the man was naturally most grateful.

As regards the children, a great deal has been talked and written lately about the contaminating influence of prison on young children. What is said is quite true. A child is utterly contaminated by prison life. But the contaminating influence is not that of the prisoners. It is that of the whole prison system – of the governor, the chaplain, the warders, the lonely cell, the isolation, the revolting food, the rules of the Prison Commissioners, the mode of discipline, as it is termed, of the life. Every care is taken to isolate a child from the sight even of all prisoners over sixteen years of age. Children sit behind a curtain in chapel, and are sent to take exercise in small sunless yards – sometimes a stone-yard, sometimes a yard at the back of the mills – rather than that they should see the elder prisoners at exercise. But the only really humanising influence in prison is the influence of the prisoners. Their cheerfulness under terrible circumstances, their sympathy for each other, their humility, their gentleness, their pleasant smiles of greeting when they meet each other, their complete acquiescence in their punishments, are all quite wonderful, and I myself learned many sound lessons from them. I am not proposing that the children should not sit behind a curtain in chapel, or that they should take exercise in a corner of the common yard. I am merely pointing out that the bad influence on children is not, and could never be, that of the prisoners, but is, and will always remain, that of the prison system itself. There is not a single man in Reading Gaol that would not gladly have done the three children's punishment for them. When I saw them last it was on the Tuesday following their conviction. I was taking exercise at half-past eleven with about twelve other men, as the three children passed near us, in charge of a warder, from the damp, dreary stone-yard in which they had been at their exercise. I saw the greatest pity and sympathy in the eyes of my companions as they looked at them. Prisoners are, as a class, extremely kind and sympathetic to each other. Suffering and the community of suffering makes people kind, and day after day as I tramped the yard I used to feel with pleasure and comfort what Carlyle calls somewhere 'the silent rhythmic charm of human companionship.' In this, as in all other things, philanthropists and people of that kind are astray. It is not the prisoners who need re-formation. It is the prisons.

Of course no child under fourteen years of age should be sent to prison at all. It is an absurdity, and, like many absurdities, of absolutely tragic results. If, however, they are to be sent to prison, during the daytime they should be in a workshop or schoolroom with a warder. At night they should sleep in a dormitory, with a night-warder to look after them. They should be allowed exercise for at least three hours a day. The dark, badly ventilated, ill-smelling prison cells are dreadful for a child, dreadful indeed for any one. One is always breathing bad air in prison. The food given to children should consist of tea and bread-and-butter and soup. Prison soup is very good and wholesome. A resolution of the House of Commons could settle the treat-ment of children in half an hour. I hope you will use your influence to have this done. The way that children are treated at present is really an outrage on humanity and common sense. It comes from stupidity.

Let me draw attention now to another terrible thing that goes on in Eng-lish prisons, indeed in prisons all over the world where the system of silence and cellular confinement is practised. I refer to the large number of men who become insane or weak-minded in prison. In convict prisons this is, of course, quite common; but in ordinary gaols also, such as that I was confined in, it is to be found.

About three months ago I noticed amongst the prisoners who took exer-cise with me a young man who seemed to me to be silly or half-witted. Every prison, of course, has its half-witted clients, who return again and again, and may be said to live in the prison. But this young man struck me as being more than usually half-witted on account of his silly grin and idiotic laughter to himself, and the peculiar restlessness of his eternally twitching hands. He was noticed by all the other prisoners on account of the strangeness of his conduct. From time to time he did not appear at exercise, which showed me that he was being punished by confinement to his cell. Finally, I discovered that he was under observation, and being watched night and day by warders. When he did appear at exercise he always seemed hysterical, and used to walk round crying or laughing. At chapel he had to sit right under the obser-vation of two warders, who carefully watched him all the time. Sometimes he would bury his head in his hands, an offence against the chapel regulations, and his head would be immediately struck up by a warder so that he should keep his eyes fixed permanently in the direction of the Communion-table. Sometimes he would cry – not making any disturbance – but with tears streaming down his face and an hysterical throbbing in the throat. Some-times he would grin idiot-like to himself and make faces. He was on more than one occasion sent out of chapel to his cell, and of course he was continu-ally punished. As the bench on which I used to sit in chapel was directly be-hind the bench at the end of which this unfortunate man was placed, I had full opportunity of observing him. I also saw him, of course, at exercise con-tinually, and I saw that he was becoming insane, and was being treated as if he was shamming.

On Saturday week last I was in my cell at about one o'clock occupied in cleaning and polishing the tins I had been using for dinner. Suddenly I was startled by the prison silence being broken by the most horrible and revolting shrieks, or rather howls, for at first I thought some animal like a bull or a cow was being unskilfully slaughtered outside the prison walls. I soon realised, however, that the howls proceeded from the basement of the prison, and I knew that some wretched man was being flogged. I need not say how hideous and terrible it was for me, and I began to wonder who it was who was being punished in this revolting manner. Suddenly it dawned upon me that they might be flogging this unfortunate lunatic. My feelings on the subject need not be chronicled; they have nothing to do with the question.

The next day, Sunday 16th, I saw the poor fellow at exercise, his weak, ugly wretched face bloated by tears and hysteria almost beyond recognition. He walked in the centre ring along with the old men, the beggars, and the lame people, so that I was able to observe him the whole time. It was my last Sunday in prison, a perfectly lovely day, the finest day we had had the whole year, and there, in the beautiful sunlight, walked this poor creature – made once in the image of God – grinning like an ape, and making with his hands the most fantastic gestures, as though he was playing in the air on some invisible stringed instrument, or arranging and dealing counters in some curious game. All the while these hysterical tears, without which none of us ever saw him, were making soiled runnels on his white swollen face. The hideous and deliberate grace of his gestures made him like an antic. He was a living grotesque. The other prisoners all watched him, and not one of them smiled. Everybody knew what had happened to him, and that he was being driven insane – was insane already. After half an hour he was ordered in by the warder, and I suppose punished. At least he was not at exercise on Monday, though I think I caught sight of him at the corner of the stone-yard, walking in charge of a warder.

On the Tuesday – my last day in prison – I saw him at exercise. He was worse than before, and again was sent in. Since then I know nothing of him, but I found out from one of the prisoners who walked with me at exercise that he had had twenty-four lashes in the cook-house on Saturday afternoon, by order of the visiting justices on the report of the doctor. The howls that had horrified us all were his.

This man is undoubtedly becoming insane. Prison doctors have no knowledge of mental disease of any kind. They are as a class ignorant men. The pathology of the mind is unknown to them. When a man grows insane, they treat him as shamming. They have him punished again and again. Naturally the man becomes worse. When ordinary punishments are exhausted, the doctor reports the case to the justices. The result is flogging. Of course the flogging is not done with a cat-of-nine-tails. It is what is called birching. The instrument is a rod; but the result on the wretched half-witted man may be imagined.

His number is, or was, A.2.11. I also managed to find out his name. It is Prince. Something should be done at once for him. He is a soldier, and his sentence is one of court-martial. The term is six months. Three have yet to run.

May I ask you to use your influence to have this case examined into, and to see that the lunatic prisoner is properly treated?

No report by the Medical Commissioners is of any avail. It is not to be trusted. The medical inspectors do not seem to understand the difference between idiocy and lunacy – between the entire absence of a function or organ and the disease of a function or organ. This man A.2.11 will, I have no doubt, be able to tell his name, the nature of his offence, the day of month, the date of the beginning of expiration of his sentence, and answer any ordinary simple question; but that his mind is diseased admits of no doubt. At present it is a horrible duel between himself and the doctor. The doctor is fighting for a theory. The man is fighting for his life. I am anxious that the man should win. But let the whole case be examined into by experts who understand brain diseases, and by people of humane feelings who have still some common sense and some pity. There is no reason that the sentimentalist should be asked to interfere. He always does harm.

The case is a special instance of the cruelty inseparable from a stupid system, for the present Governor of Reading is a man of gentle and humane character greatly liked and respected by all the prisoners. He was appointed in July last, and though he cannot alter the rules of the prison system, he has altered the spirit in which they used to be carried out under his predecessor. He is very popular with the prisoners and with the warders. Indeed he has quite altered the whole tone of the prison life. Upon the other hand, the system is, of course, beyond his reach as far as altering its rules is concerned. I have no doubt that he sees daily much of what he knows to be unjust, stupid and cruel. But his hands are tied. Of course I have no knowledge of his real views of the case of A.2.11, nor, indeed, of his views on our present system. I merely judge him by the complete change he brought about in Reading Prison. Under his predecessor the system was carried out with the greatest harshness and stupidity. – I remain, Sir, your obedient servant,

OSCAR WILDE

This letter appeared in the *Daily Chronicle*, under the heading DON'T READ THIS IF YOU WANT TO BE HAPPY TODAY, on 24 March, when the House of Commons began the debate on the second reading of the Prison Bill. The Bill introduced some of the improvements suggested by Wilde and became law in August as the Prison Act.

To the Editor of the 'Daily Chronicle' [Published 24 March 1898]

SIR, – I understand that the Home Secretary's Prison Reform Bill is to be read this week for the first or second time, and as your journal has been the one paper in England that has taken a real and vital interest in this important question, I hope that you will allow me, as one who has had long personal experience of life in an English gaol, to point out what reforms in our present stupid and barbarous system are urgently necessary.

From a leading article that appeared in your columns about a week ago, I learn that the chief reform proposed is an increase in the number of inspectors and official visitors that are to have access to our English prisons.

Such a reform as this is entirely useless. The reason is extremely simple. The inspectors and justices of the peace that visit prisons come there for the purpose of seeing that the prison regulations are duly carried out. They come for no other purpose, nor have they any power, even if they had the desire, to alter a single clause in the regulations. No prisoner has ever had the smallest relief, or attention, or care from any of the official visitors. The visitors arrive not to help the prisoners, but to see that the rules are carried out. Their object in coming is to ensure the enforcement of a foolish and inhuman code. And, as they must have some occupation, they take very good care to do it. A prisoner who has been allowed the smallest privilege dreads the arrival of the inspectors. And on the day of any prison inspection the prison officials are more than usually brutal to the prisoners. Their object is, of course, to show the splendid discipline they maintain.

The necessary reforms are very simple. They concern the needs of the body and the needs of the mind of each unfortunate prisoner.

With regard to the first, there are three permanent punishments authorised by law in English prisons: –

1. Hunger.
2. Insomnia.
3. Disease.

The food supplied to prisoners is entirely inadequate. Most of it is revolting in character. All of it is insufficient. Every prisoner suffers day and night from hunger. A certain amount of food is carefully weighed out ounce by ounce for each prisoner. It is just enough to sustain, not life exactly, but existence. But one is always racked by the pain and sickness of hunger.

The result of the food – which in most cases consists of weak gruel, suet, and water – is disease in the form of incessant diarrhoea. This malady, which ultimately with most prisoners becomes a permanent disease, is a recognised institution in every prison. At Wandsworth Prison, for instance – where I was confined for two months, till I had to be carried into hospital, where I remained for another two months – the warders go round twice or three times a day with astringent medicines, which they serve out to the prisoners as a matter of course. After about a week of such treatment it is unnecessary to say that the medicine produces no effect at all. The wretched prisoner is then left a prey to the most weakening, depressing, and humiliating malady that can be conceived: and if, as often happens, he fails from physical weakness to complete his required revolutions at the crank or the mill, he is reported for idleness, and punished with the greatest severity and brutality. Nor is this all.

Nothing can be worse than the sanitary arrangements of English prisons. In old days each cell was provided with a form of latrine. These latrines have now been suppressed. They exist no longer. A small tin vessel is supplied to each prisoner instead. Three times a day a prisoner is allowed to empty his slops. But he is not allowed to have access to the prison lavatories, except during the one hour when he is at exercise. And after five o'clock in the evening he is not allowed to leave his cell under any pretence, or for any reason. A man suffering from diarrhoea is consequently placed in a position so loathsome that it is unnecessary to dwell on it, that it would be unseemly to dwell on it. The misery and tortures that prisoners go through in consequence of the revolting sanitary arrangements are quite indescribable. And the foul air of the prison cells, increased by a system of ventilation that is utterly ineffective, is so sickening and unwholesome that it is no uncommon thing for warders, when they come in the morning out of the fresh air and open and inspect each cell, to be violently sick. I have seen this myself on more than three occasions, and several of the warders have mentioned it to me as one of the disgusting things that their office entails on them.

The food supplied to prisoners should be adequate and wholesome. It should not be of such a character as to produce the incessant diarrhoea that, at first a malady, becomes a permanent disease.

The sanitary arrangements in English prisons should be entirely altered. Every prisoner should be allowed to have access to the lavatories when necessary, and to empty his slops when necessary. The present system of ventilation in each cell is utterly useless. The air comes through choked-up gratings, and through a small ventilator in the tiny barred window, which is far too small, and too badly constructed, to admit any adequate amount of fresh air. One is only allowed out of one's cell for one hour out of the twenty-four that compose the long day, and so for twenty-three hours one is breathing the foulest possible air.

With regard to the punishment of insomnia, it only exists in Chinese and in English prisons. In China it is inflicted by placing the prisoner in a small bamboo cage; in England by means of the plank bed. The object of the plank bed is to produce insomnia. There is no other object in it, and it invariably succeeds. And even when one is subsequently allowed a hard mattress, as happens in the course of imprisonment, one still suffers from insomnia. For sleep, like all wholesome things, is a habit. Every prisoner who has been on a plank bed suffers from insomnia. It is a revolting and ignorant punishment.

With regard to the needs of the mind, I beg that you will allow me to say something.

The present prison system seems almost to have for its aim the wrecking and the destruction of the mental faculties. The production of insanity is, if not its object, certainly its result. That is a well-ascertained fact. Its causes are obvious. Deprived of books, of all human intercourse, isolated from every humane and humanising influence, condemned to eternal silence, robbed of all intercourse with the external world, treated like an unintelligent animal, brutalised below the level of any of the brute creation, the wretched man who is confined in an English prison can hardly escape becoming insane. I do not wish to dwell on these horrors; still less to excite any momentary sentimental interest in these matters. So I will merely, with your permission, point out what should be done.

Every prisoner should have an adequate supply of good books. At present, during the first three months of imprisonment, one is allowed no books at all, except a Bible, Prayer-book, and hymn-book. After that one is allowed one book a week. That is not merely inadequate, but the books that compose an ordinary prison library are perfectly useless. They consist chiefly of third-rate, badly written, religious books, so called, written apparently for children, and utterly unsuitable for children or for any one else. Prisoners should be encouraged to read, and should have whatever books they want and the books should be well chosen. At present the selection of books is made by the prison chaplain. Under the present system a prisoner is only allowed to see his friends four times a year, for twenty minutes each time. This is quite wrong. A prisoner should be allowed to see his friends once a month, and for a reasonable time. The mode at present in vogue of exhibiting a prisoner to his friends should be altered. Under the present system the prisoner is either locked up in a large iron cage or in a large wooden box with a small aperture covered with wire netting, through which he is allowed to peer. His friends are placed in a similar cage, some three or four feet distant, and two warders stand between to listen to, and if they wish, stop or interrupt the conversation, such as it may be. I propose that a prisoner should be allowed to see his relatives or friends in a room. The present regulations are inexpressibly revolting and harassing. A visit from (our) relatives or friends is to every prisoner an intensification of humiliation and mental distress. Many prisoners, rather than support such an ordeal, refuse to see their friends at all. And I cannot say I am surprised. When one sees one's solicitor, one sees him in a room with a glass door on the other side of which stands the warder. When a man sees his wife and children, or his parents, or his friends, he should be allowed the same privilege. To be exhibited, like an ape, in a cage, to people who are fond of one, and of whom one is fond, is a needless and horrible degradation.

Every prisoner should be allowed to write and receive a letter at least once a month. At present one is allowed to write only four times a year. This is quite inadequate. One of the tragedies of prison life is that it turns a man's heart to stone. The feelings of natural affection, like all other feelings, require to be fed. They die easily of inanition. A brief letter, four times a year, is not enough to keep alive the gentler and more humane affections by which ultimately the nature is kept sensitive to any fine or beautiful influences that may heal a wrecked and ruined life.

The habit of mutilating and expurgating prisoners' letters should be stopped. At present, if a prisoner in a letter makes any complaint of the prison system, that portion of his letter is cut out with a pair of scissors. If, upon the other hand, he makes any complaint when he speaks to his friends through the bars of the cage, or the aperture of the wooden box, he is brutalised by the warders, and reported for punishment every week till his next visit comes round, by which time he is expected to have learned, not wisdom, but cunning, and one always learns that. It is one of the few things that one does learn in prison. Fortunately, the other things are, in some instances, of higher import.

If I may trespass for a little longer, may I say this? You suggested in your leading article that no prison chaplain should be allowed to have any care or employment outside the prison itself. But this is a matter of no moment. The prison chaplains are entirely useless. They are, as a class, well-meaning, but foolish, indeed silly men. They are of no help to any prisoner. Once every six weeks or so a key turns in the lock of one's cell door, and the chaplain enters. One stands, of course, at attention. He asks one whether one has been reading the Bible. One answers 'Yes' or 'No,' as the case may be. He then quotes a few texts, and goes out and locks the door. Sometimes he leaves a tract.

The officials who should not be allowed to hold any employment outside the prison, or to have any private practice, are the prison doctors. At present the prison doctors have usually if not always a large private practice, and hold appointments in other institutions. The consequence is that the health of the prisoners is entirely neglected, and the sanitary condition of the prison entirely overlooked. As a class, I regard, and have always from my earliest youth regarded, doctors as by far the most humane profession in the community. But I must make an exception for prison doctors. They are, as far as I came across them, and from what I saw of them in hospital and elsewhere, brutal in manner, coarse in temperament, and utterly indifferent to the health of the prisoners or their comfort. If prison doctors were prohibited from private practice they would be compelled to take some interest in the health and sanitary condition of the people under their charge. I have tried to indicate in my letter a few of the reforms necessary to our English prison system. They are simple, practical, and humane. They are, of course, only a beginning. But it is time that a beginning should be made, and it can only be started by a strong pressure of public opinion formularised in your powerful paper, and fostered by it.

But to make even these reforms effectual, much has to be done. And the first, and perhaps the most difficult task, is to humanise the governors of prisons, to civilise the warders and to Christianise the chaplains. – Yours, etc.,

THE AUTHOR OF THE 'BALLAD OF READING GAOL'

THE DECAY OF LYING

An Observation

A Dialogue

PERSONS: *Cyril and Vivian.* SCENE: *the library of a country house in Nottinghamshire.*

CYRIL (*coming in through the open window from the terrace*): My dear Vivian, don't coop yourself up all day in the library. It is a perfectly lovely afternoon. The air is exquisite. There is a mist upon the woods, like the purple bloom upon a plum. Let us go and lie on the grass and smoke cigarettes and enjoy Nature.

VIVIAN: Enjoy Nature! I am glad to say that I have entirely lost that faculty. People tell us that Art makes us love Nature more than we loved her before; that it reveals her secrets to us; and that after a careful study of Corot and Constable we see things in her that had escaped our observation. My own experience is that the more we study Art, the less we care for Nature. What Art really reveals to us is Nature's lack of design, her curious crudities, her extraordinary monotony, her absolutely unfinished condition. Nature has good intentions, of course, but, as Aristotle once said, she cannot carry them out. When I look at a landscape I cannot help seeing all its defects. It is fortunate for us, however, that Nature is so imperfect, as otherwise we should have no art at all. Art is our spirited protest, our gallant attempt to teach Nature her proper place. As for the infinite variety of Nature, that is a pure myth. It is not to be found in Nature herself. It resides in the imagination, or fancy, or cultivated blindness of the man who looks at her.

CYRIL: Well, you need not look at the landscape. You can lie on the grass and smoke and talk.

VIVIAN: But Nature is so uncomfortable. Grass is hard and lumpy and damp, and full of dreadful black insects. Why, even Morris's poorest workman could make you a more comfortable seat than the whole of Nature can. Nature pales before the furniture of 'the street which from Oxford has borrowed its name,' as the poet you love so much once vilely phrased it. I don't complain. If Nature had been comfortable, mankind would never have invented architecture, and I prefer houses to the open air. In a house we all feel of the proper proportions. Everything is subordinated to us, fashioned for our use and our pleasure. Egotism itself, which is so necessary to a proper sense of human dignity, is entirely the result of indoor life. Out of doors one becomes abstract and impersonal. One's individuality absolutely leaves one. And then Nature is so indifferent, so unappreciative. Whenever I am walking in the park here, I always feel that I am no more to her than the cattle that browse on the slope, or the burdock that blooms in the ditch. Nothing is more evident than that Nature hates Mind. Thinking is the most unhealthy thing in the world, and people die of it just as they die of any other disease. Fortunately, in England at any rate, thought is not catching. Our splendid physique as a people is entirely due to our national stupidity. I only hope we shall be able to keep this great historic bulwark of our happiness for many years to come; but I am afraid that we are beginning to be over-educated; at least everybody who is incapable of learning has taken to teaching – that is really what our enthusiasm for education has come to. In the meantime, you had better go back to your wearisome uncomfortable Nature, and leave me to correct my proofs.

CYRIL: Writing an article! That is not very consistent after what you have just said.

VIVIAN: Who wants to be consistent? The dullard and the doctrinaire, the tedious people who carry out their principles to the bitter end of action, to the *reductio ad absurdum* of practice. Not I. Like Emerson, I write over the door of my library the word 'Whim.' Besides, my article is really a most salutary and valuable warning. If it is attended to, there may be a new Renaissance of Art.

CYRIL: What is the subject?

VIVIAN: I intend to call it 'The Decay of Lying: A Protest.'

CYRIL: Lying! I should have thought that our politicians kept up that habit.

VIVIAN: I assure you that they do not. They never rise beyond the level of misrepresentation, and actually condescend to prove, to discuss, to argue. How different from the temper of the true liar, with his frank, fearless statements, his superb irresponsibility, his healthy, natural disdain of proof of any kind! After all, what is a fine lie? Simply that which is its own evidence. If a man is sufficiently unimaginative to produce evidence in support of a lie, he might just as well speak the truth at once. No, the politicians won't do. Something may, perhaps, be urged on behalf of the Bar. The mantle of the Sophist has fallen on its members. Their feigned ardours and unreal rhetoric are delightful. They can make the worse appear the better cause, as though they were fresh from Leontine schools, and have been known to wrest from reluctant juries triumphant verdicts of acquittal for their clients, even when those clients, as often happens, were clearly and unmistakably innocent. But they are briefed by the prosaic, and are not ashamed to appeal to precedent. In spite of their endeavours, the truth will out. Newspapers, even, have degenerated. They may now be absolutely relied upon. One feels it as one wades through their columns. It is always the unreadable that occurs. I am afraid that there is not much to be said in favour of either the lawyer or the journalist. Besides, what I am pleading for is Lying in Art. Shall I read you what I have written? It might do you a great deal of good.

CYRIL: Certainly, if you give me a cigarette. Thanks. By the way, what magazine do you intend it for?

VIVIAN: For the *Retrospective Review*. I think I told you that the elect had revived it.

CYRIL: Whom do you mean by 'the elect'?

VIVIAN: Oh, The Tired Hedonists, of course. It is a club to which I belong. We are supposed to wear faded roses in our buttonholes when we meet, and to have a sort of cult for Domitian. I am afraid you are not eligible. You are too fond of simple pleasures.

CYRIL: I should be black-balled on the ground of animal spirits, I suppose?

VIVIAN: Probably. Besides, you are a little too old. We don't admit anybody who is of the usual age.

CYRIL: Well, I should fancy you are all a good deal bored with each other.

VIVIAN: We are. That is one of the objects of the club. Now, if you promise not to interrupt too often, I will read you my article.

CYRIL: You will find me all attention.

VIVIAN (*reading in a very clear voice*): 'THE DECAY OF LYING: A PROTEST – One of the chief causes that can be assigned for the curiously commonplace character of most of the literature of our age is undoubtedly the decay of Lying as an art, a science, and a social pleasure. The ancient historians gave us delightful fiction in the form of fact; the modern novelist presents us with dull facts under the guise of fiction. The Blue-Book is rapidly becoming his ideal both for method and manner. He has his tedious *document humain*, his miserable little *coin de la création*, into which he peers with his microscope. He is to be found at the Librairie Nationale, or at the British Museum, shamelessly reading up his subject. He has not even the courage of other people's ideas, but insists on going directly to life for everything, and ultimately, between encyclopaedias and personal experience, he comes to the ground, having drawn his types from the family circle or from the weekly washerwoman, and having acquired an amount of useful information from which never, even in his most meditative moments, can he thoroughly free himself.

'The loss that results to literature in general from this false ideal of our time can hardly be overestimated. People have a careless way of talking about a 'born liar,' just as they talk about a born poet. But in both cases they are wrong. Lying and poetry are arts – arts, as Plato saw, not unconnected with each other – and they require the most careful study, the most disinterested devotion. Indeed, they have their technique, just as the more material arts of painting and sculpture have their subtle secrets of form and colour, their craft-mysteries, their deliberate artistic methods. As one knows the poet by his fine music, so one can recognise the liar by his rich rhythmic utterance, and in neither case will the casual inspiration of the moment suffice. Here, as elsewhere, practice must precede perfection. But in modern days while the fashion of writing poetry has become far too common, and should, if possible, be discouraged, the fashion of lying has almost fallen into disrepute. Many a young man starts in life with a natural gift for exaggeration which, if nurtured in congenial and sympathetic surroundings, or by the imitation of the best models, might grow into something really great and wonderful. But, as a rule, he comes to nothing. He either falls into careless habits of accuracy–'

CYRIL: My dear fellow!

VIVIAN: Please don't interrupt in the middle of a sentence. 'He either falls into careless habits of accuracy, or takes to frequenting the society of the aged and the well-informed. Both things are equally fatal to his imagination, as indeed they would be fatal to the imagination of anybody, and in a short time he develops a morbid and unhealthy faculty of truth-telling, begins to verify all statements made in his presence, has no hesitation in contradicting people who are much younger than himself, and often ends by writing novels which are so life-like that no one can possibly believe in their probability. This is no isolated instance that we are giving. It is simply one example out of many; and if something cannot be done to check, or at least to modify, our monstrous worship of facts, Art will become sterile and beauty will pass away from the land.

'Even Mr. Robert Louis Stevenson, that delightful master of delicate and fanciful prose, is tainted with this modern vice, for we know positively no other name for it. There is such a thing as robbing a story of its reality by trying to make it too true, and *The Black Arrow* is so inartistic as not to contain a single anachronism to boast of, while the transformation of Dr. Jekyll reads dangerously like an experiment out of the *Lancet*. As for Mr. Rider Haggard, who really has, or had once, the makings of a perfectly magnificent liar, he is now so afraid of being suspected of genius that when he does tell us anything marvellous, he feels bound to invent a personal reminiscence, and to put it into a footnote as a kind of cowardly corroboration. Nor are our other novelists much better. Mr. Henry James writes fiction as if it were a painful duty, and wastes upon mean motives and imperceptible "points of view" his neat literary style, his felicitous phrases, his swift and caustic satire. Mr. Hall Caine, it is true, aims at the grandiose, but then he writes at the top of his voice. He is so loud that one cannot hear what he says. Mr. James Payn is an adept in the art of concealing what is not worth finding. He hunts down the obvious with the enthusiasm of a short-sighted detective. As one turns over the pages, the suspense of the author becomes almost unbearable. The horses of Mr. William Black's phæton do not soar towards the sun. They merely frighten the sky at evening into violent chromolithographic effects. On seeing them approach, the peasants take refuge in dialect. Mrs. Oliphant prattles pleasantly about curates, lawn-tennis parties, domesticity, and other wearisome things. Mr. Marion Crawford has immolated himself upon the altar of local colour. He is like the lady in the French comedy who keeps talking about *le beau ciel d'Italie*. Besides, he has fallen into the bad habit of uttering moral platitudes. He is always telling us that to be good is to be good, and that to be bad is to be wicked. At times he is almost edifying. *Robert Elsmere* is of course a masterpiece – a masterpiece of the *genre ennuyeux*, the one form of literature that the English people seems thoroughly to enjoy. A thoughtful young friend of ours once told us that it reminded him of the sort of conversation that goes on at a meat tea in the house of a serious Nonconformist family, and we can quite believe it. Indeed, it is only in England that such a book could be produced. England is the home of lost ideas. As for that great and daily increasing school of novelists for whom the sun always rises in the East-End, the only thing that can be said about them is that they find life crude, and leave it raw.

'In France, though nothing so deliberately tedious as *Robert Elsmere* had been produced, things are not much better. M. Guy de Maupassant, with his keen mordant irony and his hard vivid style, strips life of the few poor rags that still cover her, and shows us foul sore and festering wound. He writes lurid little tragedies in which everybody is ridiculous; bitter comedies at which one cannot laugh for very tears. M. Zola, true to the lofty principle that he lays down in one of his pronunciamientos on literature, *L'homme de génie n'a jamais d'esprit*, is determined to show that, if he has not got genius, he can at least be dull. And how well he succeeds! He is not without power. Indeed at times, as in *Germinal*, there is something almost epic in his work. But his work is entirely wrong from beginning to end, and wrong not on the ground of morals, but on the ground of Art. From any ethical standpoint it is just what it should be. The author is perfectly truthful, and describes things exactly as they happen. What more can any moralist desire? We have no sympathy at all with the moral indignation of our time against M. Zola. It is simply the indignation of Tartuffe on being exposed. But from the standpoint of Art, what can be said in favour of the author of *L'Assommoir, Nana* and *Pot-Bouille*? Nothing. Mr. Ruskin once described the characters in George Eliot's novels as being like the sweepings of a Pentonville omnibus, but M. Zola's characters are much worse. They have their dreary vices, and their drearier virtues. The record of their lives is absolutely without interest. Who cares what happens to them? In literature we require distinction, charm, beauty and imaginative power. We don't want to be harrowed and disgusted with an account of the doings of the lower orders. M. Daudet is better. He has wit, a light touch and an amusing style. But he has lately committed literary suicide. Nobody can possibly care for Delobelle with his *Il faut lutter pour l'art*, or for Valmajour with his eternal refrain about the nightingale, or for the poet in *Jack* with his *mots cruels*, now that we have learned from *Vingt ans de ma vie littéraire* that these characters were taken directly from life. To us they seem to have suddenly lost all their vitality, all the few qualities they ever possessed. The only real people are the people who never existed, and if a novelist is base enough to go to life for his personages he should at least pretend that they are creations, and not boast of them as copies. The justification of a character in a novel is not that other persons are what they are, but that the author is what he is. Otherwise the novel is not a work of art. As for M. Paul Bourget, the master of the *roman psychologique*, he commits the error of imagining that the men and women of modern life are capable of being infinitely analysed for an innumerable series of chapters. In point of fact what is interesting about people in good society – and M. Bourget rarely moves out of the Faubourg St. Germain, except to come to London – is the mask that each one of them wears, not the reality that lies behind the mask. It is a humiliating confession, but we are all of us made out of the same stuff. In Falstaff there is something of Hamlet, in Hamlet there is not a little of Falstaff. The fat knight has his moods of melancholy, and the young prince his moments of coarse humour. Where we differ from each other is purely in accidentals: in dress, manner, tone of voice, religious opinions, personal appearance, tricks of habit and the like. The more one analyses people, the more all reasons for analysis disappear. Sooner or later one comes to that dreadful universal thing called human nature. Indeed, as any one who has ever worked among the poor knows only too well, the brotherhood of man is no mere poet's dream, it is a most depressing and humiliating reality; and if a writer insists upon analysing the upper classes, he might just as well write of match-girls and costermongers at once.' However, my dear Cyril, I will not detain you any further just here. I quite admit that modern novels have many good points. All I insist on is that, as a class, they are quite unreadable.

CYRIL: That is certainly a very grave qualification, but I must say that I think you are rather unfair in some of your strictures. I like *The Deemster*, and *The Daughter of Heth*, and *Le Disciple*, and *Mr. Isaacs*, and as for *Robert Elsmere*, I am quite devoted to it. Not that I can look upon it as a serious work. As a statement of the problems that confront the earnest Christian it is ridiculous and antiquated. It is simply Arnold's *Literature and Dogma* with the literature left out. It is as much behind the age as Paley's *Evidences*, or Colenso's method of Biblical exegesis. Nor could anything be less impressive than the unfortunate hero gravely heralding a dawn that rose long ago, and so completely missing its true significance that he proposes to carry on the business of the old firm under the new name. On the other hand, it contains several clever caricatures, and a heap of delightful quotations, and Green's philosophy very pleasantly sugars the somewhat bitter pill of the author's fiction. I also cannot help expressing my surprise that you have said nothing about the two novelists whom you are always reading, Balzac and George Meredith. Surely they are realists, both of them?

VIVIAN: Ah! Meredith! Who can define him? His style is chaos illumined by flashes of lightning. As a writer he has mastered everything except language: as a novelist he can do everything, except tell a story: as an artist he is everything except articulate. Somebody in Shakespeare – Touchstone, I think – talks about a man who is always breaking his shins over his own wit, and it seems to me that this might serve as the basis for a criticism of Meredith's method. But whatever he is, he is not a realist. Or rather I would say that he is a child of realism who is not on speaking terms with his father. By deliberate choice he has made himself a romanticist. He has refused to bow the knee to Baal, and after all, even if the man's fine spirit did not revolt against the noisy assertions of realism, his style would be quite sufficient of itself to keep life at a respectful distance. By its means he has planted round his garden a hedge full of thorns, and red with wonderful roses. As for Balzac, he was a most remarkable combination of the artistic temperament with the scientific spirit. The latter he bequeathed to his disciples. The former was entirely his own. The difference between such a book as M. Zola's *L'Assommoir* and Balzac's *Illusions perdues* is the difference between unimaginative realism and imaginative reality. 'All Balzac's characters,' said

Baudelaire, 'are gifted with the same ardour of life that animated himself. All his fictions are as deeply coloured as dreams. Each mind is a weapon loaded to the muzzle with will. The very scullions have genius.' A steady course of Balzac reduces our living friends to shadows, and our acquaintances to the shadows of shades. His characters have a kind of fervent fiery-coloured existence. They dominate us, and defy scepticism. One of the greatest tragedies of my life is the death of Lucien de Rubempré. It is a grief from which I have never been able to completely rid myself. It haunts me in my moments of pleasure. I remember it when I laugh. But Balzac is no more a realist than Holbein was. He created life, he did not copy it. I admit, however, that he set far too high a value on modernity of form, and that, consequently, there is no book of his that, as an artistic masterpiece, can rank with *Salammbo* or *Esmond*, or *The Cloister and the Hearth*, or the *Vicomte de Bragelonne*.

CYRIL: Do you object to modernity of form, then?

VIVIAN: Yes. It is a huge price to pay for a very poor result. Pure modernity of form is always somewhat vulgarising. It cannot help being so. The public imagine that, because they are interested in their immediate surroundings, Art should be interested in them also, and should take them as her subject-matter. But the mere fact that they are interested in these things makes them unsuitable subjects for Art. The only beautiful things, as somebody once said, are the things that do not concern us. As long as a thing is useful or necessary to us, or affects us in any way, either for pain or for pleasure, or appeals strongly to our sympathies, or is a vital part of the environment in which we live, it is outside the proper sphere of Art. To Art's subject-matter we should be more or less indifferent. We should, at any rate, have no preferences, no prejudices, no partisan feeling of any kind. It is exactly because Hecuba is nothing to us that her sorrows are such an admirable motive for a tragedy. I do not know anything in the whole motive for a tragedy. I do not know anything in the whole history of literature sadder than the artistic career of Charles Reade. He wrote one beautiful book, *The Cloister and the Hearth*, a book as much above *Romola* as *Romola* is above *Daniel Deronda*, and wasted the rest of his life in a foolish attempt to be modern, to draw public attention to the state of our convict prisons, and the management of our private lunatic asylums. Charles Dickens was depressing enough in all conscience when he tried to arouse our sympathy for the victims of the poor-law administration; Charles Reade, an artist, a scholar, a man with a true sense of beauty, raging and roaring over the abuses of contemporary life like a common pamphleteer or a sensational journalist, is really a sight for the angels to weep over. Believe me, my dear Cyril, modernity of form and modernity of subject-matter are entirely and absolutely wrong. We have mistaken the common livery of the age for the vesture of the Muses, and spend our days in the sordid streets and hideous suburbs of our vile cities when we should be out on the hillside with Apollo. Certainly we are a degraded race, and have sold our birthright for a mess of facts.

CYRIL: There is something in what you say, and there is no doubt that whatever amusement we may find in reading a purely modern novel, we have rarely any artistic pleasure in re-reading it. And this is perhaps the best rough test of what is literature and what is not. If one cannot enjoy reading a book over and over again, there is no use reading it at all. But what do you say about the return to Life and Nature? This is the panacea that is always being recommended to us.

VIVIAN: I will read you what I say on that subject. The passage comes later on in the article, but I may as well give it to you now: –

'The popular cry of our time is "Let us return to Life and Nature; they will recreate Art for us, and send the red blood coursing through her veins; they will shoe her feet with swiftness and make her hand strong." But, alas! We are mistaken in our amiable and well-meaning efforts. Nature is always behind the age. And as for Life, she is the solvent that breaks up Art, the enemy that lays waste her house.'

CYRIL: What do you mean by saying that Nature is always behind the age?

VIVIAN: Well, perhaps that is rather cryptic. What I mean is this. If we take Nature to mean natural simple instinct as opposed to self-conscious culture, the work produced under this influence is always old-fashioned, antiquated, and out of date. One touch of Nature may make the whole world kin, but two touches of Nature will destroy any work of Art. If, on the other hand, we regard Nature as the collection of phenomena external to man, people only discover in her what they bring to her. She has no suggestions of her own. Wordsworth went to the lakes, but he was never a lake poet. He found in stones the sermons he had already hidden there. He went moralising about the district, but his good work was produced when he returned, not to Nature but to poetry. Poetry gave him 'Laodamia,' and the fine sonnets, and the great Ode such as it is. Nature gave him 'Martha Ray' and 'Peter Bell,' and the address to Mr. Wilkinson's spade.

CYRIL: I think that view might be questioned. I am rather inclined to believe in 'the impulse from a vernal wood,' though of course the artistic value of such an impulse depends entirely on the kind of temperament that receives it, so that the return to Nature would come to mean simply the advance to a great personality. You would agree with that, I fancy. However, proceed with your article.

VIVIAN (reading): 'Art begins with abstract decoration, with purely imaginative and pleasurable work dealing with what is unreal and non-existent. This is the first stage. Then Life becomes fascinated with this new wonder, and asks to be admitted into the charmed circle. Art takes life as part of her rough material, recreates it, and refashions it in fresh forms, is absolutely indifferent to fact, invents, imagines, dreams, and keeps between herself and reality the impenetrable barrier of beautiful style, of decorative or ideal treatment. The third stage is when Life gets the upper hand, and drives Art out into the wilderness. This is the true decadence, and it is from this that we are now suffering.

'Take the case of the English drama. At first in the hands of the monks Dramatic Art was abstract, decorative and mythological. Then she enlisted Life in her service, and using some of life's external forms, she created an entirely new race of beings, whose sorrows were more terrible than any sorrow man has ever felt, whose joys were keener than lover's joys, who had the rage of the Titans and the calm of the gods, who had monstrous and marvellous sins, monstrous and marvellous virtues. To them she gave a language different from that of actual use, a language full of resonant music and sweet rhythm, made stately by solemn cadence, or made delicate by fanciful rhythm, jewelled with wonderful words, and enriched with lofty diction. She clothed her children in strange raiment and gave them masks, and at her bidding the antique world rose from its marble tomb. A new Caesar stalked through the streets of risen Rome, and with purple sail and flute-led oars another Cleopatra passed up the river to Antioch. Old myth and legend and dream took shape and substance. History was entirely re-written, and there was hardly one of the dramatists who did not recognise that the object of Art is not simple truth but complex beauty. In this they were perfectly right. Art itself is really a form of exaggeration; and selection, which is the very spirit of Art, is nothing more than an intensified mode of over-emphasis.

'But Life soon shattered the perfection of the form. Even in Shakespeare we can see the beginning of the end. It shows itself by the gradual breaking up of the blank-verse in the later plays, by the predominance given to prose, and by the over-importance assigned to characterisation. The passages in Shakespeare – and there are many – where the language is uncouth, vulgar, exaggerated, fantastic, obscene even, are entirely due to Life calling for an echo of her own voice and rejecting the intervention of beautiful style through which alone should life be suffered to find expression. Shakespeare is not by any means a flawless artist. He is too fond of going directly to life, and borrowing life's natural utterance. He forgets that when Art surrenders her imaginative medium she surrenders everything. Goethe says, somewhere: –

In der Beschränkung zeigt sich erst der Meister[1]

It is in working within limits that the master reveals himself, and the limitation, the very condition of any art is style. However, we need not linger any longer over Shakespeare's realism. *The Tempest* is the most perfect of palinodes. All that we desired to point out was that the magnificent work of the Elizabethan and Jacobean artists contained within itself the seeds of its own dissolution, and that, if it drew some of its strength from using life as rough material, it drew all its weakness from using life as an artistic method. As the inevitable result of this substitution of an imitative for a creative medium, this surrender of an imaginative form, we have the modern English melodrama. The characters in these plays talk on the stage exactly as they would talk off it; they have neither aspirations nor aspirates; they are taken directly from life and reproduce its vulgarity down to the smallest detail; they present the gait, manner, costume and accent of real people, they would pass unnoticed in a third-class railway carriage. And yet how wearisome the

---

[1] It is in limitation that the master first reveals himself.

plays are! They do not succeed in producing even that impression of reality at which they aim, and which is their only reason for existing. As a method, realism is a complete failure.

'What is true about the drama and the novel is no less true about those arts that we call the decorative arts. The whole history of these arts in Europe is the record of the struggle between Orientalism, with its frank rejection of imitation, its love of artistic convention, its dislike to the actual representation of any object in Nature, and our own imitative spirit. Wherever the former has been paramount, as in Byzantium, Sicily and Spain, by actual contact or in the rest of Europe by the influence of the Crusades, we have had beautiful and imaginative work in which the visible things of life are transmuted into artistic conventions, and the things that Life has not are invented and fashioned for her delight. But wherever we have returned to Life and Nature, our work has always become vulgar, common and uninteresting. Modern tapestry, with its aerial effects, its elaborate perspective, its broad expanses of waste sky, its faithful and laborious realism, has no beauty whatsoever. The pictorial glass of Germany is absolutely detestable. We are beginning to weave possible carpets in England, but only because we have returned to the method and spirit of the East. Our rugs and carpets of twenty years ago, with their solemn depressing truths, their inane worship of Nature, their sordid reproductions of visible objects, have become, even to the Philistine, a source of laughter. A cultured Mahomedan once remarked to us, "You Christians are so occupied in misinterpreting the fourth commandment that you have never thought of making an artistic application of the second." He was perfectly right, and the whole truth of the matter is this: The proper school to learn art in is not Life but Art.'

And now let me read you a passage which seems to me to settle the question very completely.

'It was not always thus. We need not say anything about the poets, for they, with the unfortunate exception of Mr. Wordsworth, have been really faithful to their high mission, and are universally recognised as being absolutely unreliable. But in the works of Herodotus, who, in spite of the shallow and ungenerous attempts of modern sciolists to verify his history, may justly be called the "Father of Lies," in the published speeches of Cicero and the biographies of Suetonius; in Tacitus at his best; in Pliny's *Natural History*; in Hanno's *Periplus*; in all the early chronicles; in the Lives of the Saints; in Froissart and Sir Thomas Malory; in the travels of Marco Polo; in Olaus Magnus, and Aldrovandus, and Conrad Lycosthenes, with his magnificent *Prodigiorum et Ostentorum Chronicon*; in the autobiography of Benvenuto Cellini; in the memoirs of Casanova; in Defoe's *History of the Plague*; in Boswell's *Life of Johnson*; in Napoleon's despatches; and in the works of our own Carlyle, whose *French Revolution* is one of the most fascinating historical novels ever written, facts are either kept in their proper subordinate position, or else entirely excluded on the general ground of dullness. Now everything is changed. Facts are not merely finding a footing-place in history, but they are usurping the domain of Fancy, and have invaded the kingdom of

Romance. Their chilling touch is over everything. They are vulgarising mankind. The crude commercialism of America, its materialising spirit, its indifference to the poetical side of things, and its lack of imagination and of high unattainable ideals, are entirely due to that country having adopted for its national hero a man who, according to his own confession, was incapable of telling a lie, and it is not too much to say that the story of George Washington and the cherry-tree has done more harm, and in a shorter space of time, than any other moral tale in the whole of literature.'

CYRIL: My dear boy!

VIVIAN: I assure you it is the case, and the amusing part of the whole thing is that the story of the cherry-tree is an absolute myth. However, you must not think that I am too despondent about the artistic future either of America or of our own country. Listen to this: –

'That some change will take place before this century has drawn to its close we have no doubt whatsoever. Bored by the tedious and improving conversation of those who have neither the wit to exaggerate nor the genius to romance, tired of the intelligent person whose reminiscences are always based upon memory, whose statements are invariably limited by probability, and who is at any time liable to be corroborated by the merest Philistine who happens to be present, Society sooner or later must return to its lost leader, the cultured and fascinating liar. Who he was who first, without ever having gone out to the rude chase, told the wandering caveman at sunset how he had dragged the Megatherium from the purple darkness of its jasper cave, or slain the Mammoth in single combat and brought back its gilded tusks, we cannot tell, and not one of our modern anthropologists, for all their much-boasted science, has had the ordinary courage to tell us. Whatever was his name or race, he certainly was the true founder of social intercourse. For the aim of the liar is simply to charm, to delight, to give pleasure. He is the very basis of civilised society, and without him a dinner-party, even at the mansions of the great, is as dull as a lecture at the Royal Society, or a debate at the Incorporated Authors, or one of Mr. Burnand's farcical comedies.

'Nor will he be welcomed by society alone. Art, breaking from the prison-house of realism, will run to greet him, and will kiss his false, beautiful lips, knowing that he alone is in possession of the great secret of all her manifestations, the secret that Truth is entirely and absolutely a matter of style; while Life – poor, probable, uninteresting human life – tired of repeating herself for the benefit of Mr. Herbert Spencer, scientific historians, and the compilers of statistics in general, will follow meekly after him, and try to reproduce, in her own simple and untutored way, some of the marvels of which he talks.

'No doubt there will always be critics who, like a certain writer in the *Saturday Review*, will gravely censure the teller of fairy tales for his defective knowledge of natural history, who will measure imaginative work by their own lack of any imaginative faculty, and will hold up their ink-stained hands in horror if some honest gentleman, who has never been farther than the yew-trees of his own garden, pens a fascinating book of travels like Sir John

Mandeville, or, like great Raleigh, writes a whole history of the world, without knowing anything whatsoever about the past. To excuse themselves they will try and shelter under the shield of him who made Prospero the magician, and gave him Caliban and Ariel as his servants, who heard the Tritons blowing their horns round the coral reefs of the Enchanted Isle, and the fairies singing to each other in a wood near Athens, who led the phantom kings in dim procession across the misty Scottish heath, and hid Hecate in a cave with the weird sisters. They will call upon Shakespeare – they always do – and will quote that hackneyed passage forgetting that this unfortunate aphorism about Art holding the mirror up to Nature, is deliberately said by Hamlet in order to convince the bystanders of his absolute insanity in all art-matters.'

CYRIL: Ahem! Another cigarette, please.

VIVIAN: My dear fellow, whatever you may say, it is merely a dramatic utterance, and no more represents Shakespeare's real views upon art than the speeches of Iago represent his real views upon morals. But let me get to the end of the passage: –

'Art finds her own perfection within, and not outside of, herself. She is not to be judged by any external standard of resemblance. She is a veil, rather than a mirror. She has flowers that no forests know of, birds that no woodland possesses. She makes and unmakes many worlds, and can draw the moon from heaven with a scarlet thread. Hers are the "forms more real than living man," and hers the great archetypes of which things that have existence are but unfinished copies. Nature has, in her eyes, no laws, no uniformity. She can work miracles at her will, and when she calls monsters from the deep they come. She can bid the almond-tree blossom in winter, and send the snow upon the ripe cornfield. At her word the frost lays its silver finger on the burning mouth of June, and the winged lions creep out from the hollows of the Lydian hills. The dryads peer from the thicket as she passes by, and the brown fauns smile strangely at her when she comes near them. She has hawk-faced gods that worship her, and the centaurs gallop at her side.'

CYRIL: I like that. I can see it. Is that the end?

VIVIAN: No. There is one more passage, but it is purely practical. It simply suggests some methods by which we could revive this lost art of Lying.

CYRIL: Well, before you read it to me, I should like to ask you a question. What do you mean by saying that life, 'poor, probable, uninteresting human life,' will try to reproduce the marvels of art? I can quite understand your objection to art being treated as a mirror. You think it would reduce genius to the position of a cracked looking-glass. But you don't mean to say that you seriously believe that Life imitates Art, that Life in fact is the mirror, and Art the reality?

VIVIAN: Certainly I do. Paradox though it may seem – and paradoxes are always dangerous things – it is none the less true that Life imitates Art far more than Art imitates Life. We have all seen in our own day in England how a certain curious and fascinating type of beauty, invented and emphasised by two imaginative painters, has so influenced Life that whenever one goes to a private view or to an artistic salon one sees, here the mystic eyes of Rossetti's dream, the long ivory throat, the strange square-cut jaw, the loosened shadowy hair that he so ardently loved, there the sweet maidenhood of 'The Golden Stair,' the blossom-like mouth and weary loveliness of the 'Laus Amoris,' the passion-pale face of Andromeda, the thin hands and lithe beauty of the Vivian in 'Merlin's Dream.' And it has always been so. A great artist invents a type, and Life tries to copy it, to reproduce it in a popular form, like an enterprising publisher. Neither Holbein nor Vandyck found in England what they have given us. They brought their types with them, and Life with her keen imitative faculty set herself to supply the master with models. The Greeks, with their quick artistic instinct, understood this, and set in the bride's chamber the statue of Hermes or of Apollo, that she might bear children as lovely as the works of art that she looked at in her rapture or her pain. They knew that Life gains from Art not merely spirituality, depth of thought and feeling, soul-turmoil or soul-peace, but that she can form herself on the very lines and colours of art, and can reproduce the dignity of Pheidias as well as the grace of Praxiteles. Hence came their objection to realism. They disliked it on purely social grounds. They felt that it inevitably makes people ugly, and they were perfectly right. We try to improve the conditions of the race by means of good air, free sunlight, wholesome water, and hideous bare buildings for the better housing of the lower orders. But these things merely produce health, they do not produce beauty. For this, Art is required, and the true disciples of the great artist are not his studio-imitators, but those who become like his works of art, be they plastic as in Greek days, or pictorial as in modern times; in a word, Life is Art's best, Art's only pupil.

As it is with the visible arts, so it is with literature. The most obvious and the vulgarest form in which this is shown is in the case of the silly boys who, after reading the adventures of Jack Sheppard or Dick Turpin, pillage the stalls of unfortunate apple-women, break into sweet-shops at night, and alarm old gentlemen who are returning home from the city by leaping out on them in suburban lanes, with black masks and unloaded revolvers. This interesting phenomenon, which always occurs after the appearance of a new edition of either of the books I have alluded to, is usually attributed to the influence of literature on the imagination. But this is a mistake. The imagination is essentially creative, and always seeks for a new form. The boy-burglar is simply the inevitable result of life's imitative instinct. He is Fact, occupied as Fact usually is, with trying to reproduce Fiction, and what we see in him is repeated on an extended scale throughout the whole of life. Schopenhauer has analysed the pessimism that characterises modern thought, but Hamlet invented it. The world has become sad because a puppet was once melancholy. The Nihilist, that strange martyr who has no faith, who goes to the stake without enthusiasm, and dies for what he does not believe in, is a purely literary product. He was invented by Tourguenieff, and completed by Dostoevski. Robespierre came out of the pages of Rousseau as surely as the People's Palace rose out of the *débris* of a novel. Literature always anticipates life. It does not copy it, but moulds it to its purpose. The nineteenth century, as we know it, is largely an invention of Balzac. Our Luciens de Rubempré, our Rastignacs, and De Marsays made their first appearance on the stage of the *Comédie Humaine*. We are merely carrying out, with footnotes and unnecessary additions, the whim or fancy or creative vision of a great novelist. I once asked a lady, who knew Thackeray intimately, whether he had had any model for Becky Sharp. She told me that Becky was an invention, but that the idea of the character had been partly suggested by a governess who lived in the neighbourhood of Kensington Square, and was the companion of a very selfish and rich old woman. I inquired what became of the governess, and she replied that, oddly enough, some years after the appearance of *Vanity Fair*, she ran away with the nephew of the lady with whom she was living, and for a short time made a great splash in society, quite in Mrs. Rawdon Crawley's style, and entirely by Mrs. Rawdon Crawley's methods. Ultimately she came to grief, disappeared to the Continent, and used to be occasionally seen at Monte Carlo and other gambling places. The noble gentleman from whom the same great sentimentalist drew Colonel Newcome died, a few months after *The Newcomes* had reached a fourth edition, with the word 'Adsum' on his lips. Shortly after Mr. Stevenson published his curious psychological story of transformation, a friend of mine, called Mr. Hyde, was in the north of London, and being anxious to get to a railway station, took what he thought would be a short cut, lost his way, and found himself in a network of mean, evil-looking streets. Feeling rather nervous he began to walk extremely fast, when suddenly out of an archway ran a child right between his legs. It fell on the pavement, he tripped over it, and trampled upon it. Being, of course, very much frightened and a little hurt, it began to scream, and in a few seconds the whole street was full of rough people who came pouring out of the houses like ants. They surrounded him, and asked him his name. He was just about to give it when he suddenly remembered the opening incident in Mr. Stevenson's story. He was so filled with horror at having realised in his own person that terrible and well-written scene, and at having done accidentally, though in fact, what the Mr. Hyde of fiction had done with deliberate intent, that he ran away as hard as he could go. He was, however, very closely followed, and finally he took refuge in a surgery, the door of which happened to be open, where he explained to a young assistant, who happened to be there, exactly what had occurred. The humanitarian crowd were induced to go away on his giving them a small sum of money, and as soon as the coast was clear he left. As he passed out, the name on the brass door-plate of the surgery caught his eye. It was 'Jekyll.' At least it should have been.

Here the imitation, as far as it went, was of course accidental. In the following case the imitation was self-conscious. In the year 1879, just after I had left Oxford, I met at a reception at the house of one of the Foreign Ministers a woman of very curious exotic beauty. We became great friends, and were constantly together. And yet what interested me most in her was not her beauty, but her character, her entire vagueness of character. She seemed to have no personality at all, but simply the possibility of many types. Sometimes she would give herself up entirely to art, turn her drawing-room into a studio, and spend two or three days a week at picture galleries or museums. Then she would take to attending race-meetings, wear the most horsey clothes, and talk about nothing but betting. She abandoned religion for mesmerism, mesmerism for politics, and politics for the melodramatic excitements of philanthropy. In fact, she was a kind of Proteus, and as much a failure in all her transformations as was that wondrous sea-god when Odysseus laid hold of him. One day a serial began in one of the French magazines. At that time I used to read serial stories, and I well remember the shock of surprise I felt when I came to the description of the heroine. She was so like my friend that I brought her the magazine, and she recognised herself in it immediately, and seemed fascinated by the resemblance. I should tell you, by the way, that the story was translated from some dead Russian writer, so that the author had not taken his type from my friend. Well, to put the matter briefly, some months afterwards I was in Venice, and finding the magazine in the reading-room of the hotel, I took it up casually to see what had become of the heroine. It was a most piteous tale, as the girl had ended by running away with a man absolutely inferior to her, not merely in social station, but in character and intellect also. I wrote to my friend that evening about my views on John Bellini, and the admirable ices at Florian's, and the artistic value of gondolas, but added a postscript to the effect that her double in the story had behaved in a very silly manner. I don't know why I added that, but I remember I had a sort of dread over me that she might do the same thing. Before my letter had reached her, she had run away with a man who deserted her in six months. I saw her in 1884 in Paris, where she was living with her mother, and I asked her whether the story had had anything to do with her action. She told me that she had felt an absolutely irresistible impulse to follow the heroine step by step in her strange and fatal progress, and that it was with a feeling of real terror that she had looked forward to the last few chapters of the story. When they appeared, it seemed to her that she was compelled to reproduce them in life, and she did so. It was a most clear example of this imitative instinct of which I was speaking, and an extremely tragic one.

However, I do not wish to dwell any further upon individual instances. Personal experience is a most vicious and limited circle. All that I desire to point out is the general principle that Life imitates Art far more than Art imitates Life, and I feel sure that if you think seriously about it you will find that it is true. Life holds the mirror up to Art, and either reproduces some strange type imagined by painter or sculptor, or realises in fact what has been dreamed in fiction. Scientifically speaking, the basis of life – the energy of life, as Aristotle would call it – is simply the desire for expression, and Art is always presenting various forms through which the expression can be attained. Life seizes on them and uses them, even if they be to her own hurt. Young men have committed suicide because Rolla did so, have died by their own hand because by his own hand Werther died. Think of what we owe to the imitation of Christ, of what we owe to the imitation of Cæsar.

CYRIL: The theory is certainly a very curious one, but to make it complete you must show that Nature, no less than Life, is an imitation of Art. Are you prepared to prove that?

VIVIAN: My dear fellow, I am prepared to prove anything.

CYRIL: Nature follows the landscape painter, then, and takes her effects from him?

VIVIAN: Certainly. Where, if not from the Impressionists, do we get those wonderful brown fogs that come creeping down our streets, blurring the gas-lamps and changing the houses into monstrous shadows? To whom, if not to them and their master, do we owe the lovely silver mists that brood over our river, and turn to faint forms of fading grace curved bridge and swaying barge? The extraordinary change that has taken place in the climate of London during the last ten years is entirely due to a particular school of Art. You smile. Consider the matter from a scientific or a metaphysical point of view, and you will find that I am right. For what is Nature? Nature is no great mother who has borne us. She is our creation. It is in our brain that she quickens to life. Things are because we see them, and what we see, and how we see it, depends on the Arts that have influenced us. To look at a thing is very different from seeing a thing. One does not see anything until one sees its beauty. Then, and then only, does it come into existence. At present, people see fogs, not because there are fogs, but because poets and painters have taught them the mysterious loveliness of such effects. There may have been fogs for centuries in London. I dare say they were. But no one saw them, and so we do not know anything about them. They did not exist till Art had invented them. Now, it must be admitted, fogs are carried to excess. They have become the mere mannerism of a clique, and the exaggerated realism of their method gives dull people bronchitis. Where the cultured catch an effect, the uncultured catch cold. And so, let us be humane, and invite Art to turn her wonderful eyes elsewhere. She has done so already, indeed. That white quivering sunlight that one sees now in France, with its strange blotches of mauve, and its restless violet shadows, is her latest fancy, and, on the whole, Nature reproduces it quite admirably. Where she used to give us Corots and Daubignys, she gives us now exquisite Monets and entrancing Pissaros. Indeed there are moments, rare, it is true, but still to be observed from time to time, when Nature becomes absolutely modern. Of course she is not always to be relied upon. The fact is that she is in this unfortunate position. Art creates an incomparable and unique effect, and, having done so, passes on to other things. Nature, upon the other hand, forgetting that imitation can be made the sincerest form of insult, keeps on repeating this effect until we all become absolutely wearied of it. Nobody of any real culture, for instance, ever talks nowadays about the beauty of a sunset. Sunsets are quite old-fashioned. They belong to the time when Turner was the last note in art. To admire them is a distinct sign of provincialism of temperament. Upon the other hand they go on. Yesterday evening Mrs. Arundel insisted on my going to the window and looking at the glorious sky, as she called it. Of course I had to look at it. She is one of those absurdly pretty Philistines to whom one can deny nothing. And what was it? It was simply a very second-rate Turner, a Turner of a bad period, with all the painter's worst faults exaggerated and over-emphasised. Of course I am quite ready to admit that Life very often commits the same error. She produces her false Renés and her sham Vautrins, just as Nature gives us, on one day a doubtful Cuyp, and on another a more than questionable Rousseau. Still, Nature irritates one more when she does things of that kind. It seems so stupid, so obvious, so unnecessary. A false Vautrin might be delightful. A doubtful Cuyp is unbearable. However, I don't want to be too hard on Nature. I wish the Channel, especially at Hastings, did not look quite so often like a Henry Moore, grey pearl with yellow lights, but then, when Art is more varied, Nature will, no doubt, be more varied also. That she imitates Art, I don't think even her worst enemy would deny now. It is one thing that keeps her in touch with civilised man. But have I proved my theory to your satisfaction?

CYRIL: You have proved it to my dissatisfaction, which is better. But even admitting this strange imitative instinct in Life and Nature, surely you would acknowledge that Art expresses the temper of its age, the spirit of its time, the moral and social conditions that surround it, and under whose influence it is produced.

VIVIAN: Certainly not! Art never expresses anything but itself. This is the principle of my new æsthetics; and it is this, more than that vital connection between form and substance, on which Mr. Pater dwells, that makes basic the type of all the arts. Of course, nations and individuals, with that healthy natural vanity which is the secret of existence, are always under the impression that it is of them that the Muses are talking, always trying to find in the calm dignity of imaginative art some mirror of their own turbid passions, always forgetting that the singer of life is not Apollo but Marsyas. Remote from reality and with her eyes turned away from the shadows of the cave, Art reveals her own perfection, and the wondering crowd that watches the opening of the marvellous many-petalled rose fancies that it is its own history that is being told to it, its own spirit that is finding expression in a new form. But it is not so. The highest art rejects the burden of the human spirit, and gains more from a new medium or a fresh material than she does from any enthusiasm for art, or from any lofty passion, or from any great awakening of the human consciousness. She develops purely on her own lines. She is not symbolic of any age. It is the ages that are her symbols.

Even those who hold that Art is representative of time and place and people cannot help admitting that the more imitative an art is the less it represents to us the spirit of its age. The evil faces of the Roman emperors look out at us from the foul porphyry and spotted jasper in which the realistic artists of the day delighted to work and we fancy that in those cruel lips and heavy sensual jaws we can find the secret of the ruin of the Empire. But it was not so. The vices of Tiberius could not destroy that supreme civilisation, any more than the virtues of the Antonines could save it. It fell for other, for less interesting reasons. The sibyls and prophets of the Sistine may indeed serve to interpret for some that new birth of the emancipated spirit that we call the Renaissance; but what do the drunken boors and bawling peasants of Dutch art tell us about the great soul of Holland? The more abstract, the more ideal an art is the more it reveals to us the temper of its age. If we wish to understand a nation by means of its art, let us look at its architecture or its music.

CYRIL: I quite agree with you there. The spirit of an age may be best expressed in the abstract ideal arts, for the spirit itself is abstract and ideal. Upon the other hand, for the visible aspect of an age, for its look, as the phrase goes, we must of course go to the arts of imitation.

VIVIAN: I don't think so. After all, what the imitative arts really give us are merely the various styles of particular artists, or of certain schools of artists. Surely you don't imagine that the people of the Middle Ages bore any resemblance at all to the figures on mediaeval stained glass, or in mediaeval stone and wood carving, or on mediaeval metal-work, or tapestries, or illuminated MSS. They were probably very ordinary-looking people, with nothing grotesque, or remarkable, or fantastic in their appearance. The Middle Ages, as we know them in art, are simply a definite form of style, and there is no reason at all why an artist with this style should not be produced in the nineteenth century. No great artist ever sees things as they really are. If he did he would cease to be an artist. Take an example from our own day. I know that you are fond of Japanese things. Now, do you really imagine that the Japanese people, as they are presented to us in art, have any existence? If you do, you have never understood Japanese art at all. The Japanese people are the deliberate self-conscious creation of certain individual artists. If you set a picture by Hokusai or Hokkei, or any of the great native painters, beside a real Japanese gentleman or lady, you will see that there is not the slightest resemblance between them. The actual people who live in Japan are not unlike the general run of English people; that is to say, they are extremely commonplace, and have nothing curious or extraordinary about them. In fact, the whole of Japan is a pure invention. There is no such country, there are no such people. One of our most charming painters went recently to the Land of the Chrysanthemum in the foolish hope of seeing the Japanese. All he saw, all he had the chance of painting, were a few lanterns and some fans. He was quite unable to discover the inhabitants, as his delightful exhibition at Messrs. Dowdeswell's Gallery showed only too well. He did not know that the Japanese people are, as I have said, simply a mode of style, an exquisite fancy of art. And so, if you desire to see a Japanese effect, you will not behave like a tourist and go to Tokio. On the contrary, you will stay at home and steep yourself in the work of certain Japanese artists, and then, when you have absorbed the spirit of their style, and caught their imaginative manner of vision, you will go some afternoon and sit in the Park or stroll down Piccadilly, and if you cannot see an absolutely Japanese effect there, you will not see it anywhere. Or, to return again to the past, take as another instance the ancient Greeks. Do you think that Greek art ever tells us what the Greek people were like? Do you believe that the Athenian women were like the stately dignified figures of the Parthenon frieze, or like those marvellous goddesses who sat in the triangular pediments of the same building? If you judge from the art, they certainly were so. But read an authority like Aristophanes, for instance. You will find that the Athenian ladies laced tightly, wore high-heeled shoes, dyed their hair yellow, painted and rouged their faces and were exactly like any silly fashionable or fallen creature of our own day. The fact is that we look back on the ages entirely through the medium of art, and art, very fortunately, has never once told us the truth.

CYRIL: But modern portraits by English painters, what of them? Surely they are like the people they pretend to represent?

VIVIAN: Quite so. They are so like them that a hundred years from now no one will believe in them. The only portraits in which one believes are portraits where there is very little of the sitter and a very great deal of the artist. Holbein's drawings of the men and women of his time impress us with a sense of their absolute reality. But this is simply because Holbein compelled life to accept his conditions, to restrain itself within his limitations, to reproduce his type and to appear as he wished it to appear. It is style that makes us believe in a thing – nothing but style. Most of our modern portrait painters are doomed to absolute oblivion. They never paint what they see. They paint what the public sees, and the public never sees anything.

CYRIL: Well, after that I think I should like to hear the end of your article.

VIVIAN: With pleasure. Whether it will do any good I really cannot say. Ours is certainly the dullest and most prosaic century possible. Why, even Sleep has played us false, and has closed up the gates of ivory, and opened the gates of horn. The dreams of the great middle classes of this country, as recorded in Mr. Myers's two bulky volumes on the subject, and in the Transactions of the Psychical Society, are the most depressing things I have ever read. There is not even a fine nightmare among them. They are commonplace, sordid and tedious. As for the Church, I cannot conceive anything better for the culture of a country than the presence in it of a body of men whose duty it is to believe in the supernatural, to perform daily miracles, and to keep alive that mythopoeic faculty which is so essential for the imagination. But in the English Church a man succeeds, not through his capacity for belief, but through his capacity for disbelief. Ours is the only Church where the sceptic stands at the altar, and where St. Thomas is regarded as the ideal apostle. Many a worthy clergyman, who passes his life in admirable works of kindly charity, lives and dies unnoticed and unknown; but it is sufficient for some shallow uneducated passman out of either University to get up in his pulpit and express his doubts about Noah's ark, or Balaam's ass, or Jonah and the whale, for half of London to flock to hear him, and to sit open-mouthed in rapt admiration at his superb intellect. The growth of common sense in the English Church is a thing very much to be regretted. It is really a degrading concession to a low form of realism. It is silly, too. It springs from an entire ignorance of psychology. Man can believe the impossible, but man can never believe the improbable. However, I must read the end of my article: –

'What we have to do, what at any rate it is our duty to do, is to revive this old art of Lying. Much, of course, may be done in the way of educating the public, by amateurs in the domestic circle, at literary lunches, and at afternoon teas. But this is merely the light and graceful side of lying, such as was probably heard at Cretan dinner-parties. There are many other forms. Lying for the sake of gaining some immediate personal advantage, for instance – lying with a moral purpose, as it is usually called – though of late it has been rather looked down upon, was extremely popular with the antique world. Athena laughs when Odysseus tells her "his words of sly devising," as Mr. William Morris phrases it, and the glory of mendacity illumines the pale brow of the stainless hero of Euripidean tragedy, and sets among the noble women of the past the young bride of one of Horace's most exquisite odes. Later on, what at first had been merely a natural instinct was elevated into a self-conscious science. Elaborate rules were laid down for the guidance of mankind, and an important school of literature grew up round the subject. Indeed, when one remembers the excellent philosophical treatise of Sanchez on the whole question, one cannot help regretting that no one has ever thought of publishing a cheap and condensed edition of the works of that great casuist. A short primer, "When to Lie and How," if brought out in an attractive and not too expensive a form, would no doubt command a large sale, and would prove of real practical service to many earnest and deep-thinking people. Lying for the sake of the improvement of the young, which is the basis of home education, still lingers amongst us, and its advantages are so admirably set forth in the early books of Plato's *Republic* that it is unnecessary to dwell upon them here. It is a mode of lying for which all good mothers have peculiar capabilities, but it is capable of still further development, and has been sadly overlooked by the School Board. Lying for the sake of a monthly salary is, of course, well known in Fleet Street, and the profession of a political leader-writer is not without its advantages. But it is said to be a somewhat dull occupation, and it certainly does not lead to much beyond a kind of ostentatious obscurity. The only form of lying that is absolutely beyond reproach is lying for its own sake, and the highest development of this is, as we have already pointed out, Lying in Art. Just as those who do not love Plato more than Truth cannot pass beyond the threshold of the Academe, so those who do not love Beauty more than Truth never know the inmost shrine of Art. The solid, stolid British intellect lies in the desert sands like the Sphinx in Flaubert's marvellous tale, and fantasy, *La Chimère*, dances round it, and calls to it with her false, flute-toned voice. It may not hear her now, but surely some day, when we are all bored to death with the commonplace character of modern fiction, it will hearken to her and try to borrow her wings.

'And when that day dawns, or sunset reddens, how joyous we shall all be! Facts will be regarded as discreditable, Truth will be found mourning over her fetters, and Romance, with her temper of wonder, will return to the land. The very aspect of the world will change to our startled eyes. Out of the sea will rise Behemoth and Leviathan, and sail round the high-pooped galleys, as they do on the delightful maps of those ages when books on geography were actually readable. Dragons will wander about the waste places, and the phoenix will soar from her nest of fire into the air. We shall lay our hands upon the basilisk, and see the jewel in the toad's head. Champing his gilded oats, the Hippogriff will stand in our stalls, and over our heads will float the Blue Bird singing of beautiful and impossible things, of things that are lovely and that never happen, of things that are not and that should be. But before this comes to pass we must cultivate the lost art of Lying.'

CYRIL: Then we must entirely cultivate it at once. But in order to avoid making any error I want you to tell me briefly the doctrines of the new aesthetics.

VIVIAN: Briefly, then, they are these. Art never expresses anything but itself. It has an independent life, just as Thought has, and develops purely on its own lines. It is not necessarily realistic in an age of realism, nor spiritual in an age of faith. So far from being the creation of its time, it is usually in direct opposition to it, and the only history that it preserves for us is the history of its own progress. Sometimes it returns upon its footsteps, and revives some antique form, as happened in the archaistic movement of late Greek Art, and in the pre-Raphaelite movement of our own day. At other times it entirely anticipates its age, and produces in one century work that it takes another century to understand, to appreciate, and to enjoy. In no case does it reproduce its age. To pass from the art of a time to the time itself is the great mistake that all historians commit.

The second doctrine is this. All bad art comes from returning to Life and Nature, and elevating them into ideals. Life and Nature may sometimes be used as part of Art's rough material, but before they are of any real service to Art they must be translated into artistic conventions. The moment Art surrenders its imaginative medium it surrenders everything. As a method Realism is a complete failure, and the two things that every artist should avoid are modernity of form and modernity of subject-matter. To us, who live in the nineteenth century, any century is a suitable subject for art except our own. The only beautiful things are the things that do not concern us. It is, to have the pleasure of quoting myself, exactly because Hecuba is nothing to us that her sorrows are so suitable a motive for a tragedy. Besides, it is only the modern that ever becomes old-fashioned. M. Zola sits down to give us a picture of the Second Empire. Who cares for the Second Empire now? It is out of date. Life goes faster than Realism, but Romanticism is always in front of Life.

The third doctrine is that Life imitates Art far more than Art imitates Life. This results not merely from Life's imitative instinct, but from the fact that the self-conscious aim of Life is to find expression, and that Art offers it certain beautiful forms through which it may realise that energy. It is a theory that has never been put forward before, but it is extremely fruitful, and throws an entirely new light upon the history of Art.

It follows, as a corollary from this, that external Nature also imitates Art. The only effects that she can show us are effects that we have already seen through poetry, or in paintings. This is the secret of Nature's charm, as well as the explanation of Nature's weakness.

The final revelation is that Lying, the telling of beautiful untrue things, is the proper aim of Art. But of this I think I have spoken at sufficient length. And now let us go out on the terrace, where 'droops the milk-white peacock like a ghost,' while the evening star 'washes the dusk with silver.' At twilight nature becomes a wonderfully suggestive effect, and is not without loveliness, though perhaps its chief use is to illustrate quotations from the poets. Come! We have talked long enough.

PEN, PENCIL AND POISON

A Study in Green

It has constantly been made a subject of reproach against artists and men of letters that they are lacking in wholeness and completeness of nature. As a rule this must necessarily be so. That very concentration of vision and intensity of purpose which is the characteristic of the artistic temperament is in itself a mode of limitation. To those who are pre-occupied with the beauty of form nothing else seems of much importance. Yet there are many exceptions to this rule. Rubens served as ambassador, and Goethe as state councillor, and Milton as Latin secretary to Cromwell. Sophocles held civic office in his own city; the humorists, essayists, and novelists of modern America seem to desire nothing better than to become the diplomatic representatives of their country; and Charles Lamb's friend, Thomas Griffiths Wainewright, the subject of this brief memoir, though of an extremely artistic temperament, followed many masters other than art, being not merely a poet and a painter, an art-critic, an antiquarian, and a writer of prose, an amateur of beautiful things and a dilettante of things delightful, but also a forger of no mean or ordinary capabilities, and as a subtle and secret poisoner almost without rival in this or any age.

This remarkable man, so powerful with 'pen, pencil and poison,' as a great poet of our own day has finely said of him, was born at Chiswick, in 1794. His father was the son of a distinguished solicitor of Gray's Inn and Hatton Garden. His mother was the daughter of the celebrated Dr. Griffiths, the editor and founder of the *Monthly Review*, the partner in another literary speculation of Thomas Davis, that famous bookseller of whom Johnson said that he was not a bookseller, but 'a gentleman who dealt in books,' the friend of Goldsmith and Wedgwood, and one of the most well-known men of his day. Mrs. Wainewright died, in giving him birth, at the early age of twenty-one, and an obituary notice in the *Gentleman's Magazine* tells us of her 'amiable disposition and numerous accomplishments,' and adds somewhat quaintly that 'she is supposed to have understood the writings of Mr Locke as well as perhaps any person of either sex now living.' His father did not long survive his young wife, and the little child seems to have been brought up by his grandfather, and, on the death of the latter in 1803, by his uncle, George Edward Griffiths, whom he subsequently poisoned. His boyhood was passed at Linden House, Turnham Green, one of those many fine Georgian mansions that have unfortunately disappeared before the inroads of the suburban builder, and to its lovely gardens and well-timbered park he owed that simple and impassioned love of nature which never left him all through his life, and which made him so peculiarly susceptible to the spiritual influences of Wordsworth's poetry. He went to school at Charles Burney's academy at Hammersmith. Mr. Burney was the son of the historian of music, and the near kinsman of the artistic lad who was destined to turn out his most remarkable pupil. He seems to have been a man of a good deal of culture, and in after years Mr. Wainewright often spoke of him with much affection as a philosopher, an archaeologist, and an admirable teacher, who, while he valued the intellectual side of education, did not forget the importance of early moral training. It was under Mr. Burney that he first developed his talent as an artist, and Mr. Hazlitt tells us that a drawing-book which he used at school is still extant, and displays great talent and natural feeling. Indeed, painting was the first art that fascinated him. It was not till much later that he sought to find expression by pen or poison.

Before this, however, he seems to have been carried away by boyish dreams of the romance and chivalry of a soldier's life, and to have become a young guardsman. But the reckless dissipated life of his companions failed to satisfy the refined artistic temperament of one who was made for other things. In a short time he wearied of the service. 'Art,' he tells us, in words that still move many by their ardent sincerity and strange fervour, 'Art touched her renegade; by her pure and high influence the noisome mists were purged; my feelings, parched, hot, and tarnished, were renovated with cool, fresh bloom, simple, beautiful to the simple-hearted.' But Art was not the only cause of the change. 'The writings of Wordsworth,' he goes on to say, 'did much towards calming the confusing whirl necessarily incident to sudden mutations. I wept over them tears of happiness and gratitude.' He accordingly left the army, with its rough barrack life and coarse mess-room tittle-tattle, and returned to Linden House, full of this new-born enthusiasm for culture. A severe illness, in which, to use his own words, he was 'broken like a vessel of clay,' prostrated him for a time. His delicately strung organisation, however indifferent it might have been to inflicting pain on others, was itself most keenly sensitive to pain. He shrank from suffering as a thing that mars and maims human life, and seems to have wandered through that terrible valley of melancholia from which so many great, perhaps greater, spirits have never emerged. But he was young – only twenty-five years of age – and he soon passed out of the 'dead black waters,' as he called them, into the larger air of humanistic culture. As he was recovering from the illness that had led him almost to the gates of death, he conceived the idea of taking up literature as an art. 'I said with John Woodvil,' he cries, 'it were a life of gods to dwell in such an element,' to see and hear and write brave things: –

> These high and gusty relishes of life
> Have no allayings of mortality.

It is impossible not to feel that in this passage we have the utterance of a man who had a true passion for letters. 'To see and hear and write brave things,' this was his aim.

Scott, the editor of the *London Magazine*, struck by the young man's genius, or under the influence of the strange fascination that he exercised on every one who knew him, invited him to write a series of articles on artistic subjects, and under a series of fanciful pseudonyms he began to contribute to the literature of his day. *Janus Weathercock, Egomet Bonmot,* and *Van Vink-vooms,* were some of the grotesque masks under which he choose to hide his seriousness or to reveal his levity. A mask tells us more than a face. These disguises intensified his personality. In an incredibly short time he seems to have made his mark. Charles Lamb speaks of 'kind light-hearted Waine-wright' whose prose is 'capital.' We hear of him entertaining Macready, John Forster, Maginn, Talfourd, Sir Wentworth Dilke the poet, John Clare, and others, at a *petit-dîner*. Like Disraeli he determined to startle the town as a dandy, and his beautiful rings, his antique cameo breast-pin, and his pale lemon-coloured kid gloves, were well known and indeed were regarded by Hazlitt as being the signs of a new manner in literature: while his rich curly hair, fine eyes, and exquisite white hands gave him the dangerous and delightful distinction of being different from others. There was something in him of Balzac's Lucien de Rubempré. At times he reminds us of Julien Sorel. De Quincey saw him once. It was at a dinner at Charles Lamb's. 'Amongst the company, all literary men, sat a murderer,' he tells us, and he goes on to describe how on that day he had been ill, and had hated the face of man and woman, and yet found himself looking with intellectual interest across the table at the young writer beneath whose affectations of manner there seemed to him to lie so much unaffected sensibility, and speculates on 'what sudden growth of another interest' would have changed his mood, had he known of what terrible sin the guest to whom Lamb paid so much attention was even then guilty.

His life-work falls naturally under the three heads suggested by Mr. Swinburne, and it may be partly admitted that, if we set aside his achievements in the sphere of poison, what he has actually left to us hardly justifies his reputation.

But then it is only the Philistine who seeks to estimate a personality by the vulgar test of production. This young dandy sought to be somebody, rather than to do something. He recognised that Life itself is an art, and has its modes of style no less than the arts that seek to express it. Nor is his work without interest. We hear of William Blake stopping in the Royal Academy before one of his pictures and pronouncing it to be 'very fine.' His essays are prefiguring of much that has since been realised. He seems to have anticipated some of those accidents of modern culture that are regarded by many as true essentials. He writes about La Gioconda, and early French poets and the Italian Renaissance. He loves Greek gems, and Persian carpets, and Elizabethan translations of *Cupid and Psyche*, and the *Hypnerotomachia*, and book-bindings, and early editions, and wide-margined proofs. He is keenly sensitive to the value of beautiful surroundings, and never wearies of describing to us the rooms in which he lived or would have liked to live. He had that curious love of green, which in individuals is always the sign of a subtle artistic temperament, and in nations is said to denote a laxity, if not a decadence of morals. Like Baudelaire he was extremely fond of cats, and with Gautier, he was fascinated by that 'sweet marble monster,' of both sexes that we can still see at Florence and in the Louvre.

There is, of course, much in his descriptions, and his suggestions for decoration, that shows that he did not entirely free himself from the false taste of his time. But it is clear that he was one of the first to recognise what is, indeed, the very keynote of æsthetic eclecticism, I mean the true harmony of all really beautiful things irrespective of age or place, of school or manner. He saw that in decorating a room, which is to be, not a room for show, but a room to live in, we should never aim at any archaeological reconstruction of the past, nor burden ourselves with any fanciful necessity for historical accuracy. In this artistic perception he was perfectly right. All beautiful things belong to the same age.

And so, in his own library, as he describes it, we find the delicate fictile vase of the Greek, with its exquisitely painted figures and the faint ΚΑΛΟΣ[1] finely traced upon its side, and behind it hangs an engraving of the 'Delphic Sibyl' of Michael Angelo, or of the 'Pastoral' of Giorgione. Here is a bit of Florentine majolica, and here a rude lamp from some old Roman tomb. On the table lies a book of Hours, 'cased in a cover of solid silver gilt, wrought with quaint devices and studded with small brilliants and rubies,' and close by it 'squats a little ugly monster, a Lar, perhaps, dug up in the sunny fields of corn-bearing Sicily.' Some dark antique bronzes contrast 'with the pale gleam of two noble *Christi Crucifixi*, one carved in ivory, the other moulded in wax.' He has his trays of Tassie's gems, his tiny Louis-Quatorze *bonbonnière* with a miniature by Pettitot, his highly prized 'brown-biscuit teapots, filagree-worked,' his citron morocco letter-case, and his 'pomona-green' chair.

One can fancy him lying there in the midst of his books and casts and engravings, a true virtuoso, a subtle connoisseur turning over his fine collection of Marc Antonios, and his Turner's *Liber Studiorum*, of which he was a warm admirer, or examining with a magnifier some of his antique gems and cameos, 'the head of Alexander on an onyx of two strata,' or 'that superb *altissimo relievo* on cornelian, Jupiter Ægiochus.' He was always a great amateur of engravings, and gives some very useful suggestions as to the best means of forming a collection. Indeed, while fully appreciating modern art, he never lost sight of the importance of reproductions of the great masterpieces of the past, and all that he says about the value of plaster casts is quite admirable.

As an art-critic he concerned himself primarily with the complex impressions produced by a work of art, and certainly the first step in aesthetic criticism is to realise one's own impressions. He cared nothing for abstract discussions on the nature of the Beautiful, and the historical method, which has since yielded such rich fruit, did not belong to his day, but he never lost sight of the great truth that Art's first appeal is neither to the intellect nor to the emotions, but purely to the artistic temperament, and he more than once points out that this temperament, this 'taste,' as he calls it, being unconsciously guided and made perfect by frequent contact with the best work, becomes in the end a form of right judgment. Of course there are fashions in art just as there are fashions in dress, and perhaps none of us can ever quite free

---

[1] Beautiful.

ourselves from the influence of custom and the influence of novelty. He certainly could not, and he frankly acknowledges how difficult it is to form any fair estimate of contemporary work. But, on the whole, his taste was good and sound. He admired Turner and Constable at a time when they were not so much thought of as they are now, and saw that for the highest landscape art we require more than 'mere industry and accurate transcription.' Of Crome's 'Heath Scene near Norwich' he remarks that it shows 'how much a subtle observation of the elements, in their wild moods, does for a most uninteresting flat,' and of the popular type of landscape of his day he says that it is 'simply an enumeration of hill and dale, stumps of trees, shrubs, water, meadows, cottages and houses; little more than topography, a kind of pictorial mapwork; in which rainbows, showers, mists, haloes, large beams shooting through rifted clouds, storms, starlight, all the most valuable materials of the real painter, are not.' He had a thorough dislike of what is obvious or commonplace in art, and while he was charmed to entertain Wilkie at dinner, he cared as little for Sir David's pictures as he did for Mr. Crabbe's poems. With the imitative and realistic tendencies of his day he had no sympathy, and he tells us frankly that his great admiration for Fuseli was largely due to the fact that the little Swiss did not consider it necessary that an artist should paint only what he sees. The qualities that he sought for in a picture were composition, beauty and dignity of line, richness of colour, and imaginative power. Upon the other hand, he was not a doctrinaire. 'I hold that no work of art can be tried otherwise than by laws deduced from itself: whether or not it be consistent with itself is the question.' This is one of his excellent aphorisms. And in criticising painters so different as Landseer and Martin, Stothard and Etty, he shows that, to use a phrase now classical, he is trying 'to see the object as in itself it really is.'

However, as I pointed out before, he never feels quite at his ease in his criticisms of contemporary work. 'The present,' he says, 'is about as agreeable a confusion to me as Ariosto on the first perusal.... Modern things dazzle me. I must look at them through Time's telescope. Elia complains that to him the merit of a MS poem is uncertain; "print," as he excellently says, "settles it." Fifty years' toning does the same thing to a picture.' He is happier when he is writing about Watteau and Lancret, about Rubens and Giorgione, about Rembrandt, Corregio, and Michael Angelo; happiest of all when he is writing about Greek things. What is Gothic touched him very little, but classical art and the art of the Renaissance were always dear to him. He saw what our English school could gain from a study of Greek models, and never wearies of pointing out to the young student the artistic possibilities that lie dormant in Hellenic marbles and Hellenic methods of work. In his judgments on the great Italian Masters, says De Quincey, 'there seemed a tone of sincerity and of native sensibility, as in one who spoke for himself, and was not merely a copier from books.' The highest praise that we can give to him is that he tried to revive style as a conscious tradition. But he saw that no amount of art lectures or art congresses, or 'plans for advancing the fine arts,' will ever produce this result. The people, he says very wisely, and in the true spirit of

Toynbee Hall, must always have 'the best models constantly before their eyes.'

As is to be expected from one who was a painter, he is often extremely technical in his art criticisms. Of Tintoret's 'St. George delivering the Egyptian Princess from the Dragon,' he remarks: –

> The robe of Sabra, warmly glazed with Prussian blue, is relieved from the pale greenish background by a vermilion scarf; and the full hues of both are beautifully echoed, as it were, in a lower key by the purple-lake coloured stuffs and bluish iron armour of the saint, besides an ample balance to the vivid azure drapery on the foreground in the indigo shades of the wild wood surrounding the castle.

And elsewhere he talks learnedly of 'a delicate Schiavone, various as a tulip-bed, with rich broken tints,' of 'a glowing portrait, remarkable for *morbidezza*,[1] by the scarce Moroni,' and of another picture being 'pulpy in the carnations.'

But, as a rule, he deals with his impressions of the work as an artistic whole, and tries to translate those impressions into words, to give, as it were, the literary equivalent for the imaginative and mental effect. He was one of the first to develop what has been called the art-literature of the nineteenth century, that form of literature which has found in Mr. Ruskin and Mr. Browning its two most perfect exponents. His description of Lancret's *Repas Italien*, in which 'a dark-haired girl, "amorous of mischief," lies on the daisy-powdered grass,' is in some respects very charming. Here is his account of 'The Crucifixion,' by Rembrandt. It is extremely characteristic of his style: –

> Darkness – sooty, portentous darkness – shrouds the whole scene: only above the accursed wood, as if through a horrid rift in the murky ceiling, a rainy deluge – 'sleety-flaw, discoloured water' – streams down amain, spreading a grisly spectral light, even more horrible than that palpable night. Already the Earth pants thick and fast! The darkened Cross trembles! The winds are dropt – the air is stagnant – a muttering rumble growls underneath their feet, and some of that miserable crowd begin to fly down the hill. The horses snuff the coming terror, and become unmanageable through fear. The moment rapidly approaches when, nearly torn asunder by His own weight, fainting with loss of blood, which now runs in narrower rivulets from His slit veins, His temples and breast drowned in sweat and His black tongue parched with the fiery death-fever, Jesus cries, 'I thirst.' The deadly vinegar is elevated to Him.
>
> His head sinks, and the sacred corpse 'swings senseless of the cross.' A sheet of vermilion flame shoots sheer through the air and vanishes; the rocks of Carmel and Lebanon cleave asunder; the sea rolls on high from

---

[1] Softness.

the sands its black weltering waves. Earth yawns, and the graves give up their dwellers. The dead and the living are mingled together in unnatural conjunction and hurry through the holy city. New prodigies await them there. The veil of the temple – the unpierceable veil – is rent asunder from top to bottom, and that dreaded recess containing the Hebrew mysteries – the fatal ark with the tables and seven-branched candelabrum – is disclosed by the light of unearthly flames to the God-deserted multitude.

Rembrandt never *painted* this sketch, and he was quite right. It would have lost nearly all its charms in losing that perplexing veil of indistinctness which affords such ample range wherein the doubting imagination may speculate. At present it is like a thing in another world. A dark gulf is betwixt us. It is not tangible by the body. We can only approach it in the spirit.

In this passage, written, the author tells us, 'in awe and reverence,' there is much that is terrible, and very much that is quite horrible, but it is not without a certain crude form of power, or, at any rate, a certain crude violence of words, a quality which this age should highly appreciate, as it is its chief defect. It is pleasanter, however, to pass to this description of Giulio Romano's 'Cephalus and Procris': –

We should read Moschus's lament for Bion, the sweet shepherd, before looking at this picture, or study the picture as a preparation for the lament. We have nearly the same images in both. For either victim the high groves and forest dells murmur; the flowers exhale sad perfume from their buds; the nightingale mourns on the craggy lands, and the swallow in the long-winding vales; 'the satyrs, too, and fauns darkveiled groan,' and the fountain nymphs within the wood melt into tearful waters. The sheep and goats leave their pasture; and oreads, 'who love to scale the most inaccessible tops of all up-rightest rocks,' hurry down from the song of their wind-courting pines; while the dryads bend from the branches of the meeting trees, and the rivers moan for white Procris, 'with many-sobbing streams.'

Filling the far-seen ocean with a voice.

The golden bees are silent on the thymy Hymettus; and the knelling horn of Aurora's love no more shall scatter away the cold twilight on the top of Hymettus. The foreground of our subject is a grassy sunburnt bank, broken into swells and hollows like waves (a sort of landbreakers), rendered more uneven by many foot-tripping roots and stumps of trees stocked untimely by the axe, which are again throwing out light-green shoots. This bank rises rather suddenly on the right to a clustering grove, penetrable to no star, at the entrance of which sits the stunned Thessalian king, holding between his knees that ivory-bright body which was, but an instant agone, parting the rough boughs with her smooth forehead, and treading alike on thorns and flowers with jealously-stung foot – now helpless, heavy, void of all motion, save when

the breeze lifts her thick hair in mockery.
From between the closely-neighboured boles astonished nymphs press
forward with loud cries –

> And deerskin-vested satyrs, crowned with ivy twists, advance;
> And put strange pity in their horned countenance.

Lælaps lies beneath, and shows by his panting the rapid pace of death.
On the other side of the group, Virtuous Love with 'vans dejected' holds
forth the arrow to an approaching troop of sylvan people, fauns, rams,
goats, satyrs, and satyr-mothers, pressing their children tighter with
their fearful hands, who hurry along from the left in a sunken path be-
tween the foreground and a rocky wall, on whose lowest ridge a brook-
guardian pours from her urn her grief-telling waters. Above and more
remote than the Ephidryad, another female, rending her locks, appears
among the vine-festooned pillars of an unshorn grove. The centre of the
picture is filled by shady meadows, sinking down to a river-mouth; be-
yond is 'the vast strength of the ocean stream,' from whose floor the ex-
tinguisher of stars, rosy Aurora, drives furiously up her brine-washed
steeds to behold the death-pangs of her rival.

Were this description carefully re-written, it would be quite admirable. The
conception of making a prose poem out of paint is excellent. Much of the
best modern literature springs from the same aim. In a very ugly and sensible
age, the arts borrow, not from life, but from each other.

His sympathies, too, were wonderfully varied. In everything connected
with the stage, for instance, he was always extremely interested, and strongly
upheld the necessity for archæological accuracy in costume and scene-
painting. 'In art,' he says in one of his essays, 'whatever is worth doing at all
is worth doing well;' and he points out that once we allow the intrusion of
anachronisms, it becomes difficult to say where the line is to be drawn. In lit-
erature, again, like Lord Beaconsfield on a famous occasion, he was 'on the
side of the angels.' He was one of the first to admire Keats and Shelley – 'the
tremulously-sensitive and poetical Shelley,' as he calls him. His admiration
for Wordsworth was sincere and profound. He thoroughly appreciated Wil-
liam Blake. One of the best copies of the 'Songs of Innocence and Experi-
ence' that is now in existence was wrought specially for him. He loved Alain
Chartier, and Ronsard, and the Elizabethan dramatists, and Chaucer and
Chapman, and Petrarch. And to him all the arts were one. 'Our critics,' he
remarks with much wisdom, 'seem hardly aware of the identity of the primal
seeds of poetry and painting, nor that any true advancement in the serious
study of one art co-generates a proportionate perfection in the other;' and he
says elsewhere that if a man who does not admire Michael Angelo talks of his
love for Milton, he is deceiving either himself or his listeners. To his fellow
contributors in the *London Magazine* he was always most generous, and
praises Barry Cornwall, Allan Cunningham, Hazlitt, Elton, and Leigh Hunt

without anything of the malice of a friend. Some of his sketches of Charles Lamb are admirable in their way, and, with the art of the true comedian, borrow their style from their subject: –

What can I say of thee more than all know? That thou hadst the gaiety of a boy with the knowledge of a man: as gentle a heart as ever sent tears to the eyes.

How wittily would he mistake your meaning, and put in a conceit most seasonably out of season. His talk without affection was compressed, like his beloved Elizabethans, even unto obscurity. Like grains of fine gold, his sentences would beat out into whole sheets. He had small mercy on spurious fame, and a caustic observation on the *fashion for men of genius* was a standing dish. Sir Thomas Browne was a 'bosom cronie' of his; so was Burton, and old Fuller. In his amorous vein he dallied with that peerless Duchess of many-folio odour; and with the heyday comedies of Beaumont and Fletcher he induced light dreams. He would deliver critical touches on these, like one inspired, but it was good to let him choose his own game; if another began even on the acknowledged pets he was liable to interrupt, or rather append, in a mode difficult to define, whether as misapprehensive or mischievous. One night at C – 's, the above dramatic partners were the temporary subject of chat. Mr. X. commended the passion and haughty style of a tragedy (I don't know which of them), but was instantly taken up by Elia, who told him '*That* was nothing; the lyrics were the high things – the lyrics!'

One side of his literary career deserves especial notice. Modern journalism may be said to owe almost as much to him as to any man of the early part of this century. He was the pioneer of Asiatic prose, and delighted in pictorial epithets and pompous exaggerations. To have a style so gorgeous that it conceals the subject is one of the highest achievements of an important and much admired school of Fleet Street leader-writers, and this school *Janus Weathercock* may be said to have invented. He also saw that it was quite easy by continued reiteration to make the public interested in his own personality, and in his purely journalistic articles this extraordinary young man tells the world what he had for dinner, where he gets his clothes, what wines he likes, and in what state of health he is, just as if he were writing weekly notes for some popular newspaper of our own time. This being the least valuable side of his work, is the one that has had the most obvious influence. A publicist, nowadays, is a man who bores the community with the details of the illegalities of his private life.

Like most artificial people, he had a great love of nature. 'I hold three things in high estimation,' he says somewhere: 'to sit lazily on an eminence that commands a rich prospect; to be shadowed by thick trees while the sun shines around me; and to enjoy solitude with the consciousness of neighbourhood. The country gives them all to me.' He writes about his wandering over fragrant furze and heath, repeating Collins's 'Ode to Evening,' just to catch the fine quality of the moment; about smothering his face 'in a watery bed of cowslips, wet with May dews;' and about the pleasure of seeing the sweet-breathed kine 'pass slowly homeward through the twilight,' and hearing 'the distant clank of the sheep-bell.' One phrase of his, 'the polyanthus glowed in its cold bed of earth, like a solitary picture of Giorgione on a dark oaken panel,' is curiously characteristic of his temperament, and this passage is rather pretty in its way: –

The short tender grass was covered with marguerites – 'such that men called *daisies* in our town' – thick as stars on a summer's night. The harsh caw of the busy rooks came pleasantly mellowed from a high dusky grove of elms at some distance off, and at intervals was heard the voice of a boy scaring away the birds from the newly-sown seeds. The blue depths were the colour of the darkest ultramarine; not a cloud streaked the calm aether; only round the horizon's edge streamed a light, warm film of misty vapour, against which the near village with its ancient stone church showed sharply out with blinding whiteness. I thought of Wordsworth's 'Lines written in March'

However, we must not forget that the cultivated young man who penned these lines, and who was so susceptible to Wordsworthian influences, was also, as I said at the beginning of this memoir, one of the most subtle and secret poisoners of this or any age. How he first became fascinated by this strange sin he does not tell us, and the diary in which he carefully noted the results of his terrible experiments and the methods that he adopted, has unfortunately been lost to us. Even in later days, too, he was always reticent on the matter, and preferred to speak about 'The Excursion,' and the 'Poems founded on the Affections.' There is no doubt, however, that the poison that he used was strychnine. In one of the beautiful rings of which he was so proud, and which served to show off the fine modelling of his delicate ivory hands, he used to carry crystals of the Indian *nux vomica*, a poison, one of his biographers tells us, 'nearly tasteless, difficult of discovery, and capable of almost infinite dilution.' His murders, says De Quincey, were more than were ever made known judicially. This is no doubt so, and some of them are worthy of mention. His first victim was his uncle, Mr. Thomas Griffiths. He poisoned him in 1829 to gain possession of Linden House, a place to which he had always been very much attached. In the August of the next year he poisoned Mrs. Abercrombie, his wife's mother, and in the following December he poisoned the lovely Helen Abercrombie, his sister-in-law. Why he murdered Mrs. Abercrombie is not ascertained. It may have been for a caprice, or to quicken some hideous sense of power that was in him, or because she suspected something, or for no reason. But the murder of Helen Abercrombie was carried out by himself and his wife for the sake of a sum of about £18,000, for which they had insured her life in various offices. The circumstances were as follows. On the 12th of December, he and his wife and child came up to London from Linden House, and took lodgings at No. 12 Conduit Street, Regent Street. With them were the two sisters, Helen and Madeleine Abercrombie. On the evening of the 14th they all went to the play, and at supper that night Helen sickened. The next day she was extremely ill, and Dr. Locock, of Hanover Square, was called in to attend her. She lived till Monday, the 20th, when, after the doctor's morning visit, Mr. and Mrs. Wainewright brought her some poisoned jelly, and then went out for a walk. When they returned, Helen Abercrombie was dead. She was about twenty years of age, a tall graceful girl with fair hair. A very charming red-chalk drawing of her by her brother-in-law is still in existence, and shows how much his style as an artist was influenced by Sir Thomas Lawrence, a painter for whose work he had always entertained a great admiration. De Quincey says that Mrs. Wainewright was not really privy to the murder. Let us hope that she was not. Sin should be solitary, and have no accomplices.

The insurance companies, suspecting the real facts of the case, declined to pay the policy on the technical ground of misrepresentation and want of interest, and with curious courage the poisoner entered an action in the Court of Chancery against the Imperial, it being agreed that one decision should govern all the cases. The trial, however, did not come on for five years, when, after one disagreement, a verdict was ultimately given in the companies' favour. The judge on the occasion was Lord Abinger. *Egomet Bonmot* was represented by Mr. Erle and Sir William Follet, and the Attorney-General and Sir Frederick Pollock appeared for the other side. The plaintiff, unfortunately, was unable to be present at either of the trials. The refusal of the companies to give him the £18,000 had placed him in a position of most painful pecuniary embarrassment. Indeed, a few months after the murder of Helen Abercrombie, he had been actually arrested for debt in the streets of London while he was serenading the pretty daughter of one of his friends. This difficulty was got over at the time, but shortly afterwards he thought it better to go abroad till he could come to some practical arrangement with his creditors. He accordingly went to Boulogne on a visit to the father of the young lady in question, and while he was there induced him to insure his life with the Pelican Company for £3000. As soon as the necessary formalities had been gone through and the policy executed, he dropped some crystals of strychnine into his coffee as they sat together one evening after dinner. He himself did not gain any monetary advantage by doing this. His aim was simply to revenge himself on the first office that had refused to pay him the price of his sin. His friend died the next day in his presence, and he left Boulogne at once for a sketching tour through the most picturesque parts of Brittany, and was for a time the guest of an old French gentleman, who had a beautiful country house at St. Omer. From this he moved to Paris, where he remained for several years, living in luxury, some say, while others talk of his 'skulking with poison in his pocket, and being dreaded by all who knew him.' In 1837 he returned to England privately. Some strange mad fascination brought him back. He followed a woman whom he loved.

It was the month of June, and he was staying at one of the hotels in Covent

Garden. His sitting-room was on the ground floor, and he prudently kept the blinds down for fear of being seen. Thirteen years before, when he was making his fine collection of majolica and Marc Antonios, he had forged the names of his trustees to a power of attorney, which enabled him to get possession of some of the money which he had inherited from his mother, and had brought into marriage settlement. He knew that this forgery had been discovered, and that by returning to England he was imperilling his life. Yet he returned. Should one wonder? It was said that the woman was very beautiful. Besides, she did not love him.

It was by a mere accident that he was discovered. A noise in the street attracted his attention, and, in his artistic interest in modern life, he pushed aside the blind for a moment. Some one outside called out, 'That's Wainewright, the Bank-forger.' It was Forrester, the Bow Street runner.

On the 5th July he was brought up at the Old Bailey. The following report of the proceedings appeared in the *Times*: –

Before Mr. Justice Vaughan and Mr. Baron Alderson, Thomas Griffiths Wainewright, aged forty-two, a man of gentlemanly appearance, wearing mustachios, was indicted for forging and uttering a certain power of attorney for £2259, with intent to defraud the Governor and Company of the Bank of England.

There were five indictments against the prisoner, to all of which he pleaded not guilty, when he was arraigned before Mr. Serjeant Arabin in the course of the morning. On being brought before the judges, however, he begged to be allowed to withdraw the former plea, and then pleaded guilty to two of the indictments which were not of a capital nature.

The counsel for the Bank having explained that there were three other indictments, but that the Bank did not desire to shed blood, the plea of guilty on the two minor charges was recorded and the prisoner at the close of the session sentenced by the Recorder to transportation for life.

He was taken back to Newgate, preparatory to his removal to the colonies. In a fanciful passage in one of his early essays he had fancied himself 'lying in Horsemonger Gaol under sentence of death,' for having been unable to resist the temptation of stealing some Marc Antonios from the British Museum in order to complete his collection. The sentence now passed on him was to a man of his culture a form of death. He complained bitterly of it to his friends, and pointed out, with a good deal of reason, some people may fancy, that the money was practically his own, having come to him from his mother, and that the forgery, such as it was, had been committed thirteen years before, which, to use his own phrase, was at least a *circonstance attenuante*. The permanence of personality is a very subtle metaphysical problem, and certainly the English law solves the question in an extremely rough-and-ready manner. There is, however, something dramatic in the fact that this heavy punishment was inflicted on him for what, if we remember his fatal influence on the prose of modern journalism, was certainly not the worst of all his sins.

While he was in gaol, Dickens, Macready, and Hablot Browne came across him by chance. They had been going over the prisons of London, searching for artistic effects, and in Newgate they suddenly caught sight of Wainewright. He met them with a defiant stare, Forster tells us, but Macready was 'horrified to recognise a man familiarly known to him in former years and at whose table he had dined.'

Others had more curiosity, and his cell was for some time a kind of fashionable lounge. Many men of letters went down to visit their old literary comrade. But he was no longer the kind light-hearted Janus whom Charles Lamb admired. He seems to have grown quite cynical.

To the agent of an insurance company who was visiting him one afternoon, and thought he would improve the occasion by pointing out that, after all, crime was a bad speculation, he replied: 'Sir, you City men enter on your speculations, and take the chances of them. Some of your speculations succeed, some fail. Mine happen to have failed, yours happen to have succeeded. That is the only difference, sir, between my visitor and me. But, sir, I will tell you one thing in which I have succeeded to the last. I have been determined through life to hold the position of a gentleman. I have always done so. I do so still. It is the custom of this place that each of the inmates of a cell shall take his morning's turn of sweeping it out. I occupy a cell with a bricklayer and a sweep, but they never offer me the broom!' When a friend reproached him with the murder of Helen Abercrombie he shrugged his shoulders and said, 'Yes; it was a dreadful thing to do, but she had very thick ankles.'

From Newgate he was brought to the hulks at Portsmouth, and sent from there in the *Susan* to Van Diemen's Land along with three hundred other convicts. The voyage seems to have been most distasteful to him, and in a letter written to a friend he spoke bitterly about the ignominy of 'the companion of poets and artists' being compelled to associate with 'country bumpkins.' The phrase that he applies to his companions need not surprise us. Crime in England is rarely the result of sin. It is nearly always the result of starvation. There was probably no one on board in whom he would have found a sympathetic listener, or even a psychologically interesting nature.

His love of art, however, never deserted him. At Hobart Town he started a studio, and returned to sketching and portrait-painting, and his conversation and manners seem not to have lost their charm. Nor did he give up his habit of poisoning, and there are two cases on record in which he tried to make away with people who had offended him. But his hand seems to have lost its cunning. Both of his attempts were complete failures, and in 1844, being thoroughly dissatisfied with Tasmanian society, he presented a memorial to the governor of the settlement, Sir John Eardley Wilmot, praying for a ticket-of-leave. In it he speaks of himself as being 'tormented by ideas struggling for outward form and realisation, barred up from increase of knowledge and deprived of the exercise of profitable or even of decorous speech.' His request, however, was refused, and the associate of Coleridge consoled himself by making those marvellous *Paradis Artificiels* whose secret is only known to the eaters of opium. In 1852 he died of apoplexy, his sole living companion being a cat, for which he had evinced an extraordinary affection.

His crimes seem to have had an important effect upon his art. They gave a strong personality to his style, a quality that his early work certainly lacked. In a note to the *Life of Dickens*, Forster mentions that in 1847 Lady Blessington received from her brother, Major Powell, who held a military appointment at Hobart Town, an oil portrait of a young lady from his clever brush; and it is said that 'he had contrived to put the expression of his own wickedness into the portrait of a nice, kind-hearted girl.' M. Zola, in one of his novels, tells us of a young man who, having committed a murder, takes to art, and paints greenish impressionist portraits of perfectly respectable people, all of which bear a curious resemblance to his victim. The development of Mr. Wainewright's style seems to me far more subtle and suggestive. One can fancy an intense personality being created out of sin.

This strange and fascinating figure that for a few years dazzled literary London, and made so brilliant a *début* in life and letters, is undoubtedly a most interesting study. Mr. W. Carew Hazlitt, his latest biographer, to whom I am indebted for many of the facts contained in this memoir, and whose little book is, indeed, quite invaluable in its way, is of opinion that his love of art and nature was a mere pretence and assumption, and others have denied to him all literary power. This seems to me a shallow, or at least a mistaken, view. The fact of a man being a poisoner is nothing against his prose. The domestic virtues are not the true basis of art, though they may serve as an excellent advertisement for second-rate artists. It is possible that De Quincey exaggerated his critical powers, and I cannot help saying again that there is much in his published works that is too familiar, too common, too journalistic, in the bad sense of that bad word. Here and there he is distinctly vulgar in expression, and he is always lacking in the self-restraint of the true artist. But for some of his faults we must blame the time in which he lived, and, after all, prose that Charles Lamb thought 'capital' has no small historic interest. That he had a sincere love of art and nature seems to me quite certain. There is no essential incongruity between crime and culture. We cannot re-write the whole of history for the purpose of gratifying our moral sense of what should be.

Of course, he is far too close to our own time for us to be able to form any purely artistic judgment about him. It is impossible not to feel a strong prejudice against a man who might have poisoned Lord Tennyson, or Mr. Gladstone, or the Master of Balliol. But had the man worn a costume and spoken a language different from our own, had he lived in imperial Rome, or at the time of the Italian Renaissance, or in Spain in the seventeenth century, or in any land or any century but this century and this land, we would be quite able to arrive at a perfectly unprejudiced estimate of his position and value. I know that there are many historians, or at least writers on historical subjects, who still think it necessary to apply moral judgments to history, and who distribute their praise or blame with the solemn complacency of a successful schoolmaster. This, however, is a foolish habit, and merely shows that the moral instinct can be brought to such a pitch of perfection that it will make its appearance wherever it is not required. Nobody with the true historical sense ever dreams of blaming Nero, or scolding Tiberius, or censuring Caesar Borgia. These personages have become like the puppets of a play. They may fill us with terror, or horror, or wonder, but they do not harm us. They are not in immediate relation to us. We have nothing to fear from them. They have passed into the sphere of art and science, and neither art nor science knows anything of moral approval or disapproval. And so it may be some day with Charles Lamb's friend. At present I feel that he is just a little too modern to be treated in that fine spirit of disinterested curiosity to which we owe so many charming studies of the great criminals of the Italian Renaissance from the pens of Mr. John Addington Symonds, Miss A. Mary F. Robinson, Miss Vernon Lee, and other distinguished writers. However, Art has not forgotten him. He is the hero of Dicken's *Hunted Down*, the Varney of Bulwer's *Lucretia*; and it is gratifying to note that fiction has paid some homage to one who was so powerful with 'pen, pencil and poison.' To be suggestive for fiction is to be of more importance than a fact.

THE CRITIC AS ARTIST

Part One

With some remarks upon the importance of doing nothing

A Dialogue

PERSONS: *Gilbert and Ernest.* SCENE: *the library of a house in Piccadilly, overlooking the Green Park.*

GILBERT (*at the piano*): My dear Ernest, what you are laughing at?

ERNEST (*looking up*): At a capital story that I have just come across in this volume of Reminiscences that I have found on your table.

GILBERT: What is the book? Ah! I see. I have not read it yet. Is it good?

ERNEST: Well, while you have been playing, I have been turning over the pages with some amusement, though, as a rule, I dislike modern memoirs. They are generally written by people who have either entirely lost their memories, or have never done anything worth remembering; which, however, is, no doubt, the true explanation of their popularity, as the English public always feels perfectly at its ease when a mediocrity is talking to it.

GILBERT: Yes; the public is wonderfully tolerant. It forgives everything except genius. But I must confess that I like all memoirs. I like them for their form, just as much as for their matter. In literature mere egotism is delightful. It is what fascinates us in the letters of personalities so different as Cicero and Balzac, Flaubert and Berlioz, Byron and Madame de Sévigné. Whenever we come across it, and, strangely enough, it is rather rare, we cannot but welcome it, and do not easily forget it. Humanity will always love Rousseau for having confessed his sins, not to a priest, but to the world, and the couchant nymphs that Cellini wrought in bronze for the castle of King Francis, the green and gold Perseus, even, that in the open Loggia at Florence shows the moon the dead terror that once turned life to stone, have not given it more pleasure than has that autobiography in which the supreme scoundrel of the Renaissance relates the story of his splendour and his shame. The opinions, the character, the achievements of the man, matter very little. He may be a sceptic like the gentle Sieur de Montaigne, or a saint like the bitter son of Monica, but when he tells us his own secrets he can always charm our ears to listening and our lips to silence. The mode of thought that Cardinal Newman represented – if that can be called a mode of thought which seeks to solve intellectual problems by a denial of the supremacy of the intellect – may not, cannot, I think, survive. But the world will never weary of watching that troubled soul in its progress from darkness to darkness. The lonely church at Littlemore, where 'the breath of the morning is damp, and worshippers are few,' will always be dear to it, and whenever men see the yellow snapdragon blossoming on the wall of Trinity they will think of that gracious undergraduate who saw in the flower's sure recurrence a prophecy that he would abide for ever with the Benign Mother of his days – a prophecy that

Faith, in her wisdom or her folly, suffered not to be fulfilled. Yes; autobiography is irresistible. Poor, silly, conceited Mr. Secretary Pepys had chattered his way into the circle of the Immortals, and, conscious that indiscretion is the better part of valour, bustles about among them in that 'shaggy purple gown with gold buttons and looped lace' which he is so fond of describing to us, perfectly at his ease, and prattling, to his own and our infinite pleasure, of the Indian blue petticoat that he bought for his wife, of the 'good hog's harslet,' and the 'pleasant French fricassee of veal' that he loved to eat, of his game of bowls with Will Joyce, and his 'gadding after beauties,' and his reciting of *Hamlet* on a Sunday, and his playing of the viol on week days, and other wicked or trivial things. Even in actual life egotism is not without its attractions. When people talk to us about others they are usually dull. When they talk to us about themselves they are nearly always interesting, and if one could shut them up, when they become wearisome, as easily as one can shut up a book of which one has grown wearied, they would be perfect absolutely.

ERNEST: There is much virtue in that If, as Touchstone would say. But do you seriously propose that every man should become his own Boswell? What would become of our industrious compilers of Lives and Recollections in that case?

GILBERT: What has become of them? They are the pest of the age, nothing more and nothing less. Every great man nowadays has his disciples, and it is always Judas who writes the biography.

ERNEST: My dear fellow!

GILBERT: I am afraid it is true. Formerly we used to canonise our heroes. The modern method is to vulgarise them. Cheap editions of great books may be delightful, but cheap editions of great men are absolutely detestable.

ERNEST: May I ask, Gilbert, to whom you allude?

GILBERT: Oh! To all our second-rate *littérateurs*. We are overrun by a set of people who, when poet or painter passes away, arrive at the house along with the undertaker, and forget that their one duty is to behave as mutes. But we won't talk about them. They are the mere body-snatchers of literature. The dust is given to one, and the ashes to another, and the soul is out of their reach. And now, let me play Chopin to you, or Dvořák? Shall I play you a fantasy by Dvořák? He writes passionate, curiously-coloured things.

ERNEST: No; I don't want music just at present. It is far too indefinite. Besides, I took the Baroness Bernstein down to dinner last night, and, though absolutely charming in every other respect, she insisted on discussing music as if it were actually written in the German language. Now, whatever music sounds like, I am glad to say that it does not sound in the smallest degree like German. There are forms of patriotism that are really quite degrading. No; Gilbert, don't play any more. Turn round and talk to me. Talk to me till the white-horned day comes into the room. There is something in your voice that is wonderful.

GILBERT: (*rising from the piano*): I am not in a mood for talking to-night. How horrid of you to smile! I really am not. Where are the cigarettes?

Thanks. How exquisite these single daffodils are! They seem to be made of amber and cool ivory. They are like Greek things of the best period. What was the story in the confessions of the remorseful Academician that made you laugh? Tell it to me. After playing Chopin, I feel as if I had been weeping over sins that I had never committed, and mourning over tragedies that were not my own. Music always seems to me to produce that effect. It creates for one a past of which one has been ignorant, and fills one with a sense of sorrows that have been hidden from one's tears. I can fancy a man who had led a perfectly commonplace life, hearing by chance some curious piece of music, and suddenly discovering that his soul, without his being conscious of it, had passed through terrible experiences, and known fearful joys, or wild romantic loves, or great renunciations. And so tell me this story, Ernest. I want to be amused.

ERNEST: Oh! I don't know that it is of any importance. But I thought it a really admirable illustration of the true value of ordinary art-criticism. It seems that a lady once gravely asked the remorseful Academician, as you call him, if his celebrated picture of 'A Spring-Day at Whiteley's,' or 'Waiting for the Last Omnibus,' or some subject of that kind, was all painted by hand?

GILBERT: And was it?

ERNEST: You are quite incorrigible. But, seriously speaking, what is the use of art-criticism? Why cannot the artist be left alone, to create a new world if he wishes it, or, if not, to shadow forth the world which we already know, and of which, I fancy, we would each one of us be wearied if Art, with her fine spirit of choice and delicate instinct of selection, did not, as it were, purify it for us, and give to it a momentary perfection. It seems to me that the imagination spreads, or should spread, a solitude around it, and works best in silence and in isolation. Why should the artist be troubled by the shrill clamour of criticism? Why should those who cannot create take upon themselves to estimate the value of creative work? What can they know about it? If a man's work is easy to understand, an explanation is unnecessary. . . .

GILBERT: And if his work is incomprehensible, an explanation is wicked.

ERNEST: I did not say that.

GILBERT: Ah! But you should have. Nowadays we have so few mysteries left to us that we cannot afford to part with one of them. The members of the Browning Society, like the theologians of the Broad Church Party, or the authors of Mr. Walter Scott's Great Writers' Series, seem to me to spend their time in trying to explain their divinity away. Where one had hoped that Browning was a mystic they have sought to show that he was simply inarticulate. Where one had fancied that he had something to conceal, they have proved that he had but little to reveal. But I speak merely of his incoherent work. Taken as a whole the man was great. He did not belong to the Olympians, and had all the incompleteness of the Titan. He did not survey, and it was but rarely that he could sing. His work is marred by struggle, violence and effort, and he passed not from emotion to form, but from thought to chaos. Still, he was great. He has been called a thinker, and was certainly a man who was always thinking, and always thinking aloud; but it was not thought that fascinated him, but rather the processes by which thought moves. It was the machine he loved, not what the machine makes. The method by which the fool arrives at his folly was as dear to him as the ultimate wisdom of the wise. So much, indeed, did the subtle mechanism of mind fascinate him that he despised language, or looked upon it as an incomplete instrument of expression. Rhyme, that exquisite echo which in the Muse's hollow hill creates and answers its own voice; rhyme, which in the hands of the real artist becomes not merely a material element of metrical beauty, but a spiritual element of thought and passion also, waking a new mood, it may be, or stirring a fresh train of ideas, or opening by mere sweetness and suggestion of sound some golden door at which the Imagination itself had knocked in vain; rhyme, which can turn man's utterance to the speech of gods; rhyme, the one chord we have added to the Greek lyre, became in Robert Browning's hands a grotesque, misshapen thing, which at times made him masquerade in poetry as a low comedian, and ride Pegasus too often with his tongue in his cheek. There are moments when he wounds us by monstrous music. Nay, if he can only get his music by breaking the strings of his lute, he breaks them, and they snap in discord, and no Athenian tettix, making melody from tremulous wings, lights on the ivory horn to make the movement perfect, or the interval less harsh. Yet, he was great: and though he turned language into ignoble clay, he made from it men and women that live. He is the most Shakespearian creature since Shakespeare. If Shakespeare could sing with myriad lips, Browning could stammer through a thousand mouths. Even now, as I am speaking, and speaking not against him but for him, there glides through the room the pageant of his persons. There, creeps Fra Lippo Lippi with his cheeks still burning from some girl's hot kiss. There, stands dread Saul with the lordly male-sapphires gleaming in his turban. Mildred Tresham is there, and the Spanish monk, yellow with hatred, and Blougram, and Ben Ezra, and the Bishop of St. Praxed's. The spawn of Setebos gibbers in the corner, and Sebald, hearing Pippa pass by, looks on Ottima's haggard face, and loathes her and his own sin, and himself. Pale as the white satin of his doublet, the melancholy king watches with dreamy treacherous eyes too loyal Strafford pass forth to his doom, and Andrea shudders as he hears the cousins whistle in the garden, and bids his perfect wife go down. Yes, Browning was great. And as what will he be remembered? As a poet? Ah, not as a poet! He will be remembered as a writer of fiction, as the most supreme writer of fiction, it may be, that we have ever had. His sense of dramatic situation was unrivalled, and, if he could not answer his own problems, he could at least put problems forth, and what more should an artist do? Considered from the point of view of a creator of character he ranks next to him who made Hamlet. Had he been articulate, he might have sat beside him. The only man who can touch the hem of his garment is George Meredith. Meredith is a prose Browning, and so is Browning. He used poetry as a medium for writing in prose.

ERNEST: There is something in what you say, but there is not everything in what you say. In many points you are unjust.

GILBERT: It is difficult not to be unjust to what one loves. But let us return to the particular point at issue. What was it that you said?

ERNEST: Simply this: that in the best days of art there were no art-critics.

GILBERT: I seem to have heard that observation before, Ernest. It has all the vitality of error and all the tediousness of an old friend.

ERNEST: It is true. Yes: there is no use your tossing your head in that petulant manner. It is quite true. In the best days of art there were no art-critics. The sculptor hewed from the marble block the great white-limbed Hermes that slept within it. The waxers and gilders of images gave tone and texture to the statue, and the world, when it saw it, worshipped and was dumb. He poured the glowing bronze into the mould of sand, and the river of red metal cooled into noble curves and took the impress of the body of a god. With enamel or polished jewels he gave sight to the sightless eyes. The hyacinth-like curls grew crisp beneath his graver. And when, in some dim frescoed fane, or pillared sunlit portico, the child of Leto stood upon his pedestal, those who passed by, ἁβρῶς βαίνοντες διὰ λαμπροτάτου αἰθέρος,[1] became conscious of a new influence that had come across at their lives, and dreamily, or with a sense of strange and quickening joy, went to their homes or daily labour, or wandered, it may be, through the city gates to that nymph-haunted meadow where young Phaedrus bathed his feet, and, lying there on the soft grass, beneath the tall wind-whispering planes and flowering *agnus castus*, began to think of the wonder of beauty, and grew silent with unaccustomed awe. In those days the artist was free. From the river valley he took the fine clay in his fingers, and with a little tool of wood or bone, fashioned it into forms so exquisite that the people gave them to the dead as their playthings, and we find them still in the dusty tombs on the yellow hillside by Tanagra, with the faint gold and the fading crimson still lingering about hair and lips and raiment. On a wall of fresh plaster, stained with bright sandyx or mixed with milk and saffron, he pictured one who trod with tired feet the purple white-starred fields of asphodel, one 'in whose eyelids lay the whole of the Trojan War' Polyxena, the daughter of Priam; or figured Odysseus, the wise and cunning, bound by tight cords to the mast-step, that he might listen without hurt to the singing of the Sirens, or wandering by the clear river of Acheron, where the ghosts of fishes flitted over the pebbly bed; or showed the Persian in trews and mitre flying before the Greek at Marathon, or the galleys clashing their beaks of brass in the little Salaminian bay. He drew with silver-point and charcoal upon parchment and prepared cedar. Upon ivory and rose-coloured terra-cotta he painted with wax, making the wax fluid with juice of olives, and with heated irons making it firm. Panel and marble and linen canvas became wonderful as his brush swept across them; and life seeing her own image, was still, and dared not speak. All life, indeed, was his, from the merchants seated in the market-place to the cloaked shepherd lying on the hill; from the nymph hidden in the laurels and the faun that pipes at noon, to

---

[1] Treading delicately through the most brilliant air.

the king whom, in long green-curtained litter, slaves bore upon oil-bright shoulders, and fanned with peacock fans. Men and women, with pleasure or sorrow in their faces, passed before him. He watched them, and their secret became his. Through form and colour he re-created a world.

All subtle arts belonged to him also. He held the gem against the revolving disk, and the amethyst became the purple couch for Adonis, and across the veined sardonyx sped Artemis with her hounds. He beat out the gold into roses, and strung them together for necklace or armlet. He beat out the gold into wreaths for the conqueror's helmet, or into palmates for the Tyrian robe, or into masks for the royal dead. On the back of the silver mirror he graved Thetis borne by her Nereids, or love-sick Phædra with her nurse, or Persephone, weary of memory, putting poppies in her hair. The potter sat in his shed, and, flowerlike from the silent wheel, the vase rose up beneath his hands. He decorated the base and stem and ears with pattern of dainty olive-leaf, of foliated acanthus, or curved and crested wave. Then in black or red he painted lads wrestling, or in the race: knights in full armour, with strange heraldic shields and curious visors, leaning from shell-shaped chariot over rearing steeds: the gods seated at the feast or working their miracles: the heroes in their victory or in their pain. Sometimes he would etch in thin vermilion lines upon a ground of white the languid bridegroom and his bride, with Eros hovering round them – an Eros like one of Donatello's angels, a little laughing thing with gilded or with azure wings. On the curved side he would write the name of his friend. ΚΑΛΟΣ ΑΛΚΙΒΙΑΔΗΣ[1] or ΚΑΛΟΣ ΧΑΡΜΙΔΗΣ[2] tells us the story of his days. Again, on the rim of the wide flat cup he would draw the stag browsing, or the lion at rest, as his fancy willed it. From the tiny perfume-bottle laughed Aphrodite at her toilet, and, with bare-limbed Mænads in his train, Dionysus danced round the wine-jar on naked must-stained feet, while, satyr-like, the old Silenus sprawled upon the bloated skins, or shook that magic spear which was tipped with a fretted fir-cone, and wreathed with dark ivy. And no one came to trouble the artist at his work. No irresponsible chatter disturbed him. He was not worried by opinions. By the Ilyssus, says Arnold somewhere, there was no Higgin-botham. By the Ilyssus, my dear Gilbert, there were no silly art congresses bringing provincialism to the provinces and teaching the mediocrity how to mouth. By the Ilyssus there were no tedious magazines about art, in which the industrious prattle of what they do not understand. On the reed-grown banks of that little stream strutted no ridiculous journalism monopolising the seat of judgment when it should be apologising in the dock. The Greeks had no art-critics.

GILBERT: Ernest, you are quite delightful, but your views are terribly unsound. I am afraid that you have been listening to the conversation of some one older than yourself. That is always a dangerous thing to do, and if you allow it to degenerate into a habit you will find it absolutely fatal to any intel-

---

[1] Noble Alcibiades.
[2] Noble Charmides.

lectual development. As for modern journalism, it is not my business to defend it. It justifies its own existence by the great Darwinian principle of the survival of the vulgarest. I have merely to do with literature.

ERNEST: But what is the difference between literature and journalism?

GILBERT: Oh! Journalism is unreadable, and literature is not read. That is all. But with regard to your statement that the Greeks had no art-critics, I assure you that is quite absurd. It would be more just to say that the Greeks were a nation of art-critics.

ERNEST: Really?

GILBERT: Yes, a nation of art-critics. But I don't wish to destroy the delightfully unreal picture that you have drawn of the relation of the Hellenic artist to the intellectual spirit of his age. To give an accurate description of what has never occurred is not merely the proper occupation of the historian, but the inalienable privilege of any man of parts and culture. Still less do I desire to talk learnedly. Learned conversation is either the affectation of the ignorant or the profession of the mentally unemployed. And as for what is called improving conversation, that is merely the foolish method by which the still more foolish philanthropist feebly tries to disarm the just rancour of the criminal classes. No; let me play to you some mad scarlet thing by Dvorák. The Pallid figures on the tapestry are smiling at us, and the heavy eyelids of my bronze Narcissus are folded in sleep. Don't let us discuss anything solemnly. I am but too conscious of the fact that we are born in an age when only the dull are treated seriously, and I live in terror of not being misunderstood. Don't degrade me into the position of giving you useful information. Education is an admirable thing, but it is well to remember from time to time that nothing that is worth knowing can be taught. Through the parted curtains of the window I see the moon like a clipped piece of silver. Like gilded bees the stars cluster round her. The sky is a hard hollow sapphire. Let us go out into the night. Thought is wonderful, but adventure is more wonderful still. Who knows but we may meet Prince Florizel of Bohemia, and hear the fair Cuban tell us that she is not what she seems?

ERNEST: You are horribly wilful. I insist on your discussing this matter with me. You have said that the Greeks were a nation of art-critics. What art-criticism have they left us?

GILBERT: My dear Ernest, even if not a single fragment of art-criticism had come down to us from Hellenic or Hellenistic days, it would be none the less true that the Greeks were a nation of art-critics, and that they invented the criticism of art just as they invented the criticism of everything else. For, after all, what is our primary debt to the Greeks? Simply the critical spirit. And this spirit, which they exercised on questions of religion and science, of ethics and metaphysics, of politics and education, they exercised on questions of art also, and, indeed, of the two supreme and highest arts they have left us the most flawless system of criticism that the world has ever seen.

ERNEST: But what are the two supreme and highest arts?

GILBERT: Life and Literature, life and the perfect expression of life. The principles of the former, as laid down by the Greeks, we may not realise in an age so marred by false ideals as our own. The principles of the latter, as they laid them down, are, in many cases, so subtle that we can hardly understand them. Recognising that the most perfect art is that which most fully mirrors man in all his infinite variety, they elaborated the criticism of language, considered in the light of the mere material of that art, to a point to which we, with our accentual system of reasonable or emotional emphasis, can barely if at all attain; studying, for instance, the metrical movements of a prose as scientifically as a modern musician studies harmony and counterpoint, and, I need hardly say, with much keener æsthetic instinct. In this they were right, as they were right in all things. Since the introduction of printing, and the fatal development of the habit of reading amongst the middle and lower classes of this country, there has been a tendency in literature to appeal more and more to the eye, and less and less to the ear, which is really the sense which, from the standpoint of pure art, it should seek to please, and by whose canons of pleasure it should abide always. Even the work of Mr. Pater, who is, on the whole, the most perfect master of English prose now creating amongst us, is often far more like a piece of mosaic than a passage in music, and seems, here and there, to lack the true rhythmical life of words and the fine freedom and richness of effect that such rhythmical life produces. We, in fact, have made writing a definite mode of composition, and have treated it as a form of elaborate design. The Greeks, upon the other hand, regarded writing simply as a method of chronicling. Their test was always the spoken word in its musical and metrical relations. The voice was the medium, and the ear the critic. I have sometimes thought that the story of Homer's blindness might be really an artistic myth, created in critical days, and serving to remind us, not merely that the great poet is always a seer, seeing less with the eyes of the body than he does with the eyes of the soul, but he is a true singer also, building his song out of music, repeating each line over and over again to himself till he has caught the secret of its melody, chaunting in darkness the words that are winged with light. Certainly, whether this be so or not, it was to his blindness, as an occasion, if not as a cause, that England's great poet owed much of the majestic movement and sonorous splendour of his later verse. When Milton could no longer write he began to sing. Who would match the measures of *Comus* with the measures of *Samson Agonistes*, or of *Paradise Lost* or *Regained*? When Milton became blind he composed, as every one should compose, with the voice purely, and so the pipe or reed of earlier days became that mighty many-stopped organ whose rich reverberant music has all the stateliness of Homeric verse, if it seeks not to have its swiftness, and is the one imperishable inheritance of English literature sweeping through all the ages, because above them, and abiding with us ever, being immortal in its form. Yes: writing has done much harm to writers. We must return to the voice. That must be our test, and perhaps then we shall be able to appreciate some of the subtleties of Greek art-criticism.

As it now is, we cannot do so. Sometimes, when I have written a piece of prose that I have been modest enough to consider absolutely free from fault, a dreadful thought comes over me that I may have been guilty of the immoral effeminacy of using trochaic and tribrachic movements, a crime for which a learned critic of the Augustan age censures with most just severity the brilliant if somewhat paradoxical Hegesias. I grow cold when I think of it, and wonder to myself if the admirable ethical effect of the prose of the charming writer, who once in a spirit of reckless generosity towards the uncultivated portion of our community proclaimed the monstrous doctrine that conduct is three-fourths of life, will not some day be entirely annihilated by the discovery that the paeons have been wrongly placed.

ERNEST: Ah! Now you are flippant.

GILBERT: Who would not be flippant when he is gravely told that the Greeks had no art-critics? I can understand it being said that the constructive genius of the Greeks lost itself in criticism, but not that the race to whom we owe the critical spirit did not criticise. You will not ask me to give you a survey of Greek art-criticism from Plato to Plotinus. The night is too lovely for that, and the moon, if she heard us, would put more ashes on her face than are there already. But think merely of one perfect little work of aesthetic criticism, Aristotle's *Treatise on Poetry*. It is not perfect in form, for it is badly written, consisting perhaps of notes dotted down for an art lecture, or of isolated fragments destined for some larger book, but in temper and treatment it is perfect, absolutely. The ethical effect of art, its importance to culture, and its place in the formation of character, had been done once for all by Plato; but here we have art treated, not from the moral, but from the purely aesthetic point of view. Plato had, of course, dealt with many definitely artistic subjects, such as the importance of unity in a work of art, the necessity for tone and harmony, the æsthetic value of appearances, the relation of the visible arts to the external world, and the relation of fiction to fact. He first perhaps stirred in the soul of man that desire that we have not yet satisfied, the desire to know the connection between Beauty and Truth, and the place of Beauty in the moral and intellectual order of the Kosmos. The problems of idealism and realism, as he sets them forth, may seem to many to be somewhat barren of result in the metaphysical sphere of abstract being in which he places them, but transfer them to the sphere of art, and you will find that they are still vital and full of meaning. It may be that it is as a critic of Beauty that Plato is destined to live, and that by altering the name of the sphere of his speculation we shall find a new philosophy. But Aristotle, like Goethe, deals with art primarily in its concrete manifestations, taking Tragedy, for instance, and investigating the material it uses, which is language, its subject-matter, which is life, the method by which it works, which is action, the conditions under which it reveals itself, which are those of theatric presentation, its logical structure, which is plot, and its final aesthetic appeal, which is to the sense of beauty realised through the passions of pity and awe. That purification and spiritualising of the nature which he calls κάθαρσις[1] is, as Goethe saw, essentially æsthetic, and is not moral, as Lessing fancied. Concerning himself primarily with the impression that the work of art produces,

---

[1] Cleansing.

Aristotle sets himself to analyse that impression, to investigate its source, to see how it is engendered. As a physiologist and psychologist, he knows that the health of a function resides in energy. To have a capacity for a passion and not to realise it, is to make oneself incomplete and limited. The mimic spectacle of life that Tragedy affords cleanses the bosom of much 'perilous stuff,' and by presenting high and worthy objects for the exercise of the emotions purifies and spiritualises the man; nay, not merely does it spiritualise him, but it initiates him also into noble feelings of which he might else have known nothing, the word κάθαρσις having, it has sometimes seemed to me, a definite allusion to the rite of initiation, if indeed that be not, as I am occasionally tempted to fancy, its true and only meaning here. This is of course a mere outline of the book. But you see what a perfect piece of aesthetic criticism it is. Who indeed but a Greek could have analysed art so well? After reading it, one does not wonder any longer that Alexandria devoted itself so largely to art-criticism, and that we find the artistic temperaments of the day investigating every question of style and manner, discussing the great Academic schools of painting, for instance, such as the school of Sicyon, that sought to preserve the dignified traditions of the antique mode, or the realistic and impressionist schools, that aimed at reproducing actual life, or the elements of ideality in portraiture, or the artistic value of the epic form in an age so modern as theirs, or the proper subject-matter for the artist. Indeed, I fear that the inartistic temperaments of the day busied themselves also in matters of literature and art, for the accusations of plagiarism were endless, and such accusations proceed either from the thin colourless lips of impotence, or from the grotesque mouths of those who, possessing nothing of their own, fancy that they can gain a reputation for wealth by crying out that they have been robbed. And I assure you, my dear Ernest, that the Greeks chattered about painters quite as much as people do nowadays, and had their private views, and shilling exhibitions, and Arts and Crafts guilds, and Pre-Raphaelite movements, and movements towards realism, and lectured about art, and wrote essays on art, and produced their art-historians, and their archaeologists, and all the rest of it. Why, even the theatrical managers of travelling companies brought their dramatic critics with them when they went on tour, and paid them very handsome salaries for writing laudatory notices. Whatever, in fact, is modern in our life we owe to the Greeks. Whatever is an anachronism is due to mediaevalism. It is the Greeks who have given us the whole system of art-criticism, and how fine their critical instinct was may be seen from the fact that the material they criticised with most care was, as I have already said, language. For the material that painter or sculptor uses is meagre in comparison with that of words. Words have not merely music as sweet as that of viol and lute, colour as rich and vivid as any that makes lovely for us the canvas of the Venetian or the Spaniard, and plastic form no less sure and certain than that which reveals itself in marble or in bronze, but thought and passion and spirituality are theirs also, are theirs indeed alone. If the Greeks had criticised nothing but language, they would still have been the great art-critics of the world. To know the principles of the highest art is to know the principles of all the arts.

But I see that the moon is hiding behind a sulphur-coloured cloud. Out of a tawny mane or drift she gleams like a lion's eye. She is afraid that I will talk to you of Lucian and Longinus, of Quinctilian and Dionysius, of Pliny and Fronto and Pausanias, of all those who in the antique world wrote or lectured upon art matters. She need not be afraid. I am tired of my expedition into the dim, dull abyss of facts. There is nothing left for me now but the divine μονόχρονος ἡδονή[1] of another cigarette. Cigarettes have at least the charm of leaving one unsatisfied.

ERNEST: Try one of mine. They are rather good, I get them direct from Cairo. The only use of our *attachés* is that they supply their friends with excellent tobacco. And as the moon has hidden herself, let us talk a little longer. I am quite ready to admit that I was wrong in what I said about the Greeks. They were, as you have pointed out, a nation of art-critics. I acknowledge it, and I feel a little sorry for them. For the creative faculty is higher than the critical. There is really no comparison between them.

GILBERT: The antithesis between them is entirely arbitrary. Without the critical faculty, there is no artistic creation at all worthy of the name. You spoke a little while ago of that fine spirit of choice and delicate instinct of selection by which the artist realises life for us, and gives to it a momentary perfection. Well, that spirit of choice, that subtle tact of omission, is really the critical faculty in one of its most characteristic moods, and no one who does not possess this critical faculty can create anything at all in art. Arnold's definition of literature as a criticism of life was not very felicitous in form, but it showed how keenly he recognised the importance of the critical element in all creative work.

ERNEST: I should have said that great artists work unconsciously, that they were 'wiser than they knew,' as, I think, Emerson remarks somewhere.

GILBERT: It is really not so, Ernest. All fine imaginative work is self-conscious and deliberate. No poet sings because he must sing. At least, no great poet does. A great poet sings because he chooses to sing. It is so now, and it has always been so. We are sometimes apt to think that the voices that sounded at the dawn of poetry were simpler, fresher, and more natural than ours, and that the world which the early poets looked at, and through which they walked, had a kind of poetical quality of its own, and almost without changing could pass into song. The snow lies thick now upon Olympus, and its steep scarped sides are bleak and barren, but once, we fancy, the white feet of the Muses brushed the dew from the anemones in the morning, and at evening came Apollo to sing to the shepherds in the vale. But in this we are merely lending to other ages what we desire, or think we desire, for our own. Our historical sense is at fault. Every century that produces poetry is, so far, an artificial century, and the work that seems to us to be the most natural and simple product of its time is always the result of the most self-consciousness, and self-consciousness and the critical spirit are one.

---

[1] Momentary pleasure.

ERNEST: I see what you mean, and there is much in it. But surely you would admit that the great poems of the early world, the primitive, anonymous collective poems, were the result of the imagination of races, rather than of the imagination of individuals?

GILBERT: Not when they became poetry. Not when they received a beautiful form. For there is no art where there is no style, and no style where there is no unity, and unity is of the individual. No doubt Homer had old ballads and stories to deal with, as Shakespeare had chronicles and plays and novels from which to work, but they were merely his rough material. He took them, and shaped them into song. They become his, because he made them lovely. They were built out of music,

> And so not built at all,
> And therefore built for ever.

The longer one studies life and literature, the more strongly one feels that behind everything that is wonderful stands the individual, and that it is not the moment that makes the man, but the man who creates the age. Indeed, I am inclined to think that each myth and legend that seems to us to spring out of the wonder, or terror, or fancy of tribe and nation, was in its origin the invention of one single mind. The curiously limited number of the myths seems to me to point to this conclusion. But we must not go off into questions of comparative mythology. We must keep to criticism. And what I want to point out is this. An age that has no criticism is either an age in which art is immobile, hieratic, and confined to the reproduction of formal types, or an age that possesses no art at all. There have been critical ages that have not been creative, in the ordinary sense of the word, ages in which the spirit of man has sought to set in order the treasures of his treasure-house, to separate the gold from the silver, and the silver from the lead, to count over the jewels, and to give names to the pearls. But there has never been a creative age that has not been critical also. For it is the critical faculty that invents fresh forms. The tendency of creation is to repeat itself. It is to the critical instinct that we owe each new school that springs up, each new mould that art finds ready to its hand. There is really not a single form that art now uses that does not come to us from the critical spirit of Alexandria, where these forms were either stereotyped or invented or made perfect. I say Alexandria, not merely because it was there that the Greek spirit became most self-conscious, and indeed ultimately expired in scepticism and theology, but because it was to that city, and not to Athens, that Rome turned for her models, and it was through the survival, such as it was, of the Latin language that culture lived at all. When, at the Renaissance, Greek literature dawned upon Europe, the soil had been in some measure prepared for it. But, to get rid of the details of history, which are always wearisome and usually inaccurate, let us say generally, that the forms of art have been due to the Greek critical spirit. To it we owe the epic, the lyric, the entire drama in every one of its developments, including burlesque, the idyll, the romantic novel, the novel of adventure, the essay, the dialogue, the oration, the lecture, for which perhaps we should not forgive them, and the epigram, in all the wide meaning of that word. In fact, we owe it everything, except the sonnet, to which, however, some curious parallels of thought-movement may be traced in the Anthology, American journalism, to which no parallel can be found anywhere, and the ballad in sham Scotch dialect, which one of our most industrious writers has recently proposed should be made the basis of a final and unanimous effort on the part of our second-rate poets to make themselves really romantic. Each new school, as it appears, cries out against criticism, but it is to the critical faculty in man that it owes its origin. The mere creative instinct does not innovate, but reproduces.

ERNEST: You have been talking of criticism as an essential part of the creative spirit, and I now fully accept your theory. But what of criticism outside creation? I have a foolish habit of reading periodicals, and it seems to me that most modern criticism is perfectly valueless.

GILBERT: So is most modern creative work also. Mediocrity weighing mediocrity in the balance, and incompetence applauding its brother – that is the spectacle which the artistic activity of England affords us from time to time. And yet I feel I am a little unfair in this matter. As a rule, the critics – I speak, of course, of the higher class, of those, in fact, who write for the sixpenny papers – are far more cultured than the people whose work they are called upon to review. This is, indeed, only what one would expect, for criticism demands infinitely more cultivation than creation does.

ERNEST: Really?

GILBERT: Certainly. Anybody can write a three-volume novel. It merely requires a complete ignorance of both life and literature. The difficulty that I should fancy the reviewer feels is the difficulty of sustaining any standard. Where there is no style a standard must be impossible. The poor reviewers are apparently reduced to be the reporters of the police-court of literature, the chroniclers of the doing of the habitual criminals of art. It is sometimes said of them that they do not read all through the works they are called upon to criticise. They do not. Or at least they should not. If they did so, they would become confirmed misanthropes, or if I may borrow a phrase from one of the pretty Newnham graduates, confirmed womanthropes for the rest of their lives. Nor is it necessary. To know the vintage and quality of a wine one need not drink the whole cask. It must be perfectly easy in half an hour to say whether a book is worth anything or worth nothing. Ten minutes are really sufficient, if one has the instinct for form. Who wants to wade through a dull volume? One tastes it, and that is quite enough – more than enough, I should imagine. I am aware that there are many honest workers in painting as well as in literature who object to criticism entirely. They are quite right. Their work stands in no intellectual relation to their age. It brings us no new element of pleasure. It suggests no fresh departure of thought, or passion, or beauty. It should not be spoken of. It should be left to the oblivion that it deserves.

ERNEST: But, my dear fellow – excuse me for interrupting you – you seem to me to be allowing your passion for criticism to lead you a great deal too far.

For, after all, even you must admit that it is much more difficult to do a thing than to talk about it.

GILBERT: More difficult to do a thing than to talk about it? Not at all. That is a gross popular error. It is very much more difficult to talk about a thing than to do it. In the sphere of actual life that is of course obvious. Anybody can make history. Only a great man can write it. There is no mode of action, no form of emotion, that we do not share with the lower animals. It is only by language that we rise above them, or above each other – by language, which is the parent, and not the child, of thought. Action, indeed, is always easy, and when presented to us in its most aggravated, because most continuous form, which I take to be that of real industry, becomes simply the refuge of people who have nothing whatsoever to do. No, Ernest, don't talk about action. It is a blind thing dependent on external influences, and moved by an impulse of whose nature it is unconscious. It is a thing incomplete in its essence, because limited by accident, and ignorant of its direction, being always at variance with its aim. Its basis is the lack of imagination. It is the last resource of those who know not how to dream.

ERNEST: Gilbert, you treat the world as if it were a crystal ball. You hold it in your hand, and reverse it to please a wilful fancy. You do nothing but re-write history.

GILBERT: The one duty we owe to history is to re-write it. That is not the least of the tasks in store for the critical spirit. When we have fully discovered the scientific laws that govern life, we shall realise that the one person who has more illusions than the dreamer is the man of action. He, indeed, knows neither the origin of his deeds nor their results. From the field in which he thought that he had sown thorns, we have gathered our vintage, and the fig-tree that he planted for our pleasure is as barren as the thistle, and more bitter. It is because Humanity has never known where it was going that it has been able to find its way.

ERNEST: You think, then, that in the sphere of action a conscious aim is a delusion?

GILBERT: It is worse than a delusion. If we lived long enough to see the results of our actions it may be that those who call themselves good would be sickened with a dull remorse, and those whom the world calls evil stirred by a noble joy. Each little thing that we do passes into the great machine of life which may grind our virtues to powder and make them worthless, or transform our sins into elements of a new civilisation, more marvellous and more splendid than any that has gone before. But men are the slaves of words. They rage against Materialism, as they call it, forgetting that there has been no material improvement that has not spiritualised the world, and that there have been few, if any, spiritual awakenings that have not wasted the world's faculties in barren hopes, and fruitless aspirations, and empty or trammelling creeds. What is termed Sin is an essential element of progress. Without it the world would stagnate, or grow old, or become colourless. By its curiosity Sin increases the experience of the race. Through its intensified assertion of individualism it saves us from monotony of type. In its rejection of the current notions about morality, it is one with the higher ethics. And as for the virtues! What are the virtues? Nature, M. Renan tells us, cares little about chastity, and it may be that it is to the shame of the Magdalen, and not to their own purity, that the Lucretias of modern life owe their freedom from stain. Charity, as even those of whose religion it makes a formal part have been compelled to acknowledge, creates a multitude of evils. The mere existence of conscience, that faculty of which people prate so much nowadays, and are so ignorantly proud, is a sign of our imperfect development. It must be merged in instinct before we become fine. Self-denial is simply a method by which man arrests his progress, and self-sacrifice a survival of the mutilation of the savage, part of that old worship of pain which is so terrible a factor in the history of the world, and which even now makes its victims day by day, and has its altars in the land. Virtues! Who knows what the virtues are? Not you. Not I. Not any one. It is well for our vanity that we slay the criminal, for if we suffered him to live he might show us what we had gained by his crime. It is well for his peace that the saint goes to his martyrdom. He is spared the sight of the horror of his harvest.

ERNEST: Gilbert, you sound too harsh a note. Let us go back to the more gracious fields of literature. What was it you said? That it was more difficult to talk about a thing than to do it?

GILBERT (*after a pause*): Yes; I believe I ventured upon that simple truth. Surely you see now that I am right? When man acts he is a puppet. When he describes he is a poet. The whole secret lies in that. It was easy enough on the sandy plains by windy Ilion to send the notched arrow from the painted bow, or to hurl against the shield of hide and flame-like brass the long ash-handled spear. It was easy for the adulterous queen to spread the Tyrian carpets for her lord, and then, as he lay couched in the marble bath, to throw over his head the purple net, and call to her smooth-faced lover to stab through the meshes at the heart that should have broken at Aulis. For Antigone even, with Death waiting for her as her bridegroom, it was easy to pass through the tainted air at noon, and climb the hill, and strew with kindly earth the wretched naked corpse that had no tomb. But what of those who wrote about these things? What of those who gave them reality, and made them live for ever? Are they not greater than the men and women they sing of? 'Hector that sweet knight is dead,' and Lucian tells us how in the dim underworld Menippus saw the bleaching skull of Helen, and marvelled that it was for so grim a favour that all those horned ships were launched, those beautiful mailed men laid low, those towered cities brought to dust. Yet every day the swan-like daughter of Leda comes out on the battlements, and looks down at the tide of war. The greybeards wonder at her loveliness, and she stands by the side of the king. In his chamber of stained ivory lies her leman. He is polishing his dainty armour, and combing the scarlet plume. With squire and page, her husband passes from tent to tent. She can see his bright hair, and hears, or fancies that she hears, that clear cold voice. In the courtyard below, the son of Priam is buckling on his brazen cuirass. The white arms of Andromache are around his neck. He sets his helmet on the ground, lest their babe should be frightened. Behind the embroidered curtains of his pavilion sits Achilles, in perfumed raiment, while in harness of gilt and silver the friend of his soul arrays himself to go forth to the fight. From a curiously carven chest that his mother Thetis had brought to his ship-side, the Lord of the Myrmidons takes out that mystic chalice that the lip of man had never touched, and cleanses it with brimstone, and with fresh water cools it, and, having washed his hands, fills with black wine its burnished hollow, and spills the thick grape-blood upon the ground in honour of Him whom at Dodona barefooted prophets worshipped, and prays to Him, and knows not that he prays in vain, and that by the hands of two knights from Troy, Panthous' son, Euphorbus, whose love-locks were looped with gold, and the Priamid, the lion-hearted, Patroklus, the comrade of comrades, must meet his doom. Phantoms, are they? Heroes of mist and mountain? Shadows in a song? No; they are real. Action! What is action? It dies at the moment of its energy. It is a base concession to fact. The world is made by the singer for the dreamer.

ERNEST: While you talk it seems to me to be so.

GILBERT: It is so in truth. On the mouldering citadel of Troy lies the lizard like a thing of green bronze. The owl has built her nest in the palace of Priam. Over the empty plain wander shepherd and goatherd with their flocks, and where, on the wine-surfaced, oily sea, οἶνοψ πόντος[1] as Homer calls it, copper-prowed and streaked with vermilion, the great galleys of the Danaoi came in their gleaming crescent, the lonely tunny-fisher sits in his little boat and watches the bobbing corks of his net. Yet every morning the doors of the city are thrown open, and on foot, or in horse-drawn chariot, the warriors go forth to battle, and mock their enemies from behind their iron masks. All day long the fight rages, and when night comes the torches gleam by the tents, and the cresset burns in the hall. Those who live in marble or on painted panel, know of life but a single exquisite instant, eternal indeed in its beauty, but limited to one note of passion or one mood of calm. Those whom the poet makes live have their myriad emotions of joy and terror, of courage and despair, of pleasure and of suffering. The seasons come and go in glad or saddening pageant, and with winged or leaden feet the years pass by before them. They have their youth and their manhood, they are children, and they grow old. It is always dawn for St. Helena, as Veronese saw her at the window. Through the still morning air the angels bring her the symbol of God's pain. The cool breezes of the morning lift the gilt threads from her brow. On that little hill by the city of Florence, where the lovers of Giorgione are lying, it is always the solstice of noon, of noon made so languorous by summer suns that hardly can the slim naked girl dip into the marble tank the round bubble of clear glass, and the long fingers of the lute-player rest idly upon the chords. It is twilight always for the dancing nymphs whom Corot set free among the silver poplars of France. In eternal twilight they move, those frail diaphanous figures, whose tremulous white feet seem not to touch the dew-

---

[1] Wine-dark sea.

drenched grass they tread on. But those who walk in epos, drama, or romance, see through the labouring months the young moons wax and wane, and watch the night from evening unto morning star, and from sunrise unto sunsetting can note the shifting day with all its gold and shadow. For them, as for us, the flowers bloom and wither, and the Earth, that Green-tressed Goddess as Coleridge calls her, alters her raiment for their pleasure. The statue is concentrated to one moment of perfection. The image stained upon the canvas possesses no spiritual element of growth or change. If they know nothing of death, it is because they know little of life, for the secrets of life and death belong to those, and those only, whom the sequence of time affects, and who possess not merely the present but the future, and can rise or fall from a past of glory or of shame. Movement, that problem of the visible arts, can be truly realised by Literature alone. It is Literature that shows us the body in its swiftness and the soul in its unrest.

ERNEST: Yes; I see now what you mean. But, surely, the higher you place the creative artist, the lower must the critic rank.

GILBERT: Why so?

ERNEST: Because the best that he can give us will be but an echo of rich music, a dim shadow of clear-outlined form. It may, indeed, be that life is chaos, as you tell me that it is; that its martyrdoms are mean and its heroisms ignoble; and that it is the function of Literature to create, from the rough material of actual existence, a new world that will be more marvellous, more enduring, and more true than the world that common eyes look upon, and through which common natures seek to realise their perfection. But surely, if this new world has been made by the spirit and touch of a great artist, it will be a thing so complete and perfect that there will be nothing left for the critic to do. I quite understand now, and indeed admit most readily, that it is far more difficult to talk about a thing than to do it. But it seems to me that this sound and sensible maxim, which is really extremely soothing to one's feelings, and should be adopted as its motto by every Academy of Literature all over the world, applies only to the relations that exist between Art and Life, and not to any relations that there may be between Art and Criticism.

GILBERT: But, surely, Criticism is itself an art. And just as artistic creation implies the working of the critical faculty, and, indeed, without it cannot be said to exist at all, so Criticism is really creative in the highest sense of the word. Criticism is, in fact, both creative and independent.

ERNEST: Independent?

GILBERT: Yes; independent. Criticism is no more to be judged by any low standard of imitation or resemblance than is the work of poet or sculptor. The critic occupies the same relation to the work of art that he criticises as the artist does to the visible world of form and colour, or the unseen world of passion and of thought. He does not even require for the perfection of his art the finest materials. Anything will serve his purpose. And just as out of the sordid and sentimental amours of the silly wife of a small country doctor in the squalid village of Yonville-l'Abbaye, near Rouen, Gustave Flaubert was able to create a classic, and make a masterpiece of style, so, from subjects of little or of no importance, such as the pictures in this year's Royal Academy, or in any year's Royal Academy for that matter, Mr. Lewis Morris's poems, M. Ohnet's novels, or the plays of Mr. Henry Arthur Jones, the true critic can, if it be his pleasure so to direct or waste his faculty of contemplation, produce work that will be flawless in beauty and instinct with intellectual subtlety. Why not? Dullness is always an irresistible temptation for brilliancy, and stupidity is the permanent *Bestia Trionfans*[1] that calls wisdom from its cave. To an artist so creative as the critic, what does subject-matter signify? No more and no less than it does to the novelist and the painter. Like them, he can find his motives everywhere. Treatment is the test. There is nothing that has not in it suggestion or challenge.

ERNEST: But is Criticism really a creative art?

GILBERT: Why should it not be? It works with materials, and puts them into a form that is at once new and delightful. What more can one say of poetry? Indeed, I would call criticism a creation within a creation. For just as the great artists, from Homer and Æschylus, down to Shakespeare and Keats, did not go directly to life for their subject-matter, but sought for it in myth, and legend, and ancient tale, so the critic deals with materials that others have, as it were purified for him, and to which imaginative form and colour have been already added. Nay, more, I would say that the highest Criticism, being the purest form of personal impression, is in its way more creative than creation, as it has least reference to any standard external to itself, and is, in fact, its own reason for existing, and, as the Greeks would put it, in itself, and to itself, an end. Certainly, it is never trammelled by any shackles of verisimilitude. No ignoble considerations of probability, that cowardly concession to the tedious repetitions of domestic or public life, effect it ever. One may appeal from fiction unto fact. But from the soul there is no appeal.

ERNEST: From the soul?

GILBERT: Yes, from the soul. That is what the highest criticism really is, the record of one's own soul. It is more fascinating than history, as it is concerned simply with oneself. It is more delightful than philosophy, as its subject is concrete and not abstract, real and not vague. It is the only civilised form of autobiography, as it deals not with the events, but with the thoughts of one's life; not with life's physical accidents of deed or circumstance, but with the spiritual moods and imaginative passions of the mind. I am always amused by the silly vanity of those writers and artists of our day who seem to imagine that the primary function of the critic is to chatter about their second-rate work. The best that one can say of most modern creative art is that it is just a little less vulgar than reality, and so the critic, with his fine sense of distinction and sure instinct of delicate refinement, will prefer to look into the silver mirror or through the woven veil, and will turn his eyes away from the chaos and clamour of actual existence, though the mirror be tarnished and the veil be torn. His sole aim is to chronicle his own impressions. It is for him that pictures are painted, books written, and marble hewn into form.

---

[1] Triumphant beast.

ERNEST: I seem to have heard another theory of Criticism.

GILBERT: Yes; it has been said by one whose gracious memory we all revere, and the music of whose pipe once lured Proserpina from her Sicilian fields, and made those white feet stir, and not in vain, the Cumnor cowslips, that the proper aim of Criticism is to see the object as in itself it really is. But this is a very serious error, and takes no cognizance of Criticism's most perfect form, which is in its essence purely subjective, and seeks to reveal its own secret and not the secret of another. For the highest Criticism deals with art not as expressive but as impressive purely.

ERNEST: But is that really so?

GILBERT: Of course it is. Who cares whether Mr. Ruskin's views on Turner are sound or not? What does it matter? That mighty and majestic prose of his, so fervid and so fiery-coloured in its noble eloquence, so rich in its elaborate symphonic music, so sure and certain, at its best, in subtle choice of word and epithet, is at least as great a work of art as any of those wonderful sunsets that bleach or rot on their corrupted canvases in England's Gallery; greater indeed, one is apt to think at times, not merely because its equal beauty is more enduring, but on account of the fuller variety of its appeal, soul speaking to soul in those long-cadenced lines, not through form and colour alone, though through these, indeed, completely and without loss, but with intellectual and emotional utterance, with lofty passion and with loftier thought, with imaginative insight, and with poetic aim; greater, I always think, even as Literature is the greater art. Who, again, cares whether Mr. Pater has put into the portrait of Mona Lisa something that Leonardo never dreamed of? The painter may have been merely the slave of an archaic smile, as some have fancied, but whenever I pass into the cool galleries of the Palace of the Louvre, and stand before that strange figure 'set in its marble chair in that cirque of fantastic rocks, as in some faint light under sea,' I murmur to myself, 'She is older than the rocks among which she sits; like the vampire, she has been dead many times, and learned the secrets of the grave; and has been a diver in deep seas, and keeps their fallen day about her: and trafficked for strange webs with Eastern merchants; and, as Leda, was the mother of Helen of Troy, and, as St. Anne, the mother of Mary; and all this has been to her but as the sound of lyres and flutes, and lives only in the delicacy with which it has moulded the changing lineaments, and tinged the eyelids and the hands.' And I say to my friend, 'The presence that thus so strangely rose beside the waters is expressive of what in the ways of a thousand years man had come to desire;' and he answers me, 'Hers is the head upon which all "the ends of the world are come, " and the eyelids are a little weary.'

And so the picture becomes more wonderful to us than it really is, and reveals to us a secret of which, in truth, it knows nothing, and the music of the mystical prose is as sweet in our ears as was that flute-player's music that lent to the lips of La Gioconda those subtle and poisonous curves. Do you ask me what Leonardo would have said had any one told him of this picture that 'all the thoughts and experience of the world had etched and moulded therein that which they had of power to refine and make expressive the outward form, the animalism of Greece, the lust of Rome, the reverie of the Middle Age with its spiritual ambition and imaginative loves, the return of the Pagan world, the sins of the Borgias?' He would probably have answered that he had contemplated none of these things, but had concerned himself simply with certain arrangements of lines and masses, and with new and curious colour-harmonies of blue and green. And it is for this very reason that the criticism which I have quoted is criticism of the highest kind. It treats the work of art simply as a starting-point for a new creation. It does not confine itself – let us at least suppose so for the moment – to discovering the real intention of the artist and accepting that as final. And in this it is right, for the meaning of any beautiful created thing is, at least, as much in the soul of him who looks at it as it was in his soul who wrought it. Nay, it is rather the beholder who lends to the beautiful thing its myriad meanings, and makes it marvellous for us, and sets it in some new relation to the age, so that it becomes a vital portion of our lives, and a symbol of what we pray for, or perhaps of what, having prayed for, we fear that we may receive. The longer I study, Ernest, the more clearly I see that the beauty of the visible arts is, as the beauty of music, impressive primarily, and that it may be marred, and indeed often is so, by any excess of intellectual intention on the part of the artist. For when the work is finished it has, as it were, an independent life of its own, and may deliver a message far other than that which was put into its lips to say. Sometimes, when I listen to the overture to *Tannhäuser*, I seem indeed to see that comely knight treading delicately on the flower-strewn grass, and to hear the voice of Venus calling to him from the caverned hill. But at other times it speaks to me of a thousand different things, of myself, it may be, and my own life, or of the lives of others whom one has loved and grown weary of loving, or of the passions that man has known, or of the passions that man has not known, and so has sought for. To-night it may fill one with that ἔρως τῶν ἀδυνάτων,[1] that *Amour de l'Impossible*, which falls like a madness on many who think they live securely and out of reach of harm, so that they sicken suddenly with the poison of unlimited desire, and, in the infinite pursuit of what they may not obtain, grow faint and swoon or stumble. To-morrow, like the music of which Aristotle and Plato tell us, the noble Dorian music of the Greek, it may perform the office of a physician, and give us an anodyne against pain, and heal the spirit that is wounded, and 'bring the soul into harmony with all right things.' And what is true about music is true about all the arts. Beauty has as many meanings as man has moods. Beauty is the symbol of symbols. Beauty reveals everything, because it expresses nothing. When it shows us itself, it shows us the whole fiery-coloured world.

ERNEST: But is such work as you have talked about really criticism?

GILBERT: It is the highest Criticism, for it criticises not merely the individual work of art, but Beauty itself, and fills with wonder a form which the artist may have left void, or not understood, or understood incompletely.

---

[1] Love of the impossible.

ERNEST: The highest Criticism, then, is more creative than creation, and the primary aim of the critic is to see the object as in itself it really is not; that is your theory, I believe?

GILBERT: Yes, that is my theory. To the critic the work of art is simply a suggestion for a new work of his own, that need not necessarily bear any obvious resemblance to the thing it criticises. The one characteristic of a beautiful form is that one can put into it whatever one wishes, and see in it whatever one chooses to see; and the Beauty, that gives to creation its universal and aesthetic element, makes the critic creator in his turn, and whispers of a thousand different things which were not present in the mind of him who carved the statue or painted the panel or graved the gem.

It is sometimes said by those who understand neither the nature of the highest Criticism nor the charm of the highest Art, that the pictures that the critic loves most to write about are those that belong to the anecdotage of painting, and that deal with scenes taken out of literature or history. But this is not so. Indeed, pictures of this kind are far too intelligible. As a class they rank with illustrations, and even considered from this point of view are failures, as they do not stir the imagination, but set definite bounds to it. For the domain of the painter is, as I suggested before, widely different from that of the poet. To the latter belongs life in its full and absolutely entirety; not merely the beauty that men look at, but the beauty that men listen to also; not merely the momentary grace of form or the transient gladness of colour, but the whole sphere of feeling, the perfect cycle of thought. The painter is so far limited that it is only through the mask of the body that he can show us the mystery of the soul; only through conventional images that he can handle ideas; only through its physical equivalents that he can deal with psychology. And how inadequately does he do it then, asking us to accept the torn turban of the Moor for the noble rage of Othello, or a dotard in a storm for the wild madness of Lear! Yet it seems as if nothing could stop him. Most of our elderly English painters spend their wicked and wasted lives in preaching upon the domain of the poets, marring their motives by clumsy treatment, and striving to render, by visible form or colour, the marvel of what is invisible, the splendour of what is not seen. Their pictures are, as a natural consequence, insufferably tedious. They have degraded the invisible arts into the obvious arts, and the one thing not worth looking at is the obvious. I do not say that poet and painter may not treat of the same subject. They have always done so, and will always do so. But while the poet can be pictorial or not, as he chooses, the painter must be pictorial always. For a painter is limited, not to what he sees in nature, but to what upon canvas may be seen.

And so, my dear Ernest, pictures of this kind will not really fascinate the critic. He will turn from them to such works as made him brood and dream and fancy to works that possess the subtle quality of suggestion, and seem to tell one that even from them there is an escape into a wider world. It is sometimes said that the tragedy of an artist's life is that he cannot realise his ideal. But the true tragedy that dogs the steps of most artists is that they realise their ideal too absolutely. For, when the ideal is realised, it is robbed of its wonder and its mystery, and becomes simply a new starting-point for an ideal that is other than itself. This is the reason why music is the perfect type of art. Music can never reveal its ultimate secret. This, also, is the explanation of the value of limitations in art. The sculptor gladly surrenders imitative colour, and the painter the actual dimensions of form, because by such renunciations they are able to avoid too definite a presentation of the Real, which would be mere imitation, and too definite a realisation of the Ideal, which would be too purely intellectual. It is through its very incompleteness that Art becomes complete in beauty, and so addresses itself, not to the faculty of recognition nor to the faculty of reason, but to the aesthetic sense alone, which while accepting both reason and recognition as stages of apprehension, subordinates them both to a pure synthetic impression of the work of art as a whole, and, taking whatever alien emotional elements the work may possess, uses their very complexity as a means by which a richer unity may be added to the ultimate impression itself. You see, then, how it is that the aesthetic critic rejects these obvious modes of art that have but one message to deliver, and having delivered it become dumb and sterile, and seeks rather for such modes as suggest reverie and mood, and by their imaginative beauty make all interpretations true, and no interpretation final. Some resemblance, no doubt, the creative work of the critic will have to the work that has stirred him to creation, but it will be such resemblance as exists, not between Nature and the mirror that the painter of landscape or figure may be supposed to hold up to her, but between Nature and the work of the decorative artist. Just as on the flowerless carpets of Persia, tulip and rose blossom indeed and are lovely to look on, though they are not reproduced in visible shape or line; just as the pearl and purple of the seashell is echoed in the church of St. Mark at Venice; just as the vaulted ceiling of the wondrous chapel at Ravenna is made gorgeous by the gold and green and sapphire of the peacock's tail, though the birds of Juno fly not across it; so the critic reproduces the work that he criticises in a mode that is never imitative, and part of whose charm may really consist in the rejection of resemblance, and shows us in this way not merely the meaning but also the mystery of Beauty and, by transforming each art into literature, solves once for all the problem of Art's unity.

But I see it is time for supper. After we have discussed some Chambertin and a few ortolans, we will pass on to the question of the critic considered in the light of the interpreter.

ERNEST: Ah! You admit, then, that the critic may occasionally be allowed to see the object as in itself it really is.

GILBERT: I am not quite sure. Perhaps I may admit it after supper. There is a subtle influence in supper.

Part Two

With some remarks upon the importance of discussing everything

ERNEST: The ortolans were delightful, and the Chambertin perfect, and now let us return to the point at issue.

GILBERT: Ah! Don't let us do that. Conversation should touch everything, but should concentrate itself on nothing. Let us talk about *Moral Indignation, its Cause and Cure*, a subject on which I think of writing: or about *The Survival of Thersites*, as shown by the English comic papers; or about any topic that may turn up.

ERNEST: No; I want to discuss the critic and criticism. You have told me that the highest criticism deals with art, not as expressive, but as impressive purely, and is consequently both creative and independent, is in fact an art by itself, occupying the same relation to creative work that creative work does to the visible world of form and colour, or the unseen world of passion and of thought. Well, now, tell me, will not the critic be sometimes a real interpreter?

GILBERT: Yes; the critic will be an interpreter, if he chooses. He can pass from his synthetic impression of the work of art as a whole, to an analysis or exposition of the work itself, and in this lower sphere, as I hold it to be, there are many delightful things to be said and done. Yet his object will not always be to explain the work of art. He may seek rather to deepen its mystery, to raise round it, and round its maker, that mist of wonder which is dear to both gods and worshippers alike. Ordinary people are 'terribly at ease in Zion.' They propose to walk arm in arm with the poets, and have a glib ignorant way of saying, 'Why should we read what is written about Shakespeare and Milton? We can read the plays and the poems. That is enough.' But an appreciation of Milton is, as the late Rector of Lincoln remarked once, the reward of consummate scholarship. And he who desires to understand Shakespeare truly must understand the relations in which Shakespeare stood to the Renaissance and the Reformation, to the age of Elizabeth and the age of James; he must be familiar with the history of the struggle for supremacy between the old classical forms and the new spirit of romance, between the school of Sidney, and Daniel, and Johnson, and the school of Marlowe and Marlowe's greater son; he must know the materials that were at Shakespeare's disposal, and the method in which he used them, and the conditions of theatric presentation in the sixteenth and seventeenth century, their limitations and their opportunities for freedom, and the literary criticism of Shakespeare's day, its aims and modes and canons; he must study the English language in its progress, and blank or rhymed verse in its various developments; he must study the Greek drama, and the connection between the art of the creator of the Agamemnon and the art of the creator of Macbeth; in a word, he must be able to bind Elizabethan London to the Athens of Pericles, and to learn Shakespeare's true position in the history of European drama and the drama of the world. The critic will certainly be an interpreter, but he will not treat Art as a riddling Sphinx, whose shallow secret may be guessed and revealed by one whose feet are wounded and who knows not his name. Rather, he will look upon Art as a goddess whose mystery it is his province to intensify, and whose majesty his privilege to make more marvellous in the eyes of men.

And here, Ernest, this strange thing happens. The critic will indeed be an interpreter, but he will not be an interpreter in the sense of one who simply repeats in another form a message that has been put into his lips to say. For, just as it is only by contact with the art of foreign nations that the art of a country gains that individual and separate life that we call nationality, so, by curious inversion, it is only by intensifying his own personality that the critic can interpret the personality and work of others, and the more strongly this personality enters into the interpretation, the more real the interpretation becomes, the more satisfying, the more convincing, and the more true.

ERNEST: I would have said that personality would have been a disturbing element.

GILBERT: No; it is an element of revelation. If you wish to understand others you must intensify your own individualism.

ERNEST: What, then, is the result?

GILBERT: I will tell you, and perhaps I can tell you best by definite example. It seems to me that, while the literary critic stands of course first, as having the wider range, and larger vision, and nobler material, each of the arts has a critic, as it were, assigned to it. The actor is a critic of the drama. He shows the poet's work under new conditions, and by a method special to himself. He takes the written word, and action, gesture and voice become the media of revelation. The singer or the player on lute and viol is the critic of music. The etcher of a picture robs the painting of its fair colours, but shows us by the use of a new material its true colour-quality, its tones and values, and the relations of its masses, and so is, in his way, a critic of it, for the critic is he who exhibits to us a work of art in a form different from that of the work itself, and the employment of a new material is a critical as well as a creative element. Sculpture, too, has its critic, who may be either the carver of a gem, as he was in Greek days, or some painter like Mantegna, who sought to reproduce on canvas the beauty of plastic line and the symphonic dignity of processional bas-relief. And in the case of all these creative critics of art it is evident that personality is an absolute essential for any real interpretation. When Rubinstein plays to us the *Sonata Appassionata* of Beethoven he gives us not merely Beethoven, but also himself, and so gives us Beethoven absolutely – Beethoven reinterpreted through a rich artistic nature, and made vivid and wonderful to us by a new and intense personality. When a great actor plays Shakespeare we have the same experience. His own individuality becomes a vital part of the interpretation. People sometimes say that actors give us their own Hamlets, and not Shakespeare's; and this fallacy – for it is a fallacy – is, I regret to say, repeated by that charming and graceful writer who has lately deserted the turmoil of literature for the peace of the House of Commons; I mean the author of *Obiter Dicta*. In point of fact, there is no such thing as Shakespeare's Hamlet. If Hamlet has something of the definiteness of a work of art, he has also all the obscurity that belongs to life. There are as many Hamlets as there are melancholies.

ERNEST: As many Hamlets as there are melancholies?

GILBERT: Yes; and as art springs from personality, so it is only to personality that it can be revealed, and from the meeting of the two comes right interpretative criticism.

ERNEST: The critic, then, considered as the interpreter, will give no less than he receives, and lend as much as he borrows?

GILBERT: He will be always showing us the work of art in some new relation to our age. He will always be reminding us that great works of art are living things – are, in fact, the only things that live. So much, indeed, will he feel this, that I am certain that, as civilisation progresses and we become more highly organised, the elect spirits of each age, the critical and cultured spirits, will grow less and less interested in actual life, and *will seek to gain their impressions almost entirely from what Art has touched*. For life is terribly deficient in form. Its catastrophes happen in the wrong way and to the wrong people. There is a grotesque horror about its comedies, and its tragedies seem to culminate in farce. One is always wounded when one approaches it. Things last either too long or not long enough.

ERNEST: Poor life! Poor human life! Are you not even touched by the tears that the Roman poet tells us are part of its essence.

GILBERT: Too quickly touched by them, I fear. For when one looks back upon the life that was so vivid in its emotional intensity, and filled with such fervent moments of ecstasy or of joy, it all seems to be a dream and an illusion. What are the unreal things, but the passions that once burned one like fire? What are the incredible things, but the things that one has faithfully believed? What are the improbable things? The things that one has done oneself. No, Ernest; life cheats us with shadows, like a puppet-master. We ask it for pleasure. It gives it to us, with bitterness and disappointment in its train. We come across some noble grief that we think will lend the purple dignity of tragedy to our days, but it passes away from us, and things less noble take its place, and on some grey windy dawn, or odorous eve of silence and of silver, we find ourselves looking with callous wonder, or dull heart of stone, at the tress of gold-flecked hair that we had once so wildly worshipped and so madly kissed.

ERNEST: Life then is a failure?

GILBERT: From the artistic point of view, certainly. And the chief things that makes life a failure from this artistic point of view is the thing that lends to life its sordid security, the fact that one can never repeat exactly the same emotion. How different it is in the world of Art! On a shelf of the bookcase behind you stands the *Divine Comedy*, and I know that, if I open it at a certain place, I shall be filled with a fierce hatred of some one who has never wronged me, or stirred by a great love for some one whom I shall never see. There is no mood of passion that Art cannot give us, and those of us who have discovered her secret can settle beforehand what our experiences are going to be. We can choose our day and select our hour. We can say to ourselves, 'Tomorrow, at dawn, we shall walk with grave Virgil through the valley of the shadow of death,' and lo! The dawn finds us in the obscure wood, and the Mantuan stands by our side. We pass though the gate of the legend fatal to hope, and with pity or with joy behold the horror of another world. The hypocrites go by, with their painted faces and their cowls of gilded lead. Out of the ceaseless winds that drive them, the carnal look at us, and we watch the heretic rending his flesh, and the glutton lashed by the rain. We break the withered branches from the tree in the grove of the Harpies, and each dull-hued poisonous twig bleeds with red blood before us, and cries aloud with bitter cries. Out of a horn of fire Odysseus speaks to us, and when from his sepulcher of flame the great Ghibelline rises, the pride that triumphs over the torture of that bed becomes ours for a moment. Through the dim purple air fly those who have stained the world with the beauty of their sin, and in the pit of loathsome disease, dropsy-stricken and swollen of body into the semblance of a monstrous lute, lies Adamo di Brescia, the coiner of false coin. He bids us listen to his misery; we stop and with dry and gaping lips he tells us how he dreams day and night of the brooks of clear water that in cool dewy channels gush down the green Casentine hills. Sinon, the false Greek of Troy, mocks at him. He smites him in the face, and they wrangle. We are fascinated by their shame, and loiter, till Virgil chides us and leads us away to that city turreted by giants where great Nimrod blows his horn. Terrible things are in store for us, and we go to meet them in Dante's raiment and with Dante's heart. We traverse the marches of the Styx, and Argenti swims to the boat through the slimy waves. He calls to us, and we reject him. When we hear the voice of his agony we are glad, and Virgil praises us for the bitterness of our scorn. We tread upon the cold crystal of Cocytus, in which traitors stick like straws in glass. Our foot strikes against the head of Bocca. He will not tell us his name, and we tear the hair in handfuls from the screaming skull. Alberigo prays us to break the ice upon his face that he may weep a little. We pledge our word to him, and when he has uttered his dolorous tale we deny the word that we have spoken, and pass from him; such cruelty being courtesy, indeed, for who more base than he who was mercy for the condemned of God? In the jaws of Lucifer we see the man who sold Christ, and in the jaws of Lucifer the men who slew Cæsar. We tremble, and come forth to re-behold the stars.

In the land of Purgation the air is freer, and the holy mountain rises into the pure light of day. There is peace for us, and for those who for a season abide in it there is some peace also, though, pale from the poison of the Maremma, Madonna Pia passes before us, and Ismene, with the sorrow of earth still lingering about her, is there. Soul after soul makes us share in some repentance or some joy. He whom the mourning of his widow taught to drink the sweet wormwood of pain, tells us of Nella praying in her lonely bed, and we learn from the mouth of Buonconte how a single tear may save a dying sinner from the fiend. Sordello, that noble and disdainful Lombard, eyes us from afar like a couchant lion. When he learns that Virgil is one of Mantua's citizens, he falls upon his neck, and when he learns that he is the singer of Rome he falls before his feet. In that valley whose grass and flowers are fairer than cleft emerald and Indian wood, and brighter than scarlet and silver, they are singing who in the world were kings; but the lips of Rudolph of Hapsburg do not move to the music of the others, and Philip of France beats his breast and Henry of England sits alone. On and on we go, climbing the marvellous stair, and the stars become larger than their wont, and the song of the kings grows faint, and at length we reach the seven trees of gold and the garden of the Earthly Paradise. In a griffin-drawn chariot appears one whose brows are bound with olive, who is veiled in white, and mantled in green, and robed in a vesture that is coloured like live fire. The ancient flame wakes within us. Our blood quickens through terrible pulses. We recognise her. It is Beatrice, the woman we have worshipped. The ice congealed about our heart melts. Wild tears of anguish break from us, and we bow our forehead to the ground, for we know that we have sinned. When we have done penance, and are purified, and have drunk of the fountain of Lethe and bathed in the fountain of Eunoe, the mistress of our soul raises us to the Paradise of Heaven. Out of that eternal pearl, the moon, the face of Piccarda Donati leans to us. Her beauty troubles us for a moment, and when, like a thing that falls through water, she passes away, we gaze after her with wistful eyes. The sweet planet of Venus is full of lovers. Cunizza, the sister of Ezzelin, the lady of Sordello's heart, is there, and Folco, the passionate singer of Provence, who in sorrow for Azalais forsook the world, and the Canaanitish harlot whose soul was the first that Christ redeemed. Joachim of Flora stands in the sun, and, in the sun, Aquinas recounts the story of St. Francis and Bonaventure the story of St. Dominic. Through the burning rubies of Mars, Cacciaguida approaches. He tells us of the arrow that is shot from the bow of exile, and how salt tastes the bread of another, and how steep are the stairs in the house of a stranger. In Saturn the soul sings not, and even she who guides us dare not smile. On a ladder of gold the flames rise and fall. At last we see the pageant of the Mystical Rose. Beatrice fixes her eyes upon the face of God to turn them not again. The beatific vision is granted to us; we know the Love that moves the sun and all the stars.

Yes, we can put the earth back six hundred courses and make ourselves one with the great Florentine, kneel at the same altar with him, and share his rapture and his scorn. And if we grow tired of an antique time, and desire to realise our own age in all its weariness and sin, are there not books that can make us live more in one single hour than life can make us live in a score of shameful years? Close to your hand lies a little volume, bound in some Nile-green skin that has been powdered with gilded nenuphars, and smoothed with hard ivory. It is the book that Gautier loved, it is Baudelaire's masterpiece. Open it at the sad madrigal that begins:

> Que m'importe que tu sois sage?
> Sois belle! et sois triste![1]

and you will find yourself worshipping sorrow as you have never worshipped joy. Pass on to the poem on the man who tortures himself, let its subtle music steal into your brain and colour your thoughts, and you will become for a moment what he was who wrote it; nay, not for a moment only, but for many

---

[1] What do I care that you are wise! Be beautiful and be melancholy.

barren moonlit nights and sunless sterile days will a despair that is not your own make its dwelling within you, and the misery of another gnaw your heart away. Read the whole book, suffer it to tell even one of its secrets to your soul, and your soul will grow eager to know more, and will feed upon poisonous honey, and seek to repent of strange crimes of which it is guiltless, and to make atonement for terrible pleasures that it has never known. And then, when you are tired of these flowers of evil, turn to the flowers that grow in the garden of Perdita, and in their dew-drenched chalices cool your fevered brow, and let their loveliness heal and restore your soul; or wake from his forgotten tomb the sweet Syrian, Meleager, and bid the lover of Heliodore make you music, for he too has flowers in his song, red pomegranate blossoms, and irises that smell of myrrh, ringed daffodils and dark-blue hyacinths, and marjoram and crinkled ox-eyes. Dear to him was the perfume of the bean-field at evening, and dear to him the odorous eared-spikenard that grew on the Syrian hills, and the fresh green thyme, the wine-cup's charm. The feet of his love as she walked in the garden were like lilies set upon lilies. Softer than sleep-laden poppy petals were her lips, softer than violets and as scented. The flame-like crocus sprang from the grass to look at her. For her the slim narcissus stored the cool rain; and for her the anemones forgot the Sicilian winds that wooed them. And neither crocus, nor anemone, nor narcissus was as fair as she was.

It is a strange thing, this transference of emotion. We sicken with the same maladies as the poets, and the singer lends us his pain. Dead lips have their message for us, and hearts that have fallen to dust can communicate their joy. We run to kiss the bleeding mouth of Fantine, and we follow Manon Lescaut over the whole world. Ours is the love-madness of the Tyrian, and the terror of Orestes is ours also. There is no passion that we cannot feel, no pleasure that we may not gratify, and we can choose the time of our initiation and the time of our freedom also. Life! Life! Don't let us go to life for our fulfilment or our experience. It is a thing narrowed by circumstances, incoherent in its utterance, and without that fine correspondence of form and spirit which is the only thing that can satisfy the artistic and critical temperament. It makes us pay too high a price for its wares, and we purchase the meanest of its secrets at a cost that is monstrous and infinite.

ERNEST: Must we go, then, to Art for everything?

GILBERT: For everything. Because Art does not hurt us. The tears that we shed at a play are a type of the exquisite sterile emotions that it is the function of Art to awaken. We weep, but we are not wounded. We grieve, but our grief is not bitter. In the actual life of man, sorrow, as Spinoza says somewhere, is a passage to a lesser perfection. But the sorrow with which Art fills us both purifies and initiates, if I may quote once more from the great art critic of the Greeks. It is through Art, and through Art only, that we can realise our perfection; through Art, and through Art only, that we can shield ourselves from the sordid perils of actual existence. This results not merely from the fact that nothing that one can imagine is worth doing, and that one can imagine everything, but from the subtle law that emotional forces, like the forces of the physical sphere, are limited in extent and energy. One can feel so much, and no more. And how can it matter with what pleasure life tries to tempt one, or with what pain it seeks to maim and mar one's soul, if in the spectacle of the lives of those who have never existed one has found the true secret of joy, and wept away one's tears over their deaths who, like Cordelia and the daughter of Brabantio, can never die?

ERNEST: Stop a moment. It seems to me that in everything that you have said there is something radically immoral.

GILBERT: All art is immoral.

ERNEST: All art?

GILBERT: Yes. For emotion for the sake of emotion is the aim of art, and emotion for the sake of action is the aim of life, and of that practical organisation of life that we call society. Society, which is the beginning and basis of morals, exists simply for the concentration of human energy, and in order to ensure its own continuance and healthy stability it demands, and no doubt rightly demands, of each of its citizens that he should contribute some form of productive labour to the common weal, and toil and travail that the day's work may be done. Society often forgives the criminal; it never forgives the dreamer. The beautiful sterile emotions that art excites in us are hateful in its eyes, and so completely are people dominated by the tyranny of this dreadful social ideal that they are always coming shamelessly up to one at Private Views and other places that are open to the general public, and saying in a loud stentorian voice, 'What are you doing?' whereas 'What are you thinking?' is the only question that any single civilised being should ever be allowed to whisper to another. They mean well, no doubt, these honest beaming folk. Perhaps that is the reason why they are so excessively tedious. But some one should teach them that while, in the opinion of society, Contemplation is the gravest sin of which any citizen can be guilty, in the opinion of the highest culture it is the proper occupation of man.

ERNEST: Contemplation?

GILBERT: Contemplation. I said to you some time ago that it was far more difficult to talk about a thing than to do it. Let me say to you now that to do nothing at all is the most difficult thing in the world, the most difficult and the most intellectual. To Plato, with his passion for wisdom, this was the noblest form of energy. To Aristotle, with his passion for knowledge, this was the noblest form of energy also. It was to this that the passion for holiness led the saint and the mystic of mediaeval days.

ERNEST: We exist, then, to do nothing?

GILBERT: It is to do nothing that the elect exist. Action is limited and relative. Unlimited and absolute is the vision of him who sits at ease and watches, who walks in loneliness and dreams. But we who are born at the close of this wonderful age are at once too cultured and too critical, too intellectually subtle and too curious of exquisite pleasures, to accept any speculations about life in exchange for life itself. To us the *città divina*[1] is colourless,

---

[1] Heavenly city.

and the *fruitio Dei*[1] without meaning. Metaphysics do not satisfy our temperaments, and religious ecstasy is out of date. The world through which the Academic philosopher becomes 'the spectator of all time and of all existence' is not really an ideal world, but simply a world of abstract ideas. When we enter it, we starve amidst the chill mathematics of thought. The courts of the city of God are not open to us now. Its gates are guarded by Ignorance, and to pass them we have to surrender all that in our nature is most divine. It is enough that our fathers believed. They have exhausted the faith-faculty of the species. Their legacy to us is the scepticism of which they were afraid. Had they put it into words, it might not live within us as thought. No, Ernest, no. We cannot go back to the saint. There is far more to be learned from the sinner. We cannot go back to the philosopher, and the mystic leads us astray. Who, as Mr. Pater suggests somewhere, would exchange the curve of a single rose-leaf for that formless intangible Being which Plato rates so high? What to us is the Illumination of Philo, the Abyss of Eckhart, the vision of Böhme, the monstrous Heaven itself that was revealed to Swedenborg's blinded eyes? Such things are less than the yellow trumpet of one daffodil of the field, far less than the meanest of the visible arts; for just as Nature is matter struggling into mind, so Art is mind expressing itself under the conditions of matter, and thus, even in the lowliest of her manifestations, she speaks to both sense and soul alike. To the aesthetic temperament the vague is always repellent. The Greeks were a nation of artists, because they were spared the sense of the infinite. Like Aristotle, like Goethe after he had read Kant, we desire the concrete, and nothing but the concrete can satisfy us.

ERNEST: What then do you propose?

GILBERT: It seems to me that with the development of the critical spirit we shall be able to realise, not merely our own lives, but the collective life of the race, and so to make ourselves absolutely modern, in the true meaning of the word modernity. For he to whom the present is the only thing that is present, knows nothing of the age in which he lives. To realise the nineteenth century, one must realise every century that has proceeded it and that has contributed to its making. To know anything about oneself one must know all about others. There must be no mood with which one cannot sympathise, no dead mode of life that one cannot make alive. Is this impossible? I think not. By revealing to us the absolute mechanism of all action, and so freeing us from the self-imposed and trammelling burden of moral responsibility, the scientific principle of Heredity has become, as it were, the warrant for the contemplative life. It has shown us that we are never less free than when we try to act. It has hemmed us round with the nets of the hunter, and written upon the wall the prophecy of our doom. We may not watch it, for it is within us. We may not see it, save in a mirror that mirrors the soul. It is Nemesis without her mask. It is the last of the Fates, and the most terrible. It is the only one of the Gods whose real name we know.

And yet, while in the sphere of practical and external life it has robbed en-

---

[1] Enjoyment of God.

ergy of its freedom and activity of its choice, in the subjective sphere, where the soul is at work, it comes to us, this terrible shadow, with many gifts in its hands, gifts of strange temperaments and subtle susceptibilities, gifts of wild ardours and chill moods of indifference, complex multiform gifts of thoughts that are at variance with each other, and passions that war against themselves. And so it is not our own life that we live, but the lives of the dead, and the soul that dwells within us is no single spiritual entity, making us personal and individual, created for our service, and entering into us for our joy. It is something that has dwelt in fearful places, and in ancient sepulchres has made its abode. It is sick with many maladies, and has memories of curious sins. It is wiser than we are, and its wisdom is bitter. It fills us with impossible desires, and makes us follow what we know we cannot gain. One thing, however, Ernest, it can do for us. It can lead us away from surroundings whose beauty is dimmed to us by the mist of familiarity, or whose ignoble ugliness and sordid claims are marring the perfection of our development. It can help us to leave the age in which we were born, and to pass into other ages, and find ourselves not exiled from their air. It can teach us how to escape from our experience, and realise the experiences of those who are greater than we are. The pain of Leopardi crying out against life becomes our pain. Theocritus blows on his pipe, and we laugh with the lips of nymph and shepherd. In the wolfskin of Pierre Vidal we flee before the hounds, and in the armour of Lancelot we ride from the bower of the Queen. We have whispered the secret of our love beneath the cowl of Abelard, and in the stained raiment of Villon have put our shame into song. We can see the dawn through Shelley's eyes, and when we wander with Endymion the Moon grows amorous of our youth. Ours is the anguish of Atys, and ours the weak rage and noble sorrows of the Dane. Do you think that it is the imagination that enables us to live these countless lives? Yes; it is the imagination; and the imagination is the result of heredity. It is simply concentrated race-experience.

ERNEST: But where in this is the function of the critical spirit?

GILBERT: The culture that this transmission of racial experiences makes possible can be made perfect by the critical spirit alone, and indeed may be said to be one with it. For who is the true critic but he who bears within himself the dreams, and ideas, and feelings of myriad generations, and to whom no form of thought is alien, no emotional impulse obscure? And who the true man of culture, if not he who by fine scholarship and fastidious rejection has made instinct self-conscious and intelligent, and can separate the work that has distinction from the work that has it not, and so by contact and comparison makes himself master of the secrets of style and school, and understands their meanings, and listens to their voices, and develop that spirit of disinterested curiosity which is the real root, as it is the real flower, of the intellectual life, and thus attains to intellectual clarity, and, having learned 'the best that is known and thought in the world,' lives – it is not fanciful to say so – with those who are the Immortals.

Yes, Ernest: the contemplative life, the life that has for its aim not *doing* but *being*, and not *being* merely, but *becoming* – that is what the critical spirit can give us. The gods live thus: either brooding over their own perfection, as Aristotle tells us, or, as Epicurus fancied, watching with the calm eyes of the spectator the tragi-comedy of the world that they have made. We, too, might live like them, and set ourselves to witness with appropriate emotions the varied scenes that man and nature afford. We might make ourselves spiritual by detaching ourselves from action, and become perfect by the rejection of energy. It has often seemed to me that Browning felt something of this. Shakespeare hurls Hamlet into active life, and makes him realise his mission by effort. Browning might have given us a Hamlet who would have realised his mission by thought. Incident and event were to him unreal or unmeaning. He made the soul the protagonist of life's tragedy, and looked on action as the one undramatic element of a play. To us, at any rate, the βίος θεωρητικός[1] is the true ideal. From the high tower of Thought we can look out at the world. Calm, and self-centered, and complete, the aesthetic critic contemplates life, and no arrow drawn at a venture can pierce between the joints of his harness. He at least is safe. He has discovered how to live.

Is such a mode of life immoral? Yes; all the arts are immoral, except those baser forms of sensual or didactic art that seek to excite to action of evil or of good. For action of every kind belongs to the sphere of ethics. The aim of art is simply to create a mood. Is such a mode of life unpractical? Ah! It is not so easy to be unpractical as the ignorant Philistine imagines. It were well for England if it were so. There is no country in the world so much in need of unpractical people as this country of ours. With us, Thought is degraded by its constant association with practice. Who that moves in the stress and turmoil of actual existence, noisy politician, or brawling social reformer, or poor narrow-minded priest blinded by the sufferings of that unimportant section of the community among whom he has cast his lot, can seriously claim to be able to form a disinterested intellectual judgment about any one thing? Each of the professions means a prejudice. The necessity for a career forces every one to take sides. We live in the age of the overworked, and the under-educated; the age in which people are so industrious that they become absolutely stupid. And, harsh though it may sound, I cannot help saying that such people deserve their doom. The sure way of knowing nothing about life is to try to make oneself useful.

ERNEST: A charming doctrine, Gilbert.

GILBERT: I am not sure about that, but it has at least the minor merit of being true. That the desire to do good to others produces a plentiful crop of prigs is the least of the evils of which it is the cause. The prig is a very interesting psychological study, and though of all poses a moral pose is the most offensive, still to have a pose at all is something. It is a formal recognition of the importance of treating life from a definite and reasoned standpoint. That Humanitarian Sympathy wars against Nature, by securing the survival of the failure, may make the man of science loathe its facile virtues. The politi-

---

[1] Life of contemplation.

cal economist may cry out against it for putting the improvident on the same level as the provident, and so robbing life of the strongest, because most sordid, incentive to industry. But in the eyes of the thinker, the real harm that emotional sympathy does is that it limits knowledge, and so prevents us from solving any single social problem. We are trying at present to stave off the coming crisis, the coming revolution, as my friends the Fabianists call it, by means of doles and alms. Well, when the revolution of crisis arrives, we shall be powerless, because we shall know nothing. And so, Ernest, let us not be deceived. England will never be civilised till she has added Utopia to her dominions. There is more than one of her colonies that she might with advantage surrender for so fair a land. What we want are unpractical people who see beyond the moment, and think beyond the day. Those who try to lead the people can only do so by following the mob. It is through the voice of one crying in the wilderness that the ways of the gods must be prepared.

But perhaps you think that in beholding for the mere joy of beholding, and contemplating for the sake of contemplation, there is something that is egotistic. If you think so, do not say so. It takes a thoroughly selfish age, like our own, to deify self-sacrifice. It takes a thoroughly grasping age, such as that in which we live, to set above the fine intellectual virtues, those shallow and emotional virtues that are an immediate practical benefit to itself. They miss their aim, too, these philanthropists and sentimentalists of our day, who are always chattering to one about one's duty to one's neighbour. For the development of the race depends on the development of the individual, and where self-culture has ceased to be the ideal, the intellectual standard is instantly lowered, and, often, ultimately lost. If you meet at dinner a man who has spent his life in educating himself – a rare type in our time, I admit, but still one occasionally to be met with – you rise from table richer, and conscious that a high ideal has for a moment touched and sanctified your days. But oh! My dear Ernest, to sit next to a man who has spent his life in trying to educate others! What a dreadful experience that is! How appalling is that ignorance which is the inevitable result of the fatal habit of imparting opinions! How limited in range the creature's mind proves to be! How it wearies us, and must weary himself, with its endless repetitions and sickly reiteration! How lacking it is in any element of intellectual growth! In what a vicious circle it always moves!

ERNEST: You speak with strange feeling, Gilbert. Have you had this dreadful experience, as you call it, lately?

GILBERT: Few of us escape it. People say that the schoolmaster is abroad. I wish to goodness he were. But the type of which, after all, he is only one, and certainly the least important, of the representatives, seems to me to be really dominating our lives; and just as the philanthropist is the nuisance of the ethical sphere, so the nuisance of the intellectual sphere is the man who is so occupied in trying to educate others, that he has never had any time to educate himself. No, Ernest, self-culture is the true ideal of man. Goethe saw it, and the immediate debt that we owe to Goethe is greater than the debt we owe to any man since Greek days. The Greeks saw it, and have left us, as their legacy to modern thought, the conception of the contemplative life as well as the critical method by which alone can that life be truly realised. It was the one thing that made the Renaissance great, and gave us Humanism. It is the one thing that could make our own age great also; for the real weakness of England lies not in incomplete armaments or unfortified coasts, not in the poverty that creeps through sunless lanes, or the drunkenness that brawls in loathsome courts, but simply in the fact that her ideals are emotional and not intellectual.

I do not deny that the intellectual ideal is difficult of attainment, still less that it is, and perhaps will be for years to come, unpopular with the crowd. It is so easy for people to have sympathy with suffering. It is so difficult for them to have sympathy with thought. Indeed, so little do ordinary people understand what thought really is, that they seem to imagine that, when they have said that a theory is dangerous, they have pronounced its condemnation, whereas it is only such theories that have any true intellectual value. An idea that is not dangerous is unworthy of being called an idea at all.

ERNEST: Gilbert, you bewilder me. You have told me that all art is, in its essence, immoral. Are you going to tell me now that all thought is, in its essence, dangerous?

GILBERT: Yes, in the practical sphere it is so. The security of society lies in custom and unconscious instinct, and the basis of the stability of society, as a healthy organism, is the complete absence of any intelligence amongst its members. The great majority of people being fully aware of this, rank themselves naturally on the side of that splendid system that elevates them to the dignity of machines, and rage so wildly against the intrusion of the intellectual faculty into any question that concerns life, that one is tempted to define man as a rational animal who always loses his temper when he is called upon to act in accordance with the dictates of reason. But let us turn from the practical sphere, and say no more about the wicked philanthropists, who, indeed, may well be left to the mercy of the almond-eyed sage of the Yellow River Chuang Tsu the wise, who has proved that such well-meaning and offensive busybodies have destroyed the simple and spontaneous virtue that there is in man. They are a wearisome topic, and I am anxious to get back to the sphere in which criticism is free.

ERNEST: The sphere of the intellect?

GILBERT: Yes. You remember that I spoke of the critic as being in his own way as creative as the artist, whose work, indeed, may be merely of value in so far as it gives to the critic a suggestion for some new mood of thought and feeling which he can realise with equal, or perhaps greater, distinction of form, and, through the use of a fresh medium of expression, make differently beautiful and more perfect. Well, you seemed to be a little sceptical about the theory. But perhaps I wronged you?

ERNEST: I am not really sceptical about it, but I must admit that I feel very strongly that such work as you describe the critic producing – and creative such work must undoubtedly be admitted to be – is, of necessity, purely subjective, whereas the greatest work is objective always, objective and impersonal.

GILBERT: The difference between objective and subjective work is one of external form merely. It is accidental, not essential. All artistic creation is absolutely subjective. The very landscape that Corot looked at was, as he said himself, but a mood of his own mind; and those great figures of Greek or English drama that seem to us to possess an actual existence of their own, apart from the poets who shaped and fashioned them, are, in their ultimate analysis, simply the poets themselves, not as they thought they were, but as they thought they were not; and by such thinking came in strange manner, though but for a moment, really so to be. For out of ourselves we can never pass, nor can there be in creation what in the creator was not. Nay, I would say that the more objective a creation appears to be, the more subjective it really is. Shakespeare might have met Rosencrantz and Guildenstern in the white streets of London, or seen the serving-men of rival houses bite their thumbs at each other in the open square; but Hamlet came out of his soul, and Romeo out of his passion. They were elements of his nature to which he gave visible form, impulses that stirred so strongly within him that he had, as it were perforce, to suffer them to realise their energy, not on the lower plane of actual life, where they would have been trammelled and constrained and so made imperfect, but on that imaginative plane of art where Love can indeed find in Death its rich fulfilment, where one can stab the eavesdropper behind the arras, and wrestle in a new-made grave, and make a guilty king drink his own hurt, and see one's father's spirit, beneath the glimpses of the moon, stalking in complete steel from misty wall to wall. Action being limited would have left Shakespeare unsatisfied and unexpressed; and just, as it is because he did nothing that he has been able to achieve everything, so it is because he never speaks to us of himself in his plays that his plays reveal him to us absolutely, and show us his true nature and temperament far more completely than do those strange and exquisite sonnets, even, in which he bares to crystal eyes the secret closet of his heart. Yes, the objective form is the most subjective in matter. Man is least himself when he talks in his own person. Give him a mask, and he will tell you the truth.

ERNEST: The critic, then, being limited to the subjective form, will necessarily be less able fully to express himself than the artist, who has always at his disposal the forms that are impersonal and objective.

GILBERT: Not necessarily, and certainly not at all if he recognises that each mode of criticism is, in its highest development, simply a mood, and that we are never more true to ourselves than when we are inconsistent. The æsthetic critic, constant only to the principle of beauty in all things, will ever be looking for fresh impressions, winning from the various schools the secret of their charm, bowing, it may be, before foreign altars, or smiling, if it be his fancy, at strange new gods. What other people call one's past has, no doubt, everything to do with them, but has absolutely nothing to do with oneself. The man who regards his past is a man who deserves to have no future to look forward to. When one has found expression for a mood, one has done with it. You laugh; but believe me it is so. Yesterday it was Realism that charmed one. One gained from it that *nouveau frisson* which it was its aim to produce. One analysed it, and wearied of it. At sunset came the *Luministe* in painting, and the *Symboliste* in poetry, and the spirit of mediaevalism, that spirit which belongs not to time but to temperament, woke suddenly in wounded Russia, and stirred us for a moment by the terrible fascination of pain. To-day the cry is for Romance, and already the leaves are tremulous in the valley, and on the purple hill-tops walks Beauty with slim gilded feet. The old modes of creation linger, of course. The artists reproduce either themselves or each other, with wearisome iteration. But Criticism is always moving on, and the critic is always developing.

Nor, again, is the critic really limited to the subjective form of expression. The method of the drama is his, as well as the method of the epos. He may use dialogue, as he did who set Milton talking to Marvel on the nature of comedy and tragedy, and made Sidney and Lord Brooke discourse on letters beneath the Penshurst oaks; or adopt narration, as Mr. Pater is fond of doing, each of whose Imaginary Portraits – is not that the title of the book? – presents to us, under the fanciful guise of fiction, some fine and exquisite piece of criticism, one on the painter Watteau, another on the philosophy of Spinoza, a third on the Pagan elements of the early Renaissance, and the last, and in some respects the most suggestive, on the source of that Aufklärung, that enlightening which dawned on Germany in the last century, and to which our own culture owes so great a debt. Dialogue, certainly, that wonderful literary form which, from Plato to Lucian, and from Lucian to Giordano Bruno, and from Bruno to that grand old Pagan in whom Carlyle took such delight, the creative critics of the world have always employed, can never lose for the thinker its attraction as a mode of expression. By its means he can both reveal and conceal himself, and give form to every fancy, and reality to every mood. By its means he can exhibit the object from each point of view, and show it to us in the round, as a sculptor shows us things, gaining in this manner all the richness and reality of effect that comes from those side issues that are suddenly suggested by the central idea in its progress, and really illumine the idea more completely, or from those felicitous afterthoughts that give a fuller completeness to the central scheme, and yet convey something of the delicate charm of chance.

ERNEST: By its means, too, he can invent an imaginary antagonist, and convert him when he chooses by some absurdly sophistical argument.

GILBERT: Ah! It is so easy to convert others. It is so difficult to convert oneself. To arrive at what one really believes, one must speak through lips different from one's own. To know the truth one must imagine myriads of falsehoods. For what is Truth? In matters of religion, it is simply the opinion that has survived. In matters of science, it is the ultimate sensation. In matters of art, it is one's last mood. And you see now, Ernest, that the critic has at his disposal as many objective forms of expression as the artist has. Ruskin put his criticism into imaginative prose, and is superb in his changes and contradictions; and Browning put his into blank verse and made painter and poet yield up their secret; and M. Renan uses dialogue, and Mr. Pater fiction, and Rossetti translated into sonnet-music the colour of Giorgione and the design of Ingres, and his own design and colour also, feeling, with the instinct of one who had many modes of utterance, that the ultimate art is literature, and the finest and fullest medium that of words.

ERNEST: Well, now that you have settled that the critic has at his disposal all objective forms, I wish you would tell me what are the qualities that should characterise the true critic.

GILBERT: What would you say they were?

ERNEST: Well, I should say that a critic should above all things be fair.

GILBERT: Ah! Not fair. A critic cannot be fair in the ordinary sense of the word. It is only about things that do not interest one that one can give a really unbiased opinion, which is no doubt the reason why an unbiassed opinion is always absolutely valueless. The man who sees both sides of a question is a man who sees absolutely nothing at all. Art is a passion, and, in matters of art, Thought is inevitably coloured by emotion, and so is fluid rather than fixed, and, depending upon fine moods and exquisite moments, cannot be narrowed into the rigidity of a scientific formula or a theological dogma. It is to the soul that Art speaks, and the soul may be made the prisoner of the mind as well as of the body. One should, of course, have no prejudices; but, as a great Frenchman remarked a hundred years ago, it is one's business in such matters to have preferences, and when one has preferences one ceases to be fair. It is only an auctioneer who can equally and impartially admire all schools of Art. No; fairness is not one of the qualities of the true critic. It is not even a condition of criticism. Each form of Art with which we come in contact dominates us for the moment to the exclusion of every other form. We must surrender ourselves absolutely to the work in question, whatever it may be, if we wish to gain its secret. For the time, we must think of nothing else, can think of nothing else, indeed.

ERNEST: The true critic will be rational, at any rate, will he not?

GILBERT: Rational? There are two ways of disliking art, Ernest. One is to dislike it. The other, to like it rationally. For Art, as Plato saw, and not without regret, creates in listener and spectator a form of divine madness. It does not spring from inspiration, but it makes others inspired. Reason is not the faculty to which it appeals. If one loves Art at all, one must love it beyond all other things in the world, and against such love, the reason, if one listened to it, would cry out. There is nothing sane about the worship of beauty. It is too splendid to be sane. Those of whose lives it forms the dominant note will always seem to the world to be pure visionaries.

ERNEST: Well, at least, the critic will be sincere.

GILBERT: A little sincerity is a dangerous thing, and a great deal of it is absolutely fatal. The true critic will, indeed, always be sincere in his devotion to the principle of beauty, but he will seek for beauty in every age and in each school, and will never suffer himself to be limited to any settled custom of thought, or stereotyped mode of looking at things. He will realise himself in many forms, and by a thousand different ways, and will ever be curious of new sensations and fresh points of view. Through constant change, and through constant change alone, he will find his true unity. He will not consent to be the slave of his own opinions. For what is mind but motion in the intellectual sphere? The essence of thought, as the essence of life, is growth. You must not be frightened by words, Ernest. What people call insincerity is simply a method by which we can multiply our personalities.

ERNEST: I am afraid I have not been fortunate in my suggestions.

GILBERT: Of the three qualifications you mentioned, two, sincerity and fairness, were, if not actually moral, at least on the borderland of morals, and the first condition of criticism is that the critic should be able to recognise that the sphere of Art and the sphere of Ethics are absolutely distinct and separate. When they are confused, Chaos has come again. They are too often confused in England now, and though our modern Puritans cannot destroy a beautiful thing, yet, by means of their extraordinary prurience, they can almost taint beauty for a moment. It is chiefly, I regret to say, through journalism that such people find expression. I regret it, because there is much to be said in favour of modern journalism. By giving us the opinions of the uneducated, it keeps us in touch with the ignorance of the community. By carefully chronicling the current events of contemporary life, it shows us of what very little importance such events really are. By invariably discussing the unnecessary, it makes us understand what things are requisite for culture, and what are not. But it should not allow poor Tartuffe to write articles upon modern art. When it does this it stultifies itself. And yet Tartuffe's articles and Chadband's notes do this good, at least. They serve to show how extremely limited is the area over which ethics, and ethical considerations, can claim to exercise influence. Science is out of the reach of morals, for her eyes are fixed upon eternal truths. Art is out of the reach of morals, for her eyes are fixed upon things beautiful and immortal and ever-changing. To morals belong the lower and less intellectual spheres. However, let these mouthing Puritans pass; they have their comic side. Who can help laughing when an ordinary journalist seriously proposes to limit the subject-matter at the disposal of the artist? Some limitation might well, and will soon, I hope, be placed upon some of our newspapers and newspaper writers. For they give us the bald, sordid, disgusting facts of life. They chronicle, with degrading avidity, the sins of the second-rate, and with the conscientiousness of the illiterate give us accurate and prosaic details of the doings of people of absolutely no interest whatsoever. But the artist, who accepts the facts of life, and yet transforms them into shapes of beauty, and makes them vehicles of pity or of awe, and shows their colour-element, and their wonder, and their true ethical import also, and builds out of them a world more real than reality itself, and of loftier and more noble import – who shall set limits to him? Not the apostles of that new Journalism which is but the old vulgarity "writ large." Not the apostles of that new Puritanism, which is but the whine of the hypocrite, and is both writ and spoken badly. The mere suggestion is ridiculous. Let us leave these wicked people, and proceed to the discussion of the artistic qualifications necessary for the true critic.

ERNEST: And what are they? Tell me yourself.

GILBERT: Temperament is the primary requisite for the critic – a temperament exquisitely susceptible to beauty, and to the various impressions that beauty gives us. Under what conditions, and by what means, this temperament is engendered in race or individual, we will not discuss at present. It is sufficient to note that it exists, and that there is in us a beauty-sense, separate from the other senses and above them, separate from the reason and of nobler import, separate from the soul and of equal value – a sense that leads some to create, and others, the finer spirits as I think, to contemplate merely. But to be purified and made perfect, this sense requires some form of exquisite environment. Without this it starves, or is dulled. You remember that lovely passage in which Plato describes how a young Greek should be educated, and with what insistence he dwells upon the importance of surroundings, telling us how the lad is to be brought up in the midst of fair sights and sounds, so that the beauty of material things may prepare his soul for the reception of the beauty that is spiritual. Insensibly, and without knowing the reason why, he is to develop that real love of beauty which, as Plato is never weary of reminding us, is the true aim of education. By slow degrees there is to be engendered in him such a temperament as will lead him naturally and simply to choose the good in preference to the bad, and, rejecting what is vulgar and discordant, to follow by fine instinctive taste all that possesses grace and charm and loveliness. Ultimately, in its due course, this taste is to become critical and self-conscious, but at first it is to exist purely as a cultivated instinct, and 'he who has received this true culture of the inner man will with clear and certain vision perceive the omissions and faults in art or nature, and with a taste that cannot err, while he praises, and finds his pleasure in what is good, and receives it into his soul, and so becomes good and noble, he will rightly blame and hate the bad, now in the days of his youth, even before he is able to know the reason why': and so, when, later on, the critical and self-conscious spirit develops in him, he 'will recognise and salute it as a friend with whom his education has made him long familiar.' I need hardly say, Ernest, how far we in England have fallen short of this ideal, and I can imagine the smile that would illuminate the glossy face of the Philistine if one ventured to suggest to him that the true aim of education was the love of beauty, and that the methods by which education should work were the development of temperament, the cultivation of taste, and the creation of the critical spirit.

Yet, even for us, there is left some loveliness of environment, and the dullness of tutors and professors matters very little when one can loiter in the grey cloisters at Magdalen, and listen to some flute-like voice singing in Waynfleete's chapel, or lie in the green meadow, among the strange snake-spotted fritillaries, and watch the sunburnt noon smite to a finer gold the tower's gilded vanes, or wander up the Christ Church staircase beneath the vaulted ceiling's shadowy fans, or pass through the sculptured gateway of Laud's building in the College of St. John. Nor is it merely at Oxford, or Cambridge, that the sense of beauty can be formed and trained and perfected. All over England there is a Renaissance of the decorative Arts. Ugliness has had its day. Even in the houses of the rich there is taste, and the houses of those who are not rich have been made gracious and comely and sweet to live in. Caliban, poor noisy Caliban, thinks that when he has ceased to make mows at a thing, the thing ceases to exist. But if he mocks no longer, it is because he has been met with mockery, swifter and keener than his own, and for a moment has been bitterly schooled into that silence which should seal for ever his uncouth distorted lips. What has been done up to now has been chiefly in the clearing of the way. It is always more difficult to destroy that it is to create, and when what one has to destroy is vulgarity and stupidity, the task of destruction needs not merely courage but also contempt. Yet it seems to me to have been, in a measure, done. We have got rid of what was bad. We have now to make what is beautiful. And though the mission of the aesthetic movement is to lure people to contemplate, not to lead them to create, yet, as the creative instinct is strong in the Celt, and it is the Celt who leads in art, there is no reason why in future years this strange Renaissance should not become almost as mighty in its way as was that new birth of Art that woke many centuries ago in the cities of Italy.

Certainly, for the cultivation of temperament, we must turn to the decorative arts: to the arts that touch us, not to the arts that teach us. Modern pictures are, no doubt, delightful to look at. At least, some of them are. But they are quite impossible to live with; they are too clever, too assertive, too intellectual. Their meaning is too obvious, and their method too clearly defined. One exhausts what they have to say in a very short time, and then they become as tedious as one's relations. I am very fond of the work of many of the Impressionist painters of Paris and London. Subtlety and distinction have not yet left the school. Some of their arrangements and harmonies serve to remind one of the unapproachable beauty of Gautier's immortal *Symphonie en Blanc Majeur*, that flawless masterpiece of colour and music which may have suggested the type as well as the titles of many of their best pictures. For a class that welcomes the incompetent with sympathetic eagerness, and that confuses the bizarre with the beautiful, and vulgarity with truth, they are extremely accomplished. They can do etchings that have the brilliancy of epigrams, pastels that are as fascinating as paradoxes, and as for their portraits, whatever the commonplace may say against them, no one can deny that they possess that unique and wonderful charm which belongs to works of pure fiction. But even the Impressionists, earnest and industrious as they are, will not do. I like them. Their white keynote, with its variations in lilac, was an era in colour. Though the moment does not make the man, the moment certainly makes the Impressionist, and for the moment in art, and the 'moment's monument,' as Rossetti phrased it, what may not be said? They are suggestive also. If they have not opened the eyes of the blind, they have at least given great encouragement to the short-sighted, and while their leaders may have all the inexperience of old age, their young men are far too wise to be ever sensible. Yet they will insist on treating painting as if it were a mode of autobiography invented for the use of the illiterate, and are always prating to us on their coarse gritty canvases of their unnecessary selves and their unnecessary opinions, and spoiling by a vulgar over-emphasis that fine contempt of nature which is the best and only modest thing about them. One tires, at the end, of the work of individuals whose individuality is always noisy, and generally uninteresting. There is far more to be said in favour of that newer school at Paris, the *Archaicistes*, as they call themselves, who, refusing to leave the artist entirely at the mercy of the weather, do not find the ideal of art in mere atmospheric effect, but seek rather for the imaginative beauty of design and the loveliness of fair colour, and rejecting the tedious realism of those who merely paint what they see, try to see something worth seeing, and to see it not merely with actual and physical vision, but with that nobler vision of the soul which is as far wider in spiritual scope as it is far more splendid in artistic purpose. They, at any rate, work under those decorative conditions that each art requires for its perfection, and have sufficient aesthetic instinct to regret those sordid and stupid limitations of absolute modernity of form which have proved the ruin of so many of the Impressionists. Still, the art that is frankly decorative is the art to live with. It is, of all our visible arts, the one art that creates in us both mood and temperament. Mere colour, unspoiled by meaning, and unallied with definite form, can speak to the soul in a thousand different ways. The harmony that resides in the delicate proportions of lines and masses becomes mirrored in the mind. The repetitions of pattern give us rest. The marvels of design stir the imagination. In the mere loveliness of the materials employed there are latent elements of culture. Nor is this all. By its deliberate rejection of Nature as the ideal of beauty, as well as of the imitative method of the ordinary painter, decorative art not merely prepares the soul for the reception of true imaginative work, but develops in it that sense of form which is the basis of creative no less than of critical achievement. For the real artist is he who proceeds, not from feeling to form, but from form to thought and passion. He does not first conceive an idea, and then say to himself, 'I will put my idea into a complex metre of fourteen lines,' but realising the beauty of the sonnet-scheme, he conceives certain modes of music and methods of rhyme, and the mere form suggests what is to fill and make it intellectually and emotionally complete. From time to time the world cries out against some charming artistic poet, because, to use its hackneyed and silly phrase, he has 'nothing to say.' But if he had something to say, he would probably say it, and the result would be tedious. It is just because he had no new message that he can do beautiful work. He gains his inspiration from form, and from form purely, as an artist should. A real passion would ruin him. Whatever actually occurs is spoiled for art. All bad poetry springs from genuine feeling. To be natural is to be obvious, and to be obvious is to be inartistic.

ERNEST: I wonder do you really believe what you say?

GILBERT: Why should you wonder? It is not merely in art that the body is the soul. In every sphere of life Form is the beginning of things. The rhythmic harmonious gestures of dancing convey, Plato tells us, both rhythm and harmony into the mind. Forms are the food of faith, cried Newman in one of those great moments of sincerity that make us admire and know the man. He was right, though he may not have known how terribly right he was. The Creeds are believed, not because they are rational, but because they are repeated. Yes; Form is everything. It is the secret of life. Find expression for a sorrow, and it will become dear to you. Find expression for a joy, and you intensify its ecstasy. Do you wish to love? Use Love's Litany, and the words will create the yearning from which the world fancies that they spring. Have you a grief that corrodes your heart? Steep yourself in the language of grief, learn its utterance from Prince Hamlet and Queen Constance, and you will find that mere expression is a mode of consolation, and that Form, which is the birth of passion, is also the death of pain. And so, to return to the sphere of Art, it is Form that creates not merely the critical temperament, but also the aesthetic instinct, that unerring instinct that reveals to one all things under their conditions of beauty. Start with the worship of form, and there is no secret in art that will not be revealed to you, and remember that in criticism, as in creation, temperament is everything, and that it is, not by the time of their production, but by the temperaments to which they appeal, that the schools of art should be historically grouped.

ERNEST: Your theory of education is delightful. But what influence will your critic, brought up in these exquisite surroundings, possess? Do you really think that any artist is ever affected by criticism?

GILBERT: The influence of the critic will be the mere fact of his own existence. He will represent the flawless type. In him the culture of the century will see itself realised. You must not ask of him to have any aim other than the perfecting of himself. The demand of the intellect, as has been well said, is simply to feel itself alive. The critic may, indeed, desire to exercise influence; but, if so, he will concern himself not with the individual, but with the age, which he will seek to wake into consciousness, and to make responsive, creating in it new desires and appetites, and lending it his larger vision and his nobler moods. The actual art of to-day will occupy him less than the art of to-morrow, far less than the art of yesterday, and as for this or that person at present toiling away, what do the industrious matter? They do their best, no doubt, and consequently we get the worst from them. It is always with the best intentions that the worst work is done. And besides, my dear Ernest, when a man reaches the age of forty, or becomes a Royal Academician, or is elected a member of the Athenaeum Club, or recognised as a popular novelist, whose books are in great demand at suburban railway stations, one may have the amusement of exposing him, but one cannot have the pleasure of reforming him. And this is, I dare say, very fortunate for him; for I have no doubt that reformation is a much more painful process than punishment, is indeed punishment in its most aggravated and moral form – a fact which accounts for our entire failure as a community to reclaim that interesting phenomenon who is called the confirmed criminal.

ERNEST: But may it not be that the poet is the best judge of poetry, and the painter of painting? Each art must appeal primarily to the artist who works in it. His judgment will surely be the most valuable?

GILBERT: The appeal of all art is simply to the artistic temperament. Art does not address herself to the specialist. Her claim is that she is universal, and that in all her manifestations she is one. Indeed, so far from its being true that the artist is the best judge of art, a really great artist can never judge of other people's work at all, and can hardly, in fact, judge of his own. That very concentration of vision that makes a man an artist, limits by its sheer intensity his faculty of fine appreciation. The energy of creation hurries him blindly on to his own goal. The wheels of his chariot raise the dust as a cloud around him. The gods are hidden from each other. They can recognise their worshippers. That is all.

ERNEST: You say that a great artist cannot recognise the beauty of work different from his own.

GILBERT: It is impossible for him to do so. Wordsworth saw in *Endymion* merely a pretty piece of Paganism, and Shelley, with his dislike of activity, was deaf to Wordsworth's message, being repelled by its form, and Byron, that great passionate human incomplete creature, could appreciate neither the poet of the cloud nor the poet of the lake, and the wonder of Keats was hidden from him. The realism of Euripides was hateful to Sophokles. Those droppings of warm tears had no music for him. Milton, with his sense of the grand style, could not understand the method of Shakespeare, any more than could Sir Joshua the method of Gainsborough. Bad artists always admire each other's work. They call it being large-minded and free from prejudice. But a truly great artist cannot conceive of life being shown, or beauty fashioned, under any conditions other than those that he has selected. Creation employs all its critical faculty within its own sphere. It may not use it in the sphere that belongs to others. It is exactly because a man cannot do a thing that he is the proper judge of it.

ERNEST: Do you really mean that?

GILBERT: Yes, for creation limits, while contemplation widens, the vision.

ERNEST: But what about technique? Surely each art has its separate technique?

GILBERT: Certainly: each art has its grammar and its materials. There is no mystery about either, and the incompetent can always be correct. But while the laws upon which Art rests may be fixed and certain, to find their true realisation they must be touched by the imagination into such beauty that they will seem an exception, each one of them. Technique is really personality. That is the reason why the artist cannot teach it, why the pupil cannot learn it, and why the aesthetic critic can understand it. To the great poet, there is only one method of music – his own. To the great painter, there is only one manner of painting – that which he himself employs. The aesthetic critic, and the aesthetic critic alone, can appreciate all forms and modes. It is to him that Art makes her appeal.

ERNEST: Well, I think I have put all my questions to you. And now I must admit –

GILBERT: Ah! Don't say that you agree with me. When people agree with me I always feel that I must be wrong.

ERNEST: In that case I certainly won't tell you whether I agree with you or not. But I will put another question. You have explained to me that criticism is a creative art. What future has it?

GILBERT: It is to criticism that the future belongs. The subject-matter at the disposal of creation becomes every day more limited in extent and variety. Providence and Mr. Walter Besant have exhausted the obvious. If creation is to last at all, it can only do so on the condition of becoming far more critical than it is at present. The old roads and dusty highways have been traversed too often. Their charm has been worn away by plodding feet, and they have lost that element of novelty or surprise which is so essential for romance. He who would stir us now by fiction must either give us an entirely new background, or reveal to us the soul of man in its innermost workings. The first is for the moment being done for us by Mr. Rudyard Kipling. As one turns over the pages of his *Plain Tales from the Hills*, one feels as if one were seated under a palm-tree reading life by superb flashes of vulgarity. The bright colours of the bazaars dazzle one's eyes. The jaded, second-rate Anglo-Indians are in exquisite incongruity with their surroundings. The mere lack of style in the story-teller gives an odd journalistic realism to what he tells us. From the point of view of literature Mr. Kipling is a genius who drops his aspirates. From the point of view of life, he is a reporter who knows vulgarity better than any one has ever known it. Dickens knew its clothes and its comedy. Mr. Kipling knows its essence and its seriousness. He is our first authority on the second-rate, and has seen marvellous things through keyholes, and his backgrounds are real works of art. As for the second condition, we have had Browning, and Meredith is with us. But there is still much to be done in the sphere of introspection. People sometimes say that fiction is getting too morbid. As far as psychology is concerned, it has never been morbid enough. We have merely touched the surface of the soul, that is all. In one single ivory cell of the brain there are stored away things more marvellous and more terrible than even they have dreamed of, who, like the author of *Le Rouge et le noir*, have sought to track the soul into its most secret places, and to make life confess its dearest sins. Still, there is a limit even to the number of untried backgrounds, and it is possible that a further development of the habit of introspection may prove fatal to that creative faculty to which it seeks to supply fresh material. I myself am inclined to think that creation is doomed. It springs from too primitive, too natural an impulse. However this may be, it is certain that the subject-matter at the disposal of creation is always diminishing, while the subject-matter of criticism increases daily. There are always new attitudes for the mind, and new points of view. The duty of imposing form upon chaos does not grow less as the world advances. There was never a time when Criticism was more needed than it is now. It is only by its means that Humanity can become conscious of the point at which it has arrived.

Hours ago, Ernest, you asked me the use of Criticism. You might just as well have asked me the use of thought. It is Criticism, as Arnold points out, that creates the intellectual atmosphere of the age. It is Criticism, as I hope to point out myself some day, that makes the mind a fine instrument. We, in

our educational system, have burdened the memory with a load of uncon-
nected facts, and laboriously striven to impart our laboriously-acquired
knowledge. We teach people how to remember, we never teach them how to
grow. It has never occurred to us to try and develop in the mind a more sub-
tle quality of apprehension and discernment. The Greeks did this, and when
we come in contact with the Greek critical intellect, we cannot but be con-
scious that, while our subject-matter is in every respect larger and more var-
ied than theirs, theirs is the only method by which this subject-matter can be
interpreted. England has done one thing; it has invented and established
Public Opinion, which is an attempt to organise the ignorance of the com-
munity, and to elevate it to the dignity of physical force. But Wisdom has al-
ways been hidden from it. Considered as an instrument of thought, the
English mind is coarse and undeveloped. The only thing that can purify it is
the growth of the critical instinct.

It is Criticism, again, that by concentration makes culture possible. It takes
the cumbersome mass of creative work, and distils it into a finer essence.
Who that desires to retain any sense of form could struggle through the
monstrous multitudinous books that the world has produced, books in
which thought stammers or ignorance brawls? The thread that is to guide us
across the wearisome labyrinth is in the hands of Criticism. Nay, more,
where there is no record, and history is either lost, or was never written, Cri-
ticism can re-create the past for us from the very smallest fragment of lan-
guage or art, just as surely as the man of science can from some tiny bone, or
the mere impress of a foot upon a rock, re-create for us the winged dragon or
Titan lizard that once made the earth shake beneath its tread, can call Behe-
moth out of his cave, and make Leviathan swim once more across the startled
sea. Prehistoric history belongs to the philological and archaeological critic.
It is to him that the origins of things are revealed. The self-conscious de-
posits of an age are nearly always misleading. Through philological criticism
alone we know more of the centuries of which no actual record has been pre-
served, than we do of the centuries that have left us their scrolls. It can do for
us what can be done neither by physics nor metaphysics. It can give us the
exact science of mind in the progress of becoming. It can do for us what His-
tory cannot do. It can tell us what man thought before he learned how to
write. You have asked me about the influence of Criticism. I think I have an-
swered that question already; but there is this also to be said. It is Criticism
that makes us cosmopolitan. The Manchester school tried to make men real-
ise the brotherhood of humanity by pointing out the commercial advantages
of peace. It sought to degrade the wonderful world into a common market-
place for the buyer and the seller. It addressed itself to the lowest instincts,
and it failed. War followed upon war, and the tradesman's creed did not pre-
vent France and Germany from clashing together in bloodstained battle.
There are others of our own day, who seek to appeal to mere emotional sym-
pathies, or to the shallow dogmas of some vague system of abstract ethics.
They have their Peace Societies, so dear to the sentimentalists, and their
proposals for unarmed International Arbitration, so popular among those

who have never read history. But mere emotional sympathy will not do. It is too variable, and too closely connected with the passions; and a board of arbitrators who, for the general welfare of the race, are to be deprived of the power of putting their decisions into execution, will not be of much avail. There is only one thing worse than Injustice, and that is Justice without her sword in her hand. When Right is not Might, it is Evil.

No: the emotions will not make us cosmopolitan, any more than the greed for gain could do so. It is only by the cultivation of the habit of intellectual criticism that we shall be able to rise superior to race-prejudices. Goethe – you will not misunderstand what I say – was a German of the Germans. He loved his country – no man more so. Its people were dear to him; and he led them. Yet when the iron hoof of Napoleon trampled upon vineyard and cornfield, his lips were silent. 'How can one write songs of hatred without hating?' he said to Eckermann, 'and how could I, to whom culture and barbarism are alone of importance, hate a nation which is among the most cultivated of the earth, and to which I owe so great a part of my own cultivation?' This note, sounded in the modern world by Goethe first, will become, I think, the starting point for the cosmopolitanism of the future. Criticism will annihilate race-prejudices, by insisting upon the unity of the human mind in the variety of its forms. If we are tempted to make war upon another nation, we shall remember that we are seeking to destroy an element of our own culture, and possibly its most important element. As long as war is regarded as wicked, it will always have its fascination. When it is looked upon as vulgar, it will cease to be popular. The change will, of course, be slow, and people will not be conscious of it. They will not say 'We will not war against France because her prose is perfect,' but because the prose of France is perfect, they will not hate the land. Intellectual criticism will bind Europe together in bonds far closer than those that can be forged by shopman or sentimentalist. It will give us the peace that springs from understanding.

Nor is this all. It is Criticism that, recognising no position as final, and refusing to bind itself by the shallow shibboleths of any sect or school, creates that serene philosophic temper which loves truth for its own sake, and loves it not the less because it knows it to be unattainable. How little we have of this temper in England, and how much we need it! The English mind is always in a rage. The intellect of the race is wasted in the sordid and stupid quarrels of second-rate politicians or third-rate theologians. It was reserved for a man of science to show us the supreme example of that 'sweet reasonableness' of which Arnold spoke so wisely, and, alas! To so little effect. The author of the *Origin of Species* had, at any rate, the philosophic temper. If one contemplates the ordinary pulpits and platforms of England, one can but feel the contempt of Julian, or the indifference of Montaigne. We are dominated by the fanatic, whose worst vice is his sincerity. Anything approaching to the free play of the mind is practically unknown amongst us. People cry out against the sinner, yet it is not the sinful, but the stupid, who are our shame. There is no sin except stupidity.

ERNEST: Ah! What an antinomian you are!

GILBERT: The artistic critic, like the mystic, is an antinomian always. To be good, according to the vulgar standard of goodness, is obviously quite easy. It merely requires a certain amount of sordid terror, a certain lack of imaginative thought, and a certain low passion for middle-class respectability. Aesthetics are higher than ethics. They belong to a more spiritual sphere. To discern the beauty of a thing is the finest point to which we can arrive. Even a colour-sense is more important, in the development of the individual, than a sense of right and wrong. Aesthetics, in fact, are to Ethics in the sphere of conscious civilisation, what, in the sphere of the external world, sexual is to natural selection. Ethics, like natural selection, make existence possible. Aesthetics, like sexual selection, make life lovely and wonderful, fill it with new forms, and give it progress, and variety and change. And when we reach the true culture that is our aim, we attain to that perfection of which the saints have dreamed, the perfection of those to whom sin is impossible, not because they make the renunciations of the ascetic, but because they can do everything they wish without hurt to the soul, and can wish for nothing that can do the soul harm, the soul being an entity so divine that it is able to transform into elements of a richer experience, or a finer susceptibility, or a newer mode of thought, acts or passions that with the common would be commonplace, or with the uneducated ignoble, or with the shameful vile. Is this dangerous? Yes; it is dangerous – all ideas, as I told you, are so. But the night wearies, and the light flickers in the lamp. One more thing I cannot help saying to you. You have spoken against Criticism as being a sterile thing. The nineteenth century is a turning point in history, simply on account of the work of two men, Darwin and Renan, the one the critic of the Book of Nature, the other the critic of the books of God. Not to recognise this is to miss the meaning of one of the most important eras in the progress of the world. Creation is always behind the age. It is Criticism that leads us. The Critical Spirit and the World Spirit are one.

ERNEST: And he who is in possession of this spirit, or whom this spirit possesses, will, I suppose, do nothing?

GILBERT: Like the Persephone of whom Landor tells us, the sweet pensive Persephone around whose white feet the asphodel and amaranth are blooming, he will sit contended 'in that deep, motionless quiet which mortals pity, and which the gods enjoy.' He will look out upon the world and know its secret. By contact with divine things he will become divine. His will be the perfect life, and his only.

ERNEST: You have told me many strange things to-night, Gilbert. You have told me that it is more difficult to talk about a thing than to do it, and that to do nothing at all is the most difficult thing in the world; you have told me that all Art is immoral, and all thought dangerous; that criticism is more creative than creation, and that the highest criticism is that which reveals in the work of Art what the artist had not put there; that it is exactly because a man cannot do a thing that he is the proper judge of it; and that the true critic is unfair, insincere, and not rational. My friend, you are a dreamer.

GILBERT; Yes: I am a dreamer. For a dreamer is one who can only find his way by moonlight, and his punishment is that he sees the dawn before the rest of the world.

ERNEST: His punishment?

GILBERT: And his reward. But, see, it is dawn already. Draw back the curtains and open the windows wide. How cool the morning air is! Piccadilly lies at our feet like a long riband of silver. A faint purple mist hangs over the Park, and the shadows of the white houses are purple. It is too late to sleep. Let us go down to Covent Garden and look at the roses. Come! I am tired of thought.

THE TRUTH OF MASKS

A Note on Illusion

In many of the somewhat violent attacks that have recently been made on that splendour of mounting which now characterises our Shakespearian revivals in England, it seems to have been tacitly assumed by the critics that Shakespeare himself was more or less indifferent to the costumes of his actors, and that, could he see Mrs. Langtry's production of *Antony and Cleopatra*, he would probably say that the play, and the play only, is the thing, and that everything else is leather and prunella. While as regards any historical accuracy in dress, Lord Lytton, in an article in the *Nineteenth Century*, has laid it down as a dogma of art that archaeology is entirely out of place in the presentation of any of Shakespeare's plays, and the attempt to introduce it one of the stupidest pedantries of an age of prigs.

Lord Lytton's position I shall examine later on; but as regards the theory that Shakespeare did not busy himself much about the costume-wardrobe of his theatre, anybody who cares to study Shakespeare's method will see that there is absolutely no dramatist of the French, English, or Athenian stage who relies so much for his illusionist effects on the dress of his actors as Shakespeare does himself.

Knowing how the artistic temperament is always fascinated by beauty of costume, he constantly introduces into his plays masques and dances, purely for the sake of the pleasure which they give the eye; and we have still his stage-directions for the three great processions in *Henry the Eighth*, directions which are characterised by the most extraordinary elaborateness of detail down to the collars of S.S. and the pearls in Anne Boleyn's hair. Indeed it would be quite easy for a modern manager to reproduce these pageants absolutely as Shakespeare had them designed; and so accurate were they that one of the court officials of the time, writing an account of the last performance of the play at the Globe Theatre to a friend, actually complains of their realistic character, notably of the production on the stage of the Knights of the Garter in the robes and insignia of the order as being calculated to bring ridicule on the real ceremonies; much in the same spirit in which the French Government, some time ago, prohibited that delightful actor, M. Christian, from appearing in uniform, on the plea that it was prejudicial to the glory of the army that a colonel should be caricatured. And elsewhere the gorgeousness of apparel which distinguished the English stage under Shakespeare's influence was attacked by the contemporary critics, not as a rule, however, on the grounds of the democratic tendencies of realism, but usually on those moral grounds which are always the last refuge of people who have no sense of beauty.

The point, however, which I wish to emphasise is, not that Shakespeare appreciated the value of lovely costumes in adding picturesqueness to poetry, but that he saw how important costume is as a means of producing certain dramatic effects. Many of his plays, such as *Measure for Measure*, *Twelfth Night*, *The Two Gentlemen of Verona*, *All's Well that Ends Well*, *Cym-*

beline, and others, depend for their illusion on the character of the various dresses worn by the hero or the heroine; the delightful scene in *Henry the Sixth*, on the modern miracles of healing by faith, loses all its point unless Gloster is in black and scarlet; and the dénouement of the *Merry Wives of Windsor* hinges on the colour of Anne Page's gown. As for the uses Shakespeare makes of disguises the instances are almost numberless. Posthumous hides his passion under a peasant's garb, and Edgar his pride beneath an idiot's rags; Portia wears the apparel of a lawyer, and Rosalind is attired in 'all points as a man;' the cloak-bag of Pisanio changes Imogen to the youth Fidele; Jessica flees from her father's house in boy's dress, and Julia ties up her yellow hair in fantastic love-knots, and dons hose and doublet; Henry the Eighth woos his lady as a shepherd, and Romeo his as a pilgrim; Prince Hal and Poins appear first as footpads in buckram suits, and then in white aprons and leather jerkins as the waiters in a tavern: and as for Falstaff, does he not come on as a highwayman, as an old woman, as Herne the Hunter, and as the clothes going to the laundry?

Nor are the examples of the employment of costume as a mode of intensifying dramatic situation less numerous. After slaughter of Duncan, Macbeth appears in his night-gown as if aroused from sleep; Timon ends in rags the play he had begun in splendour; Richard flatters the London citizens in a suit of mean and shabby armour, and as soon as he has stepped in blood to the throne, marches through the streets in crown and George and Garter; the climax of *The Tempest* is reached when Prospero, throwing off his enchanter's robes, sends Ariel for his hat and rapier, and reveals himself as the great Italian Duke; the very Ghost in *Hamlet* changes his mystical apparel to produce different effects; and as for Juliet, a modern playwright would probably have laid her out in shroud, and made the scene a scene of horror merely, but Shakespeare arrays her in rich and gorgeous raiment, whose loveliness makes the vault 'a feasting presence full of light,' turns the tomb into a bridal chamber, and gives the cue and motive for Romeo's speech of the triumph of Beauty over Death.

Even small details of dress, such as the colour of a major-domo's stockings, the pattern on a wife's handkerchief, the sleeve of a young soldier, and a fashionable woman's bonnets, become in Shakespeare's hands points of actual dramatic importance, and by some of them the action of the play in question is conditioned absolutely. Many other dramatists have availed themselves of costume as a method of expressing directly to the audience the character of a person on his entrance, though hardly so brilliantly as Shakespeare has done in the case of the dandy Parolles, whose dress, by the way, only an archaeologist can understand; the fun of a master and servant exchanging coats in presence of the audience, of shipwrecked sailors squabbling over the division of a lot of fine clothes, and of a tinker dressed up like a duke while he is in his cups, may be regarded as part of that great career which costume has always played in comedy from the time of Aristophanes down to Mr. Gilbert; but nobody from the mere details of apparel and adornment has ever drawn such irony of contrast, such immediate and tragic effect, such pity and such pathos, as Shakespeare himself. Armed cap-à-pie, the dead King stalks on the battlements of Elsinore because all is not right with Denmark; Shylock's Jewish gaberdine is part of the stigma under which that wounded and embittered nature writhes; Arthur begging for his life can think of no better plea than the handkerchief he had given Hubert –

> Have you the heart! when your head did but ache,
> I knit my handkerchief about your brows,
> (The best I had, a princess wrought it me)
> And I did never ask it you again;

and Orlando's bloodstained napkin strikes the first sombre note in that exquisite woodland idyll, and shows us the depth of feeling that underlies Rosalind's fanciful wit and wilful jesting.

> Last night 'twas on my arm; I kissed it;
> I hope it be not gone to tell my lord
> That I kiss aught but he,

says Imogen, jesting on the loss of the bracelet which was already on its way to Rome to rob her of her husband's faith; the little Prince passing to the Tower plays with the dagger in his uncle's girdle; Duncan sends a ring to Lady Macbeth on the night of his own murder, and the ring of Portia turns the tragedy of the merchant into a wife's comedy. The great rebel York dies with a paper crown on his head; Hamlet's black suit is a kind of colour-motive in the piece, like the mourning of the Chimène in the *Cid*; and the climax of Antony's speech is the production of Cæsar's cloak: –

> I remember
> The first time ever Cæsar put it on.
> 'Twas on a summer's evening, in his tent,
> The day he overcame the Nervii: –
> Look, in this place ran Cassius' dagger through:
> See what a rent the envious Casca made:
> Through this the well-beloved Brutus stabbed....
> Kind souls, what, weep you when you but behold
> Our Caesar's vesture wounded?

The flowers which Ophelia carries with her in her madness are as pathetic as the violets that blossom on a grave; the effect of Lear's wandering on the heath is intensified beyond words by his fantastic attire; and when Cloten, stung by the taunt of that simile which his sister draws from her husband's raiment, arrays himself in that husband's very garb to work upon her the deed of shame, we feel that there is nothing in the whole of modern French realism, nothing even in *Thérèse Raquin*, that masterpiece of horror, which for terrible and tragic significance can compare with this strange scene in *Cymbeline*.

In the actual dialogue also some of the most vivid passages are those suggested by costume. Rosalind's

> Dost thou think, though I am caparisoned like a man, I
> have a doublet and hose in my disposition?

Constance's

> Grief fills the place of my absent child,
> Stuffs out his vacant garments with his form;

and the quick sharp cry of Elizabeth –

> Ah! cut my lace asunder! –

are only a few of the many examples one might quote. One of the finest effects I have ever seen on the stage was Salvini, in the last act of *Lear*, tearing the plume from Kent's cap and applying it to Cordelia's lips when he came to the line,

> This feather stirs; she lives!

Mr. Booth, whose Lear had many noble qualities of passion, plucked, I remember, some fur from his archaeologically-incorrect ermine for the same business; but Salvini's was the finer effect of the two, as well as the truer. And those who saw Mr. Irving in the last act of *Richard the Third* have not, I am sure, forgotten how much the agony and terror of his dream was intensified, by contrast, through the calm and quiet that preceded it, and the delivery of such lines as

> What, is my beaver easier than it was?
> And all my armour laid into my tent?
> Look that my staves be sound and not too heavy –

lines which had a double meaning for the audience, remembering the last words which Richard's mother called after him as he was marching to Bosworth: –

> Therefore take with thee my most grievous curse,
> Which in the day of battle tire thee more
> Than all the complete armour that thou wear'st.

As regards the resources which Shakespeare had at his disposal, it is to be remarked that, while he more than once complains of the smallness of the stage on which he has to produce big historical plays and of the want of scenery which obliges him to cut out many effective open-air incidents, he always writes as a dramatist who had at his disposal a most elaborate theatrical wardrobe, and who could rely on the actors taking pains about their make-up. Even now it is difficult to produce such a play as the *Comedy of Errors*; and to the picturesque accident of Miss Ellen Terry's brother resembling herself we owe the opportunity of seeing *Twelfth Night* adequately performed. Indeed, to put any play of Shakespeare's on the stage, absolutely as he himself wished it to be done, requires the services of a good property-man, a clever wig-maker, a costumier with a sense of colour and a knowledge of textures, a master of the methods of making-up, a fencing-master, a dancing-master, and an artist to direct personally the whole production. For he is most careful to tell us the dress and appearance of each character. 'Racine abhorre la réalité,' says Auguste Vacquerie somewhere; 'il ne daigne pas s'occuper de son costume. Si l'on s'en rapportait aux indications du poète, Agamemnon serait vêtu d'un sceptre et Achille d'une épée.[1]' But with Shakespeare it is very different. He gives us directions about the costumes of Perdita, Florizel, Autolycus, the Witches in *Macbeth*, and the apothecary in *Romeo and Juliet*, several elaborate descriptions of his fat knight, and a detailed account of the extraordinary garb in which Petruchio is to be married. Rosaline, he tells us, is tall, and is to carry a spear and a little dagger; Celia is smaller, and is to paint her face brown so as to look sunburnt. The children who play at fairies in Windsor Forest are to be dressed in white and green – a compliment, by the way, to Queen Elizabeth, whose favourite colours they were – and in white, with green garlands and gilded vizors, the angels are to come to Katherine in Kimbolton. Bottom is in home-spun, Lysander is distinguished from Oberon by his wearing an Athenian dress, and Launce has holes in his boots. The Duchess of Gloucester stands in a white sheet with her husband in mourning beside her. The motley of the Fool, the scarlet of the Cardinal, and the French lilies broidered on the English coats, are all made occasion for jest or taunt in the dialogue. We know the patterns on the Dauphin's armour and the Pucelle's sword, the crest on Warwick's helmet and the colour of Bardolph's nose. Portia has golden hair, Phoebe is black-haired, Orlando has chestnut curls, and Sir Andrew Aguecheek's hair hangs like flax on a distaff, and won't curl at all. Some of the characters are stout, some lean, some straight, some hunchbacked, some fair, some dark, and some are to blacken their faces. Lear has a white beard, Hamlet's father a grizzled, and Benedick is to shave his in the course of the play. Indeed, on the subject of stage beards Shakespeare is quite elaborate; tells us of the many different colours in use, and gives a hint to actors always to see that their own are properly tied on. There is a dance of reapers in rye-straw hats, and of rustics in hairy coats like satyrs; a masque of Amazons, a masque of Russians, and a classical masque; several immortal scenes over a weaver in an ass's head, a riot over the colour of a coat which it takes the Lord Mayor of London to quell, and a scene between an infuriated husband and his wife's milliner about the slashing of a sleeve.

As for the metaphors Shakespeare draws from dress, and the aphorisms he makes on it, his hits at the costume of his age, particularly at the ridiculous size of the ladies' bonnets, and the many descriptions of the *mundus muliebris*,[2] from the song of Autolycus in the *Winter's Tale* down to the account of the Duchess of Milan's gown in *Much Ado About Nothing*, they are far too

---

[1] Racine hates reality. He cannot be bothered with costume. If one went by the poet's own directions, Agamemnon would have nothing but a sceptre and Achilles a sword.

[2] The world of women.

numerous to quote; though it may be worth while to remind people that the whole of the Philosophy of Clothes is to be found in Lear's scene with Edgar – a passage which has the advantage of brevity and style over the grotesque wisdom and somewhat mouthing metaphysics of *Sartor Resartus*. But I think that from what I have already said it is quite clear that Shakespeare was very much interested in costume. I do not mean in that shallow sense by which it has been concluded from his knowledge of deeds and daffodils that he was the Blackstone and Paxton of the Elizabethan age; but that he saw that costume could be made at once impressive of a certain effect on the audience and expressive of certain types of character, and is one of the essential factors of the means which a true illusionist has at his disposal. Indeed to him the deformed figure of Richard was of as much value as Juliet's loveliness; he sets the serge of the radical beside the silks of the lord, and sees the stage effects to be got from each; he has as much delight in Caliban as he has in Ariel, in rags as he has in cloth of gold, and recognises the artistic beauty of ugliness.

The difficulty Ducis felt about translating *Othello* in consequence of the importance given to such a vulgar thing as a handkerchief, and his attempt to soften its grossness by making the Moor reiterate 'Le bandeau! le bandeau!' may be taken as an example of the difference between *la tragédie philosophique* and the drama of real life; and the introduction for the first time of the word *mouchoir* at the Théâtre Français was an era in that romantic-realistic movement of which Hugo is the father and M. Zola the *enfant terrible*, just as the classicism of the earlier part of the century was emphasised by Talma's refusal to play Greek heroes any longer in a powdered periwig – one of the many instances, by the way, of that desire for archaeological accuracy in dress which has distinguished the great actors of our age.

In criticising the importance given to money in *La Comédie Humaine*, Théophile Gautier says that Balzac may claim to have invented a new hero in fiction, *le héros métallique*. Of Shakespeare it may be said he was the first to see the dramatic value of doublets, and that a climax may depend on a crinoline.

The burning of the Globe Theatre – an event due, by the way, to the results of the passion for illusion that distinguished Shakespeare's stage-management – has unfortunately robbed us of many important documents; but in the inventory, still in existence, of the costume-wardrobe of a London theatre in Shakespeare's time, there are mentioned particular costumes for cardinals, shepherds, kings, clowns, friars, and fools; green coats for Robin Hood's men, and a green gown for Maid Marian; a white and gold doublet for Henry the Fifth, and a robe for Longshanks; besides surplices, copes, damask gowns, gowns of cloth of gold and of cloth of silver, taffeta gowns, calico gowns, velvet coats, satin coats, frieze coats, jerkins of yellow leather and of black leather, red suits, grey suits, French Pierrot suits, a robe 'for to goo invisibell,' which seems inexpensive at £3.10s., and four incomparable fardingales – all of which show a desire to give every character an appropriate dress. There are also entries of Spanish, Moorish and Danish costumes, of helmets, lances, painted shields, imperial crowns, and papal tiaras, as well as of costumes for Turkish Janissaries, Roman Senators, and all the gods and goddesses of Olympus, which evidence a good deal of archaeological research on the part of the manager of the theatre. It is true that there is a mention of a bodice for Eve, but probably the *donnée* of the play was after the Fall.

Indeed, anybody who cares to examine the age of Shakespeare will see that archæology was one of its special characteristics. After that revival of the classical forms of architecture which was one of the notes of the Renaissance, and the printing at Venice and elsewhere of the masterpieces of Greek and Latin literature, had come naturally an interest in the ornamentation and costume of the antique world. Nor was it for the learning that they could acquire, but rather for the loveliness that they might create, that the artists studied these things. The curious objects that were being constantly brought to light by excavations were not left to moulder in a museum, for the contemplation of a callous curator, and the *ennui* of a policeman bored by the absence of crime. They were used as motives for the production of a new art, which was to be not beautiful merely, but also strange.

Infessura tells us that in 1485 some workmen digging on the Appian Way came across an old Roman sarcophagus inscribed with the name 'Julia, daughter of Claudius.' On opening the coffer they found within its marble womb the body of a beautiful girl of about fifteen years of age, preserved by the embalmer's skill from corruption and the decay of time. Her eyes were half open, her hair rippled round her in crisp curling gold, and from her lips and cheek the bloom of maidenhood had not yet departed. Borne back to the Capitol, she became at once the centre of a new cult, and from all parts of the city crowded pilgrims to worship at the wonderful shrine, till the Pope, fearing lest those who had found the secret of beauty in a Pagan tomb might forget what secrets Judæa's rough and rock-hewn sepulchre contained, had the body conveyed away by night, and in secret buried. Legend though it may be, yet the story is none the less valuable as showing us the attitude of the Renaissance towards the antique world. Archæology to them was not a mere science for the antiquarian; it was a means by which they could touch the dry dust of antiquity into the very breath and beauty of life, and fill with the new wine of romanticism forms that else had been old and outworn. From the pulpit of Niccola Pisano down to Mantegna's 'Triumph of Caesar,' and the service Cellini designed for King Francis, the influence of this spirit can be traced; nor was it confined merely to the immobile arts – the arts of arrested movement – but its influence was to be seen also in the great Graeco-Roman masques which were the constant amusement of the gay courts of the time, and in the public pomps and processions with which the citizens of big commercial towns were wont to greet the princes that chanced to visit them; pageants, by the way, which were considered so important that large prints were made of them and published – a fact which is a proof of the general interest at the time in matters of such kind.

And this use of archaeology in shows, so far from being a bit of priggish pedantry, is in every way legitimate and beautiful. For the stage is not merely the meeting-place of all the arts, but is also the return of art to life. Sometimes in an archaeological novel the use of strange and obsolete terms seems to hide the reality beneath the learning, and I dare say that many of the readers of *Notre Dame de Paris* have been much puzzled over the meaning of such expressions as *la casaque à mahoitres, les voulgiers, le gallimard taché d'encre, les caraquiniers*,[1] and the like; but with the stage how different it is! The ancient world wakes from its sleep, and history moves as a pageant before our eyes, without obliging us to have recourse to a dictionary or an encyclopaedia for the perfection of our enjoyment. Indeed, there is not the slightest necessity that the public should know the authorities for the mounting of any piece. From such materials, for instance, as the disk of Theodosius, materials with which the majority of people are probably not very familiar, Mr. E. W. Godwin, one of the most artistic spirits of this century in England, created the marvellous loveliness of the first act of *Claudian*, and showed us the life of Byzantium in the fourth century, not by a dreary lecture and a set of grimy casts, not by a novel which requires a glossary to explain it, but by the visible presentation before us of all the glory of that great town. And while the costumes were true to the smallest points of colour and design, yet the details were not assigned that abnormal importance which they must necessarily be given in a piecemeal lecture, but were subordinated to the rules of lofty composition and the unity of artistic effect. Mr. Symonds, speaking of that great picture of Mantegna's, now in Hampton Court, says that the artist has converted an antiquarian motive into a theme for melodies of line. The same could have been said with equal justice of Mr. Godwin's scene. Only the foolish called it pedantry, only those who would neither look nor listen spoke of the passion of the play being killed by its paint. It was in reality a scene not merely perfect in its picturesqueness, but absolutely dramatic also, getting rid of any necessity for tedious descriptions, and showing us, by the colour and character of Claudian's dress, and the dress of his attendants, the whole nature and life of the man, from what school of philosophy he affected, down to what horses he backed on the turf.

And indeed archaeology is only really delightful when transfused into some form of art. I have no desire to underrate the services of laborious scholars, but I feel that the use Keats made of Lemprière's Dictionary is of far more value to us than Professor Max Müller's treatment of the same mythology as a disease of language. Better *Endymion* than any theory, however sound, or, as in the present instance, unsound, of an epidemic among adjectives! And who does not feel that the chief glory of Piranesi's book on Vases is that it gave Keats the suggestion for his 'Ode on a Grecian Urn'? Art, and art only, can make archaeology beautiful; and the theatric art can use it most directly and most vividly, for it can combine in one exquisite presentation the illusion of actual life with the wonder of the unreal world. But the sixteenth century was not merely the age of Vitruvius; it was the age of Vecellio also. Every nation seems suddenly to have become interested in the

---

[1] Tunic with padded sleeves, men with halberds, pen-box stained with ink, sailors of carracks.

dress of its neighbours. Europe began to investigate its own clothes, and the amount of books published on national costumes is quite extraordinary. At the beginning of the century the *Nuremberg Chronicle*, with its two thousand illustrations, reached its fifth edition, and before the century was over seventeen editions were published of Munster's *Cosmography*. Besides these two books there were also the works of Michael Colyns, of Hans Weigel, of Amman, and of Vecellio himself, all of them well illustrated, some of the drawings in Vecellio being probably from the hand of Titian.

Nor was it merely from books and treatises that they acquired their knowledge. The development of the habit of foreign travel, the increased commercial intercourse between countries, and the frequency of diplomatic missions, gave every nation many opportunities of studying the various forms of contemporary dress. After the departure from England, for instance, of the ambassadors from the Czar, the Sultan and the Prince of Morocco, Henry the Eighth and his friends gave several masques in the strange attire of their visitors. Later on London saw, perhaps too often, the sombre splendour of the Spanish Court, and to Elizabeth came envoys from all lands, whose dress, Shakespeare tells us, had an important influence on English costume.

And the interest was not confined merely to classical dress, or the dress of foreign nations; there was also a good deal of research, amongst theatrical people especially, into the ancient costume of England itself: and when Shakespeare, in the prologue to one of his plays, expresses his regret at being unable to produce helmets of the period, he is speaking as an Elizabethan manager and not merely as an Elizabethan poet. At Cambridge, for instance, during his day, a play of *Richard the Third* was performed, in which the actors were attired in real dresses of the time, procured from the great collection of historical costume in the Tower, which was always open to the inspection of managers, and sometimes placed at their disposal. And I cannot help thinking that this performance must have been far more artistic as regards costume, than Garrick's mounting of Shakespeare's own play on the subject, in which he himself appeared in a nondescript fancy dress, and everybody else in the costume of the time of George the Third, Richmond especially being much admired in the uniform of a young guardsman.

For what is the use to the stage of that archaeology which has so strangely terrified the critics, but that it, and it alone, can give us the architecture and apparel suitable to the time in which the action of the play passes? It enables us to see a Greek dressed like a Greek, and an Italian like an Italian; to enjoy the arcades of Venice and the balconies of Verona; and, if the play deals with any of the great eras in our country's history, to contemplate the age in its proper attire, and the king in his habit as he lived. And I wonder, by the way, what Lord Lytton would have said some time ago, at the Princess's Theatre, had the curtain risen on his father's Brutus reclining in a Queen Anne chair, attired in a flowing wig and a flowered dressing-gown, a costume which in the last century was considered peculiarly appropriate to an antique Roman! For in those halcyon days of the drama no archaeology troubled the stage, or

distressed the critics, and our inartistic grandfathers sat peaceably in a sti-
fling atmosphere of anachronisms, and beheld with the calm complacency of
the age of prose an Iachimo in powder and patches, a Lear in lace ruffles, and
a Lady Macbeth in a large crinoline. I can understand archaeology being at-
tacked on the ground of its excessive realism, but to attack it as pedantic
seems to be very much beside the mark. However, to attack it for any reason
is foolish; one might just as well speak disrespectfully of the equator. For
archaeology, being a science, is neither good nor bad, but a fact simply. Its
value depends entirely on how it is used, and only an artist can use it. We
look to the archaeologist for the materials, to the artist for the method.

In designing the scenery and costumes for any of Shakespeare's plays, the
first thing the artist has to settle is the best date for the drama. This should be
determined by the general spirit of the play, more than by any actual histori-
cal references which may occur in it. Most *Hamlets* I have seen were placed
far too early. Hamlet is essentially a scholar of the Revival of Learning; and if
the allusion to the recent invasion of England by the Danes puts it back to the
ninth century, the use of foils brings it down much later. Once, however,
that the date has been fixed, then the archaeologist is to supply us with the
facts which the artist is to convert into effect.

It has been said that the anachronisms in the plays themselves show us that
Shakespeare was indifferent to historical accuracy, and a great deal of capital
has been made out of Hector's indiscreet quotation from Aristotle. Upon the
other hand, the anachronisms are really few in number, and not very import-
ant, and, had Shakespeare's attention been drawn to them by a brother artist,
he would probably have corrected them. For, though they can hardly be
called blemishes, they are certainly not the great beauties of his work; or, at
least, if they are, their anachronistic charm cannot be emphasised unless the
play is accurately mounted according to its proper date. In looking at Shake-
speare's plays as a whole, however, what is really remarkable is their extra-
ordinary fidelity as regards his personages and his plots. Many of his
dramatis personae are people who actually existed, and some of them might
have been seen in real life by a portion of his audience. Indeed the most vio-
lent attack that was made on Shakespeare in his time was for his supposed
caricature of Lord Cobham. As for his plots, Shakespeare constantly draws
them either from authentic history, or from the old ballads and traditions
which served as history to the Elizabethan public, and which, even now, no
scientific historian would dismiss as absolutely untrue. And not merely did
he select fact instead of fancy as the basis of much of his imaginative work,
but he always gives to each play the general character, the social atmosphere
in a word, of the age in question. Stupidity he recognises as being one of the
permanent characteristics of all European civilisations; so he sees no differ-
ence between a London mob of his own day and a Roman mob of pagan days,
between a silly watchman in Messina and a silly Justice of the Peace in Wind-
sor. But when he deals with higher characters, with those exceptions of each
age which are so fine that they become its types, he gives them absolutely the
stamp and seal of their time. Virgilia is one of those Roman wives on whose

tomb was written *Domi mansit lanam fecit*,[1] as surely as Juliet is the romantic
girl of the Renaissance. He is even true to the characteristics of race. Hamlet
has all the imagination and irresolution of the Northern nations, and the
Princess Katharine is as entirely French as the heroine of *Divorçons*. Harry
the Fifth is a pure Englishman, and Othello a true Moor.

Again when Shakespeare treats of the history of England from the four-
teenth to the sixteenth centuries, it is wonderful how careful he is to have his
facts perfectly right – indeed he follows Holinshed with curious fidelity. The
incessant wars between France and England are described with extraordin-
ary accuracy down to the names of the besieged towns, the ports of landing
and embarkation, the sites and dates of the battles, the titles of the com-
manders on each side, and the lists of the killed and wounded. And as regards
the Civil Wars of the Roses we have many elaborate genealogies of the seven
sons of Edward the Third; the claims of the rival Houses of York and Lan-
caster to the throne are discussed at length; and if the English aristocracy will
not read Shakespeare as a poet, they should certainly read him as a sort of
early Peerage. There is hardly a single title in the Upper House, with the ex-
ception, of course, of the uninteresting titles assumed by the law lords,
which does not appear in Shakespeare along with many details of family his-
tory, creditable and discreditable. Indeed, if it be really necessary that the
School Board children should know about the Wars of the Roses, they could
learn their lessons just as well out of Shakespeare as out of shilling primers,
and learn them, I need not say, far more pleasurably. Even in Shakespeare's
own day this use of his plays was recognised. 'The historical plays teach his-
tory to those who cannot read it in the chronicles,' says Heywood in a tract
about the stage, and yet I am sure that sixteenth-century chronicles were
much more delightful reading than nineteenth-century primers are.

Of course the aesthetic value of Shakespeare's plays does not, in the slight-
est degree, depend on their facts, but on their Truth, and Truth is independ-
ent of facts always, inventing or selecting them at pleasure. But still
Shakespeare's use of facts is a most interesting part of his method of work,
and shows us his attitude towards the stage, and his relations to the great art
of illusion. Indeed he would have been very much surprised at any one class-
ing his plays with 'fairy tales,' as Lord Lytton does; for one of his aims was to
create for England a national historical drama, which should deal with inci-
dents with which the public was well acquainted, and with heroes that lived
in the memory of a people. Patriotism, I need hardly say, is not a necessary
quality of art; but it means, for the artist, the substitution of a universal for an
individual feeling, and for the public the presentation of a work of art in a
most attractive and popular form. It is worth noticing that Shakespeare's
first and last successes were both historical plays.

It may be asked, what has this to do with Shakespeare's attitude towards
costume? I answer that a dramatist who laid such stress on historical accu-
racy of fact would have welcomed historical accuracy of costume as a most

---

[1] She stayed at home and spun.

important adjunct to his illusionist method. And I have no hesitation in saying that he did so. The reference to helmets of the period in the prologue to *Henry the Fifth* may be considered fanciful, though Shakespeare must have often seen.

> The very casquer
> That did affright the air at Agincourt,

where it still hangs in the dusky gloom of Westminster Abbey, along with the saddle of that 'imp of fame,' and the dinted shield with its torn blue velvet lining and its tarnished lilies of gold; but the use of military tabards in *Henry the Sixth* is a bit of pure archaeology, as they were not worn in the sixteenth century; and the King's own tabard, I may mention, was still suspended over his tomb in St. George's Chapel, Windsor, in Shakespeare's day. For, up to the time of the unfortunate triumph of the Philistines in 1645, the chapels and cathedrals of England were the great national museums of archaeology, and in them were kept the armour and attire of the heroes of English history. A good deal was, of course, preserved in the Tower, and even in Elizabeth's day tourists were brought there to see such curious relics of the past as Charles Brandon's huge lance, which is still, I believe, the admiration of our country visitors; but the cathedrals and churches were, as a rule, selected as the most suitable shrines for the reception of the historic antiquities. Canterbury can still show us the helm of the Black Prince, Westminster the robes of our kings, and in old St. Paul's the very banner that had waved on Bosworth field was hung up by Richmond himself.

In fact, everywhere that Shakespeare turned in London, he saw the apparel and appurtenances of past ages, and it is impossible to doubt that he made use of his opportunities. The employment of lance and shield, for instance, in actual warfare, which is so frequent in his plays, is drawn from archaeology, and not from the military accoutrements of his day; and his general use of armour in battle was not a characteristic of his age, a time when it was rapidly disappearing before firearms. Again, the crest on Warwick's helmet, of which such a point is made in *Henry the Sixth*, is absolutely correct in a fifteenth-century play when crests were generally worn, but would not have been so in a play of Shakespeare's own time, when feathers and plumes had taken their place – a fashion which, as he tells us in *Henry the Eighth*, was borrowed from France. For the historical plays, then, we may be sure that archaeology was employed, and as for the others I feel certain that it was the case also. The appearance of Jupiter on his eagle, thunderbolt in hand, of Juno with her peacocks, and of Iris with her many-coloured bow; the Amazon masque and the masque of the Five Worthies, may all be regarded as archaeological; and the vision which Posthumous sees in prison of Sicilius Leonatus – 'an old man, attired like a warrior, leading an ancient matron' – is clearly so. Of the 'Athenian dress' by which Lysander is distinguished from Oberon I have already spoken; but one of the most marked instances is in the case of the dress of Coriolanus, for which Shakespeare goes directly to Plutarch. That historian, in his Life of the great Roman, tells us of the oak-wreath with which Caius Marcius was crowned, and of the curious kind of dress in which, according to ancient fashion, he had to canvass his electors; and on both of these points he enters into long disquisitions, investigating the origin and meaning of the old customs. Shakespeare, in the spirit of the true artist, accepts the facts of the antiquarian and converts them into dramatic and picturesque effects: indeed, the gown of humility, the 'wolvish gown,' as Shakespeare calls it, is the central note of the play. There are other cases I might quote, but this one is quite sufficient for my purpose; and it is evident from it at any rate that, in mounting a play in the accurate costume of the time, according to the best authorities, we are carrying out Shakespeare's own wishes and method.

Even if it were not so, there is no more reason that we should continue any imperfections which may be supposed to have characterised Shakespeare's stage mounting than that we should have Juliet played by a young man, or give up the advantage of changeable scenery. A great work of dramatic art should not merely be made expressive of modern passion by means of the actor, but should be presented to us in the form most suitable to the modern spirit. Racine produced his Roman plays in Louis Quatorze dress on a stage crowded with spectators; but we require different conditions for the enjoyment of his art. Perfect accuracy of detail, for the sake of perfect illusion, is necessary for us. What we have to see is that the details are not allowed to usurp the principal place. They must be subordinate always to the general motive of the play. But subordination in art does not mean disregard of truth; it means conversion of fact into effect, and assigning to each detail its proper relative value.

Les petits détails d'histoire et de vie domestique (says Hugo) doivent être scrupuleusement étudiés et reproduits par le poète, mais uniquement comme des moyens d'accrôitre la réalité de l'ensemble, et de faire pénétrer jusque dans les coins les plus obscurs de l'oeuvre cette vie générale et puissante au milieu de laquelle les personnages sont plus vrais, et les catastrophes, par conséquent, plus poignantes. Tout doit être subordonné à ce but. L'Homme sur le premier plan, le reste au fond.[1]

This passage is interesting as coming from the first great French dramatist who employed archaeology on the stage, and whose plays, though absolutely correct in detail, are known to all for their passion, not for their pedantry – for their life, not for their learning. It is true that he has made certain conces-

---

[1] The little details of history and of domestic life must be scrupulously studied and reproduced by the poet, but solely as a means of adding to the reality of the whole and of instilling into the darkest corners of the work this general and powerful life, in the midst of which the characters are more real and the catastrophies, as a result, more poignant. Everything must be subordinated to this end. Man in the foreground – the rest in the background.

sions in the case of the employment of curious or strange expressions. Ruy Blas talks of M. de Priego as 'sujet du roi' instead of 'noble du roi,' and Angelo Malipieri speaks of 'la croix rouge' instead of 'la croix de gueules.' But they are concessions made to the public, or rather to a section of it. 'J'en offre ici toutes mes excuses aux spectateurs intelligents,' he says in a note to one of the plays; 'espérons qu'un jour un seigneur vénitien pourra dire tout bonnement sans péril son blason sur le théâtre. C'est un progrès qui viendra'[1] And though the description of the crest is not couched in accurate language, still the crest itself was accurately right. It may, of course, be said that the public do not notice these things; upon the other hand, it should be remembered that Art has no other aim but her own perfection, and proceeds simply by her own laws, and that the play which Hamlet describes as being caviare to the general is a play he highly praises. Besides, in England at any rate, the public have undergone a transformation; there is far more appreciation of beauty now than there was a few years ago; and though they may not be familiar with the authorities and archaeological data for what is shown to them, still they enjoy whatever loveliness they look at. And this is the important thing. Better to take pleasure in a rose than to put its root under a microscope. Archaeological accuracy is merely a condition of illusionist stage effect; it is not its quality. And Lord Lytton's proposal that the dresses should merely be beautiful without being accurate is founded on a misapprehension of the nature of costume, and of its value on the stage. This value is twofold, picturesque and dramatic; the former depends on the colour of the dress, the latter on its design and character. But so inter-woven are the two that, whenever in our own day historical accuracy has been disregarded, and the various dresses in a play taken from different ages, the result has been that the stage has been turned into that chaos of costume, that caricature of the centuries, the Fancy Dress Ball, to the entire ruin of all dramatic and picturesque effect. For the dresses of one age do not artistically harmonise with the dresses of another; and, as far as dramatic value goes, to confuse the costumes is to confuse the play. Costume is a growth, an evolution, and a most important, perhaps the most important, sign of the manners, customs and mode of life of each century. The Puritan dislike of colour, adornment and grace in apparel was part of the great revolt of the middle classes against Beauty in the seventeenth century. A historian who disregarded it would give us a most inaccurate picture of the time, and a dramatist who did not avail himself of it would miss a most vital element in producing an illusionist effect. The effeminacy of dress that characterised the reign of Richard the Second was a constant theme of contemporary authors. Shakespeare, writing two hundred years after, makes the king's fondness for gay apparel and foreign fashions a point in the play, from John of Gaunt's reproaches down to Richard's own speech in the third act on his deposition from the throne. And that Shakespeare examined

---

[1] I offer here all my apologies to intelligent spectators; let us hope that one day a Venetian nobleman will be able to mention quite simply and fearlessly his coat of arms on the stage. That improvement will come.

Richard's tomb in Westminster Abbey seems to me certain from York's speech: –

> See, see, King Richard doth himself appear
> As doth the blushing discontented sun
> From out the fiery portal of the east,
> When he perceives the envious clouds are bent
> To dim his glory.

For we can still discern on the King's robe his favourite badge – the sun issuing from a cloud. In fact, in every age the social conditions are so exemplified in costume, that to produce a sixteenth-century play in fourteenth-century attire, or *vice versa*, would make the performance seem unreal because untrue. And, valuable as beauty of effect on the stage is, the highest beauty is not merely comparable with absolute accuracy of detail, but really dependent on it. To invent an entirely new costume is almost impossible except in burlesque or extravaganza, and as for combining the dress of different centuries into one, the experiment would be dangerous, and Shakespeare's opinion of the artistic value of such a medley may be gathered from his incessant satire of the Elizabethan dandies for imagining that they were well dressed because they got their doublets in Italy, their hats in Germany, and their hose in France. And it should be noted that the most lovely scenes that have been produced on our stage have been those that have been characterised by perfect accuracy, such as Mr. and Mrs. Bancroft's eighteenth-century revivals at the Haymarket, Mr. Irving's superb production of *Much Ado About Nothing* and Mr. Barrett's *Claudian*. Besides, and this is perhaps the most complete answer to Lord Lytton's theory, it must be remembered that neither in costume nor in dialogue is beauty the dramatist's primary aim at all. The true dramatist aims first at what is characteristic, and no more desires that all his personages should be beautifully attired than he desires that they should have beautiful natures or speak beautiful English. The true dramatist, in fact, shows us life under the conditions of art, not art in the form of life. The Greek dress was the loveliest dress the world has ever seen, and the English dress of the last century one of the most monstrous; yet we cannot costume a play by Sheridan as we would costume a play by Sophokles. For, as Polonius says in his excellent lecture, a lecture to which I am glad to have the opportunity of expressing my obligations, one of the first qualities of apparel is its expressiveness. And the affected style of dress in the last century was the natural characteristic of a society of affected manners and affected conversation – a characteristic which the realistic dramatist will highly value down to the smallest detail of accuracy, and the materials for which he can get only from archaeology.

But it is not enough that a dress should be accurate; it must also be appropriate to the stature and appearance of the actor and to his supposed condition, as well as to his necessary action in the play. In Mr. Hare's production of *As You Like It* at the St. James's Theatre, for instance, the whole point of Orlando's complaint that he is brought up like a peasant, and not like a gentleman, was spoiled by the gorgeousness of his dress, and the splendid apparel worn by the banished Duke and his friends was quite out of place. Mr. Lewis Wingfield's explanation that the sumptuary laws of the period necessitated their doing so, is, I am afraid, hardly sufficient. Outlaws, lurking in a forest and living by the chase, are not very likely to care much about ordinances of dress. They were probably attired like Robin Hood's men, to whom, indeed, they are compared in the course of the play. And that their dress was not that of wealthy noblemen may be seen by Orlando's words when he breaks in upon them. He mistakes them for robbers, and is amazed to find that they answer him in courteous and gentle terms. Lady Archibald Campbell's production, under Mr. E. W. Godwin's direction, of the same play in Coombe Wood was, as regards mounting, far more artistic. At least it seemed so to me. The Duke and his companions were dressed in serge tunics, leathern jerkins, high boots and gauntlets, and wore bycocket hats and hoods. And as they were playing in a real forest, they found, I am sure, their dresses extremely convenient. To every character in the play was given a perfectly appropriate attire, and the brown and green of their costumes harmonised exquisitely with the ferns through which they wandered, the trees beneath which they lay, and the lovely English landscape that surrounded the Pastoral Players. The perfect naturalness of the scene was due to the absolute accuracy and appropriateness of everything that was worn. Nor could archaeology have been put to a severer test, or come out of it more triumphantly. The whole production showed once for all that, unless a dress is archaeologically correct, and artistically appropriate, it always looks unreal, unnatural, and theatrical in the sense of artificial.

Nor, again, is it enough that there should be accurate and appropriate costumes of beautiful colours; there must be also beauty of colour on the stage as a whole, and as long as the background is painted by one artist, and the foreground figures independently designed by another, there is the danger of a want of harmony in the scene as a picture. For each scene the colour-scheme should be settled as absolutely as for the decoration of a room, and the textures which it is proposed to use should be mixed and re-mixed in every possible combination, and what is discordant removed. Then, as regards the particular kinds of colours, the stage is often too glaring, partly through the excessive use of hot, violent reds, and partly through the costumes looking too new. Shabbiness, which in modern life is merely the tendency of the lower orders towards tone, is not without its artistic value, and modern colours are often much improved by being a little faded. Blue also is too frequently used: it is not merely a dangerous colour to wear by gaslight, but it is really difficult in England to get a thoroughly good blue. The fine Chinese blue, which we all so much admire, takes two years to dye, and the English public will not wait so long for a colour. Peacock blue, of course, has been employed on the stage, notably at the Lyceum, with great advantage; but all attempts at a good light blue, or good dark blue, which I have seen have been failures. The value of black is hardly appreciated; it was used effectively by Mr. Irving in *Hamlet* as the central note of a composition, but as a tone-giving neutral its importance is not recognised. And this is curious, considering the general colour of the dress of a century in which, as Baudelaire says, 'Nous célébrons tous quelque enterrement.'[1] The archaeologist of the future will probably point to this age as the time when the beauty of black was understood; but I hardly think that, as regards stage-mounting or house decoration, it really is. Its decorative value is, of course, the same as that of white or gold; it can separate and harmonise colours. In modern plays the black frock-coat of the hero becomes important in itself, and should be given a suitable background. But it rarely is. Indeed the only good background for a play in modern dress which I have ever seen was the dark grey and cream-white scene of the first act of the *Princesse Georges* in Mrs. Langtry's production. As a rule, the hero is smothered in *bric-à-brac* and palm-trees, lost in the gilded abyss of Louis Quatorze furniture, or reduced to a mere midge in the midst of marqueterie; whereas the background should always be kept as a background, and colour subordinated to effect. This, of course, can only be done when there is one single mind directing the whole production. The facts of art are diverse, but the essence of artistic effect is unity. Monarchy, Anarchy, and Republicanism may contend for the government of nations; but a theatre should be in the power of a cultured despot. There may be division of labour, but there must be no division of mind. Whoever understands the costume of an age understands of necessity its architecture and its surroundings also, and it is easy to see from the chairs of a century whether it was a century of crinolines or not. In fact, in art there is no specialism, and a really artistic production should bear the impress of one master, and one master only, who not merely should design and arrange everything, but should have complete control over the way in which each dress is to be worn.

Mademoiselle Mars, in the first production of *Hernani*, absolutely refused to call her lover '*Mon Lion!*' unless she was allowed to wear a little fashionable *toque* then much in vogue on the Boulevards; and many young ladies on our own stage insist to the present day on wearing stiff starched petticoats under Greek dresses, to the entire ruin of all delicacy of line and fold; but these wicked things should not be allowed. And there should be far more dress rehearsals than there are now. Actors such as Mr. Forbes-Robertson, Mr. Conway, Mr. George Alexander, and others, not to mention older artists, can move with ease and elegance in the attire of any century; but there are not a few who seem dreadfully embarrassed about their hands if they have no side pockets, and who always wear their dresses as if they were costumes. Costumes, of course, they are to the designer; but dresses they should be to those that wear them. And it is time that a stop should be put to the idea, very prevalent on the stage, that the Greeks and Romans always went about bareheaded in the open air – a mistake the Elizabethan managers did not fall into, for they gave hoods as well as gowns to their Roman senators.

More dress rehearsals would also be of value in explaining to the actors that there is a form of gesture and movement that is not merely appropriate

---

[1] We are all dressed for a funeral.

to each style of dress, but really conditioned by it. The extravagant use of the arms in the eighteenth century, for instance, was the necessary result of the large hoop, and the solemn dignity of Burleigh owed as much to his ruff as to his reason. Besides, until an actor is at home in his dress, he is not at home in his part.

Of the value of beautiful costume in creating an artistic temperament in the audience, and producing that joy in beauty for beauty's sake, without which the great masterpieces of art can never be understood, I will not here speak; though it is worth while to notice how Shakespeare appreciated that side of the question in the production of his tragedies, acting them always by artificial light, and in a theatre hung with black; but what I have tried to point out is that archaeology is not a pedantic method, but a method of artistic illusion, and that costume is a means of displaying character without description, and of producing dramatic situations and dramatic effects. And I think it is a pity that so many critics should have set themselves to attack one of the most important movements on the modern stage before that movement has at all reached its proper perfection. That it will do so, however, I feel as certain as that we shall require from our dramatic critics in the future higher qualifications than that they can remember Macready or have seen Benjamin Webster; we shall require of them, indeed, that they cultivate a sense of beauty. *Pour être plus difficile, la tâche n'en est que plus glorieuse.*[1] And if they will not encourage, at least they must not oppose, a movement of which Shakespeare of all dramatists would have most approved, for it has the illusion of truth for its method, and the illusion of beauty for its result. Not that I agree with everything that I have said in this essay. There is much with which I entirely disagree. The essay simply represents an artistic standpoint, and in aesthetic criticism attitude is everything. For in art there is no such thing as a universal truth. A Truth in art is that whose contradictory is also true. And just as it is only in art-criticism, and through it, that we can apprehend the Platonic theory of ideas, so it is only in art-criticism, and through it, that we can realise Hegel's system of contraries. The truths of metaphysics are the truths of masks.

---

[1] The task is all the more glorious for being more difficult.

THE SOUL OF MAN UNDER SOCIALISM

THE chief advantage that would result from the establishment of Socialism is, undoubtedly, the fact that Socialism would relieve us from that sordid necessity of living for others which, in the present condition of things, presses so hardly upon almost everybody. In fact, scarcely any one at all escapes.

Now and then, in the course of the century, a great man of science, like Darwin; a great poet like Keats; a fine critical spirit like M. Renan; a supreme artist like Flaubert, has been able to isolate himself, to keep himself out of reach of the clamorous claims of others, to stand, 'under the shelter of the wall,' as Plato puts it, and so to realise the perfection of what was in him, to his own incomparable gain, and to the incomparable and lasting gain of the whole world. These, however, are exceptions. The majority of people spoil their lives by an unhealthy and exaggerated altruism – are forced, indeed, so to spoil them. They find themselves surrounded by hideous poverty, by hideous ugliness, by hideous starvation. It is inevitable that they should be strongly moved by all this. The emotions of man are stirred more quickly than man's intelligence; and as I pointed out some time ago in an article on the function of criticism, it is much more easy to have sympathy with suffering than it is to have sympathy with thought. Accordingly, with admirable, though misdirected intentions, they very seriously and very sentimentally set themselves to the task of remedying the evils that they see. But their remedies do not cure the disease: they merely prolong it. Indeed, their remedies are part of the disease.

They try to solve the problem of poverty, for instance, by keeping the poor alive; or, in the case of a very advanced school, by amusing the poor.

But this is not a solution; it is an aggravation of the difficulty. The proper aim is to try and reconstruct society on such a basis that poverty will be impossible. And the altruistic virtues have really prevented the carrying out of this aim. Just as the worst slave-owners were those who were kind to their slaves, and so prevented the horror of the system being realised by those who suffered from it, and understood by those who contemplated it, so, in the present state of things in England, the people who do most harm are the people who try to do most good; and at last we have had the spectacle of men who have really studied the problem and know the life – educated men who live in the East End – coming forward and imploring the community to restrain its altruistic impulses of charity, benevolence, and the like. They do so on the ground that such charity degrades and demoralises. They are perfectly right. Charity creates a multitude of sins.

There is also this to be said. It is immoral to use private property in order to alleviate the horrible evils that result from the institution of private property. It is both immoral and unfair.

Under Socialism all this will, of course, be altered. There will be no people living in fetid dens and fetid rags, and bringing up unhealthy, hunger-pinched children in the midst of impossible and absolutely repulsive surroundings. The security of society will not depend, as it does now, on the state of the weather. If a frost comes we shall not have a hundred thousand men out of work, tramping about the streets in a state of disgusting misery, or whining to their neighbours for alms, or crowding round the doors of loathsome shelters to try and secure a hunch of bread and a night's unclean lodging. Each member of the society will share in the general prosperity and happiness of the society, and if a frost comes no one will practically be anything the worse.

Upon the other hand, Socialism itself will be of value simply because it will lead to Individualism.

Socialism, Communism, or whatever one chooses to call it, by converting private property into public wealth, and substituting co-operation for competition, will restore society to its proper condition of a thoroughly healthy organism, and ensure the material well-being of each member of the community. It will, in fact, give Life its proper basis and its proper environment. But, for the full development of Life to its highest mode of perfection, something more is needed. What is needed is Individualism. If the Socialism is Authoritarian; if there are Governments armed with economic power as they are now with political power; if, in a word, we are to have Industrial Tyrannies, then the last state of man will be worse than the first. At present, in consequence of the existence of private property, a great many people are enabled to develop a certain very limited amount of Individualism. They are either under no necessity to work for their living, or are enabled to choose the sphere of activity that is really congenial to them, and gives them pleasure. These are the poets, the philosophers, the men of science, the men of culture – in a word, the real men, the men who have realised themselves, and in whom all Humanity gains a partial realisation. Upon the other hand, there are a great many people who, having no private property of their own, and being always on the brink of sheer starvation, are compelled to do the work of beasts of burden, to do work that is quite uncongenial to them, and to which they are forced by the peremptory, unreasonable, degrading Tyranny of want. These are the poor; and amongst them there is no grace of manner, or charm of speech, or civilisation or culture, or refinement in pleasures, or joy of life. From their collective force Humanity gains much in material prosperity. But it is only the material result that it gains, and the man who is poor is in himself absolutely of no importance. He is merely the infinitesimal atom of a force that, so far from regarding him, crushes him: indeed, prefers him crushed, as in that case he is far more obedient.

Of course it might be said that the Individualism generated under conditions of private property is not always, or even as a rule, of a fine or wonderful type, and that the poor, if they have not culture and charm, have still many virtues. Both these statements would be quite true. The possession of private property is very often extremely demoralising, and that is, of course, one of the reasons why Socialism wants to get rid of the institution. In fact, property is really a nuisance. Some years ago people went about the country saying that property has duties. They said it so often and so tediously that, at last, the Church has begun to say it. One hears it now from every pulpit. It is perfectly true. Property not merely has duties, but has so many duties that its possession to any large extent is a bore. It involves endless claims upon one, endless attention to business, endless bother. If property had simply pleasures, we could stand it; but its duties make it unbearable. In the interest of the rich we must get rid of it. The virtues of the poor may be readily admitted, and are much to be regretted. We are often told that the poor are grateful for charity. Some of them are, no doubt, but the best amongst the poor are never grateful. They are ungrateful, discontented, disobedient, and rebellious. They are quite right to be so. Charity they feel to be a ridiculously inadequate mode of partial restitution, or a sentimental dole, usually accompanied by some impertinent attempt on the part of the sentimentalist to tyrannise over their private lives. Why should they be grateful for the crumbs that fall from the rich man's table? They should be seated at the board, and are beginning to know it. As for being discontented, a man who would not be discontented with such surroundings and such a low mode of life would be a perfect brute. Disobedience, in the eyes of any one who has read history, is man's original virtue. It is through disobedience that progress has been made, through disobedience and through rebellion. Sometimes the poor are praised for being thrifty. But to recommend thrift to the poor is both grotesque and insulting. It is like advising a man who is starving to eat less. For a town or country labourer to practise thrift would be absolutely immoral. Man should not be ready to show that he can live like a badly fed animal. He should decline to live like that, and should either steal or go on the rates, which is considered by many to be a form of stealing. As for begging, it is safer to beg than to take, but it is finer to take than to beg. No: a poor man who is ungrateful, unthrifty, discontented, and rebellious, is probably a real personality, and has much in him. He is at any rate a healthy protest. As for the virtuous poor, one can pity them, of course, but one cannot possibly admire them. They have made private terms with the enemy, and sold their birthright for very bad pottage. They must also be extraordinarily stupid. I can quite understand a man accepting laws that protect private property, and admit of its accumulation, as long as he himself is able under those conditions to realise some form of beautiful and intellectual life. But it is almost incredible to me how a man whose life is marred and made hideous by such laws can possibly acquiesce in their continuance.

However, the explanation is not really difficult to find. It is simply this. Misery and poverty are so absolutely degrading, and exercise such a paralysing effect over the nature of men, that no class is ever really conscious of its own suffering. They have to be told of it by other people, and they often entirely disbelieve them. What is said by great employers of labour against agitators is unquestionably true. Agitators are a set of interfering, meddling people, who come down to some perfectly contented class of the community and sow the seeds of discontent amongst them. That is the reason why agitators are so absolutely necessary. Without them, in our incomplete state, there would be no advance towards civilisation. Slavery was put down in

America, not in consequence of any action on the part of the slaves, or even any express desire on their part that they should be free. It was put down entirely through the grossly illegal conduct of certain agitators in Boston and elsewhere, who were not slaves themselves, nor owners of slaves, nor had anything to do with the question really. It was, undoubtedly, the Abolitionists who set the torch alight, who began the whole thing. And it is curious to note that from the slaves themselves they received, not merely very little assistance, but hardly any sympathy even; and when at the close of the war the slaves found themselves free, found themselves indeed so absolutely free that they were free to starve, many of them bitterly regretted the new state of things. To the thinker, the most tragic fact in the whole of the French Revolution is not that Marie Antoinette was killed for being a queen, but that the starved peasant of the Vendée voluntarily went out to die for the hideous cause of feudalism.

It is clear, then, that no Authoritarian Socialism will do. For while under the present system a very large number of people can lead lives of a certain amount of freedom and expression and happiness, under an industrial-barrack system, or a system of economic tyranny, nobody would be able to have any such freedom at all. It is to be regretted that a portion of our community should be practically in slavery, but to propose to solve the problem by enslaving the entire community is childish. Every man must be left quite free to choose his own work. No form of compulsion must be exercised over him. If there is, his work will not be good for him, will not be good in itself, and will not be good for others. And by work I simply mean activity of any kind.

I hardly think that any Socialist, nowadays, would seriously propose that an inspector should call every morning at each house to see that each citizen rose up and did manual labour for eight hours. Humanity has got beyond that stage, and reserves such a form of life for the people whom, in a very arbitrary manner, it chooses to call criminals. But I confess that many of the socialistic views that I have come across seem to me to be tainted with ideas of authority, if not of actual compulsion. Of course authority and compulsion are out of the question. All association must be quite voluntary. It is only in voluntary associations that man is fine.

But it may be asked how Individualism, which is now more or less dependent on the existence of private property for its development, will benefit by the abolition of such private property. The answer is very simple. It is true that, under existing conditions, a few men who have had private means of their own, such as Byron, Shelley, Browning, Victor Hugo, Baudelaire, and others, have been able to realise their personality, more or less completely. Not one of these men ever did a single day's work for hire. They were relieved from poverty. They had an immense advantage. The question is whether it would be for the good of Individualism that such an advantage should be taken away. Let us suppose that it is taken away. What happens then to Individualism? How will it benefit?

It will benefit in this way. Under the new conditions Individualism will be far freer, far finer, and far more intensified than it is now. I am not talking of the great imaginatively realised Individualism of such poets as I have mentioned, but of the great actual Individualism latent and potential in mankind generally. For the recognition of private property has really harmed Individualism, and obscured it, by confusing a man with what he possesses. It has led Individualism entirely astray. It has made gain, not growth, its aim. So that man thought that the important thing was to have, and did not know that the important thing is to be. The true perfection of man lies, not in what man has, but in what man is. Private property has crushed true Individualism, and set up an Individualism that is false. It has debarred one part of the community from being individual by starving them. It has debarred the other part of the community from being individual by putting them on the wrong road, and encumbering them. Indeed, so completely has man's personality been absorbed by his possessions that the English law has always treated offences against a man's property with far more severity than offences against his person, and property is still the test of complete citizenship. The industry necessary for the making of money is also very demoralising. In a community like ours, where property confers immense distinction, social position, honour, respect, titles, and other pleasant things of the kind, man, being naturally ambitious, makes it his aim to accumulate this property, and goes on wearily and tediously accumulating it long after he has got far more than he wants, or can use, or enjoy, or perhaps even know of. Man will kill himself by overwork in order to secure property, and really, considering the enormous advantages that property brings, one is hardly surprised. One's regret is that society should be constructed on such a basis that man has been forced into a groove in which he cannot freely develop what is wonderful, and fascinating, and delightful in him – in which, in fact, he misses the true pleasure and joy of living. He is also, under existing conditions, very insecure. An enormously wealthy merchant may be – often is – at every moment of his life at the mercy of things that are not under his control. If the wind blows an extra point or so, or the weather suddenly changes, or some trivial thing happens, his ship may go down, his speculations may go wrong, and he finds himself a poor man, with his social position quite gone. Now, nothing should be able to harm a man except himself. Nothing should be able to rob a man at all. What a man really has, is what is in him. What is outside of him should be a matter of no importance.

With the abolition of private property, then, we shall have true, beautiful, healthy Individualism. Nobody will waste his life in accumulating things, and the symbols for things. One will live. To live is the rarest thing in the world. Most people exist, that is all.

It is a question whether we have ever seen the full expression of a personality, except on the imaginative plane of art. In action, we never have. Caesar, says Mommsen, was the complete and perfect man. But how tragically insecure was Caesar! Wherever there is a man who exercises authority, there is a man who resists authority. Caesar was very perfect, but his perfection travelled by too dangerous a road. Marcus Aurelius was the perfect man, says

Renan. Yes, the great emperor was a perfect man. But how intolerable were the endless claims upon him! He staggered under the burden of the empire. He was conscious how inadequate one man was to bear the weight of that Titan and too vast orb. What I mean by a perfect man is one who develops under perfect conditions; one who is not wounded, or worried, or maimed, or in danger. Most personalities have been obliged to be rebels. Half their strength has been wasted in friction. Byron's personality, for instance, was terribly wasted in its battle with the stupidity and hypocrisy and Philistinism of the English. Such battles do not always intensify strength; they often exaggerate weakness. Byron was never able to give us what he might have given us. Shelley escaped better. Like Byron, he got out of England as soon as possible. But he was not so well known. If the English had realised what a great poet he really was, they would have fallen on him with tooth and nail, and made his life as unbearable to him as they possibly could. But he was not a remarkable figure in society, and consequently he escaped, to a certain degree. Still, even in Shelley the note of rebellion is sometimes too strong. The note of the perfect personality is not rebellion, but peace.

It will be a marvellous thing – the true personality of man – when we see it. It will grow naturally and simply, flowerlike, or as a tree grows. It will not be at discord. It will never argue or dispute. It will not prove things. It will know everything. And yet it will not busy itself about knowledge. It will have wisdom. Its value will not be measured by material things. It will have nothing. And yet it will have everything, and whatever one takes from it, it will still have, so rich will it be. It will not be always meddling with others, or asking them to be like itself. It will love them because they will be different. And yet while it will not meddle with others, it will help all, as a beautiful thing helps us, by being what it is. The personality of man will be very wonderful. It will be as wonderful as the personality of a child.

In its development it will be assisted by Christianity, if men desire that; but if men do not desire that, it will develop none the less surely. For it will not worry itself about the past, nor care whether things happened or did not happen. Nor will it admit any laws but its own laws; nor any authority but its own authority. Yet it will love those who sought to intensify it, and speak often of them. And of these Christ was one.

'Know thyself!' was written over the portal of the antique world. Over the portal of the new world, 'Be thyself' shall be written. And the message of Christ to man was simply 'Be thyself.' That is the secret of Christ.

When Jesus talks about the poor he simply means personalities, just as when he talks about the rich he simply means people who have not developed their personalities. Jesus moved in a community that allowed the accumulation of private property just as ours does, and the gospel that he preached was, not that in such a community it is an advantage for a man to live on scanty, unwholesome food, to wear ragged, unwholesome clothes, to sleep in horrid, unwholesome dwellings, and a disadvantage for a man to live under healthy, pleasant, and decent conditions. Such a view would have been wrong there and then, and would, of course, be still more wrong now and in England; for as man moves northward the material necessities of life become of more vital importance, and our society is infinitely more complex, and displays far greater extremes of luxury and pauperism than any society of the antique world. What Jesus meant was this. He said to man, 'You have a wonderful personality. Develop it. Be yourself. Don't imagine that your perfection lies in accumulating or possessing external things. Your affection is inside of you. If only you could realise that, you would not want to be rich. Ordinary riches can be stolen from a man. Real riches cannot. In the treasury-house of your soul, there are infinitely precious things, that may not be taken from you. And so, try to so shape your life that external things will not harm you. And try also, to get rid of personal property. It involves sordid preoccupation, endless industry, continual wrong. Personal property hinders Individualism at every step.' It is to be noted that Jesus never says that impoverished people are necessarily good, or wealthy people necessarily bad. That would not have been true. Wealthy people are, as a class, better than impoverished people, more moral, more intellectual, more well-behaved. There is only one class in the community that thinks more about money than the rich, and that is the poor. The poor can think of nothing else. That is the misery of being poor. What Jesus does say, is that man reaches his perfection, not through what he has, not even through what he does, but entirely through what he is. And so the wealthy young man who comes to Jesus is represented as a thoroughly good citizen, who has broken none of the laws of his state, none of the commandments of his religion. He is quite respectable, in the ordinary sense of that extraordinary word. Jesus says to him, 'You should give up private property. It hinders you from realising your perfection. It is a drag upon you. It is a burden. Your personality does not need it. It is within you, and not outside of you, that you will find what you really are, and what you really want.' To his own friends he says the same thing. He tells them to be themselves, and not to be always worrying about other things. What do other things matter? Man is complete in himself. When they go into the world, the world will disagree with them. That is inevitable. The world hates Individualism. But that is not to trouble them. They are to be calm and self-centred. If a man takes their cloak, they are to give him their coat, just to show that material things are of no importance. If people abuse them, they are not to answer back. What does it signify? The things people say of a man do not alter a man. He is what he is. Public opinion is of no value whatsoever. Even if people employ actual violence, they are not to be violent in turn. That would be to fall to the same low level. After all, even in prison, a man can be quite free. His soul can be free. His personality can be untroubled. He can be at peace. And, above all things, they are not to interfere with other people or judge them in any way. Personality is a very mysterious thing. A man cannot always be estimated by what he does. He may keep the law, and yet be worthless. He may break the law, and yet be fine. He may be bad, without ever doing anything bad. He may commit a sin against society, and yet realise through that sin his true perfection.

There was a woman who was taken in adultery. We are not told the history of her love, but that love must have been very great; for Jesus said that her sins were forgiven her, not because she repented, but because her love was so intense and wonderful. Later on, a short time before his death, as he sat at a feast, the woman came in and poured costly perfumes on his hair. His friends tried to interfere with her, and said that it was extravagance, and that the money that the perfume cost should have been expended on charitable relief of people in want, or something of that kind. Jesus did not accept that view. He pointed out that the material needs of Man were great and very permanent, but that the spiritual needs of Man were greater still, and that in one divine moment, and by selecting its own mode of expression, a personality might make itself perfect. The world worships the woman, even now, as a saint.

Yes, there are suggestive things in Individualism. Socialism annihilates family life, for instance. With the abolition of private property, marriage in its present form must disappear. This is part of the programme. Individualism accepts this and makes it fine. It converts the abolition of legal restraint into a form of freedom that will help the full development of personality, and make the love of man and woman more wonderful, more beautiful, and more ennobling. Jesus knew this. He rejected the claims of family life, although they existed in his day and community in a very marked form. 'Who is my mother? Who are my brothers?' he said, when he was told that they wished to speak to him. When one of his followers asked leave to go and bury his father, 'Let the dead bury the dead,' was his terrible answer. He would allow no claim whatsoever to be made on personality.

And so he who would lead a Christlike life is he who is perfectly and absolutely himself. He may be a great poet, or a great man of science, or a young student at a University, or one who watches sheep upon a moor; or a maker of dramas, like Shakespeare, or a thinker about God, like Spinoza; or a child who plays in a garden, or a fisherman who throws his net into the sea. It does not matter what he is, as long as he realises the perfection of the soul that is within him. All imitation in morals and in life is wrong. Through the streets of Jerusalem at the present day crawls one who is mad and carries a wooden cross on his shoulders. He is a symbol of the lives that are marred by imitation. Father Damien was Christlike when he went out to live with the lepers, because in such service he realised fully what was best in him. But he was not more Christlike than Wagner when he realised his soul in music; or than Shelley, when he realised his soul in song. There is no one type for man. There are as many perfections as there are imperfect men. And while to the claims of charity a man may yield and yet be free, to the claims of conformity no man may yield and remain free at all.

Individualism, then, is what through Socialism we are to attain. As a natural result the State must give up all idea of government. It must give it up because, as a wise man once said many centuries before Christ, there is such a thing as leaving mankind alone; there is no such thing as governing mankind. All modes of government are failures. Despotism is unjust to everybody, including the despot, who was probably made for better things. Oligarchies are unjust to the many, and ochlocracies are unjust to the few. High hopes were once formed of democracy; but democracy means simply the bludgeoning of the people by the people for the people. It has been found out. I must say that it was high time, for all authority is quite degrading. It degrades those who exercise it, and degrades those over whom it is exercised. When it is violently, grossly, and cruelly used, it produces a good effect, by creating, or at any rate bringing out, the spirit of revolt and Individualism that is to kill it. When it is used with a certain amount of kindness, and accompanied by prizes and rewards, it is dreadfully demoralising. People, in that case, are less conscious of the horrible pressure that is being put on them, and so go through their lives in a sort of coarse comfort, like petted animals, without ever realising that they are probably thinking other people's thoughts, living by other people's standards, wearing practically what one may call other people's second-hand clothes, and never being themselves for a single moment. 'He who would be free,' says a fine thinker, 'must not conform.' And authority, by bribing people to conform, produces a very gross kind of over-fed barbarism amongst us.

With authority, punishment will pass away. This will be a great gain – a gain, in fact, of incalculable value. As one reads history, not in the expurgated editions written for schoolboys and passmen, but in the original authorities of each time, one is absolutely sickened, not by the crimes that the wicked have committed, but by the punishments that the good have inflicted; and a community is infinitely more brutalised by the habitual employment of punishment than it is by the occasional occurrence of crime. It obviously follows that the more punishment is inflicted the more crime is produced, and most modern legislation has clearly recognised this, and has made it its task to diminish punishment as far as it thinks it can. Wherever it has really diminished it, the results have always been extremely good. The less punishment, the less crime. When there is no punishment at all, crime will either cease to exist, or, if it occurs, will be treated by physicians as a very distressing form of dementia, to be cured by care and kindness. For what are called criminals nowadays are not criminals at all. Starvation, and not sin, is the parent of modern crime. That indeed is the reason why our criminals are, as a class, so absolutely uninteresting from any psychological point of view. They are not marvellous Macbeths and terrible Vautrins. They are merely what ordinary respectable, commonplace people would be if they had not got enough to eat. When private property is abolished there will be no necessity for crime, no demand for it; it will cease to exist. Of course all crimes are not crimes against property, though such are the crimes that the English law, valuing what a man has more than what a man is, punishes with the harshest and most horrible severity (if we except the crime of murder, and regard death as worse than penal servitude, a point on which our criminals, I believe, disagree). But though a crime may not be against property, it may spring from the misery and rage and depression produced by our wrong system of property-holding, and so, when that system is abolished, will disappear. When each member of the community has sufficient for his wants, and is not interfered with by his neighbour, it will not be an object of any interest to him to interfere with any one else. Jealousy, which is an extraordinary source of crime in modern life, is an emotion closely bound up with our conceptions of property, and under Socialism and Individualism will die out. It is remarkable that in communistic tribes jealousy is entirely unknown.

Now as the State is not to govern, it may be asked what the State is to do. The State is to be a voluntary manufacturer and distributor of necessary commodities. The State is to make what is useful. The individual is to make what is beautiful. And as I have mentioned the word labour, I cannot help saying that a great deal of nonsense is being written and talked nowadays about the dignity of manual labour. There is nothing necessarily dignified about manual labour at all, and most of it is absolutely degrading. It is mentally and morally injurious to man to do anything in which he does not find pleasure, and many forms of labour are quite pleasureless activities, and should be regarded as such. To sweep a slushy crossing for eight hours on a day when the east wind is blowing is a disgusting occupation. To sweep it with mental, moral, or physical dignity seems to me to be impossible. To sweep it with joy would be appalling. Man is made for something better than disturbing dirt. All work of that kind should be done by a machine.

And I have no doubt that it will be so. Up to the present, man has been, to a certain extent, the slave of machinery, and there is something tragic in the fact that as soon as man had invented a machine to do his work he began to starve. This, however, is, of course, the result of our property system and our system of competition. One man owns a machine which does the work of five hundred men. Five hundred men are, in consequence, thrown out of employment, and, having no work to do, become hungry and take to thieving. The one man secures the produce of the machine and keeps it, and has five hundred times as much as he should have, and probably, which is of much more importance, a great deal more than he really wants. Were that machine the property of all, everybody would benefit by it. It would be an immense advantage to the community. All unintellectual labour, all monotonous, dull labour, all labour that deals with dreadful things, and involves unpleasant conditions, must be done by machinery. Machinery must work for us in coal mines, and do all sanitary services, and be the stoker of steamers, and clean the streets, and run messages on wet days, and do anything that is tedious or distressing. At present machinery competes against man. Under proper conditions machinery will serve man. There is no doubt at all that this is the future of machinery; and just as trees grow while the country gentleman is asleep, so while Humanity will be amusing itself, or enjoying cultivated leisure – which, and not labour, is the aim of man – or making beautiful things, or reading beautiful things, or simply contemplating the world with admiration and delight, machinery will be doing all the necessary and unpleasant work. The fact is, that civilisation requires slaves. The Greeks were quite right there. Unless there are slaves to do the ugly, horrible, uninteresting work, culture and contemplation become almost impossible. Human slavery is wrong, insecure, and demoralising. On mechanical slavery, on the slavery of the machine, the future of the world depends. And when scientific men are no longer called upon to go down to a depressing East End and distribute bad cocoa and worse blankets to starving people, they will have delightful leisure in which to devise wonderful and marvellous things for their own joy and the joy of every one else. There will be great storages of force for every city, and for every house if required, and this force man will convert into heat, light, or motion, according to his needs. Is this Utopian? A map of the world that does not include Utopia is not worth even glancing at, for it leaves out the one country at which Humanity is always landing. And when Humanity lands there, it looks out, and, seeing a better country, sets sail. Progress is the realisation of Utopias.

Now, I have said that the community by means of organisation of machinery will supply the useful things, and that the beautiful things will be made by the individual. This is not merely necessary, but it is the only possible way by which we can get either the one or the other. An individual who has to make things for the use of others, and with reference to their wants and their wishes, does not work with interest, and consequently cannot put into his work what is best in him. Upon the other hand, whenever a community or a powerful section of a community, or a government of any kind, attempts to dictate to the artist what he is to do, Art either entirely vanishes, or becomes stereotyped, or degenerates into a low and ignoble form of craft. A work of art is the unique result of a unique temperament. Its beauty comes from the fact that the author is what he is. It has nothing to do with the fact that other people want what they want. Indeed, the moment that an artist takes notice of what other people want, and tries to supply the demand, he ceases to be an artist, and becomes a dull or an amusing craftsman, an honest or a dishonest tradesman. He has no further claim to be considered as an artist. Art is the most intense mode of Individualism that the world has known. I am inclined to say that it is the only real mode of Individualism that the world has known. Crime, which, under certain conditions, may seem to have created Individualism, must take cognisance of other people and interfere with them. It belongs to the sphere of action. But alone, without any reference to his neighbours, without any interference the artist can fashion a beautiful thing; and if he does not do it solely for his own pleasure, he is not an artist at all.

And it is to be noted that it is the fact that Art is this intense form of Individualism that makes the public try to exercise over it an authority that is as immoral as it is ridiculous, and as corrupting as it is contemptible. It is not quite their fault. The public has always, and in every age, been badly brought up. They are continually asking Art to be popular, to please their want of taste, to flatter their absurd vanity, to tell them what they have been told before, to show them what they ought to be tired of seeing, to amuse them when they feel heavy after eating too much, and to distract their thoughts when they are wearied of their own stupidity. Now Art should never try to be popular. The public should try to make itself artistic. There is a very wide difference. If a man of science were told that the results of his experiments, and the conclusions that he arrived at, should be of such a character that they would not upset the received popular notions on the subject, or disturb popular prejudice, or hurt the sensibilities of people who knew nothing about science; if a philosopher were told that he had a perfect right to speculate in the highest spheres of thought, provided that he arrived at the same conclusions as were held by those who had never thought in any sphere at all – well, nowadays the man of science and the philosopher would be considerably amused. Yet it is really a very few years since both philosophy and science were subjected to brutal popular control, to authority in fact – the authority of either the general ignorance of the community, or the terror and greed for power of an ecclesiastical or governmental class. Of course, we have to a very great extent got rid of any attempt on the part of the community, or the Church, or the Government, to interfere with the individualism of speculative thought, but the attempt to interfere with the individualism of imaginative art still lingers. In fact, it does more than linger; it is aggressive, offensive, and brutalising.

In England, the arts that have escaped best are the arts in which the public take no interest. Poetry is an instance of what I mean. We have been able to have fine poetry in England because the public do not read it, and consequently do not influence it. The public like to insult poets because they are individual, but once they have insulted them, they leave them alone. In the case of the novel and the drama, arts in which the public do take an interest, the result of the exercise of popular authority has been absolutely ridiculous. No country produces such badly written fiction, such tedious, common work in the novel form, such silly, vulgar plays as England. It must necessarily be so. The popular standard is of such a character that no artist can get to it. It is at once too easy and too difficult to be a popular novelist. It is too easy, because the requirements of the public as far as plot, style, psychology, treatment of life, and treatment of literature are concerned are within the reach of the very meanest capacity and the most uncultivated mind. It is too difficult, because to meet such requirements the artist would have to do violence to his temperament, would have to write not for the artistic joy of writing, but for the amusement of half-educated people, and so would have to suppress his individualism, forget his culture, annihilate his style, and surrender everything that is valuable in him. In the case of the drama, things are a little better; the theatre-going public like the obvious, it is true, but they do not like the tedious; and burlesque and farcical comedy, the two most popular forms, are distinct forms of art. Delightful work may be produced under burlesque and farcical conditions, and in work of this kind the artist in England is allowed very great freedom. It is when one comes to the higher forms of the drama that the result of popular control is seen. The one thing that the public dislike is novelty. Any attempt to extend the subject-matter of art is extremely distasteful to the public; and yet the vitality and progress of art depend in a large measure on the continual extension of subject-matter. The public dislike novelty because they are afraid of it. It represents to them a mode of Individualism, an assertion on the part of the artist that he selects his own subject, and treats it as he chooses. The public are quite right in their attitude. Art is Individualism, and Individualism is a disturbing and disintegrating force. Therein lies its immense value. For what it seeks to disturb is monotony of type, slavery of custom, tyranny of habit, and the reduction of man to the level of a machine. In Art, the public accept what has been, because they cannot alter it, not because they appreciate it. They swallow their classics whole, and never taste them. They endure them as the inevitable, and as they cannot mar them, they mouth about them. Strangely enough, or not strangely, according to one's own views, this acceptance of the classics does a great deal of harm. The uncritical admiration of the Bible and Shakespeare in England is an instance of what I mean. With regard to the Bible, considerations of ecclesiastical authority enter into the matter, so that I need not dwell upon the point.

But in the case of Shakespeare it is quite obvious that the public really see neither the beauties nor the defects of his plays. If they saw the beauties, they would not object to the development of the drama; and if they saw the defects, they would not object to the development of the drama either. The fact is, the public make use of the classics of a country as a means of checking the progress of Art. They degrade the classics into authorities. They use them as bludgeons for preventing the free expression of Beauty in new forms. They are always asking a writer why he does not write like somebody else, or a painter why he does not paint like somebody else, quite oblivious of the fact that if either of them did anything of the kind he would cease to be an artist. A fresh mode of Beauty is absolutely distasteful to them, and whenever it appears they get so angry and bewildered that they always use two stupid expressions – one is that the work of art is grossly unintelligible; the other, that the work of art is grossly immoral. What they mean by these words seems to me to be this. When they say a work is grossly unintelligible, they mean that the artist has said or made a beautiful thing that is new; when they describe a work as grossly immoral, they mean that the artist has said or made a beautiful thing that is true. The former expression has reference to style; the latter to subject-matter. But they probably use the words very vaguely, as an ordinary mob will use ready-made paving stones. There is not a single real poet or prose-writer of this century, for instance, on whom the British public have not solemnly conferred diplomas of immorality, and these diplomas practically take the place, with us, of what in France is the formal recognition of an Academy of Letters, and fortunately make the establishment of such an institution quite unnecessary in England. Of course, the public are very reckless in their use of the word. That they should have called Wordsworth an immoral poet, was only to be expected. Wordsworth was a poet. But that they should have called Charles Kingsley an immoral novelist is extraordinary. Kingsley's prose was not of a very fine quality. Still, there is the word, and they use it as best they can. An artist is, of course, not disturbed by it. The true artist is a man who believes absolutely in himself, because he is absolutely himself. But I can fancy that if an artist produced a work of art in England that immediately on its appearance was recognised by the public, through their medium, which is the public Press, as a work that was quite intelligible and highly moral, he would begin seriously to question whether in its creation he had really been himself at all, and consequently whether the work was not quite unworthy of him, and either of a thoroughly second-rate order, or of no artistic value whatsoever.

On the whole, an artist in England gains something by being attacked. His individuality is intensified. He becomes more completely himself. Of course, the attacks are very gross, very impertinent, and very contemptible. But then no artist expects grace from the vulgar mind, or style from the suburban intellect. Vulgarity and stupidity are two very vivid facts in modern life. One regrets them, naturally. But there they are. They are subjects for study, like everything else. And it is only fair to state, with regard to modern journalists, that they always apologise to one in private for what they have written against one in public.

Within the last few years two other adjectives, it may be mentioned, have been added to the very limited vocabulary of art-abuse that is at the disposal of the public. One is the word 'unhealthy,' the other is the word 'exotic.' The latter merely expresses the rage of the momentary mushroom against the immortal, entrancing, and exquisitely lovely orchid. It is a tribute, but a tribute of no importance. The word 'unhealthy,' however, admits of analysis. It is a rather interesting word. In fact, it is so interesting that the people who use it do not know what it means.

What does it mean? What is a healthy or an unhealthy work of art? All terms that one applies to a work of art, provided that one applies them rationally, have reference to either its style or its subject, or to both together. From the point of view of style, a healthy work of art is one whose style recognises the beauty of the material it employs, be that material one of words or of bronze, of colour or of ivory, and uses that beauty as a factor in producing the aesthetic effect. From the point of view of subject, a healthy work of art is one the choice of whose subject is conditioned by the temperament of the artist, and comes directly out of it. In fine, a healthy work of art is one that has both perfection and personality. Of course, form and substance cannot be separated in a work of art; they are always one. But for purposes of analysis, and setting the wholeness of aesthetic impression aside for a moment, we can intellectually so separate them. An unhealthy work of art, on the other hand, is a work whose style is obvious, old-fashioned and common, and whose subject is deliberately chosen, not because the artist has any pleasure in it, but because he thinks that the public will pay him for it. In fact, the popular novel that the public call healthy is always a thoroughly unhealthy production; and what the public call an unhealthy novel is always a beautiful and healthy work of art.

Perhaps, however, I have wronged the public in limiting them to such words as 'immoral,' 'unintelligible,' 'exotic,' and 'unhealthy.' There is one other word that they use. That word is 'morbid.' They do not use it often. The meaning of the word is so simple that they are afraid of using it. Still, they use it sometimes, and now, and then, one comes across it in popular newspapers. It is, of course, a ridiculous word to apply to a work of art. For what is morbidity but a mood of emotion or a mode of thought that one cannot express? The public are all morbid, because the public can never find expression for anything. The artist is never morbid. He expresses everything. He stands outside his subject, and through its medium produces incomparable and artistic effects. To call an artist morbid because he deals with morbidity as his subject-matter is as silly as if one called Shakespeare mad because he wrote *King Lear*.

I need hardly say that I am not, for a single moment, complaining that the public and the public Press misuse these words. I do not see how, with their lack of comprehension of what Art is, they could possibly use them in the proper sense. I am merely pointing out the misuse; and as for the origin of the misuse and the meaning that lies behind it all, the explanation is very simple. It comes from the barbarous conception of authority. It comes from the natural inability of a community corrupted by authority to understand or appreciate Individualism. In a word, it comes from that monstrous and ignorant thing that is called Public Opinion, which, bad and well-meaning as it is when it tries to control action, is infamous and of evil meaning when it tries to control Thought or Art.

Indeed, there is much more to be said in favour of the physical force of the public than there is in favour of the public's opinion. The former may be fine. The latter must be foolish. It is often said that force is no argument. That, however, entirely depends on what one wants to prove. Many of the most important problems of the last few centuries, such as the continuance of personal government in England, or of feudalism in France, have been solved entirely by means of physical force. The very violence of a revolution may make the public grand and splendid for a moment. It was a fatal day when the public discovered that the pen is mightier than the paving-stone, and can be made as offensive as the brickbat. They at once sought for the journalist, found him, developed him, and made him their industrious and well-paid servant. It is greatly to be regretted, for both their sakes. Behind the barricade there may be much that is noble and heroic. But what is there behind the leading-article but prejudice, stupidity, cant and twaddle? And when these four are joined together they make a terrible force, and constitute the new authority.

In old days men had the rack. Now they have the Press. That is an improvement certainly. But still it is very bad, and wrong, and demoralising. Somebody – was it Burke? – called Journalism the fourth estate. That was true at the time, no doubt. But at the present moment it really is the only estate. It has eaten up the other three. The Lords Temporal say nothing, the Lords Spiritual have nothing to say, and the House of Commons has nothing to say and says it. We are dominated by Journalism. In America the President reigns for four years, and Journalism governs for ever and ever. Fortunately, in America, Journalism has carried its authority to the grossest and most brutal extreme. As a natural consequence it has begun to create a spirit of revolt. People are amused by it, or disgusted by it, according to their temperaments. But it is no longer the real force it was. It is not seriously treated. In England, Journalism, except in a few well-known instances, not having been carried to such excesses of brutality, is still a great factor, a really remarkable power. The tyranny that it proposes to exercise over people's private lives seems to me to be quite extraordinary. The fact is that the public have an insatiable curiosity to know everything, except what is worth knowing. Journalism, conscious of this, and having tradesman-like habits, supplies their demands. In centuries before ours the public nailed the ears of journalists to the pump. That was quite hideous. In this century journalists have nailed their own ears to the keyhole. That is much worse. And what aggravates the mischief is that the journalists who are most to blame are not the amusing journalists who write for what are called Society papers. The harm is done by the serious, thoughtful, earnest journalists, who solemnly, as they are doing at present, will drag before the eyes of the public some incident in the private life of a great statesman, of a man who is a leader of political thought as he is a creator of political force, and invite the public to discuss the incident, to exercise authority in the matter, to give their views, and not merely to give their views, but to carry them into action, to dictate to the man upon all other points, to dictate to his party, to dictate to his country; in fact, to make themselves ridiculous, offensive, and harmful. The private lives of men and women should not be told to the public. The public have nothing to do with them at all.

In France they manage these things better. There they do not allow the details of the trials that take place in the divorce courts to be published for the amusement or criticism of the public. All that the public are allowed to know is that the divorce has taken place and was granted on petition of one or other or both of the married parties concerned. In France, in fact, they limit the journalist, and allow the artist almost perfect freedom. Here we allow absolute freedom to the journalist and entirely limit the artist. English public opinion, that is to say, tries to constrain and impede and warp the man who makes things that are beautiful in effect, and compels the journalist to retail things that are ugly, or disgusting, or revolting in fact, so that we have the most serious journalists in the world and the most indecent newspapers. It is no exaggeration to talk of compulsion. There are possibly some journalists who take a real pleasure in publishing horrible things, or who, being poor, look to scandals as forming a sort of permanent basis for an income. But there are other journalists, I feel certain, men of education and cultivation, who really dislike publishing these things, who know that it is wrong to do so, and only do it because the unhealthy conditions under which their occupation is carried on oblige them to supply the public with what the public wants, and to compete with other journalists in making that supply as full and satisfying to the gross popular appetite as possible. It is a very degrading position for any body of educated men to be placed in, and I have no doubt that most of them feel it acutely.

However, let us leave what is really a very sordid side of the subject, and return to the question of popular control in the matter of Art, by which I mean Public Opinion dictating to the artist the form which he is to use, the mode in which he is to use it, and the materials with which he is to work. I have pointed out that the arts which had escaped best in England are the arts in which the public have not been interested. They are, however, interested in the drama, and as a certain advance has been made in the drama within the last ten or fifteen years, it is important to point out that this advance is entirely due to a few individual artists refusing to accept the popular want of taste as their standard, and refusing to regard Art as a mere matter of demand and supply. With his marvellous and vivid personality, with a style that has really a true colour-element in it, with his extraordinary power, not over mere mimicry, but over imaginative and intellectual creation, Mr. Irving, had his sole object been to give the public what they wanted, could have produced the commonest plays in the commonest manner, and made as much success and money as a man could possibly desire. But his object was not that. His object was to realise his own perfection as an artist, under certain conditions and in certain forms of Art. At first he appealed to the few: now he has educated the many. He has created in the public both taste and temperament. The public appreciate his artistic success immensely. I often wonder, however, whether the public understand that that success is entirely due to the fact that he did not accept their standard, but realised his own. With their standard the Lyceum would have been a sort of second-rate booth, as some of the popular theatres in London are at present. Whether they understand it or not, the fact however remains, that taste and temperament have, to a certain extent, been created in the public, and that the public is capable of developing these qualities. The problem then is, why do not the public become more civilised? They have the capacity. What stops them?

The thing that stops them, it must be said again, is their desire to exercise authority over the artists and over works of art. To certain theatres, such as the Lyceum and the Haymarket, the public seem to come in a proper mood. In both of these theatres there have been individual artists, who have succeeded in creating in their audiences – and every theatre in London has its own audience – the temperament of which Art appeals. And what is that temperament? It is the temperament of receptivity. That is all.

If a man approaches a work of art with any desire to exercise authority over it and the artist, he approaches it in such a spirit that he cannot receive any artistic impression from it at all. The work of art is to dominate the spectator: the spectator is not to dominate the work of art. The spectator is to be receptive. He is to be the violin on which the master is to play. And the more completely he can suppress his own silly views, his own foolish prejudices, his own absurd ideas of what Art should be, or should not be, the more likely he is to understand and appreciate the work of art in question. This is, of course, quite obvious in the case of the vulgar theatre-going public of English men and women. But it is equally true of what are called educated people. For an educated person's ideas of Art are drawn naturally from what Art has been, whereas the new work of art is beautiful by being what Art has never been; and to measure it by the standard of the past is to measure it by a standard on the rejection of which its real perfection depends. A temperament capable of receiving, through an imaginative medium, and under imaginative conditions, new and beautiful impressions, is the only temperament that can appreciate a work of art. And true as this is in a case of appreciation of sculpture and painting, it is still more true of the appreciation of such arts as the drama. For a picture and a statue are not at war with Time. They take no account of its succession. In one moment their unity may be apprehended. In the case of literature it is different. Time must be traversed before the unity of effect is realised. And so, in the drama, there may occur in the first act of the play something whose real artistic value may not be evident to the spectator till the third or fourth act is reached. Is the silly fellow to get angry and call out, and disturb the play, and annoy the artists? No. The honest man is to sit quietly, and know the delightful emotions of wonder, curiosity, and suspense. He is not to go to the play to lose a vulgar temper. He is to go to the play to realise an artistic temperament. He is to go to the play to gain an artistic temperament. He is not the arbiter of the work of art. He is one who is admitted to contemplate the work of art, and, if the work be fine, to forget in its contemplation all the egotism that mars him – the egotism of his ignorance, or the egotism of his information. The point about the drama is hardly, I think, sufficiently recognised. I can quite understand that were *Macbeth* produced for the first time before a modern London audience, many of the people present would strongly and vigorously object to the introduction of the witches in the first act, with their grotesque phrases and their ridiculous words. But when the play is over one realises that the laughter of the witches in *Macbeth* is as terrible as the laughter of madness in *Lear*, more terrible than the laughter of Iago in the tragedy of the Moor. No spectator of art needs a more perfect mood of receptivity than the spectator of a play. The moment he seeks to exercise authority he becomes the avowed enemy of Art, and of himself. Art does not mind. It is he who suffers.

With the novel it is the same thing. Popular authority and the recognition of popular authority are fatal. Thackeray's *Esmond* is a beautiful work of art because he wrote it to please himself. In his other novels, in *Pendennis*, in *Philip*, in *Vanity Fair* even, at times, he is too conscious of the public, and spoils his work by appealing directly to the sympathies of the public, or by directly mocking at them. A true artist takes no notice whatever of the public. The public are to him non-existent. He has no poppied or honeyed cakes through which to give the monster sleep or sustenance. He leaves that to the popular novelist. One incomparable novelist we have now in England, Mr. George Meredith. There are better artists in France, but France has no one whose view of life is so large, so varied, so imaginatively true. There are tellers of stories in Russia who have a more vivid sense of what pain in fiction may be. But to him belongs philosophy in fiction. His people not merely live, but they live in thought. One can see them from myriad points of view. They are suggestive. There is soul in them and around them. They are interpretative and symbolic. And he who made them, those wonderful, quickly moving figures, made them for his own pleasure, and has never asked the public what they wanted, has never cared to know what they wanted, has never allowed the public to dictate to him or influence him in any way, but has gone on intensifying his own personality, and producing his own individual work. At first none came to him. That did not matter. Then the few came to him. That did not change him. The many have come now. He is still the same. He is an incomparable novelist.

With the decorative arts it is not different. The public clung with really pathetic tenacity to what I believe were the direct traditions of the Great Exhibition of international vulgarity, traditions that were so appalling that the houses in which people lived were only fit for blind people to live in. Beautiful things began to be made, beautiful colours came from the dyer's hand, beautiful patterns from the artist's brain, and the use of beautiful things and their value and importance were set forth. The public were really very indignant. They lost their temper. They said silly things. No one minded. No one was a whit the worse. No one accepted the authority of public opinion. And now it is almost impossible to enter any modern house without seeing some recognition of good taste, some recognition of the value of lovely surroundings, some sign of appreciation of beauty. In fact, people's houses are, as a rule, quite charming nowadays. People have been to a very great extent civilised. It is only fair to state, however, that the extraordinary success of the revolution in house-decoration and furniture and the like has not really been due to the majority of the public developing a very fine taste in such matters. It has been chiefly due to the fact that the craftsmen of things so appreciated the pleasure of making what was beautiful, and woke to such a vivid consciousness of the hideousness and vulgarity of what the public had previously wanted, that they simply starved the public out. It would be quite impossible at the present moment to furnish a room as rooms were furnished a few years ago, without going for everything to an auction of second-hand furniture from some third-rate lodging-house. The things are no longer made. However they may object to it, people must nowadays have something charming in their surroundings. Fortunately for them, their assumption of authority in these art-matters came to entire grief.

It is evident, then, that all authority in such things is bad. People sometimes inquire what form of government is most suitable for an artist to live under. To this question there is only one answer. The form of government that is most suitable to the artist is no government at all. Authority over him and his art is ridiculous. It has been stated that under despotism artists have produced lovely work. This is not quite so. Artists have visited despots, not as subjects to be tyrannised over, but as wandering wonder-makers, as fascinating vagrant personalities, to be entertained and charmed and suffered to be at peace, and allowed to create. There is this to be said in favour of the despot, that he, being an individual, may have culture, while the mob, being a monster, has none. One who is an Emperor and King may stoop down to pick up a brush for a painter, but when the democracy stoops down it is merely to throw mud. And yet the democracy have not so far to stoop as the emperor. In fact, when they want to throw mud they have not to stoop at all.

But there is no necessity to separate the monarch from the mob; all authority is equally bad.

There are three kinds of despots. There is the despot who tyrannises over the body. There is the despot who tyrannises over the soul. There is the despot who tyrannises over the soul and body alike. The first is called the Prince. The second is called the Pope. The third is called the People. The Prince may be cultivated. Many Princes have been. Yet in the Prince there is danger. One thinks of Dante at the bitter feast in Verona, of Tasso in Ferrara's madman's cell. It is better for the artist not to live with Princes. The Pope may be cultivated. Many Popes have been; the bad Popes have been. The bad Popes loved Beauty, almost as passionately, nay, with as much passion as the good Popes hated Thought. To the wickedness of the Papacy humanity owes much. The goodness of the Papacy owes a terrible debt to humanity. Yet, though the Vatican has kept the rhetoric of its thunders, and lost the rod of its lightning, it is better for the artist not to live with Popes. It was a Pope who said of Cellini to a conclave of Cardinals that common laws and common authority were not made for men such as he; but it was a Pope who thrust Cellini into prison, and kept him there till he sickened with rage, and created unreal visions for himself, and saw the gilded sun enter his room, and grew so enamoured of it that he sought to escape, and crept out from tower to tower, and falling through dizzy air at dawn, maimed himself, and was by a vine-dresser covered with vine leaves, and carried in a cart to one who, loving beautiful things, had care of him. There is danger in Popes. And as for the People, what of them and their authority? Perhaps of them and their authority one has spoken enough. Their authority is a thing blind, deaf, hideous, grotesque, tragic, amusing, serious and obscene. It is impossible for the artist to live with the People. All despots bribe. The People bribe and brutalise. Who told them to exercise authority? They were made to live, to listen, and to love. Some one has done them a great wrong. They have marred themselves by imitation of their superiors. They have taken the sceptre of the Prince. How should they use it? They have taken the triple tiara of the Pope. How should they carry its burden? They are as a clown whose heart is broken. They are as a priest whose soul is not yet born. Let all who love Beauty pity them. Though they themselves love not Beauty, yet let them pity themselves. Who taught them the trick of tyranny?

There are many other things that one might point out. One might point out how the Renaissance was great, because it sought to solve no social problem, and busied itself not about such things, but suffered the individual to develop freely, beautifully, and naturally, and so had great and individual artists, and great and individual men. One might point out how Louis XIV, by creating the modern state, destroyed the individualism of the artist, and made things monstrous in their monotony of repetition, and contemptible in their conformity to rule, and destroyed throughout all France all those fine freedoms of expression that had made tradition new in beauty, and new modes one with antique form. But the past is of no importance. The present is of no importance. It is with the future that we have to deal. For the past is what man should not have been. The present is what man ought not to be. The future is what artists are.

It will, of course, be said that such a scheme as is set forth here is quite unpractical, and goes against human nature. This is perfectly true. It is unpractical, and it goes against human nature. This is why it is worth carrying out, and that is why one proposes it. For what is a practical scheme? A practical scheme is either a scheme that is already in existence, or a scheme that could be carried out under existing conditions. But it is exactly the existing conditions that one objects to; and any scheme that could accept these conditions is wrong and foolish. The conditions will be done away with, and human nature will change. The only thing that one really knows about human nature is that it changes. Change is the one quality we can predicate of it. The systems that fail are those that rely on the permanency of human nature, and not on its growth and development. The error of Louis XIV was that he thought human nature would always be the same. The result of his error was the French Revolution. It was an admirable result. All the results of the mistakes of governments are quite admirable.

It is to be noted that Individualism does not come to the man with any sickly cant about duty, which merely means doing what other people want because they want it; or any hideous cant about self-sacrifice, which is merely a survival of savage mutilation. In fact, it does not come to a man with any claims upon him at all. It comes naturally and inevitably out of man. It is the point to which all development tends. It is the differentiation to which all organisms grow. It is the perfection that is inherent in every mode of life, and towards which every mode of life quickens. And so Individualism exercises no compulsion over man. On the contrary, it says to man that he should suffer no compulsion to be exercised over him. It does not try to force people to be good. It knows that people are good when they are let alone. Man will develop Individualism out of himself. Man is now so developing Individualism. To ask whether Individualism is practical is like asking whether Evolution is practical. Evolution is the law of life, and there is no evolution except towards individualism. Where this tendency is not expressed, it is a case of artificially arrested growth, or of disease, or of death.

Individualism will also be unselfish and unaffected. It has been pointed out that one of the results of the extraordinary tyranny of authority is that words are absolutely distorted from their proper and simple meaning, and are used to express the obverse of their right signification. What is true about Art is true about Life. A man is called affected, nowadays, if he dresses as he likes to dress. But in doing that he is acting in a perfectly natural manner. Affectation, is such matters, consists in dressing, according to the views of one's neighbour, whose views, as they are the views of the majority, will probably be extremely stupid. Or a man is called selfish if he lives in the manner that seems to him most suitable for the full realisation of his own personality; if, in fact, the primary aim of his life is self-development. But this is the way in which every one should live. Selfishness is not living as one wishes to live, it is asking others to live as one wishes to live. And unselfishness is letting other people's lives alone, not interfering with them. Selfishness always aims at creating around it an absolute uniformity of type. Unselfishness recognises infinite variety of type as a delightful thing, accepts it, acquiesces in it, enjoys it. It is not selfish to think for oneself. A man who does not think for himself does not think at all. It is grossly selfish to require of one's neighbour that he should think in the same way, and hold the same opinions. Why should he? If he can think, he will probably think differently. If he cannot think, it is monstrous to require thought of any kind from him. A red rose is not selfish because it wants to be a red rose. It would be horribly selfish if it wanted all the other flowers in the garden to be both red and roses. Under Individualism people will be quite natural and absolutely unselfish, and will know the meanings of the words, and realise them in their free, beautiful lives. Nor will men be egotistic as they are now. For the egotist is he who makes claims upon others, and the Individualist will not desire to do that. It will not give him pleasure. When man has realised Individualism, he will also realise sympathy and exercise it freely and spontaneously. Up to the present man has hardly cultivated sympathy at all. He has merely sympathy with pain, and sympathy with pain is not the highest form of sympathy. All sympathy is fine, but sympathy with suffering is the least fine mode. It is tainted with egotism. It is apt to become morbid. There is in it a certain element of terror for our own safety. We became afraid that we ourselves might be as the leper or as the blind, and that no man would have care of us. It is curiously limiting, too. One should sympathise with the entirety of life, not with life's sores and maladies merely, but with life's joy and beauty and energy and health and freedom. The wider sympathy is, of course, the more difficult. It requires more unselfishness. Anybody can sympathise with the sufferings of a friend, but it requires a very fine nature – it requires, in fact, that nature of a true Individualist – to sympathise with a friend's success.

In the modern stress of competition and struggle for place, such sympathy is naturally rare, and is also very much stifled by the immoral ideal of uniformity of type and conformity to rule which is so prevalent everywhere, and is perhaps most obnoxious in England.

Sympathy with pain there will, of course, always be. It is one of the first instincts of man. The animals which are individual, the higher animals, that is to say, share it with us. But it must be remembered that while sympathy with joy intensifies the sum of joy in the world, sympathy with pain does not really diminish the amount of pain. It may make man better able to endure evil, but the evil remains. Sympathy with consumption does not cure consumption; that is what science does. And when Socialism has solved the problem of poverty, and Science solved the problem of disease, the area of the sentimentalists will be lessened, and the sympathy of man will be large, healthy and spontaneous. Man will have joy in the contemplation of the joyous life of others.

For it is through joy that the Individualism of the future will develop itself. Christ made no attempt to reconstruct society, and consequently the Individualism that he preached to man could be realised only through pain or in solitude. The Ideals that we owe to Christ are the ideals of the man who abandons society entirely, or of the man who resists society absolutely. But man is naturally social. Even the Thebaid became peopled at last. And though the cenobite realises his personality, it is often an impoverished personality that he so realises. Upon the other hand, the terrible truth that pain is a mode through which man may realise himself exercises a wonderful fascination over the world. Shallow speakers and shallow thinkers in pulpits and on platforms often talk about the world's worship of pleasure, and whine against it. But it is rarely in the world's history that its ideal has been one of joy and beauty. The worship of pain has far more often dominated the world. Medievalism, with its saints and martyrs, its love of self-torture, its wild passion for wounding itself, its gashing with knives, and its whipping with rods – Medievalism is real Christianity, and the medieval Christ is the real Christ. When the Renaissance dawned upon the world, and brought with it the new ideals of the beauty of life and the joy of living, men could not understand Christ. Even Art shows us that. The painters of the Renaissance drew Christ as a little boy playing with another boy in a palace or a garden, or lying back in his mother's arms, smiling at her, or at a flower, or at a bright bird; or as a noble, stately figure moving nobly through the world; or as a wonderful figure rising in a sort of ecstasy from death to life. Even when they drew him crucified they drew him as a beautiful God on whom evil men had inflicted suffering. But he did not preoccupy them much. What delighted them was to paint the men and women whom they admired, and to show the loveliness of this lovely earth. They painted many religious pictures – in fact they painted far too many, and the monotony of type and motive is wearisome, and was bad for art. It was the result of the authority of the public in art-matters, and is to be deplored. But their soul was not in the subject. Raphael was a great artist when he painted his portrait of the Pope. When he painted his Madonnas and infant Christs, he was not a great artist at all. Christ had no message for the Renaissance, which was wonderful because it brought an ideal at variance with his, and to find the presentation of the real Christ we must go to medieval art. There he is one maimed and marred; one who is not comely to look on, because Beauty is a joy; one who is not in fair raiment, because that may be a joy also: he is a beggar who has a marvellous soul; he is a leper whose soul is divine; he needs neither property nor health; he is a God realising his perfection through pain.

The evolution of man is slow. The injustice of men is great. It was necessary that pain should be put forward as a mode of self-realisation. Even now, in some places in the world, the message of Christ is necessary. No one who lived in modern Russia could possibly realise his perfection except by pain. A few Russian artists have realised themselves in Art; in a fiction that is mediaeval in character, because its dominant note is the realisation of men through suffering. But for those who are not artists, and to whom there is no mode of life but the actual life of fact, pain is the only door to perfection. A Russian who lives happily under the present system of government in Russia must either believe that man has no soul, or that, if he has, it is not worth developing. A Nihilist who rejects all authority because he knows authority to be evil, and welcomes all pain, because through that he realises his personality, is a real Christian. To him the Christian ideal is a true thing.

And yet, Christ did not revolt against authority. He accepted the imperial authority of the Roman Empire and paid tribute. He endured the ecclesiastical authority of the Jewish Church, and would not repel its violence by any violence of his own. He had, as I said before, no scheme for the reconstruction of society. But the modern world has schemes. It proposes to do away with poverty, and the suffering that it entails. It desires to get rid of pain, and the suffering that pain entails. It trusts to Socialism and to Science as its methods. What it aims at is an Individualism expressing itself through joy. This Individualism will be lárger, fuller, lovelier than any Individualism has ever been. Pain is not the ultimate mode of perfection. It is merely provisional and a protest. It has reference to wrong, unhealthy, unjust surroundings. When the wrong, and the disease, and the injustice are removed, it will have no further place. It was a great work, but it is almost over. Its sphere lessens every day.

Nor will man miss it. For what man has sought for is, indeed, neither pain nor pleasure, but simply Life. Man has sought to live intensely, fully, perfectly. When he can do so without exercising restraint on others, or suffering it ever, and his activities are all pleasurable to him, he will be saner, healthier, more civilised, more himself. Pleasure is Nature's test, her sign of approval. When man is happy, he is in harmony with himself and his environment. The new Individualism, for whose service Socialism, whether it wills it or not, is working, will be perfect harmony. It will be what the Greeks sought for, but could not, except in Thought, realise completely because they had slaves, and fed them; it will be what the Renaissance sought for, but could not realise completely except in Art, because they had slaves, and starved them. It will be complete, and through it each man will attain to his perfection. The new Individualism is the new Hellenism.

THE RISE OF HISTORICAL CRITICISM

1

HISTORICAL criticism nowhere occurs as an isolated fact in the civilisation or literature of any people. It is part of that complex working towards freedom which may be described as the revolt against authority. It is merely one facet of that speculative spirit of an innovation, which in the sphere of action produces democracy and revolution, and in that of thought is the parent of philosophy and physical science; and its importance as a factor of progress is based not so much on the results it attains, as on the tone of thought which it represents, and the method by which it works.

Being thus the resultant of forces essentially revolutionary, it is not to be found in the ancient world among the material despotisms of Asia or the stationary civilisation of Egypt. The clay cylinders of Assyria and Babylon, the hieroglyphics of the pyramids, form not history but the material for history.

The Chinese annals, ascending as they do to the barbarous forest life of the nation, are marked with a soberness of judgment, a freedom from invention, which is almost unparalleled in the writings of any people; but the protective spirit which is the characteristic of that people proved as fatal to their literature as to their commerce. Free criticism is as unknown as free trade. While as regards the Hindus, their acute, analytical and logical mind is directed rather to grammar criticism and philosophy than to history or chronology. Indeed, in history their imagination seems to have run wild, legend and fact are so indissolubly mingled together that any attempt to separate them seems vain. If we except the identification of the Greek Sandracottus with the Indian Chandragupta we have really no clue by which we can test the truth of their writings or examine their method of investigation.

It is among the Hellenic branch of the Indo-Germanic race that history proper is to be found, as well as the spirit of historical criticism; among the wonderful offshoot of the primitive Aryans, whom we call by the name of Greeks and to whom, as has been well said, we owe all that moves in the world except the blind forces of nature.

For, from the day when they left the chill table-lands of Tibet and journeyed, a nomad people, to Aegean shores, the characteristic of their nature has been the search for light, and the spirit of historical criticism is part of that wonderful *Aufklärung* or illumination of the intellect which seems to have burst on the Greek race like a great flood of light about the sixth century B.C.

L'esprit d'un siècle ne nâit pas et ne meurt pas à jour fixe,[1] and the first critic is perhaps as difficult to discover as the first man. It is from democracy that the spirit of criticism borrows its intolerance of dogmatic authority, from physical science the alluring analogies of law and order, from philosophy the con-

---

[1] The spirit of an age is not born and does not die on a definite day.

ception of an essential unity underlying the complex manifestations of phenomena. It appears first as rather a changed attitude of mind than as a principle of research, and its earliest influences are to be found in the sacred writings.

For men begin to doubt in questions of religion first, and then in matters of more secular interest; and as regards the nature of the spirit of historical criticism itself in its ultimate development, it is not merely confined to the empirical method of ascertaining whether an event happened or not, but is concerned also with the investigation into the causes of events, the general relations which phenomena of life hold to one another, and in its ultimate development passes into the wider question of the philosophy of history.

Now, while the workings of historical criticism in these two spheres of sacred and uninspired history are essentially manifestations of the same spirit, yet their methods are so different, the canons of evidence so entirely separate, and the motives in each case so unconnected, that it will be necessary for a clear estimation of the progress of Greek thought, that we should consider these two questions entirely apart from one another. I shall then in both cases take the succession of writers in their chronological order as representing the rational order – not that the succession of time is always the succession of ideas, or that dialectics moves ever in the straight line in which Hegel conceives its advance. In Greek thought, as elsewhere, there are periods of stagnation and apparent retrogression, yet their intellectual development, not merely in the question of historical criticism, but in their art, their poetry and their philosophy, seems so essentially normal, so free from all disturbing external influences, so peculiarly rational, that in following in the footsteps of time we shall really be progressing in the order sanctioned by reason.

2

At an early period in their intellectual development the Greeks reached that critical point in the history of every civilised nation, when speculative invades the domain of revealed truth, when the spiritual ideas of the people can no longer be satisfied by the lower, material conceptions of their inspired writers, and when men find it impossible to pour the new wine of free thought into the old bottles of a narrow and a trammelling creed.

From their Aryan ancestors they had received the fatal legacy of a mythology stained with immoral and monstrous stories which strove to hide the rational order of nature in a chaos of miracles, and to mar by imputed wickedness the perfection of God's nature – a very shirt of Nessos in which the Heracles of rationalism barely escaped annihilation. Now while undoubtedly the speculations of Thales, and the alluring analogies of law and order afforded by physical science, were most important forces in encouraging the rise of the spirit of scepticism, yet it was on its ethical side that the Greek mythology was chiefly open to attack.

It is difficult to shake the popular belief in miracles, but no man will admit sin and immortality as attributes of the Ideal he worships; so the first symptoms of a new order of thought are shown in the passionate outcries of Xenophanes and Heraclitos against the evil things said by Homer of the sons of God; and in the story told of Pythagoras, how that he saw tortured in Hell the 'two founders of Greek theology,' we can recognise the rise of the *Aufklärung* as clearly as we see the Reformation foreshadowed in the *Inferno* of Dante.

Any honest belief, then, in the plain truth of these stories soon succumbed before the destructive effects of the *a priori* ethical criticism of this school; but the orthodox party, as is their custom, found immediately a convenient shelter under the aegis of the doctrine of metaphors and concealed meanings.

To this allegorical school the tale of the fight around the walls of Troy was a mystery, behind which, as behind a veil, were hidden certain moral and physical truths. The contest between Athena and Ares was that eternal contest between rational thought and the brute force of ignorance; the arrows which rattled in the quiver of the 'Far Darter' were no longer the instruments of vengeance shot from the golden bow of the child of God, but the common rays of the sun, which was itself nothing but a mere inert mass of burning metal.

Modern investigation, with the ruthlessness of Philistine analysis, has ultimately brought Helen of Troy down to a symbol of the dawn. There were Philistines among the Greeks also who saw in the ἄναξ ἀνδρῶν[1] a mere metaphor for atmospheric power.

Now while this tendency to look for metaphors and hidden meaning must be ranked as one of the germs of historical criticism, yet it was essentially unscientific. Its inherent weakness is clearly pointed out by Plato, who showed that while this theory will no doubt explain many of the current legends, yet, if it is to be appealed to at all, it must be as a universal principle; a position he is by no means prepared to admit.

Like many other great principles it suffered from its disciples, and furnished its own refutation when the web of Penelope was analysed into a metaphor of the rules of formal logic, the warp representing the premises, and the woof the conclusion.

Rejecting, then, the allegorical interpretation of the sacred writings as an essentially dangerous method, proving either too much or too little, Plato himself returns to the earlier mode of attack, and re-writes history with a didactic purpose, laying down certain ethical canons of historical criticism. God is good; God is just; God is true; God is without the common passions of men. There are the tests to which we are to bring the stories of the Greek religion.

God predestines no men to ruin, nor sends destruction on innocent cities; He never walks the earth in strange disguise, nor has to mourn for

---

[1] Lord of men.

the death of any well-beloved son. Away with the tears for Sarpedon, the lying dream sent to Agamemnon, and the story of the broken covenant! (Plato, *Republic*, Book ii. 380; iii. 388, 391.)

Similar ethical canons are applied to the accounts of the heroes of the days of old, and by the same *a priori* principles Achilles is rescued from the charges of avarice and insolence in a passage which may be recited as the earliest instance of that 'whitewashing of great men,' as it has been called, which is so popular in our own day, when Catilines and Clodius are represented as honest and far-seeing politicians, when *eine edle und gute Natur*[1] is claimed for Tiberius, and Nero is rescued from his heritage of infamy as an accomplished *dilettante* whose moral aberrations are more than excused by his exquisite artistic sense and charming tenor voice.

But besides the allegorising principle of interpretation, and the ethical reconstruction of history, there was a third theory, which may be called the semi-historical, and which goes by the name of Euhemeros, though he was by no means the first to propound it.

Appealing to a fictitious monument which he declared that he had discovered in the island of Panchaia, and which purported to be a column erected by Zeus, and detailing the incidents of his reign on earth, this shallow thinker attempted to show that the gods and heroes of ancient Greece were 'mere ordinary mortals, whose achievements had been a good deal exaggerated and misrepresented,' and that the proper canon of historical criticism as regards the treatment of myths was to rationalise the incredible, and to present the plausible residuum as actual truth.

To him and his school, the centaurs, for instance, those mythical sons of the storm, strange links between the lives of men and animals, were merely some youths from the village of Nephele in Thessaly, distinguished for their sporting tastes; the 'living harvest of panoplied knights,' which sprang so mystically from the dragon's teeth, a body of mercenary troops supported by the profits on a successful speculation in ivory; and Actaeon, an ordinary master of hounds, who, living before the days of subscription, was eaten out of house and home by the expenses of his kennel.

Now that under the glamour of myth and legend some substratum of historical fact may lie, is a proposition rendered extremely probable by the modern investigations into the workings of the mythopoeic spirit in post-Christian times. Charlemagne and Roland, St. Francis and William Tell, are none the less real personages because their histories are filled with much that is fictitious and incredible, but in all cases what is essentially necessary is some external corroboration, such as is afforded by the mention of Roland and Roncesvalles in the chronicles of England, or (in the sphere of Greek legend) by the excavations of Hissarlik. But to rob a mythical narrative of its kernel of supernatural elements, and to present the dry husk thus obtained as historical fact, is, as has been well said, to mistake entirely the true method of

---

[1] A noble and fine nature.

investigation and to identify plausibility with truth.

And as regards the critical point urged by Palaiphatos, Strabo, and Polybios, that pure invention on Homer's part is inconceivable, we may without scruple allow it, for myths, like constitutions, grow gradually, and are not formed in a day. But between a poet's deliberate creation and historical accuracy, there is a wide field of the mythopoeic faculty.

This Euphemeristic theory was welcomed as an essentially philosophical and critical method by the unscientific Romans, to whom it was introduced by the poet Ennius, that pioneer of cosmopolitan Hellenicism, and it continued to characterise the tone of ancient thought on the question of the treatment of mythology till the rise of Christianity, when it was turned by such writers as Augustine and Minucius Felix into a formidable weapon of attack on Paganism. It was then abandoned by all those who still bent the knee to Athena or to Zeus, and a general return, aided by the philosophic mystics of Alexandria, to the allegorising principle of interpretation took place, as the only means of saving the deities of Olympus from the Titan assaults of the new Galilean God. In what vain defence, the statue of Mary set in the heart of the Pantheon can best tell us.

Religions, however, may be absorbed, but they never are disproved, and the stories of the Greek mythology, spiritualised by the purifying influence of Christianity, reappear in many of the southern parts of Europe in our own day.

The old fable that the Greek gods took service with the new religion under assumed names has more truth in it than the many care to discover.

Having now traced the progress of historical criticism in the special treatment of myth and legend, I shall proceed to investigate the form in which the same spirit manifested itself as regards what one may term secular history and secular historians. The field traversed will be found to be in some respects the same, but the mental attitude, the spirit, the motive of investigation are all changed.

There were heroes before the son of Atreus and historians before Herodotus, yet the latter is rightly hailed as the father of history, for in him we discover not merely the empirical connection of cause and effect, but that constant reference to Laws, which is the characteristic of the historian proper.

For all history must be essentially universal; not in the sense of comprising all the synchronous events of the past time, but through the universality of the principles employed. And the great conceptions which unify the work of Herodotus are such as even modern thought has not yet rejected. The immediate government of the world by God, the nemesis and punishment which sin and pride invariably bring with them, the revealing of God's purpose to His people by signs and omens, by miracles and by prophecy; these are to Herodotus the laws which govern the phenomena of history. He is essentially the type of supernatural historian; his eyes are ever strained to discern the Spirit of God moving over the face of the waters of life; he is more concerned with final than with efficient causes.

Yet we can discern in him the rise of that *historic sense* which is the rational antecedent of the science of historical criticism, the φυσικὸν κριτήριον[1], to use the words of a Greek writer, as opposed to that which comes either τέχνη[2] or διδάχη[3].

He has passed through the valley of faith and has caught a glimpse of the sunlit heights of Reason; but like all those who, while accepting the supernatural, yet attempt to apply the canons of rationalism, he is essentially inconsistent. For the better apprehension of the character of this historic sense in Herodotus it will be necessary to examine at some length the various forms of criticism in which it manifests itself.

Such fabulous stories as that of the Phoenix, of the goat-footed men, of the headless beings with eyes in their breasts, of the men who slept six months in the year (τοῦτο οὐκ ἐνδέχομαι τὴν ἀρχήν)[4], of the wehr-wolf of the Neuri, and the like, are entirely rejected by him as being opposed to the ordinary experience of life, and to those natural laws whose universal influence the early Greek physical philosophers had already made known to the world of thought. Other legends, such as the suckling of Cyrus by a bitch, or the feather-rain of northern Europe, are rationalised and explained into a woman's name and a fall of snow. The supernatural origin of the scythian nation, from the union of Hercules and the monstrous Echidna, is set aside by him for the more probable account that they were a nomad tribe driven by the Massagetae from Asia; and he appeals to the local names of their country as proof of the fact that the Kimmerians were the original possessors.

But in the case of Herodotus it will be more instructive to pass on from points like these to those questions of general probability, the true apprehension of which depends rather on a certain quality of mind than on any possibility of formulated rules; questions which form no unimportant part of scientific history, for it must be remembered always that the canons of historical criticism are essentially different from those of judicial evidence, for they cannot, like the latter, be made plain to every ordinary mind, but appeal to a certain historical faculty founded on the experience of life. Besides, the rules for the reception of evidence in courts of law are purely stationary, while the science of historical probability is essentially progressive, and changes with the advancing spirit of each age.

Now of all the speculative canons of historical criticism, none is more important than that which rests on psychological probability.

Arguing from his knowledge of human nature, Herodotus rejects the presence of Helen within the walls of Troy. Has she been there, he says, Priam and his kinsmen would never have been so mad (φρενοβλαβεῖς) as not to give her up, when they and their children and their city were in such peril (ii. 118); and as regards the authority of Homer, some incidental passages in his

---

[1] The intuitive sense of discrimination.
[2] By art.
[3] By instruction.
[4] I don't believe a word of it.

poem show that he knew of Helen's sojourn in Egypt during the siege, but selected the other story as being a more suitable motive for an epic. Similarly he does not believe that the Alcmaeonidae family, a family who had always been the haters of tyranny (μισοτύραννοι), and to whom, even more than to Harmodios and Aristogeiton, Athens owed its liberty, would ever have been so treacherous as to hold up a shield after the battle of Marathon as a signal for the Persian host to fall on the city. A shield, he acknowledges, was held up, but it could not possibly have been done by such friends of liberty as the house of Alcmaeon; nor will he believe that a great king like Rhampsinitus would have sent his daughter κατίσαι ἐπ' οἰκήματος.[1]

Elsewhere he argues from more general consideration of probability; a Greek courtesan like Rhodopis would hardly have been rich enough to build a pyramid, and, besides, on chronological grounds the story is impossible (ii. 134).

In another passage (ii. 63), after giving an account of the forcible entry of the priests of Ares into the chapel of the god's mother, which seems to have been a sort of religious faction fight where sticks were freely used (μάχη ξύλοισι καρτερή)[2] 'I feel sure,' he says, 'that many of them died from getting their heads broken, notwithstanding the assertions of the Egyptian priests to the contrary.' There is also something charmingly naïve in the account he gives of the celebrated Greek swimmer who dived a distance of eighty stadia to give his countrymen warning of the Persian advance. 'If, however,' he says, 'I may offer an opinion on the subject, I would say that he came in a boat.'

There is, of course, something a little trivial in some of the instances I have quoted; but in a writer like Herodotus, who stands on the borderland between faith and rationalism, one likes to note even the most minute instances of the rise of the critical and sceptical spirit of inquiry.

How really strange, at base, it was with him may, I think, be shown by a reference to those passages where he applies rationalistic tests to matters connected with religion. He nowhere, indeed, grapples with the moral and scientific difficulties of the Greek Bible; and where he rejects as incredible the marvellous achievements of Hercules in Egypt, he does so on the express grounds that he had not yet been received among the gods, and so was still subject to the ordinary conditions of mortal life (ἔτι ἄνθρωπον ἐόντα)[3]

Even within these limits, however, his religious conscience seems to have been troubled at such daring rationalism, and the passage (ii. 45) concludes with a pious hope that God will pardon him for having gone so far, the great rationalistic passage being, of course, that in which he rejects the mythical account of the foundation of Dodona. 'How can a dove speak with a human voice?' he asks, and rationalises the bird into a foreign princess.

Similarly he seems more inclined to believe that the great storm at the be-

---

[1] To be a prostitute.
[2] A furious fight with staves.
[3] While still a mortal man.

ginning of the Persian War ceased from ordinary atmospheric causes, and not in consequence of the incantations of the *Magians*. He calls Melampos, whom the majority of the Greeks looked on as an inspired prophet, 'a clever man who had acquired for himself the art of prophecy'; and as regards the miracle told of the Aeginetan statues of the primeval deities of Damia and Auxesia, that they fell on their knees when the sacrilegious Athenians strove to carry them off, 'any one may believe it,' he says, 'who likes, but as for myself, I place no credence in the tale.'

So much then for the rationalistic spirit of historical criticism, as far as it appears explicitly in the works of this great and philosophic writer; but for an adequate appreciation of his position we must also note how conscious he was of the value of documentary evidence, of the use of inscriptions, of the importance of the poets as throwing light on manners and customs as well as on historical incidents. No writer of any age has more vividly recognised the fact that history is a matter of evidence, and that it is as necessary for the historian to state his authority as it is to produce one's witnesses in a court of law.

While, however, we can discern in Herodotus the rise of an historic sense, we must not blind ourselves to the large amount of instances where he receives supernatural influences as part of the ordinary forces of life. Compared to Thucydides, who succeeded him in the development of history, he appears almost like a mediaeval writer matched with a modern rationalist. For, contemporary though they were, between these two authors there is an infinite chasm of thought.

The essential difference of their methods may be best illustrated from those passages where they treat of the same subject. The execution of the Spartan heralds, Nicolaos and Aneristos, during the Peloponnesian War is regarded by Herodotus as one of the most supernatural instances of the working of nemesis and the wrath of an outraged hero; while the lengthened siege and ultimate fall of Troy was brought about by the avenging hand of God desiring to manifest unto men the mighty penalties which always follow upon mighty sins. But Thucydides either sees not, or desires not to see, in either of these events the finger of Providence, or the punishment of wicked doers. The death of the heralds is merely an Athenian retaliation for similar outrages committed by the opposite side; the long agony of ten years' siege is merely due to the want of good commissariat in the Greek army; while the fall of the city is the result of a united military attack consequent on a good supply of provisions.

Now, it is to be observed, that in this latter passage as well as elsewhere, Thucydides is in no sense of the word a sceptic as regards his attitude towards the truth of these ancient legends.

Agamemnon and Atreus, Theseus and Eurystheus, even Minos, about whom Herodotus has some doubts, are to him as real personages as Alcibiades or Gylippus. The points in his historical criticism of the past are, first, his rejection of all extra-natural interference, and, secondly, the attributing to these ancient heroes the motives and modes of thought of his own day.

The present was to him the key to the explanation of the past, as it was to the prediction of the future.

Now as regards his attitude towards the supernatural he is at one with modern science. We too know that, just as the primeval coalbeds reveal to us the traces of rain-drops and other atmospheric phenomena similar to those of our own day, so, in estimating the history of the past, the introduction of no force must be allowed whose workings we cannot observe among the phenomena around us. To lay down canons of ultra-historical credibility for the explanation of events which happen to have preceded us by a few thousand years, is as thoroughly unscientific as it is to intermingle preternatural in geological theories.

Whatever the canons of art may be, no difficulty in history is so great as to warrant the introduction of a θεὸς ἀπὸ μηχανῆς,[1] in the sense of a violation of the laws of nature.

Upon the other point, however, Thucydides falls into an anachronism. To refuse to allow the workings of chivalrous and self-denying motives among the knights of the Trojan crusade, because he saw none in the faction-loving Athenian of his own day, is to show an entire ignorance of the various characteristics of human nature developing under different circumstances, and to deny to a primitive chieftain like Agamemnon that authority founded on opinion, to which we give the name of divine right, is to fall into an historical error quite as gross as attributing to Atreus the courting of the populace (τεθεραπευκότα τόν δῆμον)[2] with a view to the Mycenean throne.

The general method of historical criticism, pursued by Thucydides having been thus indicated, it remains to proceed more into detail as regards those particular points where he claims for himself a more rational method of estimating evidence than either the public or his predecessors possessed.

'So little pains,' he remarks, 'do the vulgar take in the investigation of truth, satisfied with their preconceived opinions,' that the majority of the Greeks believe in a Pitanate cohort of the Spartan army and in a double vote being the prerogative of the Spartan kings, neither of which opinions has any foundation in fact. But the chief point on which he lays stress as evincing the 'uncritical way with which men receive legends, even the legends of their own country,' is the entire baselessness of the common Athenian tradition in which Harmodios and Aristogeiton were represented as the patriotic liberators of Athens from the Peisistratid tyranny. So far, he points out, from the love of freedom being their motive, both of them were influenced by merely personal consideration, Aristogeiton being jealous of Hipparchos' attention to Garmodios, then a beautiful boy in the flower of Greek loveliness, while the latter's indignation was aroused by an insult offered to his sister by the prince.

Their motives, then, were personal revenge, while the result of their conspiracy only served to rivet more tightly the chains of servitude which bound

---

[1] A God artificially introduced into the stage.
[2] Having courted the favour of the people.

Athens to the Peisistratid house, for Hipparchos, whom they killed, was only the tyrant's younger brother, and not the tyrant himself.

To prove his theory that Hippias was the elder, he appeals to the evidence afforded by a public inscription in which his name occurs immediately after that of his father, a point which he thinks shows that he was the eldest, and so the heir. This view he further corroborates by another inscription, on the altar of Apollo, which mentions the children of Hippias and not those of his brothers; 'for it was natural for the eldest to be married first'; and he points out that, had Hippias been the younger, he would not have so easily obtained the tyranny on the death of Hipparchos.

Now, what is important in Thucydides, as evinced in the treatment of legend generally, is not the results he arrived at, but the method by which he works. The first great rationalistic historian, he may be said to have paved the way for all those who followed after him, though it must always be remembered that, while the total absence in his pages of all the mystical paraphernalia of the supernatural theory of life is an advance in the progress of rationalism, and an era in scientific history, whose importance could never be over-estimated, yet we find along with it a total absence of any mention of those various social and economical forces which form such important factors in the evolution of the world, and to which Herodotus rightly gave great prominence in his immortal work. The history of Thucydides is essentially one-sided and incomplete. The intricate details of sieges and battles, subjects with which the historian proper has really nothing to do except so far as they may throw light on the spirit of the age, we would readily exchange for some notice of the condition of private society in Athens, or the influence and position of women.

There is an advance in the method of historical criticism; there is an advance in the conception and motive of history itself; for in Thucydides we may discern that natural reaction against the intrusion of didactic and theological considerations into the sphere of the pure intellect, the spirit of which may be found in the Euripidean treatment of tragedy and the later schools of art, as well as in the Platonic conception of science.

History, no doubt, has splendid lessons for our instruction, just as all good art comes to us as the herald of the noblest truth. But to set before either the painter or the historian the inculcation of moral lessons as an aim to be consciously pursued, is to miss entirely the true motive and characteristic of both art and history, which is in the one case the creation of beauty, in the other the discovery of the laws of the evolution of progress: *Il ne faut demander de l'Art que l'Art, du passé que le passé.*[1]

Herodotus wrote to illustrate the wonderful ways of Providence and the nemesis that falls on sin, and his work is a good example of the truth that nothing can dispense with criticism so much as a moral aim. Thucydides has no creed to preach, no doctrine to prove. He analyses the results which follow inevitably from certain antecedents, in order that on a recurrence of the same

---

[1] Only art must be asked of art, only the past of the past.

crises men may know how to act.

His object was to discover the laws of the past so as to serve as a light to illumine the future. We must not confuse the recognition of the utility of history with any ideas of a didactic aim. Two points more in Thucydides remain for our consideration: his treatment of the rise of Greek civilisation, and of the primitive condition of Hellas, as well as the question how far can he be really said to have recognised the existence of laws regulating the complex phenomena of life.

3

The investigation into the two great problems of the origin of society and the philosophy of history occupies such an important position in the evolution of Greek thought that, to obtain any clear view of the workings of the critical spirit, it will be necessary to trace at some length their rise and scientific development as evinced not merely in the works of historians proper, but also in the philosophical treaties of Plato and Aristotle. The important position which these two great thinkers occupy in the progress of historical criticism can hardly be over-estimated. I do not mean merely as regards their treatment of the Greek Bible, and Plato's endeavours to purge sacred history of its immorality by the application of ethical canons at the time when Aristotle was beginning to undermine the basis of miracles by his scientific conception of law, but with reference to these two wider questions of the rise of civil institutions and the philosophy of history.

And first, as regards the current theories of the primitive condition of society, there was a wide divergence of opinion in Hellenic society, just as there is now, for while the majority of the orthodox public, of whom Hesiod may be taken as the representative, looked back, as a great many of our own day still do, to a fabulous age of innocent happiness, a *bell' età dell' auro*[1] where sin and death were unknown and men and women were like Gods, the foremost men of intellect such as Aristotle and Plato, Æschylus and many of the other poets[2]; saw in primitive man 'a few small sparks of humanity preserved on the tops of mountains after some deluge,' 'without an idea of cities, governments or legislation,' 'living the lives of wild beasts in sunless caves,' 'their only law being the survival of the fittest.'

And this, too, was the opinion of Thucydides, whose *Archaeologia* as it is contains a most valuable disquisition on the early condition of Hellas, which it will be necessary to examine at some length.

Now as regards the means employed generally by Thucydides for the elucidation of ancient history, I have already pointed out how that, while acknowledging that 'it is the tendency of every poet to exaggerate, as it is of every chronicler to seek to be attractive at the expense of truth,' he yet as-

---

[1] Lovely golden age.
[2] *Plato's Laws; Æschylus' Prometheus Bound.*

sumes in the thoroughly euphemeristic way, that under the veil of myth and legend there does yet exist a rational basis of fact discoverable by the method of rejecting all supernatural interference as well as any extraordinary motives influencing the actors. It is in complete accordance with this spirit that he appeals, for instance, to the Homeric epithet of ἀφνειός,[1] as applied to Corinth, as a proof of the early commercial prosperity of that city; to the fact of the generic name *Hellenes* not occurring in the *Iliad* as a corroboration of his theory of the essentially disunited character of the primitive Greek tribes; and he argues from the line 'O'er many islands and all Argos ruled,' as applied to Agamemnon, that his forces must have been partially naval, 'for Agamemnon's was a continental power, and he could not have been master of any but the adjacent islands, and these would not be many but through the possession of a fleet.'

Anticipating in some measure the comparative method of research, he argues from the fact of the more barbarous Greek tribes, such as the Aetolians and Acarnanians, still carrying arms in his own day, that this custom was the case originally over the whole country. 'The fact,' he says, 'that the people in these parts of Hellas are still living in the old way points to a time when the same mode of life was equally common to all.' Similarly, in another passage, he shows how a corroboration of his theory of the respectable character of piracy in ancient days is afforded by 'the honour with which some of the inhabitants of the continent still regard a successful marauder,' as well as by the fact that the question, 'Are you a pirate?' is a common feature of primitive society as shown in the poets; and finally, after observing how the old Greek custom of wearing belts in gymnastic contests still survived among the more uncivilised Asiatic tribes, he observes that 'there are many other points in which a likeness may be shown between the life of the primitive Hellenes and that of the barbarians to-day.'

As regards the evidence afforded by ancient remains, while adducing as a proof of the insecure character of early Greek society the fact of their cities[2] being always built at some distance from the sea, he is yet careful to warn us, and the caution ought to be borne in mind by all archaeologists, that we have no right to conclude from the scanty remains of any city that its legendary greatness in primitive times was a mere exaggeration. 'We are not justified,' he says, 'in rejecting the tradition of the magnitude of the Trojan armament, because Mycenae and the other towns of that age seem to us small and insignificant. For, if Lacedemon was to become desolate, any antiquarian judging merely from its ruins would be inclined to regard the tale of the Spartan hegemony as an idle myth; for the city is a mere collection of villages after the old fashion of Hellas, and has none of those splendid public buildings and temples which characterise Athens, and whose remains, in the case of the lat-

---

[1] Prosperous.

[2] Somewhat in the same spirit Plato in his *Laws*, appeals to the local position of Ilion among the rivers of the plain, as a proof that it was not built till long after the Deluge.

ter city, would be so marvellous as to lead the superficial observer into an exaggerated estimate of the Athenian power.' Nothing can be more scientific than the archaelogical canons laid down, whose truth is so strikingly illustrated to any one who has compared the waste fields of the Eurotas plain with the lordly monuments of the Athenian acropolis.[1]

On the other hand, Thucydides is quite conscious of the value of the positive evidence afforded by archaeological remains. He appeals, for instance, to the character of the armour found in the Delian tombs and the peculiar mode of sepulture, as corroboration of his theory of the predominance of the Carian element among the primitive islanders, and to the concentration of all the temples either in the Acropolis, or in its immediate vicinity, to the name of ἄστυ[2] by which it was still known, and to the extraordinary sanctity of the spring of water there, as proof that the primitive city was originally confined to the citadel, and the district immediately beneath it (ii. 16). And lastly, in the very opening of his history, anticipating one of the most scientific of modern methods, he points out how in early states of civilisation immense fertility of the soil tends to favour the personal aggrandisement of individuals, and so to stop the normal progress of the country through 'the rise of factions, that endless source of ruin'; and also by the allurements it offers to a foreign invader, to necessitate a continual change of population, one immigration following on another. He exemplifies his theory by pointing to the endless political revolutions that characterised Arcadia, Thessaly, and Boeotia, the three richest spots in Greece, as well as by the negative instance of the undisturbed state in primitive time of Attica, which was always remarkable for the dryness and poverty of its soil.

Now, while undoubtedly in these passages we may recognise the first anticipation of many of the most modern principles of research, we must remember how essentially limited is the range of the *archaeologia*, and how no theory at all is offered on the wider questions of the general conditions of the rise and progress of humanity, a problem which is first scientifically discussed in the *Republic* of Plato.

And at the outset it must be premised that, while the study of primitive man is an essentially inductive science, resting rather on the accumulation of evidence than on speculation, among the Greeks it was prosecuted rather on deductive principles. Thucydides did, indeed, avail himself of the opportunities afforded by the unequal development of civilisation in his own day in Greece, and in the places I have pointed out seems to have anticipated the comparative method. But we do not find later writers availing themselves of the wonderfully accurate and picturesque accounts given by Herodotus of the customs of savage tribes. To take one instance, which bears a good deal

---

[1] Plutarch remarks that the *only* evidence Greece possesses of the truth that the legendary power of Athens is no 'romance or idle story,' is the public and sacred buildings. This is an instance of the exaggerated importance given to ruins against which Thucydides is warning us.

[2] Town.

on modern questions, we find in the works of this great traveller the gradual and progressive steps in the development of the family life clearly manifested in the mere gregarious herding together of the Agathyrsi, their primitive kinsmanship through women common, and the rise of a feeling of paternity from a state of polyandry. This tribe stood at that time on that borderland between umbilical relationship and the family which has been such a difficult point for modern anthropologists to find.

The ancient authors, however, are unanimous in insisting that the family is the ultimate unit of society, though, as I have said, an inductive study of primitive races, or even the accounts given of them by Herodotus, would have shown them that the νεοττία ἴδια[1] of a personal household, to use Plato's expression, is really a most complex notion appearing always in a late stage of civilisation, along with recognition of private property and the rights of individualism.

Philology also, which in the hands of modern investigators has proved such a splendid instrument of research, was in ancient days studied on too unscientific principles to be of much use. Herodotus points out that the word *Eridanos* is essentially Greek in character, that consequently the river supposed to run round the world is probably a mere Greek invention. His remarks, however, on language generally, as in the case of *Piromis*, and the ending of the Persian names, show on what unsound basis his knowledge of language rested.

In the *Bacchae* of Euripides there is an extremely interesting passage in which the immoral stories of the Greek mythology are accounted for on the principle of that misunderstanding of words and metaphors to which modern science has given the name of a disease of language. In answer to the impious rationalism of Pentheus – a sort of modern Philistine – Teiresias, who may be termed the Max Müller of the Theban cycle, points out that the story of Dionysus being inclosed in Zeus' thigh really arose from the linguistic confusion between μηρός[2] and ὅμηρος[3]

On the whole, however – for I have only quoted these two instances to show the unscientific character of early philology – we may say that this important instrument in recreating the history of the past was not really used by the ancients as a means of historical criticism. Nor did the ancients employ that other method, used to such advantage in our own day, by which in the symbolism and formulas of an advanced civilisation we can detect the unconscious survival of ancient customs: for whereas in the sham capture of the bride at a marriage feast, which was common in Wales till a recent time, we can discern the lingering reminiscence of the barbarous habit of exogamy, the ancient writers saw only the deliberate commemoration of an historical event.

Aristotle does not tell us by what method he discovered that the Greeks

---

[1] Private nest.
[2] Thigh.
[3] Homer.

used to buy their wives in primitive times, but, judging by his general principles, it was probably through some legend or myth on the subject which lasted to his own day, and not, as we would do, by arguing back from the marriage presents given to the bride and her relatives.[1]

The origin of the common proverb 'worth so many beeves,' in which we discern the unconscious survival of a purely pastoral state of society before the use of metals was known, is ascribed by Plutarch to the fact of Theseus having coined money bearing a bull's head. Similarly, the Amathusian festival, in which a young man imitated the labours of a woman in travail, is regarded by him as a rite instituted in Ariadne's honour, and the Carian adoration of asparagus as a simple commemoration of the adventure of the nymph Perigune. In the first of these *we* discern the beginning of agnation and kinsmanship through the father, which still lingers in the 'couvee' of New Zealand tribes: while the second is a relic of the totem and fetish worship of plants.

Now, in entire opposition to this modern inductive principle of research stands the philosophic Plato, whose account of primitive man is entirely speculative and deductive.

The origin of society he ascribes to necessity, the mother of all inventions, and imagines that individual man began deliberately to herd together on account of the advantages of the principle of division of labour and the rendering of mutual need.

It must, however, be borne in mind that Plato's object in this whole passage in the *Republic* was, perhaps, not so much to analyse the conditions of early society as to illustrate the importance of the division of labour, the shibboleth of his political economy, by showing what a powerful factor it must have been in the most primitive as well as in the most complex states of society; just as in the *Laws* he almost rewrites entirely the history of the Peloponnesus in order to prove the necessity of a balance of power. He surely, I mean, must have recognised himself how essentially incomplete his theory was in taking no account of the origin of family life, the position and influence of women, and other social questions, as well as in disregarding those deeper motives of religion, which are such important factors in early civilisation, and whose influence Aristotle seems to have clearly apprehended, when he says that the aim of primitive society was not merely life but the higher life, and that in the origin of society utility is not the sole motive, but that there is something spiritual in it if, at least, spiritual will bring out the meaning of that complex expression τὸ καλόν.[2] Otherwise the whole account in the *Republic* of primitive man will always remain as a warning against the intrusion of *a priori* speculations in the domain appropriate to induction.

Now, Aristotle's theory of the origin of society, like his philosophy of eth-

---

[1] The fictitious sale in the Roman marriage *per coemptionem* (by purchase) was originally, of course, a real sale.
[2] The good and beautiful.

ics, rests ultimately on the principle of final causes, not in the theological meaning of an aim or tendency imposed from without, but in the scientific sense of function corresponding to organ. 'Nature maketh no thing in vain' is the text of Aristotle in this as in other inquiries. Man being the only animal possessed of the power of rational speech is, he asserts, by nature intended to be social, more so than the bee or any other gregarious animal.

He is φύσει πολιτικός,[1] and the national tendency towards higher forms of perfection brings the 'armed savage who used to sell his wife' to the free independence of a free state, and to the ἰσότης τοῦ ἄρχειν καὶ τοῦ ἄρχεσθαι,[2] which was the test of true citizenship. The stages passed through by humanity start with the family first as the ultimate unit.

The conglomeration of families forms a village ruled by that patriarchal sway which is the oldest form of government in the world, as is shown by the fact that all men count it to be the constitution of heaven, and the villages are merged into the state, and here the progression stops.

For Aristotle, like all Greek thinkers, found his ideal within the walls of the πόλις,[3] yet perhaps in his remark that a united Greece would rule the world we may discern some anticipation of that 'federal union of free states into one consolidated empire,' which, more than the πόλις is to our eyes the ultimately perfect polity.

How far Aristotle was justified in regarding the family as the ultimate unit, with the materials afforded to him by Greek literature, I have already noticed. Besides, Aristotle, I may remark, had he reflected on the meaning of that Athenian law which, while prohibiting marriage with a uterine sister, permitted it with a sister-german, or on the common tradition in Athens that before the time of Cecrops children bore their mothers' names, or on some of the Spartan regulations, could hardly have failed to see the universality of kinsmanship through women in early days, and the late appearance of monandry. Yet, while he missed this point, in common, it must be acknowledged, with many modern writers, such as Sir Henry Maine, it is essentially as an explorer of inductive instances that we recognise his improvement on Plato. The treatise περὶ πολιτείων,[4] did it remain to us in its entirety, would have been one of the most valuable landmarks in the progress of historical criticism, and the first scientific treatise on the science of comparative politics.

A few fragments still remain to us, in one of which we find Aristotle appealing to the authority of an ancient inscription on the 'Disk of Iphitus,' one of the most celebrated Greek antiquities, to corroborate his theory of the Lycurgean revival of the Olympian festival; while his enormous research is evinced in the elaborate explanation he gives of the historical origin of pro-

---

[1] By nature adapted to living man and orderly community.
[2] The equality of the governor and the governed.
[3] City-state.
[4] Concerning forms of government.

verbs such as οὐδεὶς μέγας κακὸς ἰχθῦς,[1] of religious songs like the ἴωμεν ἐς Ἀθήνας[2] of the Botticean virgins, or the praises of love and war.

And, finally, it is to be observed how much wider than Plato's his theory of the origin of society is. They both rest on a psychological basis, but Aristotle's recognition of the capacity for progress and the tendency towards a higher life, shows how much deeper his knowledge of human nature was.

In imitation of these two philosophers, Polybios gives an account of the origin of society in the opening to his philosophy of history. Somewhat in the spirit of Plato, he imagines that after one of the cyclic deluges which sweep off mankind at stated periods and annihilate all pre-existing civilisation, the few surviving members of humanity coalesce for mutual protection, and, as in the case with ordinary animals, the one and most remarkable for physical strength is elected king. In a short time, owing to the workings of sympathy and the desire of approbation, the moral qualities begin to make their appearance, and intellectual instead of bodily excellence becomes the qualification for sovereignty.

Other points, as the rise of law and the like, are dwelt on in a somewhat modern spirit, and although Polybios seems not to have employed the inductive method of research in this question, or rather, I should say, of the hierarchical order of the rational progress of ideas in life, he is not far removed from what the laborious investigations of modern travellers have given us.

And, indeed, as regards the working of the speculative faculty in the creation of history, it is in all respects marvellous how that the most truthful accounts of the passage from barbarism to civilisation in ancient literature come from the works of poets. The elaborate researches of Mr. Taylor and Sir John Lubbock have done little more than verify the theories put forward in the *Prometheus Bound* and the *De Natura Rerum*; yet neither Aeschylus nor Lucretius followed in the modern path, but rather attained to truth by a certain almost mystic power of creative imagination, such as we now seek to banish from science as a dangerous power, though to it science seems to owe many of its most splendid generalities.[3]

Leaving then the question of the origin of society as treated by the ancients, I shall now turn to the other and the more important question of how far they may be said to have attained to what we call the philosophy of history.

Now at the outset we must note that, while the conceptions of law and order have been universally received as the governing principles of the phenomena of nature in the sphere of physical science, yet their intrusion into the domain of history and the life of man has always been met with a strong opposition, on the ground of the incalculable nature of two great forces acting on human action, a certain causeless spontaneity which men

---

[1] No big fish is bad.
[2] Let us go to Athens.
[3] Notably, of course, in the case of heat and its laws.

call free will, and the extra-natural interference which they attribute as a constant attribute to God.

Now that there is a science of the apparently variable phenomena of history is a conception which *we* have perhaps only recently begun to appreciate; yet, like all other great thoughts, it seems to have come to the Greek mind spontaneously, through a certain splendour of imagination, in the morning tide of their civilisation, before inductive research had armed them with the instruments of verification. For I think it is possible to discern in some of the mystic speculations of the early Greek thinkers that desire to discover what is that 'invariable existence of which there are variable states,' and to incorporate it in some one formula of law which may serve to explain the different manifestations of all organic bodies, *man included*, which is the germ of the philosophy of history; the germ indeed of an idea of which it is not too much to say that on it any kind of historical criticism, worthy of the name, must ultimately rest.

For the very first requisite for any scientific conception of history is the doctrine of uniform sequence: in other words, that certain events having happened, certain other events corresponding to them will happen also; that the past is the key of the future.

Now at the birth of this great conception science, it is true, presided, yet religion it was which at the outset clothed it in its own garb and familiarised men with it by appealing to their hearts first and then to their intellects; knowing that at the beginning of things it is through the moral nature, and not through the intellectual, that great truths are spread.

So in Herodotus, who may be taken as a representative of the orthodox tone of thought, the idea of the uniform sequence of cause and effect appears under the theological aspect of Nemesis and Providence, which is really the scientific conception of law, only it is viewed from an *ethical* standpoint.

Now in Thucydides the philosophy of history rests on the probability, which the uniformity of human nature affords us, that the future will in the course of human things resemble the past, if not reproduce it. He appears to contemplate a recurrence of the phenomena of history as equally certain with a return of the epidemic of the Great Plague.

Notwithstanding what German critics have written on the subject, we must beware of regarding this conception as a mere reproduction of that cyclic theory of events which sees in the world nothing but the rotation of Strophe and Antistrophe, in the eternal choir of life and death.

For, in his remarks on the excesses of the Corcyrean Revolution, Thucydides distinctly rests his idea of the recurrence of history on the psychological grounds of the general sameness of mankind.

'The sufferings,' he says, 'which revolution entailed upon the cities were many and terrible, such as have occurred and always will occur, as long as human nature remains the same, though in a severer or milder form, and varying in their symptoms according to the variety of the particular cases.

'In peace and prosperity states and individuals have better sentiments, because they are not confronted with imperious necessities; but war takes away the easy supply of men's wants, and so proves a hard taskmaster, which brings most men's characters to a level with their fortunes.'

4

It is evident that here Thucydides is ready to admit the variety of manifestations which external causes bring about in their workings on the uniform character of the nature of man. Yet, after all is said, these are perhaps but very general statements: the ordinary effects of peace and war are dwelt on, but there is no real analysis of the immediate causes and general laws of the phenomena of life, nor does Thucydides seem to recognise the truth that if humanity proceeds in circles, the circles are always widening.

Perhaps we may say that with him the philosophy of history is partly in the metaphysical stage, and see, in the progress of this idea from Herodotus to Polybius, the exemplification of the Comtian law of the three stages of thought, the theological, the metaphysical, and the scientific: for truly out of the vagueness of theological mysticism this conception which we call the Philosophy of History was raised to a scientific principle, according to which the past was explained and the future predicted by reference to general laws.

Now, just as the earliest account of the nature of the progress of humanity is to be found in Plato, so in him we find the first explicit attempt to found a universal philosophy of history upon wide rational grounds. Having created an ideally perfect state, the philosopher proceeds to give an elaborate theory of the complex causes which produce revolutions, of the moral effects of various forms of government and education, of the rise of the criminal classes and their connection with pauperism, and, in a word, to create history by the deductive method and to proceed from *a priori* psychological principles to discover the governing laws of the apparent chaos of political life.

There have been many attempts since Plato to deduce from a single philosophical principle all the phenomena which experience subsequently verifies for us. Fichte thought he could predict the world-plan from the idea of universal time. Hegel dreamed he had found the key to the mysteries of life in the development of freedom, and Krause in the categories of being. But the one scientific basis on which the true philosophy of history must rest is the complete knowledge of the laws of human nature in all its wants, its aspirations, its powers and its tendencies: and this great truth, which Thucydides may be said in some measure to have apprehended, was given to us first by Plato.

Now it cannot be accurately said of this philosopher that either his philosophy or his history is entirely and simply *a priori*. *On est de son siècle même quand on y proteste*,[1] and so we find in him continual references to the Spartan mode of life, the Pythagorean system, the general characteristics of Greek tyrannies and Greek democracies. For while, in his account of the method of

---

[1] A man belongs to his age even when he struggles against it.

forming an ideal state, he says that the political artist is indeed to fix his gaze on the sun of abstract truth in the heavens of the pure reason, but is sometimes to turn to the realisation of the ideals on earth: yet, after all, the general character of the Platonic method, which is what we are specially concerned with, is essentially deductive and *a priori*. And he himself, in the building up of his Nephelococcygia, certainly starts with a καθαρὸς πίναξ[1] making a clean sweep of all history and all experience; and it was essentially as an *a priori* theorist that he is criticised by Aristotle, as we shall see later.

To proceed to closer details regarding the actual scheme of the laws of political revolutions as drawn out by Plato, we must first note that the primary cause of the decay of the ideal state is the general principle, common to the vegetable and animal worlds as well as to the world of history, that all created things are fated to decay – a principle which, though expressed in the terms of a mere metaphysical abstraction, is yet perhaps in its essence scientific. For we too must hold that a continuous redistribution of matter and motion is the inevitable result of the normal persistence of Force, and that perfect equilibrium is as impossible in politics as it certainly is in physics.

The secondary causes which mar the perfection of the Platonic 'city of the sun' are to be found in the intellectual decay of the race consequent on injudicious marriages and in the Philistine elevation of physical achievements over mental culture: while the hierarchical succession of Timocracy and Oligarchy, Democracy and Tyranny, is dwelt on at great length and its causes analysed in a very dramatic and psychological manner, if not in that sanctioned by the actual order of history.

And indeed it is apparent at first sight that the Platonic succession of states represents rather the succession of ideas in the philosophic mind than any historical succession of time.

Aristotle meets the whole simply by an appeal to facts. If the theory of the periodic decay of all created things, he urges, be scientific, it must be universal, and so true of all the other states as well as of the ideal. Besides, a state usually changes into its contrary and not to the form next to it; so the ideal state would not change into Timocracy; while Oligarchy, more often than Tyranny, succeeds Democracy. Plato, besides, says nothing of what a Tyranny would change to. According to the cycle theory it ought to pass into the ideal state again, but as a fact one Tyranny is changed into another as at Sicyon, or into a Democracy as at Syracuse, or into an Aristocracy as at Carthage. The example of Sicily, too, shows that an Oligarchy is often followed by a Tyranny, as at Leontini and Gela. Besides, it is absurd to represent greed as the chief motive of decay, or to talk of avarice as the root of Oligarchy, when in nearly all true oligarchies money-making is forbidden by law. And finally, the Platonic theory neglects the different kinds of democracies and of tyrannies.

Now nothing can be more important than this passage in Aristotle's *Politics* (v. 12), which may be said to mark an era in the evolution of historical cri-

---

[1] Clean sheet.

ticism. For there is nothing on which Aristotle insists so strongly as that the generalisations from facts ought to be added to the data of the *a priori* method – a principle which we know to be true not merely of deductive speculative politics but of physics also: for are not the residual phenomena of chemists a valuable source of improvement in theory?

His own method is essentially historical though by no means empirical. On the contrary, this far-seeing thinker, rightly styled *il mæstro di color che sanno,*[1] may be said to have apprehended clearly that the true method is neither exclusively empirical nor exclusively speculative, but rather a union of both in the process called Analysis or the Interpretation of Facts, which has been defined as the application to facts of such general conceptions as may fix the important characteristics of the phenomena and present them permanently in their true relations. He too was the first to point out, what even in our own day is incompletely appreciated, that nature, including the development of man, is not full of incoherent episodes like a bad tragedy, that inconsistency and anomaly are as impossible in the moral as they are in the physical world, and that where the superficial observer thinks he sees a revolution the philosophical critic discerns merely the gradual and rational evolution of the inevitable results of certain antecedents.

And while admitting the necessity of a psychological basis for the philosophy of history, he added to it the important truth that man, to be apprehended in his proper position in the universe as well as in his natural powers, must be studied from below in the hierarchical progression of higher function from the lower forms of life. The important maxim, that to obtain a clear conception of anything we must 'study it in its growth from the very beginning' is formally set down in the opening of the *Politics*, where, indeed, we shall find the other characteristic features of the modern Evolutionary theory, such as the 'Differentiation of Function' and the 'Survival of the Fittest' explicitly set forth.

What a valuable step this was in the improvement of the method of historical criticism it is needless to point out. By it, one may say, the true thread was given to guide one's steps through the bewildering labyrinth of facts. For history (to use terms with which Aristotle has made us familiar) may be looked at from two essentially different standpoints; either as a work of art whose τέλος[2] or final cause is external to it and imposed on it from without; or as an organism containing the law of its own development in itself, and working out its perfection merely by the fact of being what it is. Now, if we adopt the former, which we may style the theological view, we shall be in continual danger of tripping into the pitfall of some *a priori* conclusion – that bourne from which, it has been truly said, no traveller ever returns.

The latter is the only scientific theory and was apprehended in its fulness by Aristotle, whose application of the inductive method to history, and whose employment of the evolutionary theory of humanity, show that he

---

[1] The master of those who know.

[2] End or aim.

was conscious that the philosophy of history is nothing separate from the facts of history but is contained in them, and that the rational law of the complex phenomena of life, like the ideal in the world of thought, is to be reached through the facts, not superimposed on them – κατὰ πολλῶν not παρὰ πολλά.[1]

And finally, in estimating the enormous debt which the science of historical criticism owes to Aristotle, we must not pass over his attitude towards those two great difficulties in the formation of a philosophy of history on which I have touched above. I mean the assertion of extra-natural interference with the normal development of the world and of the incalculable influence exercised by the power of free will.

Now, as regards the former, he may be said to have neglected it entirely. The special acts of providence proceeding from God's immediate government of the world, which Herodotus saw as mighty landmarks in history, would have been to him essentially disturbing elements in that universal reign of law, the extent of whose limitless empire he of all the great thinkers of antiquity was the first explicitly to recognise.

Standing aloof from the popular religion as well as from the deeper conceptions of Herodotus and the Tragic School, he no longer thought of God as of one with fair limbs and treacherous face haunting wood and glade, nor would he see in him a jealous judge continually interfering in the world's history to bring the wicked to punishment and the proud to a fall. God to him was the incarnation of the pure Intellect, a being whose activity was the contemplation of his own perfection, one whom Philosophy might imitate but whom prayers could never move, to the sublime indifference of whose passionless wisdom what were the sons of men, their desires or their sins? While as regards the other difficulty and the formation of a philosophy of history, the conflict of free will with general laws appears first in Greek thought in the usual theological form in which all great ideas seem to be cradled at their birth.

It was such legends as those of Oedipus and Adrastus exemplifying the struggles of individual humanity against the overpowering force of circumstances and necessity, which gave to the early Greeks those same lessons which we of modern days draw, in somewhat less artistic fashion, from the study of statistics and the laws of physiology.

In Aristotle, of course, there is no trace of supernatural influence. The Furies, which drive their victim into sin first and then punishment, are no longer 'viper-tressed goddesses with eyes and mouth aflame,' but those evil thoughts which harbour within the impure soul. In this, as in all other points, to arrive at Aristotle is to reach the pure atmosphere of scientific and modern thought.

But while he rejected pure necessitarianism in its crude form as essentially as *reductio ad absurdum* of life, he was fully conscious of the fact that the will is not a mysterious and ultimate unit of force beyond which we cannot go and

---

[1] Reasoning from the multiplicity of experience.

whose special characteristic is inconsistency, but a certain creative attitude of the mind which is, from the first, continually influenced by habits, education and circumstance; so absolutely modifiable, in a word, that the good and the bad man alike seem to lose the power of free will; for the one is morally unable to sin, the other physically incapacitated for reformation.

And of the influence of climate and temperature in forming the nature of man (a conception perhaps pressed too far in modern days when the 'race theory' is supposed to be a sufficient explanation of the Hindoo, and the latitude and longitude of a country the best guide to its morals[1]), Aristotle is completely unaware. I do not allude to such smaller points as the oligarchical tendencies of a horse-breeding country and the democratic influence of the proximity of the sea (important though they are for the consideration of Greek history), but rather to those wider views in the seventh book of his *Politics*, where he attributes the happy union in the Greek character of intellectual attainments with the spirit of progress to the temperate climate they enjoyed, and points out how the extreme cold of the north dulls the mental faculties of its inhabitants and renders them incapable of social organisation or extended empire; while to the enervating heat of eastern countries was due that want of spirit and bravery which then, as now, was the characteristic of the population in that quarter of the globe.

Thucydides has shown the causal connection between political revolutions and the fertility of the soil, but goes a step farther and points out the psychological influences on a people's character exercised by the various extremes of climate – in both cases the first appearance of a most valuable form of historical criticism.

To the development of Dialectic, as to God, intervals of time are of no account. From Plato and Aristotle we pass direct to Polybius.

The progress of thought from the philosopher of the Academe to the Arcadian historian may be best illustrated by a comparison of the method by which each of the three writers, whom I have selected as the highest expressions of the rationalism of his respective age, attained to his ideal state: for the latter conception may be in a measure regarded as representing the most spiritual principle which they could discern in history.

Now, Plato created his on *a priori* principles: Aristotle formed his by an analysis of existing constitutions; Polybius found his realised for him in the actual world of fact. Aristotle criticised the deductive speculations of Plato by means of inductive negative instances, but Polybius will not take the 'Cloud City' of the *Republic* into account at all. He compares it to an athlete who has never run on 'Constitution Hill,' to a statue so beautiful that it is entirely removed from the ordinary conditions of humanity, and consequently from the canons of criticism.

The Roman state had attained in his eyes, by means of the mutual counter-

---

[1] Cousin errs a good deal in this respect. To say, as he did, 'Give me the latitude and the longitude of a country, its rivers and its mountains, and I will deduce the race,' is surely a glaring exaggeration.

action of three opposing forces,[1] that stable equilibrium in politics which was the ideal of all the theoretical writers of antiquity. And in connection with this point it will be convenient to notice here how much truth there is contained in the accusation so often brought against the ancients that they knew nothing of the idea of Progress, for the meaning of many of their speculations will be hidden from us if we do not try and comprehend first what their aim was, and secondly why it was so.

Now, like all wide generalities, this statement is at least inaccurate. The prayer of Plato's ideal city – ἐξ ἀγαθῶν ἀμείνους, καὶ ἐξ ὠφελιμῶν ὠφελιμωτέρους ἀεὶ τοὺς ἐκγόνους γίγνεσθαι,[2] might be written as a text over the door of the last Temple to Humanity raised by the disciples of Fourier and Saint Simon, but it is certainly true that their ideal principle was order and permanence, not indefinite progress. For, setting aside the artistic prejudices which would have led the Greeks to reject this idea of unlimited improvement, we may note that the modern conception of progress rests partly on the new enthusiasm and worship of humanity, partly on the splendid hopes of material improvements in civilisation which applied science has held out to us, two influences from which ancient Greek thought seems to have been strangely free. For the Greeks marred the perfect humanism of the great men whom they worshipped, by imputing to them divinity and its supernatural powers; while their science was eminently speculative and often almost mystic in its character, aiming at culture and not utility, at higher spirituality and more intense reverence for law, rather than at the increased facilities of locomotion and the cheap production of common things about which our modern scientific school ceases not to boast. And lastly, and perhaps chiefly, we must remember that the 'plague spot of all Greek states,' as one of their own writers has called it, was the terrible insecurity to life and property which resulted from the factions and revolutions which ceased not to trouble Greece at all times, raising a spirit of fanaticism such as religion raised in the middle ages of Europe.

These considerations, then, will enable us to understand first how it was that, radical and unscrupulous reformers as the Greek political theorists were, yet, their end once attained, no modern conservatives raised such outcry against the slightest innovation. Even acknowledged improvements in such things as the games of children or the modes of music were regarded by them with feelings of extreme apprehension as the herald of the *drapeau rouge* of reform. And secondly, it will show us how it was that Polybius found his ideal in the commonwealth of Rome, and Aristotle, like Mr. Bright, in the middle classes. Polybius, however, is not content merely with pointing out his ideal state, but enters at considerable length into the question of those

---

[1] The monarchical, aristocratical, and democratic elements of the Roman constitution are referred to.

[2] That at the sons of good men should always be better than their fathers, and the sons of useful citizens more useful than their fathers.

general laws whose consideration forms the chief essential of the philosophy of history.

He starts by accepting the general principle that all things are fated to decay (which I noticed in the case of Plato), and that 'as iron produces rust and as wood breeds the animals that destroy it, so every state has in it the seeds of its own corruption.' He is not, however, content to rest there, but proceeds to deal with the more immediate causes of revolutions, which he says are twofold in nature, either external or internal. Now, the former, depending as they do on the synchronous conjunction of other events outside the sphere of scientific estimation, are from their very character incalculable; but the latter, though assuming many forms, always result from the overgreat preponderance of any single element to the detriment of the others, the rational law lying at the base of all varieties of political changes being that stability can result only from the statical equilibrium produced by the counteraction of opposing parts, since the more simple a constitution is the more it is insecure. Plato had pointed out before how the extreme liberty of a democracy always resulted in despotism, but Polybius analyses the law and shows the scientific principles on which it rests.

The doctrine of the instability of pure constitutions forms an important era in the philosophy of history. Its special applicability to the politics of our own day has been illustrated in the rise of the great Napoleon, when the French state had lost those divisions of caste and prejudice, of landed aristocracy and moneyed interest, institutions in which the vulgar see only barriers to Liberty but which are indeed the only possible defences against the coming of that periodic Sirius of politics, the τύραννος ἐκ προστατικῆς ῥίζης.[1]

There is a principle which Tocqueville never wearies of explaining, and which has been subsumed by Mr. Herbert Spencer under that general law common to all organic bodies which we call the Instability of the Homogeneous. The various manifestations of this law, as shown in the normal, regular revolutions and evolutions of the different forms of government,[2] are expounded with great clearness by Polybius, who claimed for his theory in the Thucydidean spirit, that it is a κτῆμα ἐς ἀεἰ,[3] not a mere ἀγώνισμα ἐς τὸ παραχρῆμα,[4] and that a knowledge of it will enable the impartial observer to discover at any time what period of its constitutional evolution any particular state has already reached and into what form it will be next differentiated, though possibly the exact time of the changes may be more or less uncertain.

Now in this necessarily incomplete account of the laws of political revolutions as expounded by Polybius enough perhaps has been said to show what is his true position in the rational development of the 'Idea' which I have called the Philosophy of History, because it is the unifying of history. Seen

---

[1] Despot of aristocratic origin.
[2] Polybius, vi. 9.
[3] Lasting possession.
[4] Prize of the immediate present.

darkly as it is through the glass of religion in the pages of Herodotus, more metaphysical than scientific with Thucydides, Plato strove to seize it by the eagle-flight of speculation, to reach it with the eager grasp of a soul impatient of those slower and surer inductive methods which Aristotle, in his trenchant criticism of his great master, showed were more brilliant than any vague theory, if the test of brilliancy is truth.

What then is the position of Polybius? Does any new method remain for him? Polybius was one of those many men who are born too late to be original. To Thucydides belongs the honour of being the first in the history of Greek thought to discern the supreme calm of law and order underlying the fitful storms of life, and Plato and Aristotle each represents a great new principle. To Polybius belongs the office – how noble an office he made it his writings show – of making more explicit the ideas which were implicit in his predecessors, of showing that they were of wider applicability and perhaps of deeper meaning than they had seemed before, of examining with more minuteness the laws which they had discovered, and finally of pointing out more clearly than any one had done the range of science and the means it offered for analysing the present and predicting what was to come. His office thus was to gather up what they had left to give their principles new life by a wider application.

Polybius ends this great diapason of Greek thought. When the Philosophy of history appears next, as in Plutarch's tract on 'Why God's anger is delayed,' the pendulum of thought had swung back to where it began. His theory was introduced to the Romans under the cultured stule of Cicero, and was welcomed by them as the philosophical panegyric of their state. The last notice of it in Latin literature is in the pages of Tacitus, who alludes to the stable polity formed out of these elements as a constitution easier to commend than to produce and in no case lasting. Yet Polybius had seen the future with no uncertain eye, and had prophesied the rise of the Empire from the unbalanced power of the ochlocracy fifty years and more before there was joy in the Julian household over the birth of that boy who, borne to power as the champion of the people, died wearing the purple of a king.

No attitude of historical criticism is more important than the means by which the ancients attained to the philosophy of history. The principle of heredity can be exemplified in literature as well as in organic life: Aristotle, Plato and Polybius are the lineal ancestors of Fichte and Hegel, of Vico and Cousin, of Montesquieu and Tocqueville.

As my aim is not to give an account of historians but to point out those great thinkers whose methods have furthered the advance of this spirit of historical criticism, I shall pass over those annalists and chroniclers who intervened between Thucydides and Polybius. Yet perhaps it may serve to throw new light on the real nature of this spirit and its intimate connection with all other forms of advanced thought if I give some estimate of the character and rise of those many influences prejudicial to the scientific study of history which cause such a wide gap between these two historians.

Foremost among these is the growing influence of rhetoric and the Isocratean school, which seems to have regarded history as an arena for the display of either pathos or paradoxes, not a scientific investigation into laws.

The new age is the age of style. The same spirit of exclusive attention to form which made Euripides often, like Swinburne, prefer music to meaning and melody to morality, which gave to the later Greek statues that refined effeminacy, that overstrained gracefulness of attitude, was felt in the sphere of history. The rules laid down for historical composition are those relating to the aesthetic value of digressions, the legality of employing more than one metaphor in the same sentence, and the like; and historians are ranked not by their power of estimating evidence but by the goodness of the Greek they write.

I must note also the important influence on literature exercised by Alexander the Great; for while his travels encouraged the more accurate research of geography, the very splendour of his achievements seems to have brought history again into the sphere of romance. The appearance of all great men in the world is followed invariably by the rise of that mythopoeic spirit and that tendency to look for the marvellous, which is so fatal to true historical criticism. An Alexander, a Napoleon, a Francis of Assisi and a Mahomet are thought to be outside the limiting conditions of rational law, just as comets were supposed to be not very long ago. While the founding of that city of Alexandria, in which Western and Eastern thought met with such strange results to both, diverted the critical tendencies of the Greek spirit into questions of grammar, philology and the like, the narrow artificial atmosphere of that University town (as we may call it) was fatal to the development of that independent and speculative spirit of research which strikes out new methods of inquiry, of which historical criticism is one.

The Alexandrines combined a great love of learning with an ignorance of the true principles of research, an enthusiastic spirit for accumulating materials with a wonderful incapacity to use them. Not among the hot sands of Egypt, or the Sophists of Athens, but from the very heart of Greece rises the man of genius on whose influence in the evolution of the philosophy of history I have a short time ago dwelt. Born in the serene and pure air of the clear uplands of Arcadia, Polybius may be said to reproduce in his work the character of the place which gave him birth. For, of all the historians – I do not say of antiquity but of all time – none is more rationalistic than he, none more free from any belief in the 'visions and omens, the monstrous legends, the grovelling superstitions and unmanly craving for the supernatural' (δεισδαιμονίας ἀγεννοῦς καὶ τερατείας γυναικώδους)[1] which he is compelled to notice himself as the characteristics of some of the historians who preceded him. Fortunate in the land which bore him, he was no less blessed in the wondrous time of his birth. For, representing in himself the spiritual supremacy of the Greek intellect and allied in bonds of chivalrous friendship to the world-conqueror of his day, he seems led as it were by the

---

[1] Base superstitious fears and that interest in the marvellous which is characteristic in women (Polybius, xii. 24).

hand of Fate 'to comprehend,' as has been said, 'more clearly than the Romans themselves the historical position of Rome,' and to discern with greater insight than all other men could those two great resultants of ancient civilisation, the material empire of the city of the seven hills, and the intellectual sovereignty of Hellas.

Before his own day, he says,[1] the events of the world were unconnected and separate and the histories confined to particular countries. Now, for the first time, the universal empire of the Romans rendered a universal history possible.[2] This, then, is the august motive of his work: to trace the gradual rise of this Italian city from the day when the first legion crossed the narrow strait of Messina and landed on the fertile fields of Sicily to the time when Corinth in the East and Carthage in the West fell before the resistless wave of empire and the eagles of Rome passed on the wings of universal victory from Calpè and the Pillars of Hercules to Syria and the Nile. At the same time he recognised that the scheme of Rome's empire was worked out under the aegis of God's will[3]. For, as one of the Middle Age scribes most truly says, the τύχη[4] of Polybius is that power which we Christians call God; the second aim, as one may call it, of his history is to point out the rational and human and natural causes which brought this result, distinguishing, as we should say, between God's mediate and immediate government of the world.

With any direct intervention of God in the normal development of Man, he will have nothing to do: still less with any idea of chance as a factor in the phenomena of life. Chance and miracles, he says, are mere expressions for our ignorance of rational causes. The spirit of rationalism which we recognised in Herodotus as a vague uncertain attitude and which appears in Thucydides as a consistent attitude of mind never argued about or even explained, is by Polybius analysed and formulated as the great instrument of historical research.

Herodotus, while believing on principle in the supernatural, yet was sceptical at times. Thucydides simply ignored the supernatural. He did not discuss it, but he annihilated it by explaining history without it. Polybius enters at length into the whole question and explains its origin and the method of treating it. Herodotus would have believed in Scipio's dream. Thucydides would have ignored it entirely. Polybius explains it. He is the culmination of the rational progression of Dialectic. 'Nothing,' he says, 'shows a foolish mind more than the attempt to account for any phenomena on the principle of chance or supernatural intervention. History is a search for rational causes, and there is nothing in the world – even those phenomena which seem to us the most remote from law and improbable – which is not the logical and inevitable result of certain rational antecedents.'

Some things, of course, are to be rejected *a priori* without entering into the

---

[1] Polybius, I. 4, viii. 4, specially; and really *passim*
[2] He makes one exception.
[3] Polybius, viii. 4.
[4] Chance.

subject: 'As regards such miracles,' he says,[1] 'as that on a certain statue of Artemis rain or snow never falls though the statue stands in the open air, or that those who enter God's shrine in Arcadia lose their natural shadows, I cannot really be expected to argue upon the subject. For these things are not only utterly improbable but absolutely impossible.'

'For us to argue reasonably on an acknowledged absurdity is as vain a task as trying to catch water in a sieve; it is really to admit the possibility of the supernatural, which is the very point at issue.'

What Polybius felt was that to admit the possibility of a miracle is to annihilate the possibility of history: for just as scientific and chemical experiments would be either impossible or useless if exposed to the chance of continued interference on the part of some foreign body, so the laws and principles which govern history, the causes of phenomena, the evolution of progress, the whole science, in a word, of man's dealings with his own race and with nature, will remain a sealed book to him who admits the possibility of extra-natural interference.

The stories of miracles, then, are to be rejected on *a priori* rational grounds, but in the case of events which we know to have happened, the scientific historian will not rest till he has discovered their natural causes, which, for instance, in the case of the wonderful rise of the Roman Empire – the most marvellous thing, Polybius says, which God ever brought about[2] – are to be found in the excellence of their constitution (τη ἰδιότητι τῆς πολιτείας)[3], the wisdom of their advisers, their splendid military arrangements, and their superstition (τη δεισιδαιμονία). For while Polybius regarded the revealed religion as, of course, objective reality of truth[4], he laid great stress on its moral subjective influence, going, in one passage on the subject, even so far as almost to excuse the introduction of the supernatural in very small quantities into history on account of the extremely good effect it would have on pious people.

But perhaps there is no passage in the whole of ancient and modern history which breathes such a manly and splendid spirit of rationalism as one preserved to us in the Vatican – strange resting-place for it! – in which he treats of the terrible decay of population which had fallen on his native land in his own day, and which by the general orthodox public was regarded as a special judgment of God, sending childlessness on women as a punishment for the sins of the people. For it was a disaster quite without parallel in the history of the land, and entirely unforeseen by any of its political-economy writers who, on the contrary, were always anticipating that danger would arise from an excess of population overrunning its means of subsistence, and becoming

---

[1] Polybius, xvi. 12.

[2] Polybius, viii. 4.

[3] The unique nature of their form of government.

[4] Polybius resembled Gibbon in many respects. Like him he held that all religions were to the philosopher equally false, to the vulgar equally true, to the statesman equally useful.

unmanageable through its size. Polybius, however, will have nothing to do with either priest or worker of miracles in this matter. He will not even seek that 'sacred Heart of Greece,' Delphi, Apollo's shrine, whose inspiration even Thucydides admitted and before whose wisdom Socrates bowed. How foolish, he says, were the men who on this matter would pray to God. We must search for the rational causes, and the causes are seen to be clear, and the method of prevention also. He then proceeds to notice how all this arose from the general reluctance to marriage and to bearing the expense of educating a large family which resulted from the carelessness and avarice of the men of his day, and he explains on entirely rational principles the whole of this apparently supernatural judgment.

Now it is to be borne in mind that while his rejection of miracles as violation of inviolable laws is entirely *a priori* – for discussion of such a matter is, of course, impossible for a rational thinker – yet his rejection of supernatural intervention rests entirely on the scientific grounds of the necessity of looking for natural causes. And he is quite logical in maintaining his position on these principles. For where it is either difficult or impossible to assign any rational cause for phenomena, or to discover their laws, he acquiesces reluctantly in the alternative of admitting some extra-natural interference which his essentially scientific method of treating the matter has logically forced on him, approving, for instance, of prayers for rain, on the express ground that the laws of meteorology had not yet been ascertained. He would, of course, have been the first to welcome our modern discoveries in the matter. The passage in question is in every way one of the most interesting in his whole work, not, of course, as signifying any inclination on his part to acquiesce in the supernatural, but because it shows how essentially logical and rational his method of argument was and how candid and fair his mind.

Having now examined Polybius's attitude towards the supernatural and the general ideas which guided his research, I will proceed to examine the method he pursued in his scientific investigation of the complex phenomena of life. For, as I have said before in the course of this essay, what is important in all great writers is not so much the results they arrive at as the methods they pursue. The increased knowledge of facts may alter any conclusion in history as in physical science, and the canons of speculative historical credibility must be acknowledged to appeal rather to that subjective attitude of mind which we call the historic sense than to any formulated objective rules. But a scientific method is a gain for all time, and the true if not the only progress of historical criticism consists in the improvement of the instruments of research.

Now first, as regards his conception of history, I have already pointed out that it was to him essentially a search for causes, a problem to be solved, not a picture to be painted, a scientific investigation into laws and tendencies, not a mere romantic account of startling incident and wondrous adventure. Thucydides, in the opening of his great work, had sounded the first note of the scientific conception of history. 'The absence of romance in my pages,' he says, 'will, I fear, detract somewhat from its value, but I have written my work not to be the exploit of a passing hour but as the possession of all time.'[1] Polybius follows with words almost entirely similar. If, he says, we banish from history the consideration of causes, methods and motives (τὸ διὰ τί, καί πῶς, καὶ τίνος χάριν[2] and refuse to consider how far the result of anything is its rational consequent, what is left is a mere, ἀγώνισμα[3], not a μάθημα[4], an oratorical essay which may give pleasure for the moment, but which is entirely without any scientific value for the explanation of the future. Elsewhere he says that 'history robbed of the exposition of its causes and laws is a profitless thing, though it may allure a fool.' And all through his history the same point is put forward and exemplified in every fashion.

So far for the conception of history. Now for the groundwork. As regards the character of the phenomena to be selected by the scientific investigator, Aristotle had laid down the general formula that nature should be studied in her normal manifestations. Polybius, true to his character of applying explicitly the principles implicit in the work of others, follows out the doctrine of Aristotle, and lays particular stress on the rational and undisturbed character of the development of the Roman constitution as affording special facilities for the discovery of the laws of its progress. Political revolutions result from causes either external or internal. The former are mere disturbing forces which lie outside the sphere of scientific calculation. It is the latter which are important for the establishing of principles and the elucidation of the sequences of rational evolution.

He thus may be said to have anticipated one of the most important truths of the modern methods of investigation: I mean that principle which lays down that just as the study of physiology should precede the study of pathology, just as the laws of disease are best discovered by the phenomena presented in health, so the method of arriving at all great social and political truths is by the investigation of those cases where development has been normal, rational and undisturbed.

The critical canon that the more a people has been interfered with, the more difficult it becomes to generalise the laws of its progress and to analyse the separate forces of its civilisation, is one the validity of which is now generally recognised by those who pretend to a scientific treatment of all history: and while we have seen that Aristotle anticipated it in a general formula, to Polybius belongs the honour of being the first to apply it explicitly in the sphere of history.

I have shown how to this great scientific historian the motive of his work was essentially the search for causes; and true to his analytical spirit he is careful to examine what a cause really is and in what part of the antecedents of any consequent it is to be looked for. To give an illustration: As regards the origin of the war with Perseus, some assigned as causes the expulsion of

---

[1] Cf. Polybius, xii. 25.

[2] The why, and how and wherefore.

[3] A discourse.

[4] A significant piece of learning.

Abrupolis by Perseus, the expedition of the latter to Delphi, the plot against Eumenes and the seizure of the ambassadors in Boetia; of these incidents the two former, Polybius points out, were merely the pretexts, the two latter merely the occasions of the war. The war was really a legacy left to Perseus by his father, who was determined to fight it out with Rome.[1]

Here as elsewhere he is not originating any new idea. Thucydides had pointed out the difference between the real and the alleged cause, and the Aristotelian dictum about revolutions, οὐ περὶ μικρῶν ἀλλ᾽ ἐκ μικρῶν[2] draws the distinction between cause and occasion with the brilliancy of an epigram. But the explicit and rational investigation of the difference between αἰτία,[3] ἀρχή[4] and πρόφασις[5] was reserved for Polybius. No canon of historical criticism can be said to be of more real value than that involved in this distinction, and the overlooking of it has filled our histories with the contemptible accounts of the intrigues of courtiers and of kings and the pretty plottings of backstairs influence – particulars interesting, no doubt, to those who would ascribe the Reformation to Anne Boleyn's pretty face, the Persian to the influence of a doctor or a curtain-lecture from Atossa, or the French Revolution to Madame de Maintenon, but without any value for those who aim at any scientific treatment of history.

But the question of method, to which I am compelled always to return, is not yet exhausted. There is another aspect in which it may be regarded, and I shall now proceed to treat of it.

One of the greatest difficulties with which the modern historian has to contend is the enormous complexity of the facts which come under his notice: D'Alembert's suggestion that at the end of every century a selection of facts should be made and the rest burned (if it was really intended seriously) could not, of course, be entertained for a moment. A problem loses all its value when it becomes simplified, and the world would be all the poorer if the Sybil of History burned her volumes. Besides, as Gibbon pointed out, 'a Montesquieu will detect in the most insignificant fact relations which the vulgar overlook.'

Nor can the scientific investigator of history isolate the particular elements, which he desires to examine, from disturbing and extraneous causes, as the experimental chemist can do (though some times, as in the case of lunatic asylums and prisons, he is enabled to observe phenomena in a certain degree of isolation). So he is compelled either to use the deductive mode of arguing from general laws or to employ the method of abstraction which gives a fictitious isolation to phenomena never so isolated in actual existence. And this is exactly what Polybius has done as well as Thucydides. For, as has been well remarked, there is in the works of these two writers a certain plastic

---

[1] Polybius, xxii. 22.
[2] Not about trivial issues but arising from trivial causes.
[3] Cause.
[4] Origin.
[5] Pretext.

unity of type and motive; whatever they write is penetrated through and through with a specific quality, a singleness and concentration of purpose, which we may contrast with the more comprehensive width as manifested not merely in the modern mind, but also in Herodotus. Thucydides, regarding society as influenced entirely by political motives, took no account of forces of a different nature, and consequently his results, like those of most modern political economists, have to be modified largely[1] before they come to correspond with what we know was the actual state of fact. Similarly, Polybius will deal only with those forces which tended to bring the civilised world under the dominion of Rome (ix. I), and in the Thucydidean spirit points out the want of picturesqueness and romance in his pages which is the result of the abstract method (τὸ μονοειδὲς τῆς συντάξεως),[2] being careful also to tell us that his rejection of all other forces is essentially deliberate and the result of a preconceived theory and by no means due to carelessness of any kind.

Now, of the general value of the abstract method and the legality of its employment in the sphere of history, this is perhaps not the suitable occasion for any discussion. It is, however, in all ways worthy of note that Polybius is not merely conscious of, but dwells with particular weight on, the fact which is usually urged as the strongest objection to the employment of the abstract method – I mean the conception of a society as a sort of human organism whose parts are indissolubly connected with one another and all affected when one member is in any way agitated. This conception of the organic nature of society appears first in Plato and Aristotle, who apply it to cities. Polybius, as his wont is, expands it to be a general characteristic of all history. It is an idea of the very highest importance, especially to a man like Polybius, whose thoughts are continually turned towards the essential unity of history and the impossibility of isolation.

Further, as regards the particular method of investigating that group of phenomena obtained for him by the abstract method, he will adopt, he tells us, neither the purely deductive nor the purely inductive mode but the union of both. In other words, he formally adopts that method of analysis upon the importance of which I have dwelt before.

And lastly, while, without doubt, enormous simplicity in the elements under consideration is the result of the employment of the abstract method, even within the limit thus obtained a certain selection must be made, and a selection involves a theory. For the facts of life cannot be tabulated with as great an ease as the colours of birds and insects can be tabulated. Now Poly-

---

[1] I mean particularly as regards his sweeping denunciation of the complete moral decadence of Greek society during the Peloponnesian War which, from what remains to us of Athenian literature, we know must have been completely exaggerated. Or, rather, he is looking at men merely in their political dealings: and in politics the man who is personally honourable and refined will not scruple to do anything for his party.

[2] Uniformity of structure.

bius points out that those phenomena particularly are to be dwelt on which may serve as a παράδειγμα[1] or sample, and show the character of the tendencies of the age as clearly as 'a single drop from a full cask will be enough to disclose the nature of the whole contents.' This recognition of the importance of single facts, not in themselves but because of the spirit they represent, is extremely scientific; for we know that from the single bone, or tooth even, the anatomist can recreate entirely the skeleton of the primeval horse and the botanist tell the characters of the flora and fauna of a district from a single specimen.

Regarding truth as 'the most divine thing in Nature,' the very 'eye and light of history without which it moves a blind thing,' Polybius spared no pains in the acquisition of historical materials or in the study of the sciences of politics and war, which he considered were so essential to the training of the scientific historian, and the labour he took is mirrored in the many ways in which he criticises other authorities.

There is something, as a rule, slightly contemptible about ancient criticism. The modern idea of the critic as the interpreter, the expounder of the beauty and excellence of the work he selects, seems quite unknown. Nothing can be more captious or unfair, for instance, than the method by which Aristotle criticised the ideal state of Plato in his ethical works, and the passages quoted by Polybius from Timaeus show that the latter historian fully deserved the punning name given to him. But in Polybius there is, I think, little of that bitterness and pettiness of spirit which characterises most other writers, and an incidental story he tells of his relations with one of the historians whom he criticised shows that he was a man of great courtesy and refinement of taste – as, indeed, befitted one who had lived always in the society of those who were of great and noble birth.

Now as regards the character of the canons by which he criticises the works of other authors, in the majority of cases he employs simply his own geographical and military knowledge, showing, for instance, the impossibility in the accounts given of Nabis's march from Sparta simply by his acquaintance with the spots in question; or the inconsistency of those of the battle of Issus; or of the accounts given by Ephorus of the battles of Leuctra and Mantinea. In the latter case he says, if any one will take the trouble to measure out the ground of the site of the battle and then test the manoeuvres given, he will find how inaccurate the accounts are.

In other cases he appeals to public documents, the importance of which he was always foremost in recognising; showing, for instance, by a document in the public archives of Rhodes how inaccurate were the accounts given of the battle of Lade by Zeno and Antisthenes. Or he appeals to psychological probability, rejecting, for instance, the scandalous stories told of Philip of Macedon, simply from the king's general greatness of character, and arguing that a boy so well educated and so respectably connected as Demochares (xii. 14) could never have been guilty of that which evil rumour accused him.

---

[1] Example.

But the chief object of his literary censure is Timaeus, who had been so unsparing of his strictures on others. The general point which he makes against him, impugning his accuracy as a historian, is that he derived his knowledge of history not from the dangerous perils of a life of action but in the secure indolence of a narrow scholastic life. There is, indeed, no point on which he is so vehement as this. 'A history,' he says, 'written in a library gives as lifeless and as inaccurate a picture of history as a painting which is copied not from a living animal but from a stuffed one.'

There is more difference, he says in another place, between the history of an eye-witness and that of one whose knowledge comes from books, than there is between the scenes of real life and the fictitious landscapes of theatrical scenery. Besides this, he enters into somewhat elaborate detailed criticism of passages where he thought Timaeus, was following a wring method and perverting truth, passages which it will be worth while to examine in detail.

Timaeus, from the fact of there being a Roman custom to shoot a war-horse on a stated day, argued back to the Trojan origin of that people. Polybius, on the other hand, points out that the inference is quite unwarrantable, because horse sacrifices are ordinary institutions common to all barbarous tribes. Timaeus here, as was so common with Greek writers, is arguing back from some custom of the present to an historical event in the past. Polybius really is employing the comparative method, showing how the custom was an ordinary step in the civilisation of every early people.

In another place he shows how illogical is the scepticism of Timaeus as regards the existence of the Bull of Phalaris simply by appealing to the statue of the Bull, which was still to be seen in Carthage; pointing out how impossible it was, on any other theory except that it belonged to Phalaris, to account for the presence in Carthage of a bull of this peculiar character with a door between his shoulders. But one of the great points which he uses against this Sicilian historian is in reference to the question of the origin of the Locrian colony. In accordance with the received tradition on the subject, Aristotle had represented the Locrian colony as founded by some Parthenidae or slaves' children, as they were called, a statement which seems to have roused the indignation of Timaeus, who went to a good deal of trouble to confute this theory. He does so on the following grounds.

First of all he points out that in the ancient days the Greeks had no slaves at all, so the mention of them in the matter is an anachronism; and next he declares that he was shown in the Greek city of Locris certain ancient inscriptions in which their relation to the Italian city was expressed in terms of the position between parent and child, which showed also that mutual rights of citizenship were accorded to each city. Besides this, he appeals to various questions of improbability as regards their international relationship, on which Polybius takes diametrically opposite grounds which hardly call for discussion. And in favour of his own view he urges two points more: first, that the Lacedaemonians being allowed furlough for the purpose of seeing their wives at home, it was unlikely that the Locrians should not have had the same privilege; and next, that the Italian Locrians knew nothing of the Aristotelian version, and had, on the contrary, very severe laws against adulterers, runaway slaves and the like. Now most of these questions rest on mere probability, which is always such a subjective canon that an appeal to it is rarely conclusive. I would note, however, as regards the inscriptions which, if genuine, would of course have settled the matter, that Polybius looks on them as a mere invention on the part of Timaeus, who, he remarks, gives no details about them, though, as a rule, he is so over-anxious to give chapter and verse for everything. A somewhat more interesting point is that where he attacks Timaeus for the introduction of fictitious speeches into his narrative; for on this point Polybius seems to be far in advance of the opinions held by literary men on the subject not merely in his own day but for centuries after.

Herodotus had introduced speeches avowedly dramatic and fictitious. Thucydides states clearly that, where he was unable to find out what people really said, he put down what they ought to have said. Sallust alludes, it is true, to the fact of the speech he puts into the mouth of the tribune Memmius being essentially genuine, but the speeches given in the senate on the occasion of the Catilinarian conspiracy are very different from the same orations as they appear in Cicero. Livy makes his ancient Romans wrangle and chop logic with all the subtlety of a Hortensius of a Scaevola. And even in later days, when shorthand reporters attended the debates of the senate and a *Daily News* was published in Rome, we find that one of the most celebrated speeches in Tacitus (that in which the Emperor Claudius gives the Gauls their freedom) is shown, by an inscription discovered recently at Lugdunum, to be entirely fabulous.

Upon the other hand, it must be borne in mind that these speeches were not intended to deceive; they were regarded merely as a certain dramatic element which it was allowable to introduce into history for the purpose of giving more life and reality to the narration, and were to be criticised, not as we should, by arguing how in an age before shorthand was known such a report was possible or how, in the failure of written documents, tradition could bring down such an accurate verbal account, but by the higher test of their psychological probability as regards the persons in whose mouths they are placed. An ancient historian in answer to modern criticism would say, probably, that these fictitious speeches were in reality more truthful than the actual ones, just as Aristotle claimed for poetry a higher degree of truth in comparison to history. The whole point is interesting as showing how far in advance of his age Polybius may be said to have been.

The last scientific historian, it is possible to gather from his writings what he considered were the characteristics of the ideal writer of history; and no small light will be thrown on the progress of historical criticism if we strive to collect and analyse what in Polybius are more or less scattered expressions. The ideal historian must be contemporary with the events he describes, or removed from them by one generation only. Where it is possible, he is to be an eye-witness of what he writes of; where that is out of his power, he is to test all traditions and stories carefully and not to be ready to accept what is plausible in place of what is true. He is to be no bookworm living aloof from the experiences of the world in the artificial isolation of a university town, but a politician, a soldier, and a traveller, a man not merely of thought but of action, one who can do great things as well as write of them, who in the sphere of history could be what Byron and Aeschylus were in the sphere of poetry, at once *le chantre et le héros*.[1]

He is to keep before his eyes the fact that chance is merely a synonym for our ignorance; that the reign of law pervades the domain of history as much as it does that of political science. He is to accustom himself to look on all occasions for rational and natural causes. And while he is to recognise the practical utility of the supernatural, in an educational point of view, he is not himself to indulge in such intellectual beating of the air as to admit the possibility of the violation of inviolable laws, or to argue in a sphere wherein argument is *a priori* annihilated. He is to be free from all bias towards friend and country; he is to be courteous and gentle in criticism; he is not to regard history as a mere opportunity for splendid and tragic writing; nor is he to falsify truth for the sake of a paradox or an epigram.

While acknowledging the importance of particular facts as samples of higher truths, he is to take a broad and general view of humanity. He is to deal with the whole race and with the world, not with particular tribes or separate countries. He is to bear in mind that the world is really an organism wherein no one part can be moved without the others being affected also. He is to distinguish between cause and occasion, between the influence of general laws and particular fancies, and he is to remember that the greatest lessons of the world are contained in history and that it is the historian's duty to manifest them so as to save nations from following those unwise policies which always lead to dishonour and ruin, and to teach individuals to apprehend by the intellectual culture of history those truths which else they would have to learn in the bitter school of experience.

Now, as regards his theory of the necessity of the historian's being contemporary with the events he describes, so far as the historian is a mere narrator the remark is undoubtedly true. But to appreciate the harmony and rational position of the facts of a great epoch, to discover its laws, the causes which produced it and the effects which it generates, the scene must be viewed from a certain height and distance to be completely apprehended. A thoroughly contemporary historian such as Lord Clarendon or Thucydides is in reality part of the history he criticises; and, in the case of such contemporary historians as Fabius and Philistus, Polybius is compelled to acknowledge that they are misled by patriotic and other considerations. Against Polybius himself no such accusation can be made. He indeed of all men is able, as from some lofty tower, to discern the whole tendency of the ancient world, the triumph of Roman institutions and of Greek thought which is the last message of the old world and, in a more spiritual sense, has become the Gospel of the new.

---

[1] The bard and the hero.

One thing indeed he did not see, or if he saw it, he thought but little of it – how from the East there was spreading over the world, as a wave spreads, a spiritual inroad of new religions from the time when the Pessinuntine mother of the gods, a shapeless mass of stone, was brought to the eternal city by her holiest citizen, to the day when the ship *Castor and Pollux* stood in at Puteoli, and St. Paul turned his face towards martyrdom and victory at Rome, Polybius was able to predict, from his knowledge of the causes of revolutions and the tendencies of the various forms of governments, the uprising of that democratic tone of thought which, as soon as a seed is sown in the murder of the Gracchi and the exile of Marius, culminated as all democratic movements do culminate, in the supreme authority of one man, the lordship of the world under the world's rightful lord Caius Julius Caesar. This, indeed, he saw in no uncertain way. But the turning of all men's hearts to the East, the first glimmering of that splendid dawn, which broke over the hills of Galilee and flooded the earth like wine, was hidden from his eyes.

There are many points in the description of the ideal historian which one may compare to the picture which Plato has given us of the ideal philosopher. They are both 'spectators of all time and all existence.' Nothing is contemptible in their eyes, for all things have a meaning, and they both walk in august reasonableness before all men, conscious of the workings of God yet free from all terror of mendicant priest or vagrant miracle-worker. But the parallel ends here. For the one stands aloof from the world-storm of sleet and hail, his eyes fixed on distant and sunlit heights, loving knowledge, for the sake of knowledge and wisdom for the joy of wisdom, while the other is an eager actor in the world ever seeking to apply his knowledge to useful things. Both equally desire truth, but the one because of its utility, the other for its beauty. This historian regards it as the rational principle of all true history, and no more. To the other it comes as an all-pervading and mystic enthusiasm, 'like the desire of strong wine, the craving of ambition, the passionate love of what is beautiful.'

Still, though we miss in the historian those higher and more practical qualities which the philosopher of the Academe alone of all men possessed, we must not blind ourselves to the merits of that great rationalist who seems to have anticipated the very latest words of modern science. Nor yet is he to be regarded merely in the narrow light in which he is estimated by most modern critics, as the explicit champion of rationalism and nothing more. For he is connected with another idea, the course of which is as the course of that great river of his native Arcadia which, springing from some arid and sun-bleached rock, gathers strength and beauty as it flows till it reaches the asphodel meadows of Olympia and the light and laughter of Ionian waters.

For in him we can discern the first notes of that great cult of the seven-hilled city which made Virgil write his epic and Livy his history, which found in Dante its highest exponent, which dreamed of an Empire where the Emperor would care for the bodies and the Pope for the souls of men, and so has passed into the conception of God's spiritual empire and the universal brotherhood of man and widened into the huge ocean of universal thought as the Peneus loses itself in the sea.

Polybius is the last scientific historian of Greece. The writer who seems fittingly to complete the progress of thought is a writer of biographies only. I will not here touch on Plutarch's employment of the inductive method as shown in his constant use of inscription and statue, of public document and building and the like, because they involve no new method. It is his attitude towards miracles of which I desire to treat.

Plutarch is philosophic enough to see that in the sense of a violation of the laws of nature a miracle is impossible. It is absurd, he says, to imagine that the statue of a saint can speak, and that an inanimate object not possessing the vocal organs should be able to utter an articulate sound. Upon the other hand, he protests against science imagining that, by explaining the natural causes of things, it has explained away their transcendental meaning. 'When the tears on the cheek of some holy statue have been analysed into the moisture which certain temperatures produce on wood and marble, it yet by no means follows that they were not a sign of grief and mourning set there by God Himself.' When Lampon saw in the prodigy of the one-horned ram the omen of the supreme rule of Pericles, and when Anaxagoras showed that the abnormal development was the rational resultant of the peculiar formation of the skull, the dreamer and the man of science were both right; it was the business of the latter to consider how the prodigy came about, of the former to show why it was so formed and what it so portended. The progression of thought is exemplified in all particulars. Herodotus had a glimmering sense of the impossibility of a violation of nature. Thucydides ignored the supernatural. Polybius rationalised it. Plutarch raises it to its mystical heights again, though he bases it on law. In a word, Plutarch felt that while science brings the supernatural down to the natural, yet ultimately all that is natural is really supernatural. To him, as to many of our own day, religion was that transcendental attitude of the mind which, contemplating a world resting on inviolable law, is yet comforted and seeks to worship God not in the violation but in the fulfilment of nature.

It may seem paradoxical to quote in connection with the priest of Chaeronea such a pure rationalist as Mr. Herbert Spencer; yet when we read as the last message of modern science that 'when the equation of life has been reduced to its lowest terms the symbols are symbols still,' mere signs, that is, of that unknown reality which underlies all matter and all spirit, we may feel how over the wide strait of centuries thought calls to thought, and how Plutarch has a higher position than is usually claimed for him in the progress of the Greek intellect.

And, indeed, it seems that not merely the importance of Plutarch himself but also that of the land of his birth in the evolution of Greek civilisation has been passed over by modern critics. To us, indeed, the bare rock to which the Parthenon serves as a crown, and which lies between Colonus and Attica's violet hills, will always be the holiest spot in the land of Greece: and Delphi will come next, and then the meadows of Eurotas where that noble people lived who represented in Hellenic thought the reaction of the law of duty against the law of beauty, the opposition of conduct to culture. Yet, as one stands on the σχιστὴ ὁδός[1] of Cithaeron and looks out on the great double plain of Boeotia, the enormous importance of the division of Hellas comes to one's mind with great force. To the north is Orchomenus and the Minyan treasure house, seat of those merchant princes of Phoenicia who brought to Greece the knowledge of letters and the art of working in gold. Thebes is at our feet with the gloom of the terrible legends of Greek tragedy still lingering about it, the birthplace of Pindar, the nurse of Epaminondas and the Sacred Band.

And from out of the plain where 'Mars loved to dance,' rises the Muses' haunt, Helicon, by whose silver streams Corinna and Hesiod sang. While far away under the white aegis of those snow-capped mountains lies Chaeronea and the Lion plain where with vain chivalry the Greeks strove to check Macedon first and afterwards Rome; Chaeronea, where in the Martinmas summer of Greek civilisation Plutarch rose from the drear waste of a dying religion as the aftermath rises when the mowers think they have left the field bare.

Greek philosophy began and ended in scepticism: the first and the last word of Greek history was Faith.

Splendid thus in its death, like winter sunsets, the Greek religion passed away into the horror of night. For the Cimmerian darkness was at hand, and when the schools of Athens were closed and the statue of Athena broken, the Greek spirit passed from the gods and the history of its own land to the subtleties of defining the doctrine of the Trinity and the mystical attempts to bring Plato into harmony with Christ and to reconcile Gethsemane and the Sermon on the Mount with the Athenian prison and the discussion in the woods of Colonus. The Greek spirit slept for wellnigh a thousand years. When it woke again, like Antaeus it had gathered strength from the earth where it lay, like Apollo it had lost none of its divinity through its long servitude.

In the history of Roman thought we nowhere find any of those characteristics of the Greek Illumination which I have pointed out are the necessary concomitants of the rise of historical criticism. The conservative respect for tradition which made the Roman people delight in the ritual and formulas of law, and is as apparent in their politics as in their religion, was fatal to any rise of that spirit of revolt against authority the importance of which, as a factor in intellectual progress, we have already seen.

The whitened tables of the Pontifices preserved carefully the records of the eclipses and other atmospherical phenomena, and what we call the art of verifying dates was known to them at an early time; but there was no spontaneous rise of physical science to suggest by its analogies of law and order a new method of research, nor any natural springing up of the questioning spirit of philosophy with its unification of all phenomena and all knowledge. At the very time when the whole tide of Eastern superstition was sweeping into the heart of the Capitol the Senate banished the Greek philosophers from

---

[1] The divided road.

Rome. And of the three systems which did at length take some root in the city, those of Zeno and Epicurus were merely used as the rule for the ordering of life, while the dogmatic scepticism of Carneades, by its very principles, annihilated the possibility of argument and encouraged a perfect indifference to research.

Nor were the Romans ever fortunate enough like the Greeks to have to face the incubus of any dogmatic system of legends and myths, the immoralities and absurdities of which might excite a revolutionary outbreak of sceptical criticism. For the Roman religion became as it were crystallised and isolated from progress at an early period of its evolution. Their gods remained mere abstractions of common-place virtues or uninteresting personifications of the useful things of life. The old primitive creed was indeed always upheld as a state institution on account of the enormous facilities it offered for cheating in politics, but as a spiritual system of belief it was unanimously rejected at a very early period both by the common people and the educated classes, for the sensible reason that it was so extremely dull. The former took refuge in the mystic sensualities of the worship of Isis, the latter in the Stoical rules of life. The Romans classified their gods carefully in their order of precedence, analysed their genealogies in the laborious spirit of modern heraldry, fenced them round with a ritual as intricate as their law, but never quite cared enough about them to believe in them. So it was of no account with them when the philosophers announced that Minerva was merely memory. She had never been much else. Nor did they protest when Lucretius dared to say of Ceres and of Liber that they were only the corn of the field and the fruit of the vine. For they had never mourned for the daughter of Demeter in the asphodel meadows of Sicily, nor traversed the glades of Cithaeron with fawn-skin and with spear.

This brief sketch of the condition of Roman thought will serve to prepare us for the almost total want of scientific historical criticism which we shall discern in their literature, and has, besides, afforded fresh corroborations of the conditions essential to the rise of this spirit, and of the modes of thought which it reflects and in which it is always to be found. Roman historical composition had its origin in the pontifical college of ecclesiastical lawyers, and preserved to its close the uncritical spirit which characterised its fountain-head. It possessed from the outset a most voluminous collection of the materials of history, which, however, produced merely antiquarians, not historians. It is so hard to use facts, so easy to accumulate them.

Wearied of the dull monotony of the pontifical annals, which dwelt on little else but the rise and fall in provisions and the eclipses of the sun, Cato wrote out a history with his own hand for the instruction of his child to which he gave the name of Origines, and before his time some aristocratic families had written histories in Greek much in the same spirit in which the Germans of the eighteenth century used French as the literary language. But the first regular Roman historian is Sallust. Between the extravagant eulogies passed on this author by the French (such as De Closset), and Dr. Mommsen's view of him as merely a political pamphleteer, it is perhaps difficult to reach the *via media*[1] of unbiassed appreciation. He has, at any rate, the credit of being a purely rationalistic historian, perhaps the only one in Roman literature. Cicero had a good many qualifications for a scientific historian, and (as he usually did) thought very highly of his own powers. On passages of ancient legend, however, he is rather unsatisfactory, for while he is too sensible to believe them he is too patriotic to reject them. And this is really the attitude of Livy, who claims for early Roman legend a certain uncritical homage from the rest of the subject world. His view in his history is that it is not worth while to examine the truth of these stories.

In his hands the history of Rome unrolls before our eyes like some gorgeous tapestry, where victory succeeds victory, where triumph treads on the heels of triumph, and the line of heroes seems never to end. It is not till we pass behind the canvas and see the slight means by which the effect is produced that we apprehend the fact that like most picturesque writers Livy is an indifferent critic. As regards his attitude towards the credibility of early Roman history he is quite as conscious as we are of its mythical and unsound nature. He will not, for instance, decide whether the Horatii were Albans or Romans; who was the first dictator; how many tribunes there were, and the like. His method, as a rule, is merely to mention all the accounts and sometimes to decide in favour of the most probable, but usually not to decide at all. No canons of historical criticism will ever discover whether the Roman women interviewed the mother of Coriolanus of their own accord or at the suggestion of the senate; whether Remus was killed for jumping over his brother's wall or because they quarrelled about birds; whether the ambassadors found Cincinnatus ploughing or only mending a hedge. Livy suspends his judgment over these important facts and history and when questioned on their truth is dumb. If he does select between two historians he chooses the one who is nearer to the facts he describes. But he is no critic, only a conscientious writer. It is mere vain waste to dwell on his critical powers, for they do not exist.

In the case of Tacitus, imagination has taken the place of history. The past lives again in his pages, but through no laborious criticism; rather through a dramatic and psychological faculty which he specially possessed.

In the philosophy of history he has no belief. He can never make up his mind what to believe as regards God's government of the world. There is no method in him and none elsewhere in Roman literature.

Nations may not have missions but they certainly have functions. And the function of ancient Italy was not merely to give us what is statical in our institutions and rational in our law, but to blend into one elemental creed the spiritual aspirations of Aryan and of Semite. Italy was not a pioneer in intellectual progress, nor a motive power in the evolution of thought. The owl of the goddess of Wisdom traversed over the whole land and found nowhere a resting-place. The dove, which is the bird of Christ, flew straight to the city of Rome and the new reign began. It was the fashion of early Italian painters

---

[1] Middle way.

to represent in mediaeval costume the soldiers who watched over the tomb of Christ, and this, which was the result of the frank anachronism of all true art, may serve to us as an allegory. For it was in vain that the middle ages strove to guard the buried spirit of progress. When the dawn of the Greek spirit arose, the sepulchre was empty, the grave-clothes laid aside. Humanity had risen from the dead.

The study of Greek, it has been well said, implies the birth of criticism, comparison and research. At the opening of that education of modern by ancient thought which we call the Renaissance, it was the words of Aristotle which sent Columbus sailing to the New World, while a fragment of Pythagorean astronomy set Copernicus thinking on that train of reasoning which has revolutionised the whole position of our planet in the universe. Then it was seen that the only meaning of progress is a return to Greek modes of thought. The monkish hymns which obscured the pages of Greek manuscripts were blotted out, the splendours of a new method were unfolded to the world, and out of the melancholy sea of mediaevalism rose the free spirit of man in all that splendour of glad adolescence, when the bodily powers seem quickened by a new vitality, when the eye sees more clearly than its wont and the mind apprehends what was beforetime hidden from it. To herald the opening of the sixteenth century, from the little Venetian printing press came forth all the great authors of antiquity, each bearing on the title-page the words ῎Αλδος ὁ Μανούτιος ῾Ρωμαῖος καὶ Φιλέλλην,[1] words which may serve to remind us with what wondrous prescience Polybius saw the world's fate when he foretold the material sovereignty of Roman institutions and exemplified in himself the intellectual empire of Greece.

The course of the study of the spirit of historical criticism has not been a profitless investigation into modes and forms of thought now antiquated and of no account. The only spirit which is entirely removed from us is the mediaeval; the Greek spirit is essentially modern. The introduction of the comparative method of research which has forced history to disclose its secrets belongs in a measure to us. Ours, too, is a more scientific knowledge of philology and the method of survival. Nor did the ancients know anything of the doctrine of averages or of crucial instances, both of which methods have proved of such importance in modern criticism, the one adding a most important proof of the statical elements of history, and exemplifying the influences of all physical surroundings on the life of man; the other, as in the single instance of the Moulin Quignon skull, serving to create a whole new science of prehistoric archaeology and to bring us back to a time when man was coeval with the stone age, the mammoth and the woolly rhinoceros. But, except these, we have added no new canon or method to the science of historical criticism. Across the drear waste of a thousand years the Greek and the modern spirit joins hands.

In the torch race which the Greek boys ran from the Cerameician field of death to the home of the goddess of Wisdom, not merely he who first reached

---

[1] Aldo Menuzio, a Roman and a lover of Greece.

the goal but he also who first started with the torch aflame received a prize. In the Lampadephoria of civilisation and free thought let us not forget to render due meed of honour to those who first lit that sacred flame, the increasing splendour of which lights our footsteps to the far-off divine event of the attainment of perfect truth.

A FEW MAXIMS FOR THE INSTRUCTION OF THE OVER-EDUCATED

(*Saturday Review*, November, 1894)

Education is an admirable thing. But it is well to remember from time to time that nothing that is worth knowing can be taught.

Public opinion exists only where there are no ideas.

The English are always degrading truths into facts. When a truth becomes a fact it loses all its intellectual value.

It is a very sad thing that nowadays there is so little useless information.

The only link between Literature and the Drama left to us in England at the present moment is the bill of the play.

In old days books were written by men of letters and read by the public. Nowadays books are written by the public and read by nobody.

Most women are so artificial that they have no sense of Art. Most men are so natural that they have no sense of Beauty.

Friendship is far more tragic than love. It lasts longer.

What is abnormal in Life stands in normal relations to Art. It is the only thing in Life that stands in normal relations to Art.

A subject that is beautiful in itself gives no suggestion to the artist. It lacks imperfection.

The only thing that the artist cannot see is the obvious. The only thing that the public can see is the obvious. The result is the Criticism of the Journalist.

Art is the only serious thing in the world. And the artist is the only person who is never serious.

To be really mediaeval one should have no body. To be really modern one should have no soul. To be really Greek one should have no clothes.

Dandyism is the assertion of the absolute modernity of Beauty.

The only thing that can console one for being poor is extravagance. The only thing that can console one for being rich is economy.

One should never listen. To listen is a sign of indifference to one's hearers.

Even the disciple has his uses. He stands behind one's throne, and at the moment of one's triumph whispers in one's ear that, after all, one is immortal.

The criminal classes are so close to us that even the policeman can see them. They are so far away from us that only the poet can understand them.

Those whom the gods love grow young.

Phrases and Philosophies for the Use of the Young

(*Chameleon*, December, 1894)

The first duty in life is to be as artificial as possible. What the second duty is no one has yet discovered.

Wickedness is a myth invented by good people to account for the curious attractiveness of others.

If the poor only had profiles there would be no difficulty in solving the problem of poverty.

Those who see any difference between soul and body have neither.

A really well-made buttonhole is the only link between Art and Nature.

Religions die when they are proved to be true. Science is the record of dead religions.

The well-bred contradict other people. The wise contradict themselves.

Nothing that actually occurs is of the smallest importance.

Dullness is the coming of age of seriousness.

In all unimportant matters, style, not sincerity, is the essential. In all important matters, style, not sincerity, is the essential.

If one tells the truth, one is sure, sooner or later, to be found out.

Pleasure is the only thing one should live for. Nothing ages like happiness.

It is only by not paying one's bills that one can hope to live in the memory of the commercial classes.

No crime is vulgar, but all vulgarity is crime. Vulgarity is the conduct of others.

Only the shallow know themselves.

Time is waste of money.

One should always be a little improbable.

There is a fatality about all good resolutions. They are invariably made too soon.

The only way to atone for being occasionally a little over-dressed is by being always absolutely over-educated.

To be premature is to be perfect.

Any preoccupation with ideas of what is right or wrong in conduct shows an arrested intellectual development.

Ambition is the last refuge of the failure.

A truth ceases to be true when more than one person believes in it.

In examinations the foolish ask questions that the wise cannot answer.

Greek dress was in its essence inartistic. Nothing should reveal the body but the body.

One should either be a work of art, or wear a work of art.

It is only the superficial qualities that last. Man's deeper nature is soon found out.

Industry is the root of all ugliness.

The ages live in history through their anachronisms.

It is only the gods who taste of death. Apollo has passed away, but Hyacinth, whom men say he slew, lives on. Nero and Narcissus are always with us.

The old believe everything: the middle-aged suspect everything: the young know everything.

The condition of perfection is idleness: the aim of perfection is youth.

Only the great masters of style ever succeed in being obscure.

There is something tragic about the enormous number of young men there are in England at the present moment who start life with perfect profiles, and end by adopting some useful profession.

To love oneself is the beginning of a life-long romance.

APPENDIX A:
CHRONOLOGICAL TABLE

1854	October 16	Oscar Wilde born at 21 Westland Row, Dublin
1855	June	Family moves to 1 Merrion Square North
1864–71		At Portora Royal School, Enniskillen
1871		Wins scholarship to Trinity College, Dublin
1873	June	Wins Trinity Foundation Scholarship
1874		Wins Berkeley Gold Medal
	June	Wins Demyship in Classics to Magdalen College, Oxford
	October	Goes up to Magdalen
1875	June	Travels in Italy with his old Trinity Classics Tutor, J. P. Mahaffy
1876	April 19	Death of father, Sir William Wilde
	July 5	Gains first class Classical Moderations (Mods)
1877	March/April	Visits Greece with Mahaffy, returning via Rome
1878	June 10	Wins Newdigate Prize with *Ravenna*
	July 19	Gains first class in Litterae Humaniores (Greats)
	November 28	Takes B.A. degree
1879	Spring	Takes rooms with Frank Miles at 13 Salisbury Street, London
1880		Writes and publishes *Vera*
	August	Moves with Miles to Keats House, Tite Street, Chelsea
1881	June	First edition of *Poems* published by David Bogue
	December 24	Sails for New York for lecture tour of the United States
1882		Lectures in U.S. and Canada all year
1883	Feb–May	In Paris, at Hôtel Voltaire where he writes *The Duchess of Padua* for the American actress Mary Anderson who then turns it down
	? July	Moves into rooms at 9 Charles Street, London
	Aug/Sept	Visits New York briefly for first production of *Vera* with Marie Prescott in the lead; it is not a success
	September	Begins lecture tour of UK which lasts off and on for a year
	November 26	Becomes engaged to Constance Lloyd while lecturing in Dublin
1884	May 29	Married to Constance Lloyd in London
	May/June	On honeymoon in Paris and Dieppe
1885	January	Moves into 16 Tite Street
	May	*The Truth of Masks* published in *The Nineteenth Century* as 'Shakespeare and Stage Costume'

1885	June 5	Cyril Wilde born
1886		Meets Robert Ross who remains life-long friend and after his death becomes his literary executor
	November 3	Vyvyan Wilde born
1887	Feb/March	*Canterville Ghost* published in *The Court & Society Review*
	May	*The Sphinx without a Secret* published in *The World*. *Lord Arthur Savile's Crime* published in *The Court & Society Review*
	June	*The Model Millionaire* published in *The World*
	November	Becomes editor of *The Woman's World*
1888	May	*The Happy Prince and Other Tales* published
	December	*The Young King* published in *The Lady's Pictorial*
1889	January	*The Decay of Lying* published in *The Nineteenth Century*. *Pen, Pencil and Poison* published in *The Fortnightly Review*
	March	*The Birthday of the Infanta* published in *Paris Illustré*
	July	Gives up editorship of *Woman's World*. *The Portrait of Mr W.H.* appears in *Blackwood's Magazine*
1890	June 20	*The Picture of Dorian Gray* appears in *Lippincott's Magazine*
	July/Sept	Both parts of *The Critic as Artist* published these months in *The Nineteenth Century* as 'The True Function and Value of Criticism'
1891	? January	Meets Lord Alfred Douglas (Bosie)
	January 26	First production of *The Duchess of Padua* under the title *Guido Ferranti*. It opens anonymously in New York and runs only for three weeks
	February	*The Soul of Man under Socialism* published in *The Fortnightly Review*
	April	*The Picture of Dorian Gray* published in book form with additional chapters and a preface
	May 2	*Intentions* published (comprising *The Truth of Masks*, *The Critic as Artist*, *Pen, Pencil & Poison*, and *The Decay of Lying*) in book form
	July	*Lord Arthur Savile's Crime and Other Stories* (the other stories being *The Sphinx without a Secret*, *The Canterville Ghost*, and *The Model Millionaire*) published in book form
	November	*A House of Pomegranates* published. It included *The Young King*, *The Birthday of the Infanta*, *The Fisherman and His Soul* and *The Star Child*, the last two of which had not been published before
	Nov/Dec	Writes *Salomé* in Paris
1892	February 20	*Lady Windermere's Fan* produced at St James's Theatre

1892	June	A production of *Salomé* with Sarah Bernhardt in the title role is banned by the Lord Chamberlain
	July	Takes cure at Homburg
	Aug/Sept	Writes *A Woman of No Importance* in Norfolk
1893	February	*The House of Judgement* published in *The Spirit Lamp*
	February 22	*Salomé* published in French
	April 19	*A Woman of No Importance* produced at Haymarket Theatre
	June	*The Disciple* published in *The Spirit Lamp*
	October	Writes *An Ideal Husband*
	November	*Lady Windermere's Fan* published
1894	February 9	*Salomé* published in English with Aubrey Beardsley's illustrations
	May	In Florence with Douglas
	June 11	*The Sphinx* published
	July	*Poems in Prose* published in *The Fortnightly Review*. *The Artist, The Doer of Good* and *The Master* are published for the first time
	Aug/Sept	Writes *The Importance of Being Earnest* at Worthing
	October 9	*A Woman of No Importance* published
	October	At Brighton with Douglas
	November	*A Few Maxims for the Instruction of the Over-Educated* published in *The Saturday Review*
	December	*Phrases and Philosophies for the Use of the Young* published in *The Chameleon*
1895	January 3	*An Ideal Husband* produced at Haymarket Theatre
	Jan/Feb	Visits Algiers with Douglas
	February 14	*The Importance of Being Earnest* produced at St James's Theatre
	February 28	Finds Queensberry's card at Albemarle Club
	March 1	Obtains warrant for Queensberry's arrest
	March 9	Queensberry remanded at Bow Street for trial at Old Bailey
	March	Visits Monte Carlo with Douglas
	April 3	Queensberry trial opens
	April 5	Queensberry acquitted. Wilde arrested at Cadogan Hotel and charged at Bow Street. Bail refused. Imprisoned at Holloway until first trial
	April 24	Sheriff's sale of all Wilde's possessions at 16 Tite Street
	April 26	First trial opens
	May 1	Jury disagree
	May 7	Released on bail
	May 20	Second trial opens
	May 25	Convicted and sentenced to two years' hard labour. Imprisoned at Pentonville

1895	May 30	*The Soul of Man under Socialism* published in book form
	July 4	Transferred to Wandsworth
	November 12	Declared bankrupt
	November 21	Transferred to Reading
1896	February 3	Death of his mother, Lady Wilde
	February 11	*Salomé* produced in Paris at the Théâtre de l'Oeuvre
1897	Jan–March	Writes *De Profundis*
	May 19	Released. Crosses to Dieppe
	May 26	Moves from Dieppe to Berneval-sur-Mer
	July–Oct	Writes and revises *The Ballad of Reading Gaol*
	August ?28	Meets Douglas in Rouen
	September 15	Leaves Dieppe for Paris
	September 20	Arrives at Naples with Douglas
1898	February	Returns to Paris
	February 13	*The Ballad of Reading Gaol* published
	end March	Moves to Hôtel d'Alsace, rue des Beaux Arts, Paris
	April 7	Death of Constance Wilde in Genoa after spinal operation
	June/July	At Nogent-sur-Marne
	August	At Chevennières-sur-Marne
	December	Invited by Frank Harris to spend three months on French Riviera at Napoule near Cannes
1899	February	*The Importance of Being Earnest* published. Leaves Napoule for Nice
	February 25	Leaves Nice to stay as Harold Mellor's guest at Gland, Switzerland
	April 1	Leaves Gland for Santa Margherita on Italian Riviera
	May	Returns to Paris. Stays at Hôtel de la Neva, then at Hôtel Marsollier
	July	*An Ideal Husband* published
	August	Moves back to the Hôtel d'Alsace
1900	April/May	Spends two weeks as Mellor's guest travelling in Italy and Sicily. After Mellor's departure Wilde stays on in Rome and visits Naples. He then passes ten days with Mellor at Gland before returning to Paris
	May	Returns to the Hôtel d'Alsace
	October 10	Undergoes ear operation in hotel room
	November 30	Dies in Hôtel d'Alsace of cerebral meningitis
1905	February	*De Profundis* first published in heavily expurgated form by Robert Ross
1906	July	Wilde's estate discharged from bankruptcy. Creditors paid 20/- in the £ and 4% from sales of books and licensing of plays
1908		First collected edition of Wilde's works published by Methuen, in which *A Florentine Tragedy, La Sainte*

1908		Courtisane, the complete *Rise of Historical Criticism* and the poem *To L.L.* were published for the first time as well as a few additional parts of *De Profundis*
1909		Wilde's remains are moved from the cemetery at Bagneux to Père Lachaise and reinterred under Epstein's monument. The manuscript of *De Profundis* is presented by Ross to the British Museum on the condition that it remains closed for 50 years
1945	March 20	Death of Lord Alfred Douglas
1949		Suppressed part of *De Profundis* published by Wilde's son, Vyvyan Holland, from Ross's typescript
1956		First publication of the original four-act version of *The Importance of Being Earnest*
1962		Publication of Wilde's *Collected Letters* including first fully correct version of *De Profundis*

APPENDIX B:
ORDER OF POEMS (1882)

ELEUTHERIA:

Sonnet to Liberty
Ave Imperatrix
To Milton
Louis Napoleon
Sonnet on the Massacre of the Christians in Bulgaria
Quantum Mutata
Libertatis Sacra Fames
Theoretikos

THE GARDEN OF EROS

ROSA MYSTICA:

Requiescat
Sonnet on approaching Italy
San Miniato
Ave Maria Gratia Plena
Italia
Sonnet written in Holy Week at Genoa
Rome Unvisited
Urbs Sacra Æterna
Sonnet on hearing the Dies Iræ sung in the Sistine Chapel
Easter Day
E Tenebris
Vita Nuova
Madonna Mia
The New Helen

THE BURDEN OF ITYS

WIND FLOWERS:

Impression du Matin
Magdalen Walks
Athanasia
Serenade
Endymion
La Bella Donna della mia Mente

Chanson

CHARMIDES

FLOWERS OF GOLD:

Impressions: I. Les Silhouettes
              II. La Fuite de la Lune
The Grave of Keats
Theocritus: A Villanelle
In the Gold Room: A Harmony
Ballade de Marguerite
The Dole of the King's Daughter
Amor Intellectualis
Santa Decca
A Vision
Impression de Voyage
The Grave of Shelley
By the Arno

IMPRESSIONS DE THÉÂTRE:
Fabien dei Franchi
Phèdre
Sonnets written at the Lyceum Theatre:
    I. Portia
    II. Queen Henrietta Maria
Camma

PANTHEA

THE FOURTH MOVEMENT:

Impression: Le Réveillon
At Verona
Apologia
Quia Multum Amavi
Silentium Amoris
Her Voice
My Voice
Tædium Vitæ

HUMANITAD

FLOWER OF LOVE:
ΓΛΥΚΥΠΙΚΡΟΣ ΕΡΩΣ

APPENDIX C:
LIST OF ORIGINAL DEDICATIONS IN WILDE'S PUBLISHED WORKS

Ravenna (1878)
To my friend George Fleming [Julia Constance Fletcher], author of 'The Nile Novel' and 'Mirage'

The Happy Prince & Other Tales (1888)
To Carlos Blacker

The House of Pomegranates (1891)
To Constance Mary Wilde
Individual stories were dedicated to:
'The Young King': To Margaret, Lady Brooke [Ranee of Sarawak]
'The Birthday of the Infanta': Mrs William H. Grenfell of Taplow Court [Lady Desborough]
'The Fisherman and His Soul': H.S.H. Alice, Princess of Monaco
'The Star-Child': To Miss Margot Tennant [Mrs H. H. Asquith]

Salomé (1893) In French
A mon ami Pierre Louÿs
        (1893) in English
To my friend Lord Alfred Bruce Douglas, the translator of my play

Lady Windermere's Fan (1893)
To the dear memory of Robert, Earl of Lytton in affection and admiration

The Sphinx (1894)
To Marcel Schwob in friendship and admiration

A Woman of No Importance (1894)
To Gladys, Countess de Grey

The Ballad of Reading Gaol (1898)
In memoriam C.T.W. [Charles Thomas Wooldridge], sometime trooper of the Royal Horse Guards. Obiit H.M. Prison, Reading, Berkshire, July 7th 1896

The Importance of Being Earnest (1899)
To Robert Baldwin Ross in appreciation, in affection

An Ideal Husband (1899)
To Frank Harris, a slight tribute to his power and distinction as an artist, his chivalry and nobility as a friend

APPENDIX D:
INDEX OF FIRST LINES OF POEMS

(*asterixes denote poems included for the first time*)

BIBLIOGRAPHY

The Works

The following is a bibliography of the works of Oscar Wilde as first published in book form. It includes privately printed first editions but not pirated editions if they predated the former. Piracy of Wilde's works between his death in 1900 and the discharge of his estate from bankruptcy in 1906 was rife and only halted by the efforts of Robbie Ross, his literary executor, once he had full control of the publishing rights.

The Ballad of Reading Gaol (London: Leonard Smithers & Co, 1898)

First published pseudonymously under Wilde's prison cell number 'C.3.3.'. Only with the seventh edition did Wilde's name appear on the title page. The first edition was 800 copies.

De Profundis (London: Methuen & Co, 1905)

Heavily expurgated by Wilde's literary executor in the first edition of 10,000 copies, this letter to Alfred Douglas was first published in its entirety only in 1962. The story is treated more fully in the introduction to the 'Essays' section of the present edition.

The Duchess of Padua (New York?/London?, 1891?)

Mystery surrounds the first printed edition. Wilde wrote the play for the American actress Mary Anderson when he was in Paris early in 1883. He sent it to her, but she turned it down. It was first played in New York in 1891. At some stage twenty acting copies were printed of which only a handful still exist. They bear the date 15 March 1883, the date he finished writing it, but given the state of Wilde's finances in 1883, it is much more likely to have been printed in time for the rehearsals in 1891.

The Happy Prince and Other Tales. Illustrated by Walter Crane and Jacomb Hood (London: David Nutt, 1888)

Containing 'The Happy Prince', 'The Selfish Giant', 'The Remarkable Rocket', 'The Devoted Friend' and 'The Nightingale and the Rose', all of which were published for the first time. 1000 copies were printed.

A House of Pomegranates. Illustrated by Charles Ricketts and Charles Shannon (London: Osgood, McIlvaine & Co, 1891)

Two of the stories 'The Young King' and 'The Birthday of the Infanta' had previously been published in periodicals (see chronology); 'The Fisherman and His Soul' and 'The Star-Child' were first published in this volume. The edition was 1000 copies.

An Ideal Husband (London: Leonard Smithers & Co, 1899)

The first edition consisted of 1000 copies. Like *The Importance of Being Earnest*, issued earlier the same year, 'By the author of *Lady Windermere's Fan*', appeared instead of Wilde's name on the title page.

The Importance of Being Earnest (London: Leonard Smithers & Co, 1899)

1000 copies were printed of the first edition. Originally written in four acts, Wilde pruned it down to three at the request of the actor-manager George Alexander who first produced it. Another copy of the four-act version had been sent to an impressario in America late in 1894 but was never staged because of Wilde's disgrace. It was discovered years later in New York and first published in 1956.

Intentions (London: Osgood, McIlvaine & Co, 1891)

Containing 'The Truth of Masks', 'The Critic as Artist', 'The Decay of Lying' and 'Pen, Pencil and Poison', all of which essays had previously been published in periodicals (see chronology) and all show considerable variations from the text as first published. The edition consisted of 1500 copies.

Lady Windermere's Fan (London: Elkin Matthews & John Lane, 1893)

An edition of 500 copies.

Lord Arthur Savile's Crime and Other Stories (London: Osgood, McIlvaine & Co, 1891)

All these stories 'Lord Arthur Savile's Crime', 'The Model Millionaire', 'The Sphinx without a Secret' and 'The Canterville Ghost' had previously been published in periodicals (see chronology). 2000 copies were printed.

Oscariana (London: Privately Printed by Arthur Humphries, 1895)

A selection of epigrams and aphorisms from Wilde's writings made by his wife, Constance. Only 50 copies were printed of this first edition.

The Picture of Dorian Gray (London: Ward, Lock & Co, 1891)

This, Wilde's only novel, was first published in 1890 in *Lippincott's Magazine* with thirteen chapters. Published a year later in book form it contained six new chapters, many alterations and much additional matter. No record of the number of copies printed. An annotated textual comparison of the two versions was edited by Donald Lawler in 1988 (London; New York: W. W. Norton).

Poems (London: David Bogue, 1881)

750 copies were printed at Wilde's expense and spread over three 'editions', each with a new title page. Another 500 were printed with minor changes as the fourth and fifth editions the following year.

The Portrait of Mr W.H. (New York: Mitchell Kennerley, 1921)

This story was first published in *Blackwood's Magazine* in 1889. Wilde projected a more elaborate version to be published in book form with publishers Elkin Matthews & John Lane who announced it 'in preparation' at the end of 1893. The manuscript was apparently returned to Wilde on the day of his arrest and then disappeared until it turned up in New York and was first published in 1921 in 1000 copies. An English edition was first published by Methuen in 1958.

Ravenna (Oxford: Thos. Shrimpton & Sons, 1878)

The long poem with which Wilde won the Newdigate Prize in 1878 was published within two weeks of the award by the Oxford booksellers Shrimpton, who traditionally published all the prize poems. Only about 170 copies were ever printed.

Salomé (French edition: Paris: Librarie de L'Art Indépendant; London: Elkin Matthews & John Lane, 1893. English edition: London: Elkin Matthews & John Lane, 1894)

Originally written in French by Wilde and 'polished' by Pierre Louÿs. The French edition appeared in 600 copies. It was then translated (badly) by Alfred Douglas, corrected (mostly by Wilde) and issued in 500 copies in English with illustrations by Aubrey Beardsley. Beardsley provided seventeen designs of which three were supressed, two bowdlerised and one omitted from this edition. All but one were finally printed as drawn in the Bodley Head edition of 1906.

The Soul of Man (London: Privately Printed, 1895)

This essay was originally published in *The Fortnightly Review* in 1891 as 'The Soul of Man Under Socialism'. This first edition in book form of only 50 copies was in fact published by Arthur Humphries within days of Wilde's final conviction and imprisonment. Humphries, a friend of the Wildes and manager of Hatchards bookshop, undertook publication as a gesture of solidarity at the time of Wilde's disgrace.

The Sphinx. Illustrated by Charles Ricketts (London: Elkin Matthews & John Lane, 1894)

Issued in 200 copies only.

Vera; or the Nihilists (London: Ranken & Co, 1880)

Almost certainly published at Wilde's expense as a very small acting edition, only a few copies are known to exist. The first performance, planned for December 1881 was cancelled for diplomatic reasons due to the assassination of Czar Alexander. Another small edition was printed and published by Wilde in 1882 when he was trying to have it staged during his American tour. It was eventually put on the following year in New York.

A Woman of No Importance (London: John Lane, 1894)

First edition in 500 copies.

The first *Collected Works* in 14 vols edited by Robert Ross, was published by Methuen & Co in 1908. It contained all the above works as well as the first non-periodical and authorised versions of: 'Poems in Prose', 'Phrases and Philosophies for the Use of the Young', previously published poems not in the editions of 1881/2, and, as far as was then known, all Wilde's reviews and published essays.

The *Collected Works* also contained a number of previously unpublished pieces: 'La Sainte Courtisane', 'A Florentine Tragedy', the full text of 'The Rise of Historical Criticism', the poem 'To L. L.' and the four lectures

'The English Renaissance', 'House Decoration', 'Art and the Handicrafts-man' and the 'Lecture to Art Students'.

Wilde's lecture 'Impressions of America' was first published by the Keystone Press in 1906.

Two previously unpublished poems 'Pan' and 'Désespoir' were first published in Methuen's second collected edition of 1909.

'A Few Maxims for the Instruction of the Over-Educated' which had been published anonymously in *The Saturday Review* in 1894 were only recognised in the 1950s and first published as Appendix B of the *Letters* in 1962.

Various small collections of Wilde's letters were published (largely by the recipients) after his death. Most were in limited bibliophile editions. One of the most impressive is *Some Letters from Lord Alfred Douglas to Oscar Wilde* (San Francisco, 1924) in which the letters are reproduced in facsimile. All, however, were superseded by the authoritative *Letters of Oscar Wilde* ed. Rupert Hart-Davis (London, 1962) and its supplement *More Letters of Oscar Wilde* (London, 1985).

The latest collection of Wilde's letters *The Complete Letters of Oscar Wilde* (London, 2000) contains all the letters published between 1962 and 1985 as well as an additional 300 and the full and accurate texts to many only previously known through auction catalogues or inaccurate type-scripts. *Oscar Wilde: A Life in Letters* (London, 2003) is a good general reader's abridgement of the *Complete Letters*.

The best generally available edition of Wilde's collected works is that published by HarperCollins, whose Centenary Edition (Glasgow, 2000) has the added advantage of being illustrated.

Oxford University Press's World's Classics Series and the Penguin Classics Series both provide the best annotated texts for the general reader grouped under 'Theatre', 'Shorter Fiction', 'Prison Writings' etc. and are generally maintained in print.

Oxford University Press also has an ongoing commitment to publish all Wilde's works in its Oxford English Texts Series with a full scholarly apparatus for each volume. So far three volumes have appeared: *Poems*, ed. Karl Beckson and Bobby Fong (2000); *De Profundis*, ed. Ian Small (2005); *The Picture of Dorian Gray* ed. Joseph Bristow (2005).

Bibliographies of Oscar Wilde

Kohl, Norbert. *Oscar Wilde* (Heidelberg, 1980; Trs. Cambridge, 1989)
    The German edition of this study contains a massive 165pp bibliography much reduced in the English translation (see below) which is an excellent supplement to Mikhail.

Mason, Stuart. *Bibliography of Oscar Wilde* (London, [1914])
A remarkable work full of biographical and other snippets. Occasional errors but still indispensable for early publications of Wilde's works. Contains valuable information on periodical publications, piracies etc.

Mikhail, E.H. *Oscar Wilde: An Annotated Bibliography of Criticism* (London, 1978)
Contains some 3500 references divided mainly into books, articles, dissertations, contemporary reviews of Wilde's works, and reviews of stage productions.

Mikolyzk, Thomas A. *Oscar Wilde: An Annotated Bibliography* (Westport, Conn., 1993)
More comprehensive than Mikhail but packed with errors, even repeating some of Mikhail's.

The Secondary Literature: Biographies, Critical Studies etc.

The following is necessarily only a small selection of the literature published on Wilde in the last 100 years. Mikhail (above) lists 375 books alone dealing entirely with Wilde. In addition to serious biographical and textual studies there have been many attempts to dramatise Wilde's life, fact/fiction novels written about him and even psychic mediums who have recorded messages from him. A small number are included here for interest. Many of the earlier works below have been reprinted but are out of print again and the reprint is as scarce as the original. Only the first date of publication is therefore given unless a later edition was revised or enlarged. Translations of foreign works into English are noted thus (Trs. London, 1967).

Amor, Anne Clark. *Mrs Oscar Wilde: A Woman of Some Importance* (London, 1983)
By far the more scholarly of two books on Constance appearing in 1983. Well researched and referenced.

Ackroyd, Peter. *The Last Testament of Oscar Wilde* (London, 1983)
A fictional account of Wilde's last days in Paris in diary form.

Beckson, Karl, (ed.). *Oscar Wilde: The Critical Heritage* (London, 1970)
Collection of contemporary and later criticism of Wilde's work.

Beckson, Karl. *The Oscar Wilde Encyclopaedia* (New York, 1998)
An indispensible tool for the serious Wildean, especially on the individual works.

Birnbaum, Martin. *Oscar Wilde: Fragments and Memories* (London, 1914)
Slim volume with reliable anecdotes.

Bloom, Harold, (ed.). *Oscar Wilde* (New York, 1985)
Mostly modern critical essays with memoir by W.B. Yeats.

Braybrooke, Patrick. *Oscar Wilde: A Study* (London, 1930)
  Literary criticism.

Brasol, Boris. *Oscar Wilde: The Man, the Artist, the Martyr* (New York, 1938)
  Best of the pre-war biographies, also attempting critique of works.

Brémont, Anna Comtesse de. *Oscar Wilde and his Mother* (London, 1911)
  Attributes Wilde's 'feminine soul' to his dominant mother.

Broad, Lewis. *The Friendships and Follies of Oscar Wilde* (London, 1954)

Byrne, Patrick. *The Wildes of Merrion Square* (London; New York, 1953)
  Noteless, chapter-headless, passable early study of the family.

Callow, Simon. *Oscar Wilde and his Circle* (London, 2000)
  Wilde from point of view of friends, lovers and family, and the whole from point of view of a leading British actor who has frequently interpreted Wilde on stage. Well illustrated.

Chamberlin, J.E. *Ripe was the Drowsy Hour: The Age of Oscar Wilde* (New York, 1977)
  Good evocation of the period, overambitious in places.

Coakley, Davis. *The Importance of Being Irish* (Dublin, 1994)
  First full-length study to examine the importance of Wilde's Irish roots.

Cohen, Philip K. *The Moral Vision of Oscar Wilde* (Cranbery, N.J., 1978)
  Literary criticism.

Conrad, Tweed. *Oscar Wilde in Quotation* (Jefferson, N.C., 2006)
  Contains 3099 Oscar Wilde quotations grouped thematically under 67 headings.

Cooper-Pritchard, A.H. *Conversations with Oscar Wilde* (London, 1931)
  Fictional conversations between Wilde and his contemporaries.

Croft-Cooke, Rupert. *Bosie: The Story of Lord Alfred Douglas* (London, 1963)

Croft-Cooke, Rupert. *The Unrecorded Life of Oscar Wilde* (London, 1972)
  Examination of Wilde's sexuality. Curious lack of sympathy with both subject and his works.

Crosland, T. W. H. *The First Stone: On Reading the Unpublished Parts of Oscar Wilde's 'De Profundis'* (London, 1912)
  A vituperative attack on Wilde by one of Douglas's cronies.

Davray, Henry-D. *Oscar Wilde: La Tragédie finale* (Paris, 1928)
  Wilde's last years chronicled by the translator of *The Ballad*.

Douglas, Lord Alfred. *Oscar Wilde and Myself* (London, 1914)
   Written with T. W. H. Crossland. Very critical of Wilde. Full of denials and fabrications about which Douglas later recanted.

Douglas, Lord Alfred. *The Autobiography* (London, 1929)
   Much taken up with attacks on Ross, Harris and Sherard.

Douglas, Lord Alfred. *Without Apology* (London, 1938)
   Recognises error of his first book in 1914.

Douglas, Lord Alfred. *Oscar Wilde: A Summing-Up* (London, 1940)
   Douglas's final withdrawal of previous criticisms of Wilde.

Edwards, Owen Dudley. *The Fireworks of Oscar Wilde* (London, 1989)
   The best excerpts from Wilde's works with a splendidly idiosyncratic index.

Ellmann, Richard. *The Artist as Critic: Critical Writings of Oscar Wilde* (New York, 1969)

Ellmann, Richard (ed.). *Oscar Wilde: A Collection of Critical Essays* (Englewood Cliffs N.J.; London, 1969)

Ellmann, Richard. *Oscar Wilde* (London, 1987)
   The best biography to date but must be read with Schroeder (see below).

Ervine, St John. *Oscar Wilde: A Present Time Appraisal* (London, 1951)
   Unbalanced, overcritical, unfair but a period piece.

Fido, Martin. *Oscar Wilde* (London, 1973)
   Copiously and sometimes interestingly illustrated but relies too heavily on dubious secondary sources.

Fletcher, Ian and John Stokes. 'Oscar Wilde' in *Anglo-Irish Literature: A Review of Research*, ed. Richard Finneran (New York, 1976), pp. 48–137

Fletcher, Ian and John Stokes. 'Oscar Wilde' in *Recent Research in Anglo-Irish Writers*, ed. Richard Finneran (New York, 1983), pp. 21–47
   Both the above give an invaluable and critical survey of published work on Wilde, editions of his works and significant manuscripts discovered.

Furnell, John. *The Stringed Lute: An Evocation in Dialogue of Oscar Wilde* (London, 1955)

Gagnier, Regenia. *Idylls of the Marketplace: Oscar Wilde and the Victorian Public* (Stanford CA, 1986)

Gide, André. *Oscar Wilde: In Memoriam* (Paris, 1910)
   Included in translation in: Stuart Mason's *Oscar Wilde: A Study* (London, 1905); Ernest La Jeunesse et al. (see below); André Gide *Oscar Wilde* (London, 1951).

Goodman, Jonathan. *The Oscar Wilde File* (London, 1988)
  Useful collection of contemporary newspaper accounts about Wilde.

[Grolleau, Charles]. *The Trial of Oscar Wilde* (Paris, 1906)
  First but somewhat inaccurate account of the trials.

Harris, Frank. *Oscar Wilde: His Life and Confessions* (London; New York, 1916)
  Often unreliable. Many anecdotes presented in dialogue form. Critical of Douglas. But a 'techicolour' account by one who knew Wilde personally. The 1918 reprint is important for Shaw's appendix 'My Memories of Oscar Wilde'.

Harris, Frank and Lord Alfred Douglas. *New Preface to* 'The Life and Confessions of Oscar Wilde' (London, 1925)
  Destined as a true preface to the above but published separately by Douglas as an 'apology' from Harris.

[Hitchens, Robert]. *The Green Carnation* (London, 1894)
  Thinly disguised satire on Wilde/Douglas relationship. Published anonymously at the time but reprinted in 1949 with Hitchens' introductory note.

Holland, Merlin. *The Wilde Album* (London, 1997)
  The most comprehensive of the pictorial biographies with around 250 illustrations, 30 of which were published for the first time.

Holland, Merlin. *Irish Peacock and Scarlet Marquess: the Real Trial of Oscar Wilde* (London, 2003)
  The full text of the Queensberry libel trial from a previously unknown contemporary transcript. Three times as long as anything previously published.

Holland, Vyvyan. *Oscar Wilde* (London, 1960)
  The first of the pictorial biographies. The first edition has superb gravure plates.

Holland, Vyvyan. *Son of Oscar Wilde* (London, 1954)
  An account of how the scandal affected Wilde's family.

Hopkins, R. Thurston. *Oscar Wilde: A Study of the Man and His Work* (London, 1913)

Housman, Laurence. *Echo de Paris* (London, 1923)
  Reconstruction in dialogue of author's last meeting with Wilde and Ross in Paris café.

Hyde, H. Montgomery. *The Trials of Oscar Wilde* (London, 1948; new enlarged edition, 1962)
  A so-called 'verbatim' edition of the proceedings of the three trials the first of which is now superseded by Holland's *Irish Peacock*.

Hyde, H. Montgomery. *Oscar Wilde*: *The Aftermath* (London, 1963)
First detailed account of Wilde's last five years from imprisonment to death.

Hyde, H. Montgomery. *Oscar Wilde* (London, 1976)
Now superseded by Ellmann. Over a quarter of the book is taken up with the trials.

Hyde, H. Montgomery. *The Annotated Oscar Wilde* (London, 1982)
Selections from the works. Annotations partly literary, partly biographical, partly helpful, partly pedantic.

Hyde, H. Montgomery. *Lord Alfred Douglas*: *A Biography* (London, 1984)

Ingleby, Leonard Cresswell. *Oscar Wilde* (London, [1907])

Ingleby, Leonard Cresswell. *Oscar Wilde*: *Some Reminiscences* (London, [1912])

Jackson, John Wise (ed.). *Aristotle at Afternoon Tea*: *The Rare Oscar Wilde* (London, 1991)
Selection of Wilde's journalism. Pick of the plums from the 'Reviews' and 'Miscellanies' vols of the 1908 *Collected Works*.

Jullian, Philippe. *Oscar Wilde* (Paris, 1967; Trs. London, 1967)
'Gossipy rehearsal of Wilde's career as wit and pederast' said a reviewer. Unscholarly and fairly lightweight.

Kenilworth, Walter Winston. *A Study of Oscar Wilde* (New York, 1912)
A semi-mystical approach.

Kohl, Norbert. *Oscar Wilde*: *Leben und Werk in Daten und Bildern* (Frankfurt, 1976)
Many unusual photographs illustrating Wilde's life and works.

Kohl, Norbert. *Oscar Wilde*: *The Works of a Conformist Rebel* (Heidelberg, 1980; Trs. Cambridge, 1989)
'Advanced' but very readable textual criticism by highly reliable German scholar.

Kronenberger, Louis. *Oscar Wilde* (Boston; Toronto, 1976)

La Jeunesse, Ernest; Franz Blei and André Gide. *Recollections of Oscar Wilde* Trs. Percival Pollard (Boston; London, 1906)

Langlade, Jacques de. *Oscar Wilde*: *écrivain francais*. (Paris, 1975)

Lemonnier, Léon. *La Vie d'Oscar Wilde* (Paris, 1931)
Interesting for view of Wilde's downfall and exile in French press.

Lemonnier, Léon. *Oscar Wilde* (Paris, 1938)

Lewis, Lloyd and Henry J. Smith. *Oscar Wilde Discovers America* [1882] (New York, 1936)

McCormack, Jerusha (ed.). *Wilde the Irishman* (New Haven & London, 1998)
 A collection of essays continuing the pioneering work by Coakley.

McKenna, Neil. *The Secret Life of Oscar Wilde* (London, 2003)
 Gay interpretation of Wilde's entire life. Contains much new source material but also much unfounded conjecture.

MacLiammóir, Micheál. *The Importance of Being Oscar* (Dublin, 1963)
 Classic dramatisation of Wilde's life by incomparable Irish actor.

Mason, Stuart [Christopher Millard]. *Oscar Wilde: Art and Morality* (London, 1908)
 Reproduction of correspondence and criticisms occasioned by publication of *The Picture of Dorian Gray* together with a bibliography of all the foreign editions published.

Mason, Stuart [Christopher Millard]. *Oscar Wilde: Three Times Tried* (London, 1912)
 First accurate account of the three trials. Superseded by Hyde who reproduces the facts in more readable form.

Mason, Stuart [Christopher Millard]. *Oscar Wilde and the Aesthetic Movement* (Dublin, 1920)

Melville, Joy. *Mother of Oscar* (London, 1994)
 Comprehensively researched biography of Oscar's mother.

Merle, Robert. *Oscar Wilde* (Paris, 1948; revised 1995)

Merle, Robert. *Oscar Wilde ou la destinée de l'homosexuel* (Paris, 1955)
 Presents the homosexual as suicidal hero.

Mikhail, E. H., (ed.). *Oscar Wilde: Interviews and Recollections* 2 vols (London, 1979)
 First hand recollections of Wilde.

Morley, Sheridan. *Oscar Wilde: An Illustrated Biography* (London, 1976)
 Competent and well written but little or no new research.

Murray, Douglas. *Bosie* (London, 2000)
 Most recent biography of Lord Alfred Douglas, largely sympathetic with some interesting new material.

Nassaar, Christopher S. *Into the Demon Universe: A Literary Exploration of Oscar Wilde* (New Haven; London, 1974)
 Unconventional approach but, some said, too far-fetched in places.

O'Brien, Kevin. *Oscar Wilde in Canada: An Apostle for the Arts* (Toronto, 1982)
 Beautifully researched account of the Canadian part of Wilde's American tour. Also valuable for the reconstructions of the lectures.

O'Sullivan, Vincent. *Aspects of Wilde* (London, 1936)
Many personal reminiscences by one who knew Wilde well.

Page, Norman. *An Oscar Wilde Chronology* (London, 1991)
Invaluable, very detailed chronology of Wilde's life in 100 pages.

Pearson, Hesketh. *The Life of Oscar Wilde* (London, 1946)
Still one of the best pre-Ellmann biographies containing much original material but infuriatingly devoid of references.

Pennington, Michael. *An Angel for a Martyr: Jacob Epstein's Tomb for Oscar Wilde* (Reading, 1987)
Account of the commissioning, creation and errecting of Wilde's tomb in Paris.

Powell, Kerry. *Oscar Wilde and the Theatre of the* 1890s (Cambridge, 1990)
Questions Wilde as 'innovative' playwright and examines other writers' influences.

Queensberry, Francis Marquis of, and Percy Colson. *Oscar Wilde and the Black Douglas* (London, 1950)
Somewhat disjointed but makes use of Queensberry family archives. Black Douglas refers to family not just to 'Bosie'.

Raby, Peter. *Oscar Wilde* (Cambridge, 1988)
Concise and useful textual criticism for the general reader.

Raby, Peter (ed.). *The Cambridge Companion to Oscar Wilde* (Cambridge, 1997)
A collection of essays on the life and works by a galaxy of Wilde scholars.

Ransome, Arthur. *Oscar Wilde: A Critical Study* (London, 1912)
The first balanced and objective account, but one for which he was sued by Douglas.

Redman, Alvin. *The Epigrams of Oscar Wilde: An Anthology* (London, 1952)
Wilde's epigrams grouped under subject headings. Useful but not entirely reliable either for the accuracy of the quotes or the stated sources.

Renier, G.J. *Oscar Wilde* (London, 1933)
Takes new liberal view of homosexuality. Attempts pseudo-scientific explanations.

Ricketts, Charles. *Oscar Wilde: Recollections* (London, 1932)
A sympathetic account in the form of letters by the illustrator of some of Wilde's works.

Saltus, Edgar. *Oscar Wilde: An Idler's Impression* (Chicago, 1917)
Personal recollections reproduced mainly as conversations.

San Juan, Epifanio. *The Art of Oscar Wilde* (Princeton, 1967)
Literary criticism.

Schmidgall, Gary. *The Stranger Wilde* (New York, 1994)
Wilde from a totally gay perspective. Many interesting insights and a valuable addition to the non-mainstream literature.

Schroeder, Horst. *Additions and Corrections to Ellmann's Oscar Wilde* (Braunschweig, 1989; revised and much enlarged edition 2002)
Corrects many slips made in Ellmann's *Oscar Wilde* and an invaluable supplement to it.

Sherard, Robert Harborough. *Oscar Wilde: The Story of an Unhappy Friendship* (London, 1902)
Sherard was the only one of Wilde's friends on whose accounts we can more or less rely. All his books contain much first-hand and anecdotal material.

Sherard, Robert Harborough. *The Life of Oscar Wilde* (London, 1906)

Sherard, Robert Harborough. *The Real Oscar Wilde* (London, [1917])

Sherard, Robert Harborough. *Oscar Wilde Twice defended from André Gide's Wicked Lies and Frank Harris's Cruel Libels* (Chicago, 1934)
Inflammatory pamphlet attempting to defend Wilde's reputation but in the end doing more harm than good.

Sherard, Robert Harborough. *Bernard Shaw, Frank Harris and Oscar Wilde* (London, 1937)

Shewan, Rodney. *Oscar Wilde: Art and Egotism* (London, 1977)
Weighty and heavy going in places but one of the first to credit Wilde with depth and sincerity of purpose.

Small, Ian. *Oscar Wilde Revalued* (Greensboro N.C., 1993)
Lists much 'new' material, long available to scholars but generally overlooked.

Small, Ian. *Oscar Wilde Recent Research* (Greenboro N.C., 2000)
A supplement to the above.

Smith, Hester Travers. *Psychic Messages from Oscar Wilde* (London, 1924)

Smith, Philip E. and Michael S. Helfand. *Oscar Wilde's Oxford Notebooks: A Portrait of Mind in the Making* (New York; Oxford, 1989)
Part of the *nouvelle vague* approach to Wilde studies, looking at the early classical influences on his writing and seeing him as a serious professional writer.

Stokes, John. *Oscar Wilde: Myths, Miracles, and Imitations* (Cambridge, 1996)

Symons, Arthur. *A Study of Oscar Wilde* (London, 1930)

Tanitch, Robert. *Oscar Wilde on Stage and Screen* (London, 1999)
An impressive listing, with casts and criticism, of Wilde's plays as well as plays and films about him. Not comprehensive, but that would take a lifetime to compile.

Whistler, James Abbott McNeill. *The Gentle Art of Making Enemies* (London, 1892)
    Contains the much publicised correspondence between Wilde and Whistler.

White, Terence de Vere. *The Parents of Oscar Wilde* (London, 1967)
    Probably the best book on both Wilde's parents to date. Maddeningly short on source references. The Speranza material is now superseded by Melville.

Winwar, Frances. *Oscar Wilde and the Yellow Nineties* (London, 1938)

Woodcock, George. *The Paradox of Oscar Wilde* (London, 1949)
    Offered at the time as critical companion to Pearson (see above).

Wright, Thomas. *Table Talk*: *Oscar Wilde* (London, 2000)
    A collection of the stories and prose-poems, which Wilde is supposed to have recounted but never committed to paper, as recalled by his contemporaries.